GARD

OF ENGLAND AND WALES

OPEN FOR CHARITY

1997

**A GUIDE TO 3,500 GARDENS
THE MAJORITY OF WHICH ARE NOT NORMALLY
OPEN TO THE PUBLIC**

THE NATIONAL GARDENS SCHEME CHARITABLE TRUST
HATCHLANDS PARK, EAST CLANDON, GUILDFORD, SURREY GU4 7RT
TEL 01483 211535   FAX 01483 211537
Reg Charity No: 279284

Thank you for your support

This year the National Gardens Scheme is celebrating its 70th anniversary.

The Chairman and Council of The National Gardens Scheme wish to express their deep gratitude to all those whose very generous support makes it possible for the Scheme to help so many worthwhile charities. We hope that you will enjoy visiting many of the beautiful gardens listed in this book and then recommend them to others.

Daphne Foulsham

Daphne Foulsham
Chairman

Her Majesty Queen Elizabeth the Queen Mother is Patron of the National Gardens Scheme

Photograph Andrew Crickmay/Camera Press London

Contents

Published by the National Gardens Scheme, Hatchlands Park, East Clandon, Guildford, Surrey GU4 7RT

Editor: The Director, National Gardens Scheme

Cover illustration of Preston Tower, Northumberland, by Val Biro

A catalogue record for this book is available from the British Library.

Typeset in Linotron Bell Centennial by Land & Unwin (Data Sciences) Limited, Bugbrooke.

Text printed and bound by Wm Clowes Ltd, Beccles.

Cover printed by George Over Limited, Rugby.

Colour illustrations printed by MN Productions, Northampton

Trade Distributor: Seymour, Windsor House, 1270 London Road, Norbury, London, SW16 4DH.

ISBN 0-900558-29-6   ISSN 1365-0572

RICHARD OGDEN
INTERNATIONAL JEWELLER

FAMOUS FOR FINE JEWELLERY
AND AN INCOMPARABLE SERVICE

WE ALSO BUY BEAUTIFUL JEWELLERY

28/29 BURLINGTON ARCADE PICCADILLY LONDON W1V 0NX
TELEPHONE 0171 493 9136/7 & 0171 493 6239
FAX 0171 355 1508

BROCHURE AVAILABLE ON REQUEST

Member of
THE NATIONAL ASSOCIATION
OF GOLDSMITHS

Member of
THE BRITISH ANTIQUE DEALERS
ASSOCIATION

The National Gardens Scheme

- *What is the National Gardens Scheme?*

  A charity founded in 1927 which raises money by opening gardens to the public.

- *How is the money raised?*

  Owners generously open their gardens to the public on specific days and money is raised from entry charges plus the sales of teas and plants.

- *How many gardens are there and where are they?*

  3,500 spread throughout England and Wales.

- *Who are the main beneficiaries?*

  The Scheme provides long-term financial assistance to the charities listed on page 13.

- *How much money is donated to the charities supported?*

  In 1996 over £1.3 million.

- *How can I help?*

  The more gardens you visit the more the National Gardens Scheme will raise for charity.

Patron, President and Council of The National Gardens Scheme Charitable Trust

Join the Royal Horticultural Society today and save £5

As a special introductory offer for readers of *Gardens of England and Wales*, we are offering a saving of £5 on your first year subscription.

For just £27, you will receive the very best advice and inspiration available to gardeners (normal price £32 – £25 plus £7 enrolment fee). Membership of the RHS is just like having a panel of experts on hand whenever you need them.

Free gardening magazine subscription

You can look forward to a monthly copy of **the** gardening magazine. *The Garden* is an entertaining combination of news, horticultural problem pages, in-depth articles about garden design and interesting plants and a range of exclusive offers for members.

Free visits

You can also start planning days out at 24 of Britain's most beautiful gardens including the RHS Gardens at Wisley in Surrey, Rosemoor in Devon and Hyde Hall in Essex. Your membership entitles you to unlimited free visits to the gardens, and you can even bring a guest in free to the RHS Gardens. You can book privileged tickets – both special prices and members-only days – to the world's top flower shows, including Chelsea and Hampton Court Palace Flower Show. You also get free entrance to the monthly Westminster Flower Shows: an ideal opportunity to buy the very best plants from Britain's top nurseries.

Free advice

Other highlights include free advice from RHS experts and free seeds from Wisley, and you'll find that *The Garden* features regular new benefits such as gardens to visit or special RHS plant offers.

Your membership is vital to Britain's gardening heritage

The Royal Horticultural Society has been promoting horticultural excellence throughout the world since 1804. Today, gardening is Britain's most popular hobby and our extensive programme of education. conservation and scientific work ensures that future generations will continue to enjoy our gardening heritage too.

As a registered charity, we are dependent on money that we raise ourselves – and your support is a vital contribution.

We are pleased to offer readers of *Gardens of England and Wales* a £5 saving when you join the RHS – or perhaps enrol a friend – today.

Please make your cheque payable to The Royal Horticultural Society and send it to the **Membership Department, The Royal Horticultural Society, PO Box 313, London SW1P 2PE**. If you are enrolling a friend, please enclose their name and address on a separate sheet; we will send the new members' pack to you to pass on. If you would prefer not to cut this coupon, please write to us with all the details required – including code 892. This offer expires 31 October 1997.

For further information please call the RHS Membership Department on 0171-821 3000.

Code 892

Apply today and save £5

Gardens of England and Wales
– special RHS membership offer

The Royal Horticultural Society, Membership Department, PO Box 313, London SW1P 2PE Tel: 0171-821 3000

❑   I would like to join the RHS.

❑   I would like to enrol a friend as an RHS member. I enclose their name and address on a separate sheet.

PLEASE COMPLETE IN BLOCK CAPITALS

Name..

Address ....

....

Postcode...Daytime Tel. No. ....

Please make your cheque for £27 per member payable to The Royal Horticultural Society

Beneficiaries

The National Gardens Scheme provides long-term financial support to the following:

- **The Queen's Nursing Institute** – for the welfare of elderly and needy district nurses

- **Cancer Relief Macmillan Fund** – for the provision and training of Macmillan cancer nurses

- **The Nurses' Welfare Service** – for assistance to nurses in personal difficulty

- **The Gardeners' Royal Benevolent Society** – for assistance to retired gardeners

- **The Royal Gardeners' Orphan Fund** – for assistance to the orphans of gardeners

- **The Gardens Fund of the National Trust** – for the restoration of historic gardens and the training of young gardeners

- **Additional Charities Nominated by Owners (ACNO)** – Over 700 charities chosen by Garden Owners

BATH SPRING FLOWER SHOW

SAT 3rd MAY - MON 5th MAY 1997
ROYAL VICTORIA PARK

Large floral marquees containing displays of spring flowers, trees and shrubs, house plants, fuchsias, cacti, bonsai, alpines, water features, herbaceous and summer plants etc.

MARQUEES CONTAINING:
- FLORAL ART ARRANGEMENTS • DEMONSTRATIONS AND LECTURES
- BEE KEEPING EXHIBITION • GARDENING SUNDRIES
- CHILDREN'S AREA • PHOTOGRAPHIC COMPETITION
- ANIMAL NURSERY • COOKERY DEMONSTRATIONS
- BRITISH FOOD AND FARMING EXHIBITION • CRAFTS
- GARDENING QUESTIONS ANSWERED
- SIT AND LISTEN TO A BAND

A WIDE SELECTION OF PLANTS AND OTHER ITEMS AVAILABLE FOR SALE

ADMISSION
Adults £4.50   Senior Citizens and Unaccompanied children £3.50
Accompanied children under 16 - Free

Group reductions by prior arrangement • Dogs not allowed • Refreshments available

OPEN SATURDAY - MONDAY 10AM - 6PM

Further details from Bath and North East Somerset Council - Parks Section Tel: Bath 01225 448433

Royal Gardens

SANDRINGHAM HOUSE AND GROUNDS Norfolk

By gracious permission of Her Majesty The Queen, the House and grounds at Sandringham will be open on the following days: from 28 March to 5 October inclusive daily. Please note that the **house only** will be **closed** to the public from 22 July to 6 August inclusive and that the house and grounds will be closed from 27 July to 6 August inclusive. Coach drivers and visitors are advised to confirm these closing and opening dates nearer the time. Picnicking and dogs are not permitted inside the grounds.

Hours

Sandringham House: 11 to 4.45; museum: 11 to 5 and grounds: 10.30 to 5.

Admission Charges

House, grounds and museum: adults £4.50, OAPs £3.50, children £2.50. Grounds and museum only: adults £3.50, OAPs £3.00; children £2.00. Advance party bookings will be accepted. There are reductions in admission fees for pre-paid parties. Free car and coach parking.

Sandringham Church

Subject to weddings, funerals and special services, when the grounds are open as stated above, opening times will be 11-5 April to October. At other times of the year the church is open by appointment only.

Sandringham Flower Show

Wednesday 30th July 1997.

Enquiries

The Public Access Manager, Estate Office, Sandringham or by telephone 9-1, 2-4.30 Monday to Friday inclusive on King's Lynn 772675.

FROGMORE GARDENS Berkshire

By gracious permission of Her Majesty The Queen, Frogmore Gardens, Windsor Castle, will be open from 10.30-7 (last admission 6.00 pm) on the following days: **Wednesday May 7 and Thursday May 8**. Entrance to gardens and mausoleum through Long Walk gate. Coaches by appointment only: apply to the National Gardens Scheme, Hatchlands Park, East Clandon, Guildford, Surrey, GU4 7RT (Telephone 01483 211535) stating whether May 7 or 8, and whether morning or afternoon. Admission £2, accompanied children free. Dogs not allowed.
Visitors are requested kindly to refrain from entering the grounds of the Home Park. Light refreshments will be available at the free car park (near the outer gate to the gardens). Also open:

Royal Mausoleum

Open, free of charge, both days.

Frogmore House

Open in aid of the Royal Collection Trust. Entrance only from Frogmore Gardens. Admission Adults £3, over 60's £2, under 17 £1, children under the age of 8 not admitted.

National Trust Gardens

Certain gardens opened by The National Trust are opened in aid of the The National Gardens Scheme on the dates shown in this book. National Trust Members are requested to note that where a National Trust property has allocated an opening day to the National Gardens Scheme which is one of its normal opening days, members can still gain entry on production of their National Trust membership card (although donations to the Scheme will be welcome). However, where the day allocated is one on which the property would not normally be open, then the payment of the National Gardens Scheme admission fee will be required.

FIRST AID FOR FLOPPY FLOWERS

◀ BEFORE

AFTER ▶

The **Easy, Unobtrusive** plant support made of strong brown pointed aluminium tube, with a pliable green plastic coated wire fork at the top.

BEND THE FORKS TO SUIT YOUR PLANTS

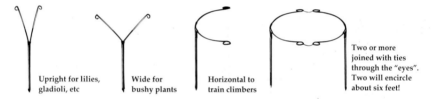

Upright for lilies, gladioli, etc

Wide for bushy plants

Horizontal to train climbers

Two or more joined with ties through the "eyes". Two will encircle about six feet!

Y-STAKES are so easy to use at any time, you do not need to put them in before a plant has fully grown. They are much tidier than netting and less obtrusive than rings. They avoid the unnatural bunched up look which can happen with other forms of staking.

SIMPLICITY. Y-Stakes can be used as a simple prop in exactly the same way as a forked stick, but you can bend the arms to suit your plant, or with a quick twist, join them together with flexible wire ties (through their eyes) **at any distance apart**.

SO EASY TO MOVE. Y-Stakes are suitable for a very wide range of plants, throughout the gardening season, from geraniums to hollyhocks. They are so easy to move, when your early plants such as peonies are over they can quickly be transferred to later plants e.g. delphiniums, dahlias or chrysanthemums.

SIZES. Y-Stakes are available in five sizes from 1ft plus 9" arms to 5ft plus 16" arms. A **Trial Set** of 3x1ft, 3x2ft, and 3x3ft (9 stakes in total) is a good way to test the lengths needed for your various plants. You will find that you have uses for all of the sizes as the season progresses.

COST. Because each stake has such a wide arm span, 28" for a 3ft stake, and as each arm can be extended by up to 24" more with the tying wire, Y-Stakes can encircle far more plants to the pound than any other comparable staking system.

The **Trial set** is available at £18.95 including postage in the UK. Please telephone, fax, or send your order with cheque or Access/Visa card number and expiry date to Pelco Fertilizers Ltd., 251 London Road East, Bath, BA1 7RL. Tel. 01225 859 962. Fax 01225 859 006. Please quote Dept YB. Or ask for free leaflet and complete price list. Orders are sent by return.

General Information and Symbols

‡ Following a garden name in the Dates of Opening list indicates that those gardens sharing the symbol are near each other and open on the same day.

‡‡ Indicates a second series of gardens near each other and open on the same day.

¶ Opening for the first time.

❀ Plants/produce for sale if available.

&. Gardens with at least the main features accessible by wheelchair.

✗ No dogs except guide dogs but otherwise dogs are usually admitted, provided they are kept on a lead.

There are three categories of garden in the National Gardens Scheme which open regularly to the public. They are indicated as follows:

● These gardens advertise their own dates in this publication although they do not nominate specific days for the NGS. Not all the money collected by these gardens comes to the NGS but they do make a guaranteed contribution.

■ These gardens nominate specific days for the NGS and advertise their own dates in this publication.

▲ These gardens open regularly to the public but they do not advertise their own dates in this publication. For further details, contact the garden directly.

Additional Charities Nominated by Owner (ACNO) Where the owners of private gardens (not normally open to the public) have nominated some other cause to receive an agreed share from the admission money, the name of the other cause is included in the descriptive entry as (Share to ....) with an ® or © to indicate whether it is a Registered Charity or a Charitable Cause.

Tea When this is available at a garden the information is given in capitals, e.g. TEAS (usually with home-made cakes) or TEA (usually with biscuits). There is, of course, an extra charge for any refreshments available at a garden. TEAS in aid of ... is used where part or all the proceeds go to another organisation.

Open by appointment Please do not be put off by this notation. The owner may consider his garden too small to accommodate the numbers associated with a normal opening or, more often, there may be a lack of car parking. The minimum size of party is either stated in the garden description or can be found out when making the appointment. If the garden has normal open days, the entrance fee is as stated in the garden description.

Coach parties Please, by appointment only unless stated otherwise.

Photographs Photographs taken in a garden may not be used for sale or reproduction without the prior permission of the garden owner.

Lavatories Private gardens do not normally have outside lavatories. Regretably, for security reasons, owners have been advised not to admit visitors into their houses to use inside toilets.

Children All children must be accompanied by an adult.

Distances and sizes In all cases these are approximate.

The Royal Horticultural Society's Garden
at
Wisley

Exclusive evening openings
in aid of the National Gardens Scheme
on the occasion of its 70th anniversary

Wednesday, 18 June, 6.30-9pm
&
Thursday, 14 August, 6.30-9pm
(Wisley Flower Show marquee open for public view 7-9pm,
with plant sales by Show Exhibitors 7-8pm)

Admission £3 in aid of the National Gardens Scheme
(admission fee also applies to RHS Members)

Coach parties must pre-book two weeks in advance, tel: (01483) 224234.
Garden accessible to the disabled. Free car and coach parking.

The Terrace Restaurant will open for pre-booked dinner reservations on
Tel: (01483) 225329.
The Conservatory Café will open for drinks and self-service buffet.
Dining services provided by Cadogan Caterers.

RHS Garden Wisley is located near the A3/M25 intersection at Junction 10.

The National Gardens Scheme

GARDENS
ILLUSTRATED

Photographic Competition

To mark the 70th anniversary of the National Gardens Scheme in 1997, the NGS, in conjunction with *Gardens Illustrated* and Pentax UK Ltd., organised a major photographic competition last year. In total, 481 individuals registered for the competition, representing every county in the UK as well as several countries from abroad, including France, Holland, Germany, Australia, New Zealand and the USA. Participants were asked to capture the spirit of a garden open for charity under the NGS in a portfolio comprising 8-12 colour transparencies. The photographic assignment was to document the layout of their chosen garden, show the excellence of its plantings and originality of its design features and provide portraits of its owner or gardeners, as appropriate.

Portfolios from 126 registered participants were received. Each was judged blindly by a panel which included Claudia Zeff, Art Director of *Gardens Illustrated*; Andrew Lawson, internationally acclaimed garden photographer; Daphne Foulsham, Chairman of the NGS; and Marilyn Dixon, Marketing Services Manager of Pentax UK Ltd.

For her excellent photographic portfolio of the garden at Upton House in Warwickshire, Rosalind Simon of London won the competition and was awarded a brand new Pentax MZ-5, the world's smallest SLR camera. The competition's runner-up was Melanie Eclare of Dorset, while commendations were given to Nada Jennett of Bristol, Jim Love of Hampshire, and Nicola Essex of Middlesex.

The results of the photographic competition were announced in an extensive feature in the February/March 1997 edition of *Gardens Illustrated*. Also, one photograph from each of the five recognised portfolios can be seen in this, the 1997 anniversary edition of *Gardens of England and Wales Open for Charity*.

The NGS would like to thank *Gardens Illustrated* and Pentax UK Ltd. for their generous support of this competition.

SPECIAL EVENTS DIARY

For further information about these events, please check relevant garden listings in county sections.

EVENING OPENINGS IN 1997

County/Garden	Date(s)	Time
BUCKINGHAMSHIRE		
Spindrift	23 July	6-9pm
CAMBRIDGESHIRE		
Fen Ditton Gardens	19 June	6.30-8pm
CUMBRIA		
Holker Hall	26 June	6.30-9pm
DORSET		
Whitefriars	22 July	7-9pm
ESSEX		
Park Farm	20, 21 June	6-9pm
Woodpeckers	13, 27 June	6-9pm
GLAMORGANS		
10 Daniel Close	19-25 July	12-8pm
HAMPSHIRE		
Mottisfont Abbey	22 June	12-8.30pm
Rowans Wood	1 June	6-8.30pm
The Vyne	20 June	from 7pm
2 Warren Farm Cottages	21 June, 19 July	6-8.30pm
KENT		
Edenbridge House	18 June	6.30-8.30pm
Beech Court Gardens	19 June	6-9pm
Lily Vale Farm	22, 25 June	2-8pm
Lodge House	22, 25 June	2-8pm
Old Tong Farm	28 June	6-9pm
Amber Green Farmhouse	2 July	6-9pm
Great Oaks House	2 July	5-8.30pm
Hookwood House	2 July	5-8pm
Cares Cross	16 July	5-8pm
LINCOLNSHIRE		
The Cottage	29 June	11-7pm
LONDON		
1F Oval Road	7, 14 June	6-9pm
Little Lodge	11 June	6.30-9pm
5 Greenaway Gardens	18 June	6-8.30pm
103 Thurleigh Road	18 June	6.30-9pm
13 Mercers Road	18, 19 June	6-9pm
Southwood Lodge	19 June	6.30-8.30pm
101 Cheyne Walk	3 July	6-8pm
2 Millfield Place	17 July	5.30-9pm
Osborne House	13 Aug	6-9.30pm

EVENING OPENINGS IN 1997

NORTHAMPTONSHIRE

Cottingham & Middleton Gardens	18 June	6-9pm
Ravensthorpe Nursery	16 July	6.30-9pm

SHROPSHIRE

Cricklewood Cottage	14 May, 11 June	6-8pm
Brown Hill House	9, 23, 30 June	6.30-8.30pm

STAFFORDSHIRE

The Covert	21 June	7-9pm

SUFFOLK

The Sun House, Long Melford Gardens	20 June	6-8pm

SURREY

Chilworth Manor	11 June, 9 July	6-8pm
Moleshill House	19 June	6.30-8.30pm
High Meadow	28 June	6-9pm

SUSSEX

Cowbeech Farm	2 June	4-8pm
Cobblers	11 June	5.30-8pm
Frith Hill	14 June	5-8pm
Frith Lodge	14 June	5-8pm
Manvilles Field	18 June	5.30-8pm
South Harting Gardens	27 June	5-7pm
Casters Brook	3 July	5.30-7.30pm
Berri Court	4 July	6-8.30pm
West Worthing Gardens	16 July	5.30-7.30pm
Denmans	31 July	5.30-8pm
Neptune House	2 Aug	5-8pm
Sennicotts	16 August	6-8pm
The White House	24, 25 Aug	5.30-7.30pm

WARWICKSHIRE

52 Tenbury Road	25 June	7-9pm
8 Vicarage Road	2 July	6.30-8.30pm

WORCESTERSHIRE

Ivytree House	21 May, 18 June, 16 July	7-9pm
The Cottage	17 June, 15 July, 19 August	3-8pm
The Elms	22 June	5-9pm
21 Swinton Lane	17 July	11-8pm

YORKSHIRE

Beningbrough Hall	12 June	6-9pm
The Old Vicarage	18 June	2-8pm
Maspin House	9 July	4-7pm

LARGE OR UNUSUAL PLANT SALES IN 1997

County/Garden	Date(s)	Time
CAMBRIDGESHIRE		
Hardwicke House	25 May	2-5.30pm
CEREDIGION/CARDIGANSHIRE		
Llwyncelyn	11 May	1-6pm
LEICESTERSHIRE		
Long Close	25 May	11-5.30pm

GARDENS

OF ENGLAND AND WALES
OPEN FOR CHARITY

1998 EDITION PUBLISHED FEB/MARCH

Price: £5.75 including UK postage. Airmail to Europe £6.75; Australia A$20.00; New Zealand NZ$24.00; USA US$20.75; Canada CDN$ 22.50

To The National Gardens Scheme, Hatchlands Park, East Clandon, Guildford, Surrey, GU4 7RT. Tel 01483 211535 (Fax 01483 211537)

Please send _____ copy/copies of *Gardens of England and Wales* for which I enclose PO/cheque for _____
Postal orders and cheques should be made payable to The National Gardens Scheme and crossed.
If sending money from abroad please use an international money order or sterling, dollar or euro cheques; other cheques are not acceptable. Add $2 to cheques for clearance.

_____

Name Mr/Mrs/Miss (Block letters)

_____

Address

_____

_____

The books will be posted on publication. If you wish to receive an acknowledgement of your order, please enclose an s.a.e.
Trade terms Supplies of this book on sale or return should be ordered direct from our trade distributors:
Seymour, 1270 London Road, Norbury, London, SW16 4DH (Tel 0181-679 1899)
The National Gardens Scheme is a registered charity, number 279284.

TO ADVERTISE IN

GARDENS OF ENGLAND AND WALES 1998

CONTACT:

AW PUBLISHING, PO BOX 38, ASHFORD, KENT TN25 6PR

TELEPHONE: 01303 813803 FAX: 01303 813737

The Art of the Garden

The *Art of the Garden* is a unique initiative between the National Gardens Scheme Charitable Trust (NGS) and the Royal Watercolour Society and the Royal Society of Painter-Printmakers, celebrating in 1997 the NGS' 70th Anniversary. Artists from the Societies have been visiting NGS gardens all around the country and using these experiences as inspiration for their watercolours and original artists' prints. Works from the project will be shown in the galleries listed below, which are hosting *The Art of the Garden* for gardens local to their area.

The Royal Watercolour Society and the Royal Society of Painter-Printmakers are the two oldest and most prestigious Societies of their kind in the world. From their headquarters at the Bankside Gallery, London, the Societies are dedicated to promoting contemporary works of art on paper. The National Gardens Scheme Charitable Trust was founded in 1927 and raises money for a number of charities through opening private gardens to the public.

15th March – 26th April
Victoria Art Gallery, Bridge Street, Bath
Telephone: 01225 477772

26th April – 4th May
Gorstella Gallery, Tudor Farm, Dodleston, Chester
Telephone: 01244 660220

19th May – 2nd June
Nevill Gallery, 43 St Peter's Street, Canterbury
Telephone: 01227 765291

22nd June – 6th July
Century Gallery, Datchet, Nr Windsor
Telephone: 01753 581284

24th June – 12th July
South Yorkshire Art Gallery at Museum of Yorkshire Life, Cusworth Hall, Doncaster
Telephone: 01302 852358

12th – 27th July
Thompson's Gallery, 175 High Street, Aldeburgh
Telephone: 01728 453743

10th – 28th September
Bankside Gallery, 48 Hopton Street, London SE1.
Telephone: 0171 928 7521

Please call the Gallery concerned to check opening details.

The Counties of England and Wales

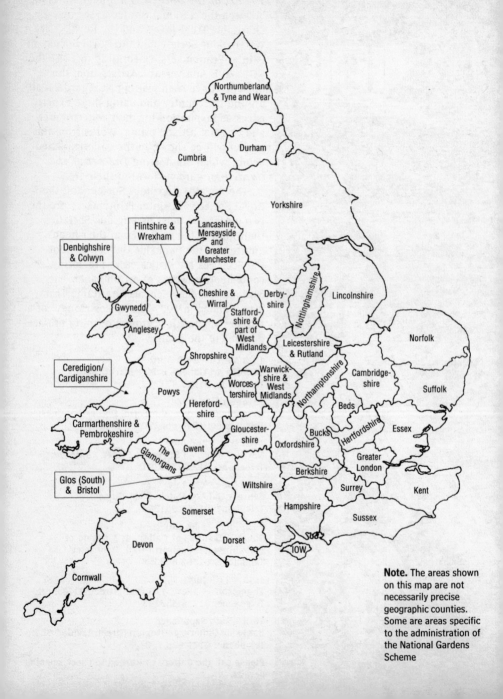

Note. The areas shown on this map are not necessarily precise geographic counties. Some are areas specific to the administration of the National Gardens Scheme

ENGLAND

Avon

See Gloucestershire (South) and Bristol

Bedfordshire

Hon County Organiser: Mr & Mrs C Izzard, Broadfields, Keysoe Row East, Bedford MK44 2JD
Hon County Treasurer: Mr Clive Thomas, FCCA, 21 Park Drive, Little Paxton, St Neots, Cambs
PE19 4NS

DATES OF OPENING

March 15 Saturday
Swiss Garden, nr Biggleswade
March 30 Sunday
King's Arms Path Garden, Ampthill
April 6 Sunday
Broadfields, Keysoe Row East
April 13 Sunday
Broadfields, Keysoe Row East
April 20 Sunday
Woburn Abbey, Woburn
April 27 Sunday
Howard's House, Cardington
The Manor House, Stevington
May 6 Tuesday
Seal Point, Luton
May 11 Sunday
Luton Hoo Gardens, Luton
May 18 Sunday
Aspley Guise Gardens
May 25 Sunday
88 Castlehill Road, Middle End,
Totternhoe
Milton House, nr Bedford
May 26 Monday
88 Castlehill Road, Middle End,
Totternhoe

6 High Street, Clophill
Woburn Abbey, Woburn
June 1 Sunday
Southill Park, nr Biggleswade
June 3 Tuesday
Seal Point, Luton
June 8 Sunday
The Old Stables, Hockliffe
June 22 Sunday
6 High Street, Clophill
The Manor House, Stevington
The Old Rectory, Yelden
June 29 Sunday
88 Castlehill Road, Middle End,
Totternhoe
Grove Lodge, 6 Deepdale, Potton
Howard's House, Cardington
The Old Rectory, Pertenhall
June 30 Monday
88 Castlehill Road, Middle End,
Totternhoe
July 1 Tuesday
Seal Point, Luton
July 6 Sunday
Swineshead Gardens
July 13 Sunday
Barton-le-Clay Gardens
Toddington Manor, Toddington

July 19 Saturday
Broadfields, Keysoe Row East
July 20 Sunday
Broadfields, Keysoe Row East
The Old Stables, Hockliffe
July 27 Sunday
Crosshall Manor, St Neots
August 5 Tuesday
Seal Point, Luton
August 31 Sunday
The Old Stables, Hockliffe
September 2 Tuesday
Seal Point, Luton
September 27 Saturday
Swiss Garden, nr Biggleswade

Regular openings

Kings Arms Path Garden, Ampthill
Luton Hoo Gardens, Luton
Toddington Manor, Toddington

DESCRIPTIONS OF GARDENS

Aspley Guise Gardens 2m SW of M1 (Exit 13) towards Woburn Sands. *Combined adm £2 Chd £1. Sun May 18 (2-6)*
   Aspley House ⚘ (Mr & Mrs C I Skipper) House on E side of village. 5 acres; shrubs and lawns. William and Mary house (not open). Woburn Sands Band and local childrens orchestra in attendance. TEAS

¶**The Old Rectory** (Sir Norman & Lady King) Small woodland area with 1640 tythe barn
The Rookery ⚘ (C R Randall Esq) 5 acres; rhododendrons and woodland

Barton-Le-Clay Gardens ⚘❀ 6m N of Luton on the B655 Barton-le-Clay to Hitchin rd. Hitchin 5m. TEAS at The Rectory. *Combined adm £2.50 Chd £1. Sun July 13 (2-6)*

47 Hexton Road ✤ (Mrs S H Horsler) ¼-acre cottage garden with mixed borders
The Rectory (Canon Peter Whittaker) 2 acres with background of Chilterns; moat, herbaceous border, mature trees, lawns; overlooked by C12 church

Broadfields ₺✤ (Mr & Mrs Chris Izzard) Keysoe Row East. Leave Bedford on Kimbolton Rd B660 approx 8½m. Turn R at Keysoe Xrds by White Horse public house ½m on R. 3 acres; herbaceous borders; spring bulbs, summer bedding, fuchsias; mature trees; shrubs; vegetable and fruit gardens. TEAS. *Adm £1.50 Chd 50p. Suns April 6, 13 (2-6) Sat July 19 (2-6) Sun July 20 (10-2). Private visits welcome, please* **Tel 01234 376326**

88 Castlehill Road ⚘✤ (Chris & Carole Jell) Middle End, Totternhoe. 2m W of Dunstable, R turn off B489 Aston-Clinton Rd. Fronting main rd approx ½m through village. Elevated position with fine views across Aylesbury Vale and Chilterns. Adjoining Totternhoe Knolls Nature Reserve. ½-acre, S sloping on limestone and clay, entirely created by owners. Plantsman garden for all seasons; designed as small gardens within a garden since 1986; shrubs; climbers and herbaceous. TEAS. *Adm £1.50 Chd free. Suns May 25, June 29; Mons May 26, June 30 (2-6). Also private visits welcome, please* **Tel 01525 220780**

Crosshall Manor ₺✤ (Mr V Constantine) Crosshall, Eaton Ford. Just off A1 on the B1048 NW of St Neots. C18 manor house situated in 1½ acres of formal lawned gardens with mature trees, mixed borders, shrubs, large pond, terrace, pools with fall fountains; formal rose gardens, pergolas, pots, trough plantings and other features. TEAS. *Adm £2 Chd 50p. Sun July 27 (2-6)*

Grove Lodge ✤ (Peter Wareing & Jean Venning) 6 Deepdale, Potton. 2m E of Sandy on 1042 towards Potton, past RSPB Reserve, downhill to Xrds. L at 'Locomotive' - lane to TV mast; first house on R. 1½-acre sandy hillside garden; conifers; heathers, shrubs, incl rhododendrons, climbing roses, herbaceous border, orchard with wild flowers, rockery banks with pond. TEAS and plant sale in aid of R.A.T.S. *Adm £1.50 Chd 50p. Sun June 29 (2-6). Private visits welcome for parties of 12 and over, please* **Tel 01767 261298**

6 High Street ₺✤ (Mrs Janice Rogers) Clophill. Midway between Bedford and Luton. Turn R just N of the A6, A507 roundabout. Limited parking on the village green, if full use the Flying Horse and Green Man car parks. ½-acre informal gardens bordering the R Flit. Beds densely planted with shrubs and herbaceous perennials, many unusual with thought given to the plant and colour combinations. Climbing roses, mature trees and bog garden containing interesting moisture loving plants. TEAS. *Adm £1.50 Chd 50p. Mon May 26; Sun June 22 (2-6). Private visits and groups welcome, please* **Tel 01525 860 853**

The National Gardens Scheme is a charity which traces its origins back to 1927. Since then it has raised a total of over £15 million for charitable purposes.

Howard's House ₺ (Humphrey Whitbread Esq) Cardington. 2m SE of Bedford. Large walled flower and vegetable gardens; flowering cherries and clematis, mature trees. *Adm £1.50 Chd 50p. Suns April 27, June 29 (2-6)*

■ **Kings Arms Path Garden** ₺⚘✤ Ampthill Town Council (Mrs N W Hudson) Ampthill. Free parking in town centre. Entrance opp old Market Place, Ampthill, down Kings Arms Yard. Small woodland garden of about 1½ acres created by plantsman the late William Nourish. Trees, shrubs, bulbs and many interesting collections. Maintained since 1987 by 'The Friends of the Garden.' Tea at adjacent Bowling Club or nearby tea shops. *Adm 50p Chd 25p. Suns Feb 16 (2-4), May 25, June 22, Aug 24, Oct 12 (2.30-5). For NGS Easter Sun March 30 (2.30-5). Private group visits welcome, please* **Tel 01525 402030/403945**

■ **Luton Hoo Gardens** ₺⚘✤ Luton; junction 10 M1. Entrance at Park St gates. The mansion house where you can view the Wernher Collection is set in a Capability Brown landscape with formal gardens and a secluded rock garden. TEAS. *Adm gardens only £2.50 OAPs £2.25 Chd £1. Easter to Oct 12, Fris, Sats, Suns (12-5). For NGS Sun May 11 (12-5)*

¶**The Manor House** ⚘✤ (Kathy Brown) Church Rd, Stevington 5m NW Bedford 1¾m off A428. Home of garden writer and designer specialising in 'garden recipes'. Features seasonal and long term containers, many incl bulbs and bedding, herbs and edible flowers, roses, cottage garden plants; an exciting collection of succulents and cacti, French style garden and long wisteria walk, newly planted; spring bulbs in orchard and grasslands; old-fashioned roses and herbaceous plants. No photography. TEAS in aid of St Mary's Restoration Fund. *Adm £1.50 Chd 50p. Guided tours available. Suns April 27, June 22 (2-6). Private parties welcome, please* **Tel 01234 822064**

Milton House ₺✤ (Mr & Mrs Clifton Ibbett) nr Bedford. N of Bedford on the A6. The drive to the house is on the R, S of the village of Milton Ernest. Formal, terrace and sunken gardens set in large grounds with lakes and waterfall. TEAS in aid of All Saints Parish Church, Milton Ernest. *Adm £2 Chd 50p. Sun May 25 (2-6)*

The Old Rectory, Pertenhall ₺✤ (Mr & Mrs F R Finston) Situated on B660 approx 10m from Bedford 1½m from Kimbolton. 4 acres of mature gardens approached through lime avenue. Walled garden with special features, ancient mulberry and medlar. Shrubberies and herbaceous borders; scented and kitchen gardens, views over large pond and paddocks. *Adm £2 Chd free. Sun June 29 (2-6)*

The Old Rectory, Yelden ₺⚘✤ (Mr & Mrs P Rushton) Beds, Northants border, 14m N of Bedford, 4m S of Rushden. Adjacent to A6 and A45. 2.5 acres of established gardens. Many fine trees, old roses, ornamental pond, herb garden, shrubberies. TEAS and plants for sale in aid of St Mary's Church. *Adm £2 Chd free. Sun June 22 (2-6)*

The Old Stables ✗❀ (Mr & Mrs D X Victor) 3m N of Dunstable. From A5 in Hockliffe, W on A4012. Turn R after ¼m (signposted Church End), then L at Church. Follow lane for ½m and take field track on R. 2 acres incl walled garden. Alpines, mixed herbaceous and shrub borders, oxalis, hardy geraniums, erodiums, dianthus, saxifrages, euphorbias, deutzias and clematis. *Adm £2 Chd £1 (Share to The Stables, Wavendon®). Suns June 8, July 20, Aug 31 (2-6). Private group visits welcome, please* **Tel 01525 210633**

Seal Point ✗❀ (Mrs Danae Johnston) 7 Wendover Way. In NE Luton, turning N off Stockingstone Rd into Felstead Way. A small sloping exciting town garden with unusual herbaceous plants, climbers and trees; water features, topiary cats and bonsai; beds representing yin and yang; original ornaments, grasses, ferns. Featured on TV 'Look East' 1996. TEA by arrangement. *Adm £2 Chd under 14 free. Tues May 6, June 3, July 1, Aug 5, Sept 2 (2-6). Private visits welcome, also small groups, please* **Tel 01582 611567**

Southill Park ᓂ❀ (Mr & Mrs S C Whitbread) 5m SW of Biggleswade. Large garden, rhododendrons, renovated conservatory. *Adm £2 Chd £1 (Share to The Tradescant Trust®). Sun June 1 (2-5.30)*

Swineshead Gardens ✗ 3m from Kimbolton between A6 and B660. TEAS in Village Hall. *Combined adm £2 Chd 50p (Share to St Nicholas Church Restoration® Village Hall Fabric Fund®). Sun July 6 (2-6)*

    Brook Farm ᓂ (Christine & Michael Whitlock) A working farm, house dating back to C17. To the rear a large family garden undergoing redevelopment, features yew hedging surrounding wide herbaceous beds. Small kitchen garden

    Chapel Close Cottage (Mrs J Smith) High St. Tiny cottage garden. Limited space has been filled with traditional, old-fashioned shrubs and perennials. Small but impressive collection of tub grown fuchsias

    ¶**Manor Bungalow** (Deborah & Steve Saville) Cottage garden specialising in herbs, vegetable deep beds and fruit, grown to be productive and attractive in limited space

    Manor Farm ❀ (Michael & Diana Marlow) High St. 3-acre garden designed and created by present owners over 18 yrs and still evolving. The yard of this C16 farm has been converted into a courtyard garden. A landscaped area with young yew hedging and lawns provides views of planted bank and stream flowing into large pond. Extensive kitchen garden, soft fruit garden and new orchard with old varieties of top fruit.

Paddock, woodland park with wildlife pond. Rare breed poultry and geese

Old School House (Cynthia & John Overland) Mature ¾-acre lawned garden flanked by established hedging, shrub and tree borders. Colourful window boxes/containers and interesting, cosy niches

Sale Cottage (Mrs K Hinde) Sandy Lane. A small enclosed garden. Significant feature is the wide variety of container grown plants in tubs, sinks, troughs and hanging baskets

Stables House ❀ (Dawn & Peter Wells) High St. Garden designed and created by owners. The former stableyard is defined by a curved wall, pergola and trellis work, with raised beds for shrubs, herbs and an ornamental pond. Sloping rear paddock is planted to frame views of open fields. Small trees, shrubs and herbaceous plants; a rockery accommodates changing levels

Swiss Garden ᓂ✗❀ (Bedfordshire County Council) Old Warden, Biggleswade. Signposted from A1 and A600. 2m W Biggleswade, next door to the Shuttleworth Collection. 9 acre landscape garden set out in 1830s alongside a further 10 acres native woodland with lakeside picnic area. Garden includes many tiny buildings, footbridges, ironwork features and intertwining ponds. Romantic landscape design highlighted by daffodils, rhododendrons and old rambling roses in season. *Adm £2.50 Concessions and Chd £1.25 (Share to Friends of the Swiss Garden®). Sats March 15, Sept 27 (1.30-5)*

■ **Toddington Manor** ᓂ❀ (Sir Neville & Lady Bowman-Shaw) Exit 12 M1. Signs in village. House and gardens restored by present owners. Walled garden with greenhouses and herb garden; roses and shrubs; lakeside walks in the woods. Rare Breeds Livestock and Vintage Tractor collection. Cricket on pitch in front of house at weekends. Gift Shop, home made TEAS. *Adm £3.50 OAP's £2.50 Chd £1.50. Special rates for parties. Open May 1-Sept 28 daily (Closed Mon & Tues incl Bank Hols) 11-5 weekdays 11-6 weekends. For NGS Sun July 13 (11-6)*

Woburn Abbey ✗ (The Marquess of Tavistock) Woburn. Woburn Abbey is situated 1½m from Woburn Village, which is on the A4012 almost midway from junctions 12 and 13 of the M1 motorway. 22 acres of private garden originally designed by Wyattville, with recent restoration of the The Duchess' rose garden. Unique hornbeam maze with C18 temple by Chambers. TEAS. *Adm £1 Chd free. Suns April 20 (gardens), Mon May 26 (gardens & maze and garden show) (11-5)*

Scotland's Gardens Scheme.

The National Gardens Scheme has a similar but quite separate counterpart in Scotland. Called Scotland's Gardens Scheme, it raises money for the Queen's Nursing Institute (Scotland), the Gardens Fund of the National Trust for Scotland and over 160 registered charities nominated by garden owners. The Handbook is available (£3.25 incl p&p) from Scotland's Gardens Scheme, 31 Castle Terrace, Edinburgh EH1 2EL.

Berkshire

Hon County Organiser:	Bob Avery Esq, 'Jingles', Derek Rd., Maidenhead, SL6 8NT Tel 01628 27580
Asst Hon County Organisers:	The Hon Mrs J A Willoughby, Buckhold Farm, Pangbourne Tel 01734 744468
	(NW) Mrs C M J Povey, Bussock Mayne, Snelsmore Common, Newbury Tel 01635 248347
	(SW) Mrs P P A Meigh, Fishponds, West Woodhay, Nr Newbury Tel 01488 668269
	(Central) Mrs M A Henderson, 'Ridings', Kentons Lane, Wargrave, RG10 8PB Tel 01734 402523
	(Publicity & Brochures) Mrs J Bewsher, Arcturus, Church Road, Bray, Berks SL6 1UR Tel 01628 22824
Hon County Treasurer:	Bob Avery Esq

DATES OF OPENING

March 9 Sunday
Foxgrove, Enborne, nr Newbury
March 31 Monday
Swallowfield Park, nr Reading
April 6 Sunday
Foxgrove, Enborne, nr Newbury
Kirby House, Inkpen ‡
Welford Park, nr Newbury
West Woodhay House, Inkpen ‡
April 12 Saturday
Sonning Village Gardens
April 13 Sunday
Bussock Mayne, nr Newbury
Folly Farm, nr Reading
April 20 Sunday
Blencathra, Finchampstead
Little Harwood, Pinkney's Green, Maidenhead
April 27 Sunday
The Harris Garden, Whiteknights, Reading
The Old Rectory, Farnborough, Wantage
Whiteknights, The Ridges, Finchampstead
April 30 Wednesday
The Old Rectory, Burghfield, nr Reading
May 4 Sunday
Bussock Wood, Snelsmore Common, nr Newbury
Simms Farm House, Mortimer, nr Reading
May 5 Monday
Simms Farm House, Mortimer, nr Reading
May 7 Wednesday
Frogmore Gardens, Windsor
May 8 Thursday
Frogmore Gardens, Windsor
May 10 Saturday
Englefield House, Theale
May 11 Sunday
Silwood Park, Ascot
May 18 Sunday
Beenham House, Beenham
Hurst Gardens, nr Reading

The Old Rectory, Farnborough, Wantage
Silwood Park, Ascot
Stone House, Brimpton
May 22 Thursday
Meadow House, nr Newbury
May 25 Sunday
Alderwood House, Greenham Common
Blencathra, Finchampstead
Little Bowden, Pangbourne
Waltham Place, White Waltham
May 26 Monday
Folly Farm, nr Reading
June 1 Sunday
Braywood House, Windsor Forest ‡
Sunningdale Park, Ascot ‡
Trunkwell Park, Beech Hill
June 5 Thursday
Meadow House, nr Newbury
June 8 Sunday
Aldermaston Park, Aldermaston
Odney Club, Cookham
Old Rectory Cottage, nr Pangbourne
Padworth Common Gardens
June 14 Saturday
Eton College, Windsor
June 15 Sunday
Bear Ash, Hare Hatch, nr Wargrave
Fox Hill, Inkpen
Stone House, Brimpton
June 22 Sunday
Alderwood House, Greenham Common
Chieveley Manor, nr Newbury ‡
Donnington Grove Country Club, Donnington
Folly Farm, nr Reading
Foxgrove, Enborne, nr Newbury
Kirby House, Inkpen ‡‡
Ockwells Manor, Maidenhead
Peasmore Gardens ‡
West Woodhay House, Inkpen ‡‡
June 25 Wednesday
Rooksnest, Lambourn
June 29 Sunday
Basildon Park, Lower Basildon

Combe Manor, Hungerford ‡
Goring-on-Thames Gardens (see Oxon)
The Old Rectory, Farnborough, Wantage
Padworth Common Gardens, Scotlands, Cockpole Green, nr Wargrave ‡‡
Summerfield House, Crazies Hill, nr Wargrave ‡‡
Withers Farmhouse, Inkpen ‡
Woolley Park, nr Wantage
July 6 Sunday
Little Bowden, Pangbourne
Old Rectory Cottage, nr Pangbourne
July 10 Thursday
Meadow House, nr Newbury
July 13 Sunday
Inkpen House, Hungerford
Stanford Dingley Village Gardens
July 24 Thursday
Meadow House, nr Newbury
July 27 Sunday
Waltham Place, White Waltham
July 30 Wednesday
The Old Rectory, Burghfield, nr Reading
August 10 Sunday
Padworth Common Gardens (Bloomsbury only)
Whiteknights, The Ridges, Finchampstead
August 21 Thursday
Meadow House, nr Newbury
September 7 Sunday
Trunkwell Park, Beech Hill
September 28 Sunday
Hurst Gardens, nr Reading
October 12 Sunday
Silwood Park, Ascot

Regular openings

Englefield House, Theale
The Old Rectory, Burghfield, nr Reading
Swallowfield Park, nr Reading
Waltham Place, White Waltham

DESCRIPTION OF GARDENS

Aldermaston Park &⚘ (Blue Circle Industries plc) Newbury 10m W; Reading 10m E; Basingstoke 8m off A340 S. 137 acres, surrounding Victorian Mansion (1849) with modern offices making interesting contrast of architecture. Fine trees; specimen rhododendrons and shrubs; large lawns; 11-acre lake with lakeside walk. TEA. *Adm £2 Chd free. Sun June 8 (1-4.30)*

Alderwood House see Stop Press page 322

▲ **Basildon Park** &⚘⚘ (Lady Iliffe; The National Trust) Lower Basildon, Reading. Between Pangbourne and Streatley, 7m NW of Reading on W of A329. Private garden designed and planted by Lady Iliffe with help of Lanning Roper. Mainly old roses but other interesting plants constantly being added by owner. TEA in NT house. *Adm to Garden only NT members 50p non members £1.50 Chd free. For NGS Sun June 29 (2-6)*

Bear Ash ⚘⚘ (Lord & Lady Remnant) Hare Hatch. 2m E of Wargrave. ½m N of A4 at Hare Hatch, between Reading and Maidenhead. 2 acres charming garden overlooking lake in parkland; silver and gold planting; shrub and specie roses. Wild flower meadow, small herb factory. TEAS. *Adm £2 Chd free. Sun June 15 (2-6)*

Beenham House &⚘ (Prof & Mrs Gerald Benney) Beenham. ½-way between Reading and Newbury, 1m N of A4; entrance off Webbs Lane. 21 acres of grounds and garden; old Lebanon cedars, oaks, hornbeams; recent plantings. Good views of park and Kennett Valley. Regency house (not open). Coach parties by appt. TEAS. *Adm £2 Chd free (Share to St Mary's Church, Beenham®). Sun May 18 (2-6)*

Blencathra &⚘ (Dr & Mrs F W Gifford) Finchampstead. Entrance at the NW end of Finchampstead Ridges on B3348. Disabled passengers may alight near the house. 11-acre garden which present owners started in 1964, laid out and maintained with minimum of help. In 'Good Gardens Guide' since 1993. Many varied mature trees; lawns; heathers; rhododendrons; azaleas; wide range of conifers; three small lakes and stream; bog areas and spring bulbs. Interesting throughout year. TEAS. *Adm £2 Chd free. Suns April 20, May 25 (2-6); also private visits welcome individuals or parties, please* **Tel 0118 9734563**

¶**Braywood House** ⚘ (Michael & Carolyn Pawson) Windsor Forest. 4 m SW of Windsor. B3022 past Legoland on R. Turn R at next roundabout. Turn R immed into Drift Rd. After 1½m Braywood House on R. Parking opp on L at New Lodge. Parking for disabled only at house. Very young 7-acre garden sharing a boundary with Windsor Forest. Planned, planted & maintained by Mrs Pawson starting in 1989. Small arboretum with specimen trees contrasting with ancient oaks. A Victorian Churchyard C1847 with interesting historical associations; Spring walk, shady walk, mulberry garden, pond garden, woodland walk, vegetable garden. Views of Windsor Castle. TEAS. *Adm 1.50 Chd free (Share to St Michael's Church, Bray®). Sun June 1 (2-6)*

Bussock Mayne ⚘⚘ (Mr & Mrs C Povey) Snelsmore Common. 3m N of Newbury on B4494. A variety of specimen trees, shrubs, fine rock and water garden. Lots of blossom and bulbs. Set in 5 acres. TEAS. *Adm £2 Chd free. Sun April 13 (2-6)*

Bussock Wood ⚘ (Mr & Mrs W A Palmer) Snelsmore Common. 3m N of Newbury. On B4494 Newbury-Wantage Rd. Bluebells, fine trees and views; sunken garden with lily pond. Early Briton Camp. TEAS in aid of St James the Less, Winterbourne. Plants for sale. *Adm £1 Chd 10p. Sun May 4 (2-5.30)*

Chieveley Manor &⚘⚘ (Mr & Mrs C J Spence) 5m N of Newbury. Take A34 N pass under M4, then L to Chieveley. After ½m L up Manor Lane. Large garden with fine views over stud farm. Walled garden containing borders, shrubs & rose garden. Listed house (not open). TEAS. *Adm £1 Chd free (Share to St St Mary's Church, Chieveley®). Sun June 22 (2-6)*

Combe Manor ⚘⚘ (Lady Mary Russell) Combe. Approx 10m from Newbury or from Andover. From M4 in Hungerford, turn L after passing under railway bridge; over cattle grid onto Hungerford Common; turn R 400yds later and follow signs to Inkpen; pass The Swan on L, bear R at junction and then almost immed L to Combe Gibbet and Combe. The Manor stands ½m from the village beside the church. 2 acres of lawns, borders, roses, shrubs and fruit trees. Walled garden with C17 gazebo, C11 church adjoining will be open. TEAS. *Combined adm with* **Withers Farm** *£2.50 Chd under 12 free. Sun June 29 (2-6)*

Donnington Grove Country Club (Shi-Tennoji Int Ltd) Donnington. Leave M4 at Junction 13; take A34 to Newbury. Leave A34 at 1st junction, turn R then L towards Donnington Castle for 2m. Cross 1st mini roundabout. At 2nd, turn R into Grove Rd. From Hungerford take the A4 Bath Rd, turn L at Oxford Rd B4494 and L into Grove Rd. Country Club 200yds on R. Buddhist Temple and water garden set within 25-acre walled English garden, being centrepiece of approx 80 acres of C18 country parkland. Lake, river and woodland walks. The temple garden contains fish ponds and wide selection of rhododendrons and azaleas. The remaining garden is laid out to herbaceous borders, shrubs and lawns with small mature yew maze. TEA. *Adm £2 Chd free (Share to Riding for the Disabled®). Sun June 22 (10.30-5)*

● **Englefield House** &⚘⚘ (Sir William and Lady Benyon) nr Theale. Entrance on A340. 7 acres of woodland garden with interesting variety of trees; shrubs; stream and water garden; formal terrace with fountain and borders. Commercial garden centre in village. Deer park. Part of garden suitable for wheelchairs. Home made TEAS Long Gallery NGS days only. *Adm £2 Chd free under 12 yrs (Share Motor Neurome Disease Society®). Open every Mon all yr and Tues, Weds, Thurs from April 1 to July 31 incl (10-dusk). For NGS Sat May 10 (2-6) (with mega plant sale). Private parties for House and Garden welcome, please* **Tel 01734 302221**

Eton College Gardens &⚘⚘ (Provost & Fellows) Stations: Windsor ¾m Eton ½m. Bus: Green Line 704 & 705 London-Windsor 1m. Luxmoore's Garden is an island garden created by a housemaster about 1880; reached by beautiful new bridge; views of college and river. Provost's and Fellows' Gardens adjoin the ancient buildings on N and E sides. Parking off B3022 Slough to Eton rd, signposted. TEAS in aid of Datchet PCC. *Combined adm £1 Chd 20p. Sat June 14 (2-6)*

Folly Farm &⚘ (The Hon Hugh & Mrs Astor) Sulhamstead, 7m SW of Reading. A4 between Reading/Newbury (2m W of M4 exit 12); take rd marked Sulhamstead at Mulligans Restaurant 1m after Theale roundabout; entrance 1m on right, through BROWN gate marked 'Folly Farm Gardens'. One of the few remaining gardens where the Lutyens architecture remains intact. Garden, laid out by Gertrude Jekyll, has been planted to owners' taste, bearing in mind Jekyll and Lutyens original design. Raised white garden, sunken rose garden; spring bulbs; herbaceous borders; ilex walk; avenues of limes, yew hedges, formal pools. House (not open). TEAS. *Adm £1.50 Chd free (Share to West Berkshire Marriage Guidance Trust®). Sun April 13, Mon May 26, Sun June 22 (2-6)*

Fox Hill &⚘ (Mrs Martin McLaren) Inkpen. Between Hungerford and Newbury, turn off A4 at sign saying Kintbury and Inkpen. Drive into Kintbury. Turn L by shop onto Inkpen Rd. After approx 1m, turn R at Xrds. After passing village signpost saying Inkpen, turn 1st L down bridle rd. Garden 2nd on L. Car park in field. 3-acre garden, blossom, bulbs, many interesting shrubs. New rose garden. Small formal garden and duck pond. TEAS. *Adm £1 Chd free. Sun June 15 (1-6)*

Foxgrove &⚘ (Miss Audrey Vockins) Enborne, 2½m SW of Newbury. From A343 turn R at 'The Gun' 2m from town centre. Bus: AV 126, 127, 128; alight Villiers Way PO 1m. Small family garden with adjoining nursery (Foxgrove Plants); interesting foliage plants, troughs, raised beds, spring bulbs, naturalised in orchard; double primroses, snowdrop species and varieties; peat bed. TEAS. *Adm £1.50 Chd free. Suns March 9, April 6, June 22 (2-6)*

Frogmore Gardens &⚘ (by gracious permission of Her Majesty The Queen) Windsor Castle; entrance via Park St gate into Long Walk (follow AA signs). Visitors are requested kindly to keep on the route to the garden and not stray into the Home Park. Station and bus stop; Windsor (20 mins walk from gardens); Green Line bus no 701, from London. Limited parking for cars only (free). 30 acres of landscaped gardens rich in history and beauty. Large lake, fine trees, lawns, flowers and flowering shrubs. The Royal Mausoleum, within the grounds, will also be open free of charge. Refreshment tent in car park on Long Walk (from where there is a 5 min walk to the gardens). **Coaches by appointment only** (apply to NGS, Hatchlands Park, East Clandon, Guildford, Surrey GU4 7RT enc. s.a.e. or **Tel 01483 211535** stating whether May 7 or 8; am or pm). *Adm £2 Chd free. Wed May 7, Thurs May 8 (10.30-7; last adm 6.30)*

The Harris Garden & Experimental Grounds &⚘⚜ (University of Reading, School of Plant Sciences) Whiteknights, Reading RG6 6AS. Off A327, Shinfield Rd, 1½m S of Reading Town Centre. Turn R just inside Pepper Lane entrance to University campus. 12-acre research and teaching garden extensively redeveloped since 1989.

Rose gardens; herbaceous borders, winter garden, herb garden etc. Flowering cherry circle, new in 1995. Jungle garden in 1996 and Gold garden planned for 1997. Extensive glasshouses. Many plants labelled. TEAS in aid of Friends of The Harris Garden. *Adm £1.50 Chd free. Sun April 27 (2-6)*

Holt End House see Hampshire

Hurst Gardens & On the A321 between Twyford and Wokingham. Both gardens are in the village of Hurst but quite a distance apart. They offer an interesting contrast in age, size and approach. TEAS at Hurst Lodge only. *Combined adm £2 Chd free (Share to Helen House Childrens Hospice®). Suns May 18, Sept 28 (2-5.30)*

Hurst Lodge ⚜ (Mr & Mrs Alan Peck) Large 5-acre old garden which has been cared for by members of the same family for over 75 yrs. It features lawns and mature trees, a recently created rockery, pond and bog garden, a formal parterre, a walled garden with herbaceous borders, a large kitchen garden as well as camellias, azaleas, rhododendrons, magnolias, flowering cherries, a variety of Japanese maples and bulbs

Reynolds Farm (Mr & Mrs Christopher Wells) Broad Common Lane. The owners freely admit to a lack of classical design, but like Topsy the garden just grew. Having been drowned in the winter of 94/95 and baked in the summer of 95 it is amazing there is anything to look at. However, 96 has been an improvement and planting has continued with many new improvements. At the moment, the moles are 40/15 up but by spring 97 hopefully they will have had a set back and many interesting plants and shrubs will be on view. But please be aware that it is a plantsman's garden and not a municipal display

Inkpen House ⚘⚜ (Mr & Mrs David Male) Lower Green, Inkpen. Between Hungerford and Newbury; turn off A4 at sign marked Kintbury and Inkpen. Drive into Kintbury. Turn L by shop onto Inkpen Rd. After approx 1m turn R at Xrds. After passing sign marked Inkpen take R fork signposted Lower Inkpen. After red telephone kiosk on R take 2nd turn on L marked C13 Ch. Car park in field on L. 4-acre garden laid out at beginning of C18 in the Versailles style with formal planting of avenues and bosquets. Pleached lime walk and walled kitchen garden. TEAS. *Adm £1.50 Chd free. Sun July 13 (2-6)*

Kirby House ⚘⚜ (Richard Astor Esq) Turn S off A4 to Kintbury; L at Xrds in Kintbury (by Corner Stores) towards Combe. 2m out of Kintbury, turn L immed beyond Crown & Garter PH, house and garden at bottom of hill. 6 acres in beautiful setting. Formal rose borders, replanted herbaceous border in kitchen garden, newly planted colour theme border between yew buttress hedges. C18 Queen Anne house (not open). TEAS at West Woodhay House. *Combined adm with **West Woodhay House** £2.50 Chd free (Share to St Swithins Church®). Suns April 6, June 22 (2-6)*

Little Bowden &⚜ (Geoffrey Verey Esq) 1½m W of Pangbourne on Pangbourne-Yattendon Rd. Large garden with fine views; woodland walk, azaleas, rhododendrons, bluebells. Heated swimming pool 50p extra. TEAS. *Adm £2 Chd free. Suns May 25, July 6 (2.30-6)*

¶**Little Harwood** ❀ (David & Margaret Harrold) Pinkneys Green. From Maidenhead take A308 towards Marlow. At Pinkneys Green turn R into Winter Hill Rd signposted to Winter Hill & Cookham Dean. Where rd forks (signposted Winter Hill L & Cookham Dean R) continue on main rd towards Cookham Dean, now Choke Lane. 500yds along Choke Lane you reach a Z bend & SLOW sign. Turn immed L through iron gates & up drive where parking will be indicated. 2 acres of mature formal & informal terraced gardens, incl water garden, rock garden, herbaceous border & herb bed. Fine views to the N & S. Large specimen trees and clipped yew & hawthorn hedges. 13 acres of bluebell woodland walk; extensive plant collection, incl bulbs, shrubs & herbaceous plants. TEAS. *Adm £1.50 Chd free (Share to Compassion in World Farming®). Sun April 20 (2-6)*

▲**Meadow House** ♿❀❀ (Mr & Mrs G A Jones) Ashford Hill is on the B3051 8m SE of Newbury. Take turning at SW end of village signposted Wolverton Common. Meadow House on R approx 300yds along lane. Approx 1¾-acre plantsman's garden. Pond with waterside planting; mixed shrub and herbaceous borders. Many unusual plants. *Adm £2 Chd free. Open for NGS Thurs May 22, June 5, July 10, July 24, Aug 21 (10-5). Private visits welcome by appt, please* **Tel 01734 816005**

North Ecchinswell House, nr Newbury see Hampshire

Ockwells Manor ♿❀❀ (Mr & Mrs B P Stein) Maidenhead. Exit 8/9 off M4. A404M towards Henley. 1st slip rd to L to Cox Green and White Waltham. R at 1st roundabout. L at 2nd roundabout. Follow rd to end and turn R. 3½ acres of formal garden around mediaeval Manor House. Listed grade 1 (not open); walled garden; new herb garden, rose garden, over 100 pots; clipped yews; small maze; lime avenue; swimming pool; peacocks, ornamental ducks and geese; farm animals; woodland walk. TEAS. *Adm £1.50 Chd free. Sun June 22 (2-6)*

Odney Club ♿❀ (John Lewis Partnership) Cookham. Car park in grounds. 120 acres; lawns, garden and meadows on R Thames; specimen trees. Cream TEAS River Room. *Adm £2 Chd free (Share to Sue Ryder Foundation Nettlebed®). Sun June 8 (2-6)*

The Old House, Silchester see Hampshire

Old Meadows, Silchester see Hampshire

■ **The Old Rectory, Burghfield** ♿❀❀ (Mr R R Merton) 5m SW of Reading. Turn S off A4 to Burghfield village; R after Hatch Gate Inn; entrance on R. Medium-sized garden; herbaceous and shrub borders; roses, hellebores, lilies, many rare and unusual plants collected by owner from Japan and China; old-fashioned cottage plants; autumn colour. Georgian house (not open). TEAS. *Adm £2 Chd free. Open 2nd and last Wed on month Feb to Oct incl (11-4). For NGS Wed April 30, July 30 (11-4)*

The Old Rectory, Farnborough ❀❀ (Mr & Mrs Michael Todhunter) 4m SE of Wantage. From B4494 Wantage-Newbury Rd, 4m from Wantage turn E at sign for Farnborough. Outstanding garden with unusual plants: fine view; old-fashioned roses, arboretum; collection of small

flowered clematis; herbaceous borders. Beautiful house (not open) built C1749. Near church with John Piper window in memory of John Betjeman who lived at The Old Rectory. Teas in village. *Adm £1.50 Chd free (Share to Farnborough PCC®). Suns April 27, May 18, June 29 (2-6). Private visits by written appt*

Old Rectory Cottage ❀ (Mr & Mrs A W A Baker) Tidmarsh, ½m S of Pangbourne, midway between Pangbourne and Tidmarsh on A340 turn E down narrow lane; L at T-junction. 2-acre cottage garden and wild garden with small lake bordered by R. Pang. Unusual plants, spring bulbs, roses climbing into old apple trees, ferns, hellebores and lilies. White doves and golden pheasants. Featured on TV and in many gardening books. *Adm £2 Chd free (Share to BBONT®). Suns June 8, July 6 (2-6)*

Padworth Common Gardens ❀❀ Rectory Rd, Padworth Common. ½-way between Reading and Newbury. 1½m S of A4 take Padworth Lane at The Courtyard Hotel. TEAS. *Combined adm £2 Chd free. Suns June 8, 29 (Bloomsbury only, adm £1.50), Aug 10 (2-6)*
    Bloomsbury (Mr & Mrs M J Oakley) 20-acre farm now grazing and gardens with plant nursery on gravel hilltop, begun from scratch 8 yrs ago. (Photo display illustrates.) Plantsmen-owners' reach exceeds grasp, but visitors' generous response encourages another attempt. Woodland beds in small orchard, roses in mixed borders, white garden. Lots of half-hardies and 'conservatory' plants. 'Teas' becoming famous. Interesting walk to C11 church with home-made lemonade
    Honeyhanger ♿ (Mrs Jenny Martin) Rectory Rd. 2-acres of traditional and woodland gardens containing many special and unusual trees, shrubs and perennials, acquired by obsessive plant collector. Courtyard with pots incl half hardies and palms: small collection of bonsai in Oriental-style garden. Tropical house, aviary, ornamental fountain pond, woodland ponds. TEAS in aid of Padworth Church

Peasemore Gardens 7m N of Newbury on A34 to M4 junction 13. N towards Oxford then immed L signed Chievely. Through Chievely and onto Peasemore approx 3½m or B4494 from Newbury 6m R signposted Peasemore. TEAS at The Old Rectory. *Combined adm £2 Chd free (Share to Invalids at Home®). Sun June 22 (2-6)*
    Hill Green House ♿ (Sir Brian McGrath) Pretty house (not open). Approx 2 acres; shrubs, roses, lily pond etc. Extensive lawns and fine views
    The Old Rectory, Peasemore ♿❀ (Mr & Mrs I D Cameron) Georgian house with fine trees in lovely setting. Shrub roses, peonies, rose garden, herbaceous border & new double mixed borders
    Paxmere House ♿❀ (The Marchioness of Lansdowne) Opp The Old Rectory. 4-acre cottage garden. Roses, shrubs, etc

Rooksnest ❀ (Dr & Mrs M D Sackler) Earls Court Farm, Lambourn Woodlands. Situated approx 3m from the A338 (Wantage) Rd along the B4000. Nearest village, Lambourn. Rooksnest signposted on the B400 in both directions, ie whether approaching from Lambourn or from the A338. Approx 10-acre exceptionally fine traditional English garden. Recently restored with help from Arabella Lennox-Boyd. Incl terraces; rose garden; lilies; herbaceous borders; herb garden; many specimen trees and fine shrubs. TEA. *Adm £1.50 Chd free. Wed June 25 (2-5)*

Scotlands &❀ (Mr Michael & The Hon Mrs Payne) In centre of triangle formed by A4130 (was A423) E of Henley-on-Thames, the A321 to Wargrave and the A4 at Knowl Hill - midway between Warren Row Village and Cockpole Green. 4 acres; clipped yews; shrub borders; grass paths through trees to woodland and pond-gardens with Repton design rustic summer house. Rocks with waterfall and new gazebo. Featured in Good Gardens Guide & several garden books. Teas at Summerfield House. *Combined adm with* **Summerfield House,** *Crazies Hill £3 Chd free. Sun June 29 (2-6). Private parties welcome, please* **Tel 01628 822648**

Silwood Park (Imperial College) Ascot. 1½m E of Ascot in the junction of A329 and the B383. Access from the B383 200 metres N of the Cannon Inn. 240 acres of parklands and natural habitats, surrounding fine C19 house by Waterhouse, architect of the Natural History Museum. Japanese garden under restoration; pinetum, young arboretum specialising in oaks and birches. Two nature walks (1m & 2m) through oak and beech woodland to lake. TEAS. *Adm £1.50 Chd free. Suns May 11, 18; Oct 12 (2-6). Parties by appt, please* **Tel 01344 23911**

Simms Farm House &❀❀ (The Rev His Hon. Christopher & Mrs Lea) Mortimer, 6m SW of Reading. At T-junction on edge of village, from Grazeley, turn R uphill; L by church into West End Rd; at next Xrd L down Drury Lane; R at T-junction. 1-acre garden with mixed shrub borders, small rockery; bog garden; formal pond; unusual plants. Lovely view. TEA. *Adm £1 Chd 50p. Sun, Mon May 4, 5 (2-6). Private visits welcome, please* **Tel 01734 332360**

Sonning Village Gardens ❀ 4m E of Reading in Sonning Lane off the A4 or 9m W of Maidenhead off the A4. TEAS. *Combined adm £2 Chd free. Sat April 12 (2-6)*
  The Dower House (Mrs J Middlemiss) Sculptured yews, a tulip tree, shrubs and bulbs
  ¶**Glendale** (Mr & Mrs D Smith) A charming small garden
  North Lodge (Mr & Mrs J Edmonds) 1 acre of informal garden and woodland around a Victorian Gothic Lodge
  ¶**Sonningdene** (Mr & Mrs R Vincent) A 2-acre garden with herbaceous border, unusual trees, flowering shrubs
  Thatched Cottage & (Dr & Mrs G Bailey) 4 acres shrub borders, lawns, specimen trees, drifts of spring flowers

Stanford Dingley Village Gardens &❀❀ Village on the Pang River, 5m from M4 junction 12. Take A4 then A340 & turn to Bradfield go through Bradfield College junction & take 1st L after bridge. Follow Back Lane into Standford Dingley N end & turn S (L) to church, pub, bridge & gardens. Gardens filmed for Granada 'Good Morning' in 1996 showing in Spring 1997 for NGS 70th Anniversary. Many footpaths, field parking at Bradfield Farm. At least three other village gardens. *Combined adm £2 Chd free. Sun July 13 (2-6) Private visits welcome, please* **Tel 01734 744113**

¶**Bradfield College** (Through main gate to W of junction). A small new garden laid out by Jane Furnly Whittingstall. Access to grounds and College Chapel
Bradfield Farm & (Mr & Mrs Newton) ½-acre wide variety of plants. Further 5-acres mixed broadleaf planting in 1990. *Private visits by appt* **Tel 01734 744113**
The Mill (Mrs P Stinton) Interesting and unusual wild garden with bog area, adjoining village green. Recently restored to former glory

Stone House &(Mr & Mrs Nigel Bingham) Brimpton. 6m E of Newbury. Turn S off A4 at junction by Coach & Horses, signed Brimpton & Aldermaston. ½m W of T-junction by War Memorial signed Newbury. Medium-sized garden in attractive park; naturalised bulbs; rhododendrons; water garden; extensive collection plants and shrubs, walled kitchen garden; picnic area. TEA. *Adm £1 Chd free (Share to St Peter's Church, Brimpton®). Suns May 18, June 15 (2-6)*

Summerfield House ❀ (Mr & Mrs R J S Palmer) Crazies Hill. Midway between Henley-on-Thames and Wargrave. 2m E of Henley on A423, take turn at top of hill signed Cockpole Green, then turn R at Green. Garden opp village hall. 7 acres, herbaceous and shrub borders, many recently planted rare trees, large working greenhouse. 1½-acre lake plus 20 acres parkland. House (not open) formerly Henley Town Hall, originally constructed in 1760 in centre of Henley and moved at end of C19. TEAS. *Combined adm with* **Scotlands** *£3 Chd free. Sun June 29 (2-6)*

Sunningdale Park ❀ (Civil Service College) Ascot. 1½m E of Ascot off A329 at Cannon Inn or take Broomhall Lane off A30 at Sunningdale. Over 20 acres of beautifully landscaped gardens designed by Capability Brown. Terrace garden and victorian rockery designed by Pulham incl cave and water features. Lake area with paved walks; extensive lawns with specimen trees and flower beds; impressive massed rhododendrons. Beautiful 1m woodland walk. Limited access for wheelchairs. Cream TEAS. *Adm £2 Chd free. Sun June 1 (2-5)*

■ **Swallowfield Park** &❀ (Country Houses Association) 5m S of Reading off B3349, entrance nr village hall. Level grounds of 25 acres which incl a large walled garden and herbaceous borders, rose beds, vegetable gardens, massed rhododendrons and many specimen trees. There are wide lawns and gravel paths, with a small lake and a wooded walk to the R Loddon. Visit dogs' graves. The distinguished house (open) was built in 1689 for Lord Clarendon. *Adm £2.50 Chd free (Share to Country Houses Association®). Weds, Thurs May 1 to Sept 30. Parties welcome, please* **Tel 01189 883815.** *Home-made TEAS. For NGS Easter Mon March 31 (2-5)*

Trunkwell Park &❀ (Trunkwell Project) Beech Hill. From Reading: M4 junction 11 follow Basingstoke sign approx. ¼m at roundabout turn L and follow Three Mile Cross-Spencers Wood. Centre of Spencers Wood look for Beech Hill Rd on R and follow into Beech Hill Village (centre) and follow signs. From Basingstoke follow A33 to

Wellington roundabout turn L following Beech Hill signs. At village turn R. Located in grounds of Trunkwell House Hotel. Parking and toilets. Conducted tours. This 3-acre site with large Victorian walled garden is run by the Charity Horticultural Therapy as a teaching and therapeutic centre where people with special needs are encouraged to participate in a wide range of horticultural activities designed to improve skills and to gain confidence. Located on Berkshire/Hants border in very attractive surroundings, Trunkwell caters to an increasing number of clients daily, so why not come and witness that disability is no handicap to rewarding and successful gardening. Part of garden dedicated to Wildlife Conservation. Plants for sale, bedding in June. TEAS. *Adm £1.50 Chd free (Share to Horticultural Therapy®). Suns June 1, Sept 7 (2-6)*

Waltham Place &෴ (Mr & Mrs N Oppenheimer) White Waltham. 3½m S of Maidenhead. Exit 8/9 on M4, the A423(M) or M40 exit 4 then A404 to A4 Maidenhead exit and follow signs to White Waltham. L at church, situated at top of hill. From the S B3024 to White Waltham. 20 acres of organic gardens with bluebell woodland and lake. Specimen trees incl splendid weeping beech and atlas cedar, herbaceous borders with planting immune to rabbits. Traditional walled garden with hot border, japanese, butterfly and iris gardens. Part of a self sufficient organic farm with kitchen garden. Dried Flowers, plants & home-made cream TEAS (May 25 & July 27 only). *Adm £2.50 Chd 50p (Share to Thames Valley Adventure Playground®). Suns May 25, July 27 (2-7). Weds during April to Sept (2-5)*

Welford Park &෴ (Mrs J L Puxley) 6m NW of Newbury on Lambourn Valley Rd. Entrance on Newbury/Lambourn Rd (fine gates with boot on top). Spacious grounds; spring flowers; walk by R. Lambourn. Queen Anne house (not open). TEAS. *Adm £2 Chd free (Share to Welford Church Council®). Sun April 6 (2-4.30)*

West Silchester Hall, nr Reading see Hampshire

West Woodhay House & (H Henderson Esq) 6m SW of Newbury. From Newbury take A343. At foot of hill turn R for East Woodhay and Ball Hill. 3½m turn L for West Woodhay. Go over Xrds in village, next fork R past Church. Gate on L. Parkland; large garden with bulbs, roses, shrubs, lake, woodland garden. Large walled kitchen garden, greenhouses. TEAS. *Combined adm £2.50 Chd 25p (Share to West Woodhay Church®) to include* **Kirby House**. *Suns April 6, June 22 (2-6)*

Whiteknights &෴෴ (Mr & Mrs P Bradly) Finchampstead. Midway along Finchampstead Ridges on B3348 between Finchampstead War Memorial and Crowthorne Station. 2½ acres, lawns, Japanese water garden, dwarf conifers, interesting plantings, fruit and vegetable garden. New Mediterranean garden. Tudor Life in Miniature Exhibition. Cream TEAS (Aug only) in aid of West Berkshire Hospital Charity Childrens Fund. *Adm £1.50 Chd 50p. Suns April 27, Aug 10 (2-5.30). Private visits and parties welcome, please* **Tel 01189 733274**

Withers Farmhouse &෴ (Mrs A L Hoare) Inkpen. Approx 3m from Hungerford. From M4 in Hungerford turn L after passing under railway bridge; over cattle grid onto Common turn R 400yds later and follow signs to Inkpen; pass Swan on L; turn R at junction by telephone kiosk and bear R, signed Ham and Shalbourne - ¼m house on L of turning L up hill to church. Car park in field. Cottage garden of 1 acre, borders, roses, shrubs. *Combined adm with* **Combe Manor** *£2.50 Chd free. Sun June 29 (2-6)*

Woolley Park &෴ (Mr & Mrs Philip Wroughton) 5m S of Wantage on A338 turn L at sign to Woolley. Large park, fine trees and views. Two linked walled gardens beautifully planted. Teas close to Old Rectory, Farnborough. *Adm £1. Sun June 29 (2-6)*

Buckinghamshire

Hon County Organiser:	Mrs Sue Wright, Brudenell House, Quainton, Aylesbury, Bucks HP22 4AW Tel 01296 655250
Assistant Hon County Organisers:	Mrs Angela Sanderson, Wellfield House, Cuddington, Aylesbury HP18 0BB (supplies) Tel 01844 291626
	Mrs Joy Try, Favershams Meadow, Mumfords Lane, Gerrards Cross, SL9 8TQ Tel 01753 882733
Hon County Treasurer:	Dr H Beric Wright

DATES OF OPENING

February 23 Sunday
  Great Barfield, High Wycombe
March 2 Sunday
  Campden Cottage, Chesham Bois
March 9 Sunday
  Springlea, Seymour Plain, Marlow
  Waddesdon Manor, nr Aylesbury

March 30 Sunday
  Turn End, Haddenham
April 6 Sunday
  Great Barfield, High Wycombe
  Springlea, Seymour Plain, Marlow
  Walmerdene, Buckingham
April 13 Sunday
  Campden Cottage, Chesham
  Bois ‡

The Old Vicarage, Padbury
  6 Oldfield Close, Little Chalfont ‡
April 20 Sunday
  Long Crendon Gardens nr Thame
  6 Oldfield Close, Little Chalfont
  Overstroud Cottage, Gt Missenden
April 27 Sunday
  Nether Winchendon House, nr
  Aylesbury

The White House, Denham Village
Whitewalls, Marlow

May 4 Sunday
The Manor House, Bledlow, nr
  Princes Risborough
Overstroud Cottage, Gt Missenden
Springlea, Seymour Plain, Marlow

May 5 Monday
Gracefield, Lacey Green
Turn End, Haddenham
Winslow Hall, nr Buckingham

May 11 Sunday
Ascott, nr Leighton Buzzard
Campden Cottage, Chesham Bois
Cliveden, Taplow
Oaklands, Main Street, Weston
  Turville
Peppers, Great Missenden
Quinton Gardens, nr Aylesbury

May 13 Tuesday
Stowe Landscape Gardens,
  Buckingham

May 18 Sunday
Chalfont St Giles Gardens ‡
Cublington Gardens
Faershams Meadow, Gerrards
  Cross ‡

May 25 Sunday
Sheredon, Longwick

May 26 Monday
The Manor Farm, Little Horwood,
  nr Winslow

May 28 Wednesday
Spindrift, Jordans, Beaconsfield

June 1 Sunday
The Edge, Chalfont St Giles
Springlea, Seymour Plain, Marlow

June 8 Sunday
Overstroud Cottage, Gt Missenden

June 11 Wednesday
Oaklands, Main Street, Weston
  Turville

June 15 Sunday
Campden Cottage, Chesham
  Bois ‡
Hillesden House, nr Buckingham
Pasture Farm, Longwick, nr
  Princes Risborough
Weir Lodge, Chesham ‡
Whitchurch Gardens

June 17 Tuesday
Pasture Farm, Longwick, nr
  Princes Risborough

June 18 Wednesday
Cublington Gardens
59 The Gables, Haddenham
Quinton Gardens, nr Aylesbury

June 22 Sunday
Askett Gardens, nr Princes
  Risborough
East & Botolph Claydon Gardens
Faershams Meadow, Gerrards
  Cross
Gipsy House, Great Missenden

The Manor House, Bledlow, nr
  Princes Risborough ‡
Sheredon, Longwick ‡
Tythrop Park, Kingsey, nr Thame

June 25 Wednesday
59 The Gables, Haddenham
The Manor Farm, Little Horwood,
  nr Winslow ‡
Old Manor Farm, Cublington ‡

June 28 Saturday
Bucksbridge House, Wendover

June 29 Sunday
Bucksbridge House, Wendover
Cheddington Gardens, nr
  Leighton Buzzard
Kingsbridge Farm, Steeple
  Claydon
Long Crendon Gardens, nr Thame
The Manor House, Hambleden, nr
  Henley-on-Thames

July 2 Wednesday
Kingsbridge Farm, Steeple
  Claydon
14 The Square, Brill

July 6 Sunday
Campden Cottage, Chesham Bois
Great Barfield, High Wycombe
Great Horwood Gardens
Overstroud Cottage, Gt Missenden
Springlea, Seymour Plain, Marlow
Watercroft, Penn
The White House, Denham Village

July 9 Wednesday
Dorneywood Garden, Burnham
14 The Square, Brill

July 13 Sunday
Marsworth Gardens

July 16 Wednesday
Dorneywood Garden, Burnham
14 The Square, Brill

July 20 Sunday
Hughenden Manor, High
  Wycombe
Nether Winchendon House, nr
  Aylesbury
Whitewalls, Marlow

July 23 Wednesday
Oaklands, Main Street, Weston
  Turville
Spindrift, Jordans, Beaconsfield
14 The Square, Brill

July 30 Wednesday
14 The Square, Brill

August 3 Sunday
Campden Cottage, Chesham Bois
Springlea, Seymour Plain, Marlow

August 6 Wednesday
14 The Square, Brill

August 9 Saturday
Dorneywood Garden, Burnham

August 13 Wednesday
14 The Square, Brill

August 16 Saturday
Dorneywood Garden, Burnham

August 17 Sunday
Ascott, nr Leighton Buzzard

August 20 Wednesday
14 The Square, Brill

August 24 Sunday
Peppers, Great Missenden
Quinton Gardens, nr Aylesbury

August 25 Monday
Spindrift, Jordans, Beaconsfield

August 27 Wednesday
14 The Square, Brill

September 7 Sunday
Campden Cottage, Chesham Bois
Overstroud Cottage, Gt Missenden
Springlea, Seymour Plain, Marlow
West Wycombe Park, West
  Wycombe

September 14 Sunday
Cliveden, Taplow
Great Barfield, High Wycombe
Turn End, Haddenham

September 21 Sunday
Whitewalls, Marlow

September 24 Wednesday
59 The Gables, Haddenham

September 28 Sunday
59 The Gables, Haddenham

October 5 Sunday
Campden Cottage, Chesham Bois

By Appointment only

Blossoms, nr Great Missenden
Hall Barn, Beaconsfield
Harewood, Chalfont St Giles
The Wheatsheaf Inn, Weedon
Wichert, Ford, nr Aylesbury

By Appointment - Parties only

*For telephone numbers and other
details see garden descriptions.
Private visits welcomed*

Campden Cottage, Chesham Bois
Faversham Meadow, Gerrards Cross
Gracefield, Lacey Green
Great Barfield, High Wycombe
Overstroud Cottage, Great
  Missenden
Sheredon, Longwick
Springlea, Seymour Plain, Marlow
Turn End, Haddenham
Whitewalls, Marlow

Regular Openings

Turn End, Haddenham

DESCRIPTIONS OF GARDENS

▲**Ascott** &⚘ (Sir Evelyn and Lady de Rothschild; The National Trust) Wing, 2m SW of Leighton Buzzard, 8m NE of Aylesbury via A418. Bus: 141 Aylesbury-Leighton Buzzard. A garden combining Victorian formality with early C20 natural style and recent plantings to lead it into the C21. Terraced lawns with specimen and ornamental trees; panoramic views to the Chilterns. Naturalised bulbs, mirror image herbaceous borders. Serpentine beech walk leading to recently restored lily pond. Impressive topiary incl box and yew sundial and Planet garden. *Adm (incl NT members) £4 Chd £2 Under 5 free. For NGS Suns May 11, Aug 17 (2-6). Last adm 5pm*

Askett Gardens &⚘⚘ 1m from Princes Risborough on A4010 to Aylesbury. At Black Horse roundabout, turn into Askett village. TEAS. Plant stall on green. *Combined adm £2 Chd free (Share to Florence Nightingale House®). Sun June 22 (2-6)*

   The Bell House (Mr & Mrs J R Hughes) **and The Bell House Barn** (Mrs Christine Ramsay) 1-acre cottage gardens with stream. Hardy perennials, shrubs and roses with backcloth of mature trees in parkland setting

   ¶**Meadowcroft Farmhouse** (Mr & Mrs N Murtagh) Walled garden with stream. Mixed borders with shrubs

   Old Rose Cottage (Mr & Mrs G A Davies) 1-acre garden with N facing walled border. Collection of hardy geraniums and old roses. Herb garden. Specimen trees. TEAS

   Three Ways Cottage (Dr & Mrs P N J Appleton) 1-acre 'surprise' garden tucked away, full of colour. Immaculate lawn, beautiful pools backing into rockeries. TEAS

Blossoms &⚘ (Dr & Mrs Frank Hytten) Cobblers Hill, 2½m NW of Great Missenden by Rignall Road (signed to Butlers Cross) to King's Lane (1½m) then to top of Cobblers Hill, R at yellow stone marker and in 50yds R at stone marked Blossoms. [Map ref SP874034]. 4-acre garden begun as hill-top fields in 1925, plus 1-acre beechwood. Lawns, trees, old apple orchard, small lake, water gardens, woodland, troughs, scree garden and several patios. Large areas of bluebells, wild daffodils, fritillaria and other spring bulbs. Flowering cherries and many interesting trees incl small collections of acer, eucalyptus and salix; foliage effects throughout the year. TEAS. *Adm £1.50. Private visits only, please* Tel 01494 863140

Bucksbridge House &⚘⚘ (Mr & Mrs J Nicholson) Heron Path, Wendover. ½m S of Wendover. Chapel Lane is 2nd turn on L off A413 towards Amersham. House is on L at bottom of lane. Georgian house with established 2-acre garden; large herbaceous border, unusual shrubs, roses, laburnum arches, an ornamental vegetable garden and 2 well stocked greenhouses. TEAS in aid of St Mary's Church. *Adm £1.50 Chd free. Sat, Sun June 28, 29 (2-6)*

Campden Cottage ⚘⚘ (Mrs P Liechti) 51 Clifton Rd, Chesham Bois, N of Amersham. From Amersham-on-the-Hill take A416; after 1m turn R (E) at Catholic Church. From Chesham take A416; and first turning L after beech woods. ½-acre derelict garden restored by owner since 1971; plantsman's garden of yr-round interest; fine collection of unusual and rare plants. Hellebores in March. Featured on 'Gardeners' World' and in the 'Good Gardens Guide 1996'. Please use car park signed on main rd. Teas Old Amersham. No push chairs. *Adm £1.50 Acc chd free. Suns March 2, April 13, May 11, June 15, July 6, Aug 3, Sept 7, Oct 5 (2-6). Also by appt for parties with TEAS. No coaches. Please* Tel 01494 726818

Chalfont St Giles Gardens ⚘⚘ Off A413. TEAS in aid of Iain Rennie Hospice. *Combined adm £3 for 3 gardens or £1.50 per garden Chd free. Sun May 18 (2-6)*

   Concordia (Mrs D E Cobb) 76 Deanway. Parking in Deanway. A small challenging garden on a difficult sloping site. Herbaceous and shrub borders; rock garden; fruit trees; collection of epiphytic orchids. *Private visits also welcome, please* Tel 01494 873671

   Halfpenny Furze (Mr & Mrs R Sadler) Mill Lane. From London take A413 signed Amersham. Mill Lane is ¼m past mini roundabouts at Chalfont St Giles. Limited parking in Mill Lane. 1-acre plantsman's garden on clay: part woodland (rhododendrons, azaleas, acers, magnolias, cercis, cercidiphyllum) part formal (catalpa, cornus, clerodendrum, unusual shrubs, roses and mixed borders). TEAS. *Private visits also welcome, please* Tel 01494 872509

   North Down (Mr & Mrs J Saunders) From Halfpenny Furze, short uphill walk L into Dodds Lane. Garden is 250yds on R. Limited parking in Dodds Lane. Approx ¾-acre garden with interest throughout yr (especially Autumn), some unusual plants, vistas. Mixed beds, shrubs, with rhododendrons, azaleas, acers; spring bulbs. Small bog garden; climbers; sempervivums; patio with water feature. *Private visits also welcome, please* Tel 01494 872928

Cheddington Gardens ⚘⚘ 11m E of Aylesbury; turn off B489 at Pitstone. 7m S of Leighton Buzzard; turn off B488 at Cheddington Station. Gardening books stall. TEAS on the green. *Combined adm £2 Chd free (Share to Methodist Chapel and St Giles Church, Cheddington®). Sun June 29 (2-6)*

   Chasea (Mr & Mrs A G Seabrook) Medium-sized garden; assorted tubs and baskets; 2 pools backing onto rockeries; conifers; perennials and bedding

   Cheddington Manor (Mr & Mrs H Hart) 3½-acres; small lake and moat in informal setting, roses, herbaceous border, and interesting mature trees

   34 Gooseacre (Mrs Barbara Smith) A well-designed partly paved small garden with magnificent views over the Chilterns. Delightful water feature, patio, mixed shrubs and climbers for all yr interest

   The Old Reading Room (Mrs M Connolley) ⅓-acre cottage garden; small fern collection; trees incl ginkgo biloba

   Rose Cottage (Mr & Mrs D G Jones) ¼-acre cottage garden planted for all yr interest with accent on colour; old roses; small scree area with unusual plants, conservatory; vegetable parterre and a camomile seat

   21 Station Road (Mr & Mrs P Jay) ½-acre informal garden with wildflower conservation area; herbaceous and shrub borders; herbs and kitchen garden

   Woodstock Cottage (Mr & Mrs D Bradford) 42 High Street. Delightful cottage garden with rear courtyard and patio

▲Cliveden ♿✂ (The National Trust) 2m N of Taplow. A number of separate gardens within extensive grounds, first laid out in the C18 incl water garden, rose garden; topiary; herbaceous borders; woodland walks and views of the Thames. Suitable for wheelchairs only in part. TEAS. *Adm grounds only £4.50 Parties £4 Chd £2.25. For NGS Suns May 11, Sept 14 (11-6)*

Cublington Gardens ♿✂❀ From Aylesbury take Buckingham Rd (A413). At Whitchurch (4m) turn R to Cublington. TEAS. *Combined adm £2.50 Chd free. Sun May 18, Wed June 18 (2-5)*

Old Manor Farm (Mr & Mrs N R Wilson) Reads Lane. Large garden recently redesigned; rose and 'yellow' gardens, herbaceous borders; swimming pool, knot garden; ha ha and walled vegetable garden. *Also open Wed June 25 Adm £2 Chd free (Share to Royal National Rose Society 2000 Appeal).* **Private visits by written appt**

The Old Rectory (Mr & Mrs J Naylor) 2-acre country garden with herbaceous border, rosebeds, shrubs and mature trees; vegetables; ponds, climbing plants

▲Dorneywood Garden ♿✂❀ (The National Trust) Dorneywood Rd, Burnham. From Burnham village take Dropmore Rd, and at end of 30mph limit take R fork into Dorneywood Rd. Dorneywood is 1m on R. From M40 junction 2, take A355 to Slough then 1st R to Burnham, 2m then 2nd L after Jolly Woodman signed Dorneywood Rd. Dorneywood is about 1m on L. 6-acre country house garden on several levels with herbaceous borders, rose garden, and cottage garden; greenhouse and kitchen garden which supply the house. Plants usually for sale. TEAS. *Adm £2.50 Chd under 15 free. Garden open* **by written appt only** *on Weds July 9, 16, Sats Aug 9, 16 (2-5.30). Apply to the Secretary, Dorneywood Trust, Dorneywood, Burnham, Bucks SL1 8PY*

East & Botolph Claydon Gardens ♿✂❀ 1 and 2m SW of Winslow. Follow signs to Claydons. Teas in village hall. *Combined adm £2 Chd free. Sun June 22 (2-6)*

Ashton (Mr & Mrs G Wylie) Botyl Rd, Botolph Claydon. ⅓-acre plot on clay with superb views on site of former barnyard. Mixed beds of shrubs and herbaceous plants

¶The Emerald (Mr & Mrs J P Elder) St Mary's Rd, E Claydon. ¾-acre garden undergoing some change. Mature trees; shrub and perennial beds. Rockery bank using sleepers and brickwork. Gravelled and paved area in front of house with pond and planting

1 Emerald Close (Mr & Mrs L B Woodhouse) E Claydon. Small garden with collection of deciduous and coniferous bonsai

Littleworth Farm (Mr & Mrs M O'Halloran) Verney Junction. Main features of the ½-acre are walled herbaceous and formal kitchen gardens

¶The Old Vicarage (Mr & Mrs N Turnbull) Church Way, E Claydon. ½-acre on clay, started 5 yrs ago and aiming at yr-round interest

Pond Cottage (Mr & Mrs B Kay) Botolph Claydon. ¼-acre garden framed by thatched C17 cottage and C19 barn

The Pump House (Mr & Mrs P M Piddington) St Mary's Rd, E Claydon. ¾-acre, trees, shrubs, borders, herbs, fishpond

The Edge ✂❀ (Mr & Mrs D Glen) London Rd, Chalfont St Giles. Garden is ¼m towards Chalfont St Peter from The Pheasant Xrds on A413 nr Kings Rd. Georgian cottage with landscaped garden of ¾ acre, created by owners. Partially enclosed with walls and yew hedges, interesting shrubs incl magnolias, wisterias, climbing and shrub roses. Small exhibition by Misbourne Art Society. TEAS. *Adm £1 Chd free. Sun June 1 (2-6)*

Favershams Meadow ♿✂❀ (Mr & Mrs H W Try) 1½m W of Gerrards Cross on A40. Turn N into Mumfords Lane opp lay-by with BT box. Garden ¼m on R. Beautiful 1½-acres with mixed herbaceous, knot, parterre and separate blue and white gardens. Wonderful roses on part C16 house and in David Austin rose garden. Very productive, brick paved vegetable area. All maintained to a high standard. Chosen to be visited by international garden groups. TEAS in aid of the Wexham Gastrointestinal Trust and the Open Door Community Church, Uxbridge. *Adm £1.50 Chd free. Suns May 18, June 22 (2-6). Group visits welcome, please* **Tel 01753 882733**

59 The Gables ♿❀ (Mrs A M Johnstone) Haddenham. Off A418 6m W of Aylesbury, 3m E of Thame. Travelling S along Churchway, The Gables is 2nd turning L after Miles' Garage. This small garden (60′ × 35′) is planted for all yr interest and incl Bonsai, ferns, a mini pond and many unusual plants. Teas available at nearby inn. *Adm £1 Chd under 10 free. Weds June 18, 25, Sept 24 (2-5); Sun Sept 28 (2-6)*

Gipsy House ✂ (Mrs F Dahl) Gt Missenden. A413 to Gt Missenden. From High St turn into Whitefield Lane, continue under railway bridge. Large Georgian house on R with family additions. York stone terrace, pleached lime walk to writing hut; shrubs, roses, herbs, small walled vegetable garden, orchard, gipsy caravan and maze for children. Limited access for wheelchairs. Teas locally. *Adm £1.50 Chd 50p (Share to Roald Dahl Foundation®). Sun June 22 (2-5)*

Gracefield ♿❀ (Mr & Mrs B Wicks) Lacey Green. Take A4010 High Wycombe to Aylesbury Rd. Turn R by Red Lion at Bradenham, up hill to Walters Ash; L at T-junction for Lacey Green. Brick and flint house on main rd beyond church facing Kiln Lane. 1½-acre mature garden; unusual plants, orchard, soft fruit, shrub borders, rockery; sink gardens. Two ponds. Ploughman's lunches, TEAS and plants in aid of local Macmillan Nurses Group. *Adm £1.50 Chd free. Bank Hol Mon May 5 (11.30-5). Parties welcome by written appt May to Sept*

Great Barfield ♿✂❀ (Richard Nutt Esq) Bradenham, A4010 4m NW of High Wycombe 4m S of Princes Risborough. At Red Lion turn into village and turn R. Park on green. Walk down No Through Road. 1½-acre garden, designed for views, lay out, contrast and colour, as background for unusual plants. Michael Gibson in 'The Rose Gardens of England' says that it is a plantsman's garden in the best possible sense of the term and not to be missed to see how all plants should be grown to the best advantage. Feb now not only famous for snowdrops and hellebores but willows and a variety of bulbs; drifts of crocus; April unique collections of pulmonarias and bergenias; also naturalised red trilliums. July old-fashioned and climbing roses, lilies including naturalised l. martagon. Sept considerable collection of colchicum, autumn colour and sorbus berries. NCCPG national collection of iris unguicularis (Feb); leucojum (spring & April). Sales of unusual plants. TEAS. *Adm £1.50 Chd under 16 free (Share to Berks, Bucks and Oxon Group of NCCPG®). Suns Feb 23 (2-5), April 6 (2-5.30), July 6 (2-6), Sept 14 (2-5). Private visits and parties welcome, please* **Tel 01494 563741.** *First opening in 1998 Sun Feb 22 (2-5), subject to unforeseen events*

¶**Great Horwood Gardens** ⌖✿❀ 2m N of Winslow, on B4033. Teas in Village Hall and at Stagsden in aid of Church Restoration Appeal. *Combined adm £2 Chd free. Sun July 6 (2-6)*

¶**2 Greenway** (Mrs Peggy Weare) Great Horwood. Small garden full of colour

¶**6 Nash Road** (Mrs Liz Whitehall) Great Horwood. Garden with many 'rooms'. Large perennial and herbaceous borders

¶**Old Vine Cottage** (Mr & Mrs M Alford) Singleborough. C15 thatched cottage with secluded back garden and terrace with pond and rockery

¶**Orchard Cottage** (Mr & Mrs Mitchell) Great Horwood. Small paved courtyard garden with pond, pots and raised beds

¶**Spring Farm** (Mr & Mrs A Heath) Great Horwood. Secluded 1-acre garden laid mainly to lawn with specimen trees

¶**Stagsden** (Mr & Mrs B A Nicholson) Singleborough. ¾-acre garden with trees, shrub and herbaceous beds, barn. Open views

Hall Barn (The Dowager Lady Burnham & The Hon Mr & Mrs Farncombe) Lodge gate 300yds S of Beaconsfield Church in town centre. One of the original gardens opening in 1927 under the National Gardens Scheme, still owned by the Burnham family. A unique landscaped garden of great historical interest, laid out in the 1680's. Vast 300-yr-old curving yew hedge. Extensive replanting in progress after severe gale damage. Formal lake. Long avenues through the Grove, each terminating in a temple, classical ornament or statue. Obelisk with fine carvings in memory of Edmund Waller's grandson who completed the garden about 1730. *Garden open* **by written appointment only**. *Applications to The Dowager Lady Burnham or The Hon Mr & Mrs Farncombe, Hall Barn, Beaconsfield, Buckinghamshire HP9 2SG*

Harewood ⌖✿ (Mr & Mrs John Heywood) Harewood Rd, Chalfont St Giles. Chalfont and Latimer Met Line tube station ¾m. From A404 Amersham-Rickmansworth Rd, at mini roundabout in Little Chalfont Village turn S down Cokes Lane. Harewood Rd is 200yds on L. 1 acre; fine yew and box hedges; established conifers; wide variety unusual shrubs and hardy plants; many climbers incl roses, clematis, wisterias; pool, sink gardens; planted for yr-round interest. Emphasis on foliage and colour contrast. Cream TEAS. *Adm £1.50 Chd free (Share to Arthritis & Rheumatism Council®). Private visits welcome, please* **Tel 01494 763553**

Hillesden House ⌖✿❀ (Mr & Mrs R M Faccenda) Hillesden, 3m S of Buckingham. 6 acres by superb Perpendicular Church 'Cathedral in the Fields'; lawns, shrubberies; rose, alpine and foliage gardens; interesting clipped hedges; conservatory; surrounded by park with red deer and highland cattle. Large lakes with ornamental duck and carp. Commanding views over countryside. TEAS in aid of Hillesden Church. *Adm £2 Chd under 12 free. Sun June 15 (2-6)*

▲**Hughenden Manor** ⌖✿❀ (The National Trust) 1½m N of High Wycombe on W side of Great Missenden Rd A4128; [Grid ref: SU866955 on OS sheet 165]. 5 acres with lawns, terraced garden, herbaceous border, formal annual bedding, orchard, walled garden and woodland walks. The Trust has undertaken restoration work in accordance with photographs taken at the time of Disraeli's death. Teas available and NT shop. *Adm House & Garden £3.80 Chd £1.90 Family £9.50. Adm garden only £1 Chd 50p. For NGS Sun July 20, Garden (12-5), House (1-5). Last adm 4.30*

¶**Kingsbridge Farm** ⌖❀ (Mr & Mrs T Aldous) Steeple Claydon. 3m S of Buckingham. Halfway between Padbury and Steeple Claydon. Xrds with sign to 'Kingsbridge Only'. 3-acre garden with ha ha, stream, mixed borders and gazebo. 1-acre shrubbery created 8-10 yrs ago from field. TEAS in aid of Crossroads and local church. *Adm £1.50 Chd free. Sun, Wed June 29, July 2 (2-6)*

Long Crendon Gardens ⌖❀ 2m N of Thame B4011 to Bicester. TEAS. *Combined adm £2.50 Chd free (Share to Long Crendon Charities®)*
Sun April 20 (2-6)
Bakers Close (Mr & Mrs R Salmon) 2 acres of sloping garden with interesting collection of trees and shrubs. Herbaceous border; spring fed pools and water garden
Manor House (Sir William & Lady Shelton) turn R by church; house through wrought iron gates. 6 acres; lawns sweep down to 2 ornamental lakes, each with small island; walk along lower lake with over 20 varieties of willow; fine views towards Chilterns. House (not open) 1675. TEAS
The Old Crown (Mr & Mrs R H Bradbury) 100yds past Chandos Inn. 1 acre on steep SW slope. Old-fashioned and other roses and climbers. Flowering shrubs, herbaceous plants. Spring bulbs, assorted colourful containers in summer; 2 vegetable patches
Springfield Cottage (Mrs Elizabeth Dorling) 6 Burts Lane. ¼-acre very secluded, mature garden. Foliage predominating all yr with primroses, bluebells, herbaceous borders, flowering shrubs and many clematis
Windacre (Mr & Mrs K Urch) 62 Chilton Rd, next to Primary School. 1-acre; roses, interesting shrubs, herbaceous plants, lenten roses, main features sunken lawns, conifers and trees. Cream TEAS
Sun June 29 (2-6)
¶**Braddens Yard** (Mr & Mrs P Simpson) ½-acre walled garden, largely created over past 7 yrs. Collection of roses, herbaceous and climbing plants. Arched walk with clematis, honeysuckle and roses; pond; small bothy garden. Cake stall

Croft House (Cdr & Mrs Peter Everett) Thame Rd. In Square. White wrought iron railings. ½-acre walled garden; plants and shrubs of botanical interest especially to flower arrangers. TEAS

8 Ketchmere Close (Mr & Mrs A Heley) Colourful split level garden with extensive views. Wide range of shrubs, conifers, rockery and water feature

Manor House (Sir William & Lady Shelton) Description with April opening

The Old Crown (Mr & Mrs R H Bradbury) Description with April opening

The Manor Farm &❀ (Mr & Mrs Peter Thorogood) Little Horwood 2m NE Winslow signposted off A413. 5m E Buckingham and 5m W Bletchley S off A421. Hilltop farmhouse garden on acid clay, laid out and replanted 1986. Wide range of alpines and plantsman's plants for yr-round interest in colour, form and foliage; good roses, pergola, 100′ hosta border, herbaceous, wild flower meadow, damp garden, lovely views. Cream TEAS in May. *Adm £2 Chd free (Share to Royal National Rose 2000 Appeal® - June only). Mon May 26, Wed June 25 (12-6). Private visits welcome May to Sept, please Tel 01296 714758*

The Manor House, Bledlow ❀ (The Lord & Lady Carrington) ½m off B4009 in middle of Bledlow village. Station: Princes Risborough, 2½m. Paved garden, parterres, shrub borders, old roses and walled kitchen garden. House (not open) C17 & C18. Water and species garden with paths, bridges and walkways, fed by 14 chalk springs. Also 2-acre garden with sculptures and landscaped planting. Partly suitable wheelchairs. TEA in aid of Bledlow Church May, TEAS June. *Adm £3 Chd free. Suns May 4, June 22 (2-6); also private visits welcome May to Sept by written application (2-4.30)*

The Manor House, Hambleden ❀ (Maria Carmela, Viscountess Hambleden) NE of Henley-on-Thames, 1m N of A4155. Conservatory; shrubs and old-fashioned rose garden. TEA at Hambleden Church. *Adm £1.50 Chd 20p. Sun June 29 (2-6)*

¶**Marsworth Gardens** ❀❀ 3m from Aston Clinton, on B489 Dunstable Rd. Small village with C12 church situated on the Grand Union Canal and adjacent to Tring Reservoirs and Bird Sanctuaries. Parking. TEAS in aid of Church Flower Festival Fund. *Combined adm £2.50 Chd free. Sun July 13 (2-6)*

¶**Gurneys Farm** (Mr D & Mrs M Nicholas) 3½-acres of great variety recently created around Rothschild stables. Courtyard. Formal rear garden extending into wild flower meadow. Ponds and vegetable garden

¶**Horseshoe Cottage** (Mr & Mrs J H White) Small garden adjacent to C17 cottage with colourful pots; separate garden across rd with variety of trees and herbaceous plants

¶**Kennels Cottage** (Mr & Mrs P G Stallabrass) A well established garden for all seasons featuring a profusion of shrubs, herbaceous plants and decorative fish pond. Approx ⅓-acre

¶**The Mill House** (Mr & Mrs D G Bellhouse) Informal country garden of interesting design. Many special features, incl stream

¶**15 Stepnells** (Mr & Mrs F Connor) Small garden full of colour and immaculately kept

¶**37 Vicarage Road** (Mr & Mrs W Layton) Rectangular plot of ¼-acre imaginatively converted into elaborate garden complete with small, gauge one, garden railway

▲**Nether Winchendon House** &❀❀ (Mr & Mrs R Spencer Bernard) Nether Winchendon, 5m SW of Aylesbury; 7m from Thame. Picturesque village, beautiful church. 5 acres; fine trees, variety of hedges; naturalised spring bulbs; shrubs; herbaceous borders. Tudor manor house (not open) home of Sir Francis Bernard, last British Governor of Massachusetts. TEA weather permitting. *Adm £1.50 Chd under 15 free. For NGS Suns April 27, July 20 (2-5.30). Private visits welcome by written application*

Oaklands &❀❀ (Mr & Mrs Roy Brunswick) 35 Main St, Weston Turville. 2m SE of Aylesbury. Turn off A413 or A41 onto B4544. Garden is opp Five Bells inn (car park). Secluded mature ½-acre offering something for everyone. A loft of tumbler pigeons overlooks the pond, which is a haven for visiting birds and animals. Flower borders, incl some of the 100 varieties of clematis in the garden, surround the bog garden and duck jacuzzi. The magic grotto and fairy paths are a delight to children and lead to the apiary where bee demonstrations can be seen, weather permitting. TEAS in aid of 14th Vale of Aylesbury Venture Sea Scouts. *Adm £1.20 Chd free. Sun May 11 (2-5.30) Weds June 11, July 23 (2-5)*

The Old Vicarage, Padbury &❀❀ (Mr & Mrs H Morley-Fletcher) Padbury 2m S of Buckingham on A413 follow signs in village. 2½ acres on 3 levels; flowering shrubs and trees. Display collection of hebes, geometric vegetable garden; pond and sunken garden; parterre; work in progress. TEAS in aid of League of Friends of Buckingham Hospital. *Adm £1.50 Chd free. Sun April 13 (2-5)*

6 Oldfield Close ❀❀ (Mr & Mrs Jolyon Lea) Little Chalfont. 3m E of Amersham. Take A404 E through Little Chalfont, turn 1st R after railway bridge, then R again into Oakington Ave. Plantsman's ⅙-acre garden of borders, peat beds, rock plants, troughs and small alpine house. Over 2,000 species and varieties of rare and unusual plants. Plant stall in aid of Bethany Village Leprosy Society, in India. Cream teas in village. *Adm £1 Chd free. Suns April 13, 20 (2-5). Private visits welcome all yr, please Tel 01494 762384*

Overstroud Cottage ❀❀ (Mr & Mrs J Brooke) The Dell, Frith Hill. Amersham 6m Aylesbury 10m. Turn E off A413 at Gt Missenden onto B485 Frith Hill to Chesham. White Gothic cottage set back in layby 100yds up hill on L. Parking on R at Parish Church. Cottage originally C16 hospital for Missenden Abbey. Artistic garden of yr-round interest; on 2 levels carved from chalk quarry. Ornamental herb/potager; lily pond; sinks; hellebores; bulbs; primulas, pulmonarias, hardy geraniums, species roses, clematis and traditional plants. Not suitable for children or push chairs. TEAS at Parish Church. *Adm £1.50 Chd 50p. Suns April 20, May 4, June 8, July 6, Sept 7 (2-6). Parties welcome by appt, please Tel 01494 862701*

General Information. For general information on the use of this book see Page 17.

Pasture Farm &⚘❀ (Mr & Mrs R Belgrove) Thame Rd. Longwick, nr Princes Risborough. 1m W of Longwick on A4129. 4m E of Thame. Farm entrance 50yds from layby. Garden at top of farm track. ½-acre plantswoman's garden. Herbaceous border, rockery and white garden. Integral nursery with perennials incl unusual white varieties. TEAS. *Adm £1 Chd free (Share to Aston Sandford Church Appeal®). Sun June 15, Tues June 17 (2-6). Also private visits welcome, please* Tel 01844 343651

Peppers &⚘❀ (Mr & Mrs J Ledger) 4 Sylvia Close, Gt Missenden. A413 Amersham to Aylesbury Rd. At Great Missenden by-pass turn at sign Great & Little Kingshill (Chiltern Hospital). After 400yds turn L, Nags Head Lane. After 300yds turn R under railway bridge. Sylvia Close 50yds on R. Approx 1 acre. Wide variety of plants, shrubs, trees, incl uncommon conifers, collection of acers, unusual containers, all year colour. TEAS. Donation from plant sale and teas to Workaid. *Adm £1 Chd free. Suns May 11, Aug 24 (10-5). Private visits welcome, please* Tel 01494 864419

Quainton Gardens 7m NW of Aylesbury. Nr Waddesdon turn N off A41
Suns May 11, Aug 24 (2-6) &❀ TEAS. *Combined adm £2 Chd free*
  Brudenell House (Dr & Mrs H Beric Wright) Opp Church. Productive 2½ acres with mature trees, new large pond, long herbaceous and mixed borders, fruit and vegetables. Dahlias in August. TEAS in aid of NGS May, Quainton Sports Club, Aug
  Capricorner (Mrs G Davis) Small garden planted for yr-round interest with many scented plants; semi-wild area with trees
  Thorngumbald (Mr & Mrs J Lydall) Lots of garden in a small space incl old-fashioned plants, organically grown; small pond, conservatory; attempts to encourage wild life
Wed June 18 (2-6) ❀ TEA *Combined adm £1 Chd free*
  Cross Farmhouse (Mr & Mrs E Viney) 1-acre garden flanking hill with old farm pond. Mixed shrub and herbaceous planting emphasising shape, texture and colour of foliage. Fine view and buildings. TEA
  Hatherways (Mr & Mrs D Moreton) A cottage garden with old-fashioned roses and clematis; intresting and unusual shrubs and herbaceous; bog garden. *Private visits welcome May and June, please* Tel 01296 655224

Sheredon &❀ (Mr & Mrs G Legg) Thame Rd, Longwick. Between Princes Risborough and Thame on A4129 next to Longwick PO. 1-acre award-winning plantsman's garden. Large fish pond with bog plants. Collection of old English and modern roses; arches leading past borders to organic vegetable plots with berries, fruits and grapes and on to orchard. Chickens and aviary. Latest mini pyramid greenhouse. Picnic and play area. Cream TEAS (June only) and plants in new meadow. *Adm £1 Chd 25p. Suns May 25, June 22 (11-5.30). Private and horticultural groups welcome, please* Tel 01844 346557

Spindrift (Norma Desmond) Jordans, nr Beaconsfield. On L of school, park in playground. Garden for all seasons on different levels full of surprises. Herbaceous border, variety of unusual hardy plants, fine hedges and specimen

trees; hosta and hardy geranium collection; dell with pond; acid-loving shrubs. Model terraced vegetable and fruit garden with greenhouses and vines. Inspired by Monet, nasturtium arches surrounded by iris, poppies and peonies. Partly suitable for wheelchairs. Member of Horticultural Research Assoc. TEAS in aid of Jordans Village School. *Adm £2 Chd under 12 20p. Weds May 28 (2-5), July 23 (6-9), Mon Aug 25 (2-5)*

Springlea &⚘❀ (Mr & Mrs M Dean) Seymour Plain. 1m from Marlow, 2½m from Lane End off B482. From Lane End pass Booker airfield on L then in 1m pass Seymour Court, L at pillar-box on grass triangle. ⅓-acre secluded garden backed by beechwoods. Flower arrangers' garden for colour, foliage and all yr interest. Spring bulbs, azaleas, rhododendrons, unusual trees, shrubs. Rockery, pond, waterfall, bog garden, hostas. Arched walkway with labelled clematis collection. 60' herbaceous border against high brick wall with many climbers, racing pigeon loft; plants labelled throughout garden. Great selection of unusual plants. TEAS by WI (not March or April). *Adm £1.50 Chd free. Suns March 9 (1-5), April 6, May 4, June 1, July 6, Aug 3, Sept 7 (2-6). Private visits and groups welcome March to October, please* Tel 01628 473366

14 The Square (Mrs Audrey Dyer) Brill. 7m N of Thame. Turn off B4011 (Thame to Bicester), or turn off A41 at Kingswood, both signed to Brill. Secret paved garden behind small terraced cottage packed with plants for yr-round interest, some in pots handbuilt by owner. *Adm £1 Chd free. Weds July and August (2-6). Small parties welcome, please* Tel 01844 237148

▲**Stowe Landscape Gardens** (The National Trust) 3m NW of Buckingham via Stowe Ave. Follow brown NT signs. One of the supreme creations of the Georgian era; the first, formal layout was adorned with many buildings by Vanbrugh, Kent and Gibbs; in the 1730s Kent designed the Elysian Fields in a more naturalistic style, one of the earliest examples of the reaction against formality leading to the evolution of the landscape garden; miraculously, this beautiful garden survives; its sheer scale must make it Britain's largest work of art. Conducted tours available. TEAS. *Adm £4.20 Chd free. For NGS Tues May 13 (10-5). Last adm 4pm*

■ **Turn End** ❀ (Mr & Mrs Peter Aldington) Townside, Haddenham. From A418 turn to Haddenham between Thame (3m) and Aylesbury (6m). Turn at Rising Sun into Townside. BR Hadd and Thame Parkway. This acre seems much more. Through archways and round corners are several secret gardens. A sweeping lawn bounded by herbaceous beds and a wooded glade with snowdrops, narcissi and bluebells. Old roses, iris and climbers abound. A sunny gravel garden has raised beds, alpine troughs and sempervivum pans. The house designed and built by the owners encloses a courtyard and fish pool. Featured in 'Country Life', 'The Garden', 'Practical Gardening'. TEAS by Stoke Mandeville Ambulance Station. *Adm £1.50 Chd 50p. Weds in June (10-4). For NGS Suns March 30, Sept 14, Bank Hol Mon May 5 (2-6). Groups by appt at other times, please* Tel 01844 291383/291817

Tythrop Park &® (Mr & Mrs Jonathan Marks) Kingsey. 2m E of Thame, via A4129; lodge gates just before Kingsey. 4 acres. Replanting of wilderness. Walled kitchen garden, fully productive. Muscat and black (Muscat) d'Hamburg vine propagated from vine at Hampton Court 150 yrs ago in vine house. Arboretum. Parterre to S of Carolean house (not open). TEAS. *Adm £1.50 Chd free (Share to NCH Action for Children®). Sun June 22 (2-6)*

▲Waddesdon Manor &✿® (The National Trust) On A41 between Aylesbury and Bicester. Follow signs to The Manor. The gardens were laid out between 1874 and 1898 under the direction of Baron Ferdinand de Rothschild. Innovative use of trees and shrubs coupled with the flamboyant displays of high Victorian bedding gives Waddesdon its own special identity. The restored Water Garden is open for the 2nd time with one of the finest displays of Pulham rockscape where naturalistic outcrops of rock, cascading water, still ponds and intricate planting provide overwhelming drama. Refreshments available all day in the Manor restaurant. *Adm Manor Gardens (10-5) £3 Chd £1.50, NT members free; Adm (incl NT members) Water and Rock garden (2-5) £1 Chd 50p (unsuitable for wheelchairs). For NGS Sun March 9 (2-5)*

Walmerdene &✿® (Mr & Mrs M T Hall) 20 London Rd Buckingham. From Town Centre take A413 (London Rd). At top of hill turn R. Park in Brookfield Lane. Cream House on corner. Medium town garden, unusual plants mostly labelled; species and hybrid hellebores; bulbs; herbaceous; euphorbias; climbing, shrub and species roses; clematis. Sink garden, rill garden, 2 ponds, white and yellow border; 2 greenhouses. TEA. *Adm £1 Acc chd free. Sun April 6 (2-5). Private visits welcome in June for roses, please* Tel 01280 817466

Watercroft ® (Mr & Mrs P Hunnings) Penn 3m N of Beaconsfield on B474, 600yds past Penn Church. Medium-sized garden on clay; white flowers, culinary herb garden planted 1993, rose walk, weeping ash; kitchen garden; pond, wild flower meadow. New Italian garden with yew hedges. Plants and honey for sale. C18 house, C19 brewhouse (not open). Cream TEAS in aid of Holy Trinity Church, Penn. *Adm £1.50 Chd 30p. Sun July 6 (2-6)*

Weir Lodge &✿® (Mr & Mrs Mungo Aldridge) Latimer Rd Chesham. 1m SE of Chesham. Turn L from A416 along Waterside at junction of Red Lion St and Amersham Rd. From A404 Rickmansworth-Amersham Rd turn R at signpost for Chenies and go for 4m. Parking at Weir House Mill (McMinns). ¾-acre garden on bank of R. Chess. Recovered from dereliction in 1983 by owners. Stream and ponds with planted banks. Gravelled terrace with sun loving plants. Assorted containers; mixed beds. Mature trees, incl fine beeches in adjoining paddock. TEAS in aid of Chesham Society. *Adm £1 Chd free. Sun June 15 (2-6)*

▲West Wycombe Park & (Sir Francis Dashwood; The National Trust). West Wycombe. 3m W of High Wycombe on A40. Bus: from High Wycombe and Victoria. Landscape garden; numerous C18 temples and follies incl Temple of the Winds, Temple of Venus, Temple of Music. Swan-shaped lake with flint bridges and cascade. *Adm (grounds only) £2.50 Chd £1.25 (incl NT members). For NGS Sun Sept 7 (2-5)*

The Wheatsheaf Inn &✿® (Mrs W Witzmann) Weedon. 2m N of Aylesbury off A413 Buckingham-Aylesbury rd. Black and White thatched Tudor Inn opp 15' brick wall of 'Lilies'. Parking in courtyard and village. 3½ acres of fields turned into formal, flower, wild and sunken gardens; with pond, roses, shrubs, perennials, spring bulbs, heather, conifers and 2 recent beds planted for deep shade. Yr-round interest and fine views. Front has a preservation 400-yr-old walnut. Recommended by Gardening 'Which' magazine and recently filmed for BBC 2's 'Gardening Britain'. *Adm £1 Chd free. Private visits welcome by appt only, please* Tel 01296 641581

Whitchurch Gardens &✿® 4m N of Aylesbury on A413. TEAS in aid of Church. *Combined adm £2 Chd free. Sun June 15 (2-6)*
  Mullions (Dr & Mrs L I Holmes-Smith) ⅓-acre picturesque cottage garden behind C17 cottage. 2 ponds and garden on 3 terraces
  The Old Cottage (Mr Roger Gwynne-Jones) ¾-acre cottage garden with herbaceous border, herb garden and wild area. Views over Vale of Aylesbury
  Quenington House (Mr & Mrs D F Ryder Richardson) 7 High Street. Paved terrace with rose beds leads to lawn. Lovely views; secret garden and new herb garden
  Yew Tree Cottage (Mr & Mrs B S Foulger) 3 tier garden with fish pond, patios and small wooded area, the whole offering sanctuary for wildlife. Panoramic views over the Vale of Aylesbury. Plants and ice cream in aid of Methodist Chapel

The White House & (Mr & Mrs P G Courtenay-Luck) Denham Village. Approx 3m NW of Uxbridge, off A40 between Uxbridge and Gerrards Cross. Denham Village is signposted from A40 or A412; nearest main line station Denham Green. Underground Uxbridge. Parking in village rd. The White House is opp the Norman church in centre of village. 17 acres comprising 6 acres formal garden and an 11-acre paddock. Old flagstone terrace surrounds 2 sides of C18/19 house, leading to new yorkstone terrace; garden being restored to former glory; rejuvenation of old yew hedges. R Misbourne meanders through lawns containing shrubberies, flower beds, orchard and developing rose garden. Large walled vegetable garden and restored Victorian greenhouses. Cream TEAS. *Adm £2 Acc chd free (Share to St Mary's Church, Denham Village®). Suns April 27, July 6 (2-5)*

Whitewalls &✿ (Mr W H Williams) Quarry Wood Rd, Marlow. From Marlow town centre cross over bridge. 1st L white garden wall, 3rd house on L. Thames-side garden approx ½-acre with spectacular view of weir. Large lily pond, interesting planting of trees, shrubs and herbaceous perennials. Many colourful containers. Sight of large conservatory with exotic plants. Teas available in

Marlow. *Adm £1.50 Chd free (Share to Crossroads, Wycombe District®). Suns April 27, July 20, Sept 21 (2-5.30). Private visits and parties welcome, please* **Tel 01628 482573**

Wichert ⅋ (Mr & Mrs C Siggers) Ford. 5m SW of Aylesbury, 5m ENE of Thame. From Aylesbury A418 towards Thame. L at Bugle Horn into Portway. After 3m L into Ford. Approx 100yds beyond Xrds L into drive immed after Old Bakehouse. Approx 1½ acres developed into separate gardens since 1990. Silver and Pearl, shade, fern, kitchen and pavement gardens; maze, pond and

wild garden with indigenous British trees. *Adm £1 Chd free. Private visits welcome, please* **Tel 01296 748431**

Winslow Hall ⅋ (Sir Edward & Lady Tomkins) Winslow. On A413 10m N of Aylesbury, 6m S of Buckingham. Free public car park. Winslow Hall (also open), built in 1700, designed by Christopher Wren, stands in a beautiful garden with distant perspectives, planted with many interesting trees and shrubs. In spring, blossom, daffodils and the contrasting foliage of trees combine to make the garden particularly attractive. TEAS. *Adm house & garden £3 garden only £1.50 Chd free. Bank Hol Mon May 5 (2-6)*

Cambridgeshire

Hon County Organisers:
South: Lady Nourse, Dullingham House, Dullingham, Newmarket CB8 9UP Tel 01638 508186
North: Mrs M Holmes, Manor House, Alwalton, Peterborough, PE7 3UU
Assistant Hon County Organisers:
South: John Drake Esq., Hardwicke House, High Ditch Road, Fen Ditton, Cambridge CB5 8TF Tel 01223 292246
Timothy Clark Esq, Netherhall Manor, Soham, Ely CB7 5AB Tel 01353 720269
Hon County Treasurers
(South Cambridgeshire): John Drake, Esq
(North Cambridgeshire): Malcolm Holmes, Esq

DATES OF OPENING

April 5 Saturday
  Moonrakers, Whittlesford
April 6 Sunday
  Barton Gardens, Cambridge
  Netherall Manor, Soham, Ely
April 13 Sunday
  Chippenham Park, nr Newmarket
April 18 Friday
  Wimpole Hall, Royston
April 20 Sunday
  Bainton House, Stamford
  Tadlow House, Tadlow
April 27 Sunday
  Downing College, Cambridge
May 4 Sunday
  Leckhampton, Cambridge
May 5 Monday
  Old Bishops Palace, Ely Gardens
  The Old Fire Engine House, Ely
    Gardens
May 11 Sunday
  Docwra's Manor, Shepreth
  Netherall Manor, Soham, Ely
May 18 Sunday
  Tadlow House, Tadlow
  Tetworth Hall, nr Sandy
May 24 Saturday
  Hyset, Horseheath
  Padlock Croft, West Wratting
  Scarlett's Farm, West Wratting

May 25 Sunday
  Fen Ditton Gardens
  Tetworth Hall, nr Sandy
May 26 Monday
  Hyset, Horseheath
  Padlock Croft, West Wratting
  Scarlett's Farm, West Wratting
June 1 Sunday
  Ramsey Gardens, nr Huntingdon
June 8 Sunday
  Ely Gardens
  Haslingfield Gardens
  Mill House, North End,
    Bassingbourn
  South Farm, Shingay-cum-
    Wendy
  Willingham Gardens
June 15 Sunday
  Alwalton Gardens
  Godmanchester Gardens ‡
  Greystones, Swaynes Lane,
    Comberton
  83 High Street, Harlton
  Madingley Hall, Cambridge
  The Manor, Hemingford Grey ‡
  Melbourn Bury, Royston
  Melbourn Lodge, Royston
  Sutton Gardens, nr Ely
  Swaffham Bulbeck Gardens
  Whittlesford Gardens
June 18 Wednesday
  Alwalton Gardens

June 19 Thursday
  Fen Ditton Gardens
June 22 Sunday
  Elm House, Elm, nr Wisbech ‡
  Grantchester Gardens,
    Grantchester
  Inglethorpe Manor, nr Wisbech ‡
  Mill House, North End,
    Bassingbourn
  Milton, Peterborough
  The Old Post Office, Brington
  South Farm, Shingay
  Sutton St Edmund Village
    Gardens see Lincs
June 28 Saturday
  Hyset, Horseheath
  Padlock Croft, West Wratting
  Scarlett's Farm, West Wratting
June 29 Sunday
  Chippenham Park, nr Newmarket
  Clare College, Cambridge
  Horningsea Gardens, Waterbeach
  Longthorpe Gardens,
    Peterborough ‡
  Mill House, North End,
    Bassingbourn
  Orton Longueville Gardens ‡
  South Farm, Shingay-cum-
    Wendy
  Waterbeach Gardens, nr
    Cambridge
  West Wratting Park, West Wratting

July 4 Friday
Elgood's Brewery Gardens,
Wisbech
July 5 Saturday
Conservatory Gallery, Cambridge
Elgood's Brewery Gardens, Wisbech
Elton Hall, Elton, Peterborough
Emmanual College & Fellows'
Gardens
July 6 Sunday
Conservatory Gallery, Cambridge
Elm House, Elm, nr Wisbech
Greystones, Swaynes Lane,
Comberton
King's College Fellow's Garden,
Cambridge
Mill House, North End, Bassingbourn
Newnham College, Cambridge
Nuns Manor, Frog End, Shepreth
South Farm, Shingay-cum-Wendy
Trinity College, Fellows' Garden,
Cambridge
July 11 Friday
Wimpole Hall, Royston

July 13 Sunday
Anglesey Abbey, Cambridge
Impington Gardens
21 Lode Road, Lode
Robinson College, Cambridge
Willingham Gardens
July 20 Sunday
Pampisford Gardens, nr
Cambridge
Whittlesford Gardens
Wytchwood, Great Stukeley
July 26 Saturday
Hyset, Horseheath
Padlock Croft, West Wratting
Scarlett's Farm, West Wratting
August 9 Saturday
Hyset, Horseheath
Padlock Croft, West Wratting
Scarlett's Farm, West Wratting
August 10 Sunday
Anglesey Abbey, Cambridge
Netherall Manor, Soham, Ely
August 16 Saturday
Unwins Seeds Trial Grounds,

Histon, Cambridge
August 17 Sunday
Netherall Manor, Soham, Ely
September 7 Sunday
Docwra's Manor, Shepreth
October 12 Sunday
Chippenham Park, nr Newmarket

Regular openings
For details see garden description

The Crossing House, Shepreth
Docwra's Manor, Shepreth

By appointment only
*For telephone numbers and other
details see garden descriptions.
Private visits welcomed*

Childerley Hall, Dry Drayton
Rose Cottage, Upton, Peterborough

DESCRIPTIONS OF GARDENS

Alwalton Gardens ⚘ Alwalton. 4m W of Peterborough, next to E of England showground. Parking at Village Hall. TEAS. *Combined adm £2 Chd free. Sun, Wed June 15, 18 (12-5)*
  The Forge ㊛ (Mr & Mrs M Watson) Cottage garden. Creative use of re-cycled materials
  Manor House ❀ (Mr & Mrs M Holmes) Walled garden divided into garden 'rooms' by yew and beech hedges. Borders and topiary surrounding C17 farmhouse (not open). Developing woodland walk with views over Nene valley
  Oak Cottage (Mr & Mrs J Wilson) Behind C17 cottage, a small, secluded garden planted for scent and atmosphere
  9 Oundle Road ㊛ (Mr & Mrs C Leary) Medium-sized garden, mixed borders, pond, shrubs, rose arbour

▲**Anglesey Abbey** ㊛⚘ (The National Trust) 6m NE of Cambridge. From A14 turn N on to B1102 through Stow-cum-Quy. 100 acres surrounding an Elizabethan manor created from the remains of a priory founded in reign of Henry I. Garden created during last 70 years; avenues of beautiful trees; groups of statuary; hedges enclosing small intimate gardens; daffodils and 4,400 white and blue hyacinths (April); magnificent herbaceous borders (June). Lunches & TEAS. *Adm house and garden £6.60; garden only £3.30 Chd £1.65. For NGS Suns July 13, Aug 10 (11-5.30). Last adm 4.30*

Bainton House ㊛ (Maj William & Hon Mrs Birkbeck) Stamford. B1443 Stamford-Helpston rd. Turn N at Bainton Church into Tallington rd. ¼m on L. 2 acres. Spring flowers, spinney and wild garden. TEAS in aid of St Mary's Church. *Adm £1.50 Chd 50p. Sun April 20 (2-5.30)*

Barton Gardens 3½m SW of Cambridge. Take A603, in village turn R for Comberton Rd. Delightful group of gardens of wide appeal and expertise. Gift and plant stalls. Teas in village hall. *Combined adm £2 Chd 50p (Share to GRBS®). Suns April 6 (2-5)*
  Farm Cottage ㊛⚘ (Dr R M Belbin) 18 High St. Cottage garden with water feature. Courtyard garden
  The Gables ㊛ (P L Harris Esq) 11 Comberton Rd. 2-acre old garden, mature trees, ha-ha, spring flowers
  14 Haslingfield Road ㊛ (J M Nairn Esq) Orchard, lawns, mixed domestic
  Kings Tythe ㊛ (Maj C H Thorne) Comberton Road. Small domestic garden; good through way to larger gardens of **Town's End** and **The Gables**
  31 New Road ㊛ (Dr D Macdonald) Cottage garden
  Orchard Cottage, 22 Haslingfield Road ㊛ (Mr J Blackhurst) Interesting mixed domestic. ½-acre garden with raised vegetable beds
  The Seven Houses ㊛⚘❀ (GRBS) Small bungalow estate on L of Comberton Rd. 1½-acre spring garden; bulbs naturalised in orchard. Colourful summer borders. Gift stall
  Town's End ㊛⚘ (B R Overton Esq) 15a Comberton Rd. 1-acre; lawns, trees, pond; extensive views. Raised vegetable beds

¶**Childerley Hall** ⚘ (Mr & Mrs John Jenkins) Dry Drayton 6m W of Cambridge on A428 opp. Caldecote turn. 4 acres of mixed planting with special emphasis on shrub roses. *Adm £2 Chd free. Private visits welcome May 16 to June 30, please Tel 01954 210271*

Chippenham Park ㊛❀ (Mr & Mrs Eustace Crawley) Chippenham 5m NE of Newmarket, 1m off A11. 3½m of walled park landscaped by Mr Eames and Mr Lapidge to incl "a beautiful sheet of water ¾m long, small stretches of canal existing from the old formal garden, 2 lines of lime trees on each side of the park said to represent the Anglo-Dutch and French fleets at the Battle of La Hogue in May 1692". Restored C18 dovecote. 7-acre garden with borders of unusual and rare shrubs, trees and perennials. Daffodils by the lake in spring, summer borders and dramatic autumn colour. Many specialist Plant Stalls. Refreshments. *Adm £2 Chd free (Share to St Margaret's Church, Chippenham®). Suns April 13, June 29, Oct 12 (11-5). Private visits welcome, please* **Tel 01638 720221**

Clare College, Fellows' Garden ✵ (Master & Fellows) Cambridge. The Master and Fellows are owners of the Fellows' Garden which is open; the Master's garden (nearby) is not open to the public. Approach from Queen's Rd or from city centre via Senate House Passage, Old Court and Clare Bridge. 2 acres; one of the most famous gardens on the Cambridge Backs. TEAS. *Adm £1.50 Chd under 13 free. Sun June 29 (2-6). Private visits welcome, please* **Tel 01223 333 222**

Conservatory Gallery ✵ (Mr & Mrs A W Barrell) 6 Hills Avenue, Cambridge. Southern outskirts of Cambridge. Hills Ave is off Hills Rd which is the main rd from railway station to Addenbrooke's Hospital. Once part of 5-acre Victorian estate, now ⅓-acre town garden with magnificent tree-line incl crataegus prunifolius. Rockery and borders incl jacobs ladder, carex pendula, macleaya cordata, 2 species ligularia, hepatica tribola etc and 2 small ponds provide interesting setting for exhibition of sculpture. TEA. *Adm £1 Chd over 10 50p. Sat, Sun July 5, 6 (10-5)*

The Crossing House ও (Mr & Mrs Douglas Fuller and Mr John Marlar) Meldreth Rd, Shepreth, 8m SW of Cambridge. ½m W of A10. King's Cross-Cambridge railway runs alongside garden. Small cottage garden with many old-fashioned plants grown in mixed beds in company with modern varieties; shrubs, bulbs, etc, many alpines in rock beds and alpine house. *Collecting box. Open daily, dawn till dusk. Parties by appt, please* **Tel 01763 261071**

■ **Docwra's Manor** ও✵❀ (Mrs John Raven) Shepreth, 8m SW of Cambridge. ½m W of A10. Cambridge-Royston bus stops at gate opposite the War Memorial in Shepreth. 2½-acres of choice plants in series of enclosed gardens. TEA May 11, Sept 7 only, in aid of Shepreth Church Funds. *Adm £2 Chd free. All year Wed, Fri (10-4), Suns April 6, May 4, June 1, July 6, Aug 3, Oct 5 (2-5). Proceeds for garden upkeep. Also private visits welcome, please* **Tel 01763 261473.** *For NGS Suns May 11, Sept 7 (2-6)*

Downing College ও✵ (The Master & Fellows of Downing College) Regent Street. Centre of Cambridge opp the University Arms Hotel to the S of Parkers's Piece. Approach from Regent St only. Fine example of 16-acre garden in a classical setting. Wilkins' Greek revival buildings frame wide lawns and paddock. Mature and newly planted rare trees. Unusual view of the Roman Catholic Church. Master's garden. Fellows' garden and walled rose garden with period roses. TEAS. *Adm £1.50 Chd 50p (Share to The Paget Gorman Society®). Sun April 27 (2-6)*

¶**Elgood's Brewery Gardens** ও❀ (Brewery Gardens Ltd) Wisbech. In the town of Wisbech on the N brink of the R Nene approx 1m W of the town centre. A garden of approx 4 acres established in the Georgian era is in the process of being restored around many of the original 200 yr-old specimen trees. Features incl lawns, a lake, rockery, rose and herb gardens and maze under construction.

TEAS. *Adm £1 Chd free (Share to Wisbech Rose Fair - Wisbech Parish Church Restoration Appeal©). Fri, Sat July 4, 5 (11-5)*

Elm House ও✵❀ (Mrs D Bullard) Elm, Wisbech. On B1101 approx 2m from Wisbech. Free parking. Walled garden approx 1½ acres with young arboretum, shrubs, perennials and annuals. (House not open). *Adm £1.50 Chd free. Suns June 22, July 6 (1-5)*

▲**Elton Hall** ✵ (Mr & Mrs William Proby) Elton, Peterborough. 8m W of Peterborough on the A605 travelling towards Oundle. Wonderful garden recreated over the last 12 yrs. Old rose garden, box walk, parterre and lawns. Sunken garden and shrub garden planted with the help of Rupert Golby. New Gothic organgery built during 1996 and herbaceous borders. TEAS. *Adm £2 Chd £1. For NGS Sat July 5 (2-6). Private visits also welcome for groups of over 10, please* **Tel 01832 280468**

Ely Gardens ও✵❀ 16m N of Cambridge on A10. (*Share to Old Palace Sue Ryder Home®)*
Mon May 5 (2-5) *Combined adm £1 Chd 50p*
  Old Bishops Palace 1½ acres with small lake and herbaceous border wonderfully restored by two expert volunteers to its original C17. Famous for its plane tree - oldest and largest in country
  The Old Fire Engine House Restaurant and Gallery (Mr & Mrs R Jarman) Delightful walled country garden with mixed herbaceous borders and wild flowers. Situated just W of the Cathedral. TEAS
Sun June 8 (2-5.30) *Combined adm £3 Chd 50p single garden [2]*
  Belmont House, 43 Prickwillow Rd ❀ (Mr & Mrs P J Stanning) Designed ½-acre garden with interesting and unusual plants
  Queen's Hall (Mr & Mrs R H Youdale) In Cathedral Close. Recently re-created in theme of "medieval garden" using as much as possible plants available pre 1600
  Rosewell House 60 Prickwillow Road (Mr & Mrs A Bullivant) Well stocked garden with emphasis on perennial planting and splendid view of cathedral and surrounding fenland
  The Bishops House To R of main Cathedral entrance. Walled garden, former cloisters of monastery. Mixed herbaceous, box hedge, rose and kitchen garden
  31 Egremont St (Mr & Mrs J N Friend-Smith) A10 Lynn Rd out of Ely. 2nd L. Approx 1 acre. Lovely views of cathedral, mixed borders, cottage garden. Ginkgo tree, tulip tree and many other fine trees
  Old Bishops Palace Description with May opening. TEAS
  48 St Mary's Street (Mr J Hardiment) Formal walled garden with a wide variety of beautiful and unusual plants

Emmanuel College Garden & Fellows' Garden ও✵ in centre of Cambridge. Car parks at Parker's Piece and Lion Yard, within 5 mins walk. One of the most beautiful gardens in Cambridge; buildings of C17 to C20 surrounding 3 large gardens with pools; also herb garden; herbaceous borders, fine trees inc Metasequoia glyptostroboides. On this date access allowed to Fellows' Garden with magnificent Oriental plane and more herbaceous borders. Teashops in Cambridge. *Adm £1 Chd free. Sat July 5 (2.30-5.30). Private visits welcome, please* **Tel 01223 334241**

Fen Ditton Gardens ⚘❀ 3½m NE of Cambridge. From A14 Cambridge-Newmarket rd turn N by Borough Cemetery into Ditton Lane; or follow Airport sign from bypass. Flower Festival in Parish Church. Teas in church hall. *Combined adm £2 Chd 50p (Share to Cambridgeshire Gardens Trust©). Sun May 25 (2-5.30) Thurs June 19 (6.30-8) (Rose smelling evening incl glass of wine)*

> **Hardwicke House** ⚘❀ (Mr J Drake) 2 acres designed to provide shelter for plants on exposed site; divided by variety of hedges; species roses; rare herbaceous plants; home of national collection of aquilegias, collection of plants grown in this country prior to 1650. Please park in road opposite. Large sale of plants in aid of NGS; rare aquilegias from National Collection; foliage plants and rare herbaceous plants. **Exceptional rare plant sale for NGS.** *Private visits welcome by appt, please* **Tel 01223 292246**

> **The Old Stables** (Mr & Mrs Zavros) Large informal garden; old trees, shrubs and roses; many interesting plants, herbs and shrubs have been introduced. House (not open) converted by owners in 1973 from C17 stables. *Private visits welcome by appt, please* **Tel 01223 292507**

> **The Rectory** (Revd & Mrs L Marsh) Small rectory garden. Largely mediterranean flowers, extensive range of climbers, Tromp l'oeil. Intensive organic vegetable garden which supplies household throughout the year, incl 34′ long decorative arch support for beans, sugar peas, spaghetti marrows, cucumbers and tomatoes

Godmanchester Gardens ⚘ TEAS in aid of Godmanchester Church Fund. *Combined adm £3 Chd free £2 per garden. Sun June 15 (1-5)*

> **Farm Hall** ❀ (Prof & Mrs Marcial Echenique) Godmanchester. Fronting West St (Offord/St Neots rd B1043) 2m S of Huntingdon, 15m NW of Cambridge (A14). Early C18 country house (not open) on edge of Godmanchester. Set in 24 acres of parkland with mature trees. Formal layout on its main axis: in front a rectangular pond or canal flanked by an avenue of poplars ending at the R Ouse; behind a long avenue of limes more than 200yrs old. Charming walled garden with formal box hedges, herbaceous borders and fruit trees. Rose garden with lily pond surrounded by yew hedge; statuary; wooded walk with wild flowers

> **Island Hall** ❀ (Mr Christopher & The Hon Mrs Vane Percy) Godmanchester. In centre of Godmanchester next to free car park, 1m S of Huntingdon (A1) 15m NW of Cambridge (A14). 3-acre grounds, of important mid C18 mansion (not open). Tranquil riverside setting with mature trees set in an area of Best Landscape. Chinese bridge over Saxon mill race to an embowered island with wild flowers. The garden has been restored over the last 12 yrs to a mid C18 formal design, with box hedging, clipped hornbeams, parterres, topiary and good vistas over borrowed landscape, punctuated with C18 wrought iron and stone urns

Grantchester Gardens ❀ 2m SW of Cambridge. A10 from S, L at Trumpington (Junction 11, M11). M11 from N, L at Junction 12. Madrigal Singers will be performing at the Old Vicarage. Craft Fair at Manor Farm, quality handmade goods; wooden toys; pottery; stained glass; glass blowing demonstration; honey and demonstrations of beekeeping. TEAS. *Combined adm £2.50 Chd 50p (Share to Grantchester Church®). Sun June 22 (2-6)*

> **Home Grove** ⚬ (Dr & Mrs C B Goodhart) 1-acre mature, orchard-type garden with shrub roses. Specimen trees and lawns and carefully planned kitchen garden

> **North End House** (Mr & Mrs A Frost) 1 acre, shrub and herbaceous borders; old-fashioned roses; water garden and rockery. Small conservatory

> **The Old Vicarage** ⚬❀ (Lord & Dr Archer) 2½ acres; house dating from C17; informal garden laid out in mid C19 with C20 conservatory; lawn with fountain; ancient mulberry tree; many other interesting trees; small lake with bridge; beyond garden is wilderness leading to river bank bordered by large old chestnut trees immortalised by Rupert Brooke, who lodged in the house 1910–1912

Greystones, Swaynes Lane ⚬⚘❀ (Dr & Mrs Lyndon Davies) Comberton. 5m W of Cambridge. From M11 take exit 12 and turn away from Cambridge on A603. Take first R B1046 through Barton to Comberton; follow signs from Xrds. Plantswoman's garden of approx ½ acre attractively planted with wide range of flowering plants framed by foliage and shrubs. Gravel bed and troughs. Water feature. TEAS. *Adm £1.50 Chd 50p (Share to Herbal Research®). Sun June 15 (2-5.30). Private visits welcome, please* **Tel 01223 264159**

Hardwicke House See Fen Ditton Gardens

¶**Haslingfield Gardens** ⚘ 5m SW of Cambridge along A10. Turn R in Harston. 1½m to car park. Teas and detailed directions at Haslingfield Village Hall. *Combined adm £1.50 Chd free. Sun June 8 (2-6)*

> ¶**15 Back Lane** (Mr & Mrs H Wiseman) On a slight slope, garden is a mixture of lawn, copse, paths, perennials and shrubs aiming at yr-round interest

> ¶**1 Chapel Hill** (Mr & Mrs A R King) A garden with mature trees, shrubs and roses. Also many herbaceous perennials, a large patio and 2 ponds

> ¶**Rowan Cottage** ⚬ (Mrs Doble) A small newly established patio garden with plants in pots

83 High Street, Harlton ⚬⚘❀ (Dr Ruth Chippindale) 7m SW of Cambridge. A603 (toward Sandy); after 6m turn L (S) for Harlton. ⅓-acre interesting design which includes many different features, colours and a wide diversity of plants. TEAS. *Adm £1 Chd free (Share to Harlton Church Restoration Fund®). Sun June 15 (2-6). Private visits welcome, please* **Tel 01223 262170**

Horningsea Gardens ⚘ Waterbeach. TEAS. *Combined adm £2 Chd 50p (Share to Village Church® & Arthur Rank Hospice®). Sun June 29 (2-5.30)*

> **15 Abbots Way** (Don & Sally Edwards) Horningsea. 4m NE of Cambridge from A1307 Cambridge Newmarket Rd. Turn N at borough cemetery to Horningsea or take B1047 N from A14. 1-acre developing plantswoman's garden on old flood bank of R Cam; overlooking river and water meadows. Spring and natural pond. Clematis and solomon's seal amongst fine collection of rare and unusual plants, shrubs and trees. Entrance to car park and garden signposted nr village hall; no access to garden via Abbots Way

The Lodge ❀ (N M Buchdal) Clayhithe Road, Horningsea. 5m NE of Cambridge to Newmarket Rd. 1½m of A14 on Clayhithe Rd (B1047), ¾m out of Horningsea on L towards R Cam. 3 acres of well landscaped garden framed by mature willows and old native trees; many shrubs and old roses; large water garden and many wide herbaceous borders. Unusual plants for sale from specialist nursery on site. Car park

32 Station Road &❀ (Mr & Mrs B D Reeve) Waterbeach. Visitors please park at station or village green. Small S facing enclosed garden. Large variety of interesting plants, conservatory with selection of vines

Hyset (Mr & Mrs S Agnew) Cardinals Green. A1307 between Linton and Haverhill. On opp side of bypass A1307 to Horseheath Village. Take turning signed 'The Camps'. Hyset is 2nd on R. ⅓-acre garden being developed by professional plantsman/horticulturist who is very able to give advice. Interesting range of herbaceous, shrubs, climbers and alpines. Attractive water feature displaying host of plants and insect life. Poly tunnel growing range of salads. *Combined adm £2 Chd 50p with* **Padlock Croft and Scarletts Farm**. *Mons, Sats May 24, 26, June 28, July 26, Aug 9 (2-6). Private visits welcome, please* **Tel 01223 892982**

¶**Impington Gardens** ✄ 2m N of Cambridge City. Very close to A14. Leave the A14 at the B1049 junction signposted to Histon and Cottenham (large roundabout). Take first L into Cambridge Rd, go round bollards, in 1 min Highfield Rd is 1st L, a cul-de-sac. Please park in the Cambridge Rd. TEA. *Combined adm £2 Chd 50p. Sun July 13 (2-6)*

¶**5 Highfield Road** (B Butcher) Medium-sized garden laid to lawn and general flower beds, conifers and roses

¶**13 Highfield Road** & (Mr & Mrs R J McCombie) Informal mixed planting borders, vegetables, fruit trees and lawn. ½-acre

¶**23 Highfield Road** ❀ (Mr & Mrs W Ward) Narrow winding paths through a well stocked medium-sized cottage garden; 2 small ponds

Inglethorpe Manor &✄❀ (Mr & Mrs Roger Hartley) Emneth, near Wisbech. 2m S of Wisbech on A1101. 200yds on L beyond 40mph derestriction sign. Entrance opp Ken Rowe's Garage. Large garden with interesting mature trees, lawns, mixed and herbaceous borders, shrub roses, rose walk and water garden. Victorian house (not open). TEAS in aid of NSPCC. *Adm £1.50 Chd free. Sun June 22 (2-6)*

King's College Fellows' Garden &✄ Cambridge. Fine example of a Victorian garden with rare specimen trees. Colour booklet available £1.50, free leaflet describing numbered trees. TEAS. *Adm £1 Chd free. Sun July 6 (2-6)*

Leckhampton &✄ (Corpus Christi College) 37 Grange Rd, Cambridge. Grange Rd is on W side of Cambridge and runs N to S between Madingley Rd (A1303) and A603; drive entrance opp Selwyn College. 10 acres; originally laid out by William Robinson as garden of Leckhampton House (built 1880); George Thomson building added 1964 (Civic Trust Award); formal lawns, rose garden, small herbaceous beds; extensive wild garden with bulbs, cowslips, prunus and fine specimen trees. TEAS. *Adm £1.50 Chd free. Sun May 4 (2-6)*

¶**21 Lode Road** ✄ (Richard P Ayres) Take B1102 from Stow cum Quy roundabout NE of Cambridge at junction with A14. Lode is 2m from roundabout. Small garden adjoining C15 thatched cottage designed by the owner (head gardener at Anglesey Abbey NT). Planted with bold groups of herbaceous plants complimenting a fine lawn and creating an element of mystery and delight. TEAS. *Adm £1 Chd 50p (Share to Lode Church®). Sun July 13 (11-5)*

¶**Longthorpe Gardens** ❀ 2m W of Peterborough city centre, off Thorpe Rd

¶**Quendale House** ❀ (Mr & Mrs P Clare) ⅓-acre garden with pond and rockery; formal paved area; lawns with a wide range of shrubs and perennials; vegetable garden with 4' beds and fruit. TEAS in aid of St Andrew's Church, Netherton. *Adm £1 Chd 50p. Sun June 29 (2-5.30)*

Thorpe Hall (See separate entry)

Madingley Hall Cambridge ✄ (University of Cambridge) 4m W, 1m from M11 Exit 13. C16 Hall set in 7½ acres of attractive grounds. Features incl landscaped walled garden with hazel walk, borders in individual colours and rose pergola. Meadow, topiary and mature trees. TEAS. *Adm £1.50 Chd free (Share to Madingley Church Restoration Fund®). Sun June 15 (2.30-5.30)*

The Manor ❀ (Mr & Mrs P S Boston) Hemingford Grey. 4m E of Huntingdon off A14. Entrance to garden by small gate off river towpath. No parking at house except disabled by arrangement with owners. Park in village. Garden designed and planted by author Lucy Boston, surrounds C12 manor house on which her Green Knowe Books were based. 4 acres with topiary; over 200 old roses and large herbaceous borders with mainly scented plants. Enclosed by river, moat and wilderness. TEAS in aid of WI. *Adm £1.50 Chd 50p. Open daily (except during June Concerts) 10% takings to NGS, rest to preservation of house. Sat June 15 (2-5.30)*

Melbourn Bury &✄❀ (Mr & Mrs Anthony Hopkinson) 2¼m N of Royston; 8m S of Cambridge; off the A10 on edge of village, Royston side. 5 acres; small ornamental lake and river with wildfowl; large herbaceous border; fine mature trees with wide lawns and rose garden. TEAS. *Combined adm with* **Melbourn Lodge** *£2 Chd free. Sun June 15 (2-6)*

Melbourn Lodge &✄❀ (J R M Keatley Esq) Melbourn 3m N of Royston, 8m S of Cambridge. House in middle of Melbourn village. 2-acre garden maintained on 9 hrs work per week in season. C19 grade II listed house (not open). TEAS at Melbourn Bury. *Combined adm with* **Melbourn Bury** *£2 Chd free. Sun June 15 (2-6)*

Mill House &✄❀ (Anthony & Valerie Jackson) Fen Road, North End. On the NW outskirts of Bassingbourn 1m from Church, on the rd to Shingay. Take North End at the war memorial in the centre of Bassingbourn which is just W of the A1198, 2m N of Royston (do not take Mill

Lane). Garden created out of open countryside by garden designer owners. Clever use of walls, pergolas, water and varying land levels provide a backdrop for many very fascinating plants notably viticella clematis, giving interest and colour throughout the year. Rare plants for sale. *Combined adm with* **South Farm** *£2.50 Chd free. Suns June 8, 22, 29, July 6 (2-5.30). Private visits welcome in July, please* **Tel 01763 243491**

Milton ✗❀ (The Hon Lady Hastings) Peterborough. Turn N off A47 just W of Peterborough into Bretton Way. Turn 1st L into Milton Park (just before entrance to Fitzwilliam Hospital). 35 acres. Pleasure grounds by Repton. Orangery by John Carr of York. Walled herbaceous and shrub garden recently replanted. Newly planted knot garden. TEA. *Adm £2 Chd free (Share to St John Ambulance, Cambridge®). Sun June 22 (2-6). Private visits welcome following written application*

Moonrakers (Mr & Mrs K Price) Whittlesford. Off A505 between Whittlesford Station and M11 junction 10, 7m S of Cambridge. 1½ acres wildlife garden, with old espalier apple trees in kitchen garden surrounded by hedgerows, trees, shrubs and pond. *Adm £1. Sat April 5 (2-6). Private visits welcome, please* **Tel 01223 832087**

Netherhall Manor ✗ (Timothy Clark) Soham. Enter Soham from Newmarket, Tanners Lane is 1st R 80yds after Webbs Store. Enter Soham from Ely, Tanners Lane is 2nd L after War Memorial. 1-acre walled garden incl courtyard featured on Geoffrey Smiths 'World of Flowers' and 'Gardeners' World'. April-Crown Imperials, Victorian hyacinths and old primroses. May-florists ranunculus (picotee and bizarre), and tulips (rose, bizarre, byblomen). Also during Aug formal beds of Victorian pelargoniums, calceolarias, lobelias and heliotropes an organic seasonal kitchen garden. *Adm £1 Chd 50p. Suns April 6, May 11, Aug 10, 17 (2-5). Private visits welcome, please* **Tel 01353 720269**

¶**Newnham College** ⅄✗❀ (The Principal & Fellows of Newnham College) Entrance from Newnham Walk. Can be approached from Sidgwick Ave or Newnham Walk, Cambridge. From City Centre via Queen's Rd or Silver St. Parking on street or College car parks. Unsuspected haven in busy city. 18 acres of Victorian and Edwardian gardens, encircled by Basil Champney's buildings. Herbaceous borders, nut walk, summer house and memorial mound. Sunken rose garden with lily pond and fountain; observatory. TEAS. *Adm £1.50 Chd free (Share to Newnham College Development Trust®). Sun July 6 (2-6)*

Nuns Manor ⅄✗❀ (Mr & Mrs J R L Brashaw) Frog End Shepreth. 8m SW of Cambridge 300yds from A10 Melbourn-Shepreth Xrds. C16 farmhouse surrounded by 2-acre garden; interesting plants, large pond, woodland walk, kitchen garden. Mixed and herbaceous borders. Unusual plants for sale. TEA in aid of Shepreth Church. *Adm £1.50 Chd free. Sun July 6 (2-5.30); also group visits by appt April to Sept, please* **Tel 01763 260313**

The Old Post Office ❀ (The Hon Mrs Sue Roe) Brington, nr Huntingdon. Turn off A14 onto B660 northbound approx 7m W of junction with A1. Then follow signs to Brington. In Brington go towards Old Weston. Last house

on L. A packed, newly planted cottage garden with plenty of unusual plants. Approx ¾-acre. The boundary between garden and countryside is deliberately left blurred to encourage wildlife. Pond, small wild flower meadow. TEA. *Adm £1. Sun June 22 (2-5). Private visits at weekends welcome April to Sept by appt, please* **Tel 01832 710223**

Orton Longueville Gardens ✗ Off 605 Oundle Rd, Peterborough, 2½m E of intersection with A1 after junction with Nene Parkway. Teas at 16 The Village. *Combined adm £2 Chd 50p. Sun June 29 (1-5)*

¶**Hemingdale** ⅄✗ (Mr & Mrs John Wilkinson) A cottage garden, incl material for flower arranging, vegetables and herbs

The Old School (Dr & Mrs Ross Gordon) The Village. A converted 1853 village school, playground, school master's house and garden. Formal layout with informal planting of ⅓-acre gardens in picturesque village

Lane End (Mr & Mrs R M Bulkeley) 9 St Botolph Lane. After junction with Nene Parkway, take 1st R into Royston Ave; park near junction with Sheringham Way take signed footway to St Botolph Lane. Please do not park in Lane. Designers secluded garden enclosed by tall hedges, contains a range of unusual small trees, shrubs and herbaceous plants. Emphasis on organic gardening and encouraging wildlife

¶**Pennard** ✗ Mr & Mrs G Stevenson) Garden developed during the past 3 yrs, featuring shrubs, herbaceous beds and arches supporting varieties of rose, honeysuckle and clematis

Padlock Croft ⅄✗❀ (Mr & Mrs P E Lewis) West Wratting. From dual carriageway on B1207 between Linton and Horseheath take turning N (Balsham W Wratting); Padlock Road is at entry to village. Plantsman's organic garden of ⅔-acre, home of the National Campanula Collection; mixed borders, troughs, alpine house etc incl rare plants; rock and scree gardens; potager with raised beds; bantams and ducks. *Combined adm £2 Chd 50p with* **Hyset** *and* **Scarletts Farm**. *Sats, Mon May 24, 26; June 28, July 26, Aug 9 (2-6). Private visits also welcome, weekdays, please* **Tel 01223 290383**

Pampisford Gardens ⅄✗❀ 8m S of Cambridge on A505. TEAS at the Old Vicarage in aid of RDA. *Combined adm £2 Chd free. Sun July 20 (2-5.30)*

Beech Corner (Dr & Mrs B E Bridgland) 22 Church Lane. Rear garden has been planned as a small paved courtyard leading round into mini woodland

The Dower House (Dr & Mrs O M Edwards) 7 High Street. Medieval house surrounded by well designed and interesting garden

Glebe Crescent A group of pensioners houses with very colourful small gardens

The Old Vicarage (Mr & Mrs Nixon) Next to Church in village. 2½-acres; mature trees; shrub and herbaceous borders with good ground cover plants; small Victorian style conservatory planted with rare species

Ramsey Gardens nr Huntingdon. TEAS at Ramsey Rural Museum in aid of Museum. *Combined adm £2 Chd free. Sun June 1 (2-6)*

The Elms (Mr & Mrs K C Shotbolt) From Ramsey travel through Ramsey Forty Foot, just before bridge over drain, turn R, 300yds on R. Large water garden beautifully landscaped with shrubs, water lilies, ferns and large tank koi carp. Mirror carp, golden orfe in lakes. 2-acres full of unusual plants; spring flowers. *Also by appt, please* **Tel 01487 812601**

77 Great Whyte ✗ (Mr & Mrs H Holden) Cottage garden 55' × 45' well stocked with trees, shrubs and flowers, many interesting plants and features. *At other times by appt, please* **Tel 01487 812529**

18 Little Whyte ✗ (Mr & Mrs R Sisman) Small garden with variety of plants, trees, shrubs and vegetable garden

Yesteryear Guest House &✿ (Mr & Mrs W Staley Grace) Small town garden full of colour with rockeries and pond, greenhouse. Patio full of hanging baskets and containers. Pergola, gazebo. TEAS in aid of Cancer Care Appeal Fund

Robinson College & (Warden & Fellows) Cambridge. Gardens surround the College and are enclosed by Grange Rd, Adams Rd, Sylvester Rd and Herschel Rd. ½m W of centre of Cambridge. Access is by Porters' Lodge on Grange Rd and Thorneycreek Gate, Herschel Rd (off Grange Rd). Ample parking in surrounding rds. From M11 turn E at Junction 12 (A603) and then turn L into Grange Rd after ½m. 8-acre garden created in 1979 by landscaping several Edwardian gardens. The site is bisected by the Bin Brook, with a pool at its centre. Wide range of trees, notably snake bark maples, parrotia persica, sequoiadendron giganteum pendulum and celtis australis. Numerous shrubs. Wide range of shade-tolerant species. TEA. *Adm £1.50 Chd free. Sun July 13 (2-6)*

Rose Cottage ✗ (Mr & Mrs K W Goodacre) Upton. 5m W of Peterborough. Turn off A47 between Castor and Wansford at roundabout signed Upton. Small cottage garden, pond, herbs, octagonal greenhouse. Many varieties cottage plants and shrubs giving colour. *Adm £1 Chd free. Private visits welcome June 1-30 incl, please* **Tel 01733 380450**

Scarlett's Farm &✗✿ (Mr & Mrs M Hicks) Padlock Rd, West Wratting. From dual carriageway on A1307 between Linton and Horseheath taking turning N (W Wratting 3½); Padlock Road is at entry to village. Scarlett's Farm at end of Padlock Road. ⅓-acre mixed country garden, planted for long season of interest; small nursery attached. TEAS. *Combined adm £2 Chd 50p with* **Hyset,** *and* **Padlock Croft.** *Sats, Mon May 24, 26; June 28, July 26, Aug 9 (2-6). Private visits welcome, April to Oct incl please* **Tel 01223 290812**

¶**South Farm** ✿✗ (Mr P Paxman) Shingay-cum-Wendy. 2m SW of A603 junction with A1198. 12m W of Cambridge. 20-yr-old garden on an exposed site with extensive windbreak planting, around a courtyard of listed farm buildings and house. Over 100 different vegetables grown. *Combined adm with* **Mill House** *£2.50 Chd free. Suns June 8, 22, 29, July 6 (2-5.30)*

Sutton Gardens &✗✿ 6m W of Ely on A142, turn L at roundabout into village. Teas at 5 Church Lane in aid of Sutton WI. *Single garden £1, Combined adm £2.50 Chd free. Sun June 15 (2-6)*

1 Church Lane &✿ (Miss B M & Miss B I Ambrose) Small garden near church with unusual trees, shrubs, climbers, perennials and alpines. Greenhouse, raised beds, troughs and tubs. Border for shade-loving plants. Teas at 5 Church Lane in aid of Sutton WI

¶**36 High Street** ✗✿ (Anna & Archie McOustra) Blending of small scale mixed plantings in an irregular ¼-acre cottage garden setting, unusual shrubs intermingling with herbaceous plants particularly hardy geraniums, incl ponds, rockery and vegetable garden

51 High Street (Mr A Wilkinson & Mr A Scott) A cottage style garden with terraced borders. Conservatory with vine, cacti and gloriosa lilies

7 Lawn Lane &✿ (Mr & Mrs R Kybird) Small garden with many hanging baskets and containers; fuchsias, penstemons, hardy geraniums, roses and clematis. Patio on two levels with pergola and water feature

8 Lawn Lane ✿ (Mr & Mrs H J Fortin) Small garden closely planted and colourful, with rockery, formal pool, terrace and curved lawns on 2 levels. Secluded vegetable corner. Meticulously cared for by plantaholic

Swaffham Bulbeck Gardens ✿ 8m E of Cambridge off B1102 past Anglesey Abbey. TEAS in aid of St Mary's Church, Swaffham Bulbeck. *Combined adm £1.50 Chd free. Sun June 15 (2-6)*

The Abbey &✿ (Dr & Mrs P Ridsdill-Smith) Abbey Lane, Commercial End. Large flower meadow surrounding historic house and small garden

Martin House (Prof & Mrs L Sealy) Station Rd. New garden with Chinese influence, designed and made by Mrs Sealy. Herb garden

The Merchant's House & (Mr & Mrs H L S Bevington) Commercial End. 1-acre walled gardens to C17 house originally used for canal-based merchanting business. Potager, orchard, old roses, mixed herbaceous borders

The Mill House &✿ (Prof J Hughes) Mill Lane. Large garden with woodland, herbaceous beds and shrubs

The Old Rectory &✿ (Mr & Mrs J Few-Mackay) High Street. English rectory garden

2 Station Road ✿ (Mr & Mrs C Rice) Small formal garden

Stocks Hill House ✿ (Mr & Mrs D Butler) Small informal garden with herbaceous borders

¶**Tadlow House** &✗ (Mr & Mrs Andrew Parkinson) Tadlow. 3½m W of Arrington on N side of B1042 adjacent to church. 2½-acre garden with spring flower walks and blossom incl tulips, narcissi, anemone blanda and fritillaria. New plantings incl recently designed water garden, parterre and circle gardens; interesting shrubs and trees. Adjacent C13 church with William Butterfield's C19 restoration. TEA in aid of Tadlow Church. *Adm £1.50 Chd free. Suns April 20, May 18 (2-5.30)*

Tetworth Hall ✿ (Lady Crossman) 4m NE of Sandy; 6m SE of St Neots off Everton-Waresley Rd. Large woodland and bog garden; rhododendrons; azaleas, unusual shrubs and plants; fine trees. Queen Anne house (not open). TEA. *Adm £1.50 Chd free (Share to Waresley Church®). Suns May 18, 25 (2- 6). Private visits welcome April 15 to June 15, please* **Tel 01767 650212**

Thorpe Hall &✗ (Sue Ryder Foundation) Thorpe Rd, Longthorpe, Peterborough. 1m W of Peterborough city centre. Thorpe Hall 1656 Grade I house in Grade II listed garden with original walls; gate piers; urns and niches. Historic planting restoration. Unique garden in course of replanting. Victorian stone parterre; iris collection; rose garden and 1650 herbaceous borders; fernery. TEA. *Adm Garden only £1 Chd 50p (Share to Sue Ryder Foundation®). Sun June 29 (2-5.30)*

Trinity College, Fellows' Garden &⚹ Queen's Road, Cambridge. Garden of 8 acres, originally laid out in the 1870s by W B Thomas; lawns with mixed borders, shrubs, specimen trees. Drifts of spring bulbs. *Adm £1 Chd free. Sun July 6 (2-6)*

Unwins Seeds Ltd ⚹ (Mr & Mrs David Unwin) Impington Lane, Histon. 3m N of Cambridge, 1m off A14 on B1049. Follow signs for Histon and Cottenham. At traffic lights nr Rose & Crown in centre of Histon, turn R into Impington Lane. Trial grounds of approx 6 acres where 4,500 varieties of annuals, biennials, perennials and vegetables from seed are assessed. Many new and experimental strains are on show. The company uses the trials to determine the garden worth of new varieties and monitor the trueness to type of strains it already lists. TEA. *Adm £1.50 Chd under 14 free. Sat Aug 16 (12-5)*

¶**Waterbeach Gardens** ⚹❀ nr Cambridge. 7m N of Cambridge on E of A10. TEA. *Combined adm £1 Chd free. Sun June 29 (2-5)*
    92 Bannold Road (Mr & Mrs R L Guy) Plantsman's tiny garden. Over 300 plants in 150 varieties. Clematis, shrubs, grasses
    ¶**Muffs Cottage** (Mr & Mrs J Runham) 7 Greenside. Small established garden behind lovely thatched cottage. Fish pond, roses, herbaceous and shrubs

West Wratting Park &⚹❀ (Mr & Mrs Henry d'Abo) 8m S of Newmarket. From A11, between Worsted Lodge and Six Mile Bottom, turn E to Balsham; then N along B1052 to West Wratting; Park is at E end of village. Georgian house (orangery shown), beautifully situated in rolling country, with fine trees; rose and herbaceous gardens. TEA. *Adm £1 Chd free. Sun June 29 (2-7)*

Whittlesford Gardens ❀ 7m S of Cambridge. 1m NE of Junction 10 of the M11 and A505. TEAS. Flowers in P church and UR church. *Combined adm £2 Chd 50p (Share to Whittlesford Memorial Hall Fund®). Suns June 15, July 20 (2-6)*
    The Guildhall ⚹ (Dr P & Dr M Spufford) North Road. *June 16 only*

Cherrytree Cottage ⚹ (Mr & Mrs J Eastwood)
58 Duxford Road & (Mr & Mrs J Bryant) *June 16 only*
13 West End ⚹ (Mr & Mrs C Taylor) *June 16 only*
15 West End (Mr & Mrs A Watson)
26 West End ⚹ (Mrs & Mrs W Wight) *July 14 only*
23 Newton Road & (Mr & Mrs F Winter) *July 14 only*
5 Parsonage Court &⚹ (Mrs L Button) Please park on main road
Brook Cottage ⚹ (R Marshall Esq & Ms J Lewis) Newton Road
11 Scotts Garden ⚹ (Mr & Mrs M Walker)
12 Swallow Croft (Miss J Woodley) *July 14 only*

Willingham Village Gardens ⚹❀ 10m N of Cambridge. TEAS. *Combined adm £2 Chd free. Sun June 8 (2-6)*
    66 Balland Field (Mr & Mrs G Burton)
    60a Church Street (Y Rutherford & M Spratling)
    15a High Street (Mr & Mrs A Robinson)
    40 Over Road (Mrs M & Mr R F Burdett)
    4 Rampton End (Mr & Mrs R Curtis)
Sun July 13 (2-6). TEAS. *Combined adm £2 Chd free*
    66 Balland Road (Mr & Mrs G Burton)
    43a Church Street (Mr & Mrs S Dyson)
    45a Church Street (Mr & Mrs K Ellwood)
    ¶**45 Church Street** (Drs P & J Leaver)

▲**Wimpole Hall** &⚹ (National Trust) Arrington. 5m N of Royston signed off A603 to Sandy 7m from Cambridge or off A1198. Part of 350-acre park. First sight of reinstatement of Victorian Parterres on N lawns. Rose garden and fine trees, marked walks in park. National Collection of Walnuts. Massed plantings of daffodil. Guided tours available 11.00, 15.00 hrs given by Head Gardener. Lunches & TEA. *Adm £2 Chd £1 (Guided Tours £3). For NGS Fris April 18, July 11 (10.30-5)*

Wytchwood ⚹❀ (Mr & Mrs David Cox) Gt Stukeley. 2m N of Huntingdon. Turn off B1043 into Owl End by Great Stukeley village hall. Parking at village hall and in Owl End. 1½ acre yr-round interest. Lawns, shrubs, perennial plants, trees, ponds, roses, area of wild plants and grasses. Vegetables and rare poultry. TEAS. *Adm £1.50 Chd 50p. Sun July 20 (1.30-5.30)*

> **By Appointment Gardens.** These owners do not have a fixed opening day usually because they cannot accommodate large numbers or have insufficient parking space.

Carmarthenshire

Ceredigion & Cardiganshire

See separate Welsh section beginning on page 323

Cheshire & Wirral

Hon County Organiser: Nicholas Payne Esq, The Mount, Whirley, Macclesfield, Cheshire SK11 9PB
Tel 01625 426730

Assistant Hon County Organisers: Mrs T R Hill, Salterswell House, Tarporley, Cheshire CW6 OED
Tel 01829 732804
Mrs N Whitbread, Lower Huxley Hall, Hargrave, Chester CH3 7RJ
Tel 01829 781481

DATES OF OPENING

April 13 Sunday
Orchard Villa, Alsager
Poulton Hall, Bebington
The Well House, Tilston
April 20 Sunday
85 Warmington Road, nr Crewe
April 27 Sunday
The Old Hall, Willaston
May 4 Sunday
Penn, Alderley Edge
Tushingham Hall, Whitchurch
Willaston Grange, S Wirral
May 5 Monday
Change Hey, Willaston, S Wirral
Penn, Alderley Edge
May 11 Sunday
Lyme Park, Disley
Orchard Villa, Alsager
Rode Hall, Scholar Green
Squirrel's Haunt, Heswall
May 16 Friday
Dunge Valley Park & Gardens
May 17 Saturday
Peover Hall, Knutsford
May 18 Sunday
Bolesworth Castle, Tattenhall
Hare Hill Gardens, Over Alderley
Haughton Hall, nr Bunbury
Peover Hall, Knutsford
May 21 Wednesday
Reaseheath, nr Nantwich
May 23 Friday
Dunge Valley Park & Gardens
May 25 Sunday
Dorfold Hall, Nantwich
Manley Knoll, Manley
Penn, Alderley Edge
Rosewood, Puddington
May 26 Monday
Ashton Hayes, Chester
Penn, Alderley Edge
May 28 Wednesday
35 Heyes Lane, Timperley
Reaseheath, nr Nantwich
June 1 Sunday
Henbury Hall, nr Macclesfield
35 Heyes Lane, Timperley
Little Moreton Hall, Congleton
Orchard Villa, Alsager
June 4 Wednesday
Reaseheath, nr Nantwich

June 7 Saturday
Arley Hall & Gardens, Northwich
June 8 Sunday
The Stray, Neston
85 Warmingham Road, nr Crewe
June 11 Wednesday
Reaseheath, nr Nantwich
June 13 Friday
Dunge Valley Park & Gardens
June 14 Saturday
The Old Parsonage, Arley Green
June 15 Sunday
Norton Priory, Runcorn
The Old Parsonage, Arley Green
Orchard Villa, Alsager
June 18 Wednesday
Reaseheath, nr Nantwich
June 20 Friday
Dunge Valley Park & Gardens
June 22 Sunday
The Old Hall, Willaston ‡
The Old Hough, Warmingham
Poulton Hall, Bebington ‡
The Well House, Tilston
June 23 Monday
Tatton Park, Knutsford
June 25 Wednesday
Reaseheath, nr Nantwich
June 29 Sunday
Burton Village Gardens ‡
Cherry Hill, Malpas
5 Pine Hey, Neston ‡
July 2 Wednesday
Reaseheath, nr Nantwich
July 6 Sunday
Greenhills Farm, Lower Whitley
73 Hill Top Avenue, Cheadle
    Hulme
Rhodewood House, Macclesfield
July 9 Wednesday
Reaseheath, nr Nantwich
July 12 Saturday
Bridgemere Nurseries Ltd
Jalna, Higher Hurdsfield
17 Poplar Grove, Sale
July 13 Sunday
Jalna, Higher Hurdsfield ‡
The Mount, Whirley ‡
17 Poplar Grove, Sale
Wood End Cottage, Whitegate
July 16 Wednesday
Cholmondeley Castle Gardens
62 Irwell Road, Warrington

Reaseheath, nr Nantwich
July 23 Wednesday
Reaseheath, nr Nantwich
July 30 Wednesday
Reaseheath, nr Nantwich
August 3 Sunday
Bluebell Cottage, Lodge Lane,
    Dutton
August 6 Wednesday
Capesthorne, Macclesfield
August 17 Sunday
Dunham Massey, Altrincham
August 25 Monday
Thornton Manor, Wirral
August 31 Sunday
Lyme Park, Disley

Regular openings
For details see garden description

Arley Hall & Gardens, Northwich
Dunge Valley Park & Gardens
Norton Priory, Runcorn
Peover Hall, Knutsford
Rode Hall, Scholar Green
Stonyford Cottage Nursery,
    Northwich

By appointment only
*For telephone numbers and other
details see garden descriptions.
Private visits welcomed*

37 Bakewell Road, Hazel Road
The Mount, Higher Kinnerton
2 Stanley Road, Heaton Moor
Willow Cottage, Prestbury

> **Regular Openers.** Open
> throughout the year. They are
> listed at the end of the Diary
> Section under 'Regular Openers'.
>
> **By Appointment Gardens.**
> These owners do not have a
> fixed opening day usually
> because they cannot
> accommodate large numbers or
> have insufficient parking space.

DESCRIPTIONS OF GARDENS

■ **Arley Hall & Gardens** &点❀ (The Viscount Ashbrook) 6m W of Knutsford. 5m from M6 junctions 19 & 20 & M56 junctions 9 & 10. 12 acres; gardens have belonged to 1 family over 500 yrs; great variety of style and design; outstanding twin herbaceous borders (one of earliest in England); unusual avenue of clipped Ilex trees, walled gardens; yew hedges; shrub roses; azaleas, rhododendrons; herb garden; scented garden; woodland garden and walk. Arley Hall and Private Chapel also open. Lunches and light refreshments (in C16 converted barn adjacent to earlier 'Cruck' barn). Gift shop. Specialist plant nursery. *Adm Gardens & Grounds only £3.30, OAP £2.90 Chd under 16 £1.70. Hall £2.30 Extra chd £1.25 (Share to Marie Curie Fund®). April to Sept (12-5) Tues to Sun & Bank Hols. Hall times vary during April & Sept. Hall closed Sats through season, last adm to gardens 4.30. For NGS Sat June 7 (11-4.30).* **Tel 01565 777353**

Ashton Hayes (Mrs J Searle) Chester. Midway between Tarvin and Kelsall on A54 Chester-Sandiway rd; take B5393 N to Ashton and Mouldsworth. Approach to Ashton Hayes can be seen halfway between Ashton and Mouldsworth. The ¾m drive is beside former lodge. About 12 acres, incl arboretum and ponds. Predominantly a valley garden of mature trees and flowering shrubs. Great variety of azaleas and rhododendrons; notable embothrium. TEAS. *Adm £1.50 OAPs £1 Chd 50p (Share to Church of St John the Evangelist, Ashton Hayes®). Mon May 26 (2-6). Private visits welcome, please* **Tel 01829 751209**

37 Bakewell Road ❀ (Mr & Mrs H Williams) Hazel Grove. From Manchester on A6 following signs to Buxton, bear R at Rising Sun Public House, Hazel Grove. Taking the Macclesfield Rd (A523) take 1st R (Haddon Rd) then 1st L into Bakewell Rd. Small suburban garden 17yds × 6½yds heavily planted with azaleas, rhododendrons (several rare and unusual varieties), hydrangeas; pool and waterfall. Excellent example of how much can be planted in a small area. TEA. *Adm £1.50 Chd free. April 13 to June 30. Private visits welcome for parties of 6 and under, please contact Mrs Williams* **Tel 01625 260592**

Bluebell Cottage &点❀ (R L & D Casey) Lodge Lane, Dutton. From M56 (junction 10) take A49 Whitchurch Rd for 3m, turn R on A533 towards Runcorn at traffic lights. Lodge Lane is the 1st turning L approx 1.5m. 1½-acre garden with ave of young trees leading to canal. The cottage garden has been developed into a series of rooms. Large lawn areas with herbaceous borders filled with wide selection of plants. Additional beds with Mediterranean theme and ornamental grasses. Adjacent is a 3-acre wild flower meadow, bluebell woodland and nursery. TEAS in aid of Cheshire Wildlife Trust. *Adm £2 Chd 50p. Sun Aug 3 (1-5.30). Private visits welcome, please* **Tel 01928 713718**

Bolesworth Castle &❀ (Mr & Mrs A G Barbour) Tattenhall. Enter by lodge on A41 8m S of Chester or 1m N of Broxton roundabout. Landscape with rhododendrons, shrubs and borders. Woodland walk replanted 1993/4. TEAS. *Adm £2 Chd free (Share to Harthill & Burwardsley Churches®). Sun May 18 (2-5.30)*

▲**Bridgemere Garden World** &点❀ On A51 7m S of Nantwich, 1m N of Woore. Follow brown tourist signs from Nantwich. The Garden Kingdom over 22 enjoyable and peaceful gardens showing many different styles of plant grouping. It includes the recreated Bridgemere Garden World prize winning exhibition gardens from Garden Festivals, Chelsea Flower Show Gold Medal gardens and the garden where the Gardeners' Diary television programme is filmed. Coffee shop and restaurant on site. *Adm £1.50 OAPs and Chd over 8yrs £1. For NGS Sat July 12 (10-6)*

Burton Village Gardens 点❀ 9m NW of Chester. Turn off A540 at Willaston-Burton Xrds (traffic lights) and follow rd for 1m to Burton. Free parking. Teas at Village Hall in aid of St John's Hospice. *Combined adm £2 Chd free. Sun June 29 (2-6)*

> **Bank Cottage** (Mr & Mrs J R Beecroft) Small, very colourful, mixed cottage garden with old roses backing on to cricket ground

> **Rake House** (Mr & Mrs R I Cowan) Enclosed sandstone courtyard, with cobbles and York stone, with pond; and old orchard

> **Briarfield** ❀ (Mr & Mrs P Carter) About an acre of rare trees and shrubs together with fruit and vegetable garden in woodland setting. Short woodland trail to

> **Lynwood** ❀ (Mr & Mrs P M Wright) On the fringe of the village on the Neston Road. ½-acre garden with shrub borders; rockery, pond with waterfall, pergola, arbour with climbers, heathers and alpines

▲**Capesthorne** 点 (Mr & Mrs W A Bromley-Davenport) 5m W of Macclesfield. 7m S of Wilmslow on A34. Varied garden; daffodil lawn; azaleas, rhododendrons; herbaceous border, arboretum and lake. Georgian chapel and memorial garden. TEAS and light lunches. Free car park. *Adm garden £2.25 OAPs £2 Chd £1. For NGS Wed Aug 6 (12-6).* **Tel 01625 861221**

¶**Change Hey** &点❀ (Mr & Mrs Keith Butcher) Willaston. A540 to W Kirby until opp new Elf garage. Turn at t-lights down B5151 to centre of Willaston. At village green turn R in direction of Hooton. Change Lane is ½m down Hooton Rd on RH-side opp garage and horseshoe store shop. Change Hey is down unadopted lane, approx 250yds on L. 2-acre garden with mature trees, developing woodland area underplanted with rhododendron and azaleas. TEAS in aid of Amnesty International. *Adm £1.50 Chd 50p. Mon May 5 (2-5)*

Cherry Hill &❀ (Mr & Mrs Miles Clarke) Malpas. 2m W of Malpas signed from B5069 to Chorlton. Massed bulbs in spring; walks through pine woods and rhododendrons to trout lake; walled garden, herbaceous borders, shrub roses. Ornamental vegetable garden. TEAS in attractive house overlooking Welsh mountains. Cricket ground. *Adm £2 Chd 50p. Sun June 29 (2-5.30)*

▲**Cholmondeley Castle Gardens** &❀ (The Marchioness of Cholmondeley) Malpas. Situated off A41 Chester/Whitchurch rd and A49 Whitchurch/Tarporley rd. Romantically landscaped gardens full of variety. Azaleas, rhododendrons, flowering shrubs; rare trees; herbaceous borders and water garden. Lakeside picnic area; rare breeds of farm animals, incl llamas; gift shop. Ancient private Chapel in the park. Tearoom offering light lunches etc. TEAS. *Adm gardens only £2.50 OAPs £2 Chd 75p. Reduced rate for coach parties over 25. For NGS Wed July 16 (12-5.30). The gardens are regularly open to the public.* Tel 01829 720383 or 720203

Dorfold Hall 米舞 (Mr & Mrs Richard Roundell) Nantwich. 1m W of Nantwich on A534 between Nantwich and Acton. 18-acre garden surrounding C17 house with formal approach; lawns and recently planted herbaceous borders; spectacular spring woodland garden with rhododendrons, azaleas, magnolias and bulbs. TEAS in aid of Acton Parish Church. *Adm £2 Chd 75p. Sun May 25 (2-5.30)*

■ **Dunge Valley Park & Gardens** 米舞 (Mr & Mrs David Ketley) Kettleshulme. Take B5470 rd from Macclesfield. Kettleshulme is 8m from Macclesfield. Turn R in village signed Dunge Valley Gardens and Goyt Valley and in ½m at Xrds, turn R down lane. Surrounded by romantic hills and set in 5 acres, at 1000ft, this is the highest garden in Cheshire; mature trees, woodland, streams, bog gardens, herbaceous borders, species rhododendrons, magnolias, acers and meconopsis plus roses. Yr-round interest an oasis in the Pennine foothills. TEAS. *Adm £3. Sats, Suns, Bank Hols £2.50 Mons to Fri Chd 50p. Open daily March 28 to Aug 31 (10.30-6). For NGS Fri May 16, 23, June 13, 20 (7pm until sunset).* Tel 01663 733787

▲**Dunham Massey** 点米舞 (The National Trust) Altrincham. 3m SW of Altrincham off A56. Well signed. Garden over 20 acres, on ancient site with moat lake, mount and orangery. Mature trees and fine lawns with extensive range of shrubs and herbaceous perennials suited to acid sand, many planted at waterside. Set in 350 acres of deer park. TEAS. *Adm £2.50 Chd free NGS day only (car entry £2.50). For NGS Sun Aug 17 (11-5)*

¶**Greenhills Farm** 点米 (Mr & Mrs Peter Johnson) Lower Whitley. From M56 take A49 S. In 1m turn R signed Dutton (Grimditch Lane), 1st L, Greenhills Lane go to end. From S go up A49 towards Warrington, turn L 1m before M56 signed Dutton etc. Approx. 1-acre of yr-round interest. Shrubs, herbaceous borders, roses, fruit and specimen trees and a small lake have made a beautifully landscaped garden which won The Best Cheshire Farm Garden 1996 Competition. TEAS. *Adm £2 Chd 50p (Share to Yorkshire Assoc for Disabled People®). Sun July 6 (2-5.30)*

▲**Hare Hill Gardens** 点米 (The National Trust) Over Alderley. Between Alderley Edge and Prestbury, turn off N at B5087 at Greyhound Rd [118:SJ85765]. Bus: Cheshire E17 Macclesfield–Wilmslow (passing BR Wilmslow and Prestbury) to within ¾m. Stations: Alderley Edge 2½m, Prestbury 2½m. Attractive spring garden featuring a fine display of rhododendrons and azaleas. A good collection of hollies and other specimen trees and shrubs. The 10-acre garden includes a walled garden which hosts many wall shrubs including clematis and vines. The borders are planted with agapanthus (African lily) and geraniums. Partially suitable for wheelchairs. *Adm £2.50 Chd £1.25. For NGS Sun May 18 (10-5.30)*

Haughton Hall 舞 (Mr & Mrs R J Posnett) Tarporley. 5m NW of Nantwich off A534 Nantwich/Wrexham Rd, 6m SE of Tarporley via A49. Medium-sized garden; species of rhododendron, azaleas, shrubs, rock garden; lake with temple; waterfall. Collection of ornamental trees. Home-made TEAS. *Adm £2 Chd 50p. Sun May 18 (2-6)*

Henbury Hall 点米 (Mr & Mrs Sebastian de Ferranti) nr Macclesfield. 2m W of Macclesfield on A537 rd. Turn down School Lane, Henbury at Blacksmiths Arms: East Lodge on R. Large garden with lake, beautifully landscaped and full of variety. Azaleas, rhododendrons, flowering shrubs, rare trees, herbaceous borders. TEAS in aid of East Cheshire Hospice. *Adm £2 Chd £1 (Share to Drugwatch®). Sun June 1 (2-5)*

35 Heyes Lane 舞 (Mr & Mrs David Eastwood) Timperley. Heyes Lane is a turning off Park Rd (B5165) 1m from the junction with the A56 Altrincham-Manchester rd 1½m N of Altrincham. Or from A560 turn W in Timperley Village for ¼m. Newsagents shop on corner. A small suburban garden 30' × 90' on sandy soil maintained by a keen plantswoman member of the Organic Movement (HDRA). An all yr round garden; trees; small pond; greenhouses; fruit and vegetables with a good collection of interesting and unusual plants. *Adm £1.50 incl TEA Chd free. Wed May 28, Sun June 1 (2-5)*

73 Hill Top Avenue 米 (Mr & Mrs Martin Land) Cheadle Hulme. Turn off A34 (new by-pass) at roundabout signed Cheadle Hulme (B5094). Take 2nd turn L into Gillbent Rd, signposted Cheadle Hulme Sports Centre. Go to end, small roundabout, turn R into Church Rd. 2nd rd on L is Hill Top Ave. No. 73 is 400yds on R. From Stockport or Bramhall turn R into Church Rd by The Church Inn. Hill Top Ave is last rd on R. ⅙-acre plantswoman's garden designed to disguise its long narrow shape. Established and new plantings of herbaceous, shrub and climbing roses, clematis, pond and damp area, shrubs and small trees. TEAS. *Adm £2 Chd free (Share to Arthritis & Rheumatism Council®). Sun July 6 (2-5)*

¶**62 Irwell Road** 米 (Mr & Mrs D Griffiths) Warrington. From Stockton Heath, N on A49 over swing bridge on to Wilderspool Causeway. L at 2nd set of lights into Gainsborough Rd. 2nd R into Irwell Rd. No 62 approx halfway down on R. Approx 1m from Warrington town centre. A small cottage garden approx 150 sq yds where colour and scent combine with sounds of trickling water and wind chimes to create a tranquil oasis in the midst of suburbia. The planting reflects the owners' interest in cottage gardening and incl traditional favourites and modern day varieties. TEAS. *Adm £1.50 Chd 50p. Wed July 16 (11-6)*

¶**Jalna** 米舞 (J Lomas & J Howell) Higher Hurdsfield. Situated 1½m outside Macclesfield on the B5470 to Whaley Bridge/Chapel-en-Frith. Turn L down Well Lane (after George & Dragon) bear R and the garden entrance is 50yds further on. This is ⅓-acre gardener's garden nestling in the hills of the Peak District. Over a 5yr period it has been transformed from a sloping grassy bank into a series of terraced beds retained by approx 1000ft of dry stone walls. The garden abounds with rare and specialist plants and is surrounded by wonderful views over the

Cheshire Plains and hills. This is a garden not to be missed. TEA. *Adm £2 Chd £1 (Share to NSPCC®). Sat, Sun, July 12, 13 (10-5)*

▲**Little Moreton Hall** &✿✤ (The National Trust) Congleton. On A34, 4m S of Congleton. 1½-acre garden surrounded by a moat and bordered by yew hedges, next to finest example of timber-framed architecture in England. Herb and historic vegetable garden, orchard and borders. Knot garden based on design in 'The English Gardener' published by Leonard Meager in 1670, though probably Elizabethan in origin. Adm includes entry to the Hall with optional free guided tours. Wheelchairs and electric mobility vehicle available. Disabled toilet. Picnic lawns. Shop and restaurant serving coffee, lunches and afternoon teas. TEAS. *Adm £3.80 Chd 1.90. For NGS Sun June 1 (12-5.30 last admission 5)*

▲**Lyme Park** &✿ (The National Trust) Disley. 6m SE of Stockport just W of Disley on A6 rd. 17-acre garden retaining many original features from Tudor and Jacobean times; high Victorian style bedding; a Dutch garden; a Gertrude Jekyll style herbaceous border; an Edwardian rose garden, a Wyatt orangery and many other features. Also rare trees, a wild flower area and lake. TEAS. Donations to NGS. *Adm £3.30 per car to estate, £2 Chd £1 to gardens. For NGS Suns May 11, Aug 31 (11-4.45)*

Manley Knoll &✤ (Mrs D G Fildes) Manley, NE of Chester. Nr Mouldsworth. B5393. Quarry garden; azaleas and rhododendrons. TEAS. *Adm £2 Chd free. Sun May 25 (2-6). Private visits welcome for parties 20 to 30, please* **Tel 01928 740226**

The Mount, Higher Kinnerton &✿ (Mr & Mrs J Major) 6m W of Chester, L off A5104 just after it crosses A55. Approx 2½-acre garden with mature trees; shrubs and lawns; kitchen garden, variety of perennial plants some interesting and unusual. *Adm £2 Chd free. Private parties welcome, please* **Tel 01244 660275.** *Best months June and July*

The Mount, Whirley &✿✤ (Mr & Mrs Nicholas Payne) The Mount is situated about 2m due W of Macclesfield along A537 rd. Opp Blacksmiths Arms at Henbury, go up Pepper St, turn L into Church Lane which becomes Andertons Lane in 100yds. The Mount is about 200yds up Andertons Lane on L. The garden is approx 1½ acres and has interesting trees including eucryphia nymansensis, fern leaved beech and sciadopitys. Shrubberies; herbaceous border; swimming pool and short vista of Irish Yews. TEAS. *Adm £2 Chd 50p. Sun July 13 (2-5.30). Parties welcome, please* **Tel 01625 426730**

■ **Norton Priory** &✤ (Norton Priory Museum Trust Ltd) Tudor Road, Manor Park, Runcorn. Runcorn New Town 1m, Warrington 5m. From M56 Junction 11 turn for Warrington and follow signs. From Warrington take A56 for Runcorn and follow signs. 16 acres well established woodland gardens; Georgian summerhouses; rock garden and stream glade; 3-acre walled garden of similar date (1760s) recently restored. Georgian and modern garden designs; fruit training; rosewalk; colour borders; herb garden, cottage garden and exhibition. Plants for sale from the Walled Garden collection. Priory remains of museum also open. TEA. *Combined adm £2.90 Chd £1.60. Daily*

April to October (12-5) weekends and bank hols (12-6) Nov to March (12-4) (Walled garden closed Nov-Feb). For NGS Sun June 15 (12-6). **Tel 01928 569895**

The Old Hall &✿ (Dr & Mrs M W W Wood) Hadlow Rd, Willaston S Wirral, 8m NW of Chester on village green. ¾-acre; mixed border; interesting plants; bulbs; winter flowering shrubs and colour. C17 house. TEAS June only. *Adm £2 Chd free (Share to Neuromuscular Centre®). Suns April 27 (2-5), June 22 (2-6); also private visits welcome, please* **Tel 0151 327 4779**

The Old Hough &✿ (Mr & Mrs D S Varey) Warmingham. 2m from Middlewich on A50 to Nantwich, turn L to Warmingham and L again at T; or L on A533 from Sandbach to Middlewich and R at T. 2½ acres owner-designed and maintained garden, enhancing period house and farm buildings. Architectural in character, with much use of reclaimed materials. Varied borders with some choice plants. Wildlife pond and interesting young trees protected by mature oak wood. Lily pond and rill amidst formal lawns and rose borders. Ample parking and WCs. TEAS in aid of Warmingham Church. *Adm £2 Chd 50p (Share to Warmingham Church®). Sun June 22 (2-6)*

The Old Parsonage &✤ (The Viscount & Viscountess Ashbrook) Arley Green; 5m NNE of Northwich and 3m Great Budworth; M6 junctions 19, 20 and M56 junction 10. Follow signposts to Arley Hall and Gardens and notices to Old Parsonage which lies across park at Arley Green. 2-acre garden yew hedges, herbaceous and mixed borders, shrub roses, climbers, woodland garden and pond, with unusual young trees and foliage shrubs. Waterplants, rhododendrons, azaleas, meconopsis. Plant stall. TEAS in aid of Red Cross June 14, NGS June 15. *Adm £2 Chd under 16 £1 (Share to Save the Children®). Sat, Sun June 14, 15 (2-6)*

Orchard Villa &✤ (Mr & Mrs J Trinder) 72 Audley Rd, Alsager. At traffic lights in Alsager town centre turn S towards Audley, house is 300yds on R beyond level Xing. Long and narrow, this ⅓-acre has been designed to be of interest through the yr; from spring bulbs and hellebores to irises and grasses. Featured in 'Surprise Gardens' TV 1996 also Amateur Gardening. TEAS. *Adm £2 Chd free. Suns April 13, May 11, June 1, 15 (1.30-5.30); also private visits welcome, please* **Tel 01270 874833**

Penn ✿✤ (R W Baldwin Esq) Macclesfield Rd, Alderley Edge. ¾m E of Alderley Edge village, on B5087, Alderley Edge-Macclesfield rd. Turn L into Woodbrook Rd for car parking. 2½ acres. This garden contains an exceptional collection of flowering shrubs and trees, on a hillside looking over the Cheshire plain. The many hundreds of rhododendron species and cultivars include some Himalayans (now small forest trees), yellow & blue species (wardii, augustinii etc.), masses of azaleas plus a wide range of camellias & magnolias including superb varieties from Cornwall, and many fairly rare trees including gingko, davidia (handkerchief tree), golden elm, embothriums, plus for added interest 2 sequoia sempervirens (now 30ft high struck in 1965 from a block of wood bought in the Muir woods across the Golden Gate in San Francisco). TEA. *Adm £2 OAPs £1.50 Chd 50p. Suns, Mons May 4, 5; 25, 26 (2-5). Parties welcome by written appt*

■ **Peover Hall** ⟐⟐ (Randle Brooks Esq) Over Peover. 3m S of Knutsford on A50, Lodge gates off Blackden Lane. 15-acres. 5 walled gardens: lily pond, rose, herb, white and pink gardens; C18 landscaped park, moat, C19 dell, rhododendron walks, large walled kitchen garden, Church walk, purple border, blue and white border, pleached lime avenues, fine topiary work. Dogs in park only. TEAS. *Adm £2 Chd £2. Mons & Thurs (2-5) May to Oct. NOT Bank Hols. Other days by appt for parties. For NGS Sat, Sun May 17, 18 (2-6)*

5 Pine Hey ⟐⟐⟐ (Mr & Mrs S J Clayton) Neston. A540 Chester to Hoylake Rd. Turn off at Shrewsbury Arms traffic lights towards Neston. Turn R at T-junction drive through Neston past cross on the L, then fork L at traffic lights and continue along Leighton Rd, Pine Hey is on L. The garden covers approx ¾ acre. It is laid out informally and incl a copse, water garden, lawns and herbaceous garden each with its own character. Featured on Granada TV in 1996. TEAS in aid of Wirral Methodist Housing Association. *Adm £1.50 Chd free (Share to Wirral Methodist Housing Association). Sun June 29 (2-5). Private parties welcome, please* **Tel 0151 3363006**

17 Poplar Grove ⟐⟐ (Gordon Cooke Esq) Sale. From the A6144 at Brooklands Station turn down Hope Rd. Poplar Grove 3rd on R. This recently englarged town garden has been created by the owner who is a potter and landscape designer. It has a special collection of unusual plants in an artistic setting with many interesting design features and details. TEAS. *Adm £1.50 Chd 75p (Share to North Manchester General Hospital®). Sat, Sun July 12, 13 (2-6)*

Poulton Hall ⟐ (The Lancelyn Green Family) Poulton Lancelyn, 2m from Bebington. From M53, exit 4 towards Bebington; at traffic lights (½m) R along Poulton Rd; house 1m on R. 2½ acres; lawns, ha-ha, wild flower meadow, shrubbery, walled gardens with literary associations. Cream TEAS. *Adm £2 Chd 20p. Suns April 13, June 22 (2-6)*

Reaseheath ⟐⟐⟐ (Reaseheath College) nr Nantwich. 1½m N of Nantwich on the A51. The Gardens, covering 12 acres, are based on a Victorian Garden surrounding Reaseheath Hall and contain many mature trees of horticultural interest. The gardens are used as a teaching resource. There are specialised features of particular interest including, glasshouses; model fruit garden; rose garden; woodland garden; lakeside bog garden and extensive shrub borders, lawns and sports facilities. TEA. *Adm £2. Weds May 21, 28, June 4, 11, 18, 25, July 2, 9, 16, 23, 30 (2-4.30). Parties welcome, please* **Tel 01270 625131**

¶**Rhodewood House** ⟐⟐ (Mr & Mrs Roger Gorvin) Prestbury Rd, Macclesfield. On the B5087 1½m NW of centre of Macclesfield. 3-acre well-stocked undulating garden with yr-round interest incl rose garden, herbaceous borders, woodland walk, wildlife pond, bridge over natural stream and a good selection of rhododendrons (over 200 recently planted species and cultivars); shrubs, conifers, clematis and hydrangeas. TEAS in aid of East Cheshire Hospice. *Adm £2 Chd 50p. Sun July 6 (11-5)*

■ **Rode Hall** ⟐ (Sir Richard & Lady Baker Wilbraham) Scholar Green [National Grid reference SJ8157] 5m SW of Congleton between A34 and A50. Nesfield's terrace and rose garden with view over Humphrey Repton's landscape is a feature of Rode gardens, as is the Victorian wild garden with a grotto and the walk to the lake past the old Stew pond. Other attractions include a restored ice house and working walled kitchen garden. TEAS. *Adm £2 Chd £1 (Share to All Saints Odd Rode and St Mary's, Astbury Parish Churches®). Tues, Weds, Thurs & Bank Hols March 31 to Sept 25 (2-5). For NGS Sun May 11 (2-5.30)*

Rosewood ⟐ (Mr & Mrs C E J Brabin) Puddington. 6m N of Chester turn L (W) off Chester to Hoylake A540 to Puddington. Bear L at village green and follow NGS signs. 1-acre garden incl small wood, pond well planted with bogside species, mixed herbaceous, shrub beds with new plantings of rhododendron, azalea species and hybrids; many unusual trees. Most of the new plantings are grown from seed by owner. TEAS. *Adm £2 Chd free (Share to St Michael's Church, Shotwick®). Sun May 25 (2-6). Private visits by appt, please* **Tel 0151353 1193**

¶**Squirrel's Haunt** ⟐⟐ (Glyn Parry Esq) Chalkwell Drive, Heswall. From 'Devon Doorway' roundabout on A540 1m S of Heswell Cross take A551 Barnston Rd. Garden 300yds on R Parking on Barnston Rd only please. 30-yr old ¼-acre suburban garden divided into 4 'rooms'. Much variegated foliage with increased colour in springtime on a level triangular site. *Adm £1.50 Chd 50p. Sun May 11 (2-5.30)*

2 Stanley Road ⟐⟐ (Mr G Leatherbarrow) Heaton Moor. Approx 1½m N of Stockport. Follow Heaton Moor Rd off A6. Stanley Rd on L. 1st house on R. Tiny town garden with all year interest, packed with interesting plants, creating a secret cottage garden atmosphere. Old species and English roses, clematis, hardy geraniums, ivies, varied evergreens, daphnes, hellebores, delphiniums, mixed herbaceous; ponds. Max no. of visitors 2 – no room for more. Not suitable for less agile. TEA. *Adm £2 Chd 75p. Private visits welcome Feb to end Sept, please* **Tel 0161 442 3828**

●**Stonyford Cottage Nursery & Garden** ⟐⟐⟐ (Mr & Mrs Anthony Overland) Cuddington. 6m W of Northwich. Turn R off A556 (Northwich to Chester). At Xrds ¾m past A49 junction (signpost Norley-Kingsley). Entrance in ½m on L. The gardens feature a 'Monet' style pool with bridges to an island, woodland walk and damp garden. Listed in Good Gardens Guide and shown on BBC Gardeners World. The adjacent nursery has herbaceous perennials and less common plants for sale. *Adm £1.50 Chd 50p. April to Oct, Wed to Sun and Bank Hols (12-5.30)*

The Stray ⟐⟐⟐ (Mr & Mrs Anthony Hannay) Neston. Approx 10m NW of Chester. ½m NW of Shrewsbury Arms (traffic lights). Turn off A540 into Upper Raby Rd. After ³⁄₁₀m turn R into unmade lane and The Stray is immediately on the L. 1½ acres of newly planted shrubs, herbaceous and mixed borders. Interesting colour schemes and unusual plants. Replanting commenced in 1991. A chance to see a new garden maturing. TEAS in aid of RNLI. *Adm £2 Chd 50p. Sun June 8 (2-5.30)*

▲**Tatton Park** & ✗❀ (Cheshire County Council: The National Trust) Knutsford. Well sign-posted on M56 junction 7 and from M6 junction 19. 2½m N of Knutsford. Considered to be the very finest and most important of all gardens within The National Trust they rank among England's 'Top Ten'. Features include orangery by Wyatt, fernery by Paxton, Japanese, Italian and rose gardens. Greek monument and African hut. Hybrid azaleas and rhododendrons, swamp cypresses, tree ferns, tall redwoods, bamboos and pines. TEAS. *Adm £2.50 Group £2 Chd £1.50 Group £1.50. For NGS Mon June 23 (10.30-5)*

Thornton Manor ❀ (The Viscount Leverhulme) Thornton Hough, Wirral. From Chester A540 to Fiveway Garage; turn R on to B5136 to Thornton Hough village. From Birkenhead B5151 then on to B5136. From M53, exit 4 to Heswall; turn L after 1m. Bus: Woodside-Parkgate; alight Thornton Hough village. Large garden of yr-round interest. TEAS. *Free car park. Adm £2 OAPs £1 Chd 50p. Bank Hol Mon Aug 25 (12-7)*

Tushingham Hall (Mr & Mrs P Moore Dutton) 3m N of Whitchurch. Signed off A41 Chester-Whitchurch Rd; Medium-sized garden in beautiful surroundings; bluebell wood alongside pool; ancient oak, girth 26ft. TEAS. *Adm £2 Chd 50p (Share to St Chad's Church, Tushingham®). Sun May 4 (2-5.30)*

85 Warmingham Road ✗❀ (Mr & Mrs A Mann) Approx 3m N of Crewe town centre on the road between Leighton Hospital and Warmingham Village. Close by White Lion Inn, Coppenhall. ⅓-acre plantsman's garden, with shrubs, perennial borders, raised beds, rock garden, peat garden, pond and greenhouse with cacti and succulents. Speciality alpines. TEAS. *Adm £2 Chd free.*

Suns April 20, June 8, (1-5). Private visits welcome March to Sept, please **Tel 01270 582030**

The Well House ✗ (Mrs S H French-Greenslade) Tilston, nr Malpas 12m S of Chester on A41, 1st turn R after Broxton roundabout, L on Malpas Rd through Tilston. House and antique shop on L. Field parking signed. 1-acre cottage garden, bridge over natural stream, many bulbs, herbs and shrubs. TEAS. *Adm £2 Chd 25p (Share to Cystic Fibrosis Trust®). Suns April 13, June 22 (2-5.30). Private visits by appt March-July, please* **Tel 01829 250332**

Willaston Grange & (Sir Derek and Lady Bibby) Willaston. A540 Chester to West Kirby until opposite the new Elf Garage. Proceed down B5151 Hadlow Rd, towards Willaston. Borders, rock garden, vegetable garden, orchard, about 3 acres. Special feature - woodland walk. TEAS. *Adm £1.50 OAPs £1 Chd free. Sun May 4 (2-6)*

Willow Cottage ✗ (Mrs Martin Tolson) Prestbury. Straight behind the Admiral Rodney Public House in Prestbury. An intensively planted small cottage garden of less than ⅒-acre. *Adm £2 Chd £1. Private visits (max of 10) welcome May to July (2.30-5), please* **Tel 01625 828697**

Wood End Cottage ✗❀ (Mr & Mrs M R Everett) Whitegate. Turn S off A556 (Northwich by-pass) to Whitegate village; opp. school follow Grange Lane for 300yds. ½-acre plantsman's garden sloping to a natural stream. Mature trees, many clematis, herbaceous, raised beds, shade and moisture loving plants. Large plant stall. TEAS. *Adm £2 Chd 50p (Share to David Lewis Centre for Epilepsy®). Sun July 13 (2-6); also by appt, please* **Tel 01606 888236**

Clwyd

See separate Welsh section beginning on page 323

SYMBOLS USED IN THIS BOOK (See also Page 17)

‡   Following a garden name in the Dates of Opening list indicates that those gardens sharing the same symbol are nearby and open on the same day.

‡‡   Indicates a second series of nearby gardens open on the same day.

¶   Opening for the first time.

❀   Plants/produce for sale if available.

&   Gardens with at least the main features accessible by wheelchair.

✗   No dogs except guide dogs but otherwise dogs are usually admitted, provided they are kept on a lead. Dogs are not admitted to houses.

●   These gardens advertise their own dates in this publication although they do not nominate specific days for the NGS. Not all the money collected by these gardens comes to the NGS but they do make a guaranteed contribution.

■   These gardens nominate specific days for the NGS and advertise their own dates in this publication.

▲   These gardens open regularly to the public but they do not advertise their own dates in this publication. For further details, contact the garden directly.

Cornwall

Hon County Organiser:	G J Holborow Esq, Ladock House, Ladock, Truro TR2 4PL
	Tel 01726 882274
Assistant Hon County Organisers:	Mrs D Morison, Boskenna, St Martin, Manaccan, Helston TR12 6BS
	Tel 01326 231 210
	Mrs Richard Jerram, Trehane, Trevanson, Wadebridge PL27 7HP
	Tel 01208 812523
	Mrs Michael Latham, Trebartha Lodge, North Hill, Launceston PL15 7PD
	Tel 01566 82373
Leaflet/Yellow Books:	Mr & Mrs Michael Cole, Nansawsan House, Ladock, Truro TR2 4PW
	Tel 01726 882392
Publicity:	Mrs Elizabeth Ann Waldron-Yeo, Pembre, Trelill Bodmin, PL30 3HZ
	Tel 01208 850793
Hon County Treasurer:	Mrs Cynthia Bassett, 5 Athelstan Park, Bodmin, PL31 1DS
	Tel 01208 73247

DATES OF OPENING

March 15 Saturday
Trengwainton, Penzance
March 16 Sunday
Burncoose Nuseries & Garden, Burncoose
March 30 Sunday
Ince Castle Gardens, Saltash
Penjerrick Garden, Budock, nr Falmouth
Watergate, Trelill
April 6 Sunday
Bodwannick, Nanstallon
Tremeer Gardens, St Tudy
April 12 Saturday
Glendurgan, Mawnan Smith
April 13 Sunday
Trelissick, Feock
April 20 Sunday
Ince Castle Gardens, Saltash
St Michael's Mount, Marazion
April 27 Sunday
Penwarne, nr Falmouth
Polgwynne, Feock
May 4 Sunday
Bodellan Farmhouse, Porthcurno
High Noon, Ladock
Ladock House, Ladock
Tregrehan, Par
Trevegean, Manor Way, Heamoor
Werrington Park, Launceston
May 7 Wednesday
Antony, Torpoint
May 11 Sunday
Bodwannick, Nanstallon
Creed House, Creed
Estray Parc, Budock
Ince Castle Gardens, Saltash
Lamorran House, Upper Castle Road, St Mawes
Pinetum, Harewood, Calstock
May 16 Friday
Cotehele House, St Dominick, Saltash

May 18 Sunday
Boconnoc, nr Lostwithiel
Carclew Gardens, Perran-ar-Worthal
Lanhydrock, Bodmin
Nansawsan House, Ladock
Trenance, Launceston
May 22 Thursday
Headland, Polruan
May 25 Sunday
Peterdale, Millbrook
Pine Lodge Gardens, Cuddra St Austell
Pinetum, Harewood, Calstock
May 29 Thursday
Headland, Polruan
May 31 Saturday
Berriow Bridge & Middlewood Gardens, Hillbrook
June 1 Sunday
Berriow Bridge & Middlewood Gardens, Hillbrook
Zoar, Mylor
June 8 Sunday
Ince Castle Gardens, Saltash
June 15 Sunday
The Hollies, Grampound, nr Truro
Kingberry, Bodmin
Newton House, Lanhydrock
Scawn Mill, nr Liskeard
Tregilliowe Farm, Ludgvan
Treloyhan Manor Hotel, St Ives
June 22 Sunday
Bodwannick, Nanstallon
Long Cross Victorian Gardens, Trelights
Manaccan Gardens, Helston
Newton House, Lanhydrock
Trevegean, Manor Way, Heamoor
June 29 Sunday
Bodellan Farmhouse, Porthcurno
Bosvigo House, Truro
Hallowarren, Carne
Northwood Farm, St Neot
Roseland House, Chacewater

Tremarkyn, Wenmouth Cross, St Neot
Water Meadow, Luxulyan
Wynlands, Manaccan
July 2 Wednesday
Treloyhan Manor Hotel, St Ives
July 6 Sunday
Trenance, Launceston
July 13 Sunday
Peterdale, Millbrook
Roseland House, Chacewater
Tregilliowe Farm, Ludgvan
July 16 Wednesday
Treloyhan Manor Hotel, St Ives
July 20 Sunday
Bonython Manor, Helston
July 27 Sunday
Scawn Mill, nr Liskeard
August 3 Sunday
Pinetum, Harewood, Calstock
August 10 Sunday
Trenarth, Constantine
August 17 Sunday
Higher Truscott, St Stephens
August 20 Wednesday
Trerice, nr Newquay
September 7 Sunday
Bodellan Farmhouse, Porthcurno
Kingberry, Bodmin
September 21 Sunday
Paradise Park, Hayle
September 28 Sunday
Trebartha, nr Launceston

Regular Openings

Bosvigo House, Truro
Carwinion, Mawnan Smith
Flambards Victorian Village Garden, Helston
Headland, Polruan
Heligan Gardens, Mevagissey
Ken Caro, Bicton, nr Liskeard
Lanterns, Restronguet, nr Mylor

Oak Lodge Woodland Garden,
    Nanstallon
Paradise Park, Hayle
Pencarrow, Bodmin
Prideaux Place, Padstow
Probus Gardens, Truro

Roseland House, Chacewater
Trebah, Mawnan Smith
Tregrehan, Par
Trevarno Gardens
Trewithen, Probus, nr Truro
Woodland Garden, Garras, nr Helston

By Appointment only

Carnowall, Black Rock, Praze
Chyverton, Zelah
Furzeball, Lanteglos-by-Fowey

DESCRIPTIONS OF GARDENS

▲**Antony** ⚲ (National Trust: Trustees of the Carew Pole Trust) 5m W of Plymouth via Torpoint car ferry; 2m NW of Torpoint, N of A374; 16m SE of Liskeard; 15m E of Looe. In a Repton landscape with fine vistas to the R Lynher. Features a formal courtyard, terraces, ornamental Japanese pond and knot garden. **Antony Woodland Garden and Woods:** an established woodland garden and natural woods extending to 100 acres. TEAS. *Woodland garden adm £2. Combined Gardens adm £3 Chd ½ price. For NGS Wed May 7 (1.30-5.30)*

Berriow Bridge & Middlewood Gardens ⚲❀ Hillbrook. [OS map ref: SX273752] Situated where the B3254 crosses R Lynher between Launceston and Liskeard. Park at Berriow where tickets and map are available. Early summer in a lovely valley below Bodmin Moor, several gardens show a variety of styles. Small cottages and a mill with secret and surprising gardens, roses, unusual plants, wildflowers, streams and natural stone and a larger riverside garden with sculptures and woodland walk. Featured on TV. TEAS in aid of North Hill Village Hall. *Combined adm £2.50 Chd free. Sat, Sun May 31, June 1 (2-6)*

Boconnoc ⚬❀ (Mr & Mrs J D G Fortescue) 2m S of A390. On main rd between middle Taphouse and Downend garage, follow signs. Privately owned gardens covering some 20 acres, surrounded by parkland and woods. Magnificent old trees, flowering shrubs and views. TEAS. *Adm £1.50 Chd free (Share to Boconnoc Church Window Fund®). Sun May 18 (2-6)*

¶**Bodellan Farmhouse** ⚲ (Richard B Webb) Porthcurno. 9m W of Penzance. On L at 30mph speed limit signs before Porthcurno. Roadside parking 100yds before these signs or at beach Carpark (10min walk). ⅔-acre exposed coastal garden on 5 levels. Rock shrubbery, ornamental ponds, sunken garden, views. Garden linked with legends of C6 Saint. Try dousing the earth energies. Teas in Porthcurno. *Adm £2 Chd free (Share to Penzance Natural Health Centre® 29 June & Tibet House Trust® Sept 7). Suns May 4, June 29, Sept 7 (2-5.30) Private visits welcome, please Tel 01736 810225*

Bodwannick ⚲ (P M & W M Appleton) Nanstallon. 2½m W Bodmin. Turn at Bodmin Trailer Centre (A30) signposted Nanstallon, L at Xrds signposted Hoopers Bridge then sharp R. Approx 1-acre compact garden incl water garden, herbaceous, granite Cornish cross, roses, shade garden and shrubs. Over 50 varieties of daffodils and narcissus. Cream TEAS. *Adm £1 Chd free. Suns April 6, May 11, June 22 (2-6). Private visits welcome, please Tel 01208 831427*

Bonython Manor ⚬ (Mr Robert & The Hon Mrs Lyle) Curry Cross Lanes. 5m S of Helston. From A3083 Helston-Lizard Rd L at Wheel Inn. Entrance 300yds on R. Bonython family recorded from 1277. Nothing remains of the mediaeval house, present fabric impressive example C18 granite construction (house not open). 10 acres surrounding gardens with walled garden, incl newly planted herb and vegetable garden, herbaceous borders, new orchard planting, shrub roses, developing water garden round 2 lakes. Cream TEAS in aid of the Red Cross. *Adm £1 Chd 50p. Sun July 20 (2-6)*

● **Bosvigo House** ⚲❀ (Mr & Mrs M Perry) Bosvigo Lane. ¾m from Truro centre. At Highertown, nr Sainsbury roundabout, turn down Dobbs Lane. After 500yds, entrance to house is on L, after nasty L-hand bend. 3-acre garden still being developed surrounding Georgian house (not open) and Victorian conservatory. Series of enclosed and walled gardens with mainly herbaceous plants for colour and foliage effect. Woodland walk. Many rare plants. Partly suitable for wheelchairs. TEAS in servants hall Sun June 29 only. *Adm £2 Chd 50p. Open Weds to Sats March to end Sept (11-6). For NGS Sun June 29 (2-5)*

Burncoose Nurseries & Garden ⚬❀ (Mr C H Williams) Burncoose, Gwennap. 3m SE of Redruth on A393 Falmouth rd, ½m beyond Lanner. 30-acre woodland garden established at turn of century. Many original plants imported from China incl collection of rare bamboos. Nursery extends over 7 acres. Involved in production of 1500 types of ornamental shrubs and trees. TEA. *Adm £2 Chd free. Sun March 16 (11-5) Teas and coaches by arrangement Tel 01209 861112*

Carclew Gardens ⚲ (Mrs Chope) Perran-ar-Worthal, nr Truro. From A39 turn E at Perran-ar-Worthal. Bus: alight Perran-ar-Worthal 1m. Large garden, rhododendron species; terraces; ornamental water. TEAS. *Adm £2 Chd 50p (Share to Barristers Benevolent Fund®). Sun May 18 (2-5.30)*

¶**Carnowall** ⚲❀ (Rod & Penny Smith) Black Rock, Praze. 5m N of Helston on B3297, take turning at Farms Common to T-junction, turn L 150 yds turn sharp L into private lane. (Map ref: 665 341). A fine example of what can be grown well at an altitude of 500'. 1½-acre garden created from fields by present owners and still developing. Enclosed gardens interconnected by sunken gravel paths, raised beds, colourful herbaceous borders, trees, shrubs and much use of local stone. Original water-colours for

---

Regular Openers. Open throughout the year. They are listed at the end of the Diary Section under 'Regular Openers'.

sale. Cream TEAS. *Adm £2. Private visits welcome mid May to end July except Sats, please* **Tel 01209 831757**

●**Carwinion** ❀ (Mr H A E Rogers) Mawnan Smith via Carwinion Rd. An unmanicured or permissive valley garden of some 10 acres with many camellias, rhododendrons and azaleas flowering in the spring. Apart from an abundance of wild flowers, grasses, ferns etc, the garden holds the premier collection of temperate bamboos in the UK. TEAS April to Oct (2-5.30). *Adm £2 Chd free. Open daily throughout the year (10-5.30). Private visits welcome, please* **Tel 01326 250258**

Chyverton (Mr N T Holman) Zelah, N of Truro. Entrance ¾m SW of Zelah on A30. Georgian landscaped garden with lake and bridge (1770); large shrub garden of great beauty; outstanding collection magnolias, acers, camellias, rhododendrons, primulas, rare and exotic trees and shrubs. Visitors personally conducted by owner. *Adm £3.50 (parties over 20 persons by arrangement Adm £3) Chd under 16 free. Private visits welcome for parties under 5 weekdays March to June by appt, please write or* **Tel 01872 540324**

▲**Cotehele House** ❤❀❀ (The National Trust) 2m E of St Dominick, 4m from Gunnislake (turn at St Ann's Chapel); 8m SW of Tavistock; 14m from Plymouth via Tamar Bridge. Terrace garden falling to sheltered valley with ponds, stream and unusual shrubs. Fine medieval house (one of the least altered in the country); armour, tapestries, furniture. Dogs in wood only and on lead. Lunches and TEAS. *Adm garden, grounds & mill £2.80 Chd half price. For NGS Fri May 16 (11-5)*

▲**Creed House** ❀ (Mr & Mrs W R Croggon) Creed. From the centre of Grampound on A390. Take rd signposted to Creed. After 1m turn L opp Creed Church and the garden is on L. Parking in lane. 5-acre landscaped Georgian Rectory garden. Tree collection; rhododendrons; sunken alpine and formal walled herbaceous gardens. Trickle stream to ponds and bog. Natural woodland walk. Restoration began 1974 – continues and incl recent planting. TEAS. *Adm £1.50 Chd free. For NGS Sun May 11 (2-5.30).* **Tel 01872 530372**

Estray Parc (Mr & Mrs J M Williams) Penjerrick. Leave Penjerrick main entrance on R follow the rd towards Mawnan Smith until entrance to The Home Hotel on L. Directly opp turn R and follow the signs. In 1983 most of this 3-acre garden was a bramble thistle-infested field. A considerable variety of plants have been introduced and continuous grass cutting has produced passable sloping lawns interspersed by a large collection of trees and shrubs. *Adm £1.50 OAPs £1 Chd over 13 50p (Share to Mermaid Appeal®). Sun May 11 (2-6)*

● ¶**Flambards Victorian Village Garden** ❤❀❀ (Mr & Mrs D Kingsford Hale) Culdrose Manor, Helston. From A394 follow official brown and white signs to Flambards, located on A3083 Helston side of Culdrose Naval Air Station. Ample free parking. A well designed and maintained 20-acre site providing an excellent family day out. Divided into many interesting sections by very colourful

award winning bedding displays and hanging baskets. Mature trees, named shrubs of varied and striking foliage. Many exciting activities incl roller coaster rides and sections of great adult interest incl an outstanding recreation of a Victorian village and several exhibitions illustrating wartime Britain. Wheelchairs available. Cafeteria. *Open most days Easter to end Oct (10.30-5). For prices and opening, please* **Tel 24hr info 01326 564093**

Furzeball ❤❀ (Phyllis & Eric Milner Kay) Pont. 1½m Fowey-Bodinnick Ferry. [Nat. Grid Ref: SX145527]. No access for coaches. 1-acre sheltered cottage garden. Outstanding views over countryside. Garden designed to exploit natural features: summer annuals and perennials, rhododendrons and azaleas, springs, small water garden, gunnera, ferns etc. Lawns, fruit trees, vegetables, also wild flower sanctuary. All areas connected by footpath/steps made from local stone. Visitors conducted by owners. *Adm £2.50. May 21 to June 19, closed Mons and Tues. By appt only, please* **Tel 01726 870600** *pref after 6pm*

▲**Glendurgan** ❀❀ (The National Trust) Mawnan Smith, take rd to Helford Passage, 5m SW of Falmouth. Follow NT signposts. Walled garden, laurel maze, giants stride, valley with specimen trees, bluebells and primulas running down to Durgan fishing village on R Helford. Large car park. Lunches and TEAS. *Adm £3 Chd half price. For NGS Sat April 12 (10.30-5.30)*

¶**Hallowarren** ❀ (Mr & Mrs Mark Osman) Carne. 1m out of the centre of Manaccan village. Down hill past Inn on R, follow signpost to Carne. House on R. Parking nearby or in drive. Approx 1½ acres set in a beautiful wooded valley bordering a meandering stream. Happy mixture of wilderness and cultivation, cottage garden with old roses, lilies and kitchen herbs, unusual shrubs and trees. TEAS in aid of St Anthony Church. *Combined adm with* **Wynlands** *£2 Chd free. Sun June 29 (2-5.30)*

■ **Headland** ❀ (Jean & John Hill) Battery Lane, Polruan. On E of Fowey estuary; leave car in public park; walk down St Saviour's Hill, turn L at Coast Guard office. 1¼-acre cliff garden with sea on 3 sides; mainly plants which withstand salty gales but incl sub-tropical. Spectacular views of Coast; cove for swimming. Cream TEAS. *Adm £1 Chd 50p. Open every Thurs June, July, Aug, Sept. For NGS Thurs May 22, 29 (2-6)*

●**Heligan Gardens** ❤❀ (Mr Tim Smit) Pentewan. From St Austell take B3273 signposted Mevagissey, follow signs. Heligan Gardens is the scene of the largest garden restoration project undertaken since the war. Of special interest in this romantic Victorian garden are; the fern ravine, 4 walled gardens with peach houses, vineries, melon grounds, a splendid collection of Bee boles, crystal grotto, Italian garden with a pool, an Elizabethan beacon 'Mount' and a large tropical Japanese valley garden. All are connected by an intricate web of over 2½m of ornamental footpaths, most unseen for more than half a century. TEAS and light refreshments. *Adm £2.90 OAPs £2.50 Chd £1.70. Open every day (10-4.30). Groups welcome,* **Tel 01726 844157**

High Noon ὠ (R E Sturdy) Ladock. 7m E of Truro on A39. 3½ acres ornamental trees, rhododendrons, camellias, and magnolias, 10yrs old; rose garden; daffodils; lawns; formal pool; S-facing slope with good views. *Combined adm with* **Ladock House** *£2 Chd free. Sun May 4 (2-5.30)*

Higher Truscott ὠ✿❀ (Mr & Mrs J C Mann) St Stephens. 3m NW of Launceston between St Stephens and Egloskerry. Signposted. Yr-round elevated garden of 1 acre in a natural setting. Trees, shrubs, climbers, herbaceous plants and alpines (many unusual). Splendid views. Ornamental vegetable garden. TEAS. *Adm £1.50 Chd free. Sun Aug 17 (2-6)*

The Hollies ὠ✿❀ (Mr J & Mrs N B Croggon) Grampound, nr Truro. In centre of village on Truro-St Austell rd. 2-acre garden of unusual design; unusual mixed planting of trees, shrubs and alpines. TEAS. *Adm £1 Chd free. Sun June 15 (2.30-5). Coach and private parties welcome by appt.* **Tel 01726 882474**

Ince Castle Gardens ὠ (Viscount & Patricia, Viscountess Boyd of Merton) 3m SW of Saltash. From A38 at Stoketon Cross take turn signed Trematon, then Elmgate. 5 acres with lawns and ornamental woods; shell house and dovecote. TEAS. *Adm £2 Chd free. Sun March 30 (Share to Cornwall Garden Soc®) April 20 (Share to Children's Hospice SW®) May 11 (Share to Cornwall Historic Churches Trust®) June 8 (Share to Titus Transport®) (2-5)*

●**Ken Caro** ✿❀ (Mr & Mrs K R Willcock) Bicton, Pensilva, 5m NE of Liskeard. From A390 to Callington turn off N at Butchers Arms, St Ive; take Pensilva Rd; at next Xrds take rd signed Bicton. 2 acres mostly planted in 1970, with a further 2-acre extension in 1993; well-designed and labelled plantsman's garden; rhododendrons, flowering shrubs, conifers and other trees; herbaceous. Panoramic views. Collection of aviary birds. Featured in NGS video 2. *Adm £2 Chd 50p. April 13 to June 30 every Sun, Mon, Tues, Wed; Tues & Weds only July & Aug (2-6).* **Tel 01579 362446**

¶**Kingberry** ❀ (Dr & Mrs M S Stead) Bodmin. N-side of town, 100yds uphill from East Cornwall Hospital. Ltd parking on hill, otherwise car parks in town centre. Approx 1-acre garden. Herbaceous borders, formal lawns, gravel terrace, ornamental pond, original stone walls, orchard and conservatory, some interesting perennials. A surprising haven in centre of Bodmin. *Adm £1.50 Chd free. Suns June 15, Sept 7 (2-6)*

Ladock House ὠ (Mr G J & Lady Mary Holborow) Ladock. 7m E of Truro on A39. Car park and entrance by church. Georgian old rectory with 4 acres of lawns, rhododendrons, camellias and azaleas with woodland garden. All planted during last 15yrs. TEAS in aid of Ladock Church. *Combined adm with* **High Noon** *£2 Chd free (Share to Ladock Church®). Sun May 4 (2-5.30)*

Lamorran House ✿❀ (Mr & Mrs Dudley-Cooke) Upper Castle Rd, St Mawes. First turning R after garage; signposted to St Mawes Castle. House ½m on L. Parking in rd. 4-acre sub-tropical hillside garden with beautiful views to St Anthonys Head. Extensive water gardens in Mediterranean and Japanese settings. Large collection of rhododendrons, azaleas, palm trees, cycads, agaves and many S hemisphere plants and trees. *Adm £2.50 Chd free. Sun May 11 (10-5).* **Tel 01326 270800**

▲**Lanhydrock** ὠ✿❀ (The National Trust) Bodmin, 2½m on B3268. Station: Bodmin Parkway 1¾m. Large-sized garden; formal garden laid out 1857; shrub garden with good specimens of rhododendrons and magnolias and fine views. Lunches and TEAS. House closed Mondays. *Adm garden only £3 Chd half price. For NGS Sun May 18 (11-5.30; last adm to house 5)*

●**Lanterns** ❀ (Mrs I Chapman) Mylor. 1m NE of Mylor. From Mylor follow the Restronguet Passage/Pandora Inn rd signs, Lanterns is on the RH-side before reaching the waterfront. ½-acre mature garden in natural setting planted by owners. Wide variety of shrubs, bulbs, herbaceous perennials, climbers, conservatory/greenhouse plants. Interesting in any season; small streams and dry areas; waterside walks. Owner always pleased to advise on plants and planting. *Collecting box (Share to Children's Hospice SW®). Open every day throughout the year (11am-dusk)*

▲**Long Cross Victorian Gardens** ὠ❀ (Mr & Mrs Crawford) Trelights, St Endellion. 7m N of Wadebridge on B3314. Charm of this garden is mazelike effect due to protecting hedges against sea winds; views of countryside and sea scapes (Port Isaac and Port Quin Bays) Garden specially designed to cope with environment of Cornwall's N Coast. Lunches and cream TEAS, coffee, evening meal. *Adm £1.25 Chd 25p. For NGS Sun June 22 (10.30-6.30). Private visits welcome for parties of 25 and over, please* **Tel 01208 880243**

¶**Manaccan Gardens** ✿❀ Manaccan is on the Lizard Peninsula E of Helston. Take A3083, at Culdrose roundabout take B3293 St Keverne rd. After Trelowarrior main entrance take L turn signposted Newtown-St Martin. Follow signs to Manaccan. [OS ref: SW764250]. Four very varied gardens situated in or near the charming village of Manaccan with C12 church and famous fig tree growing from the church wall. The gardens range from formal to cottage, one with a stream. All feature old roses, herbaceous and shrubs, showing perhaps a contrast to the spring gardens of Cornwall. Plants in aid of Manaccan church. TEAS in aid of Womens British Legion. *Combined adm £2 Chd free. Sun June 22 (2-5.30)*

Scotland's Gardens Scheme.

The National Gardens Scheme has a similar but quite separate counterpart in Scotland. Called Scotland's Gardens Scheme, it raises money for the Queen's Nursing Institute (Scotland), the Gardens Fund of the National Trust for Scotland and over 160 registered charities nominated by garden owners. The Handbook is available (£3.25 incl p&p) from Scotland's Gardens Scheme, 31 Castle Terrace, Edinburgh EH1 2EL.
Telephone 0131-229-1870, Fax 0131-229-0443

Nansawsan House ✿✤ (Mr & Mrs Michael Cole) Ladock. 7m E of Truro on B3275(A39). Parking at Falmouth Arms or Parish Hall. 1½ acres, part of a once larger Victorian garden. Rhododendrons, camellias, shrubs, trees and borders. CREAM TEAS in aid of Ladock Church. *Adm £1.50 Chd free. Sun May 18 (2-5). Also by appt* **01726 882392**

Newton House ♿✿ (Mrs Michael Trinick) Lanhydrock. 3½m SE of Bodmin on W bank of R. Fowey nr Respryn Bridge. Follow signs to Lanhydrock and Respryn. Surrounded by woods in the beautiful valley of the R. Fowey. 3 acres of old-fashioned walled garden, lawns, shrubs, herbaceous border and old shrub roses, fruit, vegetables and orchard. TEAS. *Adm £2 Chd free (Share to Lanhydrock Church®). Suns June 15, 22 (2-6)*

Northwood Farm ✿✤ (Mr & Mrs P K Cooper) St Neot. Take rd out of village to Wenmouth Cross. L and first R. Follow very narrow rd and NGS posters to Farm on R. House & garden on site of a China Clay Dri used 150 yrs ago. House rebuilt from barn and garden from old sunken pits still being developed. Discovery of several natural springs led to creation of ponds now with collection of water birds. TEAS. *Combined adm with* **Tremarkyn** *£2 Chd free. Sun June 29 (2-5.30)*

● **Oak Lodge** ✿✤ (Mr & Mrs Miller) Nanstallon, Nr Bodmin. From Bodmin, take A30 SW following signs for Redruth, for approx 2m. Turn R at top of hill and follow signs to Nanstallon. Proceed through village and take 2nd turning R on a L bend. Oak Lodge is approx 1.3m along this road on the R. Set at the edge of woodland, the 7-acre property is gradually being developed around the original trees into informal gardens, natural woodland walks carpeted with bluebells and other wild flowers in springtime, and an arboretum. *Adm £1.50 Chd free. Tues, Thurs, 1st and 3rd Sats of month April to Oct or by appt, please* **Tel 01208 831292**

■ **Paradise Park** ♿✿✤ (Mr Michael Reynolds) Hayle. Follow the A30 to Hayle, go to St Ives/St Erth roundabout then follow official brown and white signs to Paradise Park. The 2-acre walled garden is part of the 14 acres opened in 1973 as 'The rare and endangered birds breeding centre'. Much effort has been expended to make the gardens a suitable setting for a bird breeding collection of international importance. The World Parrot Trust is based here. Walled garden with pergolas, trellis and gazebos; climbing roses, clematis, lilies and passiflora are featured. TEAS. *Open throughout the yr from 10am to 5pm.* Cafe in Park. *Adm £4.95 Chd £2.95 (Share to World Parrot Trust®). For NGS Sun Sept 21 (10-5)*

●**Pencarrow** ♿✿ (Molesworth-St Aubyn Family) 4 miles N.W. Bodmin, signed off the A389. 50 acres of formal and woodland gardens laid out in the 1840's by Sir William Molesworth Bt. Marked walks past the Victorian Rockery, Italian and American Gardens, Lake and Ice House. Over 650 different varieties of rhododendrons, also an Internationally known specimen conifer collection. *House, Tearooms and Craft Centre open Sun to Thurs. Open daily Easter Sun to Oct 15. Adm garden only £2 Chd free. Gardens open daily (1.30-5)*

▲**Penjerrick Garden** ✤ (Rachel Morin) Budock. 3m SW of Falmouth between Budock and Mawnan Smith. Entrance at junction of lanes opp. Penmorvah Manor Hotel. Parking on verge along drive. Room to park one coach at gate. 15-acre garden of historical and botanical interest. Home of Barclayi and Penjerrick rhododendron hybrids. The upper garden with lovely view to the sea, contains many rhododendrons, camellias, magnolias, azaleas, bamboos, tree ferns and magnificent trees. The lower luxuriant valley garden features ponds in a wild woodland setting. *Adm £1.50 Chd 50p (Share to Parkinson's Disease Society®). For NGS Sun March 30 (11.30-4.30). Guided tours* **Tel 01872 870105**

Penwarne (Dr & Mrs H Beister) 3¼m SW of Falmouth. 1½m N of Mawnan. Garden with many varieties of flowering shrubs, rhododendrons, magnolias, New Zealand shrubs, formal and informal garden; walled garden. Ornamental ducks. *Adm £1.50 Chd 30p. Sun April 27 (2-5)*

Peterdale ✿✤ (Mrs Ann Mountfield) St John's Road, Millbrook. From Skinners Garage follow rd to mini roundabout and turn L. Straight ahead up St John's Rd Peterdale sign next to gate on wall. Last house on L. A plantsperson's garden featured on TV and Practical Garden, also Gardener's World magazine won Best Family Garden 1995. TEA. *Adm £1.50 Chd free. Suns May 25, July 13 (2-6). Groups of 10 or less by written application* **Tel 01752 823364**

Pine Lodge Gardens ♿✿✤ (Mr & Mrs R H J Clemo) Cuddra. On A390 E of St Austell between Holmbush and Tregrehan. Follow signs. 30-acre estate comprises gardens within a garden. The wide range of some 5,500 plants all of which are labelled, have been thoughtfully laid out using original designs and colour combinations to provide maximum interest for the garden lover. In addition to rhododendrons, magnolias, camellias, herbaceous borders with many rare and tender plants, marsh gardens, tranquil fish ponds, lake within the park, pinetum. TEAS. *Adm £2.50 Chd £1. Sun May 25 (1-5). Also open for groups of 20 or more by appt all year* **Tel 01726 73500**

Pinetum ♿✿✤ (Mr & Mrs G R Craw) Harewood. 6m SW of Tavistock. From A390 Tavistock-Callington Rd proceed towards Calstock. After 1m follow sign to Harewood Parish Church. At church continue straight on. 3rd house on R. Walkways meander through 2-acre pinetum full of maturing, uncommon, specimen trees of botanical and ornamental intrigue interspersed with shrubs, plants and garden features for yr-round colour and interest. TEAS. *Adm £1.50 Chd free. Suns May 11, 25; Aug 3 (2-5.30)*

Polgwynne ♿✿✤ (Mrs P Davey) Feock. 5m S of Truro via A39 (Truro-Falmouth rd) and then B3289 to 1st Xrds: straight on ½m short of Feock village. 3½-acre garden and grounds. Fruit and vegetable garden, woodlands extending to shore of Carrick Roads; magnificent Ginkgo Biloba (female, 12' girth) probably the largest female ginkgo in Britain; other beautiful trees; many rare and unusual shrubs. Lovely setting and view of Carrick Roads. TEAS. *Adm £2 Chd free. Sun April 27 (2-5).* **Tel 01872 862612**

●**Prideaux Place** & (Mr & Mrs Prideaux-Brune) Padstow. On the edge of Padstow follow brown signs for Prideaux Place, from ring rd (A389). Surrounding Elizabethan house the present main grounds were laid out in the early C18 by Edmund Prideaux. Ancient deer park with stunning views over Camel estuary; Victorian woodland walks currently under restoration. Newly restored sunken formal garden. A garden of vistas. Cream TEAS. *Adm £2 Chd £1. Easter Sunday to mid-Oct (1.30-5); Bank Hols (11-5)*

¶**Probus Gardens** &&& (Cornwall County Council) Truro. On E side of Probus village at the Trewithen roundabout. Clearly signed with brown Probus Gardens sign. 7½-acre garden started from a green field site in the early 1970's, to serve the needs of the local community as a centre for horticulture. Explains many aspects of gardening with displays of annuals, herbaceous perennials, shrubs, trees, conifers and hedges. Also layouts for fruit, vegetables and general designs. Annually, different trials are grown. A place to get ideas. TEAS. *Adm £2.70 Chd free. Daily March 15 to Oct 17 (10-5) Mons to Fris Oct 20 to 19 Dec; 1998 Jan 7 to March 13 (10-4)*

Roseland House ✿ (Charlie & Liz Pridham) Chacewater. 4m W of Truro, at Truro end of main st. Parking in village car park (100yds) or surrounding rds. 1-acre garden subdivided by walls and trellises hosting a wide range of climbers. Mixed borders of unusual plants, Victorian conservatory and greenhouse extend the gardening yr. TEAS. *Adm £1.50 Chd free. Tues June, July (1-6). Suns June 29, July 13 (2-5).* **Tel 01872 560451**

▲**St Michael's Mount** &✿ (The Rt Hon Lord St Levan; The National Trust) Marazion. ½m from shore at Marazion by Causeway; otherwise by ferry. Flowering shrubs; rock plants, castle walls; fine sea views. TEAS. *Adm Castle & gardens £3.90, Chd £1.95 (under 16). For NGS Sun April 20 (10.30-5.30) last entrance 4.45*

Scawn Mill &✿ (Mrs A Ball & Dr Julian Ball) St Keyne. From the A38 at the E end of Dobwalls take the signpost to Duloe, Herodsfoot and Looe for 1½ m. Turn R at sign for Scawn and continue for 1m down to the river. Water lily lake lying beside the West Looe River terraced with azaleas, black pines and Japanese Maples. Walks beside primulas, herbaceous border and Japanese garden. Public footpath following West Looe River through woodland to Herodsfoot. TEAS. *Adm £1.50 Chd free. Suns June 15, July 27 (2-5.30)*

●**Trebah** ✿ (Trebah Garden Trust) Mawnan Smith 4m from Falmouth. Follow tourism signs from Hillhead Roundabout on A39 approach to Falmouth. Excellent parking (free) and access for coaches. 25-acre S facing ravine garden, planted in 1850's. Extensive collection of rare and mature trees and shrubs incl glades of huge tree ferns over 100 years old and sub-tropical exotics. Hydrangea collection covers 2½ acres. Water garden with waterfalls and rock pool stocked with mature Koi Carp. A magical garden for plantsman, the artist and family. Play area and trails for children. Use of private beach. New Coffee Shop. *Adm £3 OAPs £2.80 Chd and disabled £1.*

Special group and winter prices. RHS members free. Open every day throughout year (10.30-5 last admission). **Tel 01326 250448**

Trebartha (The Latham Family) North Hill, SW of Launceston. Nr junction of B3254 & B3257. Wooded area with lake surrounded by walks of flowering shrubs; woodland trail through fine woods with cascades and waterfalls; American glade with fine trees. No coaches. TEAS. *Adm £1.50 Chd 50p. Sun Sept 28 (2-5.30)*

Tregilliowe Farm &✿ (Mr & Mrs J Richards) Penzance-Hayle A30 Rd from Penzance turn R at Crowlas Xrds. After approx 1m turn sharp L on to St Erth Rd. 2nd farm lane on R. 2-acre garden still developing. Herbaceous beds with wide range of perennials and grasses. Raised Mediterranean bed. TEAS June in aid of Save The Children. July in aid of St Julias Hospice. *Adm £1.50 Chd free. Suns June 15, July 13 (2-6).* **Tel 01736 740654**

●**Tregrehan** &&& (Mr T Hudson) Entrance on A390 opp Britannia Inn 1m W of St Blazey. Access for cars and coaches. Garden largely created since early C19. Woodland of 20 acres containing fine trees, award winning camellias raised by late owner and many interesting plants from warm temperate climes. Show greenhouses a feature containing softer species. TEA. *Adm £2.50 Chd free. Mid March to end June daily. Not open Easter Sunday. For NGS Sun May 4 (10.30-5)*

▲**Trelissick** &&& (The National Trust; Mr & Mrs Spencer Copeland) Feock, 4m S of Truro, nr King Harry Ferry. On B3289. Planted with tender shrubs; magnolias, camellias and rhododendrons with many named species characteristic of Cornish gardens. Fine woodlands encircle the gardens through which a varied circular walk can be enjoyed. Superb view over Falmouth harbour. Georgian house (not open). Lunches and TEAS. *Adm £4 Chd half price. Car park £1. For NGS Sun April 13 (12.30-5.30)*

Treloyhan Manor Hotel &✿ (Mr T Rogers) St Ives. Situated on the A3074 as you drive down into St Ives on the RH-side. Approx 7 acres of gardens overlooking St Ives bay. A pleasant garden thoughtfully laid out incl many trees, shrubs and rare ferns. Suited to the mild winter climate. TEAS. *Adm £1.50 Chd free. Sun June 15, Weds, July 2, 16 (2-5)*

Tremarkyn ✿ (Mr & Mrs J E Thomas) Wenmouth Cross, St Neot. Turn R off A38 (Liskeard and Bodmin) approx ¾m past Doublebois signposted St Neot and Carnglaze Caverns. In St Neot turn sharp R (signposted St Cleer) up steep hill; within ½m as soon as road levels out [201:194677]. ½-acre drive lined with trees and shrubs. Gardens around old granite buildings - still evolving. Bog garden, kitchen garden; unusual conifers. 2 acres of grassed areas with trees and shrubs. Cream TEAS. *Combined adm with* **Northwood Farm** *£2 Chd free. Sun June 29 (2-5.30)*

Tremeer Gardens St Tudy, 8m N of Bodmin; W of B3266, all rds signed. 7-acre garden famous for camellias and rhododendrons with water; many rare shrubs. *Adm £1 Chd 50p. Sun April 6 (2-5).* **Tel 01208 850313**

Trenance ✿✾ (Mr & Mrs J Dingle) Launceston. Follow signs for Leisure Centre along Dunheved Rd. At College end of rd take sharp L bend and immed after this take another L turning into Windmill Hill. Trenance is approx 200yds on L. A 1¾-acre garden for all seasons. A wide variety of trees and shrubs incl rhododendrons, camellias, azaleas, acers and magnolias; heathers and conifers, primulas, herbaceous borders, roses and clematis with several smaller gardens within the main garden. TEA. *Adm £1.50 Chd 50p. Suns May 18, July 6 (2-5.30)*

Trenarth ✿ (Mrs L M Nottingham) High Cross. Nearest main rds A39, A394 Truro, Falmouth, Helston. 1½m E of Constantine, 2m W of Mawnan Smith, 1½m S of Treverva. Nearest landmark High Cross Garage. From Treverva with garage on L take lane to L, then immed R down dead-end lane. Trenarth is ½m at end of lane. Diverse 2-acre gardens round old farmhouse. Courtyard, conservatory, C18 garden walls, yew hedging, herbaceous and rockery beds, shrub borders, orchard and woodland walk to Helford. Extensively replanted during past 3 yrs, with further wilderness areas awaiting reclamation. TEAS. *Adm £1.50 Chd free. Sun Aug 10 (2-5)*

▲**Trengwainton** ✿✾✿ (The National Trust) 2m N W of Penzance, ½ mile West of Heamoor on Penzance-Morvah rd (B3312), ½m off St Just rd (A3071) The garden of mainland Britain perhaps most favoured for the cultivation of exotic shrubs and trees. Plantsman's delight. *Adm £3 Chd half price. For NGS Sat March 15 (10.30-5.30)*

▲**Trerice** ✿✾✿ (The National Trust) Newlyn East 3m SE of Newquay. From Newquay via A392 and A3058; turn R at Kestle Mill (NT signposts). The summer-flowering garden is unusual in content and layout and there is an orchard planted with old varieties of fruit trees. A small museum traces the history of the lawn mower. Lunches & TEAS. *Adm house & garden £3.80 Chd £1.50. For NGS Wed Aug 20 (11-5.30). Children's Garden Trail*

●**Trevarno Gardens** ✿✾ (Mr M Sagin & Mr N Helsby) Sithney Helston. Signed from Crowntown on the B3303, 3m NW of Helston. Set within beautiful and historic Trevarno Estate dating back to 1296, one of Cornwall's most romantic and secret woodland gardens covering 40 acres. Extensive collection of rare shrubs, specimen trees, walled gardens, mysterious rockeries, grotto, enchanting lake, cascade and fountains and abundant wildlife; now subject of major restoration and replanting programme. TEAS. *Adm £2.50 Chd under 14 £1.25, under 5 free. Open daily (10-5) Jan 1 to Dec 24.* **Tel 01326 574274**

Trevegean ✿ (Mr & Mrs E C Cousins) 9 Manor Way. Take Penzance by-pass; take first L off roundabout towards Treneere and Heamoor. Sharp R turn for Manor way. ⅓-acre divided into series of enclosed areas; planting some formal, informal, topiary garden, shrubs and perennials; connected by brick and slab paths some edged with box. TEAS. *Adm £1 Chd free (Share to St Julias Hospice Hayle®). Suns May 4, June 22 (2-5)*

●**Trewithen** ✿✾ (Mr A M J Galsworthy) Truro. ½m E Probus. Entrance on A390 Truro-St Austell Rd. Signposted. Large car park. Internationally renowned garden of 30 acres laid out by Maj G Johnson between 1912 &

1960 with much of original seed and plant material collected by Ward and Forrest. Original C18 walled garden famed for towering magnolias and rhododendrons; wide range of own hybrids. Flatish ground amidst original woodland park. TEAS. *Adm £2.80 Chd £1.50 Group £2.50. Mon to Sat March 1 to Sept 30, Suns April-May only (10-4.30). Special arrangements for coaches.* **Tel 01726 883647**

Water Meadow ✾ (Philip & Rose Lamb) Luxulyan 5m NW of St Austell, 6m S of Bodmin. [Map ref SX 052582.] Park in village street between church and school. Turn by church, garden 200yds downhill on L. 1½-acre garden on sloping site with Grade II listed grotto. Large pond with waterside planting and bog garden with extensive primula, astilbe, gunnera, arum lilies etc. Gravel garden surrounded by shrub roses & herbaceous planting. Specimen trees and shrubs with recently established mixed borders. TEAS in aid of WI. *Adm £1.50 Chd free. Sun June 29 (2-5) also by appt please* **Tel 01726 851399**

Watergate Trelill ✿✾ (Lt Col & Mrs G B Browne) 5m SW of Camelford, N of St Kew highway. NE of Trelill, signposted from A39. 3-acre garden in a delightful setting with a stream running through it. In spring there is a display of many varieties of narcissus and camellias, rhododendrons and magnolias. Water garden with a variety of primulas and moisture-loving plants, also herbaceous borders, shrubs and old fashioned roses. TEAS. *Adm £1.50 Chd free. Easter Sun March 30 (2-5)*

Werrington Park (J M Williams Esq) Launceston. From A30 take the Launceston exit and follow signs to Bude. Follow the B3254 Bude rd through Yeolmbridge and up the hill to Ladycross. In the hamlet of Ladycross turn R at school ½m along lane enter drive gate with adjacent lodge situated on a sharp L-hand bend. Two gardens separated by attractive parkland valley. The Chinese garden (8 acres) contains many rare rhododendrons and magnolias, some raised from seeds sent home by Wilson and Forrest in the early 1900s from the Himalayas for Mr J C Williams. Varieties of prunus, birch and camellias. The Werrens and Bowling Green (6 acres) established during the same period, are more noted for interesting trees and are more formal but also contain many mature shrubs. Transport between the 2 gardens will be provided. TEAS in aid of Werrington Church. *Adm £2.50 Chd £1. Sun May 4 (2-5.30)*

●**Woodland Garden** ✿✾ (Mr & Mrs N Froggatt) Garras. On Helston-St Keverne Rd B3293, turn R ¼m past Garras at Woodland Garden sign. Entrance on R after ½m. Peaceful 2½-acre valley garden designed to encourage wildlife. 9 acres heather downland (Erica vagans, July/Aug). Spring succession of wild daffodils, primroses, bluebells, camellias, rhododendrons. Unusual plants set sympathetically among mature woodland. Yr-round foliage colour and form. Dogs allowed only on Downs. *Adm £1 Chd free. Sats only March 29 to Sept 27 (2-5).* **Tel 01326 221295**

General Information. For general information on the use of this book see Page 17.

¶**Wynlands** &🌸 (Mr & Mrs Henry Towner) Manaccan. W of Manaccan take Manaccan rd from Newtown St Martin. Approx 1¼m Wynlands on L. Lay-by in front. Parking in field opp farm and in lay- by. [OS ref: SW 753243]. ½-acre garden designed for maximum wind protection and yr-round interest. Wide variety of trees, shrubs and bulbs. Old fashioned climbing and new English roses, delphiniums and herbaceous perennials. Japanese corner, conservatory, greenhouse, vegetable and fruit garden. Small orchard planted and designed by owner in the last 8yrs. Plants and TEAS in aid of Manaccan Church. *Combined adm with* **Hallowarren** *£2 Chd free. Sun June 29 (2-5.30)*

Zoar &🌸 (Mrs Pixie Wells) Mylor. [O/S Map 204, ref: 807367.] From Truro take A39 to Falmouth for approx 7m. 2nd turning L after Norway Inn, follow signs to Restronguet and Mylor Bridge for 2¼m. At Xrds by large yellow house turn R, Zoar is 1st house on L. From Falmouth take A39 to Penryn. At Kessells Garage turn R, signed to Mylor. Drive through village, up Passage Hill, Zoar is last house on R. An unusual 1-acre garden mostly planted since 1986. Some mature shrubs and an interesting collection of dwarf conifers. Small pond and arboretum. Bounded on two sides by cornish hedges. *Adm £1.50 Chd free (Share to RNLI®). Sun June 1 (2-5)*

Cumbria

Hon County Organiser: (South)	Mrs R E Tongue, Paddock Barn, Winster, Windermere LA23 3NW
Assistant Hon County Organiser: (North)	Mrs E C Hicks, Scarthwaite, Grange-in-Borrowdale, Keswick CA12 5UQ
Hon County Treasurer:	Derek Farman Esq, Mill House, Winster, Windermere LA23 3NW

DATES OF OPENING

April 12 Saturday
Copt Howe, Chapel Stile
April 13 Sunday
Copt Howe, Chapel Stile
April 19 Saturday
Copt Howe, Chapel Stile
April 20 Sunday
Copt Howe, Chapel Stile
Levens Brow, Kendal
Winderwath, nr Penrith
April 21 Monday
Levens Hall, Kendal
April 26 Saturday
Copt Howe, Chapel Stile
April 27 Sunday
Copt Howe, Chapel Stile ‡
Green Bank, Grasmere ‡
May 3 Saturday
Copt Howe, Chapel Stile
May 4 Sunday
Copt Howe, Chapel Stile ‡
Dallam Tower, Milnthorpe
Green Bank, Grasmere ‡
Marton House, Long Marton
The Nook, Helton, nr Penrith
Rydal Mount, Eskdale Green, nr Gosforth
Stagshaw, Rothay Road, Ambleside ‡
May 5 Monday
Palace How, Brackenthwaite, Loweswater
May 7 Wednesday
Rydal Mount, Eskdale Green, nr Gosforth

May 10 Saturday
Acorn Bank, Temple Sowerby, nr Penrith
Copt Howe, Chapel Stile
May 11 Sunday
Copt Howe, Chapel Stile
Holme Crag, Witherslack, Grange-over-Sands
May 13 Tuesday
Browfoot, Skelwith, Ambleside
May 14 Wednesday
Browfoot, Skelwith, Ambleside
May 15 Thursday
Browfoot, Skelwith, Ambleside
May 17 Saturday
Copt Howe, Chapel Stile
May 18 Sunday
Copt Howe, Chapel Stile
Halecat, Witherslack
Holehird, Windermere ‡
Matson Ground, Windermere ‡
Winderwath, nr Penrith
May 21 Wednesday
Matthew How, Troutbeck
May 24 Saturday
Browfoot, Skelwith, Ambleside ‡
Copt Howe, Chapel Stile ‡
May 25 Sunday
Browfoot, Skelwith, Ambleside ‡
Copt Howe, Chapel Stile ‡
Fell Yeat, Kirkby Lonsdale
High Beckside Farm, Cartmel
May 26 Monday
Browfoot, Skelwith, Ambleside ‡
Green Bank, Grasmere ‡
May 28 Wednesday
Matthew How, Troutbeck ‡

Windy Hall, Windermere ‡
June 1 Sunday
Blakeholme Wray, Newby Bridge ‡
Hazelmount, Thwaites, Millom
Lindeth Fell Country House Hotel, Bowness-on-Windermere ‡
Stagshaw, Rothay Road, Ambleside ‡
Station House, Lamplugh, nr Workington
June 4 Wednesday
Brackenburn, Manesty, Keswick
Matthew How, Troutbeck
June 5 Thursday
Lingholm, Portinscale, Keswick
June 7 Saturday
Bush Green Cottage, Broughton-in-Furness
June 8 Sunday
Bush Green Cottage, Broughton-in-Furness
June 11 Wednesday
Brockhole, Windermere
June 14 Saturday
Acorn Bank, Temple Sowerby, nr Penrith
Bush Green Cottage, Broughton-in-Furness
Rannerdale Cottage, Buttermere
June 15 Sunday
Bush Green Cottage, Broughton-in-Furness
Fell Yeat, Kirkby Lonsdale
Holme Crag, Witherslack, Grange-over-Sands
Hutton-in-the-Forest, Penrith

Rannerdale Cottage, Buttermere
Tomarobandy, Blitterlees, Silloth
June 18 Wednesday
Fell Yeat, Kirkby Lonsdale
June 22 Sunday
Dallam Tower, Milnthorpe
June 26 Thursday Evening
Holker Hall & Gardens,
Cark-in-Cartmel
June 27 Friday
St Annes, Great Langdale
June 28 Saturday
St Annes, Great Langdale
Sizergh Castle, nr Kendal
June 29 Sunday
The Brown House, Maryport
Marton House, Long Marton
St Annes, Great Langdale
Whitbysteads, Askham
Windy Hall, Windermere
July 6 Sunday
Yews, Middle Entrance Drive
July 9 Wednesday
Brockhole, Windermere
July 12 Saturday
Acorn Bank, Temple Sowerby, nr
Penrith

July 13 Sunday
Tomarobandy, Blitterlees, Silloth
July 20 Sunday
Halecat, Witherslack ‡
Dallam Tower, Milnthorpe ‡
38 English Street, Longtown
Nunwick Hall, Great Salkeld
July 27 Sunday
High Cleabarrow, Windermere
August 7 Thursday
Lingholm, Portinscale, Keswick
August 17 Sunday
Holehird, Windermere
Hutton-in-the-Forest, Penrith
Tomarobandy, Blitterlees, Silloth
August 24 Sunday
Rydal Mount, Eskdale Green, nr
Gosforth
August 27 Wednesday
Rydal Mount, Eskdale Green, nr
Gosforth
September 7 Sunday
Matson Ground, Windermere
September 22 Monday
Levens Hall, Kendal

Regular openings
For details see garden description

Brockhole, Windermere
Copt Howe, Chapel Stile
Higham Hall College, Cockermouth
Holker Hall & Gardens,
Cark-in-Cartmel
Hutton-in-the-Forest, Penrith
Levens Hall, Kendal
Winderwath, nr Penrith

By appointment only
*For telephone numbers and other
details see garden descriptions.
Private visits welcomed*

High Rigg, Grange-in-Borrowdale
Langholme Mill, Woodgate, Lowick
Green
The Mill House, Sebergham
Scarthwaite, Grange-in-Borrowdale
Wood Hall, Cockermouth

DESCRIPTIONS OF GARDENS

▲**Acorn Bank** &⚘❀ (The National Trust) Temple Sowerby. 6m E of Penrith on A66; ½m N of Temple Sowerby. Bus: Penrith-Appleby or Carlisle-Darlington; alight Culgaith Rd end. Medium-sized walled garden; fine herb garden; orchard and mixed borders; wild garden with woodland/riverside walk leading to a partly restored watermill open to the public 1997. Dogs on leads only woodland walk. *Adm £2.10 Chd £1. For NGS Sats May 10, June 14, July 12 (10-5)*

Blakeholme Wray ⚘ (Mr & Mrs W T Rooney) Newby Bridge. [Grid Ref GR 384 895] Blakeholme Wray is 2m N of Newby Bridge on A592. 4 acres garden, 22 acres woodland. An outstanding position with lawns sweeping down to the shore of Windermere. Informal planting is ongoing under present owners: massed rhododendrons and azaleas, damson orchard, wild orchids, bluebell carpets, ancient woodland walk, abundant wildlife. Partially suitable for wheelchairs. TEA. *Adm £1.50 Chd free. Sun June 1 (12-5)*

Brackenburn (Prof & Mrs D C Ellwood) Manesty. Take rd signed Portinscale and Grange off A66. Follow all signs for Grange. Garden is 1½ acres on the mountainside on RH-side of rd 3½m from A66. The Garden has wonderful views of Lake Derwentwater. There are several water features planted for damp acid conditions with many rhododendrons, azaleas, ferns and primulas. Brackenburn is the former home of author Sir Hugh Walpole. *Adm £1.50 Acc chd free (Share to Scottish terrier emergency care scheme®). Wed June 4 (11-5)*

■ **Brockhole** & (Lake District National Park) Windermere. 2m NW of Windermere on A591 between Winder-

mere and Ambleside. 10 acres formal gardens, designed by Thomas Mawson. Acid soils and mild aspect, many unusual or slightly tender plants, shrub roses, herbaceous borders, scented garden. 20 acres informal grounds, wide variety of trees and shrubs. Picnic area, adventure playground, boat trips on Lake Windermere. Garden walks. Restaurant and tea rooms. *Adm free (Multi-tariff parking available, season ticket for car park. Daily March 22 to Nov 3; for NGS Wed June 11, July 9 (10-5).* **Tel 015394 46601**

Browfoot ❀ (Trevor Woodburn) Skelwith, Ambleside on A593 2½m from Ambleside. Re-vamped woodland garden approx 2 acres; collection of rhododendrons, azaleas, conifers, natural rockery, many other shrubs; delightful views of Loughrigg and the Brathay Valley. *Adm £1 Chd 40p. Tues, Wed, Thurs, Sat, Sun, Mon May 13, 14, 15, 24, 25, 26 (11-5)*

¶**The Brown House** ⚘❀ (Celia Eddy & Tim Longville) Maryport. At junction of A596 and A594, at main Maryport traffic lights by St Mary's Church, turn into Wood St, then immed R into Church St. Take 3rd L into Fleming St, which runs into Fleming Sq and Fleming Pl. Ample free parking in Fleming Sq. Small walled garden behind Victorian townhouse on Solway coast. Enthusiasts imagining a larger garden and warmer climate have crammed a warren of raised beds with a cottage garden profusion of unusual and rare plants. TEAS. *Adm £1.50 Chd free. Sun June 29 (1-5) Private visits welcome by appt, please* **Tel 01900 814959**

Bush Green Cottage &⚘❀ (Mr & Mrs James Haunch) Broughton-in-Furness. On A595 on edge of Broughton. 1½m from Foxfield on RH-side. Approx 1-acre cottage garden. Streams and pool. Originally Crossing Keepers

Cottage on Furness Railway; large collection geraniums. Wide variety hardy plants; new areas under development. *Adm £1.50 Acc chd under 12 free. Sats, Suns June 7, 8; 14, 15 (11-5). Private visits welcome from June onwards, please* **Tel after 8pm (except Mons) 01229 716 724**

Copt Howe ❀ (Professor R N Haszeldine) Chapel Stile. Great Langdale ¼m W of Chapel Stile. 2-acre plantsman's garden, newly extended. Scenic views Langdale Pikes. Extensive collections of acers (especially Japanese), camellias, azaleas, rhododendrons, quercus, fagus, rare shrubs and trees, unusual perennials; herbaceous and bulbous species; alpines and trough gardens; rare dwarf and large conifers; Expedition plants from Far East. Featured by the media, gardening magazines. *Adm £2; OAP £1.50; Chd free. Sats, Suns and Bank Holidays April 12 to end of May (12-5). Cream TEAS and plants May 4, 25 (10-5.30). Plants on many other days (Share to Langdales Society© May 4, Friends of the Lake District® other days). Private visits welcome April 1 to end Sept, please* **Tel 015394 37685**

Dallam Tower ⬥ (Brigadier & Mrs C E Tryon-Wilson) Milnthorpe, 7m S of Kendal. 7m N of Carnforth, nr junction of A6 and B5282. Station: Arnside, 4m; Lancaster, 15m. Medium-sized garden; natural rock garden, waterfalls, rambler roses and rose beds; wood walks, lawns, shrubs. C19 cast iron orangery. *Adm £1 Chd free. Suns May 4, June 22, July 20 (2-5)*

38 English Street ⬥❀ (Mr & Mrs C Thomson) Longtown, Carlisle. M6 junction 44, A7 for 6m into Longtown. 300yds on L next door to Annes Hairdressers. Entrance through open archway. Terraced house garden. Red sandstone and water features; containers and troughs, pergola and herbaceous. TEA. *Adm £1 Acc chd free (Share to Cat Protection League®). Sun July 20 (2-5). Private visits and parties welcome, please* **Tel 01228 791364**

Fell Yeat ⬥❀ (Mr & Mrs O S Benson) Casterton, nr Kirkby Lonsdale. Approx 1m E of Casterton Village on the rd to Bull Pot. Leave A65 at Devils Bridge, follow A683 for a mile, take the R fork to High Casterton at the golf course, straight across at two sets of Xrds, the house is immediately on the L about ¼m from no through rd sign. 1-acre informal country garden with mixed borders, herbaceous, old roses, small fernery, herb garden and small pond and is building up the National Collection of Ligularias. TEAS Suns only, Tea Wed only in aid of Holy Trinity Church, Casterton. *Adm £1.50 Chd 20p. Suns, Wed May 25, June 15, 18 (1.30-5)*

Green Bank ❀ (Mr & Mrs Reg Gifford) Grasmere. 4m from Ambleside off the A591 Keswick Rd. Turn R between Swan Hotel and its car park. 5-acre steep hillside garden with woodland walks and mountain stream under a 5yr renovation plan. Features a unique collection of rare trees, rhododendrons, camellias and azaleas brought to England by the late Michael Black from Bhutan, Chile, Nepal, etc. Great interest to plant enthusiasts. Teas in adjacent hotels or cafes in Grasmere. *Adm £2 Chd/OAPs £1. Suns April 27, May 4, Mon May 26 (10.30-5). Private visits welcome Mon to Fri, by appt April 1 to June 28, please* **Tel 015394 35496**

▲**Halecat** ⬥❀❀ (Mrs Michael Stanley) Witherslack, 10m SW of Kendal. From A590 turn into Witherslack following the Halecat brown signs. L in township at another brown sign and L again, signpost 'Cartmel Fell'; gates on L [map ref. 434834]. Medium-sized garden; mixed shrub and herbaceous borders, terrace, sunken garden; gazebo; daffodils and cherries in Spring, over 70 different varieties of hydrangea; beautiful view over Kent estuary to Arnside. Nursery garden attached. TEA. *Adm £1.50 Chd free. For NGS Suns May 18, July 20 (2-5). Also private parties welcome, please* **Tel 0144 852229**

Hazelmount ⬥❀❀ (Mrs J Barratt) Thwaites, Millom, 2m from Broughton-in-Furness off A595 up hill after crossing Duddon River Bridge. 5-acre woodland garden, small lake with stream and water garden; spring display of species rhododendrons, azaleas and flowering shrubs. Mature trees and exceptional views of Duddon Estuary and sea. Cream TEAS. *Adm £1.50 Chd free. Sun June 1 (2-5.30)*

High Beckside Farm ❀❀ (Mr & Mrs P J McCabe) Cartmel. 1¼m N of Cartmel. Take the Haverthwaite Rd, from the PO in the village. A newly created conservation area, a wild garden with ponds, waterfalls, waterfowl; flowering bushes and a number of rare trees. An arboretum in the very early stages of formation. 11 acres of wild flowers on a hillside with fine views. A small house garden. Approx ¼m from house to conservation area. Stout shoes. TEA. *Adm £1.25 Chd 25p. Sun May 25 (1-5). Private visits welcome, please* **Tel 015395 36528**

High Cleabarrow ⬥❀❀ (Mr & Mrs R T Brown) 3m SE of Windermere off B5284 Crook to Kendal Rd (nr Windermere Golf Course). 2-acre garden owner designed and planted comprising mixed borders, island beds, formal rose garden, old-fashioned roses, pond with waterside planting, many unusual plants. Large collection of geraniums, hostas and hydrangeas. Woodland area under development. TEAS. *Adm £1.50 Chd 50p. Sun July 27 (1.30-5.30)*

High Rigg (Miss B Newton) Grange-in-Borrowdale. From Keswick take B5289 to Grange; cross rd bridge, suitable for mini-buses. House ½m on L. ¾-acre fellside garden created over 30 yrs by Miss F M Birkett. Mixed shrub/herbaceous border, rock and bog gardens. Rhododendrons, azaleas and many other shrubs and trees. *Adm £1.50 Acc chd free. Private visits and parties welcome, please* **Tel 017687 77206**

Higham Hall College ⬥ (Alasdair Galbraith) Bassenthwaite Lake Cockermouth. 7m N of Keswick 4m SE of Cockermouth. Take rd signed Castle Inn off A66 at N end of Bassenthwaite Lake. Higham Hall is signed after ½m. 4 acres of informal Victorian gardens incl pond, woodland walk, specimen trees, lawns, sunken rose garden. Rhododendrons. Parkland views towards Skiddaw. *£1 donation in Honesty Box. Open all year, every day (9-dusk).* **Tel 017687 76276**

1927–1997

This year the National Gardens Scheme is celebrating its 70th Anniversary. Please help us celebrate by visiting a garden in 1997.

■ **Holehird (Lakeland Horticultural Society)** ✗ Patterdale Road, Windermere. ½m N of Windermere town on A591. Turn R onto A592 to Patterdale. Garden signposted on R ¾m on A592. Car park along private drive. The garden of nearly 5 acres is set on a hillside with some of the best views in Lakeland, with a great diversity of plants that grow well in this area, incl alpine and heather beds and a collection of rhododendrons and azaleas. The walled garden is mostly herbaceous. National collections of astilbes, polystichum ferns and hydrangeas. Partially suitable wheelchairs. *Garden always open. Entrance by donation £1.50 Chd free. Warden available throughout summer (11-5). Coach parties by appointment, volunteer guides available* Tel 015394 46008. *For NGS Suns May 18, Aug 17 (10-5)*

■ **Holker Hall** &✗❀ (Lord & Lady Cavendish) Cark-in-Cartmel. 4m W of Grange-over-Sands. 12m W of M6 (junction 36). Magnificent formal and woodland gardens classed as amongst the best in the world for design and content (1996 Good Gardens Guide). Exotic trees and shrubs, ancient oaks and a beech walk with a stunning display of rhododendrons, azaleas, magnolias and camellias in spring. Summer garden, rose garden and elliptical garden. Water features incl a limestone cascade. National Collection of styracaceae. Wildflower meadow. Largest slate sundial in the world. Also exhibitions and deer park, adventure playground, gift shop and cafe. Great Garden and Countryside Festival May 30, 31, June 1. *Adm £3.15 gardens only. Garden tours by arrangement. Open Sun-Fri March 28 to Oct 31 (10-6) last admission 4.30pm. For NGS Adm £3 Chd £1.75. Thurs June 26 (6.30-9)*

Holme Crag ✗ (Mr Jack Watson) Witherslack, Grange-over-Sands. Off A590 Barrow Rd through Witherslack. Turn L Helecat. Turn L at next rd on junction. Just past telephone kiosk in Newton Rd signpost approx 1m. Partially suitable for wheelchairs. 4 acres designed to encourage wildlife. Award winning bird garden with large pond and rockeries; 22 different species nest. Scree beds. Azaleas, rhododendrons and mature shrubs and trees, spring garden, primulas - species bulbs. Partially suitable for wheelchairs. *Adm £1.50 Acc chd under 12 free. Suns May 11, June 15 (1.30-5)*

■ **Hutton-in-the-Forest** (Lord Inglewood) 5m NW of Penrith. 3m from exit 41 of M6. Magnificent grounds with C18 walled flower garden, terraces and lake. C19 Low garden, specimen trees and topiary; woodland walk and dovecote. Mediaeval House with C17, C18 and C19 additions. TEAS. *Adm £2 gardens, grounds, £3.50 house, gardens & grounds Chd free gardens, grounds £1.50 house & garden & grounds. Gardens and grounds open daily all year except Sats (11-5). House open (1-4). Tearoom (12-4.30). Easter Sun, Mon; then Thurs, Fris, Suns, Bank Hols and Aug Weds May 2 to Sept 28. For NGS Suns June 15, Aug 17 (11-5)*

Langholme Mill ✗ (Dr W E Gill) Woodgate, Lowick Green. On the A5092 Greenodd to Workington rd 3m from Greenodd on a short stretch of dual carriageway. Park in front of the house. Approx ¾-acre of woodland garden with a beck running the length of it. Camellias, dwarf rhododendrons smaller rhododendrons, yak species and hybrids Japanese azaleas and azaleas; acers, bam-

boos, hostas, astilbes and waterside plants. *Adm £1.50 Chd under 12 free. Private visits welcome please write or* Tel 01229 885215

Levens Brow ✗ (Mr & Mrs O R Bagot) Kendal. 5m S of Kendal on A6. Junction 36 on M6. 1½-acre garden, mixed borders. Trees and shrubs bordered on 2 sides by Levens Park. Delightful spring garden, extensive plantings narcissus, fritillary, anemone and blossom trees. Large collection hellebores orientalis hybrids. Local limestone walling and rockeries of character. *Adm £1.50 Chd 50p (Share to NSPCC®). Sun April 20 (11.30-5)*

■ **Levens Hall** &✗❀ (C H Bagot Esq) 5m S of Kendal on Milnthorpe Rd (A6); exit 36 from M6. 10 acres incl famous topiary garden and 1st ha-ha laid out by M Beaumont in 1694. Magnificent beech circle; formal bedding; herbaceous borders. Elizabethan mansion, added to C13 pele tower, contains superb panelling, plasterwork and furniture. Steam collection. Only gardens suitable for wheelchairs. *Adm House & Garden £5 Chd £2.70. Garden only £3.70 Chd £2. Reduction for groups March 30 to Sept 30. House & garden, gift shop, tea-room, children's play area, picnic area. Sun, house (11-4.30). Mon, Tues, Wed, Thurs house (12-4.30) grounds (10.30-5), stream collection (2-5). Closed Fri & Sat. For NGS Mons April 21, Sept 22 (10.30-5)*

Lindeth Fell Country House Hotel & (Air Commodore & Mrs P A Kennedy) 1m S of Bowness on A5074. 6-acres of lawns and landscaped grounds on the hills above Lake Windermere, probably designed by Mawson around 1907; majestic conifers and specimen trees best in spring and early summer with a colourful display of rhododendrons, azaleas and Japanese maples; grounds offer splendid views to Coniston mountains. Top terrace suitable for wheelchairs. TEAS in hotel £1. *Adm £1 Chd free. Sun June 1 (2-5). Also private parties welcome, please* Tel 01539 443 286

■ **Lingholm** &✗❀ (The Viscount Rochdale) Keswick. On W shore of Derwentwater; Portinscale 1m; Keswick 3m. Turn off A66 at Portinscale; drive entrance 1m on left. Ferry: Keswick to Nicol End, 10 mins walk. Bus: Keswick to Portinscale, 1m. Formal and woodland gardens; garden walk 1m; rhododendrons, azaleas, herbaceous borders etc. Spring daffodils, autumn colours. Plant centre. Free car park. TEAS. *Adm £2.80 (incl leaflet) Chd free. March 28 to Oct 31 daily. For NGS Thurs June 5, Aug 7 (10-5)*

Marton House ✗ (Mr & Mrs M S Hardy-Bishop) Long Marton, Turn off A66 2m W of Appleby signposted Long Marton. Follow rd through village under bridge. Car park on R after house. A 6½-acre walled garden. Magnificent Cedar of Lebanon, herbaceous borders, kitchen garden. Italian garden leading to small lake, ducks, woodland walk, views. Cream TEAS in aid of Eden Animal Rescue & Friends of Long Marton School. *Adm £2 Chd 50p. Suns May 4, June 29 (1-5)*

Matson Ground &❀ (Matson Ground Trust) Windermere. From Kendal turn R off B5284 signposted Heathwaite, 100yds after Windermere Golf Club entrance. Lane joins another in ¼m. Continue straight on. Garden is on L after ¼m. From Bowness turn L onto B5284 from A5074. After ¾m turn L at Xrds follow sign to Heathwaite. Garden on L ¾m along lane. Watercourse flows through ornamental garden to large pond in the wild garden of meadow grassland, spring bulbs later wild flowers. Azaleas, rhododendrons, large mixed shrub/herbaceous borders, topiary work. Recent changes in the garden incl white garden, new spring/summer border and camomile lawn on terrace. A ½-acre walled organic kitchen garden being run on organic methods, greenhouses and dovecote. 2-acre amenity woodland. TEAS. *Adm £1.50 Chd 50p. Suns May 18, Sept 7 (1-5)*

Matthew How ✕ (Mr & Mrs John Griffiths) Troutbeck. 2½m equidistant from Windermere and Ambleside. From Windermere after Lakes school turn R up Bridge Lane off A591. From Ambleside L up Holbeck Lane between Town End (NT) and post office. 1-acre terraced fellside garden full of surprises around C17 cottage, views over peaceful Troutbeck valley High Street Range. Plantsman's garden incl rhododendrons, camellias, azaleas and magnolias. Spring bulbs especially tulips. Formal areas clipped box and yew. Collections of clematis, alpines, troughs, mixed borders unusual plants. Unique bird life incl nesting nuthatches and pied fly catchers. Red squirrels visit garden. Tea when possible next door. *Adm £1.50 Chd free (Share to Troutbeck Church®). Weds May 21, 28, June 4 (12-5). Private visits and groups welcome, please* **Tel 015394 33276**

The Mill House ✕✿ (Mr & Mrs R L Jefferson) Sebergham. Take junction 41 off M6 A5305 Penrith to Wigton Rd into Sebergham turning to L into an easily missed lane just before bridge over river Caldew. 200 yds up lane, after bungalow take L fork in drive. Available parking. ½-acre garden set in secluded valley around the water mill; features millstream and pond, a large herbaceous border and a gravel garden; fruit and vegetable garden. *Adm £1.50 Chd free. Private visits welcome by appt, please* **Tel 01697 476472**

The Nook ⚹✿ (Mr & Mrs P Freedman) Helton. Penrith N 5m from B5320, take signs to Askham-Haweswater. Turn R into Helton. ½-acre terraced rock garden, beds and tubs, alpines, ornamental pool, goldfish, bog plants, fruit and herb garden; magnificent views over R Lowther and parkland. Homemade provisions and cakes for sale. TEAS. *Adm £1.50 Chd free. Sun May 4 (11-4)*

Nunwick Hall ⚹✕✿ (Mr & Mrs C M & Mr O H Thompson) On outskirts of Great Salkeld, 5½m NE of Penrith. Parkland and walks to R Eden. 7 acres of garden, with terrace, parterre, lawns with rose garden, borders and large Victorian rockery. The original walled garden has flowers, fruit, vegetables and an orchard. Picnics in park. TEAS. *Adm £2 OAP's £1.50 Chd under 12 free (Share to St Cuthbert's Church, Great Salkeld®). Sun July 20 (1.30-5)*

Palace How ⚹✕✿ (Mr & Mrs A & K Johnson) Brackenthwaite, Loweswater, 6m SE of Cockermouth on B5292 and B5289 or from Keswick 10m over Whinlatter Pass, through Lorton village, follow signs for Loweswater. Established damp garden set in lovely situation amongst mountains. Unusual trees and shrubs, especially rhododendrons and acers. Pond with bog plants; candelabra primulas; Himalayan poppies, roses and alpines. Cream teas at Loweswater Village Hall in aid of NSPCC. *Adm £1.50 Chd free. Mon May 5 (11-5). Private visits and parties welcome, please* **Tel 01900 85648**

Rannerdale Cottage ✿ (The McElney Family) Buttermere. 8m S of Cockermouth, 10m W of Keswick. ½-acre cottage garden with beck and woodland walk overlooking Crummock Water, splendid mountain views. Herbaceous, shrubs, roses, perennial geraniums, tree peonies, pond with fish. TEAS. *Adm £1.50 Chd free. Sat, Sun June 14, 15 (11-5)*

Rydal Mount ✿ (Don & Toni Richards) Eskdale Green, Holmrook, nr Gosforth. Turn off A595 where signed 6m to Eskdale Green. Turn sharp R opp Eskdale Stores. 2nd house on R. 1½-acre garden on natural rock facing SW. Heathers and tree heaths with shrubs and small trees favouring acid soil; eucalyptus and American blueberrys; water garden. Blueberry TEAS. *Adm £1 Chd free (Share to West Cumbria Hospice at Home®). Suns, Weds May 4, 7; Aug 24, 27 (2-5). Also private visits welcome, please* **Tel 019467 23267**

St Annes ✿ (Mr & Mrs R D Furness) Great Langdale. 5m from Ambleside on B5343. Follow signs for Langdale/Old Dungeon Ghyll. At Skelwith Bridge take R hand fork and at Elterwater take R hand. Through Chapel Stile, ¾m on L hand side travelling W. 3-acre partial woodland with established variety of conifers and trees, azaleas and rhododendrons. Establishing wild flower area. Natural rock faces with alpines, streams and rocky paths. Magnificent views Langdales. Partially suitable for wheelchairs. TEAS. *Adm £1.50 Chd free. Fri, Sat, Sun June 27, 28 29 (11-4.30). Open for groups by appt, please* **Tel 015394 37271**

Scarthwaite ✕ (Mr & Mrs E C Hicks) Grange-in-Borrowdale. From Keswick take B5289 to Grange; cross on road bridge, suitable for mini buses, house ¼m on L. ¼m walk from far side of bridge for coach parties. Ferns, cottage garden plants and many others closely packed into ⅓ acre. *Adm £1.50 Acc chd free. Open Easter until end September by appt. Private visits and parties welcome, please* **Tel 01768 777 233**

▲ **Sizergh Castle** ⚹✕✿ (The National Trust) nr Kendal. Close to and W of the main A6 trunk road, 3m S of Kendal. An approach road leaves A6 close to and S of A6/A591 interchange. ⅔-acre Limestone Rock Garden largest owned by the National Trust; large collection of Japanese maples, dwarf conifers, hardy ferns, primulas, gentians and many perennials and bulbs; water garden with bog and aquatic plants; on walls around main lawn are shrubs and climbers, many half-hardy; rose garden contains specimen roses along with shrubs, climbers, ground cover and lilies; wild flower banks, herbaceous border, crab apple orchard with spring bulbs and 'Dutch' garden. *Castle & gdn adm £3.30 Chd £1.70; Gdn adm £2 Chd £1. For NGS Sat June 28 (12.30-5.30)*

▲**Stagshaw** (The National Trust) ½m S of Ambleside. Turn E off A 591, Ambleside to Windermere rd. Bus 555 Kendal-Keswick alight Waterhead. Woodland gdn incl fine collection of rhododendrons and azaleas. Ericaceous trees & shrubs incl magnolias, camellias, embothriums. Views over Windermere. *Adm £1.20 Chd 60p. For NGS Suns May 4, June 1 (10-5.30)*

Station House ⅙❀ (Mr & Mrs G H Simons) Wright Green. Lamplugh approx 6m from Workington, Whitehaven and Cockermouth signposted off A5086 Lilyhall-Workington from Cockermouth-Egremont Rd ½m under disused railway line. From Workington-Whitehaven A595 at Leyland roundabout take rd signposted Branthwaite-Loweswater. 2-acre garden created over site of disused railway line and station. Features shrubs and trees; vegetable and fruit garden. Morning coffee/TEAS. *Adm £1 Chd 50p. Sun June 1 (10.30-4.30)*

¶**Tomarobandy** ✄❀ (Mr & Mrs Tom Wrathall) Blitterlees, nr Silloth. On Silloth-Maryport Rd, B5300, centre of village on W side of rd. (Parking behind Tom Wrathall's service station). 1½-acre coastal garden, compartmented by windbreaks to form a series of twelve themed gardens. Wide variety of plants for yr-round interest. Teas at Rosebarn Restaurant in village. *Adm £2 Acc chd free. Suns June 15, July 13, Aug 17 (10-4)*

Whitbysteads ❀ (The Hon Mrs Anthony Lowther) Askham nr Penrith 8m from Penrith. Turn R at Eamont Bridge off the A6. Turn L at Y fork after Railway Bridge signed Askham. Through village, turn R at Queen's Head. 1-acre garden on several levels surrounding farmhouse on edge of fells, featuring wide variety shrub roses, unusual herbaceous plants and geraniums. Pergola; fountain. Magnificent views over Eden Valley. TEAS. *Adm £1.50 Chd free (Share to Killingbeck Heart Hospital, Leeds®). Sun June 29 (2-5)*

■ **Winderwath** ✄❀ (Miss Jane Pollock) 5m E of Penrith N of A66. Mature garden laid out at end of C19 with interesting trees and borders. Recently established rock garden; many specialist alpines. Surplus plants and secondhand garden tools for sale. Picnic area. TEA. *Adm £2 Acc chd free. March to Oct Mon-Fri (10-4). For NGS Suns April 20, May 18 (1-5)*

Windy Hall ✄ (Diane & David Kinsman) Crook Road, Windermere. 8m from Kendal on B5284 up Linthwaite Country House Hotel driveway. Garden of 3-4 acres maintained by owners and developed from a wilderness over past 16 years. Woodland, herbaceous and alpine gardens, large kitchen garden. Wide variety of plants, especially rhododendrons, camellias, magnolias, sorbus, hydrangeas and many climbers. Special collections of aconitum, aruncus and filipendula. Waterfowl gardens and rarebreed sheep. TEAS. *Adm £1.50 Chd 25p. Wed May 28, Sun June 29 (10-6). Private visits and parties by appt, please* **Tel 015394 46238**

Wood Hall ❀ (Mr & Mrs W Jackson) Cockermouth. Entrance to drive in large lay-by ¼m N (towards Carlisle) off the A595/A594 roundabout nr Cockermouth. A 5½-acre Thomas Mawson garden, with terraces, walls, small feature gardens, lawns, woods and paths. Venerable trees and newer planting. Alpines, shrubs and herbaceous plants. Partially suitable for wheelchairs. *Adm £1.50 and Acc chd free. Private visits and parties welcome, please* **Tel 01900 823585**

Yews ✄❀ (Sir Oliver & Lady Scott) Bowness-on-Windermere. Middle Entrance Drive, 50yds. Medium-sized formal Edwardian garden; fine trees, ha-ha, herbaceous borders; grenhouses. TEAS. *Adm £1.50 Chd free (Share to Marie Curie Cancer Care®). Sun July 6 (2-5.30)*

Denbighshire & Colwyn

See separate Welsh section beginning on page 323

SYMBOLS USED IN THIS BOOK (See also Page 17)

‡ Following a garden name in the Dates of Opening list indicates that those gardens sharing the same symbol are nearby and open on the same day.

‡‡ Indicates a second series of nearby gardens open on the same day.

¶ Opening for the first time.

❀ Plants/produce for sale if available.

⅙ Gardens with at least the main features accessible by wheelchair.

✄ No dogs except guide dogs but otherwise dogs are usually admitted, provided they are kept on a lead. Dogs are not admitted to houses.

● These gardens advertise their own dates in this publication although they do not nominate specific days for the NGS. Not all the money collected by these gardens comes to the NGS but they do make a guaranteed contribution.

■ These gardens nominate specific days for the NGS and advertise their own dates in this publication.

▲ These gardens open regularly to the public but they do not advertise their own dates in this publication. For further details, contact the garden directly.

Derbyshire

Hon County Organiser: Mr & Mrs R Brown, 210 Nottingham Rd, Woodlinkin, Langley Mill, Nottingham
NG16 4HG Tel 01773 714903

Hon County Treasurer: Mrs G Nutland, 4 Sadler Close, Adel, Leeds LS16 8NN

DATES OF OPENING

April 3 Thursday
Bath House Farm, Ashover

April 13 Sunday
32 Heanor Road, Codnor
Meynell Langley, Kirk Langley ‡
Radburne Hall, Kirk Langley ‡

April 16 Wednesday
Bluebell Arboretum, Smisby

April 19 Saturday
Field House Farm, Rosliston

April 20 Sunday
Bluebell Arboretum, Smisby ‡
Field House Farm, Rosliston ‡

April 27 Sunday
Bowbridge House, Mackworth
Fir Croft, Calver, nr Bakewell
The Riddings Farm, Kirk Ireton

May 1 Thursday
Gamesley Fold Cottage, Glossop

May 4 Sunday
Cherry Tree Cottage, Hilton

May 5 Monday
Cherry Tree Cottage, Hilton

May 8 Thursday
Gamesley Fold Cottage, Glossop

May 10 Saturday
Broomfield College, Morley

May 11 Sunday
Broomfield College, Morley
The Limes, Apperknowle
57 Portland Close, Mickleover

May 15 Thursday
Gamesley Fold Cottage, Glossop

May 18 Sunday
Fir Croft, Calver, nr Bakewell
The Limes, Apperknowle
Oaks Lane Farm, Brockhurst

May 21 Wednesday
Bath House Farm, Ashover ‡
Bluebell Arboretum, Smisby
Oaks Lane Farm, Brockhurst ‡

May 22 Thursday
Gamesley Fold Cottage, Glossop

May 24 Saturday
Field House Farm, Rosliston

May 25 Sunday
Bluebell Arboretum, Smisby
Bowbridge House, Mackworth
Dam Farm House, Yeldersley
Lane ‡
Dove Cottage, Clifton,
Ashbourne ‡
Field House Farm, Rosliston
The Limes, Apperknowle

Monksway, Tideswell
Mount Cottage, Ticknall

May 26 Monday
Mount Cottage, Ticknall

May 27 Tuesday
Shatton Hall Farm, Bamford

May 29 Thursday
Gamesley Fold Cottage, Glossop

June 1 Sunday
Darley House, nr Matlock
Field Farm, Kirk Ireton
Green Farm Cottage, Offcote,
Ashbourne
The Limes, Apperknowle
The Old Slaughterhouse, Shipley
Gate
Thatched Farm, Radbourne

June 5 Thursday
Gamesley Fold Cottage, Glossop
Kedleston Hall, Derby

June 8 Sunday
Cherry Tree Cottage, Hilton
Fir Croft, Calver, nr Bakewell
Locko Park, Spondon
The Poplars, Derby

June 11 Wednesday
The Poplars, Derby

June 12 Thursday
Gamesley Fold Cottage, Glossop

June 14 Saturday
Duffield House, Breaston

June 15 Sunday
Corner Cottage,
Osmaston-by-Ashbourne
Darley House, nr Matlock
32 Heanor Road, Codnor ‡
210 Nottingham Road,
Woodlinkin ‡
Park Hall House, Nether Heage
The Poplars, Derby ‡‡
57 Portland Close, Mickleover ‡‡

June 18 Wednesday
The Poplars, Derby

June 19 Thursday
Gamesley Fold Cottage, Glossop

June 21 Saturday
Field House Farm, Rosliston

June 22 Sunday
Cashel, Kirk Ireton
Dam Farm House, Yeldersley
Lane ‡
Dove Cottage, Clifton,
Ashbourne ‡
Field House Farm, Rosliston
Fir Croft, Calver, nr Bakewell
Thatched Farm, Radbourne

White Gate, Arleston Meadows

June 25 Wednesday
Bluebell Arboretum, Smisby ‡
Field House Farm, Rosliston ‡

June 26 Thursday
Gamesley Fold Cottage, Glossop

June 28 Saturday
46 Long Meadow Road, Alfreton

June 29 Sunday
Birchwood Farm, Portway
Bluebell Arboretum, Smisby
Bowbridge House, Mackworth
Cherry Tree Cottage, Hilton
Darley House, nr Matlock
32 Heanor Road, Codnor
Monksway, Tideswell
Mount Cottage, Ticknall
Tudor House Farm, Kirk Langley
White Gate, Arleston Meadows
Yew Tree Bungalow, Thatchers
Lane, Tansley

July 6 Sunday
Fanshawe Gate Hall, Holmesfield
32 Heanor Road, Codnor ‡
The Limes, Apperknowle
23 Mill Lane, Codnor ‡

July 12 Saturday
Field House Farm, Rosliston

July 13 Sunday
Dove Cottage, Clifton, Ashbourne
Fanshawe Gate Hall, Holmesfield
Field House Farm, Rosliston
Hardwick Hall, Doe Lea
Lea Hurst, nr Matlock
159 Longfield Lane, Ilkeston

July 16 Wednesday
Bath House Farm, Ashover ‡
Oaks Lane Farm, Brockhurst ‡

July 19 Saturday
Tissington Hall, nr Ashbourne

July 20 Sunday
Fanshawe Gate Hall, Holmesfield
32 Heanor Road, Codnor
The Limes, Apperknowle
Oaks Lane Farm, Brockhurst
Park Hall House, Nether Heage
Yew Tree Bungalow, Thatchers
Lane, Tansley

July 23 Wednesday
Bluebell Arboretum, Smisby
Calke Abbey, Ticknall

July 27 Sunday
Bluebell Arboretum, Smisby
Dove Cottage, Clifton, Ashbourne
The Limes, Apperknowle
Monksway, Tideswell

Shatton Hall Farm, Bamford
Stainsborough Hall, Hopton, nr
 Wirksworth
August 3 Sunday
 Field Farm, Kirk Ireton
 32 Heanor Road, Codnor ‡
 23 Mill Lane, Codnor ‡
August 13 Wednesday
 Bluebell Arboretum, Smisby
August 17 Sunday
 Bluebell Arboretum, Smisby
 Dove Cottage, Clifton, Ashbourne
 White Gate, Arleston Meadows
August 24 Sunday
 Monksway, Tideswell
August 25 Monday
 Tissington Hall, nr Ashbourne

August 31 Sunday
 The Riddings Farm, Kirk Ireton
September 4 Thursday
 Birchwood Farm, Portway
September 14 Sunday
 Broomfield College, Morley
September 17 Wednesday
 Bluebell Arboretum, Smisby
September 21 Sunday
 Bluebell Arboretum, Smisby
October 15 Wednesday
 Bluebell Arboretum, Smisby
October 19 Sunday
 Bluebell Arboretum, Smisby

Regular openings
For details see garden description

Lea Gardens, nr Matlock
Renishaw Hall, nr Sheffield

By appointment only
*For telephone numbers and other
details see garden descriptions.
Private visits welcomed*

Birchfield, Ashford in the Water
Rock House, Nether Heage

DESCRIPTION OF GARDEN

Bath House Farm &⚘ (Mr & Mrs Hetherington)
Ashover. 4½m N of Matlock on A632 Chesterfield Rd.
Take 1st R after leaving village of Kelstedge and next R
at T-junction. Overlooking Ashover and with extensive
views this garden has a wide variety of heathers and
mixed borders and a large water feature with waterfall,
pond and stream surrounded by well chosen plants and
rare shrubs and trees. Recently planted dell for spring
flowers. TEA. *Adm £1.50 Chd free. Thurs April 3, Weds
May 21, July 16.* **Tel 01246 590562**

Birchfield ⚘ (Brian Parker) Dukes Drive, Ashford in the
Water. 2m NW of Bakewell on A6 to Buxton. Beautifully
situated terraced garden of approx ¾ acre mostly constructed within last 10 yrs. Designed for all-yr-round colour, it contains a wide variety of shrubs and perennials,
bulbs, roses, water and scree gardens. Areas of copse
with wild flowers are being developed in adjacent field.
TEA. *Adm £1 Chd free (Share to Derbyshire Assoc for the
Blind®). Private visits welcome April to Sept, please* **Tel
01629 813800**

Birchwood Farm ⚘⚘ (Stuart & Janet Crooks) and
Lumley Cottage (Lisa & Jonathan Groves) Coxbench. 5m
N Derby. From A38 take B6179 by Little Chef through
Little Eaton till first Xrds. Turn L then R over railway
crossing and take rd to Holbrook. Car parking in field at
top of drive. ⅓-acre garden enclosed within old brick and
stone walls. This garden is for plant enthusiasts. The wide
range of herbaceous plants incl hardy geraniums, penstemons, silver plants, campanulas, delphiniums, English
roses and pond. Private nursery adjacent. TEA. *Adm
£1.50 Chd free. Sun June 29, Thurs Sept 4 (2-5.30). Private visits also welcome, please* **Tel 01332 880685**

Bluebell Nursery & Woodland Garden &⚘⚘ (Robert
& Suzette Vernon) Smisby. From the A50 Burton on Trent
to Ashby-de-la-Zouch Rd, turn for Smisby by the Mother
Hubbard Inn, 1m NW of Ashby. Arboretum is on L after
½m Annwell Lane. 5-acre embryo Arboretum planted in
the last 5 yrs incl many young specimens of rare trees
and shrubs. Wide range of interesting plants for sale.
Bring wellingtons in wet weather. TEA. *Adm £1 Chd free*

*(Share to MENCAP®). Suns April 20, May 25, June 29,
July 27, Aug 17, Sept 21, Oct 19; Weds April 16; May 21,
June 25, July 23, Aug 13, Sept 17, Oct 15 (10-5). Private
visits welcome, please* **Tel 01530 413700**

Bowbridge House &⚘ (Richard & Jennifer Wood)
Mackworth. On A52 Derby to Ashbourne Rd 3m W of
Derby Ring Rd, on S side, just past the Little Chef. 4½-
acre garden originally laid out in 1762 by William Eames.
Extensively informally replanted since 1978 by present
owners with rare and unusual trees, shrubs, climbers and
herbaceous plants. Flowering sized magnolia campbelli;
paulownia, numerous rhododendrons, shrub roses, 3 conservatories, ponds and vegetable garden. TEA. *Adm £1.50
Chd free. Suns April 27, May 25, June 29 (2-6)*

Broomfield College &⚘⚘ Morley on A608, 4m N of
Derby and 6m S of Heanor. Landscaped garden of 10 ha;
shrubs, trees, rose collection, herbaceous borders; glasshouses; walled garden under restoration; garden tours
and advice; demonstrations. Crafts, carvery lunches, refreshments. *Adm £1 Chd free. Sats, Suns May 10, 11,
Sept 14 (10.30-4.30)*

▲**Calke Abbey** &⚘ (The National Trust) Ticknall. 9m S
of Derby on A514 between Swadlincote and Melbourne.
Extensive walled gardens constructed in 1773. Divided
into flower garden, kitchen garden and physic garden.
Restoration commenced in 1987. Surrounding the walled
garden the pleasure ground has been re-fenced and replanting is underway. Phase 1 of orangery restoration just
completed. Phase 2 subject to further fundraising. Lunches and TEAS. *Adm £2.20 Chd £1. For NGS Wed July 23
(11-5)*

Cashel ⚘ (Anita & Jeremy Butt) Kirk Ireton. Turn off
B5023 (Duffield-Wirksworth rd). 2m S of Wirksworth. Follow rd to Kirk Ireton take sharp R turn at church corner.
Follow lane for 200 metres. Garden on R, car parking 50
metres beyond the house. 2½ acres of gradually developing garden situated on a sloping site with views of the
Ecclesbourne Valley. Many interesting trees, plants and
shrubs. TEAS in aid of local church. *Adm £1.50 Chd free.
Sun June 22 (2-5). Private visits welcome, please* **Tel
01335 370495**

Cherry Tree Cottage ✿❀ (Mr & Mrs R Hamblin) Hilton. 7m W of Derby, turn off the A516 opp The Old Talbot Inn in village centre. Parking - small public car park in Main St. A plant lover's C18 garden, about ⅓-acre with herbaceous borders; herb garden; scree garden. Many unusual and interesting plants; specie aquilegias, old dianthus. Featured in several gardening magazines, 'Gardeners World' and Good Garden Guide. *Adm £1 Chd free. Suns May 4, June 8, 29, Mon May 5 (2-5). Groups welcome by appt weekdays April, May, June only. Visitors also welcome to see snowdrops and hellebores early spring. Please* **Tel 01283 733778**

Corner Cottage ✿❀ (Alan & Lynn Poulter) Osmaston-by-Ashbourne. 2½m SE of Ashbourne in centre of village ½m off A52. Country garden of ½ acre in unspoiled Victorian estate village. Started from scratch in 1990 and aimed at providing seasonal variety and colour around every corner. Pond and bog garden, rockery, formal walled garden, shrubs, herbaceous borders and annuals. Cream TEAS in village hall in aid of Look to the Future. *Adm £1.50 Chd free. Suns June 15 (1.30-5.30). Private visits of 8 or more welcome by appt please* **Tel 01335 346112** *(1.30-5.30)*

■ **Dam Farm House** ♿✿❀ (Mrs J M Player) Yeldersley Lane, Ednaston, 5m SE of Ashbourne on A52, opp Ednaston Village turn, gate on right 500yds. 2-acre garden which has been extended beautifully situated contains mixed borders, scree. Unusual plants have been collected many are propagated for sale. TEAS (some Suns). *Adm £2 Chd free. Suns June 8, July 13, Aug 10 (1.30-4). For NGS Suns May 25, June 22 (1.30-4). Private visits and groups welcome April 1 to Oct 31, please* **Tel 01335 360291**

Darley House ♿✿❀ (Mr & Mrs G H Briscoe) Darley Dale, 2m N of Matlock. On A6 to Bakewell. 1½ acres; originally set out by Sir Joseph Paxton in 1845; being restored by present owners; many rare plants, trees; balustrade and steps separating upper and lower garden, a replica of Haddon Hall. As featured on BBC 'Gardeners World'. Picture Gallery. Plants and extensive range of seeds available. TEA. *Adm £1.50 Chd free. Suns June 1, 15, 29 (2-5) also open by appt weekdays June and Sept for private visits and groups not exceeding 15, please* **Tel 01629 733341**

Dove Cottage ✿❀ (Anne and Stephen Liverman) Clifton. 1½m SW of Ashbourne. ¾-acre garden by R Dove extensively replanted and developed since 1979. Emphasis on establishing collections of hardy plants and shrubs incl alchemillas, alliums, berberis, geraniums, euphorbias, hostas, lilies, variegated and silver foliage plants inc astrantias. Plantsmans garden featured on Channel 4 'Garden Club', 'Good Garden Guide' and 'Gardeners World Cottage Garden 1995'. TEA. *Adm £1.50 Chd free (Share to British Heart Foundation®). Suns May 25, June 22, July 13, 27, Aug 17 (1-5). Private visits welcome, please* **Tel 01335 343545**

¶**Duffield House** ♿❀ (Dr & Mrs R N Wilson) Blind Lane Breaston. Turn off A6005 opp Church and park in the Green. Walk 100yds to L. ¼ acre, newly developed. Gravel gardens, ponds, herbaceous and shrub borders. TEA

in aid of Treetops Hospice. *Adm £1 Chd free. Sat June 14 (2-6)*

Fanshawe Gate Hall ✿❀ (Mr & Mrs John Ramsden) Holmesfield. Situated on the edge of the Peak National Park. 1m E of Holmesfield Village. Follow B6054 towards Owler Bar. 1st R turn after Robin Hood Inn. Marked Old Hall on OS map. C13 seat of the Fanshawe family. Old-fashioned cottage-style garden approx 2 acres. Many stone features, fine C16 dovecote. Upper walled garden with mixed borders, shrubs, climbers, herb plantings, water features, rose beds, terracing and lawns. Lower courtyard enhanced by small formal knot garden and herb border. The garden continues to develop with particular emphasis on plantings of old-fashioned unusual varieties with interest in variegated subjects. TEAS. *Adm £1.50 Chd free (Share to Derbyshire Wildlife Trust®). Suns July 6, 13, 20 (11-5). Also private visits welcome; written application please* **Tel 0114 2890391**

Field Farm ❀ (Graham & Irene Dougan) Kirk Ireton. At top of Main St Kirk Ireton turn L signposted Hulland on sharp RH bend of Blackwall Lane. Find Field Lane, single track without passing places. Field Farm 400m parking in field. 1½-acre hilltop garden featured on ITV's 'Heart of the Country' informal planting of trees, shrubs, alpines, roses and herbaceous borders, colourful display of containers in yard. TEA in aid of local WI. *Adm £1.50 Chd free. Suns June 1, Aug 3 (2-5). Private visits welcome by appt, please* **Tel 01335 370958**

Field House Farm ♿✿❀ (Keith & Judy Thompson) Rosliston. From junction 11 (M42) take A444 NW to Castle Gresley. Turn L to Linton and Rosliston. From A38 turn E at Barton Turns fly- over on to Walton-on-Trent Rd (width restriction). From Walton follow signs to Rosliston. Farm is signposted up drive between Rosliston and Coton-in-the-Elms. An artistic plant collector's ¾-acre farmhouse garden with some unusual features. 2 ponds, mature shrubs, spring bulbs, 'dry' bog garden, secret garden, stone garden, wildlife garden and herbaceous borders. Incl many hardy geraniums, hostas and penstemons. TEAS. *Adm £1 Chd free. Sats, Suns April 19, 20, May 24, 25, June 21, 22, July 12, 13, Wed June 25 (2-6). Private visits of 10 & over welcome, please* **Tel 01283 761472**

■ **Fir Croft** ✿❀ (Dr Furness) Froggatt Rd, Calver, Via Sheffield. 4m N of Bakewell; between Q8 filling station and junction of B6001 with B6054. Plantsman's garden; rockeries; water garden and nursery; extensive collection (over 2000 varieties) of alpines, conifers. Tufa and scree beds. *Collection box. Nursery opens every Sat, Sun, Mon (1-5) March to Dec. Adjacent garden for NGS Suns April 27, May 18, June 8, 22 (2-5)*

Remember that every time you visit a National Gardens Scheme garden you are helping to raise money for the following:

The Queen's Nursing Institute
The Nurses' Welfare Service
Cancer Relief Macmillan Fund
The Gardens Fund of the National Trust
The Gardeners' Royal Benevolent Society

Gamesley Fold Cottage ✿✤ (Mr & Mrs G Carr) Glossop. Off Glossop-Marple Rd nr Charlesworth, turn down the lane directly opp St Margaret's School, Gamesley. White cottage at the bottom. Old-fashioned cottage garden down a country lane with lovely views of surrounding countryside. A spring garden planted with herbaceous borders, wild flowers and herbs in profusion to attract butterflies and wildlife. Featured in Good Housekeeping and Good Gardens Guide. TEAS. *Adm £1 Chd free. Thurs May 1, 8, 15, 22, 29, June 5, 12, 19, 26 (11-4). Private visits and groups May and June daily, please* **Tel 014578 67856**

Grafton Cottage, Barton-under-Needwood See Staffordshire

Green Farm Cottage ✿✤ (Mr & Mrs Peter Bussell) Offcote nr Ashbourne. 1½m NE of Ashbourne on T-junction Bradley-Kniveton-Ashbourne. Take Wirksworth Rd out of Ashbourne (B5035) and follow Offcote signpost (approx 1¼m from main rd). ⅓-acre plantsman's garden featured in 'Your Garden' and 'Derbyshire Life'. Designed, constructed and maintained from a wilderness in 1978 by the present owners. Flower-filled terraces, lush lawns, spring bulbs and an impressive variety of perennials, incl hellebores, shrubs and trees; greenhouse, soft fruit and small orchard area. Beautiful rural views. TEA and plants in aid of Ashbourne Animal Welfare. *Adm £1 Acc chd free. Sun June 1 (2-5). Private visits welcome April to Aug, please* **Tel 01335 343803**

▲**Hardwick Hall** ✦✿✤ (The National Trust) Doe Lea, 8m SE of Chesterfield. S of A617. Grass walks between yew and hornbeam hedges; cedar trees; herb garden; herbaceous and rose borders. Finest example of Elizabethan house in the country. Restaurant in Old Kitchens. TEAS on days the Hall is open. *Adm hall and garden £5.80 Chd £2.70 garden only £2.50 Chd £1. For NGS Sun July 13 (12-5.30 last entry 4.30)*

32 Heanor Road ✦✿✤ (Mr & Mrs Eyre) 300yds from Codnor market place (clock tower) on A6007 towards Heanor. Down lane at side of shop. Parking in adjacent field with way out on to A610 Nottingham to Ripley Rd. 1½-acre garden with yr-round interest has been constructed over many yrs from its origins of a market garden. Lawns, variety of trees, camellias, flowering shrubs, mixed borders, scree, rockery; 2 ponds and pergola. The recent development incl an arbour and stepping pond. Prize winning garden. TEA. *Adm £1 Chd free. Suns April 13, June 15, 29, July 6, 20 Aug 3 (2-5). Coach parties and private visits welcome, please* **Tel 01773 746626**

▲**Kedleston Hall** ✦✿ (The National Trust) 3m NW of Derby. Signposted from junction of A38/A52. 12-acre garden. A broad open lawn, bounded by a ha-ha, marks the C18 informal garden. A formal layout to the W was introduced early this century when the summerhouse and orangery, both designed by George Richardson late C18, were moved to their present position. The gardens are seen at their best during May and June when the azaleas and rhododendrons are one mass of colour. The Long Walk, a woodland walk of some 3m, is bright with spring flowers. Guided walk of gardens and Long Walk at 2pm. TEA. *Adm £2 Chd £1. For NGS Thurs June 5 (11-6)*

● **Lea Gardens** ✦✤ (Mr & Mrs Tye) Lea, 5m SE of Matlock off A6. A rare collection of rhododendrons, azaleas, kalmias, alpines and conifers in a delightful woodland setting. Light lunches, TEAS, home-baking. Coaches by appt. *Adm £2.50 Chd 50p daily, season ticket £3.50. Daily March 20 to July 7 (10-7)*

Lea Hurst (Residential Home) ✿✤ (Royal Surgical Aid Society) Holloway. 6m SE of Matlock off A6, nr Yew Tree Inn, Holloway. Former home (not open) of Florence Nightingale. Large garden consisting of rose beds, herbaceous borders, new shrubbery incl varieties, ornamental pond, all set in beautiful countryside. New wildlife garden 1994. TEAS in aid of RSAS. *Adm £1 Chd under 16 free. Sun July 13 (2-5)*

The Limes ✦✤ (Mr & Mrs W Belton) 6m N of Chesterfield; on A61 taking the Dronfield, Unstone turn off to Unstone, turn R at Unstone school for 1m to Apperknowle; 1st house past Unstone Grange. Bus; Chesterfield or Sheffield to Unstone. 2½-acre garden with herbaceous borders, lily ponds, roses and flowering shrubs, hundreds of naturalised daffodils and formal bedding with massed bedding of pansies and polyanthus in the spring, geraniums and bedding plants in the summer. New for 1997 a Lavender Maze, putting green and large natural pond with ducks and geese. Nature trail over 5 acres. TEAS. *Adm £1 Chd 25p. Suns May 11, 18, 25 June 1, July 6, 20 27 (2-6). Coach, private parties and evening visits welcome, please* **Tel 01246 412338**

Locko Park ✤ Spondon, 6m NE of Derby. From A52 Borrowash bypass, 2m N via B6001, turn to Spondon. Large garden; pleasure gardens; rose gardens. House by Smith of Warwick with Victorian additions. Chapel, Charles II, with original ceiling. TEA. *Adm £1 Chd 30p. Sun June 8 (2-5)*

159 Longfield Lane ✿✤ (David & Diane Bennett) Ilkeston (Stanton side) off Quarry Hill, opp Hallam Fields Junior School. A house in a garden described by visitors as an artist's garden, a large, informal over-flowing garden that works for its owners with fruit, shrubs, flowers, two small fish ponds and a conservatory. A strong emphasis on texture, colour and lots of unexpected corners. 'Beautiful Erewash' commended 1994/5. Home-made TEAS. *Adm £1 Chd free. Sun July 13 (2-5.30). Private visits of 6 and under welcome, May to July, please* **Tel 01159 325238**

¶**46 Long Meadow Road** ✦✿✤ (Rosemary Townsend) Alfreton. A38 Derby/M1. Take A61 Chesterfield and Matlock exit. At roundabout towards Alfreton through traffic light, past Swan and Salmon public house on R. Take next R, just before the church into Long Meadow Rd. Walled garden, jointly managed between 2 houses. Mainly cottage garden type with vegetable and fruit area and 2 ponds. Approx ¼-acre. Live music will be performed by students from the local Music Centre (not pop music). TEAS. *Adm £1 Chd free (Share to Avema Trust®). Sat June 28 (2-5)*

Meynell Langley ✦✤ (Godfrey Meynell Esq) Between Mackworth and Kirk Langley on A52 Derby-Ashbourne rd. Turn in at green iron gate by grey stone lodge on N side of road. Trees, lawns, daffodils, lake, views. TEAS in Regency country house. *Adm £2 Chd 50p (Share to Oxfam®). Sun April 13 (2-6)*

23 Mill Lane ঙ *&❀* (Mrs S Jackson) Codnor. 12m NW of Nottingham. A610 Ripley 10m N of Derby, A38 Ripley. 2 car parks nearby. Lawns, herbaceous borders, small pond, waterfall; fruit trees; clematis. Amber Valley 'Best Kept Garden' competition 2nd 1994. TEA. *Adm £1 Chd free. Suns July 6, Aug 3 (11-6). Private visits also welcome June to Sept, please* **Tel 01773 745707**

¶**Monksway** (Mr & Mrs R Porter) Summer Cross, Tideswell. Tideswell is situated 9m N of Buxton on the B6049. Turn up Parke Rd, between newsagent and greengrocer, off Queen St. Take a L turn at the top and then 1st R onto Summer Cross. Monksway is fourth semi-detached house on L. Well stocked gently sloping garden 1000' above sea level containing perennial and shrub borders, rose, conifer, alpine scree beds and aviary. Limited parking. *Adm £1 Chd free. Suns May 25, June 29, July 27, Aug 24 (2-5). Private visits welcome, please* **Tel 01298 871687**

Mount Cottage *&❀* (Mr & Mrs J T Oliver) 52 Main Street, Ticknall, 9m S Derby, adjacent entrance Calke Abbey NT. Medium-sized cottage garden, herbaceous borders, shrubs, lawns, new pool area, numerous roses, surrounding C18 cottage. TEAS outdoors weather permitting. *Adm £1 Chd free. Suns, Mon, May 25, June 29, May 26 (2-5)*

210 Nottingham Rd (Mr & Mrs R Brown) Woodlinkin, nr Codnor; A610. ½-acre; collections of old, modern shrub and climbing roses; shrubs; trees. TEA. *Adm £1.50 Chd free. Sun June 15 (2-5)*

Oaks Lane Farm *&❀* (Mr & Mrs J R Hunter) Brockhurst, Ashover nr Chesterfield. At Kelstedge 4m from Matlock on A632 Chesterfield Rd, just above Kelstedge Inn, turn L up narrow rd, then turn R ½m, garden is 150yds on R. ¾-acre informal plantsman's garden in beautiful situation with herbaceous borders, natural streams and pond. Small bog garden. Many varieties of hostas, euphorbia and old-fashioned roses. Spring bulbs and hellebores. Partially suitable for wheelchairs. TEA. *Adm £1.50 Chd free. Suns, Weds May 18, 21, July 16, 20 (2-5). Open by appt May 1 to Aug 31, please* **Tel 01246 590324**

The Old Slaughterhouse *&❀* (Robert & Joyce Peck) Shipley Gate. 1m S of Eastwood, take Church St from Sun Inn traffic lights, and over A610, L to narrow rd to Shipley Boat Inn; parking near Shipley Lock (Erewash Canal) and Inn. ¾-acre long, narrow garden, restored from overgrown ash tip since 1984; 200-yrs-old stone aqueduct over river; over 400 trees planted; hidden pond; pleasant extra walks in Erewash Valley (canal and river sides). TEA. *Adm £1 Chd free. Sun June 1 (2-6). Private visits welcome, please* **Tel 01773 768625**

Park Hall House *&* (Mrs P Longley) Shop Lane, Nether Heage. 200yds from Village PO towards 'Guide Post'. Village is near Ambergate by A6. Young trees, shrubs, rhododendrons, camellias and herbaceous plants. Selection of ferns, grasses and herbs. Climbers incl roses and cle-

matis, with water features and items of local interest, large collection of poppies. TEAS. *Adm £1.50 Chd free (Share to Sense). Suns June 15, July 20 (2-5). Private visits welcome, please* **Tel 01773 856900**

¶**The Poplars** ঙ *&❀* (The Clemson Family) Burleigh Drive. ½m N of Derby Cathedral. 200yds S of Broadway Inn and opp N end of Belper Rd. Late Victorian ¼ acre walled garden in the style of Edward Milner, landscape designer. Variety of herbaceous plants, shrubs, herbs, fruit. *Adm £1 Chd free. Suns, Weds June 8, 11, 15, 18 (2-6)*

57 Portland Close *&❀* (Mr & Mrs A L Ritchie) Mickleover. Approx 3m W of Derby, turn R off B5020 Cavendish Way then 2nd L into Portland Close. Small plantsman's garden, wide variety of unusual bulbs, alpines and herbaceous plants. Special interest in sink gardens, hostas, named varieties of primulas (single and double); auriculas (show, border, alpine and doubles), violas and hardy geraniums. Featured in 'Good Garden Guide'. *Adm £1 Chd free under 16. Suns, May 11, June 15 (2-5). Private visits also welcome of 10 and over, please* **Tel 01332 515450**

Radburne Hall *&* (Mrs J W Chandos-Pole) Radburne, Kirk Langley, 5m W of Derby. W of A52 Derby-Ashbourne rd; off Radburne Lane. Large landscape garden; large display of daffodils; shrubs; formal rose terraces; fine trees and view. Hall (not open) is 7-bay Palladian mansion built c1734 by Smith of Warwick. Ice-house in garden. *Adm £1 Chd 50p. Sun April 13 (2.30-6)*

● **Renishaw Hall** ঙ *&* (Sir Reresby & Lady Sitwell) Renishaw. Renishaw Hall is situated equidistant 6m from both Sheffield and Old Chesterfield on A616 2m from its junction with M1 at exit 30. Italian style garden with terraces, old ponds, yew hedges and pyramids laid out by Sir George Sitwell c1900. Interesting collection of herbaceous plants and shrubs; nature trail; museum; lakeside walk. Shop provides wine, souvenirs, antiques; also a museum. TEAS. *Adm £3 OAPs £2 Chd £1. Every Fri, Sat, Sun and Bank Hol Mons March 28 to Sept 14. Mons March 31, May 5, 26, Aug 25 (10.30-4.30). Private parties of 20 and over welcome, please* **Tel 01246 432042**

The Riddings Farm *&❀* (The Spencer Family) Kirk Ireton between Ashbourne and Wirksworth. Leave Kirk Ireton via Gorsey Lane (close to Barley Mow). Turn L at T-junction onto Broom Lane. 1st R into Hays Lane. Informal hillside garden about ¾ acre, created since 1979, with lovely views over Carsington Water. Carpets of primulas and daffodils, then rhododendrons, hardy geraniums, shrub roses, hydrangeas and fuchsias. New wildlife pond. Unusual plants propogated for adjacent nursery. TEAS in aid of Ashbourne Animal Welfare. *Adm £1 Chd free. Suns April 27, Aug 31 (2-5). Private visits welcome, please* **Tel 01335 370331**

¶**Rock House** ঙ *&❀* (Ann Taylor) Belper. [Map ref. Nether Heage - 365566.] 11m N of Derby. From the A38 at Ripley W to Heage 3m. From the A6 at Belper N to Heage 3m. From Heage to Nether Heage W on Ambergate Rd ½m. From A6 at Ambergate E to Nether Heage 1½m. Medium-size garden (approx 40 sq yds) informal cottage style. Packed with hundreds of varieties of perennials, shrubs, trees and climbers. It reflects owners artistic skills and love of plants and wildlife and is enhanced by a view of beautiful countryside incl rare six-sailed windmill. Partly accessible to wheelchair users. *Adm £1 Chd free. Private visits welcome afternoons and evenings June to Sept, please* **Tel 01773 852804**

¶Shatton Hall Farm (Mr & Mrs J Kellie) 3m W of Hathersage, take A625 from Hathersage, turn L to Shatton, after 2m (opp High Peak Roses). After ½m turn R through ford drive ½m and house is on L over cattle grids. This ½-acre garden with its ancient yew tree and C16 farmhouse in picturesque scenery is still being developed and contains many unusual plants and shrubs. Numerous informal plantings incl large natural water garden. There is access to extensive woodland and streamside walks. TEAS. *Adm £1.25 Chd 50p (Share to Save the Children®). Tues May 27, Sun July 27 (1.30-5) Private visits welcome April to September, please* **Tel 01433 620635**

Stainsborough Hall &❀ (Mr & Mrs Twogood) Wirksworth. On B5035 Wirksworth to Ashbourne Rd. 1½m W of Wirksworth take L turning to Kirk Ireton, house ¼m. The stone house and buildings merge delightfully with lawns, shrubs, roses and flower beds designed informally on different levels to provide meandering walks. Covering some 2 acres, the garden incl many young trees, shrubs, herbaceous borders and rose beds. A duck pond with a variety of domestic ducks adds to the tranquillity of the scene. Cream TEAS. *Adm £1 Chd free. Sun July 27 (2-6)*

Thatched Farm &✄❀ (Mr & Mrs R A Pegram) Radbourne. Exit A52 Derby-Ashbourne road. 2m N of Derby Ring Road. A 2-acre plant lover's garden created from meadowland since 1987 and still being developed. The garden and courtyard surround a C17 listed farmhouse set in tranquil parkland. Many rare and unusual plants grown from seed collected from around the world. Mediterranean and island beds, troughs and alpines in raised beds, wild garden. Trees, shrubs and herbaceous perennials, extensive collection of tender perennials. 2 ponds

and bog garden. As featured in Country Homes Magazine Aug 95. Home-made cream TEAS. *Adm £1.50 Chd free (Share to RELATE® June 1 & Cancer Research Campaign® June 22). Suns June 1, 22 (2-6). Private parties, min 12, also welcome, please* **Tel 01332 824507**

Tissington Hall ✄❀ (Sir Richard & Lady FitzHerbert) N of Ashbourne. E of A515. Large garden; roses, herbaceous borders. Tea available in village. Please park considerately. *Adm £1 Chd free. Sat July 19, Mon Aug 25 (2-5). Parties by written appt only on other days*

Tudor House Farm ✄❀ (Mr & Mrs G Spencer) Kirk Langley. 4½m N of Derby on A52 Ashbourne Rd. Take turning towards Dalbury Lees and Longford, garden 400yds on R. ¼-acre garden on two levels. Mixed beds of shrubs and perennials; small fish and lily pond; heathers and alpine troughs. TEAS. *Adm £1.50 Chd free. Sun June 29 (2-5)*

White Gate ✄ (Mrs Judy Beba-Thompson) Arleston Meadows, Derby. From A5111 (Ring rd), take Sinfin turn at Foresters' Leisure Park. Follow signs to Arleston for 2½m. At Xrds turn L into Wragley Way. From A5132 nr Barrow-upon-Trent take Sinfin turn, 1m and L into Wragley Way. Please park in Wragley Way. Garden signed through cutting. Very small romantic garden, recently created by owners, with over 70 varieties of rose, around 80 clematis, hardy geraniums, lilies and peonies, all in colour themed scented borders on alkaline clay. Tiny white Garden. TEAS in aid of WI. *Adm £1.50 Acc chd free. Suns June 22, 29, Aug 17 (1.30-5.30). Private visits and groups welcome June to August, please* **Tel 01332 763653**

¶Yew Tree Bungalow ✄❀ (Jayne Conquest) Thatchers Lane, Tansley. 2m W of Matlock on A615, 2nd R after Tavern at Tansley. ¾-acre informal plantswoman's garden, with herbaceous borders, vegetable and herb gardens. Incl hardy geraniums, herbaceous potentillas and campanulas. TEAS in aid of Tansley School PTA. *Adm £1 Chd free. Suns June 29, July 20 (2-6)*

SYMBOLS USED IN THIS BOOK (See also Page 17)

‡   Following a garden name in the Dates of Opening list indicates that those gardens sharing the same symbol are nearby and open on the same day.

‡‡   Indicates a second series of nearby gardens open on the same day.

¶   Opening for the first time.

❀   Plants/produce for sale if available.

&   Gardens with at least the main features accessible by wheelchair.

✄   No dogs except guide dogs but otherwise dogs are usually admitted, provided they are kept on a lead. Dogs are not admitted to houses.

●   These gardens advertise their own dates in this publication although they do not nominate specific days for the NGS. Not all the money collected by these gardens comes to the NGS but they do make a guaranteed contribution.

■   These gardens nominate specific days for the NGS and advertise their own dates in this publication.

▲   These gardens open regularly to the public but they do not advertise their own dates in this publication. For further details, contact the garden directly.

Devon

Hon County Organiser:	Mervyn T Feesey Esq., Woodside, Higher Raleigh Rd, Barnstaple EX31 4JA Tel 01271 43095
Assistant County Organisers:	
Exeter & E Devon	Mrs Ruth Charter, Ravenhill, Long Dogs Lane, Ottery St Mary EX11 1HX Tel 01404 814798
Tiverton & N E Devon	Mrs Diane Rowe, Little Southey, Northcott, Nr Cullompton EX15 3LT Tel 01884 840545
West Devon	Michael & Sarah Stone, The Cider House, Buckland Abbey, Yelverton PL20 6EZ Tel 01822 853285
Bovey Tracey & Central Devon	Miss Elizabeth Hebditch, Bibbery, Higher Bibbery, Bovey Tracey TQ13 9RT Tel 01626 833344
Torbay & Dartmouth	Major David Molloy, Mulberry House, Kingswear TQ6 OBY Tel 01803 752307
Kingsbridge & South Devon	Mrs Sheila Blake, Higher Homefield, Sherford, Kingsbridge TQ7 2AT Tel 01548 531229
Plymouth & SW Devon	Mrs Shirin Court, Westpark, Yealmpton, Nr Plymouth PL8 2HP Tel 01752 880236

DATES OF OPENING

February 23 Sunday
Little Cumbre, Exeter
Yonder Hill, Colaton Raleigh

March 16 Sunday
Bickham House, Kenn, nr Exeter
Gorwell House, nr Barnstaple
The Pines, Salcombe
Yonder Hill, Colaton Raleigh

March 19 Wednesday
Bickham House, Kenn, nr Exeter

March 23 Sunday
Fast Rabbit Farm, Ash, Dartmouth
38 Phillipps Avenue, Exmouth

March 28 Friday
Yonder Hill, Colaton Raleigh

March 30 Sunday
Fast Rabbit Farm, Ash, Dartmouth
Glebe Cottage, nr Warkleigh
Higher Knowle, nr Bovey Tracey
The Pines, Salcombe
Yonder Hill, Colaton Raleigh

March 31 Monday
Dippers, Shaugh Prior, nr
  Plymouth
1 Feebers Cottage, Westwood
Higher Knowle, nr Bovey Tracey
The Pines, Salcombe
Yonder Hill, Colaton Raleigh

April 2 Wednesday
38 Phillipps Avenue, Exmouth
Westpark, Yealmpton

April 3 Thursday
Whitmore, nr Chittlehamholt

April 6 Sunday
Higher Knowle, nr Bovey Tracey
Little Southey, Culm Valley, nr
  Culmstock
38 Phillipps Avenue, Exmouth
Westpark, Yealmpton

April 13 Sunday
Andrew's Corner, nr Okehampton

Ash Thomas & Brithem Bottom
  Gardens
Fast Rabbit Farm, Ash, Dartmouth
Gorwell House, nr Barnstaple
Higher Knowle, nr Bovey Tracey
Meadowcroft, Plympton
38 Phillipps Avenue, Exmouth
The Pines, Salcombe
Saltram House, Plymouth
Yonder Hill, Colaton Raleigh

April 14 Monday
Rock House Garden, Chudleigh

April 16 Wednesday
38 Phillipps Avenue, Exmouth

April 20 Sunday
Bickham House, Kenn, nr Exeter
Coleton Fishacre, Kingswear
Dippers, Shaugh Prior, nr Plymouth
1 Feebers Cottage, Westwood
Higher Knowle, nr Bovey Tracey
Killerton Garden, Broadclyst
Little Southey, Culmstock
Membland Villa, Newton Ferrers
38 Phillipps Avenue, Exmouth

April 23 Wednesday
Bickham House, Kenn, nr Exeter
Meadowcroft, Plympton

April 24 Thursday
Greenway Gardens, Churston
  Ferrers

April 25 Friday
Rock House Garden, Chudleigh

April 26 Saturday
Dartington Hall Gardens, nr
  Totnes

April 27 Sunday
Castle Drogo, Drewsteignton
Dartington Hall Gardens, nr Totnes
Fast Rabbit Farm, Ash, Dartmouth
Hartland Abbey, nr Bideford
Higher Knowle, nr Bovey Tracey
Knightshayes Gardens, nr Tiverton
The Pines, Salcombe

Yonder Hill, Colaton Raleigh

April 30 Wednesday
38 Phillipps Avenue, Exmouth
St Olaves, Murchington

May 1 Thursday
Greenway Gardens, Churston
  Ferrers

May 3 Saturday
Cleave House, Sticklepath
Mothecombe House, Holbeton
Shobrooke Park Gardens, Crediton

May 4 Sunday
Andrew's Corner, nr Okehampton
Broadhembury House,
  Broadhembury
Bundels, Sidbury
Cleave House, Sticklepath
Fast Rabbit Farm, Ash, Dartmouth
Hamblyn's Coombe, Dittisham
Higher Knowle, nr Bovey Tracey
Little Cumbre, Exeter
Mothecombe House, Holbeton
The Old Glebe, Eggesford
Starveacre, nr Axminster
Sunnybrook, nr Holsworthy
Wylmington Hayes, nr Honiton
Yonder Hill, Colaton Raleigh

May 5 Monday
Broadhembury House,
  Broadhembury
Hamblyn's Coombe, Ditisham
Higher Knowle, nr Bovey Tracey
Membland Villa, Newton Ferrers
The Old Glebe, Eggesford
Sunnybrook, nr Holsworthy
Wylmington Hayes, nr Honiton
Yonder Hill, Colaton Raleigh

May 7 Wednesday
Lukesland, Ivybridge
38 Phillipps Avenue, Exmouth
St Olaves, Murchington

May 11 Sunday
Arlington Court, nr Barnstaple

Castle Hill, nr South Molton
Fast Rabbit Farm, Ash, Dartmouth
Gorwell House, nr Barnstaple
Higher Knowle, nr Bovey Tracey
The Lodge, Mannamead
Lukesland, Ivybridge
Meadowcroft, Plympton
38 Phillipps Avenue, Exmouth
Saltram House, Plymouth
Wylmington Hayes, nr Honiton

May 14 Wednesday
Little Upcott Gardens, Marsh Green

May 17 Saturday
Ottery St Mary Gardens
Shobrooke Park Gardens, Crediton
Sunnybrook, nr Holsworthy
Wood Barton, Kentisbeare

May 18 Sunday
Addisford Cottage, nr Dolton
Bickham House, Kenn, nr Exeter
The Cider House, Yelverton
Coleton Fishacre, Kingswear
1 Feebers Cottage, Westwood
Higher Knowle, nr Bovey Tracey
Ottery St Mary Gardens
Sunnybrook, nr Holsworthy
Wood Barton, Kentisbeare
Woodside, Barnstaple
Wylmington Hayes, nr Honiton
Yonder Hill, Colaton Raleigh

May 21 Wednesday
Bickham House, Kenn, nr Exeter
38 Phillipps Avenue, Exmouth

May 24 Saturday
Little Upcott Gardens, Marsh Green
Monks Aish, South Brent
The Rectory, East Portlemouth
Withleigh Farm, nr Tiverton
Wolford Lodge, nr Honiton

May 25 Sunday
Addisford Cottage, nr Dolton
Andrew's Corner, nr Okehampton
Broadhembury House,
   Broadhembury
Bundels, Sidbury
Chevithorne Barton, nr Tiverton
Crosspark, Northlew
Fast Rabbit Farm, Ash, Dartmouth
The Glebe House, Whitestone, nr
   Exeter
Higher Knowle, nr Bovey Tracey
Inglewood, Newton Ferrers
Lee Ford, Budleigh Salterton
Little Upcott Gardens, Marsh Green
Monks Aish, South Brent
The Old Glebe, Eggesford
38 Phillipps Avenue, Exmouth
The Pines, Salcombe
Purple Hayes, Halberton
Rowden House, Noss Mayo
Starveacre, nr Axminster
Topsham Gardens, nr Exeter
Whitechapel Manor, nr South
   Molton
Withleigh Farm, nr Tiverton

Wylmington Hayes, nr Honiton

May 26 Monday
Alswood, George Nympton
Bicton College of Agriculture
Broadhembury House,
   Broadhembury
Crosspark, Northlew
The Croft, Yarnscombe
Higher Knowle, nr Bovey Tracey
Little Upcott Gardens, Marsh Green
Membland Villa, Newton Ferrers
The Old Glebe, Eggesford
Topsham Gardens, nr Exeter
Wylmington Hayes, nr Honiton
Yonder Hill, Colaton Raleigh

May 28 Wednesday
Little Upcott Gardens, Marsh Green
Stone Lane Gardens, nr Chagford

May 31 Saturday
Hayne Old Manor,
   Moretonhampstead
Pleasant View Nursery, nr
   Newton Abbot
Skerraton, Dean Prior

June 1 Sunday
Addisford Cottage, nr Dolton
Andrew's Corner, nr
   Okehampton ‡
Ash Thomas & Brithem Bottom
   Gardens
Blackhall Manor, South Tawton ‡
Bowcombe Gardens, Kingsbridge
Broadhembury House,
   Broadhembury
Castle Hill, nr South Molton
Crosspark, Northlew
Croftdene, Ham Dalwood
Dippers, Shaugh Prior, nr
   Plymouth
Fast Rabbit Farm, Ash, Dartmouth
1 Feebers Cottage, Westwood
Glebe Cottage, nr Warkleigh
The Glebe House, Whitestone, nr
   Exeter
Hayne Old Manor,
   Moretonhampstead
Higher Knowle, nr Bovey Tracey
Higher Spriddlestone, Brixton, nr
   Plymouth
Little Cumbre, Exeter
The Old Parsonage, Warkleigh
Overbecks, Salcombe
38 Phillipps Avenue, Exmouth
Pleasant View Nursery, nr
   Newton Abbot
Skerraton, Dean Prior
Wylmington Hayes, nr Honiton

June 4 Wednesday
Little Upcott Gardens, Marsh
   Green

June 7 Saturday
Bovey Tracey Gardens
Dicot, nr Chardstock
Little Upcott Gardens, Marsh Green
Otterton Gardens

June 8 Sunday
Addisford Cottage, nr Dolton
Bovey Tracey Gardens
Broadhembury House,
   Broadhembury
Dicot, nr Chardstock
Gidleigh Gardens
The Glebe House, Whitestone, nr
   Exeter
Gorwell House, nr Barnstaple
Higher Knowle, nr Bovey Tracey
Higher Spriddlestone, Brixton, nr
   Plymouth
Little Upcott Gardens, Marsh Green
Meadowcroft, Plympton
The Old Mill, Blakewell
Otterton Gardens
38 Phillipps Avenue, Exmouth
Stuckeridge House, Oakford, nr
   Tiverton
Wylmington Hayes, nr Honiton
Yonder Hill, Colaton Raleigh

June 11 Wednesday
Bicton College of Agriculture
Little Upcott Gardens, Marsh Green

June 14 Saturday
Brixham Gardens

June 15 Sunday
Andrew's Corner, nr Okehampton
Bickham House, Kenn, nr Exeter
Brixham Gardens
Castle Drogo, Drewsteignton
The Croft, Yarnscombe
Fast Rabbit Farm, Ash, Dartmouth
1 Feebers Cottage, Westwood
The Glebe House, Whitestone, nr
   Exeter
Heddon Hall, Parracombe
The Lodge, Mannamead
Membland Villa, Newton Ferrers
38 Phillipps Avenue, Exmouth
Rowden Gardens, Brentor
Whitechapel Manor, South Molton
Wylmington Hayes, nr Honiton

June 16 Monday
Rowden Gardens, Brentor

June 18 Wednesday
Bickham House, Kenn, nr Exeter
Cleave House, Sticklepath
Little Upcott Gardens, Marsh Green
Stone Lane Gardens, nr Chagford
Sunrise Hill, Withleigh

June 21 Saturday
Bundels, Sidbury
Kerscott House, nr Swimbridge
Little Upcott Gardens, Marsh
   Green
Sunnybrook, nr Holsworthy

June 22 Sunday
Addisford Cottage, nr Dolton
Brixham Gardens
Bundels, Sidbury
Cleave House, Sticklepath
The Glebe House, Whitestone, nr
   Exeter

Kerscott House, nr Swimbridge
Kingston House, Staverton
Little Upcott Gardens, Marsh
   Green
The Old Parsonage, Warkleigh
Overbecks, Salcombe
38 Phillipps Avenue, Exmouth
Priors, Abbotskerwell
Riversbridge, nr Dartmouth
Sowton Mill, Dunsford
Sunnybrook, nr Holsworthy
Woodside, Barnstaple
Wylmington Hayes, nr Honiton
Yonder Hill, Colaton Raleigh

June 24 Tuesday
Ash Thomas & Brithem Bottom
   Gardens

June 25 Wednesday
Ash Thomas & Brithem Bottom
   Gardens
Bicton College of Agriculture
Bundels, Sidbury
Little Upcott Gardens, Marsh Green

June 27 Friday
Dippers, Shaugh Prior, nr
   Plymouth

June 28 Saturday
Brixham Gardens
Bundels, Sidbury
Cadhay, Ottery St Mary
Dippers, Shaugh Prior, nr
   Plymouth
Little Upcott Gardens, Marsh Green
Talaton Gardens
Webbery Gardens, Alverdiscott

June 29 Sunday
Addisford Cottage, nr Dolton
Alswood, George Nympton
Brixham Gardens
Bundels, Sidbury
Cadhay, Ottery St Mary
The Croft, Yarnscombe
Dippers, Shaugh Prior, nr
   Plymouth
Fast Rabbit Farm, Ash,
   Dartmouth
1 Feebers Cottage, Westwood
Flete, Ermington, Ivybridge
The Glebe House, Whitestone, nr
   Exeter
Knightshayes Gardens, nr Tiverton
Knowle Down, Bishops Nympton
Little Upcott Gardens, Marsh
   Green
Membland Villa, Newton Ferrers
38 Phillipps Avenue, Exmouth
Priors, Abbotskerwell
Riversbridge, nr Dartmouth
Scypen, Ringmore
Talaton Gardens
Webbery Gardens, Alverdiscott
Whitechapel Manor, South Molton
Wylmington Hayes, nr Honiton

July 2 Wednesday
Little Upcott Gardens, Marsh Green

July 5 Saturday
Brixham Gardens
Wembury House, Wembury

July 6 Sunday
Addisford Cottage, nr Dolton
Arlington Court, nr Barnstaple
Brixham Gardens
Court Hall, North Molton
The Glebe House, Whitestone, nr
   Exeter
Killerton Garden, Broadclyst
38 Phillipps Avenue, Exmouth
Priors, Abbotskerwell
Rowden Gardens, Brentor
Yonder Hill, Colaton Raleigh

July 7 Monday
Rowden Gardens, Brentor

July 9 Wednesday
Stone Lane Gardens, nr Chagford

July 12 Saturday
Little Upcott Gardens, Marsh
   Green
Scypen, Ringmore
Sunnybrook, nr Holsworthy
Whitmore, nr Chittlehamholt

July 13 Sunday
The Cider House, Yelverton
The Croft, Yarnscombe
Croftdene, Ham Dalwood
Fast Rabbit Farm, Ash, Dartmouth
1 Feebers Cottage, Westwood
The Glebe House, Whitestone, nr
   Exeter
Gorwell House, nr Barnstaple
Heddon Hall, Parracombe
Kingston House, Staverton
Little Upcott Gardens, Marsh
   Green
Portington, nr Lamerton
Sowton Mill, Dunsford
Sunnybrook, nr Holsworthy

July 16 Wednesday
The Garden House, Yelverton
Little Upcott Gardens, Marsh
   Green

July 18 Friday
Court Hall, North Molton

July 20 Sunday
Addisford Cottage, nr Dolton
Andrew's Corner, nr
   Okehampton ‡
Bickham House, Kenn, nr Exeter
Blackhall Manor, South Tawton ‡
Glebe Cottage, nr Warkleigh
Kerscott House, nr Swimbridge
The Lodge, Mannamead
The Old Mill, Blakewell
The Old Parsonage, Warkleigh
Portington, nr Lamerton
Purple Hayes, Halberton
Whitechapel Manor, South Molton
Woodside, Whimple, nr Exeter
Yonder Hill, Colaton Raleigh

July 21 Monday
Fardel Manor, nr Ivybridge

July 22 Tuesday
Bickham House, (see text)

July 23 Wednesday
Bickham House, Kenn, nr Exeter
The Old Mill, Blakewell
Sunrise Hill, Withleigh

July 26 Saturday
Dicot, nr Chardstock
Little Upcott Gardens, Marsh
   Green
The Rectory, East Portlemouth

July 27 Sunday
Addisford Cottage, nr Dolton
Alswood, George Nympton
The Croft, Yarnscombe
Dicot, nr Chardstock
Glebe Cottage, nr Warkleigh
Hole Farm, Farlacombe
Little Upcott Gardens, Marsh
   Green
Membland Villa, Newton Ferrers
Oare Manor Cottage, Oare,
   Lynton

July 30 Wednesday
Little Upcott Gardens, Marsh
   Green
Sunrise Hill, Withleigh

August 3 Sunday
Glebe Cottage, nr Warkleigh
Longham, nr Lydford Gorge
38 Phillipps Avenue, Exmouth
Scypen, Ringmore
96 Wasdale Gardens, Plymouth
Whitechapel Manor, South Molton
Yonder Hill, Colaton Raleigh

August 9 Saturday
Little Upcott Gardens, Marsh
   Green

August 10 Sunday
Addisford Cottage, nr Dolton
Little Upcott Gardens, Marsh
   Green
96 Wasdale Gardens, Plymouth

August 13 Wednesday
The Garden House, Yelverton
Little Upcott Gardens, Marsh
   Green

August 17 Sunday
Bickham House, Kenn, nr Exeter
Bicton College of Agriculture
Rowden Gardens, Brentor
96 Wasdale Gardens, Plymouth
Woodside, Whimple, nr Exeter

August 18 Monday
Rowden Gardens, Brentor

August 20 Wednesday
Bickham House, Kenn, nr Exeter

August 24 Sunday
Fast Rabbit Farm, Ash, Dartmouth
Glebe Cottage, nr Warkleigh
The Old Parsonage, Warkleigh
38 Phillipps Avenue, Exmouth
96 Wasdale Gardens, Plymouth
Whitechapel Manor, South Molton
Whitmore, nr Chittlehamholt

Yonder Hill, Colaton Raleigh
August 25 Monday
  Membland Villa, Newton Ferrers
  96 Wasdale Gardens, Plymouth
  Yonder Hill, Colaton Raleigh
August 30 Saturday
  Pleasant View Nursery, nr
    Newton Abbot
August 31 Sunday
  Alswood, George Nympton
  Kerscott House, nr Swimbridge
  Pleasant View Nursery, nr
    Newton Abbot
  Starveacre, nr Axminster
September 3 Wednesday
  38 Phillipps Avenue, Exmouth
September 7 Sunday
  1 Feebers Cottage, Westwood
  Knowle Down, Bishops Nympton
  38 Phillipps Avenue, Exmouth
  Yonder Hill, Colaton Raleigh
September 14 Sunday
  Gorwell House, nr Barnstaple
  Membland Villa, Newton Ferrers
September 17 Wednesday
  Rock House Garden, Chudleigh
September 21 Sunday
  Bickham House, Kenn, nr Exeter
  1 Feebers Cottage, Westwood
  Inglewood, Newton Ferrers
  The Old Mill, Blakewell
  Rowden House, Noss Mayo
  Yonder Hill, Colaton Raleigh

September 24 Wednesday
  Bickham House, Kenn, nr Exeter
September 28 Sunday
  Ash Thomas & Brithem Bottom
    Gardens
  Rock House Garden, Chudleigh
October 5 Sunday
  Fast Rabbit Farm, Ash, Dartmouth
  1 Feebers Cottage, Westwood
  Gidleigh Gardens
  Yonder Hill, Colaton Raleigh
October 12 Sunday
  Gorwell House, nr Barnstaple
  Stuckeridge House, Oakford, nr
    Tiverton
October 19 Sunday
  Yonder Hill, Colaton Raleigh
October 26 Sunday
  Starveacre, nr Axminster
1998 February 22 Sunday
  Little Cumbre, Exeter
  Yonder Hill, Colaton Raleigh
1998 March, Mons
  Dippers, Shaugh Prior, nr
    Plymouth

Regular openings
For details see garden description

Avenue Cottage, Ashprington
Beatlands Farm, Metcombe
Burrow Farm Garden, Dalwood

Clovelly Court, Clovelly
Docton Mill and Garden
The Downes, Monkleigh
Flete, Ermington
The Garden House, Yelverton
Hill House, nr Ashburton
Lukesland, Ivybridge
Marwood Hill, nr Barnstaple
Plant World, nr Newton Abbot
Pleasant View Nursery, nr Newton
  Abbot
The Rectory, East Portlemouth
Rosemoor Garden, Great Torrington
Rowden Gardens, Brentor
Tapeley Park & Gardens, Instow

By appointment only
*For telephone numbers and other
details see garden descriptions.
Private visits welcomed*

Barton House, Nymet Rowland
The Gate House, Lee Ilfracombe
Holywell, Bratton Fleming
The Moorings, nr Lyme Regis
The Old Rectory, Woodleigh
The Orchard, Kenn
Orchard Cottage, Exmouth
Spillifords, nr Tiverton
Sweet Chestnut, Bovey Tracey
Weetwood, nr Honiton

DESCRIPTIONS OF GARDENS

Addisford Cottage ⚫✿ (Mr & Mrs R J Taylor) West Lane, Dolton. ½m W of Dolton. From village centre past Royal Oak for ½m to bottom of valley, gate on R across ford. 1½-acre garden surrounding picturesque thatched cottage in secluded wooded valley. Natural stream, large pond and water garden with hardy moisture loving and woodland plants. Extensive herbaceous borders, densely planted for sun and shade alongside many wild species. Large collection of geraniums. TEAS Suns only. *Adm £1 Chd free. Suns May 18, 25, June 1, 8, 22, 29, July 6, 20, 27, Aug 10 (11-5); also every Tues June, July (2-5). Parties welcome by appt, please* **Tel 01805 804365**

Alswood ⚫✿✿ (Bob & Marjorie Radford) George Nympton. 2m S of S Molton, halfway between the villages of George Nympton and Alswear. Ample parking, 2-acre developing garden, enthusiastically designed and maintained by owners; set in rural area with panoramic views of the Crooked Oak Valley. Many unusual specimen trees and shrubs. Well established spectacular herbaceous, erica and aquatic areas, pond and stream, unique architectural features. Cream TEAS in aid of George Nympton Church Fund. *Adm £1 Chd free. Bank Hol Mon May 26, Suns June 29, July 27, Aug 31 (2-5.30)*

Andrew's Corner ⚫✿✿ (H J & Mr & Mrs R J Hill) Belstone, 3m E of Okehampton signed to Belstone. Parking restricted but may be left on nearby common. Plants-

man's garden 1,000ft up on Dartmoor, overlooking Taw Valley; wide range unusual trees, shrubs, herbaceous plants for year round effect inc alpines, rhododendrons, bulbs, dwarf conifers; well labelled. TEAS. *Adm £1.50 Chd free. Suns April 13; May 4, 25; June 1, 15; July 20 (2.30-6); also private visits welcome, please* **Tel 01837 840332**

▲**Arlington Court** ⚫✿ (The National Trust) Shirwell, nr Barnstaple. 7m NE of Barnstaple on A39. Rolling parkland and woods with lake. Rhododendrons and azaleas; fine specimen trees; small terraced Victorian garden with herbaceous borders and conservatory. Regency house containing fascinating collections of objet d'art. Carriage collection in the stables, carriage rides. Restaurant. *Adm garden only £2.60 Chd £1.30. For NGS Suns May 11, July 6 (11-5.30)*

Ash Thomas and Brithem Bottom Gardens ✿ 5m SE of Tiverton, 2m S of Halberton. Take A361 from junction 27 on M5 signposted Tiverton but leave in ½m signposted Halberton. In 3m turn L signposted Ash Thomas. 1st garden 1m. A route map to each garden will be available on open days. TEAS at Greenlands. *Combined adm £1.50 Chd 25p. Suns April 13, June 1, Sept 28; Tues, Wed June 24, 25 (2-6)*

  Greenlands ⚫✿ (Dr & Mrs J P Anderson) Ash Thomas. ⅓-acre garden in open rural setting with far-reaching views. Alpine beds and troughs, herbaceous borders, roses and rustic screening, spring bulbs, annuals, herbs, fruit garden, vegetable plot, pond and wild areas. Parking in surrounding lanes, except disabled. Plants for sale in adjacent nursery. TEAS. *(Share to St Francis Hospital, Katete, Zambia & Royal National Rose Soc June 24 only®). Private visits also welcome March to Sept, please* **Tel 01884 821257**

Lower Beers & (Mr & Mrs G Nicholls) Brithem Bottom. Listed C16 longhouse fronts a developing 3-acre hidden garden, incl ornamental herb and vegetable garden, herbaceous beds, woodland dell and large open area leading to stream. Parking in adjoining yard. *(Share to Royal National Rose Soc June 24 only®). Private visits also welcome March to Sept, please* **Tel 01884 33096**

Lower Coombe Farm (Mr & Mrs M Weekes) Brithem Bottom. Large cottage garden with an interesting selection of plants, old roses and a ditch garden situated behind C17 farmhouse. Parking in farmyard. *(Share to Royal National Rose Soc June 24 only®). Private visits also welcome March to Sept, please* **Tel 01884 33296**

Avenue Cottage & (Mr R J Pitts & Mr R C H Soans) Ashprington. A381 from Totnes to Kingsbridge. 3m SE Totnes, from centre of village uphill past church for 400yds, drive on R. 11 acres of garden with woodland. Part of listed C18 landscape. Secluded valley site undergoing re-creation. Large collection of young and mature planting. Guided tours and tea by prior arrangement. *Adm £1.50 Chd 25p. Collecting box. Tues to Sat April 1 to Sept 27 (11-5). Private visits welcome, please* **Tel 01803 732769**. *No coaches*

Barton House ✿✿ (Mr and Mrs A T Littlewood) Nymet Rowland. 9m NW of Crediton. Follow signs to Nymet Rowland from A377 at Lapford or B3220 at Aller Bridge. Garden opposite C15 church. 1-acre garden designed and maintained by owners. Beautiful views to Dartmoor. Individual areas developed with varied character. Herbs; pond; herbaceous; yew garden; ferns, grotto, roses and fountain pool. *Adm £1 Chd 50p. Private visits welcome June, July, please* **Tel 01363 83534**

Beatlands Farm &✿✿ (Mr & Mrs D E Pounce) Metcombe, nr Tipton St John. 2½m S of Ottery St Mary. [SYO892]. 50yds N of Tipton Church take LH turn up Metcombe Vale for ½m. Instead of sharp R at Z bend, bear L up private rd. Care needed on ¼m narrow lane. Secluded 2-acre garden surrounding C17 farmhouse. Streams, waterways, large wildlife pond and wide variety of planting for colour and foliage effect. Streamside walk through woodland. Waterproof footwear advisable. Productive vegetable garden. *Adm £2 Chd 50p. Every day May 31 - July 13 (2-dusk). Private visits and coach parties only by appt, please* **Tel 01404 812968**

Bickham Barton ✿✿ (Helen Lady Roborough) Roborough, 8m N of Plymouth. Take Maristow turn on Roborough Down, ½-way between Plymouth and Tavistock, then follow poster directions. Bus stop: Maristow sign on Roborough Down; posters at Maristow turning 1m from house. Shrub garden; camellias; rhododendrons; azaleas; cherries; bulbs; trees. Lovely views. *Adm £1 Chd 50p. Every Sun April 6 to June 1, Mons April 7, May 5, Bank Hol Mon 26 (2-5.30); also private visits welcome until end of June, please* **Tel 01822 852478**

Bickham House &✿✿ (Mr & Mrs John Tremlett) Kenn. 6m W of Exeter 1m off A38. Plymouth-Torquay rd leave dual carriage-way at Kennford Services, follow signs to Kenn. 1st R in village, follow lane for ¾m to end of no-through rd. Ample parking. No shade for dogs. 5-acre garden in peaceful wooded valley. Lawns, mature trees and shrubs; naturalised bulbs, mixed borders. Conservatory, small parterre, pond garden; 1-acre walled kitchen garden; lake. Cream TEAS. *Adm £1.50 Chd 50p. Suns March 16, April 20, May 18, June 15, July 20, Aug 17, Sept 21; Wed March 19, April 23, May 21, June 18, July 23, Aug 20, Sept 24 (2-5). Special Event, 70th Anniversary NGS, July 22 (Invitation only). Private visits also welcome by appt, please* **Tel 01392 832671**

Bicton College of Agriculture ✿ Entrance is by Sidmouth Lodge, half-way between Budleigh Salterton and Newton Poppleford on B3178. Monkey puzzle avenue with fine views. Follow signs to garden car park. The gardens are linked to the old Georgian mansion and extend via the arboretum to the old walled garden and glasshouses, the centre of the Horticultural Dept. Beds and borders laid out for teaching and effect; incl NCCPG national collections of agapanthus & pittosporum; arboretum extends for ½m and incl magnolia, camellia and flowering cherries. Entrance tickets at Plant Centre or box by gate. Plant centre closes 4.30pm. Garden and arboretum guides available. TEAS. *Adm £2 Chd free (Share to Bicton Overseas Agricultural Trust®). Mon May 26; Weds June 11, 25; Sun Aug 17 (11- 4.30). Gardens also open daily throughout year, except Christmas day (11-4.30). Private parties welcome following written application using booking forms available, please* **Tel 01395 568353**

¶**Blackhall Manor** ✿✿ (Roger & Jacqueline Yeates) South Tawton. 6m E of Okehampton. Leave A30 at either Whiddon Down or Okehampton signed Sticklepath for 4m. South Tawton 2m N of Sticklepath. Small cottage garden around C16 thatched listed former farmhouse. Parking in village square. Walk through churchyard into garden. TEAS. *Adm £1.50 Chd 50p. Suns June 1, July 20 (2-6). Private visits welcome, please* **Tel 01837 840171**

Bovey Tracey Gardens Gateway to Dartmoor. A382 midway Newton Abbot to Moretonhampstead. TEAS. *Combined adm £2 Chd 30p. Sat, Sun June 7, 8 (2-6)*

    Beavers Lea (Mr & Mrs D A Pook) Bibbery. Cul-de-sac behind Coombe Cross Hotel. B3344 to Chudleigh Knighton. A very small garden on a sloping site. Shrubs, evergreens and herbaceous plants. TEAS

    Bibbery ✿ (Misses E & A Hebditch) Higher Bibbery. B3344 to Chudleigh Knighton. Cul-de-sac behind Coombe Cross Hotel. Plantspersons small garden, sheltered corners harbouring interesting shrubs and tender plants. TEAS. *Also private visits welcome, please* **Tel 01626 833344**

Church View ❀ (Mr & Mrs L Humphreys) East Street. B3344 opp St Peter & St Paul's Church. Small garden, but many unusual plants, incl secluded vegetable area. Disabled parking

¶**Lamornan** (Sally & Andrew Morgan) Furzeleigh Lane 30yds up from Bovey Hosp entrance limited parking at bottom of lane. Developing hillside garden with moorland views, mixed planting includes herbaceous alpine and vegetables

Pineholm ❀ (Dr & Mrs A A Baker) High Close. B3344 to Chudleigh Knighton. 1st L past Coombe Cross Hotel. 2-terraced garden on a steep sloping site. Wild garden with stream, wide variety of fruit grown by an expert

Sunnyside (Mr & Mrs J D Green) Hind Street. Nr town centre off A382. Opp Baptist Church. Well established enclosed garden; trees and shrubs; herbaceous and colourful conservatory; productive vegetable area. Parking nearby

¶**Bowcombe Gardens** ⚲❀ From Kingsbridge take A379 E to Torcross. In 1m before Long Bridge turn L for Bowcombe. TEAS. *Combined adm £2 Chd 50p (Share to St Mary's & St Martin's Churches®). Sun June 1 (2-5.30)*

¶**Inish** (A D Armstrong) ½-acre cottage garden with stream, shrubs and herbaceous plants

¶**Bowcombe Cottage** (C Tod) 1½-acre cottage garden with interesting hillside challenge. Surrounded by stream

Brixham Gardens ❀ *Combined adm £2 Chd free. Sat, Suns June 14, 15, 22, 28, 29; July 5, 6 (11-4)*

Rose Marie Cottage (Howard & Rosemary East) 42 Rea Barn Rd. From Brixham Town Centre take Dartmouth rd, in approx ¼m turn L at t-lights (or R if coming from Dartmouth). Garden is 150yds on L. Small secluded walled garden. Rose arbour; clematis; herbaceous borders. Beekeeping demonstration

Southdown Farm (Col & Mrs Stephen Love) Southdown Hill Rd. Take Dartmouth - Brixham rd. In Milton St, approx 1m from Brixham Town Centre follow NGS sign into Southdown Hill Rd. Farm is at end of rd in approx ½m. 1-acre garden of a working farm. Shrubs, roses and herbaceous perennials. Magnificent country views to sea. *Open on some of above dates, but please* **Tel 01803 857991**

Broadhembury House ❀ (Mr & Mrs W Drewe) Broadhembury. 5m equidistant on A373 from Honiton-Cullompton signed Broadhembury. 2-acre informal garden in C16 picturesque thatched village. A spring garden with rhododendrons and azaleas, daffodils and bluebells. Ample parking in village square. TEAS. *Adm £1.50 Chd 50p (Share to Muscular Dystrophy Group®). Suns, Mons May 4, 5, 25, 26; Suns June 1, 8 (2-5). Larger groups welcome by appt during May and June, please* **Tel 0140484 1326**

Bundels ⚲❀ (Mr & Mrs A Softly) Ridgway, Sidbury. From Sidmouth B3175 turn left at free Car Park in Sidbury. From Honiton A375, turn right. Garden 100yds up Ridgway on left. 1½-acre organic garden incl small wood and pond set round C16 thatched cottage (not open); over 100 varieties of old-fashioned and other shrub roses. Typical cottage garden with accent on preservation of

wild life. Teas in village. *Adm £1 Acc chd free. Suns May 4, 25 (2-6); Sats, Suns June 21, 22, 28, 29; Wed June 25 (10-12 2-6). Private visits also welcome May to July for large parties, please* **Tel 01395 597312**

Burrow Farm Garden ⚲❀ (Mr & Mrs John Benger) Dalwood, 4m W of Axminster. A35 Axminster-Honiton rd; 3½m from Axminster turn N near Shute Garage on to Stockland Rd; ½m on right. Secluded 5-acre garden with magnificent views has been planned for foliage effect and includes woodland garden in a dell with rhododendrons, azaleas etc; large bog garden; pergola walk with rose-herbaceous borders; many unusual plants. Nursery adjoining. Coffee, light lunch, Cream TEAS. *Adm £2 Chd 50p. Fri March 28 to Sept 30 daily (2-7), please* **Tel 01404 831285**

¶**Cadhay** ⚲❀ (Lady William-Powlett) Ottery St Mary. 1m NW of Ottery St. Mary on B3176. Ample parking. Tranquil 2-acre garden in lovely setting between the Elizabethan Manor House (not open) and ancient stew ponds. Carefully planned double herbaceous borders particularly colourful in summer. Small part-walled water garden features, roses and clematis. *Adm £1.50 Chd 50p. Sat, Sun June 28, 29 (2-5)*

▲**Castle Drogo** ⚲⚲❀ (The National Trust) Drewsteignton. W of Exeter, S of A30. Medium-sized garden with formal beds and herbaceous borders; shrubs, woodland walk overlooking Fingle Gorge. Wheelchair available. Plant centre. Restaurant. Tea room. *Adm gardens only £2.30 Chd £1.10. For NGS Suns April 27, June 15 (10.30-5.30)*

■ ¶**Castle Hill** ⚲⚲❀ (The Earl & Countess of Arran) Filleigh. 4m W of South Molton on B3227. A361 Tiverton to Barnstaple, leave at Little Chef roundabout signed Filleigh for 2m. House conspicuous by golden dome. C18 extensive landscape garden with many fine trees surrounding Palladian house. Formal grassed terraces with balustrading. Herbaceous border, arboretum and woodland with magnolias, camellias, rhododendrons, azaleas and flowering shrubs. Many C18 follies incl temples, water and an outstanding 1730 castle surmounting the hill behind the house with a fine view of the triumphal arch and distant views to Exmoor, Dartmoor and Lundy Island. TEAS. *Adm £1.50 Chd free. Suns May 4, 18, June 8, 15, 22 (2-5). For NGS Suns May 11, June 1 (2-5)*

Castle Tor (Leonard Stocks) Wellswood, Torquay. From Higher Lincombe Rd turn E into Oxlea Rd. 200yds on right, entrance identified by eagles on gate pillars. Spectacular scenic listed garden superbly designed and laid out under the influence of Lutyens in the mid-30s. Stepped terraces, orangery, paved work and ornamental water. *Adm £1 Chd 25p. Private visits welcome for parties less than 5, please* **Tel 01803 214858**

By Appointment Gardens. These owners do not have a fixed opening day usually because they cannot accommodate large numbers or have insufficient parking space.

Chevithorne Barton (Michael Heathcoat Amory) Chevithorne. 3m NE of Tiverton. A terraced walled garden and further informal planting in woodland of trees and shrubs incl NCCPG National Oak Collection. In spring the garden features magnolias, rhododendrons and azaleas. *Adm £1.50 Chd 50p (Share to CPRE®). Sun May 25 (2-6)*

The Cider House &*&* (Mr & Mrs M J Stone) Buckland Abbey, Yelverton. From A386 Plymouth-Tavistock, follow NT signs to Buckland Abbey. At Xrds before Abbey entrance turn N signed Buckland Monachorum. Drive 200yds on L, or short walk for visitors to Abbey. Peaceful and secluded garden with restrained planting complementing mediaeval house, part of a Cistercian monastery. Terrace borders and herbs, former Abbey walled kitchen garden with fruit, vegetables and flowers. Unspoilt aspect over wooded valley surrounded by NT land. Cream TEAS. *Adm £1.50 Chd 50p. Suns May 18, July 13 (2-6)*

Cleave House *&* (Ann & Roger Bowden) Sticklepath, 3½m E of Okehampton on old A30 towards Exeter. Cleave House on left in village, on main road just past small right turn for Skaigh. ½-acre garden with mixed planting for all season interest. National Collection of hostas with 500 varieties, 150 of these are for sale. Partially suitable for wheelchairs. *Adm £1 Chd free (Share to NCCPG). Wed June 18; Sat May 3; Suns May 4, June 22 (10.30-5.30). Private visits also welcome April to Oct, please* **Tel 0183784 0481**

Clovelly Court &*&* (The Hon Mrs Rous) Clovelly. 11m W of Bideford. A39 Bideford to Bude turn at Clovelly Cross Filling Station, 1m lodge gates and drive straight ahead. 25 acres parkland with beautiful open views through woodlands towards sea. 1-acre walled garden with borders, fruit and vegetables. Restored Victorian glasshouses. Medieval Manor adjacent C14 Church nr coastline. Free parking in drive. Directions at Garden entrance, nursery adjacent, blue doors in Church Path. *Adm £1 Chd 20p (Share to NSPCC®). Private visits and coach parties welcome May 1 to Sept 30 (2-5), please* **Tel 01237 431200**

▲Coleton Fishacre *&* (The National Trust) 2m NE of Kingswear. 8-ha garden planted and developed according to personal taste of the D'Oyly Carte family during 1926-1947 and unaltered by subsequent owners; wide range of tender and uncommon trees and shrubs in spectacular coastal setting. TEAS weather permitting. Unusual plants sale. *Adm £3.30 Chd £1.60. For NGS Suns April 20, May 18 (10.30-5.30)*

Court Hall *&* (Mr & Mrs C Worthington) North Molton. 2½m N from A361 Barnstaple-Tiverton rd. In N Molton drive up the hill into the square with church on your L take the only drive beside the old school buildings and Court Hall is just round the bend. A small south facing walled garden; large conservatory; rose, clematis, honeysuckle arbours surround a swimming pool garden with tender plants, rock wall and table; adjoining vegetable garden. *Adm £1 Chd 20p. Sun July 6, Fri July 18 (2.30-6)*

The Croft &*&* (Mr & Mrs Jewell) Yarnscombe. From A377, 5m S of Barnstaple turning W opposite Chapelton Railway Stn. for 3m. Drive on L at village sign. From

B3232 ¼m N of Huntshaw TV mast Xrds, turn E for 2m. 1-acre plantswoman's garden on edge of village with unspoilt distant views to West. Alpine area and wide selection of unusual plants and shrubs. Island beds, much herbaceous material, ponds and bog area. No toilets. Cream TEAS (Suns if fine). *Adm £1.25 Chd free. Mon May 26, Suns June 15, 29, July 13, 27 (2-6). Also by appt, please* **Tel 01769 560535**

Croftdene *&* (Joy and Phil Knox) Ham Dalwood. Between Axminster and Honiton. From A35 3½m W of Axminster turn N nr Shute Garage signed Dalwood and Stockland. Keep L up Stockland Hill until just past television mast. Turn R signed Ham. 1½m to Ham Cross. Park by telephone box. 1½-acre garden with further 1 acre of natural woodland. Shrubs; herbaceous; ericaceous; alpines; woodland and water plants. Island beds; rock garden; peat beds; stream-side and pond. TEAS at **Burrow Farm**. *Adm £1 Chd free. Suns June 1, July 13 (2-5.30). Private visits also welcome, please* **Tel 01404 831271**

Crosspark &*&* (Mrs G West) Northlew. From Okehampton follow A30 for 1m turn R to Holsworthy, drive for 6m past Flare Garage turn R signposted Northlew, over bridge, turn L to Kimber, we are 3m along this rd on L, or 2½m from Highampton on the Northlew Rd. 1-acre plantswoman's garden by colour theme; herbaceous borders; ponds, incl wildlife pond; bog garden; rockery heathers and conifers. Featured on BBC Gardeners World and ITV. Large variety of unusual plants for sale. TEA. *Adm 75p Chd 20p. Suns May 25; June 1; Bank Hol Mon May 26 (2-5)*

▲Dartington Hall Gardens &*&* (Dartington Hall Trust) Approx 1½m NW of Totnes. From Totnes take A384, turn R at Dartington Parish Church. 28-acre garden surrounds C14 Hall and Tiltyard. Plant sales shop and nursery. *Adm (donation) £2.00 recommended. For NGS Sat, Sun April 26, 27 (dawn to dusk)*

Dicot *&* (Mr & Mrs F Clarkson) Chardstock. Axminster to Chard A358 at Tytherleigh to Chardstock. R at George Inn, L fork to Hook, R to Burridge, 2nd house on L. 3-acre enthusiasts garden, trees unusual shrubs and conifers, bog orchids in June. Stream, mixed borders, fish pool, features. TEAS. *Adm £1.50 Chd 75p. Sats, Suns June 7, 8, July 26, 27 (2-5.30). Private visits also welcome, please* **Tel 01460 220364**

Dippers *&* (Mr & Mrs R J Hubble) Shaugh Prior. 8m NE of Plymouth. Garden 100yds down lane opp church near top of village. Park in village. No parking in lane. ¾-acre informal garden. Emphasis on foliage contrast with collection of dwarf rhododendrons, dwarf conifers and shrubs together with herbaceous and heathers. Extensive collection of alpines, in raised beds and troughs. Special interest in pinks; scented pink walk. NCCPG National collection of dianthus. Choice alpines and unusual herbaceous for sale. *Adm £1 Chd free (Share to NCCPG Devon Group). Mon March 31 (2-5) Suns April 20, June 1. Fri, Sat, Sun June 27, 28, 29 (Church Flower Festival (11-5)) 1998 Mons in March (2-4.30) for collection of hellebore cultivars and spring bulbs with hellebores for sale*

THE NATIONAL GARDENS SCHEME ROSE 'CHARITY'
This rose was bred by David Austin to celebrate the 70th anniversary of The National Gardens Scheme and will be launched at The Chelsea Flower Show in 1997. *Photograph David Austin Roses Limited*

PHOTOGRAPHIC COMPETITION

Held in conjunction with 'Gardens Illustrated'

Samples from Winning Portfolios
Above left: First prizewinner – **Rosalind Simon**
(Upton House, Warwickshire)
Above: Runner-up – **Melanie Eclare** (Goulters Mill
Farm, Wiltshire)
Below left: Highly commended – **Nada Jennett**
(Preen Manor, Shropshire)
Below: Highly commended – **Nicola Essex** (St
Michael's Convent, London)
Right: Highly commended – **Jim Love** (Little Court,
Hampshire)

Left: A quiet corner at **Frith Hill** in **Sussex**, a garden with outstanding views.
Photograph by Sheila Orme

Right: **The Queen's Nursing Institute**, the founding organisation and beneficiary of the National Gardens Scheme, assists nurses in times of difficulty; one of the recipients is seen here in her garden with a companion of many years.
Photograph by courtesy of QNI

Below: Tea-time at **Marton House, Cumbria**. Home-made teas are among the attractions of garden visiting.
Photograph by Val Corbett

Left: In 1997 **Sissinghurst Garden** in **Kent** is one of the gardens that has been opening for the National Gardens Scheme for 60 years.
Photograph by Sheila Orme

Below: Vegetable gardens are sometimes a feature of National Gardens Scheme gardens. This excellent example is at **Hean Castle, Carmarthenshire & Pembrokeshire**.
Photograph by Clive Boursnell

Right: **Hurst Lodge** in **Berkshire** first opened in 1927 and has opened every year since, apart from several years during the Second World War.
Photograph by Anne Peck

Ordered rows of vegetables seen through an arch at **Wretham Lodge, Norfolk**.
Photograph by Clive Boursnell

■ **Docton Mill and Garden** ✿ (Mr & Mrs M G Bourcier) Spekes Valley nr. Hartland. Off A39: From N Devon via Clovelly Cross & Hartland to Stoke, or from N Cornwall via Kilkhampton to the West Country Inn. On either route turn L and follow Elmscott signs towards Lymebridge in Spekes Valley for 3½m. A garden for all seasons (depicted BBC TV spring, summer and autumn) with working water mill dated 1249, 8 acres of sheltered wooded valley in one of Devon's outstanding beauty spots 1500yds from Spekes Mill Mouth coastal waterfalls and beach. Mill pond, leats, trout stream with footbridges and smaller streams. Cultivated areas incl bog garden, rockery, outcrops, woodland, and orchard. Displays of narcissi, primulas, shrub roses, specimen trees, shrubs and herbaceous plants, wild primroses, bluebells, foxgloves and ferns. Devon cream TEAS at mill. *Adm £2.50 Chd 50p. Daily March 1 to Oct 31 (10-5). For NGS every Tues. Parties by prior arrangement* **Tel 01237 441369**

The Downes ✿✿ (Mr & Mrs R C Stanley-Baker) 4½m S of Bideford; 3m NW of Torrington. On A386 to Bideford turn left (W) up drive, ¼m beyond layby. 15 acres with landscaped lawns; fine views overlooking fields and woodlands in Torridge Valley; many unusual trees and shrubs; small arboretum; woodland walks. Featured in Homes and Gardens June 1993. TEA Sats, Suns only. *Adm £1 Chd 20p. Daily March 30 to June 8 (all day). Private visits also welcome by appt June to Sept, please* **Tel 01805 622244**

Fardel Manor ♿✿✿ (Dr A G Stevens) 1¼m NW of Ivybridge; 2m SE of Cornwood; 200yds S of railway bridge. 5-acre, all organic garden, maintained with conservation and wildlife in mind. Partly reticulated. 2½ acres developed over past 12 years with stream, pond and lake. Also, small courts and walled gardens around C14 Manor, with orangery, herbaceous borders, formal pond and shrub garden. TEAS. *Adm £1.50 Chd 50p (Share to Frame®). Mon July 21 (11-4.30)*

Fast Rabbit Farm ♿✿ (Mr & Mrs Mort) Ash Cross. 1½m from Dartmouth off the Dartmouth-Totnes rd pass park and ride. Turn L at Rose Cottage. Opp direction, from Totnes or Kingsbridge, pass Woodland Park on R, drive past Norton Park on L turn R at Rose Cottage. Garden created in sheltered valley with natural stream. Several ponds and lake; partially wooded; rockery; extensively planted; extends 8 acres with new woodland planting and walks being created through woodland at head of valley. Small specialist nursery open daily. Car park. Some level walks. 'Invalids' please phone prior to visit. TEAS. *Adm £1.50 Chd 50p. Suns March 23, 30, April 13, 27, May 4, 11, 25, June 1, 15, 29, July 13, Aug 24, Oct 5 (11-5). Parties welcome by appt, please* **Tel 01803 712437**

1 Feebers Cottage ♿✿✿ (Mr & Mrs M J Squires) Westwood. 2m NE of Broadclyst from B3181 (formerly A38) Exeter-Taunton, at Dog Village bear E to Whimple, after 1½m fork left for Westwood. A modern cottage garden, a little of everything set in ¾ of an acre, with a maze of pathways; specialising in plants which tolerate heavy clay soil (alpines in raised beds) and a section of plants introduced by Amos Perry. Nursery. Cream TEAS Sun June 29 only, tea and biscuits on other days. *Adm £1 Chd free. Mon March 31 and Suns April 20, May 18, June 1, 15, 29*

(Cream TEAS), July 13, Sept 7, 21, Oct 5 (2-6). Private visits welcome, please **Tel 01404 822118**

■ **Flete** ✿ (Country Houses Association) Ermington, 2m W of Modbury on A379 Plymouth-Kingsbridge rd. Entrance adjacent to Sequers Bridge. 5 acres of gardens overlooking R Erme and valley. Landscaped in 1920's by Russell Paige and incl an Italian garden and water garden which Lawrence of Arabia helped to construct. Many fine trees and shrubs. Interesting cobbled terrace to W face of original Tudor manor. *Adm £2 Chd £1 (Share to Country Houses Assoc®). House and gardens open every Weds, Thurs pm May to end Sept. For NGS Sun June 29 (2.30-5) when TEAS will be available.* **Tel 017529 830308**

■ **The Garden House** ✿✿ (The Fortescue Garden Trust) Buckland Monachorum, Yelverton. W of A386, 10m N of Plymouth. 8-acre garden, incl a romantic, terraced walled garden surrounding the ruins of a C16 vicarage. Also incl an acer glade, spring garden, rhododendron walk, herbaceous glade, cottage garden and quarry garden. Coaches and parties by appt only, wide range of plants for sale. TEAS. *Adm £3 Chd £1 (Share to NGS®). March 1 to Oct 31 daily. For NGS Weds July 16, Aug 13 (10.30-5)*

The Gate House ✿ (Mr & Mrs D Booker) Lee Coastal Village. 3m W of Ilfracombe. Park in village car park. Take lane alongside The Grampus public house. Garden is 50yds past inn buildings. Peaceful streamside garden with a range of habitats; bog garden (National Collection of Rodgersia), woodland, herbaceous borders, patio garden with hardy 'exotics'. 2¼ acres, where no chemicals are used, only a few minutes walk from the sea and dramatic coastal scenery. Good food at the Grampus. *Collecting box. Open most days (9-12) (2-4). Please* **Tel 01271 862409** *to check*

Gidleigh Gardens From A30 take A382 for Mortonhampstead via Whiddon Down. In 100yds R to Gidleigh for 4m. Entrances adjacent C15 Church. Home made TEAS at Castle Farm. *Combined adm £2 Chd £1. Suns June 8, Oct 5 (2-5.30)*
  Castle House ✿ (Mr & Mrs M Hardy) 2 acres of hillside gardens around remains of mediaeval castle. New plantings amongst granite stones and water cascades link the gardens to the landscape
  Castle Farm ✿ (Mr & Mrs M Bell) A natural garden in one of Dartmoor's sheltered combes; stream, waterfalls and pools. Streamside walk in 6 acre wild valley. Views to deer forest and Castle Drogo

■ **Glebe Cottage** ✿✿ (Mrs Carol Klein) Warkleigh. From N Devon link rd or A377. Halfway between S Molton and Umberleigh on B3227 at Homedown Cross. S for Chittlehamolt, straight on for 2m entrance 100yds beyond Xrds. Garden featured on BBC 'Gardeners World', 'Garden Club' and ITV West Country. Chelsea Gold Medal Winners 1992/6. 1-acre cottage garden. recently redesigned with new features and exciting new plantings. S sloping, terraced. Wide collection of plants in different situations. Stumpery with ferns to sheltered formal beds and cottage garden plantings. Wide variety of unusual plants available from adjoining nursery open Tuesday to Friday. *Adm £1 Chd free. For NGS Suns March 30, June 1, July 20, 27, Aug 3, 24 (2-5)*

The Glebe House ⚹ (Mr & Mrs John West) Whitestone. 2½-acre mature garden at 650ft S facing with outstanding views ranging from Exe estuary to Dartmoor. Garden on 3 levels; lower level with extensive lawns, mature trees and lge heather garden; middle level where house walls and buildings covered by climbing roses, clematis, honeysuckles and jasmines; upper level, given over to lawns with families of trees, acer, birch and eucalyptus underplanted with species and shrub roses. Over 300 varieties of rose most notable being Rosa filipes 'Kiftsgate', probably largest rose in UK, stretching over 150ft along C14 Tithe Barn (Ancient Monument) in courtyard. Former Rectory part C14 with Georgian frontage (not open). C13/14 Church adjoins. Parking in lanes around Church, unsuitable for large coaches. *Adm £1.50 Chd free (Share to Whitestone Church®). Suns May 25, June 1, 8, 15, 22, 29, July 6, 13 (2-6). Private visits also welcome, please* **Tel 01392 811200**

Gorwell House ⬅⚹ (Dr J A Marston) 1m E of Barnstaple centre, on Bratton Fleming rd, drive entrance between two lodges on left. 4 acres of trees and shrubs, rare and tender, walled garden; mostly created since 1982; small temple; summer house with views across estuary to Lundy and Hartland Point. TEAS (except March 16, April 13, Oct 12). *Adm £1 Acc chd free. Suns March 16, April 13, May 11, June 8, July 13, Sept 14, Oct 12 (2-6)*

Greenway Gardens ⚹ (Mr & Mrs A A Hicks) Churston Ferrers, 4m W of Brixham. From B3203, Paignton-Brixham, take rd to Galmpton, thence towards Greenway Ferry. Partly suitable for wheelchairs; 30 acres; old-established garden with mature trees; shrubs; rhododendrons, magnolias and camellias. Recent plantings; commercial shrub nursery. Woodland walks by R Dart. Limited parking, partly suitable for wheelchairs. Plants in adj nursery not in aid of NGS. TEA and biscuits. *Adm £1.50 Chd 50p. Thurs April 24, May 1 (2-6).* **Tel 01803 842382**

Hamblyn's Coombe (Robert & Bridget McCrum) Dittisham. From Red Lion Inn follow the Level until it forks R up steep private road. Car park at top. 10 min pretty walk to 7-acre garden with stunning views, sloping steeply to R Dart. Extensive planting with unusual design features accompanying Bridget McCrum's stone carvings and bronzes. Wildflower meadow and woods. TEA. *Adm £1.50 Chd free (Share to National Hospital for Neurology & Neurosurgery®). Sun, Mon May 4, 5 (2-6). Private visits also welcome by appt, please* **Tel 01803 722228**

▲**Hartland Abbey** ⬅⚹ (Sir Hugh & Lady Stucley) Hartland. Turn off A39 W of Clovelly Cross. Follow signs to Hartland through town on rd to Stoke and Quay. Abbey 1m from town on right. 2 woodland shrubberies with camellias, rhododendrons; azalea and rare plants; wildflower walk through woods to remote Atlantic cove (Private walled gardens also open for NGS). Wheelchairs only on lawns around Abbey. TEAS. *Adm £1.50 Chd 50p (Share to St Nectan's Church, Hartland®). For NGS Sun April 27 (2-5.30).* **Tel 01237 441264 (The Administrator)**

Hayne Old Manor ⚹ (Mr & Mrs R L Constantine) Moretonhampstead. ¼m S of Moretonhampstead on A382. 5 acres with lake and walled garden, shrubs and herbaceous. Recent landscaping and new plantings, extensive views. Plants stall in aid of NABC. Cream TEAS. *Adm £1.50 Chd free. Sat May 31, Sun June 1 (2-5.30)*

Heddon Hall ⚹ (Mr & Mrs W H Keatley) Parracombe. 10m NE of Barnstaple off A39. 400yds N up hill from village centre. Entrance to drive on R. Ample parking 200yds. Garden of former rectory on edge of Exmoor under restoration extending to 3 acres. Walled garden with formal layout and herbaceous beds; sheltered flower garden; semi shaded S sloping shrubbery with paths leading down to natural stream and water garden. Cream TEAS. *Adm £1 Chd 50p. Suns June 15, July 13 (2-5)*

Higher Knowle (Mr & Mrs D R A Quicke) Lustleigh, 3m NW of Bovey Tracey A382 towards Moretonhampstead; in 2½m L at Kelly Cross for Lustleigh; in ¼m L/R at Brookfield along Knowle Rd; in ¼m steep drive on left. 3-acre steep woodland garden; rhododendrons, camellias, magnolias on a carpet of primroses, bluebells; water garden and good Dartmoor views. Teas in village. *Adm £2 Chd free. Suns March 30; April 6, 13, 20, 27; May 4, 11, 18, 25; June 1, 8; Mons March 31, May 5, 26 (2-6). Private visits welcome, please* **Tel 01647 277275**

Higher Spriddlestone ⬅ (Mr & Mrs David Willis) Brixton, nr Plymouth. A379 5m E from Plymouth, S at Martin's Garden Centre sign, ¾m to top of hill, R opp Spriddlestone sign, entrance 50yds on L. 1½-acre organic garden designed for shelter and low maintenance, climbing and scented plants. Produce, flowers and foliage for the house. Cream TEAS. *Adm £1 Chd free. Suns June 1, 8 (2-5.30). Private visits also welcome, please* **Tel 01752 401184**

Hill House Nursery & Gardens ⬅⚹ (Mr & Mrs R Hubbard) Landscove. Follow brown signs from A38 Ashburton or A384 Buckfastleigh to Totnes. Old Vicarage beside church both designed by John Loughborough Pearson, architect of Truro Cathedral. The 3-acre garden was the subject of 'An Englishman's Garden' by Edward Hyams, a previous owner. Also featured in 'English Vicarages and Their Gardens' and several times on TV. A fine collection of plants in adj nursery. TEAS, picnic area. *Adm - collection box. Open all year. Tea Room Mar 1 to Oct 1 (11-5)*

¶**Hole Farm** ⬅ (Rev Ian Graham-Orlebar) Farlacombe. A383 Ashburton to Newton Abbot rd 3m NE from Ashburton signed Gale, Burne, Woodland, opp turning to Bickington. At top of hill, lane on R to Hole Farm. 1½-acre valley garden, with woodland, wild garden, 2 ponds, herbaceous borders and bog areas. Old farm and buildings (not open). TEAS. *Adm £1 Chd 50p. Sun July 27 (2-5)*

Holywell ⚹⚹ (Mr & Mrs R Steele) Bratton Fleming. 7m NE of Barnstaple. Turn W beside White Hart Inn (opp White Hart Garage) signed Village Hall. At 300yds fork L for Rye Park. Entrance drive ¼m at sharp L. Parking at house. Garden on edge of Exmoor in woodland setting of mature trees, in all about 25 acres. Stream, ponds and borders. Woodland walk to Lower River meadow and old Lynton Railway Track. Many unusual plants for sale. *Adm £1 Chd free. Private visits welcome, please* **Tel 01598 710213**

¶**Inglewood** ✿❀ (Major & Mrs Stevenson) Newton Ferrers. 10m E of Plymouth. A374 Plymouth to Kingsbridge. At Yealmpton S to Newton Ferrers. At the green Xrds R into Parsonage Rd and along Court Rd for ¾m. Entrance on L. Unusual situation overlooking R Yealm. Steep garden. Recently reconstructed, with many terraces. Colour selection of plants and shrubs. TEAS. *Adm £1.50 Chd free. Suns May 25, Sept 21 (2-5.30)*

Kerscott House ♿✿❀ (Mrs Jessica Duncan) Swimbridge. Barnstaple-South Molton (former A361) 1m E of Swimbridge, R at top of hill, immediate fork L, 100yds on L, 1st gate past house. Developing 6-acre garden surrounding C16 farmhouse in peaceful rural setting. Ornamental trees, wide selection of shrubs, herbaceous and tender perennials, ponds and bog garden. Living willow constructions. 2½ acres new woodland planted 1995. *Adm £1 Chd free. Sat June 21, Suns June 22, July 20, Aug 31 (2-6). Private visits also welcome during July, please* **Tel 01271 830943**

▲**Killerton Garden** ♿✿❀ (The National Trust) 8m N of Exeter. Via B3181 Cullompton Rd (formerly A38), fork left in 7m on B3185. Garden 1m follow NT signs. 8ha of spectacular hillside gardens with naturalised bulbs sweeping down to large open lawns. Delightful walks through fine collection of rare trees and shrubs; herbaceous borders. Wheelchair and 'golf' buggy with driver available. Restaurant. Tea room, plant centre. *Adm gardens only £3.20 Chd £1.60. For NGS Suns April 20, July 6 (10.30-5.30)*

Kingston House ♿✿ (Mr & Mrs M R Corfield) Staverton. 4m NE of Totnes. A384 Totnes to Buckfastleigh, from Staverton, 1m due N of Sea Trout Inn, follow signs to Kingston. George II 1735 house grade II. Gardens are being restored in keeping with the period. Walled garden, rose garden, herbaceous borders, pleached limes and hornbeams, vegetable garden. Unusual formal garden with santolinas, lavender and camomile. Cream TEAS. *Adm £1 Chd 50p (Share to Animals in Distress, Ipplepen®). Suns June 22, July 13 (2-6). Private parties over 20 welcome by arrangement, please* **Tel 01803 762235**. No coaches

▲**Knightshayes Gardens** ♿✿❀ (The National Trust) 2m N of Tiverton. Via A396 Tiverton-Bampton; turn E in Bolham, signed Knightshayes; entrance ½m on left. Large 'Garden in the Wood', 12ha of landscaped gardens with pleasant walks and views over the Exe valley. Choice collections of unusual plants, incl acers, birches, rhododendrons, azaleas, camellias, magnolias, roses, spring bulbs, alpines and herbaceous borders; formal gardens; Wheelchair available. Restaurant. *Adm garden only £3.30 Chd £1.60. For NGS Suns April 27, June 29 (11-5.30)*

¶**Knowle Down** ♿❀ (Peter & Sue Jones) Bishops Nympton. 3½m E of South Molton. From Bishops Nympton signed Ash Mill for ½m. Adequate parking. 2½ acres on various levels. Courtyard area with rockeries and ornamental ponds. Herbaceous and shrub borders. Large patio area leads through pergola to rear gardens with stream-fed pond, ornamental shrubs and orchard area with thatched summerhouse. TEA. *Adm £1.50 Chd 50p. Suns June 29, Sept 7 (2-6)*

Lee Ford ♿❀ (Mr & Mrs N Lindsay-Fynn) Knowle, Budleigh Salterton. 40 acres parkland, formal and woodland gardens with extensive display of spring bulbs, camellias, rhododendrons, azaleas and magnolias. Traditional walled vegetable garden. Ornamental conservatory and Adam pavilion. TEAS. *Adm £1.50 OAPs £1.20 Chd 70p Special rate for groups 20 or more £1.20 (Share to the Lindsay Fynn Trust®). Sun May 25 (1.30-5.30); also by prior appt for parties of 20 or more (Light refreshments available)* **Tel 01395 445894**

Little Cumbre ✿❀ (Dr & Mrs John Lloyd) Exeter. At top of Pennsylvania Rd, 50yds below telephone kiosk on same side. Extensive views of Dartmoor and the Exe Estuary. ½-acre mixed shrub and herbaceous garden and ½ acre of woodland, newly acquired. Galanthus, hellebores, clematis and small ornamental trees chosen for bark. Ample parking in rd. *Adm £1 Chd 50p. Suns Feb 23, May 4, June 1. 1998 Sun Feb 22 (2-5)*

Little Southey ♿✿❀ (Mr & Mrs S J Rowe) Northcott, Nr Culmstock. Uffculme to Culmstock rd, through Craddock then turn R at 6'6 restriction sign, Little Southey ½m on L. Culmstock to Uffculme turn L at de-restriction sign to Blackborough, right at Xrds to Northcott. House on R. Garden surrounding C17 farmhouse. Wide variety of plants grown for round the year interest. Limited parking if wet. Plant sale partly in aid of NCCPG April 6 only. TEAS. *Adm £1 Chd free. Sun April 6 (2-6); Sun April 20 (2-5)*

Little Upcott Gardens ♿✿❀ (Mr & Mrs M Jones) Marsh Green, signposted off A30 Exeter to Honiton rd 4m E of M5 junction 29. Also signposted off B3180. Garden signposted from Marsh Green. Informal 2-acre garden. Sensitive combination of plant styles and colour and unusual varieties of conifers, shrubs, perennials and alpines, some for sale. The original cottage garden is also open and a water feature with ornamental ducks. Seats available and assistance given to disabled incl partially sighted, by prior arrangement. Parties welcomed with cream teas, available by appt. TEAS. *Adm £1.50 Chd 50p (Share to Cats Protection League, Ottery Branch®). Mons, Weds, Sat, Sun May 14, 24, 25, 26, 28, June 4, 7, 8, 11, 18, 21, 22, 25, 28, 29; July 2, 12, 13, 16, 26, 27, 30; Aug 9, 10, 13 (1.30-5.30), other times please* **Tel 01404 822797**

The Lodge ♿❀ (Mr & Mrs M H Tregaskis) Hartley Ave, Mannamead, Plymouth. 1½m from City Centre via Mutley Plain. Turn right at Henders Corner into Eggbuckland Rd, 3rd right at Tel kiosk to end of cul de sac. ½-acre S sloping aspect with variety of citrus fruits, olives, unusual shrubs, conifers, camellias and ground cover plants. Former L.A. Nursery with range of lean-to glasshouses for fruit and tender subjects. Featured on TV, 'Gardens for All'. TEA. *Adm £1.50 Chd 20p (Share to St. Luke's Hospice®). Suns May 11, June 15, July 20 (2-5.30). Private visits also welcome, please* **Tel 01752 220849**

Longham ✿❀ (Jennie Hale & Andrew Osborne) Coryton. Nr Lydford Gorge. A30, turn onto A386 Tavistock. 5m to Dartmoor Inn, signed to Lyford, past Lydford Gorge (NT). 3m R for Chillaton, 500yds R to Liddaton, downhill to Liddaton Cross, sharp R, 400yds over railway bridge, immed R into T sign rd, ½m downhill, L over small bridge, signed Longham Farm. Follow short track to the cottage. Ample parking. Small cottage garden with colourful mass herbaceous planting, ornamental grasses, shrubs, unusual perennials and climbers, vegetable garden, raised beds and polytunnel. Beautiful rural setting in wooded valley. TEAS. *Adm £1 Chd 50p. Sun Aug 3 (2-6). Private visits by appt, please* **Tel 01822 860287**

Lower Ware, Lyme Regis See Dorset

■ **Lukesland** (Mr & Mrs B N Howell) Ivybridge. 1½m N of Ivybridge on Harford Rd, E side of Erme valley. 15 acres of flowering shrubs, wild flowers and rare trees with pinetum in Dartmoor National Park. Beautiful setting of small valley around Addicombe Brook with lakes, numerous waterfalls and pools. Extensive and unusual collection of large and small leaved rhododendrons and one of the largest magnolia campbellii in country. Partially suitable for wheelchairs. TEAS. *Adm £2.50 Chd free. Suns, Weds, April 20 to June 18. Bank Hol Mons May 5, 26. For NGS Wed May 7, Sun May 11 (2-6). Coaches on application only,* **Tel 01752 893390**

●**Marwood Hill** ※ (Dr J A Smart) Marwood, 4m N of Barnstaple signed from A361 Barnstaple-Braunton rd and B3230 Barnstaple to Ilfracombe Rd. In Marwood village, opp church. 20-acre garden with 3 small lakes. Extensive collection of camellias under glass and in open; daffodils, rhododendrons, rare flowering shrubs, rock and alpine scree; waterside planting; bog garden; many clematis; Australian native plants. National Collections astilbe, iris ensata, tulbaghia. Partially suitable for wheelchairs. Plants for sale between 11-1 and 2-5. Teas in Church Room (Suns & Bank Hols or by prior arrangement for parties). *Adm £2 Acc chd under 12 free. Daily except Christmas Day (dawn-dusk)*

Meadowcroft ᵭ※ (Mrs G Thompson) 1 Downfield Way, Plympton. From Plymouth left at St Mary's Church roundabout, along Glen Rd, 3rd right into Downfield Drive; garden on right. From A38, Plympton turn-off L at 1st roundabout, R at 2nd down Hillcrest Drive and Glen Rd, L at bottom of hill. Opp Dillons into Downfield Drive. Downfield Way on R. Medium size; stream; rhododendrons, bog garden, azaleas, trees, flowering shrub borders. TEAS. *Adm £1 Chd free. Sun April 13, Wed April 23, Suns May 11, June 8 (2-5)*

Membland Villa ※※ (Mr & Mrs Jack Hockaday) Newton Ferrers. 10m E of Plymouth. A374 Plymouth-Kingsbridge. At Yealmpton, S to Newton Ferrers. Sharp L at Widey Cross to Bridgend, then L to Membland. 2nd house on L from top of Membland Hill. Small house on the former Membland Estate built 1882 by Edward Baring (Lord Revelstoke) set in country garden. Laid out and planted over 23yrs by present owner. Ornamental pond. Old roses, shrubs, climbers. Many unusual plants. Steep bluebell woods spectacular in season. TEAS. *Adm £1.25 Chd 25p. Suns April 20, June 15, 29, July 27, Sept 14; Mons May 5, 26, Aug 25 (2-5). Private visits also welcome for parties of 10 and over, please* **Tel 01752 872626**

Monks Aish ※※ (Capt & Mrs M J Garnett) 1m W of South Brent, near the hamlet of Aish, off B3372 W of village. Follow signposts to Aish. After going under Aish

railway bridge up hill, 3rd house on L next to Great Aish. [Grid Ref 688603.] A very attractive 1-acre garden with stream, a little different from most with varieties of shrubs, trees, flowers, fruit and vegetables. TEAS. *Adm £1.50 Chd under 12 50p (Share to The Missions to Seamen®). Sat, Sun May 24, 25 (2-5). Private visits of 8 or over welcome, please* **Tel 01364 73102**

The Moorings (Mr & Mrs A Marriage) Rocombe, Uplyme, 2m NW of Lyme Regis. From Lyme Regis, about 1m on A3070, turn R signposted Rocombe, over Xrds, take narrow lane signposted Rocombe 4th house on R, drive beyond house. From Axminster, straight at Hunters Lodge then fork R twice, straight at Xrds and R again. ¾m on L. 3-acre peaceful woodland garden, developed since 1965, on hillside with terraced paths, overlooking unspoilt countryside. Fine trees incl many species eucalyptus, unusual pines, nothofagus; flowering shrubs; daffodils and other spring flowers, ground cover, many ferns, autumn colour. *Adm £1 Chd free. Private visits welcome, please* **Tel 01297 443295**

Mothecombe House ᵭ※ (Mr & Mrs A Mildmay-White) Holbeton, SE of Plymouth 10m. From A379, between Yealmpton and Modbury, turn S for Holbeton. Continue 2m to Mothecombe. Queen Anne house (not open). Walled gardens, herbaceous borders. Orchard with spring bulbs; camellia walk and flowering shrubs. Newly planted bog garden; streams and pond; bluebell woods leading to private beach. Teas at beach car park, Old School tea house. *Adm garden £2 Chd free. Sat, Sun May 3, 4 (2-5.30). Parties welcome by appt, please* **Tel 01752 830444**

Oare Manor Cottage ※ (Mr & Mrs J Greenaway) Oare. 6m E of Lynton off A39. R after county gate to Oare. 50yds from Oare Church immortalized, in R D Blackmore's 'Lorna Doone'. Sheltered cottage garden in the romantic Oare Valley. Old-fashioned herbaceous borders, unusual shade plants, alpines, roses. Fine views of the moor. Parking in lower field or opp church. TEA. *Adm £1 Chd 50p (Share to Anti-Slavery International®). Sun July 27 (2-6). Private visits welcome, please* **Tel 01598 741242**

The Old Glebe ᵭ※※ (Mr & Mrs Nigel Wright) Eggesford, 4m SW of Chulmleigh. Turn S off A377 at Eggesford Station (½-way between Exeter & Barnstaple), cross railway and River Taw, drive straight uphill (signed Brushford) for ¾m; turn right into bridle path. 7-acre garden of former Georgian rectory with mature trees and several lawns, courtyard, walled herbaceous borders, bog garden and small lake; emphasis on species and hybrid rhododendrons and azaleas, 750 varieties. Specialist rhododendron nursery open daily by appt. TEAS. *Adm £1.50 Chd 50p (Share to The Abbeyfield Chulmleigh®). Suns, Mon Bank Hols May 4, 5, 25, 26 (2- 6). Parties welcome by appt, please* **Tel 01769 580632**

The Old Mill ※ (Mr & Mrs Shapland) Blakewell Muddiford, nr Barnstaple. ½m past hospital off B3230 to Ilfracombe at Blakewell Fisheries. Follow signs to Mill (grade II) at end of lane. A 3-acre south facing garden partly on slope at the rear surrounded by beautiful countryside views. Many varieties of shrubs, herbaceous, conifers and trees. Vegetable, herbs, an orchard, wildlife ponds. A young lime avenue leading to new folly. Parking in field. TEAS except July 23. *Adm £1 Chd free. Suns June 8, July 20, Sept 21 (11-5), Wed July 23 (4-8). Private visits also welcome, please* **Tel 01271 75002**

The Old Parsonage ✄❀ (Mr & Mrs Alex Hill) Warkleigh. 4m SW South Molton on B3226 past Clapworthy Mill (Hancocks Cider) R at stone barn signs to Warkleigh. From S through Chittlehamholt then 2nd R at War Memorial. Telephone kiosk marked on OS landranger sheet 180. 1-acre garden around former C16 Parsonage. Herbaceous border at entrance; enclosed stepped terraced garden behind house with wide range of plants and raised beds. Hillside above planted with trees and shrubs for autumn colour. Cream TEAS. *Adm £1 Chd 50p (Share to NCCPG®). Suns June 1, 22, July 20, Aug 24 (2-5.30)*

The Old Rectory ও✄ (Mr & Mrs H E Morton) Woodleigh nr Loddiswell. 3½m N of Kingsbridge E off Kingsbridge-Wrangaton Rd at Rake Cross (1m S of Loddiswell). 1½m to Woodleigh. Secret garden of trees, shrubs and naturalised bulbs with emphasis on rhododendrons, camellias and magnolias in spring and hydrangeas in Autumn. Chemical free. Maintained by owner. *Adm £1 Chd 10p. Private visits usually welcome at any time, please* **Tel 01548 550387**

The Orchard ❀ (Mrs Hilda M Montgomery) Kenn. 5m S of Exeter off A38. ¾ acre; mostly trees; variety of conifers, azaleas, camellias, rhododendrons, many shrubs; fishponds and flowerbeds. Masses of spring bulbs. Ample parking nr Church. *Adm £1 Chd 50p. By appointment only, please* **Tel 01392 832530**

Orchard Cottage ও❀ (Mr & Mrs W K Bradridge) 30, Hulham Rd, Exmouth, From Exeter A376 L into Hulham Road, just before 1st set of traffic lights. Entrance lane between Nos 26 and 32 Hulham Rd, opp lower end of Phillips Avenue. ¼-acre typical cottage garden. Parking in Hulham Road or Phillips Avenue. *Adm £1 Chd free. By appt only, please* **Tel 01395 278605** *(2.30-5.30)*

Otterton Gardens 3 Gardens situated in the main street of the picturesque village of Otterton between Sidmouth and Budleigh Salterton. Teas available at Otterton Mill. *Combined adm £1.50 Chd 50p. Sat, Sun June 7, 8 (2-6)*
    Basclose (Barbara & Clem Pointer) Fore St. S facing ½-acre cottage garden around C16 cob farmhouse, linhay, a small apiary and a mixed orchard and vegetable garden on a hill looking over the village
    Houstern Farmhouse (Nan & Mike Dickens) Fore St. Converted walled farmyard on 2 levels at rear of thatched cob farmhouse - mainly lawn and herbaceous beds - cottage perennials and climbing plants: very sheltered. Also orchard, vegetable garden and fruit cage
    April Cottage (Nora Butler) Fore St. Medium-sized cottage garden behind C15 cottage

Ottery St Mary Gardens Maps available at each garden. *Combined adm £1.50 Chd 50p. Sat, Sun May 17, 18 (2-6)*
    Ernespie ও (Dr & Mrs G Ward) Longdogs Lane. Next

to Ravenhill, connected by garden gate. S facing hot, dry garden, planted for easy care, cutting and continuous colour; rhododendrons, heathers, roses, level terrace. TEAS
Little Ash Farm ও (Sadie & Robert Reid) Fenny Bridges. Situated on A30, next to Esso Garage at Fenny Bridges. Park in layby. Developing ½-acre garden, trees, shrubs, large pond and borders with integrated vegetables. Handmade furniture workshop
Ravenhill ও✄❀ (Ruth & Guy Charter) Longdogs Lane. Take Sidmouth Rd from town square, 200yds up Tip Hill turn L up narrow Longdogs Lane, 5th house on R. Medium-sized garden with a wide variety of unusual plants. South aspect, country views; pond; keen NCCPG propagator. Unusual plants for sale (Share to NCCPG®)
10 Slade Close ✄❀ (Betty & Jenny Newell) From town centre take rd towards Seaton. Turn R into Slade Rd, then L into Slade Close and R again. Small garden, mixed shrubs, spring flowers, small pond, scree garden

▲**Overbecks** ✄ (The National Trust) Sharpitor 1½m SW of Salcombe. From Salcombe or Malborough follow NT signs. 2.4ha garden with rare plants and shrubs; spectacular views over Salcombe Estuary. Tea room same days as museum 12-4.15. *Adm garden only £2.40 Chd £1.20. For NGS Suns June 1, 22 (10-8 sunset if earlier)*

38 Phillipps Avenue ✄❀ (Mr & Mrs R G Stuckey) Exmouth. From Exeter, turn L into Hulham rd just before 1st set of traffic lights, 1st L into Phillipps Avenue (ample parking). Small, highly specialised alpine and rock garden containing extensive collection of rock plants and minature shrubs, many rare and unusual; peat bed; scree bed; troughs. National NCCPG Helichrysum collection. Small alpine nursery. Teashops Exmouth. *Adm 50p Chd free. Suns March 23, April 6, 13, 20, May 11, 25; June 1, 8, 15, 22, 29 (Share to NCCPG (Helichrysum Day)®), July 6, Aug 3, 24, Sept 7, Weds April 2, 16, 30, May 7, 21 Sept 3 (2-6). Private visits also welcome, please* **Tel 01395 273636**

The Pines ও (R A Bitmead) Main Rd, Salcombe. At junction of Devon and Sandhills rds; lower entrance and parking Sandhills rd. All seasons ¾-acre S facing garden; fine coastal views over Sharpitor Headland and N Sands Valley. Informal garden of surprises; many interesting and unusual shrubs, trees; water gardens; bulbs, camellias, azaleas, heathers. *Adm £2 Chd free. Suns March 16, 30 Mon March 31, Suns April 13, 27, May 25 (11-5). Private visits also welcome all year, please* **Tel 01548 842198**

Plant World ❀ (Ray & Lin Brown) St. Mary Church Rd Newton Abbot. Follow brown signs from A380 Penn Inn Roundabout. Car park on L past aquatic centre. 4-acre Hillside Garden, laid out as a map of the world with native plants. Alpines, especially primulas and gentians, shrubs, herbaceous. Himalayan and Japanese gardens. Comprehensive cottage garden with hardy geraniums, campanulas. 3 National Primula Collections. Seen on BBC Gardeners World June 1993. Rare and unusual plants sold in adjacent nursery. Picnic area, viewpoint over Dartmoor and Lyme Bay. Collecting box. *Adm £1 Chd under 12 free. Easter to end of Sept every day but Wed (9.30-5)*

Pleasant View Nursery ♿✿ (Mr & Mrs B D Yeo) Two Mile Oak, nr Denbury. 2m from Newton Abbot on A381 to Totnes. R at Two Mile Oak Public House signed Denbury. ¾m on L. Large car park. 2- acre plantsman's garden with a wide range of choice and uncommon shrubs giving colour all season. Additional 2-acre field planted with individual specimen shrubs. National Collections of Abelia and Salvia. Plants for sale in adjoining nursery (see advert). *Adm £1.50 Chd 25p. Sats, Suns May 31, June 1, Aug 30, 31 (2-6). Every Wed and Fri, May to Sept incl (2-5). Parties welcome by appt, please* **Tel 01803 813388**

Portington (Mr & Mrs I A Dingle) nr Lamerton. From Tavistock B3362 to Launceston. ¼m beyond Blacksmiths Arms, Lamerton, fork L (signed Chipshop). Over Xrds (signed Horsebridge) first L then L again (signed Portington). From Launceston R at Carrs Garage and R again (signed Horsebridge), then as above. Garden in peaceful rural setting with fine views over surrounding countryside. Mixed planting with shrubs and borders; woodland walk to small lake. TEAS. *Adm £1 Chd 20p (Share to St Luke's Hospice®). Suns July 13, 20 (2-5.30)*

Priors ♿✿ (Mrs Hunloke) Abbotskerswell. 1½m SW of Newton Abbot on Totnes-Newton Rd, signposted Abbotskerswell. Garden at bottom of village. ⅔-acre enclosed colourful garden, long herbaceous borders, old shrub roses; unusual plants. *Adm £1 Chd 50p. Suns June 22, 29, July 6 (2-5.30). Private visits welcome June to July, please* **Tel 01626 53506**

Purple Hayes ✿✿ (Kim & Bruce Thomas) Lake Farm, Halberton. B3391 ¼m SE of Halberton. Plantaholic's garden of 1 acre, started in 1987. Bold herbaceous planting, unusual plants, ornamental grasses, ponds, bog and herb garden. Pigmy goats and ducks. Cream Teas in adjoining farmhouse. *Adm £1 Chd free (Share to Cats Protection League®). Suns May 25, July 20 (11-5). Private visits welcome, please* **Tel 01884 821295**

The Rectory ♿✿✿ (Mr & Mrs T A Rhodes) East Portlemouth (Opp Salcombe). From A379 Kingsbridge to Dartmouth, at Frogmore S over bridge towards E Portlemouth for 5m, through village, R for 200yds, entrance on L. Or from Salcombe passenger ferry to E Portlemouth, L for ½m. Parking in field adjacent. Former rectory in 4-acre garden on Salcombe Estuary with lovely views to South Pool Creek. Springtime with camellias, magnolias, viburnums, bluebells and primroses. Summertime with herbaceous and mixed borders. Many unusual shrubs. Sheltered walled garden with glasshouse, roses and tender plants. TEAS on NGS days only. *Adm £1 Chd free (Share to Portlemouth Church®). For NGS Sats May 24, July 26 (2-5) Also every Thurs & Sat May 15 to Sept 21 with Collecting Box for NGS. Private visits (incl plant sales) welcome, please* **Tel 01548 842670**

Riversbridge ♿✿ (Mr & Mrs Sutton-Scott-Tucker) ½m inland from Blackpool sands and signed from A3122. Small walled gardens adjoining farmyard in lovely unspoilt valley with ponds and stream; herbaceous plants, roses and some unusual shrubs. TEAS. *Adm £1.50 Chd free. Suns June 22, 29 (2-6)*

¶Rock House Garden ✿ (Mrs D M & B Boulton) Station Hill, Chudleigh. A38 Exeter to Plymouth signed Chudleigh. S. edge of town. Entrance at Rock Nursery. Garden in ancient bishop's palace quarry with massive limestone rock. Delights for all seasons. Rare and unusual trees and shrubs. Massed daffodils in spring. Autumn brings one of the finest displays of cyclamen. Cave and ponds with Koi and Orfe. Walk with spectacular views of Dartmoor and access to Chudleigh rock, glen and waterfall. *Adm £1 Chd 50p. Mon, Fri April 14, 25, Weds Sept 17, 24 (9.30-5.0)*

●Rosemoor Garden ♿✿✿ (The Royal Horticultural Society) Great Torrington. 1m SE of Great Torrington on B3220 to Exeter. 40-acre plantsman's garden; rhododendrons (species and hybrid), ornamental trees and shrubs; dwarf conifer collection, species and old-fashioned roses, scree and raised beds with alpine plants, arboretum. 2000 roses in 200 varieties, two colour theme gardens, herb garden, potager, 200 metres of herbaceous border, a large stream and bog garden, cottage garden, foliage and plantsman's garden and a fruit and vegetable garden. Facilities for the disabled. *Adm £3.20 Chd £1 Groups £2.50 per person. Open daily all year (10-6 April to Sept. 10-5 Oct to March) (Share to NGS®).* **Tel 01805 624067**

■ ¶Rowden Gardens ♿✿✿ (Mr & Mrs John Carter) Brentor. 4m N of Tavistock. From A386 through Lydford village, or take Brentor Rd from Tavistock. Between 'Mucky Duck' and 'Brentor' Inns take rd signed Liddaton. Entrance 300yds on R. Tranquil 1-acre plantsman's garden begun in 1986 by author/lecturer John Carter. Featured in Practical Gardening '95. Ponds displaying water-lilies and many unusual aquatics. Bog gardens, grass walk, plantings of crocosmia, dierama, ligularia, rananculus, rheums. Huge collection damp loving iris incl new introductions and unique home-bred varieties. 2 NCCPG national collections. Plants for sale in adjoining nursery. Cream teas in Lydford. *Adm £1.50 Chd free. For NGS Suns, Mons June 15, 16, July 6, 7, Aug 17, 18 (10-5). Private visits welcome, please* **Tel 01822 810275**

¶Rowden House ✿ (Mr & Mrs I Hill) Noss Mayo. 10m E of Plymouth. A374 Plymouth to Kingsbridge. At Yealmpton S to Noss Mayo. At church follow signs to Stoke Beach for 1m. Entrance on R. Grade II listed farmhouse with ½-acre garden in rural setting. Developed over past 10 yrs. Exposed to salt-laden winds. Spring-fed pond. Interesting collection of plants. *Adm £1.50 Chd free. Suns May 25, Sept 21 (2-5.30)*

St Olaves ✿ (Mr & Mrs R Padley) Murchington. 1m W of Chagford. A382 1m S of Whiddon Down signed Throwleigh and Gidleigh, then signs to Murchington. From village centre, entrance to driveway adjacent house with iron railings, follow drive past cottage to open gate on L, then 50 yds for parking area. Converted, restored and replanted since 1971. Romantic landscape views over the Upper Teign Valley. Fine old trees and a large number of younger ones from round the world. Massive granite retaining walls. On a S-facing slope down which a cascade falls to the river. *Adm £2 Chd 50p (Share to Devon Gardens Trust®). Weds April 30, May 7 (2-5.30). Also private visits welcome for magnolias and camellias mid March to May, please* **Tel 01647 433415**

▲Saltram House ᴅ ✕ (The National Trust) Plympton, 3m E of Plymouth, S of A38, 2m W of Plympton. 4ha with fine specimen trees; spring garden; rhododendrons and azaleas. C18 orangery and octagonal garden house. George II mansion with magnificent plasterwork and decorations, incl 2 rooms designed by Robert Adam. Wheelchair available. Restaurant. *Adm gardens only £2.50 Chd £1.20. For NGS Suns April 13, May 11 (10.30-5.30)*

Scypen ✕✿ (Mr & Mrs John Bracey) Ringmore. From A379 Plymouth-Kingsbridge S at Harraton Cross on B3392. R at Pickwick Inn. Park in Journey's End car park on L opp church. ½-acre coastal garden, integrating design, landscaping and mixed planting for year-round effect and to take advantage of lovely views. Salt and wind tolerant plants; silver garden; chamomile and thyme lawns. Featured on BBC 'Gardener's World'. TEAS. *Adm £1 Chd 25p. Sat, Suns June 29, July 12, Aug 3 (2-5)*

Shobrooke Park Gardens ᴅ ✕ (Dr & Mrs J R Shelley) Crediton. 1m NE Crediton on A3072. 15-acre woodland gardens with old rhododendrons. Laid out in mid C19 with extensive Portland Stone terraces with views over the park and ponds. Restoration in an early stage with help from The Countryside Commission. TEAS by Posbury Chapel. *Adm £2 Chd free. Sats May 3, 17 (2-5)*

Skerraton ᴅ✿ (Mr & Mrs M Ogle) Dean Prior. 3m SW of Buckfastleigh. A38 ½m W of Buckfastleigh signed Dean. Follow signs to Skerraton for 2½m. 2 acres, 800' up on Dartmoor with views across South Hams to sea. Woodland area with azaleas, camellias and rhododendrons. Stream with marginal plants. Formal area with island and mixed borders. Pool. Most plants labelled. Dartmoor ponies and foals in paddocks and stables by house. TEAS. *Adm £1.50 Chd free (Share to Dean Prior Parish Church®). Sat, Sun May 31, June 1 (2-6)*

Sowton Mill ✿ (A Cooke and S Newton) nr Dunsford. From Dunsford take B3193 S for ½m. Entrance straight ahead off sharp R bend by bridge. From A38 N along Teign Valley for 8m. Sharp R after humpback bridge. 4 acres laid out around former mill, leat and river. Part woodland, ornamental trees and shrubs, mixed borders and scree. Yr-round interest. TEAS. *Adm £1.50 Chd free (Share to Cygnet Training Theatre®). Suns June 22, July 13 (2-6). Private visits also welcome, please* **Tel 01647 252347**

Spillifords (Dr Gavin Haig) Lower Washfield. Tiverton can be reached on A396 Tiverton to Bampton. Turn L over iron bridge signposted Stoodleigh. L again after crossing bridge marked Washfield and L again on hill following Washfield sign. The bridge is approx 2m from link rd roundabout. Spillifords is 1st house on L after Hatswell. Parking for 30 cars by annexe on same side as house. 1½-acre wildlife and wild flower garden. On steeply sloping bank of R Exe (unsuitable for disabled) wild flowers, butterflies, birds and other wildlife abound in an ideal arboreal and riverside environment. *Adm £2 Chd £1. Guided tours by appointment only. Weds, Sats pm April to Aug (3-6). Please* **Tel 01884 255353**

Starveacre ✿ (Mr and Mrs Bruce Archibold) Dalwood. Leave Axminster on A35 travelling W. After 3m (Shute Xrds) turn R at staggered Xrds follow signs to Dalwood and go through village, over stream, round sharp L bend. Follow road, ignoring L turn, up steep hill and at top turn L. Under pylons and up hill. Car park on L. A plantsman's garden of 5 acres on a hillside facing S and W with superb views. Mixed plantings of rhododendrons, camellias, conifers, acers and magnolias. TEAS. *Adm £1 Chd free. Suns May 4, 25, Aug 31, Oct 26 (2-5)*

■ Stone Lane Gardens ✿ (Kenneth & June Ashburner) Stone Farm Chagford. On NE edge of Dartmoor National park. From A30 signed Moretonhampstead, through Whiddon Down (A382) for ¼m, then signed Drewsteignton. After 1½m, 2nd R into Stone Lane. Parking in farmyards on L. 5-acre informally landscaped specialist arboretum with emphasis on foliage and bark with national collections of wild-origin birch and alder; natural streams and ponds. Views of Dartmoor. Exhibition by sculptors and designers inspired by nature, myth and folklore June-Sept. Partially suitable for wheelchairs. No coaches. TEA. *Adm £2 Chd £1. Gardens open daily mid-June to mid-Sept (2-6). For NGS Weds May 28, June 18, July 9 (2-6). Private visits also welcome, please* **Tel 01647 231311**

¶Stuckeridge House ᴅ (Major & Mrs George Llewellyn) Oakford. 6m NW of Tiverton off B3227. 1m W up hill from Black Cat garage, 1st L signed Oakford. In 200yds drive entrance on L at Thatched Lodge. ¾m wooded drive to house. 5-acre tree and shrub garden with extensive unspoilt countryside views, of particular interest to the plantsman. 1-acre walled garden and large cold greenhouse for marginally tender plants. Autumn colour. Ample parking. *Adm £1.50 Chd £1 (Share to Marie Curie Cancer Care®). Suns June 8 (2-5.30), Oct 12 (2-5). Private visits also welcome, please* **Tel 01398 351358**

¶Sunnybrook ᴅ✿ (Bill & Jean Wonnacott) Luffincott. A388 ½-way between Holsworthy and Launceston signed Luffincott at lay-by, cottage 1m on L. Small cottage garden with pond and short walk through adjacent old coppice wood. Bluebells, wild flowers and native ferns in spring. Shrubs and perennial planting around cottage and pond. Numerous containers. Cream TEAS. Ample parking. *Adm £1.50 Chd 50p (Share to Save the Children Fund®). Sun, Mon May 4, 5, Sats, Suns May 17, 18, June 21, 22, July 12, 13 (2-5). Private visits also welcome, please* **Tel 01409 271380**

Sunrise Hill ✕✿ (Chris & Sharon Britton) Withleigh. 3m W of Tiverton on B3137 rd to Witheridge and South Molton. Garden reached through Withleigh Nurseries, situated at E end of village. 1½ acres of colourful garden incl 40m 'Rainbow' border, unusual plants, shrubs, lawns and new plantings. Plants for sale in adjacent nursery (on open days 10% of plant sales for NGS). TEAS. *Adm £1 Chd free. Weds June 18, July 23, 30 (2-5.30). Parties welcome by appt, please* **Tel 01884 253351**

The National Gardens Scheme is a charity which traces its origins back to 1927. Since then it has raised a total of over £15 million for charitable purposes.

Sweet Chestnut ⚘ (P Thompson) Whisselwell Lane, Bovey Tracey. From Bovey Tracy, follow Haytor Rd to Edgemoor Hotel. Sharp L opp hotel, then 1st R, signed Whisselwell Farm. Last house on R. 1-acre woodland garden. Rhododendrons and camellias in abundance and other ericaceous plants and ground cover. Good yr-round planting and autumn colour with list available on request. *Adm £1.50 Chd 25p. Private visits welcome, please* **Tel 01626 833280**

¶**Talaton Gardens** ⚘ Leave A30 at Fairmile. Follow Talaton sign B3176 2m NW. Ample parking at Talaton Inn. Maps available. TEAS at Talaton Cottage. *Combined adm £1.50 Chd free. Sat, Sun June 28, 29 (2-5)*
  ¶**The Old Church School** (Angela & Robert Jennison) 50yds from Talaton Inn towards old village. Still developing on 2 levels. Small pool. Established trees, shrubs and herbaceous borders. Tranquil and sheltered
  ¶**The Old Post Office** (Professor & Mrs W J Moore) Follow signs up pedestrian Church Lane. Very small, low maintenance garden
  ¶**Talegarth** (Sally & Peter Smith) Opp Church Lane. 500yds from Talaton Inn. Unusual plants. Herbaceous borders densely planted for colour and foliage effect. Views. *Private visits also welcome, please* **Tel 01404 823277**
  ¶**Talaton Cottage** ♿ (Val & Vince Peterson) From Talaton Inn, keep car park on R, 300yds on R behind village hall. Herbaceous borders, vegetable garden, old fruit trees. Pool with rill. Small bog garden. TEAS
  3 Ivy Cottages ♿⚘ (Mrs N Bitschi) Towards A30 ½m from village hall on R at Public Footpath sign. Parking in rd. Limited disabled parking by cottage. ¾-acre garden in open rural setting. Still developing mixed borders. Stream with bog garden. Gravel areas with alpines and containers. *(Share to Help the Aged®)*

● **Tapeley Park & Gardens** ♿⚘ (Hector & Kirsty Christie) Instow. A39 Barnstaple-Bideford drive entrance and lodge 1m S of Instow. Italianate garden with stunning coastal views to the atlantic and Lundy Island. The terraces with long wall borders shelter many herbaceous and tender plants, replanted under the guidance of Mary Keen and Carol Klein. Walled kitchen and vegetable garden with long greenhouse for tender plants and grapes. Ice and shell houses. Lunches & cream TEAS. *Adm £2.80 OAP £2.30, Chd £1.80 (Share to NGS®). Good Fri to Sept 30 daily except Sats (10-6)*

Topsham Gardens ♿⚘ 4m from Exeter. Free parking in Holman Way car park. Teas at 20 Monmouth Ave. *Adm £1 each garden Chd free. Sun, Mon May 25, 26 (2-6)*
  4 Grove Hill (Margaret and Arthur Boyce) Off Elm Grove Rd, opp junction with Station Rd. A small town garden with some rare plants, troughs and screes with alpine plants and unusual bulbs
  20 Monmouth Avenue (Anne & Harold Lock) Access to Monmouth Ave by footpath on the L after leaving Holman Way car park. ⅓-acre level garden, wide range of unusual plants and shrubs giving year round effect, mixed curved borders, herbaceous, shrubs and bulbs incl a collection of hardy geraniums and alliums. Some old-fashioned roses. Featured on TV 'Gardens For All'. TEAS. *Private visits also welcome, please* **Tel 01392 873734**

96 Wasdale Gardens ⚘⚘ (David & Colleen Fenwick) Estover, Plymouth. Outskirts of city. From A38 Forder Valley Junction, follow Forder Valley Rd (old A38), R into Novorossisk Rd, L into Miller Way, L at 3rd mini roundabout into Keswick Crescent, 1st L into Wasdale Gardens. Car park next to 102 Wasdale Gardens, follow path along top of car park past nos 95 and 94. Garden in front of 93, with 2 dovecotes. Small council house garden 17m × 15m. Large diversity of unusual plants, mostly herbaceous. NCCPG Nat Col Crocosmia, 200 hybrids. Recycled materials used. *Adm £1 Chd 25p. Suns Aug 3, 10, 17, 24, Mon Aug 25 (11-5). Private visits also welcome at other times, please* **Tel 01752 785147**

Webbery Gardens ⚘⚘ Alverdiscott. Approx 2½m E of Bideford. Either from Bideford (E The Water) along the Alverdiscott Rd or from the Barnstaple to Torrington Rd B3232. Take the rd to Bideford at Alverdiscott and pass through Stoney Cross. TEA. *Combined adm £2 Chd free. Sat, Sun June 28, 29 (2-6).*
  Little Webbery (Mr & Mrs J A Yewdell) Webbery Cross. Parking next door field. Approx 3-acre garden with two large borders near the house with lawns running down a valley; pond, mature trees on either side and fields below, separated by 2 Ha Has. Walled garden with box hedging, partly used for fruit, vegetables, and incl a greenhouse; lawns; rose garden and trellises; shrubs and climbing plants. A tennis court below and a lake beyond
  ¶**Webbery Garden Cottage** (Mr & Mrs J Wilson) Long tree-lined drive. Herbaceous borders, specimen shrubs, roses. Special feature is old walled garden housing traditional vegetables, fruit and flowers; with small vineyard. TEA

Weetwood ♿ (Mr & Mrs J V R Birchall) Offwell, 2m from Honiton. Turn S off A35 (signed Offwell), at E end of Offwell. 1-acre all seasons garden; rhododendrons, azaleas, shrubs, ornamental pools, rock gardens, collection of dwarf conifers. Teashops Honiton. *Adm 50p Chd 10p (Share to SSAF®). Private visits usually welcome spring, summer & autumn, please* **Tel 01404 831363**

¶**Wembury House** ♿⚘ (Mr & Mrs N Hanbury) Wembury. 3m SE of Plymouth. A379 Plymouth to Kingsbridge signed Wembury at Elburton roundabout. 2m sharp R at 30mph sign. Follow lane for 200yds, R over cattle grid by Pink Lodge. Set within high walls of former Tudor mansion, giving protection to a wide range of trees and shrubs. 3 large box-edged beds of iceberg roses in front of Victorian orangery and with herbaceous borders either side of the Gerogian house. Steps leading up to Tudor perimeter ramparts. TEAS. *Adm £1.50 Chd 50p (Share to St Luke's Hospice®). Sat July 5 (2-6)*

Westpark ⚘⚘ (Mr & Mrs D Court) Yealmpton, 7m E of Plymouth; on Kingsbridge Rd (A379) Xrds centre of village, turn S on Newton Ferrers rd; park end of Torr Lane. An old-fashioned rambling 2-acre garden in peaceful country setting. Year round colour and variety. Rose pergola, mulberry (1907), unusual species of shrubs, climbers and naturalized bulbs, woodland with cyclamen, ferns, rocky outcrop. Vegetable garden. TEAS. *Adm £1.50 Chd 30p (Share to St Bartholomew's Church®). Wed, Sun April 2, 6 (2-5). Private visits also welcome mid Feb to mid Oct, please* **Tel 01752 880236**

¶**Whitechapel Manor** & (Mrs Margaret Aris) 3m NE of South Molton. A361 Tiverton to Barnstaple. At South Molton roundabout, exit N signed Whitechapel for 1m, ¾m drive through woodland. Grade I listed Elizabethan manor countryside hotel, on edge of Exmoor in tranquil woodland and pasture setting. Terraced gardens, clipped yew enclosures. Herbaceous borders and walled orchard. Woodland walk. Cream TEAS. Lunches. *Adm £1.50 Chd 50p. Suns May 25, June 15, 29, July 20, Aug 3, 24 (2-6). Small coaches only, please* **Tel 01769 573377**

Whitmore ✿✿ (Mr & Mrs Cyril Morgan) Chittlehamholt. 12m SE Barnstaple, house marked on O.S. Landranger 180. From the village take rd S past Exeter Inn and High Bullen Hotel; Whitmore is ¼m further on L down long tree-lined drive. 3-acre garden with ponds, stream and herbaceous borders. An interesting collection of trees and shrubs. Further 3 acres of woodland garden mainly ferns with pleasant sylvan walks, amongst wood warblers and box breeding pied flycatchers and nuthatches. Red and roe deer often present. A secluded peaceful garden. TEAS. *Adm £2 Chd free. Thurs April 3, Sat July 12, Sun Aug 24 (2-5)*

Withleigh Farm ✿ (T Matheson) Withleigh village. 3m W of Tiverton on B3137, 10yds W of 'Withleigh' sign, entrance to drive at white gate. Peaceful undisturbed rural setting with valley garden, 15 years in making; stream, pond and waterside plantings; bluebell wood walk under canopy of mature oak and beech; wild flower meadow, primroses and daffodils in spring, wild orchids. TEA. *Adm £1.50 Chd 50p (Share to Cancer & Arthritis Research®). Sat, Sun May 24, 25 (2-5). Private visits also welcome, please* **Tel 01884 253853**

Wolford Lodge & (The Very Rev. the Dean of Windsor and Mrs Patrick Mitchell) Dunkeswell. Take Honiton to Dunkeswell rd. L at Limer's Cross. Drive ½m on L at white entrance gate and lodge. 4 acres semi-woodland with massed rhododendrons, azaleas and camellias. Distant views to S over unspoilt Devon countryside. Woodland walks. *Adm £1 OAP/Chd 50p. Sat May 24 (2-6)*

Wood Barton &✿✿ (Mr & Mrs Richard Horton) Kentisbeare. 3m from M5 exit 28. A373 Cullompton to Honiton rd. 2m turn L signed Goodiford for 1m and turn L again at White Cottages. Farm drive, 100yds R. Bull on sign. [Landranger 192. Lat 09 Long 05/06.] 2 acres woodland garden planted 45yrs with species trees on S facing slope. Magnolias, azaleas, camellias, rhododendrons, acers; several ponds and water feature. Autumn colour. TEAS. *Adm £1 Chd 50p (Share to Action Research®). Sat, Sun May 17, 18 (2-6). Also private visits by appt* **Tel 01884 266285**

Woodside ✿ (Mr & Mrs Mervyn Feesey) Higher Raleigh Rd, Barnstaple. On outskirts of Barnstaple, A39 to Hospital and Lynton, turn R 300yds above fire station. Semi-woodland, 2 acres S sloping in suburban area with intensive planting incl many ornamental grasses, sedges, bamboos and monocots (Author of RHS Handbook on Ornamental Grasses). Parts of garden are shaded and peaceful, offering protection to unusual and tender shrubs. Special interest in New Zealand flora. Raised beds and troughs, variegated, acid loving shrubs, ornamental trees and conifers, all with emphasis on form and colour of foliage. *Adm £1.50 Chd 50p. Suns May 18, June 22 (2-5.30)*

Woodside ✿ (Mr & Mrs E J Braund) Whimple. Just off A30 rd between Honiton and Exeter. Turn N opp the B3180 turning for Exmouth. 1st L, house 1st on L, signposted Exeter 9m. Honiton 7m. ¾-acre garden 500' above sea level. Large variety of herbaceous plants, shrubs and roses. Colourful throughout the summer. TEA incl in adm. *Adm £1.50 Chd free. Suns July 20, Aug 17 (2-5.30). Private visits welcome by appt June to end Sept, please* **Tel 01404 822340**

●**Wylmington Hayes** ✿✿ (Mr and Mrs P Saunders) Wilmington. 5½m NE of Honiton on A30, turn R. Signposted Stockland 3m, Axminster 10m, after 3½m entrance gates on R (before Stockland TV Station) or from A35 3½m W of Axminster turn N nr Shute Garage on to Stockland Road for 3m, entrance on L nr TV mast. 83 acres of reclaimed gardens created 1911 and woodlands with spectacular hybrid rhododendrons, azaleas, magnolias, camellias, acers. Lakes, ponds, topiary, arboretum, woodland walks with wildlife. Collection of ornamental and domestic waterfowl including black swans. Scottish Country Dancing June 1, 15. Honiton Royal British Legion Band June 8; Accordian Music June 22, 29. TEAS. *Adm £3 Chd £1. Suns, Bank Hol Mons May 4, 5, 11, 18, 25, 26, June 1, 8, 15, 22, 29; (2-5). Coaches & parties by appt please* **Tel 01404 831751**

Yonder Hill &✿✿ (Mrs M H Herbert) Colaton Raleigh. A3052 at Newton Poppleford. B3178 towards Budleigh Salterton 1m 1st L signposted to Dotton then immed R into small lane. ¼m 1st house on R. Car parking. Part of a 4-acre smallholding set in peaceful countryside with panoramic views. Approx 2 acres with some 2000 different varieties for all-yr interest. Variety of animals and birds. Access to all parts for wheelchairs. Toilet facilities. Wheelchair available. DIY TEA. *Adm £1 Chd 50p. Suns Feb 23, March 16, 30, Apr 13, 27, May 4; 18, June 8, 22, July 6, 20, Aug 3, 24, Sept 7, 21, Oct 5, 19. Bank Hol Good Friday March 28, Mons March 31, May 5, 26, Aug 25. 1998 Sun Feb 22 (11-5). Visitors welcome on other days. Please,* **Tel 01395 567541**

Dorset

Hon County Organiser:	Mrs Hugh Lindsay, The Old Rectory, Litton Cheney, Dorchester DT2 9AH
	Tel 01308 482383
Assistant Hon County Organisers:	Mrs Raymond Boileau, Rampisham Manor, Dorchester DT2 0PT
	Tel 01935 83612
	Stanley Cherry Esq., Highbury, Woodside Rd, West Moors, Ferndown BH22 0LY
	Tel 01202 874372
	Miss Jane Bennett, The Maples, Fontmell Magna, Shaftesbury, Dorset SP7 0PF
	Tel 01747 811766
	Mr & Mrs W E Ninniss, 52 Rossmore Road, Parkstone, Poole BH12 3NL
	Tel 01202 740913
Hon Publicist:	Mrs S Henwood, The Old Rectory, West Compton, Dorchester DT2 0EY
	Tel 01300 320007
Hon County Treasurer:	Michael Gallagher Esq, 6 West Street, Chickerell, Weymouth DT3 4DY

DATES OF OPENING

March 16 Sunday
Fernhill Cottage, Witchampton ‡
Welcome Thatch, Witchampton ‡
March 23 Sunday
Langebride House, Long Bredy
Mews Cottage, Portland ‡
Witchcroft, Southwell,
    Portland ‡
March 30 Sunday
Ashley Park Farm, Damerham
Chiffchaffs, Bourton ‡
Horn Park, Beaminster
The Old Rectory, Litton Cheney
Snape Cottage, Bourton ‡
March 31 Monday
Edmondsham House, Cranborne
April 2 Wednesday
Edmondsham House, Cranborne
April 6 Sunday
Langebride House, Long Bredy
Netherbury Court, Bridport
Stour House, Blandford
April 9 Wednesday
Cranborne Manor Garden ‡
Edmondsham House, Cranborne ‡
1 Manor Close, Stratton ‡‡
Manor Orchard, Stratton ‡‡
April 12 Saturday
Glebe Cottage, Woodsford
April 13 Sunday
Bexington, Lytchett Matravers
Boveridge Farm, Cranborne
Cartref, Stalbridge
Domineys Yard, Buckland Newton
Fernhill Cottage, Witchampton ‡
Fernhill House, Witchampton ‡
1 Manor Close, Stratton ‡‡
Manor Orchard, Stratton ‡‡
Welcome Thatch, Witchampton ‡
April 16 Wednesday
Edmondsham House, Cranborne
April 19 Saturday
Knitson Old Farmhouse, nr
    Swanage

April 23 Wednesday
Edmondsham House, Cranborne
April 27 Sunday
Corfe Barn, Broadstone
Friars Way, Upwey
24a Western Avenue, Poole
April 30 Wednesday
Edmondsham House, Cranborne
Rampisham Manor, Rampisham
May 3 Saturday
Ashley Park Farm, Damerham
Lamorna, Chedington
May 4 Sunday
Chiffchaffs, Bourton
Frankham Farm, Ryme Intrinseca
Lamorna, Chedington
46 Roslin Road South,
    Bournemouth
May 7 Wednesday
Rampisham Manor, Rampisham
May 10 Saturday
Lamorna, Chedington
May 11 Sunday
Bexington, Lytchett Matravers
Bridge House, Portesham
2 Curlew Road, Bournemouth
Eurocentre Language School,
    Bournemouth
Fernhill Cottage, Witchampton ‡
Glebe House, East Lulworth
Honeybrook, Osmington
Lamorna, Chedington
The Manor House, Hinton-St-Mary
North Leigh House, nr Wimborne
Welcome Thatch, Witchampton ‡
May 14 Wednesday
Chedington Court, Chedington ‡
Lamorna, Chedington ‡
Little Platt, Plush
May 15 Thursday
Friars Way, Upwey
Melbury House, nr Yeovil
May 17 Saturday
Studland Bay House, nr Swanage
May 18 Sunday
Boveridge Farm, Cranborne

Cartref, Stalbridge
Friars Way, Upwey
Moigne Combe, nr Dorchester
52 Rossmore Road, Parkstone
Smedmore, Kimmeridge
Star Cottage, Wimborne
Studland Bay House, nr Swanage
May 21 Wednesday
Honeybrook, Osmington
Little Platt, Plush
Wincombe Park, nr Shaftesbury
May 24 Saturday
Ashley Park Farm, Damerham
Knitson Old Farmhouse, nr
    Swanage
May 25 Sunday
Corfe Barn, Broadstone
Deans Court, Wimborne Minster
Edgeways, Poole
The Friary, Hilfield
Glebe House, East Lulworth
Highwood Garden, Wareham
Lower Ware, Lyme Regis
Mews Cottage, Portland
Moigne Combe, nr Dorchester
Thornhill Park, Stalbridge
May 26 Monday
Horn Park, Beaminster
Midsummer's Cottage, Bridport
May 27 Tuesday
The Friary, Hilfield
May 28 Wednesday
The Friary, Hilfield
May 29 Thursday
Melbury House, nr Yeovil
May 31 Saturday
Lamorna, Chedington
46 Roslin Road South,
    Bournemouth
June 1 Sunday
7 Church Street, Upwey ‡
2 Greenwood Avenue, Ferndown
Highwood Garden, Wareham
Kingston Lacy, nr Wimborne
    Minster
Lamorna, Chedington

46 Roslin Road South,
Bournemouth
52 Rossmore Road, Parkstone
Slape Manor, Netherbury
Snape Cottage, Bourton
Throop Mill Cottage, Throop
West Manor, Upwey ‡
Wimborne Minster Model Town &
Gardens
June 3 Tuesday
7 Church Street, Upwey
June 7 Saturday
Lamorna, Chedington
June 8 Sunday
Ashley Park Farm, Damerham ‡
Boveridge Farm, Cranborne ‡
Friars Way, Upwey
Honeybrook, Osmington
Lamorna, Chedington
Litton Cheney Gardens
The Manor Farmhouse, Little
Windsor
The Old Rectory, Fifehead
Magdalen
Portesham House, Portesham
June 11 Wednesday
The Orchard, Blynfield Gate, nr
Shaftesbury
June 12 Thursday
Friars Way, Upwey
Melbury House, nr Yeovil
June 13 Friday
Red House Museum & Gardens,
Christchurch
June 14 Saturday
Bowhay, Iwerne Minster
Cranborne Manor Garden
June 15 Sunday
Bexington, Lytchett Matravers
Bridport Gardens
Edgeways, Poole
Frankham Farm, Ryme Intrinseca
2 Greenwood Avenue, Ferndown
Mews Cottage, Portland ‡
The Priest's House Museum &
Garden, Wimborne
Sturminster Newton Gardens
Witchcroft, Southwell, Portland ‡
June 18 Wednesday
Chilcombe House, nr Bridport
The Orchard, Blynfield Gate, nr
Shaftesbury
June 19 Thursday
Friars Way, Upwey
June 21 Saturday
Knitson Old Farmhouse, nr
Swanage
June 22 Sunday
Coombe Cottage, Shillingstone
Farriers, Puddletown ‡
Fernhill Cottage, Witchampton ‡‡
Fernhill House, Witchampton ‡‡
4 Flower Cottage, Lower
Waterston ‡

Hambledon Cottage, Child Okeford
Holworth Farmhouse, Holworth
Knitson Old Farmhouse, nr
Swanage
The Manor Farmhouse, Little
Windsor
The Manor House, Hinton St Mary
Portesham House, Portesham
Star Cottage, Wimborne
Sticky Wicket, Buckland Newton
Welcome Thatch,
Witchampton ‡‡
June 24 Tuesday
The Scented Garden, Littlebredy
June 26 Thursday
Melbury House, nr Yeovil
June 29 Sunday
7 Church Street, Upwey ‡
Coombe Cottage, Shillingstone
Corfe Barn, Broadstone
Domineys Yard, Buckland Newton
Edgeways, Poole
Honeybrook, Osmington
Loscombe Gardens
The Old Vicarage, Stinsford
Steeple Manor, nr Wareham
West Manor, Upwey ‡
Weston House, Buckhorn Weston
July 1 Tuesday
7 Church Street, Upwey
The Scented Garden, Littlebredy
July 2 Wednesday
Chilcombe House, nr Bridport
1 Manor Close, Stratton ‡
Manor Orchard, Stratton ‡
July 5 Saturday
Lamorna, Chedington
July 6 Sunday
Chiffchaffs, Bourton ‡
Lamorna, Chedington
1 Manor Close, Stratton ‡‡
Manor Orchard, Stratton ‡‡
Snape Cottage, Bourton ‡
Star Cottage, Wimborne ‡‡‡
Wimborne Minster Model Town &
Gardens ‡‡‡
July 8 Tuesday
The Scented Garden, Littlebredy
July 9 Wednesday
Honeybrook, Osmington
The Orchard, Blynfield Gate, nr
Shaftesbury
July 10 Thursday
Kingston Maurward, Dorchester
Melbury House, nr Yeovil
July 12 Saturday
Bridport Gardens
Lamorna, Chedington
July 13 Sunday
Bexington, Lytchett Matravers
2 Curlew Road, Bournemouth
Edgeways, Poole
Higher Melcombe, Melcombe
Bingham

Holworth Farmhouse, Holworth
Lamorna, Chedington
The Old Mill, Spetisbury
Stour House, Blandford
2 Winters Lane, Portesham
July 15 Tuesday
The Scented Garden, Littlebredy
July 16 Wednesday
Chedington Court, Chedington ‡
Lamorna, Chedington ‡
July 19 Saturday
Knitson Old Farmhouse, nr
Swanage
46 Roslin Road South,
Bournemouth
Tara, West Moors
Whitefriars, Dorchester
July 20 Sunday
Fernhill Cottage, Witchampton
2 Greenwood Avenue,
Ferndown ‡
Mews Cottage, Portland ‡‡
46 Roslin Road South,
Bournemouth
Tara, West Moors ‡
Thornhill Park, Stalbridge
Weston House, Buckhorn
Weston
Whitefriars, Dorchester
Witchcroft, Southwell,
Portland ‡‡
July 22 Tuesday
The Scented Garden, Littlebredy
Whitefriars, Dorchester
July 23 Wednesday
The Orchard, Blynfield Gate, nr
Shaftesbury
July 26 Saturday
Tara, West Moors
July 27 Sunday
7 Church Street, Upwey
Edgeways, Poole
Farriers, Puddletown
Hilltop Cottage, Woodville
North Leigh House, nr Wimborne
Tara, West Moors
24a Western Avenue, Poole
July 29 Tuesday
7 Church Street, Upwey
The Scented Garden, Littlebredy
July 30 Wednesday
Hilltop Cottage, Woodville
July 31 Thursday
Melbury House, nr Yeovil
August 2 Saturday
Lamorna, Chedington
August 3 Sunday
Chiffchaffs, Bourton
Frith House, Stalbridge
7 Highfield Close, Corfe Mullen
Hilltop Cottage, Woodville
Lamorna, Chedington
August 6 Wednesday
Hilltop Cottage, Woodville

August 9 Saturday
Lamorna, Chedington

August 10 Sunday
Bexington, Lytchett Matravers
Domineys Yard, Buckland Newton
Lamorna, Chedington
Stour House, Blandford

August 17 Sunday
Mews Cottage, Portland
Thornhill Park, Stalbridge
2 Winters Lane, Portesham

August 24 Sunday
7 Church Street, Upwey
Sticky Wicket, Buckland Newton

August 25 Monday
7 Church Street, Upwey

August 31 Sunday
The Old Farmhouse, Organford

September 3 Wednesday
Chedington Court, Chedington

September 6 Saturday
Bowhay, Iwerne Minster

September 7 Sunday
Aller Green, Ansty ‡
Eurocentre Language School, Bournemouth
Friars Way, Upwey
Ivy Cottage, Ansty ‡
Wimborne Minster Model Town & Gardens

September 11 Thursday
Friars Way, Upwey

September 14 Sunday
Bexington, Lytchett Matravers

September 17 Wednesday
The Orchard, Blynfield Gate, nr Shaftesbury

September 21 Sunday
Cartref, Stalbridge

September 28 Sunday
Fernhill Cottage, Witchampton ‡
Snape Cottage, Bourton
Welcome Thatch, Witchampton ‡

October 1 Wednesday
Edmondsham House, Cranborne

October 5 Sunday
Deans Court, Wimborne Minster
Mews Cottage, Portland

October 8 Wednesday
Edmondsham House, Cranborne

October 12 Sunday
The Old Rectory, Litton Cheney

October 15 Wednesday
Edmondsham House, Cranborne

October 22 Wednesday
Edmondsham House, Cranborne

October 29 Wednesday
Edmondsham House, Cranborne

Regular openings
For details see garden description

Abbotsbury Gardens, nr Weymouth
Athelhampton House & Gardens
Aurelia Gardens, West Moors
Chiffchaffs, Bourton
Compton Acres Gardens, Poole
Cranborne Manor Gardens
Deans Court, Wimborne Minster
Forde Abbey, nr Chard
Horn Park, Beaminster
Ivy Cottage, Anstey
Kingston Maurward, Dorchester
Knoll Gardens, Hampreston
Minterne, nr Cerne Abbas
The Old Mill, Spetisbury
Parnham, Beaminster
Snape Cottage, Bourton
Stapehill Abbey, Wimborne
Star Cottage, Wimborne
Sticky Wicket, Buckland Newton
Thornhill Park, Stalbridge

By appointment only
For telephone numbers and other details see garden descriptions. Private visits welcomed

Highbury, West Moors
Moulin Huet, West Moors
The Old Rectory, Seaborough
Wall Farm, Broadwindsor

DESCRIPTIONS OF GARDENS

● **Abbotsbury Gardens** ♿❀ (Ilchester Estates) 9m NW of Weymouth. 9m SW of Dorchester. From B3157 Weymouth-Bridport, turn off 200yds W of Abbotsbury village, at foot of hill. 20 acres; uniquely mild Mediterranean-type climate, started in 1760 and considerably extended in C19; much replanting during past few years; very fine collection of rhododendrons, camellias, azaleas; wide variety of unusual and tender trees and shrubs. Peacocks. Children's play area, woodland trail, aviaries and plant centre. Partly suitable for wheelchairs. TEAS. *Adm £4.20 OAPs £3.50 Chd £1.30, Family £9 Reduced rate in winter (For party rate* **Tel 01305 871387***). Easter to Oct 31 (10-6), Nov to Feb (10-dusk)*

Aller Green ✠ (A J Thomas Esq) Aller Lane, Ansty, 12m N of Dorchester. From Puddletown take A354 to Blandford; After public house, take 1st L down Long Lane signed Dewlish and Cheselbourne; through Cheselbourne to Ansty then 1st R before Fox Inn down Aller Lane. 1-acre typical Dorset cottage garden; unusual trees, shrubs and perennials in old orchard setting and many perennials grown for Autumn Colour. Teas at **Ivy Cottage**. *Combined adm with* **Ivy Cottage** *£2.50 Chd 50p (Share to the Red Cross®). Sun Sept 7 (2-5.30)*

■ **Ashley Park Farm** ♿❀ (David Dampney Esq) Damerham. Follow yellow signs off B3078, immediately W of village, 5m from Fordingbridge. Newly created gardens of 5 acres with farm and woodland walks. Many interesting trees, an arboretum in the making although now mature enough for visiting; eucalyptus grove; wild flower meadow. Many exciting plants for south facing walls, borders. TEAS, also every Sun. *Adm £1.50 Chd free (Share to Damerham Church®). For NGS Sats, Suns March 30; May 3, 24, June 8 (2-5.30). (See also* **Boveridge Farm***). Private visits welcome, please* **Tel 01725 518 200**

● **Athelhampton House & Gardens** ♿✠❀ (Patrick Cooke Esq) Dorchester. 5m E of Dorchester on A35. The Gardens date from 1891 and include collections of tulips, magnolias, roses, clematis and lilies in season. In the Great Court are 12 giant yew pyramids overlooked by 2 pavilions. This glorious Grade I garden is full of vistas and surprises and gains much from the fountains and River Piddle flowing through. The C15 Manor house is also open. New expanded conservatory restaurant serving lunches, cream teas and refreshments. *Adm House & Gardens £4.50, OAPs £4.20, Chd £1.50. Gardens only adults & OAPs £2.80 Chd free. Reduced rates for groups. Open March 23 to Oct 26 (11-5) except Saturdays,* **Tel 01305 848363**

Aurelia Gardens ♿✠❀ (Mr & Mrs Robert Knight) Newman's Lane, West Moors. N of village off B3072 Bournemouth-Verwood rd. Emphasis on coloured foliage and plumage. Heathers, dwarf conifers, grasses and alpines. Five rare breeds of poultry: white crested blue polands, partridge wyandottes, dark brahmas, salmon faverolles and buff cochins. Large natural wildlife pond. Featured on TV. 5-acre level site, incl nursery. Free parking. *Adm £1. Not suitable for children. Daily all year except Mons, Tues. Open Bank Hols (10-5)*

Bexington க்&✿✿ (Mr & Mrs Robin Crumpler) Lytchett Matravers. In Lime Kiln Rd, opp old School at W end of village. Colourful garden of ½-acre maintained by owners, with mixed borders of many interesting and unusual plants, shrubs and trees. Bog garden of primulas and hostas etc. Four rockeries of alpines, with walkways over bog area connecting two lawns, making a garden of interest from spring bulbs to autumn colour. Cream TEAS & plant stall for Alzheimer's Disease Society & gardening charities. *Adm £1 Chd 20p. Suns April 13, May 11, June 15, July 13, Aug 10, Sept 14 (2- 6). Group visits welcome by appt, please* **Tel 01202 622068**

Boveridge Farm ✿ (Mr & Mrs Michael Yarrow) Cranborne. Leave Cranborne on Martin Rd, thence take 2nd R Boveridge Farm. A plantsman's garden of 2 acres on 3 levels, part chalk and part acid; with lawns around old farmhouse, formerly manor house of the Hooper family; in rural surroundings with fine views. Fountain, fern bank and many rare and interesting trees and shrubs. Specimen acer 'Brilliantissimum', prunus 'Shidare Yoshino', prunus 'Pendula Rubra', Paulownia tomentosa. Teas at **Ashley Park**, Damerham (next village 3m). *Adm £1 Chd free (Share to Cranborne Church®). Suns April 13, May 18, June 8 (2-5). (See also* **Ashley Park Farm***). Group visits welcome by appt, please* **Tel 01725 517241**

▲**Bowhay** க்✿✿ (Stephen Ford Esq) Iwerne Minster. Iwerne Minster is connected by two roads to Shaftesbury, 6m to the N; and to Blandford, 6m to the S. Either turn up from the lower A350 rd at the village war memorial, or down from the higher rd at the signed Xrds, to the house or garden sign. Parking bottom of lane below house. Interesting and exciting 1-acre garden on hill above village, re-designed and re-built in last 5 years. Roses, rockery; pergola, ponds; cascades, terraces and sitting areas with wonderful views. 'Peaceful'. Exhibition of paintings and TEAS in aid of church lighting. *Adm £2 Chd 50p. For NGS Sats June 14, Sept 6 (10-12, 3-6.30). Visits by appt, please* **Tel 01747 811289**

Bridge House ✿ (Mr & Mrs G G Northcote) 13 Fry's Close, Portesham. 7m W of Weymouth on coast rd, B3157 to Bridport. From Dorchester take A35 W, turn L in Winterbourne Abbas and follow signs to Portesham; parking in village. Designed in Japanese manner. A popular strolling water garden and knave-sansui garden with garden planning exhibition in studio. *Adm £1.50 Chd free. Sun May 11 (2-6). Private visits welcome, please* **Tel 01305 871685**

¶**Bridport Gardens** From A35 to town centre turn into South St at Clock Tower. Park in street or nearby car park. *Combined adm £1.50 Chd 50p. Sun June 15, Sat July 12 (11-4)*

¶**Mercers Cottage** ✿ (Sandra Ferrers) 111 South St. Small cottagey town garden 12' × 54' but giving illusion of space, with pool, many roses and climbing plants

¶**Midsummer's Cottage** (S New) Next door but one to Woodman Inn on L by red telephone box. Imaginative, 16' × 50', town garden planted with roses, herbaceous plants and climbers, with green formal area and water feature. Summerhouse designed by owner. An example of what can be achieved in a small area. *Adm 75p. Also open Mon May 26 (11-4)*

▲**Cartref** ✿✿ (Nesta Ann Smith) Station Rd, Stalbridge. From A30, S at Henstridge for 1m. Turn L opp Stalbridge PO, house 80yds on R. Free car park nearby. A plantsman's garden approx ¼-acre, cottage garden and unusual plants. Small woodland area with choice shade-loving plants. Small potager, organically grown. TEA. *Adm £1.50 Chd free. For NGS Suns April 13, May 18, Sept 21 (10-5). Private visits by appt please* **Tel 01963 363705**

Chedington Court (Mr & Mrs J P H Chapman) Chedington, Beaminster. 4½m SE of Crewkerne off the A356. Turn at Winyard's Gap Inn, or 4½m NE from Beaminster via A3066. Turn R past Admiral Hood Inn in Mosterton. 10 acres. Mature Victorian garden. Magnificent situation, extensive views. Interesting trees and shrubs. Herbaceous borders, water garden and grotto, giant yew topiary, wild flowers, spring bulbs, mixture of the well-tended and the wild. TEA. *Adm £2 Chd 50p. Weds May 14, July 16, Sept 3 (11-4.30)*

■ **Chiffchaffs** ✿✿ (Mr & Mrs K R Potts) Chaffeymoor. Leave A303 (Bourton by pass) at junction signposted Gillingham, Blandford and Bourton at W end of Bourton village. A garden for all seasons with many interesting plants, bulbs, shrubs, herbaceous border, shrub roses. Attractive walk to woodland garden with far-reaching views across the Blackmore Vale. Nursery open Tues-Sat and on garden open days. TEAS in aid of church April 20, May 4, 18, 25 June 15. *Adm £2 Chd 50p (Share to St Michael's Church, Penselwood®). Open March 30 to Sept 28, 1st and 3rd Sun each month, Bank Holiday weekends, Weds & Thurs. For NGS Suns March 30, May 4, July 6, Aug 3 plus 10% of all receipts (2-5.30). Private visits by appt please* **Tel 01747 840841**

■ **Chilcombe House** ✿ (John & Caryl Hubbard) Chilcombe. Take S turning off dual carriageway on A35 4m E of Bridport, 9m W of Dorchester. 2-acre hillside garden with beautiful setting and views; wild areas; courtyards and walled garden divided into smaller sections; mixed plantings, flowers, herbs, tender perennials and old roses. TEAS on NGS days. *Adm £2.50 Chd free. Weds June 11, 25. For NGS Weds June 18, July 2 (2-6.30)*

187 Christchurch Road, Ringwood See Hampshire

7 Church Street க்✿✿ (Ann & Gordon Powell) Upwey, nr Weymouth. ½m from bottom of Ridgeway Hill on A354 Dorchester-Weymouth rd turn R B3159 (Bridport rd) L turn at bottom of hill. Please park on rd except disabled. 3 acres incl beds laid out for colour theming of foliage and flowers, vegetable garden and established woodland. Teas at Wishing Well. *Adm £1.50 Chd free. Suns June 1, 29 July 27; Aug 24; Tues June 3, July 1, 29; Mon Aug 25 (2-6)*

● **Compton Acres Gardens** ὦ ℀❀ Canford Cliffs Road, Poole. Sign from Bournemouth and Poole. Wilts & Dorset Buses 147, 150, 151. Yellow Buses nos 11 & 12 stop at entrance. Gardens with Japanese and Italian influences, rock and water, heather dell, woodland walk and sub-tropical glen. Magnificent bronze and marble statuary. Large selection of plants and stoneware garden orna-ments. Refreshments available. Large free car/coach park. *Adm £4.50 OAPs £3.50 Chd £1. March 1 to Oct 31 daily. 10.30-6.30 last admission 5.45pm.* **Tel 01202 700778**

Coombe Cottage ❀ (Mike & Jennie Adams) Blandford Rd, Shillingstone. 5m NW of Blandford on A357 next to PO Stores on main rd. Parking advised in Gunn Lane. ⅓-acre plantsman's cottage garden, enclosed by walls and hedges, with a catholic mix of herbaceous and woody perennials, climbers, bulbs and self-seeding annuals (many unusual), in broad, mostly rectangular borders, some of them colour co-ordinated. Small formal veget-able plot. TEAS. *Adm £1 Chd free. Suns June 22, 29 (2-6)*

Corfe Barn ℀❀ (John & Kathleen McDavid) Corfe Lodge Rd, Broadstone. From main roundabout in Broadstone W along Clarendon Rd, ¾m N into Roman Rd, after 50yds W into Corfe Lodge Rd. ⅔ acre on three levels on site of C19 lavender farm. Informal country garden with much to interest both gardeners and flower arrangers. Parts of the original farm have been incorporated in the design. A particular feature of the garden is the use made of old walls. TEAS. *Adm 50p Chd 25p. Suns April 27, May 25, June 29 (2-5)*

■ **Cranborne Manor Garden** ὦ ℀❀ (The Viscount & Viscountess Cranborne) Cranborne. 10m N of Wimborne on B3078. Beautiful and historic garden laid out in C17 by John Tradescant and enlarged in C20, featuring several gardens surrounded by walls and yew hedges: white gar-den, herb and mount gardens, water and wild garden. Many interesting plants, with fine trees and avenues. *Adm £3 OAPs £2 Chd 50p (Share to Holton Lee Appeal®). Weds March to Sept incl (9-5). For NGS Wed April 9, Sat June 14 (9-5)*

2 Curlew Road ὦ ℀❀ (Mr & Mrs Gerald Alford) Strouden Park, Bournemouth. From Castle Lane West turn S into East Way, thence E into Curlew Rd. Small town garden 200′ × 30′ divided into rooms and linked by arches. Conifers, acers, rhododendrons, clematis; spring and summer bedding; three water features. Seen on Pebble Mill '94 and Grass Roots '95. The owners are seri-ously disabled and their garden is thus of especial inter-est to other disabled people. *Adm £1 Chd 30p. Suns May 11, July 13 (2-6). Private visits welcome of 2 or more please* **Tel 01202 512627**

■ **Deans Court** ὦ ℀❀ (Sir Michael & Lady Hanham) Wimborne. Just off B3073 in centre of Wimborne. 13 acres; partly wild garden; water, specimen trees, free roaming peacocks. House (open by written appt) origin-ally the Deanery to the Minster. Herb garden with about 200 species chemical free plants for sale. Walled veget-able garden with chemical free produce for sale as avail-able. Free car parking. Morning coffee/TEAS. *Adm £1.50*

Chd 70p. Easter Sun (2-6) Bank Hol Mons (10-6). Suns April 6, 27 May 4, 25 July 6, 27 Aug 3, 31 Sept 7, 28 Oct 5 (2-6) other days groups by appt. Sculpture in the Gar-den Exhibition, June 7 to 29 daily (10.30-6) Adm incl cata-logue £3, Chd, Student £1.50. For NGS Suns May 25, Oct 5 (2-6)

Domineys Yard ὦ ℀❀ (Mr & Mrs W Gueterbock) Buck-land Newton, 11m from Dorchester and Sherborne 2m E of A352 or take B3143 from Sturminster Newton. Take 'no through rd' between church and 'Gaggle of Geese'. Entrance 200 metres on L. Park and picnic in field with alder lined stream and recent tree planting, or in lane if wet. 2½-acre garden on chalk, clay and greensand sur-rounding C17 thatched cottage, developed since 1961 with many unusual plants, shrubs and trees. Heated pool for summer opening. TEAS. *Adm £1.50 Chd 50p (Share to Sherborne Great West Window Appeal®). Suns April 13, June 29, Aug 10 (2-5.30). Private visits welcome, please* **Tel 01300 345295**

Edgeways ὦ ℀❀ (Mr & Mrs Gerald Andrew) 4 Green-wood Ave, Poole. From Lilliput Rd nr Compton Acres turn N into Compton Ave, W into Fairway Rd, thence L into Greenwood Ave. Please do not park by roundabout or cul-de-sac. Delightful ⅓-acre garden designed informally on a gentle slope in a setting of mature trees. Extensive range of choice perennials grouped for colour and foliage effect to provide a succession of seasonal pictures. Mixed and herbaceous borders, lawn, grass paths, arbour and a pond reaching into a steep rock area contribute to a var-iety of interesting vistas. Several seats. 'Lots to admire and inspire.' Dorset Garden Guide. Shown on ITV's Grass Roots. TEA. *Adm £1 Acc chd free. Suns May 25, June 15, 29, July 13, 27 (11.30-5)*

Edmondsham House ὦ ℀❀ (Mrs Julia Smith) Edmond-sham, nr Cranborne, off B3081 between Cranborne and Verwood. Large garden; spring bulbs, trees, shrubs; walled garden with herbaceous border; vegetables and fruit; grass cockpit. Early church nearby. TEAS Weds only. *Adm £1 Chd 50p under 5 free (Share to PRAMA®). Mon March 31, Weds April 2, 9, 16, 23, 30; Oct 1, 8, 15, 22, 29 (2-5); also private visits and parties welcome, please* **Tel 01725 517207**

Eurocentre Language School ὦ ℀ (Eurocentres (UK)) 22-28 Dean Park Rd, Bournemouth. Off Wimborne Rd (A347) ¼m N of Richmond Hill roundabout. Series of 4 linked gardens, now being restored to reflect the original surroundings of the late Victorian houses. Mature spe-cimen trees and lawns; rhododendrons, small trees and flowering shrubs; spring and summer bedding, climbers, dahlia borders and small fernery. TEA. *Adm £1 Chd 50p (Share to Wessex Childrens Hospice Appeal®). Suns May 11, Sept 7 (2.30-5)*

The National Gardens Scheme is a charity which traces its origins back to 1927. Since then it has raised a total of over £14 million for charitable purposes.

Farriers &❀ (Mr & Mrs P S Eady) 16 The Moor, Puddletown. On the A354 Puddletown-Blandford rd opp the rd to Piddlehinton, close to the Blue Vinney public house, Dorchester 5m. ⅓-acre informal country garden with much to interest gardeners and flower arrangers, designed and maintained by owners; shrubs, herbaceous, dahlias, sweet peas, vegetable plot, greenhouse with collection streptocarpus, pond. Park in village. *Joint opening with* **Flower Cottage** *on June 22 only. Adm £1 each garden Chd free also July 27 (2-6). Private visits welcome, please* **Tel 01305 848634**

Fernhill Cottage ❀❀ (Miss Shirley Forwood) Witchampton. Next to Fernhill House, directions as below. Small thatched cottage garden, uncommon perennials and old-fashioned cottage plants. *Joint opening with* **Fernhill House.** *Combined adm £1.50, £1 each garden Chd free (Share to Witchampton Village Hall®). Suns April 13, June 22 (2-5). Also Adm 50p Chd free. Suns March 16, May 11, July 20, Sept 28 (2-5). Private visits welcome, please* **Tel 01258 840321** *evenings*

Fernhill House &❀❀ (Mrs Henry Hildyard) Witchampton. 3½m E of Wimborne B3078 L to Witchampton then L up Lower St. (Blandford rd) house on R 200yds. Spring bulbs and blossom, roses and herbaceous borders, woodland walk with water garden and shrubs. Teas in aid of Village Hall, June 22. *Joint opening with* **Fernhill Cottage.** *Combined adm £1.50 Chd free (Share to Joseph Weld Hospice Trust®). Suns April 13, June 22 (2-5). Parties by appt,* **01258 840105**

4 Flower Cottage &❀❀ (Audrey Penniston) Lower Waterston. From Puddletown on the B3142 take the rd between Blue Vinney public house and Old's Garage on way to Piddletrenthide. ⅓-acre cottage garden, with herbaceous borders, scree and vegetables. TEAS. *Joint opening with* **Farriers** *Adm £1 (each garden) Chd free (Share to Dewlish Parish Church®). Sun June 22 (2-6). Private visits welcome, please* **Tel 01305 848694**

● **Forde Abbey** &❀ (M Roper Esq) 4m SE of Chard. 7m W of Crewkerne; well signed off A30. 'Christies Garden of the Year 1993'. 30 acres; many fine shrubs and some magnificent specimen trees incl post-war arboretum; herbaceous borders, rock and kitchen gardens; in bog garden one of larger collections Asiatic primulas in SW. Refreshments 11-4.30 Easter to Oct 31. *Adm £3.50 OAPs £3.25 Chd under 15 and wheelchairs free. Open daily all year (10-4.30)*

Frankham Farm &❀ (Mr & Mrs R G Earle) Ryme Intrinseca. A37 Yeovil-Dorchester; 3m S of Yeovil turn E at Xrds with garage; drive ¼m on L. 2 acres started in 1960s; plantsman's garden with shrubs, trees, spring bulbs, clematis, roses, vegetables and fruit; extensive wall planting. Recently planted unusual hardwoods. TEAS in aid of Ryme Church. *Adm £1.50 Chd free. Suns May 4, June 15 (2-5.30)*

Friars Way ❀❀ (Les & Christina Scott) 190 Church Street, Upwey. Twixt Weymouth and Dorchester on B3159, Martinstown rd. C17 thatched cottage is opp church car park. ¾-acre plantsman's garden developed by owners since 1991. Idyllic situation, sloping, S facing partially terraced site. Newly created scented inner garden. Featured on TV. Small nursery of garden propagated plants. TEAS. *Adm £1.50 Chd 50p. Suns April 27, May 18, June 8, Sept 7; Thurs May 15, June 12, 19, Sept 11 (2.30-6). Private visits and parties welcome, please* **Tel 01305 813243**

The Friary (The Society of St Francis) Hilfield, Dorchester. A352 from Dorchester to Minterne Magna, take 1st L after village, up hill round sharp L bend, take 1st turning on R signed The Friary. From Yeovil turn off A37 signed Batcombe and take 3rd turning on L. A small woodland garden begun in 1950's then neglected. Reclamation began in 1984. The Secret Garden has a number of mature trees, rhododendrons, azaleas, magnolias, camellias and other choice shrubs with a stream on all sides crossed by bridges (stout shoes recommended). TEA. *Adm £1 Chd free. Sun, Tue, Wed, May 25, 27, 28 (2-5). The Friary is happy to receive visitors every day apart from Monday*

Frith House &❀ (Urban Stephenson Esq) Stalbridge. Between Milborne Port & Stalbridge, 1m S of A30. Turn W nr PO in Stalbridge. 4 acres; self-contained hamlet: lawns; 2 small lakes; woodland walks. Terrace in front of Edwardian house, mature cedars; flower borders, excellent kitchen garden. TEAS. *Adm £1.50 Chd free. Sun Aug 3 (2-6). Groups welcome by appt, please* **Tel 01963 250 232**

¶**Glebe Cottage** (Mr F K Fletcher) Woodsford, Dorchester. Take Wareham Rd W out of Dorchester. Follow signs to Crossways and L fork to Woodsford after passing under light controlled bridge. Entrance ¼m after Woodsford Castle on L and labelled Woodsford House. Drive forks to Glebe Cottage. Approach from E by taking sign to Woodsford at Moreton/Woodsford Cross Rd on B3390. Camellias, mostly in woodland setting. 1½-acre garden with rhododendrons and azaleas and many varieties of trees. TEAS. *Adm £1 Chd 50p. Sat April 12 (2-6)*

Glebe House &❀ (Mr & Mrs J G Thompson) East Lulworth. 4m S of Wool 6m W of Wareham. Take Coombe Keynes Rd to East Lulworth. Glebe House just to E of Weld Arms and War Memorial. Shrub garden with lawns; walks and terrace, 2 acres with interesting and varied planting. TEAS. *Adm £1.25 Chd free (Share to Wool & Bovington Cancer Relief®). Suns May 11, 25 (2-6)*

2 Greenwood Avenue ❀ (Mr & Mrs P D Stogden) Ferndown. Off Woodside Rd which is between Ringwood Rd (A348) and Wimborne Rd (C50 ex-A31), E of town centre. ⅓-acre designed and maintained by owners. An interesting and informal garden, with accent on herbaceous plants; many rare and unusual. Hostas, sempervivums and penstemons are a special interest of the owners. Soft fruits and vegetable garden. Arbour and pergola. Dogs must be kept on leads. TEAS. *Adm £1 Acc chd free. Suns June 1, 15; July 20 (11-5)*

Hambledon Cottage &❀ (Mr & Mrs D W Schwier) Child Okeford. 6m W of Blandford Forum take L turn at sign for Child Okeford. Drive through village and take the R fork after passing the church. This is Shaftesbury Rd. Hambledon Cottage is ¼m on L. It is white with a red brick wall surmounted by a white picket fence. The garden was started in Oct 89 and nearly 2 acres of docks and thistles have been transformed into a series of rooms. These rooms contain 700 old English roses and modern roses, sweet pea walks, fishponds, lawns, shrubs, perennials and annuals. The garden is bounded on three sides by an ancient nut hedge and uses Hambledon Hill as a natural backdrop. *Adm £1.50 Chd free. Sun June 22 (2-6)*

Highbury ♿❀❀ (Stanley Cherry Esq) West Moors, 8m N of Bournemouth. In Woodside Rd, off B3072 Bournemouth-Verwood rd; last rd at N end of West Moors village. Woodland garden of ½ acre in mature setting surrounding interesting Edwardian house (1909 listed). Unusual plants and shrubs with ground cover. Weather station. Seen on T.V. TEAS in orchard when fine. *House and garden, organised parties Adm £1 (incl TEA); Otherwise by appt. Garden only 75p (2-6). April to Sept* **Tel 01202 874372**

Higher Melcombe ❀ (Lt Col and Mrs J M Woodhouse) Melcombe Bingham. 11m NE of Dorchester. From Puddletown A354 to Blandford. After ½m follow signs to Cheselbourne then to Melcombe. At Xrds in Melcombe Bingham follow signpost 'Private rd to Higher Melcombe'. From Sturminster Newton signs to Hazelbury Bryan, Ansty, past Fox Inn to Melcombe Bingham Xrds. 1½-acre garden, many annuals. Fine views and setting outside Elizabethan house. Parking adjoining field. TEAS in chapel. *Adm £1. Sun July 13 (1.30-5). Parties by appt in July, please* **Tel 01258 880251**

7 Highfield Close ❀❀ (Mr & Mrs Malcolm Bright) Corfe Mullen. From Wareham Rd turn E in Hanham Rd, thence ahead into Highfield Close. Colourful ⅓-acre summer garden designed and made by owners over 15yrs. Bedding plants, fuchsias and pelargoniums interplanted with shrubs; fish pond and ornamental pool. Much to interest gardeners in a small area. TEAS. *Adm 50p Chd 25p. Sun Aug 3 (2-5)*

Hightown Farm, nr Ringwood See Hampshire

Highwood Garden ❀ (H W Drax Esq) Charborough Park, Wareham, 6m E of Bere Regis behind long wall. Enter park by any lodge on A31; follow signpost to Estate Office, then Highwood Garden. Large garden with rhododendrons and azaleas in woodland setting. TEAS. *Adm £2 Chd £1 (7-16 yrs) (Share to Red Post Parish©). Suns May 25, June 1 (2.30-6)*

Hilltop Cottage ❀❀ (Mr & Mrs Emerson) approx 5m N Sturminster Newton on B3092 turn R at Stour Provost Xrds, signed Woodville. After 1¼m a thatched cottage on the RH-side. Parking in lane outside. Well established cottage garden now being extended with a wealth of different and interesting perennials. Very colourful. An inspiration to those with smaller gardens. Incl a small nursery. TEAS. *Adm £1 Chd free. Suns, Weds July 27, 30, Aug 3, 6 (2-6)*

Holt End House, Ashford Hill See Hants

Holworth Farmhouse ❀❀ (Anthony & Philippa Bush) Holworth. 7m E of Dorchester, 1m S of A352. Follow

signs to Holworth up the hill, through the farmyard, past duck pond on R. After 300yds turn L to the farmhouse. 3 acres of garden surrounding C16 grade II farmhouse on side of hill with lovely views. Main planting from 1980; considerable use of hedges as protection from exposed windy conditions; partially walled garden terraced and replanted in 1990 with a wide variety of herbaceous plants, shrubs and old roses. Also small wood, orchard, vegetable garden and pond. TEAS in aid of Joseph Weld Hospice & 'Fight for Sight'. *Adm £2 Chd free. Suns June 22, July 13 (2-7)*

¶**Honeybrook** ❀❀ (Allan & Gill Howarth) Osmington. 4m E of Weymouth on A353. Parking only at The Sunray - large car park. Proceed down Chapel Lane into village st and turn R into Church Lane. Garden 500yds from public house. Stunning views of The White Horse and village from this informal ⅓-acre garden constructed and maintained since 1991 by present owners. Pond, spring flowers, herbs, roses and herbaceous. TEAS. *Adm £1 Chd free. Suns May 11, June 8, 29, Weds May 21, July 9 (2-6)*

■ **Horn Park** ♿❀ (Mr & Mrs John Kirkpatrick) Beaminster. On A3066 1½m N of Beaminster on L before tunnel. Ample parking, toilet. Large garden; magnificent view to sea; listed house built by pupil of Lutyens in 1910 (not open). Plantsman's garden worth visiting at all seasons; many rare plants and shrubs in terraced, herbaceous, rock and water gardens. Woodland garden and walks in bluebell woods. Wild flower meadow with 162 varieties incl orchids. TEAS. *Adm £2.50 Chd under 16 free. Open every Tues, Weds, Suns, also Bank Hol Mons April to Oct 31. For NGS Easter Sun March 30, Bank Hol Mon May 26 (2-6)* **Tel 01308 862212**

■ **Ivy Cottage** ❀❀ (Anne & Alan Stevens) Aller Lane, Ansty, 12m N of Dorchester. A354 from Puddletown to Blandford; After pub take 1st L down Long Lane signed Dewlish-Cheselbourne, through Cheselbourne to Ansty 6 miles from Puddletown, then 1st R before Fox Inn, down Aller Lane. 1½-acre excellent plantsman's garden specialising in unusual perennials, moisture-loving plants; specimen trees and shrubs; well laid out vegetable garden. Featured on Meridian TV 'Grass Roots' 1994 and Ch4 'Garden Party' 1996. TEAS Sun only. *Combined adm with* **Aller Green** *£2.50 Chd 50p. Also every Thurs April to Oct incl Adm £2 (Share to NGS®) (10-5). For NGS Sun Sept 7 (Share to Red Cross®) (2-5.30).* **Tel 01258 880053**

▲**Kingston Lacy** ♿❀❀ (The National Trust) 1½m W of Wimborne Minster on the Wimborne-Blandford rd B3082. The setting landscaped in the C18, to W J Bankes's Kingston Lacy House. Magnificent trees planted over 175 years by Royal and famous visitors; avenue of limes and cedars; 9 acres of lawn; Dutch garden; sunken garden laid out to 1906 plans. TEAS and lunches in aid of NT. *Adm House & Garden £5.50, Gardens £2.20, Chd half price. For NGS Sun June 1 (11.30-6)*

■ **Kingston Maurward Gardens** ♿❀❀ 1m E of Dorchester. Follow brown Tourist Information signs. Classical Georgian mansion set in 35 acres of gardens laid out in the C18 incl a 5-acre lake. Restoration programme is nearing completion in the Edwardian gardens which are divided by hedges and stone balustrading. Stone features and interesting plants, including the National Collection of salvias and penstemons. Demonstration garden and animal park. Restaurant. *Adm £3 Chd £1.50. Open Easter to Oct 31. For NGS Thurs July 10 (10-6). Private visits welcome, please* **Tel 01305 264738** *(Mike Hancock)*

Knitson Old Farmhouse ✗✿ (Rachel & Mark Helfer) Knitson. Signposted L off A351 Knitson, approx 1m W of Swanage 3m E of Corfe Castle. Ample parking in yard or in adjacent level field. Approx 1 acre of mature cottage garden. Herbaceous borders, rockeries, climbers, shrubs – many interesting cultivars. Large organic kitchen garden, orchard. Purbeck Woodcraft Exhibition. TEAS in aid of F.A.R.M. Africa. *Adm £1.50 Chd 50p. Sats April 19, May 24, June 21, July 19, Sun June 22 (2-5). Private visits and parties welcome, please* **Tel 01929 422836**

●**Knoll Gardens** &✗✿ (Neil Lucas, Esq) Hampreston. 2½m W of Ferndown, ETB brown signs from A31. Gardens on a 6-acre site. Wide collections of trees, shrubs and herbaceous plants, continually being expanded. Under new ownership since 1994. Water gardens with waterfalls, pools and streams; mixed borders and woodland setting. NCCPG collections of phygelius and ceanothus. Tea rooms and visitor centre, to which entry is free. Large car park. Many plants shown are available in adjacent nursery. TEAS. *Adm £3.25 OAP's £2.90 Students £2.40 Chd £1.70. Group rates on application. Daily, Easter to end Oct (10-5.30). Nov to Easter, Weds to Sats, reduced prices (10-4)*

Lamorna ✗✿ (Mr & Mrs R Hewitt) Chedington. 5m N of Beaminster. Off A356 Dorchester-Crewkerne rd at Winyards Gap Inn. Lamorna is next to village hall. Nearby is a National Trust woodland walk and the Wessex Division memorial. Approx 1-acre garden in conservation village with extensive views over Axe valley. Many shrubs and plants incl pond, bog garden, dry shade garden, pergola, banks and other features. TEAS. *Adm £1 Chd free. Sats, Suns May 3, 4; 10, 11, 31; June 1, 7, 8; July 5, 6, 12, 13; Aug 2, 3; 9, 10, Weds May 14, July 16 (11-6). Private visits welcome* **Tel 01935 891410**

Langebride House ✿ (Mrs John Greener) Long Bredy. ½-way between Bridport and Dorchester, S off A35, well signed. Substantial old rectory garden with many designs for easier management. 200-yr-old beech trees, pleached limes, yew hedges, extensive collections of spring bulbs, herbaceous plants, flowering trees and shrubs. TEA in aid of Joseph Weld House. *Adm £1.50 Chd free. Suns March 23, April 6 (2-5). Private visits welcome March to end July* **Tel 01308 482257**

Little Platt (Sir Robert Williams) Plush, 9m N of Dorchester by B3143 to Piddletrenthide, then 1½m NE by rd signed Plush & Mappowder, 1st house on L entering Plush. 1-acre garden created from a wilderness since 1969; interesting collection of ornamental trees and flowering shrubs, incl several daphnes, spiraeas and viburnums; spring bulbs, hellebores, numerous hardy geraniums and unusual perennials. *Adm £1.50 Chd 50p. Weds May 14, 21 (2-5). Private visits welcome March to Aug* **Tel 01300 348320**

Litton Cheney Gardens 1m S of A35, 10m Dorchester, 6m Bridport. Small village in the beautiful Bride Valley. TEAS in Church Hall in aid of the Church. *Combined adm £2.50 Chd 50p. Sun June 8 (12-6)*

Faith House & (Commander & Mrs Larry Herrick) Small unusual walled garden of ⅔ acre, surrounded by tall mature trees. Beds of shrubs interplanted with herbaceous plants and roses. Upper reaches of the Bride river flows through one corner

2 Litton Hill ✗✿ (Patricia & Malcolm Munro) New garden on difficult site; ⅕ acre; shallow soil overlying chalk. S facing with steep slopes. Showing some plants that flourish on chalk; plants of interest to dyers

The Old Rectory ✿ (Mr & Mrs Hugh Lindsay) Small walled garden, partly paved and with a prolific quince tree. A steep path leads to 4 acres of natural woodland with many springs, streams and 2 small lakes; mostly native plants, and many primulas. Wild flower lawn; (stout shoes recommended). TEAS in aid of Red Cross on 30 March. *Adm £1.50 Chd 20p. Also open Easter Sun March 30, Oct 12 (2-5.30). Private visits welcome April to June, please* **Tel 01308 482383**

¶**Steddings** (Brian & Jennie Prentice) 1-acre immaculate garden with lawns, specimen trees, shrubs, herbaceous borders. Fine fruit and vegetable garden

¶**Swallowfield** ✗ (Geoffrey & Mary Court) Small irregular shaped garden with long herbaceous border and interesting patio. Adjoining artist's studio open

Loscombe N of Bridport. S of Beaminster. Approx 1½m E of A3066. One way traffic (narrow lanes) as signed from B3163 via Mapperton and A3066 at Melplash (opp Half Moon Inn). Leave Loscombe via West Milton. You are requested not to approach from this direction. Cream TEAS at Pear Tree Farm. *Combined adm £2 Chd free. Sun June 29 (2-6)*

Flowery Bottom ✿ (Peter Mugliston) 2½ acres reclaimed field in a tranquil setting surrounded by hills. Garden with lake, native trees and meadow area left for wild flowers

Pear Tree Farm ✗ (Major & Mrs John Poe) ½ acre garden started in 1989 making best use of limited space with sub dividing into different areas. Wide and interesting variety of shrubs, herbaceous plants, shrub roses with wild flowers and bulbs in long grass area. Conservatory with exotic plants. New developments and plants added every year

Lower Ware ✗ (Mr & Mrs J Bones) Ware Lane, Lyme Regis. Outskirts of Lyme Regis, off A3052 Sidmouth Rd. From the town E 2nd L after Holmbush Carpark; from W, app Lyme Regis, R at Xrds signposted to 'Ware'. Narrow lane, considerate parking please. Attractive 1-acre hillside garden overlooking Lyme Bay, mainly planted since 1989. Individual small gardens on three levels; mixed planting. TEAS in aid of MRI Scanner and Critical Care Appeal. *Adm £1. Sun May 25 (2-5.30)*

1927–1997

This year the National Gardens Scheme is celebrating its 70th Anniversary. Please help us celebrate by visiting a garden in 1997.

Macpenny Woodland Garden & Nurseries, Bransgore See Hampshire

1 Manor Close ♿ (Mr & Mrs W A Butcher) Stratton. 3m NW of Dorchester off A37 to Yeovil, turn into village, gardens signed at Church. ⅕-acre plantsman's garden. Alpines at front. To the rear interesting shrubs, and herbaceous beds. *Combined adm with* **Manor Orchard** *£1.50 Chd free. Suns, Weds, April 9, 13; July 2, 6 (2-5.30)*

The Manor Farmhouse ✂❀ (Mr & Mrs E Hornsby) Little Windsor. 4m NW of Beaminstser; 1m from Broadwindsor. From A3066 turn off at Mosterton, signed Drimpton. 3 acres landscaped gardens; pond and water garden; unusual trees and shrubs. TEA. *Adm £1 Chd free. Suns June 8, 22 (2-6)*

The Manor House, Hinton St Mary ♿✂ (Mr & Mrs A Pitt-Rivers) 1m NW of Sturminster Newton on B3092. Next to Church in Hinton St Mary. 5-acre garden with views over Blackmore Vale. Spring bulbs, trees and shrubs, yew and box hedges, pleached lime walk, lots of roses. Major alterations made in 1992 and 1996. C15 tithe barn. TEA. *Adm £2 Chd 50p. Suns May 11, June 22 (2-6)*

Manor Orchard ♿❀ (Mr & Mrs G B David) Stratton. 3m NW of Dorchester off A37 to Yeovil, turn into village, gardens signed at Church. 1-acre garden planted for yr-round interest. Spring bulbs, herbaceous and shrub borders, lawns, pond, roses, vine. Kitchen garden with fruit tunnel and topiary. Cream TEAS (Suns only). DIY teas on Weds. *Combined adm with* **1 Manor Close** *£1.50 Chd free. Suns, Weds, April 9, 13; July 2, 6 (2-5.30)*

Melbury House ✂❀ 6m S of Yeovil. Signed on Dorchester-Yeovil rd. 13m N of Dorchester. Large garden; very fine arboretum; shrubs and lakeside walk; beautiful deer park. Garden only. TEAS. *Adm £2 OAPs/Chd £1 (Share to CRMF®). Thurs May 15, 29, June 12, 26; July 10, 31 (2-5). Private visits welcome for parties of 15 max, please* **Tel 01935 83699** (*Andrew Clark*)

Merebimur, Mockbegger, nr Ringwood See Hampshire

Mews Cottage ✂❀ (Mr & Mrs P J Pitman) 34 Easton Street, Portland. Situated in the 1st village on the top of the Island, 50yds past the Punchbowl Inn on the L. Park in the main st and follow signs. Small cottage style garden, with a pond and a good mix of herbaceous plants and unusual shrubs, incl crinodendron hookerianum and callestemon. In spring a good collection of hellebore and spring bulbs. In summer a national collection of Penstemon (150+ named varieties incl many alpine varieties). Autumn colour is achieved with a large collection of nerine bowdenii. TEAS in aid of St Georges Church. *Adm £1 Chd free. Suns March 23, May 25, June 15, July 20, Aug 17, Oct 5 (2-5)*

● **Minterne** (The Lord Digby) Minterne Magna. On A352 Dorchester-Sherborne rd. 2m N Cerne Abbas; woodland garden set in a valley landscaped in the C18 with small lakes, cascades and rare trees; many species and hybrid rhododendrons and magnolias tower over streams and water plants. *Adm £3 Acc chd and parking free. Open daily March 28 to Nov 10 (10-7)*

Moigne Combe (Maj-Gen H M G Bond) 6m E of Dorchester. 1½m N of Owermoigne turn off A352 Dorchester-Wareham rd. Medium-sized garden; wild garden and shrubbery; heathers, azaleas, rhododendrons etc; woodland paths and lake walk. Tea Wyevale Garden Centre, Owermoigne. *Adm £1 1st chd 25p thereafter 10p. Suns May 18, 25 (2-5.30)*

Moulin Huet ♿✂❀ (Harold Judd Esq) 15 Heatherdown Rd, West Moors. 7m N of Bournemouth. Leave A31 at West Moors Garage into Pinehurst Rd, take 1st R into Uplands Rd, then 3rd L into Heatherdown Rd. thence into cul-de-sac. ⅓-acre garden made by owner from virgin heathland after retirement. Considerable botanical interest; collections of 90 dwarf conifers and bonsai; many rare plants and shrubs; alpines, sink gardens, rockeries, wood sculpture. *Adm 75p Chd free. Private visits and parties welcome April to Sept, please* **Tel 01202 875760**

Netherbury Court ♿✂❀ (Mark Culme-Seymour Esq) Bridport. In Netherbury off A3066, 2m from Beaminster 4m from Bridport. Parking in village, garden starts at gates directly past church on R. Tranquil garden of approx 4 acres; thirties lay-out incl Italian garden with canal; courtyard garden; stone paths, yew hedges and many fine mature trees; camellias and rhododendrons; splendid hellebores. Woodland garden in process of restoration. TEAS in aid of village playground equipment. *Adm £2 OAP £1 Chd free. Sun April 6 (2-6)*

North Leigh House ❀ (Mr & Mrs Stanley Walker) Colehill, 1m NE of Wimborne. Leave B3073 (formerly A31) nr Sir Winston Churchill public house into North Leigh Lane, thence ¾m. 5 acres of informal parkland with fine trees, small lake, rhododendrons; ornamental shrubs; specimen magnolia grandiflora and Green Brunswick fig; colony of orchis morio and naturalised spring bulbs in lawns; Victorian features include balustraded terrace, fountain pool, walled garden and superb conservatory, all being restored and maintained by owners. Dogs on leads welcome. Suitable wheelchairs in parts. TEAS in Bothy Cottage. *Adm £1 Chd 20p (Share to Animal Aid®). Suns May 11, July 27 (2-6). House open only to parties by appt, please* **Tel 01202 882592**

Oakdene, Sandleheath See Hampshire

¶**The Old Farmhouse** ✂❀ (Mr & Mrs D J Palmer) Organford. From A35, 1m W of The Baker's Arms roundabout, take the rd S to Organford. ½-acre garden with typical Georgian fronted old Dorset farmhouse. Date of layout is unknown but has been retained with additional planting, incl the unconventional design of the rear walled garden. Planting incl robust old-fashioned perennials, herbs, shrubs, with a vegetable and fruit area. TEAS. *Adm £1 Chd free. Sun Aug 31 (2.30-5)*

1997 Special Events. For information on special National Gardens Scheme events in 1997 see Pages 18-19.

■ **The Old Mill** &※ (The Rev & Mrs J Hamilton-Brown) Spetisbury, Spetisbury Village opposite school on A350 3m SE of Blandford. 2 acres mainly water garden by R Stour; choice trees and plants, vegetable garden, parterre and "wigloo". TEAS on Sun in aid of Spetisbury Church. *Adm £2 Chd free. Every Wed June to Aug (2-5) (Share to NGS®). For NGS Sun July 13.* **Tel 01258 453939**

The Old Rectory, Fifehead Magdalen &※ (Mrs Patricia Lidsey) 5m S of Gillingham just S of the A30. Small garden with interesting shrubs and perennials; pond; grandchildren's garden; plant stall. TEAS in aid of St Mary Magdalen. *Adm £1 Chd free. Sun June 8 (2-6) also private visits welcome, please* **Tel 01258 820293**

The Old Rectory, Litton Cheney see Litton Cheney Gardens

Old Rectory, Seaborough (Mr & Mrs C W Wright) 3m S of Crewkerne. Take B3165, after derestriction sign 2nd L, ¾m 1st R, then after 2½m 2nd L in village. 2-acre garden constructed since 1967; splendid views; rare trees, conifers, magnolias, flowering shrubs, roses, Himalayan plants, bulbs throughout the year, ferns; over 1000 species and cultivars. *Adm £1 Chd free. Private visits welcome all year, please* **Tel 01308 868426**

The Old Vicarage, Stinsford ※※ (Mr & Mrs Antony Longland) Off roundabout at E end of Dorchester bypass A35. Follow signs for Stinsford Church 400yds. 1¼ acres incl an Italianate garden, herbaceous and mixed borders with unusual plants and shrubs, nearly 200 roses, lawns, terraces with exuberant pots, and fruit. Thomas Hardy, C Day Lewis and Cecil Hanbury, creator of gardens at La Mortola and Kingston Maurward, commemorated in church next door. TEAS. *Adm £1.50 Chd 50p. Sun June 29 (2-6). Private visits welcome for parties of 6 and more, please* **Tel 01305 265827**

The Orchard ※※ (Mr & Mrs K S Ferguson) Blynfield Gate. 2m W of Shaftesbury on the rd to Stour Row. From Shaftesbury take B3091 to St James's Church then onto the Stour Row rd. A 3-acre country garden, orchard and native meadow developed since 1981. Lawns and paths link formal, informal and wild areas. Colourful mixed borders and island beds with a wide variety of plants, several chosen for their intermingling qualities and lengthy flowering period. Hedgebanks of hardy geraniums, interesting trees and shrubs, small natural pond and plenty of seats. Home-made TEAS. *Adm £2 to incl descriptive guide Chd free (Share to Red Cross®). Weds June 11, 18; July 9, 23; Sept 17 (2-6)*

● **Parnham** & (Mr & Mrs John Makepeace) ½m S of Beaminster on A3066, 5m N of Bridport. 14 acres extensively reconstructed early this century; much variety of form and interest, topiary; terraces; gazebos; spring fed water rills; small lake; fine old trees; grand herbaceous borders featured in Discovering Gardens (1990/91). Old roses in formal front courtyard; riverside walk and woodland; many unusual plants. House (Grade 1 listed, dating from 1540) exhibitions of contemporary craftsmanship, also John Makepeace furniture workshops. Restaurant, coffee, lunches. TEAS. *Adm to whole site £4 Chd 10-15 £2 under 10 free. Weds, Suns, Bank Hols Easter to Oct 29 (10-5).* **Tel 01308 862204**

Portesham House &※※ (Mrs G J Romanes) Portesham. 7m W of Weymouth on coast rd, B3157 to Bridport. From Dorchester take A35 W, turn L in Winterborne Abbas and follow signs to Portesham; parking in village. Home of Admiral Sir Thomas Masterman Hardy, with 300-yr-old mulberry tree; over an acre of family garden with modern dry stone walling, old walls and recent plantings by stream. Tree paeonies, herbaceous paeonies, unusual trees and shrubs. Teas at Millmead Country Hotel. *Adm £1 Chd free. Suns June 8, 22 (2-5.30). For early flowering tree paeonies in May please,* **Tel 01305 871300**

Potters Cot, Hightown Hill, nr Ringwood. See Hampshire

▲**The Priest's House Museum and Garden** &※ (The Priest's House Museum Trust) 23 High St, Wimborne. Public car parks nearby. Old 'borough plot' garden of ½ acre, at rear of local museum, in historic town house. Extending to mill stream and containing many unusual plants, trees and exhibits. Tea-room daily. *Adm £2 Family £5 OAP/Students £1.60 Chd 80p. For NGS Sun June 15 (2-5).* **Tel 01202 882533**

Pumpkin Patch, Ringwood. See Hampshire

Rampisham Manor ※※ (Mr & Mrs Boileau) Dorchester. 9m S of Yeovil take A37 to Dorchester. 7m turn R signed Evershot follow signs to Rampisham. 11m NW Dorchester take A37 to Yeovil, 4m turn L A356 signed Crewkerne; at start of wireless masts R to Rampisham. 3-acre garden. Mixture of formal and flowing planting in rural setting, spring bulbs, English roses amongst shrubs, grasses bed, hedged walks, water and new woodland garden. TEAS. *Adm £1.50 Chd 50p. Weds April 30, May 7 (2-5). Private visits welcome, please* **Tel 01935 83612**

▲**Red House Museum and Gardens** &※ (The Hampshire Museum Service) Quay Road, Christchurch. Tranquil setting in heart of town's conservation area. Gardens of ½ acre developed from early 1950's to complement Museum; plants of historic interest; herb and south gardens with lawns, herbaceous, peony and old rose borders and woodland walk. Gardens used as gallery display area for sculpture exhibitions. Admission to Museum and Art Gallery included. TEAS. *Adm £1 OAP/Chd 60p (under 5 free) (Share to the Mayor of Christchurch's Appeal of the Year©). For NGS Fri June 13 (10-4)*

46 Roslin Road South ※※ (Dr & Mrs Malcolm Slade) Bournemouth. W of N end of Glenferness Ave in Talbot Woods area of Bournemouth. ⅓-acre walled town garden of yr-round interest with unusual plants in attractive settings. Features include rose pergola, 2 pools, gravel garden with many colourful and mature herbaceous and shrub plantings. Carefully tended fruit and vegetable garden. *Adm 80p Chd free. Sats, Suns May 4, 31, June 1, July 19, 20 (1.30-5). Also private visits welcome from May to July, please* **Tel 01202 510243**

52 Rossmore Road ※※ (Mr & Mrs W E Ninniss) Parkstone, Poole. From A348 Poole-Ringwood rd turn SE into Rossmore Rd, ¼m. ⅓-acre country garden in a town, designed in rooms; containing many rare plants; knot garden; scree garden; herb garden; oriental; mixed and herbaceous borders; small pools; greenhouses. TEAS. *Adm £1 Chd free. Suns May 18, June 1 (2-6). Parties welcome, please* Tel 01202 740913

¶**The Scented Garden** ✿✿ (Chris & Judy Yates) Littlebredy. 10m equidistant Dorchester and Bridport. 1½m S off the A35. Park on Littlebredy village green by round bus shelter. 1-acre Victorian walled garden, in tranquil setting, being lovingly restored. Old roses and stately delphiniums form the backbone to the mixed, colour themed beds and borders, which contain many unusual plants. Display bed containing National Collection of lavender (over 60). *Adm £1 Chd 20p (Share to Littlebredy Church®). Tues June 24, July 1, 8, 15, 22, 29 (2.30-8). Private visits welcome, please* Tel 01308 482307

Slape Manor &✿ (Mr & Mrs Antony Hichens) Netherbury. 1m S of Beaminster turn W off A3066 to village of Netherbury. House ⅓m S of Netherbury on back road to Bridport. River valley garden – extensive lawns and lake. Azaleas, rhododendrons; specimen trees. TEAS partly in aid of Sherborne Window Appeal. *Adm £1.50 Chd 50p under 5 free. Sun June 1 (2-6)*

Smedmore &✿ (Dr Philip Mansel) Kimmeridge, 7m S of Wareham. Turn W off A351 (Wareham-Swanage) at sign to Kimmeridge. 2 acres of colourful herbaceous borders; display of hydrangeas; interesting plants and shrubs; walled flower gardens; herb courtyard. House also open for NGS. *Adm £2 Chd £1. Sun May 18 (2-5). Private visits welcome by appt, please* Tel 01929 480719 *(Mr T Gargett)*

■ **Snape Cottage** ✿✿ (Ian & Angela Whinfield) Chaffeymoor at W end of Bourton. Opp Chiffchaffs. ½-acre plantsman's country garden full of old-fashioned and uncommon perennials, most labelled. Organically managed and planted for yr-round interest with large collection of snowdrops, hellebores, pulmonarias, auriculas, geraniums, dianthus, iris, penstemon and asters. Special emphasis on plant history and nature conservation. Beautiful views, wildlife pond. *Adm £1.50 Chd free. Every Sun in May to July and Wed in April to Sept (closed Aug). For NGS Suns March 30, June 1, July 6, Sept 28 (2-5). Parties welcome by appt, please* Tel 01747 840330 *(evenings only)*

Spinners Boldre See Hampshire

● **Stapehill Abbey** &✿✿ Wimborne Rd West, Ferndown. 2½m W of Ferndown on the old A31, towards Wimborne, ½m E of Canford Bottom roundabout. Early C19 Abbey, its gardens and estate restored and renovated to lawns, herbaceous borders; rose and water gardens; Victorian cottage garden; lake and Victorian greenhouse. Mature trees. Busy working Craft Centre; Countryside Museum featuring the National Tractor Collection, all under cover. Refreshments available in former refectory throughout the day. Licensed coffee shop. Large free car/coach park. *Adm £4.50 OAPs £4 Chd £2.50. Open daily April to Oct (10-5); Nov to Easter (10-4); except Mons and Easter. Closed Christmas Eve to Feb 1.* Tel 01202 861686

■ **Star Cottage** ✿✿ (Lys de Bray) 8 Roman Way, Cowgrove, Wimborne. Leave B3082 at Wimborne Hospital, along Cowgrove Rd for approx 1½m to Roman Way on R. Created in 1992 from a field, the garden is rapidly becoming another 'living library' of botanical artist and author Lys de Bray, lately of Turnpike Cottage, Wimborne. An opportunity to meet Miss de Bray and see a specialised garden in the making. The owner is a RHS gold medallist whose botanical drawings and paintings are on permanent exhibition in her working studios which are open throughout the year at weekends and bank holidays. *Adm £1.50 Chd £1. Garden and Studio open Sats and Suns all year. Easter to end Oct (2-6). End Oct to end March (2-4). For NGS Suns May 18, June 22, July 6 (2-6). Private visits and parties welcome, please* Tel 01202 885130

Steeple Manor &✿✿ (Mr Julian & the Hon Mrs Cotterell) Steeple, 5m SW of Wareham in Isle of Purbeck. Take Swanage rd from Wareham, or bypass, R in Stoborough. A beautiful garden designed by Brenda Colvin 1920's round C16/17 Purbeck stone manor house (not open); lovely setting in folds of Purbeck hills in small hamlet of Steeple next to ancient church, specially decorated for the occasion. Approx 5 acres, the garden includes walls, hedges, enclosed gardens, ponds, stream, bog garden and meadow, collection old roses; many interesting and tender plants and shrubs for the plantsman. Parts garden suitable for wheelchairs. Free parking. Cream TEAS. *Adm £2.50 (to include written guide) Chd under 16 free. Sun June 29 (1.30-6)*

■ **Sticky Wicket** &✿✿ (Peter & Pam Lewis) Buckland Newton. 11m from Dorchester and Sherborne. 2m E of A352 or take B3143 from Sturminster Newton. T-junction midway Church, School and Gaggle of Geese public house. 1½-acre garden created since 1987, unusual designs, well documented, showing wild life interest; fragrant cottage garden planting with many perennials and herbs. TEAS. *Adm £2 Chd £1. Every Thurs June 5 to Sept 25 incl (10.30-8). For NGS Suns June 22, Aug 24 (2-6). Groups only by appt, please* Tel 01300 345476

Stour House &✿✿ (T S B Card Esq) East St, Blandford. On 1-way system, 100yds short of market place. 2½-acre town garden, half on a romantic island in R Stour reached by a remarkable bridge; bulbs; borders well planted with perennials and many rare shrubs; river views. TEAS (in aid of Blandford Parish Church, July). *Adm £1 Chd 20p. Suns April 6, July 13, Aug 10 (2-5)*

Studland Bay House &🌼 (Mrs Pauline Ferguson) Studland. On B3351 5m E of Corfe Castle. Through village, entrance on R after Studland Bay House. Ample parking (no coaches). From Bournemouth, take Sandbanks ferry, 2½m, garden on L after Knoll House Hotel. 6-acre spring garden overlooking Studland Bay. Planted in 1930's on heathland; magnificent rhododendrons, azalea walk, camellias, magnolias, ferns and stream; recent drainage and replanting, garden suitable for wheelchairs. Cream TEAS in aid of Joseph Weld Hospice. *Adm £2 Chd free. Sat, Sun May 17, 18 (2-5)*

Sturminster Newton Gardens &✗ Off A357 between Blandford and Sherborne take turn opp Nat West Bank. Park in car park or behind Stourcastle Lodge. Walk down Penny St for **Ham Gate** and Goughs Close for **Stourcastle Lodge**. TEAS at **Ham Gate**. *Combined adm £2 Chd free. Sun June 15 (2-6). Parties by appt, please* Tel **01258 472462** *or* **01258 472320**

   Ham Gate (Mr & Mrs H E M Barnes) Informal 2-acre garden with shrubs, trees, lawns running down to R Stour, pleasant woodland views across water meadows, over the last few years Pam Lewis of Sticky Wicket has helped redesign the garden

   Stourcastle Lodge (Jill & Ken Hookham-Bassett) S facing secluded cottage garden, with a wide selection of interesting herbs, perennials and shrubs, a dovecote and water features

Tara &🌼 (Mr & Mrs W H Adams) 66 Elmhurst Rd, West Moors. 7m N of Bournemouth. Leave A31 at Gulf Garage into Pinehurst Rd and take 4th R into Elmhurst Rd. Carefully tended garden 130′ × 40′ lawns with island beds. Bridge over bog garden with pebble pools, statuary features, ivy topiary and bonsai. Featured in Amateur Gardening and Garden News, the garden is also used in its advertising by an organic fertiliser manufacturer. Plants, Teas and other stalls in aid of animal charities. *Adm 50p Chd 20p. Sats, Suns July 19, 20; 26, 27 (10-4.30) Private visits welcome, please* Tel **01202 877686**

■ **Thornhill Park** ✗🌼 (Richard and Cary Goode) Stalbridge. 1m S of Stalbridge on A357. Gates opposite T junction. Go down drive for ¾m. 6-acre garden surrounding C18 house built by Sir James Thornhill. Garden currently being re-established and extended by Cary Goode, a professional Garden Designer. Incl formal area with small parterre, rose garden, nut walk, willow garden, 2 ponds, wild garden and beds planted in colour themes. TEAS. *Adm £2 Chd 50p. Fris (10-5) and Suns (2-5) May to Sept (Share to NGS®). For NGS (Share to Dorset Gardens Trust®) Suns May 25, July 20, Aug 17 (2-5)*

Throop Mill Cottage & (Dr & Mrs James Fisher) Throop. 4m N of Bournemouth Square. Ring Rd (Castle Lane B3060) to Broadway PH. Broadway Lane becomes Throop Rd in ¾m. Thatched cottage next to Throop Mill. 1-acre riverside garden with landscape features such as a ha-ha. Developing collection of ferns in a small valley. TEAS. *Adm £1 Chd 50p. Sun June 1 (2-5.30)*

¶**Wall Farm** (Cdr & Mrs P Corson) Broadwindsor. 1m from Broadwindsor on B3164 Axminster Rd. Turn L behind Tin Hut. Very narrow lane, beware tractors. Parking limited. 4-acre garden surrounding C17 thatched farmhouse in a hidden valley. Garden in the making, started 5 yrs ago and being continued by present owners. A mass of spring bulbs and bluebells. Herbaceous borders, small well-hedged garden. Stream and new bog garden and another pond in the making. A flower arranger's garden. Yr-round interest. *Adm £1.50 Chd free. Private visits welcome, please* Tel **01308 868203**

Welcome Thatch ✗🌼 (Mrs Diana Guy) Witchampton. 3½m E of Wimborne, B3078 L to Witchampton, thence through village past church & shop to last but one on R. Please avoid parking close village centre. Listed thatched cottage. Enthusiast's garden (⅔ acre) with unusual plants of interest from spring to autumn, ranging from the exotic and tender to hardy perennials and shrubs. Large collection of hardy geraniums. TEAS except June when in village hall. *Adm £1 Chd free. Suns March 16, April 13, May 11, June 22, Sept 28 (2-5.30). Private visits also welcome by appt, please* Tel **01258 840894**

West Manor &✗ (Mr & Mrs R Bollam) Church St, Upwey. ½m from bottom of Ridgeway Hill on A354 Dorchester-Weymouth rd. Turn R on B3159 (Bridport rd). At bottom of hill turn L, Church St. Limited parking for disabled only. ¾-acre low maintenance garden, worked on organic principles; lawns, borders, shrubs, woodland, large mulberry tree, small pond and vegetable garden. Teas at Wishing Well. *Adm £1.50 Chd free. Suns June 1, 29 (2-6)*

24a Western Avenue ✗ (Mr & Mrs Peter Jackson) Poole. Central in Branksome Park, ½m from Compton Acres. Award winning 1-acre part Mediterranean, part English garden close to sea. Formal areas incl lawns, cherry tree walk, rose garden, herbaceous beds, topiary and courtyard with tender wall plants. Tree ferns, drimys, bamboo and camellias flourish. Sunny banks are planted with eucalyptus, acacias, and a collection of callistemons, agaves, yuccas and other drought resistant plants. *Adm £1 Chd free. Suns April 27, July 27 (2-6)*

Weston House &🌼 (Mr & Mrs E A W Bullock) Buckhorn Weston. 4m W of Gillingham and 4m SE of Wincanton. From A30 turn N to Kington Magna, continue towards Buckhorn Weston and after railway bridge take L turn towards Wincanton. 2nd on L is Weston House. 1 acre plus fields; old and English roses; herbaceous and mixed borders backed by old walls with climbers. Small woodland and wild flower areas; wild-life pond; lawns and view of Blackmore Vale. TEAS in aid of Buckhorn Weston Parish Church. *Adm £1.50 Chd free. Suns June 29, July 20 (2-6)*

¶**Whitefriars** &✗ (John E Ward) Dorchester. ¾m from town centre on Wareham Rd. Turn L at Trumpet Major Inn roundabout, Friars Close on R. ⅓-acre, surrounded by beech hedge. Herbaceous border, supplemented with shrubs and annuals. Variety of tubs, beds and baskets giving very colourful show with use of annuals. TEA. *Adm 80p Chd 20p. Sat, Sun July 19, 20 (2-5), Tues evening July 22 (7-9)*

▲**Wimborne Minster Model Town & Gardens** &✗🌼 (The Wimborne Minster Model Town Trust). King St 200yds W of Minster, opp public car park. 1½-acre grounds with ¹⁄₁₀ scale models of the town in early fifties, surrounded by landscaped gardens. Herbaceous borders, alpines, herbs, heather and rose gardens, with many rare and unusual plants, with pools and fountain, making a colourful pleasure garden. Visitors' and exhibition centres. Many seats and views over Stour valley. Refreshments daily. *Adm £2.25 OAPs £1.75 Chd £1 (3-15) under 3 free. For NGS Suns June 1, July 6, Sept 7 (10-5).* **Tel 01202 881924**

Wincombe Park ❀ (The Hon M D Fortescue) 2m from Shaftesbury. Off A350 to Warminster signed to Wincombe and Donhead St Mary. Plantsman's garden surrounding house set in parkland; raised beds, shrubs, perennials; walled kitchen garden; view of valley with lake and woods. Unusual plants for sale. TEA. *Adm £1.50 Chd free. Wed May 21 (2-5.30), also private visits and groups by appt* **Tel 01747 852161**

2 Winters Lane ⚘❀ (Mr & Mrs K Draper) Portesham. 7m W of Weymouth on coast rd, B3157 to Bridport. From Dorchester take A35 W, turn L in Winterborne Abbas and follow signs to Portesham. Winters Lane is signposted in village to Coryates. ¹⁄₄-acre garden with ponds and water features. Many ideas for smaller gardens such as small herb garden; container garden. 50 varieties of clematis, wishing well and miniature village; most plants labelled. Featured in 'The Water Garden' May 95. Teas at Orchard House. *Adm 75p Chd free. Suns July 13, Aug 17 (2-6). Private visits and parties welcome June and July, please* **Tel 01305 871316**

Witchcroft ⚘❀ (Mr & Mrs Rowland & Pamela Reynolds) 1 Sweet Hill Rd, Southwell, Portland. Follow the signs for Portland Bill (A354). 'Witchcroft' is the bungalow 300yds on L, past Eight Kings public house in the village of Southwell. Small cottage garden with pond, shrubs, and herbaceous borders and open rural views. In spring there are bulbs and hellebores, in summer new and old-fashioned roses. Park in main st. TEAS in aid of Cancer and Leukaemia in Childhood Trust. *Adm £1 Chd free. Suns March 23, June 15, July 20 (2-5)*

County Durham

Hon County Organiser: Mrs Ian Bonas, Bedburn Hall, Hamsterley, Bishop Auckland DL13 3NN
Tel 01388 488231

DATES OF OPENING

May 4 Sunday
Barningham Park, nr Barnard Castle
Croft Hall, Darlington
May 18 Sunday
Wycliffe Gardens
May 25 Sunday
Westholme Hall, Winston
May 26 Monday
Birkheads Cottage Garden & Nursery
June 8 Sunday
Eggleston Hall Gardens nr Barnard Castle
June 15 Sunday
10 The Chesters, nr Consett

June 22 Sunday
The General's Wood, Harraton
June 29 Sunday
Low Walworth Hall, nr Darlington
July 6 Sunday
17 The Lyons, Hetton Le Hole
Merrybent Gardens
Westholme Hall, Winston
July 13 Sunday
Bedburn Hall, Hamsterley
July 20 Sunday
Ravensford Farm, Hamsterley
August 24 Sunday
Westholme Hall, Winston
August 25 Monday
Birkheads Cottage Garden & Nursery

Regular openings
For details see garden description

Raby Castle, Staindrop
University of Durham Botanic Garden, Durham

By appointment only
For telephone numbers and other details see garden descriptions. Private visits welcomed

173 Gilesgate, Durham

DESCRIPTIONS OF GARDENS

Barningham Park ❀ (Sir Anthony Milbank) 6m S of Barnard Castle. Turn S off A66 at Greta Bridge or A66 Motel via Newsham. Woodland walks, trees and rock garden. House (not open) built 1650. Home-made cream TEAS. *Adm £2.50 Chd 50p (under 14). Sun May 4 (2-5). Also by appt for parties, please* **Tel 01833 621202**

Bedburn Hall ⬥❀ (Ian Bonas Esq) Hamsterley, 9m NW of Bishop Auckland. From A68 at Witton-le-Wear, turn off W to Hamsterley; turn N out of Hamsterley-Bedburn and down 1m to valley. From Wolsingham on B6293 turn off SE for 3m. Medium-sized garden; terraced garden on S facing hillside with streams; lake; woodland; lawns; rhododendrons; herbaceous borders; roses. TEAS. *Adm £2 Chd 50p. Sun July 13 (2-6)*

▲**Birkheads Cottage Garden & Nursery** ⚘❀ (Christine Liddle) Nr Sunniside. From A1M N or S take A692 or A693 on to A6076 rd between Sunniside and Stanley. Birkheads Nursery is signposted 1m S of Tanfield Steam Railway. It is exactly 1m from signed junction to Nursery. Look out for the beehive! Over 4,000 different hardy plants in garden of 1½ acres incl pond, formal topiary garden, rockeries, gravel garden, herbaceous borders. Set in S facing open countryside. Beautiful views. Small specialist nursery featured on TV 3 yrs ago. *Adm £1.50 Chd 50p. For NGS Mons May 26, Aug 25 (10-5). Parties welcome, at other times by appt, please* **Tel 01207 232262**

10 The Chesters ♿❀ (Dianne Allison) Ebchester, Nr Consett. S end of village on A694, signposted, 2m from Consett. Small 'cottage-style' garden, with the National Collection of Polemoniums among a wide variety of plants. National Trust woodland walk nearby for dog walking etc. Lectures and group visits by appointment. TEAS. *Adm £1 Chd free/donation. Sun June 15 (2-5)*

Croft Hall ♿✲ (W D Chaytor) Darlington. Croft Village lies 3m S of Darlington on A167 to Northallerton and 6m from Scotch Corner. Croft Hall is 1st house on R as you enter the village from Scotch Corner. Square yellow Georgian. 3 acres incl lawn with avenue of red may, water garden with temple, shrubbery bank, herb and knot gardens, long herbaceous border sheltered by magnificent yew hedge. TEAS. *Adm £2 Chd 50p. Sun May 4 (2-6)*

Eggleston Hall Gardens ♿✲❀ (Sir William Gray) Eggleston, NW of Barnard Castle. Route B6278. Large garden with many unusual plants; large lawns, rhododendrons, greenhouses, mixed borders, fine trees, large extension of kitchen garden (all organically grown). Garden centre open. Homemade TEAS. *Adm £2 Chd free. Sun June 8 (2-5). Private visits welcome, please* **Tel 01833 650553**

17 The General's Wood ✲❀ (Bob & Doreen Wigham) Harraton. From A1M at Chester-Le-Street take rd signposted Picktree. In 1m turn R into Bonemill Lane; after lm turn R into The General's Wood. ⅓rd acre mature garden in woodland setting with large pond area. Refreshments. *Adm 50p Chd free. Sun June 22 (2-5)*

173 Gilesgate ♿✲ (Dr Anne Sullivan) Durham. Leave Durham Market Place to roundabout at top of Claypath. 3rd exit (marked Hild & Bede College) then immed 1st L. 173 is first house - phonebox outside. ½-acre garden of lawns, mixed herbaceous borders, with small formal herb garden, quiet 'cottage' garden, and small area of formal boxed beds, shade borders. *Adm £1. Private visits welcome, please* **Tel 0191 3866402**

Low Walworth Hall ♿❀ (Mr & Mrs Worrall) 3½m W of Darlington, on Staindrop Rd. B6279 (½m drive). Old walled garden; herbaceous borders, shrubs, roses; trout rearing pond. Small Japanese garden. Interesting and varied shrubs and greenhouse plants for sale. Homemade cream TEAS. *Adm £2 Chd 50p. Sun June 29 (2-5.30)*

¶17 The Lyons ✲❀ (Jim & Eileen Manwaring) Hetton Le Hole. From A1 to A690 towards Sunderland, turn R to Hetton Le Hole. At New Inn roundabout take B1285, ½m to Hetton Lyons Park. From A19 take B1285 through Murton, 1½m to Hetton Lyons Park. White cottage opp park entrance. Approx ½-acre S facing garden, with lawns, shrubbery, roses, vegetables and herbaceous borders with a wide variety of plants. Pond and greenhouses. TEAS. *Adm £1 Chd 50p (Share to St Nicholas Church®). Sun July 6 (2-6). Private visits welcome June to Sept, please* **Tel 0191 5263769**

Merrybent Gardens ♿ (David & Grace Hunter) 42 Merrybent. On A67 2½m W of Darlington within easy reach of town centre. Collection of hostas and ferns and large natural pond. An opportunity to explore a number of small and up to 1-acre private gardens of great variety close to R Tees. Home-made TEAS in aid of St Edwins Church, High Conscliffe. *Combined adm £1.50 Chd free. Sun July 6 (2-5.30)*

● **Raby Castle** ♿✲ (The Rt Hon The Lord Barnard) Staindrop, NW of Darlington. 1m N of Staindrop on A688 Barnard Castle-Bishop Auckland. Buses: 75, 77 Darlington-Barnard Castle; 8 Bishop Auckland-Barnard Castle; alight Staindrop, North Lodge, ¼m. Large walled garden; informal garden with ericas; old yew hedges; shrub and herbaceous borders; roses. Castle also open, principally C14 with alterations made 1765 and mid-C19; fine pictures and furniture. Collection of horse-drawn carriages and fire engines. Garden only suitable wheelchairs. Tearoom at Stables. Special terms for parties on application. *Adm Castle Gardens and carriages £4 OAPs £3 Chd £1.50. Family ticket £10 (2 adults, 2-3 Chd) Gardens & carriages only £1.50 OAPs/Chd £1. Open all Bank Holidays; Sat to Wed May, June; Wed, Sun July to Sept; Daily (except Sat) (Castle 1-5; garden and park 11-5.30, last adm 4.30); also by appt for parties* **Tel 01833 660202**

Ravensford Farm ✲❀ (Mr & Mrs J Peacock) 9m NW of Bishop Auckland. From A68 at Witton-le-Wear turn off W to Hamsterley. Go through village and turn L just before tennis courts. 2½-acre. Garden created since 1986 from a field containing a mass of nettles and thistles, and 1 ancient apple tree. There is now a small wood, 2 ponds, a sunken garden, a rhododendron walk and mixed borders containing flowering shrubs, roses and herbaceous perennials. TEAS. *Adm £1.50 Chd 50p. Sun July 20 (2-6)*

● **University of Durham Botanic Garden** ♿✲❀ 1m from centre of Durham. Turn off A167 (old A1) at Cock O'The North roundabout, direction Durham for 1m; turn R into Hollingside Lane which is between Grey and Collingwood Colleges; gardens 600yds on R. 18 acres on a beautiful SW facing hillside features 15-yr-old North American Arboretum planted 1980, woodland and ornamental bog garden, winter heather beds and tropical and desert display glasshouses. The Prince Bishop's garden contains 6 statues. TEAS in Visitor Centre. *Adm £1 Chd 50p. March 1 to Oct 31 (10-5). Also open* **St Aidan's College garden**, *Nov 1 to Feb 28 every afternoon weather permitting. Private parties welcome, please* **Tel 0191 374 7971**

Westholme Hall ♿❀ (Mr & Mrs J H McBain) Winston. 11m W of Darlington. From A67 Darlington-Barnard Castle, nr Winston turn N onto B6274. 5 acres of gardens and grounds laid out in 1892 surround the Jacobean house (not open). Rhododendrons, flowering shrubs, mixed borders, old-fashioned rose garden. The croquet lawn leads on to an orchard, stream and woodland. Home made TEAS. *Adm £2 Chd 50p. Suns May 25, July 6, Aug 24 (2-6)*

General Information. For general information on the use of this book see Page 17.

¶**Wycliffe Gardens** From Scotch Corner 8m NW on A66. Turn R to Thorpe and Wycliffe. TEAS. *Combined adm £2 Chd 50p. Sun May 18 (2-5)*
  ¶**Orchard Cottage** & (Miss C Scrope) ¼-acre cottage garden
  ¶**The Nest** (Mr & Mrs J Usher) ¼-acre riverside garden featuring magnolias

> The National Gardens Scheme is a charity which traces its origins back to 1927. Since then it has raised a total of over £15 million for charitable purposes.

Dyfed

See separate Welsh section beginning on page 323

Essex

Hon County Organiser:	Mrs Judy Johnson, Saling Hall, Great Saling, Braintree CM7 5DT Tel 01371 850243
Assistant Hon County Organisers:	Mrs Jill Cowley, Park Farm, Great Waltham, Chelmsford CM3 1BZ (Publicity) Tel 01245 360871
	Mrs Rosemary Kenrick, The Bailey House, Saffron Walden CB10 2EA
Hon County Treasurer:	Eric Brown Esq, 19 Chichester Road, Saffron Walden CB11 3EW

DATES OF OPENING

March 30 Sunday
  Glen Chantry, Wickham Bishops
  Lower Dairy House, Nayland
  The Magnolias, Brentwood
March 31 Monday
  Lower Dairy House, Nayland
April 6 Sunday
  Lower Dairy House, Nayland
  The Magnolias, Brentwood
April 17 Thursday
  Woodpeckers,
    Burnham-on-Crouch
April 18 Friday
  Woodpeckers,
    Burnham-on-Crouch
April 19 Saturday
  Lower Dairy House, Nayland
April 20 Sunday
  Glen Chantry, Wickham Bishops
  Lower Dairy House, Nayland
  The Magnolias, Brentwood
  Over Hall, Colne Engaine
  Saling Hall Lodge, Great Saling
April 27 Sunday
  Lower Dairy House, Nayland
  The Magnolias, Brentwood
May 1 Thursday
  Woodpeckers,
    Burnham-on-Crouch
May 2 Friday
  Woodpeckers,
    Burnham-on-Crouch
May 4 Sunday
  Glen Chantry, Wickham Bishops
  Lower Dairy House, Nayland
  Park Farm, Great Waltham

  Rose Cottage, Theydon Bois
May 5 Monday
  Carters House, Sible Hedingham
  Glen Chantry, Wickham Bishops
  Lower Dairy House, Nayland
  Park Farm, Great Waltham
  Rose Cottage, Theydon Bois
May 11 Sunday
  6 Fanners Green, Great
    Waltham ‡
  Hobbans Farm, Bobbingworth, nr
    Ongar
  Lower Dairy House, Nayland
  The Magnolias, Brentwood
  Park Farm, Great Waltham ‡
  Rose Cottage, Theydon Bois
May 12 Monday
  6 Fanners Green, Great Waltham
May 15 Thursday
  Woodpeckers,
    Burnham-on-Crouch
May 16 Friday
  Perrrymans, Boxted
  Woodpeckers,
    Burnham-on-Crouch
May 18 Sunday
  Lower Dairy House, Nayland
  The Magnolias, Brentwood
  Park Farm, Great Waltham
  Rose Cottage, Theydon Bois
  Saling Hall Lodge, Great Saling
  Shore Hall, Cornish Hall End
May 21 Wednesday
  Shore Hall, Cornish Hall End
May 23 Friday
  Perrymans, Boxted
May 24 Saturday
  Edelweiss, Hornchurch

May 25 Sunday
  Edelweiss, Hornchurch
  Glen Chantry, Wickham Bishops
  Hobbans Farm, Bobbingworth, nr
    Ongar
  Lower Dairy House, Nayland
  Park Farm, Great Waltham
  Rose Cottage, Theydon Bois
May 26 Monday
  Glen Chantry, Wickham Bishops
  Lower Dairy House, Nayland
  Park Farm, Great Waltham
  Rose Cottage, Theydon Bois
May 28 Wednesday
  Shore Hall, Cornish Hall End
May 30 Friday
  Perrymans, Boxted
May 31 Saturday
  Lower Dairy House, Nayland
June 1 Sunday
  Lower Dairy House, Nayland
  The Magnolias, Brentwood
  Park Farm, Great Waltham
  Rose Cottage, Theydon Bois
  Saling Hall Lodge, Great
    Saling
June 2 Monday
  Park Farm, Great Waltham
June 4 Wednesday
  Shore Hall, Cornish Hall End
June 6 Friday
  Perrymans, Boxted
June 8 Sunday
  Carters House, Sible
    Hedingham
  8 Dene Court, Chelmsford
  The Old Rectory, Boreham
  Over Hall, Colne Engaine

Park Farm, Great Waltham
Rose Cottage, Theydon Bois
June 9 Monday
Park Farm, Great Waltham
June 11 Wednesday
Shore Hall, Cornish Hall End
June 12 Thursday
Woodpeckers,
Burnham-on-Crouch
June 13 Friday
Perrymans, Boxted
Woodpeckers,
Burnham-on-Crouch
June 14 Saturday
Lower Dairy House, Nayland
Stamps and Crows, Layer Breton
Heath
June 15 Sunday
Barnards, Sible Hedingham ‡
The Dower House, Castle
Hedingham ‡
Fanners Farm, Great Waltham ‡‡
6 Fanners Green, Great
Waltham ‡‡
Hobbans Farm, Bobbingworth, nr
Ongar
Lower Dairy House, Nayland
Park Farm, Great Waltham ‡‡
Rose Cottage, Theydon Bois
Stamps and Crows, Layer Breton
Heath
June 16 Monday
Fanners Farm, Great Waltham ‡
6 Fanners Green, Great
Waltham ‡
Park Farm, Great Waltham ‡
June 18 Wednesday
Horkesley Hall, Colchester
Shore Hall, Cornish Hall End
Stamps and Crows, Layer Breton
Heath
June 20 Friday
Park Farm, Great Waltham (6-9)
Perrymans, Boxted
June 21 Saturday
Park Farm, Great Waltham (6-9)
June 22 Sunday
Clavering Gardens, nr Saffron
Walden
8 Dene Court, Chelmsford
Folly Faunts House, Goldhanger
Lower Dairy House, Nayland
The Magnolias, Brentwood
Park Farm, Great Waltham
Shore Hall, Cornish Hall End
June 23 Monday
Park Farm, Great Waltham
June 26 Thursday
Woodpeckers, Burnham-on-Crouch
June 27 Friday
Woodpeckers, Burnham-on-Crouch
June 28 Saturday
Edelweiss, Hornchurch
Lower Dairy Farm, Nayland

June 29 Sunday
Audley End House, Saffron
Walden ‡
Edelweiss, Hornchurch
Glen Chantry, Wickham Bishops
Hobbans Farm, Bobbingworth, nr
Ongar
Littlebury Gardens ‡
Lower Dairy House, Nayland
Park Farm, Great Waltham
Saling Hall, Great Saling ‡‡
Saling Hall Lodge, Great Saling ‡‡
June 30 Monday
Park Farm, Great Waltham
July 3 Thursday
Woodpeckers, Burnham-on-Crouch
July 4 Friday
Woodpeckers,
Burnham-on-Crouch
July 5 Saturday
Lower Dairy House, Nayland
July 6 Sunday
8 Dene Court, Chelmsford
Lower Dairy House, Nayland
The Old Vicarage, Rickling
Park Farm, Great Waltham
Rose Cottage, Theydon Bois
July 7 Monday
Park Farm, Great Waltham
July 13 Sunday
Barnards Farm, West Horndon,
Brentwood ‡
6 Fanners Green, Great
Waltham ‡‡
Hobbans Farm, Bobbingworth, nr
Ongar
The Magnolias, Brentwood ‡
Park Farm, Great Waltham ‡‡
Rose Cottage, Theydon Bois
July 14 Monday
6 Fanners Green, Great
Waltham ‡
Park Farm, Great Waltham ‡
July 16 Wednesday
Horkesley Hall, Colchester
July 20 Sunday
8 Dene Court, Chelmsford
Rose Cottage, Theydon Bois
July 26 Saturday
Edelweiss, Hornchurch
July 27 Sunday
Edelweiss, Hornchurch
Hobbans Farm, Bobbingworth, nr
Ongar
Rose Cottage, Theydon Bois
August 3 Sunday
8 Dene Court, Chelmsford
The Magnolias, Brentwood
Rose Cottage, Theydon Bois
August 10 Sunday
Audley End House, Saffron
Walden
Hobbans Farm, Bobbingworth, nr
Ongar

Rose Cottage, Theydon Bois
August 17 Sunday
Rose Cottage, Theydon Bois
August 20 Wednesday
Horkesley Hall, Colchester
August 23 Saturday
Edelweiss, Hornchurch
August 24 Sunday
Edelweiss, Hornchurch
Hobbans Farm, Bobbingworth, nr
Ongar
The Magnolias, Brentwood
Rose Cottage, Theydon Bois
August 25 Monday
Rose Cottage, Theydon Bois
August 31 Sunday
Rose Cottage, Theydon Bois
September 7 Sunday
Barnards Farm, West Horndon,
Brentwood
Deers, Clavering, nr Saffron
Walden
Glen Chantry, Wickham Bishops
Hobbans Farm, Bobbingworth, nr
Ongar
Rose Cottage, Theydon Bois
September 14 Sunday
Rose Cottage, Theydon Bois
Saling Hall Lodge, Great Saling
September 21 Sunday
Glen Chantry, Wickham Bishops
The Magnolias, Brentwood
Rose Cottage, Theydon Bois
September 28 Sunday
Rose Cottage, Theydon Bois
October 19 Sunday
Writtle College, Writtle
October 26 Sunday
The Magnolias, Brentwood

Regular openings
For details see garden description

Beth Chatto Gardens, Elmstead
Market
The Gardens of Easton Lodge, Great
Dunmow
Feeringbury Manor, Feering
Glen Chantry, Wickham Bishops
The Gibberd Garden, Harlow
Hyde Hall, RHS Garden, Rettendon
Saling Hall, Great Saling
Volpaia, Hockley

By appointment only
*For telephone numbers and other
details see garden descriptions.
Private visits welcomed*

Olivers, nr Colchester
Reed House, Great Chesterford

DESCRIPTIONS OF GARDENS

▲¶**Audley End House** ⅃⅁ (English Heritage) 1m W of Saffron Walden on the B1383 (Bishops Stortford to Cambridge rd.) 100-acre landscape park, designed by Capability Brown, surrounding Jacobean mansion. Garden incl parterre flower garden restored over last 10yrs to plans developed 1830. Fine plane, tulip trees and famous Audley End oak. Pond garden, laid out in 1868 with scented old roses and pulhamite rock garden. TEAS in restaurant. Guided tours extra charge. *Adm £3.30 Chd £1.70. For NGS Suns June 29, Aug 10 (11-5)*

Barnards ⅃⅃⅁ (Mr & Mrs Leonard Ratcliff) Sible Hedingham. 1½m from A604, on Hedingham-Wethersfield rd. Garden on L. Formal plantsman's garden of 2 acres, created since 1994 with Elizabethan 'forthright'; parterre; Mediterranean edible garden; lime walk; evergreen 'Mondrian' garden. Farm pond; rough area of old-fashioned shrub roses and grasses and walks to 5 acres of newly planted native trees. TEAS. *Adm £1.50 Chd free (Share to Halstead Hospital League of Friends®). Sun June 15 (2-5.30). Parties by appt, please Tel 01787 462293*

¶**Barnards Farm** ⅃⅃⅁ (Bernard & Sylvia Holmes) West Horndon. 6km E on A127 from junction 29, M25. 2km S on A128 on R under railway bridge. An evolving garden from open fields around Georgian house (not open), and Essex pylons, Framed by barns it is partially designed to be viewed from the air; aviators particularly welcome. Life size bronzes, sculptured pots and brick maze are special features. Herbaceous borders, 17 hectares of grounds, ponds, developing woodland, arboretum, malus collection, Japanese garden, long avenue, water course, parterre, and ornamental vegetable garden. Self drive golf buggy available. Open air religious service 5.30 to 6. TEAS. *Adm £2 Chd free (Share to St Francis Church West Horndon®). Suns July 13, Sept 7 (2-5.30)*

●**Beth Chatto Gardens** ⅃⅁ (Mrs Beth Chatto) On A133, ¼m E of Elmstead Market. 5 acres of attractively landscaped garden with many unusual plants, shown in wide range of conditions from hot and dry to water garden. The recently made gravel garden, converted from the original car park, has been planted with drought-tolerant plants to help gardeners who have hose-pipe watering bans. Books available by Beth Chatto The Dry Garden, The Damp Garden, Beth Chatto's Garden Notebook, The Green Tapestry. Adjacent nursery open. *Adm £2.50 Chd free. March 1 to Oct 31, every Mon to Sat but closed Bank Hols (9-5); Nov 1 to end of Feb every Mon to Fri but closed Bank Hols (9-4). Parties by appt*

Carters House ⅃⅃⅁ (Mrs Michael Gosling) High Street Green, Sible Hedingham. Well-marked off A604 from Sible Hedingham. Hedingham to Wethersfield Rd. ¾-acre garden, created since 1990. Many bulbs, especially tulips. Malus, cherries, lilacs, clematis and roses; white border, gold and blue border; other interesting and species plants of yr-round interest. TEAS. *Adm £1.50 Chd free. Mon May 5; Sun June 8 (2-6). Private visits welcome, please Tel 01787 461106*

General Information. For general information on the use of this book see Page 17.

Clavering Gardens ⅃⅁ Clavering. On B1038 7m N of Bishops Stortford. Turn W off B1383 (old A11) at Newport. TEAS in Cricket Pavilion on village green in aid of Clavering Cricket Club. *Adm £2.50 Chd free. Sun June 22 (1-5.30)*
> **Brooklands** (Mr & Mrs John Noble) Walled garden, herbaceous and shrub borders, rustic rose trellis, arboretum. Extended garden planting in old orchard; 1½ acres
> **Clavering Court** (Mr & Mrs S R Elvidge) Approx 1½ acres, fine trees, shrubs and borders. Walled garden, Edwardian greenhouse
> **Deers** (Mr & Mrs S Cooke) Parking in yard next to house. For details see separate entry
> **Piercewebbs** (Mr & Mrs B R William-Powlett) Includes old walled garden, shrubs, lawns, ha ha, yew and stilt hedges, pond and trellised rose garden. Extensive views. Best amateur garden in Country Gardens Competition. Plant stall
> **Shovellers** (Miss J & Miss E Ludgate) Stickling Green. 3-acre extended cottage garden, orchard and meadow

Deers ⅃ (Mr & Mrs S Cooke) Clavering. On B1038 7m N of Bishop's Stortford. Turn W off B1383 (old A11) at Newport; close to Fox & Hound Inn, centre of village. Follow signs to Langley, 2nd L on bend, sign to Ford End. Shrub and herbaceous borders; ponds; old roses in formal garden; walled vegetable garden; flower meadow; trees. 4 acres. Parking in yard next to house. Runner-up in large gardens competition 1994. *Combined adm with Clavering Gardens £2.50 Chd free. Sun June 22 (1-5.30). Also open Sun Sept 7 (2-5). Adm £2 Chd free*

8 Dene Court ⅃⅁ (Mrs Sheila Chapman) Chelmsford. W of Chelmsford (Parkway). Take A1060 Roxwell Rd for 1m. Turn R at t lights into Chignall Rd, Dene Court 3rd exit on R. Parking in Chignall Rd. Well maintained and designed compact garden (250 sq yds) circular lawn surrounded by many unusual plants incl wide variety of clematis, roses, ferns and grasses; ornamental well; three pergolas; rose-covered perimeter wall. Featured in Essex Homes and Living, Garden News and Daily Mirror. *Adm £1 Chd 50p (Share to Audrey Appleton Trust for the Terminally Ill®). Suns June 8, 22, July 6, 20, Aug 3 (2-5.30)*

The Dower House ⅃⅁ (Mr & Mrs John Allfrey) Castle Hedingham on B1058. 5m from Halstead A604. 1m NE of Sible Hedingham. Follow signs to Hedingham Castle. Garden 50yds from entrance. Terraced plantsman's garden of 1½ acres overlooking Tudor church and village. Mixed borders developed since 1987 with flower arranging in mind. TEAS. *Adm £1.50 Chd free (Share to St Nicholas Church, Castle Hedingham®). Sun June 15 (2-6)*

●**The Gardens of Easton Lodge** formerly **Warwick House** ⅃⅁ (Mr & Mrs B Creasey) Great Dunmow. Follow brown heritage signs from A120, W of Dunmow to Gardens, 1½m N of Dunmow. Home of 'Darling Daisy' Countess of Warwick, who in 1903 commissioned Harold Peto to lay out Italian and Japanese Gardens. Abandoned 1950; major restoration since 1993 incl herring bone brick and cobble courtyard, ponds, C18th dove cote, conservatory and pavilion. Work started on sunken Italian Garden. Featured Anglia's 'Homemaker' series BBC Look East and History Exhibition and occasionally American Air

Force Exhibits. Cream TEAS. *Adm £2.50 OAPs £2.25 Chd under 12 free (Share to Five Parishes®). Sats, Suns, Bank Hols March 28 to Oct 26 (2-6). Private visits welcome, please* **Tel 01371 876979**

Edelweiss (Joan H Hogg, Pat F Lowery) 20 Hartland Road, Hornchurch. From Romford E along the A124 past Tesco on L, turn R into Albany Rd opp church on corner of Park Lane on the L. Go to the bottom of Albany Rd, humps all the way down, turn L at the end into Hartland Rd. Small town garden approx 200′ × 25′. Laid out to maximise use of small narrow plot and featuring many containers, baskets, seasonal bedding and mixed borders. Tiny prize-winning garden to the front of the property. Home-made produce, eggs etc. Narrow access and steps at side and rear not suitable for push-chairs. TEAS. *Adm £1 Chd free. Sats, Suns May 24, 25, June 28, 29, July 26, 27 Aug 23, 24 (3-6). Private visits welcome, June-Aug please* **Tel 01708 454610**

Fanners Farm ♿♨ (Mr & Mrs P G Lee) 4m N of Chelmsford. In Great Waltham turn into South Street opp inn/restaurant. Garden 1¼m on R. Informal garden of approx 2 acres surrounding C14 house (not open). Conservatory featured in The Garden, Feb 1990. Small collection of vintage cars. TEAS Sun only. *Adm £1 Chd free. Sun, Mon June 15, 16 (2-6)*

6 Fanners Green ♿♨❀ (Dr & Mrs T M Pickard) 4m N of Chelmsford. In Great Waltham turn into South Street opp inn/restaurant. Garden 1¼m on R. A 15-yr-old small country garden of ⅓ acre divided into different formal areas with informal planting. Herb garden and conservatory. *Adm £1 Chd free. Suns, Mons May 11, 12; June 15, 16, July 13, 14 (2-6). Parties by appt May to July, please* **Tel 01245 360035**

Feeringbury Manor ♿ (Mr & Mrs G Coode-Adams) Coggeshall Rd, Feering, on rd between Coggeshall and Feering. 7-acre garden bordering R Blackwater. Many unusual plants including wide variety of honeysuckles, clematis, old-fashioned roses; rare bog-loving plants, border, ponds and stream; small Victorian water wheel. Contemporary sculpture exhibition during June. Featured in Country Life 1994 and The Passionate Gardener. *Adm £2 Chd free (Share to Colchester and District Visual Arts Trust®). Weekdays April 28 to Aug 1 (8-1) closed weekends and Bank Hols. Private visits welcome, please* **Tel 01376 561946**

Folly Faunts House ♿❀ (Mr & Mrs J C Jenkinson) Goldhanger. On B1026 between Colchester and Maldon. Winner best large garden in Essex award 1994. 5-acre garden around an C18 manor house (not open) created since 1963. Garden is divided into 7 different compartments each with a wide variety of unusual plants, shrubs and trees. Formal and informal water gardens. 20 acres of park and woodland, planted in 1988, is divided into 5 double avenues. Large car park. Unusual and interesting plants for sale. TEAS. *Adm £2 Chd £1. Sun June 22 (2-5). Parties of 12 or more by appt, please* **Tel 01621 788213**

●¶**The Gibberd Garden** ♿ (The Gibberd Garden Trust) Harlow. E off B183, Hatfield Heath Rd, approx 1m from junction with A414. Turn L into Marsh Lane off Gilden

Way (B183). 'Garden Open' sign at entrance to lane. ¾m down narrow lane. 7-acre C20 garden designed by Sir Frederick Gibberd, on side of small valley. Terraces, wild garden, landscaped vistas, pools and streams, 'Roman Temple', moated log castle, gazebo, tree house and large collection of modern sculpture. TEAS. *Adm £3 Concessions £2 Chd free. Suns Easter Sun to end of Sept (2-6). Weekday parties by appt, please* **Tel 01279 442112**

Glen Chantry ♿❀❀ (Mr & Mrs W G Staines) Wickham Bishops 1½m SE of Witham. Take Maldon Rd from Witham and 1st L to Wickham Bishops. Pass Benton Hall Golf Course: cross narrow bridge over R Blackwater and turn immediately L up track by side of Blue Mills. 3-acre garden, emphasis on mixed borders, unusual perennials and shrub roses. Limestone rock gardens with associated ponds form a dominant feature, formal specialist white garden and foliage beds with grasses and hostas; range of plants for sale. TEAS in aid of local charities. *Adm £1.50 Chd 50p. Suns Mar 30, April 20; May 4, 25; June 29; Sept 7, 21; Mons May 5, 26 (2-5). Fris, Sats June, July and August (10-4) (no TEAS). Also parties by appt, please* **Tel 01621 891342**

¶**Hobbans Farm** ❀❀ (Mrs Ann Webster) Bobbingworth, Ongar. N of A414 between Ongar 'Four Wantz' roundabout and N Weald 'Talbot' roundabout just past Blake Hall Gardens. 1st farm entrance on R after St Germain's Church. Mature, romantic informal garden, set in 1½ acres divided into 3 parts surrounding C15 farmhouse. Unusual plants; clematis, old roses, small herb and sink gardens. Set in pastures with fine views. TEAS in aid of Local Charities. *Adm £1 Chd free. Suns May 11, 25, June 15, 29, July 13, 27, Aug 10, 24, Sept 7 (2-6)*

Horkesley Hall ♿ (Mr & Mrs Richard Eddis) Little Horkesley, Colchester. Little Horkesley is W of A134, 3m N of Colchester. House marked on map just beyond church. A young garden of approx 5 acres within the setting of a classical house, 2 old fishponds and some fine old trees around the perimeter. Its creation began in 1990/91 and the emphasis is on shrubs and trees chosen for colour and effect and incl some which are unusual and rare. *Adm £2 Chd £1 (Share to Co-workers of Mother Theresa®). Weds June 18, July 16, Aug 20 (2-5). Parties by appt on weekdays, please* **Tel 01206 272067**

●**Hyde Hall Garden** ♿❀❀ (Royal Horticultural Society) Rettendon. 7m SE of Chelmsford; 6m NE of Wickford. Signed from A130. 20-acre garden with flowering trees, shrubs, perennials, and spring bulbs. Large cool glass house and small, alpine house. Collection of modern and shrub roses. Nat. Collection malus and viburnum. Large formal pond; enlarged lower pond and new bridge to be completed spring 1997. Thatched Barn Restaurant, (licensed). *Adm £3 Chd 70p 6-14 Chd under 6 free. Parties 10+ £2.50. Every Wed, Thurs, Fri, Sat, Sun and Bank Hols March 26 to Oct 26. March to Aug (11-6), Sept, Oct (11-5)*

Littlebury Gardens ❀❀ 2m from Saffron Walden, opp Littlebury church on B1383 1m N of Audley End House, entrance in Littlebury Green Rd. TEAS. *Combined adm £1.25 Chd free. Sun June 29 (2-5.30)*

Granta House & (Mr & Mrs R A Lloyd) Old walled garden of 2 acres; unusual shrubs, herbaceous plants and roses, plants in dry areas; courtyard

North House (Dr & Mrs B G Sanders) opp Granta House. Mixed borders, herb garden, roses, ornamental vegetable garden created by artists over 10 yrs

Lower Dairy House &&& (Mr & Mrs D J Burnett) 7m N of Colchester off A134. Turn L at bottom of hill before Nayland village into Water Lane, signed to Little Horkesley. Garden ½m on L past farm buildings. Plantsman's garden approx 1½ acres. Natural stream with waterside plantings; rockery and raised beds; lawns; herbaceous borders; roses. Many varieties of shrubs and ground cover plants. Garden made and maintained by owners for yr-round colour and variety. Good spring bulbs and blossom. Tudor House (not open). Teas in village. *Adm £1.50 Chd 50p. Sats, Suns, Mons March 30, 31, April 6, 19, 20, 27; May 4, 5, 11, 18, 25, 26, 31; June 1, 14, 15, 22, 28, 29; July 5, 6 (2-6). Also private visits welcome, please* **Tel 01206 262220**

The Magnolias && (Mr & Mrs R A Hammond) 18 St John's Ave, Brentwood. From A1023 turn S on A128; after 300yds R at traffic lights; over railway bridge; St John's Ave 3rd on R. ½-acre informal garden with particular appeal to plantsmen; good collection spring bulbs; ground-cover; trees and shrubs incl maples, rhododendrons, camellias, magnolias and pieris. Koi ponds and other water interests. Featured on Garden Club. *Adm £1 Chd 50p. Suns March 30; April 6, 20, 27; May 11, 18; June 1, 22; July 13; Aug 3, 24; Sept 21; Oct 26 (10-5). Parties by appt March to Oct incl, please* **Tel 01277 220019**

The Old Rectory &&& (Sir Jeffery & Lady Bowman) Boreham. 4m NE of Chelmsford. Take 1137 to Boreham Village, turn into Church Rd at Red Lion Public House. ½m along on R opp church. 2½-acre garden with ponds, stream, interesting trees and shrubs, herbaceous borders and kitchen garden. TEAS. *Adm £1.50 Chd free. Sun June 8 (2-6)*

The Old Vicarage && (Mr & Mrs James Jowitt) Rickling. 7m S from Saffron Walden: from Newport take B1038 W to Wicken Bonhunt. In village turn L to Rickling, The Old Vicarage is on the L after 1m. 2-acre garden divided by mature yew hedges, interesting 'hot' borders, herbaceous and mixed borders; rose garden, shrubbery, new herb garden. TEAS in aid of Rickling Church. *Adm £2 Chd free. Sun July 6 (2-6)*

Olivers &&& (Mr & Mrs D Edwards) 3m SW of Colchester, between B1022 & B1026. Follow signs to zoo and continue 1m towards Colchester. Turn R at roundabout (Cunobelin Way) and R into Olivers Lane. From Colchester via Maldon Rd turn L at roundabout, R into Olivers Lane (signed Roman River Centre). C18 house (not open) overlooks Roman R valley, surrounded by terrace and yew-backed borders; closely planted with unusual plants for varying conditions. Lawns; 3 lakes; meadow; woodland with fine trees underplanted with shrubs including rhododendrons and old roses; spring bulbs and bluebells. *Adm £2 Chd free. Parties and private visits by appt, please* **Tel 01206 330575**

¶**Over Hall** ❀ (Mr & Mrs Michael Lambert) Colne Engaine, Colchester. N of A604 signed from Earls Colne. 1m from village of Colne Engaine towards Countess Cross. 12 acres, surrounding Georgian house (not open); sloping gardens, woodland walk with ponds and watercourse; walled garden. TEAS. *Adm £1.50 Chd free. Suns April 20, June 8 (2-6)*

Park Farm && (Mrs J E M Cowley & Mr D Bracey) Great Waltham. Take B1008 N from Chelmsford through Broomfield Village. On Little Waltham bypass turn L into Chatham Hall Lane signposted Howe Street; Park Farm ½m on L. 2 acres of garden in separate 'rooms' formed by yew hedges with climber-obscured old farmhouse and dairy in centre. Many different species of bulbs; shrubs; roses and herbaceous perennials; designing still proceeding with new projects underway. Featured in magazines and on TV. TEAS. *Adm £1.25 Chd 50p. Suns, May 4, 11, 18, 25; June 1, 8, 15, 22, 29; July 6, 13. Mons May 5, June 2, 9, 16, 23, 30, July 7, 14 (2-6). Evening openings Fri, Sat June 20, 21 (6-9). Parties by appt, please* **Tel 01245 360871**

Perrymans &&& (Mr & Mrs H R J Human) Boxted. 4m NE from Colchester Station to Boxted Cross. Follow Dedham Rd, drive entrance on R 200yds past village shop. 7-acre undulating garden created from scratch since 1970, lakes, rose garden, borders, spring bulbs and selection of old and new trees; small vegetable garden. Teas by special arrangement. *Adm £2 Chd 50p. Fris May 16, 23, 30, June 6, 13, 20 (10.30-3.30). Private visits welcome, any number, please* **Tel 01206 272297**

Reed House && (Mrs W H Mason) Great Chesterford. 4m N of Saffron Walden and 1m S of Stump Cross, M 11. On B184 turn into Great Chesterford High Street. Then L at Crown & Thistle public house into Manor Lane. ¾-acre garden developed in the last 10 years with collection of unusual plants. Featured in Essex Homes and Living. *Adm £1.50. Open by appt, please* **Tel 01799 530312**

Rose Cottage && (Anne & Jack Barnard) 42 Blackacre Rd, Theydon Bois. 2m S of Epping on B172. At pedestrian crossing turn into Poplar Row (opp Bull inn). Pass village pond, turn 2nd R. Garden at top of hill on R. Small romantic garden 35' × 130', on a sloping site on verges of Epping Forest. Designed in compartments incl woodland, sundial, cottage and fountain gardens. Luxuriant planting; small collection of old-fashioned and new English roses; cottage garden; unusual plants, herbs and bulbs. TEAS. *Adm £1 Chd free. Suns May 4, 11, 18, 25; June 1, 8, 15; July 6, 13, 20, 27; Aug 3, 10, 17, 24, 31, Sept 7, 14, 21, 28; Mons May 5, 26, Aug 25 (2-6). Private visits welcome by appt May to Sept, please* **Tel 01992 814619**

Saling Hall && (Mr & Mrs H Johnson) Great Saling, 6m NW of Braintree. Turn N off A120 between Braintree and Dunmow at the Saling Oak. 12 acres; walled garden dated 1698; small park with fine trees; extensive new collection of unusual plants with emphasis on trees; water gardens. Hugh Johnson is 'Tradescant' of the RHS. TEAS Sun only. *Adm £2 Chd free (Shore to St James's Church, Great Saling®). Weds in May, June, July (2-5). Sun June 29 with **Saling Hall Lodge** Combined adm £2.50 (2-6). Parties by appt on weekdays. Written application, please*

Saling Hall Lodge ﾝ✗✿ (Mr & Mrs K Akers) Great Saling. 6m NW of Braintree. Turn N off A120 between Braintree and Dunmow at the Saling Oak. Drive at end of village on L, please park in village. Well-designed and maintained ½-acre garden with pond, limestone rock garden, small peat garden, tufa bed and sinks. As seen on Channel 4 and Anglia TV. TEAS. *Adm £1 Chd free. Suns April 20, May 18, June 1, Sept 14 for cyclamen (2-5). Combined adm with* **Saling Hall** *£2.50 Sun June 29 (2-6), Also parties by appt please,* **Tel 01371 850683**

Shore Hall ✗✿ (Mr & Mrs Peter Swete) Cornish Hall End, nr Braintree. 2½m NE of Finchingfield. ½m W of Cornish Hall End on Gt Sampford Rd. Long drive with poplars. 3½-acre garden surrounding C17 house (not open) with several enclosed formal areas and interesting shrubs. 100-yr-old box hedges enclose formal beds planted with herbaceous and old roses; rose garden surrounding lily ponds; newly planted ornamental vegetable and fruit garden and many young rare trees. TEAS in aid of local charity Suns only. *Adm £2 Chd free. Suns May 18, June 22, Weds May 21, 28, June 4, 11, 18 (2-6). Parties by appt weekdays, May to July, please* **Tel 01799 586411**

Stamps and Crows ﾝ✿ (Mr & Mrs E G Billington) Layer Breton Heath. 5½m S of Colchester on B1022 take L fork signed Birch and Layer Breton. On R side of Layer Breton Heath. 2½ acres of moated garden surrounding C15 farmhouse (not open). Herbaceous borders, mixed shrubs, old roses and good ground cover. Recently created bog garden and dovecote. Highly commended in Essex Country Garden Competition. Fine views towards Layer Marney Tower. TEAS (Sun only). *Adm £1.50 Chd free (Share to St. Mary's Church, Layer Breton®). Sat,*

Sun, Wed June 14, 15, 18 (2-6). Parties by appt, please **Tel 01206 330220**

●**Volpaia** ✗✿ (Mr & Mrs D Fox) 54 Woodlands Rd, Hockley. 2¾m NE of Rayleigh. B1013 Rayleigh-Rochford, turn S from Spa Hotel into Woodlands Rd. On E side of Hockley Woods. 1 acre containing many exotic trees, rhododendrons, camellias and other shrubs. Carpets of wood anemones and bluebells in spring, underplanting is very diverse, especially with woodland, liliaceous plants and ferns. TEA. *Adm £1 Chd 30p (Share to Essex Group of NCCPG®). All Thurs & Suns from April 13 to June 22 (2.30-6). Also private visits welcome, please* **Tel 01702 203761**

Woodpeckers ﾝ✗✿ (Mr & Mrs N J Holdaway & Mrs L M Burton) Mangapp Chase, Burnham-on-Crouch. B1010 to Burnham-on-Crouch. Just beyond town sign turn L into Green Lane. Turn L after ½m. Garden 200yds on R. 1½ acres redeveloped since 1991. Planted for long season of interest using old 'cottage' favourites as well as newer varieties of roses, shrubs and herbaceous perennials. 'Potager', rose walk, new pond all set amongst mature trees. TEAS. *Adm £1 Chd 50p. Thurs, Fris April 17, 18; May 1, 2, 15, 16; June 12, 13, 26, 27; July 3, 4 (12-6). Evening openings Fris June 13, 27 (6-9). Parties welcome by appt, please* **Tel 01621 782137**

▲**Writtle College** ﾝ✿ Lordship Rd, Writtle. On A414 W of Chelmsford, nr Writtle village, clearly signed. Approx 15 acres; informal lawns, tree collection, good autumn tints, mixed borders, alpines, formal 'Victorian' garden, aromatic garden. Small gardens designed and built by students undergoing training, bedding trial area, heather garden, ornamental and landscaped glasshouses. TEA. *Adm £2 Chd free. For NGS Sun Oct 19 (10-4)*

Flintshire & Wrexham/The Glamorgans

See separate Welsh section beginning on page 323

SYMBOLS USED IN THIS BOOK (See also Page 17)

‡   Following a garden name in the Dates of Opening list indicates that those gardens sharing the same symbol are nearby and open on the same day.

‡‡   Indicates a second series of nearby gardens open on the same day.

¶   Opening for the first time.

✿   Plants/produce for sale if available.

ﾝ   Gardens with at least the main features accessible by wheelchair.

✗   No dogs except guide dogs but otherwise dogs are usually admitted, provided they are kept on a lead. Dogs are not admitted to houses.

●   These gardens advertise their own dates in this publication although they do not nominate specific days for the NGS. Not all the money collected by these gardens comes to the NGS but they do make a guaranteed contribution.

■   These gardens nominate specific days for the NGS and advertise their own dates in this publication.

▲   These gardens open regularly to the public but they do not advertise their own dates in this publication. For further details, contact the garden directly.

Gloucestershire (North & Central)

Hon County Organiser: Mrs Stella Martin, Dundry Lodge, France Lynch, Stroud GL6 8LP
Tel 01453 883419
Assistant Hon County Organisers: Mrs Barbara Adams, Warners Court, Charfield, Wotton under Edge GL12 8TG
Mrs Jennie Davies, Applegarth, Alstone, nr Tewkesbury GL20 8JD
Mrs Sally Gough, Trevi, Over Old Road, Hartpury GL19 3BJ
Mr Tony Marlow, Greenedge, 32 Dr Browns Road, Minchinhampton GL6 9BT
Miss Anne Palmer, 10, Vineyard Street, Winchcombe GL54 5LP
Mrs Catherine Watson, Colpen House, Winson, Cirencester GL7 5EN
Hon County Treasurer: Mr Graham Baber, 11 Corinium Gate, Cirencester GL7 2PX

DATES OF OPENING

February 2 Sunday
Home Farm, Huntley, nr Newent
February 6 Thursday
Cinderdine Cottage, Dymock nr
Newent
February 11 Tuesday
Cinderdine Cottage, Dymock nr
Newent
February 13 Thursday
Cinderdine Cottage, Dymock, nr
Newent
February 16 Sunday
Minchinhampton Gardens
Cinderdine Cottage, Dymock nr
Newent
February 18 Tuesday
Cinderdine Cottage, Dymock, nr
Newent
February 20 Thursday
Cinderdine Cottage, Dymock, nr
Newent
February 24 Monday
The Old Rectory, Duntisbourne
Rous, nr Cirencester
March
Cinderdine Cottage, Dymock, nr
Newent. Every Tues & 1st &
3rd Suns
Grove Cottage, Lower Lydbrook,
Cinderford. Every Thurs
The Old Manor, Twyning,
Tewkesbury. Every Mon
except Bank Hols
March 2 Sunday
Green Cottage, Lydney
Home Farm, Huntley, nr Newent
March 9 Sunday
Green Cottage, Lydney
March 16 Sunday
Green Cottage, Lydney
March 20 Thursday
Trevi Garden, Hartpury, nr
Gloucester
March 23 Sunday
Green Cottage, Lydney
March 24 Monday
The Old Rectory, Duntisbourne
Rous, nr Cirencester

March 27 Thursday
Trevi Garden, Hartpury, nr
Gloucester
March 29 Saturday
Ashley Manor, nr Tetbury
March 30 Sunday
Beverston Castle, nr Tetbury
Brockweir Gardens,
Chepstow
Green Cottage, Lydney
Trevi Garden, Hartpury, nr
Gloucester
Westonbirt Gardens at
Westonbirt School
March 31 Monday
Ashley Manor, nr Tetbury
Beverston Castle, nr Tetbury
Brockweir Gardens, Chepstow
Trevi Garden, Hartpury, nr
Gloucester
April
Cinderdine Cottage, Dymock, nr
Newent Every Tues & 1st &
3rd Suns
Grove Cottage, Lower Lydbrook,
Cinderford. Every Thurs
The Old Manor, Twyning,
Tewkesbury. Every Mon
April 6 Sunday
Home Farm, Huntley, nr Newent
Minchinhampton Gardens
Misarden Park, Miserden, nr
Cirencester
Painswick Rococo Garden,
Painswick
Trevi Garden, Hartpury, nr
Gloucester
April 10 Thursday
Trevi Garden, Hartpury, nr
Gloucester
April 17 Thursday
Trevi Garden, Hartpury, nr
Gloucester
April 20 Sunday
Mill Dene, Blockley
Pigeon House, Southam, nr
Cheltenham
Stanway House, nr Winchcombe
Sudeley Castle Gardens,
Winchcombe

Trevi Garden, Hartpury, nr
Gloucester
Upton Wold, nr Moreton-in-Marsh
April 24 Thursday
Trevi Garden, Hartpury, nr
Gloucester
April 27 Sunday
Abbotswood, Stow-on-the-Wold
Blockley Gardens,
Moreton-in-Marsh
Brockweir Gardens, Chepstow
Lydney Park Gardens, Lydney
April 28 Monday
The Old Rectory, Duntisbourne
Rous, nr Cirencester
May
Cinderdine Cottage, Dymock, nr
Newent Every Tues & 1st &
3rd Suns
Ewen Manor nr Cirencester,
Weds, Thurs, Fris
Grove Cottage, Lower
Lydbrook, Cinderford. Every
Thurs
The Old Manor, Twyning,
Tewkesbury. Every Mon
except Bank Hols
Rodmarton Manor, nr
Cirencester. Every Sat
May 3 Saturday
Barnsley House, nr Cirencester
May 4 Sunday
Ampney Knowle, Barnsley, nr
Cirencester
Eastcombe, Bussage & Brownshill
Gardens
Ewen Manor, nr Cirencester
Green Cottage, Lydney
Hidcote Manor Garden, Chipping
Campden
Hodges Barn, nr Tetbury
Millend House, nr Newland,
Coleford
Trevi Garden, Hartpury, nr
Gloucester
May 5 Monday
Eastcombe, Bussage & Brownshill
Gardens
Millend House, nr Newland,
Coleford

Southrop Manor, nr Lechlade
Trevi Garden, Hartpury, nr
Gloucester

May 7 Wednesday
Lydney Park Gardens, Lydney

May 8 Thursday
Trevi Garden, Hartpury, nr
Gloucester

May 10 Saturday
Kiftsgate Court, nr Chipping
Campden

May 11 Sunday
Batsford Arboretum, nr
Moreton-in-Marsh
Cerney House Gardens, North
Cerney
Green Cottage, Lydney
Home Farm, Huntley, nr Newent
Snowshill Manor, nr Broadway

May 15 Thursday
Trevi Garden, Hartpury, nr
Gloucester

May 18 Sunday
Abbotswood, Stow-on-the-Wold
Green Cottage, Lydney
Mill Dene, Blockley
Millend House, nr Newland,
Coleford
Stowell Park, nr Northleach

May 21 Wednesday
Southrop Manor, nr Lechlade

May 22 Thursday
Trevi Garden, Hartpury, nr
Gloucester

May 25 Sunday
Boddington Manor, Boddington,
nr Cheltenham
Brockweir Gardens, Chepstow
Eastington Gardens, nr
Northleach
Millend House, nr Newland,
Coleford
The Red House, Staunton, nr
Gloucester
Trevi Garden, Hartpury, nr
Gloucester
Willow Lodge, nr Longhope,
Gloucester

May 26 Monday
Brackenbury, Coombe, nr
Wotton-under-Edge
Brockweir Gardens, Chepstow
Eastington Gardens, nr Northleach
Millend House, nr Newland,
Coleford
The Red House, Staunton, nr
Gloucester
Trevi Garden, Hartpury, nr
Gloucester
Willow Lodge, nr Longhope,
Gloucester

May 29 Thursday
Trevi Garden, Hartpury, nr
Gloucester

June
Cinderdine Cottage, Dymock, nr
Newent Every Tues & 1st &
3rd Suns
Ewen Manor, nr Cirencester.
Weds, Thurs, Fris
Grove Cottage, Lower Lydbrook,
Cinderford. Every Thurs
The Old Manor, Twyning,
Tewkesbury. Every Mon
Rodmarton Manor, nr
Cirencester. Every Sat

June 1 Sunday
Burnside, Prestbury
The Chestnuts, Minchinhampton
Green Cottage, Lydney
Pigeon House, Southam, nr
Cheltenham

June 4 Wednesday
Daylesford House, nr
Stow-on-the-Wold
Southrop Manor, nr Lechlade

June 7 Saturday
Barnsley House, nr Cirencester

June 8 Sunday
Green Cottage, Lydney
Home Farm, Huntley nr Newent
Hunts Court, North Nibley, nr
Dursley
Millend House, nr Newland,
Coleford
Pitt Court, North Nibley, Dursley
Tetbury Gardens
Trevi Garden, Hartpury, nr
Gloucester
Willow Lodge, nr Longhope,
Gloucester

June 9 Monday
The Old Rectory, Duntisbourne
Rous, nr Cirencester
Willow Lodge, nr Longhope,
Gloucester

June 11 Wednesday
Green Cottage, Lydney

June 12 Thursday
Church Cottage, Stinchcombe, nr
Dursley
Trevi Garden, Hartpury, nr
Gloucester

June 15 Sunday
25 Bowling Green Road,
Cirencester
Green Cottage, Lydney
Hillesley House, nr
Wotton-under-Edge
Hunts Court, North Nibley, nr
Dursley
13 Merestones Drive,
Cheltenham
Pitt Court, North Nibley, Dursley
The Red House, Staunton, nr
Gloucester

June 18 Wednesday
Green Cottage, Lydney

June 19 Thursday
Trevi Garden, Hartpury, nr
Gloucester

June 22 Sunday
Alderley Grange, Alderley
25 Bowling Green Road,
Cirencester
Grange Farm, Evenlode, nr
Moreton in Marsh
Green Cottage, Lydney
Humphrey's End House,
Randwick, nr Stroud
Hunts Court, North Nibley, nr
Dursley
Icomb Place, nr
Stow-on-the-Wold
Pitt Court, North Nibley, Dursley
20 St Peters Road, Cirencester
Southrop Manor, nr Lechlade
Sunningdale, nr
Westbury-on-Severn
Trevi Garden, Hartpury, nr
Gloucester
Upton Wold, nr Moreton-in-Marsh
Willow Lodge, nr Longhope,
Gloucester
Witcombe Gardens, nr Gloucester

June 23 Monday
Willow Lodge, nr Longhope,
Gloucester

June 23 to 28 Monday to
Saturday
The Old Chapel, nr Stroud

June 26 Thursday
Bourton House Garden,
Bourton-on-the-Hill
Trevi Garden, Hartpury, nr
Gloucester

June 28 Saturday
Ozleworth Park, nr
Wotton-under-Edge

June 29 Sunday
Beverston Gardens, nr Tetbury
Blockley Gardens,
Moreton-in-Marsh
Brackenbury, Coombe, nr
Wotton-under-Edge
Brockweir Gardens, Chepstow
Chalford Gardens, nr Stroud
Hullasey House, Tarlton, nr
Cirencester
Hunts Court, North Nibley, nr
Dursley
13 Merestones Drive, Cheltenham
Millend House, nr Newland,
Coleford
Misarden Park, Miserden, nr
Cirencester
Pitt Court, North Nibley, Dursley
Quenington Gardens, nr Fairford
Stanton Gardens, nr Broadway
Stowell Park, nr Northleach
Willow Lodge, nr Longhope,
Gloucester

June 30 Monday
Beverston Gardens, nr Tetbury
Willow Lodge, nr Longhope,
    Gloucester

July
Cinderdine Cottage, Dymock, nr
    Newent Every Tues & 1st &
    3rd Suns
Ewen Manor, nr Cirencester.
    Weds, Thurs, Fris until July 11
Grove Cottage, Lower Lydbrook,
    Cinderford. Every Thurs
The Old Manor, Twyning,
    Tewkesbury. Every Mon
Rodmarton Manor, nr Cirencester
    Every Sat

July 2 Wednesday
Moor Wood, Woodmancote, nr
    Cirencester

July 5 Saturday
Rockcliffe, nr Lower Swell

July 6 Sunday
25 Bowling Green Road,
    Cirencester
Broad Campden Gardens, nr
    Chipping Campden
The Bungalow, nr Newent
Hodges Barn, nr Tetbury
Hunts Court, North Nibley, nr
    Dursley
Rockcliffe, nr Lower Swell
20 St Peters Road, Cirencester
Sezincote, nr Moreton-in-Marsh
Willow Lodge, nr Longhope,
    Gloucester

July 7 Monday
Willow Lodge, nr Longhope,
    Gloucester

July 9 Wednesday
Rookwoods, Waterlane, nr Bisley

July 10 Thursday
Sunningdale, nr
    Westbury-on-Severn
Trevi Garden, Hartpury, nr
    Gloucester

July 13 Sunday
Bourton-on-the-Hill Gardens
Campden House, nr Chipping
    Campden
Hunts Court, North Nibley, nr
    Dursley
The Red House, Staunton, nr
    Gloucester
Stanway House, nr Winchcombe
Sunningdale, nr
    Westbury-on-Severn
Willow Lodge, nr Longhope,
    Gloucester

July 14 Monday
Willow Lodge, nr Longhope,
    Gloucester

July 16 Wednesday
Rookwoods, Waterlane, nr
    Bisley

July 17 Thursday
Church Cottage, Stinchcombe, nr
    Dursley
Trevi Garden, Hartpury, nr
    Gloucester

July 19 Saturday
Trevi Garden, Hartpury, nr
    Gloucester

July 20 Sunday
25 Bowling Green Road,
    Cirencester
Cowley Manor, nr Cheltenham
Trevi Garden, Hartpury, nr
    Gloucester

July 21 Monday
The Old Rectory, Duntisbourne
    Rous, nr Cirencester

July 24 Thursday
Trevi Garden, Hartpury, nr
    Gloucester

July 27 Sunday
25 Bowling Green Road,
    Cirencester
Brackenbury, Coombe, nr
    Wotton-under-Edge
Brockweir Gardens,
    Chepstow
Millend House, nr Newland,
    Coleford
Willow Lodge, nr Longhope,
    Gloucester

July 28 Monday
The Old Rectory,
    Duntisbourne Rous, nr
    Cirencester
Willow Lodge, nr Longhope,
    Gloucester

July 31 Thursday
Bourton House Garden,
    Bourton-on-the-Hill
Trevi Garden, Hartpury, nr
    Gloucester

August
Cinderdine Cottage, Dymock, nr
    Newent. Every Tues & 1st &
    3rd Suns
Grove Cottage, Lower Lydbrook,
    Cinderford. Every Thurs
The Old Manor, Twyning,
    Tewkesbury. Every Mon
    except Bank Hols
Rodmarton Manor, nr Cirencester
    Every Sat

August 3 Sunday
25 Bowling Green Road,
    Cirencester
Minchinhampton Gardens
Trevi Garden, Hartpury, nr
    Gloucester

August 4 Monday
Minchinhampton Gardens

August 7 Sunday
Sunningdale, nr
    Westbury-on-Severn

August 10 Sunday
Millend House, nr Newland,
    Coleford
Sunningdale, nr
    Westbury-on-Severn
Willow Lodge, nr Longhope,
    Gloucester

August 11 Monday
Willow Lodge, nr Longhope,
    Gloucester

August 14 Thursday
Trevi Garden, Hartpury, nr
    Gloucester

August 16 Saturday
Kiftsgate Court, nr Chipping
    Campden

August 17 Sunday
Westonbirt Gardens at
    Westonbirt School
Willow Lodge, nr Longhope,
    Gloucester

August 18 Monday
Willow Lodge, nr Longhope,
    Gloucester

August 21 Thursday
Trevi Garden, Hartpury, nr
    Gloucester

August 24 Sunday
Eastington Gardens, nr Northleach
Millend House, nr Newland,
    Coleford
Trevi Garden, Hartpury, nr
    Gloucester

August 25 Monday
Brackenbury, Coombe, nr
    Wotton-under-Edge
Eastington Gardens, nr Northleach
Millend House, nr Newland, Coleford
Trevi Garden, Hartpury, nr
    Gloucester

August 28 Thursday
Bourton House Garden,
    Bourton-on-the-Hill
Trevi Garden, Hartpury, nr
    Gloucester

August 31 Sunday
Brockweir Gardens, Chepstow

September
The Old Manor, Twyning,
    Tewkesbury. Every Mon

September 2 Tuesday
Cinderdine Cottage, Dymock nr
    Newent

September 4 Thursday
Sunningdale, nr
    Westbury-on-Severn

September 7 Sunday
Cinderdine Cottage, Dymock nr
    Newent
Park Farm, Alderley
Sunningdale, nr
    Westbury-on-Severn
Westbury Court Garden,
    Westbury-on-Severn

Westonbirt Gardens at
Westonbirt School

September 9 Tuesday
Cinderdine Cottage, Dymock, nr
Newent

September 11 Thursday
Trevi Garden, Hartpury, nr
Gloucester

September 14 Sunday
Green Cottage, Lydney
Sudeley Castle Gardens,
Winchcombe

September 16 Tuesday
Cinderdine Cottage, Dymock, nr
Newent

September 18 Thursday
Trevi Garden, Hartpury, nr
Gloucester

September 21 Sunday
Cowley Manor, nr Cheltenham
Green Cottage, Lydney

September 22 Monday
The Old Rectory, Duntisbourne
Rous, nr Cirencester

September 25 Thursday
Bourton House Garden,
Bourton-on-the-Hill
Cinderdine Cottage, Dymock, nr
Newent

September 28 Sunday
Laurel Cottage, Brockweir
Gardens, Chepstow

Green Cottage, Lydney
Sunningdale, nr
Westbury-on-Severn

October
The Old Manor, Twyning,
Tewkesbury. Every Mon.

October 5 Sunday
Painswick Rococo Garden,
Painswick

October 24 Thursday
Bourton House Garden,
Bourton-on-the-Hill

1998 February
Cinderdine Cottage, Dymock, nr
Newent. Tues 10, 17, Thurs 5,
12, 19, Suns 15, 22 (12-5)

Regular openings
For details see garden description

Barnsley House, nr Cirencester
Batsford Arboretum, nr
Moreton-in-Marsh
Bourton House Garden,
Bourton-on-the-Hill
Cerney House, North Cerney
Cinderdine Cottage, Dymock, nr
Newent
Cowley Manor, nr Cheltenham
Ewen Manor, nr Cirencester

Grove Cottage, Lower Lydbrook,
Cinderford
Hunts Court, North Nibley, nr Dursley
Kiftsgate Court, nr Chipping
Campden
Lydney Park Gardens, Lydney
Mill Dene, Blockley
Misarden Park, Miserden, nr
Cirencester
The Old Manor, Twyning,
Tewkesbury
Painswick Rococo Garden, Painswick
Rodmarton Manor, nr Cirencester
Sezincote, nr Moreton-in-Marsh
Stanway House, nr Winchcombe
Sudeley Castle Gardens,
Winchcombe
Trevi Garden, Hartpury, nr
Gloucester

By appointment only
*For telephone numbers and other
details see garden descriptions.
Private visits welcomed*

Amai Yume Teien, Blockley
Camp Cottage, Highleadon, nr
Newent
Cotswold Farm, Cirencester
Orchard Cottage, Gretton, nr
Winchcombe

DESCRIPTIONS OF GARDENS

Abbotswood (Dikler Farming Co) 1m W of Stow-on-the-Wold, nr Lower Swell. Several acres of massed plantings of spring bulbs, heathers, flowering shrubs and rhododendrons in dramatic, landscaped hillside stream gardens; fine herbaceous planting in elegant formal gardens with lily pond, terraced lawn and fountain created by Sir Edwin Lutyens. TEAS. Car park free. *Adm £2 Chd free. Suns April 27, May 18 (1.30-6)*

Alderley Grange ☘✗ (Mr Guy & the Hon Mrs Acloque) Alderley, 2m S of Wotton-under-Edge. Turn NW off A46, Bath-Stroud rd, at Dunkirk. Walled garden with fine trees, roses; herb gardens and aromatic plants. *Adm £2 Chd free. Sun June 22 (2-6). Private groups by written request welcome during June*

Amai Yume Teien (Garden of Sweet Dreams) ✗ (Mr Tim Brown) Blockley. On the Chipping Campden rd almost opp St Georges Hall and the School. A unique example of a Japanese kare sansui teien (dry landscape garden) set in the improbable context of an old Cotswold village. The garden is a small rectangle within a 25sq metre space bounded by two interesting types of Japanese fencing. It is crossed by rectilinear paths (an example of mino ishi) which create five sub-rectangles. Looks interesting in all weathers. *Adm £1 Chd 50p (Share to London Lesbian and Gay Switchboard®). Private visits welcome usually last Sun of each month, please* **Tel 01386 701026**

Ampney Knowle ✿ (Mr & Mrs Richard Pile) nr Cirencester. 4m NE Cirencester B4425 ¼m S of Barnsley on Ampney Crucis rd. Medium-sized garden, created by present owners, around C18 farmhouse with plant packed terrace; walled gardens, mixed borders with choice and less known plants and old shrub roses. Atmospheric woodland garden with indigenous wild flowers and 40-acre bluebell wood. TEAS in aid of Royal British Legion Women's Section. *Adm £2 Chd free. Sun May 4 (12-6). Private visits welcome, please* **Tel 01285 740230**

Ashley Manor ✿ (Mr & Mrs M J Hoskins) 3m NE of Tetbury on A433, turn R through Culkerton to Ashley. Old garden next to church redesigned by present owners and imaginatively planted. Mature yew hedges divide 4 separate gardens and are the backdrop to a collection of clematis, shrub roses and herbaceous plants. Kitchen garden. TEAS. *Adm £1.50 Chd free (Share to Ashley Church®). Sat March 29, Mon March 31 (2-5)*

■ **Barnsley House** ☘✗✿ (Mr Charles Verey) Barnsley 4m NE of Cirencester on B4425. Mature garden created and cared for by Rosmary Verey, with interesting collection of shrubs and trees; ground cover; herbaceous borders; pond garden; laburnum walk; knot and herb gardens; formal kitchen garden; C18 summer houses. C17 house (not open). *Adm £3 Chd free (no charge Dec and Jan). Mons, Weds, Thurs & Sats (10-6). Parties by appt only* **Tel 01285 740281.** *For NGS (Share to Barnsley Church®). Sats May 3, June 7 (2-6)*

■ **Batsford Arboretum** &※ (The Batsford Foundation Registered Charity No 286712) 1½m NW of Moreton-in-Marsh, off A44. Arboretum & wild gardens; over 1500 named trees (many rare) and shrubs; magnolias, flowering cherries, bulbs; beautiful views from Cotswold escarpment. House not open. TEAS at Garden Centre. *Adm £3 OAPs £2.50 Chd 11-15 £2 under 10 free. Open daily, March 1 to Nov 5 (10-5). For NGS Sun May 11 (2-5)*

Beverston Gardens ※ 2m W of Tetbury on A4135 rd to Dursley

Beverston Castle (Mrs L Rook) Overlooked by romantic C12-C15 castle ruin, the overflowingly planted paved terrace leads from C17 house across moat to sloping lawn with spring bulbs in abundance and full herbaceous and shrub borders. Large walled kitchen garden and greenhouses. TEAS June 29. *Adm £1.50 OAPs & Chd £1 (Share to Tetbury Hospital League of Friends®). Suns, Mons March 30 (2-6) 31 (11-6), June 29 (2-6), June 30 (11-6)*

Orchard Cottage ※※ (Mr & Mrs H L Pierce) On corner by memorial garden. ⅔-acre space used to the full with mixed borders, trees, shrubs, climbers, ferns and other shady plants, together with kitchen garden, wall and cordon fruit and herb interest in sheltered back garden. *Adm £1 Chd free. Sun, Mon June 29, 30 (2-6)*

Blockley Gardens ※※ NW of Moreton-in-Marsh. A44 Moreton-Broadway; turning E. Popular Cotswold hillside village with great variety of high quality gardens, some walking necessary and some gardens not safe for small children. TEAS at St George's Hall in aid of Blockley WI and Blockley Ladies Choir. *Combined adm £3 (single garden) £1 Chd free. Suns April 27, June 29 (2-6)*

Colebrook House

The Garage Garden (Mrs M Stuart-Turner) *Sun June 29 only*

Grange Cottage (Mrs J Moore) *Sun April 27 only*

Holly House (Simon Ford & Robert Ashby)

Malvern Mill (Mr & Mrs J Bourne)

Mill Dene (Mr & Mrs B S Dare) *For additional openings and full desc see main entry*

The Old Silk Mill (Mr & Mrs A Goodrick-Clarke) (Very dangerous for children.) *Sun June 29 only*

Pear Trees (Mrs J Beckwith)

Boddington Manor &※ (Robert Hitchins Ltd) Boddington 3m W of Cheltenham off the A4019 Cheltenham to Tewkesbury rd. After crossing the M5 motorway take first turning L which is signed to Boddington. Old garden sympathetically restored since 1985 incl wild flower woodland walk, mature specimen trees, extensive lawns and lakes; established Pinetum and bog garden. New planting of acers, birches, liquidambars, in meadow setting. Neogothic manor house (not open). 'Gardening with Nature Fair'. Cream TEAS in aid of Glos Macmillan Nurses. *Adm £1.50 Chd free. Sun May 25 (11-5)*

■ **Bourton House Garden** ※※ (Mr & Mrs R Paice) Bourton-on-the-Hill 2m W of Moreton-in-Marsh on A44. Intensively planted 3 acres with topiary, knot garden, potager, colour and herbaceous borders, water features and C16 Tithe Barn. Imaginative containers, vast range of unusual plants incl tender and half hardy; a plantsman's paradise. *Adm £2.50 Chd free. Every Thurs & Fri May 29*

to Oct 24. Also Bank hols Mon May 26, Mon Aug 25 (12-5). For NGS last Thurs of every month. May to Oct (12-5). Also in conjunction with **Bourton-on-the-Hill Gardens**. *Parties of 20 minimum welcome, please* Tel 01386 700121

Bourton-on-the-Hill Gardens ※※ 2m NW Moreton-in-Marsh A44 to Broadway. Wide selection of gardens of varied character in charming hillside village. Plant stall. TEAS (2-5). *Gardens adm £3 (including* **Bourton House** *as above) Chd free (Share to The Old School, Bourton®). Sun July 13 (1-6)*

¶**The Chantry** (Mr & Mrs T Martin)

Glebe House (Sir Peter & Lady Herbert)

Hillcrest (Mr & Mrs M Gaden)

Porch House (Mr & Mrs A Firth)

Springwood (Mr & Mrs D Storey)

Tawnies (Mr & Mrs P Hayes)

25 Bowling Green Road ※ (Fr John & Susan Beck) Cirencester. Take A417 to Gloucester just to traffic lights, cross or turn R into The Whiteway then 1st L to no 25 on R of rd bend. Please respect neighbours' driveways, no pavement parking. Uncontrollable enthusiasts' ever-growing semi-detached corner plot plant home. Wide range of perennials, daylilies, roses, geraniums, clematis etc. *Adm £1 Chd under 16 free. Suns June 15, 22, July 6, 20, 27, Aug 3 (2-5). Private visits welcome June to Aug, please* Tel 01285 653778

Brackenbury ※ (Mr & Mrs Peter Heaton) Coombe, 1m NE of Wotton-under-Edge. From Wotton Church ½m on Stroud rd B4058 turn R (signed Coombe); from Stroud on B4058, 300yds past Wotton-under-Edge sign turn L, (signed Coombe). Garden on R. ⅔-acre plantsman's terraced garden with multi-layer planting; foliage a special feature. Well stocked mixed borders, cottage garden, pool; 900 different hardy perennials and 200 different shrubs. Fruitcage, vegetables on deep-bed system. National Collection of Erigeron cultivars on show in June and July. Home-made TEAS. *Adm £1.50 Chd free (Share to Cotswold Care Hospice®). Mon May 26, Suns June 29, July 27, Mon Aug 25 (2-6)*

Broad Campden Gardens &※ 5m E of Broadway 1m SE of Chipping Campden. Big group of gardens of wide appeal and expertise: large and small, old and new, formal and informal, within picturesque popular village with meandering stream. Teas in aid of Village Hall. *Combined adm £3 or 80p each garden Chd free. Sun July 6 (2-6). Free car park. Coaches by appt only* Tel 01386 840467

The Angel House (Mr & Mrs Bill Boddington) Angel Lane

Briar Hill House (Sir Geoffrey and Lady Ellerton)

The Farthings (Mr & Mrs John Astbury)

Halfpenny Cottage (Mr & Mrs Kenneth Jones)

Hillside (Mr John Wilkinson)

The Malt House (Mr & Mrs Nick Brown)

Manor Barn (Mr Michael Miles & Mr Christopher Gurney) Angel Lane

Oldstones (Mr & Mrs H R Rolfe) Angel Lane

Pinders (Mr & Mrs Ian Dunnett)

Sharcomb Furlong (Mr & Mrs Basil Hasberry)

Vine Cottage (J Murray)

Withy Bank (Mr & Mrs Jim Allen)

¶**Wold Cottage** (Mr & Mrs James Jepson)

Wyldlands (Mr & Mrs John Wadey)

Brockweir Gardens ❀ (2m Tintern Abbey) From A466 Chepstow to Monmouth rd, cross R Wye to Brockweir, ¾m uphill take L turning to Coldharbour. TEAS in aid of Marie Curie Cancer Care and RSPCA at Laurel Cottage. *Adm £1 each garden. Suns March 30, April 27, May 25, June 29, July 27, Aug 31, Mons March 31, May 26 (2-6)*

    Laurel Cottage ও ✗ (David & Jean Taylor) Informal 1-acre cottage garden with lovely views over Offas Dyke. Dry stone walling creates gardens within a garden with lawns, herbaceous flowers and spring bulbs. Interesting selection of unusual shrubs and plants. *Also open Sept 28. Private visits welcome all year, please* **Tel 01291 689565**

    Threeways (Iorrie & Gwen Williams) Follow signs from A466 Brockweir Bridge or from B4228 at Hewelsfield Xrds: also on foot from Laurel Cottage. 2-acre garden with unusual shrubs and trees. Small woodland area, bog garden and stream. Formal area with water feature and well stocked herbaceous borders

¶**The Bungalow** ✗❀ (Mrs Sue Clive) Birches Lane off B4215, ½-way between Newent and Dymock, signposted Botloes Green and Pool Hill. The Bungalow is first on L on edge of Three Choirs Vineyard. Park in orchard. ½-acre garden created and maintained by professional working woman at weekends. Full of interest, incl 2 water features, sitting areas, pergolas and arches, formal and informal planting of herbaceous and wild flowers, herbs and fruit, merging into an orchard, with fine view over the Malvern Hills. *Adm £1.50 Chd free (Share to Downs Syndrome Assoc®). Sun July 6 (2-6)*

Burnside ❀ (Mr & Mrs John Anton-Smith) Prestbury. Burnside is 300yds E of B4632, up Mill Lane, in the village of Prestbury which is 3m NE of Cheltenham. 1½-acre working garden specialising in plant-breeding of hellebores, pulsatillas, geraniums, erodiums and other plants, and production of unusual herbaceous plants. Stock beds, large rockery, stream. *Adm £1 Chd free (Share to NCCPG Glos Group®). Sun June 1 (2-6). Private visits welcome, please* **Tel 01242 244645**

Camp Cottage ✗❀ (Les Holmes & Sean O'Neill) Highleadon, nr Newent. 6m NW of Gloucester. From Glos take A40 Ross rd, turn R onto B4215 Newent rd, 2½m along turn R at sign for Upleadon. The cottage is about 100yds up lane on L hand side. A much publicised plant lover's garden around C17 thatched cottage. About 1 acre overflowing with old roses, climbing plants, snowdrops, hellebores and many unusual plants from all over the world mostly grown from seed and cuttings. Pergola, arches and short shrubland walk. TEA. *Adm £1 Chd 50p. Due to long illness, no regular openings. Private visits welcome all year (2-5), please* **Tel 01452 790352**

Campden House ও❀ (Mr & Mrs Philip Smith) Chipping Campden. Drive entrance on Chipping Campden to Weston Subedge rd, about ¼m SW of Campden. 2-acre garden featuring mixed borders of plant and colour interest around Manor House and C17 Tithe Barn. Set in fine parkland in hidden valley. TEAS and plant stall in aid of Marie Curie Cancer Care. *Adm £1.50 Chd free. Sun July 13 (2-6)*

■ **Cerney House Gardens** ও✗❀ (Sir Michael & Lady Angus) North Cerney. 4m N of Cirencester on A435 Cheltenham rd. Turn L opp Bathurst Arms, past church to top of hill, pillared gates on R. Romantic walled garden filled with old-fashioned roses and herbaceous borders. There is a working kitchen garden with a scented garden and well-labelled herb garden. Spring bulbs in abundance all around the wooded grounds. TEAS. *Adm £2 Chd £1 (free on NGS day). Tues, Weds, Fris, Apr to Sept (2-6). For NGS Sun May 11 (2-6). Private visits welcome, please* **Tel 01285 831300**

Chalford Gardens ✗❀ 4m E of Stroud on A419 to Cirencester. Gardens are high above the Chalford Vale and reached on foot by steep climb from car park on main rd or from High St. *Combined adm £2.50 Chd free. Sun June 29 (2-6)*

    Marle Hill House (Mike & Leslie Doyle-Davidson) 1-acre newly reclaimed Victorian woodland garden, containing a number of interlinked secret, formal and natural areas on terraced hillside

    The Old Chapel (F J & F Owen) For description see separate entry. *Garden also open with Art Exhibition in studio Mon June 23 to Sat June 28 (10-5) Adm £2 (50% to NGS)*

    The Rock House (Mr & Mrs George Edwards) 1-acre, S facing old garden, recently reconstructed. Dramatic 40' cliff and cave provide backdrop for climbing roses, clematis, shrubbery, rockery, lawn and herbaceous borders. *Private visits welcome (May to July), please* **Tel 01453 886363**

The Chestnuts ✗❀ (Mr & Mrs E H Gwynn) Minchinhampton. From Nailsworth by Avening rd (B4014) L Weighbridge Inn ¼m up hill. From Minchinhampton 1m via New Rd or Well Hill. This peaceful ⅔-acre walled garden with lovely views offers an interesting mix of shrubs, bulbs, roses, clematis, rock garden, pool garden and wildflower lawn. ⅔-acre arboretum, with wide variety of unusual trees and shrubs. *Adm £1.50 Chd free (Share to Glos Wildlife Trust®). Sun June 1 (2-6)*

Church Cottage ✗❀ (Mr & Mrs David Leach) Stinchcombe. Off A38, 5m NW of Dursley. Peacefully situated next to the church. A plant lover's cottage garden of about ¼-acre planted since 1992 and still evolving. Good variety of hardy plants. Please use car park. *Adm £1 Chd free. Thurs June 12, July 17 (1.30-5.30). Private visits welcome, please* **Tel 01453 542116**

Cinderdine Cottage ও✗❀ (John & Daphne Chappell) Dymock. 3m NE of Newent. Off the B4215 just S of Dymock village signed Ryton/Ketford. Cottage ¾m on R of lane. ½-acre garden in the heart of daffodil country belonging to 2 plant-aholics. Combining the formal and informal, in a country garden for all seasons. Interesting and unusual snowdrop collection; hellebores, pulmonarias and a host of other spring flowering plants. Large colourful herbaceous borders summer and early autumn. TEA at Cinderdine Cottage. Refreshments at Three Choirs Vineyard 5 minutes away. *Adm £1 Chd free (Share to St Mary's Church, Dymock®). Thurs Feb 6, 13, 20, Tues Feb 11, 18, Sun Feb 16 every Tues March 4 to Sept 16, Suns March 2, 16, April 6, 20, May 4, 18 June 1, 15, July 6, 20, Aug 3, 17, Sept 7, 21, (12-5) 1998, Feb Tues, 10, 17, Thurs 5, 12, 19, Suns 15, 22 (12-5). Private parties welcome Feb to Sept, please Tel 01531 890265*

Cotswold Farm ✗ (Major & Mrs P D Birchall) 5m N of Cirencester on A417; signed immediately W of Five Mile House Inn and before Centurian Garage. Cotswold garden in lovely position on different levels with a terrace designed by Norman Jewson in 1938; shrubs and trees, mixed borders, alpine border, shrub roses. *Adm £2 Chd free. Private parties welcome by appt with adequate notice, please Tel 01285 653856*

■ **Cowley Manor** ❀ Cowley, nr Cheltenham. SE of Cheltenham off A435. 50 acres of Victorian landscaped grounds with lakes and Italianate terraces and cascade (awaiting restoration) provide a setting for innovatory herbaceous planting by Noël Kingsbury inspired by contemporary German and Dutch design. Lakeside walk. 2nd yr of a garden returning to life after a period of neglect. No dogs at weekends. TEAS in aid of Alzheimers Disease Society. *Adm £2.50 Chd free. Every day except Mon & Fri from March 1 to Oct 30. For NGS Suns July 20, Sept 21 (2-6)*

Daylesford House ♿✗ (Sir Anthony & Lady Bamford) Daylesford. Between Stow-on-the-Wold and Chipping Norton off A436. Magnificent lakeside and wooded walks amidst unusual shrubs and trees and massed bluebells. Large decorative formal fruit and vegetable walled garden with orchid house, peach house and working glasshouses. Trellised rose garden on raised terrace. Grounds immed around Grade 1 house not open. Visitors should note that this is a very large garden with substantial distances to be walked. *Adm £3 Chd free (Share to Marie Curie Cancer Care® and Katharine House Hospice®). Wed June 4 (2-5.30). No coach parties NGS days. Private visits welcome, please contact Secretary, Daylesford House GL56 0YH*

Eastcombe, Bussage & Brownshill Gardens 3m E Stroud. 2m N of A419 Stroud to Cirencester on turning signposted to Bisley and Eastcombe. Cream Teas at Eastcombe Village Hall. *Combined adm £2.75 Chd free (Share to Glos Macmillan Cancer Service®, and Cotswold Care Day Hospice®). Sun, Mon May 4, 5 (2-6)*
Eastcombe:
  Brewers Cottage ♿ (Mr & Mrs T G N Carter) Hillside garden with laburnum covered pergola, shady & sunny borders and a small hidden courtyard
  18 Farmcote Close ♿ (Mr & Mrs K Chalmers) Small garden planned for retirement
  21 Farmcote Close ♿❀ (Mr & Mrs R Bryant) Nearly 350 varieties of interesting perennials, bulbs, shrubs and old roses on various colour themes. Espalier fruit
  Fidges Hill House (Mr & Mrs R Lewis) Secluded and lovely view. No car access, please park in village. Steep descent

Highlands (Mr & Mrs J Page) Small, tranquil and colourful cottage garden
Jasmine Cottage (Mr & Mrs K Hopkins) Cottage garden with view of the beautiful Toadsmoor valley
Vatch Rise ♿❀ (Mr & Mrs R G Abbott) Interesting collection of bulbous plants, alpines and unusual perennials. A real plantsman's garden
Brownshill:
  Beechcroft ♿ (Mr & Mrs R H Salt) Mature trees, shrubs, borders, vegetables, fruit, conservatory and wild area
  Bovey End (Sir Norman & Lady Wakefield) A large, informal garden sloping steeply; many trees and shrubs
Bussage:
  Pine Corner (Mr & Mrs W Burns-Brown) ¾-acre terraced garden. Spring bulbs, shrubs, alpines; kitchen & herb garden
  Redwood ❀ (Mr & Mrs D F Collins) Terraced garden with 3 small ponds and many unusual plants. Vegetables and cordon fruit trees. Hundreds of plants for sale. *Private visits welcome April to July, please Tel 01453 882595*
  Spindrift, The Ridge ♿ (Mr & Mrs B Wilson) Small garden on housing estate devoted largely to plant breeding experiments incl a foxglove mutation

Eastington Gardens 1m SE of Northleach (A40). Charming Cotswold village with lovely views. 3 gardens of traditional appeal. TEAS at **Middle End**. *Combined adm £1.50 Chd free (Share to Northleach Church Fund®). Suns, Mons May 25, 26, Aug 24, 25 (2-6)*
  Bank Cottage (Mr & Mrs E S Holland) Lower End
  Middle End (Mr & Mrs Owen Slatter)
  Yew Tree Cottage (Mr M Bottone)

■ **Ewen Manor** ♿❀ (Lady Gibbs) 4m S of Cirencester via A429 3m from Cirencester turn at signpost Ewen 1m. Profusely planted series of gardens with architectural features, yew hedges, pattern mown lawn, terrace and containers, lily pool, cedar trees over 200yrs old and woodland area all around. Georgian Cotswold manor (not open). TEAS Sun only. *Adm £2 Chd free. Weds, Thurs, Fris May 5 to July 12 (11-4.30) (Share to NGS®). For NGS Sun May 4 (Share to Cotswold Care Hospice®) (12-6). Private visits welcome, please Tel 01285 770206*

Grange Farm ✗ (Lady Aird) Evenlode, nr Moreton in Marsh. Evenlode 3m from Moreton-in-Marsh and Stow-on-the-Wold. E of the A429 Fosseway and 1½m from Broadwell. This medium-sized atmospheric garden continues to be developed and the C17 rose-covered house and ancient apple trees provide a wonderful setting for the water garden, wide lawns, grass steps and extensive plantings. Lots of places to sit, vegetable patch and croquet. TEAS. *Adm £2 Chd free (Share to Evenlode Church®). Sun June 22 (11-6)*

Green Cottage ♿❀ (Mr & Mrs F Baber) Approaching Lydney from Gloucester DO NOT TAKE BYPASS, keep to A48 through the town. Leaving Lydney turn R into narrow lane, just after desrestriction sign. Garden 50yds on R. Shady car park. Informal country garden of approx 1 acre with planted stream bank, hostas, hellebores, iris and cottage garden. Many herbaceous paeonies, incl National Reference Collection of pre and early post 1900 cultivars in June. Hellebores at their best in March, paeonies May,

June. Large clematis montana rubens in May. *Adm £1.50 Chd free (Share to Multiple Sclerosis Research Charitable Trust®). Suns March 2, 9, 16, 23, 30 (1-4), May 4, 11, 18, June 1, 8, 15, 22, Sept 14, 21, 28, (2-6) Weds June 11, 18 (11-5). Private visits for parties in June, please* Tel **01594 841918**

Grove Cottage ⚘❀ (Graham Birkin & Allan Thomas) Forge Hill, Lower Lydbrook. 5m NW of Cinderford. Opp 'Jovial Colliers' Inn in Upper Lydbrook follow sign to Joys Green; after ¾m turn L into Forge Hill. Very steep 2-acre garden with glorious views over Wye valley. Packed with woodland and shade tolerant plants growing in raised beds, peat beds, shrub and herbaceous borders; large rockery. Extensive collections of rare N American woodland plants, irises and over 1000 hellebores. Many steps and steep paths. Not suitable for small children. TEA. *Adm £1 Chd 50p. Thurs March 6 to Aug 28 (2-6). Private visits welcome, please* Tel **01594 860544**

▲**Hidcote Manor Garden** ⚘❀ (The National Trust) 4m NE of Chipping Campden. Series of formal gardens, many enclosed within superb hedges, incl hornbeam on stems. Many rare trees, shrubs, plants. Coffee, lunches and teas. *Adm £5.30 Chd £2.60. For NGS Sun May 4 (11-6)*

Hillesley House ❀ (Mr & Mrs J Walsh) Hillesley. 3m from Wotton-under-Edge on rd to Hawkesbury Upton and the A46. Recently revived garden in 4 acres surrounding Tudor house (not open); walled garden, borders in sun and shade, roses. Innovative perennial plantings by Noël Kingsbury offer interesting ideas. TEAS. *Adm £2 Chd free. Sun June 15 (2-6)*

Hodges Barn ♿❀ (Mrs C N Hornby) Shipton Moyne 3m S of Tetbury on Malmesbury side of village. Very unusual C15 dovecot converted into a family home. Cotswold stone walls act as host to climbing and rambling roses, clematis, vines and hydrangeas; and together with yew, rose and tapestry hedges they create the formality of the area around the house; mixed shrub and herbaceous borders, shrub roses and a water garden; woodland garden planted with cherries, magnolias and spring bulbs. Featured in RHS 'The Garden' May 1996. *Adm £2.50 Chd free. Mons, Tues, Fris April 1 to Aug 19 (2-5). For NGS Suns May 4, July 6 (2-6). Adjoining garden of Hodges Farmhouse also open for NGS by kind permission of Mrs Clive Lamb*

Home Farm (Mrs T Freeman) Huntley. On the B4216 ½m from the A40 in Huntley travelling towards Newent. Set in elevated position with exceptional views. 1m walk through woods and fields to show carpets of spring flowers. Waterproof footwear advisable. *Adm £1.50 Chd free. Suns Feb 2, March 2, April 6, May 11, June 8 (2-5). Private visits welcome for parties of 2 and over, please* Tel **01452 830209**

Hullasey House ⚘❀ (Jonathan & Gail Taylor) Tarlton. Midway between Cirencester and Tetbury off A433. Newly created 2½-acre garden with exceptional views. Stone walls, many old roses, gravel gardens round the house. Walled herb and fruit potager; walled mixed shrub/herbaceous garden. *Adm £2 Chd free (Share to Tarlton Church®). Sun June 29 (2-6)*

Humphreys End House ⚘❀ (Mr & Mrs J W A Hutton) Randwick 2m W of Stroud, signed at Cainscross (White Horse Inn) off A419 (toward M5 junction 13). Different areas of contrasting mood and interesting planting in 1-acre garden surrounding listed C16 farmhouse. Wildlife pond, herbs, old roses, grasses. Organic vegetable garden. TEAS. *Adm £1.50 Chd free. Sun June 22 (2-6). Private visits welcome on Fris in May, June, July, please,* Tel **01453 765401**

■ **Hunts Court** ♿⚘❀ (Mr & Mrs T K Marshall) North Nibley, Dursley. 2m NW of Wotton-under-Edge. From Wotton B4060 Dursley rd turn R in Nibley at Black Horse; fork L after ¼m. Unusual shrubs, 450 varieties old roses, large collection of penstemons in peaceful 2½-acre garden with lawns set against tree clad hills and Tyndale monument. Superb views. House (not open) possible birth place of William Tyndale. Picnic area. Home-made TEAS (Suns only). *Adm £1.50 Chd free (Share to The Royal National Rose Soc®). Garden and Nursery open Tues-Sat all year ex Aug; also Bank Hol Mons, May 5, 26. For NGS Suns June 8, 15, 22, 29; July 6, 13 (2-6); Private visits welcome, please* Tel **01453 547440**

Icomb Place ⚘ (Mr & Mrs T L F Royle) 4m S of Stow-on-the-Wold; after 2m on A424 Burford rd turn L to Icomb village. 100-year-old sizeable garden extensively restored. Featuring woodland walk through mature & young trees in arboretum; rhododendrons & azaleas; grotto; pools, stream and water garden; parterre; lawned garden with extensive views. C14 manor house (not open). TEAS. *Adm £2 Chd £1 (Share to Deus Laudamus Trust®). Sun June 22 (2-6)*

■ **Kiftsgate Court** ⚘❀ (Mr & Mrs J G Chambers) 3m NE of Chipping Campden, adjacent to Hidcote Nat Trust Garden. 1m E of A46 and B4081. Magnificent situation and views; many unusual plants and shrubs; tree paeonies, hydrangeas, abutilons, species and old-fashioned roses, inc largest rose in England, R.filipes Kiftsgate. TEAS (April 28 to Sept 1). Lunches June and July. Buses by appt. *Adm £3.50 June, July. £3 April, May, Aug, Sept Chd £1. Suns, Weds, Thurs & Bank Hols Mons April 2 to Sept 28 (2-6). Also Suns, Weds, Thurs, Sats in June & July (12-6). For NGS (Share to Sue Ryder Home, Leckhampton Court®) Sats May 10, Aug 16, (2-6).* Tel **01386 438777**

■ **Lydney Park Gardens** ❀ (Viscount Bledisloe) Lydney. On A48 Gloucester-Chepstow rd between Lydney & Aylburton. Drive is directly off A48. 8 acres of extensive valley garden with many varieties of rhododendron, azaleas and other flowering shrubs; trees and lakes. Garden round house; magnolias and daffodils (April). Roman Temple Site and Museum. Deer park with fine trees. TEAS; also picnic area (in park). *Adm £2.20 Weds £1.20 (Acc chd & cars free). Easter Sun & Mon; Every Sun, Wed & Bank Hol from Sun March 30 to June 8. Every day May 25 to June 1 (11-6). For NGS Sun April 27, Wed May 7 (11-6).* Tel **01594 842844**

13 Merestones Drive ⚘❀ (Mr Dennis Moorcraft) Cheltenham. Merestones Drive is a turning off The Park reached by following signs to Gloscat (a technical college). Nearest main rd is A46 from Stroud. Small town garden shaded by large trees; hostas and ferns a speciality;

many unusual plants; scree garden; small brook. Limited parking. TEAS. *Adm £1.50 Chd 50p. Suns June 15, 29 (2-6). Private visits welcome, please* **Tel 01242 578678**

■ **Mill Dene,** Blockley ⌀❀ (Mr & Mrs B S Dare) School Lane. Limited parking. From A44, Bourton-on-the-Hill, take the turn to Blockley. 1m down hill turn L behind 30mph sign, labelled cul de sac. 2½-acre garden with steep lawned terraces, stream and mill-pool in a frost pocket. Vegetable potager; grotto and trompe l'oeil. Dangerous for young children. Home-made TEAS. *Adm £2 Chd 50p. Open every Mon and Fri (2-5.30) April 4 to Sept 29 and Bank Hols. For NGS Sun April 20, May 18 (2-5.30). Also open with* **Blockley Gardens**: *Combined adm £3 Chd free. Suns April 27, June 29. Private visits welcome all yr please* **Tel 01386 700457**

Millend House ❀ (Mr & Mrs J D'A Tremlett) Coleford. 1½m SW out of Coleford on the Newland rd, centre of Coleford clocktower signposted (Newland 2m). Magnificently located; the 2-acre hillside garden contains many unusual herbaceous plants and shrubs, both shade and sun loving, many of which are for sale. There are also scree and fern beds, a gazebo, ornamental pond, small vegetable and soft fruit garden, and a walk round a 200yr-old wood. TEAS in aid of Glos Macmillan Nurses. *Adm £1.50 Chd free. Suns, Mons, May 4, 5, 18, 25, 26; June 8, 29, July 27; Aug 10, 24, 25 (2-6). Private groups welcome May 1 to Sept 30, please* **Tel 01594 832128**

Minchinhampton Gardens ⌀⌀❀ Minchinhampton 4m SE Stroud. From Market Sq down High St 100yds; then R at Xrds; 300yds turn L. Cream TEAS except Feb TEA in aid of Minchinhampton Centre for the Elderly. *Combined adm £2 Chd free. Suns Feb 16, April 6, Aug 3, Mon Aug 4 (11-4.30)*

    Lammas Park (Mr & Mrs P Grover) Lawns, herbaceous borders, wild garden, restored 'hanging gardens'

    St Francis (Mr & Mrs Peter Falconer) Garden made in old park round modern Cotswold stone house. Fine beech avenue; terraced garden; trough gardens; bonsai trees; unusual plants; giant snowdrops (spring); C18 ice-house. Picnickers welcome. *Also private visits welcome, please* **Tel 01453 882188**

■ **Misarden Park** ⌀⌀❀ (Maj M T N H Wills) Miserden 6m NW of Circencester. Follow the signs off the A417 or B4070 from Stroud. Spring flowers, shrubs, fine topiary (some designed by Sir Edwin Lutyens) and herbaceous borders within a walled garden; roses; fine specimen trees; C17 manor house (not open) standing high overlooking Golden Valley. Garden Nurseries open daily except Mons. TEAS in aid of Miserden School PTA. *Adm £2.50 Chd free. April 1 to Sept 25 every Tues, Wed & Thurs (9.30-4.30). For NGS (Share to Rose 2000 Appeal®). Suns April 6, June 29 (2-6).* **Tel 01285 821303**

Moor Wood ⌀ (Mr & Mrs Henry Robinson) Woodmancote. 3½m from Circencester turn L off A435 to Cheltenham at North Cerney signed 'Woodmancote 1¼m': entrance in village on L beside lodge with white gates. 2 acres of shrub, orchard and wildflower gardens in isolated valley setting. Holder of the National Collection of rambler roses. TEA. *Adm £2 Chd free. Wed July 2 (2-6). Private visits, please* **Tel 01285 831397**

The Old Chapel ⌀ (F J & F Owen) 4m E of Stroud on A419 to Cirencester. Above Chalford Vale, steep climb from car park on main rd, up Marle Hill. 1-acre Victorian chapel garden on precipitous hillside. A tiered tapestry of herbaceous borders, formal potager, small orchard, pond and summer house, old roses. Gothic pergola and rose tunnel, many unusual plants all laid out on terraced S-facing Marle Cliff. Garden open with Art Exhibition in studio. *Adm £2 Chd free (50% to NGS). Mon to Sat June 23 to 28 (10-5). Also in conjunction with* **Chalford Gardens** *Sun June 29 (2-6)*

The Old Manor ⌀⌀❀ (Mrs Joan Wilder) Twyning. 3m N of Tewkesbury via A38 to Worcester; follow sign to Twyning; garden opposite T-junction at top end of village. 2-acre walled garden. Unusual shrubs, trees, herbaceous, alpines; two areas of developing arboretum; sunken garden; terrace plantings; troughs. Field walks for picnics. Small nursery, all stock from garden (catalogue 30p and large SAE). *Adm £1.50 Acc chd free (Share to GRBS® & RGOF®). Every Mon (except Bank Hols) March to Oct (2-5, or dusk if earlier) Private visits welcome by appt except Suns incl winter months, please* **Tel 01684 293516** *evenings*

The Old Rectory, Duntisbourne Rous ⌀ (Charles & Mary Keen) NW of Cirencester at Daglingworth take valley rd for the Duntisbournes. After ½m no through valley rd joins from R at entrance to Old Rectory. Writer and designer's own 1½-acre Cotswold family garden in the making, now in its 5th yr. Featured in recent book, Gardens Illustrated and The Times. Beautiful setting nr Saxon church. Planted for atmosphere and all-yr-interest, this small garden has ten distinct areas and moods. Winter flowers, tender plants and unusual pelargoniums a speciality. *Adm £2 Chd free. Mons Feb 24, March 24, April 28 (11-3), June 9, July 21, 28, Sept 22 (11-5). Private visits for groups by WRITTEN appt only welcome. Charges negotiable*

Orchard Cottage, Gretton ⌀ (Mr Rory Stuart) 2m N of Winchcombe. Up Duglinch Lane beside Bugatti Inn. Approx 300yds up lane turn R after magnolia grandiflora. Approx 1½-acres. Romantically overplanted, owner-maintained garden, created largely by the late Mrs Nancy Saunders. Always some interest. Teas in Winchcombe. *Adm £1.50 Open all year. Private visits welcome, please* **Tel 01242 602491**

¶**Ozleworth Park** ⌀ (Mr & Mrs M J C Stone) Wotton-under-Edge. Approach from A4135 Tetbury to Dursley rd (Dursley approx 5m). At the junction of A4135 and B4058, turn S on the single track lane signposted Ozleworth. Follow signs for Ozleworth on this lane for approx 2m until reaching new gates with eagles on gate posts. Follow signs down drive. Recently renovated over the past 5 yrs. Approx 10 acres with rose garden, Victorian Bath House, lily ponds, a small lake; also glasshouses, an orchard and vegetable area. TEA. *Adm £2 Chd under 16 free. Sat June 28 (2-5)*

■ **Painswick Rococo Garden** ❀ (Painswick Rococo Garden Trust Reg No 299792) ½m outside village on B4073. Unique C18 garden from the brief Rococo period combining contemporary buildings, vistas, ponds, kitchen garden and winding woodland walks. Coach House restaurant for coffee, lunches. 'Present Collection' shop. *Adm £2.90 OAP £2.60 Chd £1.50. Jan 8 to Nov 30. Weds to Suns and Bank Hol. July and Aug daily. Restaurant open Weds to Suns (11-5). For NGS Suns April 6, Oct 5 (11-5)* **Tel 01452 813 204**

Park Farm ♿✻ (Mr & Mrs A J V Shepherd) Alderley. 1½m S from Wotton-under-Edge, just before village. The lake with its waterside plants and large Koi carp is the pivotal attraction in a scenically designed 2½-acre garden also offering maturing herbaceous borders, young trees and a new rose garden. TEAS in aid of Alderley Church Fund. *Adm £1.50 Chd 50p. Sun Sept 7 (2- 6)*

Pigeon House ✻❀ (Mr & Mrs Julian Taylor) Southam Lane, Southam. 3m from Cheltenham off B4632 toward Winchcombe. Revitalised 2-acre garden surrounding C14 manor house. Small lake and bubbling water garden with fish and bog plants. Wide range of flowering shrubs and borders designed to create multitude of vistas and plant interest. TEAS in aid of Southam Church of the Ascension. *Adm £1.50 Chd free. Suns April 20, June 1 (2-6)*

Pitt Court ♿✻❀ (Mr & Mrs M W Hall) North Nibley. Turn off the B4060 at North Nibley past the Black Horse Inn into Barrs Lane. Continue for approx ¾m. A small garden of about ⅓ acre, making interesting and ingenious use of paving, stones and brick for walls, steps and beds as settings for increasing collection of smaller trees, conifers, shrubs and herbaceous plants. Separate lawn and alpine area. Limited car parking. Teas at **Hunts Court** open nearby with plenty of parking (½m). *Adm £1 Chd free. Suns June 8, 15, 22, 29 (2-6)*

Quenington Gardens ♿✻❀ 2m N of Fairford, E of Cirencester. Peaceful Cotswold riverside village with church renowned for Norman doorways. 7 welcoming gardens offer wide range of style, content and character. TEAS in aid of The Home Farm Trust at **The Old Rectory**. *Combined adm £2.50 Chd free. Sun June 29 (2-6)*
  Apple Tree Cottage (Mrs P Butler-Henderson)
  Court Farm (Mr & Mrs Frank Gollins)
  Mawley Field (Mr & Mrs N Collins)
  Old Post House (Mrs D Blackwood)
  The Old Rectory (Mr & Mrs David Abel-Smith)
  Pool Hay (Mr & Mrs A W Morris)
  ¶**Yew Tree Cottages** (A Watson & J Lindon)

The Red House ♿❀ (Mr & Mrs W K Turner) Pillows Green, Staunton, 8m NW of Gloucester on A417; from Staunton Xrds ½m off B4208. Split level 2 acre organic and wildlife garden with herbaceous borders; rockery and terrace with containers; parterre; also flower meadow. C17 House open by appt. Garden designed and maintained by owners. All plants for sale grown from garden stock. TEA. *Adm £1.50 Chd free (Share to Glos Wildlife Trust®). Sun, Mon May 25, 26; Suns June 15, July 13 (2-6). Private visits welcome, please* **Tel 01452 840505**

Rockcliffe ✻❀ (Mr & Mrs Simon Keswick) nr Lower Swell. On B4068. From Stow-on-the-Wold turn R into drive 1½m from Lower Swell. 5-acre garden incl herbaceous borders, pink and white and blue gardens, rose terrace, walled kitchen garden and orchard. TEAS in aid of

St Peters Church, Upper Slaughter. *Adm £2 Chd under 15 free. Sat, Sun July 5, 6 (10-6)*

●**Rodmarton Manor** ♿✻ (Mr & Mrs Simon Biddulph) Between Cirencester and Tetbury off A433. The 8-acre garden of this fine Arts and Crafts house is a series of 'outdoor rooms' each with its own distinctive character. Leisure garden, winter garden, troughery, topiary, hedges, lawns, rockery, containers, wild garden, kitchen garden; recently replanted herbaceous borders. *Adm £2 Sats, £2.50 any other time (Share to NGS®) Acc chd free. Every Sat May 17 to Aug 30 (2-5). Private visits welcome, please* **Tel 01285 841253**

Rookwoods ✻ (Mr & Mrs R Luard) Waterlane, 5m E of Stroud. Between Sapperton and Bisley. Turn down 'No Through Rd' in Waterlane then follow signs. 3-acre well structured garden with herbaceous borders to colour themes. Pleached Whitebeam around pool area. Wide variety of old-fashioned and modern climbing and shrub roses (labelled), water gardens and outstanding views. TEAS. *Adm £1.50 Chd free. Weds July 9, 16 (2-6). Coaches by appt. Private visits welcome May and July, please* **Tel 01452 770747**

20 St Peters Road ✻❀ (Meg & Jeff Blumson) Cirencester. Off Cricklade St. turn R into Ashcroft Rd then L then R. Small town garden entirely remade without grass; herbaceous, clematis, rockery, pond. Intensively planted for yr-round appeal. *Adm £1 Chd free. Suns June 22, July 6 (2-5.30). Private visits welcome, please* **Tel 01285 657696**

■ **Sezincote** ✻ (Mr & Mrs David Peake) 1½m SW of Moreton-in-Marsh. Turn W along A44 towards Evesham; after 1½m (just before Bourton-on-the-Hill) take turn L, by stone lodge with white gate. Exotic oriental water garden by Repton and Daniell with lake, pools and meandering stream, banked with massed perennial plants of interest. Large semi-circular orangery, formal Indian garden, fountain, temple and unusual trees of vast size in lawn and wooded park setting. House in Indian manner designed by Samuel Pepys Cockerell was inspiration for Brighton Pavilion. TEAS (NGS day only). *Adm £3 Chd £1 under 5 free. Open every Thurs Fri & Bank Hols (except Dec) (2-6). For NGS Sun July 6 (2-6)*

▲**Snowshill Manor** ✻ (The National Trust) 3m SW of Broadway. Small terraced garden in which organic and natural methods only are used. Highlights include tranquil ponds, old roses, old-fashioned flowers and herbaceous borders rich in plants of special interest. House contains collections of fine craftmanship incl musical instruments, clocks, toys, bicycles. Ticket office, restaurant and shop open 12 noon. TEAS. *Adm house & gdn £5.40 Chd £2.70 Garden only £2, Chd £1. Family ticket £13.50. For NGS Sun May 11 (12-5)*

¶**Southrop Manor** ♿✻❀ (Mr & Mrs G MacEchern) 3m N of Lechlade, 2m E of Fairford off A417, or 2m W off A361 before Lechlade. Large riverside garden enjoying a new period of revitalisation and replanting. Of special interest is a formal stew pond garden, lime avenue and yew hedges, informal soft-coloured borders (clematis, roses abound) and a small walled garden of herbs, box hedging, roses and unusual flowers. Also woodland, spring bulbs and sweeping lawns. Redevelopment still in progress. *Adm £2 Chd free. Mon May 5, Weds May 21, June 4, Sun June 22 (2-6). Parties by appt during May and June*

Stanton Gardens ⅃🌳 Broadway. One of the most picturesque and unspoilt C17 Cotswold villages with many gardens to explore (24 open in 1996) ranging from charming cottage to large formal gardens of appeal to visitors of all tastes. Plant stall. Car park free. TEAS from 3-5.30. *Adm £2.50 Chd free £2 for pre-booked parties of 10 or more, please* **Tel 01386 584212** *(Share to Stanton Church®). Sun June 29 (2-6)*

■ **Stanway House** (Lord Neidpath) 1m E of B4632 Cheltenham-Broadway rd on B4077 Toddington to Stow-on-the-Wold rd. 20 acres of planted landscape in early C18 formal setting. Arboretum, historic pleasure grounds with specimen trees incl pinetum; remains of ornamental canal and cascade; chestnut and oak avenue; folly. Striking C16 manor with gatehouse, tithe barn and church. Tea at The Bakehouse, Stanway. *Adm grounds only £1 Chd 50p; House and grounds £3.50 OAPs £3 Chd £1. Also house open Tues & Thurs June to Sept (2-5). For NGS (Share to The Garden History Society®) Suns April 20, July 13 (2-5).* **Tel 01386 584469**

Stowell Park ⅃🌳🌳 (The Lord & Lady Vestey) 2m SW of Northleach. Off Fosseway A429. Large garden, lawned terraces with magnificent views over the Coln Valley. Fine collection of old-fashioned roses and herbaceous plants, with a pleached lime approach to the House. Two large walled gardens contain vegetables, fruit, cut flowers and ranges of greenhouses, also a long rose pergola and wide, plant-filled borders divided into colour sections. House (not open) originally C14 with later additions. TEAS. Plant sales May 18 only. *Adm £2 Chd free (Share to St Johns Ambulance Brigade® and Royal British Legion®). Suns May 18, June 29 (2-5)*

■ **Sudeley Castle Gardens** 🌳 (Lord and Lady Ashcombe) Winchcombe. The 8 individual gardens around C15 Castle incl the Queen's Garden, with old-fashioned roses, perennials, herbs, Tudor Knot Garden with water features and recently opened Victorian Kitchen garden. Also formal pools, spring bulbs and fine trees in extensive grounds. Specialist plant centre. Restaurant. *Adm gardens and Emma Dent exhibition £4 OAPs £3.20 Chd £1.80. Open daily March 1 to 21 (10.30-4.30) March 22 to Oct 31 (10.30-5.30). For NGS Suns April 20, Sept 14 (10.30-5.30). TEAS. Group tours of gardens can be booked please,* **Tel 01242 602308**

Remember that every time you visit a National Gardens Scheme garden you are helping to raise money for the following:

**The Queen's Nursing Institute
The Nurses' Welfare Service
Cancer Relief Macmillan Fund
The Gardens Fund of the National Trust
The Gardeners' Royal Benevolent Society
The Royal Gardeners' Orphan Fund**

Sunningdale ⅃🌳🌳 (Mr J Mann Taylor) Grange Court 2m NE of Westbury-on-Severn. Turn off A48 in Chaxhill. [OS map ref. SO727 164]. ¾-acre paradise or paradox; paragon or pastiche? Why not pop in and perambulate through plants with personality and phlomis with pedigrees propagated for you. Pictures proliferate with perspectives that penetrate the perimeter. A plethora of pleasures predominate. Don't procrastinate. No password required. (The National collection of phlomis should be at its best in June/July). Teas in Westbury. *Adm £1.50 Chd 50p. Suns June 22, July 13, Aug 10, Sept 7, 28; Thurs July 10, Aug 7, Sept 4 (2-5). Private visits welcome, please* **Tel 01452 760268**

Tetbury Gardens, Tetbury. *Combined adm £2.50 Chd free. Sun June 8 (2-6)*

   The Chipping Croft 🌳 (Dr & Mrs P W Taylor) At bottom of Chipping Hill approached from market place. 2-acre, secluded, walled town garden on three levels, with mature trees, shrubs, herbaceous borders, rose beds and unusual plants; spring blossom and bulbs. A series of formal gardens, incl fruit and vegetable/flower potager all informally planted; also a water garden. C17 Cotswold house (not open). TEAS in aid of Action Research. *Private visits by arrangement welcome, please* **Tel 01666 503570**

   The Old Stables (Brigadier and Mrs J M Neilson) Enter New Church St B3124 from Long St at Xrds signed to Stroud and Dursley. Turn L at Fire station into Close Gardens. Small walled garden on two levels in old stable yard of a town house. Flowering shrubs; clematis; bonsai; water garden; paved area with alpines in troughs

Trevi Garden ⅃🌳🌳 (Gilbert & Sally Gough) Hartpury 5m NW of Gloucester via A417. In village R/L into Over Old Road before/after War Memorial. 1 acre of gardens within a garden; winding water garden; new terraced alpine garden; laburnum/clematis walk, shrubberies, herbaceous borders, collections of hardy geraniums/ penstemons, diascias and clematis. Garden completely designed by owners. TEAS. *Adm £1.50 Chd free (Share to Gurkha Welfare Trust®). Suns, Mons March 30, 31; April 6, 20; May 4, 5, 25, 26; June 8, 22; Aug 3, 24, 25; Clematis weekend Sat, Sun July 19, 20; also open every 2nd, 3rd, 4th (5th) Thurs March 20 to Sept 18 (2-6); coaches/groups by appt on other dates* **Tel 01452 700370**

Upton Wold 🌳🌳 (Mr & Mrs I R S Bond) 5m W of Moreton-in-Marsh, on A44 1m past A424 junction at Troopers Lodge Garage. Ever developing and changing garden architecturally and imaginatively laid out around C17 house with commanding views. Yew hedges; old shrub roses; herbaceous walk; some unusual plants and trees; vegetable garden; pond garden and woodland garden. Cream TEAS. *Adm £2 Chd free Suns April 20, June 22 (10-6). Private visits welcome May to July, please* **Tel 01386 700667**

▲**Westbury Court Garden** ⅃🌳 (The National Trust) Westbury-on-Severn 9m SW of Gloucester on A48. Formal Dutch style water garden, earliest remaining in England; canals, summer house, walled garden; over 100 species of plants grown in England before 1700. *Adm £2.50 Chd £1.25. For NGS Sun Sept 7 (11-6)*

Westonbirt Gardens at Westonbirt School ♿ 3m S of Tetbury. A433 Tetbury-Bristol. 22 acres. Formal Victorian Italian garden, terraced pleasure garden, rustic walks, lake redredged & stocked with carp. Rare, exotic trees and shrubs. Tea at Hare & Hounds Hotel, Westonbirt ½m, (to book tea room for parties **Tel 01666 880233**). *Adm £2 Chd 25p (Share to Westonbirt Church Organ Appeal®). Suns March 30, Aug 17, Sept 7 (2-5.30)*

Willow Lodge ♿⚹✿ (Mr & Mrs John H Wood) on A40 between May Hill & Longhope 10m W of Gloucester, 6m E of Ross-on-Wye. Plantsman's garden with unusual and rare plants with colour themed herbaceous borders, shrubs, an alpine walk, stream and pools with water features, several greenhouses, organic vegetable garden, young arboretum with over 300 trees and shrubs from around the world, and wild flowers in the 4-acre grounds. Plants labelled. Ample parking. TEAS. *Adm £1 Chd free. Suns, Mons, May 25, 26; June 8, 9, 22, 23, 29, 30; July 6, 7, 13, 14, 27, 28; Aug 10, 11, 17, 18 (2-6). Groups and private visits especially welcome between May and Aug, please* **Tel 01452 831211**

Witcombe Gardens ♿ 4m E of Gloucester. From Gloucester (crossing of A46 & A417) towards Witcombe (signed). For Gt Witcombe Gdns turn R at 12 Bells Inn (¼m). For Court Farm House straight on for ½m. Strawberry cream TEAS at Court Farm House in aid of Witcombe and Bentham Village Hall. *Combined adm £2 Chd free. Sun June 22 (2-6)*

Church Cottage ⚹✿ (Sir Christopher & Lady Lawson) Great Witcombe. More than 2 acres of country garden with shrubs, trees and lawns. Stream and two ponds. Rose arbour. Old clipped yews. Further beds of roses, herbaceous borders, and several seats for resting. Soft drinks

Court Farm House ✿ (Mr & Mrs Andrew Hope) Little Witcombe. An informal family garden of 1 acre. Shrubs, roses, herbaceous perennials and self-seeding annuals; pond, pergola; wild garden, rock garden, herb garden, scree bed, play area; children welcome

Witcombe Park ⚹ (Mrs W W Hicks Beach) Great Witcombe. A plant connoisseur's medium-sized garden set in beautiful Cotswold scenery. Richly planted borders, flowering shrubs, roses; walled garden, cottage garden area and sunken water garden; C17 gazebo

Gloucestershire (South) & Bristol

Hon County Organiser:	Mrs Mary Bailey, Quakers, Lower Hazel, Rudgeway, Bristol BS12 2QP Tel 01454 413205
Assistant Hon County Organisers:	Dr Margaret Lush, Hazel Cottage, Lower Hazel, Rudgeway, Bristol BS12 2QP Tel 01454 412112
	Mrs Amanda Osmond, Church Farm House, Hawkesbury, nr Badminton, Avon GL9 1BN Tel 01454 238533
Avon Leaflet:	Mrs Jean Damey, 2 Hawburn Close, Bristol BS4 2PB Tel 0117 9775587
Hon County Treasurer:	J K Dutson Esq., The Firs, Rockhampton, Nr Berkeley, Glos GL13 9DY Tel 01454 413210

DATES OF OPENING

February 24 Monday
The Urn Cottage, Charfield
March 16 Sunday
Algars Manor & Algars Mill, Iron Acton
10 Linden Road, Clevedon
March 31 Monday
The Urn Cottage, Charfield
April 6 Sunday
Failand Court, Lower Failand
April 9 Wednesday
Emmaus House, Clifton
April 12 Saturday
The Brake, Tockington ‡
Old Down House, Tockington ‡
April 13 Sunday
The Brake, Tockington ‡
10 Linden Road, Clevedon ‡‡

The Manor House,
Walton-in-Gordano ‡‡
Old Down House,
Tockington ‡
April 15 Tuesday
The Manor House,
Walton-in-Gordano
April 20 Sunday
Algars Manor & Algars Mill, Iron Acton
April 22 Tuesday
The Manor House,
Walton-in-Gordano
April 28 Monday
The Urn Cottage, Charfield
April 29 Tuesday
The Manor House,
Walton-in-Gordano
May 1 Thursday
Jasmine Cottage, Clevedon

May 4 Sunday
Frenchay Gardens, Bristol
May 5 Monday
Frenchay Gardens, Bristol
May 6 Tuesday
The Manor House,
Walton-in-Gordano
May 8 Thursday
Jasmine Cottage, Clevedon
May 11 Sunday
10 Linden Road, Clevedon ‡
The Manor House,
Walton-in-Gordano ‡
May 13 Tuesday
The Manor House,
Walton-in-Gordano
May 14 Wednesday
Emmaus House, Clifton
May 15 Thursday
Bristol Zoo Gardens, Clifton

Jasmine Cottage, Clevedon

May 18 Sunday
Hazel Cottage, Lower Hazel ‡
Petty France Hotel, Badminton
Quakers, Lower Hazel ‡

May 20 Tuesday
The Manor House,
    Walton-in-Gordano

May 21 Wednesday
Highview, Portishead

May 22 Thursday
Jasmine Cottage, Clevedon

May 25 Sunday
Algars Manor & Algars Mill, Iron
    Acton
Pearl's Garden, Coalpit Heath

May 26 Monday
Algars Manor & Algars Mill, Iron
    Acton
Pearl's Garden, Coalpit Heath
The Urn Cottage, Charfield

May 27 Tuesday
The Manor House,
    Walton-in-Gordano

May 28 Wednesday
The Old Rectory, Stanton Prior

May 29 Thursday
Jasmine Cottage, Clevedon

May 31 Saturday
Highview, Portishead

June 1 Sunday
The Old Rectory, Stanton Prior
The Old Vicarage, Hill, nr Berkeley

June 3 Tuesday
The Manor House,
    Walton-in-Gordano

June 4 Wednesday
74 Cowling Drive, Stockwood ‡
19 Derricke Road, Stockwood ‡

June 5 Thursday
Jasmine Cottage, Clevedon

June 8 Sunday
Clifton Gardens, Bristol
The Manor House,
    Walton-in-Gordano
Rock House, Elberton
Tranby House, Whitchurch, Bristol

June 10 Tuesday
The Manor House,
    Walton-in-Gordano

June 11 Wednesday
Highview, Portishead

June 12 Thursday
Jasmine Cottage, Clevedon

June 15 Sunday
Brocklands, Burnett
Dyrham Park, Chippenham
10 Linden Road, Clevedon

June 17 Tuesday
The Manor House,
    Walton-in-Gordano

June 18 Wednesday
Brooklands, Burnett
Emmaus House, Clifton

June 19 Thursday
Jasmine Cottage, Clevedon

June 21 Saturday
Highview, Portishead

June 22 Sunday
Badminton House, Badminton
Canok Garth, Clevedon ‡
Doynton House, Bristol ‡‡
Jasmine Cottage, Clevedon ‡
Old Rectory, Doynton ‡‡

June 24 Tuesday
The Manor House,
    Walton-in-Gordano

June 25 Wednesday
Highview, Portishead
The Old Rectory, Stanton Prior

June 26 Thursday
Jasmine Cottage, Clevedon

June 28 Saturday
Heneage Court, Falfield

June 29 Sunday
Heneage Court, Falfield
University of Bristol Botanic
    Garden

July 1 Tuesday
The Manor House,
    Walton-in-Gordano

July 3 Thursday
Jasmine Cottage, Clevedon

July 6 Sunday
Failand Court, Lower Failand
Hill House, Wickwar

July 8 Tuesday
The Manor House,
    Walton-in-Gordano

July 9 Wednesday
Highview, Portishead

July 10 Thursday
Jasmine Cottage, Clevedon

July 12 Saturday
West Tyning, Beach

July 13 Sunday
The Old Vicarage, Hill, nr
    Berkeley
The Manor House,
    Walton-in-Gordano
West Tyning, Beach

July 15 Tuesday
The Manor House,
    Walton-in-Gordano

July 16 Wednesday
Emmaus House, Clifton
Highview, Portishead

July 17 Thursday
Jasmine Cottage, Clevedon

July 18 Friday
74 Cowling Drive, Stockwood ‡
19 Derricke Road, Stockwood ‡

July 20 Sunday
Petty France Hotel, Badminton
Tranby House, Whitchurch, Bristol

July 22 Tuesday
The Manor House,
    Walton-in-Gordano

July 24 Thursday
Jasmine Cottage, Clevedon

July 26 Saturday
Highview, Portishead

July 27 Sunday
Highview, Portishead

July 29 Tuesday
The Manor House,
    Walton-in-Gordano

July 30 Wednesday
The Old Rectory, Stanton
    Prior

July 31 Thursday
Jasmine Cottage, Clevedon

August 2 Saturday
Camers, Old Sodbury

August 3 Sunday
Camers, Old Sodbury

August 5 Tuesday
The Manor House,
    Walton-in-Gordano

August 6 Wednesday
Highview, Portishead

August 7 Thursday
Jasmine Cottage, Clevedon

August 10 Sunday
The Manor House,
    Walton-in-Gordano
Quakers, Lower Hazel

August 12 Tuesday
The Manor House
    Walton-in-Gordano

August 14 Thursday
Jasmine Cottage, Clevedon

August 16 Saturday
Highview, Portishead

August 17 Sunday
Highview, Portishead
Tranby House, Whitchurch,
    Bristol

August 19 Tuesday
The Manor House,
    Walton-in-Gordano

August 20 Wednesday
Emmaus House, Clifton

August 21 Thursday
Jasmine Cottage, Clevedon

August 26 Tuesday
The Manor House,
    Walton-in-Gordano

August 27 Wednesday
Highview, Portishead
The Old Rectory, Stanton Prior

August 28 Thursday
Jasmine Cottage, Clevedon

August 30 Saturday
74 Cowling Drive, Stockwood ‡
19 Derricke Road, Stockwood ‡

August 31 Sunday
Highview, Portishead
University of Bristol Botanic
    Garden

September 2 Tuesday
The Manor House,

Walton-in-Gordano
September 9 Tuesday
The Manor House,
   Walton-in-Gordano
September 10 Wednesday
Highview, Portishead
September 13 Saturday
Old Down House, Tockington
September 14 Sunday
Highview, Portishead
Old Down House, Tockington

September 17 Wednesday
Highview, Portishead
September 20 Saturday
74 Cowling Drive, Stockwood ‡
19 Derricke Road, Stockwood ‡
September 28 Sunday
The Urn Cottage, Charfield
September 29 Monday
The Urn Cottage, Charfield
October 20 Monday
The Urn Cottage, Charfield

Regular openings
For details see garden description

Jasmine Cottage, Clevedon
Pearl's Garden, Coalpit Heath
The Manor House,
   Walton-in-Gordano
University of Bristol Botanic Garden

DESCRIPTIONS OF GARDENS

Algars Manor & Algars Mill Iron Acton 9m N of Bristol. 3m W of Yate/Chipping Sodbury. Turn S off Iron Acton bypass B4059, past village green, 200yds, then over level Xing (Station Rd). Teas at Parker's Garden Centre. *Combined adm £1.50 Chd 20p. Suns March 16, April 20, May 25, Bank Hol Mon May 26 (2-6)*
   Algars Manor ❀ (Dr & Mrs J M Naish) 3-acre woodland garden beside R Frome; mill-stream; native plants mixed with azaleas, rhododendrons, camellias, magnolias, eucalyptus. Picnic areas. Early Jacobean house (not open) and old barn. Featured in NGS video 3. *Private visits also welcome* **Tel 01454 228372**
   Algars Mill (Mr & Mrs J Wright) entrance via Algars Manor. 2-acre woodland garden beside R Frome; spring bulbs, shrubs; early spring feature of wild Newent daffodils. 300-400 yr old mill house (not open) through which mill-race still runs

Badminton ❀❀ (The Duke of Beaufort) 5m E of Chipping Sodbury. Large garden designed 12 years ago. Still in the process of being created. Mixed and herbaceous borders; many old-fashioned and climbing roses; conservatories and orangery; walled kitchen garden recreated in Victorian style ¼m from house with a new glasshouse. TEAS. *Adm £1.50 OAPs/Chd £1 under 10 free. Sun June 22 (2-6)*

The Brake (Mr & Mrs D C J Skinner) Vicarage Lane, Tockington. 10m N of Bristol. From A38 turn L signposted Tockington/Olveston after bridging M4. R at triangle in Tockington and L 50yds on - Old Down Hill. L at top of hill then immediate R. Alternatively follow brown signs to Oldown. Fine views of Severn Estuary and both bridges. Long mixed borders with emphasis on plants and shrubs that thrive on dry, exposed hillside; woodland walk with interesting ground cover, bulbs, cyclamen. *Combined adm with* **Old Down House** *£1.50 Chd free (Share to BRACE®). Sat, Sun April 12, 13 (2-6)*

¶**Bristol Zoo Garden** ❀❀ From the M5, take A4018 via junction 18, then follow brown elephant signs. These signs can also be followed from the city centre. Local bus services run regularly: 8/9, 508/509, 583/586. Please use main entrance on A4176 (Clifton Down). 12-acre garden with something for everyone, from spectacular bedding and herbaceous borders to a rose garden, rock garden, large lake and numerous trees and shrubs. Gardens established in 1835. Sorry no guide dogs. TEAS. *Adm £2 Chd £1 (Share to Zoological Society®). Thurs May 15 (6-8)*

Brooklands ❀❀❀ (Mr & Mrs Patrick Stevens) Burnett. 2m S Keynsham on B3116. Turn R into Burnett Village. 1½-acre garden; mature trees and variety of ornamental shrubs; rose garden; herbaceous border; extensive planting of shrub roses and clematis; fine views of distant Mendip Hills. Ploughman lunches and TEAS (on Sun in aid of St Michael's Church, Burnett). *Adm £1.50 Chd free. Sun June 15, Wed June 18 (11-5)*

¶**Camers** ❀ (Mrs D M Denman) Old Sodbury. Entrance in Chapel Lane off A432 at Dog Inn. Approx 2 acres, parterre, walled garden, shrubberies, herbaceous and orchard recreated in mature setting. Lovely views. TEAS. *Adm £1.50 Chd 50p. Sat, Sun Aug 2, 3 (2-6)*

Canok Garth ❀ (Mr & Mrs Peter Curtis) 9 Channel Rd Clevedon. 12m W of Bristol (Junction 20 off M5). Follow signs to seafront and pier, continue N on B3124 past Walton Park Hotel, turn R at St Mary's Church. ½-acre garden with a little of everything. Herbaceous border, interesting shrubs and trees, annuals, lawns, fruit and vegetables. Fairly intensively cultivated, but with ample room for grandchildren. *Adm £1 Chd free. Sun June 22 (2-6)*

Clifton Gardens ❀ Bristol. Close to Clifton Suspension Bridge. *Combined adm £1.50 Chd 25p (Share to Royal Hospital for Sick Children®). Sun June 8 (2-5.30)*
   9 Sion Hill ❀ (Mr & Mrs R C Begg) Entrance from Sion Lane. Small walled town garden, densely planted; climbing & herbaceous plants; herb garden; old roses
   16 Sion Hill ❀ (Drs Cameron and Ros Kennedy) Entrance via green door in Sion Lane, at side of No 16. Small pretty town garden with pond, several interesting shrubs and trees
   17 Sion Hill ❀ (Mr & Mrs Philip Gray) Entrance from Sion Lane. Town garden with trees and shrubs. TEAS

74 Cowling Drive ❀❀ (Barbara Brooks) Stockwood, Bristol. A37 Wells Rd. At Whitchurch T-lights (Black Lion) turn into Staunton Lane which runs into Stockwood Lane. Turn L at roundabout, 1st L then 5th L Cowling Rd, L into Cowling Dr, cul-de-sac. Park before entering Cowling Rd (3min walk). Peaceful small garden with bulbs for all seasons, mature trees and shrubs, some unusual plants, great variety of grasses, hostas, herbaceous perennials, conifers, tubs and hanging baskets. Twice won the Bristol in Bloom Competition. TEA. *Adm £1 (not suitable for children) (Share to NSCA®). Wed June 4, Fri July 18, Sats Aug 30, Sept 20 (2-Dusk). Private visits welcome, please* **Tel 01275 831898**

19 Derricke Rd ⚘❀ (Myra & David Tucker) Stockwood, Bristol. A37 Wells Rd. At Whitchurch T-lights (Black Lion) turn into Staunton Lane whch runs into Stockwood Lane. Over 2 white roundabouts then 2nd L and 1st R. 4-yr-old colourful, densely planted corner plot. Trees, shrubs, bulbs, herbaceous perennials, tubs, grasses, ornamentals, baskets and small pond. *Adm £1 (not suitable for children) (Share to NSCA®). Wed June 4, Fri July 18, Sats Aug 30, Sept 20 (2-dusk). Private visits welcome, please* **Tel 01275 542727**

Doynton House ⚘❀ (Mrs C E Pitman) Doynton. 8m E of Bristol 7m N of Bath, ¾m NE of A420 at E end of Wick. Mature, old-fashioned 2-acre garden with herbaceous borders, shrubs and lawns. TEAS. *Adm £1 Chd 50p. Sun June 22 (2-6)*

▲**Dyrham Park** ⚘⚘❀ (The National Trust) 8m N of Bath. 12m E of Bristol. Approached from Bath-Stroud Rd (A46), 2m S of Tormarton interchange with M4, exit 18. Situated on W side of late C17 house. Herbaceous borders, yews clipped as buttresses, ponds and cascade, Parish Church set on terrace. Niches and carved urns. Long lawn to old West entrance. Deer Park. TEAS in aid of NT. *Adm incl Deer Park £2.70 Chd £1.30. For NGS Sun June 15 (11-5.30)*

¶**Emmaus House** ⚘❀ (Sisters of La Retraite) Clifton Hill. From Clifton Downs down to Clifton Village to bottom of Regent St on R. 1½-acre with Victorian walled kitchen, fruit, formal herb and Zen gardens. Rose and herbaceous borders, lawns, secret garden, ponds with fountains and fine views towards Dundry. TEAS in aid of Enid Davies Memorial Trust. *Adm £1.50 Chd 50p. Weds April 9, May 14, June 18, July 16, Aug 20 (10-4)*

Failand Court ⚘❀ (Mr & Mrs B Nathan) Lower Failand. 6m SW of Bristol. Take B3128 from Bristol towards Clevedon. Past Long Ashton Golf Club, over T lights in Failand. 2nd turning R to Lower Failand. Or M5 junction 19 towards Bristol. 1st R through Portbury, turn L into Failand Lane. 1m to top of hill. Turn L past church first R. Park in Oxhouse Lane. 1¼-acre mature garden originally landscaped by Sir Edward Fry. Further developed by Miss Agnes Fry. Interesting trees, shrubs and vegetable garden. TEAS. *Adm £1.50 Chd free. Suns April 6, July 6 (2-5)*

Frenchay Gardens ⚘❀ 5m N of Bristol. From M32 take Exit 1 towards Downend. Follow signs towards Frenchay Hospital. At t-lights turn R, take 4th turn L at mini roundabout for parking at Church and Frenchay Common. Limited parking in Malmains Drive. TEAS in aid of Frenchay Church. *Combined adm £2.50 Chd 25p. Sun, Mon May 4, 5 (2-6)*

    Lluestowen ⚘ (Mrs B Wiltshire) Bristol Rd. 1-acre old established spacious garden with a specimen tulip tree and other unusual trees. Many flowering cherries and pine trees. Paved courtyard with moongate entrance. Large area of strawberry beds

    ¶**6 Malmains Drive** ⚘ (Robert & Karen Smith) Approx ⅓ acre incl coach house. Paved areas with bubble fountain. A variety of planted tubs and containers. Rockery with conifers and heathers

    ¶**13 Malmains Drive** (Mr & Mrs J R West) ⅔-acre with rose garden, conifer and heather beds, sunken

garden, herbaceous borders and mature shrubs, fruit and vegetable garden

    29 Malmains Drive ⚘ (Mr & Mrs G E Bayley) Approx ⅓-acre. Long narrow garden with established trees creating areas for shade loving plants leading to an open area with summerhouse. Access to neighbour's garden with fish and water features

    33 Malmains Drive ⚘❀ (Mr & Mrs Eric White) ⅓-acre plantsman's garden designed by owners since 1983 for low maintenance with unusual trees and shrubs. A yr-round garden split up into different planting areas - mixed shrub and perennial borders, heather bed with grasses, wild area, rock garden plus container planting. *Private visits also welcome, please* **Tel 0117 957 4403**

Hazel Cottage ⚘❀ (Dr & Mrs Brandon Lush) Lower Hazel 700yds W of Rudgeway from A38; 10m N of Bristol. ½-acre cottage garden in rural setting with wide variety of plants and shrubs incl alpines and some unusual varieties. *Combined adm with* **Quakers** *£1.50 Chd 50p. Sun May 18 (2-5)*

¶**Heneage Court** ⚘⚘❀ (Mrs M Durston) Falfield. Exit M5 at junction 14, turn on to A38, turn R approx 50yds, 1st R into Heneage Lane. From Bristol, A38 through Almondsbury to Falfield. From Gloucester A38 to Falfield. A well-established 3½-acre garden, large lawn with flower beds, shrubs and lily pond, small orchard, fruit and vegetable garden. Walled rose garden with small fish pond leading to swimming pool, garden of roses and rock garden, new planting of trees. Terrace overlooking 2 trout lakes. TEAS. *Adm £1.50 OAP's £1 Chd free (Share to CLIC®). Sat, Sun June 28, 29 (2-5)*

Highview ⚘ (Mike & Mary Clavey) Portishead. From Bristol take the A369 (10m) M5 Junction 19. At Portishead take the Nore Rd (Coast Rd) for 1½m, pass garden centre, then take 2nd L into Hill Crest Rd, and L to bottom of private drive. Please park in Hillcrest Rd. 1-acre garden made from scratch by owners since 1987. Large collection of heathers, variety of plants in mixed borders. Herbaceous and rockery plants, rose bed, water features. Alpine bed, various wooden pergolas. Outstanding Channel views. Garden slightly on slope. Home-made TEAS. *Adm £1 Chd free. Weds May 21, June 11, 25, July 9, 16, Aug 6, 27, Sept 10, 17, Sats May 31, June 21, July 26, Aug 16; Suns July 27, Aug 17, 31 Sept 14 (2-5.30). Also private visits welcome, please* **Tel 01275 849873**

Hill House ⚘❀ (Dr & Mrs Richard Adlam) 4m N of Chipping Sodbury on B4060. Through Wickwar, L by wall signed to M5; then 200yds on L. 7 acres of land, of which 4 acres of gardens originally designed and planted by Sally, Duchess of Westminster. Gold/silver plantings in gravel; pleached lime walk; wild flowers and bulbs; owls and pheasant aviaries, peacocks. TEAS. *Adm £2 Chd £1. Sun July 6 (2-6), private visits welcome, please* **Tel 01454 294304**

Jasmine Cottage ⚘❀ (Mr & Mrs Michael Redgrave) 26 Channel Rd, Clevedon. 12m W of Bristol (junction 20 off M5). Follow signs to seafront and pier, continue N on B3124, past Walton Park Hotel, turn R at St Mary's Church. Medium-sized garden created by owners from a wooded shelter belt for interest in all seasons. Old-fashioned roses; clematis, pergola; mixed shrub borders; island beds; gravel beds, pond and potager. Unusual climbers and tender perennials a speciality. Plants propagated from the garden available in small nursery area. Toilet facilities. TEAS, refreshments all day Thurs. *Adm £1.50 Chd free. Sun June 22 (2-6). Every Thurs May 1 to Aug 28 (11-5). Private visits welcome April to Sept, please* **Tel 01275 871850**

10 Linden Road ❀ (Ruth & William Salisbury) Clevedon. Coming from the seafront, head up Alexandra Rd opp the pier, cross the roundabout. Linden Rd is between the Midland and Barclays Banks. No 10 is 150yds on the R. A very small but richly planted seaside town garden. Over 400 different species of trees, shrubs and plants grow in 3 areas, the largest being 35' × 40'. A garden designed to maximise the use of a small space. *Adm £1 Chd free. Suns March 16, April 13, May 11, June 15 (10-4). Open by appt only other Suns March to Oct, please* **Tel 01275 874694**

The Manor House ૬⚘❀ (Mr & Mrs Simon Wills) Walton-in-Gordano, 2m NE of Clevedon. Entrance on N side of B3124, Clevedon to Portishead Rd, just by houses on roadside nearest Clevedon. Clevedon-Portishead buses stop in village. 4-acres; trees, shrubs, herbaceous and bulbs mostly labelled. Coaches by appt only. TEAS (Suns only) in aid of St Peter's Hospice Bristol. *Adm £1.50, Acc chd under 14 free (Share to St Peter's Hospice, Bristol®). Every Tues April 15 to Sept 9 (10-4); Suns April 13, May 11, June 8, July 13, Aug 10 (2-6). Private visits welcome all year, please* **Tel 01275 872067**

Old Down House ૬❀ (Mr & Mrs Robert Bernays) Tockington, 10m N of Bristol. Follow brown Tourist Board signs to Oldown from A38 at Alveston. 5 acres divided into small formal and informal gardens by hedges and walls; topiary, shrubs; extensive lawns; rock garden; fine trees (weeping beeches, etc). Herbaceous borders, semi-wild areas with spring and autumn cyclamen; fine views to Severn and Welsh hills. TEAS. *Combined adm with* **The Brake** *£1.50 Chd free (Share to BRACE®). Sat, Sun April 12, 13; Adm £1 Sept 13, 14 (2-6). Private parties welcome, please* **Tel 01454 413605**

Old Rectory, Doynton ૬❀ (Sheila & Robert Sawyer) 2-acre garden surrounding Rectory with mature woodland and walled garden. Old-fashioned roses, shrubs and herbaceous plantings in mixed borders. Some new planting over past 2 yrs. Homemade ice cream and lemonade. *Adm £1 Chd 50p (Share to Doynton Parish Church®). Sun June 22 (2-6)*

The Old Rectory, Stanton Prior ૬❀ (Lt Col & Mrs Patrick Mesquita) 6m from Bath on A39 Wells Rd; at Marksbury turn L to Stanton Prior. 1-acre garden next to Church, in beautiful countryside with medieval pond and many interesting features incl knot garden, apple and pear arches; rose pergola and productive vegetable garden. TEAS. *Adm £1.50 Chd free. Sun June 1, last Wed in every month from May to Aug (2-6). Parties by appt all yr, please* **Tel 01761 471942**

¶**The Old Vicarage** ૬⚘❀ (Dr & Mrs A Longstaff) Hill, nr Berkeley. 2m N of Thornbury. At Whitfield on A38 take B4061. Turn R at Upper Morton and follow signposts to Rockhampton then Hill. Old Vicarage on R after entrances to Church and Hill Court. Set against the backdrop of the small aboretum of Hill Court and the charming tiny Church of St Michael, this Victorian vicarage garden has in recent yrs been largely redesigned and replanted. Features incl a part-walled brick-pathed potager, with moon gate. Unusual herbaceous plants and shrubs, 2 ponds, one in a small mediterranean garden, the other next to the herb garden. TEAS. *Adm £1.50 Chd free. Suns June 1, July 13 (11-5)*

■ **Pearl's Garden** ૬⚘❀ (Pearl & Doug Watts) Coalpit Heath. NE Bristol. Take Downend (Westerleigh Rd) to Tormarton Rd past Folly Public House over motorway and garden is 500yds on L. From junction 18 on M4, turn N on the A46 and almost immed L signposted Pucklechurch. After 5½m the garden is on R shortly before bridge over motorway. 2-acre 'mini estate' mature trees; herb and terrace gardens; statuary amusing and formal; 100 different hollies. Designed and built by owners since 1966 with water features and peafowl. Plenty of seats. TEAS. *Adm £1.50 Chd free. Each Sun in May and June. For NGS Sun, Mon May 25, 26 (12-5). Ploughman's Lunch available. Also private visits welcome May and June, please* **Tel 01179 562953**

Petty France Hotel ૬❀ (W J Fraser Esq) Badminton. On A46 5m N exit 18 M4. Edge of Badminton Estate. Chipping Sodbury 5m. 2 acres of mature shrubs and trees incl specimen cedar, 200-yr-old yew hedge, medlar and tulip tree. Vegetable garden and herbs. Many spring flowers and shrubs. TEAS. *Adm £1.50 Chd free. Suns May 18, July 20 (2-5). Private parties also welcome, please* **Tel 01454 238361**

Quakers ⚘❀ (Mrs Mary Bailey) Lower Hazel. 10m N of Bristol. Turn off A38 in Rudgeway, signposted to Lower Hazel and Old Down. ¼m at bottom of hill. Mature ¾-acre garden set against a backdrop of natural woodland. A large herbaceous and other colour themed mixed borders planted for seasonal interest. Surrounding the main lawn which is dominated by a large magnolia are mature shrubs. A ¼-acre 'paddock' with large pond; marginal planting, trees and ornamental shrubs. A vegetable plot screened by roses and clematis, shade plantings and extensive climbers on the house. TEAS. *Combined adm £1.50 Chd 50p with* **Hazel Cottage**. *Sun May 18 (2-5). Adm £1.50 Chd free. Aug 10 (2- 5.30)*

Rock House ⚘❀ (Mr & Mrs John Gunnery) Elberton. From Old Severn Bridge on M48 take B4461 to Alveston. In Elberton, take 1st turning L to Littleton-on-Severn and turn immed R. 1-acre walled garden undergoing improvement. Pond and old yew tree. Mixed borders. Cottage garden plants. *Adm £1 Chd free (Share to St John's Church, Elberton®). Sun June 8 (2-6)*

By Appointment Gardens. These owners do not have a fixed opening day usually because they do not like crowds or have insufficient parking space. Owner will often give a guided tour.

Tranby House ✿❀ (Jan Barkworth) Norton Lane, Whitchurch. ½m S of Whitchurch Village. Leave Bristol on A37 Wells Rd, through Whitchurch Village 1st turning on R, signposted Norton Malreward. 1¼-acre informal garden, designed and planted to encourage wildlife. Wide variety of trees, shrubs, and flowers; ponds and wild flower meadow. Plants and pressed flower cards for sale in aid of The Wildlife Trust. Partly suitable for wheelchairs. TEA. *Adm £1.50 Chd free. Suns June 8, July 20, Aug 17 (2-5.30)*

University of Bristol Botanic Garden ఈ✿❀ Bracken Hill, North Rd, Leigh Woods, 1m W of Bristol via Clifton. Cross suspension bridge, North Rd is 1st R. As featured on Gardeners World 1993, 1994 and 1995, Superintendent Nicholas Wray, (presenter). 5-acre garden supporting approx 4,500 species; special collections incl cistus, hebe, ferns, salvia and sempervivum, plus many native plants. Range of glasshouses and large Pulhams rock garden. TEAS. *Adm £1 Chd 50p (Share to Friends of Bristol University Botanic Garden®). Private visits welcome all year, please* **Tel 01179 733682**. *For NGS Suns June 29, Aug 31 (11-5)*

The Urn Cottage ఈ✿❀ (Mr A C & Dr L A Rosser) 19 Station Road, Charfield, Wotton-under-Edge, Glos GL12 8SY. 3m E of M5 exit 14. In Charfield turn off main road at The Railway Tavern, then 400yds on L: short walk from parking. Family garden, created from scratch by owners since 1982 surrounding stone built cottage with Cotswold views. Richly planted with schemes differing in character from sunbaked flagstones to streamside shade. Experiments in plant association incl colour, foliage, grasses, groundcover, with always an emphasis on well behaved plants, continuity of interest and wildlife. TEAS in aid of CLIC and Bournstream. *Adm £1.50 Chd 30p. Mons Feb 24 (10-12) March 31 (2-5) April 28 (10-12) May 26 (2-6) Sun Sept 28 (2-5) Mons Sept 29, Oct 20 (10-12). Parties by appt all year*

West Tyning ఈ✿❀ (Mr & Mrs G S Alexander) Beach. From Bath (6m) or Bristol (7m) on A43l. From Bitton village turn N up Golden Valley Lane, signposted Beach. Continue up lane for 2m to Wick-Upton Cheyney Xrds, turn R towards Upton Cheyney for 200yds. Parking in nearby field. 1¼-acre garden; roses and clematis over a series of pergolas which separate and join different areas; lawns with curved mixed borders in both sun and shade; woodland with ferns, hellebores and other shade plants; rough grass with fruit and shrubs; rock garden and vegetable garden. TEAS with home-made cakes by Bitton WI. *Adm £1.50 Chd free. Sat, Sun July 12, 13 (2-6)*

Gwent & Gwynedd

See separate Welsh section beginning on page 323

Hampshire

Hon County Organiser:	Mrs A R Elkington, Little Court, Crawley nr Winchester SO21 2PU Tel 01962 776365 Central West
Assistant Hon County Organisers:	East: Mrs D Hart Dyke, Hambledon House, Hambledon PO7 4RU
	South-West: Wing Cdr & Mrs Peter Prior, The Little Cottage, Southampton Rd, Lymington SO41 9GZ
	South: Mrs H Sykes, The Cottage, 16 Lakewood Rd, Chandlers Ford SO53 1ES
	West: C K Thornton Esq, Merrie Cottage, Woodgreen, Nr Fordingbridge SP6 2AT
	North-West: M H Walford Esq, Little Acre, Down Farm Lane, Headbourne Worthy, Winchester SO23 7LA
	North: J J Morris Esq, The Ricks, Rotherwick, Hook RG27 9BL
	North-East: Mrs E Powell, Broadhatch House, Bentley, Nr Farnham GU10 5JJ
	Central-East: Mrs W F Richardson, Hill House, Old Alresford SO24 9DY
Hon County Treasurer:	S Every Esq, The White House, Crawley, Winchester SO21 2PR

DATES OF OPENING

February 8 Saturday
Brandy Mount House, Alresford

February 16 Sunday
Little Court, Crawley
Nikendi, Swanmore

February 17 Monday
Little Court, Crawley

Nikendi, Swanmore

February 18 Tuesday
Little Court, Crawley

March 9 Sunday
Longthatch, Warnford

March 16 Sunday
Brandy Mount House, Alresford
Longthatch, Warnford
The White Cottage, Beech

March 17 Monday
The White Cottage, Beech

March 23 Sunday
Court Lodge, West Meon
Little Court, Crawley
Longthatch, Warnford
Nikendi, Swanmore
Pennington Chase,
Lymington ‡

Sowley House, Sowley ‡

March 24 Monday
Little Court, Crawley
Nikendi, Swanmore

March 25 Tuesday
Little Court, Crawley

March 26 Wednesday
Old Meadows, Silchester

March 29 Saturday
Greatham Mill, Greatham, nr Liss

March 30 Sunday
Bramdean House, Bramdean
Durmast House, Burley

March 31 Monday
Bramdean House, Bramdean

April 6 Sunday
Abbey Cottage, Itchen Abbas
Bramley Lodge, Fyfield
Fairfield House, Hambledon
Fernlea, Chilworth, Southampton
Houghton Lodge, Stockbridge

April 7 Monday
Houghton Lodge, Stockbridge

April 9 Wednesday
Hayden Barn Cottage, Warnford

April 12 Saturday
187 Christchurch Road,
    Ringwood

April 13 Sunday
Beechenwood Farm, nr Odiham
187 Christchurch Road,
    Ringwood
Crawley Gardens, Crawley
East Lane, Ovington
Mylor Cottage, Droxford Gardens
Norsebury Gardens, Stoke Charity
The Old House, Silchester

April 14 Monday
Crawley Gardens, Crawley
Norsebury Gardens, Stoke Charity

April 15 Tuesday
Chalkwood, Ropley

April 17 Thursday
Hightown Farm, Ringwood

April 20 Sunday
Bramdean House, Bramdean
The Cottage, Chandlers Ford
Hall Place, West Meon
Longthatch, Warnford
Rowans Wood, Ampfield

April 21 Monday
The Cottage, Chandlers Ford

April 24 Thursday
Little Court, Crawley

April 25 Friday
Little Court, Crawley

April 27 Sunday
Abbey Road Gardens, Fareham
Brandy Mount House, Alresford
53 Ladywood, Eastleigh
Nikendi, Swanmore
North Ecchinswell Farm, nr
    Newbury
The Old House, Silchester

Shaldon Park House, Shaldon

April 28 Monday
Nikendi, Swanmore

April 30 Wednesday
Hayden Barn Cottage, Warnford

May 4 Sunday
Abbey Cottage, Itchen Abbas ‡
Chilland, Martyr Worthy ‡
Coles, Privett, nr Alton
The Cottage, Chandlers Ford
Fernlea, Chilworth, Southampton
Rowans Wood, Ampfield
Rumsey Gardens, Clanfield
Vernon Hill House, Bishop's
    Waltham

May 5 Monday
Abbey Cottage, Itchen Abbas ‡
Chilland, Martyr Worthy ‡
Coles, Privett, nr Alton
The Cottage, Chandlers Ford
The House-in-the-Wood, Beaulieu
Rookley Manor, Up Somborne
Rowans Wood, Ampfield
Stratfield Saye House,
    Basingstoke
Vernon Hill House, Bishop's
    Waltham

May 8 Thursday
Maurys Mount, West Wellow

May 10 Saturday
Rotherfield Park, East Tisted

May 11 Sunday
Brandy Mount House, Alresford
The Dower House, Dogmersfield
Eversley Gardens, Coopers Hill
Fairfield House, Hambledon
Greenfingers, Portsmouth
Heathlands, Locks Heath
Nikendi, Swanmore
The Old House, Silchester
Rotherfield Park, East Tisted

May 13 Tuesday
Chalkwood, Ropley

May 14 Wednesday
Hayden Barn Cottage, Warnford

May 17 Saturday
187 Christchurch Road,
    Ringwood ‡
Coles, Privett, nr Alton
Potters Cot, Ringwood ‡
3 St Helens Road, Hayling Island

May 18 Sunday
Bluebell Cottage, Froxfield ‡
Bramdean House, Bramdean
187 Christchurch Road,
    Ringwood ‡
Coles, Privett, nr Alton ‡
The Dower House, Dogmersfield
Paddocks Way, Brook ‡‡
Pennington Chase, Lymington ‡‡
Potters Cot, Ringwood
Pylewell Park, Lymington ‡‡
3 St Helens Road, Hayling
    Island

Tylney Hall Hotel, Rotherwick
Verona Cottage, Mengham
Waldrons, Brook ‡‡
Walhampton, Lymington ‡‡
2 Warren Farm Cottages, West
    Tytherley

May 19 Monday
Verona Cottage, Mengham
Waldrons, Brook

May 24 Saturday
Littlewood, Hayling Island

May 25 Sunday
Bracken Cottage, Greatham
Bramshaw Lodge, Bramshaw
Coles, Privett, nr Alton
Croylands, Romsey
Hambledon House, Hambledon
Hightown Farm, Ringwood
60 Lealand Road, Drayton
Littlewood, Hayling Island
Longhatch, Warnford
Merdon Manor, Hursley
Monxton Gardens, nr Andover
The Old House, Silchester ‡
Pumpkin Patch, Ringwood
Pylewell Park, Lymington ‡‡
Rowans Wood, Ampfield
South End House, Lymington ‡‡
West Silchester Hall, nr
    Reading ‡

May 26 Monday
Bramshaw Lodge, Bramshaw
Coles, Privett, nr Alton
Hightown Farm, Ringwood ‡
Longthatch, Warnford
Monxton Gardens, nr Andover
Pumpkin Patch, Ringwood ‡
Rowans Wood, Ampfield
West Silchester Hall, nr
    Reading

May 28 Wednesday
Croylands, Romsey

May 31 Saturday
1 Brook Cottages, East Meon

June 1 Sunday
Bluebell Cottage, Froxfield
Croylands, Romsey
Flintstones, Durley
Nikendi, Swanmore
Rowans Wood, Ampfield

June 2 Monday
Flintstones, Durley
Nikendi, Swanmore

June 4 Wednesday
Croylands, Romsey

June 7 Saturday
Coles, Privett, nr Alton
Pumpkin Patch, Ringwood

June 8 Sunday
Applecroft, Woodgreen ‡‡‡
Croft Mews, Botley ‡
Croylands, Romsey
The Garden House, Lymington ‡‡
Glevins, Lymington ‡‡

Little Barn Garden & Barnhawk
  Nursery ‡‡‡
Maurys Mount, West Wellow
Merrie Cottage, Woodgreen ‡‡‡
North Ecchinswell Farm, nr
  Newbury
Warwick House, Wickham ‡
The White Cottage, Beech
White Windows, Longparish

June 9 Monday
Applecroft, Woodgreen ‡
Croft Mews, Botley
Little Barn Garden & Barnhawk
  Nursery ‡
Merrie Cottage, Woodgreen ‡
The White Cottage, Beech

June 10 Tuesday
Chalkwood, Ropley ‡
High Paddocks, Privett ‡

June 11 Wednesday
Croylands, Romsey
High Paddocks, Privett
White Windows, Longparish

June 15 Sunday
Amport House, nr Andover
Beechenwood Farm, nr Odiham
Bluebell Cottage, Froxfield
Closewood House, Waterlooville
Cranbury Park, Otterbourne
Croylands, Romsey
Durmast House, Burley
53 Ladywood, Eastleigh
Longstock Park & Water Gardens,
  Stockbridge
Pumpkin Patch, Ringwood
Tylney Hall Hotel, Rotherwick
Upham Gardens, nr Bishops
  Waltham ‡
Vernon Hill House, Bishop's
  Waltham ‡
Wonston Lodge, Wonston

June 18 Wednesday
Closewood House, Waterlooville
Croylands, Romsey
Upham Gardens, nr Bishops
  Waltham

June 20 Friday
The Vyne, Sherborne St John

June 21 Saturday
Conholt Park, Chute
Milford Gardens, Lymington
2 Warren Farm Cottages, West
  Tytherley

June 22 Sunday
Bramdean House, Bramdean ‡
Bramdean Lodge, Bramdean ‡
Brandy Mount House, Alresford
Cliddesden Gardens, nr
  Basingstoke
Conholt Park, Chute
Croylands, Romsey
Droxford Gardens
Fairfield House, Hambledon ‡
Hambledon House, Hambledon ‡

60 Lealand Road, Drayton
Longthatch, Warnford
Mottisfont Abbey, nr Romsey
Oakdene, Sandleheath
Pumpkin Patch, Ringwood

June 23 Monday
Broadhatch House, Bentley
March End, Sherfield English,
  Romsey

June 24 Tuesday
Oakdene, Sandleheath

June 25 Wednesday
Broadhatch House, Bentley
White House, East Wellow

June 26 Thursday
White House, East Wellow

June 27 Friday
White House, East Wellow

June 28 Saturday
Pumpkin Patch, Ringwood
Springfield, Hayling Island

June 29 Sunday
Abbey Road Gardens, Fareham
Brocas Farm, Lower Froyle ‡
Crawley Gardens, Crawley
Fritham Lodge, nr Lyndhurst ‡‡
Holt End House, Ashford Hill
March End, Sherfield English
Marycourt, Odiham
Old Meadows, Silchester
The Old Vicarage, Appleshaw
Paddocks Way, Brook ‡‡
Shalden Park House, Shalden ‡
Valentine Cottage, Newnham
Vernon Hill House, Bishop's
  Waltham
Waldrons, Brook ‡‡
2 Warren Farm Cottages, West
  Tytherley
Westbrook House, Holybourne ‡

June 30 Monday
Broadhatch House, Bentley ‡
Brocas Farm, Lower Froyle ‡
March End, Sherfield English
Waldrons, Brook
2 Warren Farm Cottages, West
  Tytherley

July 2 Wednesday
Broadhatch House, Bentley
Crookley Pool, Horndean
Greatham Mill, Greatham, nr Liss
Manor Lodge, Crawley
Old Meadows, Silchester
Warwick House, Wickham

July 5 Saturday
The Little Cottage, Lymington ‡
Merebimur, Mockbeggar,
  Ringwood
Pumpkin Patch, Ringwood ‡

July 6 Sunday
1 Brook Cottages, East Meon
Copperfield, Dogmersfield
Crawley Gardens, Crawley
Crookley Pool, Horndean

Harcombe House, Ropley
Lake House, Northington ‡‡
Longparish Gardens, nr
  Andover
Marycourt, Odiham
Merebimur, Mockbeggar,
  Ringwood ‡
Moth House, nr Alresford ‡‡
Moundsmere Manor, Preston
  Candover ‡‡
Potters Cot, Hightown Hill,
  Ringwood ‡
Tunworth Old Rectory, nr
  Basingstoke
The White Cottage, Beech

July 7 Monday
Potters Cot, Hightown Hill,
  Ringwood
The White Cottage, Beech

July 8 Tuesday
16 Old Barn Crescent, Hambledon

July 9 Wednesday
16 Old Barn Crescent, Hambledon
Old Meadows, Silchester
Marycourt, Odiham

July 13 Sunday
Broadhatch House, Bentley
Forest Edge, Andover Down
Heathlands, Locks Heath
Little Court, Crawley ‡
Lithend, Crawley ‡
Longthatch, Warnford
Malt Cottage, Upper Clatford
Pumpkin Patch, Ringwood
Rose Cottage, Kingsley
  Common
12 Rozelle Close, Littleton
Swarraton Gardens
Warwick House, Wickham

July 14 Monday
Broadhatch House, Bentley
Little Court, Crawley ‡
Lithend, Crawley ‡

July 15 Tuesday
Swarraton Gardens

July 16 Wednesday
Old Meadows, Silchester

July 19 Saturday
1 Brook Cottages, East Meon
2 Warren Farm Cottages, West
  Tytherley

July 20 Sunday
Abbey Cottage, Itchen Abbas ‡‡
Bramdean House, Bramdean ‡
Bramdean Lodge, Bramdean ‡
Chilland, Martyr Worthy ‡‡
Martyr Worthy Gardens ‡‡
Pumpkin Patch, Ringwood
Tylney Hall Hotel, Rotherwick
The Vyne, Sherborne St John
2 Warren Farm Cottages, West
  Tytherley

July 21 Monday
Chilland, Martyr Worthy

2 Warren Farm Cottages, West
Tytherley
July 22 Tuesday
16 Old Barn Crescent, Hambledon
July 23 Wednesday
16 Old Barn Crescent, Hambledon
Old Meadows, Silchester
July 26 Saturday
Pumpkin Patch, Ringwood
12 Rozelle Close, Littleton
July 27 Sunday
Fernlea, Chilworth,
Southampton
Jasmine Lodge, Kempshott
Paddocks Way, Brook
12 Rozelle Close, Littleton
July 30 Wednesday
Old Meadows, Silchester
August 3 Sunday
The Barn House, Church Oakley ‡
Bohunt Manor, Liphook
Hill House, Old Alresford
Jasmine Lodge, Kempshot
53 Ladywood, Eastleigh
Oakley Manor, Church Oakley ‡
West Silchester Hall, nr Reading
August 4 Monday
West Silchester Hall, nr Reading
August 5 Tuesday
Hill House, Old Alresford
16 Old Barn Crescent, Hambledon
August 6 Wednesday
16 Old Barn Crescent, Hambledon
Old Meadows, Silchester
August 9 Saturday
Pumpkin Patch, Ringwood
August 10 Sunday
Abbey Road Gardens, Fareham
Nikendi, Swanmore
2 Warren Farm Cottages, West
Tytherley
The White Cottage, Beech
August 11 Monday
Nikendi, Swanmore
2 Warren Farm Cottages, West
Tytherley
The White Cottage, Beech
August 13 Wednesday
Hightown Farm, Ringwood
Old Meadows, Silchester
August 17 Sunday
Bramdean House, Bramdean ‡
Bramdean Lodge, Bramdean ‡
60 Lealand Road, Drayton

Little Court, Crawley
Pumpkin Patch, Ringwood
White Windows, Longparish
August 18 Monday
Little Court, Crawley
August 19 Tuesday
The Worthys Gardens,
Kingsworthy
August 20 Wednesday
Old Meadows, Silchester
White Windows, Longparish
August 23 Saturday
Pullens, West Worldham, nr Alton
August 24 Sunday
Abbey Cottage, Itchen Abbas
Norsebury House, Stoke Charity ‡
Wonston Lodge, Wonston ‡
August 25 Monday
Abbey Cottage, Itchen Abbas
Norsebury House, Stoke Charity
Pumpkin Patch, Ringwood
Wonston Lodge, Wonston
August 27 Wednesday
Old Meadows, Silchester
Setters Green, Rowlands Castle
August 31 Sunday
Longthatch, Warnford
Setters Green, Rowlands Castle
September 3 Wednesday
Setters Green, Rowlands Castle
September 7 Sunday
Hambledon House, Hambledon
White Cottage, Hambledon
September 8 Monday
White Cottage, Hambledon
September 13 Saturday
Hinton Ampner, nr Alresford
September 14 Sunday
Greenfingers, Portsmouth
Hinton Ampner, nr Alresford
Little Court, Crawley
Nikendi, Swanmore
Pumpkin Patch, Ringwood
2 Warren Farm Cottages, West
Tytherley
September 15 Monday
Little Court, Crawley
Nikendi, Swanmore
2 Warren Farm Cottages, West
Tytherley
September 20 Saturday
Conholt Park, Chute
September 21 Sunday
Conholt Park, Chute

September 24 Wednesday
Greatham Mill, Greatham, nr Liss
Old Meadows, Silchester
September 28 Sunday
Abbey Cottage, Itchen Abbas
Paddocks Way, Brook
October 5 Sunday
2 Warren Farm Cottages, West
Tytherley
Wheatley House, Nr Borden
October 12 Sunday
Coles, Privett, nr Alton
October 19 Sunday
Nikendi, Swanmore
October 20 Monday
Nikendi, Swanmore

1998
February 7 Saturday
Bramdean House, Bramdean
Brandy Mount House, Alresford
February 23, 24, 25
Little Court, Crawley

Regular openings
For details see garden description

Apple Court & Apple Court Cottage,
Lymington
Exbury Gardens
Furzey Gardens, Minstead
Hambledon House, Hambledon
Sir Harold Hillier Aboretum,
Ampfield
Houghton Lodge, Stockbridge
The Little Cottage, Lymington
Longthatch, Warnford
Longstock Park & Water Gardens,
Stockbridge
Lymore Valley Herbs, Milford-on-Sea
Macpenny Woodland Nuseries,
Bransgore
Spinners, Boldre
Stratfield Saye House, Basingstoke
2 Warren Farm Cottages, West
Tytherley

By appointment only
*For telephone numbers and other
details see garden descriptions.
Private visits welcomed*

DESCRIPTIONS OF GARDENS

Abbey Cottage &⚘❀ (Colonel P J Daniell) Rectory
Lane, Itchen Abbas. 1m E of Itchen Abbas on B3047. An
inspiring walled garden and meadow with a wide selection of plants, young trees and hedges, orchard, pond
and many features. Designed, created and maintained by
owner, BBC Gardeners World TV 94, Saga Magazine 96,
Periwinkle and Phostrogen videos. TEA. *Adm £1.50 Chd*

free *(Share to St John the Baptist. Itchen Abbas®). Sun
April 6, Sun, Mon May 4, 5, Sun July 20, Sun, Mon Aug
24, 25, Sun Sept 28 (12-5). Private visits welcome, please*
Tel 01962 779575

Abbey Road Gardens From M27 Junction 9 travel on
A27 towards Fareham. At top of hill past Titchfield Gyra-
tory, turn L at traffic lights into Highland Rd. Take 4th
turning R into Blackbrook Rd. Abbey Rd is 4th turning on

L. *Combined adm £1.50 Chd free. Suns April 27, June 29, Aug 10 (11-5)*

80 Abbey Road &&& (Brian & Vivienne Garford) Very small garden with developing collection of herbs and plants of botanical and historical interest. 2 small ponds, miniscule meadow area, but no lawn

86 Abbey Road &&& (Tricia & Don Purseglove) Small developing garden started in 1991. Mixed planting and trellis work for breezy position. Small vegetable plot and Japanese garden. Winner in 1996 Fareham in Bloom tubs and containers. TEA

¶**Amport House** &&& (Ministry of Defence) Nr Andover. 4m W of Andover. S of A303 at Thruxton exit. S through E Cholderton. 1½m R at Tee. ¼m Amport House straight ahead. Authentic Lutyens and Jekyll garden, designed for the Marquess of Winchester in 1920's. Terrace, wide steps, rills and mirror pond with view over surrounding parkland. Formal Jekyll garden with yew topiary. Large "Winchester Family Crest" Box parterre dating from 1857. Mature Pleached Lime avenue. 19 acres in all. TEAS. *Adm £3 Chd under 14 £1. Sun June 15 (2-5)*

● **Apple Court & Apple Court Cottage** &&& (Mrs D Grenfell, Mr R Grounds & Mrs M Roberts) Lymington. From the A337 between Lymington and New Milton turn N into Hordle Lane at the Royal Oak at Downton Xrds. Formal 1½-acre garden created by designer-owners within the walls of former Victorian kitchen garden. 3 National Reference Collections incl small leafed hosta. Theatrical white garden, daylily display borders, collection of ferns and grasses. Small specialist nursery. Adjoining small cottage garden with variegated catalpa. Featured in BBC 'Gardeners' World', 'Grass Roots', 'Your Garden' Sept 96 'Garden Guide' to Growing Hostas'. *Adm £1.50 Chd 25p. Thurs to Mons Feb 1 to Thurs Oct 31; every day July to Aug (10-1) (2-5)*

Applecroft && (Mr & Mrs J B Milne) Brook Lane, Woodgreen. 3m N of Fordingbridge on A338 turn E to Woodgreen. Turn R at Horse and Groom and R again along the edge of the common. Park on common and walk down through 5-barred gate. Small garden. Distant view to the SW over the Avon Valley. Mixed planting incl annuals and vegetables in the cottage style. Shady arbour and pond. TEA (Mon). *Adm £1 Chd free. Sun, Mon June 8, 9 (2-6)*

Ashley Park Farm. See Dorset

The Barn House &&& (Brigadier & Mrs H R W Vernon) Rectory Rd, Oakley. 5m W of Basingstoke. From Basingstoke towards Whitchurch on B3400. Turn L at Station Rd ½m W of Newfound and follow signs. Bus No 55a, 55b Basingstoke to Oakley. Small garden, with view of church. Borders, alpines and uncommon plants, large collection of clematis, informal planting in cottage style. Tea at Oakley Manor. *Combined adm with **Oakley Manor** £2 Chd free. Free parking at Manor. Sun Aug 3 (2-5.30) also private visits welcome, please **Tel 01256 780271***

Beechenwood Farm && (Mr & Mrs M Heber-Percy) Hillside, Odiham; turn S into King St. from Odiham High St. Turn L after cricket ground for Hillside. Take 2nd turn R for Roke after 1m. Modern house ½m. Garden in many parts incl woodland garden, rock garden, pergola, conser-vatory, herb garden with exuberant planting, belvedere with spectacular views over Odiham. Newly planted 8 acre wood, open from 1pm for picnics. WI TEAS. *Adm £1.50 Chd free. Sun April 13 (2-5); Sun June 15 (2-6); also private visits welcome March to July, please* **Tel 01256 702300**

¶**Bluebell Cottage** && (Mr & Mrs T Clarke) Broadway, Froxfield. 3½m NW of Petersfield. Between top of Stoner Hill and Froxfield Green. Take sign to Froxfield off A272 and follow yellow signs. 1-acre incl natural woodland with prolific bluebells and ferns. Also varied planting with spring shrubs, kitchen garden with raised beds and labelled corden fruit trees. Soil acid clay. *Adm £1.50 Chd 50p. Suns May 18, June 1, 15, (2-6)*

Bohunt Manor &&& (Lady Holman) Liphook. On old A3 in 30m area in Liphook nr station. Flowering shrubs, herbaceous borders, lakeside and woodland walks, rhododendrons, bulbs, wild flowers and vegetable garden. Tame waterfowl will eat out of children's hands. Specimen trees. About ¾hr to walk round, lake 3½ acres. *Adm £1.50 OAP £1 Chd free. Sun Aug 3 (10-6)*

Bracken Cottage &&& (Mr & Mrs Day) Petersfield Rd, Greatham. On A325 halfway between Petersfield and Farnham. On the RH-side 100yds S of the village PO and store. ⅓-acre cottage garden. Developed since 1987 on 3 levels by use of walling. Mixed borders intensively planted by enthusiastic amateur aiming for yr-round foliage interest combined with an informal mix of herbaceous plants. Small pond and vegetable garden. Teas at Greatham Mill. *Adm £1.50 Chd free. Sun May 25 (11-6). Private visits welcome, please* **Tel 01420 538680**

Bramdean House && (Mr & Mrs H Wakefield) In Bramdean village on A272. 6½ acres carpets of spring bulbs. Walled garden with famous herbaceous borders, 1-acre working kitchen garden, large collection of unusual plants. Featured TV Grassroots programme and many gardening books. TEAS. *Adm £2 Chd free (Share to Bramdean Parish Church®). Mon March 31, Suns March 30, April 20, May 18, June 22, July 20, Aug 17, (2-5); 1998 Feb 7, also private parties welcome, please* **Tel 01962 771214**

Bramdean Lodge & (Hon Peter & Mrs Dickinson) Bramdean village, on A272 (car park and TEAS as for Bramdean House). Disabled use Wood Lane entrance and park in yard. 1¾ acres around Victorian Gothic house. Walled garden. Borders densely planted. Style evolved rather than planned. Many oddities. Over 100 varieties of clematis, and 300 of roses, all labelled. *Adm £1.50 Chd free. Suns June 22, July 20, Aug 17 (3-6). Private parties welcome, please* **Tel 01962 771324**

The Royal Horticultural Society's Garden at Wisley

Exclusive evening openings in aid of the National Gardens Scheme on the occasion of its 70th anniversary
Wednesday 18th June & Thursday 14th August
6.30-9pm
See page 18.

Bramley Lodge &✿ (Mrs J D Ward) Fyfield. From Weyhill roundabout take Thruxton Rd. In 150yds turn R signed Fyfield. Continue ¾m under bridge 100yds on R. Long 1-acre garden framed and sheltered by old railway embankment, with many shrubs in curving beds, underplanted with drifts of spring bulbs; pond and bog garden, lime tolerant heathers and conifers. Plants in aid of St Peter in the Wood Church, Appleshaw. TEAS. *Adm £1.50 Chd free. Sun April 6 (2-5)*

Bramshaw Lodge &✿✿ (Dr, Mrs & Miss Couchman) Bramshaw, Lyndhurst. 2m from junction 1 on M27 on B3079. On L past Bramshaw Village Hall. Victorian garden of 1½ acres, circa 1850, with mature trees, rhododendrons and azaleas and expanding shrub and herbaceous planting surrounded by natural forest. Dressage manège. *Adm £2 Chd free. Sun, Mon May 25, 26 (2-6)*

Brandy Mount House &✿ (Mr & Mrs M Baron) Alresford centre, first R in East St before Sun Lane. Please leave cars in Broad St. 1-acre informal plantsman's garden, spring bulbs, hellebores, species geraniums, snowdrop collection, daphne collection, European primulas, herbaceous and woodland plants. Featured in Gardeners World Feb 1993. TEAS April 27, May 11, June 22. *Adm £1.50 Chd free. Sat Feb 8 (11-4); Suns March 16, April 27, May 11, June 22 (2-5) 1998 Sat Feb 7 (11-4). Also private visits welcome on Sats, please* **Tel 01962 732189**

Broadhatch House &✿✿ (Bruce & Lizzie Powell) Bentley; 4m NE of Alton. Turn off A31 (Bentley by-pass), right through village up School Lane. R to Perrylands, after 300yds drive on R. 3½ acres, divided by yew hedges into old-fashioned rose gardens, double herbaceous and shrub borders, with walled garden and incl wide range of perrenials and flowering shrub perennials. Illustrated in 'Rose Gardens of England'. TEA. *Adm £2 Chd free (Share to St Mary Church Bentley®). Mons, Wed June 23, 25, 30 Wed, Sun, Mon July 2, 13, 14 (2- 6). Also private visits welcome in June/July, please* **Tel 01420 23185**

Brocas Farm ✿ (Mrs A A Robertson) Lower Froyle. ½m up road to Lower Froyle from A31 turning just W of Bentley; C18 House (not open) and large old timber barn. 2-acre garden surrounded by open country views. Large yew hedges, roses, herbaceous, unusual ground cover, kitchen garden. Maturing arboretum with interesting trees. TEAS (Sun only). *Adm £2 Chd £1. Sun, Mon June 29, 30 (2-5.30)*

1 Brook Cottages ✿ (Mr & Mrs D Stapley) East Meon, Petersfield. Off A272 at Langrish turn L for East Meon. Turn L in front of church. Follow rd round L into the High Street. Brook Cottage is just past Izaak Walton Public House. ⅓-acre with over 300 herbs. Small areas with herbs for wines and liqueurs. Open knot of culinary and physic herbs. Chamomile seat and covered way of scented climbers. Medical astrology garden and circular severity. Featured on TV Grass Roots 1996 and Gardeners World. Dyes, crafts, etc. *Adm £1.50. Sats, Sun May 31, July 6, 19 (2-6). Private visits welcome, please* **Tel 01730 823376**

¶**Chalkwood** &✿✿ (Mr & Mrs Ian Shield) Stapley Lane, Ropley. From Alresford on A31 turn R to Petersfield. Stapley Lane 1½m on R. Chalkwood ½m on L. 2 acres developed entirely by owner. Plantsmen's garden, woodland areas, pond, wildflowers. Parking in paddock. *Adm £1.50 Chd free. Tues April 15, May 13, June 10 (2-5) Private visits welcome, please* **Tel 01962 772209**

Chilland & (Mr & Mrs John Impey) Martyr Worthy. Midway between Winchester and Alresford on B3047. 4-acre garden with stream at bottom overlooking R Itchen watermeadows with woods and farmland beyond. Large collection of mature shrubs planned for their yr-round colour effects. Many fine trees incl huge plane and ancient mulberry, nutwalk, spring bulbs, clematis and herbaceous borders. *Adm £1.50 Chd free. Sun, Mon May 4, 5 (2-5.30) Mon July 21 (11-6). Also Sun July 20 with* **Martyr Worthy Gardens**

¶**187 Christchurch Road** &✿✿ (Mr & Mrs C S Fryer) Ringwood. S of Ringwood on B3347, approx ¾m from the A31 turn off into Ringwood, follow signs for Kingston-Sopley. Across 3 roundabouts look L for police station. 187 4th turning L past it. Parking in Willow Dr 3rd L and in service rd by house. Small garden packed with many interesting plants, gravelled front garden with many variety of houseleeks, also pulsatillas, hardy geraniums, grasses, ferns and evergreens. TEAS (May at Potters Cottage). *Adm £1.50 Chd £1. Sats April 12, May 17 (2-5), Sun April 13 (10-4), Sun May 18 (11-5)*

Cliddesden Gardens ✿✿ 2m S of Basingstoke. Take A339 (Basingstoke to Alton Rd) Turn R into Farleigh Rd (B3046) Gardens situated about 1m on L. TEAS. *Combined adm £1.50 Chd free. Sun June 22 (12.30-5.30)*

    Yew Tree Cottage & (Jean & Peter Matthews) Cottage garden in ⅓-acre. Areas of different character. Thatched well-head with roses, white garden, stream and pool. To be featured in Period Living and Traditional Homes magazine. *(Share to Cliddesden Village Hall)*

    Sussex House & (Molly & Bob Jones) ⅓-acre garden with herbaceous borders and rose beds. Pond stocked with Koi and Orfe bordered by a small rock garden partly enclosed with dwarf conifers. *(Share to St Michael's Hospice, Basingstoke®)*

Closewood House & (Mr & Mrs Peter Clowes) Denmead. Take Closewood Rd to the W of the B2150 between Waterlooville and Denmead. L at T-junction after ½m. Signs to car park after 300 metres. 1½ acre garden with good collection of scented roses and flowering shrubs. Also 3 acre field recently planted with over 100 different trees. Car park. TEAS (Sun) TEA (Wed). *Adm £1.50 Chd free. Sun June 15, Wed June 18 (2-6)*

●**Coles** ✿✿ (Mrs Tim Watkins) Privett, nr Alton and Petersfield. Approx 6m NW of Petersfield betweeen the hamlets of Privett and High Cross. From A3 take A272 Petersfield to Winchester, turn N after 5m signposted to Privett; turn 1st R, continue past the church, 1m to entrance. From A32, S of Alton between East Tisted and West Meon Hut, turn E to Froxfield at Pig and Whistle/Lawns public house, after ½m turn L at T-junction and continue for ¾m, entrance on L. 26 acres of spectacular gardens specialising in rhododendrons and azaleas, set amongst mixed woodland with rare specimens. Undulating ground with walks and clearings opening onto views of decorative ponds and other unusual features. Spring bluebells. Wonderful Autumn leaf colours. TEAS. *Adm £3, OAP £2.50 Chd 50p (Share to NGS). Sat May 17, Suns, May 4, 18, 25, Oct 12 (2-5.30). Mons, May 5, 26 (2-5.30) Sat June 7 (5-7). Private visits welcome, please* **Tel 0171 493 2008**

¶**Conholt Park** &⚘ (Caroline Tisdall) Chute, Andover. Turn N off A342 Andover-Devizes rd at Weyhill Church. 5m N through Clanville and Tangley Bottom. Turn L at Conholt (Marked on ordinance survey) ½m on R, just off Chute causeway. 10 acres surrounding Regency House, with 4 magnificent Cedars. Recently restored walled garden of 1½ acres lined with geranium and allium collections. Potager, berry wall, rare fruit orchard, white border, Edwardian glasshouses and orchid house, collection of mahonias, rose garden, ladies walk to valley, Shire horse, Garron Ponies, Bison, Tamworth pigs. TEAS. *Adm £2.50 Chd free. Sats, Suns June 21, 22; Sept 20, 21 (12-5)*

Copperfield &⚘ (John Selfe) Dogmersfield. Turn N off Odiham-Farnham A287 to Dogmersfield. Turn L by Queens Public House. Set in 1½ acres. A true plantsman's garden; with vast beds displaying a wide range of plants and ornamental trees incl many rare and unusual varieties. Designed by nurseryman owner to provide spectacular yr-round colour and a stunning water feature. A camomile lawn and woodland walk. TEAS. *Adm £2 Chd free. Sun July 6 (12-5)*

The Cottage ⚘⚘ (Mr & Mrs H Sykes) 16 Lakewood Rd, Chandler's Ford. Leave M3 at junction 12, follow signs to Chandler's Ford. At Hanrahans on Winchester Rd, turn R into Merdon Ave, then 3rd rd on L. ¾-acre garden planted for yr-round interest with spring colour from bulbs, camellias, rhododendrons, azaleas and magnolias. Woodland, conifers, herbaceous borders, bog garden, ponds, fruit and vegetable garden. TEAS. *Adm £1.50 Chd 10p (Share to British Heart Foundation®). Suns, Mons April 20, 21; May 4, 5 (2-6)*

Court Lodge ⚘⚘ (Patricia Dale) West Meon. 8m W of Petersfield, S on A32. ¼-acre specialist cottage garden of botanical artist owner. Rich in small spring plants, anemones, erythroniums, hellebores, narcissi, primulas, etc. Many used as subjects for paintings and cards, which may be seen in the Studio. Also miniature gardens in sinks, small pond, and gravel paths with interesting edge plants. Regret not suitable for small children. Teas at church in aid of their own charity. *Adm £1.50 Chd free. Sun March 23 (2-6)* **Tel 01730 829473**

Cranbury Park &⚘ (Mr & Mrs Chamberlayne-Macdonald) Otterbourne, 5m S of Winchester. 2m N of Eastleigh; main entrance on old A33 between Winchester-Southampton, by bus stop at top of Otterbourne Hill. Entrance also in Hocombe Rd, Chandlers Ford. Extensive pleasure grounds laid out in late C18 and early C19; fountains; rose garden; specimen trees; lakeside walk. Family carriages and collection of prams will be on view. TEAS. *Adm £2 Chd 50p (Share to Church of St John the Baptist, North Baddesley®). Sun June 15 (2-6) last admission 5pm*

Crawley Gardens 5m NW of Winchester, off A272 Winchester-Stockbridge Rd. Gardens signed from centre of village. Parking at top of village nr the church. Please do not obstruct access drives. TEAS Sun only. *Combined adm £3 Chd free. Sun, Mon April 13, 14 (2-5.30)*
  Glebe House & (Lt-Col & Mrs John Andrews) 1½-acres. Shrubs incl eucalyptus collection
  Little Court &⚘⚘ (Professor & Mrs A R Elkington) See separate entry. *Also open on Sun, Mons, Tues Feb 16, 17, 18, March 23, 24, 25, Sun, Mon April 13, 14, (2-5.30) Thurs, Fris Apr 24, 25, July 13, 14, Aug 17, 18, Sept 14, 15, (Suns 2- 5.30) Mons (11-7) Feb 23, 24, 25 (1998)*
  Manor Lodge &⚘⚘ (Mr & Mrs K Wren) See separate entry. Cream teas in aid of St Mary's Church. *Also open June 29, July 6 (2-5.30) with* **Paige Cottage**
  Paige Cottage ⚘ (Mr & Mrs T W Parker) 1 acre of traditional English country garden incl grass tennis court and walled Italian style swimming pool; roses climbing into apple trees. *Sun April 13 (2-5.30). Suns June 29, July 6 (2-5.30) with* **Manor Lodge**

Croft Mews &⚘⚘ (Captain & Mrs W T T Pakenham) Botley. 2m N of Botley on B3354, on L under trees (M27 exit 7). A recently created garden about 2 acres with much older buildings and walls, in grounds of old country house. Walled garden, lawns and mixed borders, woodland area, kitchen garden. Many interesting ideas and features incl new ha ha with views over meadows. TEAS in aid of NSPCC (Sun only). *Adm £1.50 Chd free. Sun June 8 (2-6) Mon June 9 (11-5). Private visits welcome May to Aug (no coaches), please* **Tel 01703 692425**

Crookley Pool &⚘⚘ (Mr & Mrs F S K Privett) Horndean. Turn up Blendworth Lane by the main bakery from the centre of Horndean. House 200yds before church on L. Off the A3 5m S of Petersfield. 2-acre garden surrounded by parkland. Mixed borders of unusual plants and roses, with a special interest in colour and plants for hot dry situations. Wisteria and rose covered walls and pergolas. Walled kitchen garden. TEAS. *Adm £2 Chd free. Wed, Sun July 2, 6 (2-6)*

Croylands &⚘⚘ (The Hon Mrs Charles Kitchener) Old Salisbury Lane. From Romsey take A3057 Stockbridge Rd, L after 1m, Duke's Head, fork L after bridge, 1m on R. Wheelwrights Cottage on Florence Nightingales family estate. 2 acres unusual interesting trees, shrubs and plants. Paeony garden with 200 plants. 3 TV appearances. TEAS. *Adm £1.50 Chd free. Suns, Weds, May 25, 28, June 1, 4, 8, 11, 15, 18, 22, (2-6). Parties welcome May and June, please* **Tel 017945 13056**

The Dower House & (Mr Michael Hoare) Dogmersfield. Turn N off A287. 6-acre garden including bluebell wood with large and spectacular collection of rhododendrons, azaleas, magnolias and other flowering trees and shrubs; set in parkland with fine views over 20-acre lake. TEAS. *Adm £1.50 Chd free. Suns May 11, 18 (2-6)*

By Appointment Gardens. These owners do not have a fixed opening day usually because they cannot accommodate large numbers or have insufficient parking space.

Droxford Gardens 4½m N of Wickham on A32 approx mid-way between Alton-Portsmouth. TEAS at Fir Hill. *Combined adm £1.50 Chd 50p. Combined adm £3 Chd £1. Sun June 22*

Fir Hill ❀ (Mrs Derek Schreiber) 4½ acres; roses, shrubs, herbaceous and shrub borders. Home-made TEAS. Car park

The Mill House ㅴ❀ (Mrs C MacPherson) Garden of 2 acres; shrubs, climbing roses and rose garden, herbaceous borders, pond, mill stream, orchard, vegetable garden. Car park

Mylor Cottage ㅴ❀ (Dr & Mrs Martin ffrench Constant) ½m S of Droxford on the Swanmore Rd. Car park. Mature beeches set off colourful herbaceous borders, fine lawns and foliage beds. A much loved and cherished chalk garden. *Sun April 13 (2-5). Parties welcome, please* **Tel 01489 877462**

Park View Cottage ㅴ (Mrs F V D Aubert) Small town garden, flowers, shrubs and very small wooded walk. Car park

Durmast House ㅴ❀ (Mr & Mrs P E G Daubeney) 1m SE of Burley, nr White Buck Hotel. 4-acre garden designed by Gertrude Jekyll in 1907 in the process of being restored from the original plans. Formal rose garden edged with lavender, 130-yr-old Monterey pine, 100-yr-old cut leaf beech and large choisya. Victorian rockery, lily pond, coach-house, large wisteria and herbaceous border. *Adm £1.50 Chd 50p (Share to Delhi Commonwealth Women's Assoc Clinic®). Suns March 30, June 15 (2-5). Private parties welcome, please* **Tel 01425 403527**

East Lane (Sir Peter & Lady Ramsbotham) Ovington A31 from Winchester towards Alresford. Immediately after roundabout 1m west of Alresford, small sign to Ovington turn sharp L up incline, down small country rd to Ovington. East Lane is the only house on left, 500yds before Bush Inn. 4 acres, spring bulbs, mixed herbaceous and shrubs; woodland plantings; walled rose garden. Terraced water garden. Ample parking. *Adm £1.50 Chd 50p. Sun April 13 (1.30-5.30)*

Eversley Gardens ❀ On the B3016 signposted from A30 just W of Blackbush airport and from the B3272 (formerly A327) E of the cricket ground at Eversley Cross. *Combined adm £2 Chd free. Sun May 11 (2-6)*

Kiln Copse (Mr & Mrs J Rowse) 8 acres; wide variety of spring flowering bulbs, bluebell wood and foxgloves. Good collection of rhododendrons, azaleas and roses, lake side with bog-side plants large, mixed borders, round garden with gazebo and plants climbing into the trees

Little Coopers (Mr & Mrs J K Oldale) A woodland walk meanders through bluebells, rhododendrons, azaleas and many unusual shrubs, labelled. Shaded by mature trees, water and bog garden with ponds and stream, then extensive lawn surrounded by Mediterranean and rose garden. Small Japanese garden

● **Exbury Gardens** ㅴ❀ (Exbury Gardens Trust) Exbury, off B3054 3m SE of Beaulieu off A326. 200 acres of landscaped woodland gardens with world-famous Rothschild Plant Collection of rhododendrons, azaleas, magnolias and camellias. Rock garden, cascades, river walk, rose gardens, heather gardens, seasonal trails and walks.

Ample seating throughout. Luncheons and teas. Plant Centre and Gift Shop. *Spring Season: Sat Feb 17 to mid April Adm £3.30 OAPs £2.80 Chd (10-15) £2.20 mid April to mid June £4.80, OAPs £4.30 Weds/Thurs £3.80 Chd £3.80. Mid June - mid July £3.30 OAPs £2.80 Chd £2.20. Summer garden (53 acres) mid July - mid Sept £2.20 OAPs & Chd £1.70. Autumn garden (200 acres) mid Sept - 2 Nov £2.80 OAPs £2.20 Chd £1.70. Call for special event details*

Fairfield House ❀❀ (Mrs Peter Wake) Hambledon. 10m SW of Petersfield. Hambledon village. 5-acre informal garden on chalk, with extensive walls, fine mature trees; large collection of shrubs and climbing roses mixed with wide variety of small trees and interesting perennials. Adjacent car park and wild flower meadow. Featured in 'A Heritage of Roses' by Hazel Le Rougetel, 'The Rose Gardens of England' by Michael Gibson, 'The Latest Country Gardens' by George Plumptre. TEAS. *Adm £2 Chd free. Suns, April 6, May 11, June 22 (2-6). Also private visits welcome anytime by appt; suitable for groups, please* **Tel 01705 632431**

Fernlea ❀❀ (Mr & Mrs P G Philip) Chilworth. From Winchester on M3 take exit 14 to Southampton A33 at roundabout follow A27 to Romsey and Chilworth at Clump Inn turn L follow Manor Rd into Chilworth. Dr over motorway bridge turn R. Fernlea last house on L. 15 acre wildlife garden natural habitat, woodland walks, also many Mediterranean plants within informal planting, formal beds around house and newly created kitchen garden. Some plants and seasonal produce for sale. Picnics welcome. TEAS. *Adm £1.50 Chd free. Suns April 6, May 4, July 27 (12-5)*

¶**Flintstones** ㅴ (June & Bill Butler) Sciviers Lane, Durley. From M3 junction 11 follow signs Marwell Zoo. From B2177 turn R opp Woodman Inn. From M27 junction 7 follow signs Fairoak Durley turn L at Robin Hood. ¾-acre on clay developed over 3yrs, with raised beds and close tapestry effect of texture and colour. TEA. *Adm £1.50 Chd free. Sun, Mon June 1, 2 (2-6)*

¶**Forest Edge** ㅴ❀❀ (Annette & David Beeson) Andover Down. On the B3400 Andover to Whitchurch rd. Surrounding the house is a traditional garden, where herbaceous plants, shrubs and climbers blend into the surrounding trees and hedges; also gravel scree. Beyond is the wild garden with a variety of natural habitats for flora and fauna, each managed to encourage different plants and animals. Moles, voles, field mice and squirrels can be seen running about. Pond for frogs and newts. Walk in the ancient Harewood Forest accessible from the garden. *Adm £1.50 Chd free. Sun July 13 (11-5)*

Fritham Lodge ㅴ❀ (Christopher and Rosie Powell) Fritham, nr Lyndhurst. M27 junction Cadnam. Follow signs to Fritham. Parking in field. Set in heart of New Forest in 18 acres; with 1 acre old walled garden surrounding Grade II listed C17 house originally one of Charles II hunting lodges. Parterre of old roses, potager with wide variety of vegetables, herbs and fruit trees, pergola, herbaceous and blue and white mixed borders, ponds, walk across hay meadows to woodland and stream. TEAS. *Adm £1.50 Chd free. Sun June 29 (2-5)*

● **Furzey Gardens** ♿❀❀ (Furzey Gardens Charitable Trust) Minstead, 8m SW of Southampton. 1m S of A31; 2m W of Cadnam and end of M27; 3½m NW of Lyndhurst. 8 acres of informal shrub garden; comprehensive collections of azaleas and heathers; water garden; fernery; summer and winter flowering shrubs. Botanical interest at all seasons. Also open (limited in winter) Will Selwood Gallery and ancient cottage (AD 1560). High quality arts and crafts by many local craftsmen. *Adm £3 OAPs £2.50 Chd £1.50 Families £7 March to Oct. £1.50 OAPs £1 Chd 75p Families £3.50 winter (Share to Minstead Training Project and other charities). Daily except Dec 25 & 26 (10-5; dusk in winter).* **Tel 01703 812464**

The Garden House ❀ (Mr & Mrs C Kirkman) Lymington. Off Lymington High St opp Woolworths. Unusual herbaceous, roses, grasses, house leeks, agaves and shrubs, interspersed with a riot of annuals, punctuated by 2 ponds in ¾ acre. Prime example of close boscage. TEAS with extravagant portions of clotted cream. *Adm £2 Chd free (Share to the Worshipful Company of Gardeners' Charitable Trust®). Sun June 8 (2-6)*

Glevins ♿❀ (Mrs Clarke) Lymington. Situated off Lymington High St between Lloyds Bank and Nat West Bank. ½-acre small walled garden with wide view of the Solent and Yarmouth, I.O.W. Mixed borders, small rockery conservatory. TEA. *Adm £2 Chd free. Sun June 8 (2-6)*

Greatham Mill ♿❀❀ (Mr & Mrs E Groves) Greatham, nr Liss. 5m N of Petersfield. From A325, at Greatham turn onto B3006 towards Alton; after 600yds L into 'No Through Rd' lane to garden. Interesting garden with large variety of plants surrounding mill house, with mill stream. Home-made TEAS. *Adm £2 Chd free. Sat March 29, Weds July 2, Sept 24 (11-6). Private visits welcome, please* **Tel 01420 538245**

¶**Greenfingers** ❀ (St James's Hospital) Locks Way, Milton. From A27 or M27 take A2030 into Portsmouth, at traffic lights rd curves R. Continue to Velder Ave until roundabout. Take L turn into Milton Rd (A288) hospital is signposted top of Locksway Rd 8th rd from roundabout. Greenfingers Horticulture Training Therapy centre is signposted in hospital grounds. ⅔-acre approx. Display beds of all kinds, incl vegetables, nature and ornamental ponds, polytunnels and greenhouses. TEA. *Adm £1 Chd free. Suns May 11, Sept 14 (11-5)*

Hall Place ♿ (Mr & Mrs Dru Montagu) West Meon. 7m W of Petersfield. From A32 in West Meon, take rd to East Meon, garden on R. Parking in drive. Large collection of rare and unusual daffodils in 8 acres of garden designed by Lanning Roper 30 years ago. Grass walks, spring bulbs, many varieties of trees and shrubs; walled kitchen garden. Parts of the garden have recently been re-designed. *Adm £2 Chd free. Sun April 20 (2-6)*

Hambledon House ❀❀ (Capt & Mrs David Hart Dyke) Hambledon. 8m SW of Petersfield. In village centre behind George Hotel. Approx 2 acres partly walled garden with unusual plants, shrubs suited to chalk soil and to give colour and interest through the seasons. Centred around 150-yr-old copper beech. Special interest in grasses, salvias, penstemons. TEAS (Suns). *Adm £2 Chd*

free. 1st, 3rd Tues, May, June, July, Sept (2-5). Suns May 25, June 22, Sept 7 (2-6); also private visits welcome, please **Tel 01705 632380**

¶**Harcombe House** (Mr & Mrs G Bearman) Park Lane, Ropley. E of Alresford. Leave A31 Alton-Winchester Rd at The Anchor, Ropley; follow rd to West Tisted for ½m; turn up first narrow lane on R and on to Harcombe. 12-acre garden; rose garden; herbaceous borders; flowering shrubs, small water garden; good views. *Adm £1.50 Chd free. Sun July 6 (2-6)*

Hayden Barn Cottage ♿❀ (Captain & Mrs Broadbent) Take A32 to Warnford. Opp George and Falcon public house take single track rd signposted to Clanfield. Go ¾m. Red brick cottage on L. 1-acre garden on several levels developed entirely by owners. Herbaceous and mixed borders, rockery, shrubberies and good spring colour set off by extensive brick and flint walling, terraces and grassy banks. No coaches. Parking through garden not in lane. TEA. *Adm £1.50 Chd free. Weds April 9, 30, May 14 (1-5)*

Heathlands ♿❀ (Dr & Mrs John Burwell) 47 Locks Rd, Locks Heath. Locks Rd runs due S from Park Gate into Locks Heath. No 47 is 1m down on the R hand side [Grid Ref 513 069]. 1-acre garden designed & developed by the owner since 1967. Yr-round interest against a background of evergreens and mature trees. Spring bulbs, rhododendrons, paulownias. cyclamen, ferns and some less usual plants. Topiary, small herbaceous border and scree bed. National Collection of Japanese anemones. 'A treat for garden visitors' Stefan Buczacki TVS. TEAS. *Adm £1.50 Chd free. Suns May 11, July 13 (2-5.30)*

Hightown Farm (Oliver & Margaret Ziegler) Hightown Hill, Ringwood. Off A31 ¼m W of Picket Post, L at Hightown and Crow sign, cross two cattle grids, garden 100yds on L. E return from Picket Post via underpass. 3 acres of formal and woodland garden for both the plantsman and those who just like a garden in a beautiful situation. Dry and stony; one damp area with hostas, iris ensata, primulas, ferns, Large range of rhododendrons, azaleas and unusual shrubs. Plants for sale (May only). TEA (Sun only). *Adm £2 Chd free. Thurs April 17, Sun, Mon, Wed May 25, 26, Aug 13 (2-5.30). Private visits welcome by appt esp early Oct for cyclamen, please* **Tel 01425 474278**

¶**High Paddocks** ♿❀ (Mrs E Cawson) Privett. Take signs to Privett off A32 then follow yellow signs. 1-acre with surrounding countryside, on clay and 600' up. Interesting collection of plants, shrubs and small wild flower paddock. *Adm £1.50 Chd free. Tues, Weds June 10, 11 (2-6)*

Hill House, Old Alresford ♿ (Maj & Mrs W F Richardson) From Alresford 1m along B3046 towards Basingstoke, then R by church. 2 acres with large old-fashioned herbaceous border and shrub beds, set around large lawn; kitchen garden. TEAS. *Adm £1.50 Chd free. Sun, Tue Aug 3, 5 (2-5.30)*

Regular Openers. Open throughout the year. They are listed at the end of the Diary Section under 'Regular Openers'.

● **Sir Harold Hillier Arboretum** &⊗❀ Jermyns Lane, Ampfield. Situated between Ampfield and Braishfield, 3m NE of Romsey. Signposted from A31 and A3057. 166-acres containing the finest collection of hardy trees and shrubs in the UK. Home to 11 National Collections. Pond, scree beds, heather garden, peat garden, centenary border and acer valley. Wonderful spring and autumn colour with guided tours at 2pm every Suns and Weds in May and Oct. Fine collections of magnolias, azaleas and rhododendrons. TEAS. *Adm April to Oct £4 OAP £3.50 Chd £1 (Group rate 10+ £3); Nov to March £3, OAP £2.50 Chd £1. Daily April 1 to Oct 31 (10.30-6); Nov 1 to March 31 (10.30-5 or dusk)*

▲**Hinton Ampner** &⊗ (The National Trust) S of Alresford. On Petersfield-Winchester Rd A272. 1m W of Bramdean village. 12-acre C20 shrub garden designed by Ralph Dutton. Strong architectural elements using yew and box topiary, with spectacular views. Bold effects using simple plants, restrained and dramatic bedding. Orchard with spring wild flowers and bulbs within formal box hedges; magnolia and philadephus walks. Dell garden made from chalk pit. Shrub rose border dating from 1950s. Chosen for 'Alan Titchmarsh's favourite gardens' 1995. TEAS. *Adm £2.80 Chd £1.40. Sats, Suns April 20, June 22. For NGS Sat, Sun Sept 13, 14 (1.30-5.30)*

Holt End House ⊗❀ (Maj & Mrs J B B Cockcroft) Ashford Hill, Newbury. Ashford Hill is on B3051 between Kingsclere and Tadley. The garden is in the village on the R going E. 3-acre garden with extensive collection of labelled roses, with many climbers on unusual tree hosts. Substantial mature shrub planting. Large ginkgo biloba. Area of SSI woodland. TEAS. *Adm £2 Chd free (Share to St Paul's Church, Ashford Hill®). Sun June 29 (2-6.30)*

■ **Houghton Lodge** &❀ (Captain M W Busk) Stockbridge. 1½m S of Stockbridge A30 on rd to Houghton. Landscape pleasure grounds surround C18 cottage ornée overlooking the tranquil beauty of R Test. Topiary, 'Peacock' garden, walled garden, fuchsia collection. Hydoronicum, living exhibition of horticulture without soil. Location of filming 'Oscar Wilde'. TEA. *Adm £2.50 Chd free (Share to All Saints Church). Daily March 1 to Sept 30 except Weds (2-5), Sats, Suns, Bank Hols (10-5). For NGS Sun, Mon April 6, 7 (10-5)*

House-in-the-Wood ⊗ (Countess Michalowska) Well signed 1½m from Beaulieu; signed from Motor Car Museum, Beaulieu. R on B3056 Beaulieu-Lyndhurst Rd. 13-acre woodland garden; rhododendrons and azaleas. *Adm £2 Chd 50p. Mon May 5 (2.30-6.30). Parties by appt Tel 01590 612346*

Jasmine Lodge & (Nigel & Linda Murgatroyd) Jasmine Rd, Kempshott, Basingstoke. From M3, junction 7, follow Basingstoke signs. At Kempshott roundabout turn L into Heather Way, then immed R into Jasmine Rd. Park on rd away from bend. Front and back gardens each 30' × 70'. Basingstoke in Bloom winner 1996. Over 5,000 summer bedding plants, carpet bedding and over 70 containers. Featured in Amateur Gardening Oct 1996. *Adm £1.50 Chd free (Share to St Michael's Hospice, Basingstoke). Suns July 27, Aug 3 (11-5)*

53 Ladywood ⊗❀ (Mr & Mrs D Ward) Eastleigh. Leave M3 at junction 12. Follow signs to Eastleigh. R at roundabout into Woodside Ave, 2nd R into Bosville. Ladywood is 5th R off Bosville, please park in Bosville. 45' × 45', developed by the owners over 7 yrs, giving many ideas for the small garden. Featured on Grass Roots and Garden Party 1996 in Gardeners' World magazine 1997. Over 1500 different plants labelled. Rustic fences give vertical space for clematis and climbing roses. Collections of hardy geraniums, pulmonarias, and many foliage plants. TEAS (afternoon only). *Adm £1.50 Chd 75p. Suns April 27, June 15, Aug 3 (11-5.30). Private visits welcome April 1 to Sept 30 Tuesday afternoons, please Tel 01703 615389*

Lake House &❀ (Lord & Lady Ashburton) Northington, Alresford. 4m N of Alresford off B3046. Follow English heritage signs to The Grange, then directions. 2 large lakes in Candover valley set off by mature woodland with waterfalls, abundant bird life, long landscaped vistas. 1½-acre walled garden, mixed borders, long herbaceous border, rose pergola leading to moon gate. Formal kitchen garden, flowering pots, conservatory and greenhouses. Picnicking by lakes. TEAS. *Adm £2.50 Chd free (Share to Friends of St John's Church, Northington®). Sun July 6 (11-5). Group visits welcome, please Tel 01962 734820*

Landford Lodge Landford see Wiltshire

60 Lealand Road &⊗❀ (Mr F G Jacob) Drayton. 2m from Cosham E side of Portsmouth. Old A27 (Havant Rd) between Cosham and Bedhampton. Small prize winning garden created and designed by owner since 1969. Featured in National Gardening Magazines. Exotic plants with rockery, ponds, dwarf conifers and collection of grasses, cacti and other exotics in greenhouse. TEAS. *Adm £1 Chd free. Suns May 25, June 22, Aug 17 (11-5). Also private visits welcome, please Tel 01705 370030*

Lithend &⊗❀ (Mrs F L Gunner) 5m NW of Winchester, off A272 in Crawley village; small cottage garden. *Combined adm £2.50 with Little Court. Sun, Mon July 13, 14 (2-5.30)*

Little Barn Garden & Barnhawk Nursery &❀ (Drs R & V A Crawford) Woodgreen. 3m NE of Fordingbridge via A338. Turn E to Woodgreen; bear L in village; R immediately past Horse and Groom, continue for 1¼m; 2½ acres of mature informal garden with all-yr interest in form, colour and texture; rhododendron; azalea; camellia; magnolia; acer and collector's plants with peat, scree, rock, woodland, bog and water area. *Adm £1.50 Chd free. Sun, Mon June 8, 9 (2-6). Also private visits welcome, please Tel 01725 512213*

The Little Cottage ⊗❀ (Lyn & Peter Prior) On N fringe of Lymington on A337, opp Toll House Inn. Formal ¼-acre town garden arranged in seven harmoniously colour schemed rooms - soft colours surround cottage, elsewhere strong and vibrant colours are used to dramatic effect. Box edging, topiary, climbers, gazebos, arbours and interesting tender plants in pots and urns. Featured in Practical Gardening 1996. *Adm £2 (unsuitable for children) Sat July 5 (10-1 & 2-5) and Tues June to Aug (10-1 & 2-6). Private visits welcome, please Tel 01590 679395*

Little Court &&✿ (Prof & Mrs A R Elkington) Crawley 5m NW of Winchester off A272 in Crawley village; 300yds from either village pond or church. 1½ acre walled garden in 6 sections. Naturalised crocus and narcussi. Exhuberant planting of many perennials and climbers in related colours for successional interest. Victorian kitchen garden, camomile seat, bantams and geese, with beautiful view to downs. TEAS Suns only. *Adm £2 (Combined with* **Crawley Gardens** *£3; with* **Lithend** *£2.50). Sun, Mons, Tues Feb 16, 17, 18, March 23, 24, 25, Sun, Mon, April 13, 14, (2-5.30) Thurs, Fri April 24, 25 July 13, 14; Aug 17, 18; Sept 14, 15 (Suns 2-5.30, weekdays 11-7) Feb 23, 24, 25 (1998). Also private visits welcome, please* **Tel 01962 776365**

Littlewood &&✿ (Steven and Sheila Schrier) 163 West Lane, Hayling Island. From A27 Havant/Hayling Island roundabout, travel S 2m, turn R into West Lane. Travel 1m and Littlewood is on R in a wood. 2½-acre woodland garden protected from the sea winds by multi barrier hedge. Woodland walk and access to Hayling Billy harbour trail. Rhododendrons, azaleas, camellias and many other shrubs. Features incl pond, bog garden watered from roof of comfortable conservatory with many house plants. New for 97 Tree/Wendy house in woods and propagating greenhouse. Picnickers welcome. Easy access for elderly and wheelchair bound. TEAS. *Donations. Sat, Sun May 24, 25 (11-6)*

Longparish Gardens &✿ 5m E of Andover off A303 to village centre on B3048. *Combined adm £3 Chd free. Sun July 6 (12-5)*
    Longmead House &&✿ (Mr & Mrs J H Ellicock) 2½-acre organic garden. Large hedged vegetable garden with deep beds, polytunnel, fruit cage and composting display. A fishpond and wildlife pond, wildflower meadow, herbaceous and shrub borders, trees. Angora goats, dairy goat and chickens. TEAS. *Private visits welcome, please* **Tel 01264 720386**
    Longparish House ✿ (Mr & Mrs R C Kelton) Period house set in parkland. Newly planted roses in formal beds. Est shrubs and trees in lawns sweeping down to banks of the Test. Long and short riverside walks along mown paths with wonderful natural flora and fauna (Bring wellies if wet) Park and picnic in the grounds

■ **Longstock Park Gardens** &✿ (Leckford Estate Ltd; Part of John Lewis Partnership) 3m N of Stockbridge. From A30 turn N on to A3057; follow signs to Longstock. Famous water garden with extensive collection of aquatic and bog plants set in 7 acres of woodland with rhododendrons and azaleas. A walk through the park leads to an arboretum, herbaceous border and nursery. Featured in several TV programmes and gardening books. Plants and Teas at nearby garden centre. TEAS in aid of local churches. *Adm £2 Chd 50p. 1st and 3rd Sunday in month April to Sept. For NGS Sun June 15 (2-5)*

■ **Longthatch** &&✿ (Mr & Mrs P Short) Lippen Lane, Warnford. 1m S of West Meon on A32 turn R from N or L from S at George & Falcon, 100yds turn R at T-junction, continue for ¼m; thatched C17 house on R, follow signs for parking. 2-acre plantsman's garden rolling down to R. Meon. Many rare trees and shrubs. Part of the National Collection of Helleborus. Alpine bog gardens, ponds and

riverside plantings and a damp shaded area being planted up. Fine lawns and herbaceous borders, and island beds. Always being added to by the enthusiastic owners. *Adm £2 Chd free. Open for NGS Suns March 9, 16, 23, April 20; Sun, Mon May 25, 26; Suns June 22, July 13, Aug 31 (2-5). Also private visits by Societies and individuals welcome. We also open Weds March 5 to Aug 27 (10-5) please* **Tel 01730 829285**

Lymore Valley Herbs &&✿ (N M Aldridge) Braxton Farm. 3m W of Lymington. From A337 at Everton take turning to Milford-on-Sea, 70yds on L is Lymore Lane. Turn into Lane and gardens are at Braxton courtyard on L. Attractive courtyard with raised lily pool and dovecote. Restored C19 barn leading into formal walled garden. Knot garden and lawns farm walks to Keyhaven and Hurst Castle. Horticultural societies welcome. Special evening visits. TEA. Shop, nursery, no dogs in courtyard or walled garden (dog rings & water provided). *Donations. Open 9-5 all year round except Dec 25 to March 1st.* **Tel 01590 642008**

Macpenny Woodland Garden & Nurseries ✿ (Mr & Mrs T M Lowndes) Burley Road, Bransgore. Midway between Christchurch and Burley. From Christchurch via A35, at Cat and Fiddle turn left; at Xrds by The Crown, Bransgore turn R and on ¼m. From A31 (travelling towards Bournemouth) L at Picket Post, signed Burley; through Burley to Green Triangle then R for Bransgore and on 1m beyond Thorney Hill Xrds. 17 acres; 4-acre gravel pit converted into woodland garden; many choice, rare plants incl camellias, rhododendrons, azaleas, heathers. Large selection shrubs and herbaceous plants available. Tea Burley (Forest Tearooms) or Holmsley (Old Station Tea Rooms). *Collecting box. Daily except Dec 25 & 26 and Jan 1 (Mons-Sats 9-5; Suns 2-5)*

Malt Cottage ✿ (Mr & Mrs Richard Mason) Turn into Upper Clatford off the Andover-Stockbridge or Andover-Salisbury Rd. Park behind village hall. Opposite Crook & Shears Public House, 6 acres developed by designer owners. Formal garden blending into natural water meadows with ¼m chalk stream. Lakes, bog garden; uncommon trees and shrubs. TEA available in aid of another charity. *Adm £2 Chd free. Sun July 13 (2-5)*

Manor Lodge &&✿ (Mr & Mrs K Wren) Crawley, nr Winchester. Signposted from A272 and near the village pond. Rose enthusiasts garden, with collection of white climbing roses, Pauls Himalyan Musk 'Tree'. Old walled garden with scent a priority. Thatched summer house and pond. Many clematis. Cream Teas in beamed Garden Room in aid of St Mary's Crawley (April) WWF (June & July). Parking in rd only. *Adm £1.50. Suns June 29, July 6 (2-5.30) Wed July 2 (2-7). Also open with* **Crawley Gardens** *April 13, 14 (2-5.30); also private visits welcome, please* **Tel 01962 776372**

▲¶**March End** &&✿ (Dr David & Mrs Joan Thomas) Sherfield English. 5m W of Romsey on the A27 Salisbury rd, at cross roads, turn N into Branches Lane, 1st R Doctor's Hill, 1st house on right. Free parking 1-acre totally organic garden on free-draining acid sandy soil surrounding C16 thatched cottage. Large vegetable garden of 4 foot beds with different mulches and green manures. S facing garden wall with kiwi, peach, fig and grape under covered walkway. Greenhouse and polytunnel. Garden with many insect-attractant flowers. *Adm £1.50 Chd 50p (Share to the Romsey Opportunity Group®). Sun June 21. For NGS Mons, Sun June 23, 29, 30 (2-6). Private visits welcome, please* Tel 01794 340255

Martyr Worthy Gardens Midway between Winchester and Alresford on B3047. Gardens joined by Pilgrims Way through Itchen Valley, approx ½m. TEAS in Village Hall in aid of village hall. *Adm £1.50 per garden Chd free. Sun July 20 only (2-5.30)*

Chilland ¿ (Mr & Mrs John Impey) See separate entry. *Also open Sun, Mon May 4, 5, Mon July 21*

Manor House ¿ (Cdr & Mrs M J Rivett-Carnac) Large garden, roses, mixed borders, lawns, shrubs and fine trees, next to C12 church

Marycourt ¿ (Mr & Mrs M Conville) Odiham 2m S of Hartley Wintney on A30 or Exit 5 on M3; In Odiham High St. 1-acre garden and paddocks. Old garden roses; shrubs; ramblers dripping from trees. Silver/pink border, long shrubaceous and colourful herbaceous borders; hosta beds and delphinium planting. Dry stone wall with alpines thriving. Grade II starred house. *Adm £2 Chd free. Suns June 29, July 6 (2-6); Wed July 9 (all day) also group visits welcome, please* Tel 01256 702100

Maurys Mount ¿❀ (Dr & Mrs P Burrows) Slab Lane, West Wellow. On A 36 midway between Salisbury and Southampton, Slab Lane is a turning between the roundabout and Red Rover Inn on A36 in West Wellow. An Edwardian style garden created over 3 generations of family. 10-acres of woodland, garden and paddocks incl young arboretum, conservatory, formal herb and kitchen gardens and mature trees incl 300yr old oak. Woodland walk with pond, orchard and wild-flower meadow. Jacob sheep, ducks, geese, hens and horses. TEAS in aid of Imperial Cancer Research Fund. *Adm £2 Chd 50p. Thurs May 8, Sun June 8 (2-5)*

Meadow House, nr Newbury See Berkshire

Merdon Manor ¿❀❀ (Mr & Mrs J C Smith) Hursley, SW of Winchester. From A3090 Winchester-Romsey, at Standon turn on to rd to Slackstead; on 2m. 5 acres with panoramic views; herbaceous and rose borders; small secret walled water garden as seen on TV. Ha-ha and sheep. TEAS. *Adm £1.50 Chd 25p. Sun May 25 (2-6); also private visits welcome, please* Tel 01962 775215 *or* 775281

Merebimur ¿❀❀ (Mr & Mrs C Snelling) Mockbeggar. 3m N of Ringwood on the A338, turn E to Mockbeggar at The Old Beams Inn. Turn L at the next small Xrds and next L into New Rd. Limited parking at garden but parking on verge opp the end of New Rd with very short walk. ½-acre owner maintained garden with pond, lawns, pergola and mixed borders with many unusual plants. TEA. *Adm £1.50 Chd free. Sat, Sun July 5, 6 (10-5). Private visits welcome, please* Tel 01425 473116

Merrie Cottage ¿❀ (Mr & Mrs C K Thornton) Woodgreen 3m N of Fordingbridge on A338 turn E to Woodgreen. Fork R at PO towards Godshill. Entrance 200

yds on L. Limited parking for disabled or park on common and walk down footpath. The irregular sloping shape offers vistas with a profusion of iris and primulas in May and June, followed by seed-grown lilies and wide variety of moisture lovers. No hard landscape or colour theme but interest is held throughout year. TEAS (Sun) TEA (Mon) at Applecroft. TEAS on private visits for Treloar Trust. *Adm £1.50 Chd free. Sun, Mon June 8, 9 (2-6). Private visits welcome, please* Tel 01725 512273

¶**Milford Gardens** 4m W of Lymington off A337 to B3058. TEAS and plants in aid of Oakhaven Hospice. *Combined adm £2 Chd free. Sat June 21 (11-5)*

Little Brook (Mrs J Spenser) Lymore Lane. Immed on joining B3058 turn L into Lane for ½m, little Brook on L. A summer garden of approx ¼-acre, situated on a gentle S facing slope. Stocked with an abundance of perennials, shrubs and self seeded annuals. *(Share to ESPANA®)*

¶**Woodside Cottage** ❀❀ (Mr & Mrs G England) After ½m turn R into Manor Rd (almost op Milford School), 400yds R into George Rd, 4th house on R. An informal, closely planted cottage garden of approx ¼-acre with two small ponds. Wide range of perennials, some unusual, incl salvias, geraniums and grasses, many grown from seed. Owner gardens by "where can I find space for this" philosophy, some unusual combinations result. Also potted plant collections and interesting plants from seed. Parking suitable for wheelchairs. *Private visits welcome Tues June and July, please* Tel 01590 642291

Monxton Gardens ¿❀❀ 3m W of Andover, between A303 and A343; parking and teas in Village Hall. TEAS in aid of Church. *Combined adm £2.50 Chd free. Sun, Mon May 25, 26 (2-5.30)*

Bec House ¿❀ (Mr & Mrs Anthony Rushworth-Lund) Old rectory garden with spring bulbs and mature trees; rose garden, croquet lawn, orchard and new water garden

Field House (Dr & Mrs Pratt) 2-acre garden made by owners with an air of tranquillity, winding paths, 2 ponds one with frogs, herbaceous borders, foliage and kitchen garden, car park

Hutchens Cottage (Mr & Mrs R A Crick) ¾-acre cottage garden with old roses, clematis, shrubs, mature trees, small orchard; mixed thyme patch and kitchen garden

White Gables (Mrs & Mrs D Eaglesham) Cottage style garden of ⅓ acre, leading down to Pill Hill Brook. Interesting shrubs, old roses and herbaceous plants

Moth House (Mrs I R B Perkins) Brown Candover. On B3046 from Alresford to Basingstoke. 5m from Alresford, just past village green on L. 2-acre garden. Gold and silver garden. Herbaceous borders and shrub walk. Speciality roses. TEAS. *Adm £2 Chd free. Sun July 6 (11-6)*

▲**Mottisfont Abbey & Garden** ¿❀❀ (The National Trust) Mottisfont, 4½m NW of Romsey. From A3057 Romsey-Stockbridge turn W at sign to Mottisfont. 4 wheelchairs and battery car service available at garden. 30 acres; originally a C12 Priory; landscaped grounds with spacious lawns bordering R Test; magnificent trees; remarkable ancient spring pre-dating the Priory; walled garden contains NT's famous collection of old-fashioned roses. Lunch and tea available in the Abbey. *Adm £5 Chd £2.50. For NGS Sun June 22 (12-8.30), last adm 7.30 pm*

Moundsmere Manor &% (Mr & Mrs Andreae) 6m S of Basingstoke on B3046. Drive gates on L just after Preston Candover sign. Authentic Edwardian garden designed by Reginald Blomfield incl period greenhouse in full use. Formal rose garden and long herbaceous borders, unusual mature specimen trees and superb views over the Candover Valley. Coaches by appt. *Adm £2 Chd £1. Sun July 6 (2-5)*

Mylor Cottage See Droxford Gardens

¶**Nikendi** %✿ (Phil Jeffs) Broad Lane, Swanmore. Swanmore is SE of Bishop's Waltham off B2177. From church New Rd runs SW Broad Lane is off New Rd, 300yds from church 'Nikendi' is 5th house on R. The 60m x 10m garden was started in 1990. Large collection of small trees and shrubs for foliage and flower effect divided by narrow paths. *Adm £1.50 Chd 25p. Suns, Mon Feb 16, 17, March 23, 24, April 27, 28, Sun May 11, Suns, Mons June 1, 2, Aug 10, 11, Sept 14, 15, Oct 19, 20 (1-dusk)*

Norsebury Gardens % Stoke Charity, nr Winchester. Just S of A30 and W of A34 2m from Sutton Scotney. Follow signs to Stoke Charity and Hunton. TEAS. *Combined adm £2.50 Chd free. Sun, Mon April 13, 14 (2-5.30)*
   Lower Norsebury & (Mrs F Hughes-Onslow) Spring woodland walk
   Norsebury House %✿ (Mr & Mrs M Goranson) 16-acres incl paddocks. Fine views, garden in many sections incl topiary, rose garden, pergola, vines, pond, pots, orchard, poultry, pony rides. *Adm £2 Chd free. Sun, Mon Aug 24, 25 (2-6)*

North Ecchinswell Farm &✿ (Mr & Mrs Robert Henderson) Nr Newbury. Turn S off A339 Newbury-Basingstoke rd. House 1m from turning (sign-posted Ecchinswell and Bishops Green) on L-hand side. Approx 6-acre garden of which 1 acre of shrub borders, with many roses, around house. Small arboretum leading to woodland. Walks with stream and small lake; planting still being extended; carpets of wild flowers incl bluebells; bog plants and many shrubs and fine trees. TEAS. *Adm £2 Chd free. Suns April 27, June 8 (Share to Ecchinswell Village Hall Appeal®). (2-5.30)*

Oakdene &%✿ (Mr & Mrs Christopher Stanford) Sandleheath. Just into Sandleheath on the B3078, 1 from Fordingbridge on the RH-side immed beyond small church. Garden of nearly 2 acres with over 300 roses of all types incl rambler covered long pergola, 'white' and 'red' herbaceous beds, orchard with free-range hens, flower-bordered productive organic kitchen garden, dovecotes with resident doves. TEAS in aid of Friends of Fordingbridge Hospital. *Adm £2 Chd free. Sun June 22, Tue June 24 (2-5.30). Private visits welcome, please Tel 01425 652133*

Oakley Manor &%✿ (Mr & Mrs Priestley) Rectory Rd, Oakley. 5m W of Basingstoke. From Basingstoke towards Whitchurch on B3400 turn L Station Rd and follow signs. Bus 55a, 55b Basingstoke to Oakley. Large 5-acre garden surrounded by open farmland with comprehensive plant-

ing incl a conservation area. Mature trees, shrubs, perennials and annuals. Thatched Wendy House. TEA. Free parking at the Manor. *Combined adm with **The Barn House** £2 Chd free. Sun Aug 3 (2-5.30)*

16 Old Barn Crescent &% (Mr & Mrs K C Moon) West St, Hambledon 8m SW of Petersfield on B2150 opp Hartridges. Plantsman and flower arrangers intensively planted garden of ½-acre with wide range of plants and areas divided by many climbers. Featured on TV, winner of best overall garden in Hillier Levington Garden Competition 1996. *Adm £2 Chd free. Tues, Weds July 8, 9, 22, 23, Aug 5, 6 (11-6). Private visits welcome, please Tel 01705 632758*

The Old House &✿ (Mr & Mrs M Jurgens) Bramley Road, Silchester; next to Roman Museum. Queen Anne rectory with large garden dating from 1920s with pergola, dell, ponds, spring bulbs, woodland carpeted with bluebells, well labelled collection of rhododendrons, camellias, azaleas, specimen trees and shrubs; easy walk to Roman town and medieval church. TEAS in aid of St Mary the Virgin Church, Silchester. *Adm £2 Chd 50p. Suns April 13, 27, May 11, 25 (2-6). Private parties welcome March to May, please Tel 01189 700240*

Old Meadows &%✿ (Dr & Mrs J M Fowler) Silchester. Off A340 between Reading and Basingstoke. 1m S of Silchester on rd to Bramley, signposted at Xrds. 5 acres including walled potager, fine display of spring bulbs, new shrubs. Herbaceous borders, meadow walk. TEAS. *Adm £2 Chd free (Share to Basingstoke North Hampshire Medical Fund®). Wed March 26 (1-4), Sun June 29 (2-6), Weds July 2, 9, 16, 23, 30, Aug 6, 13, 20, 27, Sept 24 (2-4). Private visits welcome, July to Aug, please Tel 01256 881450*

The Old Vicarage % (Sir Dermot & Lady De Trafford) Appleshaw. Take A342 Andover to Marlborough Rd, turn to Appleshaw 1m W of Weyhill, fork L at playing field, on L in village by clock. 2-acre walled garden mature trees, bush and rambler roses, shrub borders, shrubs and trees in grass; fruit and herb garden with box hedges. TEAS. *Adm £1.50 Chd free (Share to St Peter in the Wood Church, Appleshaw®). Sun June 29 (2-5)*

Paddocks Way &%✿ (Ken & Janet Elcock) Brook. 1m W from junction 1 M27 on B3079 turn L into Canterton Manor Drive before Green Dragon. Country garden of ¾ acre, maintained solely by plant loving owners. Mixed borders and island beds containing many interesting and unusual herbaceous perennials, grasses and shrubs grown for flower and foliage effect. Kitchen garden containing vegetables, fruit, greenhouse and frames. TEAS. *Adm £1.50 Chd 50p. Suns May 18, June 29, July 27, Sept 28 (11-5.30). Private visits welcome, please Tel 01703 813297*

Pennington Chase &%✿ (Mrs V E Coates) 2m SW Lymington L off A337, at Pennington Cross roundabout. 2 acres, spring bulbs, flowering shrubs, azaleas, rhododendrons and a variety of trees. TEAS 50p. *Adm £1 Chd 50p. Suns March 23, May 18 (2-7)*

¶**Potters Cot** ✻❀ (Mr & Mrs M G Smith) Hightown Hill, Ringwood. Approaching from Southampton. A31 past Picket Post 1st L over two cattle grids. From Bournemouth to Picket Post, then underpass to Hightown 1st L. Farm Cottage with extensive views, 2½ acres on acid soil. Specimen bulbs, lilies, roses, annuals and herbaceous borders, flowing shrubs. 6yr old arboretum planted for foliage effect. Small working kitchen garden. TEAS. *Adm £2 Chd £1. Sat, Sun May 17 (2-5), 18 (11-5), Sun, Mon July 6, 7 (2-6)*

Pullens ♿✻❀ (Mr & Mrs R N Baird) W Worldham. From Alton take B3006 SE on the Selborne Rd. After 2½m turn L to W Worldham. By church turn R. Pullens 100yds on R behind wall. Approx 1-acre plantsman's garden on greensand surrounded by hedges and walls. Particular emphasis on colour and yr-round interest. Tranquil atmosphere. Featured on Channel 4 TV. TEAS. *Adm £1.50 Chd free. Sat Aug 23 (2-7). Private visits welcome Weds, June only, please Tel 01420 89158*

Pumpkin Patch ✻❀ (Richard & Jenny Henry) 41 Seymour Rd, Ringwood. From junction with A31 take A338 Salisbury turn R after 400yds sharp L after garage into Northfield Rd 3rd R Seymour Rd. ½-acre garden positively invites you up the garden path! Densely planted mixed shrubs, climbers and herbaceous. Glass houses hold varied collections of plants incl succulents, orchids and other exotics. TEAS. *Adm £1.50 Chd free (Share to Cystic Fibrosis Trust®). Suns, Mons May 25, 26, June 15, 22 July 13, 20, Aug 17, 25, Sept 14; Sats June 7, 28, July 5, 26, Aug 9 (10-5)*

Pylewell Park ♿❀ (The Lord Teynham) 2½ m E of Lymington beyond IOW car ferry. Large garden of botanical interest; good trees, flowering shrubs, rhododendrons, lake, woodland garden. *Adm £2.50 Chd 50p (Share to Wessex Regional Medical Oncology Unit®). Suns May 18, 25 (2-5.30). Private visits welcome, please Tel 01590 673010*

Rookley Manor ♿✻❀ (Lord & Lady Inchyra) Up Somborne. 6m W of Winchester. From A272 Winchester-Stockbridge Rd. At Rack and Manger turn L towards Kings Somborne. 2m on R. 2 acres; spring bulbs, flowers and blossom; herbaceous, shrub roses, kitchen garden. TEAS. *Adm £2 Chd free. Mon May 5 (2-6)*

¶**Rose Cottage** ✻❀ (Mr & Mrs I R Elliot) Kingsley Common. On B3004, 5m E of Alton. Park on green below church or in public house carpark. 150yds down the track on R. Sheltered ½-acre garden with distinctive areas. Cottage-style herbaceous borders, range of conifers and trees, ornamental pond and rockery, rose garden, grass and bamboo features, productive kitchen garden and large attractive patio with tubs and baskets. TEAS. *Adm £1.50 Chd free (Share to All Saints Church). Sun July 13 (2-6)*

Rotherfield Park ✻ (Sir James & Lady Scott) East Tisted. 4m S of Alton on A32. Picturesque 12-acre garden incl 1-acre walled garden with trained fruit trees. Ice house. The house and garden starred as Manderley in the 1997 television film of Rebecca. Picnic in the park from noon. TEAS and house open in aid of local churches. *Adm £2 Chd £1. Sat, Sun May 10, 11 (2-5)*

Rowans Wood ♿✻❀ (Mrs D C Rowan) Straight Mile, Ampfield, on A31 (S side); 2m E of Romsey. 2m W of Potters Heron Hotel. Parking on service Rd. Woodland garden developed since 1962 and planted for yr-round interest. Camellias, rhododendrons, flowering trees, spring bulbs followed by azaleas, hostas and other perennials. Views. TEAS. *Adm £1.50 Chd free (Share to Winchester & Romsey Branch RSPCA®). Suns April 20 (2-5), May 4, 25 (2-6), June 1 (6-8.30 with wine), Mon May 5, 26 (2-6). Parties welcome, mid April to early June, please Tel 01794 513072*

12 Rozelle Close ✻ (Margaret & Tom Hyatt) Littleton. Turn E off Winchester to Stockbridge Rd to Littleton. Rozelle Close is near Running Horse public house. ⅓-acre spectacular display of herbaceous and 10,000 bedding plants; tubs; troughs; hanging baskets; 2 ponds; 3 greenhouses; vegetables. *Donations (Share to Littleton and Harestock New Memorial Hall®). Suns July 13, 27, Sat July 26 (9.30-5.30)*

Rumsey Gardens ♿✻ (Mr & Mrs N R Giles) 117 Drift Rd, Clanfield, 6m S of Petersfield. Turn off A3 N of Horndean, signed Clanfield. Planting of garden from a cornfield began during 1956 in poor shallow chalk soil. Acid beds have been constructed enabling lime hating shrubs and plants to be grown. Rock garden, heather beds, pools and bog gardens have been laid out. Collection of cotoneasters. TROBI/NCCPG. *Adm £1.50 Chd 50p. Sun May 4 (11-5). Private visits by societies welcome, please Tel 01705 593367*

3 St Helens Road ♿✻❀ (Mr & Mrs Norman Vaughan) Hayling Island. From Beachlands on seafront, turn R 3rd turning on R into Staunton Avenue, then 1st L. Parking in drive. ⅓-acre ornamental garden with conifers in variety. Interesting trees and shrubs; water garden; old roses; fine lawns. Prizewinning garden featured in 'Amateur Gardening'. TEAS. *Adm by donation. Sat, Sun May 17, 18 (11-5)*

¶**Setters Green** ✻❀ (Jonathan & Jennifer Lyn Dicks) 40 Links Lane, N of Havant. Take the B2149 for about 3m, fork R to Rowlands Castle. Turn L before the village green and L again. Parking 1st R in the recreation ground or in the lane. A new contemporary garden of ⅔-acre with a backdrop of mature trees. Pond, pergola and abundant mixed planting with shrubs. Feature grasses and perennials to give form and texture through the seasons. Teas in village. *Adm £1.50 Chd 50p. Sun Aug 31, Weds Aug 27, Sept 3 (2-5)*

Shalden Park House ♿❀ (Mr & Mrs Michael Campbell) Shalden. Take B3349 from either Alton or M3 intersection 5. Turn W at Xrds by The Golden Pot Public House marked Herriard, Lasham, Shalden. Garden is ¼m on L. 4-acre woodland garden with extensive views. Pond with duckhouse. Walled kitchen garden. Herbaceous borders. Beds of annuals. Glasshouses. Embryonic arboretum with wild flower walk. Lunchtime picnickers welcome. TEAS (not June). *Adm £1.50 Chd free (Share to The Red Cross®). Suns April 27 (1-5), June 29 (11-3)*

South End House ♿✻ (Mr & Mrs Peter Watson) Lymington. At town centre, turn S opp St Thomas Church 70yds, or park free behind Waitrose and use walkway.

Walled town garden to Queen Anne house. ¼-acre, architecturally designed as philosophers' garden. Pergolas, trellises and colonnade attractively planted with vines, clematis, wisteria and roses, combine with sculpted awnings to form 'outdoor rooms', enhanced by fountains, music and lights. Featured on TV 'That's Gardening' and NGS video 2. TEAS. Plants for sale. *Adm £1.50 Chd free. Sun May 25 (2-5.30). Private groups welcome, by arrangement, please* **Tel 01590 676848**

Sowley House &⚘❀ (Mr & Mrs O Van Der Vorm) Sowley. At Lymington follow signs to I.O.W. ferry. Continue E on this rd past the ferry nearest to the Solent for 3m until Sowley pond on L. Sowley House is opp the pond. Beautiful setting overlooking Solent and I.O.W. of 19 acres at high tide and 52 acres at low tide, stream walk, wild garden with drifts of primroses and violets. Helleborus collection, woodland and walled herb garden with varied planting; roses, clematis. TEAS. *Adm £2 Chd free (Shore to Ookhaven Hospice Lymington®). Sun March 23 (2-5). Private visits welcome, (no coaches) please* **Tel 01590 626231**

Spinners ⚘❀ (Mr & Mrs P G G Chappell) Boldre. Signed off the A337 Brockenhurst-Lymington Rd (do not take sign to Boldre Church). Azaleas, rhododendrons, magnolias, hydrangeas, maples etc interplanted with a wide range of choice herbaceous plants and bulbs. Nursery specialises in the less common and rare hardy shrubs and plants. *Adm £1.50 Chd under six free. April 14 to Sept 14 daily (10-5) except Suns and Mons. Nursery and part of garden open at the same times over the winter.* **Tel 01590 673347**

Springfield ⚘ (Vice-Adm Sir John & Lady Lea) 27 Brights Lane, Hayling Island. From Havant take main rd over Hayling bridge, 3m fork R at roundabout into Manor Rd, Brights Lane ¼m on R. Bus: from Havant, ask for Manor Rd, Hayling Island, alight at Manor Rd PO. Medium-sized walled Victorian cottage garden, seen several times on TV, has been gradually altered over the years to produce borders massed with unusual as well as traditional plants surrounding central lawn and young mulberry tree. Productive vegetable areas and greenhouses keep some of the cottage garden feel. Plants for sale. Partially suited for wheelchairs. TEAS. *Adm by donation. Sat June 28 (11-5). Private visits welcome, please* **Tel 01705 463801**

■ **Stratfield Saye House** &❀ (Home of the Dukes of Wellington) Off A33, equidistant between Reading and Basingstoke. 3½-acre walled garden with fruit, vegetables, herbs and greenhouses. Large rose garden. Early C19 garden created by the 1st Duke with many plants of American origin: leading to Park with magnificent specimen trees incl Wellingtonia. Riverside walk with wild fowl. Refreshments. Also, nearby, Wellington Country Park with woodlands, meadowlands and lake. TEAS. *Adm £5 Chd £2.50 special rates for 20 or more.* **Tel 01256 882882.** *Open Sats, Sun, Bank Hol Mon; Daily except Fri in June, July and Aug. Sats, Suns in Sept and during the week in Sept by prior arrangement for groups. Grounds and exhibition open (11.30-6). House open (12-4). For NGS Adm £2 Chd £1 Mon May 5 (11.30-6)*

Swallowfield Park, nr Reading See Berkshire

Swarraton Gardens &⚘❀ 3½m N of Alresford off B3046 close to the main entrance to The Grange. Follow English Heritage signs to The Grange. TEAS. *Combined adm £2.50 Chd free. Sun, Tues July 13, 15 (2-6)*
    The Clock House (Mr & Mrs Michael Brodrick) Colourful garden of 1¼ acres which is still being developed with mixed borders, many clematis, roses and hardy geraniums. Large vegetable garden and trained fruit
    Meadow Lodge (Mr & Mrs D W Hardy) Small cottage garden, many varieties of fuchsias; hanging baskets, pergola, small fruit and vegetable plot

Tunworth Old Rectory &❀ (The Hon Mrs Julian Berry) 5m SE of Basingstoke. 3m from Basingstoke turn off A30 at sign to Tunworth. Garden laid out with yew hedges, enclosing different aspects of the garden i.e. swimming pool, double rose and mixed border; ruby wedding garden; pleached hornbeam walk; lime avenue, ornamental pond, interesting trees incl beech lined walk to church. TEAS. *Adm £2 OAP £1 Chd free (Share to All Saints Church Tunworth®). Sun July 6 (2-5.30)*

Tylney Hall Hotel ⚘❀ From M3 Exit 5 Via A287 and Newnham, M4 Exit 11 via B3349 and Rotherwick. Large garden. 67 acres surrounding Tylney Hall Hotel with extensive Woodlands and fine vistas now being fully restored with new plantings; fine avenues of Wellingtonias; rhododendron and azaleas; Italian Garden; lakes; large water and rock garden and dry stone walls originally designed with assistance of Gertrude Jekyll. Plants for sale June 15 only. TEA. *Adm £2 Chd free. Suns May 18, June 15, July 20 (10-6)*

Upham Gardens 3m Bishops Waltham on A333, small R turn to Upham by Woodmans Public House. TEAS. *Adm £1.50 per garden Chd free. Sun, Wed June 15, 18 (2-6)*
    The Old Rectory (Mr & Mrs J R Vail) Beside beautiful, part-Norman church. Painter's garden, approx 1½ acres, divided into series of rooms with different planting, knot garden, parterre, woodland area and mixed herbaceous borders, vines covering remains of Victorian glass house
    Upham Farm (Mr & Mrs J Walker) Garden made over last 15 yrs; herbaceous, trellis garden of old roses

Valentine Cottage &⚘❀ (Mr & Mrs Brown) Newnham Rd. From Hook follow A30 towards Basingstoke. After approx 1m at The Dorchester Arms turn R into School Lane signposted Newnham. At the end of School Lane turn L into Newnham Rd and 200yds on the R is the car park at Village Hall. 25yd walk along Newnham Rd to Valentine Cottage. An exuberant cottage garden of ⅔ acre, developed over last 5yrs specialising in clematis, roses and laid out into individual smaller gardens. TEAS. *Adm £1.50 Chd 50p. Sun June 29 (2-6). Also private visits welcome, please* **Tel 01256 762049**

Vernon Hill House ❀ (Mr & Mrs F C Fryer) ½m N of Bishop's Waltham roundabout, turn off B3035 into Beeches Hill and follow garden signs. Attractive 6-acre spring and summer garden; wild garden with bulbs growing informally; fine trees, roses, unusual shrubs; kitchen

garden. Picnickers welcome. TEA. *Adm £1.50 Chd 25p.
Sun, Mon May 4, 5; Suns June 15, 29 (2-7); also private
parties welcome May to early July, please* **Tel 01489
892301**

Verona Cottage ✿✿ (David J Dickinson Esq) 6 Webb
Lane, Mengham. Entrance opp the Rose in June public
house. Arranged on 3 levels; 3 contrasting but linked gardens with ideas for everyone with a small garden. Wide
range of shrubs, spring bulbs and flowers, paved areas,
iris, all within a walled garden 500 metres from the sea.
It is an oasis by a main road. TEA (Sun). *Adm £1 Chd
free. Sat, Sun May 18, 19 (11-5.30)*

▲The Vyne ✿✿ (The National Trust) Sherborne St John,
4m N of Basingstoke. Between Sherborne St John and
Bramley. From A340 turn E at NT signs. 17 acres with extensive lawns, lake, fine trees, herbaceous border. Garden
tours will incl developments made possible by NGS fund-
ing. Gardeners available to answer questions. TEAS. *Adm
£2 Chd £1. For NGS Sun July 20 (12.30-5.30). Also Evening Garden Tour and Buffet, Fri June 20 (7pm) Cost
£9.50 person (limited to 50) for details* **Tel 01256
881337**

Waldrons ✿✿✿ (Major & Mrs J Robinson) Brook, Lyndhurst. 1m W from exit 1 M27 (on A3079). 1st house L
past the Green Dragon public house and directly opp the
Bell Inn. A C18 listed cottage with a conservatory, in a
garden of 1 acre, containing a herbaceous border, shrubs
and flower beds created around old orchard trees. Small
duck pond (free roaming call ducks); herb garden, arbour,
rose trellis, raised alpine garden and a small stable yard.
TEAS. *Adm £1.50 Chd 50p. Suns, Mons May 18, 19, June
29, 30 (2-5.30)*

Walhampton ✿✿ (Walhampton School Trust) Lymington. 1m along B3054 to Beaulieu. 90 acres with azaleas;
rhododendrons; lakes; shell grotto. TEAS. *Adm £1 Chd
50p. Sun May 18 (2-6)*

2 Warren Farm Cottages ✿✿ (Dr & Mrs J G Mitchell)
2m NW of West Tytherley. From A30 (Salisbury-Stock-
bridge Rd) 2m E Lopcombe Corner, 4m W Stockbridge
take turn S signposted West Tytherley. 3rd house on R,
1.9m. Please park along rd. A working cottage garden of
⅓-acre in remote location. 100 plus hardy geraniums,
cottage plants, pots of vegetables. Shade area and conservatory. Lounging cats and busy wildlife. Good late season interest. TEAS (18 May & 5 Oct). *Adm £1 Chd 50p.
Suns, Mons May 18 (10-4), June 29, 30, July 20, 21, Aug,
10, 11, Sept 14, 15, (10-6); Sats June 21, July 19 (6-8);
every Fri May 23 to Sept 26 (10-6), Oct 5 (10-4). Evening
openings Sats June 21, July 19 (6-8.30)*

Warwick House ✿✿ (Mrs Lucy Marson) Wickham. 2½m
N of Fareham on A32. Park in square or signed car park.
Warwick House is in Bridge St. Turn R at the end of the
square furthest from the Winchester Rd. Teas available in
the Square. ⅛-acre intimate walled town garden with interesting and contrasting planting. Paved courtyard,
troughs. Ornamental vegetable and herb garden. *Adm
£1.50 Chd free. Sun June 8, Wed July 2, Sun July 13 (11-
5). Private visits welcome between May 1 and July 31,
please* **Tel 01329 832313**

West Silchester Hall ✿✿ (Mrs Jenny Jowett) Bramley
Rd, Silchester. Off A340 between Reading and Basingstoke. 1½ acres, plantsman artist's garden, a good collection of herbaceous plants, rose and shrub borders,
rhododendrons and many acid loving plants, small pond
and bog garden, and interesting display of half hardies,
kitchen garden, and owner maintained. Exhibition of botanical paintings. TEAS. *Adm £1.50 Chd 50p. Suns May
25, Aug 3, Mons May 26, Aug 4 (2-6). Parties by appt
March-Sept, please* **Tel 01734 700278**

Westbrook House ✿✿ (Andrew Lyndon-Skeggs) Howards Lane, Holybourne. Turn off A31 at roundabout
immed to NE of Alton towards Holybourne/Alton 1st R to
Holybourne. 1st L up Howards Lane house on R. 2½ acres
with continuing design and development. Mature trees
and impressive formal planting of shrubs and herbaceous
with 'maze' garden leading to orchard, woodland, stream
and unexpected view. Featured in Country Life. CREAM
TEAS. *Adm £2 Chd free. Sun June 29 (2.30-5.30)*

Wheatley House ✿✿ (Mr & Mrs Michael Adlington)
Kingsley Bordon. Wheatley is a small hamlet between
Binstead and Kingsley 4m E of Alton, 5m SW of Farnham.
From Alton follow signs to Holybourne and Binsted. At
end of Binsted turn R signed Wheatley. ¾m down lane
on the L. Magnificent setting with panoramic views over
fields and forests. Sweeping mixed borders, shrubberies,
roses and rockery. 1½ acres, designed by the artist-
owner, with particular emphasis on colour and form.
TEAS in Barn. *Adm £1.50 Chd 50p. Sun Oct 5 (11.30-
5.30)*

The White Cottage ✿✿✿ (Mr & Mrs P Conyers) 35
Wellhouse Rd. Beech, nr Alton. Leave Alton on Basingstoke Rd A339. After approx 1m turn L to Medstead and
Beech. Wellhouse Rd is 2nd turning on R. Parking at village hall at bottom of rd, limited parking outside house.
1-acre chalk garden with a wide range of unusual shrubs
and plants; many hardy geraniums, hellebores and bulbs.
Conservatory with exotics, large collection of carnivorous
plants featured on TV, pond and scree bed. TEA. *Adm
£1.50 Chd free. Suns, Mons March 16, 17 (11-5), June 8,
9, July 6, 7, Aug 10, 11 (11-6). Private visits welcome,
please* **Tel 01420 89355**

White Cottage ✿ (Mr & Mrs A W Ferdinando) Speltham
Hill, Hambledon. Find Speltham Hill 'tween George' and
shop. Park in street or at hill-top. See an ancient cottage
small, climbers clinging to its wall. Gain garden, hillside
very steep; two-fifty steps to help you peep at covered
ground, plants large and small, alpines, shrubs, trees
dwarf and tall. A tea-house of the East afar provides a
hide, also no char. Dragons, bridges, pagoda too pools and
fish, vista and view. *Donations. Sun, Mon Sept 7, 8 (2-6)*

By Appointment Gardens. These owners do not
have a fixed opening day usually because they
cannot accommodate large numbers or have
insufficient parking space.

¶**White House** ⅃⚘ (A Burn) The Frenches, East Wellow. From Romsey, take A27 towards Whiteparish. After 3m turn L at Shootash Xrds, turn immed R entrance ½m on R. 1-acre sloping country garden with distant view. Borders with varied plant collection, also hidden corners; winding paths to wild pond and bog garden, enclosed swimming pool, formal pond. Pergolas and trellis with many roses and clematis. TEA. *Adm £1.50 Chd free. Wed, Thurs, Fri June 25, 26, 27 (11-5.30)*

White Windows ⅃⚘❀ (Mr & Mrs B Sterndale-Bennett) Longparish, Nr Andover. E of Andover off A303 to village centre on B3048. ⅔-acre with unusual range of hardy perennials, trees and shrubs planted for yr-round foliage interest and colour blendings in garden rooms, incl many hellebores, hardy geraniums and euphorbias. Garden featured on TV and in books and magazines. TEAS (Suns only). *Adm £1.50 Chd free. Suns, Weds June 8, 11, Aug 17, 20 (1.30-6). Private visits welcome Weds April to Sept, please* **Tel 01264 720222**

Wonston Lodge ⅃ (Mr & Mrs N J A Wood) Wonston. A34 or A30 to Sutton Scotney. At War Memorial turn to Wonston-Stoke Charity; ¾m in Wonston centre. 3 acres, owner maintained. Pond with aquatic plants and ornamental ducks; shrub roses; clematis; topiary. TEAS (Aug only). *Adm £2 Chd free. Sun, Mon June 15, Aug 24 25 (2-6)*

¶**The Worthys Gardens** Kingsworthy. *Combined adm £2 Tues Aug 19 (2-5)*

22 Springvale Road ⚘ (Mr & Mrs Fry) Kingsworthy. N end of Springwell Rd. Kingsworthy almost opp Dairiall's shop. ¾-acre. Magnolias, snowdrops, crocuses and daffodils. From late June; a comprehensive display of agapanthus Headbourne hybrids being Lewis Palmer's stock: he lived nearby. Sept for drifts of cyclamen, heathers and fine display of foliage. *Private visits welcome, please* **Tel 01962 882288**

Little Acre (Mr M Walford) Headbourne Worthy. Just off S end of Springvale, in Down Farm Lane. 1½-acre trees and shrubs planted by owner, for foliar effect and low maintenance. TEA

The National Gardens Scheme is a charity which traces its origins back to 1927. Since then it has raised a total of over £15 million for charitable purposes.

Herefordshire

Hon County Organiser: Lady Curtis, 30 Witherington Road, London N5 1PP

Assistant County Organisers: Mr & Mrs Roger Norman, Ivy Croft, Ivington Green, Leominster HR6 0JN
Tel 01568 720344
Dr J A F Evans, The Lawns, Nunnington, Hereford HR1 3NJ
Tel 01432 850664

Hon County Treasurer: Mr M Robins, Bursar, Royal National College for the Blind, College Road, Hereford HR8 2AN

DATES OF OPENING

March 30 Sunday
  Arrow Cottage, nr Weobley
March 31 Monday
  Arrow Cottage, nr Weobley
April 2 Wednesday
  Arrow Cottage, nr Weobley
April 6 Sunday
  Arrow Cottage, nr Weobley
April 13 Sunday
  Lakeside, Whitbourne
  Lower Hope, Ullingswick
  Newcote, Moccas
April 20 Sunday
  Arrow Cottage, nr Weobley
April 26 Saturday
  Dinmore Manor, Wellington
  The Nest, Moreton, Eye

April 27 Sunday
  The Nest, Moreton, Eye
  Staunton Park, Staunton-on-Arrow
  Stone House, Scotland, Wellington
May 3 Saturday
  The Nest, Moreton, Eye
May 4 Sunday
  Arrow Cottage, nr Weobley
  Brilley Court, nr Whitney-on-Wye
  The Nest, Moreton, Eye ‡
  Strawberry Cottage, Hamnish ‡
May 5 Monday
  The Nest, Moreton, Eye
May 16 Friday
  Strawberry Cottage, Hamnish
May 17 Saturday
  Lingen Nursery & Garden, Lingen

May 18 Sunday
  Brookside, Bringsty
  Bryan's Ground, Stapleton
  Lingen Nursery & Garden, Lingen
  Torwood, Whitchurch
May 25 Sunday
  Elmbury, 98 Aylestone Hill, Hereford
  Kingstone Cottages, Ross-on-Wye
May 28 Wednesday
  Arrow Cottage, nr Weobley
May 29 Thursday
  Strawberry Cottage, Hamnish
June 1 Sunday
  Arrow Cottage, nr Weobley
  Caves Folly Nursery, Colwall Green ‡
  Frogmore, nr Ross-on-Wye
  Lingen Nursery & Garden, Lingen

Longacre, Colwall ‡
Lower Hope, Ullingswick
June 8 Sunday
Ash Farm, Much Birch
The Bannut, Bringsty, Bromyard
How Caple Court, Ross-on-Wye
Kyrle House, Peterstow
Strawberry Cottage, Hamnish
Whitfield, Wormbridge
June 14 Saturday
The Nest, Moreton, Eye
June 15 Sunday
Arrow Cottage, nr Weobley
Haynstone Orchard,
    Preston-on-Wye ‡
Kingstone Cottages, Ross-on-Wye
Moccas Court, nr Hereford ‡
The Nest, Moreton, Eye ‡‡
Newcote, Moccas
Staunton Park, Staunton-on-Arrow
Strawberry Cottage, Hamnish ‡‡
Torwood, Whitchurch
June 19 Thursday
Strawberry Cottage, Hamnish
June 21 Saturday
Hergest Croft Gardens, Kington
Overcourt Garden Nursery
June 22 Sunday
Brook Cottage, Lingen ‡
Coddington Vineyard, Coddington
Lingen Nursery & Garden,
    Lingen ‡
Overcourt Garden Nursery
Stone House, Scotland,
    Wellington
Well Cottage, Lingen ‡
June 23 Monday
Bryan's Ground, Stapleton
June 24 Tuesday
Croft Castle, Kingsland
June 29 Sunday
Arrow Cottage, nr Weobley
Berrington Hall, Leominster ‡
Brilley Court, nr Whitney-on-Wye
Grantsfield, nr Leominster ‡

Kingstone Cottages, Ross-on-Wye
Shucknall Court, Hereford
Westwood Farm, Hatfield ‡
June 30 Monday
Westwood Farm, Hatfield
July 5 Saturday
The Nest, Moreton, Eye
July 6 Sunday
Arrow Cottage, nr Weobley
Lower Hope, Ullingswick
The Nest, Moreton, Eye ‡
Strawberry Cottage, Hamnish ‡
July 13 Sunday
Arrow Cottage, nr Weobley
The Bannut, Bringsty, Bromyard
The Marsh Country Hotel, Eyton
July 18 Friday
Strawberry Cottage, Hamnish
July 20 Sunday
Arrow Cottage, nr Weobley
Torwood, Whitchurch
July 26 Saturday
Wych & Colwall Horticulture
    Society Show
July 27 Sunday
Arrow Cottage, nr Weobley
Caves Folly Nursery, Colwall
    Green
Strawberry Cottage, Hamnish
July 30 Wednesday
Arrow Cottage, nr Weobley
August 3 Sunday
Arrow Cottage, nr Weobley
August 8 Friday
Strawberry Cottage, Hamnish
August 10 Sunday
The Bannut, Bringsty, Bromyard
August 14 Thursday
Strawberry Cottage, Hamnish
August 17 Sunday
Brook House, Colwall
Coddington Vineyard, Coddington
Torwood, Whitchurch
August 23 Saturday
Monnington Court, Hereford

August 24 Sunday
Arrow Cottage, nr Weobley
Monnington Court, Hereford
The Nest, Moreton, Eye ‡
Strawberry Cottage, Hamnish ‡
August 25 Monday
Monnington Court, Hereford
The Nest, Moreton, Eye
August 31 Sunday
Arrow Cottage, nr Weobley
September 3 Wednesday
Arrow Cottage, nr Weobley
September 7 Sunday
Arrow Cottage, nr Weobley
Strawberry Cottage, Hamnish
September 11 Thursday
Strawberry Cottage, Hamnish
September 21 Sunday
Torwood, Whitchurch
September 28 Sunday
Lingen Nursery & Garden, Lingen
October 11 Saturday
Dinmore Manor, Wellington

Regular openings
For details see garden description

Abbey Dore Court, nr Hereford
Bryan's Ground, Stapleton
Dinmore Manor, Wellington
Kingstone Cottages, Ross-on-Wye
Lingen Nursery and Garden, Lingen
The Picton Garden, Colwall
Staunton Park, Staunton-on-Arrow
Strawberry Cottage, Hamnish

By appointment only
*For telephone numbers and other
details see garden descriptions.
Private visits welcomed*

Well Cottage, Blakemere

DESCRIPTIONS OF GARDENS

● **Abbey Dore Court** ⬥⚘✿ (Mrs C L Ward) 11m SW of Hereford. From A465 midway between Hereford-Abergavenny turn W, signed Abbey Dore; then 2½m. 5 acres bordered by R Dore of rambling and semi formal garden with unusual shrubs, perennials and clematis in large borders. Pond and rock garden. River walk with ferns and hellebores leading to site of an old barn and roadway, planted for foliage colour. Large collection of late summer anemones. Coffee, lunch and TEAS (11-5). *Adm £2 Chd 50p (Share to Mother Theresa®). Sat March 1 to Sun Oct 19 daily except Weds (11-6). Earlier visits for hellebores welcome, please* **Tel 01981 240419**

Arrow Cottage ⚘✿ (Mr & Mrs L Hattatt) nr Weobley. From Weobley take unclassified rd direction Wormsley (Kings Pyon/Canon Pyon). After 1m, turn L signposted

Ledgemoor. 2nd R (no through rd). 1st house on L. Formal design links garden rooms in this 2-acre plantsman's garden. A newly developed gothic garden, C19 shrub roses, white and green gardens, kitchen garden, herbaceous borders and natural stream. Incl in the Good Gardens Guide. Garden unsuitable for children. Light lunches, TEAS. *Adm £2. Mon March 31; Suns, Weds, March 30, April 2, 6, 20, May 4, 28, June 1, 15, 29, July 6, 13, 20, 27, 30, Aug 3, 24, 31, Sept 3, 7*

Ash Farm ⚘✿ (David & Alison Lewis) Much Birch. From Hereford take A49 S to Much Birch (approx 7m). After the Pilgrim Hotel take 1st turning R at Xrds into Tump Lane. Garden is on L. Ample parking. Small walled farmhouse garden and ½-acre new garden created from old fold yard for all-yr interest over past 9 yrs. Small trees, herbaceous borders, blue and white borders. TEA. *Adm £1.50 Chd free. Sun June 8 (2-6)*

The Bannut &❀ (Mr Maurice & Mrs Daphne Everett) Bringsty. 3m E of Bromyard on A44 Worcester Rd. (½m E of entrance to National Trust, Brockhampton). A 1-acre garden, planted with all-yr colour in mind, mainly established by the present owners since 1984. Mixed borders, island beds of trees, shrubs and herbaceous plants, and a small 'damp' garden and an arbour garden in shades of pink, blue and silver. Walls, pergola, and terraces display unusual climbers and colourful pots and urns. Heather garden, designed around a Herefordshire cider mill, and unusual knot garden with water feature. TEAS. *Adm £1.50 Chd free. Suns June 8, July 13, Aug 10 (2-5). Also groups by appt, please* **Tel 01885 482206**

▲**Berrington Hall** &✗ (The National Trust) 3m N of Leominster on A49. Signposted. Bus Midland Red (W) x 92, 292 alight Luston, 2m. Extensive views over Capability Brown Park; formal garden; wall plants, unusual trees, camellia collection, herbaceous plants, wisteria. Woodland walk, rhododendrons, walled garden with apple collection. Light lunches and TEAS. *Adm house & garden £3.80 Chd £1.90. Grounds only £1.70. For NGS Sun June 29 (12.30-6)*

Brilley Court &✗ (Mr & Mrs D Bulmer) nr Whitney-on-Wye 6m E Hay-on-Wye. 1½m off main A438 Hereford to Brecon Rd signposted to Brilley. Medium-sized walled garden, spring and herbaceous. Valley stream garden; spring colour. Ornamental kitchen garden. Large quantity of roses. Wonderful views. TEAS by appt only. *Adm £1.50 Chd 50p (Share to CRMF®). Suns May 4, June 29 (2-6). Also by appt, please* **Tel 01497 831467**

Brook Cottage (Dorothy Phillips) Lingen. 5m NE of Presteigne. 15m SW of Ludlow. 15m NE of Leominster. On B4362 (Mortimers Cross to Presteigne) take N turn 2m from Presteigne centre marked Kinsham and Lingen. Garden in centre of Lingen village at top of lane opp the Royal George. 1¾ acres woodland and field garden with brook developed over 10 yrs by owner for yr-round interest and low maintenance. Old apple trees draped in roses; shrubs and trees for foliage colour and shape plus herbaceous plants of the more robust type suitable for a sheltered, frost pocket garden. Parking at Lingen Nursery Garden. TEAS. *Combined adm with* **Lingen Nursery Garden** *and* **Well Cottage** *£2 Chd under 10 free (Share to Lingen Village Hall©). Sun June 22 (2-6)*

Brook House & (Mr J Milne) Colwall. 3m SW Malvern and 3m E of Ledbury on B2048. ½-way between Malvern/Ledbury via Wyche Cutting; opp Oddfellows Hotel. Water garden; flowering trees and shrubs; walled garden. Old Herefordshire farmhouse with mill stream. *Adm £1.50 Chd 50p. Sun Aug 17 (2-6). Private visits welcome, please* **Tel 01684 540283**

Brookside ✗❀ (Mr & Mrs John Dodd) Bringsty; 3m E of Bromyard via A44 10m W of Worcester; Bringsty Common turn down track to 'Live & Let Live'; at PH carpark bear L to Brookside. C16 cottage with 1½-acre garden designed by Denis Hoddy; specimen trees and shrubs in grass sloping to lake; mixed beds with all yr interest. Unusual plants. Small alpine collection. TEAS on terrace. *Adm £1.50 Chd 20p (Share to Save the Children Fund®). Sun May 18 (2-5.30). Parties and private visits welcome, please* **Tel 01886 821835**

■ **Bryan's Ground** &✗❀ (David Wheeler & Simon Dorrell) between Kinsham and Stapleton, nr Presteigne. 12m NW of Leominster. At Mortimers Cross take B4362 signposted Presteigne. After 6m, at Combe, turn R signposted Kinsham and Lingen. After ½mile turn L signed Stapleton. After 1m turn L. Restoration of 3-acre Edwardian garden. Home of Hortus, The International Garden Journal. Yew and box topiary, parterres, formal herb garden, partly walled kitchen garden, newly planted flower and shrub borders with 'Sulking House'. Shrubbery with spring bulbs, 'Heritage' apple orchard, lighthouse and Edwardian greenhouse. Featured in New York Times and The Observer. Fine views of the Lugg valley. TEAS. *Adm £1.50 Chd 50p. Suns, Mons March 30 to Sept 22. For NGS Sun May 18, Mon June 23 (2-5)*

Caves Folly Nursery &✗ (Mr Leaper & Mrs Evans) Evendine Lane, off Colwall Green. B4218 between Malvern and Ledbury. Car parking at Caves Folly. Small nursery established 12 yrs. Specialising in herbaceous and alpine plants, some unusual. All plants are grown organically in peat-free compost. Recently planted herbaceous borders and a wildflower meadow. TEAS. *Combined adm with* **Longacre** *£1.50 Chd free. Sun June 1 (2-6). Also open Sun July 27. Adm £1 Chd free (2-5). Private visits welcome, clubs, societies etc, please* **Tel 01684 540631**

Coddington Vineyard & (Drs Denis & Ann Savage) Coddington, nr Ledbury. From Ledbury take Bromyard rd, 1st R after railway bridge signposted Wellington Heath, turn R at next T-junction (oak tree on island) and follow signs to Coddington. Vineyard signposted. 5 acres incl 2-acre vineyard, listed threshing barn and cider mill. Garden and vineyard planted 1985 with terraces, woodland, pond and stream. Interesting trees and shrubs. Wine tasting incl in *Adm £2 Chd free. Suns June 22, Aug 17 (2-6)*

▲**Croft Castle** &✗ (The National Trust) 5m NW of Leominster. On B4362 (off B4361, Leominster-Ludlow). Large garden; borders; walled garden; landscaped park and walks in Fishpool Valley; fine old avenues. Special garden open for NGS (Castle closed). *Adm £1 Chd 50p. For NGS Tues June 24 (1.30-4.30)*

■ **Dinmore Manor** &✗❀ (R G Murray Esq) Hereford. 6m N of Hereford. Route A49. Bus: Midland Red Hereford-Leominster, alight Manor turning 1m. Spectacular hillside location. A range of impressive architecture dating from C14-20. Chapel; cloisters; Great hall (Music Room) and extensive roof walk giving panoramic views of countryside and beautiful gardens below; stained glass. TEAS for NGS. *Adm £2.50 Acc chd under 14 free (Share to St John Ambulance®). For NGS Sats April 26, Oct 11 (10-5.30)*

Elmbury ✗❀ (Mrs E Haines) 98 Aylestone Hill, Hereford. ¾m NE of city centre on A4103 Worcester rd. ½-acre garden on sloping site containing alpine and scree beds, herbaceous borders, 2 pools with water plants, several raised peat beds containing meconopsis, camellias and rhododendrons are a special feature. TEAS. *Adm £1 Chd free (Share to National Deaf Children's Society®). Sun May 25 (2-5.30)*

The Elms School see Wych & Colwall Horticultural Society Show

Frogmore ⅍⚘⚘ (Sir Jonathan & Lady North) Pontshill. 4m SE of Ross-on-Wye. 1m S of A40 through Pontshill. 2-acre garden with fine mature trees and many unusual young trees and shrubs. Mixed borders specialising in hardy geraniums. Nut walk and ha ha. Mown walk along stream and to spinney. TEAS in aid of Hope Mansel Church. *Adm £2 Chd free. Sun June 1 (2-6)*

Grantsfield ⅍⚘⚘ (Col & Mrs J G T Polley) nr Kimbolton, 3m NE of Leominster. A49 N from Leominster, turn R to Grantsfield. Car parking in field; not coaches which must drop and collect visitors in the village. Minibus acceptable. Contrasting styles in gardens of old stone farmhouse; wide variety of unusual plants and shrubs, old roses, climbers; herbaceous borders; superb views. 1-acre orchard and kitchen garden with flowering and specimen trees. Spring bulbs. TEAS. *Adm £1.20 Chd free (Share to St John Ambulance®). Sun June 29 (2-5.30). Private visits welcome April to end Sept, please* **Tel 01568 613338**

¶**Haynstone Orchard** ⚘⚘ (Valerie Thomas) Preston on Wye. Take A438 from Hereford W to Brecon. After approx 7m Preston on Wye signed L. Once in village take Blakemere Rd and garden is 250yds on L. Approx 2-acre country garden with mixed borders planted over last 3 yrs to give yr-round interest. Many old roses, yew enclosures and lime walk. Small woodland area currently being developed. TEAS. *Adm £1.50. Sun June 15 (2-6)*

▲**Hergest Croft Gardens** ⅍⚘ (W L Banks Esq & R A Banks Esq) ½m off A44 on Welsh side of Kington, 20m NW of Hereford: Turn L at Rhayader end of bypass; then 1st R; gardens ¼m on L. 50 acres of garden owned by Banks' family for 4 generations. Edwardian garden surrounding house; Park wood with rhododendrons up to 30ft tall; old-fashioned kitchen garden with spring and herbaceous borders. One of finest private collections of trees and shrubs; now selected to hold National Collections maples and birches. Hergest Croft celebrated its centenary in 1996. TEAS. *Adm £2.50 Chd under 15 free (Share to NCCPG®). For NGS Sat June 21 (1.30-6.30).* **Tel 01544 230160**

▲**How Caple Court** ⚘ (Mrs Peter Lee) How Caple, 5m N of Ross on Wye 10m S of Hereford on B4224; turn R at How Caple Xrds, garden 400 yds on L. 11 acres; Edwardian gardens set high above R Wye in park and woodland; formal terraces: yew hedges, statues and pools; sunken Florentine water garden under restoration; woodland walks; herbaceous and shrub borders, shrub roses, mature trees: Mediaeval Church with newly restored C16 Diptych. Nursery. TEAS. *Adm £2.50 Chd £1.25. For NGS Sun June 8 (10-5).* **Tel 01989 740612**

Kingstone Cottages ⚘⚘ (Michael & Sophie Hughes) A40 Ross- Gloucester, turn L at Weston Cross to Bollitree Castle, then L to Rudhall. Informal 1½-acre cottage garden containing National Collection of old pinks and carnations and other unusual plants. Terraced beds, ponds, grotto, summerhouse, lovely views. Some areas now replanted incl a new parterre containing the Collection. *Adm £1 Chd free (Share to Abbey de Cormeilles Venture Scouts - Ghana Project®). Mons to Fris May 6 to July 11 (except Bank Hols) (9-4); Suns May 25, June 15, 29 (10-5). Private visits welcome, please* **Tel 01989 565267**

¶**Kyrle House** ⚘ (Miss Alison Barber) Peterstow. From Ross-on-Wye take A49 N to Peterstow approx ½m. Garden on L 50yds past Yew Tree Inn. Ample parking in field on edge of village approx 200 yds from garden. 1⅓-acre country garden started from scratch in 1993 by present owners. Formal cottage style linked by a series of rooms. Many herbaceous borders, small sunken garden, herb garden, pergola and pool garden. Organic vegetable garden and fruit house, Victorian conservatory. The garden is unsuitable for children. *Adm £1 (Share to Community Hospital®). Sun June 8 (2-6). Private visits welcome by appt, please* **Tel 01989 768412**

Lakeside ⚘⚘ (Mr D Gueroult & Mr C Philip) Gaines Rd, Whitbourne. 9m W of Worcester off A44 at County boundary sign (ignore sign to Whitbourne Village). 6-acres, large walled garden with many mixed beds and borders; spring bulbs, climbers, unusual shrubs and plants, heather garden, bog garden, medieval carp lake with fountain. Steep steps and slopes. TEAS in aid of Red Cross. *Adm £2 Chd free. Sun April 13 (2-5.30). Parties of 10 or more by appt, please* **Tel 01886 821119**

■ **Lingen Nursery and Garden** ⅍⚘⚘ (Mr Kim Davis) Lingen. 5m NE of Presteigne take B4362 E from Presteigne, 2m turn L for Lingen, 3m opposite Chapel in village. Specialist alpine and herbaceous nursery and general garden, rock garden and herbaceous borders, a peat bed, raised screes and an Alpine House and stock beds incl a large collection of show auriculas. 2 acres of developing garden. Unusual plants with labelling. Nursery. Catalogue available. National collection of iris sibirica and herbaceous campanula held for NCCPG. TEAS (NGS days only). *Adm £1.50 Chd free. Feb-Oct every day (10-6). For NGS Sat, Suns May 17, 18; June 1; Sept 28 (2-6). Combined adm with* **Brook Cottage** *and* **Well Cottage** *£2 Sun June 22 (2-6). Coach parties by appt* **Tel 01544 267720**

Longacre ⅍⚘ (Mr D Pudsey & Mrs H Pudsey) Evendine Lane, off Colwall Green. 3m SW Malvern and 3m E of Ledbury on B2048. 1-acre garden developed since 1970 with ½-acre extension being developed from field in 1995. Emphasis on multi-season trees and shrubs planted to create vistas across lawns, down paths and along avenues. TEAS at Caves Folly Nursery. *Combined adm with* **Caves Folly Nursery** *£1.50 Chd free. Sun June 1 (2-6)*

Lower Hope ⅍⚘⚘ (Mr & Mrs Clive Richards) Ullingswick. From Hereford take the A465 N to Bromyard. After 6m this road meets the A417 at Burley Gate roundabout. Turn L on the A417 signed Leominster. After approx 2m take the 3rd turning on the R signed Lower Hope and Pencombe, 0.6m on the LH-side. 5-acre garden facing S and W with herbaceous borders, rose walks and gardens, laburnum tunnel, Mediterranean garden, water garden incl bog gardens, streams and ponds. Conservatories with exotic species of orchids, bourgenvilleas and other rare plants. Prize-winning herd of pedigree Hereford cattle and flock of pedigree Suffolk sheep. TEAS. *Adm £2 Chd £1 (Share to St John Ambulance®). Suns April 13, June 1, July 6 (2-6). Also private visits welcome, following written application*

The Marsh Country Hotel ⚶🏵 (Mr & Mrs Martin Gilleland) Eyton. 2m NW of Leominster. Signed Eyton and Luston off B4361 Richard Castle Rd. A 1½-acre garden created over the past 8 years. Herbaceous borders, small orchard, lily pond, herb garden and stream with planted banks and rose walk. Vegetable plot. Landscaped reed bed sewage treatment system. Featured in 'The Gardener' 1994. C14 timbered Great Hall listed grade II* (not open). TEAS. *Adm £1.50 Chd 50p. Sun July 13 (2-5)*

Moccas Court ⚶ (Trustees of Baunton Trust) 10m W of Hereford. 1m off B4352. 7-acres; Capability Brown parkland on S bank of R. Wye. House designed by Adam and built by Keck in 1775. Teas in village hall. *Adm house & garden £1.95 Chd £1 (Share to Moccas Church®). Sun June 15 (2-6). By appt for groups of 20 or over, please* **Tel 01981 500381**

Monnington Court ⚶ (Mr & Mrs John Bulmer) Monnington. The ¾m lane to Monnington on Wye to Monnington Court is on the A438 between Hereford and Hay 9m from either. Approx 20 acres. Lake, pond and river walk. Sculpture garden (Mrs Bulmer is the sculptor Angela Conner). Tree lined avenues incl Monnington Walk, one of Britain's oldest, still complete mile long avenue of Scots pines and yews, made famous by Kilvert's Diary; collection of swans and ducks; Foundation Farm of the British Morgan Horse - a living replica of ancient horses seen in statues in Trafalgar Square, etc; working cider press; FREE horse and carriage display at 3.30 each open day. The C13, C15, C17 house incl Mediaeval Moot Hall is also open. Barbecue on fine days, lunches. TEA 10.30-6.30. Indoor horse display and films on rainy days. *Adm house, garden and display £4 Chd £2.50, garden and display only £3.50 Chd £1.50 (Share to British Morgan Horse Foundation Farm©). Sat, Sun, Mon Aug 23, 24, 25 (10.30-7). Private visits for 10 or over welcome, please* **Tel 01981 500698**

¶**The Nest** ⚶⚶🏵 (Mrs Sue Evans) Moreton. N from Leominster on A49 for 3m; turn L in village of Ashton for Moreton, Eye and Luston. 1m down rd and signpost on L 'Eye Veterinary Clinic'. 1530 timber-framed Yeoman's house. Drive flanked by old canal and new chestnut trees. On the N side is an established fruit garden and a new potager. The southerly aspect is lawned with rockery and shrubberies. Informal summer flower garden and fountain. A bog garden with a variety of lobelias and primulas. TEAS. *Adm £1.50 Chd free (Share to Eye Parish Church®). Sats, Suns April 26, 27, May 3, 4, June 14, 15, July 5, 6, Aug 24, Mons May 5, Aug 25 (2-6)*

Newcote ⚶🏵 (Mr John & Lady Patricia Phipps) Moccas. From Moccas village, ⅓m on rd to Preston-on-Wye. 2½ acres incl woodland garden. Speciality shrubs and exotic trees. Water garden and new formal garden with fountain etc. *Adm £1.50 Chd 50p (Share to Moccas Village Hall®). Suns April 13, June 15 (2-6)*

Overcourt Garden Nursery ⚶⚶🏵 (Mr & Mrs Peter Harper) Sutton St Nicholas. 3m N of Hereford. Turn L at Xrds in village on rd to Marden for ¼m. A Grade II C16 house once used as a vicarage and schoolhouse, with connections dating back to the Crusader Knights of St John. Views to the Black Mountains. A 1½-acre plant enthusiast's country garden planted over last 4yrs for yr-round

interest. Large shrub and herbaceous perennial borders, ponds and small copse. Vegetable garden. Nursery. TEAS in aid of Sutton St Nicholas playing field. *Adm £1.50 Chd free (Share to CRMF®). Sat, Sun June 21, 22 (2-6). Private visits welcome, please* **Tel 01432 880845**

● **The Picton Garden** ⚶⚶🏵 (Mr & Mrs Paul Picton) Walwyn Rd, Colwall. 3m W of Malvern on B4218. 1½-acres W of Malvern Hills. A plantsman's garden extensively renovated. Rock garden using Tufa. Moist garden. Roses with scented old and modern varieties. Mature interesting shrubs. Large herbaceous borders full of colour from early summer. NCCPG collection of asters, michaelmas daisies, gives a tapestry of colour from late Aug through Sept and Oct. If wet there will be a small display of Asters under cover. *Adm £1.50 Chd free. Open Wed to Sun April 2 to Oct 31 incl. Also Mon, Tues Sept 1 to Oct 14 (10-1; 2.15-5.30). Private parties of 10 or over welcome, please* **Tel 01684 540416**

Shucknall Court ⚶ (Mr & Mrs Henry Moore) 5½m E of Hereford off A4103 signposted Weston Beggard. Garden 100yds from main rd. Large collection of specie, oldfashioned and shrub roses. Mixed borders in the old walled farmhouse garden. Wild garden, small stream garden, vegetables and fruit. Partly suitable for wheelchairs. Cream TEAS. *Adm £1.50 Chd free (Share to St John Ambulance®). Sun June 29 (2-6)*

■ **Staunton Park** ⚶🏵 (Mr E J L & Miss A Savage) Staunton-on-Arrow. 3m from Pembridge; 6m from Kington on the Titley road. 18m from Hereford. 11m from Leominster; 16m from Ludlow. Signposted. The 14-acres of garden, specimen trees, herbaceous borders, herb garden, rock garden, hosta border, lake, lakeside garden, woodland walk, spring bulbs make this an ideal place in which to spend a whole afternoon. New scented border. TEAS. *Adm £1.50 Chd free. Thurs, Suns April to end Sept. Easter and Bank Holidays. For NGS Suns April 27, June 15 (2-6)*

Stone House 🏵 (Peter & Sheila Smellie) Scotland, Wellington. A49 6m N of Hereford, end of dual carriageway, turn L for Westhope. ¾m turn R up narrow track. Parking ¼m. Parking difficult in wet conditions. 1-acre S sloping garden with magnificent views over countryside. Winding paths traverse the bank and terraced areas which contain a wide selection of unusual shrubs and herbaceous plants. Children welcome. *Adm £1.50 Chd 50p. Suns April 27, June 22 (1-6). Private visits welcome, please* **Tel 01432 830470**

■ **Strawberry Cottage** ⚶🏵 (Mr & Mrs M R Philpott) Hamnish. 3m E of Leominster. A44 E from Leominster, turn L at 1st Xrds to Hamnish. A 2-acre cottage garden created by the present owners since 1988. Part on steep slope with large rockeries. Over 250 roses. Mixed and herbaceous borders. Beds with single colour themes. Pond and wild garden area and kitchen garden. Spectacular views. Featured on BBC TV (Wales). TEAS. *Adm £1.50 Chd free (Share to St Michael's Hospice®). Garden and nursery open every Thurs, Fris, Suns and Bank Hol Mons April 27 to Sept 14. For NGS Suns, Thurs, Fris May 4, 16, 29, June 8, 15, 19, July 6, 18, 27, Aug 8, 14, 24, Sept 7, 11 (11-5). Private visits welcome, please* **Tel 01568 760319**

Torwood &&🌺 (Mr & Mrs S G Woodward) Whitchurch, Ross-on-Wye. A40 turn to Symonds Yat W. Interesting cottage garden adjacent to village school and round-about. Shrubs, conifers, herbaceous plants, etc. Featured by Central TV and in several books. TEAS. *Adm £1 Chd free (Share to Hodgkins Disease & Lymphoma Assoc®). Suns May 18, June 15, July 20, Aug 17, Sept 21 (2-6). Private visits welcome all year, please* **Tel 01600 890306**

Well Cottage, Blakemere & (R S Edwards Esq) 10m due W of Hereford. Leave Hereford on A465 (Aber-gavenny) rd. After 3m turn R towards Hay B4349 (B4348). At Clehonger keep straight on the B4352 to-wards Bredwardine. Well Cottage is on L by phone box. ¾-acre garden of mixed planting plus ½ acre of wild flower meadow suitable for picnics. There is a natural pool with gunnera and primulae. Good views over local hills and fields. Featured in Diana Saville's book 'Gardens for Small Country Houses' and Jane Taylor's 'The English Cottage Garden'. *Adm £1.50 OAPS £1 Chd free. Private visits welcome May to Aug, please* **Tel 01981 500475**

Well Cottage, Lingen 🌺 (Mrs A Turnbull) 5m NE of Presteigne. 15m SW of Ludlow. 15m NE of Leominster. On B4362 (Mortimers Cross to Presteigne), take N turn 2m from Presteigne Centre marked Kinsham and Lingen. Garden is next to Lingen Alpine Nursery. Approx ½-acre cottage garden with stream. Entirely managed by OAP! *Combined adm with* **Brook Cottage** *and* **Lingen Nurs-**ery *£2 Chd under 10 free (Share to Lingen Village Hall®). Sun June 22 (2-6)*

Westwood Farm &🌺 (Mr & Mrs Caspar Tremlett) From Bromyard take A44 towards Leominster. R turn to Hatfield and Bockleton 2m R turn down Westwood Lane. First Farm. From Leominster, take A44 toward Worcester 6m L to Hatfield and Bockleton [OS sheet 149 60.59]. ¾-acre cottage type garden with unusual plants and trees, small conservatory and pond with waterside plants. Dogs can be exercised in car park field. TEAS. *Adm £1 Chd free. Sun, Mon June 29, 30 (2-6). Private visits by appt May & June, please* **Tel 01885 410212**

Whitfield & (G M Clive Esq) Wormbridge, 8m SW of Hereford on A465 Hereford-Abergavenny Rd. Parkland, large garden, ponds, walled kitchen garden, 1780 gingko tree, 1½m woodland walk with 1851 Redwood grove. Picnic parties welcome. TEAS. *Adm £2 Chd £1 (Share to St John Ambulance®). Sun June 8 (2-6). Private visits welcome, please* **Tel 0198 121 202**

●**Wych & Colwall Horticultural Society Show** The Elms School &🌺 (L A C Ashley, Headmaster) Colwall Green. Medium-sized garden, herbaceous borders, fine views of Malvern Hills. Interesting exhibits of perennials, shrubs and crafts. Classes for flowers, vegetables, art & handicrafts. Professional Horticultural displays. TEAS. *Adm to show and garden 80p Chd 10p (Share to NGS®). Sat July 26 (2-5.30)*

Hertfordshire

Hon County Organiser: Mrs Edward Harvey, Wickham Hall, Bishop's Stortford CM23 1JQ
Assistant Hon County Organisers: Mrs Hedley Newton, Moat Farm House Much Hadham SG10 6AE
                                       Mrs Leone Ayres, Patmore Corner, Albury, Ware, Herts SG11 2LY
Hon County Treasurer: Mrs Rösli Lancaster, Manor Cottage, Aspenden, Nr Buntingford SG9 9PB

DATES OF OPENING

March 31 Monday
  23 Wroxham Way, Harpenden
April 6 Sunday
  Holwell Manor, nr Hatfield
  Pelham House, Brent Pelham
April 20 Sunday
  The Abbots House, Abbots
    Langley ‡
  Hunton Park, Hunton Bridge ‡
  St Paul's Walden Bury, Hitchin
April 27 Sunday
  Great Munden House, nr Ware
May 5 Monday
  23 Wroxham Way, Harpenden
May 11 Sunday
  Pelham House, Brent Pellham
  St Paul's Walden Bury, Hitchin

May 17 Saturday
  Cockhamsted, Braughing
May 18 Sunday
  Cockhamsted, Braughing
  Hipkins, Broxbourne
  20 Park Avenue South, Harpenden
  West Lodge Park, Hadley Wood
May 25 Sunday
  The Abbots House, Abbots
    Langley ‡
  Great Sarratt Hall,
    Rickmansworth ‡
  Queenswood School, Hatfield
May 26 Monday
  Queenswood School, Hatfield
June 1 Sunday
  St Paul's Walden Bury, Hitchin
June 7 Saturday
  Cockhamsted, Braughing

June 8 Sunday
  Cockhamsted, Braughing
  Hunton Park, Hunton Bridge
  Lamer Hill, Wheathampstead
June 15 Sunday
  Hill House, Stanstead Abbots
  Little Gaddesden Gardens
  Wickham Hall, Bishop's Stortford
  23 Wroxham Way, Harpenden
June 22 Sunday
  The Barn and Serge Hill, Abbots
    Langley
  The Gardens of Mackerye End,
    Harpenden
  Moor Place, Much Hadham ‡
  St Paul's Walden Bury, Hitchin
  Thundridge Hill House, nr Ware ‡
June 28 Saturday
  Benington Lordship, nr Stevenage

June 29 Sunday
Benington Lordship, nr Stevenage
Forge Cottage, Childwick Green ‡
High Elms Gardens, Harpenden ‡
The Manor House, Ayot St
    Lawrence
Old Hammers, Rushden
Waterdell House, Croxley Green

July 6 Sunday
The Mill House, Tewin, nr Welwyn
Wilstone Gardens, nr Tring

July 13 Sunday
20 Park Avenue South,
    Harpenden ‡
Putteridge Bury, Luton ‡‡
Rothamsted Manor, Harpenden ‡
Temple Dinsley Garden,
    Preston ‡‡

July 20 Sunday
23 Wroxham Way, Harpenden

August 24 Sunday
The Abbots House, Abbots
    Langley ‡
3 Mansion House Farm, Abbots
    Langley ‡

August 25 Monday
23 Wroxham Way, Harpenden

September 7 Sunday
Hunton Park, Hunton Bridge
20 Park Avenue South, Harpenden

September 21 Sunday
23 Wroxham Way, Harpenden

September 28 Sunday
Knebworth House, Stevenage

October 12 Sunday
Capel Manor Gardens, Enfield

October 19 Sunday
West Lodge Park, Hadley Wood

Regular openings
For details see garden description

Benington Lordship, nr Stevenage
Capel Manor Gardens, Enfield
The Manor House, Ayot St Lawrence

By Appointment Only
*For telephone numbers and other
details see garden descriptions.
Private visits welcomed*

207 East Barnet Road, New Barnet
94 Gallants Farm Road, East Barnet
May Cot, Knebworth

DESCRIPTIONS OF GARDENS

The Abbots House ♿✿❀ (Dr & Mrs Peter Tomson) 10 High Street, Abbots Langley NW of Watford (5m from Watford). Junction 20 M25, junction 6 M1. Parking in free village car park. 1¾-acre garden with interesting trees; shrubs; mixed borders; bog garden; sunken garden; ponds; conservatory. Nursery featuring plants propagated from the garden. TEAS. *Adm £1.50 Chd free (Share to British Diabetic Association®). Suns April 20, May 25, Aug 24 (2-5). Also at other times by appt* **Tel 01923 264946**

The Barn ✿❀ (Tom Stuart-Smith and family) Abbots Langley. ½m E of Bedmond in Serge Hill Lane. 1-acre plantsman's garden. Small sheltered courtyard planted with unusual shrubs and perennials, contrasts with more open formal garden with views over wild flower meadow. Teas at Serge Hill. *Combined adm £3 with* **Serge Hill** *(Share to Tibet Relief Fund UK®). Sun June 22 (2-5)*

■ **Benington Lordship** ✿❀ (Mr & Mrs C H A Bott) Benington. 5m E of Stevenage, in Benington Village. Hilltop garden on castle ruins overlooking lakes. Amazing April display of scillas, rose garden, hidden rock/water garden, spectacular borders, ornamental kitchen garden, nursery. *Adm £2.50 Chd free (Share to St Peters Church®). Spring and Summer Bank Hol Mons, Weds April to Sept 24 (12-5). Suns April to Aug 31, Sun Oct 19 (2-5). For NGS TEAS and Floral Festival in Church adjoining garden. Sat, Sun June 28, 29 (12-6). Private visits of 20 and over, please* **Tel 01438 869668**

■ **Capel Manor Gardens** ♿ (Horticultural & Environmental Centre) Bullsmoor Lane, Enfield, Middx. 3 mins from M25 junction M25/A10. Nearest station Turkey Street - Liverpool Street line (not Suns). 30 acres of historical and modern theme gardens, Japanese garden, large Italian style maze, rock and water features. 5 acre demonstration garden run by Gardening Which? Walled garden with rose collection and woodland walks. TEAS. *Adm £3 OAP £2 Chd £1.50. Open daily (10-5.30 - check for winter opening times). For NGS (Share to Horticultural Therapy©) Sun Oct 12 (10-5). For other details* **Tel 0181 3664442**

Cockhamsted ♿✿❀ (Mr & Mrs David Marques) Braughing. 2m E of village towards Braughing Friars (7m N of Ware). 2 acres; informal garden; shrub roses surrounded by open country. Island with trees surrounded by water-filled C14 moat. TEAS in aid of Leukaemia Research. *Adm £2 Chd free. Sat, Sun May 17, 18; June 7, 8 (2-6)*

207 East Barnet Road ✿❀ (Margaret Arnold) New Barnet. M25 junction 24 then A111 to Cockfosters. Underground stations High Barnet or Cockfosters. On bus route 84A and 307. This is a delightful example of a minute courtyard garden. High fences are covered with clematis, honeysuckle and passion flowers, roses and vines scramble over an arch above a seat. Small pond with goldfish and water plants. Many interesting and unusual plants mainly in pots. *Adm £1 Chd 50p. Private visits welcome, please* **Tel 0181 440 0377**

Forge Cottage ✿❀ (Mr & Mrs S Andrews) Childwick Green. Midway between St Albans and Harpenden on A1081. Entrance through wrought iron gates signposted St Mary's Church. Garden diagonally opp church. ⅓-acre plantsman's garden. Informal with rockery and pond, troughs and containers, mixed herbaceous and shrub beds, pergolas with roses and clematis. The garden has been developed to compliment a cottage dating from C17. Exhibition of paintings and plant stall. TEAS. *Adm £1.25 Chd 50p (Share to The National Autistic Society®). Sun June 29 (2-6)*

¶**94 Gallants Farm Road** ✿❀ (Mr & Mrs John Gething) East Barnet. M25 junction 24 then A111 to Cockfosters. Underground stations High Barnet, Cockfosters or Arnos Grove. On bus route 84a and 307. Small town garden 50' x 30' approx, designed to give variety of views of hidden rooms. The mixed planting of trees, shrubs and perennials is constantly changing as new plants are acquired and others outgrow their allotted space. Fishpond, rockery, obelisks and a plethora of pots provide plenty of interest. TEA. *Adm £1 Chd 50p Private visits welcome (parties max. 10) please* **Tel 0181 368 4261**

Great Munden House ✿✿ (Mr & Mrs D Wentworth-Stanley) 7m N of Ware. Off A10 on Puckeridge by-pass turn W; or turning off A602 via Dane End. 3½-acre informal garden with lawns, mixed shrub and herbaceous borders; variety shrub roses, trees; kitchen and herb garden. Plant stall. TEAS in aid of NE Herts NSPCC. *Adm £2 Chd 50p. Sun April 27 (2-5). Private visits welcome, please* **Tel 01920 438244**

Great Sarratt Hall ◬✿✿ (H M Neal Esq) Sarratt, N of Rickmansworth. From Watford N via A41 (or M1 Exit 5) to Kings Langley; and left (W) to Sarratt; garden is 1st on R after village sign. 4 acres; herbaceous and mixed shrub borders; pond, moisture-loving plants and trees; walled kitchen garden; rhododendrons, magnolias, camellias; new planting of specialist conifers and rare trees. TEAS. *Adm £2 Chd free (Share to Courtauld Institute of Art Fund®). Sun May 25 (2-6)*

High Elms Gardens ◬✿ Harpenden. On B487 (Redbourne Lane) off A1081 St Albans to Harpenden Rd. TEAS. *Adm £1.50 Chd 50p (Share to Multiple Sclerosis Society®). Sun June 29 (11-5)*
 4 High Elms (Prof & Mrs Logan) ½-acre garden featuring an extensive herbaceous border
 The Spinney, 6 High Elms (Tina & Michael Belderbos) ½-acre garden planted since 1980 with many special trees and shrubs and a recently designed herb garden

Hill House ✿✿ (Mr & Mrs R Pilkington) Stanstead Abbotts, near Ware. From A10 turn E on to A414; then B181 for Stanstead Abbotts; left at end of High St, garden 1st R past Church. Ample car parking. 8 acres incl wood; species roses, herbaceous border, water garden, conservatory, woodland walk. Lovely view over Lea Valley. Modern Art Exhibition in loft gallery (20p extra). Unusual plants for sale. Home-made TEAS. *Adm £2 Chd 50p (Share to St Andrews Parish Church of Stanstead Abbotts®). Sun June 15 (2-5.30). Private visits welcome, please* **Tel 0192 0870013**

Hipkins ◬✿ (Michael Goulding Esq) Broxbourne. From A10 to Broxbourne turn up Bell or Park Lane into Baas Lane, opposite Graham Avenue. 3-acre informal garden with spring fed ponds; azaleas and rhododendrons; shrub and herbaceous borders specialising in plants for flower arrangers; many unusual plants; fine trees and well kept kitchen garden. TEAS. *Adm £2 Chd 50p. Sun May 18 (2-6)*

Holwell Manor ◬✿✿ (Mr & Mrs J Gillum) Nr Hatfield. On W side of B1455, short lane linking A414 with B158 between Hatfield (3m) and Hertford (4m). B1455 joins the A414 roundabout and is signposted Essendon. Holwell is 500yds from this roundabout. Natural garden with large pond fed by hydraulic ram powered fountain, mature trees, river walks; approx 2-3 acres. Island in pond covered with daffodils and narcissi in spring. TEA. *Adm £1.50 Chd 50p. Sun April 6 (2-5)*

Hunton Park ✿ Hunton Bridge, nr Abbots Langley. 1m S of Junction 20 off M25 and 3m N of Watford. On exiting from Junction 20 follow signs to Watford (A41), turn L at traffic lights after ½m signposted Abbots Langley. Follow Bridge Rd for ½m up hill and Hunton Park is to be found on the RH-side. 22 acres of terraced lawns, gardens, pond and woodlands incl mature trees and ancient yews. First established in the 1840s the present grounds staff are working to return the gardens to their original setting comprising herbaceous borders, heather gardens, woodland plants and rose garden. A picnic area is provided. TEA. *Adm £1.50 Chd free. Suns April 20, June 8, Sept 7 (1-5).* **Tel 01923 261511**

▲**Knebworth House** ◬✿ (The Lord Cobbold) Knebworth. 28m N of London; direct access from A1(M) at Stevenage. Station and Bus stop: Stevenage 3m. Historic house, home of Bulwer Lytton; Victorian novelist and statesman. Lutyens garden designed for his brother-in-law, the Earl of Lytton, comprising pleached lime avenues, rose beds, herbaceous borders, yew hedges, restored maze and various small gardens in process of restoration; Gertrude Jekyll herb garden. Restaurant and TEAS. *Adm £2 Chd £1.50. For NGS Sun Sept 28 (12-5)*

Lamer Hill ✿✿ (Mrs M Flory) Wheathampstead. 1m N of Wheathampstead on B 651 to Lower Gustard Wood. Turn R opp entrance to Mid-Herts Golf Club up private rd to start of wood. Old 4-acre garden re-designed during last 10 yrs; so many areas reaching maturity. Variety of trees, mature and new incl pleached hornbeams. Mixed borders; woodland walk. Partially suitable for wheelchairs. TEAS. *Adm £2 Acc chd under 10 free. Sun June 8 (2-5)*

Little Gaddesden Gardens Approach from Hemel Hempstead along Leighton Buzzard Rd or from centre of Berkhamsted N of Station. The village hall is in Church Rd in centre of village, which is 2m N of Berkhamsted or 4½m W of Hemel Hempstead. Lunches and Teas at village hall in aid of ARC. *Combined adm £2.50 Chd 50p. Sun June 15 (11-5)*
 Ashridge Management College ◬ From hall down Church Rd to Village Rd and straight over to Ashridge Rd. Through gates into Ashridge College. 180 acreage approx/features as on map. The pleasure gardens were planned by Capability's disciple Humphry Repton (1813). Mount garden, circular rose garden and grotto. A new rock and water garden rhododendron walk
 1 Home Farm ✿ (Mr & Mrs D E A Tucker) From village hall, down to main village rd L SE towards Nettleden ¾m to Home Farm Cottage and Shepherds Cottage on L. 4yr old garden with some mature trees, herbaceous borders, roses, clematis, water feature; a cottage garden
 Nettleden Lodge ◬✿ (Mr & Mrs Allsop) From village hall down main Village Rd to Nettleden 1½m on R. Approx 4 acres comprising extensive lawns, herbaceous borders, ornamental lake and cascade, rhododendrons, magnolias, acers and many unusual plants. A plantsman's garden
 Shepherds Cottage ✿ (Mr & Mrs G A B Ward) Small walled garden of interesting design. Unusual plants, water feature

The Gardens of Mackerye End *✗❀* A1 junction 4, follow signs for Wheathampstead then Luton. Gardens ½m from Wheathampstead on R. M1 junction 10 follow Lower Luton Rd (B653) to Cherry Tree Inn. Turn L following signs to Mackereye End. Lunches and TEAS. *Adm £2.50 Chd £1 (Share to Alzheimers Research Trust®). Sun June 22 (11-5)*

> **Mackerye End House** ♿ (Mr & Mrs David Laing) A 1550 Grade 1 manor house set in 11 acres of gardens and park. Front garden set in framework of formal yew hedges with a long border and a fine C17 tulip tree. Victorian walled garden now divided into smaller sections; path maze; cutting garden; quiet garden; vegetables. Newly created W garden enclosed by pergola walk of old English roses and vines.
>
> **Hollybush Cottage** (Mr & Mrs John Coaton) Delightful cottage garden around this listed house
>
> **Eightacre** (Mr J Walker) 2-acre garden incl shrub and herbaceous beds, wild life pond, raised vegetable beds, greenhouse and orchards

■ **The Manor House** ♿*✗* (Mrs Andrew Duncan) Ayot St Lawrence. Bear R into village from Bride Hall Lane, ruined Church on L and the Brocket Arms on R. On bend there is a pair of brick piers leading to drive - go through green iron gates. The Manor house is on your L. New garden, with formal garden, mixed borders and nut grove, large walled garden and orchard. TEAS NGS day only. *Adm £2 OAP/Chd £1 (under ten free) Suns July 13, Aug 17, Mon Aug 25 (2-6). By appt for parties, please* **Tel 01438 820943.** *For NGS Sun June 29 (2-6)*

¶**3 Mansion House Farm** (Peter & Sue Avery) Abbots Langley. Sited about 150yds from small roundabout in Abbots Langley on the Watford to Leverstock Green rd. M25 junction 20 or M1 junction 6. ½-acre garden with perennial borders and rose garden. Large dewpond with water lilies and other aquatic plants; garden seats are strategically placed. *Adm £1.50 Chd free (Share to Friends of St Lawrence®). Sun Aug 24 (2-5)*

¶**May Cot** *✗❀* (Richard & Juliet Penn-Clark) 100 Pondcroft Rd, Knebworth. Running parallel to and W of B197 in Knebworth Village. Small cottage garden 100' × 20' planted in 1993 incl immature knot garden, old and English roses. Small potager started 1995 at No.98, incl in adm charge. *Adm £1 Chd 50p. Private visits welcome, please* **Tel 01438 816988**

The Mill House ♿*✗❀* (Dr and Mrs R V Knight) Tewin, nr Archers Green. 3½m W of Hertford and 3½m E of Welwyn on B1000. Parking at Archers Green which is signposted on B1000. On the banks of the R Mimram. Approx 20 acres; mature gardens incl fine hedges, woodlands, many rare trees labelled, shrub and herbaceous borders, spring fed water gardens, with an abundance of wildlife in a lovely valley setting. Plants and TEAS in aid of Isabel Hospice. *Adm £2 Chd under 10 free. Sun July 6 (2-6)*

Moor Place ♿❀ (Mr & Mrs Bryan Norman) Much Hadham. Entrance either at war memorial or at Hadham Cross. 2 C18 walled gardens. Herbaceous borders. Large area of shrubbery, lawns, hedges and trees. 2 ponds. Approx 10 acres. TEAS. *Adm £2 Chd 50p. Sun June 22 (2-5.30)*

Myddelton House see London

Old Hammers *✗❀* (Mrs G D Chalk) Rushden. Off A507 Baldock to Buntingford rd or from Royston A505. Turn L at Slip End. 1-acre garden on gentle slope with interesting trees, shrubs and herbaceous plants. Car park opp. TEAS in aid of Church. *Adm £1 Chd 50p. Sun June 29 (2-6)*

¶**20 Park Avenue South** ♿*✗❀* (Miss Isobel Leek) Harpenden. Off A1081 turn W by The Cock Inn and War Memorial up Rothamsted Ave; 3rd on L. ½-acre plantsman's garden with trees, shrub and herbaceous borders, alpine gravel bed, 2 ponds and bog garden planted for yr-long interest and colour; aviary. TEAS. *Adm £1.50 Chd 50p. Suns May 18, July 13, Sept 7 (2-6)*

Pelham House ♿*✗❀* (Mr David Haselgrove & Dr Sylvia Martinelli) Brent Pelham. On E side of Brent Pelham on B1038. When travelling from Clavering immed after the village sign. 3½-acre informal garden on alkaline clay started by present owners in 1986. Plenty of interest to the plantsman. Wide variety of trees and shrubs especially birches and oaks. Bulb frames, beds with alpines and acid-loving plants and small formal area with ponds. Many daffodils and tulips. TEAS. *Adm £1.50 Chd free (Share to Brent Pelham Church®). Suns April 6, May 11 (2-5)*

Putteridge Bury *✗* (University of Luton) On A505 Hitchin/Luton rd 2m NE of Luton on S side of dual carriageway. Gertrude Jekyll's plans for the rose garden and mixed border have been faithfully restored by the Herts Gardens Trust and are maintained by the University. Edwin Lutyens' reflecting pool and massive yew hedges are important features. Wide lawns, mature trees and new specimens make this an enjoyable garden to visit. Combined with nearby Temple Dinsley it provides an insight into garden design by Lutyens and Jekyll. TEAS. *Adm £2 Chd £1 (Share to Herts Gardens Trust®). Sun July 13 (10-5)*

Queenswood School ♿*✗❀* Shepherds Way. From S: M25 junction 24 signposted Potters Bar. In ½m at lights turn R onto A1000 signposted Hatfield. In 2m turn R onto B157. School is ½m on the R. From N: A1000 from Hatfield. In 5m turn L onto B157. 120 acres informal gardens and woodlands. Rhododendrons, fine specimen trees, shrubs and herbaceous borders. Glasshouses; fine views to Chiltern Hills. Picnic area. Lunches and TEAS. *Adm £1.50 OAP's/Chd 75p. Sun, Mon May 25, 26 (11-6)*

Rothamsted Manor と♨☀ (Rothamsted Experimental Station) 5m N of St Albans, 1m from Harpenden. Turn off A1081 at roundabout. Junction with B487 toward Redbourn. Immed take R diagonal rd across Hatching Green. 6-acre formal gardens with fine topiary, rose garden and large herbaceous border surrounding C17 house, former home of Sir John Lawes, set in parkland. Conducted tour of house. Concert band of Sir John Lawes School will play. TEAS. *Adm £2 Chd £1 (Share to Lawes Agricultural Trust®). Sun July 13 (2-5)*

St Paul's Walden Bury と (Simon Bowes Lyon and family) on B651 5m S of Hitchin; ½m N of Whitwell. Formal woodland garden listed Grade 1. Laid out about 1730, influenced by French tastes. Long rides and avenues span about 40 acres, leading to temples, statues, lake and ponds. Also more recent flower gardens and woodland garden with rhododendrons, azaleas and magnolias. Dogs on leads. TEAS. *Adm £2 Chd 50p (Share to St Pauls Walden Church®). Suns April 20, May 11, June 1, 22 (2-7). Also other times by appt Tel 01438 871218 or 871229*

Serge Hill ♨☀ (Murray & Joan Stuart-Smith) Abbots Langley. ½m E of Bedmond. The house is marked on the OS map. Regency house in parkland setting with fine kitchen garden of ½ acre. A range of unusual wall plants, mixed border of 100yds. New small courtyard garden and wall garden planted with hot coloured flowers. TEAS. *Combined adm £3 with* **The Barn** *(Share to Herts Garden Trust®). Sun June 22 (2-5)*

Temple Dinsley (Princess Helena College) Preston, nr Hitchin. B656 Hitchin/Welwyn Garden City rd. Turn off just S of St Ippolits, signed Preston and·Princess Helena College. The Herts Gardens Trust is restoring this important Edwin Lutyens garden which surrounds an altered Queen Anne house. Edwardian rose garden pergolas and architectural features are surrounded by lawns and trees. This evocative garden demonstrates the skill of Lutyens' designs and is an interesting counterpart to the gardens at Putteridge Bury. TEAS. *Adm £2 Chd £1 (Share to Princess Helena College®). Sun July 13 (10-5). Private visits welcome, please Tel 01462 432100*

¶**Thundridge Hill House** と☀ (Mr & Mrs Christopher Melluish) Ware. ¾m from The Sow & Pig Inn on A10 2m from Ware to the N. [Map Ref: OS 814 359] Well-established garden of approx 2½ acres; good variety of plants and shrubs incl old roses. Fine views down to Rib Valley. TEAS in aid of St Mary's Thundridge Parish Funds. *Adm £2 Chd 50p. Sun June 22 (2-5)*

Waterdell House と♨☀ (Mr & Mrs Peter Ward) Croxley Green. 1½m from Rickmansworth. Exit 18 from M25. Direction R'worth to join A412 towards Watford. From A412 turn left signed Sarratt, along Croxley Green, fork right past Coach & Horses, cross Baldwins Lane into Little Green Lane, then left at top. 1½-acre walled garden systematically developed over more than 40 years: mature and young trees, topiary holly hedge, herbaceous borders, modern island beds of shrubs, old-fashioned roses, vegetable, fruit and pond gardens. TEAS 80p. *Adm £1.50 OAPs/Chd £1. Sun June 29 (2-6) and private visits welcome by appt yr round, please Tel 01923 772775*

West Lodge Park と (T Edward Beale Esq) Cockfosters Rd, Hadley Wood. On A111 between Potters Bar and Southgate. Exit 24 from M25 signed Cockfosters. The 10-acre Beale Arboretum consists of over 700 varieties of trees and shrubs, incl national plant collections of eleagnus and hornbeam cultivars, with a good selection of conifers, oaks, maples and mountain ash. A network of paths has been laid out, and most specimens are labelled. Lunch or teas can be booked in West Lodge Park hotel in the grounds. *Adm £2 Chd free. Suns May 18 (2-5); Oct 19 (12-4). Organised parties anytime by appt Tel 0181 4408311*

¶**Wickham Hall** と♨☀ (Mr & Mrs Ted Harvey) 1m NW of Bishop's Stortford. From A120 roundabout W of Bishop's Stortford take exit as for town. Wickham Hall drive is 300yds on LH-side. 1-acre garden surrounding Elizabethan farm house. Mixed borders of shrubs and old-fashioned roses. Large walled garden. ¶**The Dovecote** (Mr & Mrs D Whiffen) Delightful small cottage garden with many interesting plants. TEAS. *Comb adm £1.50 Chd 50p Sun June 15 (2-6)*

¶**Wilstone Gardens** と Tring. Entering Tring on A41 from direction of Hemel Hempsted, turn R at 1st mini roundabout by Robin Hood Inn. Follow signs to Long Marston. After crossing canal over hump backed bridge, turn L into Wilstone. (Approx 1½m from Tring). *Combined adm £2 Chd free. Sun July 6 (2-6)*
¶**57 Tring Road** ☀ (Frances Warren) Garden designer's organic garden approx ⅓ acre. Densely planted with unusual trees, shrubs and perennials in informal borders. Rose pergola; pond; herbs; gravel garden and ornamental vegetable garden
¶**The Old Cow House** (Gill Glasser) Large garden with well-stocked colourful herbaceous borders, mature shrubs, many specimen trees; productive vegetable garden, wildlife pond and bog garden. Large terrace with many tubs and troughs free. TEAS

23 Wroxham Way ♨☀ (Mrs M G M Easter) Harpenden. NE Harpenden off Ox Lane. M1 Junction 6 + A1081 or Junction 10a + A1081. A1 Junction 4 or 5 and B653 Lower Luton Road. Plantsman's garden 70′ × 35′. Sloping site with steps and walls. Large mixed border at front. Planted for yr-round interest. Galanthus, crocus, helleborus, diascia, old dianthus, geranium; penstemon; alpine scree; herbs; national collection of thymus. *Adm £1 (Share to Gt Ormond St Children's Hospital®). Mons March 31 (2-5), May 5, Aug 25, Suns June 15, July 20, Sept 21 (2-5.30). Private visits welcome, please Tel 01582 768467*

Humberside

See Yorkshire

Isle of Wight

Hon County Organiser:	Mrs John Harrison, North Court, Shorwell PO30 3JG
Hon County Treasurer:	Mrs R Hillyard, The Coach House, Duver Rd, St Helens, Ryde PO33 1XY

DATES OF OPENING

March 30 Sunday
Kings Manor, Freshwater
April 20 Sunday
Woolverton House, St Lawrence
April 27 Sunday
Badminton, Carisbrooke
May 11 Sunday
Osborne House, East Cowes
May 18 Sunday
Northcourt Gardens, Shorwell
May 26 Monday
Fortunes Corner, Brighstone
Waldeck, Brighstone
June 8 Sunday
Northcourt Gardens, Shorwell

June 15 Sunday
Hamstead Grange, Yarmouth
June 18 Wednesday
Mottistone Manor Garden,
Mottistone
June 29 Sunday
Nunwell House, Brading
July 6 Sunday
Pitt House, Bembridge
July 13 Sunday
Ashknowle House, Whitwell,
Ventnor
August 31 Sunday
Crab Cottage, Shalfleet
September 7 Sunday
Osborne House, East Cowes

By appointment only
*For telephone numbers and other
details see garden descriptions.
Private visits welcomed*

Highwood, Cranmore
Owl Cottage, Mottistone
Rock Cottage, Blackwater
Waldeck, Brightstone
Westport Cottage, Yarmouth

> **By Appointment Gardens.**
> These owners do not have a
> fixed opening day usually
> because they cannot
> accommodate large numbers or
> have insufficient parking space.

DESCRIPTIONS OF GARDENS

¶**Ashknowle House** ✗✿ (Mr & Mrs K Fradgley) Whitwell. The turn for Ashknowle Lane is from the Ventnor Rd in Whitwell close to the church. The lane is unmarked and unmade. Cars can be left in the village but parking is provided in the grounds. A 3-acre mature but developing garden with trees, shrubs and lawned areas. Of special interest is the vegetable garden with glasshouses and raised beds. The garden has recently been extended by a further acre of young trees. TEA. *Adm £1.50 Chd free. Sun July 13 (2-5)*

Badminton ✿ (Mr & Mrs G S Montrose) Clatterford Shute. Parking in Carisbrooke Castle car park. Public footpath in corner of car park leads down to the garden. ¾-acre garden with natural chalk stream. Mixed borders planted by owners during last 21 yrs, for all-yr interest. Lovely views. Changes since 1995. *Adm £1.50 Chd 25p. Sun April 27 (2-5)*

¶**Crab Cottage** &✿ (Mrs Peter Scott) Shalfleet. Turn past New Inn into Mill Rd through NT gates. The entrance is first on L. Please park cars in car park before going through NT gates. Less than 5 mins walk. 1.1-acre 5-yr-old garden with good views. Croquet lawn, pond and walled garden. TEA. *Adm £1.50 Chd free (Share to St Michael, Shalfleet®). Sun Aug 31 (2-5.30)*

¶**Fortunes Corner** ✗ (Mr & Mrs Wortham) Brighstone. 5 min walk from Waldeck. Top of Moor Lane over wooden footbridge and on L. Small shady garden attractively planted with damp loving plants. *Combined adm with* **Waldeck** *£1.50 Chd free. Mon May 26 (2-5.30)*

Hamstead Grange & (Mr & Mrs Tom Young) Yarmouth. Entrance to drive on A3054 between Shalfleet and Ningwood. Rose garden with shrubs, lawns and trees and new water garden. 3 acres with superb views of Solent. Swimming pool. TEAS in aid of local charity. *Adm £1.50 Chd 20p. Sun June 15 (2.30-5)*

Highwood ✗✿ (Mr & Mrs Cooper) Cranmore Ave is approx halfway between Yarmouth and the village of Shalfleet on the A3054. From Yarmouth the turning is on the L hand side, opp a bus shelter 3m out of Yarmouth on an unmade rd. 10-acre site with several acres under cultivation. A garden for all seasons and plant enthusiasts. Pond, woodland area with hellebores, borders and island beds. TEA. *Adm £1.50 Chd free. Private visits welcome, please* Tel 01983 760550

Kings Manor &✗✿ (Mrs Jamie Sheldon) Freshwater. Head E out of Yarmouth over R Yar Bridge. Approx 1m turn L at top of Pixleys Hill. Entrance on L at top of next hill. 3-acre informal garden with shrubs and spring bulbs and frontage onto marshes. Special features - views of estuary and saltings - formal garden around lily pond. TEAS. *Adm £1.50 Chd free (Share to Marie Curie®). Sun March 30 (2.30-5)*

▲**Mottistone Manor Garden** (The National Trust) Mottistone. 8m SW Newport on B3399 between Brighstone and Brook. Medium-sized formal terraced garden, backing onto medieval and Elizabethan manor house, set in wooded valley with fine views of English Channel. *Adm £1.80 Chd 90p. For NGS Wed June 18 (2-5.30)*

Northcourt Gardens &✿ (Mrs C D Harrison, Mr & Mrs J Harrison) On entering Shorwell from Carisbrooke entrance on R. 15 acres incl bathhouse, walled kitchen garden, stream planted with candelabra primulas and bog plants. Garden rises to mediterranean terraces and new sub-tropical garden with sea views. Collection of 76 hardy geraniums. Jacobean Manor House. TEAS. *Adm £2 Chd 25p. Suns May 18, June 8 (1-5.30)*

Nunwell House ✀❀ (Col & Mrs J A Aylmer) Brading. 3m S of Ryde; signed off A3055 in Brading into Coach Lane. 5 acres beautifully set formal and shrub gardens with exceptional view of Solent. House developed over 5 centuries, full of architectural interest. Coaches by appt only. TEAS. *Adm £1.50 Chd 20p; House £2 Chd 30p extra (Share to St Johns, Isle of Wight®). Sun June 29 (2-5)*

▲¶**Osborne House** ♿✀ (English Heritage) East Cowes. Off A3021 1m SE of East Cowes. Landscaped gardens surrounding the family home of Queen Victoria and Prince Albert. Terrace gardens adorned with fountains and statues in the Renaissance manner step down towards the sea. Royal children's garden surrounding the Swiss Cottage. Restaurant available. *Adm Garden only £3.50 Concessions £2.60 Chd £1.80. House & Gardens £6 Concessions £4.50 Chd £3. Family ticket £15. For NGS Suns May 11, Sept 7 (10-6)*

Owl Cottage ♿✀ (Mrs A L Hutchinson) Hoxall Lane, Mottistone. 9m SW of Newport, from B3399 at Mottistone turn down Hoxall Lane for 200yds. Interesting cottage garden, view of sea. Home-made TEAS. Plant sale. *Adm £2 Chd free. Visits by appointment every day May until Aug, parties of 10 up to 30 (2.30-5.30), please* **Tel 01983 740433** *after 6pm*

Pitt House ♿✀ (L J Martin Esq) Bembridge. NE of Bembridge Harbour. Enter Bembridge Village, pass museum and take 1st L into Love Lane. Continue down lane (5 min walk) as far as the bend; Pitt House is on L. Enter tall wrought iron gates. If coming by car enter Ducie Ave 1st L before museum. Pitt House at bottom of ave, on the R. Parking in lane. Approx 4 acres with varied aspects and points of interest. A number of sculptures dotted around the garden; also victorian greenhouse, mini waterfall and 4 ponds. TEAS. *Adm £1.80 Chd 50p. Sun July 6 (10.30-5)*

Rock Cottage ✀ (Mary & Cliff Pain) Blackwater. From Newport take main rd to Ventnor. Park in Blackwater on/off main rd **but not** in Sandy Lane. Short walk, approx 200yds, up Sandy Lane to Rock Cottage. ⅓-acre. Cottage garden. Some flowering shrubs, spring bulbs, numerous clematis and hardy perennials; fruit and vegetables. Lawn and numerous small plots divided by grass paths. TEA. *Adm £1 Chd free. Private visits by appt for max 20, please* **Tel 01983 525845**

Waldeck ✀❀ (Mr & Mrs G R Williams) Brighstone. 8m SW of Newport. Take Carisbrooke-Shorwell rd, then B3399 to Brighstone. Through village centre, turn R off main rd into Moor Lane. Limited parking in lane. ¾-acre garden informally planted to provide some colour and interest from trees, shrubs and perennial plants throughout the year. Special emphasis placed on foliage and shade tolerant plants such as acers, ferns, hostas, etc. Teas available. *Combined adm with* **Fortunes Corner** *£1.50 Chd free (Share to Society for the Blind®). Mon May 26 (2-5.30). Also by appt during July, please* **Tel 01983 740430**

Westport Cottage ♿❀ (M Fisher & K Sharp) Tennyson Close off Tennyson Rd. ½-acre walled working garden. Semi-hardy and unusual plants. TEA. *Adm £1.50 Chd 25p (Share to St Mary's Hospital League of Friends©). Private visits welcome, especially garden groups, flower arrangers. Talks and meals by arrangement, please* **Tel 01983 760751**

Woolverton House (Mr & Mrs S H G Twining) St Lawrence. 3m W of Ventnor; Bus 16 from Ryde, Sandown, Shanklin. Flowering shrubs, bulbs, fine position. Home-made TEAS. **50th yr of opening for NGS**. *Adm £1.50 Chd 25p (Share to St Lawrence Village Hall®). Sun April 20 (2-5)*

Kent

Hon County Organiser:	Mrs Valentine Fleming, Stonewall Park, Edenbridge TN8 7DG
Assistant Hon County Organisers:	Mrs Jeremy Gibbs, Upper Kennards, Leigh, Tonbridge TN11 8RE
	Mrs Nicolas Irwin, Hoo Farmhouse, Minster, Ramsgate CT12 4JB
	Mrs Richard Latham, Stowting Hill House, nr Ashford TN25 6BE
	Miss E Napier, 447 Wateringbury Road, East Malling ME19 6JQ
	Mrs M R Streatfeild, Hoath House, Chiddingstone Hoath, Edenbridge TN8 7DB
	Mrs Simon Toynbee, Old Tong Farm, Brenchley TN12 7HT
Hon County Treasurer:	Valentine Fleming Esq, Stonewall Park, Edenbridge TN8 7DG

DATES OF OPENING

February 16 Sunday
Goodnestone Park, Wingham, nr Canterbury

February 23 Sunday
190 Maidstone Road, Chatham

February 27 Thursday
Broadview Gardens, Hadlow College

March 2 Sunday
Great Comp, Borough Green

March 9 Sunday
Great Comp, Borough Green
Weeks Farm, Egerton Forstal

March 16 Sunday
Copton Ash, Faversham
Goodnestone Park, Wingham, nr Canterbury
Great Comp, Borough Green

March 23 Sunday
Church Hill Cottage, Charing Heath
Cobham Hall, Cobham
Withersdane Hall, Wye

March 30 Easter Sunday
Church Hill Cottage, Charing Heath
Copton Ash, Faversham
Godinton Park, nr Ashford
Hault Farm, Waltham, nr Canterbury
Jessups, Mark Beech
Longacre, Selling
The Pines Garden & Bay Museum, St Margaret's Bay

March 31 Easter Monday
Church Hill Cottage, Charing Heath
Copton Ash, Faversham
Crittenden House, Matfield
Longacre, Selling

April 5 Saturday
Sissinghurst Place, Sissinghurst

April 6 Sunday
Church Hill Cottage, Charing Heath
Copton Ash, Faversham
190 Maidstone Road, Chatham
Mere House, Mereworth

Sissinghurst Place, Sissinghurst
Spilsill Court, Staplehurst

April 13 Sunday
Church Hill Cottage, Charing Heath ‡
Edenbridge House, Edenbridge
Egypt Farm, Plaxtol ‡‡
Hamptons Farm House, Plaxtol ‡‡
Hole Park, Rolvenden
Horton Priory, Sellindge
2 Thorndale Close, Chatham
39 Warwick Crescent, Borstal, nr Rochester
Weeks Farm, Egerton Forstal ‡
Yalding Gardens

April 16 Wednesday
Riverhill House, Sevenoaks

April 19 Saturday
Sissinghurst Place, Sissinghurst

April 20 Sunday
Church Hill Cottage, Charing Heath
Coldham, Little Chart Forstal
Copton Ash, Faversham
Hole Park, Rolvenden
Mount Ephraim, Hernhill, Faversham
Olantigh, Wye
Sissinghurst Place, Sissinghurst
Swan Oast, Stilebridge, Marden
Torry Hill, nr Sittingbourne

April 21 Monday
Groombridge Place, Groombridge

April 23 Wednesday
Hole Park, Rolvenden
Sissinghurst Garden, Sissinghurst
Westview, Hempstead, Gillingham

April 26 Saturday
Everden House, Alkham
Haydown, Great Buckland
Pett Place, Charing

April 27 Sunday
Bradbourne House, East Malling
Coldharbour Oast, Tenterden
Longacre, Selling
Maurice House, Broadstairs
Pett Place, Charing
St Michael's House, Roydon, Peckham Bush
Stoneacre, Otham, Maidstone
Swan Oast, Stilebridge, Marden

2 Thorndale Close, Chatham
Westview, Hempstead, Gillingham

May 2 Friday
Great Maytham Hall, Rolvenden

May 3 Saturday
Rock Farm, Nettlestead

May 4 Sunday
Church Hill Cottage, Charing Heath
Copton Ash, Faversham
Edenbridge House, Edenbridge ‡
Hole Park, Rolvenden
Ladham House, Goudhurst
Longacre, Selling ‡‡
Luton House, Selling ‡‡
Meadow Wood, Penshurst
Swan Oast, Stilebridge, Marden
Weald Cottage, Four Elms Road, Edenbridge ‡
Whitehurst, Chainhurst, Marden
Withersdane Hall, Wye

May 5 Monday
Brewhouse, Boughton Aluph
Church Hill Cottage, Charing Heath
Copton Ash, Faversham
Crittenden House, Matfield
Longacre, Selling

May 7 Wednesday
Penshurst Place, Penshurst
Rock Farm, Nettlestead

May 10 Saturday
Emmetts Garden, Ide Hill
Rock Farm, Nettlestead

May 11 Sunday
Charts Edge, Westerham
Church Hill Cottage, Charing Heath
Finchcocks, Goudhurst
Hole Park, Rolvenden
Larksfield, Crockham Hill ‡
Larksfield Cottage, Crockham Hill ‡
The Red House, Crockham Hill ‡
Stonewall Park Gardens, nr Edenbridge
Swan Oast, Stilebridge, Marden
2 Thorndale Close, Chatham
39 Warwick Crescent, Borstal, nr Sittingbourne
Whitehurst, Chainhurst, Marden

May 14 Wednesday
Riverhill House, Sevenoaks
Rock Farm, Nettlestead
Waystrode Manor, Cowden
Westview, Hempstead, Gillingham

May 17 Saturday
25 Crouch Hill Court, Lower
  Halstow
Peddars Wood, St Michaels,
  Tenterden
Rock Farm, Nettlestead

May 18 Sunday
Bilting House, nr Ashford
Brenchley Gardens
Charts Edge, Westerham
Larksfield, Crockham Hill ‡
Larksfield Cottge, Crockham Hill ‡
New Barns House, West
  Malling ‡‡
Owl House, Lamberhurst
The Red House, Crockham Hill ‡
Sea Close, Hythe
Town Hill Cottage, West
  Malling ‡‡
Westview, Hempstead, Gillingham

May 21 Wednesday
Edenbridge House, Edenbridge
Hole Park, Rolvenden
Rock Farm, Nettlestead

May 23 Friday
Kypp Cottage, Biddenden

May 24 Saturday
Abbotsmerry Barn, Penshurst
25 Crouch Hill Court, Lower
  Halstow
Doddington Place, Sittingbourne
Kypp Cottage, Biddenden
Rock Farm, Nettlestead

May 25 Sunday
Church Hill Cottage, Charing
  Heath
Copton Ash, Faversham
Crittenden House, Matfield
Doddington Place, Sittingbourne
Everden House, Alkham
Godmersham Park, Godmersham
Goudhurst Gardens
Hole Park, Rolvenden
Kypp Cottage, Biddenden
Little Trafalgar, Selling ‡
Longacre, Selling ‡
Marle Place, Brenchley
Old Buckhurst, Mark Beech
Oxon Hoath, nr Hadlow
The Pines Garden & Bay
  Museum, St Margaret's Bay
St Michaels House, Roydon,
  Peckham Bush
The Silver Spray, Sellindge
2 Thorndale Close, Chatham
Weald Cottage, Four Elms Road,
  Edenbridge

May 26 Monday
Beech Court Gardens, Challock

Brewhouse, Boughton Aluph
Church Hill Cottage, Charing
  Heath
Copton Ash, Faversham
Doddington Place, Sittingbourne
Everden House, Alkham
Forest Gate, Pluckley
Godmersham Park, Godmersham
Kypp Cottage, Biddenden
Ladham House, Goudhurst
Little Trafalgar, Selling ‡
Longacre, Selling ‡
Scotney Castle, Lamberhurst
The Silver Spray, Sellindge
Weald Cottage, Four Elms Road,
  Edenbridge

May 27 Tuesday
Doddington Place, Sittingbourne
Kypp Cottage, Biddenden

May 28 Wednesday
Doddington Place, Sittingbourne
Kypp Cottage, Biddenden
Rock Farm, Nettlestead
Waystrode Manor, Cowden

May 29 Thursday
Doddington Place, Sittingbourne

May 30 Friday
Doddington Place, Sittingbourne

May 31 Saturday
25 Crouch Hill Court, Lower
  Halstow
Doddington Place, Sittingbourne
Rock Farm, Nettlestead

June 1 Sunday
Brewhouse, Boughton Aluph
Doddington Place, Sittingbourne
Kypp Cottage, Biddenden
Northbourne Court, nr Deal
Old Buckhurst, Mark Beech
Ramhurst Manor, Leigh,
  Tonbridge
Waystrode Manor, Cowden

June 2 Monday
Kypp Cottage, Biddenden

June 3 Tuesday
Kypp Cottage, Biddenden

June 4 Wednesday
Knole, Sevenoaks
Kypp Cottage, Biddenden
Rock Farm, Nettlestead
Sissinghurst Garden, Sissinghurst
Westview, Hempstead,
  Gillingham

June 5 Thursday
Penshurst Place, Penshurst

June 7 Saturday
25 Crouch Hill Court, Lower
  Halstow
Little Combourne Farmhouse,
  Curtisden Green
Rock Farm, Nettlestead

June 8 Sunday
Abbotsmerry Barn, Penshurst
Kypp Cottage, Biddenden

Little Combourne Farmhouse,
  Curtisden Green
Little Trafalgar, Selling ‡
Longacre, Selling ‡
Northbourne Court, nr Deal
Patches, Barham
2 Thorndale Close, Chatham
Thornham Friars, Thurnham
Torry Hill, nr Sittingbourne
Westview, Hempstead,
  Gillingham
Whitehurst, Chainhurst, Marden

June 9 Monday
Kypp Cottage, Biddenden

June 10 Tuesday
Kypp Cottage, Biddenden

June 11 Wednesday
Kypp Cottage, Biddenden
Patches, Barham
Rock Farm, Nettlestead
Upper Pryors, Cowden

June 13 Friday
Smallhythe Place (Ellen Terry
  Museum), Tenterden

June 14 Saturday
25 Crouch Hill Court, Lower
  Halstow
The Old Parsonage, Sutton
  Valence
Rock Farm, Nettlestead
The Silver Spray, Sellindge

June 15 Sunday
Abbotsmerry Barn, Penshurst
The Anchorage, West Wickham
Church Hill Cottage, Charing
  Heath
Copton Ash, Faversham
Edenbridge House, Edenbridge
Goudhurst Gardens
Hartlip Gardens
Horton Priory, Sellindge
Kypp Cottage, Biddenden
Lullingstone Castle, Eynsford
Maycotts, Matfield
Mill House, Hildenborough
Northbourne Court, nr Deal
Old Place Farm, High Halden
Pevington Farm, Pluckley
Sea Close, Hythe
Town Hill Cottage, West Malling
Whitehill, Wrotham
Whitehurst, Chainhurst, Marden
Withersdane Hall, Wye

June 16 Monday
Kypp Cottage, Biddenden

June 17 Tuesday
Kypp Cottage, Biddenden
The Old Parsonage, Sutton
  Valence

June 18 Wednesday
Edenbridge House, Edenbridge
Kypp Cottage, Biddenden
Rock Farm, Nettlestead
Waystrode Manor, Cowden

June 19 Thursday
Beech Court Gardens, Challock
June 20 Friday
The Old Parsonage, Sutton
Valence
June 21 Saturday
25 Crouch Hill Court, Lower
Halstow
Downs Court, Boughton Aluph
Peddars Wood, St Michaels,
Tenterden
Rock Farm, Nettlestead
June 22 Sunday
Battel Hall, Leeds, nr Maidstone
Coldham, Little Chart Forstal
Downs Court, Boughton Aluph
Kypp Cottage, Biddenden
Lily Vale Farm, Smeeth,
Ashford ‡
Little Trafalgar, Selling ‡‡
Lodge House, Smeeth, Ashford ‡
Long Barn, Weald, Sevenoaks
Longacre, Selling ‡‡
Northbourne Court, nr Deal
Olantigh, Wye
The Old Parsonage, Sutton
Valence
Rogers Rough, Kilndown
Rose Cottage, Hartley
St Michaels House, Roydon,
Peckham Bush
Shipbourne Gardens
The Silver Spray, Sellindge
Sotts Hole Cottage, Borough
Green
2 Thorndale Close, Chatham
Weald Cottage, Four Elms Road,
nr Edenbridge
Went House, West Malling
Wyckhurst, Aldington
June 23 Monday
Kypp Cottage, Biddenden
June 24 Tuesday
Kypp Cottage, Biddenden
June 25 Wednesday
Hole Park, Rolvenden
Ightham Mote, Ivy Hatch
Kypp Cottage, Biddenden
Lily Vale Farm, Smeeth,
Ashford ‡
Lodge House, Smeeth, Ashford ‡
Rock Farm, Nettlestead
Wyckhurst, Aldington
June 27 Friday
Great Maytham Hall, Rolvenden
June 28 Saturday
25 Crouch Hill Court, Lower
Halstow
Old Tong Farm, Brenchley
Pett Place, Charing
Rock Farm, Nettlestead
Womenswold Gardens
June 29 Sunday
Aldon House, Offham ‡

Brewhouse, Boughton Aluph
Cedar House, Addington ‡
Forest Gate, Pluckley ‡‡
Kypp Cottage, Biddenden
Northbourne Court, nr Deal
Old Tong Farm, Brenchley
Pett Place, Charing
Plaxtol Gardens
Sibton Park, Lyminge
Street Cottage, Bethersden
Swan Oast, Stilebridge, Marden
Walmer Castle, Deal
Walnut Tree Gardens, Little
Chart ‡‡
Waystrode Manor, Cowden
Womenswold Gardens
June 30 Monday
Kypp Cottage, Biddenden
July 1 Tuesday
Kypp Cottage, Biddenden
July 2 Wednesday
Amber Green Farmhouse, Chart
Sutton
Great Oaks House, Shipbourne ‡
Hookwood House, Shipbourne ‡
Kypp Cottage, Biddenden
Rock Farm, Nettlestead
July 5 Saturday
25 Crouch Hill Court, Lower
Halstow
Rock Farm, Nettlestead
South Hill Farm, Hastingleigh
July 6 Sunday
Cedar House, Addington ‡
Charts Edge, Westerham
Field House, Staplehurst
Godinton Park, Ashford
Kypp Cottage, Biddenden
Little Trafalgar, Selling ‡‡
Longacre, Selling ‡‡
Nettlestead Place, Nettlestead
Northbourne Court, nr Deal
Old Tong Farm, Brenchley
Placketts Hole, Bicknor, nr
Sittingbourne
South Hill Farm, Hastingleigh
Torry Hill, nr Sittingbourne
Walnut Tree Gardens,
Little Chart
39 Warwick Crescent, Borstal, nr
Rochester
Waystrode Manor, Cowden
Went House, West Malling ‡
Worth Gardens
July 7 Monday
Kypp Cottage, Biddenden
July 8 Tuesday
Kypp Cottage, Biddenden
July 9 Wednesday
Chartwell, Westerham
Kypp Cottage, Biddenden
Rock Farm, Nettlestead
Sissinghurst Garden,
Sissinghurst

July 12 Saturday
25 Crouch Hill Court, Lower
Halstow
Rock Farm, Nettlestead
The Silver Spray, Sellindge
July 13 Sunday
Aldon House, Offham
Bilting House, nr Ashford
Church Hill Cottage, Charing
Heath
Edenbridge House, Edenbridge
115 Hadlow Road, Tonbridge
Kypp Cottage, Biddenden
Little Oast, Otford
Northbourne Court, nr Deal
Old Tong Farm, Brenchley
Sea Close, Hythe
Swan Oast, Stilebridge, Marden
Walnut Tree Gardens, Little Chart
July 14 Monday
Kypp Cottage, Biddenden
July 15 Tuesday
Kypp Cottage, Biddenden
July 16 Wednesday
Cares Cross, Chiddingstone Hoath
Kypp Cottage, Biddenden
Rock Farm, Nettlestead
July 19 Saturday
25 Crouch Hill Court, Lower
Halstow
Rock Farm, Nettlestead
July 20 Sunday
Copton Ash, Faversham
Goodnestone Park, Wingham, nr
Canterbury
Groome Farm, Egerton
Little Trafalgar, Selling ‡
Long Barn, Weald, Sevenoaks
Longacre, Selling ‡
Northbourne Court, nr Deal
Rogers Rough, Kilndown
Squerryes Court, Westerham
Walnut Tree Gardens, Little Chart
Weald Cottage, Four Elms Rd,
Edenbridge
July 23 Wednesday
Hole Park, Rolvenden
Rock Farm, Nettlestead
The Silver Spray, Sellindge
July 26 Saturday
The Beehive, Lydd
25 Crouch Hill Court, Lower
Halstow
Everden House, Alkham
Haydown, Great Buckland
Peddars Wood, St Michaels,
Tenterden
Rock Farm, Nettlestead
The Silver Spray, Sellindge
July 27 Sunday
The Beehive, Lydd
Everden House, Alkham
Northbourne Court, nr Deal
Slaney Cottage, Staplehurst ‡

Spilsill Court, Staplehurst ‡
Swan Oast, Stilebridge, Marden
Walnut Tree Gardens, Little Chart

July 28 Monday
The Beehive, Lydd

July 30 Wednesday
185 Borden Lane, Sittingbourne
Rock Farm, Nettlestead

August 2 Saturday
25 Crouch Hill Court, Lower
Halstow
Rock Farm, Nettlestead

August 3 Sunday
185 Borden Lane, Sittingbourne
Field House, Staplehurst
Groome Farm, Egerton
115 Hadlow Road, Tonbridge
Little Trafalgar, Selling ‡
Longacre, Selling ‡
190 Maidstone Road, Chatham
Northbourne Court, nr Deal
Orchard Cottage, Bickley
Walnut Tree Gardens, Little Chart

August 4 Monday
Walmer Castle, nr Deal

August 6 Wednesday
Knole, Sevenoaks
Rock Farm, Nettlestead

August 9 Saturday
25 Crouch Hill Court, Lower
Halstow
Rock Farm, Nettlestead

August 10 Sunday
Chevening, Sevenoaks
Marle Place, Brenchley
Northbourne Court, nr Deal
Sea Close, Hythe
Swan Oast, Stilebridge, Marden

August 16 Saturday
25 Crouch Hill Court, Lower
Halstow

August 17 Sunday
Beech Court Gardens, Challock
Northbourne Court, nr Deal
Squerryes Court, Westerham
West Studdal Farm, nr Dover

August 20 Wednesday
The Silver Spray, Sellindge

August 23 Saturday
25 Crouch Hill Court, Lower
Halstow

August 24 Sunday
Church Hill Cottage, Charing Heath
Copton Ash, Faversham
115 Hadlow Road, Tonbridge
Little Trafalgar, Selling ‡
Longacre, Selling ‡
Northbourne Court, nr Deal
The Pines Garden & Bay
Museum, St Margaret's Bay
Swan Oast, Stilebridge, Marden

August 25 Monday
Church Hill Cottage, Charing
Heath

Copton Ash, Faversham
Little Trafalgar, Selling ‡
Longacre, Selling ‡
The Silver Spray, Sellindge

August 30 Saturday
25 Crouch Hill Court, Lower
Halstow

August 31 Sunday
Cobham Hall, Cobham
Coldharbour Oast, Tenterden
Swan Oast, Stilebridge, Marden
Withersdane Hall, Wye

September 6 Saturday
25 Crouch Hill Court, Lower
Halstow

September 7 Sunday
185 Borden Lane, Sittingbourne
Little Trafalgar, Selling ‡
Longacre, Selling ‡
Old Buckhurst, Mark Beech
39 Warwick Crescent, Borstal, nr
Rochester

September 13 Saturday
25 Crouch Hill Court, Lower
Halstow

September 14 Sunday
Broadview Gardens, Hadlow
College
Finchcocks, Goudhurst
Nettlestead Place, Nettlestead
Old Buckhurst, Mark Beech
Sotts Hole Cottage, Borough
Green
Weeks Farm, Egerton Forstal

September 20 Saturday
25 Crouch Hill Court, Lower
Halstow

September 21 Sunday
Copton Ash, Faversham
Little Trafalgar, Selling

September 24 Wednesday
Edenbridge House, Edenbridge

September 26 Friday
Great Maytham Hall, Rolvenden

September 27 Saturday
25 Crouch Hill Court, Lower
Halstow

September 28 Sunday
Edenbridge House, Edenbridge
Mount Ephraim, Hernhill,
Faversham
Stoneacre, Otham, Maidstone

October 1 Wednesday
Sissinghurst Garden,
Sissinghurst

October 4 Saturday
Emmetts Garden, Ide Hill

October 5 Sunday
Everden House, Alkham
Marle Place, Brenchley
Sea Close, Hythe
Whitehurst, Chainhurst, Marden

October 12 Sunday
Beech Court Gardens, Challock

Hault Farm, Waltham, nr
Canterbury
Hole Park, Rolvenden
Whitehurst, Chainhurst, Marden

October 19 Sunday
Copton Ash, Faversham
Hole Park, Rolvenden
Mere House, Mereworth

October 20 Monday
Groombridge Place, Groombridge

November 2 Sunday
Great Comp, Borough Green

By appointment only
*For telephone number and other
details see garden descriptions.
Private visits welcomed.*

Greenways, Single Street, nr Downe
43 Layhams Road, West Wickham
The Pear House, Sellindge
Saltwood Castle, nr Hythe
Tanners, Brasted

Regular openings
For details see garden descriptions

Beech Court Gardens, Challock
Cobham Hall, Cobham
Doddington Hall, nr Sittingbourne
Finchcocks, Goudhurst
Goodnestone Park, Wingham, nr
Canterbury
Groombridge Place, Groombridge
Hault Farm, Waltham, nr Canterbury
Hever Castle, nr Edenbridge
Marle Place, Brenchley
Mount Ephraim, Hernhill, Faversham
The Owl House, Lamberhurst
Penshurst Place, Penshurst
The Pines Garden & Bay Museum,
St Margaret's Bay
Riverhill House, Sevenoaks
Squerryes Court, Westerham
Walmer Castle, Deal

DESCRIPTIONS OF GARDENS

Abbotsmerry Barn ⚘❀ (Mr & Mrs K H Wallis) Salmans Lane, Penshurst. Between Penshurst and Leigh on B2176: 200yds N of Penshurst turn L, 1m down lane with speed ramps. 5-acre garden with widely varied planting on S-facing slope overlooking the Eden valley. Teas in Penshurst. *Adm £2 Acc chd free (Share to James House Hospice Trust©). Sat May 24; Suns June 8, 15 (2-5.30)*

¶**Aldon House** ♿ (Mr & Mrs Robert Fawssett) Aldon Lane, Offham, 2m W of West Malling. Turn S from A20 into Aldon Lane, entrance 1st L after railway bridge. 1-acre traditional garden with wide range of shrubs, herbaceous and foliage plants, young trees. **Cedar House, Addington** (with TEAS) also open on June 29. *Adm £1.50 Acc chd free. Suns June 29, July 13 (2-6)*

Amber Green Farmhouse ⚘❀ (Mr & Mrs J Groves) Chart Sutton, 7m SE of Maidstone. Turn W off A274 onto B2163, in 1m turn L at Chart Corner, next R is Amber Lane, house ½m W. C17 listed weatherboarded farmhouse (not open) in 1-acre garden. Enchanting cottage garden with hardy perennials, old fashioned climbing and shrub roses, two ponds, bog plants, shrub borders. *Adm £2.50 (incl glass of Kentish wine) Acc chd free. Wed July 2 (6-9pm)* **NB EVENING OPENING**

The Anchorage ⚘ (Mrs Wendy Francis) 8 Croydon Road, W Wickham. 3m SW of Bromley. 100yds from A232 and A2022 roundabout; enter from A232 opp Manor House public house, as rd is one way. ⅓-acre garden, lovingly created by owner and her late husband since 1988, inspired by Sissinghurst, comprising small compartments individually designed for colour within hedges of hornbeam, beech and box; old-fashioned shrub roses, irises and large collection of unusual perennials; herb garden, walled garden, vegetables, trained fruit trees; wildlife area with pond, woodland and plants. Featured on BBC Gardeners World 1993. TEAS. *Adm £1.50 Chd 25p (Share to St Christopher's Hospice®). Sun June 15 (2-5.30)*

Battel Hall ♿⚘ (John D Money Esq) Leeds, Maidstone. From A20 Hollingbourne roundabouts take B2163 S (signed Leeds Castle), at top of hill take Burberry Lane, house 100yds on R. Garden of approx 1 acre created since 1954 around medieval house; roses, herbaceous plants, shrubs and ancient wisteria. TEAS. *Adm £2 Chd £1 (Share to Macmillan Fund for Cancer Relief®). Sun June 22 (2-6)*

■ **Beech Court Gardens** ♿⚘❀ (Mr & Mrs Vyvyan Harmsworth) Challock, W of crossroads A251/A252, off the Lees. An oasis of beauty and tranquillity in 10 acres of woodland garden surrounding medieval farmhouse; large collection of rhododendrons, azaleas, viburnums, roses, summer borders, fine collection of trees, giving colour and interest at all seasons. Picnic area, pets, children's trail, area for visually impaired people. TEAS. *Adm £2 (£3 on June 19 to incl glass of wine) Chd £1, under 5 free. Open every day March 27-October 31 (Mon-Fri 10-5.30; Sat, Sun 12-6). For NGS Mon May 26 (10-5.30); Thurs June 19 (6-9)* **NB EVENING OPENING; Suns Aug 17, Oct 12 (12-6); also private visits welcome, please** **Tel 01233 740735**

The Beehive ♿⚘ (C G Brown Esq) 10 High Street, Lydd. S of New Romney on B2075, in centre of Lydd opp Church. Small walled garden, tucked behind village street house dating from 1550, with over 200 varieties of plants. There are paths and cosy corners in this cottage garden with pond and pergola; a pool of seclusion; the busy world outside unnoticed passes by. Teas usually available in the church. *Adm £1.50 Acc chd free (Share to Horder Centre for Arthritis, Crowborough®). Sat, Sun, Mon July 26, 27, 28 (2.30-5)*

Bilting House ♿⚘❀ (John Erle-Drax Esq) A28, 5m NE of Ashford, 9m from Canterbury. Wye 1½m. Old-fashioned garden with ha-ha; rhododendrons, azaleas; shrubs. In beautiful part of Stour Valley. TEAS. *Adm £1.50 Chd 50p (Share to BRCS®). Suns May 18, July 13 (2-6)*

185 Borden Lane ♿⚘ (Mr & Mrs P A Boyce) ½m S of Sittingbourne. 1m from Sittingbourne side of A2/A249 junction. Small informal garden with many varieties of fuchsia; hardy perennials; shrubs; pond; fruit, vegetable and herb garden. Home-made TEAS. *Adm £1 Acc chd free. Wed July 30, Suns Aug 3, Sept 7 (2-5.30); also private visits welcome, please* **Tel 01795 472243**

Bradbourne House Gardens ♿ (East Malling Trust for Horticultural Research & Horticulture Research International) East Malling, 4m W of Maidstone. Entrance is E of New Road, which runs from Larkfield on A20 S to E Malling. The Hatton Fruit Garden consists of demonstration fruit gardens of particular interest to amateurs, in a walled former kitchen garden and incl intensive forms of apples and pears. Members of staff available for questions. TEAS. *Adm £2.50 (incl entry to ground floor of House) Acc chd free. Sun April 27 (2-5)*

Brenchley Gardens 6m SE of Tonbridge. From A21 1m S of Pembury turn N on to B2160, turn R at Xrds in Matfield signed Brenchley. *Combined adm £2.50 Acc chd free. Sun May 18 (2-6)*
  Holmbush ♿⚘ (Brian & Cathy Worden Hodge) 1½-acre informal garden, mainly lawns, trees and shrub borders, planted since 1960
  Portobello (Barry M Williams Esq) 1½ acres, lawn, trees, shrubs incl azaleas and shrub roses; walled garden. House (not open) built by Monckton family 1739
  Puxted House ♿❀ (P J Oliver-Smith Esq) 1½ acres with rare and coloured foliage shrubs, water and woodland plants. Alpine and rose garden all labelled. Present owner cleared 20yrs of brambles in 1981 before replanting. TEAS

Brewhouse ♿⚘❀ (Mrs R Nicholson) Malthouse Lane, Boughton Aluph, 3m N of Ashford, off Pilgrims Way. ¼m N of and signed from Boughton Lees village green, on A251 Ashford-Faversham. 1-acre plantsman's garden. C16 farmhouse (not open) with fine views of open chalkland. Collections of old roses, other old-fashioned flowers, herbaceous and foliage plants. TEAS in aid of All Saints Church. *Adm £1.50 Acc chd free. Mons May 5, 26; Suns June 1, 29 (2-5.30); also private visits welcome, please* **Tel 01233 623748**

Broadview Gardens, Hadlow College &🌿❀ Hadlow. On A26 9m SW of Maidstone and 4m NE of Tonbridge. 9 acres of ornamental planting in attractive landscape setting; island beds with mixed plantings, rock garden, lake and water gardens; series of demonstration gardens including oriental, Italian and cottage gardens. TEAS in aid of local charities. *Adm £2 Acc chd (under 16) free. Thurs Feb 27 (hellebores); Sun Sept 14 (10-5)*

Cares Cross &❀ (Mr & Mrs R L Wadsworth) Chiddingstone Hoath. [Ordnance Survey Grid ref. TQ 496 431.] Landscaped garden around C16 house (not open). Dramatic views to N Downs over fields with old oaks, restored hedgerows, wildfowl lake and vineyard. Garden features old roses; water garden; innovative ground cover; rare shrubs and trees; speciality American plants. *Adm £3 (incl glass of Kentish wine) Acc chd free (Share to Countryside Workshops®). Wed July 16 (5-8pm)* **NB EVENING OPENING;** *also by appt to groups of 5-20, weekdays only mid May to end July*

¶**Cedar House** &❀ (Mr & Mrs J W Hull) Trottiscliffe Road, Addington, 1½m W of West Malling. Turn N from A20 into Trottiscliffe Road, continue for about ½m, garden on R. ½-acre garden with wide range of trees, shrubs and perennials: still being developed towards easy and efficient management. **Aldon House** also open on June 29. TEAS. *Adm £1.50 Acc chd free. Suns June 29, July 6 (2-6)*

Charts Edge & (Mr & Mrs John Bigwood) Westerham, ½m S of Westerham on B2026 towards Chartwell. 7-acre hillside garden being restored by present owners; large collection of rhododendrons, azaleas & magnolias; specimen trees & newly-planted mixed borders; Victorian folly; walled vegetable garden; rock garden. Fine views over N Downs. Dressage display, if riders available, at 3.30pm. TEAS. *Adm £2 Chd 25p (Share to BHS Dressage Group©). Suns May 11, 18, July 6 (2-5)*

▲**Chartwell** (The National Trust) 2m S of Westerham, fork L off B2026 after 1½m, well signed. 12-acre informal gardens on a hillside with glorious views over Weald of Kent. Fishpools and lakes together with red-brick wall built by Sir Winston Churchill, the former owner of Chartwell. The avenue of golden roses given by the family on Sir Winston's golden wedding anniversary will be at its best. Self-service restaurant serving coffee, lunches and teas. *Adm to garden only £2.50 Chd £1.25. For NGS Wed July 9 (11-4.30)*

Chevening & (By permission of the Board of Trustees of Chevening Estate and The Secretary of State for Foreign and Commonwealth Affairs) 4m NW of Sevenoaks. Turn N off A25 at Sundridge traffic lights on to B2211; at Chevening Xrds 1½m turn L. 27 acres with lawns and woodland garden, lake, maze, formal rides, parterre. Garden being restored. TEAS in aid of Kent Church Social Work and overseas charities. *Adm £2 Chd £1. Sun Aug 10 (2-6)*

■ **Church Hill Cottage** &🌿❀ (Mr & Mrs Michael Metianu) Charing Heath, 10m NW of Ashford. Leave M20 at junction 8 (Lenham) if Folkestone-bound or junction 9 (Ashford West) if London-bound: then leave A20 dual carriageway ½m W of Charing signed Charing Heath and Egerton. After 1m fork R at Red Lion, then R again; cottage 250yds on R. C16 cottage surrounded by garden of 1½ acres, developed & planted by present owners since 1981. Several separate connected areas each containing island beds & borders planted with extensive range of perennials, shrubs, spring bulbs, ferns and hostas. Picnic area. Lunches/snacks at Red Lion. *Adm £1.50 Chd 50p (Share to Paula Carr Trust®). Open every day except Mon, from March 23 to Sept 30. For NGS Suns March 23, 30, April 6, 13, 20, May 4, 11, 25, June 15, July 13, Aug 24; Mons March 31, May 5, 26, Aug 25 (11-5)*

▲**Cobham Hall** &❀ (Westwood Educational Trust) Cobham. Next to A2/M2 8m E of junction 2 of M25, midway between Gravesend and Rochester. Beautiful Elizabethan mansion in 150 acres landscaped by Humphry Repton at end of C18. Acres of daffodils and flowering trees planted in 1930s; grounds now being restored by Cobham Hall Heritage Trust. TEAS. *Adm House £3 OAP/Chd £2.50 Garden £1 (Share to Cobham Hall Heritage Trust®). For NGS Suns March 23, Aug 31 (2-5). For details of other open days, please* Tel 01474 823371/824319

Coldham &🌿❀ (Dr & Mrs J G Elliott) Little Chart Forstal, 5m NW of Ashford. Leave M20 at junction 8 (Lenham) if Folkestone-bound or junction 9 (Ashford West) if London-bound: then leave A20 at Charing by road signposted to Little Chart, turn E in village, ¼m. 2-acre garden developed since 1970 in setting of old walls; good collection of rare plants, bulbs, alpines, mixed borders. C16 Kent farmhouse (not open). TEAS. *Adm £2 Chd 50p. Suns April 20, June 22 (2-5.30)*

Coldharbour Oast &❀ (Mr & Mrs A J A Pearson) Tenterden. 300yds SW of Tenterden High St (A28), take lane signed West View Hospital, after 200yds bear R on to concrete lane signed Coldharbour, proceed for 600yds. Garden started in late 1987 from ¾-acre field in exposed position. Pond; dry stream; unusual shrubs and perennials; maintained by owners. TEA in aid of League of Friends of West View Hospital. *Adm £1.25 Acc chd free. Suns April 27, Aug 31 (1.30-5.30)*

Copton Ash &🌿❀ (Mrs John Ingram & Drs Tim & Gillian Ingram) 105 Ashford Rd, Faversham, 1m. On A251 Faversham-Ashford rd opp E-bound junction with M2. 1½-acre plantsman's garden developed since 1978 on site of old cherry orchard. Wide range of plants in mixed borders and informal island beds; incl spring bulbs, alpine and herbaceous plants, shrubs, young trees and collection of fruit varieties. Special interest in plants from Mediterranean-type climates. Good autumn colour. TEAS. *Adm £1.50 Acc chd free (Share to National Schizophrenia Fellowship, East Kent Group®). Suns March 16, 30, April 6, 20, May 4, 25, June 15, July 20, Aug 24, Sept 21, Oct 19; Mons March 31, May 5, 26, Aug 25 (2-6)*

By Appointment Gardens. These owners do not have a fixed opening day usually because they cannot accommodate large numbers or have insufficient parking space.

Crittenden House ⚘ (B P Tompsett Esq) Matfield, 6m SE of Tonbridge. Bus: MD 6 or 297, alight Standings Cross, Matfield, 1m. Garden around early C17 house completely planned and planted since 1956 on labour-saving lines. Featuring spring shrubs (rhododendrons, magnolias), roses, lilies, foliage, waterside planting of ponds in old iron workings, of interest from early spring bulbs to autumn colour. *Adm £2 Chd (under 12) 25p. Mons March 31, May 5; Sun May 25 (2-6)*

¶**25 Crouch Hill Court** ⚘❀ (Mrs Sue Hartfree) Lower Halstow, 5m NW of Sittingbourne. 1m W of Newington on A2, turn N to Lower Halstow; continue to T-junc, turn R, pass The Three Tuns on R, take next R (Vicarage Lane), then first R and fork R. Please park with consideration in cul de sac. Long narrow garden (300' × 25'), landscaped on various levels with mixed borders, rock garden, small woodland area, natural stream and islands; wide range of plants, many rare and unusual. *Adm £1.50 Chd 50p. Every Sat May 17-Sept 27 (2-5.30); private visits also welcome, please* **Tel 01795 842426**

■ **Doddington Place** ⚘❀ (Richard Oldfield Esq) 6m SE of Sittingbourne. From A20 turn N opp Lenham or from A2 turn S at Teynham or Ospringe (Faversham) (all 4m). Large garden, landscaped with wide views; trees and yew hedges; woodland garden with azaleas and rhododendrons, Edwardian rock garden; formal garden with mixed borders. TEAS, restaurant, shop. *Adm £2 Chd 25p (Share to Kent Assoc for the Blind and Doddington Church®). May to Sept: Suns 2-6; Weds and Bank Hol Mons 11-6. For NGS every day from May 24 to June 1 (Bank Hol and Wed 11-6, other days 2-6)*

Downs Court ⚘❀ (Mr & Mrs M J B Green) Boughton Aluph, 4m NE of Ashford off A28. Take lane on L signed Boughton Aluph church, fork R at pillar box, garden is next drive on R. Approx 3 acres with fine downland views, and some mature trees and yew hedges. Mixed borders largely replanted by owners in last 10 years; shrub roses. TEAS Sunday only in aid of National Hospital Development Foundation®. *Adm £1.50 Chd 50p. Sat, Sun June 21, 22 (2-6)*

Edenbridge House ⚘❀ (Mrs M T Lloyd) Crockham Hill Rd, 1½m N of Edenbridge, nr Marlpit Hill, on B2026. 5-acre garden of bulbs, spring shrubs, herbaceous borders, alpines, roses and water garden. House part C16 (not open). TEAS. *Adm £1.50 Chd 25p. Suns April 13, May 4, June 15, July 13, Sept 28 (2-6); Weds May 21, Sept 24 (1-5) and June 18 (6.30-8.30)* **NB EVENING OPENING;** *£2.50 incl glass of wine; also private visits welcome for groups, please* **Tel 01732 862122**

Egypt Farm ⚘ (Mr & Mrs Francis Bullock) Hamptons, 6m N of Tonbridge, equidistant from Plaxtol & Hadlow. In Hadlow take Carpenters Lane, at small Xrds at end of Lane, turn R into Oxon Hoath Rd, next turn L (Pillar Box Lane), R at next T-junc, garden 100yds on L, 100yds N of Artichoke Inn. Undulating garden of 4 acres, designed by owners; spring bulbs, terrace, water garden, lovely views. **Hamptons Farm** open same day. *Adm £1.75 Acc chd under 12 free (Share to West Peckham Church). Sun April 13 (2-6)*

■ **Emmetts Garden** ⚘ (in parts) (The National Trust) Ide Hill, 5m SW of Sevenoaks. 1½m S of A25 on Sundridge-Ide Hill Rd. 1½m N of Ide Hill off B2042. 5-acre hillside garden. One of the highest gardens in Kent, noted for its fine collection of rare trees and shrubs; lovely spring and autumn colour. TEA. *Adm £3 Chd £1.50. Open Weds, Sats, Suns, April to end Oct (11-5.30). For NGS Sats May 10, Oct 4 (11-5.30)*

Everden Farmhouse ⚘❀ (Martinez family) Alkham, 4m W of Dover. Follow signs to Alkham Valley, turn R opp Hoptons Manor to Everden, then follow 'Garden Open' signs. Designer's garden created from field since 1990, exposed hillside, alkaline soil. Many unusual plants combined with colour and form in mind. TEAS May, July: TEA April, Oct. *Adm £1.50 Chd 50p. Suns May 25, July 27, Oct 5; Mon May 26; Sats April 26, July 26 (2-6); also private visits welcome, please* **Tel 01303 893462**

Field House ⚘❀❀ (Mr & Mrs N J Hori) Clapper Lane, Staplehurst. W of A229, 9m S of Maidstone and 1½m N of Staplehurst village centre. A 'Garden of the Mind'. Approx 2 acres designed in the tradition of contemplative and paradise gardens. Extensive plant collection on Wealden clay, also 2-acre, species-rich meadow with pond. TEAS. *Adm £1.50 Chd 50p. Suns July 6, Aug 3 (2-6)*

■ **Finchcocks** ⚘❀❀ (Mr & Mrs Richard Burnett) Goudhurst. 2m W of Goudhurst, off A262. 4-acre garden surrounding early C18 manor, well-known for its collection of historical keyboard instruments. Spring bulbs; mixed borders; autumn garden with unusual trees & rare shrubs; recently restored walled garden on lines of C18 pleasure garden. TEAS. *Adm £5.20 House & garden, £1.50 Garden, Chd £3.80 & 50p. Suns Easter to Sept 28; Bank Hol Mons; Aug every Wed, Thurs & Sun (2-6). For NGS Suns May 11, Sept 14 (2-6)*

Forest Gate ⚘❀❀ (Sir Robert & Lady Johnson) Pluckley, 8m W of Ashford. From A20 at Charing take B2077 to Pluckley village; turn L signed Bethersden, continue 1m to garden 100yds S of Pluckley station. 2-acre garden on heavy clay; well stocked mixed borders, laburnum tunnel, winter garden, ponds and interesting herb collection. Many plants labelled. C17 house (not open). TEAS in aid of Cystic Fibrosis Trust. *Adm £1.50 Acc chd free. Mon May 26, Sun June 29 (1-6); coaches by appointment, please* **Tel 0171 373 8300**

▲**Godinton Park** ⚘❀ (Godinton House Preservation Trust) Entrance 1½m W of Ashford at Potter's Corner on A20. Bus: MD/EK 10, 10A, 10B Folkestone-Ashford-Maidstone, alight Hare & Hounds, Potter's Corner. Formal garden designed c1900 by Reginald Blomfield, and wild gardens. Topiary. House closed in 1997. *Adm £1 Chd under 16 free. For NGS Suns March 30, July 6 (2-5)*

Godmersham Park ⚘ (John B Sunley Esq) off A28 midway between Canterbury and Ashford. Associations with Jane Austen. Early Georgian mansion (not open) in beautiful downland setting, 24 acres of formal and landscaped gardens, topiary, rose beds and herbaceous borders. Festival of Flowers in Godmersham Church. Refreshments all day. *Adm £2 Acc chd free (Share to Godmersham Church®). Sun, Mon May 25, 26 (11-6)*

■ **Goodnestone Park** &⚘❀ (The Lady FitzWalter) nr Wingham, Canterbury. Village lies S of B2046 rd from A2 to Wingham. Sign off B2046 says Goodnestone. Village St is 'No Through Rd', but house and garden at the terminus. Bus: EK13, 14 Canterbury-Deal; bus stop: Wingham, 2m. 5 to 6 acres; good trees; woodland garden, snowdrops, spring bulbs, walled garden with old-fashioned roses. Connections with Jane Austen who stayed here. Picnics allowed. TEAS (not in Feb, Mar). *Adm £2.50 OAP £2.20 Chd (under 12) 20p (Disabled people in wheelchair £1). Suns March 30 to Oct 19 (12-6); Mons, Weds to Fris March 24 to Oct 24 (11-5). For NGS (Share to Church of the Holy Cross, Goodnestone®) Suns Feb 16 (snowdrops), March 16 (spring bulbs and hellebores), July 20 (12-6). Closed Tues and Sats*

Goudhurst Gardens 4m W of Cranbrook on A262. TEAS at Tara and Tulip Tree Cottage. *Combined adm £2.50 Acc chd free. Suns May 25, June 15 (1-6)*
  Crowbourne Farm House &⚘ (Mrs S Coleman) 2-acre farmhouse garden in which replanting started in 1989. Established cottage garden; shrub roses; vegetable garden; and areas newly planted with trees and shrubs. Former horse pond now stocked with ornamental fish
  Garden Cottage &❀ (Mr & Mrs Peter Sowerby) ¾-acre garden with small trees, shrubs, perennials and grass, to provide year-round softly coloured foreground to outstanding views of Teise valley. First laid out in 1930s with extensive planting since 1980s
  Tara &⚘❀ (Mr & Mrs Peter Coombs) 1¼ acres redesigned in 1982 into a number of linked garden areas, including a formal herb garden, each providing a different atmosphere, using an interesting range of plants and shrubs
  Tulip Tree Cottage ⚘❀ (Mr & Mrs K A Owen) 1½ acres with sweeping lawn, established trees in herbaceous and shrub borders; 90ft Liriodendron tulipifera, said to be one of finest in country, also fine Cedrus atlantica glauca. In May azalea garden of ½-acre, established 1902; *also visitors welcome by appointment, please* Tel 01580 211423

■ **Great Comp Charitable Trust** &⚘❀ (R Cameron Esq) 2m E of Borough Green. A20 at Wrotham Heath, take Seven Mile Lane, B2016; at 1st Xrds turn R; garden on L ½m. Delightful 7-acre garden skilfully designed by the Camerons since 1957 for low maintenance and yr-round interest. Spacious setting of well-maintained lawns and paths lead visitors through a plantsman's collection of trees, shrubs, heathers and herbaceous plants. From woodland planting to more formal terraces good use is made of views to plants, ornaments and ruins. Good autumn colour. Early C17 house (not open). TEAS on Suns, Bank Hols and NGS days (2-5). *Adm £3 Chd £1. Open Suns in March and every day April 1 to Oct 31 (11-6). Open for NGS (Share to Tradescant Trust®) Suns Mar 2, 9, 16 (for hellebores, heathers and snowflakes); Nov 2 (for autumn colour) (11-6)*

Great Maytham Hall ⚘❀ (Country Houses Association) Rolvenden, 4m SW of Tenterden. On A28 in Rolvenden turn L at church towards Rolvenden Layne; Hall ½m on R. Lutyens house (not open) and garden, 18 acres of parkland with bluebells, daffodils and flowering trees in spring; formal gardens incl blue and silver border, roses, hydrangeas and autumn colour. Walled garden inspired Frances Hodgson Burnett to write her novel 'The Secret Garden'. TEAS. *Adm £1.50 Chd 75p (Share to Country Houses Association©). Fris May 2, June 27, Sept 26 (2-5)*

¶**Great Oaks House** ⚘ (Mr & Mrs Max Cohen) Puttenden Road, Shipbourne, 7m SE of Sevenoaks. Puttenden Rd joins A227 on sharp bend 3m N of Tonbridge, signed Plaxtol. Parking at **Hookwood House** (open same evening) on the RH side, Great Oaks 200yds further on. Informal romantic garden of over 2 acres designed for year-round interest with low maintenance shrubs and cottage-style planting. Wide lawns, mature trees, fruit trees, mixed borders with hardy perennials and native plants, herbs, old-fashioned and climbing roses, evergreen ground cover, gravel courtyards and terrace; wild garden with trees, meadow, grasses and pond. Landscape design studio open. *Combined adm £3 (incl glass wine) Chd 50p. Wed July 2 (5-8.30)* **NB EVENING OPENING**

Greenways &⚘ (Mr & Mrs S Lord) Single Street, nr Downe. Gardener's garden; interesting design ideas and plant collections; willows, jasmines, buddleias, honeysuckles and alpines; bonsai miniature garden display; small pool, plant house and pottery. *Adm £1.50 (Share to Save the Children Fund®). Private visits welcome, anytime, please* Tel 01959 574691

■ **Groombridge Place Gardens** ⚘❀ (Andrew de Candole Esq) 4m SW of Tunbridge Wells. Take A264 towards E. Grinstead, after 2m take B2110: Groombridge Place entrance on L, past the church. C17 formal walled gardens with medieval moat, ancient topiary and fountains. Canal boat rides to Enchanted Forest; children's garden and birds of prey displays. Restaurant. *Adm £5 OAPs £4.50 Chd £3.50. Open daily March 28 to Oct 20 (10-6). For NGS Mons April 21, Oct 20 (10-6)*

Groome Farm &⚘❀ (Mr & Mrs Michael Swatland) Egerton, 10m W of Ashford. From A20 at Charing Xrds take B2077 Biddenden Rd. Past Pluckley turn R at Blacksmiths Tea Rooms; R again, until Newland Green sign on L, house 1st on L. 1½ acres around C15 farmhouse and oast. Interesting collection trees, shrubs, roses and herbaceous plants; also water, heather and rock gardens. Picnics welcome in field. TEAS. *Adm £1.50 Acc chd free. Suns July 20, Aug 3 (2-6). Private visits welcome, please* Tel 01233 756260

115 Hadlow Road ⚘ (Mr & Mrs Richard Esdale) in Tonbridge. Take A26 from N end of High St signed Maidstone, house 1m on L in service rd. ⅓-acre unusual terraced garden with roses, island herbaceous border, clematis, hardy fuchsias, shrub borders, alpines, kitchen garden and pond; well labelled. TEA. *Adm £1.50 Acc chd free. Suns July 13, Aug 3, 24 (2-6); also private visits welcome, please* Tel 01732 353738

Hamptons Farm House &⚘ (Mr & Mrs Brian Pearce) Hamptons. Between Plaxtol, Hadlow, Shipbourne and West Peckham. In a hamlet opp Artichoke Inn; signed from nearby villages. Garden of 3 acres; stream and ponds; trees, shrubs, old barn; fine views. TEAS. **Egypt Farm** open same day. *Adm £1.75 Acc chd free. Sun April 13 (2-6)*

Hartlip Gardens 6m W of Sittingbourne, 1m S of A2 midway between Rainham and Newington. Parking for Craiglea in village hall car park and The Street. *Combined adm £2 Acc chd free. Sun June 15 (2-6)*

Craiglea &% (Mrs Ruth Bellord) The Street. Cottage garden crammed with interesting shrubs and plants; vegetable garden; small pond

Hartlip Place % (Lt-Col & Mrs J R Yerburgh) Secret garden concealed by rhododendrons, planted with old roses; shrub borders; wilderness walk; sloping lawns; pond. TEAS in aid of Kent Gardens Trust

■ **Hault Farm** &%❀ (Mr & Mrs T D Willett) 7m S of Canterbury, between Petham and Waltham. From B2068 turn R signed Petham/Waltham; 2m on L. Victorian house on site of Knights Templar property once occupied by Crusader Sir Geofrey de Hautt. Plantaholic's 4 acres of woodland, bog, herbaceous, rose and scree areas. TEAS. *Adm £2 Chd £1. Suns and Bank Hols, March 31, April 20 to June 29, Aug 3 to 31 (11-5). For NGS Suns March 30, Oct 12 (2-5). Groups welcome at any time by appt, please* **Tel 01227 700263**

Haydown %❀ (Dr & Mrs I D Edeleanu) Great Buckland, nr Cobham, 4m S of A2. Take turning for Cobham, at war memorial straight ahead down hill, under railway bridge to T-junc, turn R, after 200yds take L fork, follow narrow lane for 1½m. Entrance on L after riding stables. North Downs 9-acre hillside garden developed since 1980, with woodland and meadowland, incl native and unusual trees, shrubs, small vineyard, orchard, ponds, bog garden; patio with terracing; roses. TEAS. *Adm £1.50 Acc chd free (Share to Northfleet Rotary Club Charities). Sats April 26, July 26 (2-6)*

●**Hever Castle and Gardens** &❀ (Broadland Properties Ltd) 3m SE of Edenbridge, between Sevenoaks and E. Grinstead. Signed from junctions 5 and 6 of M25, from A21 and from A264. Reinstated 120 yds of herbaceous border, also formal Italian gardens with statuary, sculpture and fountains; large lake; 'splashing' water maze; rose garden and Tudor herb and knot garden, topiary and maze. Romantic moated castle, the childhood home of Anne Boleyn, also open. No dogs in castle, on lead only in gardens. Refreshments available. *Open every day from March 1 to Nov 30 (11-6 last adm 5, March & Nov 11-4, Castle opens 12 noon). Adm Castle and gardens £6.50, Chd £3.30, gardens only £4.90, Chd £3*

Hole Park &% (D G W Barham Esq) Rolvenden-Cranbrook on B2086. Beautiful parkland; formal garden with mixed borders, roses, yew hedges and topiary a feature, many fine trees. Natural garden with daffodils, rhododendrons, azaleas, conifers, dell and water gardens; bluebell wood in spring. Autumn colour. *Adm £2.50 Chd (under 12) 50p (Share to St Mary's Church, Rolvenden©). Suns April 13, 20, May 4, 11, 25, Oct 12, 19; Weds April 23, May 21, June 25, July 23 (2-6)*

¶**Hookwood House** &%❀ (Mr & Mrs Nicholas Ward) Puttenden Road, Shipbourne, 7m SE of Sevenoaks. S of village, Puttenden Rd joins A227 on sharp bend 3m N of Tonbridge, signed Plaxtol: house 1m on RH side. Charming country garden of 2 acres of formal and informal features; old brick paths lead through small garden rooms

enclosed by clipped native and yew hedges; mixed and herbaceous borders, perennials, old-fashioned roses, topiary, silver garden, herb garden, vegetable garden, nut plat, apple orchard, cobbled Kentish ragstone yard and planted containers. **Great Oaks House** open on same evening. *Combined adm £3 (incl glass of wine) Chd 50p. Wed July 2 (5-8)* **NB EVENING OPENING**

Horton Priory (Mrs A C Gore) Sellindge, 6m SE of Ashford. From A20 Ashford-Folkestone, 1m from Sellindge, turn E along Moorstock Lane, signed Horton Priory. Bus: EK/MD 10, 10A, 10B Maidstone-Ashford-Folkestone; alight Sellindge, 1m. Herbaceous and rose border, lawn, pond and rock garden. Priory dates back to C12; church destroyed in reign of Henry VIII, but remains of W doorway and staircase to S aisle of nave can be seen by front door. Along W front Norman buttresses (all genuine) and C14 windows (some restored); one genuine small Norman window. Outer hall only open to visitors. TEAS. *Adm £1 Chd 50p (Share to Leonora Childrens Cancer Fund®). Suns April 13, June 15 (2-6)*

▲**Ightham Mote** & (in part) %❀ (The National Trust) Ivy Hatch. 6m E of Sevenoaks, off A25 and 2½m S of Ightham [188: TQ584535]. Buses: Maidstone & District 222/3 from BR Borough Green: NU-Venture 67/8 Sevenoaks to Plaxtol passing BR Sevenoaks: alight Ivy Hatch ½m walk to Ightham Mote. 14-acre garden and moated medieval manor c.1340. Mixed borders with many unusual plants; lawns; courtyard; newly-planted orchard; water features incl small lake, leading to woodland walk with rhododendrons and shrubs. TEAS. *Adm £4 Chd £2. House and garden open as normal. Tours of garden 1.30pm, 2.30pm, 3.30pm. NT members £1 donation for tours. For NGS Wed June 25 (11.30-5.30 last admission 5pm)*

Jessups ❀ (The Hon Robin Denison-Pender) Mark Beech. 3m S of Edenbridge. From B2026 Edenbridge-Hartfield rd turn L opp Queens Arms signed Mark Beech, 100yds on L. Small established garden, spring bulbs and shrubs, fine views to Sevenoaks Weald. Small wood. Wildfowl pond (25 different breeds). TEAS. *Adm £1.50 Acc chd free. Sun March 30 (2-5)*

▲**Knole** &% (The Lord Sackville; The National Trust) Sevenoaks. Station: Sevenoaks. Pleasance, deer park, landscape garden, herb garden. TEAS. *Adm Car park £2.50: garden £1 Chd 50p; house £5 Chd £2.50. For NGS Weds June 4, Aug 6 (11-4 last adm 3)*

Kypp Cottage %❀ (Mrs Zena Grant) Woolpack Corner, Biddenden. At Tenterden Rd A262 junction with Benenden Rd. Tiny woodland garden planted by owner on rough ground, now overflowing with interesting plants. Hundreds of roses and clematis intertwine, providing shady, scented nooks. Large variety of geraniums and other ground cover plants. Subject of Meridian TV programme. Morning coffee & TEAS. *Adm £1.50 Chd 30p (Share to NSPCC®). Suns May 25, June 1, 8, 15, 22, 29, July 6, 13 (2-6); Mons May 26, June 2, 9, 16, 23, 30, July 7, 14; Tues May 27, June 3, 10, 17, 24, July 1, 8, 15: Weds May 28, June 4, 11, 18, 25, July 2, 9, 16; Fri May 23; Sat May 24 (10.30-6); also private visits including evenings welcome all season, please* **Tel 01580 291480**

Ladham House ♿❀ (Mr & Mrs A Jessel) Goudhurst. On NE of village, off A262. 10 acres with rolling lawns, fine specimen trees, rhododendrons, camellias, azaleas, shrubs and magnolias. Arboretum. Spectacular twin mixed borders; fountain and bog gardens. Fine view. Subject of many magazine articles. TEAS. *Adm £2.50 Chd (under 12) 50p. Sun May 4; Mon May 26 (11-5.30)*

Larksfield ♿❀ (Mr & Mrs P Dickinson) Crockham Hill, 3m N of Edenbridge, on B269 (Limpsfield-Oxted). Octavia Hill, a founder of the NT, lived here and helped create the original garden; fine collection of azaleas, shrubs, herbaceous plants, rose beds and woodlands; views over Weald and Ashdown Forest. **The Red House** and **Larksfield Cottage** gardens open same days. TEAS at The Red House. *Combined adm £2.50 OAPs £2 Chd 50p (Share to the Schizophrenia Association of G.B.®). Suns May 11, 18 (2-6)*

Larksfield Cottage ♿❀ (Mr & Mrs Steven Ferigno) Crockham Hill, 3m N of Edenbridge, on B269. An enchanting garden redesigned in 1981 with attractive lawns and shrubs. Views over the Weald and Ashdown Forest. **Larksfield** and **The Red House** gardens also open same days. *Combined adm £2.50 OAPs £2 Chd 50p (Share to The Schizophrenia Association of G.B.®). Suns May 11, 18 (2-6)*

43 Layhams Road ♿✗ (Mrs Dolly Robertson) West Wickham. Semi-detached house recognisable by small sunken flower garden in the front. Opp Wickham Court Farm. A raised vegetable garden, purpose-built for the disabled owner with easy access to wide terraced walkways. The owner, who maintains the entire 24′ × 70′ area herself, would be pleased to pass on her experiences as a disabled gardener so that others may share her joy and interest. *Collecting box. Private visits welcome all year, please* **Tel 0181-462 4196**

Lily Vale Farm ♿❀ (Mr & Mrs R H V Moorhead) Smeeth, 4m E of Ashford. Turn N off A20 at garage opp converter station W of Sellindge; follow lane to T-junc, turn L, entrance ½m on L. Family garden with trees and pastoral outlook; shrub roses, herbaceous borders and courtyard garden. **Lodge House** open same days. TEAS. *Adm £1.50 Acc chd free. Sun June 22; Wed June 25 (2-8:* **NB LATE OPENINGS**)

¶Little Combourne Farmhouse ♿✗ (Mr & Mrs Grant Whytock) Curtisden Green, 1½m NW of Cranbrook. Turn off A262 at Chequers Inn in Goudhurst, then 2nd R signed Curtisden Green. Family garden of 1½ acres with old-fashioned roses, set in idyllic rural countryside, created by present owners around C16 farmhouse. TEAS. *Adm £1.50 Acc chd free. Sat, Sun June 7, 8 (2-6)*

¶Little Oast ❀ (Mrs Pam Hadrill) High Street, Otford, 3m N of Seven-oaks at W end of village, just past Horns Inn, turn R into private drive. (Please park opp Bull Inn.) Half-acre garden of varied planting, designed to complement circular oast; patios, ponds, pots and 3 summer-houses. Lunches and teas in village. *Adm £1.50 Acc chd free (Share to Hospice in the Weald). Sun July 13 (2-6)*

Little Trafalgar ♿✗❀ (Mr & Mrs R J Dunnett) Selling, 4m SE of Faversham. From A2 (M2) or A251 make for Selling Church, then follow signs to garden. ¾-acre garden of great interest both for its wealth of attractive and unusual plants, and its intimate, restful design. Emphasis is placed on the creative and artistic use of plants. Featured in BBC Geoff Hamilton's Private Paradise 1997. TEAS. *Adm £1 Acc chd free. Suns May 25, June 8, 22, July 6, 20, Aug 3, 24, Sept 7, 21; Mons May 26, Aug 25 (2-6); also private visits welcome, please* **Tel 01227 752219**

Lodge House ♿❀ (Mr & Mrs J Talbot) Smeeth, 4m E of Ashford. From A20 3m E of Ashford, turn N signed Smeeth, turn R at Woolpack, continue ½m to entrance. 2-acre garden, with lawns sloping into sheepfields; shrubs; herbaceous borders and ponds in lovely setting. Field walk to **Lily Vale Farm** open same days. Picnickers welcome. Informal live music. TEAS. *Adm £1.50 Acc chd free; evening incl glass of wine £2.50 (Share to Smeeth Church©). Sun June 22; Wed June 25 (2-8)* **NB LATE OPENINGS**

Long Barn ✗ (Brandon & Sarah Gough) Weald, 3m S of Sevenoaks. Signed to Weald at junction of A21 & B245. Garden at W end of village. 1st garden of Harold Nicolson and Vita Sackville-West. 3 acres with terraces and slopes, giving considerable variety. Dutch garden designed by Lutyens, features mixed planting in raised beds. Teas in village. *Adm £2 OAP £1 Chd 50p, under 5 free (Share to Hospice in the Weald®). Suns June 22, July 20 (2-5)*

Longacre ♿✗❀ (Dr & Mrs G Thomas) Perry Wood, Selling, 5m SE of Faversham. From A2 (M2) or A251 follow signs for Selling, passing White Lion on L, 2nd R and immediately L, continue for ¼m. From A252 at Chilham, take turning signed Selling at Badgers Hill Fruit Farm. L at 2nd Xrds, next R, L and then R. Small, ¾-acre plantsman's garden with wide variety of interesting plants, created and maintained entirely by owners. Lovely walks in Perry Woods adjacent to garden. TEAS in aid of local charities. *Adm £1 Acc chd free (Share to Canterbury Pilgrims Hospice®). Suns March 30, April 27, May 4, 25, June 8, 22, July 6, 20, Aug 3, 24, Sept 7; Mons March 31, May 5, 26, Aug 25 (2-5); also private visits welcome, please* **Tel 01227 752254**

Lullingstone Castle ♿✗❀ (Mr & Mrs Guy Hart Dyke) In the Darenth Valley via Eynsford on A225. Eynsford Station ½m. All cars and coaches via Roman Villa. Lawns, woodland and lake, mixed border, small herb garden. Henry VII gateway; Church on the lawn open. TEAS. *Adm garden £2.50 OAPs/Chd £1; house 50p extra. Sun June 15 (2-6)*

Luton House ✗ (Sir John & Lady Swire) Selling, 4m SE of Faversham. From A2 (M2) or A251 make for White Lion, entrance 30yds E on same side of rd. 4 acres; C19 landscaped garden; ornamental ponds; trees underplanted with azaleas, camellias, woodland plants. *Adm £1.50 Acc chd free. Sun May 4 (2-6)*

190 Maidstone Road ✗❀ (Dr M K Douglas) Chatham. On A230 Chatham-Maidstone, about 1m out of Chatham and 7m from Maidstone. Informal ¼-acre garden; herbaceous borders on either side of former tennis court; scree garden and pool; many snowdrops and other spring bulbs. TEAS (not Feb). *Adm £1.50 Acc chd free. Suns Feb 23 (2-5) (snowdrops), April 6, Aug 3 (2-6)*

■ **Marle Place** &⌀❀ (Mr & Mrs Gerald Williams) Brenchley, 8m SE of Tonbridge, signed from Brenchley. Victorian gazebo; plantsman's shrub borders; walled scented garden, large Edwardian rockery; herbaceous borders and bog garden. Woodland walk; autumn colour. C17 listed house (not open). Specialist nursery. TEAS. *Adm £3 Chd £2.50. Every day April 1 to Oct 31 (10-5). For NGS Suns May 25, Aug 10, Oct 5 (10-6)*

Maurice House & (The Royal British Legion Care Home) Callis Court Rd, Broadstairs. From Broadstairs Broadway take St Peter's Park Rd; turn R under railway arch into Baird's Hill; join Callis Court Rd entrance on R, 100yds beyond Lanthorne Rd turning. Well-maintained 8-acre garden; lawns, flowering trees, shrubs; formal flower beds; rose and water gardens; orchard. Spring bedding displays of wallflowers, polyanthus; wide variety of herbaceous plants and shrubs especially suited to coastal conditions. TEAS. *Adm £1.50 Chd 25p (Share to the Royal British Legion®). Sun April 27 (2-5.30)*

¶**Maycotts** &⌀❀ (Mr & Mrs David Jolley) Matfield, 6m SE of Tonbridge. From A21, 1m S of Pembury, turn N onto B2160, turn R at Xrds in Matfield, and first L at Five Wents into Maycotts Lane. Medium-sized, partly walled garden around C16 farmhouse (not open) being developed by garden designer-owner. Herbaceous borders; old-fashioned and shrub roses; herb garden and potager; unusual perennials and foliage plants. TEAS if fine. *Adm £1.50 Acc chd free. Sun June 15 (2-6).*

Meadow Wood & (Mr & Mrs James Lee) Penshurst. 1¼m SE of Penshurst on B2176 in direction of Bidborough. 1920s garden, on edge of wood with long southerly views over the Weald, and with interesting trees and shrubs; azaleas, rhododendrons and naturalised bulbs in woods with mown walks. TEAS. *Adm £2 Chd £1 (Share to Relate®). Sun May 4 (2-6)*

Mere House &❀ (Mr & Mrs Andrew Wells) Mereworth, midway between Tonbridge & Maidstone. From A26 turn N on to B2016 and then into Mereworth village. 6 acre garden with C18 lake; ornamental shrubs and trees with foliage contrast; lawns, daffodils; Kentish cobnut plat. Woodland walk. TEAS. *Adm £1.50 Acc chd free. Suns April 6, Oct 19 (2-5.30)*

Mill House &⌀❀ (Dr & Mrs Brian Glaisher) Mill Lane, ½m N of Hildenborough, 5m S of Sevenoaks. From B245 turn into Mill Lane at Mill garage. 3-acre garden laid out in 1906; herbaceous and mixed borders; new secluded herb garden; old shrub roses and climbers; clematis and many fine trees. Formal garden with topiary; ruins of windmill and conservatory with exotics. TEAS. *Adm £2 Chd 25p. Sun June 15 (2-6)*

■ **Mount Ephraim** (Mrs M N Dawes and Mr & Mrs E S Dawes) Hernhill, Faversham. From M2 and A299 take Hernhill turning at Duke of Kent. Herbaceous border; topiary; daffodils and rhododendrons; rose terraces leading to a small lake; Japanese rock garden with pools;

water garden; small vineyard. TEAS daily except Tues; lunches only Bank Hol Suns & Mons. *Adm £2.50 Chd 50p. Open Easter to mid-Sept (1-6). For NGS Suns April 20 (Share to Karna Prayog Trust, Madras), Sept 28 (1-6)*

Nettlestead Place &⌀ (Mr & Mrs Roy Tucker) Nettlestead, 6m W/SW of Maidstone. Turn S off A26 onto B2015 then 1m on L (next to Nettlestead Church). C13 manor house set in 7-acre plantsman's garden on different levels with fine views over open countryside; many plant collections incl herbaceous and shrub island beds; formal garden with shrub and species roses; hardy geranium border; sunken pond garden; 4 acres in course of development as pinetum and glen garden. TEAS. *Adm £2 Acc chd free (Share to Friedrich's Ataxia Group Research®). Suns July 6, Sept 14 (2-5.30)*

New Barns House &❀ (Mr & Mrs P H Byam-Cook) West Malling. Leave M20 at Exit 4 to West Malling. In High Street turn E down Waters Lane, at T-junction turn R, take bridge over by-pass, follow lane 400yds to New Barns House. 6-acre garden with fine trees and flowering cherries. Walled garden, mixed borders and shrubs. TEAS. *Adm £2 Acc chd free. Sun May 18 (2-6)*

Northbourne Court ⌀ (The Hon Charles James) W of Deal. Signs in village. Great brick terraces, belonging to an earlier Elizabethan mansion, provide a picturesque setting for a wide range of shrubs and plants on chalk soil; geraniums, fuchsias and grey-leaved plants. *Adm £3 OAPs/Chd £2.50 (Share to National Art Collections Fund®). Suns June 1, 8, 15, 22, 29, July 6, 13, 20, 27, Aug 3, 10, 17, 24 (2-5)*

Olantigh ⌀ (Mr & Mrs J R H Loudon) Wye, 6m NE of Ashford. Turn off A28 either to Wye or at Godmersham; ¾m from Wye on rd to Godmersham. Edwardian garden in beautiful setting; water garden; rockery; shrubbery; herbaceous border; extensive lawns. TEAS in Wye village. *Adm £1.50 Chd 50p. Suns April 20, June 22 (2-5)*

Old Buckhurst (Mr & Mrs J Gladstone) Chiddingstone Hoath Road, Mark Beech. 4m E of Edenbridge via B2026, at Cowden Pound turn E to Mark Beech. First house on R after leaving Mark Beech on Penshurst Rd. 1-acre garden surrounding C15 farmhouse (not open). Part-walled ornamental and kitchen gardens; shrub roses, clematis, shrubs and wide range of herbaceous plants carefully planned and maintained by owners for all year round interest, using colour, texture and shape. *Adm £2 Acc chd free (Share to St Mary's Church, Chiddingstone©). Suns May 25, June 1, Sept 7, 14 (2-6)*

The Old Parsonage &⌀❀ (Dr & Mrs Richard Perks) Sutton Valence, 6m SE of Maidstone. A274 from Maidstone or Headcorn, turn E into village at King's Head Inn and proceed on upper rd through village; climb Tumblers Hill and entrance at top on R. 4-acre labour-saving garden planted since 1959 with emphasis on ground cover; trees, shrubs and mixed borders; cranesbills and shrub roses. Ancient nut plat now developed as a wild garden. Fine views over Low Weald. In grounds is Sutton castle, C12 ruined keep, permanently open to the public. *Adm £1.50 Chd 50p. Sat June 14, Tue June 17, Fri June 20, Sun June 22 (2-6); also private visits welcome, please* Tel 01622 842286

Old Place Farm &⚘⚘ (Mr & Mrs Jeffrey Eker) High Halden, 3m NE of Tenterden. From A28 take Woodchurch Rd (opp Chequers public house) in High Halden, and follow for ½m. 3½-acre garden, mainly designed by Anthony du Gard Pasley, surrounding period farmhouse & buildings with paved herb garden & parterres, small lake, ponds, lawns, mixed borders, cutting garden, old shrub roses, lilies & foliage plants; all created since 1969 & much new planting in 1996. TEAS in aid of St Mary's Church, High Halden. *Adm £2 Chd 50p. Sun June 15 (2-6)*

Old Tong Farm ⚘⚘ (Mr & Mrs Simon Toynbee) 1¼m S of Brenchley. Follow Horsmonden rd from Brenchley, take first R. Medium-size garden made by owners around C15 farmhouse (not open); rose garden, pond, herb parterre, nut plat; wild woodland walk. Adj cottage with newly planted garden also open. TEAS. *Adm £1.50 (£2.50 on June 28 to incl glass of wine) Acc chd free. Suns June 29, July 6, 13 (2-6); Sat June 28 (6-9)* NB **EVENING OPENING**

Orchard Cottage &⚘⚘ (Professor & Mrs C G Wall) 3 Woodlands Road, Bickley, 1½m E of Bromley, about 400 yds from the A222. From Bickley Park Road turn into Pines Road, then 1st R into Woodlands Road, no 3 is 1st house on L. Attractive ⅓-acre garden in course of development; mixed borders with many interesting herbaceous plants and shrubs; scree beds and troughs with alpines and other small plants. TEAS. *Adm £1.50 Acc chd free (Share to Downs Syndrome Association: SE Branch®). Sun Aug 3 (2-5.30)*

▲**Owl House** &(in parts)⚘ (Maureen, Marchioness of Dufferin and Ava) Lamberhurst. 1m W of A21, signposted from Lamberhurst. 16½-acre woodland garden surrounding C16 wool smuggler's cottage: water gardens, unusual roses climbing into woodland trees; daffodils, rhododendrons, azaleas, magnolias, camellias, roses, irises, good autumn colour. *Adm £3 Chd £1 (Share to Maureen's Oast House for Arthritics®). For NGS Sun May 18 (11-6)*

Oxon Hoath &⚘⚘ (Mr & Mrs Henry Bayne-Powell) nr Hadlow, 5m NE of Tonbridge. *Car essential.* Via A20, turn off S at Wrotham Heath onto Seven Mile Lane (B2016); at Mereworth Xrds turn W, through West Peckham. Or via A26, in Hadlow turn off N along Carpenters Lane. 10 acres, landscaped with fine trees, rhododendrons and azaleas; woodland walk; replanted cedar avenue; formal parterre rose garden by Nesfield. Large Kentish ragstone house (not shown) principally Georgian but dating back to C14; Victorian additions by Salvin. Once owned by Culpeppers, grandparents of Catherine Howard. View over C18 lake to Hadlow Folly. Picnickers welcome. *Adm £1.50 Chd 50p (Share to W. Peckham Church©). Sun May 25 (2-7)*

Patches ⚘ (Mrs Katherine Headley) Gravel Castle Road, Barham, 6m SE of Canterbury. From A2 (Canterbury/Dover) take exit for Folkestone/Channel Tunnel (A260), turn R at roundabout signed Folkestone/Barham, at T-junc turn R towards Barham, turn immediately L onto minor road, proceed for ¼m to Xrds, park on R. Garden is approx 50yds down Gravel Castle Hill on L. ¾-acre chalk garden sloping S, developed over 16 years, in-cluding tree and shrub planting; mixed borders, pond and small fern garden; small kitchen garden; all designed by present owners. TEAS in next door garden. *Adm £1.50 Acc chd free (Share to Friends of Barham Church). Sun June 8; Wed June 11 (2-6)*

The Pear House ⚘ (Mrs Nicholas Snowden) Stone Hill, Sellindge, 6m E of Ashford. Turn L off A20 at Sellindge Church towards Brabourne into Stone Hill. ⅔ acre developed by present owner. Contains smaller gardens with informal planting; bulbs, roses (over 100 different, mostly old-fashioned), shrubs, small orchard with climbing roses, pond garden, shady areas. *Adm £1.50 Chd 50p. Due to limited parking, visits by appointment welcome anytime between April 26 to July 27, please* Tel 01303 812147

Peddars Wood &⚘⚘ (Mr & Mrs B J Honeysett) 14 Orchard Rd, St Michaels, Tenterden. From A28, 1m N of Tenterden, turn W into Grange Rd at Crown Hotel, take 2nd R into Orchard Rd. Small plantsman's garden created by present owner since 1984. One of the best collections of rare and interesting plants in the area, incl over 100 clematis, 50 climbing roses, lilies and ferns. TEAS. *Adm £1 Chd 20p (Share to Baptist Minister's Help Society). Sats May 17, June 21, July 26 (2-6); also private visits welcome, please* Tel 015806 3994

■ **Penshurst Place** &⚘ (Viscount De L'Isle), S of Tonbridge on B2176, N of Tunbridge Wells on A26. 10 acres of garden dating back to C14; garden divided into series of 'rooms' by over a mile of clipped yew hedge; profusion of spring bulbs: herbaceous borders; formal rose garden; famous peony border. All yr interest. TEAS and light refreshments. *Adm House & Gardens £5.50 OAPs £5.10 Chd £3 Family Ticket £14.50: Gardens £4 OAPs £3.50 Chd £2.75 Family Ticket £11.50. Open daily March 28 to Sept 30. For NGS Wed May 7, Thurs June 5 (11-6)*

Pett Place ⚘⚘ (Mrs I Mills, C I Richmond-Watson Esq & A Rolla Esq) Charing, 6m NW of Ashford. From A20 turn N into Charing High St. At end turn R into Pett Lane towards Westwell. Walled gardens covering nearly 4 acres. A garden of pleasing vistas and secret places which has been featured in Country Life, House and Garden etc. There is a ruined C13 chapel as a romantic feature beside the manor house (not open), which was re-fronted about 1700 and which Pevsner describes as 'presenting grandiloquently towards the road'. TEAS. *Adm £2 Chd 50p (Share to Kent Gardens Trust®). Sats, Suns April 26, 27, June 28, 29 (2.30-5)*

Remember that every time you visit a National Gardens Scheme garden you are helping to raise money for the following:

**The Queen's Nursing Institute
The Nurses' Welfare Service
Cancer Relief Macmillan Fund
The Gardens Fund of the National Trust
The Gardeners' Royal Benevolent Society
The Royal Gardeners' Orphan Fund**

Pevington Farm &® (Mr & Mrs David Mure) Pluckley, 3m SW of Charing. From Charing take B2077 towards Pluckley, before Pluckley turn R towards Egerton, Peverton Farm ½m on. From SW go through Pluckley, turn L for Egerton. ¾-acre garden with wonderful views over the Weald. Mixed borders with many interesting plants. Tours of garden with the owner at 12pm, 2pm and 3.30pm. TEAS for Friends of St Nicholas Church, Pluckely. *Adm £1.50 Chd 50p. Sun June 15 (11-5); private visits welcome in May, June, July, please* **Tel 01233 840317**

■ **The Pines Garden & The Bay Museum** &® (The St Margaret's Bay Trust) Beach Rd, St Margaret's Bay, 4½m NE of Dover. Beautiful 6-acre seaside garden. Water garden with waterfall and lake. Statue of Sir Winston Churchill complemented by the Bay Museum opposite. Fascinating maritime and local interest. TEAS. *Adm £1.25 Chd 35p. Gardens open daily except Christmas Day. Museum open May to end Aug (closed Mon, except Bank Hols, and Tues). For NGS Suns March 30, May 25, Aug 24 (10-5)*

Placketts Hole &®® (Mr & Mrs D P Wainman) Bicknor 5m S of Sittingbourne, and W of B2163. Owners have designed and planted 2-acre garden around charming old house (C16 with Georgian additions); interesting mix of shrubs, large borders, rose garden, a formal herb garden and sweet-smelling plants. TEAS. *Adm £1.50 Acc chd free (Share to Kent Gardens Trust®). Sun July 6 (2-6.30)*

Plaxtol Gardens 5m N of Tonbridge, 6m E of Sevenoaks, turn E off A227 to Plaxtol village. TEAS. Tickets and maps available at all gardens. Parking at Spoute Cottage. *Combined adm £2.50 Acc chd free (Share to Friends of Plaxtol Church©). Sun June 29 (2-6)*
>   **Ducks Farm** ® (Mr & Mrs H Puleston Jones) Dux Lane. 2 acres, in course of restoration, surrounding medieval/Victorian farmhouse. Mixed herbaceous borders, walled garden, vegetable garden, herb garden
>   **The Retreat** ® (Mr & Mrs S Cartwright), Plaxtol Lane. Newly constructed, 2-acre garden with lake and pond, rock landscape, cottage garden; wide range of interesting trees and shrubs
>   **Spoute Cottage** &®® (Mr & Mrs Donald Forbes) situated at the bottom of Plaxtol St on L side opp Hyders Forge. ¾ acre of mixed borders of contrasting flowering and foliage plants, especially for flower arranging; small pond & stream. Japanese garden. Plant nursery attached. Large car park
>   **Watermead** ®® (Mr & Mrs Michael Scott) Long Mill Lane. Garden of ¼ acre with perennials for all year interest with flowers and foliage; fruit and vegetable plot; small pond
>   ¶**Wendings** (E E Peckham) The Street. ¼-acre garden, created and maintained by present owner; contrasting shrubs, ground cover and climbers

Ramhurst Manor & (The Lady Rosie Kindersley) Powder Mill Lane, Leigh, Tonbridge. Historic property once belonged to the Black Prince and Culpepper family. Formal gardens; roses, azaleas, rhododendrons, wild flowers. TEA. *Adm £1.50 Acc chd free. Sun June 1 (2.30-6)*

The Red House &® (K C L Webb Esq) Crockham Hill, 3m N of Edenbridge. On Limpsfield-Oxted Rd, B269. Formal features of this large garden are kept to a minimum; rose walk leads on to 3 acres of rolling lawns flanked by fine trees and shrubs incl rhododendrons, azaleas and magnolias. Views over the Weald and Ashdown Forest. TEAS. **Larksfield** and **Larksfield Cottage** gardens also open same days. *Combined adm £2.50 OAPs £2 Chd 50p (Share to The Schizophrenia Association of Great Britain®). Suns May 11, 18 (2-6)*

■ **Riverhill House** ® (The Rogers family) 2m S of Sevenoaks on A225. Mature hillside garden with extensive views; specimen trees, sheltered terraces with roses and choice shrubs; bluebell wood with rhododendrons and azaleas; picnics allowed. TEAS. *Adm £2.50 Chd 50p. Every Sun from Easter to end of June and Bank Hol weekends in this period (12-6). For NGS Weds April 16, May 14 (12-6)*

Rock Farm ®® (Mrs P A Corfe) Nettlestead. 6m W of Maidstone. Turn S off A26 onto B2015 then 1m S of Wateringbury turn R. 2-acre garden set around old Kentish farmhouse and farm buildings in beautiful setting with lovely views; created since 1968 with emphasis on all-year interest and ease of maintenance. Plantsman's collection of shrubs, trees and perennials for alkaline soil: extensive herbaceous border, vegetable area, bog garden and plantings around two large natural ponds. Plant nursery adjoining garden. *Adm £2 Chd 50p (Share to Heart of Kent Hospice and St Mary's Church, Nettlestead®). Every Wed & Sat in May, June and July, Aug 2, 6, 9 (11-5)*

Rogers Rough &®® (Richard and Hilary Bird) Kilndown, 10m S of Tonbridge. From A21 2m S of Lamberhurst turn E into Kilndown; take 1st R down Chick's Lane until rd divides. Garden writer's 1½-acre garden, mainly herbaceous borders, but also rock gardens, shrubs, a small wood and pond. Extensive views. TEAS in aid of local charities. *Adm £2 Chd 50p. Suns June 22, July 20 (2-5.30); parties welcome by appointment*

¶**Rose Cottage** &®® (Mr & Mrs Crowe) Castle Hill, Hartley, 3m NE of Swanley and 4m SE of Dartford. From B260 at Longfield, turn S at main roundabout, ½m up hill to Hartley Green with war memorial, where Castle Hill runs down to Fawkham Church: Rose Cottage garden is 100yds down Castle Hill on L. No parking on Castle Hill, please park on main road. 1-acre garden created from field since 1988, variety of shrubs and perennials, wild life pond, aviary and paved garden. TEAS in aid of Demelza Childrens Hospice. *Adm £1.50 Acc chd free. Sun June 22 (1.30-5.30): private visits also welcome, please* **Tel 01474 707376**

St Michael's House &® (Brig & Mrs W Magan) Roydon Road, Seven Mile Lane, 5m NE Tonbridge, 5m SW Maidstone. On A26 at Mereworth roundabout take S exit (A228) signed Paddock Wood, after 1m turn L at top of rise (signed Roydon). Gardens ¼m up hill on L. Old vicarage garden of ¾ acre enclosed by shaped yew hedge; tulips; roses, climbing roses, irises; 6-acre meadow with extensive views. TEAS. *Adm £2 OAPs £1 Chd 50p. Suns April 27 (tulips), May 25 (irises), June 22 (roses) (2-6)*

●**Saltwood Castle** (The Hon Mrs Clark) 2m NW of Hythe, 4m W of Folkestone; from A20 turn S at sign to Saltwood. Medieval castle, subject of quarrel between Thomas a Becket and Henry II. C13 crypt and dungeons; armoury; battlement walks and watch towers. Lovely views; spacious lawns and borders; courtyard walls covered with roses. Picnics allowed. Saltwood Castle closed to the general public in 1997. *Private parties of 20 or more weekdays only, please write for appt*

■ **Scotney Castle** ও ⚘ (Mrs Christopher Hussey; The National Trust) On A21 London-Hastings, 1¼m S of Lamberhurst. Bus: (Mon to Sat) Autopoint 256, Tunbridge Wells-Wadhurst; alight Lamberhurst Green. Famous picturesque landscape garden, created by the Hussey family in the 1840s surrounding moated C14 Castle. House (not open) by Salvin, 1837. Old Castle open May - mid-Sept (same times as garden). Gift Shop. Picnic area in car park. Tea Lamberhurst. *Adm £3.60 Chd £1.80; Family ticket £9; Pre-booked parties of 15 or more (Wed-Fri) £2.40 Chd £1.20; March 29-Nov 2, daily except Mons & Tues, but open Bank Hol Mons (closed Good Fri). Wed-Fri (11-6), Sats & Suns 2-6 or sunset if earlier; Bank Hol Mons & Suns preceding (12-6). For NGS (Share to Trinity Hospice, Clapham Common®) Mon May 26 (12-6)*

Sea Close ⚘❀ (Maj & Mrs R H Blizard) Cannongate Rd, Hythe. A259 Hythe-Folkestone; ½m from Hythe, signed. A plantsman's garden with colour throughout the year - especially autumn; 1¼ acres on steep slope overlooking the sea; designed, laid out & maintained by present owners since 1966. Approx 1000 named plants & shrubs, planted for visual effect in many varied style beds of individual character. Cold refreshments. Teas Hythe. *Adm £1.50 Acc chd free (Share to Royal Signals Benevolent Fund®). Suns May 18, June 15, July 13, Aug 10 (2-5), Oct 5 (2-4)*

Shipbourne Gardens 3m N of Tonbridge, 5m E of Sevenoaks on A227. TEAS in village hall. Maps available at gardens and village hall. Parking on village green. *Combined adm £2.50 Acc chd free. Sun June 22 (2-6)*

   1 Batey's Cottage ও (Mr & Mrs E Martin) Stumble Hill. Small cottage garden with vegetable patch, herbaceous borders, shrubs

   Brookers Cottage ও❀ (Ann & Peter Johnson) Back Lane. ⅔-acre garden with natural pond, scree bed, herbaceous borders and island beds; large collection of hardy geraniums (cranesbills); small fruit and vegetable patch

   Plantation House ❀ (Mr & Mrs A Primarolo) Reeds Lane. ¾-acre garden originally a Kent cobnut orchard, with island and herbaceous borders; conifers, heathers, roses, old apple trees, azaleas, small vegetable garden

   Yew Tree Cottage ⚘ (Susan & Ian Bowles) The Green. Small cottage garden, partially walled, with herbaceous border, small gravel garden and old roses. Studio of wild life artist Ian Bowles will be open

Sibton Park ও⚘ (Mr & Mrs C Blackwell) Lyminge, 8m NW of Folkestone. Off Elham Valley road, N of Lyminge, turn L for Rhodes Minnis, ¼m on L. Landscaped garden with spacious lawns, 30 feet high yew hedges and topiary; old walled garden; children's adventure playground

(own risk). TEAS. *Adm £1.50 OAP £1 Chd 50p. Sun June 29 (2-6)*

The Silver Spray ও⚘❀ (Mr & Mrs C T Orsbourne) Sellindge. 7m SE of Ashford on A20 opposite school. 1-acre garden developed and planted since 1983 and maintained by owners. Attractively laid out gardens and wild area combine a keen interest in conservation (especially butterflies) with a love of unusual hardy and tender plants. TEAS. *Adm £1 Acc chd free (Share to St Mary's Church, Sellindge©). Suns May 25, June 22; Mons May 26, Aug 25; Weds July 23, Aug 20; Sats June 14, July 12, 26; (2-5)*

■ **Sissinghurst Garden** ও⚘❀ (Nigel Nicolson Esq; The National Trust) Cranbrook. Station: Staplehurst. Bus: MD5 from Maidstone 14m; 297 Tunbridge Wells (not Suns) 15m. Garden created by the late V. Sackville-West and Sir Harold Nicolson. Spring garden, herb garden. Tudor building and tower, partly open to public. Moat. **Because of the limited capacity of the garden, daily visitor numbers are restricted; timed tickets are in operation and visitors may have to wait before entry.** Lunches and TEAS. *Adm £6 Chd £3. Garden open March 28 to Oct 15. (Closed Mons incl Bank Hols). Tues to Fri 1-6.30 (last adm 6pm); Sats and Suns 10-5.30 (last adm 5pm). For NGS (Share to Charleston Farmhouse Trust®) Weds April 23, June 4, July 9, Oct 1 (1-6.30)*

Sissinghurst Place ও⚘ (Mr & Mrs Simon MacLachlan) Sissinghurst, 2m NE of Cranbrook, E of Sissinghurst village ½m from Sissinghurst NT garden on A262. Large Victorian garden of herbaceous beds, lawns, fine trees, and established yew hedges; spring woodland garden with daffodils, hellebores and pond; herbs and climbers in ruin of original house. TEA. *Adm £1.50 (Share to St Georges Institute, Sissinghurst). Sats, Suns April 5, 6, 19, 20 (1.30-5.30)*

¶**Slaney Cottage** ❀ (Roger & Trisha Fermor), Headcorn Road, Staplehurst, about 1m to E of A229 (Maidstone-Hastings). Two-acre garden in the making, surrounding C18 cottage: old roses, clematis species, hardy geraniums and other herbaceous plants, both unusual and favourites: 2 wildlife ponds and new woodland area. TEAS. *Adm £1.50 Acc chd free. Sun July 27 (2-5)*

■¶**Smallhythe Place** (Ellen Terry Museum) ⚘ (The National Trust) Smallhythe Place, Tenterden. 2m S of Tenterden on E side of B2082 to Rye. Three acres of garden include old-fashioned roses and pinks, cottage garden borders, orchard, nuttery. Early C16 half-timbered house was home of actress Ellen Terry from 1899-1928; it contains many stage costumes and personal mementoes. *Adm £2.80, Chd 1.40, Family £7. Open Sat to Weds March 28-Oct 29 (2-6 or dusk). For NGS Fri June 13 (2-5.30)*

¶**Sotts Hole Cottage** ⚘ (Mr & Mrs Jim Vinson) Crouch Lane, Borough Green. Crouch Lane runs SE from A25 between Esso garage and Black Horse public house, garden at bottom of 2nd hill (approx ¾m). A redundant farmer's approach to 6 acres of undulating countryside, created over 8 years and 20,000 hours, incl many features built by owner: basically a cottage garden with extensive lawns and full of colour at its herbaceous best. *Adm £2 Chd £1. Suns June 22, Sept 14 (10-6)*

South Hill Farm と木舞 (Sir Charles Jessel Bt) Hastingleigh, E of Ashford. Turn off A28 to Wye, go through village and ascend Wye Downs, in 2m turn R at Xrds marked Brabourne and South Hill, then first L. Or from Stone Street (B2068) turn W opp Stelling Minnis, follow signs to Hastingleigh, continue towards Wye and turn L at Xrds marked Brabourne and South Hill, then first L. 2 acres high up on N Downs, C17/18 house (not open); old walls; ha-ha; formal water garden; old and new roses; unusual shrubs, perennials and foliage plants. TEAS. *Adm £1.50 Chd 25p (Share to Kent Association for the Blind®). Sat, Sun July 5, 6 (2-6)*

Spilsill Court と木舞 (Mr & Mrs C G Marshall) Frittenden Road, Staplehurst. Proceed to Staplehurst on A229 (Maidstone-Hastings). From S enter village, turn R immediately after Elf garage on R & just before 30mph sign, into Frittenden Rd; garden ½m on, on L. From N go through village to 40mph sign, immediately turn L into Frittenden Rd. Approx 4 acres of garden, orchard and paddock; series of gardens including those in blue, white and silver; roses; lawns; shrubs, trees and ponds. Small private chapel. Jacob sheep & unusual poultry. COFFEE/TEA. *Adm £1.50 Chd (under 16) 50p (Share to Gardening for the Disabled Trust®). Suns April 6, July 27 (11-5)*

■ **Squerryes Court** (Mr & Mrs John Warde) ½m W of Westerham signed from A25. 15 acres of well-documented historic garden, C18 landscape. Part of the formal garden has been restored by the family using C17 plan. Lake, spring bulbs, azaleas, herbaceous borders, C18 dovecote, cenotaph commemorating Gen Wolfe; woodland walks. TEAS on NGS days for St Mary's Church, Westerham. *Adm £2.20 Chd £1.20 (House and garden £3.70 Chd £1.80) Weds, Sats, Suns from March 29 to Sept 28 (Garden 12-5.30: House 1.30-5.30). For NGS Suns July 20, Aug 17 (12-5.30)*

■ **Stoneacre** 木舞 (Mrs Rosemary Alexander; The National Trust) Otham, 4m SE of Maidstone, between A2020 and A274. Old world garden recently replanted. Yew hedges; herbaceous borders; ginkgo tree; unusual plants. Timber-framed Hall House dated 1480. Subject of newspaper and magazine articles. (National Trust members please note that openings in aid of the NGS are on days when the property would not normally be open, therefore adm charges apply.) TEAS. *Adm £2.20 Chd 50p. Open Weds & Sats April-Oct 29 (2-5). For NGS (Share to Garden History Society®) Suns April 27, Sept 28 (2-5) and private visits welcome, please* **Tel 01622 862871**

Stonewall Park Gardens (Mr & Mrs V P Fleming) Chiddingstone Hoath, 5m SE of Edenbridge. ½-way between Mark Beech and Penshurst. Large walled garden with herbaceous borders. Extensive woodland garden, featuring species and hybrid rhododendrons, azaleas; wandering paths, lakes. **North Lodge** (Mrs Dorothy Michie) traditional cottage garden full of interest. TEAS. *Adm £2 Acc chd free. Sun May 11 (2-5)*

Street Cottage (Mr & Mrs Timothy Stubbs) The Street, Bethersden. 6m SW of Ashford, 6m NE of Tenterden, turn off A28 to village centre. 1½-acre garden in lovely setting next to St Margaret's Church. Herbaceous, shrub and rose borders, vegetables and fruit with lawns and ponds;

owner maintained. TEAS. *Adm £1.50 Acc chd free. Sun June 29 (2-6)*

Swan Oast と (Mr & Mrs Bedford) Stilebridge, Marden, 6m S of Maidstone. On A229 (Maidstone-Hastings) ½m S of Stilebridge inn, 3m N of Staplehurst. 20-year-old 1¾-acre garden, incl ¼ acre of water, landscaped with shrubberies, rockeries, with dwarf conifers and heathers, raised beds of seasonal bedding, kitchen garden; ornamental fish and small collection of waterfowl. TEAS in aid of The Mike Colinwood Trust®. *Adm £1.50 Acc chd free. Suns April 20, 27, May 4, 11, June 29, July 13, 27, Aug 10, 24, 31 (2-5)*

Tanners 木舞 (Lord & Lady Nolan) Brasted, 2m E of Westerham, A25 to Brasted; in Brasted turn off alongside the Green and up the hill to the top; 1st drive on R opp Coles Lane. Bus stop Brasted Green and White Hart 200yds. 5 acres; mature trees and shrubs; maples, magnolias, rhododendrons and foliage trees; water garden; interesting new planting. Plants mostly labelled. Teas in Village Tearoom, High Street, Brasted. *Adm £1.50 Chd 50p. Open Mons, Weds, Thurs by appointment, groups also welcome, please* **Tel 01959 563758**

2 Thorndale Close と (in parts) 木 (Mr & Mrs L O Miles) Chatham. From A229 Chatham-Maidstone rd turn E opp Forte Posthouse into Watson Ave, next R to Thorndale Close. Minute front and rear gardens of 11' × 18' and 20' × 22'. Plantsman's garden with alpines, pool, bog garden, rockery, peat and herbaceous beds. *Adm £1 Acc chd under 10 free. Suns April 13, 27, May 11, 25, June 8, 22 (2-5.30); also private visits welcome, please* **Tel 01634 863329**

Thornham Friars と (Geoffrey Fletcher Esq) Pilgrims Way, Thurnham, 4m NE of Maidstone. From M20 or M2 take A249, at bottom of Detling Hill turn into Detling 1m along Pilgrims Way to garden. 2-acre garden on chalk. 12-acre park and magnificent views. Many unusual shrubs; trees; lawns with special beds for ericaceous shrubs. Tudor house. *Adm £1.50 Chd 25p. Sun June 8 (2-5.30)*

Torry Hill と木舞 (Lord & Lady Kingsdown) 5m S of Sittingbourne. Situated in triangle formed by Frinsted, Milstead and Doddington. Leave M20 at junction 8 for A20, at Lenham turn N for Doddington; at Great Danes N for Hollingbourne and Frinsted (B2163). From M2 Intersection 5 via Bredgar and Milstead. From A2 and E turn S at Ospringe via Newnham and Doddington. 8 acres; large lawns, specimen trees, flowering cherries, rhododendrons, azaleas and naturalised daffodils; walled gardens with lawns, shrubs, roses, herbaceous borders, wild flower areas and vegetables. Extensive views to Medway and Thames estuaries. TEA. *Adm £1.50 Chd (over 12) 50p (Share to St Dunstan's Church, Frinsted©). Suns April 20, June 8, July 6 (2-5)*

Town Hill Cottage 木舞 (Mr & Mrs P Cosier) 58 Town Hill, West Malling. From A20 6m W of Maidstone, turn S onto A228. Top of Town Hill at N end of High St. Part walled small village garden of C16/C18 house, with many interesting plants. Hardy ferns for sale. TEAS. *Adm £1.50 Chd 75p. Suns May 18, June 15 (2-5)*

Upper Pryors ✗ (Mr & Mrs S G Smith) Cowden, 4½m SE of Edenbridge. From B2026 Edenbridge-Hartfield, turn R at Cowden Xrds and take 1st drive on R. 10 acres of country garden featuring variety, profusion of plants, water and magnificent lawns. TEAS. *Adm £2 Chd 50p. Wed June 11 (2-5)*

▲¶**Walmer Castle** ঙ✗ (English Heritage) nr Deal. 1m S of Deal, well signed. Gardens surrounding Walmer Castle, a tudor fortress, now an elegant home and residence of the Lord Warden of the Cinque Ports. Summer gardens with herbaceous borders and ornamental trees; new this year is the Queen Mother's Garden. *Adm £4, Concessions £3, Chd £2. For NGS (Share to English Heritage) Sun June 29; Mon Aug 4 (birthday of The Queen Mother) (10-6)*

Walnut Tree Gardens ঙ✗ (Mr & Mrs M Oldaker) Swan Lane, Little Chart. 6m NW of Ashford. Leave A20 at Charing signed to Little Chart. At Swan public house turn W for Pluckley, gardens 500yds on L. Romantic 4-acre garden set within and around walls dating from early C18. Large collection of old roses; extensive range of unusual and interesting plants, shrubs and young trees. TEAS subject to weather. *Adm £1.50 Acc chd free (Share to Green Wicket Animal Sanctuary©). Suns June 29, July 6, 13, 20, 27, Aug 3 (2-5)*

39 Warwick Crescent ✗✤ (Mr & Mrs J G Sastre) Borstal, Rochester. From A229 Maidstone-Chatham at 2nd roundabout turn W into B2097 Borstal-Rochester rd; turn L at Priestfields, follow Borstal St to Wouldham Way, 3rd turning on R is Warwick Cres. Small front & rear plantsperson's gardens; sinks and troughs; alpine terraces, peat & herbaceous beds; rockery with cascade & pool, bog garden, borders. Featured in NGS video 2. *Adm £1 Acc chd free. Suns April 13, May 11, July 6, Sept 7 (2-5.30): private visits welcome by prior arrangement, please* Tel 01634 401636

Waystrode Manor ঙ✗✤ (Mr & Mrs Peter Wright) Cowden, 4½m S of Edenbridge. From B2026 Edenbridge-Hartfield, turn off at Cowden Pound. 8 acres; sweeping lawns, borders, ponds, bulbs, shrub roses, clematis and many tender plants. Orangery. All trees, plants and shrubs labelled. House C15 (not open). Last entry ½-hour before closing time. TEAS. Gift shop. *Adm £2.50 Chd 50p. Weds May 14, 28, June 18 (1.30-5.30); Suns June 1, 29, July 6 (2-6); also open for groups of 15 or more by appt* Tel 01342 850695

¶**Weald Cottage** ঙ✤ (Mrs Pauline Abraham) Four Elms Road, just N of Edenbridge on B2027, opp Eden Valley School. Small garden with theme areas including French, Roman and Japanese; mixed planting of bulbs, herbaceous, shrubs and trees, vegetables and fruit trees, conservatory. TEAS. *Adm £1.50 Chd 25p. Suns May 4, 25, June 22, July 20; Mon May 26 (2-5)*

Weeks Farm ঙ✗✤ (Robin & Monica de Garston) Bedlam Lane, Egerton Forstal, Ashford, 3½m E of Headcorn. Take Smarden Road out of Headcorn, Bedlam Lane is 3rd turning on L, Weeks Farm approx 1½m on R. 2-acre garden on Wealden clay, showing varied use of badly drained site; double herbaceous borders flanking gateway, vista a feature; orchard with crocus & fritillaria. New

water garden, ponds with abundance of wild life. TEAS. *Adm £1.50 Acc chd free. Suns March 9 (12-5), April 13, Sept 14 (12-6). Private visits welcome, please* Tel 01233 756252 (evenings)

Went House ঙ✤ (Mrs Robin Baring) Swan Street, West Malling. From A20, 6m W of Maidstone turn S onto A228. Turn E off High Street in village towards station. Queen Anne house with secret garden surrounded by high wall. Interesting plants, water gardens, woodland, parterre and octagon potager. TEAS. *Adm £1.50 Acc chd free (Share to St Mary's Church West Malling Bell Fund®). Suns June 22, July 6 (2-6)*

West Studdal Farm ঙ✤ (Mr & Mrs Peter Lumsden) West Studdal, N of Dover half-way between Eastry and Whitfield. From Eastry take A256, after 2½m pass Plough & Harrow, then L at roundabout and 1st R, entrance ¼m on L. From Whitfield roundabout take A256, after 2½m pass High & Dry public house, then R at roundabout and 1st R, entrance ¼m on L. Medium-sized garden around old farmhouse set by itself in small valley; herbaceous borders, roses and fine lawns protected by old walls and beech hedges. TEAS in Dodecagonal folly. *Adm £1.50 Chd 50p. Sun Aug 17 (2-6)*

Westview ✤ (Mr & Mrs J G Jackson) Spekes Rd, Hempstead. From M2 take A278 to Gillingham; at 1st roundabout follow sign to Wigmore, proceed to junction with Fairview Av, turn L & park on motorway link rd bridge, walk into Spekes Rd, Westview 3rd on L. ¼-acre town garden on very sloping site with many steps; good collection of plants & shrubs suitable for a chalk soil; designed by owners for all-year interest and low maintenance. Good autumn colour. TEAS. *Adm £1 Acc chd free. Weds April 23, May 14, June 4; Suns April 27, May 18, June 8 (2-5); also private visits welcome, please* Tel 01634 230987

Whitehill ✗ (Mrs Henderson) Wrotham. On A20 at Wrotham, between junctions 2A (M26) and 2 (M20). 3-acre garden, incl 1½ acres with design by Gertrude Jekyll in 1919, now carefully restored from original plans. *Adm £1.50 Chd 50p (Share to Kent Air Ambulance©). Sun June 15 (2-5.30); private visits welcome, please* Tel 01732 882521

Whitehurst ঙ✗ (Mr & Mrs John Mercy) Chainhurst, 3m N of Marden. From Marden station turn R into Pattenden Lane and under railway bridge; at T-junc turn L; at next fork bear R to Chainhurst, then second turning on L. 1½ acres of trees, roses & water garden. Victorian spiral staircase leading to aerial walkway through the tree tops. Exhibition of root dwellings. TEAS. *Adm £2 Chd £1 (Share to Stroke Assoc®). Suns May 4, 11, June 8, 15, Oct 5, 12 (2-5.30)*

Withersdane Hall ঙ (University of London) Wye College, 3m NE of Ashford. A28 take fork signed Wye. Bus EK 601 Ashford-Canterbury via Wye. Well-labelled garden of educational and botanical interest, containing several small carefully designed gardens; flower and shrub borders; spring bulbs; herb garden. Rain-fed garden. Free guide book with map available. TEAS in Wye village. *Adm £1.50 Chd 50p. Suns March 23, May 4, June 15, Aug 31 (2-5)*

Womenswold Gardens &⚲❀ Midway between Canterbury and Dover, SE of A2, take B2046 signed Wingham at Barham crossover, after about ¼m turn R at Armada beacon, follow signs for gardens. Four diverse and colourful cottage gardens within easy walking distance. St Margaret's Church will be open, with flower festival. TEAS. *Combined adm £2 Acc chd free (Share to St Margaret's Church). Sat, Sun June 28, 29 (2-6)*

Worth Gardens &⚲❀ 2m SE of Sandwich and 5m NW of Deal, from A258 signed Worth. A group of cottage gardens in wide variety in peaceful village setting incl a new garden, recently planted. Maps and tickets available at each garden. TEA. *Combined adm £2 Acc chd free. Sun July 6 (1-5)*

Wyckhurst &⚲❀ (Mr & Mrs C D Older) Mill Road, Aldington, 4m SE of Ashford. Leave M20 at junction 10, on A20 travel S to Aldington turning; proceed 1½m to Aldington village hall, 'Walnut Tree' take rd signed to Dymchurch, after ¼m turn R into Mill Road. C16 cottage (not open) surrounded by 1-acre cottage garden; old roses; herbaceous borders; unusual perennials. Extensive views across Romney Marsh. TEAS in aid of Bonnington Church. *Adm £2 Chd 50p. Sun June 22, Wed June 25 (11-6)*

Yalding Gardens ⚲❀ 6m SW of Maidstone, three gardens S & W of village. *Combined adm £3 Chd under 12 free. Sun April 13 (2-5.30)*

Long Acre &⚲❀ (Mr & Mrs G P Fyson) is on L in Cheveney Farm Lane, just off Yalding-Hunton rd (Vicarage Road) ⅓m from Yalding War Memorial. Long, narrow garden comprising shrubberies, lawns, vegetable and fruit garden and paddock with young specimen trees. Shrubberies have been recently developed to eliminate the work in maintaining flower beds

Parsonage Oasts ⚲ (Mr & the Hon Mrs Raikes) Between Yalding village and station turn off at Anchor public house over bridge over canal, continue 100yds up the lane. ¾-acre riverside garden with walls, shrubs, daffodils. TEAS in aid of The Fifth Trust for Mentally Handicapped Adults®

Rugmer Farmhouse ⚲❀ (Mr & Mrs R Lawrence) S of village, off Benover Rd (B2162), 440yds past Woolpack Inn. 2-acre garden, surrounding C16 cottage (not open), developed by present owners since 1975; spring bulbs, mixed borders and vegetables, on Wealden clay

Lancashire, Merseyside & Greater Manchester

Hon County Organisers:	Mr & Mrs R Doldon, Old Barn Cottage, Greens Arms Road, Turton, Nr Bolton BL7 0ND Tel 01204 852139
Assistant Hon County Organiser:	J Bowker Esq, Swiss Cottage, 8 Hammond Drive, Read, Burnley

DATES OF OPENING

March 31 Sunday
Weeping Ash, Glazebury
April 20 Sunday
Lindeth Dene, Silverdale
May 4 Sunday
The Ridges, Limbrick, nr Chorley
May 5 Monday
The Ridges, Limbrick, nr Chorley
May 18 Sunday
191 Liverpool Road South, Maghull
May 25 Sunday
Catforth Gardens, Catforth
Cross Gaits Cottage, Blacko
191 Liverpool Road South, Maghull
Old Barn Cottage, Turton
May 26 Monday
Cross Gaits Cottage, Blacko
Old Barn Cottage, Turton
June 1 Sunday
Lindeth Dene, Silverdale
Woodside, Shevington

June 8 Sunday
Mill Barn, Salmesbury Bottoms
Rufford Old Hall, Rufford, nr Ormskirk
Speke Hall, The Walk, Liverpool
June 15 Sunday
Swiss Cottage, Read
June 22 Sunday
Mill Barn, Salmesbury Bottoms
June 29 Sunday
Catforth Gardens, Catforth
Clearbeck House, Higher Tatham
Hesketh Bank Village Gardens
Windle Hall, St Helens
July 5 Saturday
Newton Hall, nr Carnforth
July 6 Sunday
Bank House, Borwick
Clearbeck House, Higher Tatham
Frigham Cottage, Trawden
Newton Hall, nr Carnforth
The Ridges, Limbrick, nr Chorley
July 13 Sunday
Weeping Ash, Glazebury
July 20 Sunday

Cross Gaits Cottage, Blacko
July 27 Sunday
Catforth Gardens, Catforth
August 3 Sunday
Greyfriars, Walker Lane, Fulwood
August 25 Monday
Old Barn Cottage, Turton
September 7 Sunday
Windle Hall, St Helens
Woodside, Shevington
September 14 Sunday
Weeping Ash, Glazebury
September 21 Sunday
Hawthornes, Hesketh Bank
October 6 Sunday
Mill Barn, Salmesbury Bottoms

Regular openings
For details see garden description

Catforth Gardens, Catforth
Hawthornes, Hesketh Bank

DESCRIPTIONS OF GARDENS

Bank House ❀❁ (Mr & Mrs R G McBurnie) Borwick. 2m NE of Carnforth off A6. Leave M6 at junction 35. Plantsman's garden of 2 acres designed to provide all yr round shape, colour and form. Divided into different areas of interest incl shady borders, sunny gravel area with old-fashioned roses, arboretum, fruit and vegetables. Island beds, silver and gold borders. Collection of carnivorous plants. TEAS. *Adm £1.50 Chd free. Sun July 6 (2-6)*

■ **Catforth Gardens** ♿❀❁ Leave M6 at junction 32 turning N on A6. Turn L at 1st set of traffic lights; 2m to T-junction, turn R. Turn L at sign for Catforth, L at next T-junction, 1st R into Benson Lane. Bear L at church lane to Roots Lane. Incl adjoining gardens of **Willowbridge Farm** and **Cherry Tree Lodge** as seen on Gardeners World 1993, featured in the Good Gardens Guide. TEAS NGS days only. *Combined adm £2 OAP £1.50 Chd 50p. Gardens and adjacent nursery open March 15 to Sept 14 (10.30-5.30). For NGS Suns May 25, June 29, July 27. Parties by appt, please* **Tel 01772 690561/690269**
    Cherry Tree Lodge(Mr & Mrs T A Bradshaw) 1-acre informal country garden, planted for yr-round interest and colour. Wide variety of unusual shrubs; trees; rhododendrons, azaleas; rare herbaceous plants incl euphorbias, dicentras, pulmonarias; ground cover plants; national collection of hardy geraniums; 2 ponds with bog gardens, large rockery and woodland garden
    Willow Bridge Farm (Mr & Mrs W Moore) ¼-acre cottage garden with wide variety of herbaceous perennials. Also 1 acre summer flower garden with 3 natural clay-lined ponds and high banks. Large herbaceous borders and rose garden, shrubs, climbing roses intermingled with perennials

Clearbeck House ♿❁ (Mr & Mrs P Osborne) Higher Tatham. Signed from Wray (M6 Junction 34, A683, B6480) and Low Bentham. Partly re-landscaped garden of about 1 acre focused on larger lake and wildlife area with increasing bird species. Traditional and formal borders near house lead out through vistas to distant views. Pyramid and symbolic garden; sculptures (some for sale); varied planting incl old-fashioned roses and wet areas. A garden to walk in, with surprises. TEAS. *Adm £1 Chd free. Suns June 29, July 6 (11.30-5.30). Private visits welcome (£1.50), please* **Tel 015242 61029**

Cross Gaits Cottage ❀❁ (Mr & Mrs S J Gude) Take M65 exit junction 13. Follow Barrowford signs then Barnoldswick signs. Garden 1½m on Barnoldswick Rd opp Cross Gaits Inn. ⅔-acre walled cottage garden featured on Granada TV; shrub and herbaceous borders; 2 ornamental ponds. 700ft above sea level; fine view of Pennines. TEA. *Adm £1.50 Chd 50p. Sun, Mon May 25, 26; Sun July 20 (1-5). Private visits welcome, please* **Tel 01282 617163**

Frigham Cottage ❁ (Sue & Alec Rumbold) Trawden. 3m SE of Colne. From the A6068, follow the B6250 into Trawden. Turn L at church, then straight on for 1m. No parking at the house on open day - visitors have a 600yd walk. Garden on the lower slopes of Boulsworth Hill at 850ft above sea level. Divided into several small gardens with water features and a wide variety of plants. Started

in 1990 and changing each yr. Shown on Granada TV and listed in 1997 Good Gardens Guide. TEAS in aid of St Mary's Church. *Adm £1 Chd free. Sun July 6 (1-6). Private visits welcome May to July (with parking at the house), please* **Tel 01282 870581**

Greyfriars ♿❀❁ (Mr & Mrs William Harrison) Walker Lane, Fulwood. 2m N of Preston. Junction 32 off M6 (M55); S to Preston; at Black Bull Xrds, R to Boys Lane Xrds, entrance ½m on R. 8 acres; lawns, rose beds, fuchsias; 4 greenhouses with hybrid begonias, geraniums and carnations; fountains; koi carp pond. Music. TEAS. *Adm £2 Chd 50p. Sun Aug 3 (2-5)*

Hawthornes ❀❁ (Mr & Mrs R Hodson) Hesketh Bank. Midway between Preston and Southport. Turn off A59 at Tarleton traffic lights. Head N for 2m. Turn R into Marsh Rd at end of Station Rd. 1-acre garden. Mixed borders; island beds; shrub roses; clematis. Many perennials. Pond. Nursery attached. Also open with Hesketh Bank Village Gardens. TEAS Sept 21 only. *Adm £1. Every Thurs, Fri May, June, July, Sept (2-5), Sun Sept 21 (1-5). Also open with Hesketh Bank Village Gardens Sun June 29 (12-6). Also by appt please* **Tel 01772 812379**

Hesketh Bank Village Gardens ❀❁ Midway between Preston and Southport. From Preston take A59 towards Liverpool, then turn R at traffic lights for Tarleton village. Straight through Tarleton to Hesketh Bank. Free vintage bus between gardens. TEAS. *Combined adm £2 Chd free. Sun June 29 (12-6)*
    31 Becconsall Lane (Mr & Mrs J Baxter) Cottage style garden with pond, white and green beds and semi-woodland walk
    74 Chapel Road (Mr & Mrs T Iddon) Compact colourful garden. Wide variety of plants. Pond, arbour and gazebo
    11 Douglas Avenue (Mr & Mrs J Cook) Large established garden with lawns, mature trees, mixed herbaceous borders and naturalised areas
    Hawthornes (Mr & Mrs R Hodson) See separate entry
    Manor Farm (Mr & Mrs K Dickinson) Shore Rd. Informal cottage garden with herbs, shrub roses in naturalistic setting
    135 Station Road (Mr & Mrs G Hale) Large and interesting garden with pond, mixed herbaceous, shrub borders and climbers

Lindeth Dene ❀❁ (Mrs B M Kershaw) 38 Lindeth Rd, Silverdale. 13m N of Lancaster. Take M6 to junction 35, turn L (S) on A6 to Carnforth t-lights. Turn R follow signs Silverdale. After level Xing ¼m uphill turn L down Hollins Lane. At T junction turn R into Lindeth Rd. Garden is 4th gateway on L, park in rd. 1¼ acres overlooking Morecambe Bay. Limestone rock garden; troughs; pools; heathers; veganic kitchen garden, saxifrages, geraniums, Elizabethan primroses, N.Z. plants and hardy perennials. Teas and toilets available in village. *Adm £1.50 Acc chd free. Suns April 20, June 1 (2-5). Private visits welcome by appt, please* **Tel 01524 701314**

191 Liverpool Rd South ♿❁ (Mr & Mrs D Cheetham) Maghull. From A59 take turning for Maghull Town Centre. Turn L at traffic lights and veer R over canal bridge. Garden ¼m on R. ½-acre suburban garden; rhododendrons, azaleas, camellias, rockery, pool, sink gardens, primulas, a variety of trees (some unusual), shrubs, bulbs and herbaceous plants for all year colour in the smaller garden. Featured in Lancashire Life 1995. TEAS and coffee. *Adm £1 Acc chd free. Suns May 18, 25 (1.30-5.30)*

Mill Barn &✿ (Dr C J Mortimer) Goose Foot Close, Samlesbury Bottoms, Preston. 6m E of Preston. From M6 junction 31 2½m on A59/A677 B/burn. Turn S. Nabs Head Lane, then Goose Foot Lane 1m. 1½-acre tranquil, terraced garden on the site of C18 corn and cotton mills along the banks of the R Davwen. Varied planting with many uncommon herbaceous perennials. A maturing garden that is still being developed and extended. TEAS. *Adm £1 Chd free. Suns June 8, 22 (2-6) Oct 6 (2-5). Private visits of 4 and over welcome, please Tel 01254 853300*

¶**Newton Hall** &✗ (Mrs T R H Kimber) nr Carnforth. 12m N of Lancaster. 3m S of Kirby Lonsdale. Exit 35. Take B6254 to Kirby Lonsdale. 6m then through Arkholme, 2m to sign to Newton. Pass junction and cottage with round windows on L, street lamp on R. Entrance 150yds on L. Lodge at gate. Former shooting lodge 4 acres cultivated and 6 acres wild garden re-constructed, with yews from Thurland Castle. Rhododendrons and daffodils in spring, roses and herbaceous borders in summer. Superb views of Nene Valley and Ingleborough. TEAS. *Adm £1 Chd 50p. Sat, Sun July 5, 6 (2-5)*

Old Barn Cottage &✿ (Ray & Brenda Doldon) Greens Arms Rd, Turton. Midway between Bolton and Darwen on B6391 off A666, or through Chapeltown Village High St (B6391). 1-acre garden on moorland site. Spring flowering trees; shrubs; azaleas, rhododendrons; water gardens; heathers; conifers, herbaceous beds; moorland views. As seen on TV Garden Club 1993. TEAS in aid of St Ann's Church (May 25 and Aug 26), Beacon Counselling Service (May 26). *Adm £1 Chd free. Sun, Mon May 25, 26, Mon Aug 25 (12-5). Private visits welcome by appt (May to Aug), please Tel 01204 852139*

■ **The Ridges** &✿ (Mr & Mrs J M Barlow) Limbrick, nr Chorley. Approx 2m SE of Chorley. M61 from Manchester Chorley S junction 6 approx 6m, passing through Adlington taking Long Lane to Limbrick. Passing Black Horse follow rd to L and up hill on L. From Preston and N, junction 8 M61, take Cowling Rd out of Chorley towards Rivington approx 1½m on R. C17 house with 2¼-acre gardens. Incl old walled kitchen garden, cottage style garden with lawn, herbaceous borders, and area for growing annuals to dry. Fish pond with patio; laburnum arch leads to large formal lawn, surrounded by rhododendrons, and natural woodland. New ornamental centre pond and new 'quiet patio' as seen on Granada TV Border Patrol and Lancashire Life 1996. TEAS in aid of Chorley Stroke Club and the Diabetic Society. *Adm £1.50 Chd 50p. Suns, Mons May 25, 26, Aug 24, 25. For NGS Sun, Mon May 4, 5, Sun July 6 (11-5). Private visits for 5 & over welcome, please Tel 01257 279981*

▲**Rufford Old Hall** &✿ (The National Trust) Rufford. On A59 Liverpool to Preston rd in village of Rufford, 7m N of Ormskirk. Set in 14 acres of garden and woodland. Informal garden and walks. Spectacular in May and June for spring flowering rhododendrons and azaleas. TEAS. *Adm £1.70 Chd 85p (Garden only). For NGS Sun June 8 (12-4.30)*

▲**Speke Hall** &✗ (The National Trust) Liverpool. 8m SE of Liverpool adjacent to Liverpool Airport. Follow signs for Liverpool Airport. A formal garden with herbaceous border, rose garden; moated area with formal lawns. A stream garden now open this yr. A wild wood is included. Approx size of estate 35 acres. TEAS. *Adm £1.20 Chd 60p (Garden only). Sun June 8 (12-5). Parties of 20 or over welcome, please Tel 0151 4277231*

Swiss Cottage ✗✿ (James & Doreen Bowker) 8 Hammond Drive, Read. 3m SE of Whalley on A671 Whalley to Burnley Road, turn by Pollards Garage, up George Lane to T junction, L into Private Rd. 1½-acre hillside garden designed on 2 levels in mature woodland setting. Variety of shrubs, trees, rhododendrons, azaleas, perennials and alpines. Stream and bog garden feature. Featured in Lancashire Life. TEAS. *Adm £1.50 Chd free. Sun June 15 (1-5). Private visits welcome by appt, please Tel 01282 774853*

Weeping Ash &✗ (John Bent Esq) Glazebury. ¼m S A580 (East Lancs Rd Greyhound Motel roundabout, Leigh) on A574 Glazebury/Leigh Boundary. 2-acre garden of yr-round interest on heavy soil. A broad sweep of lawn with mixed borders of shrubs and herbaceous perennials gives way to secret areas with pools, roses and island beds, a rockery with alpines, a ruined Doric temple and elevated viewing points to enable one to see the garden, plus industrial Lancashire landscape. A hot area with mediterranean planting and a further extensive lawn. Newly planted bank 100yds long. Teas 100yds N at Garden Centre. *Adm £1.50 Chd free (Share to Macmillan Leigh Home Care Unit®). Suns March 31, July 13, Sept 14 (1-5)*

Windle Hall &✿ (The Lady Pilkington) N of E Lancs Rd, St Helens. 5m W of M6 via E Lancs Rd, nr Southport junction. Entrance by bridge over E Lancs Rd. 200yr-old walled garden surrounded by 5 acres of lawns, rock and water garden; thatched summer house. Tufa stone grotto; herbaceous borders, pergola and rose gardens containing exhibition blooms, miniature ornamental ponies, ducks; greenhouses. TEAS. *Adm £1 Chd 50p. Suns June 29, Sept 7 (2-5)*

¶**Woodside** ✗✿ (Barbara & Bill Seddon) Shevington. M6 Exit 26 or 27. Follow to Shevington. Princes Park is small side rd off Gathurst Lane almost opp Sheer Garage. ⅔-acre undulating garden with several levels. Developed by owners from dense woodland and featuring rhododendrons, azalea, camellia, magnolia, acer, eucryphia, hydrangea and specimen paeonies. Lancashire garden winner. TEAS. *Adm £1 Chd free. Suns June 1, Sept 7 (1.30-5). Private visits welcome, please Tel 01257 255255*

1927–1997

This year the National Gardens Scheme is celebrating its 70th Anniversary. Please help us celebrate by visiting a garden in 1997.

Leicestershire & Rutland

Hon County Organisers: (Leicestershire) Mr John Oakland, Old School Cottage, Oaks-in-Charnwood, nr Loughborough LE12 9YD Tel 01509 502676 or 01509 890376
(Rutland) Mrs Jennifer Wood, Townsend House, Morcott Road, Wing, LE15 8SE Tel 01572 737465

Assistant Hon County Organiser: (Rutland) Mrs Rose Dejardin, Wingwell, Top Street, Wing LE15 8SE Tel 01572 737727

Hon County Treasurer: (Rutland) Mr David Wood

DATES OF OPENING

March 23 Sunday
The Homestead, Normanton
April 1 Tuesday
Whatton House, Loughborough
April 5 Saturday
Long Close, Woodhouse Eaves
April 6 Sunday
Long Close, Woodhouse Eaves
April 10 Thursday
Burbage Gardens, Burbage
April 12 Saturday
Paddocks, Shelbrook,
Ashby-De-La-Zouch
April 13 Sunday
Gunthorpe, Oakham
Paddocks, Shelbrook,
Ashby-De-La-Zouch
April 27 Sunday
The Old Rectory, Teigh
May 4 Sunday
Burrough House, Burrough on the
Hill
May 5 Monday
Burrough House, Burrough on the
Hill
May 6 Tuesday
Whatton House, Loughborough
May 7 Wednesday
Arthingworth Manor, Market
Harborough
May 8 Thursday
Burbage Gardens, Burbage
May 11 Sunday
Burrough House, Burrough on the
Hill
The Homestead, Normanton
Market Overton Gardens ‡
Wakerley Manor, Uppingham ‡
May 14 Wednesday
Arthingworth Manor, Market
Harborough
May 17 Saturday
Holly Hayes, Birstall
May 18 Sunday
1 Cumberland Road,
Loughborough ‡
Holly Hayes, Birstall ‡
Owston Gardens, Oakham
18 Park Road, Birstall ‡
The White Lodge, Willesley,
Ashby-De-La-Zouch

May 19 Monday
18 Park Road, Birstall
May 21 Wednesday
Arthingworth Manor, Market
Harborough
May 25 Sunday
Burrough House, Burrough on the
Hill
Hambleton Gardens
Long Close, Woodhouse Eaves
May 26 Monday
Burrough House, Burrough on the
Hill
May 27 Tuesday
Whatton House, Loughborough
May 28 Wednesday
Arthingworth Manor, Market
Harborough
June 1 Sunday
The Dairy, Coleorton ‡
The Gables, Thringstone ‡
Orchards, Walton, nr Lutterworth ‡
Pine House, Gaddesby
Woodyton Farmhouse, Grace
Dieu, Coalville ‡
June 4 Wednesday
Arthingworth Manor, Market
Harborough ‡
Orchards, Walton, nr
Lutterworth ‡
Pine House, Gaddesby
June 7 Saturday
Paddocks, Shelbrook,
Ashby-De-La-Zouch
June 8 Sunday
Burbage Gardens, Burbage
Burrough House, Burrough on the
Hill
Paddocks, Shelbrook,
Ashby-De-La-Zouch
June 11 Wednesday
Arthingworth Manor, Market
Harborough
June 15 Sunday
Burrough on the Hill Gardens
Prebendal House, Empingham
June 18 Wednesday
Arthingworth Manor, Market
Harborough
June 21 Saturday
Sheepy Magna Gardens
June 22 Sunday
Arthingworth Manor, Market

Harborough
Hill House, Dunton Bassett
Preston Gardens, Uppingham
Queniborough Gardens
Sheepy Magna Gardens
June 25 Wednesday
Arthingworth Manor, Market
Harborough
June 29 Sunday
Beeby Manor, Beeby ‡
Brooksby Agricultural College, nr
Melton Mowbray ‡
Forge Cottage, Edith Weston ‡‡
Manton Gardens, Oakham ‡‡
Mill View, Shepshed ‡‡‡
Reservoir Cottage, Knipton
Sutton Bonington Hall, Sutton
Bonington ‡‡‡
July 1 Tuesday
Beeby Manor, Beeby
July 2 Wednesday
Arthingworth Manor, Market
Harborough
July 6 Sunday
Ridlington Gardens, Uppingham
July 8 Tuesday
Stoke Albany House, Market
Harborough
July 9 Wednesday
Arthingworth Manor, Market
Harborough
Stoke Albany House, Market
Harborough
July 13 Sunday
Ashwell Gardens, Oakham ‡
Burrough House, Burrough on
the Hill
South Luffenham Hall, nr
Stamford ‡
Stoke Albany House, Market
Harborough
July 15 Tuesday
Stoke Albany House, Market
Harborough
July 16 Wednesday
Arthingworth Manor, Market
Harborough
Stoke Albany House, Market
Harborough
July 19 Saturday
Fenny Drayton Gardens
Paddocks, Shelbrook,
Ashby-De-La-Zouch

July 20 Sunday
Fenny Drayton Gardens
Paddocks, Shelbrook,
  Ashby-De-La-Zouch
The Priory, Ketton
July 23 Wednesday
Arthingworth Manor, Market
  Harborough
July 27 Sunday
University of Leicester Botanic
  Garden, Oadby
The White Lodge, Willesley,
  Ashby-De-La-Zouch
July 30 Wednesday
Arthingworth Manor, Market
  Harborough
August 3 Sunday
The Dairy, Coleorton ‡
Woodyton Farmhouse, Grace
  Dieu, Coalville ‡
August 9 Saturday
Paddocks, Shelbrook,
  Ashby-De-La-Zouch

August 10 Sunday
Paddocks, Shelbrook,
  Ashby-De-La-Zouch
August 24 Sunday
Burrough House, Burrough on the
  Hill
August 25 Monday
Burrough House, Burrough on the
  Hill
August 30 Saturday
12 Church Lane, Fenny Drayton
  Gardens ‡
Little Froome, Fenny Drayton
  Gardens ‡
August 31 Sunday
12 Church Lane, Fenny Drayton
  Gardens ‡
Hill House, Market Overton
Little Froome, Fenny Drayton
  Gardens ‡
September 7 Sunday
Barnsdale Plants & Gardens,
  Exton

September 11 Thursday
Burbage Gardens
September 14 Sunday
Whatton House, Loughborough
October 5 Sunday
1700 Melton Road, Rearsby
Whatton House, Loughborough

Regular openings
For details see garden description

Brooksby College
Long Close, Woodhouse Eaves
1700 Melton Road, Rearsby
Orchards, Walton, nr Lutterworth

By appointment only
*For telephone numbers and other
details see garden descriptions.
Private visits welcomed*

Wartnaby, nr Melton Mowbray

DESCRIPTIONS OF GARDENS

Arthingworth Manor ❀ (Mr & Mrs W Guinness) 5m S of Market Harborough. From Market Harborough via A508 at 4m L to Arthingworth; from Northampton via A508. At Kelmarsh turn R at bottom of hill for Arthingworth. In village turn R at church 1st L. 6 to 7-acre beautiful garden; collection shrub roses; white garden; delphiniums, herbaceous and mixed borders; greenhouses. Newly planted 3-acre arboretum. Original house now restored. Art gallery, British Modern Pictures. TEAS only on Sunday. *Adm £1.75 Chd 50p. Weds May 7, 14, 21, 28, June 4, 11, 18, 25, July 2, 9, 16, 23, 30; Sun June 22 (2-5)*

Ashwell Gardens ❀ 3m N of Oakham, via B668 towards Cottesmore, turn L for Ashwell. TEAS at **Ashwell House**. *Combined adm £2 Chd 50p (Share to St Mary's Church®). Sun July 13 (2-6)*
  Ashwell House ❀❀ (Mr & Mrs S D Pettifer) 1½-acre vicarage garden, 1812; vegetable garden; almost original format partly given over to specialist flowers for drying. Pleasure garden with summer pavilion in classical style and architectural features by George Carter. TEAS. Plant stall and home-made produce
  The Old Hall (Mrs N L McRoberts) Medium-sized garden, mixed borders, good variety of shrubs, climbers and herbaceous plants. Good trees and view of church

Barnsdale Plants & Gardens ❀❀❀ (Nick Hamilton) The Avenue, Exton. Turn off Stamford/Oakham rd A606 at Barnsdale Lodge Hotel then 1m. 3½ acres of individual gardens laid out in the same style as the main television garden and inc the 2 gardens built and used in the Geoff Hamilton's Paradise Gardens Series. A good mix of different gardens so as to give visitors a wealth of ideas. The main TV garden will be open and will be charged as an added entry fee (Share to NGS). *Adm £1.50 Chd 25p (Share to Plant Life & Sustrans®). Sun Sept 7 (10-5)*

Beeby Manor ❀❀❀ (Mr & Mrs Philip Bland) Beeby. 8m E of Leicester. Turn off A47 in Thurnby and follow signs through Scraptoft. 3-acre mature garden with venerable yew hedges, walled herbaceous border, lily ponds, rose towers and box parterre. Plus the start of a 1-acre arboretum. C16 and C18 house (not open). TEAS. *Adm £1.80 Chd free (Share to Beeby Village Funds©). Sun June 29, Tues July 1 (2-6)*

■ **Brooksby College** ❀ 6m SW of Melton Mowbray. From A607 (9m from Leicester or 6m from Melton Mowbray) turn at Brooksby; entrance 100yds. Bus: Leicester-Melton Mowbray; alight Brooksby turn, 100yds. Grounds incl extensive lawns, lake, stream, specimen trees, shrub borders, herbaceous beds, rose garden, topiary, wildflower meadows, national plant collections, rock gardens, pergola, plant centre/nursery. Church built 1220. *Adm £1.50 Chd free. Every Sun July, Aug. For NGS Sun June 29 (1-5). Private visits welcome, please Tel 01664 434291*

Burbage Gardens ❀ From M69 junction 1, take B4109 signed Hinckley. TEAS (Thurs only). *Combined adm £1.50 Chd free (Share to Hinkley Hospital©). Thurs April 10, May 8 (2-5) Combined adm £2. Sun June 8 (11-5)*
  6 Denis Road ❀❀ (Mr & Mrs D A Dawkins) Sketchley Manor Estate. From M69 junction 1 take 1409 signposted Hinkley then 1st L after roundabout. Small garden with wide range of plants, many unusual, incl plants grown for scent, alpines in sinks. Species clematis, scree area, hellebores, spring bulbs. Featured in Amateur Gardening Magazine. *Also open Thur Sept 11 (2-5). Private visits welcome April to Sept 30 Tues afternoons, please Tel 01455 230509*
  7 Hall Road Burbage ❀ (Mr & Mrs D R Baker) Sketchley Manor Estate. From M69 roundabout take B4109 to Hinkley at 1st roundabout L then R to Sketchley Lane. 1st R; 1st R; 1st L; into Hall Rd. Medium-sized garden; mixed borders; alpines; sink gardens; scree area; collection of hellebores and hosta;

unusual plants; foliage plants. Partially suitable for wheelchairs. *Also open Thur Sept 11 (2-5). Private visits welcome, please* **Tel 01455 635616**

11 Primrose Drive ✿ (Mr & Mrs D Leach) Take 2nd turning on R into Sketchley Rd. 1st L into Azalea Drive, 1st R into Marigold Drive, 1st L Begonia Drive, 1st R into Primrose Drive. No 11 is on L on bend. Small cottage garden. Spring interest camellias, clematis and hellebores, summer interest paeonies, clematis and new English roses. *Also open Sept 11 (2-5). Private visits welcome April to July, please* **Tel 01455 250817**

The Long Close, Bullfurlong Lane ♿ (Mr & Mrs A J Hopewell) Burbage. 1st R onto Coventry Road 2nd R onto Bullfurlong Lane, garden on L. Limited parking, park if poss on Coventry Rd. ½-acre family garden. Mixed borders; 'natural' ponds; vegetable plot; greenhouse and cool orchid house. Organic vegetable plot. Cream TEAS, ploughman's lunches in aid of Childrens Society; toilets. **Open Sun June 8 only**

Burrough House ♿✿✿ (Mrs Barbara Keene) 6m W of Oakham, 5m S of Melton Mowbray. From A606 at Langham, take rd signposted to Cold Overton and Somerby, continue through Somerby to Burrough on the Hill. Approx 5 acres set in glorious countryside with special spring interest with tulips, azaleas, rhododendrons and unique wisteria wheel. A thatched timber bower house used by the Prince of Wales and Mrs Simpson; water pools, peony, delphinium and herbaceous borders. A white and rose garden offer summer attraction. Featured in The Times in 1995. TEAS & refreshments. *Adm £2 Chd free. Suns May 4, 11, 25, June 8, July 13, Aug 24, Mons May 5, 26, Aug 25 (1-6). Private visits welcome, please* **Tel 01664 454226**

Burrough on the Hill Gardens ✿ 6m W of Oakham, 5m S of Melton Mowbray. From A606 at Langham, take rd signposted to Cold Overton and Somerby, continue through Somerby to Burrough on the Hill. TEAS in village. *Combined adm £2 Chd free (Share to St Mary's Church, Burrough on the Hill®). Sun June 15 (1-6)*

Cheseldyne House (H & V J Blakebrough) Well established garden with pretty flower borders

¶**The Cottage** ✿ (Mrs H A Baylis) Attractive well garden, borders mixed shrubs

1 Gilson Greene ♿✿ (Mr & Mrs M Walton) Main Street. A small cottage garden incl vegetables, herbaceous area, annual borders and mixed shrubs

¶**Manor Farm House** ✿ (Chrystine Pettifer) Imaginatively laid out cottage garden. Lovely views

The Manor House ✿✿ (M A Chamberlain & G E Palmer) 1½-acres mainly lawns with informal mixed shrubs, trees, lawns, sunken pond, woodland walk, views

¶**Pasture Farm House** ✿ (J & S Knight) Kings Lane. Countrygarden with lovely views. Cottage garden area still under construction

The White House ✿ (Mr & Mrs D Cooper) Main Street. ¾-acre recently created garden. Many unusual plants; Japanese, wild and rock gardens; woodland walk and alpine house; views

1 Cumberland Road ♿✿ (Mr & Mrs R Peddle) Loughborough. On A512 into Loughborough, 1m E of M1 junction 23, 1st L turn 300yds after Ring rd roundabout. Parking in Cumberland Rd and adjacent streets. Plant enthusiast's small walled town garden, herbaceous borders, scree, climbers, pots. Planted for sun and shade. TEAS. *Adm £1 Chd free (Share to NCCPG®). Sun May 18 (1-5)*

The Dairy ♿✿✿ (Mr & Mrs J B Moseley) Coleorton. Moor Lane off A512 W of Peggs Green Roundabout. A garden of approx ⅓-acre with mature trees and shrubs, herbaceous borders containing some unusual plants, herb garden and pergola leading to other interesting areas. TEAS. *Adm £1 Chd 50p. Suns June 1, Aug 3 (2-6)*

Fenny Drayton Gardens Situated approx 3m N of Nun-eaton on the A444, crossing the A5 at The Royal Red Gate Inn and MSF Garage junction. Teas in St Michael's Church. *Combined adm £1.50 Chd free (Share to Mary Ann Evans Hospice Nuneaton®). Sat, Sun July 19, 20 (2-6)*

4 Drayton Lane ✿✿ (Mr & Mrs G Wright) ½ acre of lawn, with heather conifer beds, inlaid with bedding, plant areas, rockeries, pond and a wishing well

Little Froome ♿✿ (Mr & Mrs G J Cookes) Drayton Lane. 1½-acre garden, mature trees and wide variety of conifers. Landscaped with heathers at their best in Aug, Sept, large pond with bridge. TEA. *Also open Sat, Sun Aug 30, 31 (2-6)* with **12 Church Lane** *Combined adm £1 Chd free (Share to Parkinsons Disease Soc®)*

4 Rookery Close ✿✿ (Mr & Mrs J Dowse) Average sized garden with pond and waterfall. Abundance of hanging baskets and tubs. Very good selection of perennials and shrubs

Crofters ♿ (Mr & Mrs G M Heaton) 16 Rookery Close. Neat tidy garden front and rear, mostly lawns and flower beds. Open views of Leicestershire countryside at rear

19 Rookery Close ♿ (Mr & Mrs Ratcliffe) Small garden lots of colour

Gem Cottage ✿ (Alan & Jane Priest) 4 Church Lane. ⅓-acre cottage side and rear gardens. Trees, shrubs and plants with pool and fish. Chimney pots and cart filled to brim with colour

12 Church Lane ♿✿ (Mr & Mrs M Ambrose) ½-acre garden, ornamental walls and borders with rockeries, pond and waterfall. *Also open Sat, Sun, Aug 30, 31 (2-6)* with **Little Froome** *Combined adm £1 Chd free. Private visits welcome, please* **Tel 01827 713257**

Five Corners ♿✿ (Mr & Mrs Perrin) ¼-acre garden, mainly lawns with mixed shrubbery borders and evergreen hedges

Forge Cottage ♿✿✿ (Prof J Lindesay & Dr G Hall) Edith Weston. 5m E of Oakham off A6003. ¼-acre garden with an emphasis on drought-tolerant plants and vegetables. Collection of phlomis, euphorbia, cacti and succulents. Featured on Channel 4 Garden Club Sept 95. *Adm £1 Chd 50p. Sun June 29 (2-6)*

The Gables ♿✿✿ (Mr & Mrs P J Baker) Main St, Thringstone. Leave A512 Lougborough to Ashby de la Zouch rd turn at Bull's Head, signposted Thringstone. Main St is off the village green. ⅓-acre country garden. Herbaceous borders, many unusual plants, containers, clematis and old roses. Grade II listed cottage not open. TEAS. *Adm £1 Chd 25p. Sun June 1 (2-6)*

Gunthorpe ኔ (A T C Haywood Esq) 2m S of Oakham. On Uppingham Rd; entrance by 3 cottages, on R going S. Medium-sized garden; spring flowers and flowering trees in good setting. TEAS. *Adm £2 Chd 50p (Share to CRMF®). Sun April 13 (2-5.30)*

¶**Hambleton Gardens** ❀ 3m E of Oakham on A606 Oakham to Stamford rd. Turn R at signpost for Hambleton and Egleton. TEAS. *Combined adm £2 Chd free. Sun May 25 (10-5)*

¶**Orchard House** (Mr & Mrs J L Cookson) Lyndon Rd. In village, church on R, immed turn R, go to bottom of hill, house is last on R, before cattle grid. Small 4-sectioned, walled and hedged gardens, mainly herbaceous and bulbs, on the edge of Rutland Water. New terrace and further gardens at rear under development. 2 acres

¶**Stone Cottage** (Mr M Bonser) Ketton Rd. Opp Hambleton Hall. Approx 1-acre garden with interesting plants - shrubs, roses, herb garden and water features. Orchard underplanted with bulbs and shrubs. Views of Rutland Water

Hill House, Dunton Bassett ⊗❀ (Mr & Mrs M J Rowe) The Mount, Dunton Bassett, nr Lutterworth. S of Leicester via A426 (between Leicester and Lutterworth) follow signs for Dunton Bassett, then to Leire. Grade II listed former Georgian Farmhouse. Frame Knitters workshop open to public. Small ½-acre family garden planted for yr-round interest and colour; ponds, rockery, herbs, soft fruits, ferns and large mixed herbaceous beds. Owner maintained. TEAS in aid of Dunton Bassett PTA. *Adm £1.20 Chd free. Sun June 22 (2-5)*

Hill House, Market Overton ኔ❀ (Brian & Judith Taylor) Teigh Rd, Market Overton. 6m N of Oakham beyond Cottesmore, 5m from the A1 via Thistleton, 10m E from Melton Mowbray via Wymondham. ½-acre plant enthusiasts' garden consisting mainly of mixed beds designed for seasonal interest and comprising many unusual hardy and tender perennials; owner maintained. Featured on Channel 4 Garden Club Sept 95. TEAS. *Adm £1 Chd 25p. Sun Aug 31 (2-6)*

¶**Holly Hayes** ኔ❀ (Mrs Edith A Murphy) 216 Birstall Rd, Birstall. Take Birstall Rd from Redhill island. Near village hall. 4-acre garden with rhododendrons, azaleas, fine old trees incl redwoods, wisteria, pergola, flower borders and ponds. TEA. *Adm £1 Chd 20p Sat, Sun May 17, 18 (2-6)*

¶**The Homestead** ❀ (Mr & Mrs J E Palmer) Normanton. 10m W of Grantham on A52. In Bottesford turn N, signposted Normanton; last house on R before disused airfield. ¾-acre informal plant lover's garden. Vegetable garden, small orchard, woodland area, many hellebores and single paeonies. Collections of hostas and sempervivums. TEAS. *Adm £1 Chd free (Share to NCCPG®). Suns March 23, May 11 (2-6)*

Long Close ❀ (Mrs George Johnson) 60 Main St, Woodhouse Eaves, S of Loughborough nr M1 Junc 23. From A6, W in Quorn B591. 5 acres spring bulbs, rhododendrons (many varieties), azaleas, flowering shrubs, camellias, magnolias, many rare shrubs, trees, conifers, forest trees; lily ponds; terraced lawns, herbaceous borders,

wild flower meadow walk. TEAS and plant sale Sat, Sun April 5, 6 (2-5). Teas and plant fair (over 25 stalls) to celebrate 70th Anniversary of NGS Sun May 25 (11-5.30). *Adm £2 Chd 20p. Daily Mons-Sats March-June/July and autumn (9.30-1 & 2-5.30) Tickets Pené Craft Shop opp. Also private parties welcome March to June, please* **Tel 01509 890616** *business hrs*

Manton Gardens ⊗ Turn off A6003 halfway between Uppingham and Oakham to Manton village. TEAS at Manton Grange. *Combined adm £2 Chd 20p. Sun June 29 (2-6)*

The Barn House (Mr & Mrs R A Diment) Small irregular shaped plantsman's garden created from stable yard and started in 1986. Wide variety of plant associations set in gravelled area

Manton Grange ኔ❀ (Mr & Mrs M Taylor) Recently redesigned garden still undergoing improvements. Good mix of foliage, shrubs, rose garden with gazebo. New kitchen garden. Good trees and spectacular view

Market Overton Gardens ⊗ 6m N of Oakham beyond Cottesmore; 5m from the A1 via Thistleton; 10m E from Melton Mowbray via Wymondham. TEAS. *Combined adm £2 Chd 50p. Sun May 11 (2-6)*

Old Manor House ⊗ (Dr & Mrs Evans) Medium walled garden to inspire the botanical painter. Herbaceous borders, collection of old roses and Georgian house (not open)

31 Bowling Green Lane (Richard Hirst) Secluded cottage garden,approx ⅓-acre, varied plants, shrubs and bulbs

The Old Hall ኔ⊗ (Mr & Mrs T Hart) Newly designed S facing 3-acre garden, lovely views, flowing lawns on 2 levels; herbaceous borders, climbing roses; pond; unusual trees and bulbs

1700 Melton Road ኔ⊗❀ (Hazel Kaye) Rearsby, N of Leicester on A607. In Rearsby, on L.H. side from Leicester. 1-acre garden with wide range of interesting herbaceous plants; some shrubs and trees. Extensive new water garden. Nursery. *Adm £1 Chd 10p. Daily March to Oct (Tues to Sat 10-5, Sun 10-12). Also SPECIAL OPEN DAY Sun Oct 5 (2-5). TEAS Oct 5 only.* **Tel 01664 424578**

¶**Mill View** ኔ⊗❀ (Dr & Mrs P R Stableford) Tickow Lane, Shepshed. 2m W of Loughborough from junction 23 M1 on A512 for 1m take the 3rd on R; from M42 Ashby take A512 to Loughborough as entering Shepshed take first L. Victorian walled garden incl large herbaceous borders. Collection of penstemons, hosta and ferns, vegetable plot. Also a good spring garden full of bulbs etc. TEAS. *Adm £1.50 Chd free. Sun June 29 (2-5). Private visits welcome on Fris, please* **Tel 01509 503202**

The Old Rectory ኔ⊗❀ (Mr & Mrs D B Owen) Teigh. 5m N of Oakham. Between Wymondham and Ashwell; or from A1 via Thistleton and Market Overton. Medium-sized walled garden; mixed borders; good variety shrubs, herbaceous and climbing plants. Spring bulbs. Unusual C18 church next door. TEAS. *Adm £1 Chd under 12 free (Share to Teigh, PCC®). Sun April 27 (2-6)*

General Information. For general information on the use of this book see Page 17.

■ **Orchards** ✿✿ (Mr & Mrs G Cousins) Hall Lane, Walton, nr Lutterworth. 8M S of Leicester via the A50 take a R turn just after Shearsby (sign-posted Bruntingthorpe); thereafter follow signs for Walton. A garden of surprises. It is full of rare and unusual plants which are grown in colour-theme garden 'rooms'. Featured on TVs Garden Club. Views of countryside. TEAS. *Adm £1.50 Chd free. Open Suns June to Aug. For NGS Sun June 1, Wed June 4 (11-5). Also parties and private visits welcome June to Sept, please* Tel 01455 556958

Owston Gardens ✿✿ 6m W of Oakham via Knossington, 2m S of Somerby. From Leicester turn L 2m E of Tilton. TEAS. *Combined adm £1.50 Chd free. Sun May 18 (2-6)*

   The Homestead (Mr & Mrs David Penny) ⅓ acre with lawn, clematis, ponds, borders, containers, alpine garden, views and photographs. Plants and sundries stalls
   Rose Cottage (Mr & Mrs John Buchanan) Undulating 1¾ acres; shrub and flower borders; spring bulbs, roses, alpines, ponds, waterfall, fine views. *(Share to St Andrew's Church Owston©). Private visits welcome, please* Tel 01664 454545

Paddocks ✿✿✿ (Mrs Ailsa Jackson) Shelbrook. 1½m W of Ashby-de-la-Zouch on B5003 towards Moira. A plantaholic's garden with over 2000 varieties in 1 acre incl snowdrops, hellebores, astrantias and many less common herbaceous plants & shrubs. Plants propagated from garden for sale. NCCPG collection of old named double and single primulas. Silver medallist at Chelsea and Vincent Square. TEAS. *Adm £1 Chd free. Sats and Suns April 12, 13 June 7, 8, July 19, 20; Aug 9, 10 (2-5). Also private visits of 10 or more welcome, please* Tel 01530 412606

Park Farm, Normanton, see Nottinghamshire

18 Park Road ✿✿ (Dr & Mrs D R Ives) Birstall. Turn off A6 into Park Rd at crown of the hill on Leicester side of Birstall. Local buses stop at end of Park Rd. Approx 1-acre of lawn, trees, shrubs and other mixed planting incl bluebells with emphasis on foliage and scent. TEAS. *Adm £1.20 Chd 30p (Share to LOROS®). Sun, Mon May 18, 19 (2-5.30). Private visits welcome late April to mid June, please* Tel 0116 2675118

Pine House ✿✿ (Mr & Mrs T Milward) Rearsby Rd, Gaddesby. From A607 Leicester-Melton Mowbray, at Rearsby turn off for Gaddesby. 2-acre garden with fine mature trees, woodland walk and pond. Herb and potager garden with a vinery. Pleached lime trees, mixed borders and rockery and a pot garden. TEAS. *Adm £1.50 Chd 20p (Share to Gaddesby Church©). Sun, Wed June 1, 4 (2-5)*

Prebendal House ✿✿ (Mr & Mrs J Partridge) Empingham. Between Stamford & Oakham on A606. House built in 1688; summer palace for the Bishop of Lincoln. Recently improved old-fashioned gardens incl water garden, topiary and kitchen gardens. TEAS. *Adm £1.50 Chd 50p. Sun June 15 (2-6)*

Preston Gardens 2m N of Uppingham on A6003 between Uppingham & Oakham. Teas in Village Hall. *Combined adm £2 Chd free. Sun June 22 (2-6)*

   14 Main Street ✿ (Mr & Mrs J B Goldring) ¾-acre village garden; several small borders of differing aspect; tender wall shrubs; variety of climbers incl clematis, herbaceous plants, seasonal shrubs (particularly old roses) and bulbs
   Corner Cottage (Dr & Mrs T D Brentnall) Small cottage garden and newly planted herb garden
   The Dower House ✿✿ (Mrs M Norton-Fagge) Small garden; herbaceous, flowering shrubs and species roses
   Preston Hall ✿✿ (Capt & Mrs R M Micklethwait) Magnificent views on 3 sides and the garden is planned to frame and complement these. Formal rose garden, collection of shrub roses with many other shrubs and herbaceous plants
   ¶**The Granary** ✿ (Mr & Mrs A Morse) Delightful, peaceful ¾-acre garden intermixed with unusual and ordinary plants and bulbs. A small vegetable garden, swimming pool area surrounded with containers

The Priory ✿✿✿ (Mr & Mrs J Acton) Ketton. 3m W of Stamford. Take A6121 to Ketton, turn at Xrds in Ketton, down Church Rd, opp the churchyard. Newly created 2-acre garden; herbaceous border; water garden; alpines. Over 100 different roses. 2 courtyard gardens with mixed planting and cottage garden. TEA. *Adm £1.50 Chd 50p (Share to Stamford Citizens Advice Bureau®). Sun July 20 (2-6)*

Queniborough Gardens ✿✿ A607 N out of Leicester. 6m from Leicester. 9m from Melton Mowbray. *Combined adm £1 Chd 25p. Sun June 22 (11-5)*

   5 Barkby Road (Mr & Mrs A R B Wadd) Small cottage garden containing herbs, pond, herbaceous borders. Small orchard with greenhouse, collection of scented leaved pelargoniums
   21 Barkby Road (Mr & Mrs P Hemingray) Small, enclosed, organic, wildlife friendly garden. *Private visits welcome, please* Tel 0116 2605824
   40 The Ringway (Mr & Mrs W D Hall) Small garden with alpine scree, tufa bed, alpine house. Large pond and bog, herbaceous plants and greenhouse. *Private visits welcome, please* Tel 0116 2605908
   8 Syston Road (Mrs R A Smith) Plant enthusiasts cottage style garden; old and new English roses, small pond with frogs and newts; organic vegetable garden. TEAS. *Private visits welcome during July, please* Tel 0116 2605606

Reservoir Cottage ✿ (Lord & Lady John Manners) Knipton, 7m W of Grantham. W of A1; between A52 and A607; nr Belvoir Castle. Medium-sized country garden with lovely views over the lake. TEA. *Adm £1.50 Chd free. Sun June 29 (2-6)*

Ridlington Gardens ✿ 2½m N of Uppingham. Turn off A47 to Ayston from Uppingham roundabout. TEAS. *Combined adm £2 Chd free. Sun July 6 (2-6)*

   The Dower House (Mr & Mrs Peter Meakin) Holygate Road. ⅓-acre; good mix of plants and small trees
   ¶**The Old Rectory** ✿ (Mr & Mrs Sytnor) 1¼-acre garden with mature trees and formal lawns set behind yew hedges with framed apple arbour leading to kitchen garden and gravelled paths lined with clipped box hedging running down to the house and informal lawns

Ridlington House ❀ (Mr & Mrs Moubray) 1½-acres; roses; herbaceous border; flowering shrubs; vegetables; orchard

Stone Cottage ❀ (Mr & Mrs Gavin Simpson) ¾-acre informal cottage garden; wide views across Chater Valley

Sheepy Magna Gardens ও⌀ B4116 2½m N of Atherstone on Atherstone to Twycross Rd. Cream TEAS in aid of Sheepy Magna Church. *Combined adm £1.50 Chd free. Sat, Sun June 21, 22 (2-6)*

Gate Cottage ❀ (Mr & Mrs O P Hall) Church Lane. Opp church. Approx ½-acre cottage garden; mixed herbaceous borders; greenhouse; vegetable garden; several specimen trees; lawns, patio and pond

Vine Cottage ❀ (Mr & Mrs T Clark) 26 Main Rd. Opp shop. Approx ¾-acre cottage garden; mixed herbaceous borders with many unusual plants; alpine gardens; ponds; vegetable plot with greenhouse. Cream TEAS

South Luffenham Hall ⌀❀ (Dr & Mrs G Guy) South Luffenham on 6121 between Stamford and Uppingham. Turn off A47 at Morcott. 3-acre garden around 1630 house (not open), featured in 'The Perfect English Country House'. Shrubs, roses, herbaceous borders, lawns, pleached lime hedge and terrace with alpines and lilies. TEAS. *Adm £1.75 Chd 50p (Share to St Mary's Church, S Luffenham®). Sun July 13 (2-6)*

Stoke Albany House ও⌀❀ (Mr & Mrs A M Vinton) 4m E of Market Harborough via A427 to Corby; turn to Stoke Albany; R at the White Horse (B669); garden ½m on L. Large garden with fine trees; shrubs; herbaceous borders and grey garden. TEAS on Sun only. *Adm £2 Chd free. Sun July 13 (2-5.30); Tues, Weds July 8, 9, 15, 16 (2-5). Private parties welcome May to July Mons to Thurs only, please* **Tel 01858 535227**

Sutton Bonington Hall ও❀ (Anne, Lady Elton) Sutton Bonington, 5m NW of Loughborough; take A6 to Hathern; turn R (E) onto A6006; 1st L (N) for Sutton Bonington. Conservatory, formal white garden, variegated leaf borders. Queen Anne house (not open). Picnics. TEA. *Adm £1.50 Chd 50p (Share to St Michael's and St Ann's Church, Sutton Bonington®). Sun June 29 (12-5.30)*

University of Leicester Botanic Garden ও⌀❀ Stoughton Drive South, Oadby. SE outskirts of city opp race course. 16-acre garden incl grounds of Beaumont Hall, The Knoll, Southmeade and Hastings House. Wide variety of ornamental features and glasshouses laid out for educational purposes incl NCCPG collections of aubrieta, hardy fuchsia and skimmia. TEAS. *Adm £1.50 Chd free (Share to Rainbows Hospice®). Sun July 27 (1-4.30)*

Wakerley Manor ও❀ (A D A W Forbes Esq) 6m Uppingham. R off A47 Uppingham-Peterborough through Barrowden, or from A43 Stamford to Corby rd between Duddington and Bulwick. 4 acres lawns, shrubs, herbaceous; kitchen garden; 3 greenhouses. TEAS. *Adm £1.50 Chd free (Share to St Mary the Virgin Church, South Luffenham®). Sun May 11 (2-6)*

Wartnaby ও❀ (Lord & Lady King) Wartnaby. 4m NW of Melton Mowbray. From A606 turn W in Ab Kettley, from A46 at Six Hills Hotel turn E on A676. Medium-sized garden, shrubs, herbaceous borders, newly laid out rose garden with a good collection of old-fashioned roses and others; small arboretum. Formal vegetable garden. *Adm £2 Chd 20p (Share to Wartnaby Church©). Private parties welcome, please* **Tel 01664 822296 business hours**

■ **Whatton House** ও❀ (Lord Crawshaw) 4m NE of Loughborough on A6 between Hathern and Kegworth; 2½m SE of junc 24 on M1. 15 acres; shrub and herbaceous borders, lawns, rose and wild gardens, pools; arboretum. Nursery open. TEAS in Old Dining Room. Catering arrangements for pre-booked parties any day or evening. *Adm £2 OAP/Chd £1. Open Suns from Easter to end August. Also Bank Hol Mons. For NGS Tues April 1, May 6, 27 (2-6) Suns Sept 14, Oct 5 (2-6). Special plant sales Suns Sept 15, Oct 6. Also private visits welcome, please* **Tel 01509 842268**

¶**The White Lodge** ⌀❀ (Paul & Wendy Watson) Willesley. 1m SW of Ashby-de-la-Zouch. Leave A42 at junction 12 and take B5006 N towards Ashby. 100yds beyond Golf Club entrance turn sharp L signed Willesley. Garden ½m. ⅔-acre formal garden with island beds of shrubs, roses and herbaceous plants leading to walk through 3½ acres of woodland with glades, stream pools, island. Bog garden and views. TEAS. *Adm £1.50 Chd 50p (Share to Leicestershire Macmillan Cancer Service®). Suns May 18, July 27 (2-6)*

Woodyton Farmhouse ও⌀❀ (Mr & Mrs F A Slater) Grace Dieu, Coalville. On A512, 6m E of Ashby de la Zouch, 6m W of Loughborough, 3m W of M1 junction 23. ¼-acre garden, herbaceous borders, shrub roses, hydrangeas, scree and shade. TEA. *Adm £1 Chd free. Suns June 1, Aug 3 (2-6)*

Lincolnshire

Hon County Organiser: Mrs Patrick Dean, East Mere House, Lincoln LN4 2JB Tel 01522 791371
Assistant Hon County Organisers: Lady Bruce-Gardyne, The Old Rectory, Aswardby, Spilsby, Lincs PE23 4JS
Tel 01790 752652
Mrs Peter Sandberg, Croft House, Ulceby, N Lincs DN39 6SW Tel 01469 588330
Hon County Treasurer: Mrs Julian Gorst, Oxcombe Manor, Horncastle, Lincs LN9 6LU
Tel 01507 533227

DATES OF OPENING

February 15 Saturday
21 Chapel Street, Hacconby
February 16 Sunday
21 Chapel Street, Hacconby
February 22 Saturday
21 Chapel Street, Hacconby ‡
25 High Street, Rippingale ‡
Manor Farm, Keisby, Bourne ‡
February 23 Sunday
21 Chapel Street, Hacconby ‡
25 High Street, Rippingale ‡
Manor Farm, Keisby, Bourne ‡
March 30 Sunday
21 Chapel Street, Hacconby
April 10 Thursday
21 Chapel Street, Hacconby
April 13 Sunday
Croft House, Ulceby, nr Brigg
April 17 Thursday
The Old Rectory, East Keal
April 20 Sunday
Doddington Hall, nr Lincoln
Grimsthorpe Castle Gardens,
Bourne
Little Ponton Hall, Grantham
April 27 Sunday
Holton-le-Moor Hall,
Holton-le-Moor
Pinchbeck Hall, nr Spalding
May 1 Thursday
21 Chapel Street, Hacconby
May 3 Saturday
Belton House, Grantham
May 4 Sunday
The Old Rectory, Welton-le-Wold
May 15 Thursday
The Old Rectory, East Keal
June 1 Sunday
83 Halton Road, Spilsby
Harston Village Gardens
June 5 Thursday
21 Chapel Street, Hacconby

June 8 Sunday
Croft House, Ulceby, nr Brigg
Holly House, Boston ‡
Springtyme, Sibsey, Boston ‡
Toft House, Old Leake ‡
Westholme, Lincoln ‡‡
136 Yarborough Road,
Lincoln ‡‡
Ye Olde Three Tuns, Kirkby
Underwood
June 15 Sunday
The Old Rectory, East Keal
2 School House, Stixwould
June 19 Thursday
Grimsthorpe Castle Gardens,
Bourne
June 22 Sunday
Harrington Hall, Spilsby
Marston Hall, Grantham
Park Farm, Normanton - see Notts
Sutton St Edmund Village
Gardens
The Villa, South Somercotes,
Louth
June 28 Saturday
2 School House, Stixwould
June 29 Sunday
Auburn Hall, Auburn
Barnetby-le-Wold Village
Gardens ‡
Grange Cottage, Cadney, Brigg ‡
Gunby Hall, Burgh-le-Marsh
Houlton Lodge, Goxhill
Laburnum Cottage, Cadney ‡
The Old Vicarage, Holbeach
Hurn ‡‡
Old White House, Holbeach
Hurn ‡‡
2 School House, Stixwould
Willowcroft, Wilsthorpe
July 3 Thursday
21 Chapel Street, Hacconby
July 6 Sunday
Park Farm, Normanton - see Notts

July 13 Sunday
Pinefields, Bigby
July 19 Saturday
Belton House, Grantham
July 27 Sunday
Houlton Lodge, Goxhill
Park View, Holton-le-Moor
73 Saxilby Road, Sturton by Stow
August 7 Thursday
21 Chapel Street, Hacconby
August 17 Sunday
Luskentyre, Roman Bank,
Scaracens Head, nr Holbeach
September 4 Thursday
21 Chapel Street, Hacconby
September 6 Saturday
Belton House, Grantham
September 7 Sunday
Hall Farm, Harpswell
September 28 Sunday
Harlaxton Manor Gardens,
Grantham
October 12 Sunday
21 Chapel Street, Hacconby

1998
February 21, 22 Sat, Sun
21 Chapel Street, Hacconby

Regular opening
(see text for dates)
Harlaxton Manor Gardens, Grantham

By appointment only
*For telephone numbers and other
details see garden descriptions.
Private visits welcomed*

The Manor House, Bitchfield
Park House Farm, Walcott
Walnut Cottage, Careby

DESCRIPTIONS OF GARDENS

Auburn Hall &⚘❀ (Lady Nevile) Auburn. 7m SW of Lincoln. Signposted off A606 at Harmston. Approx 3 acres. Lawns, mature trees, shrubs, roses, mixed borders. C11 church adjoining. Wheelchairs in dry weather only. TEAS. *Adm £1.50 Chd 50p (Share to St. Peters Church Auburn - repairs®). Sun June 29 (2-5.30)*

¶Barnetby-le-Wold Village Gardens ❀ 4m Brigg. Off junction 5 of M180. Park at Church Hall on main rd through village. Refreshments. *Combined adm £1.50 Chd free. Sun June 29*
　　¶6 Belvoir House & (Archie & Audrey Eastcrabbe) ⅓-acre level garden. Shrubberies, flower, vegetable plots. Small pond, rose pergola - and space for grand-children! *(12-6)*

¶6 The Cottage (Mr & Mrs Rod Kicks) ½-acre garden created by owners. Informal mixed tree, shrub, perennial and wild flower borders. Climbing roses, wild life pond. Old orchard, medlar, peach. Vegetable garden. Environmentally friendly. Morning coffee. *(11-7)*

▲Belton House &✿ (The National Trust) 3m NE of Grantham on the A607 Grantham to Lincoln rd. Easily reached and signed from the A1 (Grantham N junction). 32 acres of garden incl formal Italian and Dutch gardens, and orangery by Sir Jeffrey Wyatville. TEAS. *Adm house & garden £4.80 Chd £2.40. For NGS Sats May 3, July 19, Sept 6 (11-5.30)*

21 Chapel Street ✿✿ (Cliff & Joan Curtis) A15 3m N of Bourne, turn E at Xrds into Hacconby. Cottage garden overflowing with plants for yr-round interest, special interest alpines, bulbs, herbaceous. Early opening for hellebores and snowdrop collection. Asters for late opening. Featured on TV. TEAS. *Adm £1 Chd free (Share to Marie Curie Memorial Foundation®). Sats, Suns Feb 15, 16, 22, 23 Sun March 30 (11-5) Thurs April 10, May 1, June 5, July 3, Aug 7, Sept 4 (2-6), Sun Oct 12 (11-5). Provisional 1998 Sat, Sun Feb 21, 22 (11-4). Private visits and parties welcome, please* Tel 01778 570314

Croft House &✿ (Mr & Mrs Peter Sandberg) Ulceby near Brigg. At War Memorial turn into Front Street and then into Pitmoor Lane. 2-acre garden set within a formal design filled with informal planting. Many old favourites alongside sought- after varieties. Mixed and herbaceous borders, bulbs, meadow, gravel bed, Victorian vinery. TEAS. *Adm £1.50 Chd free. Suns April 13, June 8 (2-5.30). Also by appt, please* Tel 01469 588330

▲Doddington Hall &✿ (Antony Jarvis Esq) 5m SW of Lincoln. From Lincoln via A46, turn W on to B1190 for Doddington. Superb walled gardens; thousands of spring bulbs; wild gardens; mature trees; Elizabethan mansion. Free car park. TEAS and snacks available. *Adm garden only £1.90 Chd 95p (Share to Lincolnshire Old Churches Trust© and St Peter's Church Doddington®). For NGS Sun April 20 (2-6)*

Grange Cottage ✿✿ (Mr & Mrs D Hoy) Cadney. 3m S of Brigg. In Brigg turn L into Elwes St; follow rd to Cadney. From Market Rasen to Brigg Rd, turn L in Howsham on to Cadney Rd. ⅓-acre cottage garden; many unusual and old-fashioned plants; old roses; pond; orchard; conservatory with interesting tender plants. *Adm £1 Chd free. Sun June 29 (2-5). Private visits also welcome May to July, please* Tel 01652 678771

▲Grimsthorpe Castle Gardens &✿ (Grimsthorpe and Drummond Castle Trust) 8m E of A1 on the A151 from the Colsterworth junction, 4m W of Bourne. 15 acres of formal and woodland gardens which incl bulbs and wild flowers. The formal gardens encompass fine topiary, roses, herbaceous borders and an unusual ornamental kitchen garden. TEAS. *Adm £3 OAP/Chd £2. Combined adm castle and garden £6 OAP/Chd £4 (Share to Grimsthorpe and Drummond Castle Trust®). For NGS Sun April 20, Thurs June 19 (11-6)*

▲Gunby Hall ✿ (Mr & Mrs J D Wrisdale; The National Trust) 2½m NW of Burgh-le-Marsh; S of A158. 7 acres of formal and walled gardens; old roses, herbaceous borders; herb garden; kitchen garden with fruit trees and vegetables. Tennyson's 'Haunt of Ancient Peace'. House built by Sir William Massingberd 1700. House unsuitable for wheelchairs. Plant centre, games. TEAS. *Adm House and gardens £3, gardens only £2 Chd £1. For NGS Sun June 29 (2-6) NT membership cards not valid*

Hall Farm &✿✿ (Pam & Mark Tatam) Harpswell. 7m E of Gainsborough on A631. 1½m W of Caenby Corner. ¾-acre garden with mixed borders of trees, shrubs, roses and unusual perennials. Over 100 - mainly old - varieties of rose. Sunken garden, pond, courtyard garden and recently constructed walled gravel garden. Short walk to old moat and woodland. Free seed collecting in garden Sept 7. TEAS. *Adm £1.50 Chd 50p. Sun Sept 7 (10-6). Garden open daily with collecting box (10-5); by appt in the evenings* Tel 0142 7668412

83 Halton Road ✿✿ (Jack & Joan Gunson) Spilsby. In Spilsby take B1195 towards Wainfleet; garden on L. Limited parking on Halton Rd, free car park Post Office Lane, Spilsby. ¼-acre town garden and hardy plant nursery, divided into a series of smaller gardens featuring densely planted mixed borders, incl many unusual plants and hardy geranium collection of approx 130 varieties. Spring bulbs a feature, many unusual. Featured in 'The Times' and 'Practical Gardening'. TEAS. *Adm £1 Chd free. Sun June 1 (2-6)*

■ Harlaxton Manor Gardens &✿ (University of Evansville) Grantham. 1m W of Grantham off A607 Melton Mowbray rd. Historically important 110-acre formal gardens and woodland currently undergoing major restoration. Fascinating stonework and steps. 6-acre walled gardens, extremely ornate walls; potager and theme gardens. Harlaxton Manor was built by Gregory Gregory and the house and garden built to rival anything in Europe. Alan Mason is spearheading the restoration project. Formal gardens built as a walk around European styles, Dutch canal, Italian gardens, French terracing, views. Walled garden. TEAS. *Adm £2.50 OAP £2 Chd £1.25. April 1 to Oct closed Mons except Bank Hol Mons. For NGS Sun Sept 28 (11-5)*

Harrington Hall ✿✿ (Mr & Mrs David Price) Spilsby. 6m NW of Spilsby. Turn off A158 (Lincoln-Skegness) at Hagworthingham, 2m from Harrington. Approx 5-acre Tudor & C18 walled gardens, incl recently designed kitchen garden; herbaceous borders, roses and other flowering shrubs. High terrace mentioned in Tennyson's 'Maud'. TEAS. *Adm £1.50 Chd under 14 free. Sun June 22 (2-5)*

Remember that every time you visit a National Gardens Scheme garden you are helping to raise money for the following:

The Queen's Nursing Institute
The Nurses' Welfare Service
Cancer Relief Macmillan Fund
The Gardens Fund of the National Trust
The Gardeners' Royal Benevolent Society
The Royal Gardeners' Orphan Fund

Harston Village Gardens ⚤❀ 6½m W of Grantham off A607. Turn R into Denton. Follow rd through village, fork L signposted to Harston. Cream TEAS in aid of Church. *Combined adm £1.50 Chd 50p. Sun June 1 (2-6)*

> **Bretton House** (Mr & Mrs J B Grice) 11yr old garden, built on hillside with superb view, approx ½-acre. Terraces, herbaceous borders, raised beds, fish pond, pergola etc, arranged in a semi-formal manner to compliment the Jacobean style house
>
> **Harston House** (Mr & Mrs R Gardiner) Mature peaceful hillside garden of 2½ acres with spectacular view, trees, shrubs, roses and herbaceous

25 High St, Rippingale ♿⚤❀ (Mr & Mrs R Beddington) On A15 5m N of Bourne. Turn E at Xrds into Rippingale. No 25, Westcombe is 5th house on R. ½-acre village garden. Borders, island beds, ponds and vegetable garden. Yr-round interest. Hellebores and snowdrops in spring. TEA. *Adm £1 Acc chd free. Sat, Suns Feb 22, 23 (11-4)*

Holly House ♿⚤❀ (Sally & David Grant) Fishtoft Drove, nr Frithville, Boston. Fishtoft Drove is an unclassified rd approx 3m N of Boston and 1m S of Frithville on the W side of the West Fen Drain. Approx 1-acre informal gardens with mixed borders, scree beds, old sinks with alpines and steps leading down to a large pond with cascade and stream. Softly curving beds are full of unusual and interesting herbaceous plants. *Adm £1 Chd free (Share to Pilgrim Heart and Lung Fund®). Sun June 8 (2-6)*

Holton-le-Moor Hall ♿⚤❀ (Mr & Mrs P H Gibbons) Holton-le-Moor. From A46 Market Rasen to Caistor rd, take B1434 (Brigg). In Holton-le-Moor turn E by Church. 2nd driveway on R. 2½ acres well-established garden with spring bulbs and flowering trees and shrubs. Large kitchen garden and orchard. TEAS in aid of St Luke's Church. *Adm £1.50 Chd free. Sun April 27 (2-5.30)*

Houlton Lodge ♿⚤❀ (Mr & Mrs M Dearden) Goxhill. 6m E of Barton-on-Humber. Follow signs to Goxhill, do not go into village centre but straight on over railway bridge and take 5th turning on R. Houlton Lodge is about 100yds from junction on LH-side. Park cars outside property. A well-established very neat garden approx ¾ acre. Shrub rose and mixed borders; large island bed and rockery and conifer bed. TEAS in aid of Goxhill Methodist Church. *Adm £1 Chd free. Suns June 29, July 27 (2-6). Private visits welcome, please Tel 01469 531355*

Laburnum Cottage ♿⚤ (Colin & Jessie Lynn) Cadney. 3m S of Brigg. In Brigg turn L into Elwes St, follow rd to Cadney. From Market Rasen to Brigg Rd turn L in Howsham on to Cadney Rd. 1-acre, herbaceous and mature shrub borders; island beds; smaller separate gardens within the garden; rose covered walk leading to shrub roses; small orchard; wildlife and formal pond. TEAS in aid of Cadney Church. *Adm £1 Chd free. Sun June 29 (2-5). Private parties of 10 and over welcome, please Tel 01652 678725*

Little Ponton Hall ♿❀ (Mr & Mrs Alastair McCorquodale) Grantham 3m. ½m E of A1 at S end of Grantham bypass. 3 to 4-acre garden. Spacious lawns with cedar tree over 200yrs old. Many varieties of old shrub roses; borders and young trees. Stream with spring garden; bulbs and river walk. Kitchen garden and listed dovecote. Adjacent to Little Ponton Hall is St Guthlacs Church which will be decorated and all visitors welcome. TEAS. *Adm £1.50 Chd under 12 free (Share to St Guthlacs Church, Little Ponton®). Sun April 20 (2-6)*

Luskentyre ⚤❀ (Mr & Mrs C Harris) 7m E of Spalding signed from A17 at Saracen's Head. Attractive small garden extensively planted with a wide range of interesting plants mainly chosen for their ability to withstand dry conditions and give yr-round interest. As seen in 'Inspirations'. *Adm £1 Chd free. Sun Aug 17 (1-5). Private visits welcome, please Tel 01406 423987*

Manor Farm ⚤❀ (Mr & Mrs C A Richardson) Keisby. 9m NW of Bourne, 10m E of Grantham, signed to Keisby from Lenton and Hawthorpe. ½-acre plantsman's garden. Snowdrop collection and hellebores. *Adm £1 Chd free (Share to Stamford and Bourne CRMF®). Sat, Sun Feb 22, 23 (11-4)*

The Manor House ⚤ (John Richardson Esq) Bitchfield; 6m SE of Grantham, close to Irnham and Rippingale. A52 out of Grantham to Spital Gate Hill roundabout; take B1176 to Bitchfield; house on R after public house. 1½ acres re-created in 1972; essentially a shrub rose garden (96 varieties) with shrubs and other perennials; 50 by 40ft pond planted spring 1985; small box hedged formal garden; ha-ha, new large garden room with fountain and over 100 plants. *Adm £2. Parties of 20 or more welcome by appointment June 1 to mid-July; no bookings accepted before May 1. Please Tel 01476 585261*

▲**Marston Hall** ♿❀ (The Rev Henry Thorold) 6m N of Grantham. Turn off A1, 4½m N of Grantham; on 1½m to Marston. Station: Grantham. Notable trees; wych elm and laburnum of exceptional size. House C16 continuously owned by the Thorold family. Interesting pictures and furniture. TEAS. *Adm house & garden £2.50 Chd £1 (Share to Marston Church®). For NGS Sun June 22 (2-6)*

The Old Rectory, East Keal ❀ (John & Ruth Ward) 2m SW of Spilsby on A16. Turn into Church Lane by PO. A rambling cottage garden with a variety of mixed borders, incl shrubs, roses, climbers, perennials and annuals. Ponds and rock garden. TEAS Sun only TEA Thurs. *Adm £1.20 Chd free. Sun June 15 (2-6), Thurs April 17, May 15, (2-5). Private visits welcome, please Tel 01790 752477*

The Old Rectory, Welton le Wold ❀ (Mrs M L Dickinson). 3m W of Louth in the valley between A157 Louth-Wragby rd on the S and A631 Louth-Market Rasen rd on the N. The Old Rectory is on the approach rd from A157 halfway down the hill. Situated in charming valley. Garden has been developed from an 1853 Victorian garden into the present 4 acres of woodland, mixed shrub and herbaceous borders and a water garden of 4 pools linked by a small stream. A half-walled vegetable garden, divided by a brick and timber pergola leads to a small arboretum. The adjoining park has mature trees and a young 2-acre wood with woodland walk. The nearby church is open to visitors and there are fine views. TEAS. *Adm £1.20 Chd 50p. Sun May 4 (2-5)*

The Old Vicarage ⚘⚘ (Mrs Liz Dixon-Spain) Holbeach Hurn. Turn off A17 N to Holbeach Hurn, past PO in the middle of village, turn R into Low Rd. Old Vicarage on R approx 400 yds. 2 acres of gardens incl mature trees, formal and informal areas, a croquet lawn surrounded by borders of shrubs, roses, herbaceous plants; also pond, bog garden and wild flowers; shrub roses in old paddock area. *Combined adm with* **Old White House** £1.50 Chd free (Share to Hovenden House Cheshire Home®). Sun June 29 (2-6)

Old White House ⚘⚘ (Mr & Mrs A Worth) Holbeach Hurn. Turn off A17 N to Holbeach Hurn, follow signs to village, go straight through, turn R after the Rose and Crown at Baileys Lane. 1½ acres of mature garden, featuring herbaceous borders, roses, patterned garden, and wild garden with small pond. TEAS. *Combined adm with* **The Old Vicarage** £1.50 Chd free (Share to Hovenden House, Cheshire Home®). Sun June 29 (2-6)

Park House Farm ⚘⚘⚘ (Mr & Mrs Geoffrey Grantham) Walcott. 16m S of Lincoln on B1189 between Billinghay and Metheringham. Traditional farm buildings adapted to make a series of garden rooms; half-hardy climbers, gravel. Winter and white garden. Featured in 'Living' magazine 1995 by Margot Bishop and Channel 4 with Roy Lancaster. *Adm £1.50 Chd free. Parties welcome by appt, May to July, please* **Tel 01526 860409**

¶**Park View** ⚘⚘⚘ (David & Margaret Jackson) Holton-le-Moor. 6m N of Market Rasen Turn L off A46 onto B1436 to Holton-le-Moor village. A new 2-acre garden started approx 5 yrs ago. Mixed shrubs, trees and herbaceous borders. TEAS. *Adm £1. Sun 27 July (1.30-5.30)*

Pinchbeck Hall ⚘⚘ (Mr & Mrs George Adams) Situated in centre of Pinchbeck on A16. Next door to Bull public house. 2m from Spalding. Informal country garden with some fine old-trees. Areas of bulbs in spring. Approx 6 acres. TEA. *Adm £1 Chd 50p. Sun April 27 (2-5)*

Pinefields ⚘⚘ (Reg & Madeleine Hill) Bigby. Off A1084 between Caistor 5m and Brigg 4m. At top of Smithy Lane - junction with Main St. 4th house from Church. ¾-acre plantsperson's garden. Shrubs and herbaceous borders containing some unusual plants. Roses and clematis on pergolas and trellis. Gravelled alpine area. An established wildlife pond with arches to an area of wild flowers. Featured on TV Nov '95. TEAS in aid of Bigby Village Hall Fund. *Adm £1.20 Chd free. Sun July 13 (1.30-6). Private parties welcome by appt* **Tel 01652 628327**

¶**73 Saxilby Road** ⚘⚘⚘ (Charles & Tricia Elliott) Sturton by Stow. 9m N of Lincoln on B1241. Saxilby to Lea Rd. House on RH side entering village. ⅓-acre garden and hardy plant nursery, extensively cultivated, interesting for its maximum use of available space. Ponds, gravelled areas. Beds and borders contain a broad mix of herbaceous and evergreen plants, several unusual designed to give interest and colour throughout the year. TEAS. *Adm £1 Chd free. Sun July 27 (2-6)*

2 School House ⚘⚘ (Andrew & Sheila Sankey) Stixwould. 1½m N of Woodhall Spa. ¼-acre garden, redesigned in Oct 1994 and in process of being developed to

incl front garden with unusual perennials and shrubs, herb garden, vegetable garden. Owners are garden designers. TEAS. *Adm £1 Chd free (Share to Sick Children's Trust®). Suns June 15, 29, Sat June 28 (2-6). Private visits welcome May to Sept, please* **Tel 01526 352453**

Springtyme ⚘⚘⚘ (Mr & Mrs J W Lynn) Station Rd, Sibsey. 5m N of Boston. From A16 at Sibsey turn R onto B1184, towards Old Leake, garden on R in 400yds. Approx ¼-acre informal garden with alpine house, scree beds, alpine troughs, densely planted mixed borders and pond. TEA. *Adm £1 Chd free. Sun June 8 (2-6)*

¶**Sutton St Edmund Village Gardens** ⚘⚘ Peterborough 18m - Spalding 16m - Wisbech 8m. TEAS. *Combined adm £1.50 Chd 50p (Share to Cystic Fibrosis Research Trust®). Sun June 22 (12-6)*

¶**Farmers Rest** (Mr & Mrs H Beaton) In Sutton St Edmund, if facing S turn L then L again onto Gavnock Gate, house ¼m on L, well signposted. Lovely cottage garden, flowers, vegetables, mature trees, ginko, mulberry and tulip trees. Also a life's collection of Farming Bygones will be on view

¶**Holly Tree Farm** ⚘ (Mr & Mrs C Pate) In Sutton St Edmund if facing S take R turn in village onto Church gate. Next L onto Hallgate, farm 1st house on R. 1-acre family garden, on working 4-acre on working 4-acre holding with mixed stock. Free range poultry; island beds of perennials and shrubs, vegetables, fruit, scree in cottage garden style. developed over the last 8yrs

¶**Inley Drove Farm** ⚘ (Dr & Mrs Francis Pryor) N of Sutton St Edmund, 2m straight on when rd swings R, 2nd turning on R into Inley Drove. Garden 5 acres and wood 7½ acres still under construction. Double mixed borders, dry garden, herbs, natural pond, nut walk, roses, orchard and shrubs, all on land which was arable farmland until 1992

Toft House ⚘⚘⚘ (Mr & Mrs Grant) Old Leake. 7m from Boston on A52 to Skegness, garden situated 1½m N of Church in Fold Hill. Also 4m from Sibsey on B1184. Approx 2-acre garden has evolved over 40 yrs. It has large informal beds with many unusual trees, shrubs and plants enhanced by a bowling green lawn. A formal potager is being established with rose arches and box hedging. TEAS. *Adm £1 Chd free. Sun June 8 (2-6)*

The Villa ⚘ (Michael & Judy Harry) South Somercotes. 8m E of Louth. Leave Louth by Eastfield Rd. Follow signs to S Cockerington. Take rd signposted to N & S Somercotes. House on L 100yds before church. ¼-acre densely planted in cottage style; large collection of herbs, old-fashioned and unusual perennials; orchard with interesting old varieties of fruit trees. Livestock incl flock of Lincoln Longwool Sheep. TEAS. *Adm £1 Chd free. Sun June 22 (2-6). Private visits welcome, April to end September, please* **Tel 01507 358487**

1927–1997

This year the National Gardens Scheme is celebrating its 70th Anniversary. Please help us celebrate by visiting a garden in 1997.

Walnut Cottage &❀ (Roy & Sue Grundy) Careby. 6m N of Stamford on B1176. 5m E of A1 at Stretton. Situated approx ⅓m at end of Main St on L. ½-acre developing garden with interesting herbaceous borders. Herb garden, small shade and gravel areas, water garden with S facing slope leading to small woodland feature with natural pond. Featured on Channel 4 'Garden Club'. TEA. *Adm £1 Chd free. Private visits welcome by appt only Tues and Sat, May to Sept, please* Tel 01780 410660

Westholme ❀❀ (Ian Warden & Stewart Mackenzie) 10 Yarborough Rd, Lincoln. From bypass take A57 to City. At first major t-lights continue straight ahead. After 50yds continue ahead, uphill at t-lights, house 100yds from t-lights after L-hand bend. Free car park in Hampton St 300 yds past house on L. Tiny town garden planted to reflect owners' interest in unusual herbaceous perennials and shrubs. Ponds with natural plantings. Collection of hostas; plants in containers. Unusual plants for sale. TEAS. *Combined adm with* **136 Yarborough Road** *£1.50 Chd 50p. Sun June 8 (11-6). Private visits welcome by parties of less than 10, please* Tel 01522 568401

¶**Willowcroft** ❀❀ (Mr & Mrs P Holden) Wilsthorpe. 8m E of Stamford. Signposted off A15. Between Market Deeping and Bourne. Approx ¼-acre extensively planted mixed beds and borders with many unusual plants, incl variety of roses, hostas, scented plants, gravel area, ponds and tubs. *Adm £1 Chd 50p. Sun June 29 (11-5)*

136 Yarborough Road ❀ (Mr & Mrs Colin Merry) Lincoln, 400yds uphill from Westholme. Family garden approx ⅕ acre on sloping site with wide views across West Common. Alpines, herbs, cordon fruit trees and vegetable. Bearded iris, clematis, herbaceous and mixed shrub borders. TEAS in aid of Lincoln and District Children in Need Fund. *Combined adm with* **Westholme** *£1.50 Chd 50p. Sun June 8 (11-6)*

¶**Ye Olde Three Tuns** &❀❀ (Ivan & Sadie Hall) Kirkby Underwood. A15 6m N of Bourne turn W at Xrds into Kirkby Underwood. House in centre of village. Approx ¼-acre cottage style garden developed over last 8yrs by present owners. Divided into Victorian, container and courtyard gardens. Japanese Koi carp pond, alpine trough walk, mixed borders with many unusual trees, shrubs and herbaceous plants, hostas, pulmonaries, grasses and hardy geraniums. Featured in Garden News, Lincolnshire Life and TV. TEAS. *Adm £1 Chd free. Sun June 8 (2-6)*

London (Greater London Area)

Hon County Organiser: Mrs Maurice Snell, Moleshill House, Fairmile, Cobham, Surrey KT11 1BG Tel 01932 864532

Assistant Hon County Organisers: Mrs Stuart Pollard, 17 St Alban's Rd, Kingston-upon-Thames, Surrey Tel 0181 546 6657
Mrs Joan Wall, Orchard Cottage, 3 Woodlands Road, Bickley, Kent Tel 0181 467 4190
Mrs V West, 11 Woodlands Rd, Barnes, SW13 0JZ Tel 0181 876 7030
Miss Alanna Wilson, 38 Ornan Road, London NW3 4QB Tel 0171 794 4071

DATES OF OPENING

February 23 Sunday
Myddleton House Gardens, Enfield
March 15 Saturday
The Elms, Kingston-on-Thames
March 16 Sunday
The Elms, Kingston-on-Thames
April 6 Sunday
Chelsea Physic Garden, SW3
April 13 Sunday
29 Deodar Road, SW15
29 Gilston Road, SW10
Ham House, Richmond
April 19 Saturday
The Elms, Kingston-on-Thames
April 20 Sunday
10 Chiltern Road, Pinner
The Elms, Kingston-on-Thames
16 Eyot Gardens, W6

7 The Grove, N6
21a The Little Boltons, SW10
St Mary's Convent & Nursing Home, W4
Well Cottage, NW3
7 Woodstock Road, W4
April 26 Saturday
Lambeth Palace, SE1
Trinity Hospice, SW4
April 27 Sunday
Eccleston Square, SW1
9 Eland Road, SW11
16 Hillcrest Road, E18
Trinity Hospice, SW4
7 Upper Phillimore Gardens, W8
47 Winn Road, SE12
May 4 Sunday
51 Gloucester Road, Kew
1 Hocroft Avenue, NW2
5 St Regis Close, N10

The Watergardens, Kingston-on-Thames
May 5 Monday
1 Hocroft Avenue, NW2
11 Hocroft Road, NW2
26 Nassau Road, Barnes
May 7 Wednesday
Frogmore Gardens, Windsor
May 8 Thursday
Frogmore Gardens, Windsor
May 10 Saturday
The Elms, Kingston-on-Thames
May 11 Sunday
5 Burbage Road, SE24
Chiswick Mall, W4
The Elms, Kingston-on-Thames
11 Hampstead Way, NW11
37 Heath Drive, NW3
Malvern Terrace, N1
2 Millfield Place, N6

43 Penerley Road, SE6
Southwood Lodge, N6

May 17 Saturday
Highwood Ash, NW7

May 18 Sunday
39 Boundary Road, NW8
Chumleigh Multicultural Garden,
    SE5
2 Cottesmore Gardens, W8
133 Crystal Palace Road, SE22
5 Greenaway Gardens, NW3
Hall Grange, Croydon
117 Hamilton Terrace, NW8
Highwood Ash, NW7
43 Ormeley Road, SW12
131 Upland Road, SE22

May 21 Wednesday
12 Lansdowne Road, W11

May 25 Sunday
5 Garden Close, off Portsmouth
    Road, SW15
109 Halsbury Road East, Northolt
Myddleton House Gardens, Enfield

May 31 Saturday
Roots & Shoots, SE11

June 1 Sunday
51 Cholmeley Crescent, N6
49 & 51 Etchingham Park Road,
    N3
64 Kings Road, Richmond
22 Loudoun Road, NW8
Museum of Garden History,
    Tradescant Trust SE1
15 Norcott Road, N16
Roots & Shoots, SE11

June 7 Saturday
Lambeth Community Care
    Centre, SE11
Flat 1, 1F Oval Road, NW1
Trinity Hospice, SW4

June 8 Sunday
Barnes Gardens, SW13
37 Creighton Avenue, N10
Eccleston Square, SW1
55 Falkland Road, NW5 ‡
Hyde Vale Gardens, Greenwich
Islington Gardens Group I, N1
Lambeth Community Care
    Centre, SE11
Little Lodge, Thames Ditton
9 Montpelier Grove, NW5 ‡
52 Mount Park Road, Ealing
2 Northbourne Road, SW4
Regents College, NW1
7 St George's Road, Twickenham
Southwood Lodge, N6
Trinity Hospice, SW4

June 11 Wednesday
Little Lodge, Thames Ditton

June 14 Saturday
Flat 1, 1F Oval Road, NW1
Regents College, NW1

June 15 Sunday
Albion Square Gardens, E8

The Anchorage, West Wickham
43 Brodrick Road, SW17
15a Buckland Crescent, NW3 ‡
5 Burbage Road, SE24
5 Cecil Road, N10
43 Dene Road, Northwood
Fenton House, NW3 ‡
The Ferry House, Old Isleworth
7 The Grove, N6
133 Haverstock Hill, NW3
Highgate Village, N6
10 Lawn Road, NW3
1 Lower Merton Rise, NW3
2 Mansfield Place, NW3 ‡
17a Navarino Road, E8
Osterley Park House, Isleworth
71 Palace Road, SW2
78 Palace Road, SW2
43 Penerley Road, SE6
13 Queen Elizabeth's Walk, N16
19 St Gabriel's Road, NW2
103 Thurleigh Road, SW12
Trumpeters' House & Lodge
    Garden, Richmond
66 Wallingford Avenue, W10
Wimbledon Gardens, SW19
35 Wincanton Road, SW18

June 18 Wednesday
5 Greenaway Gardens, NW3
13 Mercers Road, N1
103 Thurleigh Road, SW12

June 19 Thursday
13 Mercers Road, N1
Southwood Lodge, N6

June 21 Saturday
Frankfort House, Clapham
    Common

June 22 Sunday
133 Crystal Palace Road, SE22
9 Dalebury Road, SW17
De Beauvoir Gardens, N1
36 Downs Hill, Beckenham
Elm Tree Cottage, South Croydon
66 Floriston Avenue, Hillingdon
Frankfort House, Clapham
    Common
5 Garden Close, off Portsmouth
    Road, SW15
70 Gloucester Crescent, NW1
5 Hillcrest Avenue, NW11
125 Honor Oak Park, SE23
Islington Gardens Group II, N1
38 Killieser Avenue, SW2
Leyborne Park Gardens, Kew
Ormeley Lodge, Richmond
The Pagoda, Blackheath
48 Rommany Road, SE27
7 St George's Road, Twickenham
12a Selwood Place, SW7
40 Station Road, Hampton
3 Wellgarth Road, NW11
47 Winn Road, SE12

June 28 Saturday
St Michael's Convent, Ham

June 29 Sunday
33 Balmuir Gardens, SW15
22 Cambridge Road, Teddington
10 Charlotte Square, Richmond
105 Dulwich Village, SE21
235 Eastcote Road, Ruislip
20 Eatonville Road, SW17
Goldsborough, Blackheath
20 Lessingham Avenue, SW17
21a The Little Boltons, SW10
239 Norwood Road, SE24
39 Oxford Road, SW15
2a Penn Road, N7 ‡
9 Ranelagh Avenue, SW6
5 St Regis Close, N10
3 Somerton Avenue, Richmond
13 Trecastle Way, N7 ‡
66 Woodbourne Avenue, SW16

July 3 Thursday
101 Cheyne Walk, SW10

July 5 Saturday
10 Wildwood Road, NW11

July 6 Sunday
10 Chiltern Road, Pinner
3 Radnor Gardens, Twickenham
15 Upper Grotto Road,
    Twickenham

July 9 Wednesday
Osborne House, Long Ditton

July 12 Saturday
15 Lawrence Street, SW3

July 13 Sunday
37 Heath Drive, NW3
The Horticultural Therapy
    Demonstration Garden, SW11
15 Lawrence Street, SW3
15 Norcott Road, N16
Osborne House, Long Ditton
35 Perrymead Street, SW6
3 Radnor Gardens, Twickenham
11 Ranulf Road, NW2
Trumpeters' House & Lodge
    Garden, Richmond
15 Upper Grotto Road,
    Twickenham

July 17 Thursday
2 Millfield Place, N6

July 19 Saturday
27 Wood Vale, N10

July 20 Sunday
5 Greenaway Gardens, NW3
48 Rommany Road, SE27
27 Wood Vale, N10
23 Woodville Road, W5

July 26 Saturday
Trinity Hospice, SW4

July 27 Sunday
29 Addison Avenue, W11
29 Deodar Road, SW15
Myddleton House Gardens,
    Enfield
10A The Pavement, Chapel Road,
    SE27
57 St Quintin Avenue, W10

5 St Regis Close, N10
Trinity Hospice, SW4
August 2 Saturday
239a Hook Road, Chessington
August 3 Sunday
7 Byng Road, High Barnet
235 Eastcote Road, Ruislip
117 Hamilton Terrace, NW8
239a Hook Road, Chessington
4 Macaulay Road, SW4
Orchard Cottage, Bickley
57 St Quintin Avenue, W10
August 10 Sunday
10 Chiltern Road, Pinner
73 Forest Drive East, E11
Hornbeams, Stanmore
1 Lister Road, E11
239 Norwood Road, SE24
August 13 Wednesday
Osborne House, Long Ditton
August 17 Sunday
17a Navarino Road, E8
47 Winn Road, SE12

August 24 Sunday
2 Cottesmore Gardens, W8
70 Gloucester Crescent, NW1
September 6 Saturday
Trinity Hospice, SW4
September 7 Sunday
Trinity Hospice, SW4
September 14 Sunday
5 Garden Close, off Portsmouth
Road SW15
September 21 Sunday
26 Thompson Road, SE22
October 19 Sunday
The Watergardens,
Kingston-on-Thames
October 26 Sunday
Chelsea Physic Garden, SW3
February 24 1998
Myddleton House Gardens, Enfield

Regular Openings
Chelsea Physic Garden, SW3

Myddleton House Gardens, Enfield

Special Evening Openings

June 11 Wednesday
Little Lodge, Thames Ditton
June 18 Wednesday
5 Greenaway Gardens, NW3
13 Mercers Road, N1
103 Thurleigh Road, SW12
June 19 Thursday
13 Mercers Road, N1
Southwood Lodge, N6
July 3 Thursday
101 Cheyne Walk, SW10
July 17 Thursday
2 Millfield Place, N6
August 13 Wednesday
Osborne House, Long Ditton

DESCRIPTIONS OF GARDENS

29 Addison Avenue, W11 ⚘ (Mr & Mrs D B Nicholson) No entry for cars from Holland Park Avenue; approach via Norland Square and Queensdale Rd. Station: Holland Park. Bus 94. Small garden packed with interesting plants, winner of many prizes and photographed over the last 10yrs for several gardening magazines. Featured in the Good Garden Guide 1997. Lots of unusual wall shrubs, variegated plants and colourful perennials. Phlox paniculata (over 40 varieties) a special favourite. *Adm £1 Chd 50p (Share to the Museum of Garden History®). Sun July 27 (2-6)*

The Anchorage West Wickham. *Sun June 15 (2-5.30).* See Kent

Albion Square Gardens, E8 ⚘❀ 2m N of Liverpool St Station (BR & tube). 1m S of Dalston/Kingsland Station (BR). Buses 22, 67, 149, 243. By car approach from Queensbridge Rd northbound turning L into Albion Drive leading to Albion Square. TEAS. *Combined adm £3 for 4 or £1 each Chd £1 for 4 or 50p each. Sun June 15 (2-5.30)*
    12 Albion Square (Ann Black & David Richardson) Victorian gothic church provides backdrop to this 70′ × 60′ L-shaped garden. Brick paved herb garden leads to lawns and a terrace. Ornamental trees, shrubs and flowers. Planting is 5 yrs old and is just beginning to take shape. *(Share to The Peter Walker Trust®)*
    24 Albion Square (Mr David French) 80′ town garden designed to unfold as a series of views and focal points divided by a yew hedge. Emphasis on foliage plants rather than flowers. Secluded seating areas, fountain and through shared summer house to No 25. *(Share to St Joseph's Hospice, Hackney®)*
    25 Albion Square (Sandy Maclennan) 80′ informal walled garden on two levels with pond beside camomile patch and features ornamental shrubs and

trees creating interest in foliage, form and colour. *(Share to The Peter Walker Trust®)*
252 Haggerston Road (Heather Wilson). 60′ long, mid-terrace shady town garden. Informal, densely planted design with emphasis on unusual perennials and shrubs, incl peat bed, herbs, ferns, dry shade area, herbaceous border, soft fruit and (friendly) bee-hive. TEAS. *(Share to St Joseph's Hospice, Hackney®)*

33 Balmuir Gardens, SW15 ⚘❀ (Mrs Gay Wilson) Putney. 5 mins walk from Putney SR Station. Off the Upper Richmond Rd on corner with Howards Lane. Bus 37, 74, 14. A designer's garden on a corner plot that is continually evolving. Secluded tiny mixed borders backed by stained beams. Pots, and a formal pond with a waterfall through moose antlers. A passionate plantswoman who tries out different colour combinations before using them on clients. All crammed into 80′ × 38′ at widest only 16′ at narrowest. *Adm £2 Chd 50p (Share to Greenmead School for Severe Disability®). Sun June 29 (2-7)*

Barnes Gardens Barnes, SW13 ⚘ TEAS at 25 Castelnau. *Adm £4 for 4 gardens or £1.50 each garden, OAP £3 for 4 gardens or £1 each garden, Chd free. Sun June 8 (2-6)*
    25 Castelnau ⚘ (Dr & Mrs P W Adams) Castelnau is on the main route from Hammersmith Bridge. The garden is approx 120′ × 40′ designed in 1978 by Malcolm Hillier and the late Colin Hilton, well known for their books on flowers and garden design. The garden was planned for ease of maintenance and family living. There is a good variety of herbaceous plants, some attractive roses and a compact working vegetable area and screened swimming pool. Cream TEAS
    26 Nassau Road ⚘❀ (Mr & Mrs Anthony Hallett) 26 Nassau Road lies midway between the Thames and Barnes Pond and is approached via Lonsdale Rd or Church Rd in Barnes. Long, slim, terraced garden with tallest wisteria in Barnes. Weigela, philadelphus, pittosporum, chaemomeles, ceanothus with borders of

hebe, cistus, rose, delphiniums, potentilla and spiraea. Plants for sale. *Adm £1.50 OAP £1. Also open on Mon May 5 (2-6). Private visits welcome, please* **Tel 0181 748 5940**

8 Queen's Ride ♿ (His Honour Judge White & Mrs White) Train: Barnes Station, turn R down Rocks Lane, then L along Queen's Ride. Bus, 22 terminus at Putney Hospital; 3 minutes walk W along Queen's Ride. House is at the junction of Queen's Ride and St Mary's Grove. ⅔-acre garden facing Barnes Common. Croquet lawn with herbaceous and mixed borders and a small history of the rose garden. TEA

12 Westmoreland Road ✿❀ (Mr & Mrs Norman Moore) From Hammersmith take Bus 9, 33, or 72 to the Red Lion. Briefly retrace steps along Castelnau turn L into Ferry Rd then L at Xrds. Small garden with raised stone terrace planted with choisya, convolvulus, euonymus, honeysuckle and decorative herbs, leading to lower lawn. Borders densely planted with wide variety of flowering shrubs and pretty pool with fountain. Gravel garden with lilies, agapanthus, diascia and lady's mantle. *(Share to St Mary's Churchyard®)*

39 Boundary Road, NW8 ✿❀ (Hermoine Berton) Between Swiss Cottage and St John's Wood tube. Buses 13, 113, 82, 46, 139. Enjoy the surprises of a wild-life garden as seen on Gardeners World 1992. 'Inside Britain' 1993, London TV The Real Gardening Show 1995 and the Sunday Express Magazine 1996. *Adm £1.50 Chd 50p (Share to London Lighthouse Aids Centre®). Sun May 18 (2-6). Private visits welcome April - Sept. Please* **Tel 0171 624 3177**

43 Brodrick Road, SW17 ✿ (Helen Yemm) Wandsworth Common. Approx 1m S of Wandsworth Bridge, off Trinity Rd. A long (110′), tranquil garden of a typical Victorian terrace house, surrounded by mature trees. Its length is broken by a bank of shrubs and a pond, overhung by an ancient rose-clad apple tree. Small gravel garden, herbaceous planting for semi-shade, clematis, roses - distinctly un-urban. Featured in Sainsbury's Magazine and Sunday Times. *Adm £1.50 Chd 50p (Share to Alzheimers Disease Soc®). Sun June 15 (2-6)*

15a Buckland Crescent, NW3 ♿✿❀ (Lady Barbirolli) Swiss Cottage Tube. Bus: 46, 13 (6 mins) or Hampstead Hoppa (request stop nearby). ⅓-acre; interesting collection of shrubs and trees in well-designed garden featured in Country Life Nov 88, also in books 'Private Gardens of London' by Arabella Lennox Boyd and 'Town Gardens' by Caroline Boisset. *Adm £1.25 Chd over 12 50p (Share to RUKBA®). Sun June 15 (2.30-6.30). Private visits welcome for parties of 25 and over, please* **Tel 0171 586 2464**

5 Burbage Road, SE24 ✿❀ (Crawford & Rosemary Lindsay) Nr junction with Half Moon Lane. BR Station Herne Hill, 5 mins walk. Buses 2, 3, 37, 40, 68, 196. Garden of member of The Society of Botanical Artists. 150′ × 40′ with large and varied range of plants. Herb garden, herbaceous borders for sun and shade, climbing plants, pots, terraces, lawns. Subject of article in 'The Garden' (RHS Journal) in April 1997. TEAS. *Adm £1.50 Chd free. Suns May 11, June 15 (2-5).* **Tel 0171 274 5610**

7 Byng Road ♿✿❀ (Rhian & Julian Bishop) High Barnet. A newly-created organic garden dominated by 3 large borders: a white garden with mainly perennials and roses; a 'cool' border of pinks, blues and mauves; and a vibrant 'hot' border incl giant dahlias, sunflowers, rudbeckias and other unusual plants. Also a woodland area, fountains, many pots and a collection of unusual foxgloves. TEA. *Adm £1 Chd 25p (Share to Edgware Hospital Special Care Baby Unit®). Sun Aug 3 (12-5)*

22 Cambridge Road ♿✿ (Sheila & Roger Storr) Teddington. S turning off Teddington High St. Buses 281, 285. A family garden of approx ⅙-acre. Designed to give the long garden a feeling of width. Many unusual shrubs and herbaceous perennials. A tree house has been built around an old pear tree incl a drawbridge and flying fox. The water feature allows children to paddle in it. At the end of the garden is a large vegetable and soft fruit plot. TEA. *Adm £1 Chd 50p. Sun June 29 (2-6)*

Capel Manor Farm and Gardens See Hertfordshire

5 Cecil Road, N10 ✿ (Ben Loftus Esq) Just off Alexander Park Rd between Muswell Hill and the North Circular Rd. 70′ × 20′ garden designer's peaceful garden; old apple trees, roses, euphorbias, masses of lilies, paeonies, hellebores, ferns, bulbs and evergreens; many scented plants, rich and varied foliage; unusual plants in containers. *Adm 80p Chd free. Sun June 15 (2-5)*

¶10 Charlotte Square ✿❀ (Claire McCormack & James Cowan) Richmond. 371 Bus from Richmond Station. Slug resistant garden organically cultivated and full of herbaceous plants, fragrant climbers and shrubs (no bedding or lawns). Front 28′ × 15′, secluded rear 28′ × 18′. Tiny pool, hedgehogs, frogs, birds' nests. TEA. *Adm £1 Chd free. Sun June 29 (2-6). Private visits welcome in May and June please* **Tel 0181 255 8868**

■ Chelsea Physic Garden, SW3 ♿✿❀ (Trustees of the Garden) 66 Royal Hospital Rd, Chelsea. Bus 239 (Mon-Sat). Station: Sloane Square (10 mins). Cars: restricted parking nr garden weekdays; free Sundays, or in Battersea Park weekdays. Entrance in Swan Walk (except wheelchairs). Second oldest Botanic Garden in UK; 3.8 acres; medicinal and herb garden, incl an ethnobotanical 'Garden of World Medicine' perfumery border; family order beds; historical walk, glasshouses and over 6,000 trees, shrubs and herbaceous plants, many rare or unusual. TEAS. *Adm £3.50 Students/Chd £1.80. Suns April 6 to Oct 26 (2-6); Weds April 9 to Oct 22 (2-5); Winter Festival Suns Feb 2, 9 (11-3) also in Chelsea Flower Show week Mon-Fri May 19-23 and in Chelsea Festival Week Mon-Fri June 2-6 (12-5). For NGS Suns April 6, Oct 26 (2-6)*

101 Cheyne Walk, SW10 ⚘❀ (Malcolm Hillier Esq) Situated to the W of Battersea Bridge. Long and narrow strongly layered with a structure of evergreen hedges and topiaries. A colonnaded Mediterranean terrace with many containers leads to a winding path set about with old roses and perennials. A romantic arbour surrounded and covered by perfumed plants surveys the whole length of the garden. *Adm £3.50 incl wine and refreshments. Thurs July 3 (6-8). Private visits welcome for parties of 5 and over, please* **Tel 0171 352 9031**

10 Chiltern Road ⚘❀ (Mrs G & Mr D Cresswell) Eastcote, Pinner. Off Cheney St and Barnhill/Francis Rd which link Cuckoo Hill/Eastcote High Rd (B466) with Bridle Rd/Eastcote Rd. Please park in Francis Rd. Plantswoman's garden ⅓-acre, mature trees, mixed shrubs and herbaceous plantings. Plants for sale propagated from the garden. TEAS. *Adm £1.50 Chd free. Suns April 20, July 6, Aug 10 (2-5)*

Chiswick Mall, W4 Station: Stamford Brook (District Line). Bus: 290 to Young's Corner from Hammersmith. By car A4 Westbound turn off at Eyot Gdns S, then R into Chiswick Mall. *Sun May 11 (2-6.30)*

   16 Eyot Gardens ⚘ (Dianne Farris) Small town garden at end of Victorian terrace. Front garden white, yellow and blue flowers; back has raised beds and small terrace. TEAS. *Adm £1.20 Chd free. Also open Sun April 20 (2-6)*

   Walpole House ⚘❀ (Mr & Mrs Jeremy Benson) Plantsman's garden; specie and tree peonies; water garden; spring flowers. Features in 'The Englishman's Garden'. Mid C16 to early C18 house, once home of Barbara Villiers, Duchess of Cleveland. Seeds and some plants for sale. *Adm £1.50 OAP/Chd 50p (Share to St Mary's Convent and Nursing Home®)*

51 Cholmeley Crescent, N6 ⚘❀ (Ernst & Janet Sondheimer) Highgate. Between Highgate Hill and Archway Rd, off Cholmeley Park. Nearest tube Highgate. Approx ⅙-acre garden with many alpines in screes, peat beds, tufa, troughs and greenhouse; shrubs, rhododendrons, camellias, magnolias, pieris, ceanothus etc. Clematis, bog plants, roses, primulas, treeferns. Alpines for sale. TEA. *Adm £1 Chd 50p. Sun June 1 (2-6). Private visits welcome, please* **Tel 0181 340 6607**

¶Chumleigh Multicultural Garden ♿⚘ (Southwark Council) Situated midway along Albany Rd which runs between Old Kent Rd and Camberwell Rd. Nearest tube Elephant & Castle; buses P3, 42. Constructed around almshouses (erected in 1821 by the Friendly Female Soc) now a Parks Visitor Centre. Walled garden, nearly 1 acre divided into English, Oriental, African and Carribean, Islamic and Mediterranean styles. Many unusual plants incl tree fern, jelly palm, rice paper plant. Formal and informal water features. TEAS. *Adm £1 (Share to Bede House®). Sun May 18 (2-6)*

2 Cottesmore Gardens, W8 ⚘ (The Marchioness of Bute) From Kensington Rd turn into Victoria Rd. Cottesmore Gardens on R. A wide range of trees, shrubs and plants concentrating on foliage shapes, fragrance and unusual plant material; many spring bulbs. TEA. *Adm £2 Chd £1 (Share to Winter Garden Trust). Suns May 18, Aug 24 (2-5)*

37 Creighton Avenue, N10 ⚘❀ (Tim Elkins & Margaret Weaver) Buses 43, 134, 243 from Highgate tube to Muswell Hill Broadway-Fortis Green Rd, along Tetherdown, turn R into Creighton Ave at mini-roundabout. Mature S facing rear garden 120′ × 30′. 2 alpine beds, well stocked mixed borders, evergreen shrubs, ornamental trees and patio with pots. TEAS. *Adm £1 Chd 50p (Share to CHICS Children with Cancer Support Group®). Sun June 8 (2-5)*

133 Crystal Palace Road, SE22 ⚘❀ (Sue Hillwood-Harris & David Hardy) East Dulwich. Buses 176, 185, 12. Featured by Gay Search and in magazines in Europe and Japan. A newly-built pergola has subtly changed the character of this inspirational 17′ × 36′ Victorian garden created around a weathered brick terrace (once the garden wall). Roses, wisteria, clematis, shrubs, herbs and shade-loving plants combine in formality tempered by wilful indiscipline. TEAS. *Adm £1 Chd 50p (Share to Amnesty®). Suns May 18, June 22 (2-6). Private visits welcome, please* **Tel 0181 693 3710**

¶9 Dalebury Road, SW17 ♿⚘ (Gina Glover & Geof Rayner) 8-10 mins from Tooting Bec Tube or Wandsworth Common BR. An unusual square-ish walled garden (approx 13m sq) with some intriguing detail in the hard, architectural landscaping, good trees and evergreens, where the bold leaf shaped and strong colour schemes are clearly influenced by the creative eye of professional photographer Gina - recently struck down with a passion for gardening. Euphorbias, acanthus and angelica all add to the drama. An enlarged herbaceous mixed border is the latest development. TEA. *Adm £1 Chd 50p (Share to Photofusion Educational Trust®). Sun June 22 (2-6)*

De Beauvoir Gardens, N1 Islington-Hackney border. *Combined adm £2 Chd 50p. Sun June 22 (2-6)*

   51 Lawford Road ⚘ (Mrs Carol Lee) Lawford Rd (formerly called Culford Rd) is a cul-de-sac with entrance for cars from Downham Rd. Parking fairly restricted. Downham Rd runs between Kingsland and Southgate Rd. Buses Kingsland Rd 149, 243, 22A/B and 67, Southgate Rd 141. A small garden 16′ × 45′ at rear of a typical Victorian terraced house. Bricked with different levels, lots of pots and a pond with waterfalls. Hostas, ferns and fuchsias greatly favoured. TEAS. *(Share to National Deaf Children's Soc®)*

   26 Northchurch Road ⚘ (Mrs Kathy Lynam) Angel tube then Buses 38, 73, 56, 30, 171A down Essex Rd, alight bus stop after Essex Rd Station just before Northchurch Rd. Cross over and proceed down Northchurch Rd (petrol stn on corner) to lower end near church. House on L. By car from Angel down Essex Rd. R into Halliford St past lights at Southgate Rd. Turn L 1st rd Upton Rd, then R at bottom, house on L. Walled back garden, approx 70′ × 30′ with 2 old apple trees, greenhouse and lawn, mixed borders with clematis, roses and lots of perennials. Places to sit and ponder. TEA. *Private visits welcome, please* **Tel 0171 254 8993**

43 Dene Road ⚘❀ (Mr & Mrs M Hillman) Northwood. 10 min walk from Northwood Station (Met line). Turn L into Green Lane 2nd R Dene Rd. Car park, RNIB Sunshine House next door. Access also from Rickmansworth Rd. ⅓-acre S facing garden yr-round interest, large lawn surrounded by wide borders; island beds filled with shrubs and perennials with a backdrop of colourful trees. Terrace with many containers. TEAS. *Adm £1 Chd free (Share to RNIB Sunshine House®). Sun June 15 (2-6)*

29 Deodar Road, SW15 ⚘❀ (Peter & Marigold Assinder) Putney. Off Putney Bridge Rd Bus: 14, 22, 37, 74, 80, 85, 93, 220. Tubes: Putney Bridge and East Putney. Small garden 130ft × 25ft running down to Thames with lovely view. Camellias, wide range of variegated shrubs, hardy geraniums and hydrangeas. TEA. *Adm £1 Chd 50p (Share to All Saints Church Putney Restoration Appeal®). Suns April 13, July 27 (2-5). Cuttings and visits at other times by arrangement* Tel 0181 788 7976.

¶**36 Downs Hill** ⚘❀ (Janet & Marc Berlin) Beckenham. 2 mins from Ravensbourne Station near top of Foxgrove Rd. Long 2/3-acre E facing garden sloping steeply away from the house. Ponds and waterfalls with patio garden. Wooded area. Dense planting. Varied collection of trees, shrubs and flowers. TEAS. *Adm £1 Chd free (Share to NSPCC®). Sun June 22 (2.30-5)*

¶**105 Dulwich Village**, SE21 ⚘❀ (Andrew & Ann Rutherford) BR trains to North Dulwich and West Dulwich and then 10-15 mins walk. P4 bus passes the house. About ¼-acre, mostly herbaceous with lawns and lots of old-fashioned roses. Ornamental pond. A very pretty garden with many unusual plants. *Adm £2 Chd free. Sun June 29 (2-5)*

235 Eastcote Road ⚘❀ (T & J Hall) Ruislip. From Ruislip High Street take the B466 (Eastcote Road) nearest tube Ruislip Manor. Parking off Eastcote Rd in Evelyn Ave please. Medium sized suburban garden. 115ft × 80ft. Contains a wide variety of herbaceous perennials and shrubs, shady patio area and pond. Home-made TEAS. *Adm £1 Chd free. Suns June 29, Aug 3 (2-6)*

20 Eatonville Road, SW17 ❀ (Pamela Johnson & Gethyn Davies) Tooting. 400yds from Tooting Bec tube (Northern Line). Bus stop Trinity Rd nr Police Station. Nos. 249, 219, 349 or 155 and 355 on Balham High Rd at tube station. Garden designer's own 42′ × 23′ S facing garden. Interesting plant combinations and an imaginative use of containers shows just how much can fit into a small space. Tiny front garden. Excellent plant sale and delicious home-made cakes. TEAS. *Adm £1 Chd 50p. Sun June 29 (2-6)*

Eccleston Square, SW1 ⚘❀ (Garden Manager Roger Phillips) Central London; just off Belgrave Rd near Victoria Station, parking allowed on Suns. 3-acre square was planned by Cubitt in 1828. The present Garden Committee have worked intensively over the last 16 years to see what can be created despite the inner city problems of drought, dust, fumes, shade and developers. Within the formal structure the garden is sub-divided into mini-gardens incl camellia, iris, rose, fern, and container garden. A national collection of ceanothus incl more than 50 species and cultivars is held in the square. TEAS. *Adm £1.50 Chd 75p. Suns April 27, June 8 (2-5)*

9 Eland Road, SW11 ⚘ (Nancye Nosworthy) Battersea. Off Lavender Hill backing onto Battersea Arts Centre. 345,

77 and 77a bus stop at top of st. Clapham Junction Station and buses 19, 49, 319, 239, 249, 295, 137a nearby. 50′ courtyard on slopes of Lavender Hill designed by Christopher Masson. Terraces with unusual shrubs; a pergola covered in vitis coignetiae and pink and white jasmine. Pool with fountain. *Adm £1 Chd free. Sun April 27 (2-5)*

Elm Tree Cottage ⚘ (Wendy Witherick & Michael Wilkinson) 85 Croham Rd, S Croydon, off B275 from Croydon, off A2022 from Selsdon 64 Bus Route. A gently sloping plantsperson's garden with fine views of Croham Hurst and Valley. Cottage garden full of rare and unusual roses, perennials, climbers and shrubs. Pond and bog garden in pots. Unsuitable for those unsteady on their feet and pushchairs. *Adm £2 Chd free. Sun June 22 (10-5). Private visits welcome, please* Tel 0181 681 8622

The Elms ⚘❀ (Prof & Mrs R Rawlings) Kingston-on-Thames entry via Manorgate Rd. Im E Kingston on A308. Buses to Kingston Hospital: LT 213, 85, 57, K3, K5, K6, K8, K10, 718: BR Norbiton Station 100yds. Enter via garages in Manorgate Rd which is off A308 at foot of Kingston Hill. Wheelchairs limited to the tea area. 55′ × 25′ garden owned by 'plantaholic!' Trees, shrubs, climbers, herbaceous and ground cover plants, some rare and unusual. Pool with geyser; fruit trees and soft fruits. In Good Garden Guide. Seed and plants. TEAS. *Adm £1 Chd 50p (Share to Princess Alice Hospice/Home Form Trust®). Sats, Suns March 15, 16 April 19, 20; May 10, 11 (2-5). Private groups welcome, please* Tel 0181 546 7624

49 & 51 Etchingham Park Rd, N3 ♿⚘❀ (Robert Double, Gilbert Cook and Diane & Alan Langleben) Finchley. Off Ballards Lane overlooking Victoria Park. Station: Finchley Central. 2 rear gardens. ⅝-acre; lawn, small orchard, shrubs, large selection of hostas. Sculpture by Wm Mitchell, new ornamental vegetable garden as seen on TV. Exhibition and sale of water colour paintings by Robert Double. TEAS. Live music. *Adm £1 Chd free. Sun June 1 (2-6)*

¶**55 Falkland Road**, NW5 ⚘❀ (Carol Bateman) Kentish Town tube station and buses C2, 135, 134, 214 5 mins. By car approach from Lady Margaret Rd or Montpelier Grove. Small walled garden 40′ × 20′ plus raised shade bed. A cottage-style garden crammed with plants. *Adm £1 Chd 50p. Sun June 8 (2-5.30)*

▲**Fenton House**, NW3 ⚘ (The National Trust) 300yds from Hampstead Underground. Entrances: top of Holly Hill and Hampstead Grove. 1½-acre walled garden in its first decade of development. It is on three levels with compartments concealed by yew hedges and containing different plantings, some still in the experimental stage. The herbaceous borders are being planned to give yr-round interest while the recently brick paved sunken rose garden is already donning the patina of age. The formal lawn area contrasts agreeably with the rustic charm of the orchard and kitchen garden. *Adm £1.50 Chd 50p. For NGS Sun June 15 (11-6)*

¶**The Ferry House** ♿❀ Old Isleworth (Lady Caroline Gilmour) Bus 37 from Richmond and Hounslow, Bus 267 from Hammersmith to Bush Corner. Train to Syon Lane

Station. By car follow signs to Syon Park. Parking available inside Syon Gate on L. 3 acres of mature gardens. Terrace with urns and troughs filled with unusual plants. Borders with old-fashioned roses, climbers, paeonies and shrubs. Lawn leads down to Thames wall. Adjacent garden bordering Syon Park with old trees, groups of unusual shrubs and herbaceous borders. Vegetable and fruit cage. Shaded areas for sitting and observing wildlife etc. TEAS. *Adm £2.50 OAPs £1.50 Chd 50p. Sun June 15 (2-6)*

66 Floriston Avenue ✂❀ (Jean Goodall) Hillingdon. From A40 at Master Brewer Motel into Long Lane (to Hillingdon) 2nd L by church (Ryefield Ave), L after shops. Pedestrian entrance to garden by lane rear of shops. Plantswoman's long narrow garden (90′ × 17′) with many design features, Auricular theatre, species iris and alliums, herbs, colour themed borders. TEAS. *Adm £1 Chd 50p. Sun June 22 (2-5). Private visits welcome, please* **Tel 01895 251036**

Frogmore Gardens, Windsor. *Wed, Thurs May 7, 8 (10.30-7).* See Berkshire

73 Forest Drive East, E11 ✂❀ (A J Wyllie) Leytonstone. Into Whipps Cross Rd, then SW into James Lane. 1st L into Clare Rd, 1st R into Forest Drive East. By bus to Whipps Cross Hospital or tube to Leytonstone and bus to James Lane. 20′ × 65′ country garden in miniature, but with full-sized plants, behind a terraced house. Small lawn with mixed borders leading to a shrub and woodland area. 2 fountains and various unusual plants. Also 20′ front garden informally planted round formal paths and centrepiece. TEA. *Adm £1 Chd 50p (Share to The Margaret Centre, Whipps Cross Hospital®). Sun Aug 10 (11-5)*

¶Frankfort House ✂❀ (Mr & Mrs Richard Roxburgh) Clapham Common. 100yds off The Avenue. South Circular Rd across grass. 10mins walk from Clapham South tube station, 20 mins walk from Clapham Junction. Close to junction with Wynsham Grove. One of the largest gardens remaining on Clapham Common. Partly walled 245′ × 90′. Neglected condition when bought by present owners in 1993. Redesigned to make the most of existing mature trees incl fine cedar. Peaceful shady oasis in a busy area. Laurels, shrubs, pergola walks and large lawn. Lots of climbers, old roses, etc. Large terrace with formal box-edged beds and trellis surround new 'English' roses. Plenty of seating. TEAS. *Adm £1.50 Chd free (Share to Trinity Hospice®). Sat, Sun June 21, 22 (2-6)*

¶5 Garden Close ♿✂ (Vivien & Tom Jestico) off Portsmouth Rd, SW15 7-10 mins walk from the Green Man Public House, Putney Hill. ¼-acre walled garden which serves as a backdrop to architect's all glass house. Oriental inspiration with black bamboos, and swathes of box, hebe, lavender and rhododendrons. Ponds and timber decks surround the house. *Adm £1.50. Suns May 25, June 22, Sept 14 (11-5)*

¶29 Gilston Road, SW10 ✂ (James & Margaret Macnair) Gilston Rd is a short street leading N from Fulham Rd to the Boltons. Medium sized garden (34′ × 75′) with large plane tree at far end. Many spring flowering bulbs and shrubs. *Adm £1.50 Sun April 13 (2-6)*

70 Gloucester Crescent, NW1 ✂ (Lucy Gent & Malcolm Turner) Nr junction Gloucester Crescent and Oval Rd 600yds SW of Camden Town Tube Station. A square in front; plants growing into shingle. A triangle at the side; a wedge at the back - from Mediterranean to woodland. Strong geometry on the ground plays off against extensive plant interest. *Adm £1.50 Chd 50p. Suns June 22, Aug 24 (11-3). Private visits welcome, please* **Tel 0171 485 6906**

51 Gloucester Road ❀ (Mrs Lindsay Smith) Kew. 10 mins walk from Kew Gardens Tube Station. Travel towards S Circular along Leybourne Park Rd, cross main rd, down Forest Rd 1st L into Gloucester Rd. House ½-way down on R. A small square cottage garden. Many interesting plants and shrubs. Wallflowers and bulbs in spring. TEA. *Adm £1.50 Chd 75p. Sun May 4 (2-6)*

Goldsborough, SE3 ♿✂ 112 Westcombe Park Rd, Blackheath. Nearest BR Westcombe Park (10 mins walk) or Maze Hill (15 mins walk). Buses to the Standard from Central London and surrounding areas. Car parking available. Community garden for close care and nursing home residents. Approx ½ acre of landscaped gardens, incl walkways of rose-covered pergolas; fish ponds; herbaceous borders and colourful annuals. A very sheltered and peaceful garden. TEAS available. *Adm £1 Chd 50p. Sun June 29 (2-5)*

5 Greenaway Gardens, NW3 ✂ (Mrs Marcus) Tube (½ mile) Hampstead or Finchley Road Stations. Buses: Finchley Road, West End Lane stop, nos. 13, 82, 113, off Frognal Lane. Large and varied garden on three levels with yr-round interest. Terrace with climbing plants; water feature and swimming pool; large lawn surrounded by herbaceous borders, wide variety of trees and shrubs, decorative urns and furniture. Partially suitable for wheelchairs. TEAS July 20 only. *Adm £1 Chd free. Suns May 18, July 20 (2-6). Special evening opening Wed June 18 (6-8.30) £2.50 incl canapes and wine*

7 The Grove, N6 ♿✂ (Thomas Lyttelton Esq) The Grove is between Highgate West Hill & Hampstead Lane. Stations: Archway or Highgate (Northern Line, Barnet trains) Bus: 210, 271 to Highgate Village. ½-acre designed for maximum all-yr interest with minimum upkeep. Water garden restructured in Autumn 1996. TEAS on June 15 only at No. 5. *Adm £1.50 per garden or £3 for 3 gardens OAPs/Chd £1 per garden or £2 for 3 gardens. Suns April 20, June 15 (2-5.30). Private visits welcome, please* **Tel 0181 340 7205**

Hall Grange ♿✂ (Methodist Homes) Croydon. Situated in Shirley Church Rd near to junction with Upper Shirley Rd. From N leave A232 at junction of Shirley Rd and Wickham Rd. From S leave A212 at junction of Gravel Hill and Shirley Hills Rd. The garden, laid out circa 1913 by Rev W Wilks secretary to RHS, comprises 5 acres of natural heathland planted with azaleas, rhododendrons, heathers and shrubs and is unchanged. Parking nearby. TEA. *Adm £1.30 Chd free. Sun May 18 (2-5)*

¶109 Halsbury Road East ✂❀ (Don Fuller) Northolt. Nearest underground Sudbury Hill. L out of station, first L Cavendish Avenue. Turn L at the end, over small bridge and first R. Prize winning town garden (160' × 40') Herbaceous and mixed borders giving yr-round interest, particularly delightful in spring and summer. Many unusual plants grown and propagated for sale. TEA. *Adm £1 Chd free (Share to Greater Ealing Old People's Home®). Sun May 25 (2-6)*

▲**Ham House** ბ⚭✿ (The National Trust) Richmond. Mid-way between Richmond and Kingston W of A307 on the Surrey bank of the R Thames. Signposted with Tourism brown signs. Restored C17 garden, gravel terrace, paths dividing eight large grass plats; wilderness; parterre. TEAS. *Adm House £4.50 Chd £2 Garden free. For NGS Sun April 13 (10.30-6)*

117 Hamilton Terrace, NW8 ბ⚭ (Mrs K Herbert and the Tenants Association) Hamilton Terrace, where there is room for parking, is parallel with Maida Vale. Buses from Marble Arch 16, 16a, 98 go to Elgin Avenue which is near. This is a large garden, part of the back is kept wild and there is a tiny garden in memory of Dame Anna Neagle, who lived in the house. TEA. *Adm £1 Chd 20p (Share to the SCOPE®). Suns May 18, Aug 3 (2-6)*

11 Hampstead Way, NW11 ⚭✿ (Mr & Mrs R L Bristow) Nearest tube station Golders Green, 10 min walk up North End Rd, L into Wellgarth Road, R up Hampstead Way. ¼-acre prize winning garden, water features, unusual plants around lawns in the front and patio at the back. TEAS. *Adm £1.50 Chd 50p. Sun May 11 (2-6)*

133 Haverstock Hill, NW3 ⚭✿ (Mrs Catherine Horwood) Belsize Park Tube Station turn L out of station. Buses C11, C12, 168 (Haverstock Arms stop). Prizewinning 120ft long narrow garden divided into rooms. Packed planting of old and English roses, clematis, cottage garden perennials from balconied terrace to mini-orchard. Many unusual tender perennials and scented plants. Featured in Country Life and Wonderful Window-boxes. *Adm £1 Chd 50p. Sun June 15 (2-5.30). Private visits welcome, please Tel 0171 586 0908*

37 Heath Drive, NW3 ბ⚭✿ (C Caplin Esq) Station: Finchley Rd; buses: 82, 13 & 113 Heath Drive. Many uncommon plants; lawn; pond; rockery; ferns. Unusual treatment of fruit trees, greenhouse and conservatory. 1982, 1983, 1987, 1988, 1989, 1991, 1993, 1995 winner of Frankland Moore Trophy. Featured in Arabella Lennox-Boyd's Private Gardens of London. TEAS. *Adm £1 Chd 50p (Share to Royal Marsden®). Suns May 11, July 13 (2.30-6)*

Highgate Village, N6 ⚭✿ The Grove is between Highgate West Hill and Hampstead Lane Stations: Archway or Highgate (Northern Line, Barnet trains). Bus: 210, 271, 211 to Highgate Village. TEAS at 5 The Grove. *Adm £3 for 3 gardens £1.50 each garden Chd/OAP £2 for 3 gardens or £1 each garden. Sun June 15 (2-5)*

    4 The Grove ✿ (Cob Stenham Esq) 2-tiered with formal upper garden; view across Heath; orchard in lower garden

    5 The Grove (Mr & Mrs A J Hines) Newly-designed garden on 2 levels *(Share to local Scouts)*

    7 The Grove see separate entry

Highwood Ash, NW7 ✿ (Mr & Mrs R Gluckstein) Highwood Hill, Mill Hill. From London via A41 (Watford Way) to Mill Hill Circus; turn R up Lawrence St; at top bear L up Highwood Hill; house at top on R. Stations Totteridge and Whetstone or Edgware (Northern Line). Stanmore (Jubilee Line) Arnos Grove (Piccadilly Line). Bus from all these 251. House not within walking distance of stations. 3¼-acre incl rose garden, shrub and herbaceous borders, rhododendrons, azaleas, lake with waterfall, a mixture of formal and informal. TEAS. *Adm £1.50 Chd 50p (Share to The North London Hospice®). Sat, Sun May 17, 18 (2-6)*

5 Hillcrest Avenue, NW11 ⚭✿ (Mrs R M Rees) Hillcrest Ave is off Bridge Lane. By bus to Temple Fortune, Buses 82, 102, 260. Nearest Tube Golders Green or Finchley Central. Walk down Bridge Lane. Small labour saving colourful garden with many interesting features; rockery, fish pond, conservatory, tree fern. Secluded patio, auriculum theatre, acid bed. Cycas Revoluta Cypressus, Sempervirens. TEAS. *Adm £1 Chd 50p (Share to ADS®). Sun June 22 (2-6) Private visits welcome, please Tel 0181 455 0419*

¶**16 Hillcrest Road**, E18 ბ⚭ (Stanley Killingback) N from London on A11 (Woodford High Rd) L into Hillcrest, last lamp on L. S from M25 or North Circular, R into Grove Hill Rd into Hillcrest from South Woodford Station (Central Line). Short walk W uphill. Small suburban garden dedicated exclusively to the display of 10,000 tulips in rows - 400 different varieties. Featured in The Oldie magazine. *Adm £1 Chd 50p (Share to Emma Killingback Memorial Fund®). Sun April 27 (2-6)*

1 Hocroft Avenue, NW2 ბ⚭✿ (Dr & Mrs Derek Bunn) 113 bus (stop at Cricklewood Lane). Easy parking. Prizewinning garden with yr-round interest, especially in the spring. Front garden shown on BBC Gardeners' World, in their Front Garden series. Black and white bed featured in The Independent and The Evening Standard. Mixed borders in the back garden with a wide variety of plants. Subject of an article by Tony Venison in Country Life focusing on plant sales in the NGS. TEAS. *Adm £1.50 Chd free (Share to Hampstead Counselling Service®) Sun, Mon May 4, 5 (2.30-6.00)*

¶**11 Hocroft Road**, NW2 ბ⚭ (Richard & Louise Graham) 2nd L off Hendon Way from Finchley Rd. 113 bus to Cricklewood Lane on Finchley Rd (Buses 13, 28, 82) or on Cricklewood Lane (Buses 245, 260). An organic, ½-acre, formal garden on 3 levels, enclosed by tall yew hedges and designed for all-yr interest and easy maintenance. Large lawns bordered by roses, perennials and evergreens; long paths and architectural features create colourful vistas. Small orchard and vegetable garden. Pergolas create a stunning clematis and rose walk. TEAS. *Adm £2 Chd free. Mon May 5 (2-5.30)*

The Holme ბ⚭ (Lessees of The Crown Estate Commissioners) Positioned in Inner Circle, Regents Park opp Open Air Theatre. Nearest tube stations Regents Park and Baker St. 4-acre garden filled with interesting and unusual plants, with magnificent view over Regents Park Lake to the Nash terraces. Originally designed by J C Loudon, the Regency layout has been used to guide recent improvements. Sweeping lakeside lawns intersected by islands of herbaceous beds. Extensive rock garden recently rebuilt with waterfall, stream and pool. Formal flower garden with unusual annual and half hardy plants, sunken lawn, fountain pool and arbour. Teas available in Park Cafe adjacent. *Adm £2.50 Chd £1. For opening dates see local press or* **Tel NGS 01483 211535**

125 Honor Oak Park, SE23 &❀ (Mrs Heather West) Off South Circular (A205) via Honor Oak Rd. Multifarious plant collection on 2 levels; the lower a shady, informally planted knot garden, the upper sunny with lawn, pond, pots and verandah. York stone steps flank this approx 4,000 sq.ft 'secret' retreat. Strawberry TEAS. *Adm £1 Chd 50p. (Share to BHHI). Sun June 22 (2-6)*

239a Hook Road & (Mr & Mrs D St Romaine) Chessington. A3 from London, turn L at Hook underpass onto A243 Hook Rd. Garden is approx. 300yds on L. Parking opp. in park. Bus 71, K4 from Kingston and Surbiton to North Star Pub. ¼-acre developing garden divided into 2. The flower garden contains a specimen Albizia julibrissin, a Robbinia Hispida, and a good mix of herbaceous plants, shrubs and climbers. Also a gravel garden, rose tunnel and pond. The potager divided by paths into small beds has many vegetables, soft fruit, fruit trees, and herbs all inter-planted with flowers. TEAS. *Adm £1 Chd 50p. Sat, Sun Aug 2, 3 (2-5)*

Hornbeams &&❀ (Dr & Mrs R B Stalbow) Priory Drive, Stanmore. 5m SE of Watford. Nearest underground Stanmore. Priory Drive private rd off Stanmore Hill (A4140 Stanmore-Bushey Heath Rd). ½-acre informal garden where everyday plants mingle happily with rare treasures. Kitchen garden, fruit-cage, greenhouse and conservatory shaded by Muscat grapevine. Extensive new design and planting. Unusual plants for sale. TEAS. *Adm £1.50 Chd free (Share to Friends of Hebrew University Botanical Gardens Group®) Sun Aug 10 (2.30-6) Private visits welcome, please* **Tel 0181 954 2218**

The Horticultural Therapy Demonstration Garden, SW11 &❀ East Carriage Drive, Battersea Park, opp Tennis Courts. ⅓-acre; fully accessible garden with heated greenhouse, wildlife meadow and pond; vegetable and herb gardens, raised beds and containers, herbaceous beds, pergola and raised pond. Horticultural Therapy staff on hand for advice and information on accessible gardening tools, techniques and therapeutic gardening. TEAS. *Adm £1 Chd free (Share to Horticultural Therapy®). Sun July 13 (10-4)*

¶**Hyde Vale Gardens** & Greenwich. Parking is allowed at the top of Hyde Vale and in the Royal Hill car park. From Greenwich BR station turn L towards town centre. Turn R on Royal Hill just before Pelican crossing. Turn L at 4th street (Hyde Vale). No parking outside residences. TEAS. *Combined adm £2. Sun June 8 (11-2)*
  ¶**31 Hyde Vale** (Alison & John Taylor) Newly planted formal garden, with Mediterranean style terrace - accented with many pots
  ¶**51 Hyde Vale** (Jane Baker) Newly designed N facing garden (20' × 60') behind terraced house. Very vertiginous steps requiring great care

Islington Gardens Group I, &❀ Station: Highbury and Islington. Bus: 4, 19, 30, 43, 104, 279 to Highbury Corner or Islington Town Hall, 30 to New Crown public house stops outside 60 St Paul's Rd. A1 runs through Canonbury Sq. *Combined adm £4 or £1.50 each garden Chd £2 or 75p each garden. Sun June 8 (2-6)*
  37 Alwyne Road, N1 &&❀ (Mr & Mrs J Lambert) Bordering the New River. Views over the river and the park would make you think you are in the country; an enclosed formal garden reminds you that you are in town. Some flowers that are green; some leaves that are not. Some fun with topiary; some old-fashioned roses. TEAS. *(Share to SOS Children's Villages®)*
  28 Barnsbury Square, N1 & (F T Gardner Esq) Islington. 1¾m N of King's Cross off Thornhill Rd. Bus stop: Islington Town Hall, Upper St or Offord Rd, Caledonian Rd. Tube Highbury and Islington. Small prize-winning Victorian garden; gazebo; pond; grotto; roses, shrubs, plants of interest throughout year. *(Share to CRMF®)*
  60 St Paul's Road, N1 & (John & Pat Wardroper) This typical back-of-terrace town garden has been planted chiefly for shade, and to create a quiet, green enclosed atmosphere just off a busy street; designed on 3 levels with paved patios, border of flowering shrubs

Islington Gardens Group II *Combined adm £3 or £1.25 each garden Chd £1 or 50p each garden. Sun June 22 (2-6)*
  8 College Cross & (Ms Anne Weyman & Chris Bulford Esq) Walled town garden, 70' × 20' with over 400 different plants incl many unusual shrubs and herbaceous plants; walls covered with climbers. List of plants in the garden available. TEAS. *(Share to Family Planning Association®)*
  13 College Cross & (Diana & Stephen Yakeley) A small town garden behind a Georgian terrace house, measuring 5.2m x 16.8m enclosed by evergreen climbers with bay, box and fig trees. Paved areas with plants chosen for form and texture in shades of green. Large pots of white flowers incl lilies and Daturas, provide the only colour
  ¶**36 Thornhill Square** ❀ (Anna & Christopher McKane) Prize-winning 120' long informal garden, with unusual herbaceous plants and shrubs in curved beds giving a country garden atmosphere. Clematis and old roses, incl a rambler covering the Wendy House. TEAS. *(Share to St Mary's Church)*

¶**38 Killieser Avenue**, SW2 &&❀ (Mrs Winkle Haworth) 5 min walk from Streatham Hill BR Station. Buses 159, 137, 133 to Telford Avenue. Killieser Ave 2nd turning L off Telford Ave. Exuberantly planted 90' × 28' garden containing many unusual perennial plants, violas and viticella clematis. Classical rose arch, obelisk and Gothic arbour. Also L off main garden with vegetables, fruit etc. TEAS. *Adm £1 Chd 50p. Sun June 22 (2-6). Private visits welcome for 5 or more. Please,* **Tel 0181 671 4196**

Regular Openers. Open throughout the year. They are listed at the end of the Diary Section under 'Regular Openers'.

64 Kings Road ✿❀ (Jill & Ged Guinness) Richmond. 15 mins walk from Richmond Stn (District, N London & BR) or Buses 33, 337 to Belvedere PH and walk up Kings Rd. Nearly ½ an acre of slightly unkempt grass, vegetable, fruit and flower gardens. Mature trees from the original 1881 lay-out and numerous more recently planted trees and shrubs. Not much bedding out. TEAS. *Adm £1 Chd 50p. Sun June 1 (2.30-6)*

Lambeth Community Care Centre, SE11 ♿✿❀ Monkton Street. Tube or buses to Elephant and Castle, cut behind Leisure Centre to Brook Drive. Turn into Sullivan Rd at Bakery, passage to Monkton St. (or drive) to Kennington Rd buses 3, 109 159. At The Ship turn into Bishop's Terrace, 1st R to Monkton St. ⅔-acre garden. Mixed shrubs, trees, small rose garden, herbs, interesting walkways and mixed borders. Prize winner in London Hospital Gardens Competition. TEAS. *Adm £1 OAP/Chd 50p (Share to St. Thomas's Trustees for the garden®). Sat, Sun June 7, 8 (2-5)*

Lambeth Palace, SE1 ♿✿❀ (The Archbishop of Canterbury & Mrs Carey) Waterloo main line and underground, Westminster, Lambeth and Vauxhall tubes all about 10 mins walk. 3, 10, 44, 76, 77, 159, 170, 507 buses go near garden. Entry to garden on Lambeth Palace Rd (not at gatehouse) 2nd largest private garden in London. Land in hand of Archbishops of Canterbury since end C12. Work on garden carried out over last 100 years but significant renewal has taken place during last 10 years. *Adm £2 OAP/Chd 10-16 £1 (Share to Lambeth Palace Garden©). Sat April 26 (2-5.30)*

12 Lansdowne Rd, W11 ♿ (The Lady Amabel Lindsay) Holland Park. Turn N off Holland Park Ave nr Holland Park Station; or W off Ladbroke Grove ½-way along. Bus: 12, 88, GL 711, 715. Bus stop & station: Holland Park, 4 mins. Medium-sized fairly wild garden; border, climbing roses, shrubs; mulberry tree 200 yrs old. *Adm £2 Chd £1. Wed May 21 (2-6)*

10 Lawn Road, NW3 ♿✿❀ (Mrs P Findlay) Tube to Belsize Park or go up Haverstock Hill. Turn R at Haverstock Arms then L. House 200yds on R, with blue door. ¹⁄₁₀-acre approx; uniquely curvaceous design of intersecting circles, set in rectangular format. Organically cultured garden, very heavily stocked; many unusual and native species plants. *Adm £1 Chd 50p. Sun June 15 (2.30-6)*

15 Lawrence Street, SW3 (John Casson Esq) Between King's Rd and the river parallel to Old Church St. Nearest tubes: Sloane Square and South Kensington. Buses 11, 19, 22, 211, 319, 49. Prize-winning small Chelsea cottage garden (featured in Secret Garden Walks): clematis, roses, herbaceous perennials and shrubs, all yr-round interest; some unusual plants. House (built c1790), not open except for access to garden. *Adm £1 Chd 50p (Share to Chelsea Physic Garden®). Sat, Sun July 12, 13 (2-6)*

20 Lessingham Avenue, SW17 ✿ (George Hards) Tooting Bec underground (Northern Line). Buses 155, 219. Tranquil green and white small town garden 20′ × 40′ with water feature. Closely planted to provide yr-round variety, interesting plants incl trachelospermum jasmi-

noides, catalpa bungei, auralia elata variegata, romneya coulteri. TEAS. *Adm 50p (Share to Imperial Cancer Research Fund®). Sun June 29 (2-6)*

Leyborne Park Gardens ✿❀ 2 min walk from Kew Gardens station. Take exit signposted Kew Gardens. On leaving station forecourt bear R past shops. Leyborne Park is 1st rd on R. Bus 391, R68 to Kew Gdns station. Bus 65 to Kew Gdns, Victoria Gate. Access by car is from Sandycombe Rd. TEAS. *Combined adm £1.50 Chd free (Share to Arthritis and Rheumatism Council for Research®). Sun June 22 (2-5.30)*

    36 Leyborne Park (David & Frances Hopwood) 120ft long mature, family garden; architect designed for minimum upkeep with maximum foliage effects; patio; imaginative children's play area; huge eucalyptus. TEAS

    38 Leyborne Park ❀ (Mr & Mrs A Sandall) 120ft long organic garden; lawn with mixed borders; containers; long established vine; alliums, lavenders, eryngiums, scented pelargoniums, bamboos; plants for the dry garden

    40 Leyborne Park (Debbie Pointon-Taylor) 120ft long garden; lawn and mixed borders; mature shrubs; conifers; patio with containers

1 Lister Road, E11 ✿❀ (Myles Challis Esq) Leytonstone underground station (central line). 5 mins to High Rd Leytonstone. Hills garage marks corner of Lister Rd which is directly off High Rd. Garden designer's unexpected, densely planted sub-tropical garden containing a mixture of tender plants such as daturas, gingers, cannas, tree ferns, bananas and hardy exotics including gunneras, bamboos, cordylines, phormiums and large leaved perennials in a space unbelievably only 40′ × 20′. *Adm £1 Chd 50p. Sun Aug 10 (11-4)*

21a The Little Boltons, SW10 ❀ (Mrs D Capron) Between Fulham and Old Brompton Rd off Tregunter Rd. Nearest tube Earls Court, buses 30, 14, 74. 70ft prize winning herbaceous plant collection. Portrayed in the book 'Private Gardens of London' by Arabella Lennox-Boyd and House and Garden Magazine. *Adm £1 Chd 25p. Suns April 20 (2-5.30), June 29 (2-6)*

Little Lodge ♿✿❀ (Mr & Mrs P Hickman) Watts Rd, Thames Ditton (Station 5 mins). A3 from London; after Hook underpass turn left to Esher; at Scilly Isles turn R towards Kingston; after 2nd railway bridge turn L to Thames Ditton village; house opp library after Giggs Hill Green. A cottage style informal garden within 15m of central London. Many British native plants. Garden has an atmosphere of tranquillity, featuring plants with subtle colours and fragrance; small brick-pathed vegetable plot. TEAS. *Adm £1.50 Chd free (Share to Cancer Research®). Sun June 8 (11.30-6). Special evening opening Wed June 11 (6.30-9) £2.50 incl wine and light refreshments. Private visits welcome, please* **Tel 0181 339 0931**

22 Loudoun Road, NW8 ✿ (Ruth Barclay) 3 to 4 min walk to St. John's Wood tube station. Lies between Abbey Road and Finchley Rd serviced by buses, mins from bus stop. A strong emphasis on design, water, arbour garden within a garden. Back Italianate courtyard, romantic and mysterious. Interesting water features, incl grotto with water cascading down mussel shells surrounded by ferns and tree ferns. Prizewinner for 4 consecutive years. Featured in 'Town Gardens'. TEAS. *Adm £1 Chd 25p. Sun June 1 (2-6)*

1 Lower Merton Rise, NW3 ✤ (Mr & Mrs Paul Findlay) Between Swiss Cottage and Chalk Farm, Primrose Hill. Approx ¼-acre. Redesigned in 1995 with many new features; sunken courtyard, cascade, pergolas and herbaceous borders. TEAS. *Adm £1.50 Chd 50p. Sun June 15 (2-6)*

4 Macaulay Road, SW4 ♿✤ (Mrs Diana Ross) Clapham Common Tube. Buses 88, 77, 77A, 137, 137A, 37, 45. Prize-winning garden featured in House and Gardens 1996 and belonging to a garden writer. Mature now after a redesign job in 1994, it consists of jungle, grotto and lots of things in pots and containers. It measures about 85' × 50' but seems bigger. *Adm £1.50 Chd free. Sun Aug 3 (2-6) or by appt please,* **Tel 0171 627 1137**

Malvern Terrace, N1 ♿✤ Barnsbury. Approach from S via Pentonville Rd into Penton St, Barnsbury Rd; from N via Thornhill Rd opp Albion public house. Tube: Highbury & Islington. Bus: 19, 30 to Upper St Town Hall. Unique London terrace of 1830s houses built on site of Thos Oldfield's dairy and cricket field. Cottage-style gardens in cobbled cul-de-sac; music. Victorian plant stall. Homemade TEAS. Music. *Combined adm £1.50 Chd free (Share to International Spinal Research Trust®). Sun May 11 (2-5.30)*

    1 Malvern Terrace (Mr & Mrs Martin Leman)
    2 Malvern Terrace (Mr & Mrs K McDowall)
    3 Malvern Terrace (Mr & Mrs A Robertson)
    4 Malvern Terrace
    5 Malvern Terrace
    6 Malvern Terrace (Dr B A Lynch)
    7 Malvern Terrace (Mr & Mrs Mark Vanhegan)
    8 Malvern Terrace (Mr & Mrs R Le Fanu)
    10 Malvern Terrace (Dr & Mrs P Sherwood)

¶**2 Mansfield Place**, NW3 ✤ (Ruth & Adam Townsend) 50yds up Heath St from Hampstead underground. At top of Back Lane, alley to Streatley Place leading to Mansfield Place. This small secret garden is divided into rooms, with the sound of water trickling from a well-shaped fountain. A mulberry tree gives shade and beauty in summer and has become the dominant feature. It is a surprisingly peaceful retreat from the bustle of Hampstead Town. 1996 winner of 'Seen from the Street' competition. TEA. *Adm £1. Sun June 15 (2-5.30)*

13 Mercers Road, N19 ✤❀ (Dr & Mrs N Millward) off Holloway Rd (A1) N of Odeon Cinema. 30' × 15' front garden featuring cool whites, greys and greens. 30' × 20' rear garden on two levels. Profusion of pastel shades from April to Sept. Many small-flowered clematis, pink schizophragma, rosa soulieana and other interesting climbers and perennials. Featured on Channel 4 Garden Club, May 1994. Wine and nibbles available. *Adm £2.50 Wed, Thurs June 18, 19 (6-9). Private visits welcome for small groups and individuals, please* **Tel 0171 281 2674**

2 Millfield Place, N6 ♿✤ Garden is off Highgate West Hill, E side of Hampstead Heath. Buses 210, 271 to Highgate Village or C2, C11, C12, 214 to Parliament Hill. 1½-acre spring and woodland garden with camellias and rhododendrons. Spring bulbs; herbaceous border; small orchard. TEAS. *Adm £1.50 Chd 50p. Sun May 11 (2-6), Thurs July 17 (5.30-9) Adm £2.50 incl wine*

¶**9 Montpelier Grove**, NW5 ✤❀ (Sara Feilden & Rod Harper) Kentish Town 7 mins walk from Tufnell Park & Kentish Town Tube Stations, off Lady Margaret Rd. Parking in st (no restrictions). Narrow 60' garden behind terrace house. Designed for use by family with working parents. Variety of plants for interest and backdrop of greenery. Colour co-ordination and combination of particular interest. *Adm £1 Chd 50p. Sun June 8 (2-5.30)*

52 Mount Park Road, Ealing, W5 ✤ (Paddy & Judith O'Hagan) Ealing Broadway Stn. Bus 65 from Kingston and Richmond. 100' × 50' triangular garden on 2 levels. Designed for wildlife by Chris Baines in 1989, the garden has developed and matured to absorb a passion for architectural and tender plants. Woodland walk, terrace, decorative vegetable plot, glass fountain and pond with bog area. All leading to more eccentric and contemplative gardening - shell grotto, Turkish kiosk, wishing tree and spirit house. Conservatory with unusual euphorbias. Classical music. *Adm £1 Chd 50p. Sun June 8 (2-6)*

▲**Museum of Garden History** ♿✤❀ (The Tradescant Trust) Lambeth Palace Road, SE1. Bus: 507 Red Arrow from Victoria or Waterloo, alight Lambeth Palace. 7,450 sq ft. replica of C17 garden planted in churchyard with flowers known and grown by John Tradescant. Tombs of the Tradescants and Admiral Bligh of the 'Bounty' in the garden. Opened by HM the Queen Mother in 1983. Museum being established in restored church of St Mary-at-Lambeth saved from demolition by The Trust. The new garden at The Ark, 220 Lambeth Road, also open. TEAS. *Adm £1 OAPs/Chd 25p (Share to Museum of Garden History®). For NGS Sun June 1 (10.30-5)*

■ **Myddelton House Gardens** ♿✤❀ (Lee Valley Park) Bulls Cross, Enfield. Junction 25 (A10) off M25 S towards Enfield. 1st set of lights turn R into Bullsmoor Lane, L at end along Bulls Cross, garden signed on R. The 4 acres of garden were created by Edward A Bowles. The gardens feature a diverse and unusual plant collection incl a large selection of naturalised bulbs, as well as the national collection of award winning bearded irises. The grounds have a large pond with terrace, two conservatories and interesting historical artefacts. TEAS and plants for sale on NGS days and selected Suns. *Adm £1.50 Concessions 75p. Open Mon-Fri (10-3.30)(except Bank Hols) (2-5) selected Suns. For NGS Suns Feb 23, May 25, July 27; Feb 24 1998 (2-5). No concessions on NGS days & Suns*

17A Navarino Road, E8 ✤ (John Tordoff Esq) situated between Dalston and Hackney and connects Graham Rd with Richmond Rd. Buses 38, 22A, 22B, 277, 30. Winner of the 1996 BBC Gardener's World competition to find 'the most beautiful small garden in Britain'. A formal Italian garden of clipped box and yew. Rambler roses make a spectacular display over arches and a pergola. The Japanese garden begun 3yrs ago features a large informal pond, tea house, ornamental bridge, and miniature Mount Fuji. Plantings of azaleas, acers and bamboo. *Adm £1.50 Chd 50p. Suns June 15, Aug 17 (12-6). Private visits welcome, please* **Tel 0171 254 5622**

15 Norcott Road, N16 &✿ (Amanda & John Welch) Buses 73, 149, 76, 67, 243 Clapton or Stoke Newington Stations (Rectory Rd closed Suns). Largish (for Hackney) walled back garden. Pond, herbs, herbaceous plants especially irises, geraniums and campanulas. TEAS. *Adm £1 Chd 50p (Share to St Joseph's Hospice®). Suns June 1, July 13 (2-6)*

2 Northbourne Road, SW4 &✿ (Mr & Mrs Edward A Holmes) Clapham Common tube. Buses 137, 137A, 37. W facing, walled garden 36' × 56' with good architectural planting and rose pergola. Featured in Sainsbury's Magazine. Patio extended and improved. Planting revised following major renovations to the house during the latter part of 1996, garden designed by Judith Sharpe. *Adm £1.50 OAPs/Chd 50p (Share to the Foundation for the Study of Infant Deaths®). Sun June 8 (2-6)*

¶239 Norwood Road, SE24 (Mr & Mrs J Baillie) Just off South Circular between Tulse Hill and Herne Hill BR Stations. Best parking in Trinity Rise, opp house. Approx 100' × 25'. Garden designer's romantic garden with a Mediterranean feel combined with the formal English garden. The garden has several brick and york stone seating areas; one with Golden Hop covered arbour, 10' Trachycarpus, large Urn and 400 yr-old Xanthorrhea. It then progresses to a formal lawn with weeping pears, weeping mulberry tree and many interesting climbing plants and painted pots. From the lawn you enter a romantic seating area with tree fern and many other shade loving plants. The far end incl a formal topiary box garden. Finalist in Daily Mail Garden Comp 1966 as seen at Hampton Court Flower Show. *Adm £1.50 Chd free. Suns June 29, Aug 10 (2-6)*

Orchard Cottage, Bickley. *Sun Aug 3 (2-5.30)*. See Kent

Ormeley Lodge ✿ (Lady Annabel Goldsmith) Ham Gate Avenue, Richmond. From Richmond Park, exit at Ham Gate into Ham Gate Avenue. 1st house on R. From Richmond A307, 1½m past New Inn on R, first turning on L. House is last on L. Bus: 65. Large walled garden in delightful rural setting on Ham Common. Newly designed formal garden, wide herbaceous borders, box hedges. Walk through to newly planted orchard with wild flowers. Vegetable garden. Secluded swimming pool area, trellised tennis court with roses and climbers. TEA. *Adm £1 Chd 50p. Sun June 22 (3-6)*

43 Ormeley Road, SW12 ✿ (Richard Glassborow & Susan Venner) Nearest tube and BR station Balham, 5 mins walk, off Balham High Rd. Big ideas in a small garden 30' × 18' approx, SW facing, full of unusual plants. *Adm £1 Chd free (Share to Friends of the Earth®) Sun May 18 (2-6)*

¶Osborne House &✿ (Jane & John Legate) 54 Herne Road, Long Ditton. Off A3 at Hook Junction (no exit coming from Guildford), R towards Surbiton, L into Herne Rd before zebra crossing. Please park considerately. 100' × 50' garden with roses, clematis, hydrangeas, herbaceous plants. Raised formal pool. Conservatory with water feature. Low level York stone terrace. New 'wild' area with informal water feature. Display of garden photography. Evening opening with lighting. TEAS. *Adm £1 Chd 50p.* *Wed July 9, Sun July 13 (10-5). Wed Aug 13 (6-9.30) £2.50 to include wine and light refreshments.*

▲Osterley Park House & (The National Trust) Jersey Rd, Isleworth. Access is via Thornbury Rd on N side of A4 (Great West Rd) between Gillette Corner and Osterley Tube Station. Nearest station Osterley (Piccadilly Line). Car Park £2 (NT Members free). Osterley is one of the last great houses with an intact estate in Greater London. The Pleasure Grounds are being restored. The NGS fund is contributing a substantial part of the cost of replanting the early C19 garden which stood in front of Robert Adams' elegant semi-circular garden house. Private walled garden open and opportunity to meet the gardeners. TEAS. *Adm £1 Chd free. For NGS Sun June 15 (11-4)*

Flat 1, 1F Oval Road, NW1 ✿ (Sheila Jackson) Tube station Camden Town. Buses: any bus to Camden Town, C2 and 274 stop very near. Parking difficult near centre on Sunday. A small side garden approaches an illustrator's very small hidden back garden approx 24ft × 20ft which abuts the Euston railway line. A great variety of plants, mainly in pots, are banked to create interesting shapes, making use of a variety of levels. This garden is the subject of the book 'Blooming Small, A City Dwellers Garden'. *Adm £1 Chd 50p. Sats June 7, 14 (6-9) or private visits welcome, please* Tel 0171 267 0655

¶39 Oxford Road, SW15 &✿ (Jennifer Adey) 3 mins walk from E Putney Tube, L out of station then 1st R off Upper Richmond Rd. 5 mins from Putney Br, turn L out of station, L again into Upper Richmond Rd, first L or cross Putney Br, first L then 3rd R. Buses 14, 74 and 37. Enchanting small box-edged formal garden 40' × 35'. Arched walk covered with hops, small cobbled planted areas. Curious summerhouse and imaginative views through wrought iron gates. *Adm £1 Chd 50p. Sun June 29 (2-6)*

¶The Pagoda ✿ (Caroline Cooper) Pagoda Gardens, Blackheath. BR Blackheath or Lewisham, 10 mins walk. ½-acre historic garden of historic house, being restored and revived. TEAS. *Adm £1.50 Chd free (Share to Greenwich & Lewisham Newpin®). Sun June 22 (2-5.30)*

¶71 Palace Road, SW2 (Mr & Mrs Jeremy Nieboer) Tulse Hill, Brixton Tube. Buses 2A, 2B. By car enter Palace Rd from Norwood High St or Hillside Rd. 45' × 40' front garden formal and enclosed on a theme of blue and white. 90' × 45' rear garden laid out with herbaceous borders and brick terracing. TEAS. *Adm £1.50 Chd 50p. Sun June 15 (1-6)*

78 Palace Road, SW2 &✿ (Mr & Mrs D S Senior) BR station Streatham Hill 15min walk (NB Tulse Hill BR closed Sundays). Buses 2, 68, 196 to Tulse Hill station. By car S Circular Rd, just W of Tulse Hill one-way system. Located corner Palace Rd and Northstead Rd. 90' × 60' garden planted mainly for foliage effect and yr-round interest. Shrubs, bamboos, grasses, some interesting small trees. Part planted with Mediterranean plants to suit hot dry conditions, areas left wild to encourage wildlife, pond. *Adm £1.50 Chd free. Sun June 15 (2-6)*

10A The Pavement, SE27 ❀ (Brendan Byrne) Chapel Rd. Located off Ladas Rd down alleyway behind All Seasons Fish Bar. Buses 68 to Knights Hill alight at S London College. No. 2 to Norwood bus garage. BR W Norwood. Come out Knights Hill, turn L. Chapel Rd is 10 mins walk on L after passing bus garage. Smallest garden in London (entry restricted to 5 people at any one time). A hidden oasis behind houses and shops. Country type of garden, mostly in containers. Shrubs, herbaceous, bedding and rare plants continually changing. Featured in 'The Observer'. *Adm £1 Acc chd free with adult (Share to Horses & Ponies Protection Assoc®). Sun July 27 (10-12, 2-6)*

43 Penerley Rd, SE6 ⅍✿❀ (Mr & Mrs E Thorp) BR stations Catford, Catford Bridge (15 mins walk). Many bus routes to Catford. Off A21 just S of S Circular Rd. Plant lover's shady garden 33' × 100', full of interesting and unusual plants. Formal lawns, informal planting, paved areas with ferns, hostas and other foliage plants in pots. TEAS in aid of St Laurence Church. *Adm £1 Acc chd free. Suns May 11, June 15 (2-5.30)*

¶2a Penn Road, N7 ⅍ (Judy & Paul Garvey) Caledonian Rd Underground. Turn L out of station and continue N up Caledonian Rd for approx 700 yds. Penn Rd is on LHS. House is opp Penn Rd Gardens. Buses 17, 91, 259 along Caledonian Rd; 29, 253 to nearby Nags Head. 100' × 30' walled garden, plus long side-entrance border and small front garden; colourful, well-stocked borders, mature trees, containers, arches, vegetable garden. Prizewinner in local garden competition. TEA. *Adm £1 Chd free. Sun June 29 (2-6)*

35 Perrymead Street, SW6 ✿ (Mr & Mrs Richard Chilton) Fulham. New King's Rd W from Chelsea; 1st on L after Wandsworth Bridge Rd. Stations: Fulham Broadway or Parsons Green; bus 22 from Chelsea; 28 from Kensington. Small paved garden with ornamental feature; surrounded by mature trees. Shrubs, climbers (especially clematis) interspersed with summer planting suitable for shade. *Adm £1.25 Chd 60p. Sun July 13 (2-6)*

13 Queen Elizabeth's Walk, N16 ✿ (Lucy Sommers) From Manor House tube go S down Green Lanes, then take 2nd L off Lordship Park. 100' × 25' plantperson's garden backing onto a woody wilderness. Many interesting shrubs, climbers, perennials set in a series of flowing borders around pergola, arch, pond and sculpture, in both sunny and woodland areas. Created by owner 4½ yrs ago to provide interest through all seasons. TEA. *Adm £1 OAP/Chd 50p. Sun June 15 (2-6)*

3 Radnor Gardens ✿❀ (Ms Jill Payne) Twickenham. A-Z 2k 103. Train: Twickenham, Turn L 10 min walk. Train/tube: Richmond then bus 90, R70 to Heath Rd or 33, R68 to King St. From Heath Rd turn into Radnor Rd by Tamplins then R into Radnor Gardens. A narrow, green and secluded garden, 12' × 54' of a small terraced house; crammed with a wide range of plants. Tiny ponds and water features, small conservatory. *Adm 50p Chd 20p. Suns July 6, 13 (2-6)*

9 Ranelagh Avenue, SW6 ✿ (Mrs P Tham) Nearest tube Putney Bridge. Approx 60' × 40'. A semi-formal two level garden featuring shade tolerant plants, incl many hostas

and trees; arbutus, judas, magnolia, crab apple. Small patio with container grown plants. *Adm £1.20 Chd 50p. Sun June 29 (2-6)*

11 Ranulf Road, NW2 ✿❀ (Mr & Mrs Jonathan Bates) 13, 82, or 113 bus to Platts Lane from Golders Green or Swiss Cottage; 28 from Golders Green or West Hampstead. Nearest stations Finchley Rd, W Hampstead and Golders Green. Take Ardwick Rd at junction of Finchley Rd and Fortune Green Rd, bear L into Ranulf Rd. No 11 is on L at brow of hill. Medium-sized garden, surrounded by trees, full of colour; herbaceous borders, roses, lilies, fuchsias, bedding plants and many geranium filled pots. Home-made TEAS. *Adm £1 Chd free. Sun July 13 (2-6)*

Regents College, NW1 ❀ Regents Park. Regents College is located at the junction of York Bridge and the Inner Circle opp Queen Mary's Rose Garden in Regents Park. Baker Street tube is 5 mins walk. Buses: 1, 2, 2B, 13, 18, 27, 30, 74, 159. Enter gate or the Garden Gate which is reached via the footbridge at Clarence Gate. Within the 10-acre grounds of Regent's College is the Botany garden - a secret garden of charm. Layout and features have been sympathetically adapted and developed to create garden areas of pleasing atmosphere and form. Rock, water, a pergola and arbour, sun and shade offers homes to a large range of plants. TEA. *Adm £1.50 Concessions/Chd 50p. Sun June 8, Sat June 14 (12-5). Private visits welcome, please **Tel 0171 487 7494***

48 Rommany Rd, SE27 ✿❀ (Dr Belinda I Barnes & Mr Ronald Stuart-Moonlight). BR Gipsy Hill Stn. Buses 3, 322. Easiest access to Rommany Rd via Gipsy Rd. A luscious small 30' × 20' walled town garden created in 1995 by present owners. Ferns and hostas lead towards the York stone patio and herbaceous borders. A vine and rose covered pergola forms the entrance to the rear secret garden with fountain and trachelospernum arch. For benefit of all max 15 persons at any one time. TEAS. *Adm 80p Chd 50p (Share to RNLI®). Suns June 22, July 20 (1-6). Private visits by written appointment, welcome*

Roots & Shoots, SE11 ⅍❀ (Roots & Shoots Training Scheme) Vauxhall Centre, Walnut Tree Walk. Tube: Lambeth North; Buses 159, 109, 3. Just off Kennington Rd, 5 mins from War Museum. Derelict site used by Civil Defence during the war, transformed by 'Roots & Shoots' Training Scheme (for young people with disabilities) into a garden. Mixed borders, plant nursery, ½ acre wildlife garden, superb walnut tree, acacia dealbata and other unusual shrubs. TEAS. *Adm £1 Chd 50p (Share to Roots & Shoots, Lady Margaret Hall Settlement®). Sat, Sun May 31, Jun 1 (11-4)*

19 St Gabriel's Road, NW2 ⅍❀ (Mrs Penelope Mortimer) St Gabriel's Rd is a short walk from Willesden Green Tube (Jubilee Line). When Penelope Mortimer moved here in 1991 she brought two van-loads of plants from her Cotswold garden. With the help of a splendid balsam poplar, a great deal of muck and hard work, what was 150ft of exhausted grass and rubbish is now a miniature country garden brimming with roses and rare herbaceous plants. 'A sanctuary!' *Adm £2 Chd under 14 free. Sun June 15 (2-6). Private visits welcome, please **Tel 0181 452 8551***

7 St George's Rd ⚘❀ (Mr & Mrs Richard Raworth) St Margaret's, Twickenham. Off A316 between Twickenham Bridge and St Margarets roundabout. ½-acre maturing town garden backing onto private parkland. Garden divided into 'rooms'. Unusual shrubs, clematis and old English roses. Large conservatory with rare plants and climbers. Parterre garden. Sink garden, pergola, paved garden. Mist propagated specimens and unusual plants for sale. Featured in Penelope Hobhouse's 'Garden Style' and the The Conservatory Gardener by Anne Swithenbank. TEAS. *Adm £1.50 Chd 50p. Suns June 8, 22 (2-6) or private visits welcome, please* **Tel 0181 892 3713**

St Mary's Convent & Nursing Home, W4 ♿❀ (Sister Jennifer Anne) Chiswick. Exit W from London on A4 to Hogarth roundabout. Take A316 signposted Richmond. St Mary's is 500yds down on L. Parking in Corney Rd, 1st turning L after Convent. 2½-acre walled garden with fine specimen trees; herbaceous borders and shrub borders being planted for yr-round interest, incl spring flowering shrubs and bulbs. TEAS. *Adm £1 Chd free. Sun April 20 (2-5)*

St Michael's Convent, Ham ⚘❀ (Community of The Sisters of The Church) 56 Ham Common. From Richmond or Kingston, A307, turn onto the common at traffic lights nr the New Inn, 100 yds on the R adjacent to Martingales Close. 4-acre walled organic garden. Bible garden and circle garden of meditation. Extensive herbaceous borders, two orchards, wild life areas, working kitchen garden, vinehouse and ancient mulberry tree. Wheelchairs with difficulty. TEAS. *Collection Box. Sat June 28 (11-3).*

57 St Quintin Avenue, W10 ⚘❀ (H Groffman Esq) 1m from Ladbroke Grove/White City Underground. From Ladbroke Grove station; bus; 7 to North Pole Road, 30ft × 40ft walled garden; wide selection of plant material. Patio; small pond; hanging baskets; special features. Regular prizewinner in garden competitions. Featured on TV and in horticultural press. Special 50th Anniversary floral display for 1997. TEAS. *Adm £1.50 Chd 80p. Suns July 27, Aug 3 (2-7). Private visits welcome for parties of 10 and over, please* **Tel 0181 969 8292**

5 St Regis Close, N10 ⚘❀ (Susan Bennett & Earl Hyde) Muswell Hill. 2nd turning on L in Alexandra Park Rd, coming from Colney Hatch Lane Tube: Bounds Green then Buses 102, 299 to Curzon Rd or East Finchley then Bus 102. Maureen Lipman's favourite garden chosen for an exhibition at Museum of Garden History, features architectural constructions, ponds, waterfalls and container planting; lawns, well-stocked borders and collection of antique chimney pots. Oriental Raku-tiled mirrored enclosure made and designed by owner in garden studio, conceals plant nursery. Cover feature 'Practical Gardening' Magazine; filmed for BBC 2 'Gardener's World' and Sky TV 'One to Three'. TEAS. *Adm £1.50 Chd 50p. Suns May 4, June 29, July 27 (2-8)*

12a Selwood Place, SW7 ♿ (Mrs Anthony Crossley) South Kensington, entrance opp 92 Onslow Gardens. South Kensington tube 8 mins walk, no. 14 bus down Fulham Rd (Elm Place request stop). Long green and white border; pink border in L-shaped walled garden; collection of roses, peonies, camellias, iris, lilies, poppies, vegetables; terraced herb garden. Suitable for wheelchairs only if dry. *Adm £1 Chd 50p. Sun June 22 (2.30-6)*

¶3 Somerton Avenue ❀ (Nigel & Philippa Palmer) Richmond. By junction of Clifford Ave and A316. Tiny suburban trellised garden crammed with plants, pots and scents. Conservatory, terrace, pool, miniature borders, fernery and 'Mediterranean garden' all packed into 30' × 20'. TEAS. *Adm £1 Chd 50p. Sun June 29 (2-6)*

Southwood Lodge, N6 ⚘❀ (Mr & Mrs C Whittington) 33 Kingsley Place. Off Southwood Lane. Buses 210, 271. Tube Highgate. A romantic, hidden garden laid out last century on a steeply sloping site, now densely planted with a wide variety of shrubs, bulbs, roses and perennials. Pond, waterfall, frogs. Many unusual plants are grown and propagated for sale. Featured in Gardens Illustrated (1994) and Sunday Express Colour Magazine (1996). *Adm £1 Chd 50p (Share to Wednesday's Child©). Suns May 11, June 8 (2-6). Special evening opening, Thurs June 19 (6.30-8.30) £2.50 incl wine. Private visits welcome, please* **Tel 0181 348 2785**

¶40 Station Road ⚘ (Marianne Cartwright) Hampton. Buses 267 and 68 to Hampton Church. 1st turning on L of High St. From river end 5 mins walk. Buses 111 and 216 pass the house. Alight Police Station 100yds. Hampton BR Station 5 mins. Small secluded cottage garden romantically planted in pinks, blues and mauves. Ferns, trachelospermum jasminoides, pond. Front planted for winter and spring interest. TEA. *Adm £1 Chd 50p. Sun June 22 (2-6)*

¶26 Thompson Road, SE22 ⚘ (Anthony Noel Esq) A205 South Circular from Clapham Common, L into Lordship Lane. R into Crystal Palace Rd. 1st L Landcroft Rd, 1st R Thompson Rd. Anthony Noel's new garden - approx 15' × 38'. L shaped. Elegant white garden in its early stages with promise of Regency romance. Old roses, rare plants and a theatrical twist. *Adm £2, OAP £1. Sun Sept 21 (2.30-6)*

103 Thurleigh Road, SW12 ♿⚘❀ (Charles MacKinnon Esq) Clapham S Tube Station (Northern Line) is 5 mins walk. Thurleigh Rd runs between Clapham Common (Wside) and Wandsworth Common (Bollingbroke Grove). A 100' × 100' walled garden surrounded by limes. Formal new courtyard with box and lavender balances deep herbaceous borders and secret areas. Careful planting to minimise upkeep and to balance my dreams of Sissinghurst with my children's footballs. TEAS. *Adm £1.50 Chd 50p. Sun June 15 (1-6). Special evening opening, Wed June 18 (6.30-9) £2.50 incl wine and light refreshments (Share to Queen Mary's Clothing Guild®)*

13 Trecastle Way, N7 ⚘❀ (Mrs Vera Quick) Carleton Rd. Camden Rd buses 29, 253 to Dalmeny Ave. 1st R from Dalmeny Ave into Trecastle Way (nr Holloway Prison). A very pretty garden. Small in size approx 60' × 30'. Full of colour, lots of interesting plants, ornamental pond and waterfall. Bedding plants grown from seeds and cuttings. TEAS. *Adm 80p Chd free. Sun June 29 (2-6)*

Trinity Hospice ♿⚘❀ 30 Clapham Common North Side, SW4. Tube: Clapham Common. Bus: 37, 137, 35 stop outside. 2-acre park-like garden restored by Lanning Roper's friends as a memorial to him and designed by John Medhurst. Ricky's sculpture a feature. TEAS. *Adm £1 Chd free. Sats, Suns April 26, 27; June 7, 8; July 26 27; Sept 6, 7 (2-5)*

Trumpeters' House (Miss Sarah Franklyn) and **Trumpeters' Lodge** ᯥᯥ❀ (Mrs Pamela Franklyn) Old Palace Yard, Richmond. Off Richmond Green on S side. Car parking on the green and in car parks. Approx 3 acres, lawns, established old trees. Old roses; shrubs; ponds; knot garden; mixed borders. **Gazebo garden**. Redesigned in '95/'96. Now a drought-resistant experimental garden. Lush plantings of Eucalyptus, Acacia, Pyrus, Eleagnus, Pittosporum, Artemesia, Euphorbia, grasses and Dianthus etc. Emphasis on bold silver foliage shrubs and perennials interspersed with vibrant seasonal colour from tender perennials and annuals. Nigella, Papaver, Verbena, Eschscholzia, Salvia, Aquilegia etc. Features incl raised Georgian gazebo overlooking the river. Planted knot garden. Silver pergola walk. Long border. Raised terrace area. Extensive use of old railway sleepers. Small orchard with picket fence. The garden's centrepiece is a white wrought iron aviary housing white doves. Featured in House & Garden, Country Life and in NGS Calendar 1995 (July). NCCPG collection of old-fashioned pinks (Dianthus). TEAS. *Adm £2.50 OAPs £1.50 Chd 50p. Suns June 15, July 13 (2-6)*

131 Upland Road ᯥᯥ❀ (Ms G Payne & Ms P Harvey) East Dulwich. Nearest BR Peckham Rye. Buses 78, 12, 63. 78, 12 to Barry Rd. Get off 1st stop opp Peckham Rye Common. Upland Rd 50yds on L. 63 to Peckham Rye Common. Get off Forest Hill Rd. Cross over to Piermont Green leading to Upland Rd. Small garden full of surprises. Unusual, semi-oriental-style stone rear garden with pond and waterfall. Informal planted areas. 20' × 40' designed for effect and low maintenance. Front and side areas incl shade loving plants, bamboos, camellias, magnolias and viticellas. TEAS. *Adm £1 Chd 25p. Sun May 18 (2-5.30)*

15 Upper Grotto Road ❀ (Jeane Rankin) Twickenham. Stations Strawberry Hill or Twickenham. Buses R68, 33 to Pope's Grotto; 90B, 267, 281, 290 to Heath Rd/Radnor Rd, 2nd R into Upper Grotto Rd. Small sunken suntrap courtyard garden designed and constructed with advancing age and arthritis in mind; raised borders with small shrubs, herbaceous perennials, self sown annuals; wall shrubs, other climbers; plants in pots and tiny fountain over pebbles. TEA. *Adm 75p Chd 25p. Suns July 6, 13 (2-6). Private visits welcome, please Tel 0181 891 4454*

7 Upper Phillimore Gardens, W8 ᯥ (Mr & Mrs B Ritchie) From Kensington High St take either Phillimore Gdns or Camden Hill Rd; entrance Duchess of Bedford Walk. 100' × 35' garden; rockery, sunken garden; Italian wall fountain, ground cover planting, pergola. TEA. *Adm £1 Chd 50p. Sun April 27 (2.30-6)*

66 Wallingford Avenue (off Oxford Gdns), W10 ᯥ (Mrs R Andrups) Nearest underground station: Latimer Rd and Ladbroke Grove. Nearest bus stop Oxford Gdns (7) or Ladbroke Grove (7, 52, 70, 295, 302). Small garden 20' × 40'. Raised beds, mixed borders, ponds, conservatory. Yr-

round garden. 7 times winner Brighter Kensington & Chelsea Gardens Competition. Refreshments. *Adm £1 Chd 50p. Sun June 15 (2-6)*

The Watergardens ᯥ Warren Road, Kingston (Residents' Association). From Kingston take the A308 (Kingston Hill) towards London about ½m on R turn R into Warren Road. Japanese landscaped garden originally part of the Coombe Wood Nursery, approx 9 acres with water cascade features. *Adm £2 OAP £1 Chd 50p. Suns May 4, Oct 19 (2-5)*

¶**Well Cottage**, NW3 ᯥ❀ (Lynne & Ian Engel) 22D East Heath Rd, 5 mins walk from Hampstead station and a similar distance from the 268 bus stop at the Whitestone Pond. An interesting garden dating from the 50's within the sound of Christchurch clock chimes. One of the highest gardens in Hampstead with water, trees, and an old vine from the days when the cottage was part of a Chapel attached to a convent. Interesting new area to the side of the cottage created by Evelyn Hannah 2 yrs ago. Fenton House and Kenwood are within easy walking distance. TEAS. *Adm £1. Sun April 20 (2-6)*

3 Wellgarth Road, NW11 ᯥ❀ (Mrs A M Gear) Hampstead Garden Suburb. Turning off the North End Rd. Golders Green tube 6 mins walk. Buses, 268, 210. A walk all round the house, swathe of grass with long borders of bushes, trees and climbers. Close planting, herbaceous beds, roses, heathers, lavenders: herbs, mints, some uncommon plants. Paving, pots, and old oak tree; small pond with bubbling water. Winner in Hampstead Gardens Competition and All London Championship 1996. Homemade TEAS. *Adm £1.50. Sun June 22 (2-6)*

10 Wildwood Rd, NW11 ᯥ (Dr J W McLean) Hampstead. Wildwood Rd is between Hampstead Golf Course and N end of Hampstead Heath. From North End Rd turn by Manor House Hospital into Hampstead Way, then fork R. Garden planned and maintained by owner; one of finest herbaceous borders in North London, pond, HT roses; owner-grown prize winning delphiniums and seedlings. TEA. *Adm £1.50 Chd free. Sat July 5 (2-7)*

Wimbledon Gardens, SW19 ᯥᯥ Train: BR or underground. TEAS Somerset Rd and Murray Rd. *Combined adm £2 or £1 per garden Chd 50p. Sun June 15 (2-6)*
¶**2 Denmark Avenue** (John & Gillian Quenzer) Modest town garden (60' × 27') dominated by a 30 yr-old magnolia tree. Informal shrub and flower beds with sculptures by the owner emerging from the plants and hanging on the wall by the veranda
10 Denmark Road (Mr & Mrs Eadie) Tiny courtyard garden of interesting design with raised beds and containers. Wall fountain and pool; dovecote. Denmark Rd is a street of mid C19 cottages, with interesting front gardens
3 Murray Road ᯥ (Mr & Mrs Michael Waugh) On the corner of St Johns Rd opp St Johns Church. A continuous narrow plot approx 308 sq yds, round 3 sides of house. Informal cottage-garden planting of small shrubs, fruit trees, climbing roses, herbaceous and ground cover plants easy to grow and maintain in sunny position and very dry soil. Redesigned pond; some replanting. TEAS and morning coffee

21 Somerset Road ㅵ (Mr & Mrs John Perring) BR train or underground, 93 Bus up Wimbledon Hill to Calonne Rd. Walk on, next R, garden shortly on L. A new layout for the front garden; also new planting in the conservatory. Partly walled garden in ⅓-acre with 2 fine specimen cedars, shrubs, herbaceous, groundcover, climbing plants and small herb area around a lawn with lots of pine needles in it! TEAS

35 Wincanton Rd, SW18 ❀ (Helen Faulls) Off Wimbledon Park Rd, Southfields Tube. Bus 39. Sunny garden 17′ × 45′ located in a conservation area. Created by densely planting a wide variety of shrubs and herbaceous plants, incl many from the southern hemisphere. Colour, form and flowers yr-round. Terrace enclosed by mixed planting and fences clothed with shrubs and climbers to form a luxuriant setting for outdoor living. *Adm £1 Chd 50p (Share to International Spinal Research Trust®). Sun June 15 (2-6)*

47 Winn Road, SE12 ㅵ❀ (Mr & Mrs G Smith) Lee. 8m SE central London. 15mins walk from either BR Lee station (Sidcup Line to Dartford) or Grove Park (Orpington Line) from Charing Cross. By car, ½m from A20 Sidcup bypass or A205 S Circular. ⅓-acre mature plantsman's garden maintained by owners. Mixed borders, alpine beds, fruit and vegetables, 3 greenhouses featuring colourful displays of pelargoniums, fuchsias, begonias, cacti and succulents and other interesting plants. TEAS. *Adm £1 Chd free (Share to The Fifth Trust©). Suns April 27, June 22, Aug 17 (2-5)*

27 Wood Vale, N10 ♨❀ (Mr & Mrs A W Dallman) Muswell Hill 1m. A1 to Woodman public house; signed Muswell Hill; Muswell Hill Rd sharp R Wood Lane leading to Wood Vale; Highgate tube station. ¾-acre garden with herbaceous borders; ponds; orchard and kitchen garden. Unusual layout full of surprises. Numerous shrubs, roses, trees and conifers; greenhouses. Visitors may also wander in neighbouring gardens, all of which are of high standard. TEAS. *Adm £1.50 Chd 50p under 5yrs free (Share to British Legion and Meeting Point For St Georges Church®). Sat, Sun July 19, 20 (2-6)*

66 Woodbourne Avenue ♨ (Bryan d'Alberg & Keith Simmonds) Streatham. Cars enter from Garrads Rd by Tooting Bec Common. Easy parking. Garden designer's garden constantly evolving. Busy cottage style front garden 40′ × 60′ containing roses, irises and herbaceous plants. Rear garden approx 40′ × 80′ created over the last 6 yrs. Features shrubs, trees, gazebo and pool, creating a tranquil oasis in an urban setting. TEAS. *Adm £1 Chd 50p (Share to Crusaid®). Sun June 29 (1-6.30)*

7 Woodstock Road, W4 ♨ (Mr & Mrs L A Darke) Buses E3, 94, 27. Underground to Turnham Green 5 mins. Unusual garden created by present owners over 45 yrs behind Norman Shaw house in Bedford Park, the earliest garden suburb. Original rockery and wide selection of fine flowering trees, shrubs, herbaceous plants, roses, bulbs and recently planted ferns. Featured in 'London Pride', the 1990 exhibition of the history of the capital's gardens in the Museum of London. *Adm £1.25 Chd free. Sun April 20 (2-5)*

23 Woodville Road, W5 ♨❀ (Jill & Taki Argyropoulos) Close to Ealing Broadway Station (Central and District Lines). Bus 65 from Kingston and Richmond. Prize winner in 1995 and 1996 Ealing in Bloom competition. Front garden brick-paved, colourfully and densely planted borders and pots. Secluded, walled garden at rear 100′ × 40′ well stocked with flowering shrubs, climbers and many herbaceous plants. Alpine bed, small ornamental pond with waterfall and bog garden; also raised water trough with fish and frogs. Vegetable, herb and fruit areas. TEAS. *Adm £1. Sun July 20 (2-6)*

SYMBOLS USED IN THIS BOOK (See also Page 17)

‡   Following a garden name in the Dates of Opening list indicates that those gardens sharing the same symbol are nearby and open on the same day.

‡‡   Indicates a second series of nearby gardens open on the same day.

¶   Opening for the first time.

❀   Plants/produce for sale if available.

ㅵ   Gardens with at least the main features accessible by wheelchair.

♨   No dogs except guide dogs but otherwise dogs are usually admitted, provided they are kept on a lead. Dogs are not admitted to houses.

●   These gardens advertise their own dates in this publication although they do not nominate specific days for the NGS. Not all the money collected by these gardens comes to the NGS but they do make a guaranteed contribution.

■   These gardens nominate specific days for the NGS and advertise their own dates in this publication.

▲   These gardens open regularly to the public but they do not advertise their own dates in this publication. For further details, contact the garden directly.

Norfolk

Hon County Organisers: Mrs Neil Foster, Lexham Hall, King's Lynn PE32 2QJ
Tel 01328 701 341
Mrs David McCosh, Baconsthorpe Old Rectory, Holt NR25 6LU
Tel 01263 577611
Assistant County Organisers: Mrs David Mcleod, Gate House Farm, Salle NR10 4SD Tel 01603 870 897
The Hon Mrs Julian Darling, Intwood Hall, Norwich NR4 6TG
Hon Treasurer: Denzil Newton Esq OBE, Briar House, Gt Dunham, King's Lynn PE32 2LX

DATES OF OPENING

February 23 Sunday
Rainthorpe Hall, Tasburgh
March 30 Sunday
Lake House, Brundall
Wretham Lodge, East Wretham
March 31 Monday
Lake House, Brundall
April 13 Sunday
Desert World, Thetford Road,
Santon Downham
Gayton Hall, nr King's Lynn
Mannington Hall, Norwich
April 20 Sunday
Alby Crafts Gardens, Erpingham
The Old House, Ranworth
The Plantation Garden, Norwich
April 30 Wednesday
Hoveton Hall Gardens
May 4 Sunday
Lake House, Brundall
May 5 Monday
Lake House, Brundall
May 11 Sunday
How Hill Farm, Ludham ‡
Minns Cottage, Chapel Road,
Potter Heigham ‡
The Mowle, Ludham ‡
May 18 Sunday
Desert World, Thetford Road,
Santon Downham
Elmham House, North Elmham
86 Hungate Street, Aylsham ‡
The Old Vicarage, East Ruston
Rippon Hall, Hevingham, nr
Norwich ‡
Sheringham Park, Upper
Sheringham
Wretham Lodge, East Wretham
May 25 Sunday
Aylsham Gardens
Lexham Hall, nr Swaffham
Orchard House, Ringstead
May 26 Monday
Dell Farm, Aylsham
June 1 Sunday
Hoveton House, nr Wroxham
Letheringsett Gardens
Sheringham Park, Upper
Sheringham
Stow Hall, Stow Bardolph

June 8 Sunday
Alby Crafts Gardens, Erpingham
Besthorpe Hall, Attleborough
Gillingham Hall, nr Beccles
June 15 Sunday
Conifer Hill, Starston
Cubitt Cottage, Sloley
The Garden in an Orchard, Bergh
Apton
Hoveton House, nr Wroxham
Lawn Farm, Holt
Rainthorpe Hall, Tasburgh
Southacre Old Rectory
Southgate House, South Creake
June 22 Sunday
Bayfield Hall, nr Holt
Congham Hall Herb Gardens,
Grimston
13 Drapers Lane, Ditchingham
The Dutch House, Ludham
Felbrigg Hall, nr Cromer
Lexham Hall, nr Swaffham
Raveningham Hall
Wretham Lodge, East
Wretham
June 25 Wednesday
Congham Hall Herb Gardens,
Grimston
June 29 Sunday
Bradenham Hall, East
Dereham
Cubitt Cottage, Sloley
Elsing Hall, nr Dereham
Intwood Hall, nr Norwich
Stow Hall, Stow Bardolph
Wicken House, Castle Acre
July 2 Wednesday
Congham Hall Herb Gardens,
Grimston
July 6 Sunday
Cossey Corner Farm,
Raveningham
Orchards, Raveningham
July 13 Sunday
Easton Lodge, Easton
Minns Cottage, Chapel Road,
Potter Heigham
Town Close House School,
Norwich
July 18 Friday
The Lodge, Old Lakenham,
Norwich

July 20 Sunday
Burlingham Gardens, North
Burlingham
Hoveton House, nr Wroxham
The Lodge, Old Lakenham,
Norwich ‡
Oak Tree House, Thorpe,
Norwich ‡
Oxburgh Hall Garden, Oxburgh
July 25 Friday
Blickling Hall, Norwich
July 27 Sunday
Baconsthorpe Old Rectory, Holt
The Garden in an Orchard, Bergh
Apton
August 9 Saturday
Blickling Hall, Norwich
August 10 Sunday
Hoveton Hall Gardens
Oxburgh Hall Garden, Oxburgh
August 31 Sunday
The Plantation Garden, Norwich
September 3 Wednesday
The Old Vicarage, East Ruston
September 28 Sunday
Felbrigg Hall, nr Cromer
October 5 Sunday
Mannington Hall, Aylsham

Regular openings
For details see garden description

Bradenham Hall, East Dereham
Congham Hall Herb Gardens
Hoveton Hall Gardens, nr Wroxham
Magpies, Green Lane, Mundford
Mannington Hall, Norwich
Norfolk Lavender Ltd, Heacham
The Old Vicarage, East Ruston
The Plantation Garden, Norwich
Raveningham Hall
Sandringham Grounds

By appointment only
*For telephone numbers and other
details see garden descriptions.
Private visits welcomed*

Lanehead, Garboldisham

DESCRIPTIONS OF GARDENS

▲**Alby Crafts Gardens** ♿❀ (Mr & Mrs John Alston) Erpingham. On A140 4m N Aylsham, parking by Alby Crafts car park. 4-acre garden. Primroses, spring bulbs, irises, hellebores, old-fashioned roses, mixed borders, 4 ponds (1 with wild flower and conservation area). Plantsman's garden. TEAS. *Adm £1.50 Chd free. For NGS Suns April 20, June 8 (11-5). Parties welcome, please* **Tel 01263 761226**

Aylsham Gardens *Combined adm £3 Chd free*
   5 Cromer Road ♿ (Dr & Mrs James) Aylsham. 100yds N of Aylsham Parish Church down old Cromer Rd on LH-side. Approx 1 acre of semi-wild garden nr town centre with large willow trees and grass. Mixed borders and shrubs. Small natural pond, hostas and primulas. Vegetables. *Adm £1 Chd free. Sun May 25 (2-6)*
   10 St Michael's Close ❀❀ (M I Davies Esq) Aylsham NW on B1354 towards Blickling Hall; 500yds from market place, turn R, Rawlinsons Lane, then R again. Front gravelled area with mixed shrub and herbaceous border; small rockery. Back garden with large variety of shrubs, herbaceous plants, bulbs, small lawn, roses, azaleas. Plants, pond. Aviary, guinea pigs. TEAS. *Adm £1 Chd free. Sun May 25 (11-6). Private visits welcome, please* **Tel 01263 732174**
   West Lodge ♿ (Mr & Mrs Jonathan Hirst) Aylsham. ¼m NW of market square on N side of B1354 (entrance in Rawlinsons Lane) Large 9-acre garden with lawns, mature trees, rose garden, herbaceous borders, ornamental pond and walled kitchen garden; Georgian House (not open) and outbuildings incl a well-stocked toolshed (open) and greenhouses. TEAS in aid of Aylsham Church. *Adm £1.50 Chd free. Sun May 25 (2-5.30)*

Baconsthorpe Old Rectory ♿❀❀ (Mr & Mrs David McCosh) Holt. Follow sign to Baconsthorpe from Holt bypass for 3m. Rectory is beside church at far end of village. Overgrown 3-acre garden undergoing excavation and restoration. Extensive box hedges dividing kitchen garden and newly planted herbaceous borders. 30ft conservatory. Thatched summer house, rosebeds and mulberry trees; lawns and large trees; decorative outbuildings. TEAS. *Adm £1.50 Chd free (Share to St Mary's PCC®). Sun July 27 (2-6)*

Bayfield Hall ❀ (Mr & Mrs R H Combe) 1m N of Holt, off A148. Formal but simple pleasure gardens with medieval church ruin. Old-fashioned roses, herbaceous and shrub borders; magnificent view over lake and park. Wildflower centre adjacent to garden. Mini-Antiques Road Show, Mongrel's Crufts (all dogs welcome) various stalls and family entertainment, in aid of St Martins Church, Glandford. Free TEAS. *Adm £1.50 Chd 50p. Sun June 22 (2-5)*

Besthorpe Hall ♿❀❀ (John Alston Esq) 1m E of Attleborough. On Attleborough-Bunwell Rd; adjacent to Besthorpe Church. Garden with shrubs, trees and herbaceous borders within Tudor enclosures; walled kitchen garden; tilting ground. Coach parties by appt. TEAS. *Adm £2 Chd free (Share to Besthorpe Church®). Sun June 8 (2-5). Also private visits welcome, please* **Tel 01953 452138**

▲**Blickling Hall** ♿❀ (The National Trust) 1¼ miles NW of Aylsham on N side of B1354. 15m N of Norwich (A140). Large garden, orangery, crescent lake, azaleas, rhododendrons, herbaceous borders. Historic Jacobean house. Wheelchairs available. Cream TEAS and lunches. *Adm £3.20 Chd £1.70. For NGS Fri July 25, Sat Aug 9 (10.30-5)*

■ **Bradenham Hall** ♿❀❀ (Lt Col & Mrs R C Allhusen) West Bradenham, Thetford. Off A47 6m E Swaffham, 3m W of East Dereham. Turn S signed Wendling and Longham. Turn S 1m signed Bradenham, 2m. Follow NGS signs. A garden for all seasons with massed daffodil plantings, in varieties all labelled. Arboretum of over 1000 species and varieties all labelled. Rose garden, herbaceous borders and mixed plantings, wall shrubs and roses, fruit and vegetable garden, glasshouses. Featured in Country Life, House and Garden and Sunday Telegraph. TEAS. *Adm £3 Chd free (Share to Bradenham PCC and SCBU, Q Elizabeth Hospital, Kings Lynn®). Open 2nd, 4th and 5th Sun of every month from April to Sept (2-5.30). For NGS Suns June 29 (11-5.30). Coaches at other times by appt only* **Tel 01362 687279**

Burlingham Gardens ♿❀ (Easton College) North Burlingham, 10mE of Norwich off A47 at Burlingham. Horticultural Educational Gardens founded in 1926, with a range of continually varying features. Fine lawns and herbaceous borders with specimen trees and mature shrubs. Winter gardens with demonstration hedges. Glasshouses open for viewing with plants and crops on display. TEAS. *Adm £1.50 Chd free. Sun July 20 (1.30-5.30)*

■ ¶**Congham Hall Herb Gardens** ♿❀❀ (Mr & Mrs Forecast) Grimston, King's Lynn. From A149/A148 interchange NE of King's Lynn, follow A148 to Sandringham/Fakenham. 100yds on, turn R to Grimston. The hotel and herb garden are 2½m on L. Set in 40 acres of parkland, this working herb garden contains over 650 herbs. Cultivated gardens, new 'woodery garden' and orchards. TEAS. *Adm £1.50 Chd 50p. Open from April 1 to Sept 30 (2-4). For NGS Sun June 22 (1.30-5). Weds June 25, July 2 (10-4)*

Conifer Hill ♿❀ (Mr & Mrs Richard Lombe Taylor) Starston, Harleston. 18m S of Norwich. A140 to Pulham Xrds. Turn L to B1134. 1m NW of Harleston, off B1134. Take Redenhall Rd out of Starston. Conifer Hill on L ½m out of village. Steep bend and white gates. 4-acre Victorian garden. Lawns, shrubs, roses, herbaceous and kitchen garden. ½-acre pinetum, in steep escarpment of old quarry. TEAS. *Adm £1.50 Chd free. Sun June 15 (2-6)*

Cubitt Cottage &&& (Mrs Janie Foulkes) Sloley. 11m N of Norwich just off B1150 Coltishall to North Walsham Rd. 2nd R after Three Horseshoes public house at Scottow. Into village, then Low Street, R at next signpost. 1-acre garden with lawns, herbaceous and shrub border, over 100 varieties of old roses, clematis and unusual plants; wildflower meadow; wild life pond and bog garden; vegetable garden and greenhouses. Cream TEAS. *Adm £2 Chd free. Suns June 15, 29 (2-6). Also private visits welcome, please* Tel 01692 538295

Dell Farm &&& (Mrs M J Monk) Aylsham. Approx ¼m W of centre of Aylsham. Turn L off Blickling Rd on to Heydon Rd (signposted Oulton). 400yds on to copper beech arching rd. Turn R through gate. 4-acre garden; mature trees and shrubs. Various rose collections, rhododendrons, azaleas, heathers. Spring bulbs, primroses etc in old orchard and wild flower garden. TEAS. *Adm £1.50 Chd 50p. Mon May 26 (2-6). Also private visits welcome especially for spring bulbs, please* Tel 01263 732277

Desert World &&& (Mr & Mrs Barry Gayton) Santon Downham. On B1107. Thetford 4m, Brandon 2m. 1¼ acres landscaped plantsman's garden, specialising in alpines, herbaceous and spring bulbs, incl semperviviums. Glasshouses containing 12,500 cacti and succulents. Viewing of glasshouses by appt only. Featured on radio and TV. TEAS. *Adm £1.50 Chd free. Suns April 13, May 18 (1-6). Private, group visits and gardening lectures by appt. Please,* Tel 01842 765861

13 Drapers Lane &&& (Mr & Mrs Borrett) Ditchingham. 1m Bungay off the B1332 towards Norwich. ⅓-acre containing many interesting, unusual plants incl 100 plus varieties of hardy geraniums, climbers and shrubs. Herbaceous perennials a speciality. Owner maintained. TEAS. *Adm £1.50 Chd free. Sun June 22 (12-4). Also opening for Suffolk May 4, 5*

The Dutch House && (Mrs Peter Seymour) Ludham. B1062 Wroxham to Ludham 7m. Turn R by Ludham village church into Staithe Rd. Gardens ¼m from village. Long, narrow garden designed and planted by the painter Edward Seago, leading through marsh to Womack Water. Approx 2½ acres. Newly replanted herbaceous borders and alterations in hand. TEAS. *Adm £2 Chd free. Sun June 22 (2-5.30)*

Easton Lodge ✿ (J M Rampton Esq) Easton, 6m W Norwich. Cross the new Southern Norwich Bypass at the Easton Roundabout and take the Ringland Rd. Large garden in magnificent setting above river surrounded by fine trees; walks amongst interesting shrubs, roses, plants; herbaceous border; walled kitchen garden. Late Georgian house with Jacobean centre portion (not open). TEAS. *Adm £1.50 Chd free. Sun July 13 (2.30-5.30)*

Ellingham Hall nr Bungay. See Suffolk for details

Elmham House &&& (Mr & Mrs R S Don) North Elmham, 5m N of East Dereham, on B1110. Entrance opp Church. Medium-sized garden; wild garden; C18 walled garden; view of park and lake; vineyard, tours of winery. TEAS. *Adm £2 Chd free (Share to St Mary's Church N Elmham®). Sun May 18 (2-6). Private visits by appt only to incl vineyard, please* Tel 01362 668363

Elsing Hall ✿ (Mrs D Cargill) Dereham. 2m E of Dereham off A47; sign to Elsing. Medieval house surrounded by moat. Over 200 varieties of old-fashioned roses; wild flower lawn, walled kitchen garden with roses, fruit trees & clematis. Many water plants by moat and fish stew. Rare and interesting trees in arboretum; formal garden with clipped box, lavender, sage, santolina and thyme. Suitable wheelchairs in places. TEAS in aid of Elsing Church. *Adm £3 Chd free. Sun June 29 (2-6). Private parties welcome, please* Tel 01362 637224

▲**Felbrigg Hall** &&& (The National Trust) Roughton, 2½m SW of Cromer, S of A148; main entrance from B1436; signed from Felbrigg village. Large pleasure gardens; mainly lawns and shrubs; orangery with camellias; large walled garden restored and restocked as fruit, vegetable, herb and flower garden; vine house; dovecote; dahlias; superb colchicum; wooded parks. 1 Electric and 3 manual wheelchairs available. Lunches, pre booking essential. TEAS. *Adm £2 Chd £1 Family ticket £4. For NGS Suns June 22, Sept 28 (11-5)*

The Garden in an Orchard &&& (Mr & Mrs R W Boardman) Bergh Apton, Norwich. 6m SE of Norwich off A146 at Hellington Corner signed to Bergh Apton. Down Mill Rd 300 yds. 3½-acre garden set in an old orchard. Many rare and unusual plants set out in an informal pattern of wandering paths. ½-acre of wild flower meadows, many bamboos, specie roses, 9 species of eucalyptus. In all a plantsman's garden. TEAS. *Adm £1.50 Chd free. Suns June 15, July 27 (11-6)*

Gayton Hall &&& (Mr & Mrs Julian Marsham) 6m E of King's Lynn off B1145; signs in Gayton village. 20 acres; wild woodland, water garden. Bulbs, TEAS. *Adm £2 Chd free (Share to NSPCC®). Sun April 13 (2-5). Private visits welcome, please* Tel 01553 636259

Gillingham Hall &&& (Mr & Mrs Robin Bramley) Beccles. 16m SE of Norwich, 1½m from Beccles off A146. 14-acre garden with lake, lawns, borders, rose garden, specimen plane trees, wild flower areas, bulbs; Mansion house (not open) c1600. TEAS/Plants in aid of Church Restoration Funds. *Adm £2 Chd free. Sun June 8 (2-5). Parties welcome, please* Tel 01502 713294

■ **Hoveton Hall Gardens** &&& (Mr & Mrs Andrew Buxton) 8m N of Norwich; 1m N of Wroxham Bridge on A1151 Stalham Rd. Approx 10-acre gardens and grounds featuring principally daffodils, azaleas, rhododendrons and hydrangeas in a woodland setting and a large, mature, walled herbaceous garden. Water plants, a lakeside walk and walled kitchen garden provide additional interest. Early C19 house (not open). TEAS. *Adm £2.50 Chd £1. Gardens open, every Wed, Fri, Sun and Bank Hols, Easter Sun to Sept 14 incl (11.30- 5.30). For NGS Weds April 30, Sun Aug 10 (Share to Multiple Sclerosis Society Research®) (11.30-5.30)*

Hoveton House &&& (Sir John & Lady Blofeld) 9m N Norwich, ½m Wroxham on B1062, Horning-Ludham Rd. Old-fashioned walled garden; magnificent herbaceous and other borders full of unusual plants and bulbs; rock garden. Established rhododendron grove. Kitchen garden. Park; lawns, walks with magnificent view. William & Mary House (not open.) Plants for sale June only. TEAS. *Adm £2 Chd free (Share to St John's Church®). Suns June 15, July 20 (2-5.30)*

How Hill Farm ❀ (P D S Boardman Esq) 2m W of Ludham on A1062; then follow signs to How Hill; Farm Garden - S of How Hill. Very pretty garden started in 1968 in water garden setting with three ponds; recent 3-acre broad (dug as conservation project) with variety of water lilies and view over the R Ant; fine old mill. Winding paths through rare conifers; unusual and rare rhododendrons with massed azaleas; other ornamental trees and shrubs; a few herbaceous plants; collection of English holly, ilex aquifolium (over 100 varieties). Collection of bamboos. Partly suitable for wheelchairs. TEA. *Adm £2 Chd free (Share to How Hill Trust©). Sun May 11 (2-5)*

86 Hungate Street ✿❀ (Mrs Sue Ellis) Aylsham. From Norwich towards Cromer on A140. Turn L at roundabout S of Aylsham towards Stonegate, turn R into Hungate St. Proceed along for ¾m to row of white cottages on L. A small town garden 95' × 45' laid out in a semi-formal style, consisting of sunken lawns, raised beds and pergolas. A plantswoman's garden densely planted with small specimen trees/shrubs. Rhododendrons, roses, primulas, ornamental pond. Raised vegetable area with propagation frame, greenhouse, enclosed by beech and laurel hedge. *Adm £1.50 Chd free. Sun May 18 (12-5)*

Intwood Hall ♿❀ (The Hon Julian & Mrs Darling) 3½m SW Norwich, via A11 to Cringleford, fork L (avoid dual carriageway), over Cringleford bridge, L turn, over Xrds, level crossing, bypass for ½m. On R by thatched lodge. Tudor walled water garden and walled Victorian rose garden; herbaceous borders; 2 woodland walks, 1 to Saxon Church; park with lovely trees; walled kitchen garden with greenhousing. TEAS. *Adm £2 Chd free. Sun June 29 (2-5.30)*

Lake House ❀ (Mr & Mrs Garry Muter) Brundall. Approx 5m E of Norwich on A47; take Brundall turn at Roundabout. Turn R into Postwick Lane at T-junction. An acre of water gardens set among magnificent trees in a steep cleft in the river escarpment. Informal flower beds with interesting plants; a naturalist's paradise; unsuitable for young children or the infirm. Wellingtons advisable. 'Unusual plants for sale.' TEAS. *Adm £2 Chd free (Share to Water Aid®). Easter Sun & Mon March 30, 31; Sun, Mon May 4, 5 (11-5). Private parties welcome, please* **Tel 01603 712933**

Lanehead ♿ (Mrs N A Laurie) Garboldisham, 8m W of Diss off A1066 at village Xrds take the A1111 for ½m to 1st R. Medium-sized garden created by owner; featured in a television programme, visited by many horticultural groups; well designed natural walks with shrubs and specimen trees; colour co-ordinated borders for all-year interest; water and bog garden; roses and woodland. Coffee, TEA. *Adm £2 Chd free (Share to Garboldisham Church Fabric Fund®). Private visits welcome by appt April to Sept, please* **Tel 01953 81380**

¶**Lawn Farm** ♿❀❀ (Mrs G W Deterding) Holt. Leave Holt on Cley Rd (opp. King's Head) 1m on R. 6½-acre garden with ponds and mediaeval courtyard gardens. Interesting trees and spectacular roses. TEAS in aid of Norwich Blind Association. *Adm £1.50 Chd free. Sun June 15 (2-5)*

Letheringsett Gardens ♿ 1m W of Holt on A148. Car park King's Head Meadow or disabled near church. TEAS. *Combined adm £2 Chd free. Sun June 1 (2-5.30)*
> **The Glebe** ♿❀ (The Hon Beryl Cozens-Hardy) Medium-sized riverside garden, with island, wild flowers, water garden, shrub borders
> **Letheringsett Hall** (Mrs English) Home for the Elderly; medium-sized garden and river
> **Letheringsett Estate Garden** (Mr & Mrs Robert Carter) Large garden; wooded walks, fountain, lake, water plants, wild flowers. Hydraulic rams 1852 and 1905

Lexham Hall ♿❀❀ (Mr & Mrs Neil Foster) 2m W of Litcham off B1145. Fine 17th/18th century Hall (not open); parkland with lake and river walks. Formal garden with terraces, yew hedges, roses and mixed borders. Traditional kitchen garden with crinkle-crankle wall. 3-acre woodland garden with azaleas, rhododendrons, spring bulbs and rare trees. TEAS. *Adm £2.50 Chd free (Share to St Andrews Church, E. Lexham® May, All Saints Church, Litcham® June). Suns May 25, June 22 (2-6). Also groups (min 20) by appt May 1 to July 31 (weekdays only), please* **Tel 01328 701288**

The Lodge ❀❀ (Mr & Mrs P J E Smith) Sandy Lane, Old Lakenham. SE of Norwich just off ring rd (Barrett Rd). Turn out of city at Mansfield Lane traffic lights. 200yds on L opp St John's Church (also open). 1½-acres of contoured garden in beautiful setting leading down to R Yare. Herbaceous and shrub borders, enclosed croquet lawn, 1920's sunken garden, ducks, ancient mulberry tree. TEAS. *Adm £2 Chd free (Share to St John's Church®). Sun July 20 (2-6). Fri July 18 (6-8.30) Adm £3.50 Chd free with Music and wine*

Magpies ♿❀❀ (Mr & Mrs Dennis Cooper) Green Lane Mundford. From main Mundford roundabout take A1065 to Swaffham. After ¼m turn L down Green Lane. Divided into 'rooms' giving a cottage garden effect, a 1-acre garden filled with island beds, intensively planted with unusual perennials, ornamental grasses and cottage garden plants. Ponds and planted gravel areas. A wilder margin and tree belt encourages an abundance of birds throughout the year. Featured in 'Amateur Gardening'. Wide variety of unusual plants available from adjoining nursery. *Adm £1 Chd free. Open every day in June (12-6). Private visits welcome, please* **Tel 01842 878496**

■ **Mannington Hall** ♿❀❀ (The Lord & Lady Walpole) 2m N of Saxthorpe; 18m NW of Norwich via B1149 towards Holt. At Saxthorpe (B1149 & B1354) turn NE signed Mannington. 20 acres feature roses, shrubs, lake and trees. Daffodil lined drive. Extensive countryside walks and trails. Moated manor house (not open). Saxon church with C19 follies. Lunches and TEAS in aid of St Mary's Church, Itteringham. *Gardens open Suns May to Sept, Weds, Thurs, Fris June to Aug. Adm £3 OAPs/students £2.50 Chd free. For NGS Sun April 13, Oct 5 (12-5)*

Minns Cottage &&& (Mr & Mrs Derek Brown) Chapel Rd, Potter Heigham. From Norwich take A1151 then A149 to Potter Heigham Xrds. Turn L into Station Rd on to T junction, turn L into School Rd, turning into Green Lane. At telephone box turn R into Chapel Rd. Approx 1¼-acres winding lawns leading through pergolas to rose garden with old English roses and other small gardens with mixed borders, recently planted woodland area with rhododendrons and bulbs. A garden to walk round peacefully at all seasons. TEAS. *Adm £2 Chd free. Suns May 11 (2-5), July 13 (2-6)*

The Mowle &&& (Mrs N N Green) Ludham. B1062 Wroxham to Ludham 7m. Turn R by Ludham village church into Staithe Rd. Gardens ¼m from village. Approx 2½ acres running down to marshes. Interesting shrub borders, unusual trees etc incl tulip trees and a golden catalpa. TEAS. *Adm £1.50 Chd free. Sun May 11 (2-6); also private visits welcome, please.* **Tel 01692 678213**

●**Norfolk Lavender Ltd** &&& Caley Mill, Heacham. On A149 13m N of Kings Lynn. National collection of lavenders set in 2 acres (lavender harvest July-Aug); fragrant meadow and herb garden. New conservatory opens as fragrant plant centre this yr. TEAS. *Adm free. Collecting box. Daily to Christmas (10-5). Reopens Jan 10.* **Tel 01485 570384**

Oak Tree House &&& (W R S Giles Esq) 6 Cotman Rd, Thorpe. E of Norwich off A47 Thorpe Rd. ¼m from Norwich Thorpe Station. From Yarmouth direction follow one way system towards City Centre, turn R at traffic lights opposite Min. of Fisheries & Agric. Approx 300yds on, turn L opposite Barclays Bank. Botanical illustrators interesting plantsmans garden, of approx ½-acre on a hillside. Containing a mixture of hardy and tender plants giving a strong subtropical Mediterranean influence, containing tree ferns, bamboos, palms, bananas, cannas, agaves and many more. Also traditional herbaceous borders and a woodland garden with fernery. This garden has appeared in various TV programmes, magazines and books. TEAS. *Adm £2.50, Chd free. Sun July 20 (1.30-5.30)*

The Old House, Ranworth &&& (Mr Francis & The Hon Mrs Cator) 9m NE of Norwich off B1140. Turn L in S Walsham to Ranworth, below church. Attractive linked and walled gardens alongside beautiful, peaceful Ranworth inner broad. Bulbs, shrubs, potager, mown rides through recently established arboretum where dogs may be walked on leads, pond with many species of ducks and geese. ½m of woodland walk. Norfolk Wildlife Trust Conservation Centre, and historic Church nearby. TEA. *Adm £2 Chd free. Sun April 20 (2-5)*

Remember that every time you visit a National Gardens Scheme garden you are helping to raise money for the following:
**The Queen's Nursing Institute
The Nurses' Welfare Service
Cancer Relief Macmillan Fund
The Gardens Fund of the National Trust
The Gardeners' Royal Benevolent Society
The Royal Gardeners' Orphan Fund**

■ **The Old Vicarage** &&& (Alan Gray and Graham Robeson) East Ruston. 3m N of Stalham on Stalham to Happisburgh/Walcott Rd (ignore all 3 signposts to East Ruston). Turn R 200 yds just N of East Ruston Church. 12-acre exotic coastal garden and grounds incl impressive herbaceous borders, autumn border, tropical border incl bananas and palms, sunken garden, walled garden, Mediterranean garden and wild flower meadows and walks. TEAS. *Adm £3 Chd £1. Open every Sun and Wed from May 4 to Oct 29 incl. For NGS Sun May 18, Wed Sept 3 (2-5)*

¶**Orchard House** ❀ (Mr & Mrs M G T Hart) Ringstead. A149 13m N from King's Lynn. Turn R to Ringstead shortly after Norfolk Lavender. Follow signs to Docking. Orchard House is 3rd last on way out of village. ¾-acre shrubs and herbaceous. Mixed and themed borders and beds, small pond, water feature, herb and vegetable gardens. Sunken garden and small wild area. TEA. *Adm £1 Chd free (Share to International Glaucoma Assoc®). Sun May 25 (2-6)*

▲**Oxburgh Hall Garden** &&& (The National Trust) 7m SW of Swaffham, at Oxburgh on Stoke Ferry rd. Hall and moat surrounded by lawns, fine trees, colourful borders; charming parterre garden of French design. Lunches. Cream TEAS. *Adm £2 Chd 50p. For NGS Suns July 20, Aug 10 (11-5)*

■ **The Plantation Garden** &&& (Plantation Garden Preservation Trust) 4 Earlham Rd, Norwich. Entrance between Crofters and Beeches Hotels, nr St John's R C Cathedral. 3-acre Victorian town garden created 1856-96 in former medieval chalk quarry. Still undergoing restoration by volunteers, remarkable architectural features include 60ft Italianate terrace and unique 30ft Gothic fountain. Surrounded by mature trees. 10 min walk city centre, beautifully tranquil atmosphere. *Adm £1.50 Chd free (Share to Plantation Garden Preservation Trust®). Suns mid April to mid Oct (2-5). For NGS TEAS Suns April 20, Aug 31 (2-5). Private visits welcome, please* **Tel 01603 621868**

Rainthorpe Hall &&& (Mr & Mrs Alastair Wilson) Tasburgh. Approx 8m S of Norwich, just off the A140 - turn by garage in Newton Flotman. On 1m to red brick pillars and gates on L. Elizabethan/Victorian/Country House (not open) prettily set in interesting variety of gardens, incl knot hedge (said to be as old as the house) and hazel coppice (said to be older). Fine trees and collection of bamboos. [Croquet and bowls available, but *not* to high standard]. TEAS. *Adm £2.50 OAP £1.50 Chd free. Suns Feb 23 (1-4) June 15 (2-5.30). Private visits welcome, please* **Tel 01508 470618**

Raveningham Gardens &&& 14m SE of Norwich, 4m from Beccles off B1136. *Combined adm £2 Chd free. Sun July 6 (2-5)*
　　Cossey Corner Farm (Mr & Mrs M Myhill) From Norwich, ¼m before Hall. ¼-acre herbaceous and large variety of bedding plants. Colourful and delightful garden
　　Orchards (Priscilla Lady Bacon) From Norwich, ¼m before Raveningham Hall. Plantsman's garden, rare shrubs and plants. *Private visits welcome, by arrangement please* **Tel 01508 548 322/206**

■ **Raveningham Hall** ﹩✿ (Sir Nicholas Bacon) Large garden specialising in rare shrubs, herbaceous plants, especially euphorbia, agapanthus and shrub roses. Victorian conservatory and walled vegetable garden, newly planted Arboretum. *Adm £2 Chd free. Garden open every Sunday, Bank Hols May, June, July (2-5). For NGS TEAS Sun June 22 (2-5)*

Rippon Hall ﹩✿ (Miss Diana Birkbeck) Hevingham, 8m N of Norwich. From A140 Norwich-Aylsham rd, turn R (E) at Xrds just N of Hevingham Church. Rhododendrons and azalea borders. Large herd of rare breed of British White Cattle. TEAS. *Adm £1.50 Chd 25p. Sun May 18 (2-5.30)*

● **Sandringham Grounds** ﹩✿✿ By gracious permission of H.M. The Queen, the House, Museum and Grounds at Sandringham will be open. 60 acres of informal gardens, woodland and lakes, with rare plants and trees. Donations are given from the Estate to various charities. For further information see p 15. TEAS. *Adm House and Grounds £4.50 OAPs £3.50 Chd £2.50; Grounds only £3.50 OAPs £3 Chd £2 March 28 to Oct 5 daily. House closed July 22 to Aug 6 incl & Grounds closed July 27 to Aug 6 incl. (Hours House 11-4.45; Grounds 10.30-5)*

▲**Sheringham Park** ﹩✿ (The National Trust) 2m SW of Sheringham. Access for cars off A148 Cromer to Holt Road, 5m W of Cromer, 6m E of Holt (signs in Sheringham Town). 50-acres of species rhododendron, azalea and magnolia. Also numerous specimen trees incl handkerchief tree. Viewing towers, waymarked walks, sea and parkland views. Special walk way and WCs for disabled. TEAS. *Adm £2.50 per car. For NGS Suns May 18, June 1 (dawn to dusk).* **Tel 01263 823778**

Southacre Old Rectory ﹩✿ (Mrs Clive Hardcastle) 3m NW of Swaffham off A1065 opp Southacre Church. 3-acre garden with splendid views of Castle Acre Priory. Mixed borders, shrubs, vineyard, herb garden, pool and old-fashioned rose garden. Interesting C15 church. TEAS in aid of Southacre Church Restoration Fund. *Adm £2 Chd free. Sun June 15 (2-5.30). Private visits welcome May, June and July, please* **Tel 01760 755469**

Southgate House ﹩✿✿ (Mr & Mrs Harry Schulman) South Creake. 5m NW of Fakenham. Follow B1355 towards Burnham Market. Just after sign to Waterden on R, turn L at signs. Entrance approx 200yds. A challenging garden of 1½ acres with new developments annually.

Many interesting trees, shrubs, plants and bulbs. A must for anyone discouraged by wind and lack of shelter. Cream TEAS. *Adm £1.50 Chd free (Share to St Mary's Church, N Creake®). Sun June 15 (2-5.30)*

Stow Hall ﹩✿ (Lady Rose Hare) Stow Bardolph. 2m N of Downham Market on A10, village of Stow Bardolph signposted to the E of the A10. Approx 20 acres of garden and grounds with many mature trees, high walls, climbing plants and shrub roses. Walled kitchen garden contains very old varieties of apple and pear trees one of which - Golden Noble Apple is mentioned in The English Apple by Rosanne Sanders as having been raised at Stow in 1820. Young apple trees with East Anglian interest are being planted. Newly landscaped gardens on site of old Hall. TEAS. *Adm £2 Chd free (Share to Holy Trinity Church, Stow Bardolph®). Suns June 1, 29 (2-6). Private parties welcome, please* **Tel 01366 383194**

Town Close House School ﹩✿ 14 Ipswich Rd. On A140 between Norwich outer ring rd and St Stephen's roundabout; entrance opp City College. Approx 4 acres of gardens of C18 Town Close House (now prep school). Part laid out to shrubs, flower and heather beds, part woodland with paths. Ponds, large lawn. TEAS. *Adm £1.50 Chd free. Sun July 13 (1-5)*

Wicken House ﹩✿✿ (Lord & Lady Keith) Castle Acre, 5m N of Swaffham off A1065; W at Newton to Castle Acre; then 2m N off the rd to Massingham. Large walled garden planted in sections with many roses and unusual herbaceous plants; gravel paths and greenhouses; swimming pool garden; spring and wild gardens. Fine views. Approx 6 acres. Rare plants for sale. Home-made cream TEAS. *Adm £2 Chd free (Share to the Friends of Castle Acre Church®). Sun June 29 (2-5)*

Wretham Lodge ﹩✿✿ (Mrs Anne Hoellering) East Wretham. A11 E from Thetford; L up A1075; L by village sign; R at Xrds then bear L. In spring masses of specie tulips, hellebores, fritillaries, daffodils and narcissi; bluebell walk. In June hundreds of old roses. Walled garden, with fruit and interesting vegetable plots. Mixed borders and fine old trees. Wild flower meadows. Featured in Peter Beales' Vision of Roses. TEAS. *Adm £2 (£1 March) Chd free (Share to St Johns Ambulance in May, and Wretham Church in June®). Suns March 30 (11-6) May 18, June 22 (2.30-5.30). Also private visits and coach parties welcome, please write or* **Tel 01953 498366**

1927–1997

This year the National Gardens Scheme is celebrating its 70th Anniversary.

Please help us celebrate by visiting a garden in 1997.

Northamptonshire

Hon County Organiser:	Mrs E T Smyth-Osbourne, Versions Farm, Brackley NN13 5JY
	Tel 01280 702412
Asst Hon County Organisers:	Mrs John Bussens, Glebe Cottage, Titchmarsh, Kettering NN14 3DB
	Tel 01832 732510
	Mrs R H N Dashwood, Farthinghoe Lodge, Nr Brackley, Northants NN13 5NX
	Mrs R Blake, Lodge Lawn, Fotheringhay, Peterborough PE8 5HZ
Hon County Treasurer	R H N Dashwood Esq, Farthinghoe Lodge, nr Brackley,
	Northants NN13 5NX
	Tel 01295 710377

DATES OF OPENING

March 30 Sunday
Evenley Wood Garden, nr Brackley
March 31 Monday
Evenley Wood Garden, nr Brackley
April 6 Sunday
Charlton, nr Banbury
The Nursery Gardens, Geddington
The Old Rectory, Sudborough
April 20 Sunday
Maidwell Hall, Northampton
May 4 Sunday
Evenley Wood Garden, Brackley
The Haddonstone Show Garden,
nr Northampton
May 5 Monday
Evenley Wood Garden, Brackley
The Haddonstone Show Garden,
nr Northampton
Titchmarsh Gardens, nr Thrapston
May 11 Sunday
Aldwincle Gardens, nr Thrapston
Great Brington Gardens,
Northampton
The Walnuts, King's Cliffe
Holdenby House Garden and
Falconry Centre
May 14 Wednesday
The Walnuts, King's Cliffe
May 18 Sunday
Deene Park, nr Corby
Guilsborough and Hollowell
Gardens
May 25 Sunday
4 Elmington Cottages, nr Oundle
Evenley Wood Garden, Brackley
Falcutt House, nr Brackley
Lois Weedon House, Weedon
Lois, nr Towcester
Newnham Gardens, nr Daventry
The Old Barn, Weedon Lois
May 26 Monday
Evenley Wood Garden, Brackley
Titchmarsh Gardens, nr Thrapston
May 28 Wednesday
Newnham Gardens, nr Daventry
June 1 Sunday
Litchborough Gardens
The Old Rectory, Sudborough

Sholebroke Lodge, Towcester
Steane Park, Brackley
June 7 Saturday
Canons Ashby House, nr Daventry
June 8 Sunday
Benefield House, Lower
Benefield, nr Oundle
The Nursery Gardens,
Geddington
Preston Capes Gardens
Slapton Gardens, nr Towcester
Stoke Park, Stoke Bruerne,
Towcester
Turweston Mill, Brackley
Versions Farm, nr Brackley
June 10 Tuesday
Coton Manor, Guilsborough
June 11 Wednesday
Badby Gardens, nr Daventry
June 14 Saturday
Evenley Gardens, nr Brackley
June 15 Sunday
Badby Gardens, nr Daventry
Cottingham & Middleton Gardens
Evenley Gardens, nr Brackley
Kilsby Gardens, nr Rugby
Maidwell Gardens
Sulgrave Gardens, Banbury
June 18 Wednesday
Cottingham & Middleton
Gardens
Maidwell Gardens
June 21 Saturday
Flore Gardens, nr Northampton
The Old Vicarage, Great Cransley,
nr Kettering
June 22 Sunday
Culworth Gardens, nr Banbury
Flore Gardens, nr Northampton
Great Addington Manor, nr
Kettering ‡
Irthlingborough, 49 Finedon
Road, nr Wellingborough ‡
The Menagerie, Horton, nr
Northampton
The Old Vicarage, Great Cransley,
nr Kettering
June 25 Wednesday
The Old Barn, Weedon Lois
Bradden House, nr Towcester

June 29 Sunday
Bulwick Rectory, Bulwick
Cottesbrooke Hall, nr Creaton
Easton Neston, Towcester
Finedon Gardens, nr
Wellingborough ‡
Gamekeepers Cottage, nr Creaton
Harpole Gardens, Northampton
Turweston Gardens, nr Brackley
Wilby Gardens, nr
Wellingborough ‡
July 2 Wednesday
The Old Barn, Weedon Lois
July 6 Sunday
Mill House, Stoke Doyle, nr
Oundle
Newnham Gardens, nr Daventry
West Haddon Gardens, nr
Northants
July 9 Wednesday
The Old Barn, Weedon Lois
July 12 Saturday
The Prebendal Manor House,
Nassington
July 13 Sunday
Cranford Gardens, nr Kettering
Ravensthorpe Gardens
July 16 Wednesday
Ravensthorpe Nursery
July 20 Sunday
Castle Ashby House, nr
Northampton
1 The Green, Kingsthorpe Village
July 23 Wednesday
1 The Green, Kingsthorpe Village
July 27 Sunday
Cottesbrooke Hall, nr Creaton
Gamekeepers Cottage, nr Creaton
August 3 Sunday
Bulwick Gardens, nr Corby
August 17 Sunday
The Old Rectory, Sudborough
August 24 Sunday
4 Elmington Cottages, nr Oundle
September 4 Thursday
Coton Manor, Guilsborough
September 7 Sunday
Canons Ashby House, nr Daventry
The Haddonstone Show Garden,
nr Northampton

The Nursery Gardens,
   Geddington
September 14 Sunday
   Deene Park, nr Corby
September 28 Sunday
   Evenley Gardens, nr Brackley
October 5 Sunday
   Bulwick Rectory, Bulwick

Regular openings
For details see garden description

Coton Manor, Guilsborough
Cottesbrooke Hall, nr Creaton
Evenley Wood Garden, Brackley
The Menagerie, Horton, nr
   Northampton
The Old Rectory, Sudborough
The Walnuts, King's Cliffe

By appointment only
*For telephone numbers and other
details see garden descriptions.
Private visits welcomed*

Spring House, nr Banbury

DESCRIPTIONS OF GARDENS

Aldwincle Gardens ♿✗ 4m S of Oundle; 3m N of Thrapston on A605. Turn at The Fox at Thorpe Waterville. Aldwincle village 1½m. TEAS. *Combined adm £2 Chd free. Sun May 11 (2-6)*
   The Maltings (Mr & Mrs N Faulkner) ¾-acre old farmhouse garden incl farmyard; walled garden, lawns, mixed border, scree bed, tender wall shrubs; many plants in containers; spring bulbs, small tree plantation
   The Manor House (Mr & Mrs G Anderson) 3 acres of garden in process of being replanned and replanted; orchard with bulbs and wild spring flowers, herbaceous beds, wooded area, sweeping lawns overlooking nature reserve and Nene Valley

Badby Gardens ✗✿ 3m S of Daventry on E side of A361. TEAS at Church Hill. *Combined adm £2 (Share to St Mary's Church®). Wed June 11, Sun June 15 (2-6)*
   Church Hill ✗ (Dr & Mrs C M Cripps) Close to Badby Woods and Fawsley Park (suitable for walks and picnics). Medium-sized country garden on an irregular sloping site, parts of which have been recently redesigned. Yew hedges, mixed borders thickly planted in colour groups. Some interesting plants, shady border, greenhouse and conservatory
   The Old House ♿ (Dr & Mrs C Rose) A medium-sized open garden overlooking Badby Woods. Mostly stone raised beds recently designed and planted with a good variety of traditional herbaceous plants, featuring many David Austin roses as a speciality
   ¶**Stone Way** (Mr & Mrs C Howes) ⅝-acre open-plan family garden containing: flower beds, bushes, annual and perennial plants; gazebo and patio with rockeries, small orchard, greenhouse, vegetable plot; aviary with canaries

Benefield House ♿✗ ✿ (Mr & Mrs John Nicholson) Lower Benefield. 3m W Oundle off A427. Oundle-Corby Rd. 2½-acre garden. Shrubbery and large herbaceous border with interesting plants. Old walled kitchen garden containing vegetables and flowers. TEA in aid of St Mary's Church. *Adm £1.50 Chd free. Sun June 8 (2-6)*

Bradden House ✿✗ (Keith Barwell Esq) Bradden. 5m W of Towcester. 25 acres of garden with ornamental woodland and lake, the walled garden of Edwardian origin, the rest has been laid out by present owners since 1991. Good mixed borders with colour themes, long rose pergola and rose garden planted with new English roses around an ornamental pool, vegetable, herb and fruit gardens. Walk through newly planted park and flower meadow with ponds. TEAS. *Adm £2 Chd 50p (Share to Home Farm Trust®). Wed June 25 (2-6)*

Bulwick Gardens 7m NE of Corby, 10m SW of Stamford, ½m off A43. TEAS. *Combined adm £2 Chd free (Share to Multiple Sclerosis®). Sun Aug 3 (2-5.30)*
   Bulwick Hall ♿ (Mr & Mrs G T G Conant) In Bulwick Village turn in Red Lodge Rd, enter park over cattle grid. Formal terraced 8-acre walled garden leading to river and island. 50 metre double herbaceous borders. 100 metre holly walk ending at attractive C18 wrought iron gates. C19 orangery and colonnade; large newly planned kitchen garden; fine mature trees; peacocks. TEAS
   Hollyberry Barn ♿✿ (Colin McAlpine) A newly planted cottage garden in an old cowyard; herbaceous plants, shrubs, old-fashioned roses and climbers; raised vegetable beds; greenhouse; cold frames; gravelled area with alpine plants and pots
   The Shambles ✗ (Mr & Mrs M R Glithero) Approx ⅓-acre garden, mixed herbaceous borders; vegetable garden with fruit and an original village well; variety of flowering plants in pots and tubs

Bulwick Rectory ♿✗✿ (Revd & Mrs Mervyn Wilson) Bulwick. 8m NE of Corby; 13m NE of Kettering; next to Bulwick Church. 1½-acre old rectory garden largely remade and replanted since 1978 as a number of gardens with vistas and surprises. Dovecote; folly; stonewalls. Shrubs, old roses, mixed borders with wide variety of plants. Fruit trees 35 varieties of apple, 15 of pear and 12 of plum in various forms of training and quince medlar and vegetables cultivated on organic principles. TEAS and plants May only. *Adm £1 Chd 50p (Share to Bulwick Parish Church®). Suns June 29, Oct 5 (2-5). Private visits welcome, please* **Tel 01780 450 249**

▲**Canons Ashby House** ♿✗✿ (The National Trust) nr Daventry. Formal gardens enclosed by walls being developed. Gate piers from 1710; fine topiary; axial arrangement of paths and terraces; wild flowers, old varieties of fruit trees, newly planted gardens. Home of the Dryden family since C16, Manor House 1550 with contemporary wall paintings and Jacobean plastering. TEAS. *Adm £3.50 Chd £1.70 (includes house). Reduced party rate. For NGS Sat June 7, Sun Sept 7 (12-5.30)*

▲**Castle Ashby House** ♿✿ (The Marquis of Northampton) 6m E of Northampton. 1½m N of A428 Northampton-Bedford; turn off between Denton and Yardley Hastings. Parkland incl avenue planted at suggestion of William III in 1695; lakes etc by Capability Brown; Italian gardens with orangery; extensive lawns and trees. Nature trail. Elizabethan house (not open). TEA. *Adm £2.50 Chd & OAPs £1. For NGS Sun July 20 (11-5)*

Charlton & 7m SE of Banbury, 5m W of Brackley. From A41 turn off N at Aynho; or from A422 turn off S at Farthinghoe. Home-made TEAS **The Cottage**. *Combined adm £2 Chd £1 (Share to Friends of Charlton Primary School©).* Sun April 6 (2-6)

   The Cottage (Lady Juliet Townsend) Flowering shrubs, spring bulbs, roses, lawns, woodland walk, stream and lakes. House in village street

   Holly House (The Hon Nicholas Berry) Walled garden with beautiful views. C18 house (not open)

■ **Coton Manor** &❀❀ (Mr & Mrs Ian Pasley-Tyler) 10m N of Northampton. 11m SE of Rugby nr Ravensthorpe Reservoir. From A428 & A50 follow Tourist signs. C17 stone manor house with old yew and holly hedges, extensive herbaceous borders, rose garden, water garden, herb garden, woodland garden, famous bluebell wood (early May) and newly planted wildflower meadow. Home-made Lunches and TEAS. *Adm £3 OAPs £2.40 Chd £1. Open daily Weds to Suns & Bank Hols Easter to end Sept. For NGS Sun June 10, Thurs Sept 4 (12-5.30). Private parties welcome, please Tel 01604 740219*

■ **Cottesbrooke Hall Gardens** &❀❀ (Captain & Mrs J Macdonald-Buchanan) 10m N of Northampton, nr Creaton on A50 and Brixworth on A508. (A14 link rd A1/M1). Notable gardens of great variety incl fine old cedars and specimen trees, herbaceous borders, water and wild gardens. TEAS. *Adm house & gardens £4 Gardens only £2.50 Chd half price. Open Easter to end Sept. House and Gardens open Thursdays and Bank Hol Mons plus all Sun afternoons in Sept (2-5). Garden only open on Wed and Fri afternoons. For NGS Combined adm with* **Gamekeepers Cottage** *£2.50 Chd £1.25 (Share to All Saints Church®). Suns June 29, July 27 (2-6). House NOT open on these days. Tel 01604 505808*

Cottingham & Middleton Gardens ❀❀ 4m W of Corby on B607 Corby to Market Harborough rd. TEAS at Cannam House. *Combined adm £2 Chd free. Sun June 15 (2-6) Wed June 18 (6-9)*

   ¶**Cannam House** & (Mr & Mrs R Pollard) 15 Main Street. ¾-acre walled garden with formal herb garden and colour-themed borders

   Fosse Way House (Mr & Mrs Robert Newman) School Lane. Informal country garden stocked with trees, herbaceous borders and vegetables; wide range of fruit; greenhouse with vines; fish pond; hidden areas reached by an intriguing network of paths

   5 School Hill (Mr & Mrs N J Henson) ½-acre garden on a steep slope with magnificent views over the Welland valley. Island beds with many unusual shrubs and plants

   ¶**10 School Hill** & (Mrs P Carson) Newly planted small garden with established rose walk; sunken garden created from the old swimming pool

Cranford Gardens 4½m E of Kettering. A14 Kettering-Thrapston. TEAS, Station House, Oakrise. Car parking available. *Combined adm £2 Chd 50p (Share to Cranford Churches Restoration Fund®). Sun July 13 (2-6)*

   16 Duck End (Miss Margaret Thomson) Very small cottage garden overlooking the church. Borders of perennials and shrubs

   ¶**45 High Street** (Mr & Mrs M Naylor) A flower ar-

ranger's garden consisting of many herbaceous plants, fernery, herb garden, ponds and fruit and vegetables

   Oakrise & (Mr & Mrs G T Oakes) 5 The Green. ½-acre with variety of shrubs, perennials, dwarf conifers; Japanese water garden with Koi Carp and water plants; lovely view

   Station House &❀ (Mr & Mrs A Bates) Garden created from the original railway station. Old platform now a walled patio with fish pond and rockery. Many varieties of trees, new planting of shrubs, herbaceous perennials. Natural wildlife pond

   Also 3 small cottage gardens – "Over the garden wall"

   4 The Green

   6 The Green

   8 The Green

¶**Culworth Gardens** ❀ 7m NE Banbury. Follow B4525 Banbury to Northampton rd. TEAS. *Combined adm £3 Chd free (Share to St Mary's Church, Culworth®). Sun June 22 (2-6)*

   Fulford Farm (Mr & Mrs M Moerman) Unusual continental garden, featuring ponds, a terraced garden, a birds' wood, mixed borders and beautiful views of the surrounding countryside. This garden has been developed since 1984 on a 3-acre site. New developments incl pond, woodland garden, shady walk and Mediterranean rock garden

   Fulford House (Mr & Mrs Stephen Wills) Old-fashioned 1-acre garden on 3 levels with flowering trees and shrubs surrounding 2 classical herbaceous borders. Informal paths lead through lower garden to paved look-out point

   The Manor House (Mr & Mrs Richard Soar) Country house garden with lovely views set in 2½ acres. C17 enclosed central courtyard and pretty traditional herb garden

   Thorpe View (Sir Anthony & Lady Dawson) ¼-acre walled cottage garden of mixed borders, bog and pond; alliums, clematis, hellebores, herbs, roses

Deene Park &❀ (Edmund Brudenell Esq) 5m N of Corby on A43 Stamford-Kettering Rd. Large garden; long mixed borders, old-fashioned roses, rare mature trees, shrubs, natural garden, large lake and waterside walks. Parterre designed by David Hicks echoing the C16 decoration on the porch stonework. Interesting Church and Brudenell Chapel with fine tombs and brasses. TEAS. *Adm £2 Chd 50p. Suns May 18, Sept 14 (2-5)*

Easton Neston & (The Lord & Lady Hesketh) Towcester. Entrance on Northampton Rd (old A43). Hawkesmoor's only Private house. Large formal garden; ornamental water, topiary; walled garden; woodland walk with C14 church (not open) in grounds. TEA. *Adm £2.50 Chd 50p. Sun June 29 (2-6)*

¶**4 Elmington Cottages** ❀ (Mr & Mrs D L Welman) Elmington. Proceed N along A605 from Oundle. Garden ½m on R. 4 acres started 1992. Herbaceous border, shrubbery, orchard, native and ornamental trees, kitchen garden, lavender and yew walks. *Adm £1.50 Chd free. Suns May 25, Aug 24 (2-6)*

Evenley Gardens From Brackley 1m S on A43. Teas at Evenley Hall. *Combined adm £2 (June) £1.50 (Sept) Chd 50p. Sat, Suns June 14, 15, Sept 28 (2-6)*

15 Church Lane (Mr & Mrs K O'Regan) ⅓-acre garden with pond, mixed borders and vegetables. Terrace and herb garden on S side of house *(Not open Sept 28)*

Five Gables ⚘❀ (Mr & Mrs M Bosher) Constantly developing plantsman's garden of 1½ acres sloping to pond. Old-fashioned roses, mixed borders, masses of pots. *Also Sun Sept 28 (2-6)*

Hill Grounds ⚘❀ (Mr & Mrs C F Cropley) Garden designer and lecturer's mainspring of inspiration. Plantsman's garden of 2 acres sheltered by 200yds C19 yew hedge. Many rare plants. *Also Sun Sept 28 (2-6)*

The Manor House (Mr & Mrs H Bentley) Established garden on ½-acre sloping site; topiary and an ambience in harmony with fine Elizabethan Manor House (not open). *(Not open Sept 28)*

■ **Evenley Wood Garden** ⅍ (R T Whiteley) Brackley. A43 ¾m S turn L to Evenley straight through village towards Mixbury 1st turning L. A woodland garden spread over a 60-acre mature wood. Acid and alkaline soil. Magnolias, rhododendrons, azaleas, malus, quercus, acers, euonymus collection and many other species. A large collection of bulbous plants. TEAS. *Adm £2 Chd £1. Suns, Mons May 4, 5; 25, 26 (2-7). For NGS Sun, Mon March 30, 31 (2-6). Proceeds from all dates to NGS and Mixbury Church. Private visits welcome, please* **Tel 01280 703329**

Falcutt House ⅍⚘❀ (Paul & Charlotte Sandilands) Falcutt, Helmdon. 4m N of Brackley, 2m to the W of A43, ½m SE of Helmdon Church. 3-acre garden in secluded rural setting; fine hedges incl yew topiary; mixed borders; lilacs, ancient mulberry tree; garden in process of being restored; young tree plantation. Small nursery with unusual plants. TEAS in aid of St Mary Magdalen, Helmdon. *Adm £1.50 Chd free. Sun May 25 (1.30-5). Private visits welcome by prior appt, please* **Tel 01280 850204**

Finedon Gardens ⚘ Wellingborough. 2m NE of Wellingborough on the A510, 6m SE Kettering on the A6. Teas in aid of Finedon Church, at Finedon Antique Centre. *Combined adm £1.50 Chd free. Sun June 29 (2-6)*

Great Harrowden Lodge ⅍❀ (Mrs J & Mr R M Green) 1¼-acre garden on a dry exposed site, recently extended. Wide variety of herbaceous perennials

¶**1 Grove Way** ⅍ (Mr & Mrs P J Sibley) Small recently established plantsman's garden with containers, herb beds and columnar fruit trees

4 Harrowden Lane ⅍ (Mr & Mrs D J West) ½-acre garden on a steep slope, created since 1982 from waste land; lawns, rose and flower beds; ornamental fish pond with cascade fountain, aviary and greenhouses

23 Regent Street ⚘❀ (Mr & Mrs G Perkins) ½-acre garden with raised lawn, mature trees, fruit trees. 2 large ponds with koi carp, golden orfe and terrapins; incl filter system. Aviaries, ducks and numerous pets. Free-flying budgerigars

Thingdon Cottage ⅍ (Mrs M A Leach) 4½ acres of garden, originally belonged to Finedon Hall. Lawns, ancient trees, shrubs, brook, hillside pasture with unique view of Finedon Hall and Church

Flore Gardens 7m W of Northampton, 5m E of Daventry on A45. Flower Festival at All Saints Church and U.R Chapel incl light lunches, Teas, plants, etc. *Combined adm £2 Chd free (Share to Flore Flower Festival®). Sat, Sun June 21, 22 (11-6)*

Beech Hill ⚘ (Dr & Mrs R B White) 1 acre facing S over the Nene Valley. Lawns, herbaceous and shrub borders with mature trees. There is a vegetable garden, an orchard, alpine house, cool greenhouse. Hanging baskets and tubs

The Croft (John & Dorothy Boast) ⅓-acre garden of C17 cottage with mature trees, shrubs, lawns and interesting perennials

¶**28 High Street** ⚘❀ (Mr & Mrs P Harrison) ¾-acre informal garden with views over the Nene valley. Incl mature trees, pond and vegetable garden

The Manor House ⚘ (Richard & Wendy Amos) 1-acre garden with established lawns and herbaceous border surrounded by mature trees. Formal pond and walled kitchen garden. Partly suitable for wheelchairs

The Old Manor ⚘ (Mr & Mrs Keith Boyd) Medium-sized garden of early C18 house comprising lawn, herbaceous border, rose garden, vegetables, fruit and paddock with pond and shrubs

6 Thornton Close ❀ (Mr & Mrs D L Lobb) Medium sized garden; trees, shrubs, herbaceous plants, conifers and alpines. 2 fish ponds

9 Thornton Close ⚘ (Mr & Mrs Dinsdale) Informal flowering shrub garden, incl rhododendrons. Variety of conifers and beginnings of a cranesbill collection

Gamekeepers Cottage Garden ⅍⚘❀ (Mr & Mrs D R Daw) Cottesbrooke. 10m W of Northampton, nr Creaton on A50; nr Brixworth on A508. Cottage garden featuring unusual herbaceous plants, flowers for drying, fruit, vegetables, native plants with a difference. Strictly organic. Featured on Ch4 Garden Club and in various publications. *For NGS only Combined adm £2.50 Chd £1.25 with* **Cottesbrooke Hall**. *Suns June 29, July 27 (2-6)*

Great Addington Manor (Mr & Mrs G E Groome) Great Addington. 7m SE of Kettering, 4m W Thrapston, A510 exit off A14 signed Finedon and Wellingborough. Turn 2nd L to the Addingtons. 4½-acre manor gardens with lawns, mature trees, mulberry, yew hedges, pond and spinney. A garden being rejuvenated. Teas in Village Hall. *Adm £2 Chd over 5yrs 50p (Share to Great Addington Church Maintenance Fund®). Sun June 22 (2-5.30)*

Great Brington Gardens ⚘ 7m NW of Northampton off A428 Rugby rd. 1st L turn past main gates of Althorp. Tickets/maps at church. Gardens signed in village. Parking facilities. Lunches, TEAS. Exhibition and plant stall at various village venues in aid of St Mary's Church. *Combined adm £2 Chd free (Share to St Mary's Church®). Sun May 11 (11-5)*

¶**Beard's Cottage** ❀ (Capt & Mrs L G Bellamy) Designed and planted by Ann and Bill Bellamy, formerly at Folly House. A very new garden, mainly shrubs and herbaceous borders

Brington Lodge ⅍ (Mr & Mrs P J Cooch) An old garden on the edge of the village, approx ¾ acre, partially walled with a number of spring flowering trees and shrubs

30 Great Brington &. (Mr & Mrs John Kimbell) Interesting small garden attached to old stone cottage, well-stocked with shrubs, climbers and perennials. Small pond with bog area, secret garden
New Cross &. (R J Kimbell) ½-acre old country garden surrounding a mellow Northamptonshire stone house. Mature trees and shrubs with many spring flowering bulbs
¶The Old Rectory &. (Mr & Mrs R Thomas) 3-acre garden with mature trees, yew hedging, formal rose garden, vegetable and small herb gardens. ½-acre orchard
Ridgway House (Mr & Mrs John Gale) 1½ acres with lawns, herbaceous borders and many spring-flowering shrubs and bulbs
Rose Cottage &. (Mr David Green) 2-yr-old estate cottage garden designed, built and planted by owner. Variety of fan fruit trees, rockery and brick terrace with pagoda

1 The Green Kingsthorpe Village ✿✸ (Mrs D Nightingale). 2m N of Northampton Town Centre. Turn off A508 into Mill Lane at Cock Hotel Junction, taking 2nd turn R. ⅓-acre well-established garden on steep slope, partly terraced. Planned for yr-round interest with a variety of shrubs, herbaceous and climbing plants; to be explored with many surprises. TEAS. *Adm £1.20 Chd 50p. Sun July 20 (12-5), Wed July 23 (2-6)*

Guilsborough and Hollowell Gardens 10m NW of Northampton between A50 - A428. 10m E of Rugby. Cream TEAS at **Dripwell House** by Guilsborough WI. Teas at Hollowell Village Hall. *Combined adm £2 Chd free. Sun May 18 (2-6). Private visits welcome for parties of 12 and over*
Dripwell House, Guilsborough ✿✸ (Mr & Mrs J W Langfield, Dr C Moss, Mr & Mrs P G Moss) 2½-acre mature garden; many fine trees and shrubs on partly terraced slope. Rock garden, herbaceous border, herb garden. Some unusual shrubs and many rhododendrons and azaleas in woodland garden. Cream TEAS in garden. **Tel 01604 740140**
Gower House ✸ (Peter & Ann Moss) Small garden evolving since 1991 on part of Dripwell vegetable garden. A plantsman's garden with herbaceous alpine, climbing plants and shrubs. **Tel 01604 740755**
Rosemount, Hollowell &.✿✸ (Mr & Mrs J Leatherland) In centre of village, up hill behind bus shelter towards Church, entrance 100yds on R. ½-acre plantsman's garden reconstructed in 1982, unusual plants and shrubs, alpine garden, fish pond, small collections of clematis, conifers, camellias, daphne and abutilons. Partly suitable for wheelchairs. Car parking and Teas at village hall behind Church, **Tel 01604 740354**

The Haddonstone Show Garden, East Haddon Manor &.✿✸ (Mr & Mrs R Barrow) 10m N of Northampton, 12m S of Rugby, from A428. Walled garden on different levels, old shrub roses, ground cover plants, conifers, clematis and climbers; swimming pool surrounded by Haddonstone Colonnade, over 30 planted pots and containers. TEAS. Refreshments. Specialist plant stands and exhibition of flower paintings (May). *Adm £2 Chd free (Share to NSPCC®). Garden Festival Weekend Sun, Mon May 4, 5, (10-5). Early Autumn opening Sun Sept 7 (2-5)*

Harpole Gardens 4m W Northampton on A45 towards Weedon. Turn R at The Turnpike Hotel into Harpole. TEAS and stalls at The Close. The Gardens below are varied and unique, incl an old fashioned country garden, cactus and succulents, water gardens and unusual plants. *Combined adm £2 Chd free. Sun June 29 (2-6)*
The Close &.✸ (Mr & Mrs M Orton-Jones) 68 High St. Old-fashioned English country garden with large lawns, herbaceous borders and mature trees, stone house
¶The Cottage (Angie & John Roan) 23 Park Lane. An informal cottage garden transformed from a rubbish tip
¶7 High Street (Mr & Mrs R Fountain) A walled cottage garden with many unusual plants and sunken water feature created by the present owners
33 High Street (Mr S Orton-Jones) A thatched cottage with walled garden featuring many unusual plants
47b High Street (Mr & Mrs Peter Rixon) An enclosed ⅙-acre garden consisting of cottage borders, a rockery, pond, rose and herb areas; a Japanese style feature and a large collection of cacti and succulents
¶74 Larkhall Lane (Mr & Mrs J Leahy) Medium-sized garden in 'The Process of Change' from an overgrown untidy plot 3½ yrs ago to an informal garden with a wide variety of plants, shrubs, some mature trees, climbers, alpines, pond and small vegetable plot
19 Manor Close (Mr & Mrs E Kemshed) 40yds × 10yds flower arranger's garden on new estate, cultivated by present owners since 1975
¶Millers (Mr & Mrs M Still) 56 Upper High St. Old stone farmhouse with about an acre of lawns and mixed borders mainly shrubs; some mature trees; good views overlooking the farm and strawberry field

▲Holdenby House ✸ (Mr & Mrs James Lowther) 7m NW of Northampton. Signposted from A50 and A428. Impressive house and garden built from the Elizabethan remains of what was the largest house in England and former prison of Charles 1; Elizabethan garden reproduced in miniature by Rosemary Verey; fragrant and silver borders. Rare breeds farm animals; museum, falconry centre, working armoury, C17 farmstead and rare breeds of farm animals bring this historical garden to life. TEAS and shop (on Suns) *Adm £2.75 (groups of 25 or more £2.25) OAP £2.25 Chd £1.75. For NGS Sun May 11 (2-6)*

Irthlingborough &.✿✸ (Mr & Mrs D Ingall) 49 Finedon Rd. 5m E of Wellingborough, off the A6. A garden of approx 1 acre full of interest and unusual plants, incl spring bulbs, herbaceous border, shrubs, pools, gravel bed and rock garden, wild and scented areas. Also fruit and vegetables. TEAS in aid of Barnardos. *Adm £1.50 Chd free. For NGS Sun June 22 (2-6). Private visits welcome between Easter and end of July, please* **Tel 01933 650343**

Kilsby Gardens 5m SE of Rugby on A428 turn R on B4038 through village. 6m N of Daventry on A361. Exhibition of embroidery in Kilsby Room. Teas in village hall in aid of Village Hall funds. *Combined adm £2 Chd free. Sun June 15 (2-6)*
Croft Close ✿ (Mr & Mrs P Couldrey) Rugby Rd. Herbaceous beds, shrubs, pond and rockery. Productive vegetable garden, soft fruit, greenhouse

Lawn House ✗ (Mr & Mrs Morris) 7 The Lawns. Small walled garden; formal pond; mixture of surfaces; paving, cobbles, shingle; climbing and rock plants; variety of containers

Lynn Cottage ✗ (Mr & Mrs G Burton) Manor Rd. Small cottage garden with pond, thatched summer house, containers and hanging baskets

¶**Mayville** ⅍✗ (Mr & Mrs R Dobson) 15 Main Rd. Derelict wilderness in the process of restoration over past 2 yrs. Formal and informal areas and vegetable garden

The Old Vicarage ⅍✗ (Mr & Mrs P G B Jackson) On A5 opp George Hotel. 1-acre; lawns, mature trees, shrubs, herbaceous border, small water garden, vegetable garden

Pytchley House ⅍✗ (Mr & Mrs T F Clay) 14 Main Rd. 1-acre mature garden; lawns; trees; island beds; vegetable garden; 3 fish ponds; wild garden. *Private visits welcome by written appt only*

Rainbow's End ⅍✗ (Mr & Mrs J J Madigan) Middle St. Approx ⅛-acre mixed garden with large pond feature and own design of pergola patio

15 Smarts Estate ⅍✿ (Mr & Mrs R Collins) Mature, small garden with shrubs, climbers, herbaceous border, pond and vegetable garden, fruit. Greenhouse

The White House ⅍ (John & Lesley Loader) Chapel St. ½-acre partly walled garden with ponds and stream, heather bed, herbaceous border, vegetable garden with raised beds

Litchborough Gardens ✗ Nr Towcester, Litchborough village is mid-way between Northampton and Banbury. Teas in WI Hall. *Combined adm £2.50 Chd free (Share to St Martin's Church®). Sun June 1 (2-6)*

   Bruyere Court, Farthingstone Rd ⅍ (Mr & Mrs R Martin) 4 acres of landscaped garden featuring lawns; 2 ornamental lakes with rock streams and fountain; shrub borders; rhododendron and azalea borders; herbaceous border; old-fashioned rose hedge; ornamental trees and conifers

   The Hall ⅍ (Mr & Mrs A R Heygate) Large garden with open views of parkland; laid to lawns and borders with clipped hedges around the house; the extensive woodland garden has large numbers of specimen trees and shrubs; walks wind through this area and round the lakes

   The Old Rectory (Mr & Mrs T R Sykes) Partly walled garden approx 1 acre with herbaceous and shrub borders, established heather bank surrounds raised beds planted with alpines. Small kitchen garden area and recently constructed water garden

   Orchard House ✿ (Mr & Mrs B Smith) Banbury Rd, Landscape architects country garden designed for low maintenance; orchard, pools, conservatory and working pump. *Private visits welcome by parties of less than 5, please* **Tel 01327 830144**

   The House on the Green (Mr & Mrs K E Ellis) 1 Ivens Lane. ¼-acre cottage garden which includes well, summerhouse, water feature, rockery, variety of trees, shrubs, roses and bulbs; unusual garden foliage, flowering plants, herbs, soft fruit and apple, pear and plum trees

   The Firs ⅍ (Leslie Brooks) 6 Ivens Lane. Organic vegetable and ornamental garden of ¼ acre; cold greenhouse

¶**The Barn** (John Newman & Mary Cave) Towcester Rd. New country garden based around ancient ponds

2 Kiln Lane (Anna Steiner) Semi-wild garden originally built over a farmyard; features include artists studio and bog garden

Lois Weedon House (Sir John & Lady Greenaway) Weedon Lois. 7m from Towcester on the edge of Weedon Lois village. Pass through village going E towards Wappenham; as you leave village entrance on R. Large garden with terraces and fine views; lawns; pergola; water garden; mature yew hedges; pond. TEAS. *Combined adm with* **The Old Barn** *£2 Chd free (Share to Lois Weedon PCC®). Sun May 25 (2-6)*

Maidwell Gardens ✗ 8m N of Northampton on A508, 6m S of Market Harborough. TEAS. *Adm £2.50 Chd free. Sun June 15 (2-6), Wed June 18 (10-6)*

   The Old Bake House (Ken & Angela Palmer) Small walled garden with herbaceous borders, shrubs, old fruit trees and a large gravel courtyard under redevelopment. Many plants are grown for preserving or drying for arrangements

   The Old Barn ⅍✿ (Mr & Mrs John Groocock) ¾-acre garden developed around an old stone barn. Mixed herbaceous and shrub borders. Newly-planted area surrounding gazebo with clematis and roses

   School Farmhouse ⅍ (Mr & Mrs D J Carter-Johnson) ¾-acre walled cottage garden brimful of traditional mid-summer flowering perennials

   Wisteria Cottage ✗✿ (Mr & Mrs P J Montgomery) A plantsman's cottage garden of approx ½ acre, developed over the last 7yrs. A series of rooms in themed colours, sunken garden, water feature, knot garden, herbaceous borders. *Open daily for NGS April 27 to Sept 28* **Tel 01604 686308**

Maidwell Hall ⅍✿ (Mr & Mrs P R Whitton, Maidwell Hall School) A508 N from Northampton, 6m S of Market Harborough, entrance via cattle grid on S fringe of Maidwell village. 45 acres of lawns, playing fields, woodland. Colourful display of spring bulbs, magnolias and early flowering shrubs; mature rose garden; lake and arboretum. TEA. *Adm £2.50 Chd free (Share to St Mary's Church, Maidwell®). Sun April 20 (2-5). Private visits welcome April to July, Sept to Oct, please* **Tel 01604 686234**

■ **The Menagerie** ⅍✗✿ (The Executors of the late G Jackson-Stops) On B526, 6m S of Northampton, 1m S of Horton, turn E at lay-by, across field. These newly developed gardens are set around an C18 folly. Most recently completed is the exotic bog garden to complement the native wetland garden. Also rose garden, shrubberies, herbaceous borders and vernal garden with spring bulbs. TEAS. *Adm £2.75 Chd £1.25. Thurs June 22 (10-4). House, garden and shell grotto open to parties by written appt. For NGS Sun June 22 (2-6)*

Mill House ✗✿ (Mr & Mrs H Faure Walker) Stoke Doyle. 1½m SW of Oundle. Walled garden, vegetable and fruit garden; small gravel garden. Former field area with continuous planting since 1989 of trees, shrubs and roses. Cream teas available at Wadenhoe Village Hall. *Adm £1.50 Chd free. Sun July 6 (2-6)*

Newnham Gardens & 1m E of Daventry on B4037. Cream Teas in Village Hall. *Combined adm £2 Chd free. Sun May 25 (2-6), Wed May 28, Sun July 6 (2-5)*

The Cross ❀ (M Dawkins) Manor Lane. A cottage garden incl wall plants, perennials, a few unusual plants and pond. TEAS. *Adm £1.50 Chd free. Sun July 6*

Newnham Grounds (Mr & Mrs Roy Hodges) 2-acres nature garden planted in late 20's on 3 levels with lovely view. Interesting shapes and paths, lime avenue, rose garden, early spring rockery. *Not open July 6*

Newnham Fields ❀ (Mr & Mrs E R Mobbs) Church St. Mature garden with many unusual and rare plants, climbers and conifers, next to church with valley view and small pond. *Adm £1.50 Chd free. Sun July 6*

¶**The Nursery Gardens** &❀ (Christine Sturman) Geddington. 3m N of Kettering on A43. Turn into village. Follow brown tourist signs for 'Boughton House'. Nursery gardens approx ½m on R. 1-acre garden, set in 2½ acres which incl a spinney, paddock and nursery. New owners presently restoring the garden to incl shrub and herbaceous borders, sunken garden, pergola walk and orchard. Planned new features incl a cottage garden, mediterranean area and display beds. TEAS. *Adm £2 Chd free. Suns April 8, June 8, Sept 7 (2-5)*

The Old Barn ⚘⚘ (Mr & Mrs John Gregory) Weedon Lois. Small plantsman's garden designed by the owners to compliment converted C18 barn; with interesting selection of herbaceous perennials. Other features incl clematis, shrub roses and gravel gardens, incl euphorbia, hardy geraniums and violas. Unusual plants for sale. *Combined adm with* **Lois Weedon House** *£2 Chd free. Sun May 25 (2-6), Adm £1 Chd free incl TEA Weds June 25, July 2, 9 (2-6)*

■ **The Old Rectory, Sudborough** &⚘ (Mr & Mrs A Huntington) Corby exit 12 off A14. Village just off A6116 between Thrapston & Brigstock. Classic English country garden containing many rare and unusual plants which fill this 3-acre plantsman's garden surrounding a fine Georgian Rectory (not open). Features incl colour themed mixed and herbaceous borders; formal rose garden; shrubberies and pond; woodland walk; intricate potager designed by Rosemary Verey and developed by the owners with Rupert Golby. Many well planted containers; in March a comprehensive display of helleborus x orientalis (Lenten Rose) can be seen massed with spring bulbs. TEA (depending on weather) April 6, TEAS June 1, Aug 17. *Adm £2.50 (March) £2.50 (June and Aug) Chd free (Share to All Saints Church, Sudborough®). Suns March 23, Easter March 30 & 31. Bank hol Mons May 4, 5, 25, 26, Suns June 8 to July 13 (2-6). For NGS Suns April 6, June 1, Aug 17 (2-6). Private visits welcome, please* **Tel 01832 733247**

The Old Vicarage ⚘ (Mr & Mrs M J Percival) Great Cransley. 3m SW of Kettering off A43 signposted to Broughton and 1m to Great Cransley. 1½ acres of English country garden with lawns, mature trees and hedges; mixed herbaceous and shrub borders. TEAS. *Adm £1.50 Chd free (Share to St Andrews Church, Great Cransley®). Sat, Sun June 21, 22 (2-6)*

¶**The Prebendal Manor House Gardens** &⚘ (Mrs J Baile) Church Street, Nassington off c14 Wansford to Oundle Rd. 6m N of Oundle, 8m W of Peterborough, 6m S of Stamford. Unique to E Anglia are the 6 acres of recreated mediaeval gardens set within the grounds of an early C13 manor house. Incl are the mediaeval fish ponds, rose arbour, herber, trellised raised herb beds, turf seat and mediaeval garden historical tithe barn display. TEAS. *Adm £2 Chd 50p (Share to The Martin House Memorial Fund©). Sat July 12 (2-5.30)*

Preston Capes Gardens ⚘ Approx 7m S of Daventry, 3m N of Canon's Ashby. Homemade TEAS at **Old West Farm**. TEAS and plants in aid of St Peter's & St Paul's Church. *Combined adm £2.50 Chd free. Sun June 8 (2-6)*

Archway Cottage (Mr & Mrs D King) Approx ½-acre garden, with outstanding views. Lawns with specimen shrubs, herbaceous borders and ornamental fish pond. Sloping plot converted to nature garden, with natural pond, marginal plants and berry-bearing trees and shrubs

City Cottage &❀ (Mr & Mrs Gavin Cowen) A mature garden in the middle of an attractive village, with a walled herbaceous border, rose beds, flowering shrubs, wisteria and a newly planted garden with unusual shrubs

Old West Farm &❀ (Mr & Mrs Gerard Hoare) Little Preston. 2-acre garden re-designed since 1980. Woodland area underplanted with shrubs and bulbs. Roses and borders designed for yr-round interest

¶**Fernlea** ⚘⚘ (Mr & Mrs B Firmin) Small garden designed by RHS for easy maintenance and yr-round interest. Pergola and water feature

Ravensthorpe Gardens Halfway between Rugby and Northampton. Signposted Ravensthorpe 1½m from the A428. TEAS in aid of Guilsborough School PTA. *Combined adm £2 Chd free. Sun July 13 (2-6)*

32 The High St &⚘ (Mr & Mrs J Patrick) Moderate size garden planted over the last 8yrs. Mostly perennials but some shrubs and roses; also greenhouse and vegetables

Ravensthorpe Nursery &❀ (Mr & Mrs Richard Wiseman) Approx 1-acre new show garden being developed to display plants; wide range of shrubs, trees and hardy perennials, incl shrub rose and mixed borders with fine views; also private ¼-acre owners' plantsman's garden. *Also open Wed July 16 (6.30-9).* **Tel 01604 770548**

¶**Wigley Cottage** &⚘ (Mr & Mrs Dennis Patrick) Small flower arrangers' and plantsman's garden with many interesting and unusual plants, shrubs and trees; water features, greenhouse and gravel terrace with outstanding view over Ravensthorpe Reservoir

¶**Woodslea** &⚘ (Mr & Mrs L Highton) Small neat garden planted with many colourful bedding plants, hanging baskets; planted pots and containers, pond with koi carp

Sholebroke Lodge &❀ (A B X Fenwick Esq) Whittlebury, 3m S of Towcester. Turn off A413 Towcester end of Whittlebury village. 5-acre informal garden. Many interesting plants and walks through flowering shrubs. Pond planting and wall plants. Garden shop in old barn. Homemade TEAS. *Adm £2 Chd free. Sun June 1 (1-6)*

Slapton Gardens Slapton, a tiny village 4m W of Towcester ¼m N of the Towcester to Wappenham Rd. Superb small 13/14th century church, public footpath round village passing the Old Mill and stream. TEAS at Slapton Lodge. Car park by church. *Combined adm £2 Chd free. Sun June 8 (2-6)*

¶**Boxes Farm** ঙ় ⚇ (Mary & James Miller) Approx ¼-acre completely new garden around a rebuilt typical 'Grafton' farmhouse. Garden had not been touched for over 30 yrs. Formal rose garden; herbaceous border surrounded by yews

Fellyard ঙ়❀ (Mr & Mrs R Owen) Mature 1½-acre garden with orchard, herbaceous and walled garden areas. Stream walk, ha-ha and new rose plantings. Some unusual specimen trees and shrubs. Large vegetable garden and new herb parterre with espaliered fruit trees. *Private visits welcome, please* **Tel 01327 860214**

The Old Royal Oak ❀ (Mrs David Mumford) This garden is maturing well after 8 yrs on a very exposed site; trees and flowering shrubs create a partial windbreak interspersed with many hardy herbaceous plants giving colour throughout the summer. A large scree bed and a difficult clay bank all make up approx ⅓ acre

Slapton Lodge (Mr & Mrs Webster) In beautiful grounds and parkland

The Spring House ⚇ (Mr & Mrs C Shepley-Cuthbert) Mill Lane, Chipping Warden on A361 between Banbury and Daventry. Garden originally laid out by Miss Kitty Lloyd Jones in the thirties and now mature. Approx 3 acres app through a 16′ tapestry hedge. April-May spring flowers, bulbs and blossom. June-Sept bog and water garden at its most colourful. Other times unconventional borders, shrub roses and specimen trees with many new plantings. Ploughmans lunches and Teas available for groups & clubs by arrangement. *Private visits welcome April to Oct, please* **Tel 01295 660261**

Steane Park ⚇ (Sir Michael & Lady Connell) Brackley. On the N side of the A422 6m E of Banbury 3m W of Brackley. Beautiful trees in 80 acres of parkland, old waterways and fish pond, 1620 church in the garden. The garden has been remade over last 5 yrs, designed in sympathy with the old, stone house and church. TEAS. *Adm £1.50 Chd 50p (Share to St Peter's Steane®). Sun June 1 (11-6)*

▲**Stoke Park** ঙ় (A S Chancellor Esq) Stoke Bruerne, Towcester. 1m off A508 between Northampton and Stony Stratford. Stoke Park is down a private road ¾m, 1st turning L, ¼m beyond village. Approx 3 acres. Terraced lawn with ornamental basin, orchard, herb garden, shrub and other borders, as setting to two C17 pavillions and colonnade. TEA. *Adm £2 Chd £1. For NGS Sun June 8 (2-6)*

Sulgrave Gardens ⚇ Sulgrave is situated just off B4525 Banbury to Northampton rd, 7m from junction 11 of M40. Village garden map given to all visitors on arrival. Teas at The Cottage and Sulgrave Manor. *Combined adm £2.50 Chd free. Sun June 15 (2-6)*

Ferns ঙ়❀ (George & Julia Metcalfe) ⅙-acre garden. Trees, shrubs, unusual herbaceous perennials. A new feature is a mediterranean gravelled area with drought resistant species

¶**Corner House** ঙ় (Mr & Mrs K Tattersall) Walled garden with shrubs, roses and herbaceous borders

Church Cottage (Mr & Mrs H R Lloyd) ½-acre garden with some unusual shrubs and trees; old roses and ramblers; mixed planting for colour, form and scent throughout the yr

¶**Mertyne** ঙ় (Mrs E Roberts) Medium-sized garden with shrubs, roses, herbaceous borders and containers

Forge Cottage ঙ় (Mrs B Burke) Informal cottage garden, tubs and containers

Mayfield ঙ় (Mr & Mrs Brian Hart) Approx ½-acre family garden, mixed borders, fruit and vegetable gardens, greenhouse, small stream, lovely setting

Apple Acre ঙ় (Mr & Mrs P Flynn) Medium-sized garden comprising lawns, shrubs, mixed borders, pond, pergola and fruit trees

Harry's Cottage ঙ় (Mr & Mrs R Jeffery) Tiny walled cottage garden

Titchmarsh Gardens 2m N of Thrapston, 6m S of Oundle on A605, Titchmarsh signposted as turning to E. TEAS. *Combined adm £2 Chd free (Share to St Marys Church, Titchmarsh©). Mons May 5, 26 (2-6)*

Glebe Cottage ঙ়⚇ (Mr & Mrs J Bussens) ⅓ acre; NE aspect; informal herbaceous and shrub borders and beds. Clematis in a variety of situations

16 Polopit ⚇ (Mr & Mrs C Millard) ½ acre. Developed since 1984; rockeries, ornamental and herbaceous borders; fruit decorative shrubs

Titchmarsh House ঙ়⚇ (Mr & Mrs Ewan Harper) 4 acres extended and laid out since 1972; cherries, magnolias, herbaceous irises; shrub roses, clematis, range of wall shrubs, walled borders

Turweston Gardens A43 from Oxford, in Brackley turn R at traffic lights. A422 towards Buckingham, 1m turn L signposted Turweston. Teas in village hall. *Combined adm £2 Chd free 50p (Share to Friends of Turweston Church®). Sun June 29 (2-6)*

The Old School House ⚇ (Mr & Mrs Hugh Carey) ¼-acre walled garden. Formal with potager and featuring planters

Spring Valley ⚇❀ (Mr & Mrs A Wildish) 1-acre terraced garden leading to formal and informal ponds, bog garden, herbaceous borders

Turweston Barn (Mr & Mrs A Kirkland) 2 acres informal planting, lawns, woodland and walled garden

Turweston House (Mrs Octavian von Hofmannsthal) 5½ acres landscaped garden; walled garden and lake

Turweston Lodge ঙ়⚇ ½-acre walled garden with stone terraces; herbaceous borders and unusual trees; new enclosed wall garden

Turweston Mill ঙ়⚇ (Mr & Mrs Harry Leventis) 5 acres, mill stream, water garden, lawns. *Also open with Versions Farm. Combined adm £2 Chd free. Sun June 8 (2-6)*

Versions Farm ঙ়⚇❀ (Mrs E T Smyth-Osbourne) Brackley 2m N of Brackley on the Turweston Rd. 3-acres plantsman's garden; wide-range of unusual plants; shrubs and trees; old stone walls; terraces; old-fashioned rose garden; iris border; pond. Conservatory. Cream TEAS. *Combined adm £2 Chd free with* **Turweston Mill** *(Share to Whitfield Church®). Sun June 8 (2-6). Parties welcome by appt May to July, please* **Tel 01280 702412**

■ **The Walnuts, King's Cliffe** (Mr & Mrs Martin Lawrence). 7m NE of Oundle, 7m SW of Stamford, 4m W of Wansford from A1 and A47; last house on L leaving King's Cliffe on rd to Apethorpe. 2½-acre country garden with lawns, mature trees and hedges, mixed herbaceous and shrub borders, sunken rose garden. Mown pathway through meadow to pond, R Willowbrook and woodland walk. Children's play area in orchard. TEAS in aid of All Saints Church. *Adm £1.50 Chd free. Every Wed April to July. For NGS Sun May 11, Wed May 14 (2-6). Private visits welcome, please* Tel 01780 470312

West Haddon Gardens As seen on BBC TV in 1992. The village is on the A428 between Rugby and Northampton and lies 4m E of M1 exit 18. Teas in village hall. *Combined adm £2.50 Chd free (Share to West Haddon Parish Church and West Haddon Baptist Church©). Sun July 6 (2-6)*

Beech Trees ✗ (Gerald & Daphne Kennaird) Small partially walled garden with views over rolling Northamptonshire countryside. Terrace, lawns, mixed borders and small pond

Hardays House ♿ (Guy & Anne Ballantyne) 1½ acres, lawns and shrubbery on sloping ground with S-facing views, pond, vegetable garden, flower beds

Lime House ✗ (Lesley and David Roberts) ½-acre of walled garden with rockeries, herbaceous borders, walk-through shrubbery, rose beds; croquet lawn. Summerhouse and patio with greenhouse

The Mews ✗ (Rob and Jane Dadley) ½-acre of secluded walled garden including lawns, secret garden, herbaceous border, formal and informal ponds, statuary and pergolas

The Shambles ✗ (Jan & Frank Penrose) Large country garden on several levels with mixed beds and borders, pond with ducks and small cottage garden

Well Cottage ✗ (Sandra and Roger Woodcock) Very small walled garden on various levels displaying many containers, pond and a variety of plants

¶**Wesleyan Cottage** (Stephanie & Paul Russell) Small walled garden with walkways and paved sitting areas. Colourful borders and containers and newly built pond

West Cottage (Geoff & Rosemary Sage) ⅔-acre of mixed borders and lawns; informal ponds; lawn tennis court; kitchen garden and greenhouses; many containers and baskets

6 West End ✗ (Jill & Graham Lord) Large informal gardens with greenhouses, pond and many baskets and containers; good sized vegetable garden

Wilby Gardens. 3m SW of Wellingborough on the A4500 to Northampton signposted Wilby. TEAS at The Old Chapel. *Combined adm £1.80 Chd free. Sun June 29 (2-6)*

The Farm ♿ (Mr & Mrs R H Thompson) ½-acre old-walled farm garden to its original pattern. Herbs, vegetable garden, fruit trees, roses and clematis

7 Mears Ashby Road ✗ (Mr & Mrs K H Coleman) Small garden containing shrubs and herbaceous borders. Variety of plants in containers, plenty of colour

Wilby Cottage ✤ (Mrs B K Gale) Well established cottage garden, surrounded by walls and hedge, shrubs, herbaceous border, rockery and tubs, a plantsman's garden

Northumberland & Tyne and Wear

Hon County Organiser:	Mrs G Baker Cresswell, Preston Tower, Chathill, Northumberland NE67 5DH Tel 01665 589210
Assistant Hon County Organisers:	Mrs T Sale, Ilderton Glebe, Ilderton, Alnwick, Northumberland NE66 4YD Tel 01668 217293
	Mrs Susan White, Hexham Herbs, Chesters Walled Garden, Chollerford, Hexham NE46 4BQ Tel 01434 681483

DATES OF OPENING

April 26 Saturday
Bide-a-Wee Cottage, Stanton, Netherwitton, Morpeth
April 27 Sunday
Preston Tower, Chathill
May 11 Sunday
Wallington, Scots Gap
May 18 Sunday
Chesters, Humshaugh
66 Darras Road, Ponteland
Hexham Herbs, Chester Walled Garden, Chollerford
May 26 Monday
Berryburn, Ancroft

May 28 Wednesday
Bide-a-Wee Cottage, Stanton, Netherwitton, Morpeth
June 15 Sunday
66 Darras Road, Ponteland
June 19 Thursday
Herterton House, Cambo, Morpeth
June 22 Sunday
Chillingham Castle, Chillingham
June 29 Sunday
Belsay Hall, Castle & Gardens
Mindrum, Cornhill on Tweed
July 6 Sunday
Northumbria Nurseries, Ford, Berwick on Tweed

Ravenside, East Heddon, Heddon-on-the-Wall
July 13 Sunday
Kirkley Hall Gardens, Ponteland
Kirkwhelpington Village Gardens
July 17 Thursday
Herterton House, Cambo, Morpeth
July 20 Sunday
Cragside, Rothbury
Lilburn Tower, Alnwick
July 23 Wednesday
Bide-a-Wee Cottage, Stanton, Netherwitton,
July 27 Sunday
Kiwi Cottage, Scremerston

August 7 Thursday
Herterton House, Cambo,
Morpeth
August 17 Sunday
66 Darras Road, Ponteland
September 7 Sunday
Belsay Hall, Castle & Gardens

Regular Openings
For details see garden description

Northumbria Nurseries, Ford,
Berwick on Tweed

By appointment only
For telephone numbers and other details see garden descriptions. Private visits welcomed

Ashfield, Hebron

DESCRIPTIONS OF GARDENS

Ashfield ѽ೫ (B & R McWilliam) Hebron. 3m N of Morpeth, Hebron is ½m E of A1. The 5-acre garden is developing with a further herbaceous border, more woodland plantings and tree and shrub groupings. The area closest to the house has many bulbs, a collection of alpines, dwarf conifers, herbaceous and mixed borders. The woodland garden stretches along the W boundary incl collections of sorbus, acer and betula. TEAS. *Adm £1.50 Chd free. Private visits welcome, please* **Tel 01670 515616**

Belsay Hall, Castle & Gardens ѽ೫ (English Heritage) Ponteland. Belsay village lies 14m NW of Newcastle-upon-Tyne, on the A696 [OS map 88. Ref NZ 082785]. 30 acres newly restored C19 garden incl formal terraces; large heather garden; rhododendrons, rare trees & shrubs. Crag wood walk. Quarry garden covering several acres. Belsay Hall & Castle within the grounds. TEAS and refreshments. *Adm (incl Hall and Castle) £3.50 Concessions £2.60 Chd £1.80. Suns June 29, Sept 7 (10-6). Private parties welcome, please* **Tel 01661 881636**

Berryburn ѽ೫ (Mr & Mrs W J Rogers-Coltman) Ancroft. 5m S of Berwick. Take Ancroft Mill Rd off A1 for 1m; drive entrance 2nd turn on R beside council bridge. 4 acres created from wilderness since 1981. Mixed borders; shrubs; shrub roses; woodland walk alongside burn with developing wood garden. Partially suited for wheelchairs. TEA. *Adm £1.50 Chd free. Mon May 26 (2-5). Private visits welcome, please* **Tel 01289 387332**

Bide-a-Wee Cottage ѽ೫ (M Robson) Stanton. 7m NNW of Morpeth. Turn L off A192 out of Morpeth at Fairmoor. Stanton is 6m along this road. Both a formal and informal garden developed out of a small stone quarry as well as some surrounding higher land. Natural rock is featured as are water and marsh areas. Garden contains mixed planting with a large number of perennial species. *Adm £1.75. Sats April 26 (1.30-4), Weds May 28, July 23 (2-5)*

Chesters ѽ೫ (Mr & Mrs G J K Benson) Humshaugh. 5m N of Hexham. ½m W of Chollerford on B6318. Curved terraced border in front of C18 house with 1891 wings designed by Norman Shaw. Herbaceous borders, rock garden, lawns overlooking ha-ha and parkland with fine views over the North Tyne. TEA. *Combined adm with* **Hexham Herbs, Chesters Walled Garden** *£1.50 Chd under 10 free. Sun May 18 (1-5)*

▲Chillingham Castle ѽ೫ (Sir Humphry Wakefield) Chillingham. Approx 16m N of Alnwick. Signposted from A1 and A697. Romantic grounds laid out by Sir Jeffrey

Wyatville, fresh from his triumphs at Windsor Castle. Command views over the Cheviots and incl topiary gardens and woodland walk. Parkland and lake. TEAS. *Adm £2 Chd free. For NGS Sun June 22 (12-5)*

▲Cragside ೫ (The National Trust) Rothbury, 13m SW of Alnwick (B6341); 15m NW of Morpeth (B6344). Formal garden in the 'High Victorian' style created by the 1st Lord Armstrong with special features incl fully restored orchard house, carpet bedding, dahlia walk and fernery. 3½ acres of rock garden surrounding the House and a pinetum and valley garden beside the Debdon Burn. Extensive grounds of over 1000 acres famous for rhododendrons and beautiful lakes. House designed by Richard Norman Shaw, containing original furniture and paintings. The 1st house in the world to be lit by electricity generated by water power. Restaurant. Shop. Grounds, Power Circuit and Armstrong Energy Centre. TEAS. *Adm House, Garden & Grounds £5.80; Garden & Grounds £3.80 Chd £1.90. Family ticket House, Garden & Grounds (2 adults & 2 chd) £15. For NGS Sun July 20 (10.30-6.30). Large parties by appt, please* **Tel 01669 620333**

66 Darras Road ѽ೫ (Mr & Mrs D J Goodchild) Ponteland. SW of A696 at Ponteland. Turn L after crossing the R Pont. Travelling W, signposted Darras Hall. 1m on R. Medium-sized garden, owner designed and maintained, with herbaceous and shrub borders incl some unusual varieties. Conifers, kitchen garden, water garden and greenhouses. Bulbs in spring. TEA. *Adm £1.50 Chd free. Suns May 18, June 15, Aug 17 (2-6)*

▲Herterton House ೫ (Frank Lawley Esq) Hartington. Cambo, Morpeth. 2m N of Cambo on the B6342 signposted to Hartington. (23m NW of Newcastle-on-Tyne). 1 acre of formal garden in stone walls around a C16 farmhouse. Incl a small topiary garden, physic garden, flower garden and a nursery garden. Planted since 1976. *Adm £1.80 Chd free. For NGS Thurs June 19, July 17, Aug 7 (1.30-5.30)*

Scotland's Gardens Scheme. The National Gardens Scheme has a similar but quite separate counterpart in Scotland. Called Scotland's Gardens Scheme, it raises money for the Queen's Nursing Institute (Scotland), the Gardens Fund of the National Trust for Scotland and over 160 registered charities nominated by garden owners. The Handbook is available (£3.25 incl p&p) from Scotland's Gardens Scheme, 31 Castle Terrace, Edinburgh EH1 2EL. Telephone 0131-229-1870, Fax 0131-229-0443

Hexham Herbs, Chesters Walled Garden &✿❀ Chollerford. 6m N of Hexham, just off the B6318. ½m W of Chollerford roundabout, past the entrance to Chesters Roman Fort, take L turning signposted Fourstones and immediately L through stone gateposts. 2-acre walled garden containing a very extensive collection of herbs. Raised thyme bank, home to the National Thyme Collection, Roman garden; National Collection of Marjoram. Elizabethan-style knot garden, gold and silver garden and collection of dye plants. Herbaceous borders contain many unusual plants and old-fashioned roses. Woodland walk with wildflowers and pond. Hexham Herbs won a large gold medal at National Garden Festival, Gateshead 1990 and featured on BBC2's 'Gardener's World' and Channel 4's 'Over the Garden Wall'. Shop sells herbal gifts, honey and dried flowers. TEA. *Combined adm with Chesters £1.50 Chd under 10 free. Sun May 18 (1-5)*

Kirkley Hall Gardens &✿❀ Ponteland. 2½m NW of Ponteland on C151 to Morpeth. Turn L at main college entrance. Car park. These beautiful gardens and Victorian walled garden form a showcase for the gardening enthusiast. Walled garden with climbers, wall-trained fruit trees, borders and unusual and colourful herbaceous plants all grouped and labelled. Grounds contain shaped island beds following the contours of the land each composed for variety of profile and continuity of colour. TEA. *Adm £1.50 OAPs 70p family £3 Chd under 8 free. Sun July 13 (10-4). Private visits welcome, please* **Tel 01661 860808**

Kirkwhelpington Village Gardens ✿❀ On A696 approx 10m N of Belsay. Turn R into village. A number of small gardens in an attractive village. Each garden entirely different with something of interest for everyone. Teas in village hall. *Combined adm £1.50 Chd 50p tickets at village hall (Share to village hall fund®). Sun July 13 (1.30-5.30)*

    Cliff House (Mr & Mrs I Elliot)
    1 Meadowland (Mr & Mrs K Hodgson)
    6 Meadowlands (Mr & Mrs A Rogerson)
    The School House (Mr & Mrs F Young)
    Sike View (Prof & Mrs D Kinniment)
    Welburn (Prof D Wise)
    West House (Mr & Mrs C Scott)
    Whitridge House (Mr & Dr C Keating)

Kiwi Cottage &✿❀ (Mrs D Smail) Scremerston. Kiwi Cottage is in the village of Scremerston, about 2½m due S of Berwick-upon-Tweed. It is the 1st house on the R hand side of the village, off the A1 rd coming from the S and the last house on the L hand side of the village when travelling S from Berwick-upon-Tweed. Entrance through gateway next to War Memorial. Please drive in and do not park on the rd. 3-acre garden with lawns, annuals, herbaceous plants, providing colour and interest throughout the year. Shrubs, orchard and large vegetable garden. *Adm £1.50 Chd 50p. Sun July 27 (2.30-5)*

Lilburn Tower ✿❀ (Mr & Mrs D Davidson) Alnwick. 3m S of Wooler on A697. 10 acres of walled and formal gardens incl conservatory and large glass house. About 30 acres of woodland with walks and pond garden. Also ruins of Pele Tower and C15 Chapel. Rhododendrons and azaleas. TEAS. *Adm £1.50 Chd 50p under 8 free. Sun July 20 (2-6)*

Loughbrow House &✿❀ (Mrs K A Clark) Hexham. Take B6306 from Hexham fork R, lodge gates in intersection of 2nd fork, ½m up drive. 5 acres; woodland garden; herbaceous borders, roses, wide lawns; kitchen garden. *Adm £1.50 Chd 50p. Private visits welcome, please* **Tel 01434 603351**

Mindrum ❀ (Hon P J Fairfax) Cornhill on Tweed. On B6352, 4m from Yetholm, 5m from Cornhill on Tweed. Old-fashioned roses; rock and water garden; shrub borders. Wonderful views along Bowmont Valley. Approx 3 acres. TEAS. *Adm £1.50 Chd 50p. Sun June 29 (2-6). Private visits welcome, please* **Tel 01890 850246**

■ **Northumbria Nurseries** &❀ (Northumbria Nurseries) Ford, Berwick upon Tweed. Follow the flower signs on the brown Ford Etal Heritage signs to Ford village, 10m N of Wooler, off A697. 1¾-acre walled garden incl display beds and growing areas. Teas available in village. *Open all year Mon to Fri (8-6, or dusk), March to Oct Sat, Sun (10-6, or dusk). Donations for NGS Sun July 6 (10-6)*

Preston Tower &✿❀ (Maj & Mrs T Baker Cresswell) Chathill. 7m N of Alnwick, take the turn signed to Preston and Chathill. Preston Tower is at the top of a hill, in 1¼m. Mostly shrubs and woodland; daffodils and azaleas. C14 Pele Tower with great views from the top. TEAS. *Adm £1.50 Chd 50p (Share to local church®). Sun April 27 (2.30-5). Parties by appt, please* **Tel 016655 89210**

Ravenside ✿❀ (Mrs J Barber) East Heddon. 9m from Newcastle on the A69 take the Heddon on the Wall B6528 turn off, at end of slip rd turn R under bridge then L to East Heddon. 3rd house on R. ⅓-acre plantswoman's garden filled with shrubs, shrub roses, herbaceous borders, alpine, many in troughs and pond with bog area. TEAS. *Adm £1.50 Chd free. Sun July 6 (2-5). Private visits welcome, please* **Tel 01661 825242**

▲**Wallington** &❀ (The National Trust) Cambo. From N 12m W of Morpeth (B6343); from S via A696 from Newcastle, 6m W of Belsay, B6342 to Cambo. Walled, terraced garden with fine shrubs and species roses; conservatory with magnificent fuchsias; 100 acres woodland and lakes. House dates from 1688 but altered and interior greatly changed c.1740; exceptional rococo plasterwork by Francini brothers; fine porcelain, furniture, pictures, needlework, dolls' houses, museum, display of coaches. Tearoom. Shop. *Adm to Walled garden, garden and grounds £2.80 Chd £1.40. Last admission (5). For NGS Sun May 11 (10-7). Free guided walk at 2pm*

By Appointment Gardens. These owners do not have a fixed opening day usually because they cannot accommodate large numbers or have insufficient parking space.

Nottinghamshire

Hon County Organisers: Mr & Mrs A R Hill, The White House, Nicker Hill, Keyworth, Nottinghamshire
NG12 5EA Tel 0115 9372049

Assistant Hon County Organisers: Mr & Mrs J Nicholson, 38 Green Lane, Lambley, Nottingham NG4 4QE
Tel 0115 9312998

Hon County Treasurer: Mr J Gray, 43 Cliffway, Radcliffe-on-Trent, Nottinghamshire NG12 1AQ
Tel 0115 9334272

DATES OF OPENING

March 23 Sunday
The Homestead (see Leics)

March 31 Monday
Gateford Hill Nursing Home
Holme Pierrepont Hall,
Nottingham

April 2 Wednesday
The Willows, Radcliffe-on-Trent

April 6 Sunday
Skreton Cottage, Screveton
Springwell House, Brinkley
Woodpecker Cottage, Girton

April 9 Wednesday
Woodpecker Cottage, Girton

April 13 Sunday
Felley Priory, Underwood
Morton Hall, Retford

April 16 Wednesday
Mill Hill House, East Stoke

April 27 Sunday
37 Loughborough Road,
Ruddington

May 1 Thursday
Springwell House, Brinkley

May 4 Sunday
Dumbleside, 17 Bridle Road,
Burton Joyce
Mill Hill House, East Stoke
14 Temple Drive, Nuthall

May 5 Monday
Holme Pierrepont Hall,
Nottingham

May 7 Wednesday
Hazel Cottage, Treswell, Nr
Retford

May 11 Sunday
Greenways, Bathley
The Homestead (see Leics)
Hodsock Priory, Blyth
Morton Grange, Babworth

May 13 Tuesday
Hodsock Priory, Blyth

May 14 Wednesday
Hodsock Priory, Blyth

May 15 Thursday
Hodsock Priory, Blyth

May 18 Sunday
Brackenhurst College, Southwell

May 21 Wednesday
The Beeches, Milton
Rose Cottage, Underwood

May 24 Saturday
The Beeches, Milton

May 25 Sunday
Long Close (see Leics)
Springwell House, Brinkley
147 Tollerton Lane, Tollerton

May 26 Monday
Mill Hill House, East Stoke
The White House, Keyworth

May 28 Wednesday
38 Green Lane, Lambley

June 1 Sunday
144 Lambley Lane, Burton Joyce
Morton Hall, Retford
The Old Slaughterhouse (see
Derbyshire)

June 8 Sunday
Southwell, Bishops Manor

June 15 Sunday
Bracken House, Caythorpe ‡
Gardeners Cottage, Papplewick
The Manor House, Gonalston ‡
Rose Cottage, Underwood
Upton and Headon Gardens, Nr
Retford

June 18 Wednesday
Mill Hill House, East Stoke

June 22 Sunday
Askham Gardens
Baxter Farm,
Willoughby-on-the-Wolds ‡
Granby Gardens
The Old Rectory, Hickling ‡
Park Farm, Normanton

June 25 Wednesday
Hazel Cottage, Treswell, Nr
Retford

June 29 Sunday
Canal Turn, Retford
12 Dunster Road, West Bridgford
Felley Priory, Underwood
Norwell Gardens
Skreton Cottage, Screveton

July 2 Wednesday
Springwell House, Brinkley

July 6 Sunday
Park Farm, Normanton
Sutton Bonington Hall ‡
14 Temple Drive, Nuthall
Thrumpton Hall, Nottingham ‡
Woodpecker Cottage, Girton

July 9 Wednesday
Woodpecker Cottage, Girton

July 13 Sunday
Brackenhurst College, Southwell
Landyke, Lowdham
Mill Hill House, East Stoke

July 20 Sunday
Dumbleside, 17 Bridle Road,
Burton Joyce
Rose Cottage, Underwood
The White House, Keyworth

July 27 Sunday
Canal Turn, Retford

August 10 Sunday
Rose Cottage, Underwood

August 25 Monday
Mill Hill House, East Stoke

September 7 Sunday
Rose Cottage, Underwood

September 14 Sunday
Springwell House, Brinkley

September 24 Wednesday
Mill Hill House, East Stoke

October 12 Sunday
Springwell House, Brinkley

October 19 Sunday
Morton Hall, Retford

Regular openings
For details see garden description

Felley Priory, Underwood
Hodsock Priory, Blyth
Holme Pierrepont Hall, Nottingham

By appointment only
For telephone numbers and other
details see garden descriptions.
Private visits welcomed

Oakland House, Oxton Road,
Southwell
St Helen's Croft, Halam

By Appointment Gardens.
These owners do not have a
fixed opening day usually
because they cannot
accommodate large numbers or
have insufficient parking space.

DESCRIPTIONS OF GARDENS

Askham Gardens &✿ Markham Moor. On A638 between Markham Moor and Gamston, in Rockley village turn E to Askham. Wide variety of pleasant English village gardens. TEAS at Manor Lodge. *Combined adm £2 Chd free (Share to Askham Church®). Sun June 22 (2-6)*
   Nursery House (Mr & Mrs D Bird)
   ¶Canmore Lodge (Mr & Mrs P Partridge)
   ¶Stone Lea (Mr & Mrs J Kelly)
   Villosa ✿ (Mr & Mrs T Townrow)
   Manor Lodge (Mr & Mrs Kelly Bloom)

¶Baxter Farm &✿ (Dr & Mrs Peter Tatham) Willoughby on the Wolds. 10m S of Nottingham, 12m N of Leicester. About ½m off A46 at the E end of Main St. Old farmhouse and barns. 1-acre garden planted last 20 yrs. Conservatory, old cattle drinking pond now planted, herbaceous borders, informal plantings of old roses, irises, hardy geraniums and many climbers. Pergola in beech and yew hedged walks. Kitchen garden. TEAS. *Adm £1.20 Chd free. Sun June 22 (2-6)*

¶The Beeches &✿✿ (Margaret & Jim Swindin) Milton, Tuxford. 12m N of Newark. Off A1 at Markham Moor roundabout take Walesby sign into village (1m). Garden for all seasons developed organically from a wilderness with wild life in mind. 1 acre with 2-acre hay meadow. Mature trees, shrubs, herbaceous, climbing and alpine plants. Pond, small woodland with bulbs and shade loving plants. Vegetables in raised beds and tunnel. Top and soft fruit. Adj Mausoleum grounds also open. TEAS. *Adm £1.20 Chd free. Wed, Sat May 21 (2-6), 24 (2-5)*

Bracken House &✿ (Mr & Mrs A Wheelhouse) Caythorpe. Approx 9m NE Nottingham. A612 to Lowdham at Magna Carta Inn. Follow signs Caythorpe, immed over level-Xing turn L Caythorpe Rd. Through village 1½m past Black Horse Inn, Brackenhill on L. Park at bottom on main rd. Last house up Brackenhill. Approx ¼-acre garden. Re-designed 1991. Colourful densely planted mixed borders and rockeries with shrubs and bulbs, small pond. Picturesque views over open countryside and Trent valley. TEAS in aid of St Aidans Church, Caythorpe. *Adm £1.20 Chd free. Sun June 15 (2-5)*

Brackenhurst College &✿ (The Secretary) Southwell. Brackenhurst 1m S of Southwell on A612. Ornamental shrubs, lawns, rose, sunken, and walled gardens, glasshouses, views. Organic vegetable plot. Wheelchair users please notify in advance. Careers information. TEAS. *Adm £1.50 Chd 50p. Suns May 18 (12-4.30) July 13 (12-5)*

¶Canal Turn &✿✿ (Mr & Mrs H M Healey) Welham Rd, Retford. A620 Retford to Gainsborough Rd, nearly opp 'Hop Pole' public house 1m from Retford roundabout. True plantsman's garden of 3¼ acres incl developing arboretum of over 1,000 trees, shrubs with interesting characteristics of leaf, flower, berry and bark. Water features incl a large wild life pond. Shrubberies, rockeries, herb, rose and conifer beds. Gazebo, pergola, trellis, many honeysuckle, clematis. Various materials for mulches used to conserve moisture. Large fruit and veg area. TEA in aid of Bassetlaw Hospice. *Adm £1.50 Chd 50p. Suns June 29, July 27 (2-5)*

Dumbleside, 17 Bridle Road &✿ (Mr & Mrs C P Bates) Burton Joyce. In Burton Joyce turn N off A612, Nottingham to Southwell Rd, into Lambley Lane, Bridle Rd ½m on R, an impassable looking rd. 1-acre mixed borders, woodland slopes, stream and water garden with naturalised ferns, primulas, hostas and moisture loving plants. Terrace and orchard with spring and summer bulbs in grass. *Adm £1.20 Chd 50p (Share to St Helens Church, Burton Joyce®). Sun May 4, July 20 (2-6). Private visits welcome at weekends, please Tel 0115 9313725*

12 Dunster Road ✿✿ (Mr & Mrs M Jones) West Bridgford. Approx 2m S of Nottingham. From Trent Bridge follow A606 Melton Rd. Approx 1m turn L into Burleigh Rd, 400yds turn 4th R into Dunster Rd. 90' × 30' garden developed since 1989. Mixed borders with varied trees, shrubs and perennials especially penstemons, rhododendrons, alpines and climbers. Small woodland bed, patio and summerhouse. Ornamental pond, bog area and numerous containers. *Adm £1 Chd 25p (Share to Alzheimer's Disease Society®). Sun June 29 (2-5)*

■ Felley Priory &✿ (The Hon Mrs Chaworth Musters) Underwood. 8m SW Mansfield, off A608 ½m W of M1 junction 27. Old-fashioned garden round Elizabethan house. Orchard of daffodils, herbaceous borders, pond. Topiary, rose garden, featured in Good Garden Guide and Gardeners Year Book; unusual plants for sale. Refreshments. *Adm £1.50 Chd free. (Share to Marie Curie Cancer Care®). Weds Feb 12, 26, March 12, 26, April 9, 23, May 14, 28, June 11, 25, July 9, 23, Aug 13, 27, Sept 10, 24, Oct 8, 22 (9-4). For NGS Suns April 13, June 29 (11-4). Private visits welcome for parties of 15 min, please Tel 01773 810230*

Gardeners Cottage &✿✿ (Mr & Mrs J Hildyard) Papplewick; nr Papplewick Hall. 6m N of Nottingham off A60. Interesting old-fashioned garden of 1½ acres with 150yd long border, shrub and rhododendrons; shrub rose garden. Large rockery and water feature; scree beds. TEAS. *Adm £1.50 Chd 25p. Sun June 15 (2-6)*

Gateford Hill Nursing Home &✿ 1m N of Worksop on A57. Nursing home is well signed from main rd. Impressive house built 1860. Large walled garden. Spectacular display of daffodils with many varieties. A fine collection of mature, native and evergreen trees. Cream TEAS and plants incl specialist alpines. *Adm £1.20 Chd 50p. Mon March 31 (10-4.30)*

Granby Gardens 14m E of Nottingham on A52 Nottingham-Grantham. Turn S 1m E of Bingham signposted Granby 2½m. TEAS at The Old Vicarage in aid of All Saints' Church, Granby. *Adm £2 Chd free. Sun June 22 (1.30-5.30)*
   The Old Vicarage ✿✿ (Dr & Mrs M A Hutson) Large country garden, old-fashioned and English roses, herbaceous borders, conservatory, water and kitchen gardens
   ¶Woodbine Cottage ✿ (Erika & Stuart Humphreys) Small, developing, traditional cottage garden, closely planted, unusual plants

---

General Information. For general information on the use of this book see Page 17.

38 Green Lane ✻❀ (Mr & Mrs J E Nicholson) Lambley. 6m N of Nottingham. Take B684 Woodborough Rd turn R to Lambley. Main St turn L into Church St, R into Green Lane. Buses hourly from Nottingham. Barton No 7a. Small cottage garden densely planted, spring bulbs, herbaceous beds, varied climbers. Separate formal vegetable garden. Beautiful views across open countryside. Morning coffee and TEA pm. *Adm £1.20 Chd free. Weds May 28 (11-5). Private group visits welcome May and June, please* **Tel 0115 9312998**

Greenways ❀✻❀ (Mr & Mrs D Smith) Bathley. 1m A1. B6325 North Newark. 1½-acre. Mixed trees and shrubs, orchard and vegetables. Profuse cherry and fruit blossom. Tennis court. Formal beds with masses of spring bulbs and flowers. Rose garden, golden laburnum pergola. Plenty of seating and quiet spots. TEAS. *Adm £1.50 Chd free (Share to Arthritis Care, Newark®). Sun May 11 (2-6)*

Hazel Cottage ❀✻❀ (Jean & Mike Rush) Treswell. Treswell is approx 6m E of Retford; 4½m NW of A57 at Dunham-on-Trent. Parking in village st. A packed plantperson's garden now extended to almost 1 acre. Containing many unusual trees, shrubs and herbaceous plants, spring bulbs, old roses. Many interesting features incl newly developed gravel garden linked by bridge over beck. Paintings by garden owners for sale in small gallery. Featured in Yorks TV Great Little Gardens and 'Practical Gardening' Oct 1996. TEAS. *Adm £1 Chd free. Weds May 7, June 25 (1-5.30) Private visits and parties welcome, please* **Tel 01777 248089**

■ **Hodsock Priory** ❀✻ (Sir Andrew & Lady Buchanan) Blyth. Off B6045, Blyth-Worksop rd approx 2m from A1. We invite you to share the beauty and peace of a traditional 5-acre private garden on the historic domesday site. Sensational snowdrops, massed daffodils, bluebell wood, fine trees, mixed borders, roses, lilies, ponds. *Adm £2.50 Chd free and visitors in wheelchairs. Open daily for 4 weeks Feb/March (10-4). Dates depend on weather, check by tel first. Hot refreshments. Every Tues, Wed & Thurs April to Aug, Sun April 13 (1-5). For the NGS Sun, Tues, Wed, Thurs May 11, 13, 14, 15 (1-5) All enquiries to Lady Buchanan* **Tel: 01909 591204**

■ **Holme Pierrepont Hall** ❀❀ (Mr & Mrs Robin Brackenbury). Follow signs from A52 Nottingham-Grantham rd to National Water Sports centre continue for 1½m. The courtyard garden enclosed on 3 sides by early Tudor house with church on 4th side is a formal, listed garden laid out in 1875 with lawns, flower beds and elaborate box parterre probably influenced by Nesfield. In this 'Secret Garden' repeat flowering shrub roses, herbs and herbaceous plants, shows how contemporary planting fits into an earlier authentic framework. Second garden to the E of the house, with clipped yews and shrubs and a long June border of old-fashioned roses. Parkland is grazed by Jacob sheep with Easter lambs. TEAS. *Adm £1.50 Chd 50p (Share to Holme Pierrepont Church Fabric Fund®). Every Sun June; Thurs, Suns July; Tues, Thurs, Fris, Suns Aug. For NGS Mons March 31, May 5 (2-5.30). Private visits welcome, for groups, please* **Tel 0115 933 2371**

144 Lambley Lane ❀ (Mr & Mrs B P Collyer) Burton Joyce. In Burton Joyce turn N off A612 Nottingham to Southwell Rd, up Lambley Lane to top. Parking in field close by. Sloping ½-acre garden with mature trees, spring flowering shrubs, conifers, rockeries, troughs, containers. TEA. *Adm £1 Chd free (Share to St Helens Church®). Sun June 1. Private visits welcome, please* **Tel 0115 9313170**

¶**Landyke** ✻❀ (Dr & Mrs Peter Smith) Ton Lane, Lowdham. 10m NE of Nottingham off A6097 in Lowdham. ½-acre mature tranquil closely planted garden. Wide variety unusual, trees, shrubs and herbaceous. Pond and water features. Many climbers. Park in main street. *Adm £1.20 Chd free (Share to Riding for the Disabled (South Notts & Locko Park Group®). Sun July 13 (2-5)*

37 Loughborough Road ✻ (Mr & Mrs B H C Theobald) Ruddington. 4m S of Nottingham via A60 Loughborough Rd, cross A52 Ring Rd at Nottingham Knight. Take 1st L 400yds beyond roundabout and immed L again up Old Loughborough Rd. 1-acre garden with many unusual varieties of spring bulbs, perennials, shrubs and trees in borders, island beds, shady walk and walled patio. *Adm £1.50 Chd free. Sun April 27 (2-5). Private visits welcome by appt, please* **Tel 0115 984 1152**

The Manor House ❀❀ (Mr & Mrs John Langford) Gonalston. ⅛m on the N-side of A612 between Lowdham and Southwell. Walled C17 farmhouse in centre of village. ¾-acre garden made from farmyard over past 25yrs by present owners. Pergolas, terraces, obelisks, Irish yews, box hedges, ponds used to give formality and to divide garden into separate areas. Enthusiasm for herbaceous plants, climbers, shrubs and their propagation. TEAS and plants in aid of Amnesty International (British Section). *Adm £1.50 Chd 50p. Sun June 15 (2-5)*

Mill Hill House ❀❀ (Mr & Mrs R J Gregory) Elston Lane, East Stoke. 5m S of Newark on A46 turn to Elston. Garden ½m on R. Entrance through nursery car park. ½-acre country garden close to the site of the Battle of East Stoke (1487). A series of small gardens closely planted with many unusual hardy/half hardy plants provide yr-round interest and a tranquil atmosphere. Teas in Newark. *Adm £1.20 Chd free. Weds April 16, June 18, Sept 24, Suns May 4, July 13, Mons May 26, Aug 25 (10-6). Private visits welcome, please* **Tel 01636 525460**

Morton Grange ❀✻❀ (Mr & Mrs F Morrell) Babworth. 4m W of Retford. From A1 take B6240; after one field turn R 2½m down private rd. 2-acre garden created since 1975; large mixed herbaceous and shrub borders, roses, lily pond, rockery and sunken garden. Rhododendrons and woodland walks. TEAS partly in aid of Babworth Church. *Adm £1 Chd free. Sun May 11 (2-5)*

Morton Hall ❀❀ (Lady Mason) Retford, 4m W of Retford. Entrance on Link Rd from A620 S bound A1. Spring woodland garden, flowering shrubs, rhododendrons, azaleas, specimen trees; pinetum in park, cedars and cypresses. Bulbs, autumn colour. Picnics. Partly suitable for wheelchairs. TEAS in aid of Ranby Church. *Adm £2.50 per car or £1.50 per person whichever is least. Suns April 13, June 1, Oct 19 (2-6). Also groups by appt, please* **Tel 01777 701142**

¶**Norwell Gardens** ⅃⚹ 6m N of Newark off A1 at Cromwell turning. Gardens incorporating colourful planting schemes, unusual perennials, well stocked ponds, landscaped woodland and stream walk. TEAS in aid of St Laurance Church. *Combined adm £1.80 Chd free. Sun June 29 (2-5.30)*

¶**Norwell Nurseries** ⚘ (Andrew Ward)
¶**1 Marston Cottage** (Mr & Mrs B Shaw)
¶**Climsland** (C Read)
¶ **Scotts Cottage** (J & A Roddis)
¶ **Watermill Farm** (Mrs Patricia Foulds)

Oakland House ⚹ (Dr & Mrs D Skelton) Southwell. 12m NE of Nottingham, 12m E Newark. From Southwell E on B6386 to Oxton. 3m on from Southwell on R. Maturing 2½-acre flower arranger's garden incl large water feature, cottage and alpine areas, woodland walk, fruit and vegetable patch. *Adm £1.25 Chd free. Private visits welcome, please* **Tel 0115 9652030**

The Old Rectory ⅃⚘ (Cdr & Mrs Cadogan-Rawlinson) Hickling. 10m SE of Nottingham. From junction of A46 and A606 head for Melton Mowbray. At Hickling Pastures turn L Hickling 2m, in village turn L. 1-acre developing old-fashioned style country garden round lovely mellow old building. Features herbaceous borders and in keeping with atmosphere, old and new English roses incl the new rose 'Charity', fruit arch and newly created puddled pond. TEAS. *Adm £1.20 Chd free. Sun June 22 (2-6). Also groups by appt, please,* **Tel 01664 823260**

Park Farm ⅃⚹ (Mr & Mrs John E Rose) Normanton, Bottesford. Half way between Bottesford and Long Bennington on A1 side of Normanton village on old Normanton Airfield. 2½-acre garden, developed since 1987; formal and mixed borders; natural and formal ponds; small lakes seeded with wild flowers scree gardens and small woodland area. Mature trees moved to flat open field prior to the creation of garden. Large scented, colour co-ordinated herb garden, now 2yrs old. *Adm £1.50 Chd free. Suns June 22, July 6 (2-6)*

Rose Cottage ⚹⚘ (Mr & Mrs Allan Lowe) 82 Main Rd, Underwood. 1½m from junction 27 M1. Take B608 to Heanor. Join B600; after about 200-300yds turn R into Main Rd by large sign for 'the Hole in the Wall' Inn. Flower arranger's cottage garden with ponds; shrubs; small secret garden. Rear garden of approx 1,000 sq yds with surprise features, partly developed from a field over last few years; goat and other animals. Bed of show spray chrysanthemums; greenhouses. TEAS. *Adm £1.20 Chd free. Wed May 21, Suns June 15, July 20, Aug 10, Sept 7 (2-6)*

St Helen's Croft ⅃⚹⚘ (Mrs E Ninnis) Halam. A614 Nottingham-Doncaster, turn off at White Post roundabout towards Southwell. Mid-way Edingley-Halam. 9 acres in all, tranquil plantsman country garden, beside an English meadow; trees for leaf and berry colour, twice televised. *Adm £1.20 Chd free. Private visits welcome, please Tel* **01636 813219**

Skreton Cottage ⅃⚘ (Mr & Mrs J S Taylor) Screveton, 8m SW of Newark, 12m E of Nottingham. From A46 Fosse Rd turn E to Car Colston; L at green and on for 1m.

1¾-acre mature garden, created during the last 30yrs to be a 'garden for all seasons' with separate areas of different character. Fine display spring bulbs old and English roses, wide variety of trees, shrubs herbaceous plants; spacious lawns, pool, orchard, kitchen garden, greenhouses and many interesting design features. TEAS and plants in aid of St Wilfrid's Church, Screveton. *Adm £1.50 Chd free. Suns April 6, June 29 (2-6)*

Southwell, Bishops Manor ⅃ (The Rt Rev the Lord Bishop of Southwell & Mrs Harris) End of Bishops Drive on S side of Minster. The house is built into a part of the old medieval Palace of the Archbishops of York. The ruins form a delightful enclosed garden, lawns, 4 seasons tree garden, orchard and vegetable garden. Rockery, attractive borders in an unusual setting. TEAS in aid of Mirasol Charitable Trust. *Adm £1.50 Chd free. Sun June 8 (2-5)*

Springwell House ⚹⚘ (Mrs Celia Steven) Brinkley. In Southwell turn off A612 by The White Lion towards Fiskerton. Springwell House ¾m on RH-side. Approx 2 acres, many unusual trees, shrubs; perennials in informal beds. Pond, waterfall, collection of daffodils supplied by the late Mrs Abel Smith with local names. New camomile walk and seat. Autumn foliage colour. *Adm £1 Chd free. Thurs May 1, Suns April 6, May 25, Sept 14, Oct 12, Wed July 2 (2-5). Private visits welcome, please* **Tel 01636 814501**

Sutton Bonington Hall ⅃⚘ (Anne, Lady Elton) 5m NW of Loughborough, take A6 to Kegworth, turn R (E) onto A6006. 1st L (N) for Sutton Bonington into Main St. Conservatory, formal white garden, variegated leaf borders. Queen Anne house (not open). Plant stall with shrubs, herbaceous and alpines. Picnics. TEA. *Adm £1.50 50p (Share to St Michael's & St Ann's Church, Sutton Bonington®). Sun July 6 (12-5.30). Also open for Leicestershire*

14 Temple Drive ⅃⚹⚘ (Tom & Margaret Leafe) Nuthall. 4m NW of Nottingham. From M1 leave at junction 26 and take A610 towards Nottingham. Circle 1st roundabout in A6002 then Nottm Rd lane and leave on minor rd marked 'Cedarlands and Horsendale'. From Nottingham take A610, turning off at the Broxtowe Inn, Cinderhill. Parking restricted, use Nottingham rd. ⅓-acre garden with herbaceous borders; informal island beds, ornamental trees and shrubs; troughs; old-fashioned roses; clematis. Mostly labelled. Fruit and vegetable garden. TEAS and cake stall in aid of Cats Protection League. *Adm £1.20 Chd 50p. Suns May 4, July 6 (2-5.30). Also private visits by appt, please* **Tel 0115 9271118**

Thrumpton Hall ⅃⚘ (The Hon Mrs Rosemary Seymour) 8m SW of Nottingham. W of A453; 3m from M1 at Exit 24. Large lawns; massive yew hedges; rare shrubs; C17 larches, cedars, planted to commemorate historic events since George III. Lake. Early Jacobean house shown. NO DOGS in house. TEA. *Adm to Garden £1 Chd 50p; House £2 extra Chd £1 (Share to Museum of Garden History®). Sun July 6 (2.30-6)*

¶**147 Tollerton Lane** ⅃⚘ (Simon & Elizabeth Fradd) Tollerton. 4m SW Nottingham. Off A606 in Tollerton turn N along Tollerton Lane (1m), opposite church. Almost 1 acre intensively cultivated. Wide variety different areas incl rose, herb, vegetable, gardens, rockeries, waterfalls, extensive greenhouses. All bedding plants home grown from seeds/cuttings (also for sale). Roses propagated by grafting. Demonstration of planting hanging baskets. TEAS. *Adm £1.25 Chd 50p. Sun May 25 (2-6)*

Upton & Headon Gardens &❀ South Retford on A638 and turn L to Grove or in Eaton Village turn L to Upton. Adjoining villages, varied cottage gardens, incl wild flower meadow, specialist herb garden. TEAS. *Combined adm £1.50 Chd free. Sun 15 June (2-6)*

Headon
> **Greenspotts** (Mr & Mrs Dolby)
> **The Homestead** (Mr & Mrs Brailsford)

Upton
> **Manor House** (Mr & Mrs Walker) Plants in aid of Headon Church
> **Willowholme Herb Farm** (Mr & Mrs Farr) *Private visits welcome, please* **Tel 01777 248053**

The White House ❀❀ (Mr & Mrs A R Hill) Nicker Hill, Keyworth. Approx 8m SE Nottingham. From A606 at Stanton-on-the-Wolds, by Fina Garage, turn into Browns Lane. Follow Keyworth signs into Stanton Lane, and continue into Nicker Hill. ¾-acre mixed borders with emphasis on unusual plants, trees, shrubs. Water, bog garden. Climbing plants. Tender and borderline hardy plants a speciality. Plants propagated from garden for

very large plant stall. *Adm £1.20 Chd free. Bank Hol Mon May 26, Sun July 20 (2-5). Also private visits welcome, March (esp primulas, named hellebores) to Sept (esp asters and tender perennials) incl, please* **Tel 0115 9372049**

The Willows ❀❀ (Mr & Mrs R A Grout) 5 Rockley Ave, Radcliffe-on-Trent. 6m E of Nottingham; Radcliffe-on-Trent is N of A52; from High St turn into Shelford Rd; over railway bridge, 300yds opp green seat turn L into Cliff Way, then 2nd R. Restricted parking. Designed 1982 62yds × 12yds garden; a quart in a pint plot; featured 'Gardeners World' and 'Great Little Gardens'. Many rare and unusual plants; collections of hostas, hellebores, pulmonarias, paeonies, clematis, snowdrops. Colour planned island beds throughout the year. TEAS. *Adm £1 Chd free. Wed April 2 (2-5.30) Coaches strictly by appt* **Tel 0115 9333621**

¶**Woodpecker Cottage** &❀❀ (Mr & Mrs Roy Hill) Girton. 6m N of Newark W off A1133. 1st cottage on R in village. Approx 1 acre interestingly designed and developed by owners, many unusual plants, trees, shrubs, water garden. Delphiniums and roses feature in summer, gravel and grass paths lead to secluded areas. French potage garden, field with indigenous trees, wild flowers. TEAS in aid of St Cecilia's Church, Girton. *Adm £1.20 Chd free. Suns, Weds April 6, 9, July 6, 9 (2-6). Private visits welcome, please* **Tel 01522 778759**

Oxfordshire

Hon County Organisers:	Col & Mrs J C M Baker, Hartford Greys, Sandy Lane, Boars Hill Oxford, OX1 5HN Tel 01865 739360
Hon County Treasurer:	Col J C M Baker

Assistant Hon County Organisers:

Vale of the White Horse & SW Oxon (Abingdon, Bampton, Faringdon & Wantage areas)	Mrs D J Faulkner, Haugh House, Longworth, Abingdon, Oxon OX13 5DX Tel 01865 820286
N Oxon (Banbury, Charlbury and Chipping Norton areas)	Mr & Mrs B A Murphy, Hundley Cottage, Hundley Way, Charlbury OX7 3QU Tel 01608 810549
S Oxon (Didcot, Goring, Henley and Wallingford areas)	Mr & Mrs R J Baldwin, Northfield Cottage, High Street, Long Wittenham, Oxon OX14 4QJ Tel 01865 407258
E Oxon (Headington, Iffley, Bicester, Steeple Aston & Thame areas)	Mr & Mrs J Lankester, Park Wall, Otmoor Lane, Beckley, Oxford OX3 9TB Tel 01865 351312
W Oxon (Witney, Burford & Woodstock areas), Central Oxford & Colleges	Mrs M Curtis, Bradwell, Blackditch, Stanton Harcourt, Witney OX8 1SB Tel 01865 881957

DATES OF OPENING

February 16 Friday
> Broadwell House, nr Lechlade

March 9 Sunday
> Greystone Cottage, Kingwood Common, nr Henley

March 23 Sunday
> Ashbrook House, Blewbury
> Magdalen College, Oxford ‡
> St Hilda's College, Oxford ‡
> Wadham College, Oxford

March 30 Sunday
> Clifton Hampden Manor

April 6 Sunday
> Bampton & Weald Gardens
> Broughton Poggs & Filkins Gardens
> Epwell Mill, nr Banbury ‡
> The Mill House, Sutton Courtenay
> Pettifers, Wardington ‡

Shotover House, nr Wheatley
Swyncombe House, nr Nettlebed
Taynton House, nr Burford
April 12 Saturday
Blenheim Palace, Woodstock
April 13 Sunday
Blenheim Palace, Woodstock
Broadwell Gardens, nr Lechlade
Buckland, Nr Faringdon
Kencot Gardens, nr Lechlade
The Mill House, Stadhampton
Tadmarton Gardens
April 20 Sunday
Kingston Bagpuize House
Lime Close, Drayton
The Old Rectory, Coleshill
April 27 Sunday
Garsington Manor. nr S Oxford
Kingstone Lisle Park, Wantage
Stanton Harcourt Manor
Town Farm Cottage, Kingston
Blount
Wick Hall, Radley, nr Abingdon
May 4 Sunday
Adderbury Gardens
Barton Abbey, Steeple Barton
The Priory, Charlbury
May 11 Sunday
Greystone Cottage, Kingwood
Common, nr Henley
The Manor House, Sutton
Courtenay
Troy & Gould's Grove Farmhouse,
Ewelme
May 16 Friday
Hearns House, Gallows Tree
Common
May 17 Saturday
Hearns House, Gallows Tree
Common
May 18 Sunday
Checkendon Court, nr Reading ‡
The Clock House, Coleshill
Headington Gardens, Oxford
Hearns House, Gallows Tree
Common ‡
Pettifers, Wardington ‡
Wardington Manor,
Wardington ‡
May 25 Sunday
Bellevue, Hornton
Dundon House, Minster Lovell
Foxcombe End Boars Hill ‡
Nutford Lodge, nr Faringdon
Wood Croft Boars Hill ‡
May 26 Monday
Epwell Mill, nr Banbury ‡
Nutford Lodge, nr Faringdon
Sparsholt Manor, nr Wantage
Swerford Park, nr Chipping
Norton
Wroxton Gardens ‡
May 27 Tuesday
Nutford Lodge, nr Faringdon

May 28 Wednesday
Nutford Lodge, nr Faringdon
May 29 Thursday
Nutford Lodge, nr Faringdon
May 30 Friday
Nutford Lodge, nr Faringdon
May 31 Saturday
Greys Court, nr Henley
Nutford Lodge, nr Faringdon
June 1 Sunday
Balscote Gardens, nr Banbury
Manor Farm, Old Minster Lovell
Nutford Lodge, nr Faringdon
South Newington Gardens, nr
Banbury
Stansfield, Stanford-in-the-Vale
University Arboretum, Nuneham
Courtenay
Wolfson College, Oxford
June 8 Sunday
Bloxham Gardens, nr Banbury ‡
Nettlebed Gardens
Sibford Ferris Gardens ‡
Steeple & Middle Aston Gardens
Waterperry Gardens, nr Wheatley
June 14 Saturday
Hill Court, Tackley
June 15 Sunday
Chalkhouse Green Farm, Kidmore
End
The Clock House, Coleshill
Hill Court, Tackley
The Mill House, Sutton Courtenay
Stratton Audley Gardens
Swalcliffe Lea House
Town Farm Cottage, Kingston
Blount
White's Farm House, Letcombe
Bassett
June 18 Wednesday
Towersey Manor, nr Thame
June 22 Sunday
Broughton Castle, nr Banbury ‡
Green College, Oxford
Lime Close, Drayton
Querns, Goring Heath
Sibford Gower Gardens ‡
Souldern Gardens
Stanton Harcourt Manor
June 25 Wednesday
Balscote Gardens, nr Banbury ‡
Sibford Gower Gardens
Wroxton Gardens ‡
June 29 Sunday
Adwell House, nr Tetsworth
East Hagbourne Gardens, nr
Didcot
Exeter & New Colleges, Oxford
Goring-on-Thames Gardens
Green Place, Rotherfield Greys
Holywell Manor, Oxford
Iffley Gardens, S Oxford
Kencot Gardens, nr Lechlade
Longworth Gardens

The Manor House, Wheatley
New College, Oxford
July 6 Sunday
Kiddington Hall, nr Woodstock ‡
The Priory, Charlbury ‡
Shotover House, nr Wheatley
Westwell Manor, Nr Burford
July 13 Sunday
Balscote Gardens, nr Banbury ‡
Benson Gardens
Chastleton Glebe, nr
Moreton-in-Marsh
Fiveways Cottage, Shutford ‡
Headington Gardens, Oxford
Heron's Reach, Whitchurch, nr
Pangbourne
25 Newfield Road, Sonning
Common
Sibford Gower Gardens
Stansfield, Stanford-in-the-Vale
Stonewalls, Hempton, nr
Deddington
July 19 Saturday
Highmoor Hall, nr Nettlebed
July 20 Sunday
Adwell House, nr Tetsworth
Queen's & Wadham Colleges,
Oxford
Rewley House, Oxford
Swinbrook House, nr Burford
White's Farm House, Letcombe
Bassett
July 27 Sunday
Ashbrook House, Blewbury
Tusmore Park, between Bicester
& Brackley
August 3 Sunday
Broughton Castle, nr Banbury
East Oxford Gardens
August 10 Sunday
Headington Gardens, Oxford
Stansfield, Stanford-in-the-Vale
Trinity College, Oxford
Waterperry Gardens, nr
Wheatley
August 17 Sunday
Chalkhouse Green Farm, Kidmore
End
Christ Church & Corpus Christi
Colleges, Oxford
Colegrave Seeds Ltd
August 24 Sunday
Salford Gardens, nr Chipping
Norton
Wootton Hill, Boars Hill
August 25 Monday
Broadwell Gardens, nr
Lechlade
Kencot Gardens, nr Lechlade
September 7 Sunday
Chivel Farm, Heythrop, nr
Chipping Norton
September 14 Sunday
The Clock House, Coleshill

Epwell Mill, nr Banbury
The Old Rectory, Coleshill
Rofford Manor, Little Milton
September 21 Sunday
Kingston Bagpuize House
Tadmarton Gardens
September 27 Saturday
Nutford Lodge, nr Faringdon
September 28 Sunday
The Mill House, Sutton Courtenay
Nutford Lodge, nr Faringdon
Pettifers, Wardington
October 5 Sunday
Garsington Manor. nr S Oxford
Hook Norton Manor, Nr Banbury
October 12 Sunday
The Clock House, Coleshill

October 19 Sunday
Templeton College, Kennington,
Oxford

Regular openings
*For telephone number and other
details see garden descriptions.
Private visits welcomed.*

Brook Cottage, Alkerton, nr
Banbury
The Clock House, Coleshill
Kingston Bagpuize House
4 Northfield Cottages, Oxford
Old Church House, Wantage
Stansfield, Stanford-in-the-Vale

Stanton Harcourt Manor
Waterperry Gardens, nr Wheatley

By appointment only
For details see garden descriptions

23 Beech Croft Road, Summertown,
Oxford
Clematis Corner, Shillingford
Home Close, Garsington
14 Lavender Place, Carterton
The Mill House, Sutton Courtenay
Mount Skippet, Ramsden
Wilcote House, nr Finstock
Yeomans, Tadmarton

DESCRIPTIONS OF GARDENS

Adderbury Gardens West of A423 on A4260, 3m S of
Banbury. A large village with many quaint lanes and a
beautiful church. TEAS at Church House. *Combined adm
£2 Chd free. Sun May 4 (2-6)*
   Berry Hill House ও ✿✿ (Mr & Mrs J P Pollard) Berry
   Hill Rd, off A4260 signed Milton, Bloxham, W Adderbury. 2-acre garden reclaimed since 1982. Mature
   trees; lawns; shrubbery; mixed herbaceous and shrub
   borders. Kitchen garden
   Crosshill House ও (Mr & Mrs Gurth Hoyer Millar)
   Manor Rd. 4-acre classic Victorian walled gardens
   around stone Georgian House
   Sorbrook Manor (Mr & Mrs R Thistlethwayte) 3
   acres, lawns with mature trees and shrubs running
   down to the bridge over the Sorbrook

Adwell House ও (Mr & Mrs W R A Birch-Reynardson) Nr
Tetsworth, 4m SW of Thame. From London leave M40 at
exit 6, turn L in Lewknor. From Oxford A40, turn R after
Tetsworth. Roses, formal and water gardens, ornamental
lakes, fine trees, lawns; new tree and shrub planting.
Commemorative garden with monument. Recently designed potager. TEAS. Plant sale (subject to availability of
home produced plants). *Adm £2 Chd free (Share to Adwell Church PCC© & National Asthma Campaign®). Suns
June 29, July 20 (2.30-5.30)*

Arboretum See Oxford University Gardens under University Arboretum

Ashbrook House ও✿ (Mr & Mrs S A Barrett) Blewbury.
4m SE of Didcot on A417; 3½-acre chalk garden with
small lake, stream, spring bulbs. TEAS. *Adm £1.50 Chd
free. Suns March 23, July 27 (2-6)*

Balscote Gardens Pretty hill village ½m off A422 5m W
of Banbury. TEAS June 1 in Balscote in aid of Church
(C14 St Mary Magdalene), June 25 at Wroxton, July 13 at
Fiveways Cottage, Shutford. *Combined adm (4 gdns) £2
Chd free. Suns June 1, July 13 (2-6). Wed June 25 (11-5)*
   ¶**Colbar** ✿ (Mr & Mrs C Neville) Small terrace with
   prolifically planted pots. Water cascade with pool,
   shrubs, herbaceous plants, alpines and lawn. Well
   stocked vegetable garden

Home Farm ও✿ (Mr & Mrs G C Royle) C17 house
and barn with attractive views from ½-acre closely
planted elevated garden designed for yr-round interest
with unusual plants, contrasting foliage, flowering
shrubs, bulbs and perennials. Featured in Sunday Express Magazine 1995, Good Gardens Guide 1996 and
97. *Adm £1.50. Private visits also welcome by appt,
please* **Tel 01295 738194**
Homeland ✿ (Dr & Mrs J S Rivers) ¾-acre, developed
since 1982 with shrubs, roses, perennials and rock garden, incl field adjacent to church, planted with trees
Manor Cottage (Mrs P M Jesson) This is both a ⅓-
acre garden crafted from a steep slope using local
stone and treated timbers and a ⅔-acre woodland
scheme. Variety of decorative trees and shrubs. 250
broad-leaved indigenous trees

Bampton & Weald Gardens On A4095 Witney-Faring-
don rd. TEAS at **Weald Manor**. *Combined adm £1.50
Chd free. Sun April 6 (2-5.30)*
   Bampton Manor ও✿ (Earl & Countess of Donoughmore)
   Interesting wild spring garden with beautiful views of
   church. Masses of varied spring flowers. *(Share to Dr
   Clark Memorial Fund®)*
   Weald Manor ও (Maj & Mrs R A Colvile) Medium-
   sized old garden; woodland area with many spring bulbs;
   topiary and shrub borders; fine trees; small lake. *(Share
   to Friends of St Mary's Church, Bampton®)*

Barton Abbey ও✿ (Mrs R Fleming) On B4030; 1m
Middle Barton; ½m from junction of A4260 and B4030. 4
acres lawns & garden under restoration; 3 acres of lake; fine
trees; kitchen garden and glasshouses. Plants and home
produce stall. TEAS. *Adm £2 Chd free. Sun May 4 (2-5)*

23 Beech Croft Road ✿ (Mrs A Dexter) Summertown,
Oxford. A 23yd by 7yd, south-facing, plant lover's paved
garden of a terraced house has been made secluded by
planting evergreen shrubs, roses and clematis all round
the brick walls; the 2 herbaceous, 2 alpine, 2 shady beds
all contain many unusual plants, shrubs, ferns; troughs
filled with small alpines. NO push-chairs. *Adm £3. Private
visits welcome April to Sept 30* **Tel 01865 56020**

Bellevue ✿✿ (Mr & Mrs E W Turner) Bell St, Hornton.
6m NW of Banbury. Between A422 and B4100. Approx

1½-acre hillside garden of many aspects. Bordered walks; a 'surprise' garden leading to water falling to pools, flower beds and the finest views of Hornton Village. Added attraction miniature windmill ⅓ scale of original at Hornton. TEAS in aid of Hornton School. *Adm £1 Chd free. Sun May 25 (2-6). Private group visits welcome, please* **Tel 01295 670304**

Benson Gardens Off High St. Benson off A4074 Oxford-Henley, 2m from Wallingford. Parking in High St. TEAS at **Mill Lane House** in aid of Benson Volunteer Help-Line. *Combined adm £1.50 Chd free. Sun July 13 (2-6)*

Hethersett ❀ (Dr Anne Millar) ½-acre garden on natural chalk stream; climbing plants and bog area; colour co-ordination and plant-form a feature of mixed beds. *Private visits welcome for parties of 15 or under, please* **Tel 01491 838116**

Mill Lane House ✗ (Marion & Geoff Heywood) ¼-acre garden with alpine rockeries and banks sloping to stream, pond, small island and spring. Dried flower crafts display

▲**Blenheim Palace** ⟡✗ (His Grace the Duke of Marlborough) Woodstock, 8m N of Oxford. Bus: 20 Oxford-Chipping Norton-Stratford, alight Woodstock. Original grounds and garden plan by Henry Wise. Park landscaped and lake created by 'Capability' Brown in late C18. Maze. Lavender and herb garden; formal gardens by Achille Duchene; Butterfly house. Restaurant, Cafeteria. Adventure Play Area. *Adm charge not available on going to press. For NGS Sat, Sun April 12, 13 (10.30-4.45)*

Bloxham Gardens ✗ A large village near Banbury on A361 to Chipping Norton. Has a fine church with a 198ft spire. TEAS in village by WI. *Combined adm £2 Chd free. Sun June 8 (2-6)*

25 The Avenue (Miss E Bell-Walker) A small informal garden with emphasis on small shrubs; sub shrubs and herbaceous plants

¶**113 Courtington Lane** (Mr P C Bury) Sheltered garden with emphasis on herbaceous borders, shrubs and tubs. Winding paths giving attractive rural views

71 Courtington Lane (Mr P Sheasby) About ¼ acre with herbaceous borders, shrubs, rockeries and small peat beds; there is a small pond and a series of alpine troughs; the greenhouse contains cacti and a large succulent collection especially Lithops, Haworthia and Echeveria; a wide range of herbaceous species are grown

Frog Lane Cottage (Mr & Mrs R Owen) An artists and a plantsmans garden. Steeply terraced on many levels, extending to the brook. Mixture of shrubs and herbaceous plants, incl camomile lawn, wonderful views across valley (approx ½ acre)

Broadwell Gardens 5m NE Lechlade, E of A361 to Burford. Delightful Cotswold village with interesting church. TEAS. *Combined adm with* **Kencot Gardens** *£2 Chd free. Sun April 13 (2-4). Mon Aug 25 (2-6). Adm* **Broadwell House** *£1.50 Chd free. Sun Feb 16 (2-4)*

Broadwell House ⟡❀ (Brigadier & Mrs C F Cox) Mature 2-acre garden planted for colour throughout the year. Many interesting trees and shrubs including wellingtonia, ginkgo, acers, aralias, salix, clematis. Topiary, rare plants, many golden, silver and variegated; unusual grasses, penstemons and osteospermums, also

many hardy geraniums. Featured in 'Over the Hills from Broadway'. Listed house and old barn. Gardening clubs welcome. *Adm £1.50 Chd free. Suns Feb 16 (2-4); April 13 (2-4), Mon Aug 25 (2-6). Private visits welcome, please* **Tel 01367 860230**

Broadwell Old Manor ⟡❀ (Mr & Mrs M Chinnery) 1-acre garden with listed house. Shrub borders, courtyard and topiary garden. Pleached lime hedge, old mulberry tree, young tulip and sorbus trees. *April 13 only (2-6)*

●**Brook Cottage** ❀ (Mr & Mrs D Hodges) Alkerton, 6m W of Banbury. From A422, Banbury-Stratford, turn W at sign to Alkerton, L opp Alkerton War Memorial, into Well Lane, R at fork. 4-acre hillside garden, formed since 1964, surrounding C17 house. Wide variety of trees, shrubs and plants of all kinds in areas of differing character; water garden; alpine scree; one-colour borders; over 200 shrub and climbing roses; many clematis. Interesting throughout season. DIY Tea & Coffee. Refreshments for groups by arrangement. *Adm £2 OAPs £1.50 Chd free. Mon to Fri March 31 to Oct 31 incl Bank Hols (9-6). Evenings, weekends and all group visits by appt* **Tel 01295 670303** *or* **670590**

▲**Broughton Castle** ⟡❀ (Lord Saye & Sele) 2 ½m W of Banbury on Shipston-on-Stour rd (B4035). 1-acre shrub, herbaceous borders, walled garden, roses, climbers seen against background of C14-C16 castle surrounded by moat in open parkland. House also open, extra charge. TEAS. *Adm Garden only £2 Chd £1. For NGS Suns June 22, Aug 3 (2-5)*

Broughton Poggs & Filkins Gardens ⟡ Enchanting limestone villages between Burford and Lechlade, just E of A361. A number of gardens varying in size from traditional cottage garden to over 2 acres, growing wide variety of plants. TEAS. *Combined adm £2 Chd free. Tickets from* **The Court House, Broughton Hall** *or* **Little Peacocks** *(Share to Broughton & Filkins Church Funds®). Sun April 6 (2-5.30)*

Broughton Poggs :

Broughton Hall (Mr & Mrs C B S Dobson)

Corner Cottage (Mr & Mrs E Stephenson)

The Court House ❀ (Richard Burls Esq)

The Garden Cottage (Mr & Mrs R Chennells)

Rose Cottage (Mr & Mrs R Groves)

¶**Manor Farm Cottage** (Mr & Mrs E R Venn)

Filkins:

St Peter's House (John Cambridge Esq)

Little Peacocks (Colvin & Moggridge, Landscape Consultants)

Buckland ❀ (Mrs Richard Wellesley) Signposted to Buckland off A420, lane between two churches. Beautiful lakeside walk; fine trees; daffodils; shrubs. Norman church adjoins garden. TEAS. *Adm £1 Chd free (Share to Buckland Church Restoration Fund®). Sun April 13 (2-7). Private visits welcome Tues and Thurs, please* **Tel 01367 870235**

¶**Chalkhouse Green Farm** ⟡❀ (Mr & Mrs J Hall) Kidmore End. Situated 2m N of Reading between A4074 (Wallingford-Reading rd) and B481 (Sonning Common-Caversham rd). Approx 1.5m SE of Kidmore End. 1-acre garden and traditional farmstead on chalk soil. Herbaceous borders, herb garden, shrubs, old-fashioned roses, trees incl medlar, quince and mulberries. 10 different types of farm animal ranging from an ancient breed of British White cattle, donkey, pigs, piglets and ducks, to a ferret. Farm trail available. TEAS in aid of "Music for disabled children appeal", Friends of Ormerod School. *Adm £1.50 Chd under 16 and wheelchairs free. Suns June 15, Aug 17 (2-6)*

Chastleton Glebe &❀ (Prue Leith) 3m SE of Moreton-in-Marsh and W of Chipping Norton off A44 5 acres; old trees; terraces (one all red); small lake, island; Chinese-style bridge, pagoda; formal vegetable garden; views; rose tunnel. TEAS in aid of Chastleton Church. *Adm £2 Chd free. Sun July 13 (2-6)*

Checkendon Court &✄ (Sir Nigel Broackes) Checkendon, NW of Reading. 2m NE of Woodcote off A4074 nr Checkendon church. 15 acres, attractively laid out with yew hedges, herbaceous borders, roses, kitchen garden. New rhododendrons and azalea planting and new laburnum pergola walk now complete. Teas at Checkendon Village Hall in aid of Checkendon School Assoc. *Adm £2 Chd free. Sun May 18 (2-5)*

Chivel Farm &✄❀ (Mr & Mrs J D Sword) Heythrop, 4m E of Chipping Norton, off A44 or A361. High and open to extensive view, medium-sized garden designed for continuous interest. Colour schemed borders with many unusual shrubs, roses, herbaceous plants; small formal white garden, conservatory. TEAS in aid of St Nicholas Church, Heythrop. *Adm £1.50 Chd free. Sun Sept 7 (2-6)*

Christ Church see Oxford University Gardens

Clematis Corner &❀ (Mike & Dorothy Brown) 15 Plough Close. At Shillingford roundabout (10m S of Oxford on A4074), take A329 towards Warborough and Thame. Clematis Corner is 200yds from roundabout, 1st on L inside Plough Close, just round sharp L bend. ¼ acre garden specialising in clematis (over 200 varieties) grown in a variety of ways, within mixed flower beds. Beautiful views of the Chilterns. TEAS. *Adm £1.50 Chd 50p (Share to ICRF®). Private visits welcome by appt May 1 to Sept 30, please* Tel 01865 858721

Clifton Hampden Manor &❀ (Mr C Gibbs) 4m E of Abingdon on A415. 4-acre romantic C19 garden above R Thames with statuary and far-reaching views; long pergola, lime tunnel, herbaceous borders, bulbs, wild riverside walks, much new planting in progress. TEAS in aid of St Michael's and All Angels Church. *Adm £2 Chd free. Sun March 30 (2.30-5.30). Parties welcome, please* Tel 01865 407720

Clock House &✄❀ (Denny Wickham & Peter Fox) Coleshill, 3½m SW of Faringdon on B4019. Garden at top of village. Planted around site of Coleshill House, which was burnt down in the 50s, the main floor plan has been laid out and is being planted as a memorial to this famous house. Walled garden in old laundry drying ground; with big greenhouse, unusual plants with emphasis on foliage, vegetables and herbs; good views across Vale of the White Horse and parkland. Toilets not suitable disabled. TEAS. *Adm £1.50 Chd free. Open every Thurs April to Sept (2-5). Suns May 18, June 15, Sept 14, Oct 12 (2-6). Private visits welcome, please* Tel 01793 762476

Colegrave Seeds Ltd & Milton Rd, West Adderbury off A423 Banbury-Oxford rd. From M40 travelling S leave at junction 11: travelling N leave at junction 10. In Adderbury head for Milton and Bloxham. Trial grounds ½m on R. Seed trial grounds and patio display gardens containing thousands of summer flowering annuals and perennials. Many new items in trial prior to introduction. A festival of colour unique in Oxfordshire. Covered display. TEAS. *Adm £2 Chd £1 (Share to The David Colegrave Foundation®). Sun Aug 17 (10-5)*

Corpus Christi College see Oxford University Gardens

Dundon House &✄❀ (Mr & Mrs W Pack) In Minster Lovell, charming Cotswold village on R Windrush. Off B4047 Witney-Burford Rd opp White Hart, signed to Minster Lovell Hall, 1st drive on R, parking in field to L. Disabled parking at house. Mainly C16 house, (not open), owned in C18 by the Dundons, a notorious family of highwaymen; moved in 1930s to old quarry. Beautiful views across Windrush valley. 4-acre terraced garden. Yew hedges and stone walls enclose flower, shrub rose and wild gardens. Planted pool and new woodland gardens. TEAS by WI. *Adm £2 OAPs £1.50 Chd free. Sun May 25 (2-6). Parties welcome by appt, please* Tel 01993 775092

East Hagbourne Gardens & 1½m SE of Didcot. 6 gardens in exceptionally pretty village Best kept village winners. Flower Festival in C11-12 Church. Renowned Bell-Ringers viewable (3-5). Art Galleries. TEAS at Manor Farm. *Combined adm £3 Chd free. Sun June 29 (2-6)*
    1 Church Close ❀ (Mr & Mrs N V Linklater) ¼-acre, cottage garden, Elizabethan house. Plant sale in aid BBONT
    Kingsholm (Mr & Mrs J Lawson) Partly Elizabethan, partly C17 house (with mediaeval origins). ¾-acre garden with fine topiary in Box and Yew. Herbaceous and shrub borders
    ¶Knights Barn (Mr & Mrs A D Knox) ½-acre walled garden with fine shrubs and herbaceous border
    Lime Tree Cottage (Mr & Mrs R K Evans) ¼-acre old cottage garden, with stream
    Manor Farm (Mr & Mrs R W Harries) 2-acre garden, water surrounds the main house in the form of a moat and full use has been made of this feature. TEAS in aid of Church & Village Hall
    Willowbrae Barn (Mr & Mrs R Turner) 1-acre garden, interesting tree planting and herbaceous border

East Oxford Gardens &✄❀ Off Cowley Rd, Oxford 1m E from the Plain. Parking at **Restore**. TEAS at **Restore** and **St John's Home**. *Combined adm £1.50 OAPs £1 Chd free (Share to Society of All Saints Sisters of the Poor®). Sun Aug 3 (2-5)*
    Restore, Manzil Way N off Cowley Rd leading to E Oxford Health Centre. A town garden and plant nursery run as a mental health rehabilitation project. Sample beds of shrubs, perennials, herbs, alpines and annuals. Large range of plants for sale, also hand-made crafts and cards
    St John's Home, St Mary's Rd, off Leopold St S of Cowley Rd. 3-acre grounds of All Saints Convent and St John's Home for the Elderly. Mature trees, lawns, secluded prayer garden and vegetable garden. Comper chapel open

Epwell Mill ⅋❀ (Mrs William Graham & Mrs David Long) Epwell, 7m W of Banbury, between Shutford and Epwell. Medium-sized garden, interestingly landscaped in open country, based on former water-mill; terraced pools; bulbs; azaleas. Home-made TEAS. *Adm £1 Chd free (Share to Epwell Parochial Church Council®). Suns April 6, Sept 14, Mons May 26 (2-6). Please apply in writing for groups outside opening dates*

Exeter College see Oxford University Gardens

Fiveways Cottage ⅋❀ (Dr & Mrs M R Aldous) Shutford. 5m W of Banbury between A422 to Shutford & B4035 to Shipston on the Tadmarton Rd. Just over ½ acre, started 1986. Essentially cottage garden style, with shrubs, roses, small woodland areas, herbaceous borders and ponds. Many clematis varieties grown. TEAS. *Adm £2 (Share to Rangapara Hospital Trust®). Sun July 13 (2-6)*

Foxcombe End ⅋❀ (Mr & Mrs R Stevens) Foxcombe Lane, Boars Hill, 3 m S of Oxford. From roundabout at junction of ring rd with A34 follow signs to Wootton and Boars Hill. Foxcombe Lane is 1st on L after entering Boars Hill. Parking in garden reserved for infirm **only**. 7 acres oak woodland, 4 acres natural garden. Garden trail, donkey, wild orchids, azaleas, rhododendrons, magnolias and extensive yew hedges. TEAS in aid of Sobell House Hospice. *Adm £1 Chd free. Sun May 25 (2-6)*

Garsington Manor ⅋❀ (Mr & Mrs L V Ingrams) SE of Oxford N of B480. House C17 of architectural interest (not open). Monastic fish ponds, water garden, dovecot c.1700; flower parterre and Italian garden laid out by Philip and Lady Ottoline Morrell; fine trees and yew hedges. Free car park. TEAS in aid of local churches. *Adm £2 Chd free. Sun April 27 (2-6), Sun Oct 5 (2-5)*

Goring-on-Thames Gardens 5m S of Wallingford where B4009 crosses wooden bridge over Thames. A beautiful old village backed by steep wooded hills. TEAS at **The Old Farm House & Streatley Farm**. *Combined adm £2.50 Chd free. Sun June 29 (2-6)*

> **Manor Field** ⅋❀❀ (Mr & Mrs D L Watts) Manor Road. An interesting ½-acre garden of a modern bungalow. Collection of rock plants, cactus, bonsai, unusual shrubs and tender plants, vegetable garden. *(Share to The Reading Abbeyfield House Society®)*
> **The Mill Cottage** ⅋ (Mr & Mrs M J H Weedon) 1-acre riverside garden between C11 St Thomas Church and Goring Mill. Dramatic views of the R Thames and the Berkshire Downs
> **The Old Farmhouse** ⅋❀ (Mr & Mrs J F Denny) Station Road. 1-acre walled village garden around early C19 house. Features herbaceous borders, roses, shrubs, swimming pool (available at 50p). Kitchen garden and lily pond. *(Share to Sue Ryder & St John Ambulance®)*
> ¶**Streatley Farm** ⅋❀ (Mr & Mrs R Bishop) E of A329 between Streatley and Moulsford. 1½-acre garden. Brick and flint farmhouse, young walnut orchard; herbaceous borders, roses on flint walls, small cobbled fountain garden. TEAS in aid of Solden Hill House

Green College see Oxford University Gardens

Green Place ⅋❀❀ (Mr & Mrs R P Tatman) Rotherfield Greys. 3m W of Henley-on-Thames next to Greys War Memorial. Extensive views towards the E from secluded 1-acre garden containing a pergola walk, herbaceous borders, rose beds and many varieties of fuchsia. Teas in aid of WI in nearby village hall. *Adm £1 Chd free. Sun June 29 (2-6)*

▲**Greys Court** ❀❀ (Lady Brunner; The National Trust) Rotherfield Greys, 3m W of Henley-on-Thames on rd to Peppard. 8 acres amongst which are the ruined walls and buildings of original fortified manor. Rose, cherry, wisteria and white gardens; lawns; kitchen garden; ice house; Archbishop's maze. Jacobean house open with C18 alterations on site of original C13 house fortified by Lord Grey in C14. Donkey wheel and tower. Large sale of unusual plants. TEAS. *Adm garden £3 Chd £1.50 House & Garden £4 Chd £2. For NGS Sat May 31 (2-5.30)*

Greystone Cottage ⅋❀❀ (Mr & Mrs W Roxburgh) Colmore Lane, Kingwood Common. Signposted from B481 Nettlebed-Reading rd. 2 acres in woodland setting, collections of hellebores, snowdrops, hostas and ferns. Geraniums and many unusual plants, shrubs and conifers. Fritillary and wildflower meadow, new wildlife ponds and marsh area. Old roses and azaleas, mediterranean areas. Edwardian pear tree walk. Featured in 'Good Gardens Guide' and 'RHS Gardeners Year Book'. Nursery. TEAS in aid of Oxfam (March)' Peppard C of E School (May). *Adm £2 Chd free. Suns March 9, May 11 (2-6). Private visits welcome March 1 to Sept 1 by appt, please Tel 01491 628559*

Headington Gardens East Oxford, off London Road, ¾m W of ring road. Teas in Parish Hall, Dunstan Rd in aid of WI. *Combined adm £2 Chd free. Suns May 18, July 13, Aug 10 (2-6)*

> **2 Fortnam Close** ❀ (Mr & Mrs D Holt) Off Headley Way. Multi-award winner, featured on TV and radio. ¼-acre garden on 3 levels, trees, shrubs, heathers, azaleas and a large wisteria. Roses, bearded iris and other herbaceous plants in a planned layout which includes a pond and pergola. Watercolour paintings and pressed flower arrangements to view if you wish
> **40 Osler Road** ❀❀ (Mr & Mrs N Coote) ⅔-acre 'secret garden' on the edge of Old Headington. Semi-formal design; tender shrubs and plants in pots supporting Mediterranean atmosphere of house. Luxuriant spring display. Plants for dry soil, many chosen for foliage effect, some rare or unusual, many late flowering. Featured on 'Gardeners World' and in many publications. *Private visits for groups welcome, please Tel 01865 67680 (after dark)*
> **Pumpkin Cottage** ⅋❀ (Mr & Mrs M Davis) 6 St Andrew's Lane, Old Headington, off St Andrew's Rd, nr to Church. Small garden, 20m × 16m, enclosed within stone walls situated at rear of Grade II listed cottage. Small pool and rockery; mixed planting; paved areas with some container grown plants. Small cobble paved front garden. Wheelchair access possible by arrangement
> **1 Stoke Place** ❀ (Mr & Mrs M Carrington) The garden takes its shape from a network of old stone walls which happen to have survived in the area. A scattering of trees blending with stone work provides a

framework for a linked series of paths and flower beds which gives an atmosphere of seclusion. A number of small pools and many contrasting shrubs and plants provide variety and do not diminish the sense of privacy of the whole garden. The area is just short of an acre. *Open May 18 only (Share to RSPCA®)*

Hearns House ᕁ❀ (Mr & Mrs J Pumfrey) Gallows Tree Common, 5m N of Reading, 5m W of Henley. From A4074 turn E at The Fox, Cane End. Limited car parking in the garden so additional Friday and Saturday openings. Architects house in 2-acre garden in woodland setting. Designed for maintenance by two people with full time careers. Featured in Amateur Gardening. Emphasis on design, good foliage and single colour areas with paved courtyard and shady walks. New small garden. Unusual plants for sale. TEAS or coffee in aid of Oxfam. *Adm £2 Chd free. Fri, Sat, Sun May 16, 17, 18 (10-12; 2-5)*

Heron's Reach ᕁ❀ (Mr & Mrs B Vorhaus) Eastfield Lane, Whitchurch-on-Thames. From Pangbourne take tollbridge rd over Thames to Whitchurch-on-Thames; at The Greyhound turn R into Eastfield Lane. 1 acre in beautiful Thames-side setting with views to the Chiltern hills; woodland garden with pond, stream, shrubs, and herbaceous borders. TEAS. *Adm £2 Chd free. Sun July 13 (2-6). Private visits also welcome in July, please* Tel 01734 843140 or 0171 722 1458

Highmoor Hall ᕁ❀❀ (Mr & Mrs P D Persson) Highmoor. 1m S of Nettlebed on B481 to Reading. 6-acre garden in a peaceful setting: open views across ha-ha; secluded areas; mature trees; water garden; walled kitchen garden; shrubberies and herbaceous borders with an accent on colour blending. Arts Centre within the grounds. Home grown plants for sale. TEAS. *Adm £2 Chd free (Share to TEAR Fund®). Sat July 19 (2-6)*

Hill Court ᕁ❀❀ (Mr & Mrs Andrew Peake) Tackley. 9m N of Oxford. Turn off A4260 at Sturdy's Castle. Walled garden of 2 acres with clipped yew cones at the top of the terrace as a design feature by Russell Page in the 1960s. Terraces incl silver, pink and blue plantings, white garden, herbaceous borders, shrubberies, orangery. Many rare and unusual plants. Entry incl History Trail (not suitable for wheelchairs) with illustrated leaflet giving notes on unique geometric fishponds (1620), C17 stables and pigeon house, C18 lakes, icehouse etc (stroll of at least 1hr). TEAS. Pied Pipers recorder group (Sun only). *Adm £1.50 Chd free (Share to Tackley History Group & Tackley Pre-School®). Sat, Sun June 14, 15 (2-6)*

Holywell Manor see Oxford University Gardens

Home Close ❀ (Dr P Giangrande and Miss M Waud) Southend, Garsington. SE of Oxford, N of B480. 2-acre garden with listed house and granary. Interesting trees, shrubs and perennials planted for all yr interest. Terraces, walls and hedges divide the garden into ten distinct areas. *Adm £1.50 Chd free. Private visits welcome April 1 to Sept 30, please* Tel 01865 361394

Home Farm, Balscote see Balscote Gardens

Hook Norton Manor ❀ (Mr & Mrs Nicholas Holmes) SW of Banbury. From A361, 1m from Chipping Norton turn N and follow signs. 2½-acres terraced lawns leading down to streams; trees, shrubs and bog garden. TEAS in aid of St Peter's Church. *Adm £1 Chd free. Sun Oct 5 (2-5.30)*

Iffley Gardens ᕁ❀ S Oxford. Secluded old village within Oxford's ring road, off A4158 from Magdalen Bridge to Littlemore roundabout. Renowned Norman church, featured on cover of Pevsner's Oxon guide. Short footpath from Mill Lane leads to scenic Iffley Lock and Sandford to Oxford towpath. Teas from 3-5 at thatched village hall, Church Way. Two plant stalls, one in aid of NGS, the other for The White House Nursery. *Combined adm £2 OAPs £1.50 Chd free. Sun June 29 (2-6)*
    8 Abberbury Road ᕁ (F S Tordoff Esq) Off Church Way. ½-acre plantsman's garden developed since 1971. Mature trees, shrubs, coloured and variegated foliage, many old and modern shrub roses and climbers. *Private visits welcome, please* Tel 01865 778644
    24 Abberbury Road ᕁ (Mr & Mrs E Townsend-Coles) ½-acre family garden with fruit, flowers and vegetables
    65 Church Way ❀ (Mrs J Woodfill) Small cottage garden planted with shrubs, perennials and herbs, many of them grown for their historical associations. *Private visits welcome, please* Tel 01865 770537
    71 Church Way (Mrs M L Harrison) A small, low maintenance professionally designed, front garden with mixed shrubs and herbaceous plantings. *Private visits welcome, please* Tel 01865 718224
    122 Church Way (Sir John & Lady Elliott) Small secluded cottage style garden with trees, shrubs, roses and herbaceous plants behind listed house with view of church tower
    ¶**11 Iffley Turn** ᕁ (Ann & Matthew Ellett) A well established garden of ½-acre containing many mature trees
    The Mill House (Mrs P A Lawrence) 30 Mill Lane. A terraced garden dropping westwards to the river at the old mill-race
    Rosedale ❀ (Mrs T Bennett) Mill Lane, off Church Way. ½-acre garden on different levels, hidden behind walls. A mixture of trees, shrubs, roses and herbaceous plants with a large rockery and tiny woodland garden. Private visits welcome, please Tel 01865 714151

Kencot Gardens 5m NE of Lechlade, E of A361 to Burford. A most charming Cotswold village with interesting church. TEAS. *Combined adm with* **Broadwell Gardens** *£2 Chd free. Sun April 13; Mon Aug 25. Also* **Kencot House** *and* **Manor Farm** *open Sun June 29. Combined adm £2 Chd free*
    De Rougemont ᕁ (Mr & Mrs D Portergill) ½-acre garden with very varied planting: over 350 named plants; beds for perennials, conifers, fuchsias, herbs and roses; spring bulbs; vegetables and fruit trees; soft fruit cage; greenhouse with vine; well
    The Gardens ᕁ (Lt-Col & Mrs J Barstow) ¼-acre cottage garden featuring spring bulbs, iris, roses, herbaceous, rock plants, old apple trees and a well
    Ivy Nook (Mr & Mrs W Gasson) Cottage garden; rockeries, lawns, mixed borders. *Sun April 13, Mon Aug 25*
    Kencot Cottage ❀ (Mrs M Foster) Very small garden with spring bulbs and bedding, also bonsai trees

Kencot House ❀ (Mr & Mrs A Patrick) 2-acre garden with lawns, trees, borders; quantities of daffodils and other spring bulbs; roses and over 50 different clematis; notable ginkgo tree. Interesting carved C13 archway. *Also open Sun June 29. Adm £2*

Manor Farm (Mr & Mrs J R Fyson) 2-acre garden with lawns and herbaceous borders; naturalised spring bulbs; incl long-established fritillaries; clipped yew, pleached lime walk, pergola with rambling and gallica roses. Mature orchards. C17 listed farmhouse. *Suns April 13, June 29 only*

Kiddington Hall ✄❀ (Hon Maurice & Mrs Robson) 4m NW of Woodstock. From A44 Oxford-Stratford, R at Xrds in Kiddington and down hill; entrance on L. Partly suitable for wheelchairs. Large grounds with lake, parkland designed by Capability Brown; terraced rose garden and orangery beside house designed by Sir Charles Barry; C12 church, C16 dovecote and large walled kitchen garden. TEAS in aid of St Nicholas Church, Kiddington. *Adm £2 Chd free. Sun July 6 (2-6)*

■ **Kingston Bagpuize House** ✆✄❀ (Mr & Mrs Francis Grant) Kingston Bagpuize, A415, 5½m W of Abingdon. The gardens contain a notable collection of unusual trees, shrubs, perennials and bulbs. Guided tours of Manor House not suitable for wheelchairs. *Adm garden only £1. House and garden £3 OAP's £2.50 Chd £2 (under 5's free to garden, not admitted to the house). Open Bank Hol weekends Sat, Sun, Mon and also April 12, 13, 16, 19, 20; June 11, 14, 15; July 9, 12, 13; Aug 6, 9, 10 and Sept 3, 6, 7, 17, 20, 21 (2.30-5.30) last adm 5pm. TEAS. Plants NGS days only. For NGS Suns April 20, Sept 21. Groups welcome by written appt Feb to Nov, please* **Tel 01865 820259**

▲**Kingstone Lisle Park** ✆ (Mr & Mrs J L S Lonsdale) nr Wantage. 5m W of Wantage along B4507. 12 acres of gardens incl a shrubbery, pleeched limes, an avenue leading up to an ornamental pond and a replica of Queen Mary's rose garden in Regents Park. 3 acres of lakes. TEAS. *Adm for NGS garden only £2.50 Chd free (Share to St John the Baptist Church, Kingstone Lisle®). Sun April 27 (2-5)*

14 Lavender Place ✄❀ (Mrs Angela Chambers) Carterton. 4m SE of Burford on B4020. After entering Carterton from Burford, turn R at lights into Upavon Way (towards Alvescot & Faringdon). Lavender Place fourth L. Plant enthusiast's tiny 35 ft square garden behind small modern house. Clematis and other climbers provide secluded setting for densely packed collection of unusual and exotic perennials. Small pond, shaded area, raised beds. Colour and interest all year. *Adm 80p Chd free (Share to Association for International Cancer Research®). Private visits welcome by appt June 1 to Aug 31, please* **Tel 01993 843216**

By Appointment Gardens. These owners do not have a fixed opening day usually because they cannot accommodate large numbers or have insufficient parking space.

Lime Close ✆❀ (M-C de Laubarede) 35 Henleys Lane, Drayton. 2m S of Abingdon. 3-acre mature garden with very rare trees, shrubs, perennials and bulbs. New unusual topiary; raised beds; rock garden and troughs with alpines. Newly reclaimed border planted with interesting shade lovers, pond and much new planting in progress. Ornamental kitchen garden with pergola. Herb garden designed by Rosemary Verey. Listed C16 house (not open). Unusual plants for sale from Green Farm Plants. TEAS. *Adm £2 Chd free. Suns April 20, June 22 (2-6)*

¶**Longworth Gardens** ✆ Longworth is N of A420 between Kingston Bagpuise and Faringdon. TEAS at Longworth Manor. *Combined adm £2 Chd free. Sun June 29 (2-6)*

Longworth Manor ❀ (Col & Mrs John Walton) A medium size garden with roses, borders, shrubs and ornamental ponds. C17 house (not open) with good views over R Thames. Special features are wild flower meadow and a new formal garden

¶**The Old Rectory** ✆✄ (Mrs Axtell) C18 house in garden of mature trees with lime avenue. Quatrefoil pond surrounded by brick paths and intensely planted borders

Magdalen College see Oxford University Gardens

Manor Farm ✆❀ (Sir Peter & Lady Parker), Old Minster Lovell. Off B4047 Witney-Burford rd; turn R at sign to Old Minster Lovell and Leafield; in ¼m cross Windrush bridge, turn R at Old Swan; no parking in village, follow signs to large free car park. Adjoining churchyard and ruins of Minster (open); C14 dovecote. Owner is author of book about her garden: 'Purest of Pleasures'. TEAS by WI. *Adm £2 Chd free. Sun June 1 (2-5). Parties welcome by appt*

The Manor House, Sutton Courtenay ✆✄❀ (The Hon David Astor) 4m S of Abingdon. Out of Abingdon on the A415. Turn off to Culham - Sutton Courtenay. From A34 going N come into Milton Village take last rd on R to Sutton Courtenay. 10 acres of garden approx 35 acres of land. ½m R Thames Bank. TEAS. *Adm £1.50 Chd 50p. Sun May 11 (2-6)*

The Manor House, Wheatley ✆✄❀ (Mr & Mrs T G Hassall) 26 High St, Wheatley. Off A40 E of Oxford. 1½-acre garden of Elizabethan manor house; formal box walk; herb garden, cottage garden with rose arches and a shrubbery with old roses. A romantic oasis in this busy village. TEAS in aid of Wheatley Windmill Restoration Society. *Adm £1.50 Acc chd free. Sun June 29 (2-6)*

The Mill House, Sutton Courtenay ✆✄❀ (Mrs J Stevens) Abingdon, Oxon, OX14 4NH. Approx 8½ acres; R Thames runs through garden which is on several islands with mill pond and old paper mill. TEAS. *Adm, (ONLY BY APPT IN WRITING), £2 Chd £1, under 4 free. Suns April 6, June 15, Sept 28 (2-6). Parties of 10 and over also welcome on other days by appt in writing*

The Mill House, Stadhampton ✆❀ (Mr & Mrs F A Peet) A329/B480, 8m SE of Oxford. 1-acre family garden with old mill and stream. Mill not working but machinery largely intact and wheel turning with pumped water.

Parking on green; parking for disabled only at house. TEAS in aid of Stadhampton Church Restoration Fund. *Adm £1 Chd free. Sun April 13 (2-5.30)*

Mount Skippet &⊛ (Dr & Mrs M A T Rogers) Ramsden, 4m N of Witney. At Xrds turn E towards Finstock; after 30yds, turn R (sign-post Mount Skippet). After 400yds turn L (No Through Way sign) for 75yds. 2 acres; 2 rock gardens; alpine house; stone troughs; shrubs; herbaceous beds; primulas; conservatory; many rare plants. Fine views. Cotswold stone house largely C17. Teas for groups by prior arrangement. *Adm £1 Chd free (Share to Finstock Church®). Private visits welcome April 1 to Sept 30, please* **Tel 01993 868253**

Nettlebed Gardens On A4130, some 5m NW of Henley-on-Thames. Take B481 towards Reading and after 200yds turn R into Sue Ryder Home where there is ample parking. Teas and Plant sales in aid of Sue Ryder Home. *Combined adm £2 Chd free. Sun June 8 (2-5.30)*
    Red Lion House &⊛ (Mr & Mrs G Freeman)
    Sue Ryder Home &⊛ (The Sue Ryder Foundation) 26-acre garden surrounding large Edwardian house (not open). Fine rhododendrons and rare trees. Large lawns, pond and Italian terrace. The dell and secret garden are in the course of replanting

New College see Oxford University Gardens

¶25 Newfield Road &⊛ (Joyce & David Brewer) Sonning Common. 5m N of Reading on B481 Nettlebed Rd, on leaving village turn L past Catholic Church, Shiplake Bottom then immed L into Newfield Rd. Free car parking available behind village hall Wood Lane. Garden 5 mins walk N. Small interesting garden of ¼ acre. In excess of 110 different varieties of clematis; shrubs, annuals and containers; mature trees and vegetable garden. Bantams and fish pond, winter shrubs, heathers and spring bulbs. TEAS. *Adm £1.50 Chd under 16 free (Share to Action Against Breast Cancer®). Sun July 13 (2-6). Private visits welcome, please Tel* **01734 723611**

4 Northfield Cottages &⊛⊛ (Miss S E Bedwell) Water Eaton, nr Kidlington. From Sainsbury Roundabout S of Kidlington on A4260 take exit for A34 N. Take 1st R Water Eaton lane opp Kings Arms. Then 1st L following signs for Northfield Farm. A cottage garden of approx ¼-acre designed over last 7-8 yrs. Mainly herbaceous, unusual plants, fruit, vegetables and greenhouse extending into two further gardens, woodland garden. *Adm £1. Every Tues, Fri, Sat, March 16 to Aug 31 (2-5). Private visits welcome all year, please* **Tel 01865 378910**

Nutford Lodge &⊛ (Mr & Mrs K Elmore) In Longcot Village next to The King & Queen public house. S of A420 between Faringdon and Shrivenham. 1½-acre sculpture garden with accent on fragrance, for the blind. Ponds, rockeries, colour schemed borders, potager, views to White Horse; indoor gallery. *Adm £1 Chd free (Share to Headway in Oxford®). May 25 to June 1 (2-8) daily; Sat, Sun Sept 27, 28 (2-6). Also private visits welcome, please Tel 01793 782258*

Old Church House, Wantage &⊛ (Dr & Mrs Dick Squires). At the crossway of A417 and A338. Situated next to Parish Church nr the Wantage market square. An

unusual town garden running down to the Letcombe brook. Much interest with different levels, follies, water, mature trees and many special plants. Tickets and teas at Vale & Downland Museum close by in Church St. *Adm £1 Chd free (Share to Vale & Downland Trust®). Tues to Fris. Private visits also welcome, please* **Tel 01235 762785**

The Old Rectory, Coleshill & (Sir George & Lady Martin) 3m W of Faringdon. Coleshill (NT village) is on B4019 midway between Faringdon and Highworth. Medium-sized garden; lawns and informal shrub beds; wide variety shrubs, incl old fashioned roses, 40-yr-old standard wisteria. Distant views of Berkshire and Wiltshire Downs. House dates from late C14. TEAS. *Adm £1 Chd free. Suns April 20 (2-6), Sept 14 (2-5)*

The Old Rectory, Farnborough, nr Wantage see Berkshire

Oxford see also 23 Beech Croft Road, East Oxford, Headington, Iffley

Oxford University Gardens
    Christ Church ⊛ **Masters' Garden** Entrance on Christ Church Meadow (through War Memorial garden on St Aldate's). Created in 1926, has herbaceous borders and a new border with some unusual shrubs. A walk through the newly designed and replanted Pocock Garden, past Pocock's plane, an oriental plane planted in 1636, leads to the Cathedral Garden. *Adm £1 Chd free Combined adm £1.50 with* **Corpus Christi** *garden. Sun Aug 17 (2-5)*
    Corpus Christi &⊛ Entrance from Merton St or **Christ Church Fellows' garden.** Several small gardens and courtyards overlooking Christchurch meadows. Fellows' private garden not normally open to the public. TEAS in aid of 'Breakthrough Breast Cancer'. *Adm £1. Combined adm £1.50 with* **Christ Church** *garden. Sun Aug 17 (2-5)*
    Exeter College, Rector's Lodgings ⊛ The Turl, between High & Broad Sts, Oxford. Small enclosed garden, herbaceous and shrubs, especially clematis. Fellows' Garden and Chapel also open. *Combined adm with* **New College** *£1.50 Chd free. Sun June 29 (2-5)*
    Green College &⊛ Woodstock Rd, next to Radcliffe Infirmary. 3 acres; lawns, herbaceous borders, medicinal garden with notes on traditional usage of plants. Radcliffe Observatory (Tower of the Winds) open for views of Oxford and TEAS. *Adm £1 Chd free (incl Observatory). Sun June 22 (2-6)*
    Holywell Manor ⊛⊛ (Balliol College) Central Oxford at corner of Manor Rd & St Cross Rd on L of St Cross Church opp law library. College garden of about 1 acre, not normally open to the public. Imaginatively laid out 50 yrs ago around horse chestnut to give formal and informal areas. Mature ginkgo avenue, spinney with spring flowers and bulbs. *Adm £1 Chd free. Sun June 29 (2-6). Private visits welcome, please Tel* **01865 271501**
    Magdalen College and Fellows' Garden (and **President's Garden** not normally open to the public) &⊛ High Street Oxford. Entrance in High St. 60 acres incl deer park, college lawns, numerous trees 150-200 yrs old, notable herbaceous and shrub plantings; Magdalen Meadows are surrounded by Addison's Walk, a tree lined circuit by the R Cherwell developed since

the late C18. An ancient herd of 60 deer is located in the grounds. TEAS. *Adm £2 Chd £1. Sun March 23 (1-5). Private visits welcome by arrangement with Home Bursar* **Tel 01865 276050**

New College & & **Warden's Garden** Entered from New College Lane, off Catte St. Secret walled garden, re-planted 1988 with interesting mix of herbaceous and shrubs. *Adm £1 Acc chd free. Combined adm with* **Exeter College** *£1.50. Sun June 29 (2-5). Private visits welcome for parties of 4 and over, please* **Tel 01865 249002**

Queen's College, Provost's, Fellows' and Nuns' Gardens & High Street. ½-acre with splendid herbaceous borders, rose garden, high old stone walls; large ilex tree. Magnificent statues set in wall of Hawksmoor's library (viewed from Provost's garden). *Combined adm with* **Wadham College** *£1.50. Sun July 20 (2-5)*

Rewley House & & (Oxford University Dept for Continuing Education) Wellington Sq., St John Street. Courtyard gardens, planted by townscaper, Jeanne Bliss, with variegated shrubs, climbers, trailing plants in mobile boxes on wheels. Landscaped gardens designed and maintained by Walter Sawyer, head of the University Parks. TEA. *Adm £1 Chd free. Sun July 20 (2-5). Private visits welcome, please* **Tel 01865 270375**

St Hilda's College & & & Approx 15 mins walk E from city centre. Cross Magdalen Bridge and turn R at roundabout into Cowley Place. College Lodge at end on R. Or park in public car park at St Clements. Approx 5 acres laid to lawns and flower beds with flood plain meadow containing interesting wild flowers. TEAS. *Adm £1 Chd under 12 free. Sun March 23 (2-5)*

Templeton College & & Kennington. 37 acre grounds form a triangle between Oxford S Ring & A34. (First Autumn colour opening). Entering between clumps of Ace of Spades trees, Dawyk Beech and Gingko, this low maintenance scheme by the late Alan Mitchell, author of Collins 'Field Guide to the Trees' will surely be one of the great landscapes this century. 20,000 trees planted since 1969 incl Liquidambar, Black Walnut, Oaks in variety, Cricket Bat Willow avenue etc. Also pond and cottage gardens and formal courtyard herb garden. Exceptional Plant Stall in aid of British Heart Foundation. TEAS in aid of Kennington Overseas Aid Week. *Adm £2 Acc chd free. Sun Oct 19 (11-3)*

Trinity College & & & **President's Garden** Entrance in Broad St. Surrounded by high old stone walls, has mixed borders of herbaeous, shrubs and statuary. Historic Main College Gardens with specimen trees incl 250-yr-old forked catalpa, fine long herbaceous border and handsome garden quad originally designed by Wren. **Fellows' Garden** Small walled terrace, herbaceous borders; water feature formed by Jacobean stone heraldic beasts. TEAS in aid of local charities. *Adm £1.50 Chd free. Sun Aug 10 (2-5)*

University Arboretum & & & 6m S of Oxford on A4074 (formerly A423), 400yds S of Nuneham Courtenay. 55 acres incl informal rhododendron walks, camellia, bamboo and acer collections, natural woodland and oak woodland, meadow with pond and associated aquatics and marginals; fine collection of mature conifers; many 150 yrs old. Staff available to answer queries. Large sale of unusual plants. Plant stall in aid of Oxford University Botanic Garden. *Adm £1 Chd under 12 free. Sun June 1 (2-5)*

Wadham College & & **Fellows' Private Garden & Warden's Garden** Parks Rd. 5 acres, best known for trees and herbaceous borders. In the Fellows' main garden, fine ginkgo and Magnolia acuminata, etc; in the Back Quadrangle very large Tilia tomentosa 'Petiolaris'; in Mallam Court white scented garden est 1994; in the Warden's garden an ancient tulip tree; in the Fellows' private garden Civil War embankment with period fruit tree cultivars, recently established shrubbery with unusual trees and ground cover amongst older plantings. *Adm £1 Chd free. Sun March 23. Combined adm with* **Queen's College** *£1.50. Sun July 20 (2-5)*

Wolfson College & & End of Linton Rd, off Banbury Rd, between city centre and Summertown shops. 9 acres by R Cherwell; garden developed in recent years with comprehensive plant collection tolerant of alkaline soils, grown in interesting and varied habitats both formal and informal, around a framework of fine mature trees; award winning building designed by Powell & Moya; President's garden. TEAS. *Adm £1 Chd free. Sun June 1 (2-6)*

Pettifers & & & (Mr J & the Hon Mrs Price) Lower Wardington. 5m NE of Banbury. C17 village house. 12 yr-old 1-acre plantsman's garden frames an exceptional view of sheep pastures and wooded hills. New Autumn border, with some areas reaching maturity. Unusual plants for sale. TEAS. *Adm £1.50 Chd free. Suns April 6, Sept 28 (2-6). Also open with* **Wardington Manor** *Combined adm £2.50 Chd free. Sun May 18 (2-6). Private visits welcome by appt*

The Priory & (Dr D El Kabir and others) Charlbury, large historic village on B4022 Witney-Enstone. Adjacent church. Formal terraced topiary gardens with Italianate features, incl foliage colour schemes, parterres, specimen trees and shrubs, water features and over 3 acres of recently planted arboretum. Teas at the Church. *Adm £1.50 Chd 50p (Share to Wytham Hall Sick Bay for Homeless, Medical Care®). Suns May 4, July 6 (2-6)*

Queen's College see Oxford University Gardens

Querns & & & (Mr M & the Hon Mrs Whitfeld) Goring Heath. 3m NE of Pangbourne. Take B4526 from A4074 Reading-Oxford Rd. After ½m follow signs. 2-acre garden: shrub and herbaceous borders, rose garden, shrub rose garden, courtyard and formal pond. Listed house dating from early C16 with large thatched C17 barn. TEAS. *Adm £1.50 Chd free. Sun June 22 (2-6)*

Rewley House see Oxford University Gardens

Rofford Manor & & & (Mr & Mrs J L Mogford) Little Milton. 10m SE of Oxford. 1m from Little Milton on Chalgrove Rd. Signposted Rofford only. 2 acres of gardens, within old walls laid out since 1985. Vegetable, herb, rose and swimming pool gardens. Box garden with raised pool. Yew hedges and pleached limes. Twin herbaceous borders planted Autumn 1989 flanking lawn leading to recently constructed ha-ha. TEAS. *Adm £2 Chd free. Sun Sept 14 (2-6). Private visits welcome following written application*

St Hilda's College see Oxford University Gardens

Salford Gardens ⚘ 2m W of Chipping Norton. Off A44 Oxford-Worcester. TEAS. *Combined adm £1.50 Chd free. Sun Aug 24 (2-6)*

Old Rectory ♿⚘ (Mr & Mrs N M Chambers) 1½-acre garden mainly enclosed by walls. A garden of year round interest with unusual plants in mixed borders, many old roses, orchard and vegetable garden

Willow Tree Cottage ⚘ (Mr & Mrs J Shapley) Small walled twin gardens; one created by owners since 1979 with shrub and herbaceous borders, many clematis; other created 1985 from old farmyard with large alpine garden. Featured in 'Successful Gardening'

Shotover House ♿⚘ (Lt-Col Sir John Miller) Wheatley, 6m E of Oxford on A40. Bus: Oxford to Thame or Oxford to High Wycombe to London; alight Islip turn. Large unaltered landscape garden with ornamental temples, lawns and specimen trees. Also small collection of rare cattle, sheep and birds. TEAS (in arcade with view of lake). *Adm £1.50 Chd free. Suns April 6, July 6 (2-6)*

Sibford Ferris Gardens ⚘ Near the Warwickshire border, S of B4035 (Banbury 6 ½m, Shipston-on-Stour 7½m). TEAS in aid of Sibford Primary School PTA. *Combined adm £1.50 Chd free. Sun June 8 (2-6)*

Back Acre ⚘ (Mr & Mrs F A Lamb) Almost an acre, much of which is wild woodland and rough grass with wild flowers; rockery and pond, constructed about 100 years ago and restored over the last few years

Home Close (Mr & Mrs P A Randall) Cotswold stone house fronting formal 1¼-acre garden designed by Baillie-Scott in 1911, under restoration. Courtyard with ornamental fountain and Roman-style stone recesses. Terraced garden, large variety of shrubs including rare species

Maria's House ♿ (Mr & Mrs B R Mills) ¼-acre old cottage garden, surrounded and subdivided by low stone walling. Features incl box hedge porch, small pond, rockeries and herbaceous borders

Sibford School ⚘ (The Manor Walled Gardens) 1½ acres of walled gardens, completely reconstructed and replanted since 1984. Designed with central pergola covered pathways, with many varieties of climbing roses and clematis. The garden is subdivided to provide vegetable plots, soft fruit, greenhouses and herb garden. The gardens are used for the teaching of horticulture and are maintained by students at the school

Sibford Gower Gardens Near the Warwickshire border, S of B4035 (Banbury 7m, Shipston-on-Stour 7m) Superlative views and numerous intriguing tucked away lanes are features of this village. TEAS in aid of Sibford Primary School. **Handy Water Farm** & **Meadow Cottage** *Combined adm for 2 gardens £2 Chd free Sun, Wed June 22, 25 (2-6);* **Carters Yard, The Manor House, Temple Close** *Combined adm for 3 gardens £2 Acc chd free. Sun July 13 (2-6)*

Carters Yard (Mr & Mrs W J S Clutterbuck) Next to Wykeham Arms. ⅓-acre very private cottage garden. Various beds and rockeries in soft colours

Handywater Farm ⚘⚘ (Mr & Mrs W B Colquhoun) ½m N of Sibford Gower on rd to Epwell; 1½ acre family garden in process of creation since 1980. Lovely setting in open rolling countryside. Westerly sloping lawns, stream and ponds, shrub and herbaceous beds

The Manor House ♿ (Mr & Mrs Roger Garner) Opp Wykeham Arms. Completely reconstructed May 1989, the gardens (under 1 acre) are already well established and compliment the romantic atmosphere of this recently renovated rambling thatched manor house

Meadow Cottage ♿⚘⚘ (Mr & Mrs Roger Powell) 6 The Colony. At S end of village. A 1.3-acre garden started from a field in 1988. Large 'shrubaceous' borders; over 1300 different plants; many unusual. Conifers; shrub roses and alpines in raised beds; budding arboretum and series of waterfalls leading to stream. Views

Temple Close ♿⚘ (Mrs Vera Jones) E of Wykham Arms. 1¼ acres with rockery, various beds of shrubs, roses, perennials and herbs; paved stream-side walk running through extensive water garden between two ponds with fountains; pets paddock; good view

Souldern Gardens Between Banbury (8m) and Bicester (7m) off B4100. 4 gardens in picturesque 'Best Kept' prizewinning village. TEAS. *Combined adm £2 Chd free (Share to Souldern Trust®). Sun June 22 (2-6)*

Great House Close ♿⚘ (Mrs C E Thornton) Long, varied garden and orchard framed by old farm buildings

The Old Forge (Mr & Mrs D Duthie) Resourceful, densely planted cottage garden with stone walling

¶Park Lodge ♿⚘ (Mrs J Bellinger) End of village, last house on R, opp Manor Gates. Garden retrieved from woodland with pond and flower borders

Souldern Manor ♿⚘ (Mr & Dr C Sanders) 25 acres of C17 house with much fresh development. Linked ponds, rock garden, waterfall, fountains, temple, pavillions and view of Cherwell valley are enhanced by many newly planted mature trees. Children's play area

South Newington Gardens A small village 1½m from Bloxham, nr Banbury on A361 to Chipping Norton. It has a fine church, with superb mediaeval wall paintings. TEA at the village hall with stalls. 3 gardens within easy walking distance. *Combined adm £1.50 Chd free. Sun June 1 (2-6)*

Applegarth ⚘⚘ (Mr & Mrs Andrew Edgar) ¾-acre cottage garden with a rose walk featuring old-fashioned roses and lavenders; herbaceous borders and mixed borders with some unusual shrubs and young trees; small water garden and pond

The Barn ♿⚘ (Mrs Rosemary Clark) Green Lane. 1 acre of lawns and mixed borders with outdoor chess game, croquet lawn, trompe l'oeuil, vine walk and vegetable patch

The Little Forge ♿ (Mr M B Pritchard) Small garden with shrubs; trees and vegetable patch

Sparsholt Manor (Sir Adrian & Lady Judith Swire) Off B4507 Ashbury Rd 3 ½m W of Wantage. Spring garden, lakes and wilderness. Teas in village hall in aid of Sparsholt Church. *Adm £1.50 Chd free (Share to St John Ambulance, Wantage Division®). Mon May 26 (2-6)*

Stansfield ⚘⚘ (Mr & Mrs D Keeble) 49 High St, Stanford-in-the-Vale. 3½m SE of Faringdon. Park in street. Plantsman's 1¼-acre garden on alkaline soil. Wide range of plants, many uncommon. Scree bed, sinks and troughs, damp garden, herbaceous borders, ornamental grasses. Copse underplanted with hellebores and shade loving plants. Aromatic plants. Unusual trees and shrubs. Yr-round interest. Wide range of plants for sale. Listed in Good Gardens Guide. Featured in TV's Secret Garden 95. TEAS. *Adm £1 Chd free. Every Tues April 1 to Sept 23 (10-4); Suns June 1, July 13, Aug 10 (2-6). Private visits also welcome, please* Tel 01367 710340

■ **Stanton Harcourt Manor** ৬❀ (Mr Crispin & The Hon Mrs Gascoigne) W of Oxford on B4449. Picturesque stone manor house with unique C15 Great Kitchen, Chapel and Pope's Tower. Formal gardens leading to woodland area with remains of moat and medieval stew ponds. TEAS. *Adm House and garden £4 Chd/OAP's £2. Garden only £2.50 Chd/OAP's £1.50. Thurs April 10, 24, May 15, June 5, 19, July 3, 17, 31; Aug 14, Sept 11, 25; Suns March 30, April 13, May 4, 18, 25, June 8, July 6, 20, Aug 3, 17, 24, Sept 14, 28, Bank hol Mons March 31, May 5, 26, Aug 25. For NGS Suns April 27, June 22 (2-6)*

Steeple & Middle Aston Gardens Beautiful stone villages midway between Oxford & Banbury, ½m off A4260. Villages bordering Cherwell valley; interesting church and winding lanes with a variety of charming stone houses and cottages. Map available at all gardens. TEAS at Canterbury House in aid of local scout group. *Combined adm £2 Chd free. Sun June 8 (1-6)*

    Canterbury House ৬✕❀ (Mr & Mrs M G Norris) Former rectory in 2-acre garden with mature trees and intersected by walls. The garden is continually being redeveloped for ease of maintenance, interest and attraction of wildlife. *(Share to Specialcare Baby Unit, John Radcliffe®)*

    Home Farm House ✕❀ (Mr & Mrs T J G Parsons) ¾m N of Steeple Aston, opp Middle Aston House. 1-acre informal garden surrounding C17 farmhouse, fine view. Mixed planting, incl unusual perennials, shrubs and roses. Interesting small nursery. *Private visits welcome May to Oct, please* Tel 018693 40666

    Kralingen (Mr & Mrs Roderick Nicholson) 2-acre informal garden designed for low maintenance without professional help. Great variety of interesting trees and shrubs. Water garden and wild flower area

    The Longbyre (Mr & Mrs V Billings) Hornton stone house in ¼ acre. Garden constructed out of old orchard. Water feature, mixed perennials, shrubs, tubs on different levels

    Middle Aston House ✕ (Pera Group) ¾m N of Steeple Aston. 20 acres of grounds landscaped in C18 by William Kent, incl 2 lakes, granary and icehouse

    Rowans ৬❀ (Mr & Mrs M J Clist) The Dickredge, opp White Lion. An acre of orchard and mixed garden, incl shrubs, herbaceous borders, alpines, vegetables

    Willow Cottage ✕❀ (Mr & Mrs M Vivian) The Dickredge, opp White Lion. Hornton stone cottage with ½-acre garden. Old-fashioned shrub roses, many unusual plants in garden and conservatory. Fish pond with Koi

Stonewalls ৬✕ (Mr & Mrs B Shafighian) Hempton. 1½m W of Deddington on B4031. A plantsman's garden of 1½ acres divided into many interesting areas, incl shrubbery, herbaceous border, conifer and heather bed, nearly 200 clematis and climbers. Sunken pool. TEAS in aid of St John's Church, Hempton. *Adm £1 Chd free. Sun July 13 (2-6)*

Stratton Audley Gardens 3m NE of Bicester, off A421 to Buckingham. Village dates from Roman times. Church is largely mediaeval with spectacular late C17 tomb. TEAS at Stratton House. *Combined adm £2 Chd free (Share to Helen House Hospice®). Sun June 15 (2-6)*

    1 Church Cottages ৬❀ (Mr & Mrs L Sweetman) About ½-acre. A proper country cottage garden with rockery pools and stonework, vegetables, seasonal bedding, orchids

    Mallories ৬❀ (Mr P Boyd) Mainly walled garden of ¾ acre behind row of C17 cottages converted to house. Sunny and shady herbaceous borders, bearded irises, old roses and other shrubs, wall plants and climbers, small conservatory. Plant stall in aid of Stratton Audley Church

    Stratton House ৬✕ (Mr & Mrs P J Bailey) A quiet and peaceful walled garden, set in ¾-acre with terraces, paved area with fountain, herbaceous border, shrubs, heathers, ornamental pond, topiary, a black walnut tree and a yew, said to be over 400 yrs old

Swalcliffe Lea House ✕❀ (Jeffrey & Christine Demmar) Swalcliffe Lea. Situated between Tadmarton and Shutford The garden has been developed during the last 8 yrs. It covers 7 acres with lawns, flower beds, water, herb garden, pergola, vegetables, orchard and 'nature reserve', There is a wide range of young trees, shrubs and plants. TEAS. *Adm £1.50 Chd free. Sun June 15 (2-6)*

Swerford Park (Mr & Mrs J W Law) 4m NE of Chipping Norton, just off A361 to Banbury, ½m W of Swerford Church. In extensive parkland setting with lakeside walks, garden of Georgian house overlooks spectacular wooded valley with series of lakes linked by waterfalls. Approach along front drive where signed; parking at rear only, may not be very close. TEAS. *Adm £1.50 Chd free (Share to Swan Lifeline, Windsor®). Mon May 26 (2-6)*

Swinbrook House ৬✕ (Mr & Mrs J D Mackinnon) 1½m N of Swinbrook on Shipton-under-Wychwood Rd. Large garden; herbaceous border; shrubs; shrub roses; large kitchen garden; fine views. Picnics allowed. TEA. *Adm £1.50 Chd free. Sun July 20 (2-6)*

Swyncombe House ৬❀ (Mr & Mrs W J Christie-Miller) Follow main rd from Cookley Green towards Ewelme. Turn L at Rectory corner. Parkland with mature trees, flowers and spring bulbs. TEA and plants in aid of St Botolph Church. *Adm £1 Chd free. Sun April 6 (2-7)*

Tadmarton Gardens 5m SW of Banbury on B4035. Refreshments at village hall in aid of St Nicholas Church, Tadmarton. *Combined adm £2 Chd free. Suns April 13, Sept 21 (2-5)*

    The Arches ৬✕ (Mr & Mrs J Bolland) ⅕-acre garden hidden at back of 30s house, designed and created by present owners since 1983. Lovingly adapted for disabled occupant. Stone paths, open air 'rooms', summer houses. A garden for sitting in

    Buxton House ৬✕ (Mr & Mrs J Steele) Small garden created in last 10 yrs incl a waterfall and two fountains

    Tadmarton Manor ৬❀ (Mr & Mrs R K Asser) Old established 2½-acre garden; beautiful views of unspoilt countryside; fine trees, great variety of perennial plants and shrubs; hardy cyclamen, tunnel arbour; C15 barn and C18 dovecote

¶**Tile Cottage** (Mr & Mrs D Woodward) Traditional country garden. Flowers, vegetables and orchard

Taynton House &☀ (Mr & Mrs David Mackenzie) Taynton, off A424 Burford to Stow-on-the-Wold. Medium-sized garden behind listed stone house in delightful Cotswold village with interesting church. Stream and copse with thousands of daffodils and spring flowers. TEAS. *Adm £1.50 Chd free (Share to St John's Church, Taynton®). Sun April 6 (2-5)*

Templeton College see Oxford University Gardens

Towersey Manor &☀ (Mr & Mrs U D Barnett) Towersey, 1½m SE of Thame, 300 yds down Manor Rd from Xrds in middle of village. Main garden of 2 acres lies behind house. Within the last 22 yrs this once open and flat site has been transformed by the present owners. Formal hornbeam hedges frame smaller informal areas incorporating many shrubs, trees and old-fashioned and modern shrub roses. *Adm £1.50 Chd free. Wed June 18 (2-6). Private visits welcome on weekdays May to July, please Tel 01844 212077*

Town Farm Cottage &☀☀ (Mr & Mrs J Clark) Kingston Blount. 4m S of Thame. 4m NE of Watlington. 1½m NE of junction 6, M40 on B4009. 1¼-acre colourful garden bursting with many unusual plants. Totally developed over last 8 yrs by present plantaholic owners incl large rockery, large herbaceous borders, scree beds full of 'little treasures'. Rare English mature black poplar trees by small lake, full of fish and frequent sightings of the red kite overhead. TEAS. *Adm £1.50 Chd under 14 free. Suns April 27, June 15 (2-6). Private visits also welcome, please Tel 01844 352152*

Trinity College see Oxford University Gardens

Troy & Gould's Grove Farmhouse &☀ (Mr & Mrs D Ruck Keene & Mr T Ruck Keene). Ewelme. 3m NE of Wallingford. From roundabout on A4074/A4130 take exit signed Ewelme, RAF Benson (Clacks Lane). Approx 1½m turn R at T-junction towards Henley. 1½-acre garden featuring grey and herb gardens, daffodils; summer houses used by Jerome K Jerome (former owner). Small flocks of Jacob and Hebridean sheep with lambs. Small garden adjacent with interesting shrubs and fine views of The Chilterns. TEAS in aid of Marie Curie Foundation. *Adm £2.50 Chd free. Sun May 11 (2-6)*

Tusmore Park &☀ (Tusmore Park Holdings) Off A43. 3½ m S of Brackley. Approx 20 acres of lawns, herbaceous borders, woodland garden and terraces. 6-acre lake, 3 greenhouses; walled garden. TEAS *Adm £1.50 Chd free. Sun July 27 (2-6)*

Wadham College see Oxford University Gardens

Wardington Manor & (The Lord & Lady Wardington) Wardington. 5m NE of Banbury. 5-acre garden with topiary, rock garden, flowering shrub walk to pond. Carolean manor house 1665. TEAS. *Combined adm with Pettifers £2.50 Chd free. Sun May 18 (2-5.30). Private visits by parties also welcome adm £2, please Tel 01295 750202*

■**Waterperry Gardens** &☀ 2½m from Wheatley M40 Junction 8. 50m from London, 62m from Birmingham, 9m E of Oxford. Gardens well signed locally with Tourist Board 'rose' symbol. 20 acres; ornamental gardens, nurseries, parkland; many interesting plants; shrub, herbaceous and alpine nurseries; glasshouses and comprehensive fruit section. High quality plant centre, garden shop (Tel **01844 339226**). TEA SHOP, Art and Craft Gallery. Saxon church with famous glasses and brasses in grounds. *Adm Gardens & Nurseries £2.40 OAPs £1.90 Chd £1.10 under 10 free.* **OPEN DAILY** *except Christmas and New Year hols and July 17 to 20. Coach parties by appt only Tel* 01844 339254 *. For NGS (Share to NCCPG®). Suns June 8, Aug 10 (10-6)*

Weald Manor see Bampton & Weald Gardens

Westwell Manor ☀☀ (Mr & Mrs T H Gibson) 2m SW of Burford, from A40 Burford-Cheltenham, turn L after ½m on narrow rd signposted Westwell. Unspoilt hamlet with delightful church. 6 acres surrounding old Cotswold manor house, knot and water gardens, potager, shrub roses, herbaceous borders, topiary, moonlight garden. *Adm £2 Chd 50p (Share to St Mary's Church Westwell®). Sun July 6 (2-6.30)*

White's Farm House &☀ (Dr & Mrs M Shone) Letcombe Bassett 3m SW of Wantage. Take B4507 signed Ashbury, then through Letcombe Regis. 2½ acres; mixed borders; wild garden with 30 yrs growth of chalk-tolerant trees, shrubs, unusual herbaceous plants, summer bulbs. Gravel scree bed, plants in pots and tubs, pond, playground and monster adventure walk. New wood and willow features. TEAS in C18 barn. *Adm £1.50 Chd free. Suns June 15, July 20 (2-6)*

Wick Hall & Nurseries &☀☀ (Mr & Mrs P Drysdale) Between Abingdon & Radley on Audlett Drive. Parking for disabled at house, some off-street parking. Approx 10 acres lawns and wild garden; topiary; pond garden; rockeries; walled garden enclosing knot garden; young arboretum. Early C18 house (not open), barn and greenhouses, garden restored and developed since 1982. TEAS in aid of Radley WI. *Adm £1.50 Chd free. Sun April 27 (2-5)*

Wilcote House &☀ (The Hon C E & Mrs Cecil) Finstock. Between Finstock & North Leigh. East of B4022 Witney-Charlbury Road. Approx 7 acres set in parkland surrounding an early C17-C19 Cotswold stone house. Shrub and herbaceous borders, old-fashioned rose garden and 40yd laburnum walk (planted 1984). Old orchard being replanted as an arboretum. Spring bulbs, flowering trees, sheep and lovely views. *Adm £2. Private visits welcome on weekdays, please contact Mr Pollard on Tel 01993 868 606 and confirm in writing*

Wolfson College see Oxford University Gardens

Wood Croft ☀ (St Cross College) Foxcombe Lane, Boars Hill, S of Oxford. From ring rd follow signs to Wootton and Boars Hill. From junction at top Hinksey Hill, house 1st on L. 1½ acres designed and planted by the late Prof G E Blackman FRS. Rhododendrons, camellias, azaleas, many varieties primula in woodland and surrounding natural pond; fine trees. TEA. *Adm £1 Chd free (Share to Royal Marsden Hospital Development Appeal®). Sun May 25 (2-6)*

Wootton Hill &❀ (Mr & Mrs A Ellis) Boars Hill. From B4017 to Abingdon Rd take 1st L 50 yds after Bystander PH (Wootton Village). Colourful 7 acres with large herbaceous border. Extensive lawns, pond and natural woodland. Wonderful mulberry tree; beautiful views to The Ridgeway. TEAS in aid of Sir Michael Sobell House Hospice. *Adm £2 Chd 50p. Sun Aug 24 (2-6)*

Wroxton Gardens &❀ 3m NW of Banbury off A422. Grounds of Wroxton Abbey open free. Teas at village fete May. TEAS in aid of Wroxton Church Bell Fund, **Laurels Farm** Aug. *Combined adm £1.30 Chd free. Mon May 26 (1-6). Also open with* **Home Farm, Balscote** *Adm £2 Chd free. Wed June 25 (11-5)*

6 The Firs Stratford Rd (Mr & Mrs D J Allen) Approx ⅓-acre family garden with island beds, shrubs, herbaceous perennials incl large collection of cranesbill geraniums

Laurels Farm (Mr & Mrs R Fox) ½-acre with island beds, shrubs, old roses and herbaceous perennials. *(Share to Katherine House Hospice)*

Yeomans ❀ (Mrs M E Pedder) Tadmarton 5m SW of Banbury on B4035. Small garden on 4 levels, featured in 'Easy Plants for Difficult Places' by Geoffrey Smith; C16 thatched cottage. Colourful from spring to autumn; wide variety annuals, perennials, shrubs; many climbers incl roses, clematis; shrub roses with hips. *Adm £1 Chd free (Share to Katharine House Hospice Trust®). Private visits welcome for 2 and over, by appt, please. April to Sept* **Tel 01295 780285**

Powys

See separate Welsh section beginning on page 323

Rutland

See Leicestershire

Shropshire

Hon County Organisers:	Mrs J H M Stafford, The Old Rectory, Fitz, Shrewsbury SY4 3AS
	Tel 01743 850555
	Mr & Mrs James Goodall, Rectory Cottage, Chetton, Bridgnorth, Shropshire WV16 6UF
	Mrs K Cooke, Harnage Farm, Cound, Shropshire SY5 6EJ
Hon County Treasurer:	Mrs P Trevor-Jones, Preen Manor, Church Preen, nr Church Stretton SY6 7LQ

DATES OF OPENING

February 23 Sunday
Erway Farm House, Dudleston Heath

March 29 Saturday
Erway Farm House, Dudleston Heath

March 30 Sunday
Erway Farm House, Dudleston Heath

March 31 Monday
Erway Farm House, Dudleston Heath
Hundred House Hotel, Norton

April 1 Tuesday
Radnor Cottage, Clun

April 6 Sunday
Erway Farm House, Dudleston Heath

April 13 Sunday
Badger Farmhouse, Badger nr Shifnal
Erway Farm House, Dudleston Heath

April 20 Sunday
Astley Abbotts House, Bridgnorth
Erway Farm House, Dudleston Heath

April 27 Sunday
Erway Farm House, Dudleston Heath
Swallow Hayes, Albrighton

May 2 Friday
Wollerton Old Hall, Market Drayton

May 3 Saturday
Field House, Clee St Margaret, nr Ludlow

May 4 Sunday
Field House, Clee St Margaret, nr Ludlow

May 5 Monday
Millichope Park, Munslow

May 6 Tuesday
Radnor Cottage, Clun

May 9 Friday
Wollerton Old Hall, Market Drayton

May 11 Sunday
Adcote School, nr Shrewsbury
Gatacre Park, Six Ashes
Swallow Hayes, Albrighton

May 12 Monday
Mawley Hall, Cleobury Mortimer

May 14 Wednesday
Cricklewood Cottage, Plox Green

May 16 Friday
Wollerton Old Hall, Market
Drayton
May 18 Sunday
Adcote School, nr Shrewsbury
Brimstry, Albrighton
Brownhill House, Ruyton XI
Towns
Gatacre Park, Six Ashes
Ridgway Wood, Edgton
May 23 Friday
Wollerton Old Hall, Market
Drayton
May 25 Sunday
Erway Farm House, Dudleston
Heath
Hatton Grange, Shifnal
Longnor Hall, nr Dorrington
Ridgway Wood, Edgton
Walcot Hall, Lydbury North
May 26 Monday
Dudmaston, nr Bridgnorth
Longnor Hall, nr Dorrington
Oteley, Ellesmere
Ridgway Wood, Edgton
Walcot Hall, Lydbury North
May 27 Tuesday
Hundred House Hotel, Norton
Radnor Cottage, Clun
May 29 Thursday
Preen Manor, nr Church Stretton
May 30 Friday
Wollerton Old Hall, Market
Drayton
May 31 Saturday
Brownhill House, Ruyton XI
Towns
June 1 Sunday
Adcote School, nr Shrewsbury
Brownhill House, Ruyton XI
Towns
The Lyth, Ellesmere
Willey Park, Broseley
June 6 Friday
Wollerton Old Hall, Market
Drayton
June 8 Sunday
Gate Cottage, nr Ellesmere
The Old Rectory, Fitz
The Old Vicarage, Cardington
The Patch, Acton Pigot
June 9 Monday
Brownhill House, Ruyton XI
Towns
June 10 Tuesday
Radnor Cottage, Clun
June 11 Wednesday
Cricklewood Cottage, Plox Green
June 12 Thursday
Preen Manor, nr Church
Stretton
June 13 Friday
Wollerton Old Hall, Market
Drayton

June 14 Saturday
Moortown, nr Wellington
Peplow Hall, Hodnet
June 15 Sunday
Adcote School, nr Shrewsbury
Brownhill House, Ruyton XI
Towns
Moortown, nr Wellington
Nordybank Nurseries, nr Ludlow
The Old Vicarage, Cardington
The Patch, Acton Pigot
Peplow Hall, Hodnet
June 16 Monday
Mawley Hall, Cleobury Mortimer
June 17 Tuesday
Weston Park, Shifnal
June 19 Thursday
Triscombe, Wellington
June 20 Friday
Wollerton Old Hall, Market
Drayton
June 21 Saturday
Hartshill Gardens, Oakengates
Whittington Village Gardens, nr
Oswestry
June 22 Sunday
Hartshill Gardens, Oakengates
Lower Hall, Worfield
Millichope Park, Munslow
Nordybank Nurseries, nr Ludlow
Whittington Village Gardens, nr
Oswestry
June 23 Monday
Brownhill House, Ruyton XI
Towns
June 24 Tuesday
Hundred House Hotel, Norton
June 26 Thursday
Preen Manor, nr Church
Stretton
June 27 Friday
Morville Dower House, nr
Bridgnorth
Wollerton Old Hall, Market
Drayton
June 29 Sunday
Benthall Hall, Broseley
Bitterley Court, Ludlow
David Austin Roses, Albrighton
Erway Farm House, Dudleston
Heath
Hatton Grange, Shifnal
Limeburners, Ironbridge
Madeley Gardens, Telford
Ruthall Manor, Ditton Priors
June 30 Monday
Brownhill House, Ruyton XI
Towns
July 4 Friday
Wollerton Old Hall, Market
Drayton
July 5 Saturday
Field House, Clee St Margaret, nr
Ludlow

July 6 Sunday
Field House, Clee St Margaret, nr
Ludlow
Harnage Farm, Cound,
Shrewsbury ‡
The Mill Cottage, Cound,
Shrewsbury ‡
The Old Vicarage, Cardington
July 8 Tuesday
Radnor Cottage, Clun
July 9 Wednesday
Burford House Gardens, nr
Tenbury Wells
Cricklewood Cottage, Plox
Green
July 10 Thursday
Preen Manor, nr Church
Stretton
July 11 Friday
Wollerton Old Hall, Market
Drayton
July 12 Saturday
Brownhill House, Ruyton XI
Towns
July 13 Sunday
Brownhill House, Ruyton XI
Towns
The Old Vicarage, Cardington
July 14 Monday
Mawley Hall, Cleobury Mortimer
July 15 Tuesday
Hundred House Hotel, Norton
Weston Park, Shifnal
July 17 Thursday
Triscombe, Wellington
July 18 Friday
Wollerton Old Hall, Market
Drayton
July 20 Sunday
Astley Abbotts House, Bridgnorth
Church Bank, Westbury
July 24 Thursday
Preen Manor, nr Church Stretton
July 25 Friday
Wollerton Old Hall, Market
Drayton
July 27 Sunday
Erway Farm House, Dudleston
Heath
July 29 Tuesday
Radnor Cottage, Clun
August 1 Friday
Wollerton Old Hall, Market
Drayton
August 2 Saturday
Hodnet Hall Gardens, nr Market
Drayton
August 5 Tuesday
Hawkstone Hall, Shrewsbury
August 6 Wednesday
Hawkstone Hall, Shrewsbury
August 8 Friday
Wollerton Old Hall, Market
Drayton

August 9 Saturday
Hodnet Hall Gardens, nr Market
Drayton
August 13 Wednesday
Burford House Gardens, nr
Tenbury Wells
Cricklewood Cottage, Plox Green
August 15 Friday
Wollerton Old Hall, Market
Drayton
August 17 Sunday
Church Bank, Westbury
Madeley Gardens, Telford
August 22 Friday
Wollerton Old Hall, Market
Drayton
August 29 Friday
Wollerton Old Hall, Market
Drayton

August 31 Sunday
Brownhill House, Ruyton XI
Towns
September 10 Wednesday
Cricklewood Cottage, Plox
Green
October 5 Sunday
Preen Manor, nr Church
Stretton

Regular openings
For details see garden description

Burford House Gardens, nr Tenbury
Wells
Field House, Clee St Margaret, nr
Ludlow
Hawkstone Hall, Shrewsbury

Hodnet Hall Gardens, nr Market
Drayton
Weston Park, Shifnal
Wollerton Old Hall, Market Drayton

By appointment only
For telephone numbers and other
details see garden descriptions.
Private visits welcomed

Ashford Manor, Ashford Carbonel
Fairfield, Oldbury, Bridgnorth
Farley House, Much Wenlock
Haye House, nr Bridgnorth

DESCRIPTIONS OF GARDENS

Adcote School ✗ (Adcote School Educational Trust Ltd)
Little Ness, 8m NW of Shrewsbury via A5 to Montford
Bridge, turn off NE follow signs to Little Ness. 20-acres;
fine trees incl beeches, tulip trees, oaks (American and
Evergreen); atlas cedars, Wellingtonia etc; rhododendrons, azaleas; small lake; landscaped garden. House
(part shown) designed by Norman Shaw RA; Grade I
listed building; William Morris windows; De Morgan tiles.
TEAS. *Adm £1.50 Acc chd free. Suns May 11, 18, June 1,
15 (2-5). Other times strictly by appt only* **Tel 01939
260202**

Ashford Manor ⅄ (Kit Hall Esq) Ashford Carbonel, 2¾m
S of Ludlow. E of A49 Ludlow-Leominster. Garden of 2
acres, herbaceous foliage and shrubs grown in the hope
of maintaining interest through the entire year, hence
very few flowers. Worked entirely by owner. Picnic area –
Dogs welcomed. Reasonably level ground. *Adm 50p.
Private visits welcome all year, please* **Tel 01584 872100**

Astley Abbotts House ❀ (Mrs H E Hodgson) 2m NW of
Bridgnorth. B4373 from Bridgnorth turn R at Cross Lane
Head. 10 acres, 5 acres PYO lavender, bee village; herbs;
wild woodland garden; fine trees; lawns; rhododendrons.
Only partly suitable for wheelchairs. TEAS. *Adm £1.50
Chd free (Share to Wolverhampton Eye Infirmary®). Suns
April 20 (2-6), July 20 (11-6)*

Badger Farmhouse ⅄❀ (Mr & Mrs N J D Foster) Badger. From A464 Shifnal to Wolverhampton Rd turn S to
Burnhill Green. In Burnhill Green turn W to Beckbury. At
T junction in Beckbury turn S, ¾m on R. 3-acre garden.
Over 300 varieties of daffodils and narcissi in a mature
setting. Mainly in three orchards, one of apple one pear
and plum and one of cherry. Also fine trees, shrubs and
roses. TEAS. *Adm £1.50 Chd free (Share to Riding for the
Disabled, Brockton Group®). Sun April 13 (2-6). Private
visits welcome, please* **Tel 01746 783222**

▲**Benthall Hall** ⅄✗ (The National Trust) 1m NW of
Broseley, 4m NE of Much Wenlock (B4375); turning up
lane marked with brown sign. Garden 3 acres; shrub
roses; rockery banks; lawns; former kitchen garden; wild
garden. Interesting plants and fine trees. C16 house also
open. *Adm £2 Chd £1. For NGS Sun June 29 (1.30-5.30)*

Bitterley Court ⅄❀ (Mr & Mrs J V T Wheeler) Ludlow.
Next to Bitterley Church. Follow A4117 E from Ludlow
and turn off to Bitterley after about 2m. 5m from Ludlow
altogether. A 6-acre garden featuring specimen and rare
trees, shrubs, woodland walks, ornamental kitchen garden and herbaceous borders. TEAS in aid of The Shropshire and Mid-Wales Hospice. *Adm £2 Chd free. Sun June
29 (2-6)*

Brimstry ⅄ (Dr & Mrs H V Hughes) Shaw Lane, Albrighton. 7m NW of Wolverhampton. At Albrighton on
A41 turn off into Station Rd. 1st turning L is Shaw Lane.
2⅓-acre garden. Created and maintained by the owners
since 1981. Rhododendrons, azaleas, camellias, magnolias. A wide variety of trees. TEAS. *Adm £1.50 Chd free
(Share to Albrighton Parish Church®). Sun May 18 (2-6)*

Brownhill House ✗❀ (Roger & Yoland Brown) Ruyton
XI Towns. 10m NW of Shrewsbury on B4397. Park at
Bridge Inn. Unusual and distinctive hillside garden bordering River Perry featured on TV and in magazines. Great
variety of plants and styles from laburnum walk and formal terraces to woodland paths plus large kitchen garden. 200 varieties of plants for sale, proceeds to NGS.
TEAS. *Adm £1.50 Chd free. Sun May 18; Sat, Sun May 31,
June 1; Sun June 15, Sat, Sun July 12, 13, Sun Aug 31
(1.30-5.30) Mons June 9, 23, 30 (6.30-8.30). Also by appt
May-Aug please* **Tel/Fax 01939 260626**

■ **Burford House Gardens** ⅄✗❀ (Treasures of Tenbury) 1m W of Tenbury Wells on A456. 4 acres of sweeping lawns and serpentine borders, set in beautiful
surroundings in the Teme Valley, around an elegant
Georgian house. National Clematis Collection and over
2,000 other kinds of plants in wonderful combinations of
colours and textures. Nursery offers over 200 varieties of
clematis and comprehensive range of usual and unusual
plants. Fine church, gallery and gift shop. DOGS on lead,
nursery only. TEAS. *Adm £2.50 Chd £1. Open every day,
all yr-round 10-5. For NGS Weds July 9, Aug 13 (10-5)*

Church Bank ✿❀ (Mr & Mrs B P Kavanagh) Rowley 12m SW of Shrewsbury on B4386 Montgomery Rd continuing through Westbury. After ⅓m turn R for Rowley. After 3½m turn L at Xrds for Brockton. Church Bank is on L after 120yds. A S-facing, steeply sloping garden in one of Shropshire's most beautiful and least known corners; packed with interesting and unusual plants, predominantly perennial, and has a large area of young woodland and 'natural' planting which incl 2 pools - 1 established, the other newly made and a newly created bog garden. *Adm £1.50 Chd free (Share to Action Aid®). Suns July 20, Aug 17 (2-6); also private visits welcome May to Sept, please* **Tel 01743 891661**

Cricklewood Cottage ✿❀ (Paul & Debbie Costello) Plox Green. On A488 1m SW of Minsterley. Park on grass verge opposite. Pretty ⅓-acre cottage garden, bordered by trout stream with waterfalls and natural bog garden; colour-schemed borders of shrubs and perennials, all packed with plants, particularly shrub roses, day lilies and hardy geraniums. Featured in Your Garden magazine. TEAS. *Adm £1.50 Chd free (Share to Hope House Children's Respite Hospice®). Weds May 14, June 11, July 9, Aug 13, Sept 10 (1.30-5); Weds May 14, June 11 (6-8) with home-made soup. Private visits also welcome, please* **Tel 01743 791229**

▲**David Austin Roses** ♿❀ (Mr & Mrs David Austin) Bowling Green Lane, Albrighton, 8m NW of Wolverhampton. 4m from Shifnal (A464) L into Bowling Green Lane; or junction 3, M54 to Albrighton, R at sign 'Roses & Shrubs', Bowling Green Lane 2nd R. Breeders of the famous English roses. Gardens; 900 varieties old roses, shrub, species and climbing roses; herbaceous display garden, semi-wild. Private garden, trees and water garden with many plants. Variety of plants for sale. Sculpture by Pat Austin. TEAS. *Adm £1.50 Chd free. For NGS Sun June 29 (2-6)*

▲**Dudmaston** ♿✿ (The National Trust; Sir George Labouchere) 4m SE of Bridgnorth on A442. Bus stop at gates ½m. 8 acres with fine trees, shrubs; lovely views over Dudmaston Pool and surrounding country. Dingle walk. TEAS. *Adm £2.50 Chd £1. For NGS Mon May 26 (2-6)*

Erway Farm House ✿❀ (Mr & Mrs A A Palmer) 3m N of Ellesmere, 2m S of Overton on Dee. Signposted from B5068 Ellesmere-St Martins Rd and B5069 Overton- Oswestry rd. 1-acre Plantswoman's garden packed with rare and interesting plants. Hellebores in profusion, many varieties of snowdrop. Later, hardy geranium and other shade loving plants. Sunny gravel garden with shrub roses. Permanent display of garden sculpture. Unusual plants from garden for sale. *Adm £1.50 Chd free. Sat, Sun, Mon March 29, 30, 31 (2-6), also last Sun in every month Feb to July (2-6) (February 1-5) and every Sun in April (2-6). Coach parties by appt, please* **Tel 01691 690479**

Fairfield ♿✿ (Mr & Mrs G P Beardsley) Oldbury, Bridgnorth. Take B4363 from Bridgnorth to Cleobury Mortimer Rd 100 yds from SVR railway bridge - over bypass turn L. Informal landscaped garden of approx 3½ acres, containing sweeping lawns, many interesting trees and shrubs, water garden and woodland area. *Adm £1.50 Chd free. April to end July Mon to Fri incl (2-6), strictly by appt please,* **Tel 01746 763291**

Farley House ✿ (Mr & Mrs R W Collingwood) From A458 at Much Wenlock turn N on to A4169 signed Ironbridge; house 1m on L. 1-acre garden made since 1980 by owners; alpines, herbaceous island beds, shrubs and trees. Coach parties welcome. *Adm £2 Chd free. Open by appt April to Oct, please* **Tel 01952 727017**

■ **Field House** ♿✿❀ (Dr & Mrs John Bell) Clee St Margaret. 8m NE of Ludlow. Turning to Stoke St Milborough and Clee St Margaret. 5m from Ludlow, 10m from Bridgnorth along B4364. Through Stoke St Milborough to Clee St Margaret. Ignore R turn to Clee Village. Carry on to Field House on L. Parking. 1-acre garden created since 1982 for yr-round interest. Mixed borders; rose walk; pool garden; herbaceous borders; organic vegetable garden; spring bulbs and autumn colours. TEAS in aid of Village Hall Fund on NGS days and Suns only. *Adm £1.50 Chd 50p. Garden and nursery open 1st Sat, Sun in month from April 5 to Oct 5. For NGS Sat, Sun May 3, 4 and July 5, 6 (12-6). Private visits welcome, please* **Tel 01584 823242**

Gatacre Park ♿❀ (Lady Thompson) Six Ashes, 6m SE of Bridgnorth on A458. Stourbridge-Bridgnorth Rd. 8 acres. Originally a Victorian garden partly redeveloped over the last 56 years by present owner. Flowering shrubs, fine trees, incl 100ft tulip tree and manna ash; topiary walk; large woodland garden with pieris, azaleas, rhododendrons incl many interesting species now fully grown. Lovely views over Park. TEAS. *Adm £2 Chd free (Share to Tuck Hill Church, Six Ashes®). Suns May 11, 18 (2-6)*

Gate Cottage ✿❀ (G W Nicholson & Kevin Gunnell) nr Ellesmere 10m N of Shrewsbury on A528. At village of Cockshutt take rd signposted English Frankton. Garden is 1m on R. Parking in adjacent field. A developing garden at present about 2 acres. Informal mixed plantings of trees, shrubs, herbaceous of interest to flower arrangers and plantsmen. Pool and rock garden; informal pools. Large collection of hostas; old orchard with roses. TEA. *Adm £1.50 Chd 50p. Sun June 8 (1-5). Parties by appt at other times, please* **Tel 01939-270606**

Harnage Farm ♿✿ (Mr & Mrs Ken Cooke) Cound. 8m SE of Shrewsbury on A458. Turn to Cound 1m S of Cross Houses. Harnage Farm 1m, bearing L past church. ½-acre farmhouse garden; well stocked with herbaceous plants, shrubs and climbers and a collection of old roses. Extensive views over beautiful Severn Valley. TEAS. *Combined adm with* **The Mill Cottage** *£2 Chd 50p (Share to Ward 21, Nurses Fund, Shrewsbury Hospital©). Sun July 6 (2-6)*

Hartshill Gardens ♿✿❀ Oakengates E of Shrewsbury. Once within the Telford/Wrekin district. Follow local signs to Oakengates. TEAS. *Combined adm £1 Chd free. Sat, Sun June 21, 22 (2-5.30)*

   Longmede (Mr & Mrs D J Steele) 13 Hartshill Road. Approx ½-acre ornamental garden with specimen trees, shrubs and raised alpine beds. Yr-round interest. *Private visits welcome (April-Oct), please* **Tel 01952 612710**

Northcote (Mr & Mrs R A Woolley) 15 Hartshill Road. ¼-acre garden with vegetables, flowers and shrubs. *Private visits welcome (April-Oct), please* **Tel 01952 613644**

Hatton Grange &❀ (Mrs Peter Afia) Shifnal. Lodge gate entrance on A464, 2m S of Shifnal. 1m up drive. Large dingle with pools, rhododendrons, azaleas, fine old trees; shrubbery; roses; lily pond garden. TEAS. *Adm £2 Chd free (Share to BACUP®). Suns May 25, June 29 (2-7). Parties by appt, please* **Tel 01952 460415**

■ **Hawkstone Hall** (Redemptorist Study Centre) 13m NE of Shrewsbury. 6m SW of Market Drayton on A442. Entrance from Marchamley. Large formally laid out garden. Features incl ornamental flower beds; herbaceous border; rockery; pools and magnificent trees. Georgian mansion (open) with courtyard garden and winter garden. TEAS. *Adm garden only £1.50 Chd £1. Open Aug 5 to 31. For NGS Tues, Wed Aug 5, 6 (2-5)*

Haye House &❀❀ (Mrs Paradise) Eardington. 2m S of Bridgnorth, sign Highley B4555. 1m through village Eardington. 1-acre garden especially planted by the owner, for her work as a National & International flower demonstrator. Grade 2 listed house (not open). TEAS. *Adm £2 Chd free. Private visits welcome, April to Oct (10-6), also open in the evening by appt, please* **Tel 01746 764884**

■ **Hodnet Hall Gardens** &❀ (Mr & the Hon Mrs A Heber-Percy) 5½m SW of Market Drayton; 12m NE Shrewsbury; at junc of A53 and A442. 60-acre landscaped garden with series of lakes and pools; magnificent forest trees, great variety of flowers, shrubs providing colour throughout season; featured on TV and Radio. Unique collection of big-game trophies in C17 tearooms. Gift shop and kitchen garden. TEAS; parties to pre-book. Free car-coach park. *Adm £2.80 OAP £2.30 Chd £1. April to end of Sept (Tues to Sat 2-5; Suns & Bank Hols 12-5.30). Reduced rates for organised parties of 25 or over* **Tel 01630 685 202**. *For NGS Sats Aug 2, 9 (2-5)*

¶**Hundred House Hotel** &❀ (Sylvia & Henry Phillips) Norton. Situated on the A442 in the village of Norton. Midway between Bridgnorth and Telford. Large cottage garden created by Sylvia Phillips since 1986. Unusual stone placements, recently completed memorial garden, herbaceous borders, bulbs, old-fashioned roses and climbers, young acers and betulas. Also features a working herb garden for the hotel. Teas and lunches in hotel. *Adm £1.50 Chd £1. Mon March 31, Tues May 27, June 24, July 15 (12-6)*

Limeburners &❀ (Mr & Mrs J E Derry) Lincoln Hill. On outskirts of Ironbridge, Telford. From Traffic Island in Ironbridge take Church Hill and proceed up hill for ½m, garden on L 300yds below The Beeches Hospital. Prize-winning garden formerly site of a rubbish tip developed by owners as a Nature garden to attract wildlife. Many unusual shrubs giving year round interest. Featured on TV Channel 4, Garden Club. TEAS in aid of Arthritis & Rheumatism Council for Research. *Adm £1.50 Chd free. Sun June 29 (2-6). Private visits also welcome April to Sept, please* **Tel 01952 433715**

Lingen Nursery, Lingen Village See Hereford and Worcester

Longnor Hall &❀ (Mr & Mrs A V Nicholson) Longnor. Take A49 road S of Shrewsbury to Longnor. Entry to Longnor Hall garden through grounds of Longnor Church. 70-acre garden and parkland. Interesting varieties of trees; herbaceous borders, yew and beech hedges; walled kitchen garden; stable yard and C17 house (not open); sheep and deer; Cound Brook; views of The Lawley and Caer Caradoc hills. Adjacent C13 Longnor Church. TEAS. *Adm £1.50 Chd 50p (Share to St. Mary's Church, Longnor®). Sun, Mon May 25, 26 (2-6)*

Lower Hall &❀ (Mr & Mrs C F Dumbell) Worfield, E of Bridgnorth. ½m N of A454 in village centre. 4 acres on R Worfe. Garden developed by present owners. Courtyard with fountain, walled garden with old-fashioned roses, clematis and iris. Water garden with pool, primula island and rock garden. Woodland garden incl rare magnolias and paper bark trees. Plant sales to local charity. WI TEAS. *Adm £2 Chd free. Sun June 22 (2-6). Private visits welcome. Coach and evening parties by appt, local catering can be arranged.* **Tel 01746 716607**

The Lyth &❀❀ (Mr & Mrs L R Jebb) 1m SE of Ellesmere; entrance between Whitemere and junction of A528/A495. 2-acre garden, rhododendrons, azaleas; good outlook on parkland; heath bed, shrub borders. Regency colonial house (not open), birthplace of founder of Save The Children, Eglantyne Jebb. Meres nearby worth a visit. TEAS by local Save the Children Fund. *Adm £1.75 Chd 50p. Sun June 1 (2-6)*

¶**Madeley Gardens** ❀❀ (℅ Dr & Mrs G Richards) Telford. From Ironbridge up steep hill towards Madeley (B4373) R at roundabout into Glendinning Way. Group of gardens of various sizes up to 1¼ acres. Differing styles and planting incl water features, herbaceous borders and vegetables. Also woodland walk with views across Ironbridge Gorge. TEAS. *Adm £1.50 Chd 50p. Suns June 29, Aug 17 (2-6)*

Mawley Hall &❀ (Mr & Mrs R A Galliers-Pratt) 2m NE of Cleobury Mortimer. On A4117 Bewdley-Ludlow Rd. Bus: X92, alight at gate. A natural garden in beautiful country with magnificent views; designed for wandering amongst roses, herbs, flowering shrubs; fine old trees. TEAS. *Adm £1.50 OAPs £1 Chd under 15, 50p. Mons May 12, June 16, July 14 (2-6)*

The Mill Cottage &❀❀ (Mrs A J Wisden & Miss J M Hawkes) Cound. 8m SE of Shrewsbury on A458. Turn to Cound 1m S of Cross Houses. Mill Cottage 300yds on L. ¼-acre cottage garden. Many unusual & lovely herbaceous & alpine plants. Good & varied collection of hostas and ferns; also a variety of clematis. *Combined adm with* **Harnage Farm** *£2 Chd 50p (Share to Ward 21, Nurses Fund, Shrewsbury Hospital©). Sun July 6 (2-6)*

Regular Openers. Open throughout the year. They are listed at the end of the Diary Section under 'Regular Openers'.

Millichope Park (Mr & Mrs L Bury) Munslow, 8m NE of Craven Arms. From Ludlow (11m) turn L off B4368, ¾m out of Munslow. 13-acre garden with lakes; woodland walks; fine specimen trees, wild flowers; herbaceous borders. TEAS. *Adm £2 Chd 50p. Mon May 5, Sun June 22 (2-6). Private visits welcome, please* Tel 01584 841234

Moortown ✗✿ (David Bromley Esq) 5m N of Wellington. Take B5062 signed Moortown 1m between High Ercall and Crudgington. Approx 1-acre plantsman's garden. Here may be found the old-fashioned, the unusual and even the oddities of plant life, in mixed borders of 'controlled' confusion. *Adm £2 Chd 50p. Sat, Sun June 14, 15 (2-5.30)*

Morville Dower House ♿✿ (Dr K Swift) nr Bridgnorth. 3m NW of Bridgnorth on A458 at junction with B4368. 1½-acre sequence of gardens in various historical styles, begun in 1989: medieval garden, Elizabethan knot garden, Victorian rose border, formal vegetable garden, canal garden, wild garden. TEAS. *Adm £1.50 Chd 50p (Share to Morville Church®). Fri Jun 27 (12-6)*

▲**Nordybank Nurseries** ✿ (P Bolton) Clee St Margaret. 7½m NE of Ludlow. Turning to Stoke St Milborough and Clee St Margaret 5m from Ludlow, 10m from Bridgnorth along B4364, through Stoke St Milborough on the Lane to Clee St Margaret. 1-acre cottage garden on sloping site. Informal plantings of trees, shrubs and unusual herbaceous, incl herbs and wildflowers. Also 'Rose Garden' with over 60 varieties of old roses and 'Field Garden' with 700 varieties of herbaceous plants. TEAS. *Adm £1.50 Chd free. For NGS Suns June 15, 22 (12-6)*

The Old Rectory ✗✿ (Mrs J H M Stafford) Fitz; A5 NW of Shrewsbury; turn off at Montford Bridge, follow signs; from B5067 turn off at Leaton, follow signs. 1¼-acre botantist's garden; shrubs, vegetables; water garden. Partially suitable for wheelchairs. TEAS. *Adm £1.50 Chd 50p. Sun June 8 (12-6)*

The Old Vicarage ♿ (W B Hutchinson Esq) Cardington, 2m N of B4371 Church Stretton/Much Wenlock rd, signed, or turn off A49 Shrewsbury-Ludlow rd at Leebotwood, 2½-acre scenic garden; trees, shrubs, roses, primulas, alpines, water and bog garden. Picnics allowed; on site parking. *Adm £1.50 Chd free. Suns June 8, 15; July 6, 13 (12-5.30). Private visits welcome, June, July, Aug, please* Tel 01694 771354

Oteley ✿ (Mr & Mrs R K Mainwaring) Ellesmere 1m. Entrance out of Ellesmere past Mere, opp Convent nr to A528/495 junc. 10 acres running down to Mere, incl walled kitchen garden; architectural features many interesting trees, rhododendrons and azaleas, views across Mere to Ellesmere Church. Wheelchairs only if dry. TEAS in aid of NSPCC. *Adm £1.50 Chd 50p. Mon May 26 (2-6). Private visits also welcome, please* Tel 01691 622514

The Patch ♿✗✿ (Mrs J G Owen) Acton Pigot. 8m SE of Shrewsbury between A49 and A458. Take Cressage Rd from Acton Burnell. Turn L after ½m, signpost Acton Pigot. This is not a garden in the strict sense but an unconventional developing patch for the plant connoisseur

in excess of ½ acre. June early herbaceous, shrubs and trees. Plants in aid of St. Anthony's Cheshire Home. *Adm £1.50 Chd free. Suns June 8, 15 (2-6). Private visits for groups over 5 welcome, please* Tel 01743 362139

Peplow Hall ♿✿ (The Hon & Mrs R V Wynn) 3m S of Hodnet via A442; turn off E. 10-acre garden with lawns, azaleas, rhododendrons, etc; roses, herbaceous borders; walled kitchen garden; 7-acre lake. TEAS. *Adm £2.50 Chd 50p. Sat, Sun June 14, 15 (2-5.30)*

Preen Manor ✗✿ (Mr & Mrs P Trevor-Jones) Church Preen, nr Church Stretton; signposted from B4371 Much Wenlock-Church Stretton Rd. Not suitable for wheelchairs. 6-acre garden on site of Cluniac monastery and Norman Shaw mansion. Kitchen; chess; water and wild gardens. Fine trees in park; woodland walks. Featured in NGS video 1. Replanning still in progress. TEAS (except Oct TEA). *Adm £2 Chd 50p. Thurs May 29, June 12, 26, July 10, 24 (2-6); Sun Oct 5 (2-5) 4.30 Harvest Thanksgiving. Private visits of min 15 and coach parties by appt June & July only* Tel 01694 771207

Radnor Cottage ✗✿ (Pam and David Pittwood) Clun. 8m W of Craven Arms, 1m E of Clun on B4368 midway between Clunton and Clun. 2 acres S-facing slope, overlooking Clun Valley. Recently developed for all-year-round interest. Daffodils; cottage garden borders; dry stone wall and terracing with herbs and alpines; stream and bog garden with willow collection; native trees, orchard, wild flower meadow. TEAS. *Adm £1.50 Chd 50p (Share to Abbeyfield Bishop's Castle and District®). Tues April 1, May 6, 27, June 10, July 8, 29 (2-6). Private visits welcome, please* Tel 01588 640451

Ridgway Wood ✗✿ (Mr & Mrs A S Rankine) Edgton 4m NW of Craven Arms. Turn W off A49 on to A489, 2½m, then left towards Edgton ¾m, drive on right. Informal 2½-acre garden created and maintained for all yr round colour and set in 20 acres of mixed woodland. Mixed borders, heather beds, woodland garden, azaleas, shrubs and trees. Woodland walks. TEAS. *Adm £2 Chd 50p (Share to Shropshire and Mid Wales Hospice®). Suns May 18, 25; Mon May 26 (11-6)*

Ruthall Manor ♿✗ (Mr & Mrs G T Clarke) Ditton Priors, Bridgnorth. Ruthall Rd signed nr garage. 1-acre garden with pool and specimen trees. Designed for easy maintenance with lots of ground-covering and unusual plants. Tea Room in village. *Adm £1.50 Chd free. Sun June 29 (2.30-6). Parties welcome April to Sept, please* Tel 01746 712608

Swallow Hayes ♿✿ (Mrs P Edwards) Rectory Rd, Albrighton WV7, 7m NW of Wolverhampton. M54 exit 3 Rectory Rd 1m towards Wolverhampton off A41 just past Roses and Shrubs Garden Centre. 2-acres; planted since 1968 with emphasis on all-the-year interest and ease of maintenance; National collection of Hamamellis and Russell Lupins. Nearly 3000 different plants, most labelled. TEAS. *Adm £1.50 Chd 10p (Share to Compton Hospice®). Suns April 27, May 11 (2-6); also by appt for parties, please* Tel 01902 372624

¶**Triscombe** ⚘🌸 (Dr & Mrs J Calvert) Wellington. Roslyn Rd is close to Wrekin College which is well signposted. Approx ¾-acre town garden with access via steps. Features well stocked herbaceous and shrub borders, pond and bog garden, pergolas, alpine house, rockery and container plants. TEAS in aid of Shropshire & Mid Wales Hospice, Telford Day Centre. *Adm £1.50 Chd 50p. Thurs June 19, July 17 (1.30-5)*

Walcot Hall &🌸 (The Hon Mrs E C Parish) Bishops Castle 3m. B4385 Craven Arms to Bishops Castle, turn L by Powis Arms, in Lydbury N. Arboretum planted by Lord Clive of India's son. Cascades of rhododendrons, azaleas amongst specimen trees and pools. Fine views of Sir William Chambers' Clock Towers, with lake and hills beyond. TEAS. *Adm £2 Chd 15 and under free. Sun, Mon May 25, 26 (2-6). Also by appt for parties, please* **Tel 01588 680232**

■ **Weston Park** & (The Weston Park Foundation) Shifnal. 7m E of Telford on the A5 in the village of Weston-under-Lizard. Easy access junction 12 M6 and junction 3 M54. Free car/coach park. 28 acres Capability Brown landscaped gardens and arboretum, incl fine collection of nothofagus, rhododendrons and azaleas. Formal gardens of SW terrace restored to original C19 design, with new rose garden and long border together with colourful adjacent Broderie Garden. Wide variety of trees, shrubs and flowers provides colour throughout the season. C17 house open (adm £1.50). TEAS and light meals available in The Old Stables restaurant. *Adm £3.50, OAP's £2.50, Chd £2, reduced rates for parties of 20 or more. Open Easter to September (enquiries for dates and times,* **Tel 01952 850207***). For NGS Tues June 17, July 15 (11-5)*

Whittington Village Gardens &🌸 Daisy Lane Whittington. 2½m NE of Oswestry. Turn off B5009 150yds NW of church into Top St then into Daisy Lane. Car parking at Whittington Castle and Top St. A group of next-door country gardens, ranging from small cottage to 1-acre, newly landscaped. Imaginative ideas for tubs and baskets. Herbaceous borders, water features and kitchen gardens. The group hope to celebrate the 10th Anniversary of opening for the Scheme with some 'special happenings'. TEAS at **The Bramleys**; Top St. *Adm £2 Chd free. Sat, Sun June 21, 22 (1-5.30)*

Willey Park ⚘🌸 (The Lord & Lady Forester) Broseley 5m NW of Bridgnorth. Turn W off B4373. Much Wenlock 4m. 6-acre formal garden set in extensive parkland. Fine views. 10-acre woodland rhododendron/azalea walk. Magnificent mature trees. Recently planted herbaceous borders. Spectacular azalea bed near house. TEAS. *Adm £2 Chd/OAP £1 (Share to Willey & District Village Hall®). Sun June 1 (2-6)*

■ **Wollerton Old Hall** &⚘🌸 (John & Lesley Jenkins) Wollerton, nr Market Drayton on A53 between Hodnet and A53/A41 junction. From S turn R after 'Wollerton' sign. From N & E turn L after 'Wollerton' sign. Both rds lead to a brick pound. Garden ahead on L. Award-winning 3-acre garden created around C16 house (not open). Featured in Homes & Gardens, House & Garden, NGS Video 1. A combination of formal design and intensive cultivation of perennials. A painter's garden using planting combinations with an emphasis on colour and form. Lunches, Teas (teas only May). *Adm £2.50 Chd 50p. Every Sun May 2 to Aug 31 (12-5). For NGS, Every Fri May 2 to Aug 29. Parties, min 20, by appt, please* **Tel 01630 685760**

SYMBOLS USED IN THIS BOOK (See also Page 17)

‡   Following a garden name in the Dates of Opening list indicates that those gardens sharing the same symbol are nearby and open on the same day.

‡‡   Indicates a second series of nearby gardens open on the same day.

¶   Opening for the first time.

🌸   Plants/produce for sale if available.

&   Gardens with at least the main features accessible by wheelchair.

⚘   No dogs except guide dogs but otherwise dogs are usually admitted, provided they are kept on a lead. Dogs are not admitted to houses.

●   These gardens advertise their own dates in this publication although they do not nominate specific days for the NGS. Not all the money collected by these gardens comes to the NGS but they do make a guaranteed contribution.

■   These gardens nominate specific days for the NGS and advertise their own dates in this publication.

▲   These gardens open regularly to the public but they do not advertise their own dates in this publication. For further details, contact the garden directly.

Somerset (incorporating South Avon)

Hon County Organiser:	Miss P Davies-Gilbert, Coombe Quarry, West Monkton, Taunton TA2 8RE Tel 01823 412187
Assistant Hon County Organisers: **Somerset Leaflet:**	Mrs M R Cooper, Quarry House, 21 Lower St, Merriott TA16 5NL Tel 01460 76105
	Mrs B Hudspith, Rookwood, West St, Hinton St George, TA17 8SA Tel 01460 73450
	Mrs Judy Kendall, Barle House, 17 High St, Chew Magna, BS18 8PR Tel 01275 332459
	Mrs Shirley Gyles, Rose Cottage, Flax Bourton, BS19 3QE Tel 01275 462680
	Richard D Armitage Esq, Dormers, Park Lane, Carhampton, TA24 6NN Tel 01643 821386
Publicity:	Mrs Alison Kelly, The Mount, Wincanton, Tel 01963 32487
Tour Advisor and Talks:	Mrs Lyn Spencer-Mills, Hooper's Holding, Hinton St George, TA17 8SE Tel 01460 76389
Treasurer:	John A Spurrier Esq, Tudor Cottage, 19 Comeytrowe Lane, Taunton TA1 5PA Tel 01823 333827

DATES OF OPENING

March 15 Saturday
Langford Court, Langford

March 16 Sunday
Elworthy Cottage, Elworthy
Langford Court, Langford

March 28 Friday
Beryl, Wells

March 30 Sunday
Broadview, Crewkerne
Fairfield, Stogursey

March 31 Monday
Broadview, Crewkerne

April 6 Sunday
Elworthy Cottage, Elworthy
Glencot House, Wookey Hole
Manor Farm, Stone Allerton
Smocombe House, Enmore

April 12 Saturday
Greencombe, Porlock
Stowleys, Bossington Lane,
    Porlock

April 13 Sunday
Wayford Manor, Crewkerne

April 20 Sunday
Barrington Court, Ilminster
Coley Court & The Little Manor,
    East Harptree
Crowe Hall, Widcombe
Hangeridge Farm, Wellington
The Time-Trail of Roses, Wells

April 26 Saturday
Brackenwood Garden Centre,
    Portishead
The Mount, West Hill, Wincanton

April 27 Sunday
Brackenwood Garden Centre,
    Portishead
Broadview, Crewkerne
The Mount, West Hill, Wincanton

The Old Rectory, Limington, nr
    Ilchester

April 29 Tuesday
Tone Dale House, Wellington

May 3 Saturday
Woodborough, Porlock Weir

May 4 Sunday
Broadview, Crewkerne ‡
Higher Luxton Farm, Churchinford
The Old Mill House, Spaxton
Pear Tree Cottage, Stapley
Wayford Manor, Crewkerne ‡

May 5 Monday
Broadview, Crewkerne ‡
Clapton Court, Crewkerne ‡
Forge House, Oake
Higher Luxton Farm, Churchinford
Ilminster Gardens
Pear Tree Cottage, Stapley

May 6 Tuesday
Tone Dale House, Wellington

May 10 Saturday
Hadspen Garden, nr Castle Cary
The Mount, West Hill, Wincanton

May 11 Sunday
Court House, East Quantoxhead
7 Little Keyford Lane, Frome
Milton Lodge, Wells
The Mount, West Hill, Wincanton

May 13 Tuesday
Hestercombe Gardens

May 14 Wednesday
Windmill Cottage, Backwell

May 17 Saturday
Kingsdon, Somerton
The Mill, Cannington
Parsonage Farm, Publow

May 18 Sunday
Cannington College Gardens
Hangeridge Farm, Wellington
Kingsdon, Somerton

The Mill, Cannington
Parsonage Farm, Publow
Smocombe House, Enmore
Wayford Manor, Crewkerne

May 25 Sunday
Broadview, Crewkerne ‡
Chinnock House, Middle Chinnock
Greencombe, Porlock
Hinton St George Gardens,
    Crewkerne ‡
The Mill House, Castle Cary
Milton Lodge, Wells
Stonewell House, Churchill Green
Woodborough, Porlock Weir

May 26 Monday
Broadview, Crewkerne ‡
Chinnock House, Middle Chinnock
Elworthy Cottage, Elworthy
Forge House, Oake
Hinton St George Gardens,
    Crewkerne ‡
The Mill House, Castle Cary
Woodborough, Porlock Weir

June 1 Sunday
Barrow Court, Barrow Gurney
Gaulden Manor, Tolland
Harptree Court, East Harptree
Holt Farm, Blagdon
Kites Croft, Westbury-sub-Mendip
Sherborne Garden, Litton
Stone Allerton Gardens, nr
    Wedmore
Wayford Manor, Crewkerne

June 4 Wednesday
Kites Croft, Westbury-sub-Mendip

June 7 Saturday
Kingsdon, Somerton

June 8 Sunday
Broadview, Crewkerne
Kingsdon, Somerton
Landacre Farm, Withypool

7 Little Keyford Lane, Frome
Lovibonds Farm, Burrowbridge
Lower Severalls, Crewkerne
Milton Lodge, Wells
The Mount, Chelston
Pear Tree Cottage, Stapley
Sherborne Garden, Litton
Stone Allerton Gardens, nr
   Wedmore
June 14 Saturday
Hestercombe Gardens
The Mount, West Hill, Wincanton
Pendower House, Taunton
June 15 Sunday
Crowe Hall, Widcombe
Darkey Pang Too Gang, Oakhill
Goblin Combe, Cleeve
Hangeridge Farm, Wellington
Little Weston Gardens
The Mount, West Hill, Wincanton
Montacute Gardens, nr Yeovil
Pendower House, Taunton
Rose Cottage, Henstridge,
   Templecombe
Sherborne Garden, Litton
Stogumber Gardens, Taunton
The Time-Trail of Roses, Wells
June 18 Wednesday
Windmill Cottage, Backwell
June 21 Saturday
190 Goldcroft, Yeovil
Greencombe, Porlock
The Old Rectory, Swell Fivehead
Wellesley Park Gardens,
   Wellington
June 22 Sunday
Brewers Cottage, Isle Brewers
Dodington Hall, Nether Stowey
Elworthy Cottage, Elworthy
Forge House, Oake
190 Goldcroft, Yeovil
Hatch Beauchamp Gardens,
   Taunton
The Old Rectory, Swell Fivehead
Sherborne Garden, Litton
Thurloxton Gardens
Wellesley Park Gardens,
   Wellington
June 24 Tuesday
2 Old Tarnwell, Upper Stanton
   Drew
June 25 Wednesday
Thurloxton Gardens
Wellesley Park Gardens,
   Wellington
June 28 Saturday
Kingsdon, Somerton
The Mount, West Hill, Wincanton
Pendower House, Taunton
Stowleys, Bossington Lane,
   Porlock
June 29 Sunday
Bourne House, Burrington
Butleigh House, Butleigh

Cothay Manor, Greenham
Highfield House, Chew Magna
Kingsdon, Somerton
Milverton Gardens
Montacute House, Montacute
The Mount, West Hill, Wincanton
The Old Rectory, Limington, nr
   Ilchester
Pear Tree Cottage, Stapley
Pendower House, Taunton
Rimpton Gardens, nr Yeovil
Sherborne Garden, Litton
Stanton Drew Gardens
Walnut Farm, Yarley, nr Wells
July 3 Thursday
2 Old Tarnwell, Upper Stanton
   Drew
July 6 Sunday
Broadview, Crewkerne
Church Farm & The Gables,
   Stanton Prior
Milton Lodge, Wells
Popinjays & Little Norton Mill,
   Stoke-sub-Hamdon
Rumwell Gardens ‡
Sherborne Garden, Litton
Taunton Gardens ‡
Wall House, Staplegrove ‡
July 8 Tuesday
2 Old Tarnwell, Upper Stanton
   Drew
July 11 Friday
Lufton Manor College, Lufton
July 13 Sunday
Barford Park, nr Bridgwater
Barrington Court, Ilminster
Brewers Cottage, Isle Brewers
Fernhill, nr Wellington
7 Little Keyford Lane, Frome
Lufton Manor College, Lufton
Moorland Gardens
Sherborne Garden, Litton
Sutton Hosey Manor, Long
   Sutton
July 16 Wednesday
Fernhill, nr Wellington
Tintinhull House, nr Yeovil
Windmill Cottage, Backwell
July 17 Thursday
2 Old Tarnwell, Upper Stanton
   Drew
July 20 Sunday
Brent Knoll Gardens, Highbridge
Chinnock House, Middle
   Chinnock ‡
Elworthy Cottage, Elworthy
Forge House, Oake
Greencombe, Porlock
Hangeridge Farm, Wellington
Manor Farm, Middle Chinnock ‡
Sherborne Garden, Litton
July 27 Sunday
Broadview, Crewkerne
Cothay Manor, Greenham

Keymer Cottage, Buckland St
   Mary
Sherborne Garden, Litton
August 2 Saturday
The Mill, Cannington
August 3 Sunday
Landacre Farm, Withypool
The Mill, Cannington
Sherborne Garden, Litton
August 7 Thursday
Dunster Castle, nr Minehead
August 10 Sunday
Hangeridge Farm, Wellington
7 Little Keyford Lane, Frome
Lower Severalls, Crewkerne
Sherborne Garden, Litton
August 16 Saturday
Hooper's Holding, Hinton St
   George
August 17 Sunday
Fernhill, nr Wellington
Highfield House, Chew Magna,
   Bristol
Hooper's Holding, Hinton St
   George
Sherborne Garden, Litton
August 20 Wednesday
Fernhill, nr Wellington
Windmill Cottage, Backwell
August 24 Sunday
Broadview, Crewkerne
Lady Farm, Chelwood
Sherborne Garden, Litton
August 25 Monday
Beryl, Wells
Broadview, Crewkerne
August 31 Sunday
Kites Croft, Westbury-sub-
   Mendip
Sherborne Garden, Litton
September 3 Wednesday
Kites Croft, Westbury-sub-
   Mendip
September 7 Sunday
Fernhill, nr Wellington
7 Little Keyford Lane, Frome
September 10 Wednesday
Fernhill, nr Wellington
September 13 Saturday
Pondarosa, Wayford
September 14 Sunday
Harptree Court, East Harptree
Ponda Rosa, Wayford
September 21 Sunday
Elworthy Cottage, Elworthy
Windmill Cottage, Backwell
October 5 Sunday
7 Little Keyford Lane, Frome
October 12 Sunday
Elworthy Cottage, Elworthy
Stonewell House, Churchill
   Green
October 25 Saturday
Pendower House, Taunton

October 26 Sunday
Pendower House, Taunton

Regular openings
For details see garden description

Church Farm & The Gables, Stanton Prior
Clapton Court, Crewkerne
Cothay Manor, Greenham
Crowe Hall, Widcombe
Elworthy Cottage, Elworthy
Greencombe, Porlock
Hadspen Garden, Castle Cary
Hatch Court, Hatch Beauchamp
Hestrcombe Garden, Nr Taunton
Kingsdom, Somerton
Lower Severells, Crewkerne
Milton Lodge, Wells
Sherbourne Garden, Litton
Time Trail of Roses, Wells

By appointment only
For telephone numbers and other details see garden descriptions. Private visits welcomed

Benchmark, Wells
Brewery House, Bath
Littlecourt, West Bagborough
Madron, Bathford
The Mill, Henley Lane, Wookey
2 Old Tarnwell, Upper Stanton Drew
Withey Lane Farmhouse, Barton St David

By Appointment Gardens. These owners do not have a fixed opening day usually because they cannot accommodate large numbers or have insufficient parking space.

DESCRIPTIONS OF GARDENS

Barford Park ♿ (Mr & Mrs M Stancomb) Spaxton. 4½m W of Bridgwater, midway between Enmore and Spaxton. 10 acres including woodland walk. Formal garden, wild garden and water garden, surrounding a Queen Anne house with park and ha ha. TEAS. *Adm £2 Chd free (Share to Somerset Garden Trust®). Sun July 13 (2-5.30)*

▲Barrington Court ♿✿❀ (The National Trust) Ilminster. NE of Ilminster. Well known garden constructed in 1920 by Col Arthur Lyle from derelict farmland (the C19 cattle stalls still exist). Gertrude Jekyll suggested planting schemes for the layout; paved paths with walled rose and iris, white and lily gardens, large kitchen garden. Licensed restaurant, plant sales and garden shop. Lunches and TEAS. *Adm £3.10 Chd £1.50. Suns April 20, July 13 (11-5.30)*

Barrow Court ❀ Barrow Gurney 5m SW Bristol. From Bristol take A370 and turn E onto B3130 towards Barrow Gurney; immediate right, Barrow Court Lane, then ½m, turn R through Lodge archway. 2 acres of formal gardens, designed by Inigo Thomas in 1890. Architectural garden, with sculpture and pavilions; arboretum; ongoing renovations to stonework; replanted yew hedging and parterres. C17 E-shaped house (not open). Parking limited. TEAS. *Adm £1.50 Chd 50p (Share to Barrow Gurney Church®). Sun June 1 (2-6)*

Benchmark ✿❀ (Mr & Mrs Terence Whitman) 99 Portway, Wells. On A371 Cheddar Rd out of Wells, ½m from city centre on L. ¾-acre mature garden with mixed borders and potager, interesting perennials incl more than 100 varieties of penstemon. *Adm £1. Private visits and groups welcome, please* **Tel 01749 677155**

Beryl ♿❀ (Mr & Mrs E Nowell) 1m N of Wells off B3139 to Bath. Left at Hawkers Lane. Victorian park created in 1842. Walled vegetable garden broken into quadrangles with box hedging and double flower picking borders. More recent planting of trees and shrubs and creation of walks and vistas. Morning coffee and TEAS. *Adm £1 OAP/Chd 50p. Fri, March 28, Mon, Aug 25 (11-5.30).* **Tel 01749 678738**

Bourne House ♿✿❀ (Mr & Mrs Christopher Thomas) Burrington nr Bristol 12m S Bristol. N of Burrington. Turning off A38 signposted Blagdon-Burrington; 2nd turning L. 4 acres, and 2 paddocks. Stream with waterfalls & lily pond; new pergola; mature trees, and shrubs. New mixed borders; roses; bulbs. TEAS in aid of St Peters Hospice, Bristol. *Adm £1.50 Chd free. Sun June 29 (2-6). Private visits welcome by appt please,* **Tel 01761 462494**

▲Brackenwood Garden Centre Woodland Garden ✿❀ (Mr & Mrs John Maycock) 131 Nore Rd, Portishead. From Bristol A369 (10m). M5 Junc 19. 1m from Portishead on coast rd to Clevedon. 8-acre woodland garden. Rhododendrons, camellias, Japanese maples and pieris; secluded woodland pools with waterfowl; many rare trees and shrubs. Magnificent coastal views. Japanese maples in full colour in the Autumn. Restaurant and Tea Room open every day. *Adm £1.50 OAPs £1.25 Chd 60p (Share to NT®). For NGS Sat, Sun, April 26, 27 (9-5),* **Tel 01275 843484**

Brent Knoll Gardens ❀ off A38 2m N of Highbridge and M5 exit 22. A mixture of 3 colourful country gardens. TEAS at Copse Hall in aid of Parish Hall. *Combined adm £2.50 Chd free. Sun July 20 (2-6)*

Copse Hall ❀ (Mrs S Boss & A J Hill Esq) Terraced gardens, crinkle crankle kitchen garden wall, kiwi fruit. Shrubs, trees and Beechwood. Partly suitable for wheelchairs. *Private visits welcome, please* **Tel 01278 760301** *evenings*

¶Hays ♿ (Dr & Mrs M Barry) Homeopath's relaxing organic garden. New native wood

Talbelands ♿ (Drs Gavin & Meg Stoddart) Collection of cactii. Garden matured since opening 1993

¶Brewers Cottage ♿✿❀ (Mr & Mrs J A Clements) Isle Brewers. 9m ESE of Taunton. 1½m from A378 at Fivehead. ¾-acre garden hidden behind a pretty cottage. Newly designed over the last 3 years, features incl a formal herb garden, pergola with old roses, and colour themed borders around old apple trees. Further areas of woodland, 'secret' yew enclosed garden and iris walk still being developed. TEAS in aid of Village Church. *Adm £1.50 Chd free. Suns June 22, July 13 (2-6.30) Private visits welcome,* **please Tel 01460 281395**

Brewery House ✿ (John & Ursula Brooke) 2½m S of Bath off A367, L onto B3110, take 2nd R to Southstoke or bus to Cross Keys. House is ¼m down Southstoke Lane. ⅔-acre garden on 2 levels. Fine views; top garden walled. Many unusual plants. Water garden. All organic. Cream TEAS in aid of Village Hall. *Adm £1.50 Chd free. Private or group visits welcome, May - Sept by appt please* **Tel 01225 833153**

Broadview Gardens ✿ (Mr & Mrs R Swann) East, Crewkerne. A30 Yeovil Rd only enter by turning R. Garden that is a bit different with interesting and time saving features. Over 1 acre of terraced garden planted with hundreds of unusual plants. Some for sale. *Adm £1.50 Chd free. Suns, Mons March 30, 31 April 27, May 4, 5, 25, 26, June 8, July 6, 27, August 24, 25 (11-4.30). Also private visits welcome, please* **Tel 01460 73424**

Butleigh House ♿✿ (Sir Dawson & Lady Bates) Butleigh. 4m SE of Glastonbury and N of B3153 at Kingweston. Turn down High St in centre of village. About 3 acres of well laid out garden. Large herbaceous borders with chosen colours; fine trees; high semi-circular yew hedge; many roses and other good plants. TEAS in aid of St Leonard's Church, Butleigh. *Adm £1.50 Acc chd free. Sun June 29 (2-6). Private visits welcome June, July, please.* **Tel 01458 850383**

Brooklands, Burnett see Glos (South) and Bristol

▲**Cannington College Gardens** ♿✕✿ Cannington, 3m NW of Bridgwater. On A39 Bridgwater-Minehead Rd. Old College: Benedictine Priory 1138; fine Elizabethan W front; 7 old sandstone walled gardens protect wide range of plants, incl many less hardy subjects, ceanothus, Fremontias, Wistarias etc; 10 very large greenhouses contain exceptionally wide range of ornamental plants. New College (built 1970); magnificent views to Quantocks; tree and shrub collections; ground cover plantings; lawn grass collection and trials; one of the largest collections of ornamental plants in SW England incl 4 national plant collections. TEA. *Adm for both College grounds £1.50 Chd (& organised parties of OAPs) 75p. Special rates for party bookings. For NGS Sun May 18 (2-5)*

Chinnock House ♿✕✿ (Guy & Charmian Smith) Middle Chinnock. Off A30 between Crewkerne and Yeovil. 1½-acre walled gardens, silver, white and herbaceous; recently redesigned. TEAS in aid of West Chinnock Primary School. *Adm £1.50 Chd free. Sun, Mon May 25, 26 (2-6). Also open July 20 (2-6) with* **Manor Farm**. *Comb adm £2.50 Chd free. Private visits welcome for parties of 2 or over, please* **Tel 01935 881229**

■ **Church Farm & The Gables, Stanton Prior** ♿✕✿ 6m from Bath on A39 Wells Rd; at Marksbury turn L to Stanton Prior; gardens set in beautiful countryside in unspoilt village. Ploughman's lunch & cream TEAS July 6 in aid of St Lawrence Church. *Combined adm £2 Chd free. 1st and 2nd Weds May to Sept (11-5). For NGS Sun July 6 (11-6). Open by appt all year, please* **Tel 01761 470384/472690**

Church Farm (Mr & Mrs Lesley Hardwick) Herbaceous borders, rock garden, scree garden; shrub roses, many unusual plants, wild area with ¼-acre pond
The Gables (Mr & Mrs Alistair Hardwick) Newly created cottage garden open for NGS day only

■ **Clapton Court** ✕ (Mr & Mrs P Giffin) 3m S of Crewkerne on B3165 to Lyme Regis in Clapton village. 10 acres of beautiful gardens, under new ownership. Woodland garden with streams, the largest Ash tree in Gt Britain. Many rare and interesting plants. Terraced formal gardens with ornamental lily pond, white border, yellow border, mixed herbaceous and rose garden, rockery and fine collection of narcissus and other bulbs. *Adm £3 Chd free. Tues, Weds, Thurs April to Sept incl (2-5). For NGS Mon May 5 (2-5) Coach parties by appt, please* **Tel Mike & Penny Cox 01460 73220**

Coley Court & The Little Manor ✕✿ Teas at **Manor Farm**. *Combined adm £1.50 Chd free. Sun April 20 (2-6)*
Coley Court (Mrs M J Hill) East Harptree, 8m N of Wells from A34. At Chewton Mendip take B3114 for 2m. Well before East Harptree turn R at sign Coley and Hinton Blewitt before bridge. 1-acre garden, stone walls, spring bulbs; 1-acre old mixed orchard. Early Jacobean house (not open)
The Little Manor (Mrs K P P Goldschmidt) Farrington Gurney on A39. Turn E in village on to A362 towards Radstock-600yds turn L. ¾-acre spring garden; many varieties of bulbs, flowering trees, many rare shrubs; rose garden. Early C17 house with attractive courtyard

■ **Cothay Manor** ♿✕✿ (Mr & Mrs A H B Robb) Greenham. 5m W of Wellington. From A38 at Beambridge Hotel turn R signposted Thorne St Margaret. Go straight for 1½m turn R signposted Cothay. 1½m keep L, entrance on L. Over the last 3yrs this plantsman's garden of 7 acres has been reconstructed and replanted within the original framework. Set with a backdrop of a medieval house (not open). Imaginatively planted courtyard, garden rooms, 200yd yew walk. An oxbow bog garden. 5 acres have been newly planted with specimen trees. The R Tone runs through the gardens. Cream TEAS. *Adm £2 Chd free. Every Thurs and 1st Sun May to Sept. For NGS Suns June 29, July 27 (2-6)*

Court House ♿✿ (Sir Walter & Lady Luttrell) East Quantoxhead 12m W of Bridgwater off A39; house at end of village past duck pond. Lovely 5-acre garden; trees, shrubs, roses and herbaceous. Woodland garden started 1992. Views to sea and Quantocks. Partly suitable for wheelchairs. Teas in Village Hall. *Adm £2 Chd free. Sun May 11 (2-5.30)*

▲**Crowe Hall** ♿ (John Barratt Esq) Widcombe. 1m SE of Bath. L up Widcombe Hill, off A36, leaving White Hart on R. Large varied garden; fine trees, lawns, spring bulbs, series of enclosed gardens cascading down steep hillside. Italianate terracing and Gothic Victorian grotto contrast with park-like upper garden. Dramatic setting, with spectacular views of Bath. New trellis and water garden created in 1995. Featured in NGS gardens video 2. Dogs welcome. TEAS. *Adm £1.50 Chd 50p. For NGS Suns April 20, June 15 (2-6). Also private visits welcome, please* **Tel 01225 310322**

Darkey Pang Too Gang ✿✿ (Graham & Chrissy Price) Oakhill. 3m N of Shepton Mallet off A367 in Oakhill High St opp converted chapel. ¾-acre. Creatively designed and landscaped by owner since 1981. Crammed with trees, shrubs, herbaceous and climbers, with a lushness of greens and leaf combinations. Winding path link wild and cultivated areas with grotto, pergola, wildlife pond and bog garden. TEAS. *Adm £1.50 Chd free (Share to Somerset Wildlife Trust®). Sun June 15 (2-6). Private visits welcome Weds only June 25 to July 23 (9.30-dusk), please* **Tel 01749 840795**

Dodington Hall ✿✿ (Grania & Paul Quinn) A39 Bridgwater-Minehead. 2m W of Nether Stowey turn at signpost opp Castle of Comfort. ¼m turn R. Entrance through churchyard. Reclaimed 1½-acre terrace garden; clematis, shrub roses, bulbs; Tudor house (part open). TEAS in aid of Life. *Adm £2 Chd free. Sun June 22 (2.30-5.30). Private visits welcome, please* **Tel 01278 741400**

▲**Dunster Castle** ♿✿ (The National Trust) On A396 3m SE of Minehead. Terraces of sub-tropical plants, shrubs and camellias surrounding the fortified house of the Luttrells for 600 yrs; fine views. Self-drive battery operated car available. Teas in village. *Adm Garden Only £2.70 Chd £1.30. Family ticket £6.50.* ▲*For NGS Thurs Aug 7 (10-6)*

■ **Elworthy Cottage** ✿✿ (Mike & Jenny Spiller) Elworthy, 12m NW of Taunton. Leave Taunton on A358 signed Minehead. In 5m turn L onto B3224 signed Monksilver. After 6m turn R into Elworthy village. 1-acre garden, cottage-style plantings, island beds. Many unusual herbaceous plants. Large collection of hardy geraniums (over 200 varieties); pulmonarias, campanulas, penstemons, grasses and plants for foliage effect. Wide selection of plants from the garden for sale. *Adm £1 Chd free (Share to Cancer and Leukaemia in Childhood Trust®). Nursery and Garden open Tues, Thurs and Fri afternoons mid March to mid Oct. For NGS Suns March 16, April 6, June 22, July 20, Sept 21, Oct 12; Mon May 26 (2-5.30). Parties welcome, please* **Tel 01984 656427**

Fairfield Court - see Glos (South) and Bristol

Fairfield ♿✿ (Lady Gass) Stogursey, 11m NW of Bridgwater 7m E of Williton. From A39 Bridgwater-Minehead turn N; garden 1½m W of Stogursey. Woodland garden with bulbs and shrubs; paved maze. Views of Quantocks. Dogs in park and field only. TEA. *Adm £1.50 Chd free (Share to Stogursey Church®). Easter Sun March 30 (2-5.30)*

Fernhill ✿✿ (Peter & Audrey Bowler) White Ball Hill nr Wellington. W on A38 from Wellington. Past Beam Bridge Hotel and at top of Hill follow signs into garden. Mature wooded garden in approx 2 acres with rose, herbaeous and mixed borders thoughtfully planted to provide interest and colour throughout the season. Alpine and bog garden with waterfalls and pools leading to shady arbour. Fine views over ha-ha to Black Downs and Mendips. Good plant collection. TEAS. *Adm £1.50 Chd free. Suns, Weds July 13, 16, Aug 17, 20, Sept 7, 10 (2-6). Private visits welcome* **Tel 01823 672423**

Forge House ♿✿✿ (Peter & Eloise McGregor) Oake. On A38 midway between Taunton & Wellington. Take signpost for Oake. 1st house on R entering village. ¾-acre informal country garden with emphasis on colour borders. Bee and butterfly plants and fragrance. Unmanaged wildlife area and pond. TEAS if fine. *Adm £1 Chd 50p. Mons May 5, 26, Suns June 22, July 20 (2-5.30). Disabled & parties welcome following written application by appt weekends May to June, please* **Tel 01823 461 500 after 7**

Gaulden Manor ♿✿✿ (Mr & Mrs J Le G Starkie) Tolland. Nr Lydeard St Lawrence. 9m NW Taunton off A358. Medium-sized garden made by owners. Herb; bog; scent and butterfly gardens. Bog plants, primulas and scented geraniums. Partly suitable for wheelchairs. Cream TEAS. *Adm house & garden £3.50, garden only £1.75, Chd £1.75. Sun June 1 (2-5.30)*

Glencot House ✿✿ (Mrs Jenny Attia) Wookey Hole. ½m SW of Wells. From Wells follow the signs to Wookey Hole. Through the village, past the Wookey Hole Caves and take 1st turning L into Titlands Lane. Proceed for approx ½m and the entrance to Glencot Cricket field is on LH-side. Drive across field and park to L of bridge. 18 acres of parkland of which approx 4 acres are formal gardens with frontage to R Axe. Herbaceous borders, rose walk and terraced walk with a water feature. TEAS. *Adm £1.50 Chd 50p. Sun April 6 (2-5)*

Goblin Combe ✿✿ (Mrs H R Burn) Cleeve. 10m S of Bristol on A370, turn L onto Cleeve Hill Rd just before Lord Nelson Inn. After 300 yds turn L onto Plunder St, first drive on R. Car parking near the bottom of the drive just beyond the Plunder St turning. 2 acre terraced garden with interesting collection of trees, shrubs and borders, surrounded by orchards, fields and woodlands. Magnificent views. TEAS. *Adm £1.50 Chd free (Share to The Music Space Trust®). Sun June 15 (2-5.30)*

190 Goldcroft ♿✿✿ (Mr & Mrs E Crate) Yeovil. Take A359 from roundabout by Yeovil College, then 1st R. ¼-acre. Colour-themed shrub and herbaceous borders and island beds, rose garden, raised ponds, vegetable garden designed for the visually impaired. TEAS in aid of Somerset Association for the blind. *Adm £1.50 Chd 50p. Sat, Sun June 21, 22 (2-5). Groups welcome by appt* **Tel 01935 75535**

■ **Greencombe** ♿✿✿ (Miss Joan Loraine, Greencombe Garden Trust) ½m W of Porlock, left off road to Porlock Weir. 51-yr-old garden on edge of ancient woodland, overlooking Porlock Bay. Choice rhododendrons, azaleas, camellias, maples, roses, hydrangeas, ferns, small woodland plants and clematis. National collections of Polystichum, (the 'thumbs up' fern), Erythronium (sping-time lilies), Vaccinium (blue berries) and Gaultheria. Completely organic, with compost heaps on show. TEA. *Adm £3 Chd under 16 50p. Sats, Suns, Mons, Tues, April, May, June, July (2-6); private visits, please* **Tel 01643 862363**. *For NGS Sats, Suns, April 12, May 25, June 21, July 20 (2-6)*

1997 Special Events. For information on special National Gardens Scheme events in 1997 see Pages 18-19.

● **Hadspen Garden** ఉ⚘❀ (N & S Pope) 2m SE of Castle Cary on A371 to Wincanton. 5-acre Edwardian garden featuring a 2-acre curved walled garden with extensive colourist borders of shrub roses and choice herbaceous plants; woodland of fine specimen trees. National Rodgersia Collection. Lunches, TEAS. *Adm £2.50 Chd 50p (Share to Friends of the Earth®). Garden and Nursery open Thurs, Fri, Sat, Sun & Bank Hol Mon (9-6); private visits welcome, March 6 to Sept 28 (9-6) please* Tel 01749 813707 *(after 6pm). For NGS Sun May 10 (9-6)*

Hangeridge Farm ఉ⚘❀ (Mrs J M Chave) Wrangway. Wellington, 1m off A38 bypass signposted Wrangway. 1st L towards Wellington Monument over motorway bridge 1st R. 1-acre garden, herbaceous borders, flowering shrubs and heathers, raised rockeries, spring bulbs. Lovely setting under Blackdown Hills. Wide selection of plants available from garden. TEAS. *Adm £1 Chd free. Suns April 20, May 18, June 15, July 20, Aug 10 (2-7)*

Harptree Court ఉ❀ (Mr & Mrs Richard Hill) East Harptree. 8m N of Wells via A39 Bristol Rd to Chewton Mendip, then B3114 to East Harptree, gates on L. From Bath via A368 Weston-super-Mare Rd to West Harptree. Large garden in beautiful setting. Many exotic plants and newly designed herbaceous borders in walled garden. Fine trees, 18C stone bridge, subterranean passage, lily pond, paved garden. TEAS. *Adm £1.50 Chd free. Suns June 1, Sept 14 (2-6)*

Hatch Beauchamp Gardens 5m SE of Taunton (M5 junction 25) off A358 to Ilminster. Turn L in village of Hatch Beauchamp at Hatch Inn. Parking at Hatch Court. TEAS. *Combined adm £2 Chd £1 under 12 free. Sun June 22 (2.30-5.30)*

● **Hatch Court** ఉ⚘❀ (Dr & Mrs Robin Odgers) Hatch Beauchamp. 5-acre garden with 30 acres of parkland and deer park surrounding a perfect 1750 Palladian mansion. Extensive, recent and continuing restoration redesign and replanting. Magnificent walled kitchen garden, fine display of roses, shrubs, clematis and many young trees. Glorious views and a lovely setting. 1995 Historic Garden Restoration Award. TEAS Thurs only. *Combined adm Garden only £2.50 Chd £1 under 12 free, house and garden £3. Every day April 14 to June 30. Mon to Fri July 1 to Sept 30 (10-5.30). (garden) Thurs June 12 to Sept 11 (house) (2.30-5.30). For NGS Sun June 22 (2.30-5.30)*

Hatch Court Farm ఉ⚘ (John Townson Esq) ⅓-acre walled garden with mixed borders created over recent yrs from derelict farm buildings. Also wild area with mediaeval pond surrounded by wood and parkland. Woodland walk

■ **Hestercombe Gardens** ❀ (SCC/Hestercombe Gardens Project) 4m N of Taunton. Follow Tourist Information 'Daisy' symbol. Encompasses over 3 centuries of garden history in 50 acres of formal gardens and parkland. Famous Edwardian gardens designed by Sir Edwin Lutyens and planted by Gertrude Jekyll created 1904-6. The terraces and borders are based on Jekyll's original planting scheme and are considered the supreme example of their famous partnership. Secret Landscape Garden opening this yr for the first time in over 100 yrs by Coplestone Warre Bampfylde in the 1750's. Georgian pleasure

grounds comprise 40 acres of lakes, temples and woodland walks. TEAS. *Combined adm £3 Chd £1.50 under 5 free. (Share to Fire Brigade Benevolent Fund®). Open every day (10-6) For NGS Tues, Sat May 13, June 14 (10-5)*

Higher Luxton Farm ⚘ (Mr & Mrs Peter Hopcraft) 1½m out of Churchingford on Honiton Rd. Over county boundary into Devon past thatched farmhouse on R; next turning on L before Xrds. 9m S of Taunton, 9m N of Honiton. Approx 1 acre with species trees and bulbs; walls with clematis; ponds with primula; lovely views. Pony stud. Partly suitable for wheelchairs. TEAS in aid of Churchstanton Church. *Adm £1 Chd free. Sun, Mon May 4, 5 (2-6)*

¶**Highfield House** ఉ⚘❀ (Mr & Mrs R A Webb) Chew Magna. Top of Chew Magna High Street, between fork of roads to Chew Stoke and Winford. Large C19 garden extensively replanted during the last 6yrs by present owners. Mixed shrub and herbaceous borders containing some unusual specimens. Open lawns; fine stone walled flower and vegetable garden. Small flock award-winning Hampshire Down pedigree sheep. TEAS. *Adm £1.50 Chd free. Suns June 29, Aug 17 (11-6)*

Highview - see Glos (South) and Bristol

Hinton St George Gardens 2m NW of Crewkerne. N of A30 Crewkerne-Chard; S of A303 Ilminster Town Rd, at roundabout signed Lopen & Merriott, then R to one of Somerset's prettiest villages. TEAS in aid of Cats Protection League, dog park provided at Hooper's Holding. *Combined adm £3 Chd free. Sat, Sun May 25, 26 (2-6)*

   Fig Tree Cottage ఉ⚘ (Mr & Mrs Whitworth) Old walled cottage garden and courtyard of stables made from kitchen garden of neighbouring rectory, over the past 18 years by owners inspired by Margery Fish. Ground cover, shrubs, old-fashioned roses. Three giant fig trees, all perennials. *Private visits welcome, please* Tel 01460 73548

   The Firs ⚘ (Mr & Mrs B Cable) ½-acre informal garden mixture of shrubs, herbaceous borders and climbing plants

   Holly Oak House (Mr & Mrs M O'Loughlin). ½-acre garden in lovely setting. Walled herbaceous border, shrubs, pergola and heather

   Hooper's Holding ఉ❀ (Ken & Lyn Spencer-Mills) ⅓-acre garden, in a formal design; lily pool; dwarf conifers, rare herbaceous and shrubby plants; NCCPG National Collection of Hedychiums; fancy cats and poultry. (Hedychiums flowering Sept and Oct). *Also open Sat, Sun Aug 16, 17 (2-6). Adm £1.50. Private visits welcome, please* Tel 01460 76389

   Rookwood (Ian & Betty Hudspith) ¼-acre, modern garden, herbaceous borders, pond, greenhouse, vegetable garden and fruit cage. Accommodation available Tel 01460 73450

   Springfield House ఉ⚘ (Capt & Mrs T Hardy) 1½-acres; semi-wild wooded dell, mature trees framing view to Mendips, shrubs, herbaceous plants, bulbs

¶**Holt Farm** ఉ⚘❀ (Mrs Sarah Mead) Blagdon. Approx 12m S of Bristol, located off the A368 Weston-Super-Mare to Bath Rd, between the villages of Blagdon and Ubley. The entrance to Holt Farm is approx ½m outside Blagdon, on the L-hand side. A developing farmhouse garden bordering Blagdon lake with wild flower meadow, stream, woodland walk and sunken walled garden. Extensive herbaceous planting throughout the 3-acre site, with several new projects underway. TEAS. *Adm £1.50 Chd free (Share to The Home Farm Trust®) Sun June 1 (2-6)*

Ilminster Gardens ⚤❀ TEA. *Combined adm £1.50 Chd free. Mon May 5 (2-5.30)*
¶**Hill Rise** (Christine Akhurst) Garden wedge shaped 85' long. South sloping, clay soil cottage garden; some mature fruit trees. Interesting shrubs and many tubs. *Private visits also welcome, please Tel 01460 53032*
¶**65 Summerlands Park Avenue** (Katherine Saunders) Ilminster. 400 metres W of town centre. Station Rd, turn S into Summerlands Park Drive. 50 metres into the Avenue. 90' long sloping suburban back garden, designed and built by owner from bare plot since 1990. Railway sleeper and gravel terraces, mixed borders, living willow fence and arch, camomile walk, salad bed. *Private visits also welcome, please Tel 01460 53284*

Iford Manor See Wiltshire

Jasmine Cottage - see Glos (South) and Bristol

¶**Keymer Cottage** ⚤ (Hilary & Ian Cumming) Buckland St Mary. Take A303 to Eagle Cross, turn towards Taunton-Wellington. Victorian "reclaimed" garden with many interesting shrubs and flower beds. Established trees and pretty courtyards. TEAS. *Adm £2 Chd free (Share to RUKBA®). Sun July 27 (2-6)*

Kingsdon ♿⚤❀ (Mr & Mrs Charles Marrow) 2m SE of Somerton off B3151 Ilchester Rd. From Ilchester roundabout on A303 follow NT signs to Lytes Cary; left opp gates ½m to Kingsdon. 2-acre plantsman's garden and nursery garden. Over 500 varieties of unusual plants for sale. Teas in Village Hall. *Adm £2 Chd free. Sats, Suns May 17, 18; June 7, 8, 28, 29 (2-7). Private visits welcome, please Tel 01935 840 232*

Kites Croft ⚤❀ (Dr & Mrs W I Stanton) Westbury-sub-Mendip 5m NW of Wells. At Westbury Cross on A371 turn uphill, R to square and L up Free Hill to Kites Croft 2-acre garden with fine views to Glastonbury Tor. Winding paths lead from the terrace to different levels; lawn, ponds, rockery, herbaceous borders, shrubs and wood. As featured on TV. *Adm £1.50 Chd free. Sun June 1, Wed June 4, Sun Aug 31, Wed Sept 3 (2-5). Private visits welcome for parties of 2 or over, please Tel 01749 870328.*

Lady Farm ♿❀ (Mr & Mrs M Pearce) Chelwood. On the A368 ½m E of Chelwood roundabout (A37 & A368) 9m S of Bristol and 9m W of Bath. The existing garden, started 11 yrs ago, covers an area of 1 acre, but a further 6 acres were reclaimed from farm building 6 yrs ago. Surrounding the farmhouse and courtyard are shrub and rambling roses, 2 recently planted, herbaceous borders, and a terrace overlooking a spring fed watercourse now in its third yr which flows into a lake in the valley with adjacent rock features. Woodland walks are in the early stages of development. New perennial planting with prairie and steppe plants and a variety of grasses. This garden is

NOT recommended for children under 14. Ample parking. TEAS in aid of Chelwood Church. *Adm £2 Chd free. Sun August 24 (2-6). Private parties welcome, please Tel 01761 490770*

Landacre Farm ⚤❀ (Mr & Mrs Peter Hudson) Withypool, nr Minehead. On the B3223 Exford/S. Molton Rd 3m W of Exford not in Withypool village. 9m NW of Dulverton ¼m above Landacre Bridge. ½-acre terraced garden 1000ft up on Exmoor. Developed from a field over past 19yrs by present owners; rockery, stream and bog garden, octagonal pergola, rhododendrons and shrub roses. Exposed position with fantastic views of Barle Valley and open moorland; specializing in climbers and hardy perennials. TEAS. *Adm £1 Chd free. Suns June 8, Aug 3 (2-5.30). Private visits welcome, please Tel 0164 383 1223*

Langford Court ♿⚤❀ (Sir John & Lady Wills) Langford. 150yds S of A38 Bristol-Bridgwater rd. 11½m S of Bristol. 1½m N of Churchill traffic lights. Signpost marked Upper Langford. 3½ acres. Lawns and trees, good display of daffodil and crocus. Topiary. Pleasant setting and outlook. TEAS. *Adm £1.50 Chd free (Share to Marie Curie Cancer Care, Somerset®) Sat, Sun March 15, 16 (2-6)*

10 Linden Road see Glos (South) and Bristol

7 Little Keyford Lane ⚤❀ (Duncan Skene). Frome. B3092 to Frome outskirts. 1st major L. Follow signs. Windswept ½-acre garden started 1988. Distinct areas eg native flower patch. Intensive organic cultivation. Herbaceous perennial emphasis. Several unusual plants propogated for sale. Collections of siberian iris (June) lavender; (July); daylilies (August) crocosmia (Sept) and michaelmas daisies (Oct). Reference collection of purple loosestrifes (Lythrum). TEA. *Adm £1 Chd free (Share to Amnesty International®). Suns May 11, June 8, July 13, Aug 10, Sept 7, Oct 5 (2-6). Private visits, please Tel 01373 472879*

Littlecourt ♿⚤ (Jane Kimber & John Clothier) West Bagborough. 7m N of Taunton signed from A358. 6-acre garden in fine setting with woodland and water; spectacular new borders, interesting and extensive planting; wonderful views. *Adm £2. Private visits very welcome any time, please Tel 01823 432281*

¶**Little Weston Gardens** 1m E of Sparkford on the old A303 towards Wincanton; turning to Little Weston on R. *Combined adm £2.50 Chd under 14 free (Share to Weston Bamfylde Church®) June 15 (2-6)*
¶**Cider Press House** ♿⚤ (Mr & Mrs Alastair Ralston Saul) ½-acre garden, planted 6 yrs previously, surrounded by old established cider apple orchard. Charming views across the Sparkford Vale *(Share to Mark Davies Injured Riders Fund®)*
¶**Little Weston House** ⚤❀ (Mr & Mrs Colin Rae) A colourful garden on different levels with a variety of interesting plants, roses and abutilon, and other flowering shrubs
¶**Middle Farmhouse** ⚤❀ (Mrs E Clapp) 1-acre garden partly newly planted, mixed herbaceous borders and many shrub roses. Beautiful area with views to Cadbury Hill

¶**The Priest's House** &❀ (Diana Hunter) ½-acre garden surrounding medieval house (not open). Mixed planting, roses, shrubs and herbaceous

Lovibonds Farm &✿❀ (Mr & Mrs J A Griffiths) Burrowbridge. A361 from Taunton to Glastonbury, in village of Burrowbridge. Turn L immed over bridge. ½m on. 3 acre garden created from derelict farm 9 yrs ago. Delightful herbaceous and shrub borders. Gravel, bog and woodland gardens. Wildlife area. Ponds, stream and small lake with wild and ornamental water birds. TEAS in aid of Burrowbridge WI. *Adm £1.50 Chd free. Sun June 8 (2-5.30) Private/group visits welcome in June, please* **Tel 01823 698173**

■ **Lower Severalls** &✿❀ (Howard & Audrey Pring) 1½m NE of Crewkerne. Turning for Merriott off A30; or Haselbury from A356. 2½-acre plantsman's garden beside early Ham stone farmhouse. Herbaceous borders and island beds with collections of unusual plants, shrubs and interesting features. Herb gardens. Nursery (open daily March 1 to Oct 31 10-5, Suns 2-5. Closed all day Thurs.) Sells herbs, herbaceous plants and half-hardy conservatory plants. TEAS on Suns June 8, Aug 10. *Adm £1.50 Chd free. Coaches by appointment. Garden open daily April 1 to Sept 30 (10-5). For NGS Suns June 8, Aug 10 (2-6).* **Tel 01460 73234**

¶**Lufton Manor College** &❀ (The Principal) Lufton. 2m W of Yeovil towards Montacute, 3rd exit at Houndstone roundabout, 1m signposted on R Lufton Manor College. Approx 5 acres. Formal Edwardian gardens presently undergoing restoration. Special features incl many interesting and rare trees, lily pond with koi carp. Beautiful lake with ducks and some rare birds; woodland walk. TEAS and plants in aid of MENCAP. *Adm £1.50 Chd free. Fri, Sun July 11, 13 (10-5)*

Madron ✿❀ (Mr & Mrs Martin Carr) Ostlings Lane, Bathford. Approx 3½m E of Bath close to A4. At Batheaston roundabout take A363 Bradford-upon-Avon Rd; then 1st turning L, Ostlings Lane is immediately on R alongside Crown Inn. At top of short rise 100yds, stone pillars on L are entrance to Madron - 2nd house on L along drive. 1½ acres overlooking Avon valley. Conifers, trees, hardy and tender perennials, water garden and fine lawns. Designed with an artist's eye for plant and colour associations. Featured in RHS book 'Planting your Garden'. TEAS. *Adm £1.50 Chd free. June 15 to July 20 by prior appt only. Parties and painters welcome, please* **Tel 01225 859792**

¶**Manor Farm** ✿ (Simon & Antonia Johnson) Middle Chinnock. Off A30 between Crewkerne and Yeovil. 2-acre newly planted garden; mixed borders. *Combined adm with Chinnock House £2.50 Chd free, Sun July 20 (2-6)*

The Manor House see Glos (South) and Bristol

The Mill, Cannington ✿❀ (Mr & Mrs J E Hudson) 21 Mill Lane. 4m W of Bridgwater on A39. Turn opposite Rose & Crown. ¼-acre cottage type plantsman's garden with waterfall and pond, over 80 clematis and National Caltha Collection. Featured in NGS video 1. TEA in aid of Cannington W.I. *Adm £1.50 Chd free (Share to NCCPG®). Sats May 17, Aug 2 (2-5), Suns May 18, Aug 3 (11-5). Private visits welcome by appt, please* **Tel 01278 652304**

The Mill, Wookey &✿❀ (Peter & Sally Gregson). 2m W from Wells off A371. Turn L into Henley Lane, driveway 50 yds on L. 2½ acres beside R Axe. Traditional and unusual cottage plants informally planted in formal beds with roses, pergola, lawns and 'hot red border'. Ornamental kitchen garden. Wide selection of plants seen in garden for sale in nursery. TEA for pre-arranged groups. *Adm £1 Chd free. Please* **Tel 01749 676966**

The Mill House &✿❀ (Mr & Mrs P J Davies) Castle Cary. Do not go into Castle Cary Town Centre, but follow signs to Torbay Rd Industrial Estate (W). Entrances to Trading Estate on L proceed E along Torbay Rd about 200yds. Garden on the R. Approx 1-acre terraced sloping garden, with stream and waterfalls. Emphasis on Natural look. Many interesting plants mingled with native flora. Bog garden; and vegetable plot. TEAS and plants in aid of Oncology Centre BRI Bristol. *Adm £1.50 Chd free. Sun, Mon May 25, 26 (2-6)*

●**Milton Lodge** ✿❀ (D C Tudway Quilter Esq) ½m N of Wells. From A39 Bristol-Wells, turn N up Old Bristol Rd; car park first gate on L. Mature Grade II listed terraced garden with outstanding views of Wells Cathedral and Vale of Avalon. Mixed borders; roses; fine trees. Separate 7-acre arboretum. TEAS in aid of Children's Society. Suns & Bank Hol Mons April to Sept. *Adm £2 Chd under 14 free. Open daily (2-6) ex Sats, Good Friday to end Oct; parties by arrangement. Share to NGS Suns May 11, 25, June 8, July 6 (2-6). Share to Rose Society. Private visits welcome, please* **Tel 01749 672168**

Milverton Gardens 9m W of Taunton on the new B3227 (old A361) L at roundabout to Milverton. TEAS in aid of Milverton Surgery. *Combined adm £2 Chd free. Sun June 29 (2-6)*

    Barn Elms &✿ L at Globe Inn, down Rosebank Rd, R at Houndsmoor Lane. 1-acre wild garden and ponds. Small formal garden; many interesting plants; imaginative design

    Cobbleside &✿ (Mr & Mrs C Pine) ¾-acre walled garden incl herb garden and potagere. Completely redesigned, with photographs illustrating the old layout. *Private visits by appt May to Sept, please* **Tel 01823 400404**

    3 The College &✿ (Mr Eric Thresher) Small interesting garden, featuring fireplaces amongst shrubs and borders; interesting water features. *Private visits welcome, please* **Tel 01823 400956**

    New Halls ✿ (Mr M Priscott) A Victorian walled garden developed as market garden; vegetables, fruit and flowers. *Private visits welcome by appt only,* **Tel 01823 400018. Outside WC**

Montacute Gardens 4m from Yeovil follow A3088, take slip road to Montacute, turn L at T-junction into village. TEAS in aid of St Catherines Church Fund at both gardens. *Combined adm £2 Chd free. Sun June 15 (2-5.30)*

Abbey Farm &✿ (Mr & Mrs G Jenkins) Turn R between Church and Kings Arms (no through Rd). 2½-acre of mainly walled gardens on sloping site provide setting for mediaeval Priory gatehouse. Roses; herbaceous borders. Clematis, white garden. Parking available. *Private visits welcome, please* Tel 01935 823572

Park House &✿✿ (Mr & Mrs Ian McNab) Turn L (signposted Tintinhull) after red brick council houses and immediately R. Approx 2-acres, spacious lawns; shrubs; walled garden with herbaceous borders and vegetable garden. The literary Powys family lived here during their father's lifetime

▲Montacute House &✿✿ (The National Trust) Montacute. NT signs off A3088 4m W of Yeovil and A303. Magnificent Tudor House with contemporary garden layout. Fine stonework provides setting for informally planted mixed borders and old roses; range of garden features illustrates its long history. Lunch and TEAS. *Adm Garden only £2.80 Chd £1.20. For NGS Sun June 29 (11-5.30)*

¶Moorland Gardens ✿ 3m SE of junction 24 (M5) roundabout or A38 Taunton Rd from Bridgwater. Follow directions to Moorland. From Burrowbridge, turn towards Bridgwater on Taunton side of river. Car Park and Teas at Village Hall. *Combined adm £1.50 Chd free (Share to Moorland & District Village Hall®) Sun July 13 (2-6)*

¶Bell-View Cottage &✿ (R J & L E Smithen) Planting scheme to create the feeling of a 'sunken garden' with minimum maintenance. Pergola, conservatory and summerhouse

¶Cherry Cob &✿ (Mrs Beryl Richardson) ¼-acre easy maintenance rectangular plot made interesting

¶Fern Villa &✿ (Kate & Richard Symonds) ½-acre organic family garden with fruit and vegetables

¶Glebe House &✿ (Malcolm & Barbara Davies) Ex-vicarage. ¾-acre. Some plants remain from original garden incl 2 varieties of hazel nuts and a highly scented cream shrub rose and interesting mature trees

Green End ✿ (Mr & Mrs S B Tunstall) 1-acre garden and orchard. "Rhyne" garden incl marginal plants and shrubs. Flat shoes recommended

¶Old Orchard &✿ (David & Vivien Berkley) Family garden with an emphasis on food production incl peaches, mulberries, figs, etc. Propogating bench, pond, flowers and shrubs. Bees

¶Waverley &✿ (Mrs J Yates) ⅓-acre country cottage garden

¶Winslade Farm House &✿ (Pete & Tess Stocks) Old farm garden recently extended to incl the paddock. Newly planted trees, shrubs (3 yrs). Pergola

The Mount, Chelston ✿✿ (Jim & Gilly Tilden) Chelston. Off M5 1m NW of junction 26. At A38 Chelston roundabout take Wellington rd. After 200yds turn R to Chelston. 1st house on R. Enclosed garden with herbaceous borders and shrubs; trees, old roses, more shrubs and small bog garden outside. 1 acre altogether. TEAS in aid of Wellington Stroke Club. *Adm £1 Chd free. Sun June 8 (2-6)*

The Mount, Wincanton ✿✿ (Alison & Peter Kelly) Follow one-way system round lower half of town, bear L at signposted Castle Cary, on up hill, house on L. 1¼-acre. Plantswoman's garden with hidden suprises. Speciality an alpine lawn and garden, half terraced shrub borders, gravel bed, rock garden and pond. Cream TEAS Suns in aid of Friends of Verrington Hospital. *Adm £1.50 Chd free. Sats, Suns April 26, 27, May 10, 11, June 14, 15, 28, 29 (2-5.30). Private visits welcome at weekends April to end June, please* Tel 01963 32487 *after sundown*

Oare Manor Cottage See Devon

The Old Mill House, Spaxton ✿✿ (Mr & Mrs W Bryant) Take A39 and Spaxton Rd. W from Bridgwater. In village take Splatt Lane opp school for car park. 2-acre peaceful plantsman's garden beside weir and trout stream. Plant stall in aid of St Mary's Church, Bridgwater. Teas in village hall in aid of Spaxton Church Rectory rooms. *Adm £1 Chd free. Sun May 4 (2-5.30)*

The Old Rectory Limington &✿✿ (David Mendel & Keith Anderson) From A303 or A37 turn off at Ilchester. Follow signpost to Limington. House in centre of village next to church. Approx 1-acre. Recently replanted garden surrounding Georgian Rectory. Mixed borders containing some unusual plants, shrub roses, small knot and ornamental kitchen gardens are set within existing old walls, fruit trees and box hedges. TEA, July in aid of St Mary's Church. *Adm £1.50 Chd free. Sun April 27. Combined adm with other village gardens £2 June 29 (11-6) Map available. Private visits welcome, please* Tel 01935 840035

The Old Rectory &✿✿ (Cdr & Mrs J R Hoover) Swell, Fivehead. 4m W of Langport on A378, signposted "Swell". ½m S of A378. Mature, informal garden of approx. 1½ acres. Good trees; natural pond with water and bog plants. Old-fashioned roses. Stone belfry from ancient church of St Catherine. TEAS in aid of St Martin's Church, Fivehead. *Adm £2. Sat, Sun June 21, 22 (2-5.30)*

The Old Rectory Stanton Prior - see Glos (South) and Bristol

2 Old Tarnwell ✿✿ (Ken & Mary Payne) Upper Stanton Drew. Lies 6m S of Bristol between the B3130 and A368 just W of Pensford. Detailed directions given when appt. is made. A quart of good plants poured into a quarter pint sized plot featuring various colour themed borders, ornamental grasses, ferns, clematis and a well stocked "puddle"! Possibly the smallest, most intensively planted garden in the Yellow Book (total 0.02 acres). Plenty of ideas for small gardeners! Regret not suitable for children. Gold Award Garden (Garden News). *Adm £1.50. Only by appt. Tues June 24, Thurs July 3, 17, Tues July 8 (10-8), please* Tel 01275 333146

Parsonage Farm ✿✿ (Mr & Mrs Andrew Reid) Publow. 9m S of Bristol. A37 Bristol-Wells; at top of Pensford Hill, almost opp B3130 to Chew Magna, take lane which runs down side of row of houses; 250yds on R. 3½-acre woodland garden with large collection of trees and shrubs incl rhododendrons, azaleas and conifers; tuffa-stone rockery. Partly suitable for wheelchairs. TEAS in aid of All Saints, Publow. *Adm £1.50 Chd free. Sat, Sun May 17, 18 (2-5)*

Pear Tree Cottage ✿ (Mr & Mrs Colvin Parry) Stapley. 9m S of Taunton nr Churchingford. Charming cottage garden leading to 2½-acre newly made park; well planted with interesting trees and shrubs leading to old leat and mill pond. Cream TEAS. *Adm £1 Chd 50p. Sun, Mon May 4, 5, Suns June 8, 29 (2-6)*

Pendower House ♿✿ (Mrs O M Maggs) Hillcommon. 5m W of Taunton off B3227 (old A361) turn R at Oake Xrds. 1st on R, parking on L verge. 1-acre landscaped garden created since 1980 on fairly level site. Shrub and herbaceous borders, collection of ceonothus. Fine display of roses, incl old-fashioned. Lge variety of young specimen and mature trees incl acers. Good autumn colour. Cream TEAS in aid of International Tree Foundation. TEA only in Oct. *Adm £1.50 Chd free. Sats, Suns June 14, 15, 28, 29 (2-5.30) Oct 25, 26 (2-4)*

¶**Pondarosa** ✿✿ (Gordon & Pearl Brown) Wayford. Approx 2½m S of Crewkerne off the B3165 Lyme Regis Rd Dunsham Lane. Approx 2-acre garden being transformed from field. Water garden. Mixed borders. Collection of ornamental water fowl. TEA. *Adm £1.50 Chd free. Sat, Sun Sept 13, 14 (2-6)*

¶**Popinjays & Little Norton Mill** Little Norton. 6m W of Yeovil. From A303 take A356. L to Norton-sub-Hamdon. Through village and follow signs. *Combined adm £2.50 Chd free. Sun July 6 (2-6)*
    ¶**Popinjays** (Eric & Jean Dunkley) Hamstone house with courtyard and ½-acre sloping garden. Herbaceous planting, water features, seating areas; fruit, vegetables and orchard, plus paddock with views from Ham Hill treeline across Little Norton valley and beyond. No parking: use field as for Little Norton Mill
    ¶**Little Norton Mill** (Tom & Lynn Hart) 3 acres of landscaped gardens, meadow and orchard. Mill pond, ornamental ponds, marsh garden. Many mature rare trees and shrubs

Rimpton Gardens ♿✿ Rimpton. 3m from Sherborne turn off B3148 at White Post Inn down hill to Rimpton. TEAS. *Combined adm £2 Chd free. Sun June 29 (2-6)*
    Ash House (Mr & Mrs Malcolm Shennan) 1st house on L after ½m. Garden planted in 1988/89. 1½ acres, mixed borders, small pond, collection of ornamental garden trees. Many rare and interesting plants. *Private visits welcome May to Sept, please Tel 01935 851179*
    Red House (Mr & Mrs Colin Lloyd) 1st on R after ½m. Cottage style with mixed borders and vegetable garden. Exceptional spinney areas comprised of native trees and shrubs which provide ideal habitat for wildlife

¶**Rose Cottage** ♿✿ (Mr & Mrs J A Perrett) Henstridge. Approx 7m between Sherborne and Shaftesbury on A30. Turn into village at traffic lights and take second R into Church St and Rose Cottage is on R. ¼-acre cottage garden, edged by stream, planted to create a romantic mood full of evocative scents, in threads of gentle colour combinations. TEAS in aid of British Red Cross. *Adm £1 Chd free. Sun June 15 (2-6)*

¶**Rumwell Gardens** SW Taunton. A38 to Wellington. Park at Rumwell Inn. *Combined adm £1.50 Chd free (Shore to Alzheimers Disease Soc®) Sun July 6 (2-6)*
    ¶**Grants** ✿ (Col D N Lowe & Mrs Lowe) Cottage garden in a lovely setting. Pond and paddock
    ¶**Little Thatch** ♿✿✿ (Derek & Joan Smalley) Garden of colour and interest in grounds of C16 thatched cottage. Many planted troughs and baskets. TEAS
    ¶**Summerhayes** ♿✿ (Mr & Mrs J E B Kyte) Beautiful large formal garden. Interesting shrubs, trees and plants. Georgian House (not open)

■ **Sherbourne Garden** ♿✿ (Mr & Mrs John Southwell) Litton. 15m S of Bristol 15m W of Bath, 7m N of Wells. On B3114 Litton to Harptree, ½m past Ye Olde Kings Arms. 4½ acre landscaped garden of horticultural interest. Wide selection of trees, shrubs and herbaceous plants; collection of hollies (150), hardy ferns (250); hostas, rose species, grasses and hemerocallis - well labelled. Ponds, pinetum. Picnic area. Tea, coffee and biscuits. *Adm £1.50 Chd free. Every Mon June to Sept. For NGS every Sun June to Sept (11-6). Private visits and groups welcome throughout year, please Tel 01761 241220*

Smocombe House ✿✿ (Mr & Mrs Dermot Wellesley Wesley) Enmore. 4m W of Bridgwater take Enmore Rd, 3rd L after Tynte Arms. 5-acres S facing in Quantock Hills. Lovely woodland garden; views down to stream and pool; waterside stocked with interesting plants for spring display; arboretum designed by Roy Lancaster; charming old kitchen garden. TEAS in aid of Enmore Parish Church. *Adm £1.50 Chd free. Suns April 6, May 18 (2-6)*

Stanton Drew Gardens ♿✿✿ 7m S Bristol A37 Bristol-Wells; at top of Pensford Hill take B3130 to Chew Magna. After 1m turn towards Stanton Drew at thatched round house. Cautiously negotiate humpbacked bridge and the gardens are just after the bridge. Parking is supervised. Refreshments in aid of Village Funds. Songs of Praise in Church 5pm. *Combined adm £2 Chd free. Sun June 29 (12-6)*
    Hall Cottage (Ivor & Kate Watkins) This small garden is typically cottage, with a strong emphasis on vegetables neatly set in plots surrounded by grass paths, with colour from herbaceous and bedding borders, pond and fruit areas. 2 greenhouses provide the facilities for raising all the stock and many more interesting plants are available for sale
    Rectory Farm House (Dr & Mrs J P Telling) ½- acre garden surrounding C15 Church House later used as a farmhouse. Garden completely redesigned and replanted over the past 5yrs. Trees, shrubs, mixed borders, pond and new rock garden
    Stanton Court (Dr R J Price & Partners) A new garden established from 1986 to complement the recreational needs of a Nursing Home. Ideal for disabled visitors. Access for elderly persons a priority. Our aim is minimal maintenance with maximum variety. The wide range of plants have been largely donated by the locality. Pond; terrace garden; patio; large sweeping borders; cut flower beds and fruits in season. Mature copper beech and cedars

Stogumber Gardens ❀ A358 NW from Taunton for 11m. Sign to Stogumber W near Crowcombe. Seven delightful gardens of interest to plantsmen in lovely village at edge of Quantocks. TEAS. *Combined adm £2.50 Chd free. Sun June 15 (2-6)*

Brook Cottage ♿✄ (Mrs M Field) Good plants incl lilies in a lovely setting; small pond for added interest
Butts Cottage (Mr & Mrs J A Morrison) Cottage garden with old roses, old-fashioned perennials, alpines, pond, small vine house and vegetable garden
Cridlands Steep (Mrs A M Leitch) Large and interesting garden with collection of trees and wildlife pond
Manor House (Mr & Mrs R W Lawrence) Large garden with borders and beds planted to give yr-round interest and colour
Manor Linney (Dr F R Wallace) A medium-sized walled garden full of colour and interest
Manor Mill (Mr G Dyke) A colourful garden on a slope bounded by a stream
Wynes ✄ (Mr & Mrs L Simms) Large garden with orchard; shrubs; ponds; perennials; alpines and vegetable garden

Stone Allerton Gardens 11m NW of Wells, 2m from A38, signposted from Lower Weare. TEAS. *Combined adm £2 Chd free. Suns June 1, 8 (2-6)*

Fallowdene ❀ (Prof & Mrs G H Arthur) ½-acre of walled garden. Rose and honeysuckle pergola, mixed shrub and herbaceous borders, lawns, kitchen garden. Splendid views over levels to Quantocks.
Greenfield House (Mr & Mrs D K Bull) ½-acre walled garden, colourful mixed planting, further ½-acre to explore
Manor Farm ♿❀ (Mr & Mrs P Coate) More than 1-acre of mixed herbaceous and shrub beds. Old orchard and many climbing plants, a painter's garden. *Also open Sun April 6 (2-5) Adm £1.50. Private groups welcome, please* **Tel 01934 713015**

Stonewell House ♿✄❀ (Mr & Mrs John Dornton) Churchill. 16m SW of Bristol. Take A368 towards Weston-super-Mare at Xrds on A38. Branch R at clock tower; continue for 1m, pass Sports Centre. Well laid out; 12 yrs old; 1½ acres; borders, trees, shrubs, bulbs in Spring; species roses; good colour in Autumn. TEAS in aid of St John the Baptist Church. *Adm £1.50 Chd free. Suns May 25, Oct 12 (2-6) Private visits also welcome, please* **Tel 01934 852919**

Stowleys ♿❀ (Rev R L Hancock) Bossington Lane, Porlock. NE of Porlock off A39. 6m W of Minehead. Medium-size garden, approx 2 acres with magnificent views across Porlock Bay and Bristol Channel. Daffodils, roses, unusual tender plants incl leptospermum, drimys and embothrium. Parking in paddock next door to garden. TEAS. *Adm £1 Chd free. Sats April 12, June 28 Plants June only (2-6)*

Sutton Hosey Manor ♿✄❀ (Roger Bramble Esq) On A372 just E of Long Sutton. 2-acres; ornamental kitchen garden, lily pond, pleached limes leading to amelanchier walk past duck pond; rose and juniper walk from Italian terrace; Judas tree avenue; new ptelea walk. TEA. *Adm £2 Chd over 3 yrs 50p. Sun July 13 (2.30-6)*

¶**Taunton Gardens** ✄❀ SW Taunton A38 signposted Trull and opp Queens College. TEAS at **4 Batts Park.** *Combined adm. £2 Chd free (Share to Alzheimers Disease Society®) Sun July 6 (2-6)*

¶**Applecroft Cottage** ✄❀ (Jack & Cynthia Law) 103 Galmington Rd. Small secret garden set on site of old orchard. Some parts recently redesigned; 2 large prize-winning allotments (organic)
¶**4 Batts Park** ✄❀ (Jan & David Stearn) off Queen's Drive. Old-fashioned garden: roses, shrubs, poppies. TEAS
¶**4 The Drive** ♿✄❀ (Cecil Best) Batts Park. Large town garden. Colourful borders. Rose pergola, numerous shrubs. 2 large horse chestnut trees, with flowers in a riot of colour growing underneath

¶**Thurloxton Gardens** A38 between Taunton & Bridgwater. Well signed. Ample parking available. Picnics welcome and bicycles. TEAS in aid of St Giles, Thurloxton. *Combined adm £2 Chd free. Sun, Wed June 22, 25 (2-6)*

¶**Coombe Mill** ✄ (Mr & Mrs Hugh Pollard) Newly created gardens situated around a C17 Mill in an area of outstanding natural beauty. The total area of approx. 2 acres incl a newly planted lime walk, an avenue of ornamental pears set in the formal section of the garden and a woodland walk through the quarry from which stone was obtained for the Mill and other buildings in the area. The latest project is a water garden now in its 2nd yr
Coombe Quarry (Patricia Davies-Gilbert) Cottage garden with quarry walk. Roses, shrubs, vegetables and animals
¶**The Cottage** (Jane & Colin Stott) Thurloxton. ¾-acre mixed garden. Herbaceous, shrubs and roses. *Open Sun June 22 only*
¶**Magnolias** ♿✄ (Margaret & Peter Brown) Thurloxton. 1½ acres of informal mixed borders planted since 1986. Very wide range of plants incl many rare varieties
The Old Rectory ♿✄ (Mr & Mrs Peter Comer) 2½ acres. Mixed borders; shrubs; conservatory; plants, tubs and hanging baskets. Beautiful views over Somerset Levels

◼ **The Time-Trail of Roses** ✄ (Mrs Susan Lee). Wells. No on-site parking. Use free car park in Tucker St and walk to entrance at top of Westfield Rd. Magnificent collection of 1500 different roses, planted in ½-acre garden in date order of their introduction to show their beauty, diversity and evolution; plus NCCPG collection of 250 miniatures. Also many spring bulbs, lilies, fruit and herbs. TEA Suns Easter to Sept 28 also Thurs, Fris, Sats June and July (2-6). Closed Aug. *For NGS Suns April 20 (daffodils), June 15 (old roses). Adm £2.50 June, July, £1.50 other times Chd free. Parties by appt* **Tel 01749 674677**

▲ **Tintinhull House** ✄ (The National Trust) NW of Yeovil. Tintinhull Village, Yeovil. Signs on A303, W of Ilchester. Famous 2-acre garden in compartments, developed 1900-1960, influenced by Gertrude Jekyll and Hidcote; many good and uncommon plants. C17 & C18 house (not open). TEAS in aid of St Margaret's Church. *Adm £3.50 Chd £1.60. For NGS Wed July 16 (12-6)*

¶**Tone Dale House** (Victoria & Ben Fox) Wellington. Just outside Wellington on the Milverton to Wellington Rd. 3-acre garden first planned in early C18 beside a mill-stream. Many interesting trees and various plantings. Parking limited. TEA. *Adm £2.50 Chd free. Tues April 29, May 6 (2-5.30)*

Tranby House - see Glos (South) and Bristol

University of Bristol Botanic Garden - see Glos (South) and Bristol

¶**Wall House** &⚸ (Mr & Mrs I Polley) Staplegrove. On the outskirts of Taunton on the A358 Staplegrove Rd towards Norton Fitzwarren. ½-acre garden with trees, shrubs, perennials, roses and mediterranean plants in borders, beds and containers for yr-round colour. *Adm £1 Chd 50p. Sun July 6 (2-6)*

Walnut Farm ⚸❀ (Angela & John Marsh) Yarley. 3m W of Wells. On B3139 turn L at Yarley Cross. Island site 200yds up Yarley Hill. ⅔-acre garden with many unusual perennials mixed with shrubs, roses and climbers. 2 ponds and bog garden. Yr-round interest. Splendid views of Mendips. Conservatory. Small conservation area in adjoining field. TEAS and plants in aid of British Diabetic Assoc. *Adm £1.50 Chd 50p. Sun Jun 29 (2-6). Private visits welcome, please* **Tel 01749 676942**

Wayford Manor ❀ (Mr & Mrs Robin L Goffe) SW of Crewkerne. Turning on B3165 at Clapton; or on A30 Chard-Crewkerne. 3 acres, noted for magnolias and acers. Bulbs; flowering trees, shrubs; rhododendrons. Garden redesigned by Harold Peto in 1902. Fine Elizabethan manor house (not open). TEAS in aid of local charities. *Adm £2 Chd 50p. Suns April 13, May 4, 18, June 1 (2-6); also private parties welcome, but please* **Tel 01460 73253**

Wellesley Park Gardens &⚸ Wellington. ½m from centre of Wellington on S side, or can be found by turning down Hoyles Rd off the Wellington Relief Rd and taking 3rd rd L. 4 gardens situated just below the brow of the hill. TEAS. *Combined adm £2 Chd free. Sat, Sun, Wed June 21, 22, 25 (2-6)*
   Greenlands, 46 Wellesley Park ❀ (Jack & Pat Kenney) A ½-acre 1930's town garden in process of refurbishment, planted in cottage garden style with herbaceous plants and shrubs, all organically grown. Small wildlife pond. TEA and plants

Miraflores, 49 Wellesley Park (Dr & Mrs R W Phillips) ½-acre town garden with more than 60 specimens of old roses, lawn with pond, herbaceous border, vegetable garden and small orchard

48 Wellesley Park (John & Julie Morton) Approx ⅕-acre small town garden. Front low maintenance with trees. Rear designed for pleasing views from house and to give breadth to garden. Central rockery and pond. Trees, shrubs and herbaceous plants augmented by pots and baskets. Screened fruit and vegetable area

Windmill Cottage ⚸❀ (Alan & Pam Harwood) Hillside Rd, Backwell. 8m SW of Bristol. Take A370 out of Bristol to Backwell, ½m past Xrds/traffic lights, turn L into Hillside Rd. Parking available in Backwell and New Inn (10 min walk). Hillside Rd is single track lane with no parking (unless for special reasons). Into a 2-acre plot put a plentiful variety of plants, add to this a pinch of knowledge and a sprinkling of wildflowers, together with a reasonable amount of ground cover; blend in some colour and a generous dash of fragrance. Bind the whole thing together with a large collection of clematis. TEAS. *Adm £1.50 Chd free. Weds May 14, June 18, July 16; Aug 20, Sun Sept 21 (2-5.30). Groups welcome by appt, please* **Tel 01275 463492**

Withey Lane Farmhouse ⚸❀ (Sqn Ldr & Mrs H C Tomblin) Barton St David. 4m E of Somerton, turn off B3153 in Keinton Mandeville. Turn R in Barton 100yds past Barton Inn. 200yds turn L at Manor House. 300yds turn R into small lane; farmhouse 300yds on right. ½-acre plantswoman's garden with many unusual and interesting plants; herbaceous beds with shrubs; raised alpine beds; old roses; climbing plants; 1½-acre old cider orchard. *Adm £1 Chd 50p. Private visits and groups welcome April to Sept, please* **Tel 01458 850875**

¶**Woodborough** (R D Milne) Porlock Weir. From Porlock proceed towards Porlock Weir. After passing through West Porlock take the very first turning L opposite the gates of Porlock Vale House & Equitation Centre. Woodborough is the only house up this lane through woodland (2m from Porlock). 2-3 acres with a wide variety of shrubs, mainly ericaceous and an excellent collection of Ghent azaleas and loderi rhododendron. On a steep slope, in oak woodland, with magnificent views over Porlock Bay. Interesting water features. TEAS on May 25 & 26 only. *Adm £2 Chd under 12 free (Share to British & International Sailors' Soc®). Sat, Sun, Mon May 3, 25, 26 (12-5.30)*

The Royal Horticultural Society's Garden at Wisley

Exclusive evening openings in aid of the National Gardens Scheme on the occasion of its 70th anniversary

Wednesday 18th June & Thursday 14th August 6.30-9pm

See page 18.

Staffordshire & part of West Midlands

Hon County Organisers: Mr & Mrs D K Hewitt, Arbour Cottage, Napley, Market Drayton, Shropshire TF9 4AJ Tel 01630 672852

DATES OF OPENING

March 31 Monday
Manor Cottage, Chapel Chorlton, Newcastle

April
The Covert, nr Market Drayton Every Thurs (2-5)
Manor Cottage, Chapel Chorlton, Newcastle Every Mon (2-5)

April 18 Friday
Arbour Cottage, Napley, Market Drayton

April 25 Friday
Arbour Cottage, Napley, Market Drayton

April 30 Wednesday
38 Park Avenue, Stafford

May
The Covert, nr Market Drayton Every Thurs (2-5)
Manor Cottage, Chapel Chorlton, Newcastle Every Mon (2-5)

May 2 Friday
Arbour Cottage, Napley, Market Drayton

May 7 Wednesday
The Old Doctors House, Loggerheads

May 11 Sunday
Edgewood House, nr Kinver

May 16 Friday
Arbour Cottage, Napley, Market Drayton

May 18 Sunday
Hales Hall, nr Market Drayton
Little Onn Hall, Church Eaton, nr Stafford
Wightwick Manor, Compton

May 20 Tuesday
Grapevine, Kings Bromley

May 25 Sunday
Heath House, nr Eccleshall

May 28 Wednesday
The Old Doctors House, Loggerheads
38 Park Avenue, Stafford

May 30 Friday
Arbour Cottage, Napley, Market Drayton

June
The Covert, nr Market Drayton Every Thurs (2-5)
Manor Cottage, Chapel Chorlton, Newcastle Every Mon (2-5)

June 1 Sunday
The Garth, Milford, Stafford

Stonehill, Great Gate, nr Hollington
The Wombourne Wodehouse

June 3 Tuesday
Grapevine, Kings Bromley

June 7 Saturday
Westward Ho, Rugeley

June 8 Sunday
Little Onn Hall, Church Eaton, nr Stafford

June 11 Wednesday
Thornfold, Leek

June 13 Friday
Arbour Cottage, Napley, Market Drayton

June 14 Saturday
Lower House, Sugnall Parva, Eccleshall

June 15 Sunday
The Hollies Farm, Pattingham
Lower House, Sugnall Parva, Eccleshall
Thornfold, Leek

June 17 Tuesday
Grapevine, Kings Bromley

June 18 Wednesday
Thornfold, Leek

June 21 Saturday
The Covert, nr Market Drayton

June 22 Sunday
12 Darges Lane, Great Wyrley
Flashbrook Lodge, Flashbrook
Grafton Cottage, Barton-u-Needwood

June 25 Wednesday
38 Park Avenue, Stafford

June 27 Friday
Arbour Cottage, Napley, Market Drayton

June 28 Saturday
The Old Doctors House, Loggerheads
Woodside House, Barton-u-Needwood

June 29 Sunday
Flashbrook Lodge, Flashbrook
The Garth, Milford, Stafford
Grafton Cottage, Barton-u-Needwood
Stretton Hall, Stafford

July
The Covert, nr Market Drayton Every Thurs (2-5)
Manor Cottage, Chapel Chorlton, Newcastle Every Mon (2-5)

July 5 Saturday
Stonehill, Great Gate, nr Hollington

July 6 Sunday
Bleak House, Bagnall
The Covert, nr Market Drayton
Kings Bromley Gardens
Moseley Old Hall, Fordhouses, Wolverhampton
98 Walsall Road, Aldridge

July 9 Wednesday
The Old Doctors House, Loggerheads

July 13 Sunday
12 Darges Lane, Great Wyrley
Strawberry Fields, Hill Ridware
Woodside House, Barton-u-Needwood

July 15 Tuesday
Grapevine, Kings Bromley

July 16 Wednesday
Strawberry Fields, Hill Ridware

July 19 Saturday
Westward Ho, Rugeley

July 20 Sunday
Heath House, nr Eccleshall
Strawberry Fields, Hill Ridware

July 26 Saturday
Inglenook, 25 Clifford St, Glascote, Tamworth
The Old Doctors House, Loggerheads

July 27 Sunday
Biddulph Grange Garden, Biddulph
Brookside, Abbots Bromley

July 30 Wednesday
Brookside, Abbots Bromley
38 Park Avenue, Stafford

August
The Covert, nr Market Drayton Every Thurs (2-5)
Manor Cottage, Chapel Chorlton, Newcastle Every Mon (2-5)

August 2 Saturday
Inglenook, 25 Clifford St, Glascote, Tamworth

August 3 Sunday
Woodside House, Barton-u-Needwood

August 10 Sunday
Brookside, Abbots Bromley
Grafton Cottage, Barton-u-Needwood
The Willows, Trysull

August 17 Sunday
The Covert, nr Market Drayton

Grafton Cottage, Barton-u-Needwood

August 24 Sunday

Woodside House, Barton-u-Needwood

September 9 Tuesday

Grapevine, Kings Bromley

September 23 Tuesday

Grapevine, Kings Bromley

September 28 Sunday

Biddulph Grange Garden, Biddulph

October 12 Sunday

Wightwick Manor, Compton

Regular Openings

For details see garden description

The Covert, nr Market Drayton

Manor Cottage, Chapel Chorlton, Newcastle

By Appointment only

For telephone numbers and other details see garden descriptions. Private visits welcomed

Eastfield House, Kings Bromley

DESCRIPTIONS OF GARDENS

Arbour Cottage ♿✂❀ (Mr & Mrs D K Hewitt) Napley. 4m N of Market Drayton. Take A53 then B5415 signed Woore, turn L 1¾m at telephone box. Cottage garden 2 acres of alpine screes, grasses, shrub roses and many paeonias, bamboos etc. Colour all yr from shrubs and trees of many species. TEAS. *Adm £2 Chd free. Fris April 18, 25, May 2, 16, 30, June 13, 27 (2-5.30). Private visits welcome, please* **Tel 01630 672852**

▲Biddulph Grange Garden ✂❀ (The National Trust) Biddulph. 3½m SE of Congleton, 7m N of Stoke-on-Trent on A527. An exciting and rare survival of a high Victorian garden extensively restored since 1988. Conceived by James Bateman, the 15 acres are divided into a number of smaller gardens designed to house specimens from his extensive plant collection. An Egyptian Court; Chinese Pagoda, Willow Pattern Bridge; Pinetum and Arboretum together with many other settings all combine to make the garden a miniature tour of the world. TEAS. *Adm £4 Chd £2 Family £10. March 29 to Nov 2, Wed to Fri (12-6), Sat to Sun (11-6). For NGS Suns July 27, Sept 28 (11-6)* **Tel 01782 517999**

Bleak House ✂❀ (Mr & Mrs J H Beynon) Bagnall. A5009 to Milton Xrds turn for Bagnall. 2m up hill past golf course to corner opp Highlands Hospital. 1-acre plantswoman's garden on 3 levels with roses, herbaceous borders. Terraces leading to informal garden incl stone quarry with pool and waterfall. TEAS. *Adm £1.50 Chd free. Sun July 6 (1-5). Parties welcome, please* **Tel 01782 534713**

Brookside ✂ (Mr & Mrs L Harvey) Abbots Bromley. Approach village from Uttoxeter or Rugeley via B5013; from Burton via B5017. Turn opp Bagot Arms Inn situated in the main st. Small village garden comprising shrubs, herbaceous and bedding plants, rose and herb gardens with brook running along the Northern Boundary. TEAS in nearby C17 hall. *Adm £1.50 Chd free. Suns July 27, Aug 10, Wed July 30 (1-5)*

The Covert ♿✂❀ (Mr & Mrs Leslie Standeven) Burntwood Loggerheads. On Staffs/Shrops borders. Turn off A53 Newcastle-Market Drayton Rd onto Burntwood at Loggerheads Xrds. Approx ¾-acre of plantsperson's garden featuring many rare and unusual plants. Mediterranean scree, tuffa, peat and mixed beds. Alpine house, featured Gardeners World magazine 1996. Partially suitable for wheelchairs. TEAS. *Adm £2 Chd 50p. Suns July 6, Aug 17 (2-5.30). TEA. Thurs April 3 to Aug 28 incl (2-5). Adm £2.50 incl wine, Sat June 21 (7-9)*

12 Darges Lane ✂❀ (Mr & Mrs K Hackett) Great Wyrley. From A5 take A34 towards Walsall. Darges Lane is 1st turning on R (over brow of hill). House on R on corner of Cherrington Drive. ¼-acre well stocked plantsman's and flower arranger's garden. Foliage plants a special feature. Mixed borders incl trees, shrubs and rare plants giving yr-round interest. Features constantly changing. As featured in Channel 4 Garden Club Aug 95. TEAS. *Adm £1.50 Chd 50p. Suns June 22, July 13 (2-6). Also private visits welcome, please* **Tel 01922 415064**

Eastfield House ♿ (Mr & Mrs A Rogers) Kings Bromley. Kings Bromley lies 5m N of Lichfield on A515 Lichfield to Ashbourne rd and 3m W of the A38 on the A513 Tamworth to Rugeley rd. Eastfield House is ½m E of the village centre on the A513. 2-acre garden surrounding a Victorian House, shrubs, lawns herbaceous plants, pond and bog garden. *Adm £1.50 Chd 50p. Private visits welcome June to Sept, please* **Tel 01543 472315**

Edgewood House ❀ (Mr & Mrs G E Fletcher) Stourton. 4m W of Stourbridge 11m E of Bridgnorth. Take A458 from Stew Poney Junction on A449 (Wolverhampton/Kidderminster) towards Bridgnorth. 1st lane on R (Greensforge Lane). ¾m along lane on L. 12 acres of woodland with winding paths through bluebells and trees from cultivated natural garden with small pools. Rhododendrons and azaleas. TEAS. *Adm £2 Chd free. Sun May 11 (2-6)*

Flashbrook Lodge ✂ (Mrs Minnie A Mansell) Flashbrook. On A41 4m N of Newport, take rd signed Knighton. A garden established in 1992 from green field site of approx 1 acre. Features large pool, rockery, waterfall, pergola, gazebo, arbour, trees, shrubs, old-fashioned shrub roses and herbaceous perennials with all yr interest. TEAS. *Adm £1.50 Chd 50p (Share to St Michael and All Angels Church, Adbaston®). Suns June 22, 29 (2-6)*

The Garth ❀ (Mr & Mrs David Wright) 2 Broc Hill Way, Milford, 4½m SE of Stafford. A513 Stafford-Rugeley Rd; at Barley Mow turn R (S) to Brocton; L after 1m. ½-acre; shrubs, rhododendrons, azaleas, mixed herbaceous borders, naturalized bulbs; plants of interest to flower arrangers. Rock hewn caves. Fine landscape setting. Coach parties by appt. TEAS. *Adm £1.50 Chd 50p. Suns June 1, 29 (2-6). Private parties welcome, please* **Tel 01785 661182**

Grafton Cottage ✂❀ (Mr & Mrs P Hargreaves) Bar Lane, Barton-under-Needwood. 5m NE of Lichfield. Take B5016 between Barton-under-Needwood and Yoxall. Bar Lane is ½m W of Top Bell public house. ¾m along lane. A plant lover's cottage garden. ¼-acre. Trellises covered with many old roses over 50 varieties of clematis; wide range of unusual perennials with all-summer interest, stream and vegetables. Winner of E Staffs Borough in Bloom competition. Featured in Aug 96 Practical Gardening. TEAS. *Adm £1.50 Chd free (Share to Arthritis Rheumatism Council for Research®). Suns June 22, 29, Aug 10, 17 (1.30-5.30). Parties welcome, please* **Tel 01283 713639**

Grapevine ⚫⚫ (Mr & Mrs B Harber) 37 Leofric Close, Kings Bromley. A515 5m N of Lichfield. Voted best village garden 1992-6 incl. Front, rear and side gardens with many unusual plants, interest and colour throughout summer. Collection of succulents and pelargoniums. Plans for 97 incl new dry and shade beds. TEA. *Adm £1 Chd free. Tues May 20, June 3, 17, July 15, Sept 9, 23 (1-3.30). Also open with* **Kings Bromley Gardens** *Sun July 6 (1-6) Private visits welcome for not more than 24, please* **Tel 01543 472762**

Hales Hall ⚫⚫ (Mr & Mrs R Hall) Hales. Signposted to Hales due S from A53 between Market Drayton and Loggerheads. C18 house (not open) in beautiful setting. 15 acres of mixed garden particularly rhododendrons, azaleas, woodland and wild garden. Partially suitable for wheelchairs by prior arrangement. Bring picnic lunches to have in park beforehand. TEAS. *Adm £2 Chd free. Sun May 18 (2-5.30)*

Heath House ⚫⚫ (Dr & Mrs D W Eyre-Walker) Nr Eccleshall. 3m W of Eccleshall. Take B5026 towards Woore. At Sugnall turn L, after 1½m turn R immediately by stone garden wall. After 1m straight across Xrds. 1½-acre garden. Borders, bog garden, woodland garden and alpine bed. Many unusual plants. Car parking limited and difficult if wet. TEAS. *Adm £2 Chd free (Share to Parish Church®). Suns May 25, July 20 (2-6). Also private visits welcome, please* **Tel 01785 280318**

The Hollies Farm ⚫⚫ (Mr & Mrs J Shanks) Pattingham. From Wolverhampton A454 W, follow signs to Pattingham. Cross t-lights at Perton, 1½m R for Hollies Lane. From Pattingham take Wolverhampton Rd 1m turn L to Hollies Lane. 2-acre plantsman's landscaped garden with interesting trees and shrubs in lovely countryside setting. TEAS in aid of NSPCC. *Adm £1.50 Chd free. Sun June 15 (2-6)*

Inglenook ⚫⚫⚫ (Mr & Mrs J Sippitts) Glascote, Tamworth. From new A5 bypass, take B5440 signed Glascote to B5000 approx ½m. Follow sign for town centre at roundabout for 300yds. Clifford St 1st R opp Glascote WMC. Extra parking opp WMC. ¼-acre garden of mixed borders, shrubs and trees; small wildlife pond, ornamental pond. Arbours and gazebo. Featured in 'Garden News' and Thompson & Morgan Gardeners of the Year 1996. TEA. *Adm £1 Chd 25p. Sats July 26; Aug 2 (1-5)*

Kings Bromley Gardens ⚫⚫ A515. 5m N of Lichfield. Teas at Village Hall on Alrewas Rd. *Adm £1.50 Chd free. Sun July 6 (1-6)*
  Fairfield (Mr & Mrs K Smith) Church Farm Mews. L-shaped garden with open views to rear of C16 barn. Mature mixed planting and large Koi carp pond
  Forge House (Mr & Mrs A Reid) Adjacent to War

Memorial. Cottage garden, roses, mixed borders, annuals
  Grapevine (Mr & Mrs B Harber) see separate entry
  21 Manor Road (Mr & Mrs D O'Dea) Perennials, shrubs, mixed borders
  Wych Tree (Mr & Mrs P Booth) Manor Park. ½-acre woodland garden containing part of the original walled garden of Kings Bromley Manor, mature shrubs, lawns, roses and perennial beds

Little Onn Hall ⚫ (Mr & Mrs I H Kidson) Church Eaton, 6m SW of Stafford. A449 Wolverhampton-Stafford; at Gailey roundabout turn W on to A5 for 1¼m; turn R to Stretton; 200yds turn L for Church Eaton; or Bradford Arms - Wheaton Aston and Marston 1¼m. 6-acre garden; herbaceous lined drive; abundance of rhododendrons; formal paved rose garden with pavilions at front; large lawns with lily pond around house; old moat garden with fish tanks and small ruin; fine trees; walkways. Paddock open for picnics. TEAS. *Adm £2 Chd 50p. Suns May 18, June 8 (2-6)*

Lower House ⚫⚫ (Mr & Mrs J M Treanor) Sugnall Parva, Eccleshall. 2m W of Eccleshall. On B5026 Loggerheads Rd turn R at sharp double bend. House ½m on L. Large cottage garden with all yr colour and interest, mixed borders, shrubs, pond and rockery in rural setting. TEAS. *Adm £2 Chd free. Sat, Sun June 14, 15 (1-6). Also private visits welcome, please* **Tel 01785 851 378**

Manor Cottage ⚫⚫ (Mrs Joyce Heywood) Chapel Chorlton. 6m S of Newcastle-U-Lyme. On A51 Nantwich to Stone Rd turn behind Cock Inn at Stableford; white house on village green. The garden is full of interesting and unusual plants especially fern, euphorbias, grasses and geraniums. TEAS. *Adm £1.50 Chd 50p. Every Mon March 31 to Aug 25 (2-5). Also private visits welcome, please* **Tel 01782 680206**

▲**Moseley Old Hall** ⚫⚫ (The National Trust) Fordhouses, 4m N of Wolverhampton, between A460 & A449 south of M54 motorway; follow signs. Small modern reconstruction of C17 garden with formal box parterre; mainly includes plants grown in England before 1700; old roses, herbaceous plants, small herb garden, arbour. Late Elizabethan house. TEAS. *Adm Garden £1.70 Chd 85p. For NGS Sun July 6 (1.30-5.30)*

The Old Doctors House ⚫⚫⚫ (Mr & Mrs David Ainsworth) The Burntwood, Loggerheads. On Staffs/Shrops border. Turn off A53 Newcastle to Market Drayton rd onto Kestrel Drive/The Burntwood nr Loggerheads Xrds, adjacent hotel. A garden of approx ¾ acre with mature trees and shrubs; mixed borders and woodland plantings give interest over many months. Pool, waterfall and kitchen garden. TEAS. *Adm £1.50 Chd 50p (Share to Ashley and Loggerheads Day Centre/Luncheon Club©). Weds May 7, 28; July 9; Sats June 28, July 26 (1-5). Group visits welcome for 10 and over, please* **Tel 01630 673363**

38 Park Avenue ⚫⚫ (Mr & Mrs Eric Aspin) Rising Brook. Leave M6 at junction 13, A449 towards Stafford, approx 2m, past Royal Oak on R, past Westway on L, next turn L. From Stafford take A449 over railway bridge, 4th turn on R. ⅛-acre small town garden with interesting design features and varied planting. 'Every corner's a mini masterpiece', Express and Star, June 1996. Secluded white garden, good selection of old roses and clematis. TEA. *Adm £1.50 Chd free. Weds April 30, May 28, June 25, July 30 (2-6). Private visits welcome, please* **Tel 01785 212762**

Stonehill &⚘❀ (Mr & Mrs D Raymont) Great Gate. 4m NW Uttoxeter. A50 to Uttoxeter. R onto B5030 to JCB Rocester, L to Hollington. Third R to Croxden Abbey and Gt Gate. L to Stonehill [SKO53402]. 5 acres of developing quarry gardens. Light woodland with azaleas and rhododendrons, spring bulbs, herbaceous and bog gardens. Parking for disabled. Regret children to remain with parents at all times - ground nesting birds. TEAS in aid of St Giles Church. *Adm £1.50 Chd free. Sun June 1, Sat July 5 (2-6). Private visits welcome, please* **Tel 01889 507202**

Strawberry Fields ⚘ (Mr & Mrs T Adams) Hill Ridware. 5m N of Lichfield. B5014 Lichfield/Abbots Bromley. At Hill Ridware turn into Church Lane by Royal Oak Inn, then 1st R. This delightful ⅓-acre award winning garden has a water trail and a succession of focal points that draw you round this plant person's paradise. Pleasing country views. TEAS. *Adm £1.50 Chd free. Suns July 13, 20; Wed July 16 (11-5). Group visits welcome, please* **Tel 01543 490516**

¶**Stretton Hall** &⚘❀ (Mr & Mrs A Monckton) Stretton village, Stafford 1m N of A5 approx 2m W of Gailey roundabout (junction A449). 7 acres with formal rose garden, landscaped garden with many species of trees and shrubs, woodland garden and walk. TEAS in aid of CRMF. *Adm £2 Chd 50p. Sun June 29 (2-5.30)*

¶**Thornfold** ⚘❀ (Mrs Patricia Machin) A523. 1m from Leek. L at hospital Moorland Rd, 2nd R Thornfield Ave, Arden Close on R. Please park with consideration in the Avenue. New small cottage garden, yr-round colour from mixed herbaceous borders, trellises with roses and clematis. Pond, unusual plants. TEAS. *Adm £1.50 Chd free. Weds June 11, 18, Sun June 15 (2-5.30)*

¶**98 Walsall Road** ⚘❀ (Mr & Mrs T Atkins) Aldridge. 3m NW of Walsall on A454, 300yds past White Horse Inn. ⅓-acre well stocked small town garden, mostly shrubs and perennials with informal pond. *Adm £1.50 Chd 50p. Sun July 6 (2-6)*

¶**Westward Ho** &⚘❀ (Mr & Mrs A Hargreaves) Rugeley. From N: Proceed from junction A513 and A51 towards Rugeley. After 1m turn R into Bower Lane after 1.8m turn R into Kingsley Wood Rd. From S: At large island in Rugeley take N A51 to Stone/Stafford. After 300yds turn L at t-lights towards Penkridge after 1.7m turn R into Stafford Brook Rd, 1st L into Kingsley Wood Rd. Large car park at rear of garden. Set in the heart of Cannock Chase, this large garden offers peaceful surroundings and places to sit and enjoy herbaceous beds, shrubs, trees, pool, pagoda, pergola and vegetable garden. TEAS. *Adm £1 Chd 50p (Share to Chadsmoor Methodist Church®). Sats June 7, July 19 (1-5.30)*

▲**Wightwick Manor** & (The National Trust) Compton, 3m W of Wolverhampton A454, Wolverhampton-Bridgnorth, just to N of rd, up Wightwick Bank, beside Mermaid Inn. Partly suitable for wheelchairs. 17-acre, Victorian-style garden laid out by Thomas Mawson; yew hedges; topiary; terraces; 2 pools; rhododendrons; azaleas. House closed. TEAS. *Adm £2 Chd £1. For NGS Suns May 18, Oct 12 (2-6)*

The Willows &⚘❀ (Mr & Mrs Nigel Hanson) Trysull. 7m SW of Wolverhampton. From A449 at Himley B4176 towards Bridgnorth, 2¼m turn R to Trysull. ¾m on L. 2-acre garden created and maintained by owners since 1981. Natural pool, hostas, rhododendrons, salvias, old-fashioned roses, colour theme borders with a wide range of interesting and unusual plants. Teas in village hall in aid of Trysull Church. *Adm £1.50 Chd free. Sun Aug 10 (2-6). Private parties welcome, please* **Tel 01902 897557**

The Wombourne Wodehouse &⚘❀ (Mr & Mrs J Phillips) 4m S of Wolverhampton just off A449 on A463 to Sedgley. 18-acre garden laid out in 1750. Mainly rhododendrons, herbaceous and iris border, woodland walk, water garden. TEAS. *Adm £2 Chd free. Sun June 1 (2-5.30); also private visits welcome in May, June, July, please* **Tel 01902 892202**

Woodside House ⚘❀(Mr & Mrs R C Webster) Barton-under-Needwood. Take B5016 out of Barton-under-Needwood. Turn R at Top Bell public house, 300yds turn R into signed gravel drive. 1-acre plantsman's garden incl Japanese garden with stream, waterfalls and lily pond; rose walk; cottage garden. Large Koi pond with rockery. Rare plants. TEAS. *Adm £1.50 Chd free (Share to RNIB®). Sat June 28, Suns July 13, Aug 3, 24 (1.30-6). Private visits welcome by appt June 29 to Aug 30 (1.30-6), please* **Tel 01283 716046**

Scotland's Gardens Scheme. The National Gardens Scheme has a similar but quite separate counterpart in Scotland. Called Scotland's Gardens Scheme, it raises money for the Queen's Nursing Institute (Scotland), the Gardens Fund of the National Trust for Scotland and over 160 registered charities nominated by garden owners. The Handbook is available (£3.25 incl p&p) from Scotland's Gardens Scheme, 31 Castle Terrace, Edinburgh EH1 2EL. Telephone 0131-229-1870, Fax 0131-229-0443

Suffolk

Hon County Organisers:
(East) Mrs Robert Stone, Washbrook Grange, Washbrook, Nr Ipswich IP8 3HQ
Tel 01473 730244

(West) Lady Mowbray, Hill House, Glemsford, Nr Sudbury CO 10 7PP
Tel 01787 281930

Asst Hon County Organiser: (East) Mrs T W Ingram, Orchard House, Chattisham Lane, Hintlesham, Suffolk
IP8 3NW Tel 01473 652 282
Mrs R I Johnson, 13 Trinity St, Bungay NR35 1EH Tel 01986 894586

Asst Hon County Organiser: (West) Mrs M Pampanini, The Old Rectory, Hawstead, Bury St Edmunds IP29 5NT
Tel 01284 386 613
Mrs A Kelsey, The Priory, Church Road, Little Waldingfield, Suffolk CO10 0SW
Tel 01787 2477335

Hon County Treasurer: (West) Sir John Mowbray

DATES OF OPENING

March 31 Monday
East Bergholt Place, East
Bergholt
April 6 Sunday
Barham Hall, Barham, Ipswich
Great Thurlow Hall, Haverhill
April 13 Sunday
The White House, Clare
April 20 Sunday
East Bergholt Place, East
Bergholt
April 27 Sunday
Garden House Farm, Drinkstone
Giffords Hall, Wickhambrook
Tollemache Hall, Offton, nr
Ipswich
May 4 Sunday
Blakenham Woodland Garden,
Little Blakenham
13 Drapers Lane, Ditchingham
The Old Hall, Beccles
May 5 Monday
Bucklesham Hall, Bucklesham
13 Drapers Lane, Ditchingham
Letheringham Watermill,
Woodbridge
The Old Hall, Beccles
May 7 Wednesday
Blakenham Woodland Garden,
Little Blakenham
May 11 Sunday
Somerleyton Hall, Lowestoft
May 18 Sunday
The Priory, Stoke by Nayland
May 25 Sunday
Felsham House, Bury St
Edmunds
Thrift Farm, Cowlinge, nr
Newmarket
Windmill Cottage, Capel St Mary,
Ipswich
May 26 Monday
Thrift Farm, Cowlinge, nr
Newmarket

June 1 Sunday
Aldeburgh Gardens
Rosedale, Colchester Road,
Bures, nr Sudbury
June 7 Saturday
Wyken Hall, Stanton
June 8 Sunday
Bucklesham Hall, Bucklesham
Hengrave Hall, Hengrave
Rosemary, East Bergholt
St Stephens Cottage, Spexhall
June 15 Sunday
The Lawn, Walsham le
Willows
Magnolia House, Yoxford
Washbrook Grange, nr Ipswich
Windmill Cottage, Capel St Mary,
Ipswich
June 21 Saturday
Sun House, Long Melford
June 22 Sunday
Cavendish Hall, Cavendish
Ellingham Hall, nr Bungay
Gable House, Redisham
The Rookery, Eyke
Sun House, Long Melford
June 29 Sunday
Boxted Hall, nr Bury St
Edmunds ‡
Clipt Bushes, Cockfield ‡
2 Factory Cottages, Cowlinge
Hill House, Glemsford
Moat Cottage, Great Green,
Cockfield
North Cove Hall, Beccles
Reydon Grove House,
Reydon
Thrift Farm, Cowlinge, nr
Newmarket
July 6 Sunday
Denston Hall, Denston, nr
Wickhambrook
The Dhoon, Barton Mills
Giffords Hall, Wickhambrook
The Old Hall, Beccles
The Spong, Groton

July 12 Saturday
Thumbit, Walsham-le-Willows
July 13 Sunday
Garden House, Moulton nr
Newmarket
Holbecks, Hadleigh
Redisham Hall, Beccles
Thumbit, Walsham-le-Willows
Western House, Cavendish
July 20 Sunday
Highfield Farm Bures
The Jockey Club, Newmarket
Rosedale, Colchester Road,
Bures, nr Sudbury
July 23 Wednesday
Highfield Farm Bures
July 27 Sunday
2 Factory Cottages, Cowlinge
Porters Lodge, Cavenham
Riverside House, Stoke Road,
Clare
August 3 Sunday
The Beeches, Walsham-le-
Willows
Highfield Farm Bures
August 10 Sunday
Akenfield, Charsfield
August 17 Sunday
Thrift Farm, Cowlinge, nr
Newmarket
August 24 Sunday
Rosedale, Colchester Road,
Bures, nr Sudbury
St Stephens Cottage, Spexhall
August 25 Monday
Letheringham Watermill,
Woodbridge
September 7 Sunday
Rosedale, Colchester Road,
Bures, nr Sudbury
September 14 Sunday
Ickworth House, Horringer
The Old Hall, Beccles
October 19 Sunday
East Bergholt Place, East
Bergholt

Regular openings
For details see garden description

Blakenham Woodland Garden
Euston Hall, nr Thetford
Somerleyton Hall

By appointment only
For telephone numbers and other details see garden descriptions.
Private visits welcomed

Battlies House, Rougham
Grundisburgh Hall, Woodbridge
Rumah Kita, Bedfield
Woottens, Wenhaston

By Appointment Gardens. These owners do not have a fixed opening day usually because they cannot accommodate large numbers or have insufficient parking space.

DESCRIPTIONS OF GARDENS

■ **Akenfield, 1 Park Lane** &⚘ (Mrs E E Cole) Charsfield, 6m N of Woodbridge. On B1078, 3m W of Wickham Market. ½-acre council house garden; vegetables, flowers for drying, 2 greenhouses; small fishponds with water wheel; many pot plants etc. In village of Charsfield (known to many readers and viewers as Akenfield). *Adm £2 OAPs 75p Chd free. Daily from Easter to Sept 30. For NGS Sun Aug 10 (10.30-7). Parties welcome by appt, please* **Tel 01473 737402**

¶**Aldeburgh Gardens** ⚘ From A12 take A1094 to Aldeburgh. On approach to town go over 1st roundabout then almost immed R into Park Rd. At tennis courts on the R turn R into Priors Hill Rd. TEAS and tickets at Stanford House. *Combined adm £3.50 Chd free. Sun June 1 (2-5.30)*
    ¶**Stanford House** (Lady Cave) 1½ acres of terraced garden with waterfall, water garden and wide variety of rare plants and specimen shrubs luxuriating in a mild maritime climate. Beautiful views over riverside and sea
    ¶**Westcroft** (Mr & Mrs H Jenkyns) Informal and peaceful garden sloping towards river with southern aspect allowing mimosa, pittosporum, a Judas tree and tender plants to flourish
    ¶**Heron House** (Mr & Mrs J Hale) 1¾ acres with views over coastline, river and marshes. Unusual trees, herbaceous beds, many shrubs, ponds and a waterfall in a large rock garden

Barham Hall &⚘⚘ (Mr & Mrs Richard Burrows) Barham. From Ipswich A45 going W. 4m sign Great Blakenham to roundabout beneath motorway. Leave by 3rd turning to Claydon. Through Claydon, after decontrolled signs turn R up Church Lane to Barham Green. ½m up Church Lane. 7 acres of undulating gardens mainly recreated during the last 5yrs. 3 herbaceous borders, a lake surrounded by azaleas and bog plants, a woodland shrub garden full of spring flowers; a very considerable collection of victorian roses set in well kept lawns with mature trees; a water garden and many other interesting features. St Mary's and St Peter's Church open with famous Henry Moore sculpture. TEA. *Adm £2 OAPs £1 Chd 25p (Share to St Mary's & St Peters Church Barham®). Sun April 6 (2-5)*

Battlies House &⚘ (Mr & Mrs John Barrell) Bury St Edmunds. Turn N off A14 at GT Barton and Rougham industrial estate turning, 3m E of Bury St Edmunds. In ½m turn R by lodge. 8-acre garden, lawns; shrubberies, woodland walk with a variety of old trees; rhododendrons; elms and conifers. *Adm £2 Chd free. Private visits welcome, please* **Tel 01284 787397**

The Beeches & (Dr & Mrs A J Russell) Walsham-le-Willows. 10m NE of Bury St Edmunds; signed Walsham-le-Willows off A143. At Xrds in village pass Church on L, after 50yds turn L along Grove Rd. Pink house behind Church. 3 acres; lawns, herbaceous border, mature and newly-planted trees. Potager, thatched summer house with ornamental pond, gazebo and wild garden by stream. TEAS. *Adm £2 Chd under 14 free (Share to St Mary's Church, Walsham-le-Willows®). Sun Aug 3 (2-6)*

■ **Blakenham Woodland Garden** ⚘ Little Blakenham. 4m NW of Ipswich. Follow signs from 'The Beeches' at Lt Blakenham, 1m off the old A1100, now called B1113. 5-acre bluebell wood densely planted with fine collection of trees and shrubs; camellias, magnolias, cornus, azaleas, rhododendrons, roses, hydrangeas. *Adm £1 Chd £1. Open daily (1-5) except Sats, March 1 to June 30. For NGS Sun Wed May 4, 7 (1-5). Parties by appt, please* **Tel 0171 411 2201**

Boxted Hall &⚘ (Mrs Weller-Poley) Bury St Edmunds. Boxted Hall is approached by a drive off the B1066 Bury St Edmunds-Long Melford back rd ½m S of Boxted Village. Moated House (not open) with 4 acres of grounds, extensive lawns, trees and roses in outstanding setting. Strawberry TEAS. *Adm £2 Chd free. Sun June 29 (2-6)*

Bucklesham Hall ⚘⚘ (Mr & Mrs D R Brightwell) Bucklesham. 6m SE of Ipswich, 1m E of village opp to Bucklesham School. 7 acres created by previous owners in 1973 and maintained by present owners since 1994. Unusual plants, shrubs and trees. Shrub/rose garden, water and woodland gardens. TEAS in aid of Village Hall Fund, Bucklesham. *Adm £2 Chd £1. Mon May 5, Sun June 8 (2-6). Private visits welcome by parties of 4 or more, please* **Tel 01473 659263**

Cavendish Hall & (Mrs T S Matthews) Cavendish. Entrance on A1092 midway between Cavendish and Clare, about 7m NW of Sudbury. 30 acres incl park and woodland. Fine views overlooking Stour Valley woodland walks, old roses, paeonies, shrubs in encircling borders. TEAS. *Adm £2 Chd free. Sun June 22 (2-6)*

Clipt Bushes &⚘ (Mr & Mrs H W A Ruffell) Cockfield. Just off the A1141 8m S of Bury St Edmunds and 3m N of Lavenham. Ample parking. Farmhouse gardens, approx 3 acres designed for easy maintenance. Shrubberies, specimen trees and old roses. TEAS. *Combined adm with* **Moat Cottage** *£3 OAP £1.50 Chd free. Sun June 29 (2-6)*

Denston Hall &⚘ (Mr & Mrs R Macaire) Denston. Approx 10m from Bury St Edmunds and Newmarket. Denston is 1m SE of A143. Denston Hall is situated at end of cul-de-sac in centre of village. Approx 10 acre garden recently renovated to a very high standard set in parkland with large walled garden, lake, old fish ponds and many fine trees. *Adm £2 Chd free. Sun July 6 (2-6)*

The Dhoon ᕓᵛ❀ (Mr & Mrs H H Morriss) 19 The Street, Barton Mills. Opp the PO in the Old Street in Barton Mills, take signs off the A11 to Barton Mills. New garden of 7 yrs going down to the R Lark. 2 × 65' herbaceous borders, pergola, conservatory and raised vegetable beds. Sir Alexander Fleming's former country house. TEAS. *Adm £2 Chd free (Share to Newmarket Day Centre©). Sun July 6 (2-6)*

13 Drapers Lane ᵛ❀ (Mr & Mrs Borrett) Ditchingham. 1¼m Bungay off the B1332 towards Norwich. ⅓-acre containing many interesting, unusual plants including 100 plus varieties of hardy geraniums, climbers and shrubs. Herbaceous perennials a speciality. Owner maintained. TEAS. *Adm £1.50 Chd free. Sun, Mon May 4, 5 (12-4) also open on Sun June 22 under Ditchingham Gardens, Norfolk*

East Bergholt Place Garden ᕓᵛ❀ (Mr & Mrs Rupert Eley) East Bergholt. On the B1070 towards Manningtree, 2m E of A12. 15-acre garden originally laid out at the beginning of the century by the present owner's great Grandfather. Full of many fine trees and shrubs some of which are rarely seen in East Anglia. Particularly beautiful in spring when the rhododendrons, magnolias and camellias are in full flower, and in Autumn, with newly cut topiary and Autumn colours. TEAS. *Adm £2 Chd free. Mon, Sun March 31, April 20 (2-5.30) Oct 19 (1-dusk)*

Ellingham Hall ᕓᵛ❀ (Col & Mrs H M L Smith) On A143 between Beccles 3m and Bungay 2m. Georgian house set in parkland. The 2-acre garden, designed by Sue Gill (see Great Campston, Gwent) is planted in deep borders with a wide and unusual variety of plants and trees. The recently planted 'Terracotta Garden' has a Mediterranean atmosphere. The walled garden includes fan trained fruit trees and a nuttery. TEAS. *Adm £2 Chd under 12 free. Sun June 22 (2-6)*

●**Euston Hall** ᵛ (The Duke & Duchess of Grafton) on the A1088 12m N of Bury St Edmunds. 3m S of Thetford. Terraced lawns; herbaceous borders, rose garden, C17 pleasure grounds, lake and watermill. C18 house open; famous collection of paintings. C17 church; temple by William Kent. Craft shop. Wheelchair access to gardens, tea-room and shop only. TEAS in Old Kitchen. *Adm house & garden £3 OAPs £2, Chd 50p Parties of 12 or more £2 per head (Share to NGS®). Thurs June 5 to Sept 25; Suns June 29 & Sept 7 (2.30-5)*

¶**2 Factory Cottages** ❀ (Mrs Annie Hayes) Cowlinge. Situated on the main rd through Cowlinge village, 7m from Haverhill, 10yds from turning to Hobbles Green. Small country garden set in ⅓-acre with pond, pavilion and many interesting plants. TEAS. *Adm £1.50 Chd free. Suns June 29, July 27 (2-6)*

Regular Openers. Open throughout the year. They are listed at the end of the Diary Section under 'Regular Openers'.

Felsham House ᕓᵛ❀ (The Hon Mrs Erskine) Felsham 7m SE of Bury St Edmunds off A134, 8m W of Stowmarket via Rattlesden. 5 acres incl meadow with wild flowers, established trees, shrubs, roses; herb garden. TEAS. *Adm £2 Chd free. Sun May 25 (2-6)*

Gable House ᕓᵛ❀ (Mr & Mrs John Foster) Redisham. 3½m S of Beccles. Mid-way between Beccles and Halesworth on Ringsfield-Ilketshall St Lawrence Rd. Garden of 1 acre, mixed borders, alpines. Greenhouses. Home-made TEAS. *Adm £2 (Share to St Peters Church Redisham, Beccles, Suffolk®). Sun June 22 (2-5.30). Private visits welcome Suns from May to Sept Tel 01502 575298*

Garden House ᕓᵛ❀ (Mr & Mrs John Maskelyne) Brookside. Moulton is 3m due E of Newmarket on B1085. The garden is close to the Pack Horse Bridge and faces the village green. Interesting ¾-acre plantsman's garden, roses, small woodland area, alpines and mixed borders. Small water feature, pergola; large number of clematis. Past chairman of British Clematis Society; maintained by owners. TEAS in aid of Riding for the Disabled. *Adm £2 Chd free. Sun July 13 (2-6)*

Garden House Farm ᵛ❀ (Mr & Mrs Seiffer) Drinkstone. A14 was A45. Turn off at Woolpit, go through village and follow signs to Drinkstone and then Drinkstone Green, past Cherry Tree Inn and then 1st L, Rattlesden Rd. After ¾m turn L down lane and drive to end. 3m from Woolpit. Formerly the gardens of Barcock's Nursery. The woodland garden is particularly delightful in Spring with many camellias, magnolias and Spring flowers. This is a plantsman's garden with many rare and unusual plants, trees and shrubs. 11 acres incl pond and lake. New owners are currently creating new areas of interest. TEAS and plant stall in aid of NACC. *Adm £2 Chd free. Sun April 27 (2-5.30). Private visits welcome, please Tel 01449 736434*

Giffords Hall ᕓ (Sir David and Lady Rowland) Wickhambrook. 10m SW of Bury St Edmunds, 10m NE of Haverhill. ¾m from Plumber's Arms, Wickhambrook in direction of Bury St Edmunds on A143. Garden ¾m up lane signposted Giffords Hall. C15 moated Suffolk Hall (not open). Gardens with herbaceous borders and rose beds. TEAS. *Adm £2 Chd free. Suns April 27, July 6 (2-5.30)*

Great Thurlow Hall ᕓ (Mr & Mrs George Vestey) N of Haverhill. Great Thurlow village on B1061 from Newmarket; 3½m N of junction with A143 Haverhill-Bury St Edmunds rd. 20 acres. Herbaceous borders, shrubs, roses, spacious lawns, river walk, trout lake. Daffodils and blossom. Walled kitchen garden. New inspired gardener. TEA. *Adm £2 Chd free. Sun April 6 (2-5)*

Grundisburgh Hall ᕓᵛ (Lady Cranworth) 3m W of Woodbridge on B1079, ¼m S of Grundisburgh on Grundisburgh to Ipswich Rd. Approx 5 acres walled garden with yew hedges; wisteria walk and mixed borders. Old rose garden; lawns and ponds. *Adm £2.50 Chd free (Share to St Marys Grundisburgh, St Botolphs Culpho®). Private visits welcome May 20 to July 20, please Tel 01473 735 485*

Hengrave Hall &⚘✿ Hengrave. 3½m NW Bury St Edmunds on A1101. Tudor mansion (tours available). Lake and woodland path. 5-acre formal garden with spacious lawns. Mixed borders with some unusual plants. Kitchen garden. TEAS in aid of Hengrave Bursary Fund. *Adm £2 OAPs £1 Chd free. Sun June 8 (2-6)*

Highfields Farm &✿ (Mr & Mrs John Ineson) Bures. 6m SE of Sudbury. From Bures Church take Nayland Rd. In 2m turn L signposted Assington. Take 1st R Tarmac Drive. From other directions take Assington-Wormingford rd. Approx 1½-acre plantsman's garden started in 1984 with mixed borders, shrubs, chamomile lawn and herbaceous beds. Various features incl lily pond, wildlife pond and folly. No WCs. TEAS. *Adm £2 Chd free. Suns July 20, Aug 3, Wed July 23 (2-6). Private visits welcome in July, please* **Tel 01787 227136**

The Hill House & (Sir John and Lady Mowbray) Glemsford. 100yds N of village of Glemsford on the back rd to Hawkedon and Boxted. Lately renovated garden of 1 acre with interesting mixed borders and conservatory. Strawberry teas at Boxted Hall. *Adm £2 Chd free. Sun June 29 (2-6)*

Holbecks ✿ (Sir Joshua & Lady Rowley) Hadleigh. From Hadleigh High St turn into Duke St signed to Lower Layham; immediately over bridge go right up concrete rd to top of hill. 3 acres; early C19 landscape terraced and walled gardens, flowerbeds, roses and ornamental shrubs. TEAS. *Adm £2 Chd free (Share to Suffolk Historic Churches Trust®). Sun July 13 (2-5.30)*

▲**Ickworth House, Park & Gardens** &⚘ (The National Trust) Horringer. 3m SW of Bury St. Edmunds on W side of A143 [155:TL8161] 70 acres of garden. South gardens restored to stylized Italian landscape to reflect extraordinary design of the house. Fine orangery, agapanthus, geraniums and fatsias. North gardens informal wild flower lawns with wooded walk; the Buxus collection, great variety of evergreens and Victorian stumpery. New planting of cedars. The Albana Wood, a C18 feature, initially laid out by Capability Brown, incorporates a fine circular walk. Restaurant TEAS. *Adm £4.75 (house, park and garden) Chd £2. £1.75 (park and garden) Chd 50p. For NGS Sun Sept 14 (10-5.30). Private visits of 15 and over welcome, please* **Tel 01284 735270**

¶**The Jockey Club** &⚘ Newmarket. The entrance is in Newmarket High St. next to the Post Office and opp. the White Hart Hotel. The entrance gates open automatically when approached by vehicle; there is also a pedestrian gate. Well stocked 70 metre long herbaceous border and extensive lawn area. *Adm £2 Chd free. Sun July 20 (2-5)*

The Lawn & (Mr & Mrs R Martineau) Walsham-le-Willows. NE from Bury St Edmunds on A143 about 6m to Ixworth bypass R at 2nd roundabout to Walsham-le-Willows. 3½m house on R, ½m short of village. About 3½ acres of lawns, herbaceous borders and shrubs overlooking parkland. Also a woodland walk around an 8-acre wood. TEAS. *Adm £2 Chd free. Sun June 15 (2.30-6)*

■ **Letheringham Watermill** &⚘✿ (Mr & Mrs Rod Allen) nr Easton. 7m N of Woodbridge. Letheringham turn off

B1078, 1m W of Wickham Market. 5 acres of garden with the rare lathraea clandestina and river walks. Aviary. Watermill has picture gallery and restored waterwheel. Unusual plants for sale. Home-made TEAS. *Adm £2 OAP's £1 Chd free (Share to St Elizabeth Hospice©). Open Suns, Bank Hols Mons (2-6). For NGS Mons May 5, Aug 25 (2-6)*

Magnolia House ⚘ (Mr Mark Rumary) On A1120 in centre of Yoxford. Small, completely walled village garden. Mixed borders with flowering trees, shrubs, climbers, bulbs, hardy and tender plants. Featured in UK and foreign gardening books and magazines. TEA. *Adm £2 Chd free. Sun June 15 (2-6)*

Moat Cottage ⚘ (Stephen & Lesley Ingerson) Great Green. Cockfield. Take A134 S from Bury St Edmunds. After Sicklesmere village turn sharp L for Cockfield Green and R at 1st Xrds. Follow winding rd through Bradfield St Clare. At Great Green fork L Moat Cottage is opp garage at far end. 1 acre of enchanting cottage garden created over the last 10yrs and forever changing. The garden is divided into smaller areas incl white, herb, herbaceous borders and water features, with a kitchen garden that provides the owners with all year round vegetables. Teas at Clipt Bushes (½m). *Combined adm with* **Clipt Bushes** *£3 OAPs £1 Chd free. Sun June 29 (2-6)*

North Cove Hall &✿ (Mr & Mrs B Blower) Beccles. Just off A146 3½m E of Beccles on Lowestoft Rd. Take sign to North Cove. 5 acres of garden; large pond; new water feature; mature and interesting young trees. Walled kitchen garden; shrub roses; herbaceous borders; woodland walks. Home-made TEAS. *Adm £2 Chd free. Sun June 29 (2-5.30)*

The Old Hall &✿ (Mr & Mrs Maurice Elliott) Barsham. Off B1062 1½m W of Beccles. Recently restored C16 Hall, Civic Trust Award 1994. Young garden, many unusual trees, shrubs and climbers. 85 clematis, herb garden (over 400 different grown); greenhouse. Small nursery. TEAS. *Adm £2 OAP £1 Chd free. Suns, Mons May 4, 5, July 6, Sept 14 (2-5). Private visits welcome, please* **Tel 01502 717475**

Porters Lodge & (Mr Craig Wyncoll) Cavenham. 5m W of Bury St Edmunds; 1m SW of Cavenham on the rd to Kentford. 2 acres of woodland walks surrounding and linked into an acre of semi-formal lawns with mixed borders and ponds. An unusual and interesting garden designed as a series of interlinked spaces enlivened by fountains, statutary and architectural 'follies'. TEAS. *Adm £2 Chd free. Sun July 27 (2-6)*

The Priory &✿ (Mr & Mrs H F A Engleheart) Stoke-by-Nayland (1m); 8m N of Colchester, entrance on B1068 rd to Sudbury. Interesting 9-acre garden with fine views over Constable countryside, with lawns sloping down to small lakes & water garden; fine trees, rhododendrons & azaleas; walled garden; mixed borders & ornamental greenhouse. Wide variety of plants; peafowl. TEAS. *Adm £2 Chd free. Sun May 18 (2-6)*

Redisham Hall &⚘ (Mr Palgrave Brown) SW of Beccles. From A145 1½m S of Beccles, turn W on to Ringsfield-Bungay Rd. Beccles, Halesworth or Bungay, all within 6m.

5 acres; parkland and woods 400 acres. Georgian house C18 (not shown). Safari rides. TEAS (3.30-5 only). *Adm £2 Chd free (Share to East Suffolk Macmillan Nurses®). Sun July 13 (2-6)*

Reydon Grove House &❀ (Cmdr & Mrs J Swinley) Reydon. Situated ½m N of Reydon Church. Turnings off the Wangford-Southwold rd. 1½-acre mature garden. Large herbaceous borders, many interesting and unusual shrubs, plants, old-fashioned roses. Large vegetable garden. TEAS in aid of Reydon Church. *Adm £2 Chd free. Sun June 29 (2-5.30) Private visits welcome June to Sept, please* **Tel 01502 723655**

Riverside House ✕ (Mr & Mrs A C W Bone) Clare. On the A1092 leading out of Clare, towards Haverhill. A peaceful walled garden of 1 acre, bordering the R Stour, with lawns, trees, mixed herbaceous beds and shrubs. Spot the stone pig! Teas at Kate's Kitchen in Clare opp Town Hall. *Adm £2 Chd free. Sun July 27 (2-5.30)*

The Rookery &✕❀ (Captain & Mrs Sheepshanks) Eyke. 5m E of Woodbridge turn N off B1084 Woodbridge-Orford Rd when sign says Rendlesham. 10-acre garden; planted as an arboretum with many rare specimen trees and shrubs; landscaped on differing levels, providing views and vistas; the visitor's curiosity is constantly aroused by what is round the next corner; ponds, bog garden, shrubbery, alpines, garden stream, bulbs, herbaceous borders and a 1-acre vineyard. Wine tastings and farm shop. Home-made TEAS. *Adm £2 Chd 50p. Sun June 22 (2-5.30). Private visits welcome for parties of 10 and over, please* **Tel 01394 460271**

Rosedale ✕❀ (Mr & Mrs Colin Lorking) 40 Colchester Rd, Bures. 9m NW of Colchester on B1508. As you enter the village of Bures, garden is on the L or 5m SE of Sudbury on B1508, follow signs through village towards Colchester, garden is on the R as you leave village. Approx ⅓-acre, plantsman's garden; many unusual plants, herbaceous borders, pond, woodland area, rose beds. Featured in Daily Mail Weekend Magazine. TEA. *Adm £2 Acc chd free. Suns June 1, July 20, Aug 24, Sept 7 (12-6). Private visits welcome, please* **Tel 01787 227619**

Rosemary &✕❀ (Mrs N E M Finch) Rectory Hill. Turn off the A12 at East Bergholt and follow rd round to church. Rosemary is 100yds down from the church on L. Mature 1-acre garden adapted over 20yrs from an old orchard loosely divided into several smaller gardens; mixed borders; herb garden; over 80 old roses, unusual plants. TEAS. *Adm £2 Chd free. Sun June 8 (2-6) and private visits welcome June and July, please* **Tel 01206 298241**

Rumah Kita & (Mr & Mrs I R Dickings) Bedfield is situated 2½m NW of the A1120 on secondary rd turning between Earl Soham and Saxted Green. 1½-acre garden designed and planted by owners; mixed borders of many unusual plants. Parterre, scree, peat and raised alpine beds. *Adm £2 Chd free. Private visits welcome, individual or parties, please* **Tel 01728 628401**

St Stephens Cottage ✕❀ (Mrs D Gibbs) Spexhall. 2m from Halesworth off A144 Halesworth to Bungay Rd take signposted lane to Spexhall Church. 1-acre cottage garden with island beds surrounding mature trees, natural pond, unusual plants. New 3 acres which incl formal scented garden, rosary and newly planted arboretum. Large conservatory featured on TV and national journals. TEA. *Adm £2 Chd free. Suns June 8, Aug 24 (2-5). Parties welcome by appt May-Aug, please* **Tel 01986 873394**

■ **Somerleyton Hall** &✕ (The Lord & Lady Somerleyton) 5m NW of Lowestoft. Off B1074. Large garden; famous maze, beautiful trees and borders. House C16 150 yrs old lavishly remodelled in 1840's. Grinling Gibbons' carving, library, tapestries. Mentioned in Domesday Book. Miniature railway. Light lunches & TEAS. *Adm £4.20 OAP £3.80 Chd £1.95. House open 1.30-5 Gardens 12.30-5.30: Sun April 28 Easter Sun to end Sept, Thurs, Suns, Bank Hol Mons; in addition Tues, Weds, July and Aug; miniature railway will be running on most days. For NGS Sun May 11. Group private visits welcome by prior arrangement (Min 20)*

The Spong ❀ (Joseph Barrett Esq & John Kirby Esq) Groton, Boxford. 5m W of Hadleigh on A1071. Leave Boxford via Swan Street, bear R at Fox and Hounds follow main road past Groton Church, take next R. The Spong is the pink house at the bottom of the hill. Approached over stream; planned as a series of small gardens due to irregular shape; ever changing with mixed herbaceous/shrubs; ponds; pergola. *Adm £2 Chd free. Sun July 6 (2-6)*

Sun House &✕❀ (Mr & Mrs John Thompson) Long Melford. Centre of village, 3½m N of Sudbury on A134 opp Cock & Bell Inn. 2 attractive adjacent walled gardens with roses, shrubs, hostas, ferns and many rare herbaceous plants - over 100 clematis, water and architectural features, folly and paved courtyards. Runner up Daily Mail /RHS Garden Competition 1995 - Winner Best Garden in East Anglia - Look East TV. TEAS. *Adm £2 Chd free. Sat, Sun June 21, 22 (2-6)*

Thrift Farm &✕❀ (Mrs J Oddy) Cowlinge. 7m SE of Newmarket, centrally between Cowlinge, Kirtling and Gt Bradley. On the Gt Bradley rd from Kirtling. Picturesque thatched house set in a cottage style garden extending to approx 1½ acres. Forever changing island beds filled with herbaceous plants amongst shrubs and ornamental trees in great variety. It is a garden which encourages you to walk round. Owner maintained. TEA. *Adm £2. Suns, Mon May 25, 26, June 29, Aug 17 (2-6). Private visits welcome (lunch/teas if required), please* **Tel 01440 783274**

Thumbit & (Mrs Ann James) Walsham-le-Willows. 10m NE of Bury St Edmunds. Leave A143 at Walsham-le-Willows sign and continue to Xrds by church at centre of village. Take Badwell Rd to outskirts of village (½m). House is part of thatched C16 one-time inn. Shared driveway - (please do not drive in). Small informal garden with strong emphasis on design and plant association. Pergola, pool, topiary. 500 choice herbaceous plants and shrubs, roses and climbers. Featured in Weekend Telegraph and Practical Gardening. TEA, lunches by arrangement. *Adm £2 OAP £1 Chd free. Sat, Sun July 12, 13 (2-6). Private visits welcome, please* **Tel 01359 259 414**

Tollemache Hall ⟨&⟩⟨✗⟩ (Mr & Mrs M Tollemache) Offton, nr Ipswich. S of the B1078 opp the Ringshall turning. 4 acres of recently renovated garden in a lovely rural setting. Shrubs, rose and knot gardens. A large walled garden with interesting herbaceous borders. Also woodland walk planted with many conifer species. Suffolk punches, TEAS. *Adm £2 Chd free. Sun April 27 (2-6)*

Washbrook Grange ⟨✗⟩⟨❀⟩ (Mr & Mrs Robert Stone) From Ipswich take A1071 to Hadleigh. L at 1st roundabout and then 1st R to Chattisham. ½m on L. 5 acres with small lake, ornamental vegetable garden, maple walk, herbaceous borders, roses, iris, shrubs and trees both old and new; woodland walk and river garden. TEAS. *Adm £2 Chd free. Sun June 15 (2-6)*

Western House (Mr & Mrs Marshall) Cavendish. On the A1092 between Clare and Long Melford in village of Cavendish. Signposted 'Full of Beans B & B', garden to the rear. Very pretty rambling cottage. 1-acre garden divided into three sections. It has shrubs and herbaceous plants, a small herb garden. *Adm £2 Chd free. Sun July 13 (2-6)*

The White House ⟨&⟩ (Mrs Perina Fordham) Clare. Situated in Nethergate St, opp the Clare Hotel. Medium sized garden planted liberally with spring bulbs surrounded by trees and bordering R Stour. TEAS. *Adm £2 Chd free. Sun April 13 (2-6)*

¶**Windmill Cottage** ⟨✗⟩⟨❀⟩ (Mr & Mrs G A Cox) Capel St Mary. Approx 3m S of Ipswich. Turn off at Capel St Mary. At far end of village on R after 1.2m. ½-acre plantsman's cottage style garden. Island beds, pergolas with clematis and other climbers. Many trees and shrubs, iris bed, ponds and vegetable area. TEAS. *Adm £2 Chd free. Suns May 25, June 15 (2-6)*

Woottens ⟨&⟩⟨✗⟩⟨❀⟩ (M Loftus) Blackheath Rd. Woottens is situated between A12 and B1123 follow signposts to Wenhaston. Woottens is a small romantic garden with attached plantsman nursery, in all about 1-acre; scented leafed pelargoniums, violas, cranesbills, lilies, salvias, penstemons primulas, etc. Featured in Gardens Illustrated and RHS Journal. *Adm £1.50 OAPs 50p Chd 20p. Weds May to Sept (9.30-3)*

Wyken Hall ⟨&⟩⟨❀⟩ (Sir Kenneth and Lady Carlisle) Stanton, 9m NE from Bury St Edmunds along A143. Follow signs to Wyken vineyards on A143 between Ixworth and Stanton. 4-acre garden much developed recently; with knot and herb gardens; old-fashioned rose garden; wild garden; nuttery, gazebo and maze, herbaceous borders and old orchard. Woodland walk, vineyard. TEAS. *Adm £2 OAPs £1.50 Chd free. Sat June 7 (10-6)*

SYMBOLS USED IN THIS BOOK (See also Page 17)

‡   Following a garden name in the Dates of Opening list indicates that those gardens sharing the same symbol are nearby and open on the same day.

‡‡   Indicates a second series of nearby gardens open on the same day.

¶   Opening for the first time.

❀   Plants/produce for sale if available.

&   Gardens with at least the main features accessible by wheelchair.

✗   No dogs except guide dogs but otherwise dogs are usually admitted, provided they are kept on a lead. Dogs are not admitted to houses.

●   These gardens advertise their own dates in this publication although they do not nominate specific days for the NGS. Not all the money collected by these gardens comes to the NGS but they do make a guaranteed contribution.

■   These gardens nominate specific days for the NGS and advertise their own dates in this publication.

▲   These gardens open regularly to the public but they do not advertise their own dates in this publication. For further details, contact the garden directly.

Surrey

Hon County Organiser:	Lady Heald, Chilworth Manor, Guildford GU4 8NL Tel 01483 561414
Assistant Hon County Organisers:	Mrs J Foulsham, Vale End, Albury, Guildford GU5 9BE Tel 01483 202296
	Miss C Collins, Knightsmead, Rickman Hill Rd, Chipstead CR5 3LB Tel 01737 551694
	Mrs P Karslake, Oakfield Cottage, Guildford Road, Cranleigh GU6 8PF Tel 01483 273010
	Mrs D E Norman, Spring Cottage, Mannings Hill, Cranleigh GU6 8QN Tel 01483 272620
	Mrs J M Leader, Stuart Cottage, East Clandon GU4 7SF Tel 01483 222689
	Mrs J Pearcy, Far End, Pilgrims Way, Guildford GU4 8AD Tel 01483 563093
Hon County Treasurer:	Mr Ray Young, Paddock View, 144 Dorking Road, Chilworth, Guildford GU4 8RJ Tel 01483 569597

DATES OF OPENING

February 23 Sunday
9 Raymead Close, Fetcham

March 23 Sunday
Albury Park Garden, Albury

April 5 to 9 Saturday to Wednesday
Chilworth Manor, Guildford

April 6 Sunday
Street House, Thursley
Vann, Hambledon

April 7 to 12 Monday to Saturday
Vann, Hambledon

April 13 Sunday
Lodkin, Hascombe

April 16 Wednesday
Hookwood Farmhouse, West Horsley

April 19 Saturday
Woodside, Send

April 20 Sunday
Coverwood Lakes and Gardens, Ewhurst
Woodside, Send

April 23 Wednesday
The Coppice, Reigate
41 Shelvers Way, Tadworth

April 27 Sunday
Coverwood Lakes and Gardens, Ewhurst

April 30 Wednesday
Hookwood Farmhouse, West Horsley

May 3 to 7 Saturday to Wednesday
Chilworth Manor, Guildford

May 4 Sunday
Compton Lodge, Moor Park, Farnham
Coverwood Lakes and Gardens, Ewhurst
Feathercombe, nr Hambledon ‡‡
High Meadow, Churt ‡
Highlands, Leatherhead ‡‡

22 Knoll Road, Dorking ‡‡
Street House, Thursley ‡
Winkworth Arboretum, Hascombe ‡‡‡

May 5 Monday
Feathercombe, nr Hambledon ‡
High Meadow, Churt
Vann, Hambledon ‡
Walton Poor, Ranmore Common

May 6 to 11 Tuesday to Sunday
Vann, Hambledon

May 7 Wednesday
Highlands, Leatherhead ‡
22 Knoll Road, Dorking ‡

May 10 Saturday
Greathed Manor, Lingfield
The Old Croft, South Holmwood

May 11 Sunday
Coverwood Lakes and Gardens, Ewhurst
Dunsborough Park, Ripley
The Old Croft, South Holmwood
Polesden Lacey, Bookham
Postford House, Chilworth
Vann, Hambledon
Wintershall Manor, Bramley

May 14 Wednesday
Hookwood Farmhouse, West Horsley
Unicorns, Farnham

May 18 Sunday
Compton Lodge, Moor Park, Farnham
Coverwood Lakes and Gardens, Ewhurst
Montfleury, Virginia Water ‡‡
Postford House, Chilworth ‡
Snowdenham House, Bramley ‡
Stonywood, Haslemere
87 Upland Road, Sutton
Westbourn, Virginia Water ‡
Windlesham Park, nr Bagshot

May 21 Wednesday
Brook Lodge Farm Cottage, Blackbrook

May 24 Saturday

Crosswater Farm, Churt
Merrist Wood, Worplesdon
Vann, Hambledon

May 25 Sunday
Copt Hill Shaw, Kingswood, Tadworth
Coverwood Lakes and Gardens, Ewhurst
Crosswater Farm, Churt
Feathercombe, nr Hambledon ‡
Halnacker Hill, Bowlhead Green
Loseley Park, Guildford
Merrist Wood, Worplesdon
Munstead Wood, nr Godalming ‡

May 26 Monday
Brockhurst, Chiddingfold
Crosswater Farm, Churt
Feathercombe, nr Hambledon
Merrist Wood, Worplesdon

May 28 Wednesday
Coverwood Lakes and Gardens, Ewhurst
Hookwood Farmhouse, West Horsley

June 1 Sunday
Alderbrook, Cranleigh
Claremont Landscape Garden, Esher ‡‡
The Copse Lodge, Burgh Heath ‡
Dovecote, Cobham ‡‡
Ridings, 56 Cross Road, Tadworth

June 1 to 7 Sunday to Saturday
Vann, Hambledon

June 4 Wednesday
Rise Top Cottage, Mayford, Woking
Unicorns, Farnham

June 7 Saturday
Vann, Hambledon

June 8 Sunday
Hatchlands Park, East Clandon
Lodkin, Hascombe
Ridings, 56 Cross Road, Tadworth
Street House, Thursley
Walton Poor, Ranmore Common
Wintershall Manor, Bramley

June 11 Wednesday
Chilworth Manor, Guildford ‡
Hookwood Farmhouse, West
  Horsley
Sutton Place, Guildford ‡
Walton Poor, Ranmore Common
**June 14 to 18 Saturday to
Wednesday**
Chilworth Manor, Guildford
June 15 Sunday
Brook Lodge Farm Cottage,
  Blackbrook ‡‡
Halnacker Hill, Bowlhead Green
Haslehurst, Haslemere ‡
High Hazard, Blackheath
Moleshill House, Cobham
Rickleden, Maddox Lane, Bookham
Spring Cottage, Cranleigh
6 Upper Rose Hill, Dorking ‡‡
Yew Tree Cottage, Haslemere ‡
June 18 Wednesday
Brook Lodge Farm Cottage,
  Blackbrook
RHS Garden, Wisley
Spring Cottage, Cranleigh
June 19 Thursday
Moleshill House, Cobham
June 21 Saturday
Thanescroft, Shamley Green
June 22 Sunday
Brockhurst, Chiddingfold
Chinthurst Lodge, Wonersh ‡‡
Four Aces, Pirbright ‡
Merrist Wood, Worplesdon ‡
South Park, Blechingley
Thanescroft, Shamley Green ‡‡
Vale End, Albury ‡‡
June 23 Monday
Four Aces, Pirbright
67 Shepherds Lane, Guildford
June 25 Wednesday
The Coppice, Reigate
Hookwood Farmhouse, West
  Horsley
41 Shelvers Way, Tadworth
June 28 Saturday
High Meadow, Churt
South Park Farm, South Godstone
June 29 Sunday
Addlestone Gardens
Four Aces, Pirbright
High Meadow, Churt
Olivers, Church Road,
  Hascombe
South Park Farm, South Godstone
June 30 Monday
Four Aces, Pirbright
South Park Farm, South Godstone
July 2 Wednesday
67 Shepherds Lane, Guildford
July 5 Saturday
Little Mynthurst Farm, Norwood
  Hill
Tanyard Farmhouse, Horley

**July 6 to 12 Sunday to
Saturday**
Vann, Hambledon
July 6 Sunday
Little Mynthurst Farm, Norwood
  Hill
Loseley Park, Guildford
Rickleden, Maddox Lane,
  Bookham
Tanyard Farmhouse, Horley
July 9 Wednesday
Chilworth Manor, Guildford
**July 12 to 16 Saturday to
Wednesday**
Chilworth Manor, Guildford
July 13 Sunday
Ashcombe Cottage, Ranmore
  Common
Brockhurst, Chiddingfold
41 Shelvers Way, Tadworth
July 16 Wednesday
41 Shelvers Way, Tadworth
67 Shepherds Lane, Guildford
July 20 Sunday
Brook Lodge Farm Cottage,
  Blackbrook
The Copse Lodge, Burgh Heath
Munstead Wood, nr Godalming
July 23 Wednesday
Brook Lodge Farm Cottage,
  Blackbrook
York Road Gardens, Cheam
July 26 Saturday
Stuart Cottage, East Clandon
Street House, Thursley
July 27 Sunday
47 Harvest Road, Englefield Green
73 Ottways Lane, Ashtead
Stuart Cottage, East Clandon ‡
Vale End, Albury ‡
York Road Gardens, Cheam
July 30 Wednesday
73 Ottways Lane, Ashtead ‡
9 Raymead Close, Fetcham ‡
August 2 Saturday
South Cheam Gardens
August 3 Sunday
Odstock, Bletchingley
South Cheam Gardens
**August 9 to 13 Saturday to
Wednesday**
Chilworth Manor, Guildford
August 10 Sunday
105 Fairway, Chertsey
47 Harvest Road, Englefield Green
August 14 Thursday
Dunsborough Park, Ripley
RHS Garden, Wisley
August 16 Saturday
The Old Croft, South Holmwood
August 17 Sunday
Brook Lodge Farm Cottage,
  Blackbrook ‡
The Old Croft, South Holmwood ‡

August 20 Wednesday
Brook Lodge Farm Cottage,
  Blackbrook
August 24 Sunday
Haslehurst, Haslemere
High Meadow, Churt ‡
Street House, Thursley ‡
August 25 Monday
High Meadow, Churt
August 31 Sunday
Brook Lodge Farm Cottage,
  Blackbrook
September 7 Sunday
Valedown, nr Woking
September 14 Sunday
6 Upper Rose Hill, Dorking
September 21 Sunday
Claremont Landscape Garden,
  Esher
September 28 Sunday
Munstead Wood, nr Godalming
October 1 Wednesday
9 Raymead Close, Fetcham
October 5 Sunday
Albury Park Garden, Albury
October 12 Sunday
Walton Poor, Ranmore Common
Winkworth Arboretum, Hascombe
October 15 Wednesday
The Old Croft, South Holmwood
October 26 Sunday
Coverwood Lakes and Gardens,
  Ewhurst
January 1 1998 Thursday
Claremont Landscape Garden,
  Esher

Regular openings
For details see garden description

Crosswater Farm, Churt
Ramster, Chiddingfold
Titsey Place Gardens
Walton Poor

By appointment only
*For telephone numbers and other
details see garden descriptions.
Private visits welcomed*

Brookwell, Bramley
Coverwood Lakes and Gardens,
  Ewhurst
Chauffeur's Flat, Tandridge
Dunsborough Park, Ripley
Knightsmead, Chipstead
Lansdowne House, West Ewell, nr
  Epsom
Pinewood House, Heath House
  Road, Woking

DESCRIPTIONS OF GARDENS

Addlestone Gardens ✿✿❀ Situated within ½m of each other, 5m NE of Woking off B3121. From M25 junction 11 take A320 signposted Woking then L into B3121 or A317 signposted Weybridge and R into B3121 and follow yellow signs. Maps available at each garden. Light snacks and TEAS in aid of St Paul's Church Roof Fund. *Combined adm £2 Chd free. Sun June 29 (11-5)*

Charton (Daphne & John Clarke-Williams) Ongar Hill. ⅓-acre upward sloping mature garden, with trees, shrubs, climbing plants, hardy perennials and sink gardens, pond and vegetable garden. Extensive use of home-made compost

106 Liberty Lane (Mrs Ann Masters) 100' × 30' suburban garden belonging to self confessed 'plantaholic' imaginatively laid out containing an interesting mix of shrubs, grasses, hardy perennials, climbers and hardy geraniums, a pond and some unusual plants. Very interested in propagation

St Keverne (Lynne & Julian Clarke-Willams) ⅓-acre garden created by owners. Inspired use of companion planting. Hardy perennials - specialising in geraniums and alliums; many trees, shrubs and roses. Gravel and pots a feature

Albury Park Garden ✿✿ (Trustees of Albury Estate) Albury 5m SE of Guildford. From A25 take A248 towards Albury for ¼m, then L up New Rd, entrance to Albury Park immediately on L. 14-acre pleasure grounds laid out in 1670s by John Evelyn for Henry Howard, later 6th Duke of Norfolk. ¼m terraces, fine collection of trees, lake and river. The gardens of Albury Park Mansion also open (by kind permission of Country Houses Association Ltd). TEAS. *Adm £1.50 Chd 50p. Suns March 23, Oct 5 (2-5)*

Alderbrook (Mr & Mrs P Van den Bergh) Smithwood Common. Cranleigh. A281 from Guildford turn L 1m out of Bramley. Turn R at roundabout then immediately L. Drive on L just beyond far end of Smithwood Common. Approx 8 acres of woodland walks with azaleas and rhododendrons. Terraces with magnificent views to S Downs. TEA. *Adm £1.50 Chd free. Sun June 1 (2-6)*

¶**Ashcombe Cottage** ✿✿❀ (Mrs B Davis) Ranmore Common. 2m NW of Dorking. From Dorking turn R at the top of Ranmore Hill signed Bookham, Westhumble. Pass Parish Church. In ½m go straight ahead down private drive. Cottage is at end of lane. ¾-acre garden of old game-keeper's cottage. Mixed beds of shrubs, perennials and annuals. Many unusual plants. Interesting water feature with view over valley. Fruit trees and vegetable garden. Greenhouse. Small nursery selling hardy perennial plants. TEAS. *Adm £1.50 Chd free. Sun 13 July (10-5). Private visits welcome, please* Tel 01306 881599

Brockhurst ❀ (Prof & Mrs C F Phelps) Chiddingfold. On the Green at Chiddingfold A283. Entrance through small gate RH-side of Manor House. Parking around Village Green. A series of gardens, tucked behind the village green. An old walled cottage border leading into 2½ acres of lawns, shrubs, walkways, flower beds and watergarden. Within the garden created over the last 11 yrs by the present owners are many species and foliage plants, incl lilies and clematis;

fruit and vegetable garden. TEAS in aid of charities. *Adm £2 Chd 25p. Mon May 26, Suns June 22, July 13 (2-5). Private visits welcome for parties of 10 and over April, May, June, July, Aug, please* Tel 01428 683092

Brook Lodge Farm Cottage ✿✿❀ (Mrs Basil Kingham) Blackbrook, 3m S of Dorking. Take L-hand turning for Blackbrook off A24, 1m S of Dorking 500yds past Plough Inn. 3½-acre 50-yr-old plantsman's garden made by present owner. Collection of hardy and tender plants, especially flowering shrubs, herbaceous, shrub roses, climbers, conifers and bulbs. Emphasis on foliage and plant association. Large kitchen garden and fruit cage, attractive herb garden and large heated greenhouse leading to smaller gardener's cottage garden. Featured in various magazines. TEAS. *Adm £2 Chd free (Share to St Catherine's Hospice, Crawley®). Weds May 21, June 18, July 23, Aug 20, Suns June 15, July 20, Aug 17, 31 (2-5)*

Brookwell ✿✿❀ (Mr & Mrs P R Styles) 1½m S of Bramley on A281; turn R into private road-bridleway in Birtley Green. 2-acre garden with lake and woodland. Mixed borders, sunken garden, and knot garden planted with scented flowers and herbs. Collection of old roses, fruit tunnel and vegetable garden; greenhouses and conservatory. *Adm £1.50 Chd 25p. Private visits welcome by appointment. June, July and September, please* Tel 01483 893423 *(evenings)*

Chauffeur's Flat ✿ (Mr & Mrs Richins) Tandridge. Tandridge Lane lies 1m W of Oxted off the A25. Drive adjacent to church ½m from A25. Pass Lodge to your R. Fork R. Continue through to Courtyard. Surprise yourself with this 1 acre eclectic, romantic, artists' garden with superb views. Only for the surefooted. *Adm £1.50 Chd 25p. Private visits welcome Sat to Fri May 24 to 30, Mon to Sun June 23 to 29 please* Tel 01883 715937 *between 7-9.30am or 7-9.30pm*

Chilworth Manor ✿✿ (Lady Heald) 3½m SE of Guildford. From A248, in centre of Chilworth village, turn up Blacksmith Lane. House C17 with C18 wing on site of C11 monastery recorded in Domesday Book; stewponds in garden date from monastic period. Garden laid out in C17; C18 walled garden added by Sarah, Duchess of Marlborough; spring flowers; flowering shrubs; newly designed herbaceous border. Flower decorations in house (Sats, Suns) May; Bookham Flower Arrangement Group, June; Walton & Weybridge Flower Club, July; Merrow Floral Club. Free car park in attractive surroundings open from 12.30 for picnicking. TEAS (Sat, Sun, only). *Adm to garden £2 Chd free. Adm to house £1 Sat & Sun only (Share to Marie Curie Foundation Guildford Branch®); Open Sats to Weds April 5 to 9, May 3 to 7, June 14 to 18, July 12 to 16, Aug 9 to 13 (2-6). Evening Adm £2.50 (glass of wine) Weds June 11, July 9 (6-8) also private visits welcome, please* Tel 01483 561414

Chinthurst Lodge ✿✿❀ (Mr & Mrs M R Goodridge) Wonersh. 4m S Guildford, A281 Guildford-Horsham. At Shalford turn E onto B2128 towards Wonersh. Just after Wonersh rd sign, before village, garden on R. 1-acre yr-round garden, herbaceous borders, white garden, large variety specimen trees and shrubs; kitchen garden; fruit cage; two wells; ornamental pond. TEAS. *Adm £1.50 Chd free (Share to Guildford Branch Arthritis & Rheumatism Council®). Sun June 22 (12-6)*

▲**Claremont Landscape Garden** ప (The National Trust) 1m SE of Esher; on E side of A307 (No access from A3 by-pass). Station: Esher. Bus GL 415, alight at entrance gates. One of the earliest surviving English landscape gardens; begun by Vanbrugh and Bridgeman before 1720; extended and naturalized by Kent; lake; island with pavilion; grotto and turf amphitheatre; viewpoints and avenues. TEAS 11-5. *Adm £3 Chd £1.50. For NGS Suns June 1, Sept 21 (10-7). 1998 Thurs Jan 1 (1-4), no teas but dogs on leads*

Compton Lodge ⚘❀ (Mr & Mrs K J Kent) Farnham. 2m E of Farnham along A31 Hogs Back (new rd) follow signs Runfold. Turn S down Crooksbury Rd at Barfield School signposted Milford & Elstead. 1m on R Compton Way, Compton Lodge 2nd house on R. 1¼-acre S-facing sloping mixed garden. Mature rhododendrons, heather bed, azaleas. TEAS. *Adm £1.50 Chd 50p. Suns May 4, 18 (11-5)*

Cooksbridge, Fernhurst (See Sussex)

The Coppice ❀ (Mr & Mrs Bob Bushby) Reigate. M25 to junction 8. A217 (direction Reigate) down Reigate Hill, immediately before level Xing turn R into Somers Rd cont as Manor Rd. At very end turn R into Coppice Lane. Please park carefully. 'The Coppice' approx 200yds on L. Partly suitable wheelchairs. 6½ acres redeveloped in last 9yrs. Mixed borders with interesting and unusual plants giving yr-round interest. Pergola, 2 large ornamental ponds. Thousands of fritillarias and spring bulbs, April. Cream TEAS. *Adm £1.50 Chd 50p (Share to Winged Fellowship®). Weds April 23; June 25 (2-5)*

The Copse Lodge ప⚘❀ (Marian & Eddie Wallbank) Burgh Heath. 6m S of Sutton on A217 dual carriageway. Heathside Hotel car park 200yds on L from traffic lights at junction A217 with Reigate Rd. Please park in overflow car park at rear of hotel (our thanks to Heathside Hotel). Garden 100yds on L from hotel. ½-acre architectural garden with unusual planting featuring yuccas, palms and grasses; large tender specimens in pots; Japanese garden with bamboos, acers and Tea House; ornamental pond with waterfalls, rock garden, conservatory with specimen palms. Designed, built and maintained by owners. TEAS. *Adm £1.50 Chd free. Suns June 1, July 20 (10-5)*

Copt Hill Shaw ప⚘❀ (Mr & Mrs M Barlow) Alcocks Lane, Kingswood. 6m S of Sutton off the A217. 1st turn on L after Burgh Heath traffic lights, Waterhouse Lane, signposted Kingswood Station and Coulsdon. Alcocks Lane 1st on L. Parking in Furze Hill, courtesy of Legal and General. A formal garden of 1½ acres laid out in 1906. Fine yew hedges and topiary with azaleas, mature trees and rhododendrons and pergola of old roses and clematis, spring bulbs, geraniums, alliums, small collection of unusual plants. Fruit and vegetable garden. TEAS. *Adm £1.50 Chd free (Share to National Asthma Campaign®). Sun May 25 (2-5.30)*

●**Coverwood Lakes and Gardens** ప⚘❀ (Mr & Mrs C G Metson) Peaslake Rd, Ewhurst. 7m SW of Dorking.

From A25 follow signs for Peaslake; garden ½m beyond Peaslake. Landscaped water, bog garden and cottage gardens in lovely setting between Holmbury Hill and Pitch Hill; rhododendrons, azaleas, primulas, fine trees. 3½-acre Arboretum planted March 1990. Featured in NGS video 1. Marked trail through working farm to see herd of pedigree Poll Hereford cattle and flock of sheep. (Mr & Mrs Nigel Metson). Home-made TEAS. *Adm £2.50 Chd £1 car park and Chd under 5 free (Share to NGS®). Suns April 20, 27, May 4, 11, 18, 25; Wed May 28 (2-6); Sun Oct 26 hot soup and sandwiches (11-4.30). Also private visits welcome, please* Tel 01306 731103/1

■ **Crosswater Farm** ప⚘❀ (Mr & Mrs E G Millais) Churt. Farnham and Haslemere 6m, from A287 turn E into Jumps Road ½m N of Churt village centre. After ¼m turn acute L into Crosswater Lane and follow signs for Millais Nurseries. 6-acre woodland garden surrounded by NT heathland. Plantsman's collection of rhododendrons and azaleas including many rare species collected in the Himalayas, and hybrids raised by the owners. Ponds, stream and companion plantings. Plants for sale from specialist Rhododendron nursery. TEAS on NGS days only. *Adm £1.50 Chd free. Daily May 1 to June 7. For NGS Sat, Sun, Mon May 24, 25, 26 (10-5) + 25% other receipts. Private parties welcome, please* Tel 01252 792698

Dovecote ⚘❀ (Mr & Mrs R Stanley) Cobham. Off A307 Esher to Cobham rd near A3 bridge. Turn R from Cobham, L from Esher into Fairmile Lane. Then 4th L into Green Lane. ⅓-acre plot surrounding extended bothy. Secluded plant lovers yr-round garden with natural boundaries of mature trees, shrubs and hedges developed by present owners to incl many hardy plants on light sandy soil. TEA. *Adm £1.50 Chd free. Sun June 1 (10.30-5.30)*

■ **Dunsborough Park** ⚘❀ (Baron & Baroness Sweerts De Landas Wyborgh) Ripley. Entrance across Ripley Green. Bus GL 715 alight Ripley village. Extensive walled gardens redesigned by Penelope Hobhouse; herbaceous borders; 70ft gingko hedge, ancient mulberry tree, water garden. Victorian wooden glasshouses (under restoration). Part suitable for wheelchairs. TEAS. *Adm £2.50 Chd £1.25. Wed June 18, Suns June 29, July 20, Aug 3, Sept 21 (2-6). For NGS Sun May 11, Thurs Aug 14 (2-6)*

The Elms Kingston-on-Thames (see London)

¶**105 Fairway** ⚘❀ (Tony Keating) Chertsey. Junction 11 M25 to Chertsey. Off free Prae Rd. Opp. RC School. Sub-tropical garden containing palms, bananas, tree ferns, cannas, cacti, hardy exotics, passion flowers in a front and rear garden of semi-detached house. TEA. *Adm £1 Chd 50p. Sun Aug 10 (11-5)*

The Royal Horticultural Society's Garden at Wisley
Exclusive evening openings in aid of the National Gardens Scheme on the occasion of its 70th anniversary
Wednesday 18th June & Thursday 14th August
6.30-9pm
See page 18.

Feathercombe ✿ (Wieler & Campbell families) Hambledon, S of Godalming. 2m from Milford Station off Hambledon Rd, between Hydestile Xrds and Merry Harriers. 12-acre garden of mature rhododendrons, azaleas, shrubs and topiary. Fine views of Blackdown, Hindhead and Hogs Back. House by Ernest Newton. Garden designed and made from 1910 by Surrey author and journalist Eric Parker and his wife Ruth (neé Messel) of Nymans. Now maintained by his grandchildren. *Adm £1.50 Chd 10p (Share to St Peter's Church, Hambledon®). Suns, Mons May 4, 5; 25, 26 (2-6)*

Four Aces ✗✿ (Mr & Mrs R V St John Wright) 5m NW of Guildford on A322 Bagshot Road. Just before Brookwood arch, directly opp West Hill Golf Club, turn L into Cemetery Pales. After ⁹⁄₁₀m turn sharp L after village sign into Chapel Lane. Four Aces is 5th house on R. Overflow parking in village green car park, 250yds. Approx ²⁄₃-acre 12yr-old garden with 2 ponds, terraces with pergolas, loggias and pots; mixed borders with shrubs, perennials, new herb garden and old roses planted in informal cottage garden style. Appeared in 'BBC Gardeners' World' Magazine and 'Country Homes'. TEAS. *Adm £1.50 Chd 50p. Suns June 22, 29; Mons June 23, 30 (11-5). Private visits welcome May to July, please* **Tel 01483 476226**

Greathed Manor ✗ (Country Houses Association) Lingfield. 2½m SE of Lingfield, follow the B2028, Lingfield/Edenbridge rd to the Plough Inn, Dormansland and take the private rd, Ford Manor Rd opp and follow the signs for about 1m to Greathed Manor (not open) and Gardens. Parkland with sunken garden. Stepped terraces and flower beds surround an oval pool set in decorative paving which is enclosed by a balustraded sandstone wall attributed to Harold Peto early this century. 4 acres of attractive garden set in parkland with rhododendrons, azaleas, specimen trees, and many other spring flowers. TEAS. *Adm £2.50 Chd free (Share to Country Houses Association®). Sat May 10 (2-5)*

Hall Grange, Croydon (see London)

Halnacker Hill ✗✿ (Mr & Mrs C N Daubeny) Bowlhead Green. From A3 southbound turn L signposted Bowlhead Green (opp Thursley exit); at Xrds turn R and go 0.7m. From A286 turn off just S of Brook into Park Lane; after 2m turn R signposted Bowlhead Green. 1-acre terraced cottage garden designed as series of small informal plantsman's gardens maintained by the owners. Large variety of trees, shrubs, perennials, old roses and many tender and less common plants. 5 acres of woodland with walks and fine views. TEAS. *Adm £1.50 Chd free (Share to Thursley Horticultural Society©). Suns May 25, June 15 (2-6)*

47 Harvest Road ✗ (Mr Tony Faulkner) Englefield Green. Directly opp Royal Holloway College on A30. Nearest BR station is Egham. Car parking facilities are a short walk away in Victoria Street. Small cottage garden, shrubs, mixed borders and ornamental trees; gazebo and small pond. TEAS. *Adm £1 Chd free. Suns July 27, August 10 (2-6)*

Haslehurst ✗✿ (Mrs W H Whitbread) Bunch Lane, Haslemere. Turn off High St into Church Lane, leave church on L, carry on to T-junction, turn R, Hazelhurst, 2nd on L. 2½ acres; lawns, superb trees, rhododendrons, azaleas, various shrubs; paved rose garden, double herbaceous border; woodland rockery & waterfall. C15 Barn. *June TEA. Adm £1.50 Chd 50p (Share to Queen Mary's Clothing Guild®). Suns June 15 (also* **Yew Tree Cottage**), *Aug 24 (2.15-6). Private visits welcome, please* **Tel 01428 643471**

▲**Hatchlands Park** ♿✗ (The National Trust) Situated near East Clandon, off A246. If using A3 from London direction, follow signposts to Ripley to join A247 and proceed via West Clandon to A246. If coming from Guildford take A25 and then A246 towards Leatherhead at West Clandon. The garden and park were designed by Repton in 1800 and there are 3 newly restored walks in the park. On the S side of the house is a small parterre designed by Gertrude Jekyll in 1913. This has been restored to Jekyll's original design with May/June flowering. The house is open to the public on this day. TEA. *Adm £1.50 Chd 75p gardens only. For NGS Sun June 8 (11.30-5.30)*

High Hazard ♿✿ (Mr & Mrs P C Venning) Blackheath, Guildford. 4½m SE of Guildford from A281 Guildford to Horsham at Shalford turn E on B2128 towards Wonersh, at entry to Wonersh, turn L into Blackheath Lane, straight on at Xrds in village. Access to garden is 300yds on R. Park in Heath car park a further 150yds up lane. (No access to front of house which faces the cricket ground in use). ½-acre garden designed and laid out by the present owners. Herbaceous and mixed borders containing interesting and some unusual herbaceous perennial plants, a large number of which are for sale on the premises. TEAS. *Adm £1.50 Chd free (Share to St Joseph's Centre for Addiction, Holy Cross Hospital, Haslemere®). Sun June 15 (2-6)*

High Meadow ✗✿ (Mr & Mrs J Humphries) Tilford Rd, Churt. From Hindhead A3 Xrds take A287 signposted Farnham. After ½m take R fork signposted Tilford. 1.9m to Avalon PYO farm. Park here, short walk to garden. Disabled visitors park on grass verge in drive. Approx 1 acre maintained by owners. Large collection of rare and unusual plants attractively planted to provide all-year interest; large collection of old and modern shrub roses and David Austin English Roses; pergola walk, sunken garden with pond, colour co-ordinated borders, alpines in troughs; featured in Channel 4 Garden Party. TEAS. *Adm £2 Chd free (Share to G.U.T.S. at Royal Surrey County Hospital). Suns, Mons May 4, 5; June 29; Aug 24, 25 (11-4). Evening Sat June 28 (6-9) Adm £3 incl wine and snacks. Groups welcome, please* **Tel 01428 606129**

Highlands ✗✿ (Mr & Mrs R B McDaniel) Givons Grove, Leatherhead. From Leatherhead By-pass (A24) at roundabout by Texaco garage 1m S of Leatherhead turn into Givons Grove and proceed up hill (The Downs) for ¾m, ignoring side turnings. Highlands is on the R. Chalk garden of 1 acre on a steep slope. Large rock garden, alpine house and sinks; mixed borders; orchard; pond; fruit and vegetable garden. Fine views over Mole Valley. TEAS in aid of Cystic Fibrosis. *Adm £1.50 Chd free. Sun, Wed May 4, 7 (2-6)*

Hookwood Farmhouse &&& (Eric & Sarah Mason) West Horsley. From Guildford turn R into Staple Lane (signposted Shere). At top turn L then first L into Shere Rd and first L into Fullers Fm Rd. From Leatherhead turn L into Greendene, after approx 2.5 miles turn R into Shere Rd then first L. The 1.5 acre garden made by the owners is on S facing slope of N Downs. Wide range of plants and large collection of hardy Geraniums. Walled garden in old farmyard. *Adm £1.50 Chd free. Weds April 16, 30, May 14, 28, June 11, 25 (1-5). Private visits April-July, please* **Tel 01483 284760**

Knightsmead &&& (Mrs Jones & Miss Collins) Rickman Hill Rd, Chipstead. From A23 in Coulsdon turn W onto B2032. Through traffic lights, L fork into Portnalls Rd. Top of hill at Xrds, turn R into Holymead Rd. R into Lissoms Rd. R into Bouverie Rd. ½-acre plantsman's garden, designed and maintained by owners. Wide variety of shrubs and perennials for yr-round interest; hellebores, spring bulbs and woodland plants; pond; scented roses; raised alpine and peat beds, clematis, hostas, hardy geraniums etc. *Adm £1.50 Chd 50p. Private visits welcome July onwards, please* **Tel 01737 551694**

22 Knoll Road &&& (David & Anne Drummond) Dorking. From one way system after May's Garage turn L up the Horsham rd (A2003 which runs to N Holmwood roundabout A24). Knoll Road is on R just beyond The Bush Inn. ⅓-acre town garden with many interesting and unusual plants with notes available. Mixed borders, raised beds, sinks, mini-meadow and peat bed, fern alley and some fruit and vegetables, a surprising front garden; conservatory. (Mostly suitable for wheelchairs if driven to front door.) TEAS in aid of Amnesty. *Adm £1 Chd free. Sun, Wed May 4, 7 (10.30-5.30). Private visits welcome, please* **Tel 01306 883280**

Lansdowne House && (Mr & Mrs J Lucas) West Ewell. Between Chessington and Ewell on the B2200 opposite Hook Rd Arena. Parking and entrance in Lansdowne Rd. Lansdowne House is on corner of Chessington Rd and Lansdowne Rd; small garden (0.18 acre) developed over past 10yrs by garden designer, lecturer, broadcaster and author John Lucas. Planted mainly with shrubs and small trees, the garden is divided into rooms of various styles and atmospheres. A garden of texture with interesting focal points, for the 'green' garden lover. *Adm £1 Chd 50p. By appt groups of 10 to 35 during June, please* **Tel 0181 393 9946**

Little Lodge, Thames Ditton (see London)

Little Mynthurst Farm &&& (Mr & Mrs G Chilton) Norwood Hill. Between Leigh (2m) and Charlwood (3m); from Reigate take A217 to Horley; after 2m turn R just after river bridge at Sidlowbridge; 1st R signed Dean Oak Lane; then L at T junction. 12- acre garden; walled, old-fashioned roses, herbaceous borders and shrubs around old farm house (not open), rose beds and lake setting; Tudor courtyard and orchard; bird and butterfly garden; rose walk. Kitchen garden with greenhouses and secret garden. TEAS in aid of Leigh and District Cottage Garden Society per cent to NGS. *Adm £2 Chd free. Sat, Sun July*

5, 6 (12-5). Coach parties welcome on NGS days only by prior arrangement please contact Head Gardener Mark Dobell **Tel 01293 862639 or 863318**

Lodkin ※ (Mr & Mrs W N Bolt) Lodkin Hill, Hascombe, 3m S of Godalming. Just off B2130 Godalming-Cranleigh, on outskirts of Hascombe; take narrow lane off signposted Thorncombe Street. Country garden of 5½ acres incl woodland, stream, 4 Victorian greenhouses rebuilt to produce fruit, flowers and vegetables. Much of the old cast staging etc has been retained. In parts suitable for wheel chairs. TEAS. *Adm £1.50 Chd 20p. Suns April 13, June 8 (2-6). Sun Nov 2 (2-4) Adm £1 Chd free (No TEAS). Private parties welcome, please* **Tel 01483 208 323**

▲¶**Loseley Park** &&& (Mr & Mrs M G More-Molyneux) Guildford. Leave A3 at Compton, S of Guildford, on B3000 for 2m. Signposted. Guildford Station 2m, Godalming Station 3m. 2½-acre walled garden transformed from an organic vegetable garden to a formal garden. Features a rose garden with over 1,000 bushes, mainly old-fashioned varieties. Herb garden with sections for culinary, medicinal, ornamental and dyeing. Also a flower garden. Moat walk, terrace, herbaceous borders and ancient wisteria. TEAS. *Adm £2 Chd £1. For NGS Suns May 25, July 6 (1-5)*

▲**Merrist Wood College** &&& Worplesdon 4m NW of Guildford. 40 acres of amenity areas, landscape demonstration gardens, 16 acres nursery stock, house a listed building (Norman Shaw 1877). Only reception hall open. TEAS. Rare plants for sale % to NGS. *Adm by donation. For NGS Sat, Sun, Mon, May 24, 25, 26, June 22 (10-6) with Surrey Horticultural Federation Summer Flower Show June 22 only. Parties welcome, please* **Tel 01483 232424**

Moleshill House &&& (Mr & Mrs M Snell) Cobham. House is on A307 Esher to Cobham Rd next to free car park by A3 bridge. Flower arranger's walled romantic garden. Topiary and garlanded cisterns around house; circular lawn surrounded by informal borders; gravel bed; dovecote; bee alcoves; sorbus lutescens avenue, bog garden, paving and pots. TEAS. *Adm £1.50 Chd free. Sun June 15 (2.30-5.30). Thurs June 19 (6.30-8.30) Adm £3 incl wine and light refreshment*

Montfleury &&& (Cdr & Mrs Innes Hamilton) Christchurch Rd, Virginia Water. From A30 at Virginia Water, opp Wheatsheaf Restaurant, turn down B389. Over roundabout. Last house on R before village. English Tourist Board award winner's new spring, garden interesting plant sales. Unlimited parking. TEA. *Adm £1 Chd 10p. Sun May 18 (2-6)*

Munstead Wood &&& (Sir Robert & Lady Clark) nr Godalming. Take B2130 Brighton Rd out of Godalming towards Horsham. After 1m church on R, Heath Lane just thereafter on L. 400yds on R is entrance to Munstead Wood. Parking on L of Heath Lane. 10 acres of rhododendrons, azaleas, woods and shrub and flower beds. Home until 1931 of Gertrude Jekyll and recently restored to her plans. The architect for the house (not open) was Edwin Lutyens. TEAS. *Adm £2 OAPs £1 Chd free (Share to Godalming Musueum Trust®). Suns May 25, July 20, Sept 28 (2-6)*

Odstock &✿❀ (Mr & Mrs J F H Trott) Bletchingley. Between Godstone 2m and Redhill 3m on A25, at top of village nr Red Lion pub. Parking in village, no parking in Castle Square. ⅔ of an acre maintained by owners and developed for all-yr interest. Covered walk created by training old apple trees plus other climbers. Interesting variety of plants and shrubs with imaginative complementary and contrasting groupings of form and colour. Japanese features; dahlias. No dig, low maintenance vegetable garden. TEAS. Adm £1.50 Chd free (Share to St Mary's Church, Bletchingley®). Sun Aug 3 (1-5.30). (Disabled welcome – please telephone first **Tel 01883 743100)**

The Old Croft ❀ (David and Virginia Lardner-Burke) South Holmwood. 3m S of Dorking. From Dorking take A24 S for 3m. Turn L at sign to Leigh-Brockham into Mill Road. ¾m on L, 2 free car parks in NT Holmwood Common. Follow directional signs for 400yds along woodland walk. 5-acre parkland garden with lake, stream, ponds, woodland, wild and formal areas, herb garden, wide variety of specimen trees and shrubs; more new developments. Garden designed by owner. TEAS. *Adm £2 Chd free (Share to St Catherine's Hospice, Crawley®). Sats, Suns May 10, 11; Aug 16, 17 (2-6). Wed Oct 15 (11-4)*

Olivers ❀ (Mr & Mrs Charles Watson) Church Road, Hascombe. On B2130, Godalming to Cranleigh Road (Godalming 3m). Park by White Horse in Hascombe village. Olivers is 50yds up Church Rd, between public house and pond. 2½-acre informal country garden; wide variety, herbaceous borders, interesting trees, shrubs and perennials, some new development areas. See what can be done on 1 day a week! Beautiful village location by historic church. TEAS. *Adm £1.50 Chd free (Share to Hascombe Church Fabric Fund®). Sun June 29 (2-6)*

¶73 Ottways Lane &✿❀ (Mr & Mrs Peter Gray) Ashtead. From A24 Ashtead to Leatherhead rd turn into Ottways Lane just S of Ashtead Village or into Grange Rd at traffic lights N of M25 by Downsend School. Approx ⅓-acre. Large herbaceous border, shrubs and fuchsias. Patio with pergola, hanging baskets and troughs. TEAS in aid of Family Focus. *Adm £1.50 Chd free. Sun July 27 (11-6), Wed July 30 (2- 6)*

Pinewood House &✿ (Mr & Mrs J Van Zwanenberg) Heath House Rd. 3m Woking, 5m Guildford off A322 opp Brookwood Cemetery Wall. 4 acres. Walled garden and arboretum; water garden; bulbs in April. Interesting new house finished in Dec '86 with indoor plants. *Adm house & gardens £2. Private visits welcome for parties of 2-30 April to Oct, please* **Tel 01483 473241**

▲**Polesden Lacey** &✿❀ (The National Trust) Bookham, nr Dorking. 1½m S of Great Bookham off A246 Leatherhead-Guildford rd. 60 acres formal gardens; extensive grounds, walled rose garden, winter garden, lavender garden, iris garden, lawns; good views on landscape walks. Regency villa dating early 1820's, remodelled after 1906 by the Hon Mrs Ronald Greville, King George VI and Queen Elizabeth (now the Queen Mother) spent part of their honeymoon here. For wheelchair details **Tel 01372 458203**. Plants in aid of NT. Lunch and TEAS in licensed restaurant in grounds (11-5). *Adm garden and grounds*

£3, Chd £1.50; family ticket £7.50. For NGS garden only Sun May 11 (11-6)

Postford House &✿ (Mrs R Litler-Jones) Chilworth. 4m SE Guildford Route A248 Bus LC 425 Guildford-Dorking alight nr entrance. 25 acres woodland; bog garden; stream; rose garden; vegetable garden; rhododendrons, azaleas and shrubs; swimming pool open. Home-made TEAS. *Adm £2 Chd free. Suns May 11, 18 (2-6). Private visits welcome, please* **Tel 01483 202657**

●**Ramster** &✿ (Mr & Mrs Paul Gunn) Chiddingfold. On A283, 1½m S of Chiddingfold; large iron gates on R. Mature 20-acre woodland garden of exceptional interest with lakes, ponds and woodland walks. Laid out by Gauntlett Nurseries of Chiddingfold in early 1900s. Fine rhododendrons, azaleas, camellias, magnolias, trees and shrubs. Picnic area. Ramster Embroidery Exhibition May 10-26. TEAS daily in May. *Adm £2.50 Chd under 16 free (Share to NGS®). Daily from April 19 to July 20 (11-5.30). Parties welcome, please* **Tel 01428 644422**

¶9 Raymead Close ✿ (Mrs Susan Kirkby) Fetcham. Take A245 out of Cobham, through Stoke D'Abernon on Cobham rd over motorway, through Fetcham, then L at Raymead Way, then 2nd L. From B2122 Gt Bookham to Leatherhead rd, turn L into Cobham Rd, R into Raymead Way then 2nd L. ⅓-acre plantsman's garden of unusual design with narrow paths, small sunken garden, ponds and cosy secluded corners. Wide range of trees, shrubs, perennials and annuals with an emphasis on yr-round colour. Also interesting berries, winter's bark and some tender plants. TEA in aid of RNLI. *Adm £1.50 Chd £1. Sun Feb 23 (12-4), Wed July 30 (2- 5.30), Wed Oct 1 (12-4)*

¶Rickleden &✿❀ (Mr & Mrs Trevor Sokell) Bookham. 3m W of Leatherhead, past Bookham, N of A246. Turn into Rectory Lane opp Dobbe's nursery. Continue over crossroads for ⅔m to Maddox Lane on L. Limited parking at end of lane. Additonal parking at Bookham Station 400yds. 1½ acres, redesigned and developed by present owners, much of it in the last 5 yrs. Garden of variety, many unusual and good foliage plants. Mature trees incl 90-yr-old liriodendron, silver herb garden, colour schemed borders, pond, curved pergola, gazebo, apiary, orchard with bulbs, greenhouses. TEAS. *Adm £1.50 Chd free (Share to The National Meningitis Trust®). Suns June 15, July 6 (2-6)*

▲**¶RHS Garden Wisley** &✿ (Royal Horticultural Society) 1m from Ripley, W of London on A3 and M25 (Junction 10). Follow signs with flower logo. The primary garden of the RHS and centre of its scientific and educational activities. Arboretum, alpine and wild garden, rock garden, mixed borders, model gardens, fruit and vegetable garden, rose garden, glasshouses, orchard, formal gardens, canal, woodland garden and trial grounds. For further details see page 18. *Ticket prices (incl RHS members): £3 (admission only). For NGS Wed, June 18, Thurs Aug 14 (6.30-9)*

Ridings &✿❀ (Mr & Mrs K Dutton) Tadworth. On A217 at large roundabout 6m S of Sutton and 3m N of junction 8 on M25 take B2220 sign posted Tadworth. Take 2nd R into Tadorne Rd; L into Cross Rd. House on corner of

Epsom Lane S. ¾-acre informal garden containing interesting trees, shrubs and herbaceous plants with emphasis on colour, texture and foliage; vegetable plot. TEA. *Adm £1.50 Chd free. Suns June 1, 8 (2-5.30). Private visits welcome (May to July), please* **Tel 01737 813962**

Rise Top Cottage ✿✿ (Trevor Bath) Mayford. Midway between Woking and Guildford, off A320. On entering Maybourne Rise, take immed L. At top of Rise turn L along rough track about 100yds. Please park tactfully in Maybourne Rise. ⅓-acre approx. Profusely planted in a cottage garden style with both old and new varieties. Special interests incl aquilegias, pulmonarias, herbs, old roses, white flowers and particularly hardy geraniums. TEAS. *Adm £1 Chd free. Wed June 4 (11-4)*

41 Shelvers Way ✿✿ (Mr & Mrs K G Lewis) Tadworth. 6m S of Sutton off the A217. !st turning on R after Burgh Heath traffic lights heading S. 400yds down Shelvers Way on L. ⅓-acre plantsman's garden. Attractive cobbled area leading to a wide variety of herbaceous and other plants. Many spring bulbs followed by azaleas and old roses. Designed and developed by owners. Coffee and TEAS. *Adm £1.50 Chd free. Weds April 23, June 25, July 16, Sun July 13 (10.30-5). Private visits welcome, please* **Tel 01737 210707**

67 Shepherds Lane ✿✿ (Mr & Mrs C Graham) Stoughton, Guildford. From Guildford, 1m from A3 on A322 Worplesdon Rd. Turn L at traffic lights at Emmanuel Church, Stoughton into Shepherds Lane. Garden is on L on brow of hill. Alternatively, via A323 Aldershot Rd and Rydes Hill Rd, Shepherds Lane is 2nd R. ¼-acre suburban garden with mixed borders, lawn, specimen small trees, pond, alpine bed, fruit garden with dwarf trees; Guildford in Bloom award winners. TEAS *Adm £1 Chd free (Share to Abbeyfield®) Mon June 23 (11-5) Weds July 2, 16 (1.30-5). Private visits welcome, please* **Tel 01483 566445**

Snowdenham House &✿ (The Hon Lady Hamilton) Snowdenham Lane, Bramley. S of Guildford A281 from Guildford, R at Bramley mini-roundabout. House is ½m on L. Georgian house, outbuildings and water mill (not open). 9 acres of water, woodland, formal and walled gardens. Wide range of rhododendrons, azaleas and specimen trees and shrubs in woodland garden bordering stream. TEAS in aid of Bramley Church. *Adm £2.50 Chd free. Sun May 18 (11.30-5)*

South Cheam Gardens ✿✿ Situated approx 1m S of Cheam village. *Combined adm £2 Chd 50p. Sat, Sun Aug 2, 3 (11-5)*
   87 Sandy Lane (Mr & Mrs B West & Mr & Mrs L West) ⅓-acre garden featuring sub-tropical plants, incl palm trees, a tree fern, bananas, agaves, bamboos and acers. Large collection of cannas; rockery with small water feature. Fruit trees, dahlia borders, vegetable garden and three greenhouses. TEAS in aid of NSPCC
   89 Sandy Lane (Mr & Mrs Jeff Jones) ⅓-acre with a lower, middle and upper garden. Lower garden features conifers, bedding plants and pots; the middle garden has a pond, rockery, dahlia and sweet pea

beds and herbaceous border. The upper garden is devoted to all vegetables with 30 feet of greenhouse space. Plants in aid of Shere & Peaslake Cubs & Venture Scouts

South Park &✿ (Mr & Mrs E Wetter Sanchez) Blechingley. Take A25 Godstone to Redhill rd and before Blechingley village, turn L into Rabys Heath Rd, continue for ½m, turn R into South Park Lane, ½m to clock tower. Edwardian garden with herbaceous border. Advice from Jim Russell in 60's. Extensive views to Kent and Sussex. C17 chapel. TEAS. *Adm £2 Chd 50p (Share to Childline®). Sun June 22 (2-5)*

South Park Farm & (Mrs P J Stewart-Smith) South Godstone. Take A22 London to East Grinstead rd and 1m S of railway bridge at South Godstone turn R into Carlton Rd just before Walker's Garden Centre; follow signs for 1m. Medium-sized garden; wide variety of roses; herbaceous border; fine trees and landscape; small lake. C17 (listed) farm house (not open). Peacocks. Home-made TEAS till 6 in large C17 barn. *Adm £2 Chd free (Share to RNLI®). Sat, Sun, Mon June 28, 29, 30 (2-6). Also private visits welcome, please* **Tel 01342 892141**

Spring Cottage &✿✿ (Mr & Mrs D E Norman) Cranleigh. A281 from Guildford turn L 1m out of Bramley. Turn R at roundabout then immed L, into Smithwood Common Rd; garden 1m on R. 1-acre garden with lovely view; cottage garden; small woodland garden, old roses, pond and new greenhouse area. TEAS. *Adm £1.50 Chd free. Sun, Wed June 15, 18 (2-6); private visits welcome, please* **Tel 01483 272620**

Spur Point, nr Fernhurst (See Sussex)

Stonywood ✿✿ (Mr & Mrs Noble) Chase Lane, Haslemere. From centre of town take B2131 E towards Petworth. Take 2nd turning R for Blackdown. At junction of 5 lanes go towards Tennyson's Lane. At next junction (150yds) go straight on. House on L, ⅓m down lane. Parking space very limited in narrow lane. ⅓-acre steeply sloping garden. Many rhododendrons, azaleas, shrubs, spring bulbs; pleasant views across Chase Valley and NT woods. TEAS. *Adm £1 Chd 50p (Share to Foundation for the study of Infant Deaths®). Sun May 18 (2-5). Private visits welcome for parties of 10 and over following written application*

Street House &✿ (Mr & Mrs B M Francis) Thursley. From London take A3. 8m past Guildford turn R at sign Thursley/Churt/Frensham, 50yds past Three Horseshoes inn, bear L at fork signed The Street and No through road. Garden ahead. From Portsmouth/Petersfield turn L from A3 into Thursley village. Parking on recreation ground 100yds past house. Please park carefully in wet weather. Street House (not open), a listed Regency building and childhood home of Sir Edwin Lutyens where he first met Gertrude Jekyll. Garden of 1¼ acres divided into three gardens. Beautiful views. Ancient wall; specimen cornus kousa; Japanese snowball tree; rare old roses; special rhododendrons and camellias; rubus tridel. Astrological garden. Home-made TEAS. *Adm £1.50 Chd 50p. Suns April 6, May 4, June 8, Aug 24 (2-6), Sat July 26 (11-6)*

Stuart Cottage &❀ (Mr & Mrs J M Leader) East Clandon. This C16 hamlet, public house and C12 church is well worth a visit. Situated 4m E of Guildford on the A246 or from A3 via Ripley turning L in centre of Ripley, Rose Lane, then 2nd R. East Clandon is 4m. ½-acre partly walled cottage garden with well-stocked herbaceous beds. Rose and clematis walk, water features and paved areas with planting. Victorian chimney pots used as planters add to the charm of this C16 cottage. Home-made TEAS in aid of Cherry Trees. *Adm £1.50 Chd free. Sat, Sun July 26, 27 (2-6)*

▲**Sutton Place** &✄ (Sutton Place Foundation) Guildford. From A320 (Guildford-Woking) turn into Clay Lane. At Xrds take Blanchards Hill towards Sutton Green. Lodge gates approx ¼m on R. 60 acres, around Tudor Manor House. A series of individual gardens each with its own theme and interest. A woodland garden which runs down to the R Wey. Many of the gardens were designed by Sir Geoffrey Jellicoe and the more recently established gardens were designed by Patrick Bowe. TEAS. *Adm £6 Chd £2. For NGS Wed June 11 (10-4) Suitable for wheelchairs in parts. NO COACH PARTIES ON JUNE 11. Private visits welcome by prior appt. for parties of 12-40 please* Tel 01483 504455

Tanyard Farmhouse &❀ (Mr & Mrs E Epson) Langshott, Horley. At edge of Horley on A23. Travelling from Redhill turn L into Ladbroke Rd at Chequers Hotel roundabout. Continue ½m, garden on L. Park in Lake Lane. ⅓-acre 3-yr-old garden designed by owners on a flat site, with heavy clay, around a C15/17 wealden farmhouse. Formal layout, with informal planting, incl small white garden with pond, scented rose garden with lavender and clematis, rustic trellises and arches. Mixed borders with shrubs and perennials, some unusual. Terrace with pots and baskets containing herbs, perennials and annuals. TEAS. *Adm £1.50 Chd free. Sat, Sun July 5, 6 (2-6)*

Thanescroft &✄❀ (Mr & Mrs Peter Talbot-Willcox) Shamley Green. 5m S of Guildford, A281 Guildford-Horsham rd, at Shalford turn E onto B2128 to Wonersh and Shamley Green. At Shamley Green Village sign turn R to Lord's Hill, ¾m on L. 4-acres. Pool garden with shrubberies and Rowan avenue. Lower level kitchen garden integrated with roses, mixed borders, yew and box hedges. Orchard with shrub roses. Lawns and fine old trees. Rhododendrons and primula walk. Ice house. TEAS. *Adm £2 Chd free. Sat, Sun June 21, 22 (2-6)*

●**Titsey Place and Gardens** &✄ (The Trustees of the Titsey Foundation) Oxted. 2m N of Oxted. On A25 between Oxted and Westerham, turn L into Limpsfield Village. On bend at end of village, turn L (straight on) into Bluehouse Lane and follow signs to Titsey Place and Gardens. An ancestral home of the Greshams since 1534. 18 acres of landscaped gardens and lakes surrounded by parkland. A recently restored Victorian walled garden. *Adm £4 House and Garden, £2 Garden only. Weds and Suns May 21 to Sept 28 (1-5). Private visits welcome if pre-booked, please* Tel 01883 712124

Unicorns ✄ (Mr & Mrs Eric Roberts) Long Hill, The Sands, Farnham. Approx 4½m E of Farnham take A31 towards Guildford. 1st slip rd to Runfold turn R, then L into Crooksbury Rd through 's' bend then L turn to The Sands through village past Barley Mow public house on R. Park tactfully in Littleworth Rd. Long Hill 1st turning on R. Partly woodland garden on a sloping site, rhododendrons, azaleas, ferns, plants for ground cover and many other interesting and unusual plants and shrubs. Teas at Manor Farm, Seale. *Adm £1 Chd free. Weds May 14, June 4 (2-5). Private visits welcome from mid April to end of August please* Tel 01252 782778 after 6pm

87 Upland Road &✄❀ (Mr & Mrs David Nunn) 50yds S Carshalton Beeches station into Waverley Way, at shops into Downside Rd, then 1st on L. 0.4-acre secluded suburban plantsman's garden overlaying chalk. Shrubs; herbaceous; orchard; fruit and vegetable garden. Developed and maintained by owners. Exhibition of botanical watercolour paintings. TEAS. *Adm £1.50 Chd free. Sun May 18 (2-6)*

6 Upper Rose Hill ✄❀ (Peter & Julia Williams) Dorking. From roundabout at A24/A25 junction follow signs to town centre and Horsham. ½m S of town centre turn L after Pizza Piazza and 2nd R at top of hill. Parking available in rd and in large car park behind Sainsbury's (5 min walk). ½-acre informal suburban terraced garden on dry sand. Wide range of foliage and form; fruit and vegetables; some unusual plants; good autumn colour. TEAS in aid of Mole Valley Crossroads. *Adm £1.50 Chd free. Sun June 15, Sept 14 (2-6). Private visits welcome, please* Tel 01306 881315

Vale End ❀ (Mr & Mrs John Foulsham) Albury, 4½m SE of Guildford. From Albury take A248 W for ¼m. 1-acre walled garden on many levels in beautiful setting; views from terrace across sloping lawns to mill pond and woodland; wide variety herbaceous plants and old roses; attractive courtyard. Fruit, vegetable and herb garden. Featured in NGS video 2. Morning coffee and home-made TEAS in aid of GUTS at Royal Surrey County Hospital. *Adm £2 Chd free. Suns June 22, July 27 (10-5)*

¶**Valedown** &✄ (Clare Palgrave) Mayford. Off A320 3m S of Woking. Garden is on unmade track at top of Maybourne Rise. Please park courteously on metalled rd either side of Maybourne Rise. No parking on unmade track. ¼-acre garden owned and designed by practising garden designer. Interesting ideas to overcome challenging aspect and unusual shape of plot. Yr-round interest achieved with dense structural planting, colour and texture achieved with foliage. Drought resistant planting on sandy soil. Mainly developed over past 5 years. TEA. *Adm £1.50 Chd free. Sun Sept 7 (2-6)*

Vann ✄❀ (Mr & Mrs M B Caroe) Hambledon, 6m S of Godalming. A283 to Wormley. Turn L at Hambledon Xrds signed 'Vann Lane'. Follow yellow 'Vann' signs for 2m. House on L. An English Heritage Registered garden of 4½ acres surrounding Tudor/William & Mary house with later additions and alterations incorporating old farm buildings by W D Caröe 1907-1909. Formal yew walk, ¼-acre pond, Gertrude Jekyll water garden 1911, pergola, old cottage garden. Spring bulbs, woodland, azaleas. New vegetable garden borders. Featured in Country Life and Gardeners World 1995. Maintained by family with 2 days assistance per week. Part of garden suitable for wheelchairs. Guided garden tours, morning coffee, lunches, home-made teas in house from Easter-July by prior arrangement. TEAS (April 6, May 5 only). Plant sales weekends only. *Adm £2.50 Chd 50p (Share to Hambledon Village Hall®). Sun April 6 (2-7), Mon to Sat April 7 to 12 (10-6), Bank Hol Mon May 5 (2-7) Tues to Sun May 6 to 11, Sat May 24, Suns to Sats June 1 to 7, July 6 to 12 (10-6). Private visits welcome, please Tel 01428 683413*

Walton Poor &⚘ (Mr & Mrs Nicholas Calvert) 4m W of Ranmore. From N and W off A246 on outskirts of East Horsley turn R to Greendene 1st fork L Crocknorth Rd. From E take A2003 to Ranmore Rd from Dorking to E Horsley. Approx 3 acres; tranquil, rather secret garden; paths winding between areas of ornamental shrubs; landscaped sunken garden; pond; herb garden. Autumn colour. Extensive range of foliage, scented plants and herbs for sale; garden nr forest paths leading to North Downs with fine views over Tillingbourne valley. TEAS (May and June) (from 3pm). *Adm £1.50 Chd 50p (Share to Leukaemia Research®). Mon May 5, Sun, Wed June 8, 11 (11-6) Sun Oct 12 (11-5). Herb garden open daily Wed to Sun Easter to Sept 30. Private visits of 10 and over welcome to the main garden, please Tel 01483 282273*

Westbourn ⚘ (Mrs John Camden) Virginia Water. From Egham 3m S on A30. Turn L into Christchurch Rd opp the Wheatsheaf Hotel. After 200yds turn R into Pinewood Rd; Westbourn is 50yds on the R. 4 acres landscaped woodland on 2 levels extensively planted with unusual trees and shrubs. Rhododendrons and azaleas predominate with over 80 different species and as many hybrids. The R Bourne, a narrow, winding rivulet, forms the southern boundary of the garden. TEA. *Adm £1 Chd free. Sun May 18 (2-6)*

Windlesham Park &⚘ (Mr & Mrs Peter Dimmock) Woodlands Lane. 2m E of Bagshot. S of Sunningdale, NW of Chobham; from Windlesham Church S to T-junction, turn L into Thorndown Lane becoming Woodlands Lane over M3; entrance 100yds on R, white pillars. 9-acre parkland setting with many and varied well established azaleas and rhododendrons. Fine cedars and mature trees; wet areas. WC not suitable for wheelchairs. TEAS. *Adm £2 Chd 50p (Share to St John the Baptist Church®). Sun May 18 (2-6)*

▲**Winkworth Arboretum** (The National Trust) Hascombe, Godalming. Entrances with car parks; Upper 3m SE of Godalming on E side of B2130; Lower 2¼m S of Bramley on Bramley-Hascombe rd, turn R off A281 from Guildford at Bramley Xrds, up Snowdenham Lane. Coaches (by written arrangement) should use Upper car park on B2130. Station: Godalming 3m. 95 acres of hillside planted with rare trees and shrubs; 2 lakes; many wild birds; view over N Downs. Tours on both days with Eric Barrs, Head of Arboretum from kiosk. 10.30; £2 extra, chd free. Limited suitability for wheelchairs. Disabled visitors use lower car park. Disabled WC. TEAS 11-5.30. *Adm £2.50 Chd 5-16 £1.25 Family ticket £6.25. All NT members donation please. For NGS Suns May 4, Oct 12 (daylight hrs)*

Wintershall Manor ⚘ (Mr & Mrs Peter Hutley) 3m S of Bramley village on A281 turn R, then next R. Wintershall drive next on L. Bus: AV 33 Guildford-Horsham; alight Palmers Cross, 1m. 2-acre garden and 200 acres of park and woodland; snowdrop walk, acres of bluebell walks in spring; banks of wild daffodils; rhododendrons; specimen trees; several acres of lakes and flight ponds; path to Chapel of St Mary. Queen of Peace has Stations of Cross by contemporary sculptors. Newly opened Rosary Walk and St Francis Chapel by lakes. Superb views. Partially suitable for wheelchairs. TEA from 3.30 pm. *Adm £2 OAPs £1.50 Chd 4-14 50p (Share to Wintershall Charitable Trust®). Suns May 11, June 8 (2-5). Private parties welcome, please Tel 01483 892167*

Wisley see RHS Garden Wisley

Woodside ⚘⚘ (Mr & Mrs J A Colmer) Send Barns Lane, Send, nr Ripley, 4m NE of Guildford; on A247 (Woking/Dorking Rd) 200yds west (Send side) at junction with B2215. If travelling via M25 leave at junction 10. ⅓-acre garden; main feature rock garden and alpine house; many shrubs incl rhododendrons, ericaceous species etc; herbaceous planting; specialist collection of alpines. *Adm £1.50 Chd free. Sat, Sun April 19, 20 (2-6). Private visits welcome in May, please Tel 01483 223073*

Yew Tree Cottage ⚘⚘ (Mr & Mrs E E Bowyer) Bunch Lane, Haslemere. Turn off High St into Church Lane, leave church on L, carry on to T junction, turn L, 1st house on L. 2-acre garden created by owners since 1976 on hillside. Large variety of trees and shrubs, water garden, kitchen garden, Jacob and Shetland sheep, rare breed poultry, Shetland pony in paddock beyond garden. Partially suitable wheelchairs. See **Haslehurst.** Tea at Haslehurst. *Adm £1.50 Chd 50p (Share to Haslemere Educational Museum®). Sun June 15 (2-6). Coach parties by prior arrangement. Private visits welcome, please Tel 01428 644130*

York Road Gardens &⚘⚘ Situated in the Sutton/Cheam area and runs between Cheam Rd and Dorset Rd. Nos 67 and 70 are opp. each other at S end of York Rd towards the junction with Dorset Rd, which is a turning off Belmont Rise (A217). Dried flowers for sale. TEAS at No. 70 in aid of Salvation Army. *Combined adm £2 Chd free. Wed, Sun July 23, 27 (10-4)*
¶**Pathside** (Mr & Mrs F Wood) No. 70. Mature garden with good range of trees, shrubs, herbaceous plants, lawn, pond etc. A footpath pattern has been laid round the garden by new owner forming views, vistas and planted 'rooms' with landscaping. Interesting sunken dell garden, which is being rebuilt, featuring stone walls, arches and raised beds. New planting, landscaping, etc. will continue to provide varieties of colour, form and contrast
Woodland (Prof & Mrs S Hilton) No. 67. Mainly walled suburban garden just under 0.2 acres. 2 lawned terraces with interesting hard landscaping and footpath patterns, incl raised shrub heather and flower beds. Good range of plants incl viburnums, hollies, ferns, ivys and conifers, plus 75ft herbaceous border with wide range of hardy plants. 2 raised ponds, 1 with open roofed water pavilion. Good selection of wall climbers

Sussex

Hon County Organisers:	(East & Mid-Sussex)
	Mrs Janet Goldsmith, Sunnymead, Tapsells Lane, Wadhurst TN5 6RS
	Tel 01892 783264
	(West Sussex)
	Mrs Consie Dunn, Wildham, Stoughton, Chichester PO18 9JG
	Tel 01243 535202
Deputy County Organiser:	(East & Mid-Sussex)
	Mrs Jo Charlesworth, Snape Cottage, Snape Lane, Wadhurst TN5 6NS
Assistant Hon County Organisers:	(East & Mid-Sussex)
	Mrs Miriam Book, Appledore, 50 Hill Drive, Hove BN3 6QL
	Mrs Anne Bramall, Lea Farm, Peasmarsh, Rye TN31 7ST
	Mrs Rosemary Collins, Windwhistle, Faircrouch Lane, Wadhurst TN5 6PP
	Mrs Judy Emrich, Old Mill Barn, Argos Hill, Rotherfield TN6 3QF
	Mrs Sophie Neal, Legsheath Farm, nr East Grinstead RH19 4JN
	Mrs Lynn Neligan, Old School House, Church Lane, Northiam TN31 6NN
	Mrs Jan Newman, Graywood House, Graywood, East Hoathly BN8 6QP
	Mrs Nikola Sly, Lilac Cottage, High Hurstwood, Uckfield,
	Mrs Carolyn Steel, Beeches, Cuckfield Lane, Warninglid RH17 5UB
	(West Sussex)
	Mrs Nigel Azis, Coke's Barn, West Burton, Pulborough RH20 1HD
	Tel 01798 831636
	Mrs Jane Burton, Church Farmhouse, Lavant, nr Chichester PO18 0AL
	Mrs Louise Pollard, 6 Holbrook Park, Northlands Rd, Horsham RH12 5PW
	Mrs Claudia Pearce, 12 Belsize Rd, Worthing BN11 4RH
	Mrs Jenny Woodall, Nyewood House, nr Petersfield, Hants GU31 5JL
Hon County Treasurers:	(East & Mid-Sussex)
	D C Goldsmith Esq, Sunnymead, Tapsells Lane, Wadhurst TN5 6RS
	(West Sussex)
	W M Caldwell Esq, The Grange, Fittleworth, Pulborough RH20 1EW

DATES OF OPENING

March 9 Sunday
Champs Hill, Coldwaltham, nr Pulborough

March 12 Wednesday
Champs Hill, Coldwaltham, nr Pulborough

March 16 Sunday
Champs Hill, Coldwaltham, nr Pulborough

March 19 Wednesday
Champs Hill, Coldwaltham, nr Pulborough

March 22 Saturday
Manor of Dean, Tillington, Petworth

March 23 Sunday
Berri Court, Yapton
Champs Hill, Coldwaltham, nr Pulborough
Manor of Dean, Tillington, Petworth

March 24 Monday
Berri Court, Yapton
Manor of Dean, Tillington, Petworth

March 31 Monday
Orchards, Rowfant

April 6 Sunday
Bates Green , Arlington
Cooke's House, West Burton

April 7 Monday
Bates Green , Arlington
Cooke's House, West Burton
Little Thakeham, Storrington

April 8 Tuesday
Cooke's House, West Burton
Little Thakeham, Storrington

April 12 Saturday
Manor of Dean, Tillington, Petworth
Rymans, Apuldram, nr Chichester

April 13 Sunday
Chidmere House, Chidham
Cooke's House, West Burton
Hurston Place, Pulborough
Manor of Dean, Tillington, Petworth
Penns in the Rocks, Groombridge

April 14 Monday
Chidmere House, Chidham
Cooke's House, West Burton
Manor of Dean, Tillington, Petworth
Northwood Farmhouse, Pulborough

April 15 Tuesday
Cooke's House, West Burton
Northwood Farmhouse, Pulborough

April 16 Wednesday
Orchards, Rowfant

April 19 Saturday
King Edward VII Hospital, nr Midhurst
Rymans, Apuldram, nr Chichester

April 20 Sunday
Ghyll Farm, Sweethaws, Crowborough
High Beeches Gardens, Handcross
New Grove, Petworth
Stonehurst, Ardingly

April 23 Wednesday
Houghton Farm, nr Arundel

April 24 Thursday
Duckyls, Sharpthorne

April 26 Saturday
Cedar Tree Cottage, Washington

April 27 Sunday
Hurst Mill, Petersfield ‡
Malt House, Chithurst, nr Rogate ‡
Newtimber Place, Newtimber
Offham House, Offham

April 30 Wednesday
Cedar Tree Cottage, Washington
May 1 Thursday
Borde Hill Garden, nr Haywards
Heath
May 2 Friday
Borde Hill Garden, nr Haywards
Heath
May 4 Sunday
Bignor Park, nr Pulborough
Cedar Tree Cottage, Washington
Champs Hill, Coldwaltham, nr
Pulborough
Malt House, Chithurst, nr Rogate
Warren House, Crowborough
May 5 Monday
Bignor Park, nr Pulborough
Champs Hill, Coldwaltham, nr
Pulborough
Highdown Gardens, Goring-by-Sea
Malt House, Chithurst, nr Rogate
Orchards, Rowfant
Stonehurst, Ardingly
May 7 Wednesday
Champs Hill, Coldwaltham, nr
Pulborough
Nyewood House, Nyewood, nr
Rogate
May 10 Saturday
Manor of Dean, Tillington,
Petworth ‡
New Grove, Petworth ‡
May 11 Sunday
Ansty Gardens
Berri Court, Yapton
Champs Hill, Coldwaltham, nr
Pulborough
Ghyll Farm, Sweethaws,
Crowborough
Hammerwood House, Iping ‡
Malt House, Chithurst, nr
Rogate ‡
Manor of Dean, Tillington,
Petworth ‡‡
New Grove, Petworth ‡‡
Standen, East Grinstead
Tinkers Bridge Cottage, Ticehurst
May 12 Monday
Berri Court, Yapton
Manor of Dean, Tillington,
Petworth
May 14 Wednesday
Champs Hill, Coldwaltham, nr
Pulborough
Sheffield Park Garden, nr Uckfield
May 15 Thursday
Duckyls, Sharpthorne
May 18 Sunday
Champs Hill, Coldwaltham, nr
Pulborough
Fittleworth Gardens, nr
Pulborough
Hammerwood House, Iping ‡
1 & 6 Holbrook Park, Horsham

Legsheath Farm, nr Forest
Row
Malt House, Chithurst, nr
Rogate ‡
Mountfield Court, nr
Robertsbridge
Selehurst, Lower Beeding, nr
Horsham
Trotton Old Rectory, nr Rogate ‡‡
Trotton Place, nr Rogate ‡‡
Warren House, Crowborough
The White Magpie, Lamberhurst
May 19 Monday
Mountfield Court, nr
Robertsbridge
May 21 Wednesday
Champs Hill, Coldwaltham, nr
Pulborough
May 22 Thursday
Duckyls, Sharpthorne
Petworth House Pleasure Ground
May 24 Saturday
Lane End, Midhurst
May 25 Sunday
Baker's Farm, Shipley, nr Horsham
Chidmere House, Chidham
Cookscroft, Earnley
Cowdray Park Gardens,
Midhurst ‡
Ghyll Farm, Sweethaws,
Crowborough ‡‡
Hurst Mill, Petersfield
Lane End, Midhurst ‡
Malt House, Chithurst, nr
Rogate ‡
Moorlands, nr Crowborough ‡‡
Rose Cottage, Hadlow Down
May 26 Monday
Chidmere House, Chidham
Cobblers, Crowborough ‡‡
Cookscroft, Earnley
Highdown Gardens, Goring-by-Sea
Lane End, Midhurst ‡
Malt House, Chithurst, nr
Rogate ‡
Orchards, Rowfant
Roundhill Cottage, East Dean
Stonehurst, Ardingly
Warren House, Crowborough ‡‡
May 27 Tuesday
Roundhill Cottage, East Dean
May 28 Wednesday
Houghton Farm, nr Arundel
May 29 Thursday
Duckyls Holt, West Hoathly ‡
The Priest House, West Hoathly ‡
May 31 Saturday
Coombland, Coneyhurst,
Billingshurst
Gaywood Farm, Pulborough
Lane End, Midhurst
June 1 Sunday
Cowbeech Farm, Cowbeech
Fitzhall, Iping, nr Midhurst ‡

The Garden In Mind, Stansted
Park
Gaywood Farm, Pulborough
Lane End, Midhurst ‡
Malt House, Chithurst, nr
Rogate ‡
Morris Down, Piltdown
Neptune House, Cutmill,
Bosham ‡‡
Nymans, Handcross
Sennicotts, nr Chichester ‡‡
Warren House, Crowborough
June 2 Monday
Cowbeech Farm, Cowbeech
Lane End, Midhurst
Morris Down, Piltdown
Sennicotts, nr Chichester
June 4 Wednesday
Orchards, Rowfant
Wilderness Farm, Cabbages and
Kings Garden, Hadlow Down
June 6 Friday
Uppark, South Harting
June 7 Saturday
King John's Lodge, Etchingham
June 8 Sunday
Ashdown Park Hotel, Wych Cross
Hailsham Grange, Hailsham
King John's Lodge, Etchingham
Kingston Gardens, nr Lewes
Little Hutchings, Etchingham
Manvilles Field, Fittleworth
Merriments Gardens, Hurst Green
Moorlands, nr Crowborough
North Manor, Flansham, Bognor
Regis
Nyewood House, Nyewood, nr
Rogate
June 9 Monday
Little Thakeham, Storrington
Merriments Gardens, Hurst Green
June 10 Tuesday
Coombland, Coneyhurst,
Billingshurst
Little Thakeham, Storrington
June 11 Wednesday
Ashburnham Place, Battle
Cobblers, Crowborough
North Manor, Flansham, Bognor
Regis
Nyewood House, Nyewood, nr
Rogate
Somerset Lodge, North St,
Petworth
West Dean Gardens, nr
Chichester
June 12 Thursday
Ashburnham Place, Battle
Duckyls Holt, West Hoathly ‡
The Priest House, West Hoathly ‡
Somerset Lodge, North St,
Petworth
June 13 Friday
Ashburnham Place, Battle

Somerset Lodge, North St,
Petworth

June 14 Saturday
Chantry Green House, Steyning
Coombland, Coneyhurst,
Billingshurst
Frith Hill, Northchapel ‡
Frith Lodge, Northchapel ‡
Lilac Cottage, Duncton
Somerset Lodge, North St,
Petworth

June 15 Sunday
Ashburnham Place, Battle
Chantry Green House, Steyning
Clinton Lodge, Fletching ‡‡
Fittleworth Gardens, nr
Pulborough
Knabbs Farmhouse, Fletching ‡‡
Lilac Cottage, Duncton ‡
Mount Harry Gardens, Offham
New Barn, Egdean, nr Petworth ‡
Sherburne House, Eartham
Somerset Lodge, North St,
Petworth ‡

June 16 Monday
Clinton Lodge, Fletching ‡
Knabbs Farmhouse, Fletching ‡
New Barn, Egdean, nr Petworth

June 17 Tuesday
Coombland, Coneyhurst,
Billingshurst
New Barn, Egdean, nr Petworth

June 18 Wednesday
Clinton Lodge, Fletching
Lilac Cottage, Duncton
Manvilles Field, Fittleworth
Ringmer Park, Lewes

June 19 Thursday
Doucegrove Farm, Northiam
Town Place, Freshfield, nr
Sheffield Park

June 20 Friday
Doucegrove Farm, Northiam
Down Place, South Harting

June 21 Saturday
Bankton Cottage, Crawley Down
Buckhurst Park, Withyham
Coombland, Coneyhurst,
Billingshurst
Down Place, South Harting ‡
Gaywood Farm, Pulborough
Hurston Place, Pulborough
Manor of Dean, Tillington,
Petworth
Telegraph House, North Marden,
nr Chichester ‡
Uppark, South Harling
Winchelsea Gardens

June 22 Sunday
Bankton Cottage, Crawley Down
Cobblers, Crowborough
Down Place, South Harting ‡
Ebbsworth, Nutbourne nr
Pulborough ‡‡

Gaywood Farm, Pulborough ‡‡
Hammerwood House, Iping ‡
Hurston Place, Pulborough
Ketches, Newick
Manor of Dean, Tillington,
Petworth
Manvilles Field, Fittleworth
Moat Mill Farm, Mayfield
Offham House, Offham ‡‡‡‡
The Old Vicarage, Firle ‡‡‡‡
Priesthawes Farm, Polegate
Telegraph House, North Marden,
nr Chichester ‡
Town Place, Freshfield, nr
Sheffield Park
Trotton Old Rectory, nr
Rogate ‡‡‡
Trotton Place, nr Rogate ‡‡‡

June 23 Monday
Ebbsworth, Nutbourne nr
Pulborough
Hurston Place, Pulborough
Manor of Dean, Tillington,
Petworth
Priesthawes Farm, Polegate

June 25 Wednesday
Bateman's, Burwash
Clinton Lodge, Fletching
Houghton Farm, nr Arundel
Middle Coombe, East Grinstead ‡
Orchards, Rowfant ‡

June 26 Thursday
Town Place, Freshfield, nr
Sheffield Park

June 27 Friday
Dallington Cottage Gardens
South Harting Gardens
Uppark, South Harling

June 28 Saturday
Coombland, Coneyhurst,
Billingshurst
Dallington Cottage Gardens
Frith Hill, Northchapel ‡
Frith Lodge, Northchapel ‡
South Harting Gardens

June 29 Sunday
Baker's Farm, Shipley, nr
Horsham
Bates Green , Arlington
Berri Court, Yapton
Casters Brook, Cocking, nr
Midhurst
Church Farm, Aldingbourne
Home Farm House, Isfield, nr
Uckfield ‡‡
Hurst Mill, Petersfield ‡
Mayfield Cottage Gardens,
Mayfield
North Springs, Fittleworth
Pheasants Hatch, Newick ‡‡
Rose Cottage, Hadlow Down
South Harting Gardens ‡
Warren House, Crowborough
West Worthing Gardens

June 30 Monday
Bates Green , Arlington
Berri Court, Yapton
Home Farm House, Isfield, nr
Uckfield ‡
Northwood Farmhouse,
Pulborough
Pheasants Hatch, Newick ‡

July 1 Tuesday
Northwood Farmhouse,
Pulborough

July 2 Wednesday
Clinton Lodge, Fletching
Parham House & Gardens, nr
Pulborough

July 3 Thursday
Casters Brook, Cocking, nr
Midhurst
Parham House & Gardens, nr
Pulborough

July 4 Friday
Berri Court, Yapton

July 5 Saturday
North Springs, Fittleworth

July 6 Sunday
Ansty Gardens
Casters Brook, Cocking, nr
Midhurst
Hailsham Grange, Hailsham
The Lodge Garden, Westfield
Merriments Gardens, Hurst
Green
North Springs, Fittleworth
Town Place, Freshfield, nr
Sheffield Park
Whiligh, Shovers Green
8 Wimblehurst Road, Horsham

July 7 Monday
The Lodge Garden, Westfield
Whiligh, Shovers Green

July 9 Wednesday
Orchards, Rowfant

July 10 Thursday
8 Wimblehurst Road, Horsham

July 12 Saturday
Crown House, Eridge
Manor of Dean, Tillington,
Petworth
Palmer's Lodge, West Chiltington
Village
Telegraph House, North Marden,
nr Chichester

July 13 Sunday
Ambrose Place Back Gardens,
Worthing
Cobblers, Crowborough
Crown House, Eridge
Manor of Dean, Tillington,
Petworth
Nyewood House, Nyewood, nr
Rogate ‡
Nymans, Handcross
Palmer's Lodge, West Chiltington
Village

Telegraph House, North Marden,
nr Chichester ‡
Town Place, Freshfield, nr
Sheffield Park
July 14 Monday
Manor of Dean, Tillington,
Petworth
July 16 Wednesday
Houghton Farm, nr Arundel
Nyewood House, Nyewood, nr
Rogate
West Worthing Gardens
July 18 Friday
Pashley Manor, Ticehurst
Wakehurst Place, Ardingly
July 19 Saturday
Bumble Cottage, West
Chiltington ‡
Palmer's Lodge, West Chiltington
Village ‡
July 20 Sunday
Bumble Cottage, West
Chiltington ‡
Fitzhall, Iping, nr Midhurst
Moorlands, nr Crowborough
Palmer's Lodge, West Chiltington
Village ‡
Wadhurst Gardens
July 21 Monday
Wadhurst Gardens
July 23 Wednesday
Middle Coombe, East Grinstead ‡
Orchards, Rowfant ‡
July 25 Friday
Rye Gardens, Rye
July 26 Saturday
Bumble Cottage, West Chiltington
July 27 Sunday
Bumble Cottage, West Chiltington
Frewen College, Northiam
Kingston Gardens, nr Lewes
West Worthing Gardens
July 31 Thursday
Denmans, Fontwell, nr Arundel
August 1 Friday
St Mary's House, Bramber
August 2 Saturday
Cooksbridge, Fernhurst
Neptune House, Cutmill, Bosham
St Mary's House, Bramber
August 3 Sunday
Champs Hill, Coldwaltham, nr
Pulborough
Cobblers, Crowborough
Cooksbridge, Fernhurst
August 6 Wednesday
Champs Hill, Coldwaltham, nr
Pulborough
August 10 Sunday
Ashdown Park Hotel, Wych Cross
Champs Hill, Coldwaltham, nr
Pulborough
The White Magpie,
Lamberhurst

August 13 Wednesday
Champs Hill, Coldwaltham, nr
Pulborough
August 15 Friday
Latchetts, Dane Hill
August 16 Saturday
Latchetts, Dane Hill
Manor of Dean, Tillington,
Petworth
Sennicotts, nr Chichester
August 17 Sunday
Champs Hill, Coldwaltham, nr
Pulborough
Manor of Dean, Tillington,
Petworth
August 18 Monday
Manor of Dean, Tillington,
Petworth
August 20 Wednesday
Champs Hill, Coldwaltham, nr
Pulborough
August 24 Sunday
Chidmere House, Chidham
Merriments Gardens, Hurst Green
Newtimber Place, Newtimber
Warren House, Crowborough
The White House, Burpham, nr
Arundel
August 25 Monday
Chidmere House, Chidham
Cobblers, Crowborough
Highdown Gardens, Goring-by-Sea
Merriments Gardens, Hurst Green
New Barn, Egdean, nr Petworth
Orchards, Rowfant
Penns in the Rocks, Groombridge
The White House, Burpham, nr
Arundel
August 31 Sunday
Round Oak, Old Station Road,
Wadhurst
September 3 Wednesday
Round Oak, Old Station Road,
Wadhurst
September 4 Thursday
Petworth House Pleasure Ground
Round Oak, Old Station Road,
Wadhurst
September 5 Friday
Wilderness Farm, Cabbages and
Kings Garden, Hadlow Down
September 6 Saturday
Wilderness Farm, Cabbages and
Kings Garden, Hadlow Down
September 7 Sunday
Bates Green, Arlington
Fitzhall, Iping, nr Midhurst
High Beeches Gardens, Handcross
The Lodge Garden, Westfield
Wadhurst Park
Wilderness Farm, Cabbages and
Kings Garden, Hadlow Down
September 8 Monday
Bates Green, Arlington

The Lodge Garden, Westfield
September 10 Wednesday
Orchards, Rowfant
September 13 Saturday
Manor of Dean, Tillington,
Petworth
September 14 Sunday
Manor of Dean, Tillington,
Petworth
Merriments Gardens, Hurst Green
Standen, East Grinstead
September 15 Monday
Manor of Dean, Tillington,
Petworth
September 17 Wednesday
Ringmer Park, Lewes
September 18 Thursday
Denmans, Fontwell, nr Arundel
8 Wimblehurst Road, Horsham
September 21 Sunday
The Garden In Mind, Stansted
Park
September 24 Wednesday
Orchards, Rowfant
September 28 Sunday
Cowbeech Farm, Cowbeech
October 4 Saturday
Manor of Dean, Tillington,
Petworth
October 5 Sunday
Manor of Dean, Tillington,
Petworth
October 6 Monday
Manor of Dean, Tillington,
Petworth
October 8 Wednesday
Orchards, Rowfant
October 15 Wednesday
Sheffield Park Garden, nr Uckfield
October 19 Sunday
Coates Manor, Fittleworth
October 20 Monday
Coates Manor, Fittleworth

Regular openings
For details see garden description

Great Dixter, Northiam
High Beeches Gardens, Handcross
Little Dene, Chelwood Gate
Merriments Gardens, Hurst Green
Michelham Priory, Upper Dicker
Moorlands, nr Crowborough
Pashley Manor Ticehurst
The Priest House, West Hoathly
Wilderness Farm, Cabbages and
Kings Garden, Hatlow Down

> **Regular Openers.** Open
> throughout the year. They are
> listed at the end of the Diary
> Section under 'Regular Openers'.

By appointment only

Combehurst, Frant
Greenacres, Crowborough
The Old Chalk Pit, Hove
The Old Rectory, Newtimber
64 Old Shoreham Road, Hove
Rosemary Cottage, Rotherfield
Spur Point, nr Fernhurst
93 Wayland Avenue, Brighton
46 Westup Farm Cottages, Balcombe
Whitehouse Cottage, Haywards Heath
Yew Tree Cottage, Crawley Down

By Appointment Gardens. These owners do not have a fixed opening day usually because they cannot accommodate large numbers or have insufficient parking space.

DESCRIPTIONS OF GARDENS

Ambrose Place Back Gardens, Richmond Rd ✿❀ Worthing. Take Broadwater Rd into town centre, turn R at traffic lights into Richmond Rd opp Library; small town gardens with entrances on left; parking in rds. TEAS. *Combined adm £1.50 Chd 50p (Share to Christ Church and St Paul's Worthing®). Sun July 13 (11-1, 2-5)*

No 1 (Mrs M M Rosenberg) Walled garden; shrubs, pond, climbing plants
No 3 (Mr & Mrs M Smyth) Paved garden with climbing plants, lawn & pond
No 4 (Mr & Mrs T J Worley) Paved garden raised herbaceous borders, lawn & flowering summer plants
No 5 (Mr & Mrs P Owen) Paved with borders
No 6 (Mrs Leslie Roberts) Attractive garden with conservatory
No 7 (Mr & Mrs M Frost) Patio garden, with conservatory
No 8 (Mr & Mrs P McMonagle) Summer flowering plants and lawn
No 10 (Mrs C F Demuth) Paved garden with roses and interesting trees
No 11 (Mrs M Stewart) Roses, summerhouse, flowering plants
No 12 (Mr & Mrs P Bennett) Original paved small garden with trees
No 14 (Mr & Mrs A H P Humphrey) Roses, flowering plants, greenhouse and bonsai collection
Ambrose Villa (Mr & Mrs Frank Leocadi) Italian style small town garden

Ansty Gardens ✿❀ On A272. 3m W of Haywards Heath. 1m E of A23. Start in car park signposted in Ansty village. Coffee, Ploughmans, TEAS & plants in aid of Riding for the Disabled, St Catherines, St James & St Peters Hospice, Ansty Village Hall Trust. *Combined adm £2.50 Chd free. Suns May 11, July 6 (11-6)*

Apple Tree Cottage (Mr & Mrs Longfield) Cottage garden, herbaceous borders, mature trees
Brenfield (Mr & Mrs Mace) Major private collection of cacti and succulents
Greenacre (Mr & Mrs Owen) 2½-acre mixed garden
Netherby (Mr & Mrs Gilbert) Cottage garden
Whydown Cottage (Mr & Mrs Gibson) 1-acre woodland garden. TEAS

Ashburnham Place ♿✿❀ (Ashburnham Christian Trust) Battle. 5m W of Battle on A271 (formerly B2204). 220 acres of beautifully landscaped gardens, with glorious views over 3 lakes, designed by George Dance and Capability Brown. Extensive 4-acre walled garden being restored incl recently planted scented garden and kitchen gardens. Peaceful woodland walks. Features from several centuries. Cream TEAS in C18 orangery. *Adm £2.50 Chd 50p (Share to Ashburnham Christian Trust®). Wed, Thurs, Fri, Sun June 11, 12, 13, 15 (2-5.30)*

¶Ashdown Park Hotel ✿ 6m S of Grinstead. Take A22, 3m S of Forest Row, turn L at Wych Cross by garage, 1m on R. From M25 take M23 S and leave at junction 10 taking A264 to E Grinstead. Approach from S on A22, turn R at Wych Cross. 186 acres surrounding Ashdown Park hotel. Parkland setting where wild deer roam freely, a mixture of woodland walks, water gardens and walled garden. (New Victorian glasshouse due to open in Spring 1997). Fine mature specimen trees, gardens and grounds now being restored, newly cleared pond in woods and a restored 'Secret Garden' due for completion during 1997. TEA. *Adm £2.50 Chd free. Suns June 8, Aug 10 (2-6)*

Baker's Farm ✿❀ (Mr & Mrs Mark Burrell) Shipley, 5m S of Horsham. Take A24 then A272 W, 2nd turn to Dragon's Green, L at George and Dragon then 300yds on L. Large Wealden garden; lake; laburnum tunnel; shrubs, trees, rose walks of old-fashioned roses; scented knot garden and bog gardens. TEAS. *Adm £1.50 Chd 30p (Share to St Mary the Virgin, Shipley®). Suns May 25, June 29 (2-6). Parties by appt, please* **Tel 01403 741215**

Bankton Cottage ♿✿❀ (Mr & Mrs Robin Lloyd) Crawley Down. 4m W of East Grinstead. 2½m E of M23 (J.10). On B2028 1m N of Turners Hill Xrds. 3½-acre partially walled cottage garden, herbaceous borders, shrub and climbing roses, small lake and pond with bog gardens. Enormous number of terracotta pots planted up, many seconds for sale. TEAS in aid of Cheshire Homes. *Adm £1.50 Chd free. Sat, Sun June 21, 22 (2-6). Parties welcome by appt May to July, please* **Tel 01342 718907 or 714793**

▲Bateman's ♿✿ (The National Trust) Burwash ½m S (A265). From rd leading S from W end of village. Home of Rudyard Kipling from 1902-1936. Garden laid out before he lived in house and planted yew hedges, rose garden, laid paths and made pond. Bridge to mill which grinds local wheat into flour. LUNCHES & TEAS. *Adm £4.50 Groups 15 or more £3.50 Chd £2.25. For NGS Wed June 25 (11-5.30) last entry 4.30. Parties welcome by appt on open days, please* **Tel 01435 882302**

Bates Green ♿✿❀ (Mr & Mrs J R McCutchan) Arlington. 2½m SW of A22 at Hailsham and 2m S Michelham Priory, Upper Dicker. Approach Arlington passing the 'Old Oak Inn' on R continue for 350yds then turn R along a small lane. [TQ5507] Plantsman's tranquil garden of over 1 acre gives year-round interest; rockery; water; mixed borders with colour themes, and shaded foliage garden. B & B accommodation. TEAS (Suns) TEA (Mons). *Adm £2 Chd free. Suns April 6, June 29, Sept 7 (2.30-5). Mons April 7, June 30, Sept 8 (10-5) Private visits welcome, please* **Tel 01323 482039**

Berri Court &❀ (Mr & Mrs J C Turner) Yapton, 5m SW of Arundel. In centre of village between PO & Black Dog public house. A2024 Littlehampton-Chichester rd passes. Intensely planted 2-acre garden of wide interest; trees, flowering shrubs, heathers, eucalyptus, daffodils, shrub roses, hydrangeas and lily pond. *Adm £1.50 Chd free. Suns, Mons March 23, 24, May 11, 12; June 29, 30, (2-5); Fri July 4 (6-8.30) with a glass of wine. Private visits welcome for 4 and more, please* Tel 01243 551663

Bignor Park (The Viscount & Viscountess Mersey) Pulborough, 5m from Petworth on West Burton rd. Nearest village Sutton (Sussex). 11 acres of trees, shrubs, flowers and magnificent views of the South Downs, from Chanctonbury Ring to Bignor Hill. Music in the temple. TEAS. *Adm £2 Chd free. Sun, Mon May 4, 5 (2-5)*

Bohunt Manor, Liphook see Hampshire

▲**Borde Hill Garden** &❀ 1½m N of Haywards Heath on Balcombe Rd. Borde Hill is Britain's best private collection of champion trees. Tranquil gardens with rich variety of all season colour set in 200 acres of parkland and woods. Attractions incl the rhododendrons, azaleas, new Autumn borders, rose and herbaceous garden. Woodland walks and lakes with picnic area; children's trout fishing; "Pirates" adventure playground; Tea room, restaurant, gift shop & plant centre. *Adm £2.50 Chd £1. For NGS Thurs, Fri May 1, 2 (10-6)* Tel 01444 450326

Buckhurst Park ✄ (Earl & Countess De La Warr) Withyham. On B2110 between Hartfield and Groombridge. Drive adjacent to Dorset Arms public house. Historic garden undergoing complete restoration. Repton park, large lake with woodland walk and ornamental waterfall and rocks created by James Pulham. Terraces, lily pond and pergolas designed by Lutyens and originally planted by Jekyll. Shetland pony stud. TEAS. *Adm £2.50 Chd £1 (Share to Sussex Historic Churches©). Sat June 21 (2-5.30). Private visits welcome, please* Tel 01892 770790 or 770220

Bumble Cottage ✄ (Mr & Mrs D Salisbury-Jones) West Chiltington. 2m E of Pulborough, 2m N of Storrington. From Pulborough turn off A283 E of Pulborough into W Chiltington Rd then R into Monkmead Lane (signed Roundabout Hotel) follow yellow signs. From Storrington take B2139 W into Greenhurst Lane, R at T Junction 100yds fork L into Monkmead Lanel. Charming 'all seasons' garden of 1 acre created from a sandy slope. Wide variety of interesting trees, shrubs and plants combined with ponds all set off by very fine lawn. Featured on Grassroots TV programme. *Adm £1.50 Chd 25p. Sats, Suns July 19, 20, 26, 27 (2-6)*

Cabbages & Kings see Wilderness Farm

Casters Brook &✄ (Mr & Mrs John Whitehorn) Cocking; 3m S of Midhurst at Cocking PO on A286 take sharp turn E; garden is 100yds to right. Extensive ponds with islands, trout and a small bridge distinguish this 2-acre site, sloping past lawns and rose beds down to the ponds with a huge gunnera under a massive plain tree Near the house are a fig court and a herb garden, by the churchyard a secret garden and a shady walk. Dramatic sculptures by Philip Jackson on loan add the finishing touch. TEAS.

Adm £1.50 Chd free (Share to Cocking Church®). Suns June 29, July 6 (2-6) Thurs July 3 with licensed bar (5.30-7.30). Private visits welcome, please Tel 01730 813537

Cedar Tree Cottage ✄❀ (Mr & Mrs G Goatcher) Rock Rd, Washington. Turn W off A24 ¼m N. of Washington Roundabout. Park in 'Old Nursery' Car Park. Mixed borders with many unusual shrubs and perennials, leading into newly developing 5 acre arboretum with many rare subjects and also some fine mature trees and shrubs dating from early C20. Good views of S Downs. Picnics welcome. TEAS in aid of Sussex Wildlife Trust. *Adm £1.50 Chd free. Sat, Wed April 26, 30, Sun May 4 (2-5.30)*

Champs Hill &✄❀ (Mr & Mrs David Bowerman) Coldwaltham, S of Pulborough. From Pulborough on A29, in Coldwaltham turn R to Fittleworth Rd; garden 300yds on R. From Petworth turn off B2138 just S of Fittleworth to Coldwaltham, garden approx ½m on L. 27 acres of formal garden and woodland walks around old sand pit. Conifers and acid-loving plants, many specie heathers labelled. Superb views across Arun valley. Special features. March - Winter heathers and spring flowers. May - rhododendrons, azaleas, wild flowers. August - heathers and other specialities. TEAS (Suns, Mon only). *Adm £2 Chd free. Suns, Weds March 9, 12, 16, 19, 23; Bank Hol Mon May 5, Suns, Weds, May 4, 7, 11, 14, 18, 21 Aug, 3, 6, 10, 13, 17, 20. Suns (2-6), Weds (11-4). Private visits welcome for parties of 10 and over, please* Tel 01798 831868

Chantry Green House ✄❀ (Mr R S Forrow & Mrs J B McNeil) Steyning. 5m N of Worthing, 10m NW of Brighton off A283. Turn into Church St from High St opp White Horse Inn. Garden 150yds down on LH-side. Parking on Fletchers Croft car park, entrance opp church. An interesting 1-acre garden, recently redesigned by Jack Grant White. Features incl a wall fountain, herbaceous borders and extensive shrub borders with a predominance of colourful evergreens providing interest throughout the year. There is also a small arboretum and rock and water garden. TEAS and plants in aid of NSPCC. *Adm £1.50 Chd 50p. Sat, Sun June 14, 15 (2-5)*

Chidmere House & (Thomas Baxendale Esq) Chidham, 6m W of Chichester. A259 1m Bus: SD276/200 Chichester-Emsworth. Interesting garden; subject of article in 'Country Life'; yew and hornbeam hedges; bulbs, and flowering shrubs bounded by large mere, now a private nature reserve. C16 house (not open). TEAS Suns only. *Adm £2 Chd free under 12 (Share to Chidham Parish Church®). Suns, Mons April 13, 14, May 25, 26 (2-6) Aug 24, 25 (2-7). Parties welcome, please* Tel 01243 572287 or 573096

¶**Church Farm** &✄❀ (Mr Jerome O'Hea) 4¼ miles E of Chichester. Take B2233 off A27. Turn into Oving Rd. Entrance 250yds on L. 4 acres designed by John Brookes. Shrub and climbing roses, herbaceous borders, partially walled garden, pond, conservatory. TEAS. *Adm £1.50 Chd 50p. Sun June 29 (2-6)*

Clinton Lodge &✄❀ (Mr & Mrs H Collum) Fletching, 4m NW of Uckfield; from A272 turn N at Piltdown for Fletching, 1½m. 6-acre formal and romantic garden, overlooking parkland, with old roses, double herbaceous borders, yew hedges, pleached lime walks, copy of C17 scented herb garden, medieval-style potager, vine and rose allee, wild flower garden. Carolean and Georgian house (not open). Plant Stall on June 15, 16. TEAS. *Adm £2.50 Chd £1 (Share to Fletching Church Fabric Fund®). Sun June 15; Mon June 16, Weds June 18, 25, July 2 (2-6). Parties over 20 welcome, please* **Tel 01825 722952**

Coates Manor ✕✿ (Mrs G H Thorp) nr Fittleworth. ½m S of Fittleworth; turn off B2138 at signpost marked 'Coates'. 1 acre, mainly shrubs and foliage of special interest. Small walled garden with tender and scented plants. Often featured in UK and foreign gardening magazines. Elizabethan house (not open) scheduled of historic interest. TEAS in aid of Children's Society *Adm £1.50 Chd 20p. Sun, Mon, Oct 19, 20 (11-5). Private visits welcome, please* **Tel 01798 865356**

Cobblers &✕✿ (Mr & Mrs Martin Furniss) Mount Pleasant, Jarvis Brook, Crowborough. A26, at Crowborough Cross take B2100 towards Crowborough Station. At 2nd Xrds turn into Tollwood Rd for ¼m. 2-acre sloping site designed by present owners since 1968 to display outstanding range of herbaceous and shrub species and water garden, giving all season colour. Subject of numerous articles. *Adm £3.50 Chd £1 (incl home-made TEAS). Mons May 26, Aug 25, Suns June 22, July 13, Aug 3 (2.30-5.30). Wed June 11, Wine (5.30-8). Groups welcome by appt, please* **Tel 01892 655969**

Combehurst ✿ (Mrs E E Roberts) 3m S of Tunbridge Wells off A267, 400yds S of B2099. 2½-acre beautifully laid out garden; shrubs, trees, plants. TEAS. *Adm £2 Chd free. Private visits and small coach parties welcome by appt, April to Sept (2-5). Please* **Tel 01892 750367**

Cooke's House &✕ (Miss J B Courtauld) West Burton, 5m SW of Pulborough. Turn off A29 at White Horse, Bury, ¾m. Old garden with views of the Downs, Elizabethan house (not open); varied interest, spring flowers, topiary, herbaceous borders, herbs. Tea. *Adm £1.50 Chd free under 14. Suns, Mons, Tues April 6, 7, 8, 13, 14, 15 (2-6). Private visits welcome, please* **Tel 01798 831353**

Cooksbridge ✕ (Mr & Mrs N Tonkin) Fernhurst. On A286 between Haslemere and Midhurst, ¾m S of Fernhurst Xrds. 6 acres, and adjoining bluebell wood beside the R Lodd. Pictured in GRBS 1992 & 93 calendars this is a plantsman's garden for all seasons. Features incl the herbaceous border, vine and ornamental plant houses, lily pond and lake with waterfowl. TEAS. *Adm £2 Chd 50p 5 and under free (Share to Sussex Wildlife Trust®). Sat, Sun Aug 2, 3 (2-6). Private visits and groups welcome by appt, please* **Tel 01428 652212**

Cookscroft &✿ (Mr & Mrs John Williams) Earnley. 6m S of Chichester. At end of Birdham Straight take L fork to E Wittering. 1m on, before sharp bend turn L into Bookers Lane. 2nd house on L. 5-acre garden started from fields 7yrs ago. Many trees grown from provenance seeds or liners. Collections of eucalyptus, birch, snake bark maples and unusual shrubs. 3 ponds with waterfalls and a Japanese garden. An interesting and developing garden, incl a woodland area. TEAS in aid of St Wilfrids Hospice.

Adm £1.50 Chd free. Sun, Mon May 25, 26 (2-6). Private visits welcome by appt, please **Tel 01243 513671**

Coombland &✕✿ (Mr & Mrs Neville Lee) Coneyhurst. In Billingshurst turn off A29 onto A272 to Haywards Heath; approx 2m, in Coneyhurst, turn S for further ¾m. Large garden of 5 acres developed since 1981 with the help and advice of Graham Stuart Thomas. Undulating site on heavy clay. Old shrub-rose beds, rose species and ramblers scrambling up ageing fruit trees; extensive planting of hardy geraniums; herbaceous border with interesting planting. Oak woodland; orchard dell with hybrid rhododendrons; hostas; primulas and woodland plants. Nightingale wood with water area. Large planting of iris, water wheel. Featured in magazines and TV. National collection of hardy geraniums held here. TEAS. *Adm £1.50 Chd 50p (Share to NCCPG May 31 only). Sats May 31 June 14, 21, 28 (10-5) Tues June 10, 17 (2-5). Nursery open Mon to Fri (2-4). Parties welcome, please* **Tel 01403 741727**

Cowbeech Farm ✕✿ (Mrs M Huiskamp) Cowbeech. 4m NE of Hailsham. A271 to Amberstone, turn off N for Cowbeech. 5-acre garden with knot herb garden and water feature. Bog garden with many unusual plants, Japanese garden with bridge, moongate and waterfall - carp and koi carp. Beautiful colours in spring and autumn. New yellow and red borders. Farmhouse TEAS. *Adm £2.50 Chd £1.25. Suns June 1, Sept 28 (2-5) Mon June 2 (4-8) wine. Private visits welcome by appt for minimum of 10 May to Oct, please* **Tel 01323 832134**

Cowdray Park Gardens ✕ (The Viscount Cowdray) S of A272. 1m E of Midhurst. Entrance by East Front. Avenue of Wellingtonias; rhododendrons; azaleas; sunken garden with large variety trees and shrubs, Lebanon cedar 300 yrs old; pleasure garden surrounded by ha-ha, new water garden. TEA. *Adm £2 Chd free. Sun May 25 (2-6)*

Crown House &✕✿ (Maj L Cave) Eridge, 3m SW of Tunbridge Wells. A26 Tunbridge Wells-Crowborough rd; in Eridge take Rotherfield turn S, then take 1st R, house 1st on L. 1½ acres with pools; rose garden & rose walk; herbaceous border; herb garden. Full size croquet lawn. Prize winner in Sunday Express garden of the year competition. Plant and produce stalls. TEAS. *Adm £1.50 Chd under 14 free (Share to Multiple Sclerosis®). Sat, Sun July 12, 13 (2-6). Private visits welcome May to Aug, please* **Tel 01892 864389 or 864605**

Dallington Cottage Gardens 6m NW of Battle. 5m E of Heathfield. Turn S off B2096 for ¼m nr school. Lunches & Cream TEAS. *Combined adm £2.50 Chd under 12 free. Fri, Sat June 27, 28 (11-6)*

    Brookfield (Mr & Mrs John Britten) Approx ⅔-acre, lawns, varied shrubs and clematis collection

    Staces (Mr & Mrs J Steel) Approx ⅔-acre, terraced hillside garden with extensive downland views, old roses, rockery with waterfall

▲**Denmans** &✕✿ (The Executors of the late Mrs J H Robinson & Mr John Brookes) Denmans Lane, Fontwell. Chichester and Arundel 5m. Turn S on A27 at Denmans Lane, W of Fontwell Racecourse. Renowned gardens extravagantly planted for overall, all-year interest in form, colour and texture; areas of glass for tender species. TEAS. *Adm £2.50 OAPs £2.25 Chd £1.50 (Share to Friends of the Aldingbourne Trust®). For NGS Thurs July 31 (5.30-8) Sept 18 (9-5)* **Tel 01243 542808**

¶**Doucegrove Farm** ✣ (Mr P M Camp) Northiam. 9m N Hastings, 9m W Rye. From Northiam take A28 S 1½m to Horns Cross ¼m S turn L at sign to Catholic Church, 100 yds turn L, on R. Park in church car park before gates to Private Rd. 2 acres of formal garden incl four ponds, two rose gardens and many interesting varieties of trees, shrubs and plants. *Adm £3 Chd £1. Thurs, Fri June 19, 20 (10-4)*

Down Place ✣✣ (Mr & Mrs D M Thistleton-Smith) 1m E of South Harting. B2124 to Chichester, turn L down unmarked lane below top of hill. This large hillside, chalk garden is surrounded by woodlands, with fine views of surrounding countryside. The garden sweeps down through terraced herbaceous, shrub and rose borders to a natural meadow containing many wild flowers incl several species of orchid. Woodland walks and interesting kitchen and cottage gardens. TEAS. *Adm £1.50 Chd 50p (Share to Harting Parish Church®). Fri, Sat, Sun June 20, 21, 22 (2-6)*

Duckyls ✤ (Lady Taylor) Sharpthorne. 4m SW of E Grinstead. 6m E of Crawley. At Turners Hill take B2028 S 1m fork left to W Hoathly, turn L signed Gravetye Manor. Interesting old 12-acre woodland garden. Partly suitable for wheelchairs. TEAS. *Adm £3 Chd £1 (Share to Elizabeth Fitzroy Homes®). Thurs April 24, May 15, 22 (12-6). Parties welcome by appt, please* **Fax/Tel 01342 811038**

¶**Duckyls Holt** ✤ (Mr & Mrs Kenneth Hill) West Hoathly. 4m SW of E Grinstead. 6m E of Crawley. At Turners Hill take B2028 S 1m fork left to W Hoathly, 2m on R. A surprisingly intimate cottage garden of about 2 acres on many different levels. Small herb garden, formal and informal plantings. Herbaceous borders and rose border. Heated swimming pool, which visitors are welcome to use. TEAS. *Adm £1.50 Chd free. Thurs May 29, June 12 (11-5.30) Also open within walking distance* **The Priest House**

Ebbsworth ✣✣ (Mrs F Lambert) Nutbourne nr Pulborough. Take A283 E from junction with A29 (Swan Corner) 2m with 2 L forks signposted Nutbourne. Pass Rising Sun and follow signs to garden. Charming, well-planted, owner maintained cottage garden, surrounding old cottage. Roses and lilies, together with herbaceous borders. Manmade stream and ponds planted with water plants. Flower arranging demonstration by Brinsbury College students. TEAS. *Adm £1.50 Chd free. Sun, Mon June 22, 23 (2-5)*

Fittleworth Gardens ✤✣✤ Fittleworth A283 midway Petworth-Pulborough; in Fittleworth turn onto B2138 then turn W at Swan. Car parking available. TEAS and plants in aid of NSPCC and St Wilfred's Hospice, Chichester. *Combined adm £2 Chd free. Suns May 18, June 15 (2-6)*

    The Grange (Mr & Mrs W M Caldwell) 3-acre garden; spring flowering shrubs, specimen trees, herbaceous borders; pond and stream; small walled garden redesigned and replanted 1995. Old roses, clematis and herbaceous. Small formal vegetable & cutting garden, swimming pool garden designed & planted 1996-1997

The Hermitage (Mr & Mrs P F Dutton) Charming informal garden; azaleas, rhododendrons sloping to the R Rother with riverside walk and lovely views to the S Downs. Guide Dogs only

Lowerstreet House (L J Holloway Esq) Small garden with shrubs, bulbs, herbaceous

▲**Fitzhall** ✣✤ (Mr & Mrs G F Bridger) Iping, 3m W of Midhurst. 1m off A272, signposted Harting Elsted. 9 acres; herb garden; herbaceous and shrub borders; vegetable garden. Farm adjoining. House (not open) originally built 1550. TEAS. *Adm £2 Chd £1. For NGS Suns June 1, July 20, Sept 7 (2-6). Private visits welcome, please* **Tel 01730 813634**

Frewen College (Brickwall) ♿ (Frewen Charitable Trust) Northiam. 8m NW of Rye on B2088. Tudor home of Frewen family since 1666. Featured in the filming of 'Cold Comfort Farm'. Gardens and walls built and laid out by Jane Frewen c1680; chess and knot gardens; arboretum. Cream TEAS (scones & cream only). *Adm £2 Chd £1 under 10 free. Sun July 27 (2-5). Parties welcome of 30 to 50, please* **Tel 01797 223329**

Frith Hill ✣✤ (Mr & Mrs Peter Warne) Northchapel 7m N of Petworth on A283 turn E in centre of Northchapel into Pipers Lane (by Deep Well Inn) after ¾m turn L into bridleway immed past Peacocks Farm. 1-acre garden, comprising walled gardens with herbaceous border; shrubbery; pond; old-fashioned rose garden and arbour. Herb garden leading to white garden with gazebo. Outstanding views of Sussex Weald. Wine (June 14). *Adm £2.50 Chd free (Share to 1st Northchapel Scouts®). Sats June 14 (5-8), 28 (2-6)*

Frith Lodge (Mr & Mrs Geoffrey Cridland) Northchapel. 7m N of Petworth on A283 turn E in centre of Northchapel into Pipers Lane (by Deep Well Inn) after ¾m turn L into bridleway immediately past Peacocks Farm. 1-acre cottage style garden created around pair of Victorian game-keepers cottages. Undulating ground with roses, informal planting with paved and hedged areas; outstanding views of Sussex Weald. *Adm £1.50 Chd 50p. Sats June 14 (5-8) 28 (2-6). Parties welcome by appt only, please write to Frith Lodge, Northchapel, W Sussex, GU28 9JE*

The Garden in Mind ✣ (Mr & Mrs Ivan Hicks - Stansted Park Foundation) The Lower Walled Garden. Stansted Park, Rowlands Castle. Follow brown signs. Stansted is 3m NE of Havant, 7m W of Chichester. A surreal symbolic ½-acre walled garden. Began in 1991 as a concept for BBC2 Dream Garden series. Extravagent planting combined with sculpture, assemblage, found objects, mirrors and chance encounters. Wide range of plants; sequioa to sempervivum, marigolds to meliathus, grasses, foliage plants, topiary and tree sculpture. Featured in numerous publications and TV. Come with an open mind. *Adm £2 Chd donation. Suns June 1, Sept 21 (2-6)*

Gaywood Farm ♿✣ (Mrs Anthony Charles) nr Pulborough. 3m S of Billingshurst turn L off A29 into Gay Street Lane. After railway bridge at 2nd junction fork L and at T junction turn L signed 'no through rd'. 2-acre garden, surrounding ancient farm house, built between

C14 and C18. Fine weeping Ash, black Mulberry, Irish yews and extravagantly planted borders with interesting plant assoc. Large pond surrounded by good planting. *Adm £2 Chd free. Sats, Suns May 31, June 1, 21, 22 (2-5). Private visits groups only welcome, please* **Tel 01798 812223**

Ghyll Farm, Sweethaws Lane ✿ (Mr & Mrs I Ball) Crowborough. 1m S of Crowborough centre on A26. L into Sheep Plain Lane immed R Sweethaws Lane ½m. 'The Permissive Garden' planted by the late Lady Pearce. 1-acre, azaleas, camellias, woodland bluebell walk; spectacular views. TEAS. *Adm £1.50 Chd 50p. Suns April 20, May 11, 25 (2-5.30) Private visits welcome, April to end July, please* Tel 01892 655505

● **Great Dixter** ✿✿ (Christopher Lloyd) Northiam, ½m N of Northiam, off A28 8m NW of Rye. For bus information call 01797 223053. Topiary; wide variety of plants. Historical house open (2-5). *Adm house & garden £4 Chd 50p OAPs & NT members (Fris only) £3.50; garden only £3 Chd 25p. March 28 to Oct 15 daily except Mons but open on Bank Hols (2-5).*

Greenacres ✿✿ (Mr & Mrs John Hindley) Crowborough. From A26 at Crowborough Cross take B2100 S. At 1st Xrd R into Montagis Way, then 2nd L into Luxford Rd for ⅓m. 2-acre sloping woodland garden maintained wholly by present owners. Developed over the years with interesting water features fed by natural springs: ponds, bog area, naturalised area, raised island beds. Many trees, shrubs and foliage plants. A tranquil garden with views over countryside. TEA. *Adm £2 Chd free. Private visits welcome, please* **Tel 01892 653069**

Hailsham Grange ✿✿✿ (Noel Thompson Esq) Hailsham. Turn off Hailsham High St into Vicarage Rd, park in public car park. Formal garden designed and planted since 1988 in grounds of former C17 Vicarage (not open). A series of garden areas representing a modern interpretation of C18 formality; Gothic summerhouse; pleached hedges; herbaceous borders; romantic planting in separate garden compartments. Featured in Country Living and Grass Roots. Teas in adjacent church in aid of The Hailsham Church Clock Restoration Fund. *Adm £1.50 Chd free. Suns June 8, July 6 (2-5.30). Floral Festival in Adjacent Church July 6*

Hammerwood House ✿✿ (The Hon Mrs J Lakin) Iping, 1m N of A272 Midhurst to Petersfield Rd. Approx 3m W of Midhurst. Well signposted. Large informal garden; fine trees, rhododendrons, azaleas, acers, cornus, magnolias; wild garden (¼m away), bluebells, stream. TEAS (May only). *Adm £2 Chd free (Share to King Edward VII Hospital, Midhurst®). Suns May 11, 18 (1.30-5.30) June 22 (2-5.30)*

■ **High Beeches Gardens** ✿ (High Beeches Gardens Conservation Trust) Situated on B2110 1m E of A23 at Handcross. 20-acres of enchanting landscaped woodland and water gardens; spring daffodils; bluebell and azalea walks; many rare and beautiful plants; wild flower meadows, glorious autumn colours. Picnic area. Car park. *Daily April, May, June, Sept, Oct (1-5) closed on Weds. In July & Aug Mons & Tues only. Adm £3 Acc chd free (Share*

to St Mary's Church, Slaugham®). For NGS Suns April 20, Sept 7 (1-5). Also by appt for organised groups at any time, please Tel 01444 400589

▲**Highdown, Goring-by-Sea** ✿✿ (Worthing Borough Council) Littlehampton Rd (A259), 3m W of Worthing. Station: Goring-by-Sea, 1m. Famous garden created by Sir F Stern situated in chalk pit and downland area containing a wide collection of plants. Spring bulbs, paeonies, shrubs and trees. Many plants were raised from seed brought from China by great collectors like Wilson, Farrer and Kingdon-Ward. TEAS. *Collecting box. For NGS Mons May 5, 26, Aug 25 (10-8). Parties by appt, please* **Tel 01903 239999 ext 2544**

1 & 6 Holbrook Park ✿✿✿ (Mr & Mrs Paul Leithsmith & Louise & John Pollard) From Horsham take A24 Dorking direction. At roundabout take A264 signposted Gatwick. Follow dual carriageway then 2nd lane on L marked Old Holbrook, formerly Northlands Rd. Please park carefully on RH-side of lane. 10 acres Victorian parkland garden with fine trees, azaleas and rhododendrons. Informal areas provide colour and interest throughout the year, shrub and herbaceous walk, two ponds, conservatory, Pergola, recently planted Bamboo walk. Coffee, Ploughman's Lunches, TEAS. *Adm £2 Chd free. Sun May 18 (11-5). No 6 only Plantswomen and designers garden, private visits welcome Thurs April - end October (1-4) please* **Tel 01403 252491**

Home Farm House ✿ (Mrs P Cooper) Buckham Hill. Uckfield-Isfield back rd. Small attractive cottage garden; interesting shrubs. *Adm £1.25 Chd free. Sun, Mon June 29, 30 (2-5.30). Private visits also welcome Jan to March to see 20ft mimosa, please* **Tel 01825 763960**. *Also open* **Pheasants Hatch**

Houghton Farm ✿✿ (Mr & Mrs Michael Lock) Arundel. Turn E off A29 at top of Bury Hill onto B2139 or W from Storrington onto B2139 to Houghton. 1-acre garden with wide variety of shrubs and plants, interesting corners and beautiful views. Tea Houghton Bridge Tea Gardens. *Adm £1.50 Chd free. Weds April 23, May 28, June 25, July 16 (2-5)*

Hurst Mill ✿ Hurst. 2m SE of Petersfield on B2146 midway between Petersfield and S Harting. 8-acre garden on many levels in lovely position overlooking 4-acre lake in wooded valley with wildfowl. Waterfall and Japanese water garden beside historic mill. Bog garden; large rock garden with orientally inspired plantings; acers, camellias, rhododendrons, azaleas, magnolias, hydrangeas and ferns; shrubs and climbing roses; forest and ornamental trees. TEAS. *Adm £2 Chd free. Suns April 27, May 25, June 29 (2-5)*

The Royal Horticultural Society's Garden at Wisley

Exclusive evening openings in aid of the National Gardens Scheme on the occasion of its 70th anniversary

Wednesday 18th June & Thursday 14th August
6.30-9pm
See page 18.

¶**Hurston Place** (Mrs David Bigham) Pulborough. Off the A283 between Pulborough and Storrington approx 3m. From Pulborough going towards Storrington at 2 cottages turn L. Straight down lane, over small bridge round to R and garden on L behind mature yew hedge. A garden divided into 2 parts: One a walled, semi formal garden with boxed edged beds, vegetables and borders. Two herbaceous wall beds, planted mainly in the cottage garden style. Orchard and wild part of garden has good daffodils and narcissi in April. TEAS in aid of Parham Church. *Adm 1.50 Chd 50p. Sun April 13, Sat, Sun, Mon June 21, 22, 23 (2-6)*

Ketches &❀ (David Manwaring Robertson Esq) Newick, 5m W of Uckfield on A272. Take Barcombe Rd S out of Newick, house is on right opp turning to Newick Church. 3 acres; lovely old-fashioned roses; specimen trees; shrub and herbaceous borders. TEAS. *Adm £1.50 Chd under 12 free. Sun June 22 (2-6). Parties welcome by appt, mid May to mid July, please* **Tel 01825 722679**

King Edward VII Hospital & Midhurst. 3m NW of Midhurst. Hospital built early this century, stands in grounds of 152 acres elevated position of great natural beauty; extensive views across Downs. Gardens by Gertrude Jekyll. Aspect over gardens and pine woods little changed. TEAS. *Collecting box. Sat April 19 (10-4)*

King John's Lodge &❀❀ (Mr & Mrs R A Cunningham) Etchingham. Burwash to Etchingham on the A265 turn L before Etchingham Church into Church Lane which leads into Sheepstreet Lane after ½m. L after 1m. 3-acre romantic garden surrounding a listed house. Formal garden with water features, wild garden, rose walk, large herbaceous borders, old shrub roses and secret garden. B & B accommodation. Garden Statuary for sale. TEAS. *Adm £2 Chd free. Sat June 7 (2-6), Sun June 8 (11-6). Also private visits welcome, please* **Tel 01580 819232**

Kingston Gardens ❀ 2½m SW of Lewes. Turn off A27 signposted Kingston at roundabout; at 30 mph sign turn R. Home-made TEAS **Nightingales**. *Combined adm (payable at* **Nightingales** *only) £2 Chd free. Suns June 8, July 27 (2-6)*

> **Nightingales** (Geoff & Jean Hudson) The Avenue. Informal sloping ½-acre garden for all-year interest; wide range of plants incl shrub roses, hardy geraniums, perennials, ground cover. Mediterranean plants, conservatory. Childrens play area. Short steep walk or drive, parking limited, to:-
> **The White House** (John & Sheila Maynard Smith) The Ridge. ½-acre garden on a chalk ridge. Shrubs, herbaceous border, alpines; greenhouse with unusual plants

Knabbs's Farmhouse &❀ (Mrs W G Graham) 4m NW of Uckfield; from A272 turn N at Pildown for Fletching, 1 ½m. Garden at N end of village and farm. ½-acre informal garden; mixed beds and borders; shrubs, roses, perennials, foliage plants. Good views over ha-ha. Teas at Clinton Lodge. *Adm £1 Chd 20p. Sun, Mon June 15, 16 (2-6)*

Lane End ❀ (Mrs C J Epril) Sheep Lane, Midhurst. In North St turn L at Knock-hundred Row, L into Sheep lane, L to garden. Park at church or in lane. 2 acres incl wild garden; alpine rockery with pools; rhododendrons, azaleas, heath border. Below ramparts of original castle with fine views over water meadows to ruins of Cowdray House. Tea Midhurst. *Adm £1 Chd free. Sats, Suns, Mons May 24, 25, 26; 31, June 1, 2 (11-6)*

Latchetts ❀❀ (Mr & Mrs Laurence Hardy) Dane Hill. 5m NE Haywards Heath. SW off A275 into Freshfield Lane. 1m on R. Parking in field. 3-4 acre well maintained country garden still being developed bordering fields and woods. Overlooking lake. Lawns, shrubs, mixed borders, terraces with interesting brick and stone paving, water features, vegetable garden. TEAS. *Adm £2 Chd 50p. Fri, Sat Aug 15, 16, (2-5.30)*

Legsheath Farm &❀ (Mr & Mrs Michael Neal) Legsheath Lane. 2m W of Forest Row, 1m S of Weirwood Reservoir. Panoramic views over reservoir. Exciting 10-acre garden with woodland walks, water gardens and formal borders. Of particular interest, clumps of wild orchids, a fine davidia, acers, eucryphia and rhododendrons. TEAS. *Adm £2 Chd free. Sun May 18 (2-6)*

Lilac Cottage ❀ (Mrs G A Hawkins) Willet Close, Duncton. 3m S of Petworth on the W side of A285 opp entrance to Burton Park. Park in Close. ¼-acre village garden on several levels with shrubs, small trees and approx 100 varieties of shrub and climbing roses and herb garden. TEAS. *Adm 80p. Sat, Sun, Wed June 14, 15, 18 (2-6). Private visits welcome, please* **Tel 01798 343006**

Little Dene ❀❀ (Prof & Mrs D Anderson) Chelwood Gate. 8m S of East Grinstead. Take A275 off A22 at Wych Cross, then 1st L and 2nd R. Plantsman's garden yr-round interest. Many unusual shrubs and climbers, over 100 clematis, raised alpine bed. Wheelchairs if dry. *Adm £1.50. First Thurs in month May-Aug (11-5). Private visits and parties welcome, please* **Tel 01825 740657**

Little Hutchings &❀❀ (Mr & Mrs P Hayes) Fontridge Lane, Etchingham.[TQ 708248.]Take A265 to Etchingham from A21 at Hurst Green. 1st turning L after level crossing. R after ½m. Colourful 1½-acre old-fashioned cottage garden laid out over 21 years. At least 300 different roses, over 100 metres of tightly packed herbaceous borders full of many different perennials. Large collection of clematis. Shrubberies containing specimen trees and shrubs. Kitchen garden. TEAS. *Adm £2.10 Chd free. Sun June 8 (11-5)*

Little Thakeham ❀❀ (Mr & Mrs T Ractliff) Storrington. Take A24 S to Worthing and at roundabout 2m S of Ashington return N up A24 for 200yds. Turn L into Rock Rd for 1m. At staggered Xrds turn R into Merrywood Lane and garden is 300yds on R. From Storrington take B2139 to Thakeham. After 1m turn R into Merrywood Lane and garden is 400yds on L. 4-acre garden with paved walks, rose pergola, flowering shrubs, specimen trees, herbaceous borders and carpets of daffodils in spring. The garden laid out to the basic design of Sir Edward Lutyens in 1902 and planted by his his client Ernest Blackburn. No toilet fac. House closed to public. Partially suitable for wheelchairs. TEAS. *Adm £2 Chd £1. Mons, Tues April 7, 8, June 9, 10 (2-5)*

¶**The Lodge Garden** ✿✱ (Sandra Worley & Danny Butler) Westfield. Between Westfield & Sedlescombe. From Hastings take A28 Ashford Rd to Westfield Village. Just past car showroom turn L into Cottage Lane past post office approx 2m on L adjacent to Westfield Place. The garden has been completely redesigned by the present occupiers over the last 4 yrs into a plantsman's cottage style garden and nursery. Boasting a wide range of unusual herbaceous plants & shrubs completely surrounded by deciduous woodland. It also holds several garden features incl pond, arches, gazebo & an 1860 working hand pump. TEAS. *Adm £1.50. Nursery open Wed to Sun. Suns Mons July 6, 7, Sept 7, 8 (10.30-5) Parties welcome by appt, please* **Tel 01424 870186**

Malt House ✱ (Mr & Mrs Graham Ferguson) Chithurst, Rogate. From A272, 3½m W of Midhurst turn N signposted Chithurst then 1½m; or at Liphook turn off A3 onto old A3 for 2m before turning L to Milland, then follow signs to Chithurst for 1½m. 5 acres; flowering shrubs incl exceptional rhododendrons and azaleas, leading to 50 acres of lovely woodland walks. TEA. *Adm £2 Chd 50p (Share to Friends of King Edward VII Hospital Midhurst®). Suns April 27, May 4, 11, 18, 25, June 1, Mons May 5, 26 (2-6); also private visits welcome for parties or plant sales, please* **Tel 01730 821433**

The Manor of Dean ✱✱ (Miss S M Mitford) Tillington, 2m W of Petworth. Turn off A272 N at NGS sign. Flowers, shrubs, specimen trees, bulbs in all seasons. A miniature pony, 2 pigmy goats, Vietnamese pigs, tame lambs. House (not open) 1400-1613. TEA 50p. *Adm £1 Chd over 5 50p. Sats, Suns, Mons March 22, 23, 24, April 12, 13, 14, May 10, 11, 12, June 21, 22, 23, July 12, 13, 14, Aug 16, 17, 18, Sept 13, 14, 15, Oct 4, 5, 6 (2-6). Private visits welcome, please* **Tel 01798 861247**

Manvilles Field ఉ✱✱ (Mrs P J Aschan & Mrs J M Wilson) 2m W of Pulborough take A283 to Fittleworth, turn R on sharp L-hand bend. 2 acres of garden with orchard, many interesting shrubs, clematis, roses, other herbaceous plants. Beautiful views surrounding garden. TEAS. Wine June 18. *Adm £1.50 Chd free. Suns June 8, 22 (2-6). Wed June 18 (5.30-8)*

Mayfield Cottage Gardens ✿ 8m S of Tunbridge Wells on A267. In Fletching St E off A267 by Marchants Garage signposted Witherenden. Flower Festival at St Dunstan's Church. *Combined adm £2 Chd 20p. Sun June 29 (2-5.30)*
  Courtney Cottage (Mr & Mrs D Clark) ⅕-acre steeply sloping garden
  Hopton (E Stuart Ogg Esq) ½-acre, Delphinium specialist
  ¶**Maryhill** ఉ (Mr & Mrs I A D Lyle) Knowle Park, off West Street, S of High Street by Barclays Bank. Approx 1 acre, pergola, formal garden and wild area
  The Oast ✱ (Mr & Mrs R G F Henderson) Charming ½-acre sloping garden, fine views
  The Vicarage St Dunstans Church ✱ (Fr Grant Holmes) High St. ¼-acre terraced. TEAS in aid of St Dunstan's Church

■ **Merriments Gardens** ఉ (Mark & Mandy Buchele & Mr David Weeks) Hawkhurst Rd, Hurst Green. Situated between Hawkhurst & Hurst Green. 4-acre garden with richly planted mixed borders in country setting. Ponds, streams and rare plants give beautiful display all season. TEAS. *Adm £1.50 Chd free under 12. Open daily Easter Weekend to Oct. For NGS Suns June 8, July 6, Aug 24, Sept 14; Mons June 9, Aug 25 (12-5). Parties welcome by appt, please* **Tel 01580 860666**

● **Michelham Priory** ఉ✱✱ (Sussex Past) Upper Dicker. 2m W Hailsham, 8m NW Eastbourne. Signposted from A22 and A27. Cradled in beautiful Cuckmere Valley, guarded by the Sussex Downs, the gardens have been carefully designed to allow visitors to relax and enjoy their informal splendour. The 7-acre island site is enclosed by a C14 moat nearly 1 mile long. The gardens incl an orchard, kitchen and water gardens; physic herb garden and a recreated mediaeval cloister garden. TEAS. *Adm House and Garden £4 Chd £2 other concessions available. (Share to Sussex Archaeological Society®). Open Wed to Suns & Bank Hols March 15 to Oct 31 (11-5). March & Oct (11-4) Aug daily (10.30-5.30).* **Tel 01323 844224**

Middle Coombe ఉ✱✱ (Andrew & Ann Kennedy) From E Grinstead 1½m SW on B2110. Turn L into Coombe Hill Rd. ¼m on L. 4½-acre garden and woodland walk with small lake. Garden designed in Victorian rooms using Agriframes. Formal and informal planting to give all year colour. TEAS. *Adm £2 Chd free. Weds June 25, July 23 (2-5). Parties welcome by appt, please write to Middle Coombe, Coombe Hill Rd, E Grinstead, W Sussex RH19 4LZ*

Moat Mill Farm ✱ (Mr & Mrs C Marshall) Newick Lane, Mayfield. 1m S on Mayfield-Broadoak Rd. 8 acres, formal rose garden, herbaceous border and wild gardens. Nature Trail for Children. Picnic area (12.30-2). TEAS and ice creams. *Adm £1.50 Chd 50p. Sun June 22 (2-5.30)*

Moorlands ✱ (Dr & Mrs Steven Smith) Friar's Gate, 2m N of Crowborough. St Johns Rd to Friar's Gate. Or turn L off B2188 at Friar's Gate. 3 acres set in lush valley adjoining Ashdown Forest; water garden with ponds and streams; primulas, rhododendrons, azaleas, many unusual trees and shrubs. New river walk. TEAS. *Adm £2 OAPs £1.50 Chd free. Every Wed April to Oct 1 (11-5). Suns May 25, June 8, July 20 (2-6). Private visits welcome, please* **Tel 01892 652474**

Morris Down ✱✱ (Mr & Mrs Hugh Dibley) Down St, Piltdown. 8m E Haywards Heath, 3m N Uckfield turn N off A272 for 1m. Parking in field. Established 2-acre garden with outstanding panoramic views, mature and ornamental trees, azalea and rhododendron walk, colourful mixed borders and feature pond. TEAS in aid of Isfield WI and NGS. *Adm £1.50 Chd free. Sun, Mon June 1, 2 (2-6)*

Mount Harry House (Mr & Mrs R T Renton) & **Mount Harry Lodge** ✿ (Mr & Mrs A K Stewart-Roberts) (2 adjoining gardens). 2m NW of Lewes on S of Ditchling Rd B2116, ½m W of A275 (sign Mount Harry Trees at entrance to drive). Coach parking. 7 acres and 1-acre terraced gardens on chalk, herbaceous and shrubbery borders, specimen trees, laburnum walks, walled garden, dell garden, conservatory, ornamental tree nursery in beautiful downland setting. *Combined adm £3 Chd free (Share to St John Ambulance, Sussex®). Sun June 15 (2-6)*

Mountfield Court ✿❀ (Mr & Mrs Simon Fraser) 2m S of Robertsbridge. On A21 London-Hastings; ½m from Johns Cross. 2-3-acre wild garden; flowering shrubs, rhododendrons, azaleas and camellias; fine trees. Homemade TEAS. *Adm £2 Chd free (Share to All Saints Church Mountfield®). Sun, Mon May 18, 19, (2-6)*

Neptune House ✿❀ (The Hon & Mrs Robin Borwick) Cutmill. From Chichester take A259 to Bosham roundabout, after ½m move into reservation in rd and turn R into Newells Lane. 150yds turn L and park (sufficient space). From W take A259 through Emsworth. Turn L after Bosham Inn at Chidham into Newells Lane. Garden extends to 6 acres incl a lake. The R Cut runs through the garden feeding 3 ponds. Planting is being increased, particularly around the lake which is home to various waterfowl. Live classical music. TEAS with strawberries and cream Sun only. Sat, bring a picnic. *Adm £1.50 Chd 50p. Evening party £2.50 Chd £1. Sun June 1 (2-6), Sat Aug 2 (5-8). Private visits and coach tours welcome April 4 to Sept 30, please* **Tel 01243 576900**

New Barn ❀✿ (Mr & Mrs Adrian Tuck) Egdean. 1m S of Petworth turn L off A285, at 2nd Xrds turn R into lane or 1m W of Fittleworth take L fork to Midhurst off A283. 200yds turn L. 2 acres, owner maintained garden round converted C18 barn in beautiful farmland setting. Large natural pond and stream, water irises, roses, shrubs and herbaceous; lawns and woodland area. Seats in garden, picnic area, Autumn colour. *Adm £1.50 Chd 20p. Sun, Mon, Tues June 15, 16, 17; Bank Hol Mon Aug 25 (12-5.30). Private visits for parties of 4 & over weekdays 12-19 May & 6-19 Oct, please* **Tel 01798 865502**

New Grove ❀✿ (Mr & Mrs Robert de Pass) Petworth. 1m S of Petworth turn L off A285 and take next L. Follow signs. From the N at Xrds in Petworth straight across into Middle Street then L into High Street follow signs. A mature garden of about 3 acres. Mainly composed of shrubs with all year interest incl a small parterre; magnolias, camellias, azaleas, cornuses, roses etc. lovely views to the South Downs. TEAS in aid of King Edward VII Hospital, Midhurst. *Adm £1.50 Chd free. Sat, Suns April 20, May 10, 11 (2-6)*

Newtimber Place ❀❀ (Andrew Clay Esq) Newtimber. 7m N of Brighton off A281 between Poynings and Pyecombe. Beautiful C17 moated house. Wild garden, roses, mixed borders and water plants. TEAS in aid of Newtimber Church. *Adm £1.50 Chd 50p. Suns April 27, Aug 24 (2-5.30)*

¶**North Manor** ❀✿❀ (Mr & Mrs Derek Bingley) Flansham. Hoe Lane is a turning off the NW side of the A259 and is approx 2½m E of Bognor Regis and 4m W of Littlehampton. A small old English garden ¼-acre, with box and yew hedges, oriental poppies, herbaceous borders with special attention to blending of colours. TEAS. *Adm £1.50 Sun, Wed June 8, 11 (2-6)*

1927–1997

This year the National Gardens Scheme is celebrating its 70th Anniversary. Please help us celebrate by visiting a garden in 1997.

North Springs ❀❀ (Mr & Mrs Michael Waring) Fittleworth. Approach either from A272 outside Wisborough Green or A283 at Fittleworth and follow signs. Steep hillside garden with walls, terraces, water gardens and pools, mixed borders containing wide variety of trees, shrubs, herbaceous plants, roses and clematis; surrounded by woodland, spectacular views Featured in numerous periodicals. *Adm £2 Chd £1. Sat, Suns June 29, July 5, 6 (2-6). Private visits welcome May to Sept please,* **Tel 01798 865731**

Northwood Farmhouse ❀✿ (Mrs P Hill) Pulborough. 1m N of Pulborough on A29. turn NW into Blackgate Lane and follow lane for 2m then follow the signs. Cottage garden with bulbs, roses, pasture with wild flowers and pond all on Wealded clay surrounding Sussex farmhouse dating from 1420. TEA. *Adm £1.50 Chd £1. Mon, Tues April 14, 15, June 30, July 1 (2-5)*

Nyewood House ❀❀ (Mr & Mrs Timothy Woodall) Nyewood. From A272 at Rogate take rd signposted Nyewood, S for approx 1¼m. At 40 mph sign on outskirts of Nyewood, turn L signposted Trotton. Garden approx 500yds on R. 3-acre S facing garden recently renovated, with colour planted herbaceous borders, newly planted knot garden, pleaching, rose walk, water feature, and new potager. TEAS. *Adm £1.50 Chd free. Weds May 7, June 11, July 16; Suns June 8, July 13 (2-5.30)*

▲**Nymans** ❀✿❀ (The National Trust) Handcross. On B2114 at Handcross signposted off M23/A23 London-Brighton rd, SE of Handcross. Bus: 137 from Crawley & Haywards Heath [TQ265294]. Glorious herbaceous borders, June borders, old-fashioned rose garden, rare trees and shrubs. New Tea Rooms and shop. *Adm £4.50 Chd £2.25. For NGS Suns June 1, July 13 (11-6)*

Offham House ❀❀ (Mr & Mrs H N A Goodman; Mrs H S Taylor) Offham, 2m N of Lewes on A275. Cooksbridge station ½m. Fountains; flowering trees; double herbaceous border; long paeony bed. Queen Anne house (not open) 1676 with well-knapped flint facade. Featured in George Plumptre's Guide to 200 Gardens in Britain. Home-made TEAS. *Adm £2 Chd over 14 25p (Share to Offham Churches®). Suns April 27, June 22 (2-6)*

The Old Chalk Pit ❀✿❀ (Mr & Mrs Hugo Martin) 27 Old Shoreham Road, Hove, E Sussex BN3 6NR. A270. Unexpected, romantic oasis for chalk loving plants, old roses and climbers forming different areas incl white garden, ponds, wildlife and shady spots. *Adm £1 Chd 50p. Private visits by written request very welcome for afternoons & summer evenings*

The Old Rectory, Newtimber ❀ (Lambert & Rosalyn Coles) 7m N of Brighton off A281 between Poynings and Pyecombe. 2 acres with views of South Downs and Newtimber Church. Pond garden, fine tulip tree, perennial borders; combined kitchen and flower garden. *Adm £1.50 Chd 50p. Parties welcome by appt, please* **Tel 01273 857288**

64 Old Shoreham Road ❀✿ (Brian & Muriel Bailey) Hove. A270. Mainly walled garden 12.6 metres by 33.6 metres on flint and chalk. Alpine bed, arches, bog garden, conservatory, fruit bushes and trees, herb parterre, 2 ponds with fountain and waterfall, pergola, rose arbour, trellises, vegetables. Over 800 different varieties of plants - all named. 100 pots, many containing chalk hating plants. *Adm £1 Chd 50p or £2 with owner as guide. Private visits by appt welcome evenings and weekends, please* **Tel 01273 889247**

The Old Vicarage &✿ (Arabella & Charlie Bridge) Firle. 5m SE Lewes on A27 towards Eastbourne. Sign to Firle. 3½-acre garden with downland views. Walled garden with mixed vegetable and flower borders. Partially suitable for wheelchairs. TEAS. *Adm £1.50 Chd 20p. Sun June 22 (2-5)*

Orchards ✿✿ (Penelope S Hellyer) Rowfant. Wallage Lane off B2028. 1½m N of Turners Hill Xrds. 3m E of M23 junction 10. Woodland garden created by the late renowned horticulturist Arthur and Gay Hellyer. 7-acre woodland garden, mature trees, herbaceous & mixed borders, orchards, bluebell wood, wild orchard meadow, heather/conifer garden, rhododendrons and camellias. Yr-round interest. Continuing restoration, redesign and replanting by their daughter. Garden owners nursery Tel 01342 718280. TEA. *Adm £2 Acc chd free. Mons March 31, May 5, 26, Aug 25 (12-4). Weds April 16, June 4, 25, July 9, 23, Sept 10, 24, Oct 8 (2-4)*

Palmer's Lodge ✿ (R Hodgson Esq) West Chiltington Village. At Xrds in centre of West Chiltington Village opp Queens Head. 2m E of Pulborough 3m N Storrington. A charming plantsman's ½-acre garden with herbaceous and shrub borders. TEAS in aid of Motor Neurone. *Adm £1.50 Chd free. Sats, Suns July 12, 13, 19, 20, (2-6). Private visits welcome following written application (July only)*

▲**Parham House and Gardens** &(gdns) ✿ (Hse)✿ 4m SE of Pulborough on A283 Pulborough-Storrington Rd. Beautiful Elizabethan House with fine collection of portraits, furniture, rare needlework. 4 acres of walled garden; 7 acres pleasure grounds with lake. Veronica's Maze a brick and turf maze designed with the young visitor in mind. Picnic area. Suitable for wheelchairs on dry days. Cream TEAS. *Adm £3 Chd 50p. For the NGS Wed, Thurs July 2, 3 (12-6)* **Tel 01903 744888**

■ **Pashley Manor** ✿✿ (J Sellick Esq) Ticehurst. 10m S of Tunbridge Wells. 1½m SE Ticehurst on B2099. Pashley Manor is a grade 1 Tudor timber-framed ironmaster's house. Standing in a well timbered park with magnificent views across to Brightling Beacon. The 8 acres of formal garden, dating from the C18, were created in true English romantic style and are planted with many ancient trees and fine shrubs, new plantings over the past decade give additional interest and subtle colouring throughout the year. Waterfalls, ponds and a moat which encircled the original house built 1262. TEAS. *Adm £3.50 OAPs £2.50 Chd £1 6 to 14 years, under 6 free. Tues, Wed, Thurs, Sat and Bank Hols April 12 to Sept 27. For NGS Fri July 18 (11-5).* **Tel 01580 200692**

Penns in the Rocks &✿✿ (Lord & Lady Gibson) Groombridge. 7m SW of Tunbridge Wells on Groombridge-Crowborough Rd just S of Plumeyfeather corner. Bus: MD 291 Tunbridge Wells-East Grinstead, alight Plumeyfeather corner, ¾m. Large wild garden with rocks;

lake; C18 temple; old walled garden. House (not open) part C18. Dogs under control in park only (no shade in car park). TEAS. *Adm £2 Up to two chd 50p each, further chd free. Sun April 13, Mon Aug 25 (2.30-5.30). Parties welcome, please* **Tel 01892 864244**

▲**Petworth House** &✿ (The National Trust) Petworth. In centre of Petworth A272/A283. Car park on A283 Northchapel Rd. 30-acre woodland garden of Elizabethan origin and redesigned by 'Capability Brown' in 1751. New wild walks through 10,000 trees and shrubs planted since Great Storm. Park also open. 1 guided walk. (Adm £2) with NT head gardener and staff at 2pm (about 1½hr) starting from car park kiosk. (House closed). May 22, young azaleas, flower trees & shrubs. Sept 4, fruits of the Pleasure Grounds. *Adm £1.50 Chd free. For the NGS Thurs May 22, Sept 4 (1-4.30)*

Pheasants Hatch &✿ (Mrs G E Thubron) Piltdown. 3m NW of Uckfield on A272. 2 acres, rose gardens with ponds and fountains; beautiful herbaceous borders; foliage; wild garden; peacocks. TEAS. *Adm £1.50 Chd free. Sun, Mon June 29, 30 (2-6.30). Parties welcome June to July, please* **Tel 01825 722960**. *Also open* **Home Farm, Buckham Hill**

▲**The Priest House** ✿ (Sussex Past, Sussex Archaeological Society) West Hoathly. 4m SW of East Grinstead, 6m E Crawley. At Turners Hill take B2028 S, 1m fork L to West Hoathly, 2m S turn R into North Lane. C15 timber-framed house with small cottage garden. Features large selection of herbs in formal garden plus mixed herbaceous borders with long established yew topiary, box hedges and espalier fruit trees. *Adm £1 Chd free. For NGS Thurs May 29, June 12 (11-5.30). Also open within walking distance* **Duckyls Holt**

Priesthawes Farm &✿✿ (Mr & Mrs A Wadham) Polegate. On B2104 2½m. S Hailsham 4m N Eastbourne. 1m N of Stone Cross. C15 listed house of historical interest (not open) surrounded by 2½acres. Walls used to full advantage with large clematis collection, climbers, old roses, herbaceous borders and pergola. Mainly replanted in the last 15 yrs. Lovely views over farmland. TEAS in aid of St Lukes Church. *Adm £2 Chd free (Shore to St Wilfreds Hospice®). Sun, Mon June 22, 23 (2-5). Private visits also welcome mid May to July please.* **Tel 01323 763228**

¶**Ringmer Park** &✿ (Mr & Mrs Michael Bedford) Ringmer. Situated on A26 1½m NE of Lewes and 5m S of Uckfield. 5-acre garden with extensive rose gardens incl 100ft pergola and substantial mixed border featuring many old-fashioned roses. 100ft double herbaceous border. White garden, hot garden, incl dahlia display, Autumn border under development. Mature trees and lawns, kitchen and fruit garden. *Adm £2 Chd free. Weds June 18, Sept 17 (2-5.30)*

¶**Rose Cottage** ✿✿ (Ken & Heather Mines) Hadlow Down, Uckfield. Off A272 6m NE of Uckfield & 4m NW of Heathfield A previous 'Yellow Book' gardener with a small London garden, moved to Sussex in 1993 and now making a new garden from ½ acre of wilderness. Shoestring budget requires imaginative use of reclaimed materials to leave sufficient funds to satisfy a confirmed plantaholic's passion for interesting and unusual plants. Tiny woodland garden, pond, mouldering carvings from a demolished Victorian church and organic vegetable garden. TEAS in aid of Breakthrough to Breast Cancer. *Adm £1.50 Chd 50p. Suns May 25, June 29 (2-6)*

Rosemary Cottage ✿ (Mr & Mrs D R Coe) Bletchinglye Lane, nr Rotherfield. From Mark Cross on the A267, 9m S of Tunbridge Wells, turn W on the B2100 towards Crowborough, after 1m turn L into Bletchinglye Lane signed as no through rd. 150yds on R. ⅓-acre informal garden with mixed borders, herbs, ponds and paved pathways. The garden is managed following organic principles and incl planting for beneficial insects and wildlife. Interesting vegetable garden based on 4 ft beds with extensive compost area. TEAS. *Adm £1 Chd 50p. Open by appt May to Sept, please* **Tel 01892 852584**

Round Oak ♿✿❀ (Mr & Mrs B J Mitchell) Wadhurst. 6m SE Tunbridge Wells. At Lamberhurst take B2100 off A21. ⅓m after Wadhurst sign turn R at 30mph sign, L into Gloucester Rd, turn R, 200yds on R. 1-acre garden in the early yrs of restoration. Designed to provide all season interest. Wide variety of shrubs, roses and perennials with interesting features incl a secret garden, rockeries and pond. TEAS Sun only, Ploughmans Lunch Wed, Thurs. *Adm £1.50 Chd free. Wed, Thurs Sept 3, 4 (10.30-4.30). Sun Aug 31 (2-5)*

Roundhill Cottage ✿ (Mr Jeremy Adams) East Dean. Take A286 Chichester-Midhurst. At Singleton follow signs to Charlton/East Dean. In East Dean turn R at Hurdlemakers Inn and Roundhill is approx 100yds on R. 1-acre country garden of surprises set in tranquil fold of the South Downs, designed in 1980 by Judith Adams whose inspiration came from French impressionists. *Adm £1.50 Chd free. Mon, Tues May 26, 27 (2-6). Private visits welcome, please* **Tel 01243 811 550**

Rye Gardens ✿ 3 gardens in the centre of Rye. Cars must be left in public car parks. Ploughman's Lunch and TEAS at 11 High Street. *Combined adm £2.50 Chd free. Fri July 25 (12.30-5)*

11 High Street (Mr & Mrs C Festing) One way street on RH-side next to Midland Bank. ⅓-acre old walled garden, many trees incl gingko by pond. Vinery and vine covered pergola

Lamb House (The National Trust) West Street nr church. 1-acre walled garden; variety of herbaceous plants, shrubs, trees, herbs. Home of Henry James 1898-1916 and E F Benson 1918-1940

¶The Old House (Rev'd & Mrs W Buxton) The Mint continuation of High Street. A modest-sized well stocked colourful cottage garden on different levels adjoining C15 cottage. *Private visits welcome, please* **Tel 01797 223952**

Rymans ♿ (Michael & Suzanna Gayford) Apuldram. 1½m SW of Chichester. Witterings Rd out of Chichester; at 1½m SW turn R signposted Apuldram; garden down rd on L. Walled and other gardens surrounding lovely C15 stone house (not open); bulbs, flowering shrubs, roses. Lunch (soup & roll) in aid of Leukemia Research Fund. *Adm £1.50 Chd 50p. Sats April 12, 19 (12-3)*

▲St Mary's House ♿✿ (Mr Peter Thorogood) Bramber. 10m NW of Brighton in Bramber Village off A283 or 1m E of Steyning. Medium-sized formal gardens with amusing topiary, large example of living-fossil Gingko tree and Magnolia Grandiflora; pools and fountains, ancient ivy-clad 'Monk's Walk', all surrounding listed Grade 1 C15 timber framed medieval house, once a monastic inn. TEAS. *Adm 1 Chd 50p. Fri, Sat Aug 1, 2 (2-5.30)* **Tel 01903 816205**

Selehurst ✿❀ (Mr & Mrs M Prideaux) Lower Beeding, 4½m S of Horsham on A281 opp Leonardslee. Woodland garden in romantic valley. Sham-Gothic tower on the skyline above a pebblework waterfall, chain of five ponds, further waterfalls, pretty bridge. Fine trees, tree-like rhododendrons, eucryphias, azaleas, camellias, stewartias. Formal features incl walled garden with borders semi-circular arbour of cytissus battandieri, 60′ rose and laburnum tunnel underplanted with ferns, artichokes, grasses and hostas. Newly planted box and herb parterre. Fine views of the South Downs. TEAS. *Adm £1.50 Chd free (Share to St. John's Church, Coolhurst®). Sun May 18 (1-5)*

Setters Green, Rowlands Castle see Hampshire

Sennicotts ♿❀ (John Rank Esq) Chichester. From Chichester take B2178 signed to Funtington for 2m. Entrance on R. Long drive ample parking near house. From Fishbourne turn N marked Roman Palace then straight on until T junction. Entrance opp. 6-acre mature garden with intriguing spaces, lawns, rhododendrons and azaleas. Large walled kitchen and cutting garden, greenhouses and orchard. TEAS. *Adm £2 Chd free. Sun, Mon June 1, 2 (2-6) Sat Aug 16 (6-8)*

▲Sheffield Park Garden ♿✿ (The National Trust) Midway between E Grinstead and Lewes, 5m NW of Uckfield; E of A275. The garden, with 4 lakes, was laid out by Capability Brown in C18, greatly modified early in the C20. Many rare trees, shrubs and fine waterlilies; the garden is beautiful at all times of year. TEAS Oak Hall (not NT). *Adm £4 Chd £2. For NGS Weds May 14, Oct 15 (11-6) last adm 5*

Sherburne House ♿✿❀ (Mr & Mrs Angus Hewat) Eartham, 6m NE of Chichester, approach from A27 Chichester-Arundel Rd or A285 Chichester-Petworth Rd, nr centre of village, 200yds S of church. Chalk garden of about 2 acres facing SW. Shrub and climbing roses; lime-tolerant shrubs; herbaceous, grey-leaved and foliage plants, pots; water feature; small herb garden, kitchen garden potager and conservatory. TEAS. *Adm £1.50 Chd 50p. Sun June 15 (2-6)*

Somerset Lodge (Mr & Mrs R Harris) North St, Petworth. On A283 and A272 100yds N of church. Parking in town car park. Charming ½-acre town garden with ponds and walled kitchen garden, small collections of old and English roses and wildflower garden. Cleverly landscaped on slope with beautiful views. TEAS in aid of Petworth Parish Council. *Adm £1.25 Chd 20p. Wed, Thurs, Fri, Sat, Sun June 11, 12, 13, 14, 15 (12-6). Parties by appointment, please* **Tel 01798 343842**

South Harting Gardens 4m SE of Petersfield on B2146. Cream TEAS at Pyramids. *Combined adm £1.50 Chd 50p Fri adm £2.50 incl glass of wine. Fri June 27 (5-7) Sat, Sun June 28, 29 (2-6)*

Ivy House ♿✿ (Mr & Mrs David Summerhayes) At S end of village opp Harting Church on B2136. 1½-acre terraced village garden, sloping down to brook with orchard and paddock beyond, Specimen trees, shrubs and roses. Views to Harting Down

The Old House (Captain & Mrs Duncan Knight) Next to the White Hart Inn. The Street. Small village walled garden. Herbaceous borders, roses and delphiniums

Pyramids ♿❀ (Mrs S J Morgan) 200yds on R up North Lane. ½-acre with mainly chalk loving plants; old-fashioned roses, rose arbour; pool; uniquely shaped old apple trees. Interesting modern house (designed 1965 by Stout & Lichfield) linked to garden by paved areas. Fine views

Spur Point ✿❀ (Mr & Mrs T D Bishop) Marley Heights, Kingsley Green. Plantsman's garden created by owners since 1970. 3 acres of S facing terraces containing rhododendrons, azaleas, roses, mixed borders and scree beds. Not suitable for children. *Adm £2. Private visits welcome May and June by individuals, and parties of no more than 20, please*

▲Standen ✿ (The National Trust) 1½m from East Grinstead. Signed from B2110 and A22 at Felbridge. Hillside garden of 10½-acres with beautiful views over the Medway Valley. Partly suitable for wheelchairs. TEAS. in aid of NT Enterprises. *Adm Garden £3 Chd £1.50. For NGS Suns May 11, Sept 14 (12.30-6 Last adm 5pm)*

Stonehurst ❀ (Mr D R Strauss) Ardingly. 1m N of Ardingly. Entrance 800yds N of S of England showground, on B2028. 30-acre garden set in secluded woodland valley. Many interesting and unusual landscape features; chain of man made lakes and waterfalls; natural sandstone rock outcrops and a fine collection of trees and shrubs. TEAS. *Adm £2.50 Chd £1 (Share to Homelife®). Sun April 20, Mons May 5, 26, (11-5)*

Telegraph House ♿❀ (Mr & Mrs David Gault) North Marden, 9m NW of Chichester. Entrance on B2141. From Petersfield to South Harting for 2m. From Chichester via A286 for 4m N of Lavant turn W on to B2141. 1-acre enclosed chalk garden 700 ft asl; chalk-tolerant shrubs, shrub roses, herbaceous plants; 1m avenue of copper beeches; walks through 150-acre yew wood; lovely views. TEAS. *Adm £1.50 Chd 75p. Sats, Suns June 21, 22, July 12, 13, (2-6). Also private visits welcome May to Aug (2-5), please* **Tel 01730 825206**

Tinkers Bridge Cottage ❀ (Mr & Mrs Michael Landsberg) Ticehurst. From B2099 1m W Ticehurst; turn N to Three Leg Cross for 1m; R after Bull Inn. House at bottom of hill. 12 acres attractively landscaped; stream garden nr the house leading to herbaceous borders, newly planted trees and shrubs, pond, wild flower meadow and woodland with bluebell walk. *Adm £2 to incl TEA Chd 50p. Sun May 11 (2.30-5.30)*

Town Place ♿✿❀ (Mr & Mrs A C O McGrath) Freshfield. 3m E Haywards Heath. From A275 turn W at Sheffield Green into Ketches Lane for Lindfield. 1¾m on L. 3 acres with sunken rose garden, herbaceous border, walled herb and shrub rose gardens, 150′ herbaceous border, shrubbery, ancient hollow oak, orchard and spring-cabbage patch. C17 Sussex farmhouse (not open). TEAS. *Adm £2 Chd free (Share to St Peter & St James Hospice®). Thurs June 19, 26, Suns June 22, July 6, 13 (2-6) Groups welcome by appt, please* **Tel 01825 790221**

Trotton Old Rectory ✿❀ (Captain & Mrs John Pilley) nr Petersfield 3m W of Midhurst on A272. This typical English garden with its rose beds designed by Hazel Le Rougetel, framed in box and yew, has 2 levels with beautiful and interesting trees and shrubs running down to a lake and the R Rother. Plants for sale in the adjoining vegetable garden. *Adm £1.50 Chd 50p. Suns May 18, June 22 (2-6)*

Trotton Place ♿✿ (Mr & Mrs N J F Cartwright) 3½m W of Midhurst on A272. Entrance next to church. Garden of over 4 acres surrounding C18 house (not open). Walled fruit and vegetable garden; C17 dovecote. Fine trees; mature borders with shrub roses; lake and woodland walk. TEAS in aid of Trotton Church PCC. *Adm £1.50 Chd free. Suns May 18, June 22 (2-5.30)*

▲Uppark ♿✿ (The National Trust) 5m SE of Petersfield on B2146, 1½m S of S Harting. Fine late C17 house situated high on the South Downs with magnificent views towards the Solent. Reptonian garden replanned and replanted since major fire in 1989. Woodland walk. Shop. House not open. Gardener Guided Tours. Post Fire Restoration Exhibition. Surrey Sculpture Exhibition in Garden. TEAS. *Collection for NGS Adm £2.50 Chd £1.25. Fri June 21, 27 (2-6)*

Wadhurst Gardens ✿❀ 6m SE of Tunbridge Wells. 3 gardens all created by present owners. *Combined adm £2 Chd free. Sun, Mon July 20, 21 (2-5.30)*

Millstones (Mr H W Johnson) next door to Sunnymead ½-acre plantsman's garden featuring an exceptionally wide range of shrubs and perennial plants

The Robins (Mr & Mrs D G Leney) Mayfield Lane. ⅓m on L on B2100 going SW to Mark Cross from junction with B2099. ¾-acre garden created in 1991 with many unusual shrubs and beautifully planted pond

Sunnymead (Mr & Mrs D Goldsmith) On B2099 ¾m SE Wadhurst Station at junction of Tapsells Lane. 1¼-acre landscaped garden imaginatively designed for the sporting family, small kitchen garden

Wadhurst Park ✿❀ (Dr & Mrs H Rausing) Wadhurst. 6m SE of Tunbridge Wells. Turn R along Mayfield Lane off B2099 at NW end of Wadhurst. L by Best Beech public house, L at Riseden Rd. A chance to see this magnificent garden much later in the season. It was re-created on C19 site with restored conservatories and is situated within an 800 acre park, stocked with 7 species of deer. Trailer rides into park. Partly suitable for wheelchairs. TEAS. *Adm £2 Chd 50p. Sun Sept 7 (2-5.30)*

▲**Wakehurst Place** & & (National Trust & Royal Botanic Gardens, Kew) Ardingly, 5m N of Haywards Heath on B2028. National botanic garden noted for one of the finest collections of rare trees and flowering shrubs amidst exceptional natural beauty. Walled gardens, heath garden, Pinetum, scenic walks through steep wooded valley with lakes, attractive water courses and large bog garden. Guided tours 11.30 & 2.30 most weekends, also prebooked tours. The ranger **Tel 01444 894067**. Restaurant. *Adm £4.50 Concessions £3 Chd £2.50 under 5's free. For NGS Fri July 18 (10-7)*

Warren House & & (Mr & Mrs M J Hands) Warren Rd, Crowborough. From Crowborough Cross take A26 towards Uckfield. 4th turning on R. 1m down Warren Rd. Beware speed ramps. 9-acre garden with views over Ashdown Forest. Series of gardens old and new, displaying a wealth of azaleas, rhododendrons, impressive trees and shrubs. Sweeping lawns framed by delightful walls and terraces, woodlands, ponds and ducks. Planted and maintained solely by owner. TEAS. *Adm £2 Chd free. Suns May 4, 18, June 1, 29, Aug 24, Mon May 26 (2-5). Groups welcome by appt, please* **Tel 01892 663502**

93 Wayland Avenue & (Brian & Sylvia Jackson) off Dyke Road Avenue (above Withdean Stadium). Creatively designed small garden, with mixed borders and raised beds, with emphasis on dense, informal planting, incl some unusual plants, shrubs, grasses and many clematis, tender perennials and climbers. Focal points are provided by rose arch and water features with cascades and pools in rockery and bog garden areas. The whole garden is designed to encourage wild life. *Adm £1 Chd 50p. Private visits by appt welcome evenings & weekends June & July, please* **Tel 01273 501027**

▲**West Dean Gardens** & & & (Edward James Foundation) On A286, 5m N of Chichester. Historic garden of 35 acres in tranquil downland setting. Noted for its 300ft long Harold Peto pergola, mixed and herbaceous borders, rustic summerhouses, water garden and specimen trees. Newly restored 2½-acre walled garden contains fruit collection, 13 Victorian glasshouses, apple store, large working kitchen garden and a tool and mower collection. Circuit walk (2¼m) climbs through parkland to 45-acre St Roches Arboretum with its varied collection of trees and shrubs. TEAS. *Adm £3.50 OAP £3 Chd £1.50. For NGS Wed June 11 (11-5)* **Tel 01243 818209**

West Worthing Gardens & & 10m W of Brighton, 6m E of Littlehampton, off A259. From Brighton follow signs for Worthing town centre then A259 at traffic lights (Richmond Rd). Continue for approx 1m to traffic lights/junction with Heene Rd. Carry straight on and take 2nd turning on R for Belsize Rd and 5th turning on L for Grand Avenue. Medium-sized part walled town gardens. TEAS at Belsize Rd only. *Combined adm £2 Chd 50p. Suns June 29, July 27 (1-5). Weds 16 July (5.30-7.30)*
　No 10 Belsize Rd (Mr Robin Spare) Combined ornamental and vegetable garden, newly built small pond with fountain, green house & conservatory with vine
　No. 12 Belsize Rd (Claudia & Peter Pearce) Ornamental garden with large variety of perennials, shrubs and climbers, some unusual. Many pots and hanging baskets

¶**72 Grand Avenue** (Mr & Mrs D Marshall) Begun in 1976. Cottage garden feel, closely planted with old roses, clematis, perennials, decorative foliage trees and shrubs, post and statuary. *Private visits welcome, please* **Tel 01903 501323**

46 Westup Farm Cottages & & (Chris & Pat Cornwell) Balcombe. Midway Cuckfield and Crawley. 1¼m Balcombe Station off B2036. Telephone for further directions. Well stocked cottage garden, designed to provide yr-round interest in idyllic setting. *Adm £1 Chd free. Private visits incl parties welcome all yr, please* **Tel 01444 811891**

Whiligh & (Mr & Mrs John Hardcastle) Shovers Green. 1½m E of Wadhurst on N side of B2099. Old garden of 3½ acres with some new features. Mature trees and shrubs and wide selection of herbaceous plants chosen for colour and form. TEAS. *Adm £2. Sun, Mon July 6, 7 (2-5.30)*

The White House & (Elizabeth Woodhouse) Burpham. Turn off A27 Arundel-Worthing Rd ½m S of Arundel. Proceed through Wepham to Burpham for 2m. Charming garden planned and planted by practicing garden designer artist. Great attention to plant forms and colour associations. Small wild garden with pond, not suitable for children. Wine. *Adm £2.50 (Share to Arundel Cathedral Organ Fund & The Weald & Downland Open Air Museum.®). Sun, Mon Aug 24, 25 (5.30- 7.30). Private visits welcome, please write for appt*

¶**The White Magpie** (Mr Ronald J Wootton) Lamberhurst. From Lamberhurst, on B2100 signposted Wadhurst 1m approx turn R (Hog Hole Lane) for ½m. A small estate with approx 5 acres of garden, surrounded by farmland, valley views, series of interlinking ponds, walled garden. All to the memory of Mrs J P Wootton. TEAS. *Adm £1.50 Chd free (Share to The Hodgkins Disease Association®). Suns May 18, Aug 10 (1-6)*

Whitehouse Cottage (Barry Gray Esq) Staplefield Lane, Staplefield 5m NW of Haywards Heath. Garden is ⅓m. E of A23; and 2m S of Handcross. In Staplefield at Xrds by cricket pavilion take turning marked Staplefield Lane for 1m. 4-acre woodland garden with mixed shrubs, old roses; paths beside stream linked by ponds; interesting paved and planted areas around house. TEAS. *Adm £1.50 Chd 50p. Private visits welcome, please* **Tel 01444 461229**

■ **Wilderness Farm** & & (Andrew & Ryl Nowell of Cabbages & Kings) Hadlow Down. ½m S of A272 from village. An imaginative garden developed by designer Ryl Nowell to demonstrate the art of garden design and to help people realise the full potential of their own gardens. A stunning transformation has been achieved from a windswept E facing slope to a richly planted, interlinking series of small terraced gardens. The garden opens out to the beautiful High Weald landscape. Spacious buildings afford shelter and house exhibitions to inspire visiting gardeners. TEAS. *Adm £2.50 OAPs & Chd £2. Under 5 free. Open Fri, Sat, Sun Bank Hols Easter to Sept (11-6). For NGS Wed June 4 (2-6) Fri, Sat, Sun Sept 5, 6, 7 (11-6) Group visits by appt welcome, please* **Tel 01825 830552**

¶8 Wimblehurst Road ᏓᏯ☺ (Dr & Mrs S J Dean) ½m N of town centre. From A24 Horsham Bypass take B2237 Warnham Rd into Horsham. Turn L at 1st set of traffic lights. Please park in side rds. Disabled badge holders only may park in driveway. ⅓-acre walled town garden with a backdrop of mature trees. A plantswoman's garden with deep herbaceous borders incorporating a range of plants to give all year interest. Secluded areas for contemplation. Brick terrace with many containers luxuriantly planted. Greenhouse vegetable and cut flower garden. TEAS in aid of The Church of St Mary The Virgin Restoration Appeal. *Adm £2 Chd free. Sun, Thurs July 6, 10, Sept 18 (11-5). Private visits, small groups welcome by appt, please* Tel 01403 268166

Winchelsea Gardens ☺ S of Rye. TEAS at Five Chimneys. *Combined adm £2 Chd 75p. Sat June 21 (2-6)*
  Cleveland House (Mr & Mrs S Jempson) 1½-acre semi-formal walled garden, many varied plants, ornamental trees, water feature, beautiful views, swimming in heated pool
  Cooks Green (Mr & Mrs Roger Neaves) Cottage garden with views to Rye Bay

Firebrand (Mr & Mrs R Comotto) Well hidden from street, visitors will be surprised to find this newly planted garden, roses, wooded glade around lawn
Five Chimneys (Mr & Mrs Dominic Leahy) Formal town garden
Nesbit (Mr & Mrs G Botterell) Formal enclosed ¼-acre garden, many and varied plants
No 1 Trojans Plat (Mr & Mrs Norman Turner) C13 Grade 11 listed archway providing access to small garden of great variety
Old Castle House (Mr & Mrs R Packard) Walled garden with roses, varied trees and shrubs
The Old Rectory (June & Denis Hyson) ½-acre of open lawn garden with views overlooking the Brede Valley

Yew Tree Cottage ❀ (Mrs K Hudson) Crawley Down. 4m W of East Grinstead. 2½m E of M23 (J10). On B2028 N of Turners Hill. ¼-acre garden planted for yr round interest and easy management. Featured in RHS 1989 and book 'Cottage Garden'. *Adm £1 Chd free. Parties welcome May to July (10-6), please* Tel 01342 714633

Warwickshire & West Midlands

Hon County Organiser: Mrs D L Burbidge, Cedar House, Wasperton, Warwick CV35 8EB
Assistant Hon County Organiser: Mrs C R King-Farlow, 8 Vicarage Road, Edgbaston, Birmingham B15 3EF
                           Mrs Michael Perry, Sherbourne Manor, Sherbourne, Warwick CV35 8AP
Hon County Treasurer: Michael Pitts, Hickecroft, Mill Lane, Rowington, Warwickshire CV35 7DQ

DATES OF OPENING

March 2 Sunday
  Birmingham Botanic Gardens & Glasshouses, Edgbaston
March 30 Sunday
  Compton Scorpion Farm, Shipston-on-Stour
April 6 Sunday
  Elm Close, Welford-on-Avon
April 7 Monday
  Elm Close, Welford-on-Avon
April 12 Saturday
  Baddesley Clinton
  Castle Bromwich Hall Garden Trust, Castle Bromwich
April 13 Sunday
  Ilmington Gardens, Shipston-on-Stour
April 20 Sunday
  Elm Close, Welford-on-Avon
  Greenlands, Wellesbourne
  Ivy Lodge, Radway
  The Mill Garden, Warwick
  Moseley Gardens, Birmingham

April 21 Monday
  Elm Close, Welford-on-Avon
April 27 Sunday
  The Hiller Garden & Dunnington Heath Farm, Alcester
  Ryton Organic Gardens, nr Coventry
  52 Tenbury Road, Kings Heath, Birmingham
May 4 Sunday
  Elm Close, Welford-on-Avon
  Hunningham Village Gardens, nr Leamington Spa
  Idlicote Gardens, nr Shipston-on-Stour
May 5 Monday
  Elm Close, Welford-on-Avon
  Hunningham Village Gardens, nr Leamington Spa
May 11 Sunday
  Elizabeth Road Gardens, Moseley, Birmingham
  The Mill Garden, Warwick
  Pereira Road Gardens, Birmingham

May 14 Wednesday
  Arbury Hall, Nuneaton
  The Folly Lodge, Halford
  89 Harts Green Road, Harborne
May 18 Sunday
  Elm Close, Welford-on-Avon
  Ilmington Manor, Shipston-on-Stour
  Pear Tree Cottage, Shipston-on-Stour
May 25 Sunday
  Ashover, 25 Burnett Rd, Streetly
June 1 Sunday
  Barton House, Barton-on-the-Heath
  Maxstoke Castle, nr Coleshill
  Warwickshire Constabulary Headquarters, Leek Wootton
June 8 Sunday
  Cedar House, Wasperton, nr Warwick
  Packington Hall, Meriden, nr Coventry
  Packwood House, nr Hockley Heath

June 11 Wednesday
The Folly Lodge, Halford
89 Harts Green Road, Harborne
June 15 Sunday
Alscot Park, nr Stratford-on-Avon
Dorsington Gardens,
Stratford-on-Avon
Greenlands, Wellesbourne
Holywell Gardens, nr Claverden ‡
Shrewley Pools Farm, Haseley,
Warwick ‡
Whichford & Ascott Gardens,
Shipston-on-Stour
June 21 Saturday
Compton Scorpion Farm,
Shipston-on-Stour
17 Gerrard Street, Warwick
Hickecroft, Rowington
The Master's Garden, Lord
Leycester Hospital, Warwick
June 22 Sunday
The Bevingtons, Ilmington
Gardens
Compton Scorpion Farm,
Shipston-on-Stour
Foxgloves, Dunchurch, Rugby
17 Gerrard Street, Warwick
Hickecroft, Rowington
Ilmington Manor,
Shipston-on-Stour
Maxgate, 103 Bilton Road,
Rugby ‡
The Mill Garden, Warwick
2 Paddox House, Hillmorton ‡
Paxford, Leamington Road,
Princethorpe
Pereira Road Gardens,
Birmingham
Warmington Village Gardens
50 Wellington Road, Edgbaston
June 25 Wednesday
The Folly Lodge, Halford
52 Tenbury Road, Kings Heath,
Birmingham
June 28 Saturday
Coughton Court, Alcester
June 29 Sunday
Balsall Common Gardens, Balsall
Common
The Earlsdon Gardens, Coventry
The Hiller Garden & Dunnington
Heath Farm, Alcester

Honington Village Gardens,
Shipston-on-Stour
Roseberry Cottage, Fillongley
8 Vicarage Rd, Edgbaston
July 2 Wednesday
8 Vicarage Rd, Edgbaston
July 5 Saturday
Upton House, nr Banbury
July 6 Sunday
Alscot Park, nr Stratford-on-Avon
Avon Dassett Gardens, Avon Dassett
Ivy Lodge, Radway
Ilmington Manor,
Shipston-on-Stour
Sherbourne Manor, nr Warwick
52 Tenbury Road, Kings Heath,
Birmingham
July 9 Wednesday
Arbury Hall, Nuneaton
The Folly Lodge, Halford
July 12 Saturday
Charlecote Park, Warwick
Orchard Cottage, Hurley
July 13 Sunday
Ashover, 25 Burnett Rd, Streetly
Elm Close, Welford-on-Avon
Moseley Gardens, Birmingham
Orchard Cottage, Hurley
July 14 Monday
Elm Close, Welford-on-Avon
July 20 Sunday
Martineau Centre Gardens,
Edgbaston
The Mill Garden, Warwick
Paxford, Leamington Road,
Princethorpe
26 Sunnybank Road, Wylde Green
July 27 Sunday
Elizabeth Road Gardens, Moseley,
Birmingham
August 3 Sunday
Alne View, Pathlow
August 10 Sunday
Ashover, 25 Burnett Rd, Streetly
The Mill Garden, Warwick
August 13 Wednesday
The Folly Lodge, Halford
August 17 Sunday
The Hiller Garden & Dunnington
Heath Farm, Alcester
August 24 Sunday
Greenlands, Wellesbourne

September 7 Sunday
Sherbourne Manor, nr Warwick
Wheelwright House, Long
Compton
September 10 Wednesday
The Folly Lodge, Halford
September 14 Sunday
Tysoe Manor, Warwick
September 20 Sunday
The Mill Garden, Warwick
September 21 Sunday
Elm Close, Welford-on-Avon
September 22 Monday
Elm Close, Welford-on-Avon
September 27 Saturday
Castle Bromwich Hall Garden
Trust, Castle Bromwich
September 28 Sunday
Birmingham Botanic Gardens &
Glasshouses, Edgbaston
Ryton Organic Gardens, nr
Coventry
October 5 Sunday
The Hiller Garden & Dunnington
Heath Farm, Alcester
October 12 Sunday
The Mill Garden, Warwick

Regular openings
For details see garden description

Arbury Hall, Nuneaton
Birmingham Botanical Gardens and
Glasshouses, Edgbaston
89 Harts Green Road, Harborne
The Master's Garden, Lord Leycester
Hospital, Warwick
The Mill Garden, nr Warwick
Ryton Organic Gardens, nr Coventry

By appointment only
*For telephone numbers and other
details see garden descriptions.
Private visits welcomed*

11 Hillwood Common Road, Four
Oaks
Parham Lodge, Alveston
Sherbourne Park, nr Warwick
Woodpeckers, Bidford-on-Avon

DESCRIPTIONS OF GARDENS

Alne View &⚘❀ (Mrs E Butterworth) Pathlow 5m from Henley-in-Arden; 3m N of Stratford on the A3400. Approx ⅓-acre. Shrubs, perennials, 2 small ponds and rockery. Aviary, collection of fuchsia, greenhouses. TEAS. *Adm £1.50 Chd free (Share to Wilmcote CE J & I School©). Sun Aug 3 (2-5)*

Alscot Park &❀ (Mrs James West) 2½m S of Stratford-on-Avon A3400. Fairly large garden; extensive lawns,

shrub roses, new lavender parterre planted in 1995. fine trees, orangery, with C18 Gothic house (not open), river, deer park, lakes. TEAS in aid of Warwickshire Assoc of Boys Clubs. *Adm £1.50 Chd free. Suns June 15, July 6 (2-6)*

■ **Arbury Hall** & (Rt Hon The Viscount Daventry) Nuneaton, 3m SW of Nuneaton off the B4102 (Junction 3 M6/A444). Free Car Park. Delightful 10-acre garden with a sense of peace. Bulbs at start of season, followed by rhododendrons, azalea and wisteria, then roses in June and autumn colours from trees and shrubs. Formal rose garden. Lakes with wildfowl. Bluebell woods. Pollarded limes and arboretum in old walled garden. *Adm to Hall & Gardens £4 Chd £2.50. Gardens only £2.50 Chd £1.50. Easter Sun to last Sun in Sept. Hall, Suns and Bank Hol Mons. Gardens as Hall and Weds in May, June and July. For NGS Mons May 14, July 9 (2-6). Last admission 5pm.*

¶Ashover ✿✿ (Jackie & Martin Harvey) 25 Burnett Rd. Streetly. 8m N of Birmingham. Take A452 towards Streetly, turn R at Queslett island taking the B4138 alongside Sutton Park. Carry on for approx 1m and turn L at shops into Burnett Rd. ⅓-acre well stocked plant lovers' garden. Cottage-style mixed plantings planned for yr round interest with the use of bulbs, shrubs and herbaceous plants. Features constantly changing. Particular emphasis in May with azaleas and other late spring colour, also in summer with shrubs, roses, climbers and a wide range of perennials. *Adm £1.50 Chd 50p. Suns May 25, July 13, Aug 10 (1.30-5.30)*

Avon Dassett Gardens ♿✿ 7m N of Banbury off B4100 (use Exit 12 of M40). Car parking in the village and in car park at top of hill. TEAS at **Old Mill Cottage**. *Combined adm £2 Chd free (Share to Myton Hamlet Hospice®). Sun July 6 (2-6). Coaches welcome, please* **Tel 01295 690643**

  Hill Top Farm (Mrs N & Mr D Hicks) 1-acre garden. Dramatic display of bedding plants, perennials and roses. Extensive kitchen garden. Greenhouses

  ¶**The Limes** (Mr & Mrs J Baylis) Large garden, herbaceous borders, mature trees and roses

  Old Mill Cottage (Mr & Mrs M Lewis) Conservation garden of ½ acre with shrubs, perennial borders and rockeries. Collection alpines and herbs. Two ponds and kitchen garden. Newly planted tropical garden

  Old Pumphouse Cottage (Mr & Mrs W Wormell) Cottage garden with mixed borders featuring varieties of pinks and shrub roses and clematis. Kitchen garden and greenhouse

  The Old Rectory (Mrs L Hope-Frost) 2-acre garden surrounding listed building mentioned in Doomsday Book (not open). Large variety of fine trees and shrubs. Small wood

  The Coach House (Mr & Mrs G Rice) 2-acre former Victorian kitchen garden. Woodland area. Extensive new planting

▲**Baddesley Clinton** ♿✿ (The National Trust) ¾m W off A4141 Warwick-Birmingham rd near Chadwick End. 7½m NW of Warwick. Mediaeval moated manor house little changed since 1633; walled garden and herbaceous borders; natural areas; lakeside walk. Lunches and TEAS. *Adm Grounds only £2.30 Chd £1.15. Shop and restaurant open from noon. For NGS Sat April 12 (12-5)*

Balsall Common Gardens ♿✿✿ Balsall Common. 5m S of M42/M6 intersection, 6m W of Coventry, 10m N of Warwick, junction of A452 and B4101. From traffic lights of this intersection go W along B4101 towards Knowle for ¾m. Map available for each garden. TEAS at **White Cottage and Silver Trees Farm**. *Combined adm £2 Chd 50p (Share to The Helen Ley Home®). Sun June 29 (1.30-6). Private visits welcome May & June, please* **Tel 01676 533143**

The Bungalow (Mr & Mrs G Johnson) Table Oak Lane, Fen End. 2 acres mixed borders, pond and lawn. New areas developing

Firs Farm (Mr & Mrs C Ellis) Windmill Lane. ½-acre garden, courtyard with tubs, walled garden, formal garden with rose bed and mixed borders

Meriglen (Mr & Mrs J Webb) Windmill Lane, Balsall Common. ¾-acre mixed borders, small woodland

The Pines (Mr & Mrs C Davis) Hodgetts Lane. 1½-acre formal garden. Avenue of flowering trees, series of small gardens, vegetable, herb garden and rose walk

Silver Trees Farm (Mr & Mrs B Hitchens) Balsall Street. 1½ acres, mixed borders, orchard, bog area, woodland garden. Large formal pond

¶**Fen End House** (Mr & Mrs W Husselby) Fen End. 1-acre garden, with lawns interspersed with borders containing formal and informal planting schemes

White Cottage Farm (Mr & Mrs J Edwards) Holly Lane. 1½ acres cottage garden, mixed borders, pond, sunken garden

32 Wootton Green Lane (Dr & Mrs Leeming) Balsall Common. Lawns, water features, greenhouses

¶**Barton House** ♿✿✿ (Mr & Mrs I H B Cathie) Barton-on-the-Heath. 2m W of Long Compton which lies on the A3400 Stratford-upon-Avon to Oxford Rd. 5-acre garden with mature trees, species and hybrid rhododendrons, azaleas, magnolias and moutan paeonies. Japanese garden, catalpa walk, rose garden, secret garden and many rare and exotic plants. Manor House by Inigo Jones. TEAS. *Adm £2 Chd £1 (Share to St Lawrence Church®). Sun June 1 (2-6). Private visits for groups by appt only, please* **Tel 01608 674303**

The Bevingtons ✿ (Mr & Mrs N Tustain) Ilmington. 8m S of Stratford-on-Avon, 4m NW of Shipston-on-Stour. Cottage garden with many old favourites, old roses, shrubs, herb garden. TEA at **Ilmington Manor**. *Adm £1 Chd free. Sun June 22 (2-6). Also open Sun April 13 with* **Ilmington Gardens**

■ **Birmingham Botanical Gardens & Glasshouses** ♿✿✿ 2m SW of Birmingham City Centre, signposted from Hagley Rd (A456). 15 acres; Tropical House with large lily pond and many economic plants. Palm House; Orangery; Cactus House. Outside-bedding displays; rhododendrons and azaleas; rose garden; rock garden; 200 trees. Theme, herb, historic and cottage gardens. National Bonsai Collection. Fun area for children. Plant centre. Bands play Sun afternoon Easter to Sept. TEAS in the Pavilion. *Adm £3.80 Chd, Students & OAPs £2.10 (Share to Birmingham Botanical & Hort Soc Ltd®). Open daily. For NGS Suns March 2, Sept 28 (10-6)*

▲**Castle Bromwich Hall Garden Trust** Chester Rd ♿✿ Chester Rd 4m E of Birmingham. 1m from junction 5 of the M6 (exit Northbound). An example of the Formal English Garden of the C18. The ongoing restoration, started 10 yrs ago now provides visitors, academics and horticulturalists opportunity of seeing a unique collection of historic plants, shrubs, medicinal and culinary herbs and a fascinating vegetable collection. Guided tours Weds, Sats & Suns. Shop. Refreshments available; meals by arrangement. TEAS. *Adm £2 OAPs £1.50 Chd 50p. For NGS Sats April 12, Sept 27 (2-6)*

Cedar House ⭑⭑ (Mr & Mrs D L Burbidge) Wasperton. 4m S of Warwick on A429, turn R between Barford and Wellesbourne, Cedar House at end of village. 3-acre mixed garden; shrubs, herbaceous borders, ornamental trees, woodland walk. TEAS. *Adm £1.50 Chd free (Share to St John's Church, Wasperton®). Sun June 8 (2-6)*

▲**Charlecote Park** ⭑⭑ (The National Trust) Warwick. 1m W of Wellesbourne signed off A 429. 6m S of Warwick, 5m E of Stratford upon Avon. Landscaped gardens featuring clipped yews and terraces with urns, contain a C19 orangery; a rustic thatched summer house by the cedar lawn; a River Parterre and a Wilderness garden under development. A 1m walk follows a route round the park along the banks of the R Avon, giving fine vistas to two churches. TEAS in Orangery. *Adm £4.60 Chd £2.30. For NGS Sat July 12 (11-6)*

Compton Scorpion Farm ⭑ (Mrs T M Karlsen) nr Ilmington. As for Ilmington Manor then fork L at village hall; after 1½m L down steep narrow lane, house on L. Garden designed and created by owners in 1989 from meadow hillside, aiming at Jekyll single colour schemes. *Adm £1.25 Chd free. Sun March 30, Sat, Sun June 21, 22 (2-6)*

▲**Coughton Court** ⭑⭑⭑ (Mrs C Throckmorton) Alcester. On A435 2m N of Alcester. 12 acres of garden designed by Christina Birch with a courtyard containing an Elizabethan knot garden; beyond are lime walks and a yew rotunda with views of parkland; a new walled garden, continuing by the lake a new rose labyrinth. There are a series of 'rooms' culminating in an herbaceous garden; a walk planted with willows and native shrubs and trees beside the River Arrow; a new bog garden and a formal orchard. TEAS. *Adm £3.50 Chd £1.75 (Share to Coughton Catholic Church Restoration Appeal®). For NGS Sat June 28 (11-5.30)*

Dorsington Gardens ⭑⭑ 6m SW of Stratford-on-Avon. On B439 from Stratford turn L to Welford-on-Avon, then R to Dorsington. TEAS. *Combined adm £2.50 Chd free (Share to St Peter's Church, Dorsington®). Sun June 15 (2-5.30)*

> **Aberfoyle** (Mr & Mrs B Clarke) Well established cottage garden, fine trees and shrubs
> **Knowle Thatch** (Mr & Mrs P Turner) Large garden, mature trees, shrubs and herbaceous borders
> **Milfield** (Mr & Mrs P Carey) Typical cottage garden with pond and access to
> **Whitegates** (Mrs A Turner) Shrubs, mature trees and shrub roses
> **The Moat House** (Mr & Mrs I Kolodotschko) 6-acre moated garden incl walled vegetable garden, conservatory with mediterranean plants
> **New House Farm** (Mr & Mrs G Wood-Hill) Walled garden, climbing roses, herbaceous borders
> **The Old Manor** (Mr F Dennis) 3 acres with fairy walk, herb garden, Japanese dry garden, willow walk, and rare arboretum, Oz Maze and Udde Well. TEAS
> **The Old Rectory** (Mr & Mrs N Phillips) 2-acre Victorian garden with mature trees incl old espalier fruit trees, box hedges, herbaceous borders, many old roses, large pool, small wood
> **Windrush** (Mrs M Mills) Country garden with shrubs, cottage plants and roses

¶**The Earlsdon Gardens, Coventry** ⭑ Turn towards Coventry at the A45/A429 traffic lights. Take 3rd L turn into Beechwood Ave, to St Barbara's Church. Maps available. Other gardens also open. TEAS. *Combined adm £1.50 Chd free. Sun June 29 (2-5)*

> ¶**40 Hartington Crescent** (Viv and George Buss) An unusually large garden with interest for all ages
> ¶**144 Hartington Crescent** (Liz Campbell and Dennis Crowley). A medium-sized garden on 2 levels with water feature, herbaceous border and small trees
> ¶**22 Radcliffe Road** (Sondra and John Halliday) A small suburban garden exploiting a range of habitats - conservatory, pond, bogs and shade
> ¶**15 Shaftsbury Road** (Elaine and Mike Tierney) A small suburban garden shared by plantswoman and young family

Elizabeth Road Gardens ⭑⭑ Moseley. 4m S of Birmingham City centre, halfway between Kings Heath Centre & Edgbaston Cricket Ground. Off Moor Green Lane. TEAS at No 63 in aid of Cats-in-Care. *Combined adm £1.20 Chd 50p. Suns May 11, July 27 (2-5)*

> **No 55** (Rob & Diane Cole) Plantsman's garden 100' × 30' on 3 levels, with scree area and mixed borders of alpines, rhododendrons, primulas and perennials, many unusual. Alpine House, and tubs
> **No 63** (Barbara & Derek Colley) Informal garden, 115' × 120' with mature trees, lawns and island beds containing shrubs, herbaceous borders and rockery plants

Elm Close ⭑⭑⭑ (Mr & Mrs E W Dyer) Binton Rd, Welford-on-Avon. 5m from Stratford off A4390. Elm Close is between Welford Garage and The Bell Inn. ⅔-acre plantsman's garden designed and maintained by owners and stocked for yr-round effect. Bulbs, alpines, clematis and hellebores a particular speciality. Listed in The Good Gardens Guide. TEAS Suns only in aid of Red Cross. *Adm £1.50 Chd free. Suns, Mons April 6, 7, 20, 21, May 4, 5, 18, July 13, 14, Sept 21, 22 (2-6). Parties welcome by appointment, please* **Tel 01789 490803**

The Folly Lodge ⭑⭑ (Mrs Susan Solomon) Halford. On A429 (Fosse Way) 9m NE Moreton in Marsh. 9m SE Stratford on Avon. In Halford take turning opp PO to Idlicote. House is 300yds down on R. ⅓-acre designed, constructed and maintained by owners since 1983. Colour themed borders, roses, shrubs and small pond; wide variety of plants many unusual. TEA. *Adm £1.50 Chd free. Weds May 14, June 11, 25, July 9, Aug 13, Sept 10 (2-5). Private visits welcome, please* **Tel 01789 740183**

¶**Foxgloves** ⭑⭑ (Eve Hessey & George Andrews) 35 Rugby Rd, Dunchurch. On A426 nr village centre. Small gardens with ornamental potager, fruit cage, cordon fruit trees, grapes, figs, kiwi fruit, herb garden, lawn with colour themed herbaceous borders, ornamental shrubs, climbing roses and collections of foxgloves and hardy geraniums, nut tunnel. TEA. *Adm £1 Chd free. Sun June 22 (2-5). Private visits also welcome, please* **Tel 01788 817643**. *Other village gardens may be open ring for details*

1997 Special Events. For information on special National Gardens Scheme events in 1997 see Pages 18-19.

17 Gerrard Street (Mr T K Meredith) Warwick. 100yds from castle main gate. Car park at St Nicholas. Small town garden with interesting plants. *Adm 40p Chd free. Sat, Sun June 21, 22 (11-1 & 2-6). Private visits welcome, please* Tel 01926 496305

Greenlands &⚘ (Mr Eric T Bartlett) Wellesbourne. Leave Statford-upon-Avon due E on the B4086. Garden on Xrds at Loxley/Charlecote by airfield. An acre of mature trees; shrubs; shrub roses and herbaceous borders. TEAS. *Adm £1 Chd free (Share to Intermediate Technology®). Suns April 20, June 15, Aug 24 (11-5). Parties welcome, please* Tel 01789 840327

■ **89 Harts Green Road** ⚘⚘ (Mrs Barbara Richardson) Harborne. 3m Birmingham City Centre [A-Z A2 p88] off Fellows Lane/War Lane. ½-acre split level informal garden with troughs, scree, rockery and mixed borders of unusual plants, shrubs and climbers. Pond and vegetable garden. Adjoining orchard contains small nursery offering wide range of plants, many propagated from garden. *Adm £1 Chd free. Open every Wed in May, June, July and Sept. For NGS Weds May 14, June 11 (2-5). Private visits and groups welcome, please* Tel 0121 427 5200

Hickecroft &⚘ (Mr J M Pitts) Rowington. 6m NW of Warwick, 15m SE of Birmingham on B4439 between Hockley Heath and Hatton. Turn into Finwood Rd (signed Lowsonford); at Rowington Xrds 1st L into Mill Lane. 2-acre garden reaching maturity following redesigning and replanting. Interesting plants, mixed borders. Home to part of the NCCPG Digitalis collection. TEAS. *Adm £1.50 Chd 50p (Share to St Laurence Church®). Sat, Sun June 21, 22 (2-5.30)*

▲**The Hiller Garden & Dunnington Heath Farm** &⚘⚘ (Mr & Mrs R Beach) Alcester. On B4088 (was A435), 3m S Alcester. 2-acre garden of all-yr interest displaying unusual herbaceous perennials, old-fashioned species roses, and English roses. TEAS. *Adm by donation. Open all yr. For NGS Suns April 27, June 29, Aug 17, Oct 5 (10-4). Private gardens of Dunnington Heath Farm (adjacent) also open on NGS days. Adm £1 Chd free*

11 Hillwood Common Road ⚘⚘ (Mr & Mrs C T Smith) Four Oaks, Sutton Coldfield. From A5127 at Mere Green traffic island take Hill Village Rd. 2nd R into Sherifoot Lane and follow L bend. Straight on into Hill Wood Common Rd. [AZ ref 27.4H.] ½-acre Japanese style garden with tea house; stone and water feature; Japanese courtyard. Low heeled shoes, please. *Adm £2. Private visits welcome, please* Tel 0121 3081180

Holywell Gardens &⚘⚘ 5m E of Henley-in-Arden, nearest village Claverdon. Coffee and TEAS in aid of Myton Hospice. *Combined adm £2 Chd free. Sun June 15 (11-6)*

　Holywell Farm (Mr & Mrs Ian Harper) 2½-acre natural garden; lawn, trees, shrubs. Laid out in 1963 for easy maintenance, surrounding C16 half timbered house

　Manor Farm (Mr & Mrs Donald Hanson) Cottage type garden surrounding C16 farmhouse with natural duck pond, yew and box hedges, herb garden; white and grey border

Honington Village Gardens &⚘⚘ 1½m N of Shipston-on-Stour. Take A3400 towards Stratford then R signed Honington. TEAS **Honington Hall**. *Combined adm £2 Chd free (Share to All Saints Church, Honington®). Sun June 29 (2.15-5.30)*

　Feldon Cottage (Mr & Mrs H James)
　Holts Cottage (Mr M Harvey)
　Honington Glebe (Mr & Mrs John Orchard) Over 2 acres of informal garden interesting ornamental trees; shrubs and foliage. Parterre and raised lily pool recently laid out in old walled garden
　Honington Hall (Lady Wiggin) Extensive lawns; fine trees. Carolean house (not open); Parish Church adjoining house
　Honington Lodge (Lord & Lady Tombs)
　The Old House (Mr & Mrs R S Smith)
　Old Mullions (Mr & Mrs R Lawton)

Hunningham Village Gardens &⚘⚘ Hunningham. From Leamington Spa B4453 to Rugby. Signposted Hunningham R after Weston-under-Wetherley. Or A425 to Southam at Fosseway (B4455) turn L. At Hunningham Hill turn L then follow signs to church (open). Teas at Vicarage in aid of St Margarets Church. *Adm £2 Chd free. Sun, Mon May 4, 5 (2-5)*

　High Cross (Mr & Mrs T Chalk) Secluded garden
　Moat Cottage (Mr & Mrs Murchek) New garden with interesting features and planting
　The Olde School House (Mr & Mrs G Longstaff) 1 acre of borders, shrubs, pond and wilflife paddock area
　Sandford Cottage (Mr & Mrs A Phillips) Village cottage garden
　Other gardens may open

Idlicote Gardens &⚘ 3m NE of Shipston-on-Stour. TEAS. *Combined adm £2 OAPs £1 Chd free (Share to Parish Church of St James the Great®). Sun May 4 (2-6)*

　Idlicote House (Mrs R P G Dill) About 4 acres. Fine views. Small Norman church in grounds. House C18 (not open) listed Grade II
　Badgers Farm (Sir Derek & Lady Hornby)
　1 Bickerstaff Cottages (Mr & Mrs C Balchin)
　Bickerstaff Farm (Sir John & Lady Owen)
　Home Farm (Mr & Mrs G Menzies-Kitchen)
　Mews Cottage (Mr & Mrs D Colton)
　The Old Rectory (Mr & Mrs G Thomson)
　Stone Cottage (Mr & Mrs M Batsford)
　Woodlands (Capt & Mrs P R Doyne)

Ilmington Gardens ⚘ 8m S of Stratford-on-Avon, 4m NW of Shipston-on-Stour. Ilmington traditional Morris dancers. Teas in the Village Hall. Start anywhere, all gardens well signed and within walking distance. *Combined adm £3 Chd free (Share to GRBS®). Sun April 13 (2-6)*

　Crab Mill (L & J Hodgkins)
　The Bevingtons (N & F Tustain) See individual entry
　Foxcote Hill (M & S Dingley)
　Foxcote Hill Cottage (A Terry)
　Frog Orchard (M Naish)
　The Manor (D Flower) (see next entry)
　Pear Tree Cottage (Dr & Mrs A F Hobson) See individual entry

Ilmington Manor &❀ (Mr D & Lady Flower) 4m NW of Shipston-on-Stour, 8m S of Stratford-on-Avon. Daffodils in profusion (April). Hundreds of old and new roses, ornamental trees, shrub and herbaceous borders, rock garden, pond garden, topiary, fish pond with Koi. House (not open) built 1600. TEAS. *Adm £2 Chd free (Share to The Gardeners Royal Benevolent Society®). Suns May 18, June 22, July 6 (2-6). Also open Sun April 13 with* **Ilmington Gardens.** *Private visits welcome, please* **Tel 01608 682230**

Ivy Lodge & (Mrs M A Willis) Radway 7m NW of Banbury via A41 and B4086, turn R down Edgehill; 14m SE of Stratford via A422. L below Edgehill. 4-acres; spring bulbs and blossom; wildflower area; climbing roses; site Battle of Edgehill. TEAS. *Adm £1.50 OAP £1 Chd free (Share to the Katherine House Hospice Trust®). Sun April 20, July 6 (2-6). Also parties welcome April to July and throughout Oct (Autumn colours), please* **Tel 01295 670371 or 670580**

▲**Martineau Centre Gardens** &❀❀ (City of Birmingham Education Dept) Priory Rd, Edgbaston. From Birmingham S via A38; R at Priory Rd (lights and box junction); entrance 100yds on R opp Priory Hospital. 2-acre demonstration gardens; hardy ornamentals, vegetables, small orchard; glasshouses; nature reserve/wild garden. TEAS. *Adm £1 Chd 50p. For NGS Sun July 20 (10-6)*

■ **The Master's Garden, Lord Leycester Hospital** ❀ (Susan Rhodes for the Patron and Governors) High Street, Warwick. Town centre beside West Gate. Garden adjoins historic C14 Guildhall, Chapel, courtyard, Great Hall and Museum of the Queen's Own Hussars also open to public. 1-acre walled garden, including Norman arch and ancient finial of Nilometer. TEAS. *Adm £1 Chd free. Open daily except Mons, Easter to Sept 30 (10-4.30). For NGS Sat June 21 (11-5). Parties welcome, please* **Tel 01926 491422**

¶**Max Gate** ❀❀ (Mr & Mrs C W Bolt) 103 Bilton Rd. On A4071, Rugby to Leamington Rd, ½m from Rugby town centre. A ⅓-acre sloping town garden filled with a wide range of plants, bulbs, trees and shrubs many of which are unusual. Secluded back garden incl a large mixed border, 2 orchard areas, a dell and pool, and a hidden cottage garden. Recently re-designed in 1995, the large front garden is devoted to a succession of seasonal colour and interest in 4 separate, linked areas. TEAS in aid of RELATE, Rugby and NE Warwickshire. *Combined adm with* **2 Paddock House** *£2.50 Chd free. Sun June 22 (2-6)*

Maxstoke Castle &❀❀ (Mr & Mrs M C Fetherston-Dilke) nr Coleshill, E of Birmingham, 2½m E of Coleshill on B4114 take R turn down Castle Lane; Castle Dr 1¼m on R. 4 to 5 acres of garden and pleasure grounds with flowers, shrubs and trees in the immediate surroundings of the castle and inside courtyard; water-filled moat round castle. *Adm £2.50 OAP/Chd £1.50 under 6 free. Sun June 1 (2-5)*

■ **The Mill Garden** &❀❀ (Mr A B Measures) 55 Mill St, Warwick off A425 beside castle gate. 1 acre; series of informal, partially enclosed areas, on river next to castle.

Superb setting; herb garden; raised beds; small trees, shrubs, cottage plants and some unusual plants. Use St Nicholas Car Park. Tea in Warwick. *Adm £1 Chd free (Share to Lord Leycester Hospital®). Open daily 9 till dusk. Open for NGS Suns April 20, May 11, June 22, July 20, Aug 10, Sept 20, Oct 12. Parties welcome, please* **Tel 01926 492877**

Moseley Gardens ❀❀ Approx 3m from Birmingham City Centre halfway between Kings Heath Centre & Moseley Village. TEA April 20. TEAS July 13. *Combined adm £1.50 Chd free. Suns April 20, July 13 (2-6)*

   7 Ashfield Rd (Mr & Mrs Bartlett) Small garden with secluded, cottage feel. Attractive pond with rockery, waterfall and shingle bank

   No 16 Prospect Rd ❀ (Mrs S M & Mr R J Londesborough) Small garden with wide range of plants. Large collection of containers. *Also private visits welcome all year, please* **Tel 0121 449 8457**

   No 19 Prospect Rd (Mr A White) Well planted spring suburban garden. *April 20 only*

   No 20 Prospect Rd (Martin Page & Annie Sofiano) Large town garden on 3 levels. *July 13 only*

   No 30 Prospect Rd (Mrs J Taylor) South-facing terraced garden incorporating rockery-covered air-raid shelter

   No 33 School Rd (Ms J Warr-Arnold) Mixed garden containing plants with interesting histories. *Sun July 13 only*

   No 65 School Rd (Mrs W Weston) Small shady garden with patio, pergola and pond. *Sun July 13 only*

Orchard Cottage &❀ (Mr & Mrs G Roberts) Hurley. M42, junction 9, take A4097 to Kingsbury. 2nd island, R to Coventry, 1st L to Hurley. Approx 1½m, R into Dexter Lane cottage at end of lane. C17 property in ¾ acre. Cottage garden with informal plantings of mixed beds and borders containing many interesting plants, original water feature, evolving meadow orchard. A 10-yr-old garden that thinks it's 50! TEAS. *Adm £1 Chd under 12 free. Sat, Sun July 12, 13 (2-6)*

Packington Hall &❀ (Lord & Lady Guernsey) Meriden. On A45, towards Coventry, after Stonebridge Roundabout. Packington's pleasure grounds were laid out in 1750 by Capability Brown. The lawns run down to the 18 acre Hall Pool and are studded with clumps of azaleas and rhododendrons, together with specimen trees. The more formal area around the House has recently been replanted. TEAS. *Adm £2.50 Chd £1.50 (Share to Assoc for Brain Damaged Children, Coventry®). Sun June 8 (2-5.30)*

▲**Packwood House** &❀❀ (The National Trust) 11m SE of Birmingham. 2m E of Hockley Heath. Carolean yew garden representing the Sermon on the Mount. Tudor house with tapestries, needlework and furniture of the period. Teas at Baddesley Clinton (NT) Henley in Arden or Knowle. *Adm garden only £4 Chd £2. For NGS June 8 (1.30-5.30)*

2 Paddock House ❀❀ (Anne Sutton) Hillmorton. From Rugby take A428 to Hillmorton signed Northampton M1. Approx 1½m from town centre turn R opposite Do It All into Rainsbrook Avenue, which leads to Dunsmore Ave. Garden on R. From Motorway junction 18 follow signs to

Rugby. For **Max Gate** take A428 towards town centre. A small town garden designed by the owner. Some unusual plants and shrubs. Paved area with pots and informal pool/bog garden. Herbaceous borders, climbers and ivy mound for wildlife - an organic garden. *Combined adm with* **Max Gate** *£2.50 Chd free. Sun June 22 (2-6)*

Parham Lodge ♿✂❀ (Mr & Mrs K C Edwards) Alveston 2m E of Stratford upon Avon off B4086. Turn L at Memorial Cross into Alveston Lane. At post box on green continue 30yds. 1-acre flower arranger's country garden, designed by owners for colour, texture and scent at all seasons, large pond and terrace with grasses, alpines and heathers. Island beds, spring and summer bulbs, rose beds and wild flower orchard producing apples for most months of the year. Old cedars and hornbeams with short woodland walk. Herb and cutting gardens. Beehives so no sprays for 20 years. Butterflies, hedgehogs, toads all find a home. *Adm £1.50 Chd 50p. Private visits and parties welcome by appt May, Sept and Oct please* **Tel 01789 268955**

Paxford ♿✂❀ (Mr & Mrs A M Parsons) Princethorpe. 7m SE of Coventry, on B4453 Leamington Rd approx 200yds from junction with A423. A flower arranger's garden with heathers and fuchsias which has been designed and maintained by the owners as a series of rooms. Parking on road on one side only please. TEA. *Adm £1 (Share to Stretton-on-Dunsmore Parish Church®). Suns June 22, July 20 (2-6)*

Pear Tree Cottage ❀ (Dr & Mrs A F Hobson) Ilmington 8m S of Stratford-on-Avon, 4m NW of Shipston-on-Stour. Cottage garden with many interesting plants and bulbs. Designed and maintained by owners; rock garden and terrace. Partially suitable for wheelchairs. Teas in Village Hall April 13 and Ilmington Manor May 18. *Adm £1 Chd free. Sun May 18 (2-6). Also open Sun April 13 (2-6) with* **Ilmington Gardens**

Pereira Road Gardens ✂❀ Birmingham A-Z 5c p.72 between Gillhurst Rd and Margaret Grove, ¼m from Hagley Rd or ½m Harborne High St. TEAS June 22 at **No. 84** in aid of St Joseph's Home. *Combined adm £1.50 Chd 30p. Suns May 11, June 22 (2-5)*

No. 45 (Wyn & Alfred White) Harborne. ⅙ acre on four levels. Spring bulbs, rhododendrons, roses, shrubs, herbaceous borders and fruit trees in formal and informal areas. Harborne Nature Reserve and Bird Sanctuary can be visited. *(Share to Break Through Trust for the Deaf®). June 22 only*

No. 50 ❀ (Prof M Peil) About ⅕ acre on several levels, with approx 1000 shrubs; perennials and for all seasons and fruit and vegetables. Large bed of plants with African connections. (Plants sold in aid of Catholic Fund for Overseas Development.)

No. 84 ♿ (Mrs R E Barnett) ⅕ acre with 30 degree sloping concreted bank, now extensive rockery, interesting shrubs, herbaceous borders. *June 22 only*

Roseberry Cottage ♿✂❀ (Mr & Mrs Richard G Bastow) Fillongley. 6m N of Coventry on B4098 Tamworth Road. Go under motorway bridge to top of hill, take Woodend Lane, sign on R. Turn L into Sandy Lane, opp triangle of beech trees. 1st house on R in Sandy Lane. Please use one way system due to restricted parking. Garden of 1¾ acres incl herbaceous border, rock garden, pool, peat and bog area, scree and small herb garden. Stone troughs, orchard with wild flowers, organically grown fruit and vegetables. Herbs for sale, thymes a speciality. TEA. *Adm £1 Chd 30p (Share to NCCPG®). Sun June 29 (2-5)*

■ **Ryton Organic Gardens** ♿✂❀ 5m SE of Coventry (off A45 to Wolston). In the heart of the Warwickshire countryside, ten beautiful acres of flowers, formal roses, shrubs, alpines, top and soft fruit, herbs and many old and unusual vegetables, all grown in harmony with nature. Listed in the good food guide. TEAS. *Adm £2.50 Concessions £2, Chd £1.25. Open daily except Christmas period. For NGS Suns April 27, Sept 28 (10-5)*

Sheepy Magna Gardens, nr Atherstone see Leicestershire

Sherbourne Manor ♿✂❀ (Mr & Mrs M Perry) 2m S of Warwick just off A429 Barford Rd. Large garden contains herbaceous borders; stream; old fish pond and large variety of established trees and many new trees. TEAS in aid of All Saints Church, Sherbourne. *Adm £3 OAPs £1 Chd up to 12 free. Suns July 6, Sept 7 (2-5.30)*

Sherbourne Park ♿ (Mr R C Smith-Ryland) 3m S of Warwick off A429; ½m N of Barford. Medium-sized garden; lawns, shrubs, borders, roses, lilies; lake; temple; church by Gilbert Scott 1863 adjacent to early Georgian House (not open) 1730. Featured in 'New Englishwoman's Garden' (R Verey) and 'English Gardens' (P Coats). Featured in 1991 & 1992 Gardeners Royal Benevolent Society Calendar. Lunches, teas or coffee for private tours by arrangement. Free car park. *Adm £3 OAPs and Chd (13-16) £2, under 12 free (Share to All Saints Church, Sherbourne®). Open for private tours and coaches by appt only, please* **Tel Mrs Farey 01926 624506**

Shrewley Pools Farm ✂ (Mrs C W Dodd) Haseley. 4m NW of Warwick through Hatton. At roundabout turn L along Five Ways Rd, after approx ¾m farm entrance on L opp Audholi poultry farm. ¾m off A4177 from Falcon Inn (Warwick). 1-acre garden, herbaceous borders, rhododendrons, roses, irises, peonies etc. Many interesting shrubs and trees, terrace and garden pool. Farm animals and C17 farmhouse and barn. TEAS. *Adm £1.50 Chd 30p (Share to Saltisford Evangelical Church®). Sun June 15 (2-6). Private visits welcome for 4 and over, please* **Tel 01926 484315**

26 Sunnybank Road ✂❀ (Chris & Margaret Jones) Wylde Green. ¾m S of Sutton Coldfield. Turn off A5127 towards Wylde Green Station then; 2nd L. Medium-sized town garden on sandy soil, redesigned by present owners as a series of 'rooms'. Yr-long interest achieved by use of bulbs, shrubs and herbaceous plants. Featured on Garden Club Aug 93 (Channel 4), Secret Gardens (BBC) Spring 96, and 'Your Garden' magazine Dec 93. TEAS in aid of John Willnott School PTA. *Adm £1 OAPs 50p Chd free. Sun July 20 (2-6)*

52 Tenbury Road ♿✂❀ (Mr G & Mrs V Grace Darby) Kings Heath. 5m S of city centre off A435 (Alcester Rd). 4¾m from junction 3 off M40. ⅛ of an acre suburban garden in cottage garden style. Informal plantings of mixed beds and borders with interesting and unusual plants, shrubs, climbers. Small vegetable and fruit area, minimum use of chemical pest control. TEAS in aid of South Birmingham Talking Newspaper (for the Blind) April 27 and Muscular Dystrophy Wed June 25, Sun July 6 (2-5.30). *Adm £1.50 Chd free. Suns April 27, July 6 (2-5.30), Wed June 25 (2-5 & 7-9). Private and group visits welcome April to July, please* Tel 0121 444 6456

Tysoe Manor &⚅⚘ (Mr & Mrs W A C Wield) Tysoe. 5m NE of Shipston-on-Stour. Take the 4035 to Banbury. In Brailes turn L to Tysoe. The Manor is the 1st house on the L after reaching Upper Tysoe. 4-acre garden, large lawns with stone walls, herbaceous and flower borders, shrubs and mature ornamental and fruit trees. TEAS in aid of Tysoe Church. *Adm £1.50 Chd free. Sun Sept 14 (2-6)*

▲**Upton House** ⚅⚘ (The National Trust) 7m NW of Banbury on A422; 2m S of Edgehill. Terraced garden, rockeries, herbaceous borders, roses, water gardens, lawns. House contains a connoisseur's collection of porcelain, tapestries and paintings. Partially suitable for wheelchairs. Coaches by appt. TEAS. *Adm garden only £2.40 Chd £1.20. For NGS Sat July 5 (2-6 last adm 5.30)*

8 **Vicarage Rd** &⚅⚘ (Charles & Tessa King-Farlow) Edgbaston, 1½m W of City Centre off A456 (Hagley Rd). ¾-acre retaining in part its Victorian layout but informally planted with mixed borders of interesting and unusual plants; shrub rose border; walled potager and conservatory. Featured in House and Garden Sept 1995. TEAS in aid of St George's Church. *Adm £1.50 Chd free. Sun June 29 (2-6). Special evening opening Adm £2.50 to include a glass of wine, Wed July 2 (6.30-8.30) Private visits very welcome, please* Tel 0121 455 0902

Warmington Village Gardens &⚅⚘ 5m NW of Banbury on B4100. Teas at **The Village Hall**. *Combined adm £2 Chd free (Share to Warmington PCC Restoration Fund®). Sun June 22 (2-6) Car park; coaches welcome, please* Tel 01295 690 318
  Berka (Mr & Mrs B J Castle) Chapel Street
  3 Court Close (Mr & Mrs C J Crocker)
  The Glebe House (Mr & Mrs G Thornton) Village Road
  Holly Cottage (Dr & Mrs T W Martin) The Green
  ¶**The Manor House** (Mr & Mrs G Lewis) The Green
  ¶**The Old Rectory** (Sir Wilfred & Lady Cockcroft) The Green
  Rotherwood (Miss M R Goodison) Soot Lane
  Sunnyside (Mr & Mrs M Borlenghi) Chapel Street
  Underedge (Mr & Mrs J Dixon) 1 Church Hill
  Woodcote (Mrs S Mellor) School Lane

Warwickshire Constabulary, Police HQ ⚘ Leek Wootton. Mid-way between Warwick and Kenilworth, 1m N of the Gaveston Island, on the Kenilworth Rd, off the A46 Warwick to Coventry by-pass. From Warwick, turn L after Anchor Public House in centre of village, signposted Police Headquarters. Approx 6 acres of mixed garden, large and small shrubs, herbaceous borders, Chinese garden, walk around lakes. TEAS. *Adm £1.50 Chd free (Share to Victim Support®). Sun June 1 (1.30-5)*

50 Wellington Rd &⚅⚘ (Mrs Anne Lee) Edgbaston. Corner of Ampton Rd and Wellington Rd. 1-acre walled town garden. York stone, paving, brick paths and architectural features. 100-yr-old rhododendrons and mature trees with woodland walk. Two long mixed borders, shrub roses, fountain, croquet lawn. TEAS. *Adm £1.50 Chd free. Sun June 22 (2-6). Private visits also welcome April to Oct, please* Tel 0121 440 1744

Wheelwright House &⚘ (Richard & Suzanne Shacklock) Long Compton. 6m S of Shipston-on-Stour on A3400; at S end of Long Compton village take rd signed to Little Compton; Wheelwright House is 300yds on L. 1-acre garden surrounding C18 house. Stream with attractive bridges forms centrepiece. Bog garden, shade gardens, colourful mixed borders with wide variety of traditional and unusual plants. Formal lily pool with rose pergola. Mediterranean garden. TEAS in aid of Long Compton Church. *Adm £1.50 Chd free. Sun Sept 7 (2-5.30). Private visits welcome, please* Tel 01608 684478

Whichford & Ascott Gardens ⚅⚘ 6m SE of Shipston-on-Stour. Turn E off A3400 at Long Compton for Whichford. Cream TEAS. Car park and picnic area. *Combined adm £2 Chd free. Sun June 15 (2-6)*
  Brook Hollow (Mr & Mrs J A Round) Garden on a bank, stream and large variety of plants
  Combe House (Mr & Mrs D C Seel) Hidden garden surrounding house; mature fine trees
  The Gateway (Mrs M W Thorne) Large garden in attractive setting with magnificent trees and small stream. Lawn enclosed with fine box hedges
  The Old House (Mr & Mrs T A Maher) Undulating garden. Natural ponds, trees and shrubs
  Roman Row (Mr & Mrs S C Langdon) Beautiful well kept cottage garden
  Stone Walls (Mrs J Scott-Cockburn) Walled garden; paved garden in foundations of old stable
  Whichford House (Mr & Mrs J W Oakes) Large undulating garden with extensive views. Mainly shrubs and trees
  The Whichford Pottery (Mr & Mrs J B M Keeling) Secret walled garden, unusual plants, large vegetable garden and rambling cottage garden. Adjoining pottery

Woodpeckers &⚅⚘ (Dr & Mrs A J Cox) The Bank, Marlcliff, nr Bidford-on-Avon 7m SW of Stratford-on-Avon. Off the B4085 between Bidford-on-Avon and Cleeve Prior. 2½-acre plantsman's country garden designed and maintained by owners; colour-schemed borders, old roses, meadow garden, alpines in troughs and gravel, pool, knot garden, potager. Featured on BBC2 'Gardener's World' and in 'Practical Gardening' and 'Period Living'. *Adm £2. Private visits by Societies or individuals welcome at all seasons, please* Tel 01789 773416

Remember that every time you visit a National Gardens Scheme garden you are helping to raise money for the following:
The Queen's Nursing Institute
The Nurses' Welfare Service
Cancer Relief Macmillan Fund
The Gardens Fund of the National Trust
The Gardeners' Royal Benevolent Society
The Royal Gardeners' Orphan Fund

Wiltshire

Hon County Organiser: Brigadier Arthur Gooch, Manor Farmhouse, Chitterne, Warminster BA12 OLG

Assistant Hon County Organisers: Mrs David Armytage, Sharcott Manor, Pewsey
Mrs Anthony Heywood, Monkton House, Monkton Deverell, Warminster
Mrs Colin Shand, Ashton House, Worton, Devizes

DATES OF OPENING

February 15 Saturday
Lacock Abbey, nr Chippenham
February 16 Sunday
Lacock Abbey, nr Chippenham
February 22 Saturday
Lacock Abbey, nr Chippenham
February 23 Sunday
Great Chalfield Manor, nr
Melksham ‡
Lacock Abbey, nr Chippenham ‡
March 16 Sunday
Lower House, Whiteparish
March 23 Sunday
Corsham Court, nr Chippenham
March 31 Monday
Hyde's House, Dinton, nr
Salisbury
April 2 Wednesday
Sharcott Manor, nr Pewsey
April 6 Sunday
Upper Chelworth Farm, nr
Cricklade
April 13 Sunday
Broadleas, nr Devizes
Crudwell Court Hotel, nr
Malmesbury
Fonthill House, nr Tisbury ‡
Manor House Farm, Hanging
Langford ‡
April 20 Sunday
Easton Grey House, nr
Malmesbury
Sharcott Manor, nr Pewsey
April 27 Sunday
Baynton House, Coulston
Iford Manor, nr Bradford-on-Avon
Luckington Manor, nr
Malmesbury ‡
Oare House, nr Pewsey
Ridleys Cheer, Mountain Bower ‡
May 4 Sunday
Spye Park, nr Chippenham
Stowell Park Gardens, nr Pewsey
Upper Chelworth Farm, nr
Cricklade
May 7 Wednesday
Sharcott Manor, nr Pewsey
May 11 Sunday
Home Covert, Devizes
Inwoods, nr Bradford-on-Avon
Little Durnford Manor, nr
Salisbury

Waterdale House, East Knoyle
May 18 Sunday
Conock Manor, nr Devizes
Luckington Court, nr
Chippenham ‡
7 Norton Bavant, nr Warminster
Ridleys Cheer, Mountain Bower ‡
May 28 Wednesday
Bryher, Bromham
June 1 Sunday
Bowood Rhododendron Walks, nr
Chippenham
The Close, Pewsey
Hyde's House, Dinton, nr
Salisbury
Landford Lodge, nr Salisbury
Stourhead Garden, Stourton, Mere
Upper Chelworth Farm, nr
Cricklade
June 4 Wednesday
Sharcott Manor, nr Pewsey
June 7 Saturday
Mompesson House, The Close,
Salisbury
June 8 Sunday
Corsham Court, nr Chippenham
13 Kingsdown Road, Stratton St
Margaret
Mallards, Chirton, nr Devizes
Martins, Whitehill, Bradford on
Avon
June 14 Saturday
Stourton House, Mere
June 15 Sunday
Ark Farm, Old Wardour, nr
Tisbury
Avebury Manor Garden,
Avebury
Bryher, Bromham
Chisenbury Priory, nr Upavon
Edington Gardens
Foscote Gardens, Grittleton ‡
Guyers House, Pickwick, nr
Corsham ‡‡
The Old Rectory, Stockton
Ridleys Cheer, Mountain Bower ‡
Sheldon Manor, nr
Chippenham ‡‡
June 21 Saturday
Hannington Hall, Highworth, nr
Swindon
June 22 Sunday
Avon Farm House, Stratford sub
Castle, Salisbury ‡

Biddestone Manor, Biddestone,
nr Corsham
Coulston Gardens, Coulston
The Courts, nr Bradford-on-Avon
Goulters Mill Farm, Nettleton
Great Durnford Gardens, nr
Salisbury ‡
Hannington Hall, Highworth, nr
Swindon
Hillbarn House, Great Bedwyn
Long Hall Gardens & Nursery,
Stockton, nr Warminster
Manor Farm, Monkton Deverill ‡‡
Pertwood Manor, Hindon ‡‡
June 28 Saturday
Hazelbury Manor, nr Box
June 29 Sunday
Beech Knoll House, Aldbourne
Bolehyde Manor, nr Chippenham
Chisenbury Priory, nr Upavon
Faulstone House, Bishopstone, nr
Salisbury
Garden House, Sandridge Park,
nr Melksham
The Grange, Winterbourne
Dauntsey
Green Hall, East Grafton
Hazelbury Manor, nr Box
Little Durnford Manor, nr
Salisbury
Pound Hill House, West Kington
July 2 Wednesday
Sharcott Manor, nr Pewsey
July 6 Sunday
Job's Mill, Crockerton, nr
Warminster
Ridleys Cheer, Mountain Bower
Upper Chelworth Farm, nr
Cricklade
July 9 Wednesday
Green Hall, East Grafton
July 12 Saturday
The Abbey House, Malmesbury
Great Somerford Gardens,
Chippenham
July 13 Sunday
The Abbey House, Malmesbury ‡
Crudwell Court Hotel, nr
Malmesbury ‡
Great Somerford Gardens,
Chippenham
Lackham Gardens, nr Chippenham
Mallards, Chirton, nr Devizes ‡‡
Sharcott Manor, nr Pewsey ‡‡

Waterdale House, East Knoyle
July 20 Sunday
Home Covert, Devizes ‡
13 Kingsdown Road, Stratton St
Margaret
Luckington Manor, nr Malmesbury
Worton Gardens, Devizes ‡
July 27 Sunday
Oare House, nr Pewsey
August 3 Sunday
Courtlands, nr Corsham
Heale Gardens & Plant Centre,
Middle Woodford
Lower Farm House, Milton
Lilbourne ‡
The Old Bakery, Milton
Lilbourne ‡
Upper Chelworth Farm, nr
Cricklade
August 10 Sunday
The Mead Nursery, Brokerswood
August 17 Sunday
Broadleas, nr Devizes

Luckington Manor, nr Malmesbury
August 30 Saturday
Stourton House, Mere
August 31 Sunday
The Courts, nr Bradford-on-Avon
September 3 Wednesday
Sharcott Manor, nr Pewsey
September 7 Sunday
Upper Chelworth Farm, nr
Cricklade
September 14 Sunday
Avebury Manor Garden, Avebury
September 21 Sunday
Hillbarn House, Great Bedwyn
October 1 Wednesday
Sharcott Manor, nr Pewsey
October 5 Sunday
Great Chalfield Manor, nr
Melksham ‡
Lackham Gardens, nr
Chippenham ‡

1998
**February 14, 15, 21, 22 Sats,
Suns**
Lacock Abbey, nr Chippenham

Regular openings
For details see garden description

Bowood House & Gardens, nr
Chippenham
Broadleas, nr Devizes
Heale Gardens & Plant Centre,
Middle Woodford
Iford Manor, nr Bradford-on-Avon
Lackham Gardens, nr Chippenham
Long Hall Gardens & Nursery,
Stockton, nr Warminster
The Mead Nursery, Brokerswood
Pound Hill House, West Kington
Sheldon Manor, nr Chippenham
Stourton House, Mere

DESCRIPTIONS OF GARDENS

¶**The Abbey House** ⚲❀ (Barbara & Ian Pollard) Market Cross. Malmesbury (hilltop town) centre location, NNE of Market Cross and immed adjoining the C12 Abbey Church. Parking in car park N of town (garden also adjoins). The gardens are being developed and enlarged in the 5-acre grounds of the C16 house built upon the C13 remains of the Abbotts house (not open). Planting for the millennium incl 2000 different roses in the formal gardens, 2000 different herbs in the old orchard, parterre, pergola, laburnum tunnel, woodland walk down to the river and St Aldhelm's pool with rhododendrons, maples, bog garden and a growing collection of rare shrubs and trees. TEA. *Adm £2 Chd £1. Sat, Sun July 12, 13 (10-6)*

Ark Farm ⚲ (Mr & Mrs Edmund Neville-Rolfe) Tisbury. 9m from Shaftesbury. 2½m from Tisbury. From Tisbury follow English Heritage signs to Old Wardour Castle. Private rd from Castle car park to Ark Farm. 1¼ acres incl water and woodland gardens, as featured in Country Life and the Daily Telegraph. TEAS. *Adm £2 Chd free (Share to The Mental Health Foundation®). Sun June 15 (2-6)*

▲**Avebury Manor Garden** ⚲❀ (The National Trust) Avebury on A4361 9m N of Devizes 2m from Beckhampton roundabout on A4. Use main car park and follow signs to Manor. 5-acre garden undergoing restoration to planting, hedges and walls. Ancient walled garden on site of former priory, divided by stone walls and topiary hedges, incl a rose garden, herbaceous border, new orchard, topiary garden, herb garden. Italian walk and half moon garden. Late mediaeval manor house under restoration (open). Plant sales Sept only. *Adm House and Garden £3.50 Chd £1.75; Garden only £2.20 Chd £1.40. Suns June 15, Sept 14 (Garden 11-5) (House 2-5)*

Avon Farm House ⚅⚲ (Mr & Mrs Ian Wilson) Stratford-sub-Castle. 2m NW of Salisbury in Avon Valley. Following rd to Stratford sub-Castle out of Salisbury; through village, turn L over R Avon bridges, garden 1st on L. Chalk garden of 2 acres looking up to Old Sarum. Shrub roses, wild garden, pleached limes, double herbaceous borders. TEAS in aid of Salisbury & District Samaritans. *Adm £1 Chd free. Sun June 22 (2-6)*

Beech Knoll House ⚲❀ (Mr & Mrs Richard Price) Aldbourne. 8m NW of Hungerford, 8m NE of Marlborough M4 exit 14 via Blaydon or Hungerford. Up lane to R of church around 'Crooked Corner'. Beech Knoll is on the R. Signs from church. Park in field opp house. 2-acre garden with walled entrance, which opens onto large terraced lawns with huge purple beech trees. This yrs improvements incl 2 sets of steps from the upper lawn and large S facing border. Terrace has small pool and fountain with borders tumbling down behind the house. Walled Victorian garden contains several unusual tree peonies, large rose bed, soft fruit cages, fruit trees, beehives. Clipped hedges, bushes and a wide variety of recently planted shrubs. Guide available at gate. TEAS in aid of Home Farm Trust. *Adm £1.50 Chd 50p. Sun June 29 (2-6)*

Biddestone Manor ⚅⚲❀ (Mr H Astrup) Biddestone, nr Corsham, 5m W of Chippenham, 3m N of Corsham. On A4 between Chippenham and Corsham turn N, from A420, 5m W of Chippenham, turn S. Large garden with extensive lawns, small lake, topiary, swimming pool. Recently planted mini arboretum with few specimen trees. Walled kitchen garden. Orchard, herb garden and fine C17 manor house (not open) with interesting outbuildings. TEAS. *Adm £1.20 Chd 60p. Sun June 22 (2-5)*

Bolehyde Manor ⚅❀ (Earl and Countess Cairns) Allington. 1½m W of Chippenham on Bristol Rd (A420). Turn N at Allington Xrds. ½m on R. Parking in field. A series of gardens around C16 Manor House; enclosed by walls and topiary, densely planted with many interesting shrubs and climbers, mixed rose and herbaceous beds; inner courtyard with troughs full of tender plants; wild flower orchard, vegetable, fruit garden and greenhouse yard. TEAS. *Adm £1.50 Chd 50p (Share to Kingston St Michael Church©). Sun June 29 (2.30-6). Also private visits welcome, please Tel 01249 652105*

■ **Bowood Rhododendron Walks** ✗ (The Earl of Shelburne) nr Chippenham. Entrance off A342 between Sandy Lane and Derry Hill villages. A breath-taking display of rhododendrons and azaleas from the minute detail of the individual flower to the grand sweep of colour formed by hundreds of shrubs, surrounded by a carpet of bluebells. *Open May & June. For NGS Adm £2.50 Chd free. Sun June 1 (11-6). Tel 01249 812102. Also open* **Bowood House & Gardens** *Luncheon and Teas. Garden centre. Adm £5 OAP £4.20 Chd £2.80. March 22 to Nov 2 (11-6)*

■ **Broadleas** ❀ (Lady Anne Cowdray) S of Devizes on A360. Bus: Devizes-Salisbury, alight Potterne Rd. Medium-sized garden; attractive dell planted with unusual trees, shrubs, azaleas and rhododendrons; many rare plants in secret and winter gardens. Home-made TEAS (on Suns). *Adm £2.50 Chd £1. April 2 to Oct 29 every Sun, Wed & Thurs. For NGS Suns April 13, Aug 17 (2-6)*

Bryher Ꮭ✗❀ (Mr & Mrs Richard Packham) Yard Lane Bromham. 4m N of Devizes on A342 to Chippenham turn R into Yard Lane at Xrds. A compact level garden, approx ⅔ acre created around a bungalow home. Borders planted mainly for foliage effect using a wide range of red, gold, silver and variegated plants, with many unusual varieties; short wildlife walk; display greenhouse with small nursery beds. *Adm £1 Chd free. Wed May 28; Sun June 15 (2-6). Also private visits welcome, please Tel 01380 850455*

Chisenbury Priory Ꮭ✗❀ (Mr & Mrs John Manser) 6m SW of Pewsey, turn E from A345 at Enford then N to E Chisenbury, main gates 1m on R. Mediaeval Priory with Queen Anne face and early C17 rear (not open) in middle of 5-acre garden on chalk; mature garden with fine trees within clump and flint walls, herbaceous borders, shrubs, roses. Moisture loving plants along mill leat and carp pond, orchard and wild garden, many unusual plants. TEAS. *Adm £2 Chd free. Suns June 15, 29 (2-6)*

¶**The Close** Ꮭ✗❀ (Simon Courtauld) Pewsey. 6m S of Marlborough, S end of Pewsey, off A345. Turn L at builders yard, then R before R Avon. 7 acres, informal herbaceous borders, shrubs, climbers, river walk and water meadow. TEAS in aid of Pewsey Church. *Adm £2 Chd free. Sun June 1 (2-6)*

Conholt Park, Chute See Hants

Conock Manor Ꮭ✗❀ (Mr & Mrs Bonar Sykes) 5m SE of Devizes off A342. Mixed borders, flowering shrubs; extensive replanting incl new arboretum and woodland walk; collection of eucalyptus trees. C18 house in Bath stone (not shown). Cream TEAS. *Adm £1.50 Chd free under 16 (Share to St John the Baptist Church). Sun May 18 (2-6)*

▲**Corsham Court** Ꮭ❀ (James Methuen-Campbell Esq) 4m W of Chippenham. S of A4. Park and gardens laid out

by Capability Brown and Repton. Large lawns with fine specimens of ornamental trees; rose garden; lily pond with Indian bean trees; spring bulbs; young arboretum; C18 bath house; Elizabethan mansion with alterations. TEAS. *Adm gardens £2 OAP £1.50 Chd £1. For NGS Suns March 23, June 8 (2-6)*

Coulston Gardens ✗❀ TEAS in aid of Coulston Church. *Combined adm £3 Chd free. Sun June 22 (2-6)*

> **Baynton House** Coulston. 4m E of Westbury on B3098 between Edington and Erlestoke. 4 acres with spring bulbs, rock garden, wild woodland and water garden. C17 Georgian house (not open). TEAS in aid of Coulston Church. *Adm £2 Chd free. Also open Sun April 27 (2-6)*
>
> **Font House** (Mr & Mrs R S Hicks) Coulston. 1½m E of Edington on B3098 take 1st L to Coulston, 1st house on L. 1-acre garden in rural surroundings which has been restored from a wilderness over past 30yrs and is still evolving; on 2 levels with courtyard, herbaceous borders, shrubs, herb and small specimen trees

Courtlands Ꮭ✗❀ (Mr Julius Silman) 4m S of Chippenham on Corsham-Lacock Road, 2m E of Corsham. 4-acre formal garden divided by splendid yew hedges into three connecting lawned gardens. Features include 2 gazebos; sunken lily pond with fountain, large fish pond with waterfall; walled kitchen garden; greenhouse with vines. Use of heated swimming pool available £1. TEAS. *Adm £2 Chd under 10 free. Sun Aug 3 (2-6)*

▲**The Courts** Ꮭ✗❀ (National Trust) Holt, 2m E of Bradford-on-Avon, S of B3107 to Melksham. In Holt follow National Trust signs, park at Village Hall. 3½-acres different formal gardens divided by yew hedges, raised terraces and shrubberies. Features incl conservatory, lily pond, herbaceous borders, pleached limes with interesting stone pillars, venetian gates and stone ornaments. 3½ acres wildflower and arboretum; many fine trees. NT C15 House (not shown). Plant sales in Aug in aid of Bath Cancer Research Unit. Teas (on NGS days only) in church hall in aid of Church Hall Fund. *Adm £2.80 Chd £1.40. For NGS Suns June 22, Aug 31 (2-5)*

Crudwell Court Hotel Ꮭ❀ (Nicholas Bristow Esq) Crudwell. On the A429 between Cirencester and Malmesbury. E of the rd, beside the church. 2½-acre garden surrounding C17 Rectory (now a hotel). Fine specimen 'rivers' beech, blue atlas cedar, magnolias, C12 dovecote surrounded by ancient yew hedges; Victorian sunken pond with wrought iron surround and lavender hedging. Rose garden and spring colour border outside conservatory. Recently planted apothecary (herb) garden; climbing roses; espaliered fruit trees and an Edwardian wooded walk; also spectrum and pastel coloured herbaceous border in rose garden. Swimming pool available in July; July opening with village strawberry fayre and craft fete. Coffee, lunch TEAS. *Adm £1.50 Chd free. Suns April 13, July 13 (11-5). Private visits welcome, please Tel 01666 577194*

Easton Grey House ❀ (Mr & Mrs Sheldon Gordon) 3½m W of Malmesbury on B4040. Intensively cultivated 9-acre garden of beautiful C18 house. Also contains Easton Grey Church with its interesting Norman tower, font etc. Superb situation overlooking R Avon and surrounding countryside; lime-tolerant shrubs; tremendous display of spring bulbs, clematis, many roses; large walled garden containing traditional kitchen garden, large greenhouses, rose garden and borders. Home-made TEAS; produce, cake, and other stalls in aid of Easton Grey Parish Church. *Adm £2.50 Chd free. Sun April 20 (2-6)*

Edington Gardens 4m Westbury on B3098 halfway between Westbury and West Lavington. Follow signs and park outside The Monastery Garden for the Priory or in Church car park for The Grange, and walk through churchyard and along path, and for The Old Vicarage walk up hill to B3098. Teas in Parish Hall. *Combined adm £3.50 Chd free (Share to Wiltshire Garden Trust®). Sun June 15 (2-6)*

Bonshommes Cottage (Michael Jones Esq) Through Old Vicarage garden. ¼-acre garden with mixed herbaceous, roses, shrubs. There is renewed effort to reduce the dominant Japanese knotweed, long established in this part of the former Vicarage garden
Edington Priory ⓑ (Mr & Mrs Rupert Cooper) 4-acre gardens with medieval well, walls and carp lake. Herbaceous borders, kitchen garden and extensive lawns with shrubs and roses
The Grange ⓑ (Col J S Douglas) ¾-acre garden of elegant design containing a variety of interesting shrubs and herbaceous plants with several unusual mature trees
The Monastery Garden ⓑ (Mr & Mrs Allanson-Bailey) 2½-acre garden with many varieties of spring bulbs; orchard and shrub roses; mediaeval walls of national importance
The Old Vicarage ⓑ✿❀ (J N d'Arcy Esq) A 2-acre garden on greensand situated on hillside with fine views; intensively planted with herbaceous borders; newly built wall borders, gravel garden; shrubs; a small arboretum with a growing range of trees; woodland plants; bulbs; lilies and recently introduced species from abroad. NCCPG National Collection of Evening primroses, over 20 species

¶Faulstone House ⓑ✿❀ (Miss Freya Watkinson) Bishopstone. Take minor rd W off A354 at Coombe Bissett 3m SW of Salisbury, after 2m turn S into Harvest Lane 300yds E of White Hart Inn. Separate smaller gardens in large garden surrounding Old Manor House. C14 Defence Tower converted to pigeon loft in C18. Many old-fashioned roses, herbaceous plants (some unusual), large vegetable garden. Meadow with river frontage set in rural surroundings. TEAS in aid of Bishopstone Church. *Adm £1.50 Chd free. Sun June 29 (2-6)*

Fonthill House ❀ (The Lord Margadale) 3m N of Tisbury. W of Salisbury via B3089 in Fonthill Bishop. Large woodland garden; daffodils, rhododendrons, azaleas, shrubs, bulbs; magnificent views; formal garden, limited for wheelchairs. TEAS. *Adm £1.50 Chd 30p (Share to Fonthill Bishop Church®). Sun April 13 (2-6)*

Foscote Gardens ✿❀ Grittleton, 5m NW of Chippenham. A420 Chippenham-Bristol; after 2m turn R on B4039 to Watton Keynell, fork R for Grittleton; in village for 2m, just over motorway turn R at Xrds; house on right. Home-made TEAS. *Combined adm £1.50 Chd 30p. Sun June 15 (2-6)*

Foscote Stables (Mr & Mrs Barry Ratcliffe) 2½-acres; many clematis; shrub roses; unusual shrubs, trees; small collection ornamental ducks
Foscote Stables Cottage (Mrs Beresford Worswick) This adjoining garden has been re-designed and replanted but still retains its cottage character. Unusual and some rare plants for sale

Garden House ⓑ✿❀ (J Reeve) Sandridge Park. 2m E of Melksham on A3102 (Calne) Rd. Walled garden, approx 1 acre with mixed borders, shrub roses and pond. TEAS in aid of WI. *Adm £1 Chd free. Sun June 29 (2-6)*

Goulters Mill Farm ✿❀ (Mr & Mrs Michael Harvey) the Gibb, Burton. On B4039 5m W of Chippenham; 2m NW of Castle Combe, through the Gibb. Park at top of 300 metre drive and walk down to garden. Approx ¾-acre cottage garden; mixed perennials, eremurus, old-fashioned roses; water garden and woodland walk. Home-made cream TEAS in aid of Russian Immigrants to Israel. *Adm £1.50 Chd 20p. Sun June 22 (2-5)*

The Grange ⓑ✿❀ (Mr & Mrs Rebdi) Winterbourne Dauntsey. Winterbourne Dauntsey is 4m NNE of Salisbury on the A338. Spacious 6-acre garden, still being developed, with R Bourne running through. Immaculate lawns, clipped box, borders. Laburnum, rose and clematis arched walk; lily pond; vegetable and herb garden. Wild natural area with peacocks. Restored C17 thatched barn (open). TEAS in aid of Winterbourne Glebe Hall. *Adm £1.50 Chd under 16 free. Sun June 29 (2-6)*

▲Great Chalfield Manor ✿❀ (The National Trust; Mr & Mrs Robert Floyd) 4m from Melksham. Take B3107 from Melksham then 1st R to Broughton Gifford signed Atworth, turn L for 1m to Manor. Park on grass outside. Garden and grounds of 7 acres laid out 1905-12 by Robert Fuller and his wife. Garden paths, steps, dry walls relaid and rebuilt in 1985 and roses replanted; daffodils, spring flowers; topiary houses, borders, terraces, gazebo, orchard, autumn border. C15 moated manor (not open) and adjoining Church. Evensong Service 6pm Oct 5. TEAS. *Adm £2 Chd free (Share to All Saints Church®). For NGS Suns Feb 23 (2-4) Oct 5 (2-5)*

¶Great Durnford Gardens ⓑ✿ Midway between Salisbury and Amesbury on the A345. Turn W at High Post Petrol Station to Woodfords. After 1m take 1st R to Great Durnford. Into village turn L and park next to Black Horse Inn (as signed). Lunches and Teas at Black Horse. *Combined adm £2.50. Sun June 22 (2-6)*
¶Old Hall ❀ (Mr & Mrs M Snell) An established part cob walled 2-acre village garden with lawns, herbaceous borders, featured vegetable patch and conservatory. Staddle barn, thatched barn, chickens and Herdwick sheep
¶Swaynes Mead (Major & Mrs Simon Poett) 1-acre of intensive garden established over last 20yrs. C17 thatched cottage with climbing roses. Many unusual plants, shrubs and trees

> The National Gardens Scheme is a charity which traces its origins back to 1927. Since then it has raised a total of over £15 million for charitable purposes.

Great Somerford Gardens &⚘☀ 2m N of M4 between junctions 17 and 18; 2m S of B4042 MalmesburyWootton Bassett rd; 3m E of A429 Circencester-Chippenham rd. TEAS. *Combined adm £3, Chd under 13 free (Share to Spring Board®). Sat, Sun July 12, 13 (1.30-6)*
   Clematis (Mr & Mrs Arthur Scott) A small but active, charming village garden created about 5yrs ago. Very well-stocked herbaceous borders, shrubs, fruit trees and a pond, with a collection of approx 25 clematis
   Old Church School (Cdr & Mrs Peter Neate) A ¾-acre garden created over the last 4 yrs from the school playing field. It is centred around a formal yew-hedged area containing a flourishing pool, parterre and shrubs, surrounded by herbaceous, hebe and rose beds, pergolas and arches, rockery and heathers as well as a good collection of trees and shrubs. TEAS
   The Old Maltings (Dr & Mrs S Jevons) The front garden has been recently designed with extensive and interesting herbaceous and shrub borders. Behind the house there is a walk down to and across the R Avon into a conservation area with plantations of young native trees and shrubs
   ¶**The Mount House** (C Kirkham-Sandy) 3 acres of lawns, shrubs. Large traditional fruit and vegetable garden. Approx 100 roses
   Somerford House (Mr & Mrs Derek Bayliss) The owners and their family over the past 15 yrs have designed and developed a 3-acre garden, which incorporates the original orchard and features roses, shrubs, old wisteria, perennials, rockery and pool, vegetables and soft fruit. A flower arranger's delight
   White Lodge, Startley (Major & Mrs Jonathan Oliphant) A partially-walled garden, developed gradually over the last 25 yrs. Old-fashioned roses, clematis and herbaceous borders, incl unusual plants. Topiary and catalpa tree. TEAS

Green Hall &⚘☀ (Mr & Mrs John Inge) East Grafton. 8m S of Marlborough, 2m E of Burbage on A338 signposted Hungerford and East Grafton, 8m W of Hungerford. 2½ acres of herbaceous borders, mixed shrub beds, pond area and water garden. Small kitchen garden, dried flower business run from garden. Plants and dried flowers for sale. TEAS in converted barn. *Adm £1.50 Chd under 16 50p (Share to East Grafton School and Village Hall©). Sun June 29, Wed July 9 (2-5.30) Private visits welcome, please Tel 01672 810242*

Guyers House &⚘☀ (Mr & Mrs Guy Hungerford) Pickwick, Corsham. Guyers Lane directly off A4 opp B3109 Bradford-on-Avon turning. A garden which has been recently restored and is being extended. 5 acres of herbaceous borders, new yew walks, lawns, pond, walled garden, rose hoops, climbing and shrub roses; walled garden; kitchen garden. TEA. *Adm £1.50 Chd free. Sun June 15 (2-5.30)*

Hannington Hall &☀ (Mrs A F Hussey-Freke) Hannington. 5m N of Swindon. 2m NW of Highworth, from B4019 Highworth-Blunsdon, at Freke Arms, turn N for Hannington. 3 acres. Interesting trees and shrubs. Walled kitchen garden. Well preserved ice house. Very interesting house built in 1653. Flower festival in church. TEAS. *Adm £1.50 Chd free. Sat June 21 (2-6) Sun June 22 (2-5)*

▲**Hazelbury Manor Gardens** &⚘☀ Wadswick, nr Box. 5m SW of Chippenham; 5m NE of Bath; 3m N of Bradford-on-Avon. From A4 at Box, take A365 to Melksham, L onto B3109; L again at Chapel Plaister; drive immed on R. 8 acres of Grade II landscaped formal gardens surrounding a charming C15 fortified manor house. An impressive yew topiary and clipped beeches surround the large lawn; herbaceous and mixed borders blaze in summer; laburnums and limes form splendid walkways. Other features incl rose garden, stone ring, an enchanting fountain and rockery. *Adm Gardens only £2.80 OAP £2 Chd £1. For NGS Sat, Sun June 28, 29 (2-6). Private visits welcome, please Tel 01225 812952/812088*

■**Heale Gardens & Plant Centre** &☀ (Guy Rasch Esq) Middle Woodford, 4m N of Salisbury on Woodford Valley Rd between A360 and A345. 8 acres beside R Avon; interesting and varied collection of plants, shrubs; and roses in formal setting of clipped hedges and mellow stonework surrounding C17 manorhouse where Charles II hid after the battle of Worcester. Water garden with magnolia and acer frames, an authentic Japanese Tea House and Nikki bridge. Well stocked plant centre. Gift shop. Open all year. TEAS in the house on NGS Sunday pm only. *Adm £2.75 Acc chd under 14 free (Share to Salisbury Hospice®). For NGS Sun Aug 3 (10-5). Tel 01722 782504*

Hillbarn House ⚘☀ (Mr & Mrs A J Buchanan) Great Bedwyn, SW of Hungerford. S of A4 Hungerford-Marlborough. Medium-sized garden on chalk with hornbeam tunnel, pleached limes, herb garden; some planting by Lanning Roper; a series of gardens within a garden. Swimming pool may be used (under 12) Topiary. TEA. *Adm £2 Chd 50p. Suns June 22, Sept 21 (2-6). Private visits of 10 and over welcome, please Tel 01672 870207*

Home Covert &☀ (Mr & Mrs John F Phillips) Roundway, Devizes. 1m N of Devizes on minor rd signed Roundway linking A361 to A342. 1m from each main rd, house signed. An extensive garden on greensand created out of ancient woodland by present owners since 1960. Situated below the Downs with distant views. The formal borders adjoining a large lawn are in distinct contrast to water gardens in the valleys below. The planting is of wide botanical interest. Optional bluebell walk ¾m. Featured in The Garden, Country Life, and TV. TEAS on May 11 in aid of Wilts Wildlife Trust, July 20 in aid of St James Church Repair Fund. *Adm £2 Chd free. Suns May 11, July 20 (2-6). Private parties welcome, please Tel 01380 723407*

Hyde's House ☀ (George Cruddas Esq) Dinton. 5m W of Wilton, off B3089, next to church. 2 acres of wild and formal garden in beautiful situation with series of hedged garden rooms. Numerous spring bulbs and blossom. Open in June for first time to catch garden at its best. Large walled kitchen garden, herb garden and C13 dovecote (open). Charming C16/18 Grade 1 listed house (not open), with lovely courtyard. NT walks around park and lake. TEAS in adjacent thatched 'old school room'. *Adm £1.75 Chd under 14 free (Share to St Mary's Church, Dinton®). Mon March 31, Sun June 1 (2-5). Private visits of 20 and over welcome, please Tel 01722 716203*

■ **Iford Manor** (Mr & Mrs Hignett) Off A36 7 miles S of Bath – sign to Iford 1m or from Bradford-on-Avon/Trowbridge via Lower Westwood village (brown signs). Entrance and free parking at Iford Bridge. Very romantic Italian-style terraced garden, listed Grade 1, home of Harold Peto between 1899 and 1933. House not shown. TEAS May to Sept, Sats, Suns and Bank Hol Mons. *Adm £2.20 OAPs/Student/Chd 10+ £1.60. Open daily May to Sept (except Mons & Fris), April & Oct Suns only. For NGS Sun April 27 (2-5). Private visits for groups welcome, please* **Tel 01225 863146, 862364 messages**

Inwoods ఈ❀ (Mr & Mrs D S Whitehead) Farleigh Wick, 3m NW of Bradford-on-Avon. From Bath via A363 towards Bradford-on-Avon; at Farleigh Wick, 100yds past Fox & Hounds, R into drive. 5 acres with lawns, borders, flowering shrubs, wild garden, bluebell wood. TEAS in aid of Monkton Farleigh Church. *Adm £1.50 Chd 50p. Sun May 11 (2-6)*

Job's Mill ❀ (Virginia, Marchioness of Bath) Crockerton, 1½m S of Warminster. Bus: Salisbury-Bath, alight Warminster. Medium-sized garden; small terraced garden, through which R Wylye flows; swimming pool; kitchen garden. TEAS. *Adm £1.50 Chd 50p (Share to WWF®). Sun July 6 (2-6)*

13 Kingsdown Road ⌀❀ (Mr & Mrs Kenneth Tomlin) Stratton St Margaret. Approach from S on A419. L at Kennedys Garden Centre (signposted Upper Stratton). ½m turn L at t-lights and park opp Kingsdown inn. Long and narrow garden on edge of town closely planted with shrubs and herbaceous plants. Vegetable garden. Unusual plants with some for sale. O-gauge model railway added attraction 4.30 to 5.30. Example of maximum use of space available. TEA. *Adm £1 Chd free (Share to ARC® July 20 only). Suns June 8, July 20 (2-6)*

■ **Lackham Gardens** ఈ❀ (Lackham College Principal D E Williams) Lacock, 2m S of Chippenham. Signposted N of Notton on A350. Few mins S of junction 17 on M4. Station: Chippenham. Bus: Chippenham-Trowbridge, alight drive entrance, 1m. Walled garden with greenhouses, lawn paths separating plots, labelled with variety of interesting shrubs, unusual vegetables, herbaceous plants, fruit. Pleasure gardens with historical collection of roses, mixed borders, lawns; woodland walks down to river. 17, 18, 19th century gardens, maze, pond and shrub collections. Museum of Agricultural Horticultural Equipment, RARE breeds. Adventure playground. Coffee shop; TEAS Bookable menu (11-4). *Adm £3 Chd £1 (Share to Horticultural Therapy of Frome, Somerset®). For NGS Suns July 13, Oct 5 (2-5)*

▲ **Lacock Abbey Gardens** ఈ⌀❀ (National Trust) Chippenham. A350 midway between Melksham-Chippenham. Follow National Trust signs. Use public car park just outside the Abbey. 9 acres of parkland surrounding the Abbey with a pond and exotic tree specimens. Display of early spring flowers with carpets of aconites; snowdrops; crocuses and daffodils. C13 Abbey with C18 gothic additions. (Mediaeval cloisters open on NGS days, house closed until April). Teas available in village. *Adm £1.50 Chd free. For NGS Sats, Suns Feb 15, 16; 22, 23 (2-5). 1998 Sats, Suns Feb 14, 15; 21, 22 (2-5). Parties welcome, please* **Tel 01249 730227/730459**

Landford Lodge ఈ❀ (Mr & Mrs Christopher Pilkington) 9m SE of Salisbury turn W off A36; garden ½m N of Landford. C18 House (not open) in lovely parkland overlooking lake; many fine trees. Special feature 3-acre wood with rhododendrons and azaleas. Herbaceous; ornamental terrace and swimming pool (open). Tree nursery. 500 varieties of trees planted in alphabetical order in walled garden. TEAS. *Adm £1.50 Chd 50p (Share to Salisbury Mencap Horticultural Trust®). Sun June 1 (2-5). Private parties of 10 and over welcome, please* **Tel 01794 390247**

Little Durnford Manor ఈ❀ (Earl & Countess of Chichester) 3m N of Salisbury, just beyond Stratford-sub-Castle. Extensive lawns with cedars; walled gardens, fruit trees, large vegetable garden; small knot and herb gardens, terraces, borders, gravel garden, water garden, lake with islands, river walks. Cottage Garden also on view. Home-made TEAS. *Adm £1.50 Chd 50p (Share to Wessex Medical School Trust®). Suns May 11, June 29 (2-6)*

■ **Long Hall Gardens and Nursery** ఈ⌀❀ (Mr & Mrs N H Yeatman-Biggs) Stockton 7m SE of Warminster; S of A36; W of A303 Wylye interchange. Follow signs to church in Stockton. 4-acre mainly formal garden featured recently in House and Garden; a series of gardens within a garden; clipped yews; flowering shrubs, fine old trees; masses of spring bulbs; fine hellebore walk. C13 Hall with later additions (not open). TEAS. *Adm £2 Chd free (Share to St John the Baptist's Church, Stockton). 1st Sat of the month from May 3 to August 2 (2-6). Private visits welcome, please* **Tel 01985 850424.** *For NGS Sun June 22 (2-6).* Adjacent nursery specialising in chalk tolerant plants, all organically grown, many uncommon varieties and new introductions. *Wed (9.30-5.30) to Sat (9.30-7), March 19 to Sept 27*

Lower Farm House ఈ⌀❀ (Mrs John Agate) Milton Lilbourne. E of Pewsey on B3087. Turn down village street by garage at Xrds. Garden down street on L. An enlarged and developing 5-acre garden designed by Tim Rees. Winter garden; water garden; shrubs and herbaceous borders; young trees chosen for their bark; spring bulbs; gazebo; and conservatory. *Adm £1.50 Chd free (Share to Milton Lilbourne Parish Church®). Sun Aug 3 (2-6). Private visits welcome March to Sept, please* **Tel 01672 562911**

Lower House ఈ⌀❀ (D J Wood Esq) Whiteparish. On A27 between Salisbury and Romsey (7m). Garden is N side of A27, Salisbury end of village, opp Newton Bungalows. Informal garden of 1 acre containing part of National Collection of Hellebores. *Adm £1.50 Chd free. Sun March 16 (2-4) Private visits welcome by appt Mon to Sat, March 10 to 24 (10-12 and 2-4), please* **Tel 01794 884306**

Luckington Court ఈ❀ (The Hon Mrs Trevor Horn) Luckington village, 10m NW of Chippenham; 6m W of Malmesbury. Turn S off B4040 Malmesbury-Bristol. Bus: Bristol-Swindon, alight Luckington. Medium-sized garden, mainly formal, well-designed, amid exquisite group of ancient buildings; fine collection of ornamental cherries; other flowering shrubs. House much altered in Queen Anne times but ancient origins evident; Queen Anne hall and drawing-room shown. TEAS in aid of Luckington Parish Church. *Collecting box. Sun May 18 (2.30-6)*

Luckington Manor ⌂❀❀ (Mr & Mrs K Stanbridge) NW of Chippenham 7½m SW of Malmesbury on the B4040 Malmesbury-Bristol. Park behind The Old Royal Ship pub. 3½ acres, walled flower gardens; unusual plants, shrubberies; arboretum, sunken rose garden, well garden, herbs and healing plants. Special Spring feature. Garden organically run attracting more and more wildlife. C17 Manor House (not open). Home-made TEAS. *Adm £2 Senior Citizens £1 Chd free (Share to Luckington Parish Church®). Suns April 27, July 20, Aug 17 (2-6)*

Mallards ⌂❀❀ (Mr & Mrs T Papé) Chirton. 4½m SE of Devizes just N of A342. Through village and garden is on R. 1-acre garden with several distinct areas: hot sunny borders, rose garden, woodland glades and bog garden. All informally planted and tucked into woodland on the banks of the upper R Avon. Also a woodland walk. TEAS in aid of Chirton & Marden Parish Churches. *Adm £1.50 Chd free. Suns June 8, July 13 (2-6)*

¶**Manor Farm** ⌂❀ (W G M Wood) Monkton Deverill. 5m S of Warminster. Take Mere rd off A350 at Longbridge Deverill. Monkton Deverill 2m. C18 and C19 village farmhouse garden at an early stage of reconstruction. Walled kitchen garden. New orchards and hedging, formal and informal planting. Box nursery. Picnics welcome. TEAS. *Adm £1 Chd free. Sun June 22 (2-6)*

Manor House Farm ⌂ (Miss Anne Dixon) Hanging Langford. 9m NW of Salisbury S of A36 Salisbury-Warminster. 3m SE of A303 Wylye interchange. Follow signs from Steeple Langford. Series of walled gardens with masses of bulbs, herbaceous plants, many shrubs, old-fashioned roses, collection of clematis, peonies and delphiniums. Ornamental pond, secret garden in walls of shearing barn, superb walnut, C14/16 Wiltshire manor house (not open). Teas Hanging Langford Village Hall in aid of Village Hall Fund. *Adm £2 Chd free. Sun April 13 (2-6)*

March End, Sherfield English See Hants

¶**Martins** ❀❀ (Mrs Diana Young) Whitehill Bradford-on-Avon. The top of Whitehill is off New Rd (N side of town) and Martins is the 4th house down from the top. Whitehill is 200yds from Castle Inn and Christ Church. No Parking at garden. Parking in nearby streets and town centre car parks. Surprisingly spacious garden on several levels with magnificent S facing views. Restful but full of colour and character, incl a small orchard and meadow, ancient lime and mulberry. TEAS in aid of Dorothy House Foundation. *Adm £1.50 Chd free. Sun June 8 (2-6)*

■ **The Mead Nursery** ⌂❀❀ (Mr & Mrs S Lewis-Dale) Brokerswood. Equidistant Frome and Westbury E of Rudge. Follow signs for Woodland Park. Halfway between Rudge and Woodland Park. 1¼-acre nursery with over 1,000 varieties of herbaceous perennials, alpines and bulbs, many unusual. Display beds for colour and design ideas. Raised beds, sink garden, and bog bed. TEAS on NGS day only. *Adm £1.50 Chd £1 to incl teas. Nursery open Feb 1 to Oct 31 Wed to Sat (9-5), Sun (12-5). For NGS Sun Aug 10 (12-5), please* Tel 01373 859990

▲**Mompesson House** ⌂❀❀ (The National Trust) The Close. Enter Salisbury Cathedral Close via High St Gate and Mompesson House is on the R. The appeal of this comparatively small but attractive garden is the lovely setting in Salisbury Cathedral Close and with a well-known Queen Anne House. Planting as for an old English garden with raised rose and herbaceous beds around the lawn. Climbers on pergola and walls; shrubs and small lavender walk. TEAS. *Adm £1 Chd free. For NGS Sat June 7 (11-5)*

7 Norton Bavant ⌂❀ (Mr & Mrs J M Royds) nr Warminster. 2m E of Warminster on A36 turn W to Sutton Veny on Cotley Hill roundabout at Heytesbury, then R to Norton Bavant. Turn R in village, 1st house on R after tall conifer hedge. Alpine plant collector's garden with numerous varieties (many rare). Spring bulbs, alpine house, many troughs, borders, dwarf conifers and specialised collection of daphnes. Members of AGS especially welcome. TEAS in aid of Norton Bavant Church. *Adm £1.50 Chd free. Sun May 18 (2-5). Private visits and parties welcome March to June, please* Tel 01985 840491

Oare House ⌂ (Henry Keswick Esq) 2m N of Pewsey on Marlborough Rd (A345). Fine house (not open) in large garden with fine trees, hedges, spring flowers, woodlands; extensive lawns and kitchen garden. TEA. *Adm £2 Chd free (Share to The Order of St John®). Suns April 27, July 27 (2-6)*

The Old Bakery ⌂❀❀ (Joyce, Lady Crossley) Milton Lilbourne E of Pewsey on B3087. Turn down village st by garage at Xrds. The Old Bakery is opp churchyard. Fairly intensive 1-acre garden. Mixed shrub and herbaceous plantings. 3 small glasshouses; small rock garden; some rare plants. Home-made TEAS. *Adm £1 Chd free. Sun Aug 3 (2-6). Private parties welcome, please* Tel 01672 562716

The Old Rectory ⌂❀ (Mr & Mrs David Harrison) Stockton 7m SE of Warminster, S of A36 W of A303 Wylye interchange. Just beyond the church. The 2-acre garden surrounds a C18 house, with lawns and fine old trees incl a cedar and a beech, in the front. To the S it splits into several smaller gardens; an entirely walled herb garden with a variety of herbs, with climbers, fine roses and vines. The orchard, dominated by a stunning walnut tree leads to 3 smaller walled gardens with a variety of plants incl roses and peonies. Featured recently on TV. TEAS *Adm £1.50 Chd free. Sun June 15 (2-6). Private visits welcome, please* Tel 01985 850607

¶**Pertwood Manor** ⌂❀ (Mr & Mrs James Giles) Hindon Off A350 (1m N of A303) 7m Shaftesbury, 8m Warminster. Take signs marked Pertwood Manor farm. 1½-acre part walled garden surrounding manor house (not open) in elevated position with lovely views. Herbaceous borders, various trees and shrubs. Sunken rose garden. Short woodland walk, small vegetable garden. Recently restored Church of St Peter. Home-made TEAS. *Adm £1.50 Chd free (Share to NSPCC®). Sun June 22 (2-6)*

■ **Pound Hill House** ⌂❀ (Mr & Mrs P Stockitt) West Kington. From A420 Chippenham-Bristol rd turn R by Shoe Inn, then 2nd L, 2nd R into village, entrance at nursery. Series of small gardens, charmingly set around

£15 Cotswold house, to provide interest throughout yr. Old-fashioned rose garden with clipped box, small Victorian vegetable garden, old shrub roses, herbaceous borders, water garden, courtyard garden with beautifully planted pots and containers. Imaginatively planted paved area, also buxus, taxus, topiary. Retail plant area with extensive range of connoisseur plants from adj nursery. TEAS in aid of West Kington Church. *Open Tues to Sun and Bank Hol Mon Feb to Dec. Adm £2. For NGS Sun June 29 (2-6). Private visits welcome, please* **Tel 01249 782781**

Ridleys Cheer ⅛⅜✿ (Mr & Mrs A J Young) Mountain Bower, N Wraxall. 8m NW of Chippenham. At 'The Shoe' on A420 8m W of Chippenham turn N then take 2nd L and 1st R. 1½-acre informal garden with unusual trees and shrubs; incl acers, liriodendrons, magnolias, salix and zelkova. Some 75 different shrub rose varieties incl hybrid musks, albas and species roses; planted progressively over past 21 yrs; also potager and 2 acres woodland planted 1989, with more than 20 different oak species suitable for limestone soils. Cream TEAS in aid of N Wraxall Church and Dorothy House Foundation. *Adm £1.50 Chd under 14 free. Suns April 27, May 18, June 15, July 6 (2-6). Private visits welcome, please* **Tel 01225 891204**

Sharcott Manor ⅛⅜✿ (Capt & Mrs David Armytage) 1m SW of Pewsey via A345. 5-acre garden with water planted for yr-round interest. Many young trees, bulbs, climbers and densely planted mixed borders of shrubs, roses, perennials and unusual plants, some of which are for sale in the small garden nursery. TEAS in aid of IFAW and Wiltshire Air Ambulance appeal. *Adm £2 Chd free. First Weds in every month from April to Oct (Except Aug) (11-5). Suns April 20, July 13 (2-6) all for NGS. Also private visits welcome, please* **Tel 01672 563485**

■ **Sheldon Manor** ⅛⅜✿ (Antony Gibbs Esq) Chippenham. 1½m W of Chippenham turn S off A420 at Allington Xrds. Eastbound traffic signed also from A4. Signed also from A350 Chippenham bypass. Formal garden around C13 house (700-yrs-old), collection of old-fashioned roses in profusion, very old yew trees, many interesting trees and shrubs. Home-made Buffet Lunches (licensed) and cream TEAS. *Adm house and garden £3.50 OAP's £3 Chd 11-16 £1. Garden only £2, OAP's £1.75 (Share to Kiloran Trust®). Easter Sun & Mon then every Sun, Thur & Bank Hol to Oct 5 incl. For NGS Sun June 15 (12.30-6). Private visits welcome, please* **Tel 01249 653120**

Spye Park ✿ (Mr & Mrs Simon Spicer) nr Chippenham. Take A342 Chippenham and Devizes rd, turn E at Sandy Lane opp 'The George' public house. Turn S after ½m at White Lodge. Follow signs to car park. Exit only through the village of Chittoe. 25-acre woodland walk through carpets of bluebells with paths cut through the wood. Some fine old trees mostly oak and beech, survivors of the 1989 hurricane, incl the remnants of 1000-yr-old Judy Oak with the 900-yr-old Queen still alive. TEAS. *Adm £1 Chd free (Share to Southmead Hospital Special Care Baby Unit©). Sun May 4 (11-5). Private parties welcome when bluebells are out, please* **Tel 01249 730247**

▲**Stourhead Garden** ⅛✿ (The National Trust) Stourton, 3m NW of Mere on B3092. One of earliest and greatest landscape gardens in the world; creation of banker Henry Hoare in 1740s on his return from the Grand Tour, inspired by paintings of Claude and Poussin; planted with rare trees, rhododendrons and azaleas over last 240yrs. Open every day of year. Lunch, tea and supper Spread Eagle Inn at entrance. NT shop. Teas (Buffet service Village Hall). *Adm March to Oct £4.30 Chd £2.30 parties of 15 or over £3.70. Nov to Feb £3.30 Chd 1.50. For NGS Sun June 1 (9-7)*

■ **Stourton House** ⅛⅜✿ (Mrs Anthony Bullivant) Stourton. 3m NW of Mere (A303) on rd to Stourhead. Park in NT car park. 4½-acres informal gardens; much to attract plantsmen and idea seekers. Interesting bulbs, plants and shrubs, through all seasons. Speciality daffodils and hydrangeas. Well known for 'Stourton Dried Flowers' whose production interest visitors (BBC Gardeners World '92). Coffee, lunch, TEAS in Stourton House Garden. *March 31 to November 30, Sun, Wed, Thurs and Bank Hol Mons. Adm £2 Chd 50p (Share to St Peters Church, Stourton®). For NGS Sats June 14, Aug 30 (11-6). Private visits welcome for parties of 12 and over, please* **Tel 01747 840417**

¶**Stowell Park Gardens** ⅛✿ Nr Pewsey. Turn W off A345 1m N of Pewsey, then immed R. Gardens 1m on L. Early C19 house (not open) in traditional English parkland with ha-ha, large thatched walled kitchen garden with traditional fruit and vegetables, herbaceous garden, wild garden, greenhouse, woodland walk to incl Head Gardener's garden at **1 New Cottage**. TEAS. *Adm £2.50 OAP's £1 Chd free (Share to Prospect Hospice, Wroughton®). Sun May 4 (2-6)*

Upper Chelworth Farm ⅛⅜✿ (Mr & Mrs Hopkins) nr Cricklade. Take B4040 off A419, through Cricklade, L at 1st Xrds, 1st house on L. Approx ½-acre garden of mixed perennials, shrubs and water garden. Small nursery. TEAS. *Adm £1 Chd free. Suns April 6, May 4, June 1, July 6, Aug 3, Sept 7 (2-6)*

2 Warren Farm Cottages, West Tytherley See Hants

Waterdale House ✿ (Mr & Mrs Julian Seymour) Milton, East Knoyle. North of East Knoyle on A350 turn W signed Milton, garden signed from village. 4-acre mature woodland garden with rhododendrons, azaleas, camellias, maples, magnolias, ornamental water redesigned with new terrace, bog garden; herbaceous borders. Gravelled pot garden. TEAS if fine. *Adm £1.50 Chd free. Suns May 11, July 13 (2-5). Private visits welcome April to July, lunches for parties up to 20 if required, please* **Tel 01747 830262**

The Royal Horticultural Society's Garden at Wisley

Exclusive evening openings in aid of the National Gardens Scheme on the occasion of its 70th anniversary

Wednesday 18th June & Thursday 14th August

6.30-9pm

See page 18.

Worton Gardens ♿ ✗ Devizes 3m. Devizes-Salisbury A360 turn W in Potterne or just N of West Lavington. From Seend turn S at Bell Inn, follow signs to Worton. TEAS at Ivy House. *Combined adm £2 Chd free. Sun July 20 (2-6)*

Ashton House ✾ (Mrs Colin Shand) ½-acre garden in 3 sections with herbaceous borders, many shrubs and birch grove; walled courtyard and raised vegetable garden; lovely views across Avon Vale

Brookfield House ♿ ✗ (Mr & Mrs Graham Cannon) A new 1-acre garden owned since 1993, and being developed with small children in mind. Part-walled garden with mixed borders and separate fruit and vegetable garden

Ivy House (Lt Gen Sir Maurice and Lady Johnston) 2 acre series of gardens separated by yew hedges and walls; herbaceous borders; shrubs; pond garden with maples and many fine trees incl swamp cypress, holm and red oak, medlar and mulberry; interesting vegetable garden and large greenhouse

Oakley House ✾ (Mr & Mrs Michael Brierley) ½-acre village garden with herbaceous borders, roses, many shrubs; small pond and bog garden within a rockery planted by owners since 1974

Worcestershire

Hon County Organiser: Mrs Barbara Phillips, Cedar Lodge, Blakeshall, Wolverley, nr Kidderminster DY11 5XR Tel 01562 850238

Assistant County Organisers: Mrs Jeanie Neil, Viewlands, Blakeshall, Wolverley, nr Kidderminster DY11 5XL Tel 01562 850360

Mrs Jane Carr, Conderton Manor, nr Tewkesbury, Glos GL20 7PR Tel 01386 725389

Mrs Julia Beldam, East Lodge Farm, Stanton, Broadway WR12 7NE Tel 01386 784478

Hon County Treasurer: Mrs Elizabeth Anton, Summerway, Torton, nr Kidderminster DY11 7SE Tel 01299 250388

DATES OF OPENING

February 20 Thursday
Dial Park, Chaddesley Corbett
March
Eastgrove Cottage Garden Nursery, nr Shrawley. From 27 - Thurs to Mons (2-5)
Stone House Cottage Gardens, Stone. Every Weds, Thurs, Fris, Sats (10-5.30)
March 19 Wednesday
The Cottage, Broughton Green, nr Hanbury
March 23 Sunday
Holland House, Cropthorne
Kyre Park, Tenbury Wells
Little Malvern Court, nr Malvern
March 28 Friday
Spetchley Park, nr Worcester
White Cottage, Stock Green, nr Inkberrow
March 30 Sunday
Whitlenge House Cottage, Hartlebury
March 31 Monday
Stone House Cottage Gardens, Stone ‡
Whitlenge House Cottage, Hartlebury ‡

April
Barnard's Green House, Malvern. Every Thurs (2-6)
Eastgrove Cottage Garden Nursery, nr Shrawley. Thurs to Mons (2-5)
The Elms, Lower Broadheath. Every Tues, Weds (2-5)
Stone House Cottage Gardens, Stone. Every Weds, Thurs, Fris, Sats (10-5.30)
White Cottage, Stock Green, nr Inkberrow. Every Fris to Tues, except 2nd & 4th Suns (10-5)
April 6 Sunday
Ripple Hall, nr Tewkesbury
April 13 Sunday
Eastgrove Cottage Garden Nursery, nr Shrawley
April 16 Wednesday
The Cottage, Broughton Green, nr Hanbury
April 20 Sunday
Astley Horticultural Society Barbers, Martley, nr Worcester
Holland House, Cropthorne
April 22 Tuesday
The Elms, Lower Broadheath
April 27 Sunday
Barnard's Green House, Malvern

Eastgrove Cottage Garden Nursery, nr Shrawley
May
Barnard's Green House, Malvern. Every Thurs (2-6)
Eastgrove Cottage Garden Nursery, nr Shrawley. Thurs to Mons (2-5)
The Elms, Lower Broadheath. Every Tues, Weds (2-5)
The Manor House, Birlingham, nr Pershore. Every Thurs
Stone House Cottage Gardens, Stone. Every Weds, Thurs, Fris, Sats (10-5.30)
White Cottage, Stock Green, nr Inkberrow. Every Fris to Tues, except 2nd & 4th Suns (10-5)
May 1 Thursday
Monsieurs Hall, Bromsgrove
May 4 Sunday
Arley House, Upper Arley, nr Bewdley
The Cottage Herbery, Boraston, Tenbury Wells
Stone House Cottage Gardens, Stone
White Cottage, Stock Green, nr Inkberrow

Sandringham in **Norfolk**, open by gracious permission of HM The Queen, is the only garden which has opened for The National Gardens Scheme every year since 1927. *Photograph by Brian Chapple*

The Old Vicarage, Grantchester, Cambridgeshire. Tom Gamble of the Royal Watercolour Society painting in Lord & Lady Archer's garden for the exhibition to be held in association with the National Gardens Scheme in 1997. *Photograph by Richard Hanson*

Right: The **Royal Gardeners' Orphan Fund**, a beneficiary of the National Gardens Scheme, helps both orphaned and needy children of professional horticulturists. Here a handicapped child plays with her family in their garden.

Photograph by Anita Corbin

Below: Visitors enjoying an evening opening at **Neptune House, Sussex**.

Photograph by Ian Jackson

Left: A dead pear tree covered with golden hops provides an interesting feature in this farmhouse garden at **Field House Farm, Derbyshire**.
Photograph by Ron Evans

Below: The Chairman of the National Gardens Scheme, Mrs Daphne Foulsham, presents a cheque for £738,500 to HRH the Duchess of Kent, Patron and The Marchioness of Zetland, President of the **Cancer Relief Macmillan Fund.**
Photograph by courtesy of CRMF

Left: Gardens in the Scheme encompass all sizes and styles. **Bankfield** in **Yorkshire** is one of many cottage-style gardens containing rare and unusual plants.
Photograph by Brian Chapple

Below: The shrubs and hedges at **The Crossing House, Cambridgeshire** conceal the fact that an operating railway line runs through the garden!
Photograph by Dona Haycraft

Right: Often all members of the family are involved in a garden opening. Here children help on the gate at **Whitbysteads, Cumbria.**
Photograph by Val Corbett

Below: **17 Navarino Road, London** winner of the 1996 BBC Gardener's World competition for the most beautiful small garden in Britain.
Photograph by John Tordoff

Argoed Cottage, Flintshire & Wrexham, one of the many delightful Welsh gardens that open for the National Gardens Scheme. *Photograph by Ron Evans*

Drifts of daffodils at **Wyken Hall** in **Suffolk**.
Photograph by Brian Chapple

May 5 Monday
The Manor House, Birlingham, nr
  Pershore
Stone House Cottage Gardens,
  Stone
May 9 Friday
The Manor House, Birlingham, nr
  Pershore
May 11 Sunday
Priors Court, Long Green
Spetchley Park, nr Worcester
Windyridge, Kidderminster
May 18 Sunday
24 Alexander Avenue, Droitwich
  Spa
The Cockshoot, Castle Morton,
  Malvern
The Cottage Herbery, Boraston,
  Tenbury Wells
Nafford House, Eckington
Windyridge, Kidderminster
May 19 Monday
Ivytree House, Clent
May 21 Wednesday
The Cottage, Broughton Green,
  nr Hanbury
Ivytree House, Clent
May 22 Thursday
Barnard's Green House, Malvern
Red House Farm, Bradley Green,
  nr Redditch
May 25 Sunday
The Cottage Herbery, Boraston,
  Tenbury Wells
The Priory, Kemerton
Stone House Cottage Gardens,
  Stone ‡
Whitlenge House Cottage,
  Hartlebury ‡
May 26 Monday
The Manor House, Birlingham, nr
  Pershore
Stone House Cottage Gardens,
  Stone ‡
Whitlenge House Cottage,
  Hartlebury ‡
May 28 Wednesday
The Elms, Lower Broadheath
St Egwins Cottage, Norton,
  Evesham
May 29 Thursday
The Cockshoot, Castle Morton,
  Malvern
The Priory, Kemerton
21 Swinton Lane, Worcester
May 31 Saturday
White Cottage, Stock Green, nr
  Inkberrow
June
Barnard's Green House, Malvern.
  Every Thurs (2-6)
Eastgrove Cottage Garden
  Nursery, nr Shrawley. Thurs to
  Mons (2-5)

The Elms, Lower Broadheath.
  Every Tues, Weds (2-5)
The Manor House, Birlingham, nr
  Pershore. Weds, Thurs
The Priory, Kemerton. Every
  Thurs (2-6)
Stone House Cottage Gardens,
  Stone. Every Weds, Thurs,
  Fris, Sats (10-5.30)
White Cottage, Stock Green, nr
  Inkberrow. Every Fris to
  Tues, except 2nd & 4th Suns
  (10-5)
June 1 Sunday
The Cottage Herbery, Boraston,
  Tenbury Wells
St Egwins Cottage, Norton,
  Evesham
White Cottage, Stock Green, nr
  Inkberrow
Woodmancote, Wadborough
June 4 Wednesday
St Egwins Cottage, Norton,
  Evesham
June 8 Sunday
Cedar Lodge, Blakeshall, nr
  Wolverley
The Cottage Herbery, Boraston,
  Tenbury Wells
Madresfield Court, nr Malvern
June 11 Wednesday
The Elms, Lower Broadheath
The Manor House, Birlingham, nr
  Pershore
June 12 Thursday
Barnard's Green House, Malvern
The Priory, Kemerton
Red House Farm, Bradley Green,
  nr Redditch
June 15 Sunday
24 Alexander Avenue, Droitwich
  Spa
Bell's Castle, Kemerton
Charlton House, Lulsley,
  Knightwick
The Cockshoot, Castle Morton,
  Malvern
Pershore College of Horticulture
Upper Court, Kemerton
Woodmancote, Wadborough
June 16 Monday
Ivytree House, Clent
June 17 Tuesday
The Cottage, Broughton Green,
  nr Hanbury
June 18 Wednesday
The Cottage, Broughton Green,
  nr Hanbury
Ivytree House, Clent
St Egwins Cottage, Norton,
  Evesham
June 19 Thursday
The Manor House, Birlingham, nr
  Pershore

June 22 Sunday
Birtsmorton Court, nr Malvern
Broadway, Church Street Gardens
Charlton House, Lulsley,
  Knightwick
Eastgrove Cottage Garden
  Nursery, nr Shrawley
The Elms, Lower Broadheath
The Priory, Kemerton
Stone House Cottage Gardens,
  Stone
21 Swinton Lane, Worcester
Witley Park House, Great
  Witley
June 26 Thursday
Barnard's Green House, Malvern
The Cockshoot, Castle Morton,
  Malvern
Dial Park, Chaddesley Corbett ‡
Eldersfield Court, Eldersfield
Monsieurs Hall, Bromsgrove ‡
June 28 Saturday
White Cottage, Stock Green, nr
  Inkberrow
June 29 Sunday
The Cottage Herbery, Boraston,
  Tenbury Wells
Eldersfield Court, Eldersfield
Orchard Bungalow, Bishops Frome
White Cottage, Stock Green, nr
  Inkberrow
Woodmancote, Wadborough
July
Barnard's Green House, Malvern.
  Every Thurs (2-6)
Eastgrove Cottage Garden
  Nursery, nr Shrawley. Thurs to
  Mons (2-5)
The Elms, Lower Broadheath.
  Every Tues, Weds (2-5)
The Manor House, Birlingham, nr
  Pershore. Weds, Thurs to 17
The Priory, Kemerton. Every
  Thurs (2-6)
Stone House Cottage Gardens,
  Stone. Every Weds, Thurs,
  Fris, Sats (10-5.30)
White Cottage, Stock Green, nr
  Inkberrow. Every Fris to Tues,
  except 2nd & 4th Suns (10-5)
July 2 Wednesday
The Manor House, Birlingham, nr
  Pershore
July 3 Thursday
Red House Farm, Bradley Green,
  nr Redditch
July 6 Sunday
Broadway, Snowshill Road
  Gardens
Hanbury Hall, nr Droitwich
St Egwins Cottage, Norton,
  Evesham
Spetchley Park, nr Worcester
Yew Tree House, Ombersley

July 9 Wednesday
St Egwins Cottage, Norton,
Evesham
July 10 Thursday
Barnard's Green House, Malvern
Monsieur's Hall, Bromsgrove
July 13 Sunday
Arley Cottage, Upper Arley, nr
Bewdley
The Cockshoot, Castle Morton,
Malvern
Eastgrove Cottage Garden
Nursery, nr Shrawley
The Priory, Kemerton
Woollas Hall, Eckington, nr
Pershore
July 14 Monday
Ivytree House, Clent
July 15 Tuesday
The Cottage, Broughton Green,
nr Hanbury
The Elms, Lower Broadheath
July 16 Wednesday
The Cottage, Broughton Green,
nr Hanbury
Ivytree House, Clent
July 17 Thursday
The Manor House, Birlingham, nr
Pershore
21 Swinton Lane, Worcester
July 20 Sunday
24 Alexander Avenue, Droitwich Spa
The Cottage Herbery, Boraston,
Tenbury Wells
July 24 Thursday
Barnard's Green House, Malvern
The Cockshoot, Castle Morton,
Malvern
July 27 Sunday
Eastgrove Cottage Garden
Nursery, nr Shrawley
Orchard Bungalow, Bishops Frome
July 30 Wednesday
The Elms, Lower Broadheath
August
Barnard's Green House, Malvern.
Every Thurs (2-6)
The Elms, Lower Broadheath.
Every Tues, Weds (2-5)
The Priory, Kemerton. Every
Thurs (2-6)
Stone House Cottage Gardens,
Stone. Every Weds, Thurs,
Fris, Sats (10-5.30)
White Cottage, Stock Green, nr
Inkberrow. Every Fris to Tues,
except 2nd & 4th Suns (10-5)
August 3 Sunday
The Priory, Kemerton
St Egwins Cottage, Norton,
Evesham
August 6 Wednesday
St Egwins Cottage, Norton,
Evesham

August 10 Sunday
21 Swinton Lane, Worcester
August 19 Tuesday
The Cottage, Broughton Green,
nr Hanbury
The Elms, Lower Broadheath
August 20 Wednesday
The Cottage, Broughton Green,
nr Hanbury
August 21 Thursday
Barnard's Green House, Malvern
August 24 Sunday
The Priory, Kemerton
Stone House Cottage Gardens,
Stone ‡
Whitlenge House Cottage,
Hartlebury ‡
August 25 Monday
Stone House Cottage Gardens,
Stone ‡
Whitlenge House Cottage,
Hartlebury ‡
August 31 Sunday
Barnard's Green House,
Malvern
September
Barnard's Green House, Malvern.
Every Thurs (2-6)
Eastgrove Cottage Garden
Nursery, nr Shrawley. Thurs,
Fris, Sats (2 -5)
The Elms, Lower Broadheath.
Every Tues, Weds (2-5)
The Manor House, Birlingham, nr
Pershore. Every Thurs (11-
5.30)
The Priory, Kemerton. Every
Thurs (2-6)
Stone House Cottage Gardens,
Stone. Every Weds, Thurs,
Fris, Sats (10-5.30)
White Cottage, Stock Green, nr
Inkberrow. Every Fris to Tues,
except 2nd & 4th Suns (10-5)
September 4 Thursday
21 Swinton Lane, Worcester
September 7 Sunday
The Priory, Kemerton
September 11 Thursday
The Manor House, Birlingham, nr
Pershore
September 14 Sunday
Eastgrove Cottage Garden
Nursery, nr Shrawley
Woollas Hall, Eckington, nr
Pershore
September 16 Tuesday
The Elms, Lower Broadheath
September 17 Wednesday
The Cottage, Broughton Green,
nr Hanbury
September 20 Saturday
White Cottage, Stock Green, nr
Inkberrow

September 21 Sunday
Kyre Park, Tenbury Wells
White Cottage, Stock Green, nr
Inkberrow
September 25 Thursday
Dial Park, Chaddesley Corbett
September 28 Sunday
Eastgrove Cottage Garden
Nursery, nr Shrawley
October
Eastgrove Cottage Garden
Nursery, nr Shrawley. Thurs,
Fris, Sats to 18 (2 -5)
Stone House Cottage Gardens,
Stone. Every Weds, Thurs,
Fris, Sats to 18 (10-5.30)
October 12 Sunday
Eastgrove Cottage Garden
Nursery, nr Shrawley
October 19 Sunday
Bodenham Arboretum, Wolverley
Nerine Nursery, Welland
1988 February 19 Thursday
Dial Park, Chaddesley Corbett

Regular openings
For details see garden description

Barn House, Broadway
Barnard's Green House, Malvern
Eastgrove Cottage Garden Nursery,
nr Shrawley
The Elms, Lower Broadheath
Kyre Park, Tenbury Wells
The Manor House, Birlingham, nr
Pershore
The Priory, Kemerton
Red House Farm, Bradley Green, nr
Redditch
Spetchley Park, nr Worcester
Stone House Cottage Gardens, Stone
White Cottage, Stock Green, nr
Inkberrow

By appointment only
*For telephone numbers and other
details see garden descriptions.
Private visits welcomed*

Conderton Manor, nr Tewkesbury
Keepers Cottage, Alvechurch
Overbury Court, nr Tewkesbury

By Appointment Gardens.
These owners do not have a
fixed opening day usually
because they cannot
accommodate large numbers or
have insufficient parking space.

DESCRIPTIONS OF GARDENS

¶**24 Alexander Avenue** &.&⊛ (Malley & David Terry) Droitwich Spa. South from Droitwich Spa towards Worcester A38, town centre approx 1m. Or from junction 6 M5 to Droitwich Town centre. A new garden 140' × 40' for yr-round interest, planted April 1996. Unusual shrubs, herbaceous perennials, ferns and shade loving plants. Clematis, and pillar roses in the herbaceous borders; alpine troughs and small alpine house. Superb lawn developed without re-seeding or re-turfing. Scree garden at the front. *Adm £1.50 Chd free. Suns May 18, June 15, July 20 (2-6). Private visits welcome by appt, please* **Tel 01905 774907**

Arley Cottage &. (Woodward family) Upper Arley, nr Bewdley. 5m N of Kidderminster off A442. Small country garden with lawns bordered by interesting shrubs and collection of rare trees. Cream TEAS. *Adm £1 Chd free (Share to Lane-Fox Unit, St Thomas' Hospital, London®). Sun July 13 (2-5)*

Arley House ⊛ (R D Turner Esq) Upper Arley, 5m N of Kidderminster. A442. Arboretum containing specimen conifers and hardwoods, rhododendrons, camellias, magnolias, heathers; Italianate garden; greenhouses with orchids, alpines. Aviary with ornamental pheasants, budgerigars. TEA. *Adm £2 Chd free (Share to St Peter's, Upper Arley®). Sun May 4 (2-7)*

Astley Horticultural Society &.⊛ 4m W of Stourport-on-Severn on the A451 to Tenbury Wells. 2nd L for Astley just before farm shop. Little Yarhampton is ¼m on R. Treasure hunt for families. Start at Little Yarhampton, selected gardens on a circular route, map provided. *Combined adm £2 Chd free. Sun April 20 (1-5.30)*
    Little Yarhampton Extensive formal gardens, small arboretum and lovely woodland walk. Magnificent views
    Astley Towne House Recently constructed family garden to a very ambitious design of the owners. Formal kitchen garden with central fountain. Grass paths winding through shrubs and herbaceous borders
    Pool House Beautiful Strawberry Hill style house, surrounded by extensive grass with bulbs and wild flowers, leading down to 3 large pools with tame carp. Old walled garden with rare climbers. Many unusual shrubs
    Koi Cottage Small village garden imaginatively transformed into classic Japanese garden with superb collection of Koi carp
    The Sytch Immaculately maintained terraced garden with fine views over ha-ha. Fine kitchen garden
    The White House Eccentric garden with follies, pergolas and ornaments. Long herbaceous border inspired by Christopher Lloyd's theories, bulbs beneath shrubs

Barbers &.&⊛ (Mr & the Hon Mrs Richard Webb) Martley 7m NW of Worcester on B4204. Medium-sized garden with lawns, trees, shrubs, pools and wild garden. Cowslip and fritillary lawn. Home-made TEAS. *Adm £1.50 Chd free (Share to Martley Church®). Sun April 20 (2-6)*

¶**Barn House** &. (Mark & Jane Ricketts) Broadway. Situated in beautiful Cotswold village of Broadway in the High St nr bottom of Fish Hill. Large C17 country house set in 16 acres of garden and paddocks. The well maintained gardens contain large variety of shrubs. TEAS. *Adm £1.50 Chd free (Share to Sue Ryder Home, Cheltenham®). Open every day, except occasional Sats (10-6)*

Barnard's Green House &.&⊛ (Mr & Mrs Philip Nicholls) 10 Poolbrook Rd, Malvern. On E side of Malvern at junction of B4211 and B4208. 3-acre garden, with mature trees, herbaceous border, rockery, heather beds, woodland, vegetable garden with old brick paths and box hedges maintained to pre-war standards. Unusual plants and shrubs propagated for sale. Featured in Practical Gardening 1996. Mrs Nicholls is a specialist and writer on dried flowers. 1635 half-timbered house (not open). Coach parties by appt. TEAS. *Adm £1.50 Acc chd free (Share to Save the Children Fund®). Suns April 27, Aug 31 and every Thursday April to Sept incl. (2-6). Also private visits welcome, please* **Tel 01684 574446**

Bell's Castle ⊛ (Lady Holland-Martin) Kemerton, NE of Tewkesbury. 3 small terraces with battlements; wild garden outside wall. The small Gothic castellated folly was built by Edmund Bell (Smuggler) c1820; very fine views. TEAS. *Adm £1 Chd free. Sun June 15 (2-6). Parties welcome, please* **Tel 01386 725333**

Birtsmorton Court &.⊛ (Mr & Mrs N G K Dawes) nr Malvern. 7m E of Ledbury on A438. Fortified manor house (not open) dating from C12; moat; Westminster pool, laid down in Henry V11's reign at time of consecration of Westminster Abbey; large tree under which Cardinal Wolsey reputedly slept in shadow of ragged stone. Newly planted white garden. Topiary. Motor Museum extra. TEAS in aid of Birtsmorton Church. *Adm £2 Chd 50p (Share to St Michael's Hospice®). Sun June 22 (2-6)*

Bodenham Arboretum ⊛ (Mr & Mrs J D Binnian) 2m N of Wolverley; 5m N of Kidderminster. From Wolverley Church Island follow signs. 134 acres landscaped and planted during the past 24 years; 2 chains of lakes and pools; woods and glades with over 2000 species of trees and shrubs; Laburnum tunnel; grove of dawn redwoods (Chinese water fir) in shallows of 3-acre lake. Bring wellingtons or strong boots. Partly suitable for wheelchairs. TEA. NO COACHES. *Adm £2 Chd free (Share to Kew Gardens Millennium Seed Bank Appeal©). Sun Oct 19 (2-6). Private visits welcome for parties of 10 and over at other times of the year* **Tel 01562 850382**

¶**Broadway, Church Street Gardens** Rd from the Green towards Snowshill. Public car park nearby, via Church Close. Cream TEAS and home-made cakes at **Bannits**. *Combined adm £2 Chd free. Sun June 22 (2-5.30)*
    ¶**Bannits** (Dr & Mrs R Juckes) C18 Cotswold stone house. 1-acre of formal terraced garden with herbaceous borders and lavender walk. 1½ acres old orchard and 1½ acres wild garden with path to stream
    St Michael's Cottage (Mr & Mrs K R Barling) Thatched cottage with approx ⅓-acre intensively planted cottage style and herbaceous garden planned in colour groups, incl a small white sunken garden

Broadway, Snowshill Road Gardens ✂❀ All six gardens are on Snowshill Rd. TEAS at **Far Bunchers**. *Combined adm £2 Chd free (Share to Lifford Hall, Broadway®). Sun July 6 (2-6)*

Far Bunchers (Mrs A Pallant) A recently developed mixed garden of about 1 acre. Emphasis on shrub roses and organic vegetable growing

Meadowside (Mrs P Bomford) A very pleasing and compact cottage garden that slopes down to the stream

The Old Orchard (Major & Mrs I Gregory) A cottage garden that slopes down to the stream together with an old orchard and shrub rose garden adjacent to the rd

Mill Hay Cottage (Dr & Mrs W J A Payne) The 2-acre garden is of relatively recent origin and is still being developed. A special feature is the number of unusual trees, incl many fruiting species

The Mill (Mr & Mrs H Verney) A 2½-acre paddock, bounded by 2 streams has been transformed since 1975 into an attractive garden that will support a variety of wildlife. Informal planting of trees, shrub roses and other shrubs, moisture loving plants and bulbs

Mill Hay House (Mr & Mrs H Will) The large mill pond is a centre for attention in a well laid out and interesting garden

Cedar Lodge ✂❀ (Malcolm & Barbara Phillips) Blakeshall. 4m N of Kidderminster off B4189. 1½m from Wolverley village. ¾-acre garden with extensive range of trees, shrubs and plants. Shade borders, gravel garden, pools and large mixed borders. Beautiful rural setting adjoining Kinver Edge. TEAS. *Adm £2 Chd free. Sun June 8 (2-5.30)*

Charlton House ✂ (Mr & Mrs S Driver-White) Lulsley, Knightwick. 9m W of Worcester via A44, turn 1st L after Knightsford Bridge towards Alfrick, 1st L after Fox & Hounds signed Hill Rd, Lulsley; 1m at end of lane. ⅔-acre intimate garden of shrubs, shrub roses created by owner since 1970. Fine barns. No children. *Adm £1.50. Suns June 15, 22 (1-5). Coach parties by appt, please* **Tel 01886 821220**

¶The Cockshoot ❀ (Clive & Elizabeth Wilkins) Castle Morton. 7m S of Malvern. [OS map ref: 50773379]. B4208 turn into New Rd opp Robin Hood pub. Take 1st L (½m). At 200yds bear L at fork. Keep on narrow rd until track. Straight along track. The house is 1st on R. ¾-acre garden set in common land below the Malvern Hills. Surrounds a Georgian cottage built about 1721 (not open). Garden divided into areas around circular lawns and incls hazel walk, pond, bog garden, courtyard with gazebo, hanging baskets and pots. Crafts and plants for sale, mostly propagated from the garden. TEAS. *Adm £1.50 Chd 50p. Suns, Thurs May 18, 29, June 15, 26, July 13, 24 (10-5). Parties by appt evenings only, please* **Tel 01684 833331**

Conderton Manor ♿✂ (Mr & Mrs William Carr) 5½m NE of Tewkesbury. 7-acre garden with magnificent views of Cotswolds; many trees and shrubs of botanical interest. 100yd long mixed borders, rose walks and formal terrace. Teas available at the Silk Shop in the village. *Adm £2. Private visits by appt only, yr-round, please* **Tel 01386 725389**

The Cottage ✂❀ (Mr Terry Dagley) Broughton Green, nr Hanbury. 4½m E of Droitwich. 3½m via B4090, turn S at sign, 1m. Park on side of rd. The Cottage 250yds up farm track. Approx ½-acre plantsman's country garden, stocked with extensive range of hardy perennials, bulbs, shrubs and trees to give yr-round interest. The quiet rural setting encourages abundant wildlife. *Adm £1.50 Chd free. Weds March 19, April 16, May 21, June 18, July 16, Aug 20, Sept 17 (11-5), Tues June 17, July 15, Aug 19 (3-8). Private visits welcome, please* **Tel 01905 391670**

The Cottage Herbery ✂❀ (Mr & Mrs R E Hurst) 1m E of Tenbury Wells on A456, turn for Boraston at Peacock Inn, turn R in village, signposted to garden. Half timbered C16 farmhouse with fast-flowing Cornbrook running close to its side and over ford at the bottom of garden. 1-acre garden specializing in a wide range of herbs, aromatic and scented foliage plants, planted on a cottage garden theme; also unusual hardy perennial and variegated plants. New features added each yr. Organic garden. Chelsea Medallists. Featured in Central TV Gardening Time. Gold Medal Winners '94 and '95. TEAS (served in garden and barn). Week days by appt. *Adm £1.50 Chd free. Suns May 4, 18, 25, June 1, 8, 29, July 20 (11-5). Groups welcome by appt, please* **Tel 01584 781575**

Dial Park ✂❀ (Mr & Mrs David Mason) Chaddesley Corbett. 4½m from Kidderminster, 4½m from Bromsgrove on A448. 150yds towards Kidderminster from turn into Chaddesley Corbett village. Approx ¾-acre garden developed since 1990 containing interesting and unusual plants with yr-round interest. Incl collections of snowdrops, sambucus and hardy ferns. Also small collection of country bygones. TEA. *Adm £1 Chd free. Thurs Feb 20 (1-5) June 26, Sept 25 (2-6). 1988 Thurs Feb 19 (1-5). Private visits welcome, please* **Tel 01562 777451**

●Eastgrove Cottage Garden Nursery ♿✂❀ (Mr & Mrs J Malcolm Skinner) Sankyns Green, Shrawley. 8m NW of Worcester on rd between Shrawley (on B4196) and Great Witley (on A443). Set in 5 acres unspoilt meadow and woodland, this unique 1-acre garden and nursery is of interest to the plantsman. Fine collection of hardy and tender perennial plants in old world country flower garden with thought given to planting combinations of colour and form. Garden and nursery maintained since 1970 by owners who give help and advice. Featured in The Times, The Telegraph and BBC TV. Wide range of well grown less usual plants for sale, at Nursery. *Adm £2 Chd free. March 27 to July 31 Thurs, Fri, Sat, Sun, Mon Sept 4 to Oct 18 Thurs, Fris, Sats (2-5). Suns Sept 14, 28, Oct 12 (2-5)*

¶Eldersfield Court ✂ ❀ (Mr & Mrs E C Watkins) Eldersfield. Opp the church. 6m W of Tewkesbury A438/B4211 or 12m S of Malvern B4208 past Pendock. Queen Anne house (not open). 2 acres mostly created by present owners since 1984 with formal borders, classic English rose garden, ridge walk with views, steps, slopes. *Adm £2 Chd free. Thurs June 26, Sun June 29 (1-5)*

The Elms ✂❀ (Mr & Mrs Marshall Stewart) Lower Broadheath. 4m W of Worcester, B4204 turn opp school into Frenchlands Lane. After ½m (drive with care) through farm gate, lane becomes a track. Isolated setting, lovely views in Elgar country. 1½-acre garden surrounding late Georgian farmhouse, begun by present owners in 1988. Mixed colour-themed borders, lily pool, rose walk. Nursery specialising in hardy cottage garden plants set in ornamental kitchen garden created from old fold yard. Rare breed sheep. Farming bygones. TEAS. *Adm £1.50 Chd free April, Aug, Sept; Adm £2 Chd free May, June, July (Share to Shropshire Sheep Breeders' Assoc®). Sun June 22 (5-9); Tues, Weds April 1 - Sept 30 (2-5)*

▲**Hanbury Hall** ♿⚘❀ (The National Trust) Hanbury, 3m NE of Droitwich, 6m S of Bromsgrove. Signed off B4090. Recreation of C18 formal garden by George London incl sunken parterre, fruit garden and wilderness. Victorian forecourt with detailed planting. William & Mary style house of 1701; contemporary Orangery and Ice House. TEAS. *Adm garden only £2.50 Chd £1. For NGS Sun July 6 (2-6)*

Holland House (Warden: Mr Peter Middlemiss) Main St, Cropthorne, Pershore. Between Pershore and Evesham, off A44. Car park at rear of house. Gardens laid out by Lutyens in 1904; thatched house dating back to 1636 (not open). TEAS. *Adm £1 Chd free (Share to USPG®). Suns March 23, April 20 (2.30-5)*

Ivytree House (Mrs L Eggins) [OS139 91.79] Bromsgrove Rd, Clent. 3m SE of Stourbridge and 5m NW of Bromsgrove, off A491 Stourbridge to Bromsgrove dual carriageway. Car parking next door behind the Woodman Hotel. Over 1,000 varieties of small trees, shrubs and herbaceous plants in approx ½-acre plantsman's cottage garden; tree ivies and ivytrees, collection of aucubas, small conservatory with fuchsia trees, pond garden, fruit and vegetables, bantams and bees. *Adm £1.50 Chd free. Mons, Weds May 19, 21, June 16, 18, July 14, 16 Mons (2-5), Weds (2-5 & 7-9). Also private visits welcome, please Tel 01562 884171*

Keepers Cottage ⚘❀ (Mrs Diana Scott) Alvechurch. Take main rd through Alvechurch towards Redditch. Turn opp sign to Cobley Hill and Bromsgrove for 1m over 2 humpback bridges. 3-acre garden at 600ft with fine views towards the Cotswolds; rhododendrons, camellias; old-fashioned roses; unusual trees and shrubs; rock garden; 2 alpine houses and new potager; paddock with donkeys. *Adm £2 Chd £1. Private visits welcome in May and June, please Tel 01214 455885*

■ **Kyre Park** ♿❀ (Mr & Mrs M H Rickard & Mr & Mrs J N Sellers) Kyre. 4m S of Tenbury Wells or 7m N of Bromyard. Follow signs to Kyre Church off B4214. Approx 29 acres, shrubbery walk, 5 lakes, waterfalls, hermitage, picturesque views, mature trees, Norman dovecote and Jacobean tithe barn. Largely landscaped in 1754 but neglected for several decades, now under restoration. A rare example of a Georgian shrubbery hardly touched for 240yrs. Stout shoes advised. Ferns for sale at Rickards Hardy Fern Nursery. RHS gold medal winners since 1992. TEAS, light lunches. *Adm £1.50 Chd 50p. Open daily Easter to Oct. For NGS Suns March 23, Sept 21 (11-6). Coach parties by appt, please Tel 01885 410282*

Little Malvern Court ⚘❀ (Mrs T M Berington) 4m S of Malvern on A4104 S of junction with A449. 10 acres attached to former Benedictine Priory, magnificent views over Severn valley. An intriguing layout of garden rooms, and terrace round house. Water garden below, feeding into chain of lakes. Wide variety of spring bulbs, flowering trees and shrubs. Notable collection of old-fashioned roses. TEAS. *Adm £3 Chd 50p (5-14) (Share to SSAFA®). Sun March 23 (2-5)*

Madresfield Court ♿ (The Hon Lady Morrison) Nr Malvern. 60 acres formal and parkland garden incl rare species of mature trees, Pulhamite rock garden, maze, majestic avenues and a mass of wild flowers. TEAS. *Adm £2 Chd 50p (Share to Madresfield Primary School©). Sun June 8 (2-5.30)*

The Manor House ⚘❀ (Mr & Mrs David Williams-Thomas) Birlingham, nr Pershore off A4104. Very fine views of Bredon Hill with short walk to R Avon for picnics. Walled white and silver garden, gazebo and many herbaceous borders of special interest to the plantsman. A large selection of plants propagated from the garden on sale. Featured in 'House & Garden' 1994 and 'Sunday Express' 1995. TEAS. *Adm £1.50 Chd free. Every Thurs May 1 to May 29. Every Wed, Thurs June 4 to July 17. Closed Aug. Every Thurs Sept 4 to Sept 25. Also Mons May 5, 26; Fri May 9; Weds June 11, July 2; Thurs June 19, July 17, Sept 11 (11-5.30). Private visits welcome, please Tel 01386 750005*

Monsieurs Hall ⚘❀ (Dr & Mrs A Cowan) Bromsgrove. A448 1½m W Bromsgrove. L into Monsieurs Hall Lane. 400yds on L. Hilltop acre with extensive views. Newly created parterre and formal garden around C16 farmhouse (not open). Informal mixed borders rockeries with many unusual plants, leading to wilder area and spinney. Conservatory. Featured on central TV. *Adm £1 Chd free. Thurs May 1, June 26, July 10 (2-6). Private visits welcome, please Tel 01527 831747*

Nafford House ⚘ (Mr & Mrs John Wheatley) Eckington. On entering Eckington from A4104 take 1st L, follow lane for ¾m. Nafford House on sharp R-hand bend. Georgian house set in elevated position overlooking R Avon. Features incl extensive lawns, well established herbaceous borders, many young specimen trees, small formal rose garden and copse recently replanted. TEA. *Adm £2 Chd free. Sun May 18 (2-6)*

Nerine Nursery ⚘❀ (Mr & Mrs I L Carmichael) Brookend House, Welland, ½m towards Upton-on-Severn from Welland Xrds (A4104 × B4208). Internationally famous National Collection of Nerines, 30 species and some 800 named varieties in 5 greenhouses and traditional walled garden with raised beds, hardy nerines. Coaches by appt only. TEAS. *Adm £1.50 Chd free. Sun Oct 19 (2-5). Private visits welcome, please Tel 01684 594005*

Orchard Bungalow ⚘❀ (Mr & Mrs Robert Humphries) Bishops Frome. 14m W of Worcester. A4103 turn R at bottom of Fromes Hill, through village of Bishops Frome on B4214. Turn R immediately after de-regulation signs along narrow track for 250yds. Ample parking in field 200yds from garden. ½-acre garden with conifers, trees, shrubs and herbaceous borders. Over 200 roses incl many old varieties, 4 ponds, small stream, 3 aviaries and do-vecote. 1993 winner of Garden News water garden competition. TEAS. *Adm £1 Chd free. Suns June 29, July 27 (2-6). Private visits welcome, please* Tel 01885 490273

Overbury Court ℞ (Mr & Mrs Bruce Bossom) nr Tewkesbury, Glos GL20 7NP. 5m NE of Tewkesbury, 2½m N of Teddington Hands Roundabout, where A438 crosses A435. Georgian house 1740 (not open); landscape gardening of same date with stream and pools. Daffodil bank and grotto. Plane trees, yew hedges. Shrub, cut flower, coloured foliage, gold and silver, shrub rose borders. Norman church adjoins garden. *Adm £1.50 Chd free. Private visits welcome by parties of 10 or more following written application or* Fax 01386 725528

Pershore College of Horticulture ℞✿❀ 1m S of Pershore on A44, 7m from M5 junction 7. 180-acre estate; ornamental grounds; arboretum; fruit, vegetables; amenity glasshouses; wholesale hardy stock nursery. RHS Regional Centre at Pershore. Plant Centre open for sales and gardening advice. TEA. *Adm £1 Chd 50p. Sun June 15 (2-4)*

Priors Court ℞✿❀ (Robert Philipson-Stow) Long Green. From Tewkesbury take A438 to Ledbury. Exactly 5m pass under M50. Garden on hill on L of A438. From Ledbury, Worcester or Gloucester aim for Rye Cross (A438 and B4208) then take A438 for Tewkesbury. Priors Court is approx 3m from Rye Cross on R. 3-acre garden established in 1920s by owner's parents surrounding C15 house (not open). Rock, herb and vegetable gardens, also mature trees and shrubs, herbaceous and rose borders; stunning views. Norman church 250yds over field will be open. TEAS. *Adm £1.50 Chd 50p (Share to Berrow & Pendock Parish Church®). Sun May 11 (2-6). Private visits by appt for parties of less than 20, please* Tel 01684 833221

The Priory ℞❀ (The Hon Mrs Peter Healing) Kemerton, NE of Tewkesbury B4080. Main features of this 4-acre garden are long herbaceous borders planned in colour groups; stream, fern and sunken gardens. Many unusual plants, shrubs and trees. Featured in BBC2 'Gardeners' World', 'The Garden magazine', Channel 4 Garden Party 1996. Small nursery. TEAS Suns only. *Adm £1.50 May and June, £2 July to Sept Chd free. (Share to St Richard's Hospice® Aug 24, SSAFA® Sept 7). Every Thurs May 29 to Sept 25, Suns May 25, June 22, July 13, Aug 3, 24, Sept 7 (2-6) Thurs May 29, June 12, Oct by appt only. Private visits welcome for 20 and over, please* Tel 01386 725258

Red House Farm ℞❀ (Mrs M M Weaver) Flying Horse Lane, Bradley Green. 7m NW of Redditch on B4090 Alcester to Droitwich Spa. Ignore signpost to Bradley Green. Turn opp The Red Lion. Approx ½-acre plant enthusiast's cottage garden containing wide range of interesting herbaceous perennials; roses; shrubs; alpines. Garden and small nursery open daily offering wide variety of plants mainly propagated from garden. *Adm £1 Chd free. Thurs May 22, June 12, July 3 (11-5). Private visits welcome, please,* Tel 01527 821269

Ripple Hall ℞ (Sir Hugo Huntington-Whiteley) 4m N of Tewkesbury. Off A38 Worcester-Tewkesbury (nr junction with motorway); Ripple village well signed. 6 acres; lawns

and paddocks; walled vegetable garden; cork tree and orangery. TEAS. *Adm £1.50 Acc chd free (Share to St John Ambulance®). Sun April 6 (2-5)*

St Egwins Cottage ✿❀ (Mr & Mrs Brian Dudley) Norton. 2m N of Evesham on B4088 (was A435). Park in St Egwins Church car park. Walk through churchyard to Church Lane (50yds). Please do not park in Church Lane. ⅕-acre plantsman's garden, many unusual plants; mainly perennials incl hardy geraniums, campanulas and salvias. Small thatched cottage next to C12 church (open). TEAS Suns only. TEA Weds only. *Adm £1 Chd free. Suns, June 1, July 6, Aug 3; Weds May 28, June 4, 18, July 9; Aug 6(2-5). Also private visits welcome June and July, please* Tel 01386 870486

■ **Spetchley Park** ℞✿ (R J Berkeley Esq) 2m E of Worcester on A422. 30-acre garden containing large collection of trees, shrubs and plants, many rare and unusual. New garden within kitchen garden. Red and fallow deer in nearby park. TEAS. *Adm £2.70 Chd £1.30. Open weekdays, Bank Hol Mons (11-5) Suns (2-5). For NGS Fri March 28 (11-5), Suns May 11, July 6 (2-5)*

●**Stone House Cottage Gardens** ℞✿❀ (Maj & the Hon Mrs Arbuthnott) Stone, 2m SE of Kidderminster via A448 towards Bromsgrove next to church, turn up drive. 1-acre sheltered walled plantsman's garden with towers; rare wall shrubs, climbers and interesting herbaceous plants. In adjacent nursery large selection of unusual shrubs and climbers for sale. Featured in The Garden, Country Life and Hortus. Coaches by appt only. *Adm £2 Chd free. Suns May 4, 25; June 22; Aug 24; Mons March 31, May 5, 26; Aug 25; also open March 1 to Oct 18 every Wed, Thurs, Fri, Sat (10-5.30). Private visits welcome Oct 18 to March 1, please* Tel 01562 69902

21 Swinton Lane ✿❀ (Mr A Poulton & Mr B Stenlake) Worcester. 1½m W of City Centre off A4103 Hereford Rd turning into Swinton Lane between Portabello public house and Worcester Golf Course. ⅓-acre town garden featuring a wide variety of plants in colour theme borders and containers. The intimate silver and white garden is surrounded by old roses on trellis work. Interesting and rare tender plants are a delight during the summer months. The garden holds the NCCPG National Collection of lobelia. *Adm £1.50 Chd free. Thurs, Suns May 29, June 22 (11-6), July 17 (11-8) Aug 10, Sept 4 (11-6). Parties welcome by appt, please* Tel 01905 422265

Upper Court ℞ (Mr & Mrs W Herford) Kemerton, NE of Tewkesbury B4080. Take turning to Parish Church from War Memorial; Manor behind church. Approx 13 acres of garden and grounds incl a 2-acre lake where visitors would be welcome to bring picnics. The garden was mostly landscaped and planted in 1930s. TEAS. *Adm £2 Chd free. Sun June 15 (2-6)*

White Cottage ℞✿❀ (Mr & Mrs S M Bates) Earls Common Rd, Stock Green. A422 Worcester-Alcester; turn L at Red Hart public house (Dormston) 1½m to junction in Stock Green. Turn L. 2-acre garden, developed since

.981; large herbaceous and shrub borders, many unusual varieties; specialist collection of hardy geraniums; stream and natural garden carpeted with primroses, cowslips and other wild flowers; nursery featuring plants propagated from the garden. Teas at Coneybury Plant Centre. *Adm £1.50 OAPs 75p Chd free. Open daily March 28 to Sept 28 except Weds, Thurs and 2nd and 4th Suns each month. For NGS March 28, 29, 30, 31, May 3, 4, 5, 17, 18, 31, June 1, 14, 15, 28, 29, Sept 20, 21 (10-5). Private visits welcome by prior appt only, please* **Tel 01386 792414**

Whitlenge House Cottage &⚹❀ (Mr & Mrs K J Southall) Whitlenge Lane, Hartlebury. S of Kidderminster on A449. Take A442 (signposted Droitwich) over small island, ¼m, 1st R into Whitlenge Lane. Follow signs. Home of Creative Landscapes, RHS medal winners. Professional landscaper's demonstration garden with over 600 varieties of trees and shrubs etc. Water features, twisted pillar pergola, gravel gardens rockeries. Evolved over 12 years. 2 acres of informal plantsman's garden incorporating adjacent nursery specialising in large specimen shrubs. TEA. *Adm £1.50 Chd free. Suns, Mons March 30, 31, May 25, 26, Aug 24, 25 (10-5). Private visits welcome for parties of 10 and over, please* **Tel 01299 250720**

Windyridge ⚹❀ (Mr P Brazier) Kidderminster. Turn off Chester Rd N (A449) into Hurcott Rd, then into Imperial Avenue. 1-acre spring garden containing azaleas, magnolias, camellias, rhododendrons, mature flowering cherries and davidia. Please wear sensible shoes. *Adm £1 Chd free. Suns May 11, 18 (2-6). Private visits welcome, please* **Tel 01562 824994**

Woodmancote &❀ (Ila & Ian Walmsley) Wadborough. 1½ m S of Stoulton, which is on A44 between Worcester and Pershore. ¾-acres acquired and developed in stages over the last 10yrs. 2 ponds lawn and wide variety of shrubs and herbaceous plants. Please park considerately at The Mason Arms (400yds). Bar meals available. TEAS in aid of St Peter's Church. *Adm £1.50 Chd free. Suns June 1, 15, 29 (11-5). Private visits welcome May, June and July, please* **Tel 01905 840391**

¶**Woollas Hall** (Mr & Mrs Clive Jennings) Eckington. On Bredon Hill, off B4080 Bredon to Pershore rd. From Eckington take the rd to the Combertons and Woollas Hall. Drive past farm over cattle grid, up drive marked private and park in field, before 2nd cattle grid, no cars past this point please. The Jacobean Manor house (not open) is the setting for the 1-acre garden on several levels, created and maintained by owners, since 1984. Numerous walkways featuring separate enclosures with fine trees, shrubs, mixed and herbaceous borders. Fine views over Bredon Hill and surrounding countryside. *Adm £2 Chd 50p. Suns July 13 (2-6), Sept 14 (2-5)*

Yew Tree House & (Mr & Mrs W D Moyle) Ombersley. Turn off A449 up Woodfield Lane R at T-junction. 2½-acre garden with many rare herbaceous plants and shrubs. Pretty walled garden with alpines and lily pond, numerous old-fashioned roses. Mature plantings of blue, pink and white borders around tennis court and other yellow and white beds. Orchard, copse and lawns with lovely views set around c1640 timber framed house. TEA. *Adm £2 OAPs £1.50 Chd free. Sun July 6 (2-6)*

SYMBOLS USED IN THIS BOOK (See also Page 17)

‡   Following a garden name in the Dates of Opening list indicates that those gardens sharing the same symbol are nearby and open on the same day.

‡‡   Indicates a second series of nearby gardens open on the same day.

¶   Opening for the first time.

❀   Plants/produce for sale if available.

&   Gardens with at least the main features accessible by wheelchair.

⚹   No dogs except guide dogs but otherwise dogs are usually admitted, provided they are kept on a lead. Dogs are not admitted to houses.

●   These gardens advertise their own dates in this publication although they do not nominate specific days for the NGS. Not all the money collected by these gardens comes to the NGS but they do make a guaranteed contribution.

■   These gardens nominate specific days for the NGS and advertise their own dates in this publication.

▲   These gardens open regularly to the public but they do not advertise their own dates in this publication. For further details, contact the garden directly.

Yorkshire

Hon County Organisers:

(N Yorks - Districts of Hambleton, Richmond, Ryedale, Scarborough & Cleveland)

Mrs William Baldwin, Riverside Farm, Sinnington, York YO6 6RY
Tel 01751 431764

(West & South Yorks & North Yorks Districts of Craven, Harrogate, Selby & York)

Mrs Roger Marshall, The Old Vicarage, Whixley, York YO5 8AR
Tel 01423 330474

(E Yorks)

Mrs Philip Bean, Saltmarshe Hall, Howden, Goole, Yorkshire DN14 7RX
Tel 01430 430199

DATES OF OPENING

March 5 Wednesday
Joan Royd House, Penistone
March 30 Sunday
Netherwood House, Ilkley
April 2 Wednesday
Joan Royd House, Penistone
April 6 Sunday
Harlow Carr, Harrogate
April 13 Sunday
Betula & Bolton Percy Cemetery ‡
Victoria Cottage, Stainland
Windy Ridge, Bolton Percy ‡
April 20 Sunday
Aske, Richmond
April 27 Sunday
Boston Spa Gardens, nr Wetherby
Hallgarth, Ottringham, nr Hull ‡
The White Cottage, Halsham, nr Hull ‡
Wytherstone House, nr Helmsley
May 4 Sunday
Il Giardino, Bilton
54a Keldgate, Beverley
Shandy Hall, Coxwold
Sinnington Gardens
May 5 Monday
Old Sleningford, nr Ripon
May 7 Wednesday
Joan Royd House, Penistone
May 10 Saturday
The Chimney Place, Bilton Grange
May 11 Sunday
Blackbird Cottage, Scampston
Hemble Hill Farm, Guisborough
Hillbark, Bardsey
Victoria Cottage, Stainland
The Spaniels, Hensall
May 18 Sunday
Fairview, nr Summerbridge
Stillingfleet Lodge, nr York
Woodlands Cottage, Summerbridge
May 24 Saturday
Nawton Tower Garden, Nawton
May 25 Sunday
Castle Farm Nurseries
High Farm, Bilton ‡
Il Giardino, Bilton ‡
Nawton Tower Garden, Nawton

Old Sleningford, nr Ripon
Shandy Hall, Coxwold
May 26 Monday
Nawton Tower Garden, Nawton
Old Sleningford, nr Ripon
May 31 Saturday
Pennyholme, Fadmoor ‡
Sleightholme Dale Lodge, Fadmoor ‡
June 1 Sunday
Castle Farm Nurseries
Pennyholme, Fadmoor ‡
Plants of Special Interest Nursery, Braithwell
Sleightholme Dale Lodge, Fadmoor ‡
Springfield House, Tockwith
Victoria Cottage, Stainland
June 4 Wednesday
Joan Royd House, Penistone
June 7 Saturday
Burton Agnes Hall, Driffield
Pennyholme, Fadmoor
York Gate, Adel, Leeds 16
June 8 Sunday
Burton Agnes Hall, Driffield
Brookfield, Oxenhope
Creskeld Hall, Arthington ‡
Elvington Gardens, nr York ‡‡
Hunmanby Grange, nr Scarborough
Kelberdale, Knaresborough
Pennyholme, Fadmoor
55 Rawcliffe Drive, York ‡‡
Secret Garden, York ‡‡
Snilesworth, Northallerton
York Gate, Adel, Leeds 16 ‡
June 11 Wednesday
Brookfield, Oxenhope
June 12 Thursday
Beningbrough Hall, nr York
June 14 Saturday
The Chimney Place, Bilton Grange
June 15 Sunday
Derwent House, Osbaldwick ‡
Helmsley Gardens ‡‡
32 Holly Bank Road, York ‡
Littlethorpe Gardens, nr Ripon ‡‡‡
Lullaby, Hull

Norton Conyers, nr Ripon ‡‡‡
Parkview, South Cave
Saltmarshe Hall, Saltmarshe
Scampston Hall, Malton
Wytherstone House, nr Helmsley ‡‡
June 18 Wednesday
The Old Vicarage, Whixley
June 22 Sunday
Betula & Bolton Percy Cemetery ‡
Hallgarth, Ottringham, nr Hull ‡‡
Hillbark, Bardsey
Hovingham Hall, Hovingham
Low Askew, Cropton, Pickering
Parcevall Hall, nr Skipton
Victoria Cottage, Stainland
Windy Ridge, Bolton Percy ‡
The White Cottage, Halsham, nr Hull ‡‡
June 25 Wednesday
The Mews Cottage, 1 Brunswick Drive, Harrogate
Shandy Hall, Coxwold ‡
Wass Gardens ‡
June 29 Sunday
Bankfield, Huddersfield
Brodsworth Hall, nr Doncaster
High Farm, Bilton ‡
Il Giardino, Bilton ‡
Kelberdale, Knaresborough ‡‡‡
54a Keldgate, Beverley ‡‡
80 Lairgate, Beverley ‡‡
30 Latchmere Road, Leeds 16 ‡‡‡‡
5 Lockington Road, Lund
Mount Grace Priory, nr Osmotherly
Park House, Moreby, nr York ‡‡‡‡
The Old Rectory, Nunburnholme
Stillingfleet Lodge, nr York ‡‡‡‡
Stockeld Park, Wetherby ‡‡‡
5 Wharfe Close, Leeds 16 ‡‡‡‡
July 2 Wednesday
Rye Hill, Helmsley
July 6 Sunday
8 Dunstarn Lane, Adel
Evergreens, 119 Main Road, Bilton ‡
Fernwood, Cropton

Grimston Gardens, Gilling East
Hunmanby Grange, nr
  Scarborough
Lullaby, Hull ‡
Maspin House, Hillam, nr Selby
Millgate House, Richmond
The Old Rectory, Mirfield
Shandy Hall, Coxwold
Victoria Cottage, Stainland
26 West End, Walkington
Woodcock, Thirsk
July 9 Wednesday
Maspin House, Hillam, nr Selby
Shandy Hall, Coxwold
July 10 Thursday
Grimston Gardens, Gilling East
July 12 Saturday
The Chimney Place, Bilton
  Grange
July 13 Sunday
Beamsley Hall, nr Skipton
Holly Cottage, Wressle, nr Selby
30 Latchmere Road, Leeds 16
Manor Farm, Thixendale
Plants of Special Interest
  Nursery, Braithwell
Rudston House, Rudston, nr
  Driffield
Shandy Hall, Coxwold
July 19 Saturday
Sleightholme Dale Lodge,
  Fadmoor
July 20 Sunday
Bishopscroft, Sheffield
Bridge Cottage, Rievaulx
8 Dunstarn Lane, Adel ‡
Grey Shaw Syke Cottage, Ogden,
  nr Halifax
32 Holly Bank Road, York
30 Latchmere Road, Leeds 16 ‡
Sleightholme Dale Lodge,
  Fadmoor

July 23 Wednesday
Beacon Hill House, nr Ilkley
Bridge Cottage, Rievaulx
July 27 Sunday
Bridge Cottage, Rievaulx
Joan Royd House, Penistone
30 Latchmere Road, Leeds 16 ‡‡
55 Rawcliffe Drive, York ‡
Secret Garden, York ‡
The Spaniels, Hensall
Three Gables, Markington
5 Wharfe Close, Leeds 16 ‡‡
August 3 Sunday
30 Latchmere Road, Leeds 16
August 10 Sunday
Woodlands Cottage,
  Summerbridge
August 13 Wednesday
Three Gables, Markington
August 17 Sunday
Hallgarth, Ottringham nr Hull ‡
Oliver Lodge, 10 Heads Lane,
  Hessle
The White Cottage, Halsham, nr
  Hull ‡
September 3 Wednesday
Joan Royd House, Penistone
September 7 Sunday
Evergreens, 119 Main Road, Bilton
Hillbark, Bardsey
September 10 Wednesday
32 Holly Bank Rd, Holgate
September 14 Sunday
Plants of Special Interest
  Nursery, Braithwell
September 21 Sunday
Brodsworth Hall, nr Doncaster
September 28 Sunday
Betula & Bolton Percy Cemetery
Fairview, nr Summerbridge
October 1 Wednesday
Joan Royd House, Penistone

October 4 Sunday
Harlow Carr, Harrogate
October 12 Sunday
Mount Grace Priory, nr
  Osmotherly

Regular openings
For details see garden description

Brodsworth Hall, nr Doncaster
Burton Agnes Hall, Driffield
Castle Howard, nr York
Constable Burton Hall, nr Leyburn
Gilling Castle, Gilling East
Harewood House, nr Leeds
Harlow Carr, Harrogate
Land Farm, nr Hebden Bridge
Newby Hall, Ripon
Plants of Special Interest Nursery,
  Braithwell
Shandy Hall, Coxwold
Stockeld Park, Wetherby

By appointment only
*For telephone numbers and other
details see garden descriptions.
Private visits welcomed*

Holly Cottgae, Scholes
Lanhydrock Cottage, Skerne
Ling Beeches, Scarcroft, nr Leeds
Les Palmiers, Barnsley
Newby Hall & Gardens, Ripon
Tan Cottage, Cononley, nr Skipton
8 Welton Old Road, Welton
The White House, Husthwaite

DESCRIPTIONS OF GARDENS

¶**Aske** ᕷ✻ (Marquess & Marchioness of Zetland) Richmond. Aske is between the town of Richmond and village of Gilling West on the B6274. Capability Brown park with lake. Wonderful trees. Lots of daffodils, large walled garden, lovely woodland walks. Brand new formal terraced gardens designed by Martin Lane Fox. TEAS. *Adm £2 Chd under 12 £1. Sun April 20 (2-6)*

Bankfield ✻✻ (Norma & Mike Hardy) Edgerton. 1m N of Huddersfield. From Huddersfield ring rd follow A629 towards Halifax for ½m. Cross traffic lights at Blacker Rd, turn R after 100yds into Queens Rd. From M62, turn S at junction 24 towards Huddersfield on A629. After ¾m pass 30mph sign, turn L after 200yds into Queens Rd. ⅔-acre cottage style garden which has evolved over 14yrs from a neglected Victorian town garden. Large number of perennials incl many unusual and rare of interest to plant collectors. Rambling paths, informal beds, pond, gazebo, conifer arch, terraced beds around lawn. Huddersfield Examiner 'Best Kept Garden'. Featured in Amateur Gardening 1994. TEAS. *Adm £1 Chd 50p. Sun June 29 (11-5). Private visits also by appt, please Tel 01484 535830*

Beacon Hill House ✻✻ (Mr & Mrs D H Boyle) Langbar. 4m NW of Ilkley. 1¼m SE of A59 at Bolton Bridge. Fairly large garden sheltered by woodland 900′ up, on the southern slope of Beamsley Beacon. Several features of interest to garden historians survive from the original Victorian garden. Early flowering rhododendrons, large shrub roses, mixed borders, unusual hardy and half-hardy shrubs and climbers making use of south facing walls. TEAS. *Adm £1.50. Wed July 23 (2-6.30)*

Beamsley Hall ᕷ✻ (Marquess & Marchioness of Hartington) Beamsley. 5m E of Skipton. 6-acre traditional English garden with new plantings; including extensive herbaceous border and kitchen garden. Minor restrictions for wheelchairs. TEAS. Also at Bolton Abbey or at Devonshire Arms. *Adm £2 OAPs £1.50 Chd under 15 free. Sun July 13 (1-5)*

▲¶Beningbrough Hall ঐ᯽ (National Trust) 8m NW of York, off A19 to Thirsk. Signs from York ringroad. 7 acres surrounding early Georgian Country house. Recently restored and replanted walled kitchen garden. Double herbaceous borders, old roses and American garden. Come and picnic in the gardens. Guided garden tours. Head Gardener John Thallon. Special evening opening for NGS. *Adm £2.50 NT members £2 Chd 50p. Thurs June 12 (6-9)*

Betula & Bolton Percy Cemetery ঐ᯽❀ (Roger Brook Esq) Tadcaster. 5m E of Tadcaster 10m SW of York. Follow Bolton Percy signs off A64. An acre of old village churchyard gardened by Roger Brook, in which garden plants are naturalised and grow wild. Featured in numerous TV programmes, national magazines and publications. The National Dicentra Collection will be on view in Roger Brook's garden and allotment. Light lunches and TEAS in aid of Church. *Combined adm with* **Windy Ridge** *£2 Chd free. Sun April 13, June 22. Adm £1 Chd free. Sun Sept 28 (1- 5)*

Bishopscroft ঐ᯽ (Bishop of Sheffield) Sheffield. 3m W of centre of Sheffield. Follow A57 (signposted Glossop) to Broomhill then along Fulwood Road to traffic lights past Ranmoor Church. Turn Right up Gladstone Rd and then L into Snaithing Lane. Bishopscroft on R at top of hill. 1¼ acres of well-established suburban woodland garden. Small lake and stream; the aim is to present something of the feeling of countryside in the nearby Rivelin Valley; a good variety of elders, brambles and hollies; herbaceous, shrub and rose borders. TEAS. *Adm £1 Chd free (Share to the Church Urban Fund©). Sun July 20 (2-6)*

Blackbird Cottage ঐ❀ (Mrs Hazel Hoad) Scampston. 5m from Malton off A64 to Scarborough through Rillington turn L signposted Scampston only, follow signs. ⅓-acre plantswoman's garden made from scratch since 1986. A great wealth of interesting plants, with shrub, herbaceous border. Alpines are a speciality. Please visit throughout the day to ease pressure on a small but inspirational garden. Unusual plants for sale. Morning coffee and TEAS in aid of Scampston Village Hall & Church. *Adm £1.50 Chd free. Sun May 11 (10-5). Private visits welcome, please* **Tel 01944 758256**

Boston Spa Gardens ᯽❀ A659 1m S of Wetherby. Church St immed opp Central Garage. TEA at Acorn Cottage. *Combined adm £2.50 incl coffee/tea Chd 50p (Share to Northern Horticultural Society®). Sun April 27 (11-4)*

> **Acorn Cottage** (Mr & Mrs C M Froggatt) Garden adjacent to **Four Oaks**. A small walled Alpine rock garden with the plant collection spanning 70 yrs - 2 generations. *Also by appt April to May, please* **Tel 01937 842519**
>
> **Four Oaks** (Richard Bothamley & Glenn Hamilton) A medium-sized established flower and foliage garden of particular interest to flower arrangers. Pergolas and a series of garden 'rooms' on differing levels create a sense of intimacy. A wide selection of the genera - acer. Terrace with pots and a pool with good waterside plantings

Bridge Cottage ❀ (Mr & Mrs H Scott) Rievaulx. From Helmsley take the B1257 Stokesley rd then 1st turning on L to Scawton-Old Byland. Follow rd to bridge and cottage

is over bridge on R. Cottage garden with a wide variety of planting on different levels on both sides of Nettlebeck which is crossed by 3 foot bridges and joins R Rye nr C18 stone bridge. Newly developed bog garden and wild flower lawn on streamside. ¼m from the ruins of Cistercian Abbey. TEA. *Adm £1.50 Chd free. Suns July 20, 27 (10.30-5.30), Wed July 23 (2-5.30)*

■¶Brodsworth Hall ঐ᯽ (English Heritage) Nr Doncaster. Exit junction 37 A1 (M). A major continuing restoration of a large Victorian garden of special interest to garden historians. Scrub cleared to reveal vistas with statues, temple, summerhouse, ferndell, target range and rock garden newly planted with a collection of thymes. 1860 rose garden with pergola replanted with Portland roses. Formal garden mass planted with seasonal bedding, unique lawns maintained in traditional manner allowing proliferation and seeding of wild flowers. TEAS. *Adm £2.50 OAP £1.90 Chd £1.30. Open March 22 to October daily except Mons (unless Bank Hols). For further information* **Tel Martin Coss 01302 725108.** *For NGS Suns June 29, Sept 21 (12-5)*

Brookfield ᯽❀ (Dr & Mrs R L Belsey) Oxenhope. 5m SW of Keighley, take A629 towards Halifax. Fork R onto A6033 towards Haworth. Follow signs to Oxenhope. Turn L at Xrds in village. 200yds after P O fork R, Jew Lane. A little over 1 acre, intimate garden, including large pond with island and mallards. Many varieties of candelabra primulas and florindaes, azaleas, rhododendrons. Unusual trees and shrubs; screes; greenhouse and conservatory. TEA 50p. *Adm £1.50 Chd free. Sun, Wed June 8, 11 (2-6). Also by appt, please* **Tel 01535 643070**

●Burton Agnes Hall ঐ᯽ (Mrs S Cunliffe-Lister) nr Driffield. Burton Agnes is on A166 between Driffield & Bridlington. 8 acres of gardens incl lawns with clipped yew and fountains, woodland gardens and a walled garden containing a potager, herbaceous and mixed borders; maze with a thyme garden; jungle garden; campanula collection garden and coloured gardens containing giant games boards also collections of hardy geraniums, clematis, penstemons and many unusual perennials. 'Gardeners' Fair' *Adm £2.50 Chd £1 Sat, Sun June 7, 8;* specialist nurseries; gardening advice; dried flower & herb craft. TEAS. *Adm £2 Chd £1. April 1 to Oct 31 (11-5)*

Castle Farm Nurseries ঐ᯽❀ (Mr & Mrs K Wilson) Barmby Moor. Turn off A1079 Hull/York rd, ¾m from Barmby Moor at Hewson & Robinson's Garage, towards Thornton; ½m on R is sign for nursery. 1¼-acre garden created in 1978, which is constantly changing will be gradually extended to 2 acres. Incl trees, shrubs, mixed borders, scree and rock garden. Rhododendrons, water garden, heathers and conifers. Nursery open. Cream TEAS in aid of local Methodist Church. *Adm £1 Chd free. Suns May 25, June 1 (2-5.30)*

● Castle Howard ঐ᯽ (The Hon Simon Howard & Castle Howard Estate Ltd) York. 15m NE of York off the A64. 6m W of Malton. Partially suitable for wheelchairs. 300 acres of formal and woodland gardens laid out from the C18 to present day, including fountains, lakes, cascades and waterfalls. Ray Wood covers 50 acres and has a large and increasing collection of rhododendron species and hybrids amounting to 600 varieties. There is also a notable collection of acers, nothofagus, arbutus, styrax, magnolia and a number of conifers. There are walks covering spring, summer and autumn. Two formal rose gardens planted in the mid 1970's include a large assembly of old roses, china roses, bourbon roses, hybrid teas and floribunda. Refreshments are available in the House Restaurant, in the Lakeside Cafe and the Stables Cafe. During the summer months there are boat trips on the lake in an electric launch. There are gift shops in the House and Stable courtyard. Plant centre by the car park. TEAS. *Adm Grounds and Gardens £4 Chd £2. Every day March 14 to Nov 2 (10-4.30)*

The Chimney Place, 23 Parthian Road ⚘❀ (Mrs Paddy Forsberg) Bilton Grange, E Hull. Take Holderness Rd, R into Marfleet Lane, R at roundabout into Staveley Rd, L into Griffin Rd, Parthian Rd 1st on R. A small secluded, hedge enclosed, 30-yr-old garden, designed and maintained by owner, for the welfare of birds, fish, frogs and butterflies. 10 Victorian chimneys used as containers for alpines and rockery plants, many other containers. Recent features added, obelisk, wildlife pool, stumpery, summerhouse and rockery pool cascade. *Adm £1 Acc chd free. Sats May 10, June 14, July 12 (1.30-4.30). Private visits welcome, please* **Tel 01482 783804**

● **Constable Burton Hall Gardens** ⚘ (Charles Wyvill Esq) 3m E of Leyburn on A684, 6m W of A1. Large romantic garden, with terraced woodland walks; garden and nature trails. An array of naturalized daffodils set amidst ancient trees. Rock garden with choice plants. Fine John Carr house (not open) set in splendour of Wensleydale countryside. *Adm £2 OAPs £1.50 Chd 50p. March 22 to Oct 20 daily (9-6). Guided tours of gardens by appt, please* **Tel 01677 460225**

Creskeld Hall ⚘⚘❀ (The Trustees of Lady Stoddart-Scott) Arthington. 5m E of Otley on A659. Well established 3-4-acre large garden with woodland plantings; rhododendrons, azaleas, attractive water garden with canals, walled kitchen and flower garden. TEA. *Adm £1.50 Chd 50p. Sun June 8 (12-5)*

Derwent House ⚘⚘❀ (Dr & Mrs D G Lethem) Osbaldwick. On village green at Osbaldwick. 2m E of York city centre off A1079. Approx ¾ acre, a most attractive village garden extended in 1984 to provide a new walled garden with yew hedges and box parterres. Conservatories, terraces and herbaceous borders. TEAS. *Adm £1.50 Chd free. Sun June 15 (1.30-5)*

8 Dunstarn Lane ⚘ (Mr & Mrs R Wainwright) Adel. Leeds 16. From Leeds ring rd A6120 exit Adel, up Long Causeway. 4th junction R into Dunstarn Lane, entrance 1st R. 28 bus from Leeds centre stops near gate. Entire garden formerly known as The Heath. Featured on YTV and BBC TV. 2 acres of long herbaceous and rose borders incl 60 varieties of delphiniums. Large lawns for picnics. *Adm £1 Chd free. Suns July 6, 20 (2-6)*

By Appointment Gardens. These owners do not have a fixed opening day usually because they cannot accommodate large numbers or have insufficient parking space.

Elvington Gardens ⚘❀ 8m SE of York. From A1079, immed after leaving York's outer ring road turn S onto B1228 for Elvington. Light lunches and Teas in Village Hall in aid of village hall. *Combined adm £2.50 Chd free. Sun June 8 (11-5)*

   Brook House (Mr & Mrs Christopher Bundy) Old established garden with fine trees; herb garden with rustic summer house; kitchen garden and new pond garden

   Elvington Hall (Mr & Mrs Pontefract) 3-4-acre garden; terrace overlooking lawns with fine trees and views; sanctuary with fish pond

   Eversfield (David & Helga Hopkinson) Modest sized garden with a wide variety of unusual perennials; grasses and ferns divided by curved lawns and gravel beds. Small nursery. **Tel 01904 608332**

   Red House Farm (Dr & Mrs Euan Macphail) Entirely new garden created from a field 12 years ago. Fine collection of hardy perennials shrubs and roses. Courtyard with interesting plantings and half-acre young wood

Evergreens ⚘⚘❀ (Phil & Brenda Brock) Bilton. 5m E of Hull. Leave city by A165. Exit B1238. Bungalow ¼m on L nearly opposite the Asda Store. Over 1 acre developed since 1984. Features incl mosaics and sundials; tower; raised beds; rockeries and landscaped pond; Japanese garden; conifer, heather and mixed beds. Collection of dwarf conifers, many labelled. Photographs showing development of garden; small conifer/plant nursery open. Cream TEAS in aid of Dove House Hospice. *Adm £1 Acc chd free. Suns July 6, Sept 7 (2-5). Private visits welcome May to Sept* **Tel 01482 811365**

Fairview ⚘❀ (Michael D Myers) Smelthouses nr Summerbridge. From B6165 12m NW of Harrogate turn R in Wilsill Village to Smelthouses. Fairview is immed after the bridge on the R. A ¼-acre small plantsman's garden recently extended on a steep slope, packed with unusual bulbs, alpines and woodland plants. 3 NCCPG National Collections; anemone nemorosa, hepatica and primula marginata; alpine house, fernery and large pond; small nursery. Due to the situation of the garden there may be some necessary restrictions to entry if busy. TEA. *Adm £1.50 Chd free. Suns May 18, Sept 28 (2-6). Private visits by appt, please* **Tel 01423 780291**

Fernwood ⚘❀ (Dick & Jean Feaster) Cropton. 4m NW of Pickering. From A170 turn at Wrelton signed Cropton. 1-acre garden created by the owners in the last 9yrs, containing herbaceous borders, a white garden, a scented garden, species and old roses, a wide variety of interesting plants, with a view of the N Yorkshire moors beyond. Morning coffee & TEAS. *Adm £1.50 Chd free. Sun July 6 (11-5)*

Gilling Castle ⚘ (The Rt Revd the Abbot of Ampleforth) Gilling East, 18m N of York. Medium-sized terraced garden with steep steps overlooking golf course. Unsuitable for handicapped or elderly. *Adm £1.50 Chd free. For NGS July & Aug daily dawn to dusk. Large parties welcome, please* **Tel 014393 206**

¶**Grey Shaw Syke Cottage** ❀❀ (John & Cynthia Wareing) Ogden. 4m N of Halifax on A629. Please park in Ogden Water car park. Pretty ⅓-acre cottage garden with many attractive features developed from a field and maintained by present owners. Good collection of old roses, wide range of herbaceous perennials, wildlife pond and small vegetable plot. The garden is set within magnificent moorland scenery at over 1000'. TEAS. *Adm £1 Chd 50p. Sun July 20 (11-5) Private visits welcome summer weekends, please* Tel 01422 240148

Grimston Gardens ❀ The hamlet of Grimston is 1m S of Gilling East 7m S of Helmsley 17m N of York on B1363. Follow sign 1m S of Gilling East. TEA. *Adm £2 Chd free. Sun, Thurs July 6, 10 (1.30-5.30)*

Bankside House (Clive & Jean Sheridan) ½-acre garden established some thirty years ago. Mature plantings together with newer developments, incl semi-formal beds, Japanese area, shaded walk and recently created parterre

Grimston Manor Farm (Richard & Heather Kelsey) ½-acre garden with recent extension. The intricate design is profusely planted with a wide collection of herbaceous plants; trees and shrubs incorporating fine country views and old farm buildings

¶**Hallgarth** ⅋❀(Mr & Mrs John Hinchliffe) Ottringham. Turn N in Otteringham on A1033 Hull to Withernsea rd, signed Halsham. ¾m 1st L over former railway crossing. 1-acre informal country garden developed and maintained by owners from an initial design for part by John Brookes. Interesting trees, shrubs and plants, many for use by flower arrangers. New pond garden, flowering cherries, dwarf rhododendrons, bush roses, irises etc. Cakes and preserves stall. Teas at **The White Cottage, Halsham**. *Adm £1.50 Chd free. Suns April 27, June 22, Aug 17 (2-5)*

●**Harewood House** ⅋❀ (Harewood House Trust) Leeds. 9m N of Leeds on A61. Approx 80 acres of gardens within 1000 acres of Lancelot 'Capability' Brown landscaped parkland, formal terraces recently restored to original Sir Charles Barry design, 2m of box edging surrounding seasonal displays of Victorian bedding enhanced by Italianate fountains and statues, charming informal walks through woods around the lake to the cascade and rock garden with collections of hosta and rhododendrons. TEAS Cafeteria. *Adm gardens and grounds £4 OAPs £3 Chd £2. Daily March 15 to Oct 26 (10-4.30). Weekends Nov to Dec. For NGS private groups by appt, please* Tel Trevor Nicholson 0113 288 6331

■ ¶**Harlow Carr Botanical Gardens** ❀ (Northern Horticultural Society) Harrogate. On B6162 (Harrogate - Otley) 1m W of town centre. 68 acres developed over past 50yrs as a Botanic garden ("A Wisley for the North") incl 5 national collections. Landscaped to incl heather, bulb, rock, scented and foliage gardens, herbaceous borders, vegetable, fruit and flower trials, alpine houses. Extensive woodland and streamside plantings, winter garden and wild flower meadow. Museum of Gardening, library and model village. Restaurant. *Adm £3.40 OAP £2.60 Chd free. Open all year. For NGS Suns April 6, Oct 4 (9.30-6)*

Helmsley Gardens ⅋ Teashops in Helmsley. *Adm £1 each gdn. Chd free. Sun June 15 (2-6)*

Ryedale House (Dr & Mrs J A Storrow) 41 Bridge Street. On A170, 3rd house on R after bridge into Helmsley from Thirsk and York. ¼-acre walled garden; varieties of flowers, shrubs, trees, herbs. *Private visits welcome, please* Tel 01439 770231

Rye Hill ❀❀ (Dr & Mrs C Briske) 15 Station Rd. Follow yellow signs from bridge on A170. ¼-acre site interestingly divided into compartments. Intensely planted with many unusual varieties of flowering shrubs, roses, clematis and perennials. Baskets, containers, pond and well stocked conservatory. TEA. *Also open Wed July 2 (2-6). Private visits welcome: please write*

Hemble Hill Farm ⅋❀ (Miss S K Edwards) Guisborough, on A171 between Nunthorpe and Guisborough opp the Cross Keys Inn. Dogs welcome, 7-acre garden facing the Cleveland Hills with formal and informal areas incl lake; young arboretum; heather, rhododendrons, large conservatory. TEAS. *Adm £1.50 Chd free. Sun May 11 (2-5.30). Private visits welcome June to Sept, please* Tel 01287 632511

High Farm ❀❀ (Mr & Mrs G R Cooper) Bilton. 5m E of Hull City Centre, take A165 Brid Rd, turn off at Ganstead Lane, onto B1238 to Bilton. Turn L opp Church. High Farm is at the bottom of Limetree Lane. Drive straight up the drive past the house, where parking is available in paddock. A mature garden of approx 1½ acres, harmoniously created and maintained by its present owners around a Georgian farmhouse. Many trees, shrubs, old species and climbing roses, herbaceous plants, as well as the thriving traditional kitchen garden. Flower arrangers will find much to interest them in the many unusual and rare plants to be found in the numerous beds and borders. TEAS. *Adm £1.50 Chd free (Share to RBL®). Suns May 25, June 29 (1-5)*

Hillbark ❀❀ (Malcom Simm & Tim Gittins) Bardsey. 4m SW of Wetherby, turn W off A58 into Church Lane. The garden is 150yds on L just before Church. Please use village hall car park (turn R opp Church into Woodacre Lane). A young 1-acre country garden. Past winner Sunday Express 'Large Garden of the Year'. Mixed planting with some English roses; paved and gravel terraces; descending to ponds and stream with ducks and marginal planting. TEAS. *Adm £1.50 Chd 50p (Share to Cookridge Hospital Cancer Research®). Suns May 11, June 22, Sept 7 (11-5). Private visits welcome by appt May to July, please* Tel 01937 572065

Holly Cottage, Leas Gardens (Mr & Mrs John Dixon) Scholes. 8m S of Huddersfield on A616. Turn W at signpost to Scholes. ½-acre sloping garden of interest created from a field in 1988 with raised alpine bed and paved area with troughs; pond with small bog garden, rockery and herbaceous borders with good selection of plants. *Adm £1.50 Chd free. Private visits welcome Feb to end Oct, please* Tel 01484 684083/662614

Holly Cottage, Wressle ⅋❀❀ (Maureen Read) 1m N of the A63 between Howden and Selby. From an overgrown field and orchard in 1986 to what is a seemingly long-established ¾-acre garden with ponds, grass walks and woodland area. Mixed beds and borders feature many uncommon perennial plants. TEA. *Adm £1.50 Chd free. Sun July 13 (2-5)*

32 Holly Bank Road ✿ (Mr & Mrs D Matthews) Holgate. A59 (Harrogate Rd) from York centre. Cross iron bridge, turn L after Kilima hotel (Hamilton Drive East). Fork slightly L (Hollybank Rd) after 400yds. Garden designer's small town garden planted for yr-round interest. Shrubs, small trees, climbers, clematis and container plants. Cobbled fountain, 4 separate patio areas, small pond. Finalist in Daily Mail National Gardens Competition. *Adm £1.50 incl tea Chd free. Suns June 15, July 20 (11-5), Wed Sept 10 (2-6.30). Private visits for parties of 6-10 by appt, please* **Tel 01904 627533**

Hovingham Hall ✿✿ (Sir Marcus & Lady Worsley) 8m W of Malton. In Hovingham village, 20m N of York; on B1257 midway between Malton and Helmsley. Medium-sized garden; yew hedges, shrubs and herbaceous borders. C18 dovecote and riding school; cricket ground. TEAS in aid of Hovingham Church. *Adm £2 Chd free. Sun June 22 (2-6). Enquiries* **Tel 01653 628206**

Hunmanby Grange ✿✿✿ (Mr & Mrs T Mellor) Wold Newton. Hunmanby Grange is a farm 12½m SE of Scarborough, situated between Wold Newton and Hunmanby on the rd from Burton Fleming to Fordon. The garden has been created from exposed open field over 13 yrs, on top of the Yorkshire Wolds near the coast, satisfying a plantswoman's and a young family's needs. Foliage colour, shape and texture have been most important in forming mixed borders, a gravel garden, pond garden, orchard and laburnum tunnel. TEAS in aid of St Cuthbert's Church, Burton Fleming. *Adm £1.50 Chd free. Suns June 8, July 6 (11-5). Private visits welcome, Wed afternoons April to Sept please* **Tel 01723 891636**

Il Giardino ✿✿✿ (Peter & Marian Fowler) Bilton. 5m E of Hull City Centre. Take A165 Hull to Bridlington Rd. Turn off; take B1238 to Bilton Village. Turn L opp. St Peter's Church. "Il Giardino" is at bottom of Limetree Lane on L. No. 63. Once neglected garden approx ⅓ acre redesigned and revived over last 9yrs by present owners. Features incl mixed borders and island beds stocked with many old-fashioned pinks, erodiums, hardy geraniums and other unusual plants, shrubs and trees. Attractive beech hedge, small allotment, herb garden, orchard of old apple trees; pear; plum; cherries; medlar and filberts; entwined with many types of clematis. Cedarwood greenhouse with a collection of named pelargoniums; potted citrus; fig tree and other less common plants. TEAS. *Adm £1 Chd free. Suns May 4, 25, June 29 (12-5)*

Joan Royd House ✿✿ (Mrs M Griffiths & Dr A Owen Griffiths) Penistone. 13m NW of Sheffield. M1 junction 37 A628 (Manchester), through Penistone on Stocksbridge rd. 1st R at derestriction sign. An 'all the yr' plantsman's garden of 1½ acres at 900' close to Peak Park and Holmfirth (Last of the Summer Wine). It offers styles from formal to wild and wooded. Various gardens incl old, single and English roses. Topiary, interesting borders incl many varieties of hosta, hedera, campanula, hardy geranium, hardy fuchsia and the genus polypodiaceae. Greenhouses,

shady garden room and small pinetum. The dell has large species and shrub roses by a small stream. Seats and gazebos abound. TEAS July 27 only. *Adm £2 Chd £1. Sun July 27 (11-5). Weds March 5, April 2, May 7, June 4, Sept 3, Oct 1 (2-5)*

Kelberdale ✿✿✿ (Stan & Chris Abbott) Knaresborough. 1m from Knaresborough on B6164 Wetherby rd. House on L immed after new ring rd roundabout. Attractive owner-made and maintained, medium-sized plantsman's garden with river views. Full of yr-round interest with large herbaceous border, conifer and colour beds. Alpines and pond. TEA. *Adm £1.50 Chd free. Suns June 8, 29 (10-6) Group visits welcome, please* **Tel 01423 862140**

54a Keldgate ✿✿ (Lenore & Peter Greensides) Beverley. Half-way between the double mini roundabout at SW entrance to Beverley on the B1230 and Beverley Minster. No private parking. ½-acre 'secret' garden within the charming town of Beverley. Largely created and solely maintained by the present owners over the last 18yrs. Clematis in variety, herbaceous plantings and shrubs, an inner garden of old roses, underplanted with peonies and geraniums; kitchen garden, fruit trees and irises, spring bulbs in season. TEAS in aid of Shelter on June 29 only. Plant stall on May 4. *Adm £1 Chd free. Suns May 4, June 29 (2-5). Group visits welcome, please* **Tel 01482 866708**

80 Lairgate ✿✿ (Mary & David Palliser) Beverley. In town centre on 1-way system. Enclosed ⅓-acre garden developed and maintained since 1986 by present owners, with many plants of interest to flower arrangers. Shrubs, climbers, old roses, bulbs, herbaceous and tender perennials, to provide yr-round and horticultural interest. *Adm £1 Acc chd free. Sun June 29 (2-5)*

●**Land Farm** ✿✿ (J Williams Esq) Colden, nr Hebden Bridge. From Halifax at Hebden Bridge go through 2 sets traffic lights; take turning circle to Heptonstall. Follow signs to Colden. After 2¾m turn R at 'no thru' road, follow signs to garden. 4 acres incl alpine; herbaceous, heather, formal and newly developing woodland garden. Elevation 1000ft N facing. Has featured on 'Gardeners' World'. C17 house (not open). Art Gallery. *Adm £2 Chd free. May to end Aug; Open weekends and Bank Hols (10-5). By appt parties welcome evenings during week. Adm £3 incl refreshments, please* **Tel 01422 842260**

Lanhydrock Cottage ✿✿ (Mrs Jan Joyce) Skerne. 3m SE Driffield; follow signs to Skerne. Delightful small cottage garden of much interest and love, old-fashioned roses, herbs, fragrant perennials and wild flowers etc. Light refreshments. *Adm £1 Chd free. Private visits welcome, please* **Tel 01377 253727**

30 Latchmere Rd ✿✿ (Mr & Mrs Joe Brown) Moor Grange, Leeds 16. A660 from City Centre to Lawnswood Ring Rd roundabout; turn sharp left on to ring rd A6120 for ⅓m to 3rd opening on left Fillingfir Drive; right to top of hill, turn right at top by pillar box, then left almost opposite into Latchmere Road, 3rd house on left. Bus stop at gate (Bus every 15 mins); 74 & 76 from City Centre; 54 from Briggate; 73 from Greenthorpe. Cars and coaches to park in Latchmere Drive please. A small garden full of interest; fern garden; herbaceous borders; alpine garden; glade; 2 pools; patio built of local York stone; sink gardens; collection of 80 clematis. *Adm £1.50 Chd 50p. Suns June 29, July 13, 20, 27, Aug 3 (2-5). Parties welcome, by written appt*

'Les Palmiers' 106 Vaughan Road ❀❀ (Richard Darlow & Christine Hopkins) Barnsley. 2m NW Barnsley Town centre. From M1 junction 37 take A628 towards Barnsley. After ½m turn L at major Xrds to hospital. Turn L at hospital Xrds into Gawber Rd, after ½m turn L into Vernon Way. Vaughan Rd is 1st cul-de-sac on R. Mediterranean garden to rear 60ft by 30ft. Planted entirely with 'warm climate' trees, shrubs, perennials, incl many tender subjects permanently planted eg palms, cordylines, yuccas, cacti and eucalyptus; spectacular flowering shrubs and exotic plants in pots. Mainly evergreen but most colourful April to Oct. Featured in BBC 2 Gardeners World, and many national magazine publications incl Journal of the European Palm Society and Practical Gardening Magazine. TEA. *Adm £1.50 OAP £1. Private visits welcome by appt only, weekends all yr, also evenings mid summer please* **Tel 01226 291474.** *Not suitable for young children due to many spiky plants!*

Ling Beeches ♿❀❀ (Mrs Arnold Rakusen) Ling Lane, Scarcroft 7m NE of Leeds. A58 mid-way between Leeds and Wetherby; at Scarcroft turn W into Ling Lane, signed to Wike on brow of hill; garden ⅓m on right. 2-acre woodland garden designed by owner emphasis on labour-saving planting; unusual trees and shrubs; ericaceous plants, some species roses, conifers, ferns, interesting climbers. Featured in The English Woman's Garden other publications and TV. *Private visits welcome by appt, please* **Tel 01132 892450**

Littlethorpe Gardens ♿❀❀ nr Ripon. Littlethorpe lies 1½m SE of Ripon indicated by signpost close to Ripon Racecourse on the B6265 twixt Ripon and the A1. Teas at Littlethorpe Village Hall (nr Church). *Combined adm £2.50 Chd free. Sun June 15 (1.30-5.30)*
  Deanswood (Mrs J Barber) Garden of approx 1½ acres created during the last 10 years. Herbaceous borders; shrubs; special features streamside garden; 3 ponds with many unusual bog/marginal plants. Adjacent nursery open. *Private visits also welcome, please* **Tel 01765 603441**
  Field Cottage (Mr & Mrs Richard Tite) A 6yr-old 1-acre plantsman's garden with walled garden, small pond, raised sleeper beds, gravel garden, vegetable plot, herbs, Victorian style greenhouse and extensive range of unusual plants in containers
  Littlethorpe House (Mr & Mrs James Hare) 2 acres with many beautiful varieties of old-fashioned roses; extensive established mixed herbaceous and shrub borders

5 Lockington Road ♿ (Miss E Stephenson) Lund. Lund is off B1248 Beverley-Malton Rd. Small walled garden converted from old fold yard on edge of village with old-fashioned roses and cottage garden plants. "Charmingly English". *Adm £1 Chd free. Sun June 29 (2-5). Private parties of 10 and over welcome, please* **Tel 01377 217284**

Low Askew ❀❀ (Mr & Mrs Martin Dawson-Brown) Cropton. 5m NW of Pickering between the villages of Cropton and Lastingham. Situated in beautiful valley with stream and walk to R Seven. A garden with a huge wealth of plants, shrubs and trees. Old-fashioned and species pelargoniums a speciality. Plant stalls by local nurserymen. Picnic area by river. Morning coffee, light lunches & TEAS in aid of NSPCC. *Adm £2 Chd free. Sun June 22 (11-5)*

Lullaby ❀❀ (Michael Whitton) Hull. From the A165 (Holderness Rd), travel along Saltshouse Rd towards Sutton Village. Turn R into Dunvegan Rd, R into Barra Close and R again, no 22 on L. Created by the owners from a building site, this compact 40′ × 60′ garden has developed into a peaceful retreat welcoming fox, squirrel, butterflies, frogs and a large variety of birds. A curving lawn leads the eye from a paved terrace, around herbaceous borders and an island bed and incl a pergola and a summerhouse. A small courtyard garden and a water feature. TEA. *Adm £1 Chd free. Suns June 15, July 6 (2-5). Private visits of minimum 10 people, please* **Tel 01482 783517**

¶**Manor Farm** ♿❀❀ (Mrs Gilda Brader) Thixendale. 10m SE of Malton, unclassified rd through Birdsall, ½m up hill, turn L at Xrds for Thixendale - 3m, 1st farm on R. 17m E of York, turn off A166 rd at the top of Garrowby Hill follow signs for Thixendale, 4m turn into village, drive through to end, farm on L. Created in the last 8yrs, nestling in a frost pocket and wind tunnel! 1-acre garden featuring a pergola, rose garden, alpine area, courtyard, small knot garden and large lawns surrounded by mixed beds. TEA. *Adm £1.50 Chd free. Sun July 13 (11-5)*

Maspin House ♿❀❀ (Dr & Mrs H Ferguson) Hillam Common Lane. 4m E of A1 on A63. Turn R in Monk Fryston after Thrust Garage. L at T junction. Continue for 1m. Please park in field behind house. Garden of 1½ acres started in 1985. Created and maintained by enthusiastic plant collector and handy husband. Beautiful and unusual plants plus many interesting features incl ponds. TEAS July 6 in aid of Monk Fryston School. *Adm £1.50 Chd free. Sun July 6 (2-6) Wed July 9 (4-7). Private visits welcome, by appt please,* **Tel 01977 684922**

The Mews Cottage ❀❀ (Mrs Pat Clarke) 1 Brunswick Drive, Harrogate. W of town centre. From Cornwall Rd, N side of Valley Gardens, 1st R (Clarence Dr), 1st L (York Rd), first L (Brunswick Dr). A small garden on a sloping site of particular interest to hardy planters. Full of unusual and familiar plants but retaining a feeling of restfulness. A courtyard with trompe l'oeil and a gravelled area enclosed by trellising, provide sites for part of a large collection of clematis. Winner Daily Mail/RHS National Garden Competition 96. TEAS. *Adm £1.50 Chd 50p. Wed June 25 (2-5.30). Private visits for groups, societies and parties welcome, please* **Tel 01423 566292**

Millgate House ❀❀ (Austin Lynch & Tim Culkin) Richmond Market Place. House is located at bottom of Market Place opp Barclays Bank. SE walled town garden overlooking the R Swale. Although small the garden is full of character, enchantingly secluded with plants and shrubs. Foliage plants incl ferns, hostas; old roses and interesting selection of clematis, small trees and shrubs. Featured in

'Homes & Gardens', 'Yorkshire Life', 'Daily Mail' and 'The Sunday Times'. Winner of 'Daily Mail'/RHS 1995 National Garden Competition. Full of ideas for small gardens. *Adm £1.50 Chd 50p. Sun July 6 (8am-8pm). Parties welcome, please* **Tel 01748 823571**

▲¶**Mount Grace Priory** ✿❀ (English Heritage) Saddlebridge. 9m N of Thirsk A19. Founded in 1398 the Priory is the best preserved Carthusian Charter House. Monks lived hermit-like in their own cell, private herb garden (now restored). Nature trail fruit trees, medieval fish ponds, rhododendron, acer collections, wildflowers, spring bulbs, Victorian herbaceous border. Plentiful wildlife. *Adm £2.50 Concessions £1.80 Chd £1.20. For NGS Suns June 29, Oct 12 (10-6) last admission 5.30*

Nawton Tower Garden ♿❀ (Douglas Ward Trust No. 4) Nawton, 5m NE of Helmsley. From A170, between Helmsley and Nawton village, at Beadlam turn N 2½m to Nawton Tower. Large garden; heathers, rhododendrons, azaleas, shrubs. Tea Helmsley and Kirbymoorside. *Adm £1.50 Chd 50p. Sat, Sun, Mon May 24, 25, 26 (2-6); private visits welcome, please* **Tel 01439 771218**

Netherwood House ♿❀ (Mr & Mrs Peter Marshall) 1m W of Ilkley on A65 towards Skipton; drive on L, car parking adjacent to house. Daffodils, spring flowering shrubs, duck pond; new rockery; bulb and stream plantings. Lovely views up Wharfedale. TEAS. *Adm £1.50 Chd free. Easter Sun March 30 (2-5.30)*

● **Newby Hall & Gardens** ♿✿❀ (R E J Compton Esq) Ripon. 40-acres extensive gardens laid out in 1920s; full of rare and beautiful plants. Winner of HHA/Christie's Garden of the Year Award 1987. Formal seasonal gardens, reputed longest double herbaceous borders to R. Ure and National Collection holder Genus Cornus. C19 statue walk; woodland discovery walk. Miniature railway and adventure gardens for children. Lunches & TEAS in licensed Garden Restaurant. The Newby shop and plant stall. *Adm Garden only £4, OAPs £3.30, Disabled/Chd £2.70. Easter to Sept daily ex Mons (Open Bank Hols) (Gardens 11-5.30; House 12-5). Group bookings and further details from Administrator* **Tel 01423 322583**

▲**Norton Conyers** ♿❀ (Sir James & Lady Graham) Ripon. 4m NW of Ripon. Take Melmerby and Wath sign off A61 Ripon-Thirsk. Large C18 walled garden of interest to garden historians. Interesting borders and orangery; some hardy plants for sale. House which was visited by Charlotte Bronte, the original of 'Thornfield Hall' in 'Jane Eyre', also open. TEA. *Collecting box for NGS (£1 Chd free). For NGS Sun June 15 (2-5)*

The Old Rectory, Mirfield ♿✿❀ (G Bottomley Esq) Exit 25 of M62; take A62 then A644 thru Mirfield Village; after approx ½m turn L up Blake Hall Drive, then 1st L, Rectory at top of hill. 1-acre garden surrounding Elizabethan Rectory. Mixed borders, Mulberry tree dating from C16; well, pergola and small ornamental pond. TEA. *Adm £1 Chd free. Sun July 6 (2-5)*

The Old Rectory, Nunburnholme ♿✿ (Mr & Mrs M Stringer) A1079 Hull-York rd, turn to Nunburnholm in Hayton and follow signposts. Field parking. Owner maintained, large garden for chalk loving plants, with stream and herbaceous borders blending into surrounding countryside. TEAS in aid of RNLI. *Adm £1 Chd free. Sun June 29 (1.30-5)*

Old Sleningford ♿❀ (Mr & Mrs James Ramsden) 5m W of Ripon, off B6108. After North Stainley take 1st or 2nd L, follow sign to Mickley for 1m. An excellent example of an early C19 house and garden with original layout of interest to garden historians. Many acres with extensive lawns, interesting trees; woodland walk and Victorian fernery; exceptionally lovely lake and islands, streamside walk; watermill in the walled kitchen garden; long herbaceous border; yew and huge beech hedges. Flowers and grasses grown for drying. Several plant and other stalls. Home-made TEAS. *Adm £2 Chd 50p (Share to N of England Christian Healing Trust®). Bank Hol Mon May 5, Sun May 25, Mon May 26 (1-5). Groups catered for, also private visits by appt, please* **Tel 01765 635229**

The Old Vicarage ✿❀ (Mr & Mrs R Marshall) Whixley, between York and Harrogate. ¾m from A59 3m E of A1. A delightful ¾-acre walled flower garden with mixed borders, unusual shrubs, climbers, roses, hardy and half-hardy perennials, bulbs. Paths and garden structures leading to new vistas using the gardens natural contours. Courtyard with small herb garden. TEAS. *Adm £1.50 Chd free. Wed June 18 (2-8)*

¶**Oliver Lodge** ♿✿ (Mrs M Beaulah) Hessle. ¼m from Humber Bridge roundabout, take exit marked A1105 signposted Hessle. 2nd turning on L, Lodge 100yds on L. The garden site is an old chalk pit, approx 1½ acres, with large trees and lawns. Planned in the C18 style with gazebo, mount and statuary. The banks are planted with shrubs chosen for their leaf colour and form. *Adm £1.50 Chd free. Sun 17 Aug (11-5)*

▲**Parcevall Hall Gardens** ❀ (Walsingham College (Yorkshire Properties) Ltd) Skyreholme, 9m N of Skipton signs from B6160 Burnsall rd or off B6265 Grassington-Pateley Bridge rd. 20-acres in Wharfedale; shelter belts of mixed woodland, fine trees; terraces; fishponds; rock garden; tender shrubs incl desfontainea; crinodendron; camellia; bulbs; rhododendrons; orchard for picnics, old varieties of apples; autumn colour; birds in woodland; splendid views. TEA. *Adm £2 Chd (5-12 yrs) 50p. For NGS Sun June 22 (10-5)*

Park House ♿❀ (Mr & Mrs A T Preston) Moreby. 6m S of York. Between Naburn and Stillingfleet on B1222. Approx ½-acre, gardened since 1988, set within a 2-acre walled garden using some of the 16' walls to display a wide variety of wall shrubs and climbers. Some herbaceous and mixed shrub borders. Large conservatory. TEAS. *Adm £1.20 Chd free (Share to Asthma Research Campaign®). Sun June 29 (2-5.30)*

Parkview ♿✿❀ (Mr & Mrs Christopher Powell) 45 Church Street, South Cave. 12m W of Hull on A63 turn N to S Cave on A1034. In centre of village turn L by chemists, 250yds on L black gates under arch. ⅓-acre shel-

General Information. For general information on the use of this book see Page 17.

tered garden of perennial and shrub packed beds, pond and bog bed. Rose/honeysuckle pergola underplanted with 70+ varieties of hosta. Organic fruit and vegetable garden. TEAS. *Adm £1 Chd free if on lead (Share to Church Yard Fund©). Sun June 15 (2-5). Private visits welcome, please* Tel 01430 423739

Pennyholme (Mr C J Wills) Fadmoor, 5m NW of Kirbymoorside. From A170 between Kirbymoorside and Nawton, turn N, ½m before Fadmoor turn L, signed 'Sleightholmedale only' continue N up dale, across 3 cattlegrids, to garden. No Buses. Large, wild garden on edge of moor with rhododendrons, azaleas, primulas, shrubs. TEAS in aid of St Nicolas, Barnsdale. *Adm £2 Chd £1 (Share to St Nicolas, Barnsdale®). Sats, Suns May 31, June 1, 7, 8 (11.30-5)*

■ **Plants of Special Interest Nursery** &❀ (Mr & Mrs Peter Dunstan) Braithwell. A1(M) junction 36 through Old Edington. From M18 Junction 1 take A631. Turn L in Maltby to Braithwell. Nursery in centre of village. ¼-acre Mediterranean-style garden with patio and water feature adjacent to recently planted raised beds in small walled cottage garden. Nursery with excellent half-hardy unusual plants and bulbs incl zantedeschia Green Goddess. From August a colourful display of ornamental gourds, squashes and pumpkins growing behind the nursery. Menu featuring edible gourds in Tea-room. Lunches/ TEAS. *Adm £1 Chd 50p. Nursery open March to Dec Tues to Sats (9-5.30). Suns and Bank Hol Mons 10-5. For NGS Suns June 1, July 13, Sept 14 (10-5). Group bookings, please* Tel 01709 812328

55 Rawcliffe Drive ✄❀ (Mr & Mrs J Goodyer) Clifton. A19 from York centre, turn R at Clifton Green traffic lights (Water Lane). Rawcliffe Drive is 1st L after Clifton Hotel. A 30yd by 10yd suburban garden on 2 levels. Planted for yr-round interest with excellent use of foliage and colour. Many unusual shrubs, herbaceous plants and bulbs; around 90 clematis. *Adm £1.50 Chd free incl TEA. Suns June 8, July 27 (11-5). Also private visits welcome April to July, please* Tel 01904 638489

Rudston House (Mr & Mrs Simon Dawson) Rudston, nr Driffield. On B1253 5m W of Bridlington. S at Bosville Arms for approx 300yds. Birthplace of authoress Winifred Holtby. Victorian farmhouse (not open) and 2 acres of garden with fine old trees, lawns, paths with clipped box hedges, interesting potager with named vegetable varieties, roses, hosta bed and short woodland walk. Plenty of seats. TEAS in aid of Rudston Church. *Adm £1.50 Chd free. Sun July 13 (11-5)*

Saltmarshe Hall &✄❀ (Mr & Mrs Philip Bean) Howden. From Howden (M62, Jct 37) follow signs to Howden, Howdendyke and Saltmarshe. House in park W of Saltmarshe village. Large lawns, fine old trees, R Ouse and a Regency house with courtyards provide a setting for shrubs, climbers, herbaceous plants and roses. Of special interest to plantsmen and garden designers are a pond garden, a walled garden and a large herbaceous border. Approx 10 acres. TEAS in aid of Laxton Church. *Adm £1.50 Acc chd free. Sun June 15 (2-5.30). Private visits welcome, please* Tel 01430 430199

¶**Scampston Hall** &✄❀ (Sir Charles & Lady Legard) Malton. 5m E of Malton off A64 Leeds to Scarborough rd. Through Rillington turn L signed Scampston only. Follow signs. 8 acres of garden in process of refurbishment; includes woodland walk by lakes created by Capability Brown with palladian bridge, restored walk-in rock garden built in C19 and part of a walled garden with glass houses, double herbaceous borders, formal rose garden. *Adm £2 Chd under 12 free. Sun June 15 (1-5)*

Secret Garden, 10 Sherwood Grove ✄❀ (Mr & Mrs A C Downes) Acomb. From York on A59, turn L into Beckfield Lane opp Manor School, ¼m before Western Ring Rd. Take 1st R, 2nd L. ¾-acre garden hidden behind suburban semi, developed and extended over 15 yrs. Features rockeries, pond, fruit cage but primarily extensive mixed plantings incl many unusual plants. 4 greenhouses with vines, cactus, succulent & tender plant collections. Small Nursery. TEA. *Adm £1 Chd free. Suns June 8, July 27 (10-5). Also private visits welcome, please* Tel 01904 796360

■ **Shandy Hall** ✄❀ (The Laurence Sterne Trust) Coxwold, N of York. From A19. 7m from both Easingwold and Thirsk turn E signed Coxwold. Home of C18 author Laurence Sterne. Walled gardens, 1 acre of bulbs, unusual perennials, old roses in low walled beds. Another acre in old quarry of trees, shrubs, bulbs, climbers and wild flowers. Season long interest. Featured in the Good Garden Guide, Country Life and Period Living. Shop. Unusual plants for sale. Wheelchairs with help. Teas in Coxwold (School house Tea Room; home baking). *Adm £1.50 Chd 75p (Share to Laurence Sterne Trust®). House open Wed & Sun (2-4.30) May 1 to Sept 30. Groups by appt. For NGS Suns May 4, 25, July 13, Weds June 25, July 9 (2-5).* Tel 01347 868465

Sinnington Gardens ✄ 4m W of Pickering on A170. A small group of gardens which featured in Channel 4 series 'Nature Perfected', will be open in picturesque village. Tickets and parking on village green. TEAS. *Combined adm £2.50 Chd free. Sun May 4 (11-5)*

Sleightholme Dale Lodge ❀ (Mrs Gordon Foster; Dr & Mrs O James) Fadmoor, 3m N of Kirkbymoorside. 1m from Fadmoor. Hillside garden; walled rose garden; herbaceous borders. *Not* suitable for wheelchairs. No coaches. TEAS and plants not available May 31, June 1). *Adm £1.50 Chd 50p. Sat, Sun May 31, June 1 (11.30-5) Sat, Sun July 19, 20 (2-7)*

Snilesworth &❀ (Viscount Ingleby) Halfway between Osmotherley and Hawnby. From Osmotherley bear L sign posted Snilesworth, continue for 4½m across the moor. 4½m from Hawnby on Osmotherley Rd. Turn R at top of hill. Garden created from moorland in 1957 by present owners father; rhododendrons and azaleas in a 30 acre woodland setting with magnificent views of the Hambleton and Cleveland hills; snowgums grown from seed flourish in a sheltered corner. TEAS. *Adm £1.50 Chd 50p (Share to Hawnby Church®). Sun June 8 (2-5)*

The Spaniels &✄❀ (Janet & Dennis Tredgett) Hensall. 2m N of M62, 5m S of Selby. Turn E off A19 to Hensall. Field Lane is last turn on R in Hensall Village. A new ⅔-

acre garden planted over the last 4yrs on previous farmland. Long mixed borders in colour themes, incl young conifers, trees and shrubs, divided by curved lawns with island beds. Small wildlife pond. TEAS. *Adm £1 Chd 50p. Suns May 11, July 27 (12-5). Private visits welcome, please* **Tel 01977 661858**

Springfield House &✿❀ (Mr & Mrs S B Milner) Tockwith. 5m E of Wetherby; 1m off B1224. Garden at west end of village. 1½ acres. Well established walled garden with herbaceous borders, water and rock gardens. Rose and conifer garden; shrub walk. Wide variety of plants. TEA. *Adm £1.50 Chd free. Sun June 1 (2-5)*

Stillingfleet Lodge &✿❀ (Mr & Mrs J Cook) Stillingfleet 6m S of York, from A19 York-Selby take B1222 signed Sherburn in Elmet. ½-acre plantsman's garden subdivided into smaller gardens, each one based on a colour theme with emphasis on the use of foliage plants. Wild flower meadow and natural pond; new 50 metre double herbaceous borders, holders of National Collection of Pulmonaria. Adjacent nursery will be open. Homemade Teas May 18 in village hall in aid of local church. *Adm £1.50 Chd over 5yrs 50p. Suns May 18, June 29 (1.30-5.30)*

■ **Stockeld Park** &✿❀ (Mr & Mrs P G F Grant) 2m NW of Wetherby. On A661 Wetherby-Harrogate Rd; from Wetherby after 2m entrance 2nd lodge on left. Bus: Wetherby-Harrogate, alight Stockeld lodge gates (¼m drive). 4-acres with lawns, grove and flowers, fine trees and roses. House built 1758 for Col Middleton by James Paine (listed Grade 1). C18 pigeon cote. Chapel 1890. *Open Thurs only April 3 to Oct 9 (2-5). For NGS Sun June 29. TEAS. Adm £2 Chd £1. Gardens only £2 Chd £1 (2-5)*

Tan Cottage ✿ (Mr & Mrs D L Shaw) West Lane, Cononley. Take A629; turn off to Cononley 2¾m S of Skipton; top of village turn right onto Skipton rd. ¾-acre plantsman's garden, featured twice on TV, adjoining C17 house (not open). Interesting plants, many old varieties; national collection of primroses. *Adm £1.50. Private visits by appt only, please* **Tel 01535 632030**

Three Gables (Jack Muirhead Esq) The Barrows, Markington, nr Harrogate. 1m from Wormald Green (A61 Harrogate-Ripon). ¾-acre garden set in woodland, approached over bridge of chinoiserie design crossing trout stream. On one side, herbaceous border with streamside plantings, the other a terrace garden with many container plants and pergola. Steep bank garden to rear. Some choice trees, shrubs; many unusual plants, sculptures and wood carvings. TEAS. *Adm £2 Chd free. Sun July 27, Wed Aug 13 (1.30-6). Private visits by groups and societies welcome, please* **Tel 01765 677481**

Victoria Cottage ✿ (John Bearder Esq) Beestonley Lane, Stainland. 6m SW of Halifax. From Halifax (A629 - Huddersfield) fork R B6112 (Stainland). Turn R at 2nd set traffic lights (B6114), after 1m fork L (Branch Rd), after 1m turn L by mills continue up hill. From A640 Huddersfield (M62 junction 23) follow signs to Sowood. Just before Stainland take L Barkisland fork passing Black Horse Garage. Continue for 1m down Beestonley Lane. ¾-acre plantsman garden, created by the owner from a NE slop-

ing field since 1950. Daffodils; roses, flowering shrubs and trees, some unusual for a hilly and wild part of the Pennines. Scenic setting. *Adm £1 Chd 30p. Suns April 13, May 11, June 1, 22; July 6 (10-5). Private visits welcome and parties by appt only, please* **Tel 01422 365215/374280**

Wass Gardens ✿❀ Nr Coxwold ¼m from Byland Abbey on Coxwold-Ampleforth rd. 6m SW of Helmsley turning from A170. 9m E of Thirsk; turn from A19 signed Coxwold. A variety of gardens in a picturesque hamlet set amid a broad cleft of deep wooded slopes. TEAS in aid of Wass Village Institute. *Adm £2 Chd free. Wed June 25 (12-5)*

8 Welton Old Road ❀ (Dr & Mrs O G Jones) Welton. In village of Welton 10m W of Hull off A63. Coming E turn L to village. Past church turn R along Parliament St. and up hill. House 50yds on R opp Temple Close. From E take A63 and turn off at flyover to Brough; turn R for Welton and follow above instructions. Roadside parking in village. Informal 1-acre garden developed by owners over 30yrs. Imaginative planting with unusual shrubs, plants and less common trees; natural pond and lily pond. *Adm £1 Chd free. Private visits welcome May to July* **Tel 01482 667488**

26 West End ✿ (Miss Jennifer Hall) Walkington. 2m from Beverley on the B1230, 100yds beyond Xrds in centre of village on the R. Interesting ½-acre cottage garden opening into an old wooded gravel pit still being developed by the owner single-handedly. Many rare plants collected over 15yrs. TEA. *Adm £1.50 Chd free. Sun July 6 (1.30-5)*

5 Wharfe Close ✿❀ (Mr & Mrs C V Lightman) Adel. Signposted off Leeds ring rd A6120 ¼m E of A660 Leeds-Otley rd. Follow Long Causeway into Sir George Martin Drive. Wharfe Close adjacent to bus terminus. Please park on main rd. Medium-sized well stocked garden created from sloping site incorporating pools, rock gardens and mixed borders, small woodland walk filled with unusual plants grown on predominantly acid soil. TEAS in aid of Cat Protection League. *Adm £1 Chd free. Suns June 29, July 27 (2-5)*

The White Cottage &✿❀ (Mr & Mrs John Oldham) Halsham. 1m E of Halsham Arms on B1362. Concealed wooded entrance on R. Ample parking. The garden was created by its owners 25yrs ago. Delightful specialised and unusual planting in island beds. Natural pond and water feature; small woodland area, vegetable and herb garden; architect designed sunken conservatory. Traditional pergola. Featured with Geoffrey Smith on BBC2 in 1992. Teas by Halsham Church. *Adm £1.50 Chd free (Share to Halsham Church Restoration Fund®). Suns April 27, June 22, Aug 17 (2-5). Private visits welcome by appt, please* **Tel 01964 612296**

The White House &✿❀ (Dr & Mrs A H Raper) Husthwaite. 3m N of Easingwold. Turn R off A19 signposted Husthwaite 1½m to centre of village opposite parish church. 1-acre garden created from scratch in 7 years now maturing and of particular interest to the plantswoman, containing herb garden, conservatory, gardens within the garden; herbaceous, particularly a hot summer border; shrubs; borders and many fascinating unusual plants. New landscaping and planting in the old orchard. *Adm £2. Private visits for groups and parties welcome, please* **Tel 01347 868 688**

Windy Ridge ✿✿ (Mr & Mrs J S Giles) Marsh Lane, Bolton Percy. 5m E of Tadcaster. Follow Bolton Percy signs off A64. 10m SW of York. Features a large collection of Barnhaven and Elizabethan primroses; Hose-in-Hose, Jack-in-the-Green, etc. Also wild and unusual hardy plants, grown in a natural cottage garden style sloping down to the Ings, greatly influenced by Margery Fish. Featured in Channel 4 'Over the Garden Wall' 1994. Light lunches and teas available in village hall in aid of All Saints Church. *Combined adm with* **Betula and Bolton Percy Cemetery** *£2 Chd free. Suns April 13, June 22 (1-5)*

Woodcock ✿✿✿ (Mr & Mrs David Price) ¾m E of Thirsk off A170 (Sutton Bank Rd). Turn R up bridle track. Proceed for 1m. 1½-acre garden laid out with some mature areas, always of interest. Plantings of shrubs, herbaceous, old-fashioned roses, spring bulbs, scree bed and developing camellia walk. Small woodland garden under construction. TEAS. *Adm £2 Chd free. Sun July 6 (2-5.30)*

Woodlands Cottage ✿ (Mr & Mrs Stark) Summerbridge. ½m W of Summerbridge on the B6165 (Ripley-Pateley Bridge). 1-acre country garden constructed and developed over the past 10yrs by the owners from a sloping

site incorporating part of the existing woodland edge, field and natural stone outcrops with an attractive enclosed cottage style garden; herbaceous, formal herb garden, unusual hardy plants and separate vegetable area. Small nursery. TEAS in aid of Muscular Dystrophy Society. *Adm £1.50 Chd 50p. Suns May 18, Aug 10 (1.30-5). Private visits welcome by appt* **Tel 01423 780765**

Wytherstone House ✿✿✿ (Maj N & Lady Clarissa Collin) Pockley, 3m NE of Helmsley from A170 signpost. Large garden, constantly being improved, consisting of shrubs (some choice and hard to find) shrub roses, perennials, terracotta pots, mediterranean garden, beech hedges and magnificent views. The arboretum consisting of rare interesting trees has recently been landscaped with pond and small water garden. Suitable for wheelchairs if someone strong to push. TEAS in aid of Pockley Church and Village Hall. *Adm £2.50 Chd 75p under 6 free. Suns April 27, June 15 (1-5). Parties welcome, please* **Tel 01439 770012**

York Gate ✿✿ (GRBS) Back Church Lane, Adel, Leeds 16. Behind Adel Church on Otley Rd out of Leeds (A660). Bus: WY 34 Leeds-Ilkley; alight Lawnswood Arms, ½m. A garden created by the Spencer family and bequeathed to The Gardeners' Royal Benevolent Society. 1-acre plantsman's garden, divided into 8 individual gardens, each with unique architectural features. TEA. *Adm £2.50 Chd free (Share to GRBS®). Sat, Sun June 7, 8 (2-6). Private visits welcome, please* **Tel 0113 2678240**

Stop Press

BERKSHIRE

Alderwood House ✿✿ (Mr & Mrs P B Trier) Greenham Common. S of Newbury take A 339 towards Basingstoke for approx 3m. Turn L towards New Greenham Park. Turn R immediately before gate along track to house. Interesting 2½-acre garden started in 1904. On many levels with a number of rare trees and shrubs. Old roses, herbaceous border, conservatory and fine vegetable garden. TEAS. *Adm £1 Chd 50p. Suns May 25, June 22 (2-6)*

WALES

Carmarthenshire & Pembrokeshire

Hon County Organiser:	Mrs Duncan Drew, Cwm-Pibau, New Moat, Clarbeston Road, Haverfordwest, Pembrokeshire SA63 4RE Tel 01437 532454
Hon County Treasurer:	Mr N Edmunds, Parc-y-Robert, New Moat, Clarbeston Road, Haverfordwest, Pembrokeshire SA63 4RY

DATES OF OPENING

April 24 Saturday
Colby Woodland Garden, Narberth
May 11 Sunday
Brynsifi, nr Trimsaran
May 18 Sunday
Picton Castle, Haverfordwest
Post House, Cwmbach, St Clears
May 25 Sunday
Ffynone, Boncath
Hean Castle, Saundersfoot
Post House, Cwmbach, St Clears
May 27 Sunday
Picton Castle, Haverfordwest
June 1 Sunday
Great Griggs, Llanteg, nr Amroth
June 7 Saturday
Bryngoleu, Llannon

June 8 Sunday
Bryngoleu, Llannon
June 21 Saturday
Slebech Park, Haverfordwest
June 22 Sunday
Cilwern Plants, Talley, Llandeilo
Living Garden, Bryn
July 6 Sunday
Llysnewydd, Llangadog
July 12 Saturday
Maesyrynn, Nantycaws,
  Carmarthen
July 13 Sunday
Maesyrynn, Nantycaws,
  Carmarthen
July 27 Sunday
Great Griggs, Llanteg, nr Amroth
August 17 Sunday
Llysnewydd, Llangadog

Regular Openings
For details see garden description

The Dingle, Crundale
Hilton Court Nurseries, Roch
Picton Castle, Haverfordwest
Saundersfoot Bay Leisure Park

By appointment only
*For telephone numbers and other
details see garden descriptions.
Private visits welcomed*

Blaengwrfach Isaf, nr Llandysul
Cwm Pibau, Haverfordwest
The Forge, Landshipping

DESCRIPTIONS OF GARDENS

Blaengwrfach Isaf ✿✿ (Mrs Gail M Farmer) Bancyffordd, 2m W of Llandysul. Leaving Llandysul on Cardigan rd, by Half Moon pub fork left; continue on this road; approx 1½m, after village sign Bancyffordd farm track on right. ¾-acre garden incorporating woodland, wild and cottage garden aspects within a secluded and sheltered area. Areas specially created with bees, butterflies and birds in mind; new pathway bordered by wild-flower meadow. Incl in 'English Private Gardens'. *Adm £1 Chd free. Private visits welcome April, May, June, Oct (10-4), please* Tel 01559 362604

Bryngoleu ✿✿ (Mr & Mrs Ivor Russell) Llannon. 13m from Swansea, 7m from Llanelli. From junction 49 (Pont Abraham) on M4 take A48(T) in the direction of Cross Hands. Turn L after approx 3kms towards Village of Llwyn Teg. At [map ref SN 56 E on OS 159.] 1-acre garden with converted stable block, leading to extensive choice of walks each about ½m long in mature and newly developing woodlands and alongside natural streams. 5 acres overall incl 2 lakes; fine views of the surrounding countryside. Ample seating. TEA. *Adm £1.50 Chd 50p. Sat, Sun June 7, 8 (11-5). Private parties welcome, please* Tel 01269 842343

¶**Brynsifi** ✿✿ (A C & B Grabham) Llanelli. 3m W of Llanelli on B4308 Llanelli to Trimsaran rd. Signed off main rd. Medium-sized organic garden created on shale bank with natural stone retaining walls planted to give yr-round interest. TEA. *Adm £1.50 (Share to Charlie's Rescue home for older dogs®) Sun May 11(2-6)*

¶**Cilwern** ✿✿✿ (Mrs Anne Knatchbull-Hugessen) Talley. 6m NE of Llandeilo off B4302. Turn L by large sign on main rd. Garden on L 200yds down lane. Tranquil 1½-acre garden in valley. Created over 15yrs by owner from marshy scrubland. Wide range young and mature trees, shrubs and perennials; also new plantings. Hardy geraniums in variety. Collection of grasses being established. Large wisteria festooning an ash tree spectacular in bloom. Pond, stream and small woodland area. Adjoining nursery. TEAS. *Adm £1 Chd free. Sun June 22 (2-6)*

▲**Colby Woodland Garden** ✿ (The National Trust) ½m inland from Amroth and 2m E of Saundersfoot. Signposted by Brown Tourist Signs on the coast rd and the A477. 8-acre woodland garden in a secluded and tranquil valley with a fine collection of rhododendrons and azaleas. Tea rooms and gallery. Walled garden open by kind permission of Mr & Mrs A Scourfield Lewis. TEAS. *Adm £2.60 Chd £1.30. For NGS Sat April 26 (10-5). Large parties by appt, please* Tel 01834 811885

Cwm Pibau (Mrs Duncan Drew) New Moat. 10m NE of Haverfordwest. 4-acre garden bordered by streams and created since 1978; mainly young rare shrubs on a hillside. *Adm £1 Chd free. Private visits welcome, please* **Tel 01437 532 454**

●**The Dingle** &⅍✿ (Mrs A J Jones) Crundale. On approaching Haverfordwest from Carmarthen on A40, take R turn at 1st roundabout signed Fishguard & Cardigan. At next roundabout take R turn on to B4329. ½m on fork R opp General Picton; then 1st right into Dingle Lane. 3-acres plantsman's garden; rose garden; formal beds; scree; herbaceous border; unusual shrubs; water garden; woodland walk. Picturesque and secluded; free roaming peacocks. Nursery adjoining. Tearoom. *Adm £1 Chd 50p (Share to CRMF®). Weds to Suns March 12 to Oct 12 (10-6)*

Ffynone (Earl & Countess Lloyd George of Dwyfor) Boncath. From Newcastle Emlyn take A484 to Cenarth, turn L on B4332, turn L again at Xrds just before Newchapel. Large woodland garden in process of restoration. Lovely views, fine specimen trees, rhododendrons, azaleas. Ask for descriptive leaflet. House by John Nash (1793), not shown. Later additions and garden terraces by F Inigo Thomas c1904. TEAS in aid of Fishguard Sea Cadets. *Adm £1.50 Chd under 14 free. Sun May 25 (2-6)*

The Forge & (I & S Mcleod-Baikie) Landshipping. Nearest town Narbeth. Landshipping well sign posted. Pass New Park with pillar box; 200yds further on, gate on R. Approx 2½ acres recently planted woodland garden with many varieties of bulbs, trees and shrub roses. Small, pretty very charming. Featured in NGS video 2. *Private visits welcome mid-March to mid-April and also in June, please* **Tel 01834 891279**

Great Griggs &✿ (M A & W A Owen) Llanteg. A477 from St Clears through Red Roses, next village Llanteg. Signposted on L 'Colby Woodland Garden', turn L immed; 2nd entrance on R. Approx 1-acre plantsman's garden created and maintained by owners, consisting of lawns bounded by shrub borders and interspersed with scree beds full of alpines. Two ponds, one for ornamental ducks and natural stonework incl seating, all leading to cottage garden with summerhouse, in turn leading to semi-wild garden with pond and shrubs. TEAS. *Adm £1.50 Chd 50p Suns June 1, July 27 (2-6)*

Hean Castle &⅍✿ (Mr & Mrs T Lewis) Saundersfoot. 1m N of Saundersfoot. 1½m SE of Kilgetty. Take Amroth road from Saundersfoot or the Sardis road from Kilgetty. 2-acres; mixed borders with some unusual plants and shrubs; rose garden; walled garden and greenhouse; conifers; pot plants and troughs. Good view. TEAS. *Adm £1.50 Chd free. Sun May 25 (11-5). Also private visits welcome, please* **Tel 01834 812222**

1927–1997

This year the National Gardens Scheme is celebrating its 70th Anniversary. Please help us celebrate by visiting a garden in 1997.

Hilton Court Nurseries &⅍✿ (Mrs Cheryl Lynch) Roch. From Haverfordwest take the A487 to St Davids. 6m from Haverfordwest signs L to Hilton Court Nurseries. 4 acres of garden with superb setting overlooking ponds and woodlands. Spectacular lily ponds in July and August; wild flower walks; unusual trees and shrubs giving colour throughout the year. Nursery adjoining. TEAS. *Collecting box. Daily March to October 1 (9.30-5.30), October (10.30-4).* **Tel 01437 710262**

Living Garden ⅍✿ (Alan & Justine Clarke) 4a Brynmorlais Bryn, Llanelli; 2½m NE of town on B4297. Parking in lay-by on main rd please. Long, slender plantsman's garden subdivided for interest. Rare and attractive collection of plants, containers, water features and pools, one under redevelopment. TEAS. *Adm £1 Chd 25p. Sun June 22 (2-5); also private visits welcome, please* **Tel 01554 821274** *April to Sept*

¶**Llysnewydd** &⅍✿ (Jan Jones & Nick Voyle) Llangadog. Midway between Llandeilo and Llandovery. Turn off A40 into centre of Llangadog. Bear L in front of village shop. Turn 1st R. After approx ½m turn R. Garden approx 600yds on R. 1 acre oasis of tranquility set in scenic Towy Valley. Quiet, relaxing garden evolving from the need to prevent river erosion. Planted for yr-round interest in areas ranging from full sun to deep shade. Productive vegetable garden with greenhouses. Unsuitable for children and mobile phones. TEAS. *Adm £1 Suns July 6, Aug 17 (11-5) Private visits welcome, please* **Tel 01550 777432**

Maesyrynn &✿ (Mr & Mrs Thomas) Nantycaws. From Carmarthen take A48 dual carriageway E towards Swansea. After approx 3m turn L for Nantycaws. From Swansea, sign reads Police HQ and Nantycaws. Drive 300yds BP garage on L. Turn R into lane opp; 2nd bungalow on L. Plantsman's cottage garden approx ½ acre. Mainly herbaceous beds and shrubs. Pond and water feature, pergolas and raised beds. Highly productive vegetable garden with greenhouses. Lovely views in rural setting. TEAS. *Adm £1 Chd free (Share to the British Heart Foundation®). Sat, Sun July 12, 13 (10-6). Parties welcome June to Sept, please* **Tel 01267 234198**

■ **Picton Castle** &✿ (Picton Castle Trust) The Rhos. 3m E of Haverfordwest on A40 to Carmarthen, signposted off main rd. Mature 40-acre woodland garden with unique collection of rhododendrons and azaleas, many bred over 35yrs producing hybrids of great merit and beauty; rare and tender shrubs and trees like magnolia, myrtle, embothrium and eucryphia. Wild flowers abound. Walled garden with roses, fernery, herbaceous and climbing plants and large clearly labelled collection of herbs. Restaurant, craft shop gallery and garden nursery. *Adm £2.50 Chd £1, under 5 free. Open daily except Mons, April to Sept and Bank Hols. For NGS Suns May 18, July 27 (10.30-5).* **Tel 01437 751326**

▲**Post House** ⅍✿ (Mrs Jo Kenaghan) Cwmbach 6m N of St Clears. From Carmarthen W on A40. Take B4298 through Meidrim; leave by centre lane signed Llanboidy. Turn right at Xrds signed Blaenwaun; right at Xrds to Cwmbach; garden bottom of hill. From Whitland E on A40, left at Ivydean nurseries, right at 3rd Xrds signed Cwmbach. 4-acre valley garden; rhododendrons, azaleas, camellias, unusual trees and shrubs underplanted with hardy orchids, anemones, trilliums, wild snowdrops, bluebells, etc. Large pool, bog garden. Old roses, herbaceous plants. Greenhouses and conservatory. Plants for sale. TEAS. *Adm £1.50 OAP's & Chd £1. For NGS Suns May 18, 25 (2pm until dusk). Private parties welcome, please* **Tel 01994 484213**

Saundersfoot Bay Leisure Park ⅍❀ (Ian Shuttleworth Esq) Broadfield, Saundersfoot. On B4316, ¾m S from centre of Saundersfoot. Interesting layout of lawns, shrubs and herbaceous borders with many plants of bo-

tanical interest in 20-acre modern holiday leisure park. Large rock garden and water feature; laburnum walk; Japanese Garden. Holders of a National collection of Pontentilla fruticosa. Tea Saundersfoot. *Adm free. April 1 to Oct 28 daily (10-5)*

Slebech Park ⍟❀ (Mr Geoffrey Philipps) 5m E of Haverfordwest, S of A40. Terraced walled garden on site of commandery overlooking Eastern Cleddau. TEAS. *Adm £1 Chd 50p. Sat June 21 (2-6)*

Ceredigion/Cardiganshire

Hon County Organiser: Mrs Joy Neal, Llwyncelyn, Glandyfi, Machynlleth, SY20 8SS
Tel 01654 781203
Treasurer: Mrs Sheila Latham, Garreg, Glandyfi, Machynlleth, SY20 8SS

DATES OF OPENING

April 27 Sunday
  Pant-yr-Holiad, Rhydlewis
May 11 Sunday
  Llwyncelyn, Glandyfi
  The Mill House, Glandyfi
May 18 Sunday
  Cae Hir, Cribyn
May 24 Saturday
  Dyffryn, Pennant, Llanon
May 25 Sunday
  Dyffryn, Pennant, Llanon
June 1 Sunday
  Crynfryn & Tynewydd Gardens,
    midway, Aberaeron and
    Tregaron
June 8 Sunday
  The Walled Garden at
    Pigeonsford, Llangranog
June 22 Sunday
  Cae Hir, Cribyn
  Plas Llidiardau, Llanilar

June 28 Saturday
  Felindre, Aberarth,
    Aberaeron
June 29 Sunday
  Llanllyr, Talsarn
July 6 Sunday
  Crynfryn & Tynewydd Gardens,
    midway, Aberaeron and
    Tregaron
July 20 Sunday
  Cae Hir, Cribyn
July 27 Sunday
  The Walled Garden at
    Pigeonsford, Llangranog
August 6 Wednesday
  7 Maes-yr-Awel, Ponterwyd
August 10 Sunday
  7 Maes-yr-Awel, Ponterwyd
August 24 Sunday
  Llanerchaeron, Ciliau Aeron,
    Aberaeron

Regular openings
For details see garden description

The Walled Garden at Pigeonsford,
  Llangranog
Winllan, nr Lampeter
Ynyshir Hall, Eglwysfach,
  Machyhlleth

By appointment only
For telephone numbers and other details see garden descriptions. Private visits welcomed

Coetmor, Talybont, nr Aberystwyth
Garreg, Glandyfi
The Mill House, Glandyfi
Old Cilgwyn Gardens

DESCRIPTIONS OF GARDENS

▲**Cae Hir** ⍟❀ (Mr Wil Akkermans) Cribyn. W on A482 from Lampeter. After 5m turn S on B4337. Cae Hir is 2m on L. Beautiful and peaceful 6-acre garden. Entirely created and maintained by owner since 1985 from 4 overgrown fields of rough grazing. Many unusual features found unexpectedly around each corner incl red, yellow and blue sub-gardens, bonsai 'room', stonework, ponds, lovely views; new water and bog garden and white garden. As featured on radio and national and regional TV. TEA. *Adm £2 Chd 50p. For NGS Suns May 18, June 22, July 20 (1-6)*

¶**Coetmor** ❀ (Dr & Mrs G Hughes) Talybont. From Aberystwyth take A487 towards Machynlleth, 7m N to Taly-

bont. 2nd turn L after shop on village green. House visible in the trees 300yds straight up lane. 2-acre garden extended and planted during last 10yrs with interesting trees and shrubs incl embothrium, styrax japonica, ptelea aurea, zelkova, rhododendrons, azaleas, acers and a range of sorbus. Also an increasing collection of less common conifers. *Collecting box. Private visits and parties welcome April to June and Sept to Nov, please* **Tel 01970 832365**

Crynfryn & Tynewydd Gardens ⍟❀ TEAS. *Combined adm £2 Chd free. Suns June 1, July 6 (10.30-6)*
  Crynfryn (Mr & Mrs Tom Murton) Penuwch on B4576 between Penuwch and Bwlchllan, 8m Aberaeron, 8m Tregaron. 1-acre woodland garden with mature trees, pond, bog plants, meconopsis and primulas, herba-

ceous borders and collection of old shrub roses overlooking Cambrian Mts

Tynewydd (Mr & Mrs Robin Edwards) Bwlchllan. 1m S of Crynfryn. 2-acre garden, 2 large ponds, herbaceous planting, pergola, maturing trees and shrubs. Extensive mountain views

Dyffryn ✿✿ (Mr & Mrs O P J Richards) Pennant. SN 520, 637. From Aberarth, continue 100yds up hill, turn R, B4577 to Pennant. Xrds at centre of village turn L. Follow rd up hill past school. R fork, 250yds turn R. ⅔-acre partly woodland; many shrubs for flower arranging; small ponds; small Japanese garden; open perennial border; interesting plants, local bird life. TEAS. *Adm £1.50. Sat, Sun May 24, 25 (12-6)*

Felindre ✿✿ (Mr & Mrs Peter Davis) Felindre, Aberarth. 1m N of Aberaeron on A487. Turn L towards sea after bridge. Roadside parking. 1-acre informal garden, partly hillside with coastal trees and shrubs and unusual herbaceous plants; pond, pavement, kitchen garden; pines, mulberry, salvias, geraniums and euphorbias. TEA. *Adm £1.50 Sat June 28 (11-5)*

Garreg ✿ (Lt Col & Mrs P A Latham) On A487 at Glandyfi. Between Aberystwyth (12m) and Machynlleth (5m). Old farm complex. 1st buildings on river side approaching from Machynlleth. Approx 1-acre garden courtyard surrounding old Welsh farmhouse. *Adm £1.50 Chd free. Private visits welcome May 1 to July 31, please* **Tel 01654 781251**

▲**Llanerchaeron** ◐✿✿ (The National Trust) Lampeter. 2m inland from Aberaeron, to the N of the A482 Lampeter to Aberaeron rd. Formerly the pleasure grounds and kitchen gardens to Llanerchaeron House, these 12-acre gardens are undergoing restoration by volunteers and others under the direction of The NT with very limited resources. The lake and surrounding woods and paths are yet to be restored. Visitors can see restoration at a very early stage. TEA. *Adm £2 Chd free. For NGS Sun Aug 24 (11-5)*

Llanllyr ◐✿✿ (Mr & Mrs Robert Gee) Talsarn [SA48 8QB]. 6m NW of Lampeter on B4337 to Llanrhystud. Garden of about 4 acres, originally laid out in 1830s, renovated, replanted and extended since 1986. Mixed borders, lawns, bulbs, large fish pond with bog and water plants. Formal water garden. Shrub rose borders; foliage, species and old-fashioned plants. TEAS *Adm £1.50 Chd 50p (Share to Llanfihangel Church Ystrad Aeron Restoration Fund®). Sun June 29 (2-6). Private visits welcome April to Oct. Please write*

Llwyncelyn ✿✿ (Mr & Mrs Stewart Neal) and **The Mill House** (Prof & Mrs John Pollock) Glandyfi. On A487 from Aberystwyth (12m) Machynlleth (6m). Coming from Aberystwyth pass through Eglwysfach. Turn R just before Glandyfi sign. Part of old estate. 10-acre shrub and woodland gardens with waterfalls and mill pond. More recent specialised plantings. TEAS. *Combined adm £2 Chd 50p Sun May 11 (1-6)*

7 Maes yr Awel ✿✿ (Mrs Beryl Birch) Ponterwyd. From Aberystwyth take A44 towards Llangurig. At Ponterwyd

Village, turn R on to A4120 Devil's Bridge rd, then turn 1st L almost immed. ½-acre hillside garden in mountainous surroundings; sheltered 'hidden' gardens, pools fountain, herbaceous plantings, flowering shrubs and specimen trees. Large conservatory for refreshments. TEAS. *Adm £1 Acc chd free (Share to Haematology Fund, Bronglais Hospital®). Wed, Sun Aug 6, 10 (12-5)*

The Mill House ✿ (Prof & Mrs J M Pollock) Glandyfi. On main A487 to Machynlleth, 5½m from Machynlleth. Coming from Aberystwyth direction pass through Eglwysfach village; turn R up lane, almost directly opp sign for Glandyfi (on L). Mill House is 2nd house up lane, approx 150yds. [OS 691963]. Approx 1-acre garden of a former water mill. Collecting Box. *Also open with* **Llwyncelyn**. *Combined adm £2 Chd 50p. Private visits welcome in May, please* **Tel 01654 781342**

Old Cilgwyn Gardens ◐ (Mr & Mrs Edward Fitzwilliams) Newcastle Emlyn. Situated 1m N of Newcastle Emlyn on the B4571, turn R into entrance. A mixed garden mainly woodland of 14 acres set in 900 acres of parkland, 53 acres of which are Sites of Special Scientific Interest; snowdrops, daffodils, bluebells, rhododendrons. For those prepared to walk, a large tulip tree and the site of the last duel fought in Wales can be seen in Cae Hislop field. *Adm £1.50 Chd free. Private visits welcome all year, please* **Tel 01239 710244**

▲**Pant-yr-Holiad** ✿✿ (Mr & Mrs G H Taylor) Rhydlewis, 12m NW Llandysul. NE Cardigan. From coast rd take B4334 at Brynhoffnant S towards Rhydlewis; after 1m turn left; driveway 2nd L. 5-acres embracing walled garden housing tender plants, alpine beds, water features, rare trees and shrubs in woodland setting; extensive collection rhododendron species; fancy water-fowl. Collections of birch and unusual herbaceous plants. TEA. *Adm £2 Chd £1. For NGS Sun April 27 (2-5)*

Plas Llidiardau ◐✿✿ (L A Stalbow & G Taylor) Llanilar. 7m SE of Aberystwyth. Turn off A487 3m S of Aberystwyth onto A485 to Tregaron and Llanilar. From Llanilar take B4575 to Trawsgoed. Plas Llidiardau is ¾m on R. 7-acre old landscaped site redeveloped and planted since 1985. Wide selection of unusual plants and environments. Double herbaceous borders, formal pond, gravel garden, walled garden, organic raised beds, wooded areas, stream, wildlife pond. TEAS. *Adm £1.50 Chd 50p. Sun June 22 (1-6). Private visits welcome May to July, please* **Tel 01974 241434**

■ ¶**The Walled Garden at Pigeonsford** ✿ (Mr David & Dr Hilary Pritchard) nr Llangranog. On A487 14m from Cardigan, at Pentregat turn N on B4321 for Pontgarreg. Follow signs for Urdd Centre/Ski slope through edge of Pontgarreg. ¾m past Pontgarreg turn L at Xrds. (Ski slope is R turn). Down 100yds over bridge, up 50yds. Entrance signposted R. 1½ acres of natural woodland, river walks and 2 acres of ambitious new planting of trees and shrubs. On S-facing slope, now a working nursery garden with 1 acre of pre-Victorian walled garden, choice herbaceous, shrubs, fruit and vegetables. TEAS. *Adm £1.50 Chd under 16 free. Open March 27 to 31. Also Wed to Sun May 25 to Sept 28 (10-6). For NGS Sun June 8, July 27 (10-6)*

Winllan (Mr & Mrs Ian Callan) Talsarn. 8m NNW of Lampeter on B4342, Talsarn-Llangeitho rd. 6-acres wildlife garden with large pond, herb-rich meadow, small woodland and 600 yds of river bank walk. Over 200 species of wildflowers with attendant butterflies, dragonflies and birds. Limited suitability for wheelchairs. *Adm £1.50 Chd 50p (under 12 free). Open May & June daily (12-6). Also private visits welcome July & Aug, please* **Tel 01570-470612**

Ynyshir Hall Hotel (Mr & Mrs R J Reen) Machynlleth. Situated off main A487 in Eglwysfach Village, Ynyshir Hall has 14-acre landscaped gardens; mature ornamental trees. The mild climate allows many tender and unusual trees and shrubs; fine collection of rhododendrons and azaleas built up over many decades. TEAS. *Adm £1.50 Chd 50p. May 1 to 31 (9-5)*

Clwyd

Now Denbighshire & Colwyn and Flintshire & Wrexham

Denbighshire & Colwyn

Hon County Organiser:	Mrs Susan Rathbone, Bryn Celyn, Ruthin LL15 1TT Tel 01824 702077
Assistant Hon County Organiser:	Miss Marion MacNicoll, Trosyffordd, Ystrad Rd, Denbigh LL16 4RL Tel 01745 812247
Hon County Treasurer:	Mr Alan Challoner, 13, The Village, Bodelwyddan LL18 5UR Tel 01745 583451

DATES OF OPENING

April 20 Sunday
Coed-y-Gawen, Ruthin
April 27 Sunday
Plas Ffordd Ddwr, Llandyrnog
May 4 Sunday
Rug, Corwen
May 25 Sunday
Plas Nantglyn, nr Denbigh
May 26 Monday
Plas Nantglyn, nr Denbigh
June 1 Sunday
Eyarth House, nr Ruthin
June 4 Wednesday
Dibleys Nurseries, Llanelidan
June 8 Sunday
33 Bryn Twr, Abergele
June 11 Wednesday
Dibleys Nurseries, Llanelidan

June 15 Sunday
Trosyffordd, Ystrad, Denbigh
June 18 Wednesday
Dibleys Nurseries, Llanelidan
June 22 Sunday
Gwaenynog, Denbigh
Nantclwyd Hall, Ruthin
June 25 Wednesday
Dibleys Nurseries, Llanelidan
June 29 Sunday
Bryn Celyn, Llanbedr ‡
17 Broclywedog, Rhewl ‡
July 3 Thursday
17 Broclywedog, Rhewl
July 6 Sunday
Rhyllon, St Asaph
July 12 Saturday
Cerrigllwydion Hall, Llandyrnog
July 13 Sunday
Stella Maris, Llanrhaeadr, Denbigh

July 27 Sunday
Caereuni, Godre'r Gaer, Corwen

By appointment only
For telephone numbers and other details see garden descriptions. Private visits welcomed

Byrgoed, Llandderfel, nr Bala
Castanwydden, Llandyrnog
Merlyn, Moelfre, Abergele
Tal-y-Bryn Farm, Llannefydd
Trem-Ar-For, Dyserth
Tyn yr Odyn, Llannefydd

DESCRIPTIONS OF GARDENS

17 Broclywedog ✿✿ (Mel Royles) Rhewl, Ruthin. From Ruthin take A525 to Denbigh. Turn R in Rhewl onto Llandyrnog Rd. 2nd rd on R. A small attractive plantsmans garden packed with unusual varieties of geranium, erodium, sisyrinchium, alpine and others. TEA. *Adm £1 Chd 25p. Sun June 29 (1-5) Thurs July 3 (2-6). Private visits welcome, please* **Tel 01824 702139**

Bryn Celyn ♿✿✿ (Mr & Mrs S Rathbone) Llanbedr, Ruthin. [OS Ref SJ 133 603]. From Ruthin take A494 towards Mold. After 1½m at the Griffin Inn turn L onto

B5429. 1¼m house and garden on R. 1-acre garden; mixed borders; walled garden; old-fashioned roses. TEAS. *Adm £1.50 Chd 25p (Share to Ruthin School Assoc®). Sun June 29 (2-6). Private visits welcome, please* **Tel 01824 702077**

Bryn Meifod, see Gwynedd gardens

33 Bryn Twr ✿✿ (Mr & Mrs K Knowlson) Abergele. (To incl adjoining garden, '**Lynton**') A55 W take slip rd to Abergele. Turn L at roundabout then over traffic lights; 1st L signed Llanfair T H. 3rd rd on L, no. 33 is on L. There are 2 connected gardens (Lynton) of approx ¾ acre in total, containing patio and pond areas; mixed herbaceous and shrub borders. TEAS. *Combined adm £2.50 OAPs £2 Chd free (Share to St Michaels, Abergele Scout Group©). Sun June 8 (2-6)*

Byrgoed (Alan & Joy Byrne) Llandderfel. 4½m NE Bala. Off B4401 Bala-Corwen rd. L into village 1st R over stream and up hill. Fork R at old chapel, Byrgoed is ⅝m on L [OS 125 990 372]. Densely stocked terraced cottage garden; thyme lawn, rockery, alpines, roses and fuschias. Yr-round interest. *Adm £1 Chd 50p. Parties and private visits welcome April to Oct. Please* **Tel 01678 530 270**

¶**Caereuni** ैं.⚭❀ (Mr & Mrs Steve Williams) Godre'r Gaer. Take A5 Corwen to Bala rd. R at t-lights onto A494 to Chester. 1st R after layby; house ¼m on L. Microcosm of exotic styles, mainly oriental and Mediterranean, full of unusual plants and with wonderful views. TEAS. *Adm £1 Chd 25p (Share to Melin-y-Wig Chapel©). Sun July 27 (11-5)*

Castanwydden ैं❀ (A M Burrows Esq) Fforddlas, Llandyrnog. Take rd from Denbigh due E to Llandyrnog approx 4m. From Ruthin take B5429 due N to Llandyrnog. [OS ref 1264 (sheet 116).] Approx 1-acre cottage garden with a considerable variety of plants and bulbs. Small nursery growing plants from the garden. TEA. *Adm £1.50 Chd 50p. Private visits welcome, please* **Tel 01824 790404**

Cerrigllwydion Hall ⚭❀ (Mr & Mrs D Howard) Llandyrnog. E of Denbigh. B5429 ½m from Llandyrnog village on Ruthin Road. Extensive grounds with mature trees; herbaceous borders; vegetables and greenhouses. TEAS. *Adm £1.50 Chd 25p (Share to Llanynys Church®). Sat July 12 (2-6)*

¶**Coed-y-Gawen** ैं.⚭❀ (Mary & John Scott) Ruthin. A494 1m S of Ruthin Castle on Ruthin to Corwen rd. Total of 2 acres; 1⅓-acre garden and ⅔-acre orchard. Many unusual trees; lawns and shrubs; walled garden and small water garden. TEA. *Adm £1 Chd 25p (Share to Tenovus®). Sun April 20 (2-5)*

Dibleys Nurseries ⚭❀ (Mr & Mrs R Dibley) Cefn-rhydd, Llanelidan. Take A525 to Xrds by Llysfasi Agricultural College (4m from Ruthin, 14m from Wrexham). Turn along B5429 towards Llanelidan. After 1½m turn L at Xrds with houses on the corner. Continue up lane for 1m. Nursery and gardens on L. 8 acres of trees and shrubs, some recently planted. Spectacular views across to Clwydian range. ¾ acre of glasshouses containing mostly streptocarpus. *Adm £1 Chd 50p (Share to Action Aid®). Weds June 4, 11, 18, 25 (10-5)*

Dinbren Isaf, see Flintshire and Wrexham

Eyarth House ⚭❀ (Mrs J T Fleming) 2m S of Ruthin off A525. Bus: Ruthin-Corwen, Ruthin-Wrexham. Large garden; rock garden; shrubs and ornamental trees. TEAS. *Adm £1.50 Chd 50p (Share to St Mary's Church®). Sun June 1 (2.30-6). Private visits welcome, please* **Tel 01824 702745**

Gwaenynog ैं.⚭❀ (Maj & Mrs Tom Smith & Mrs Frances Williams) Denbigh. 1m W of Denbigh on A543, Lodge on left. 2-acre garden incl the restored kitchen garden where Beatrix Potter wrote the Tale of the Flopsy Bunnies. Small exhibition of some of her work. C16 house visited by Dr Samuel Johnson during his Tour of Wales. Coffee and biscuits 11-12.30pm. Refreshments available Broadleys Farm Restaurant. TEAS in aid of St James's Church, Nantglyn. *Adm £1.50 Chd 25p. Sun June 22 (11-6)*

Merlyn ⚭ (Drs J E & B E J Riding) Moelfre, Abergele. Leave A55 (Conwy or Chester direction) at Bodelwyddan Castle, proceed uphill by castle wall 1m to Xrds. 0.1m to T-junction. (white bungalow) R B5381 towards Betws yn Rhos for 2m, then fork L (signed Llanfair TH) after telephone box garden 0.4m on R. 2-acre garden developed from a field since 1987. Long mixed border; damp and gravel garden; many shrubs and old roses; rhododendrons and azaleas; spring garden. Views of sea. *Adm £1.50 Chd 25p. Private parties welcome Feb to Nov incl by prior arrangement, please* **Tel 01745 824435**

Nantclwyd Hall ⚭❀ (Sir Phillip & Lady Isabella Naylor-Leyland) Ruthin. Take A494 from Ruthin to Corwen. The garden is 1½m from Pwllglas on L. Approx 3 acres of formal gardens and further grounds. Temples and follies by Sir Clough Williams-Ellis. Grotto by Belinda Eade. Refreshments available Leyland Arms, Llanelidan. *Adm £2 Chd 50p. Sun June 22 (2-6). Private visits welcome following written application*

Pen-y-Bryn, see Flintshire and Wrexham

Plas Ffordd Ddwr ैं.⚭❀ (Mr & Mrs D J Thomas) Llandyrnog. 2m E of Denbigh. Follow signs to Llandyrnog from roundabout at Ruthin end of Denbigh bypass A525. House 2m on R. 2½-acre country garden, elevated position in Vale of Clwyd. Established shrubs, lawns and mature trees. Small woodland and pond. Bring wellies if wet. TEAS. *Adm £1.50 Chd 50p (Share to Arthritis Care®). Sun April 27 (2-5)*

Plas Nantglyn ैं.⚭❀ (Mr & Mrs Richard Welch) Nantglyn. From Denbigh follow signs for Nantglyn in SW direction; nr phone box in Nantglyn straight over Xrds and bear R at fork, house 300yds on L. [OS Ref 116 003 613.] Large old established gardens with azaleas, rhododendrons, topiary, roses and herbaceous borders; fine trees; good views. Pond and new summerhouse. TEAS. *Adm £1.50 Chd 50p. (Share to Hope House Children's Hospice®). Sun, Mon May 25, 26 (2-6)*

Rhyllon ैं.⚭❀ (Mr & Mrs M Dodd & Mrs D M Dodd) From St Asaph take A55 towards Chester then 1st L and 1st house on R. 1-acre garden with herbaceous borders, pond area with mature trees and shrubs. Dried flower section. TEA. *Adm £1.50 Chd 25p. Sun July 6 (2-6)*

Rug ैं.❀ (The Lord & Lady Newborough) Corwen. Follow A5 from Corwen over R Dee Bridge to t-lights. About ¼m turn R off A5 by Lodge. Mainly beautiful trees, shrubs, bulbs and woodland garden to walk through. Dogs cemetery. 7-acre lake with RNLI and other model boats being sailed on open day; replanting of small grass and shrubs. TEAS. *Adm £1.50 OAP's £1 Chd 50p (Share to RNLI and Orthopaedic Hospital Gobowen®). Sun May 4 (2-6)*

¶**Stella Maris** ⚘❀ (Mr & Mrs W Moore) Llanrhaeadr. Take A525 Denbigh to Ruthin rd. After 3m from Denbigh, or 4m from Ruthin turn W to Mynydd Llech. Garden ½m on L. ¾-acre garden enjoying wonderful views over Vale of Clwyd. Trees, shrubs, borders and some interesting features. TEAS. *Adm £1.50 Chd 25p (Share to Denbigh High School PTA©). Sun July 13 (2-6)*

Tal-y-Bryn Farm ⚬⚘ (Mr & Mrs Gareth Roberts) Llannefydd. From Henllan take rd signed Llannefydd. After 2½m turn R signed Bont Newydd. Garden ½m on L. Newly designed working farmhouse garden planted to make best use of existing buildings and features framing wonderful views. *Adm £1 Chd 25p. Private visits welcome by appt, please* Tel 01745 540 256

Trem-Ar-For (Mr & Mrs L Whittaker) Dyserth. 125 Cwm Rd, Dyserth. From Dyserth to Rhuddlan rd A5151. Turn L at Xrds signed Cwm, fork L and at traffic de-restriction

sign house on L. ¾-acre limestone terraced hillside garden with dramatic views towards Snowdon and Anglesey. A highly specialised garden with many rare and interesting plants with special emphasis on alpines, daphnes and specie paeonies. *Adm £1 Chd 50p. Private visits welcome April to Sept, please* Tel 01745 570349

¶**Trosyffordd** ⚬⚘❀ (Miss Marion MacNicoll) Ystrad. From A525 to Denbigh, turn by swimming pool. Ystrad Rd sign Prion and Saron 1½m on R after 1st hill. Medium-sized, old established garden. Beds, shrubs and special plants. TEA. *Adm £1.50 Chd 25p. Sun June 15 (2-6). Private visits welcome, please* Tel 01745 812247

Tyn yr Odyn ⚬⚘ (Mr & Mrs J S Buchanan) Llannefydd. 8m from Denbigh. B5382 signed Henllan and Llansannan. In Bryn Rhyd yr Arian, turn sharp R signed Llannefydd and Aled Plants. Garden ½m on L. Approx ⅔-acre cottage garden on the bank of R Aled, with stream, ponds and alpine garden; conifers, heathers, roses, shrubs, greenhouses and alpine house. Small nursery adjacent. *Adm £1.50 Chd 50p. Private visits welcome any day April to September, please* Tel 01745 870394

Dyfed

Now Carmarthenshire & Pembrokeshire and Ceredigion/Cardiganshire

Flintshire & Wrexham

Hon County Organiser:	Mrs J R Forbes, Pen-y-Wern, Pontblyddyn, nr Mold Flintshire CH7 4HN Tel 01978-760531
Assistant Hon County Organiser:	Mrs Gwen Manuel, Tir-y-Fron, Llangollen Rd, Ruabon, LL14 6RW Tel 01978 821633
Hon County Treasurer:	Mr Peter Manuel, Tir-y-Fron, Llangollen Rd, Ruabon, LL14 6RW Tel 01978 821633

DATES OF OPENING

March 16 Sunday
  Erddig Hall Garden, Wrexham
April 20 Sunday
  Hartsheath, Pontblyddyn
  Hawarden Castle, Hawarden
April 23 Wednesday
  Hartsheath, Pontblyddyn
April 27 Sunday
  Hartsheath, Pontblyddyn
May 18 Sunday
  Hawarden Castle, Hawarden
  Three Chimneys, Rhostyllen
May 20 Tuesday
  Chirk Castle, nr Wrexham
May 25 Sunday
  Argoed Cottage, nr
    Overton-on-Dee ‡

River House, Erbistock ‡
May 28 Wednesday
  Pen-y-Bryn, Llangollen
June 1 Sunday
  Brambles, Garth, nr Llangollen
June 8 Sunday
  The Garden House, Erbistock
  Pen-y-Bryn, Llangollen
June 14 Saturday
  Tir-y-Fron, Ruabon
June 15 Sunday
  Bryn Tirion, Pen-y-Felin, Nannerch
  Tir-y-Fron, Ruabon
June 22 Sunday
  Argoed Cottage, nr
    Overton-on-Dee
  The Garden House, Erbistock
June28 Saturday
  Dinbren Isaf, Llangollen

June 29 Sunday
  Dinbren Isaf, Llangollen
  Dolwen, Cefn Coch
July 6 Sunday
  Cartref Babell ‡
  Donadea Lodge, Babell ‡
  Welsh College of Horticulture,
    Northop
July 13 Sunday
  The Garden House, Erbistock
  Pen-y-Wern, Pontblyddyn
  Tri Thy, Pontybodkin, nr Mold
July 16 Wednesday
  Bryn Tirion, Pen-y-Felin,
    Nannerch
July 17 Thursday
  Bryn Hafod, Treuddyn
July 20 Sunday
  The Garden House, Erbistock

July 24 Thursday
Bryn Hafod, Treuddyn
September 14 Sunday
The Garden House, Erbistock
September 28 Sunday
Dolwen, Cefn Coch
October 18 Saturday
Three Chimneys, Rhostyllen

October 19 Sunday
Three Chimneys, Rhostyllen

By appointment only
For details see garden description

Alyn View, nr Mold

> **By Appointment Gardens.**
> These owners do not have a fixed opening day usually because they cannot accommodate large numbers or have insufficient parking space.

DESCRIPTIONS OF GARDENS

Alyn View, Rhydymwyn ✗ (Mr & Mrs Smith) nr Mold. Directions on appointment. A cottage garden of 1 acre. A shady private garden and a very sunny open garden. Both areas full of established trees, shrubs and herbaceous borders. *Adm £1.50 Chd 50p. Private visits welcome, please* **Tel 01352 741771**

Argoed Cottage &✿ (Mr & Mrs C J Billington) Overton-on-Dee. App Overton-on-Dee from Wrexham on A528 cross over Overton Bridge and in about ¾m on brow of hill turn L into Argoed Lane. 1¾-acre garden. Interesting trees and shrubs. Herbaceous beds; roses and vegetable garden. TEAS in aid of Dolywern Cheshire Home, June 22 only. *Adm £1.50 Chd free. Suns May 25, June 22 (2-5).*

¶Brambles ✿ (Tony & Deb Jones) Garth, Trevor. Wrexham to Llangollen A483, A539. Turn R in Trevor at Australia Arms Inn. ½m on R. ¾-acre tiered garden on hillside. Mixture of shrubs, conifers and rhododendrons; pond, aviary and featuring dry-stone walls. TEAS. *Adm £1.50 Chd free (Share to Garth C P School®). Sun June 1 (1-5)*

Bryn Hafod ✗✿ (Rosemary & David Ffoulkes Jones) Treuddyn, Mold. Turn S off A5104 1m W of Treuddyn into Ffordd y Blaenau (signed). Follow lane for 1¼m. Country garden in elevated position of about 1 acre created from pasture 10yrs ago. A wide variety of plants in mixed borders and varied situations. TEAS in aid of St Mary's Church Treuddyn. *Adm £1 Chd 50p. Thurs July 17, 24 (11-5)*

¶Bryn Tirion ✗✿ (Julia White) Pen-y-Felin. Nannerch 6m W of Mold, off A541 (Mold to Denbigh rd) into Nannerch Village. Turn opp Cross Foxes Inn into Pen-y-Felin Rd. 7/10m along rd. Small picturesque country garden on SW-facing hillside. Steps lead down through terraced areas which have been densely planted in cottage style with many varieties of old fashioned plants and herbs. TEAS. *Adm £1.50 Chd 50p (Share to Capricorn Animal Rescue®). Sun June 15, Wed July 16 (11-6). Private visits also welcome by prior appt only, please* **Tel 01352 741498**

Cartref &✗✿ (Mrs D Jones) Caerwys Rd Babell, Holywell. Turn off A541 Mold to Denbigh rd at Afonwen signposted Babell. At T-junction turn R, Black Lion Inn turn L, 1st L. 4th house. From Holywell old A55, turn L for Gorsedd then L again. L at Gorsedd Church for Babell, 2m down that rd turn R at Babell Chapel which is now Chapel House, 4th house. Very attractive well-stocked cottage garden; clematis, climbers, vegetables and roses. TEA. *Adm £1 Chd 25p (Share to Cancer Research®). Sun July 6 (2-6)*

▲**Chirk Castle** & (The National Trust) Chirk 7m SE of Llangollen. Off A5 in Chirk by War Memorial. 4½ acres trees and flowering shrubs, rhododendrons, azaleas, rockery, yew topiary. TEAS. *Adm to garden £2.20 OAPs/Chd £1.10. For NGS Tues May 20 (12-5)*

Dinbren Isaf ✗✿ (Mr & Mrs P Ault Walker) 1¾m N of Llangollen on rd to Worlds End and Minera. 1-acre garden. Wide variety of herbaceous plants and shrubs in alkaline soil at 850′ in woodland setting, as featured on S4C. TEAS. *Adm £1.50 Chd free (Share to Vale of Llangollen Canal Boat Trust For The Disabled®). Sat, Sun June 28, 29 (2-6)*

■ **Dolwen** ✗✿ (Mrs F Denby) Cefn Coch Llanrhaeadrym-Mochnant. From Oswestry take the B4580 going W to Llanrhaeadr. Turn R in village and up narrow lane for 1m. Garden on R. 14m from Oswestry. 4 acres of hillside garden with pools, stream, small wood and many different types of plant and unusual annuals all backed by a stupendous mountain view. TEAS. *Adm £1.50 Chd free (Share to Oswestry Orthopaedic Hospital®). Every Fri and last Sun in month from May to Sept in aid of local charities. For NGS Sun June 29, Sept 28 (2-5). Private parties welcome, please* **Tel 01691 780 411**

Donadea Lodge &✗✿ (Mr & Mrs Patrick Beaumont) Babell. Turn off A541 Mold to Denbigh at Afonwen, signposted Babell; T-junction turn L. A55 Chester to St Asaph take B5122 to Caerwys, 3rd turn on L. Shady garden with unusual plants, shrubs; shrub and climbing roses; clematis; pink, yellow and white beds. Featured in Homes and Gardens 1994, and in The Good Gardens Guide 1997. Also on S4C 1996. Cream TEAS. *Adm £1.50 Chd 30p (Share to St Mary's Church Ysceifiog®). Sun July 6 (2-6). Private visits welcome from May 1 to Aug 1, please* **Tel 01352 720204**

▲**Erddig Hall** &✗ (The National Trust) 2m S of Wrexham. Signed from A483/A5125 Oswestry Road; also from A525 Whitchurch Road. Garden restored to its C18 formal design incl varieties of fruit known to have been grown there during that period and now incl the National Ivy Collection. TEA. Tours of the garden by Head Gardener at 1pm, 2pm. *Adm £2 Chd free. For NGS Sun March 16 (12-3) Garden only*

The Garden House &✿ (S Dyson-Wingett) Erbistock. 5m S of Wrexham on A528 Wrexham to Shrewsbury. Follow signs at Overton Bridge to Erbistock Church. Shrub and herbaceous plantings in monochromatic, analogous and complementary colour schemes. Rose pergolas and hydrangea avenue (over 200 species and cultivars). Victorian dovecote. Nursery plant centre. TEAS. *Adm £1 Chd free (Share to Frank Wingett Cancer Appeal©). Suns June 8, 22, July 13, 20, Sept 14 (2-6) Private visits welcome, please Tel 01978 780958*

Hartsheath ✿✿ (Dr M C Jones-Mortimer) Pontblyddyn. ½m S of intersection with A5104. Red brick lodge on E side of A541. Large woodland garden; many varieties of flowering cherries and crab apples. Tidy picnic lunchers welcomed. Lunch & Tea at Bridge Inn, Pontblyddyn. *Adm £1.50 Chd £1 (Share to Pontblyddyn Church®). Sun April 20 (12-5) Wed April 23 (2-5) Sun April 27 (12-5). Also private visits welcome weekdays Feb-May, Sept-Oct, please* Tel 01352 770 204

Hawarden Castle ♿✿ (Sir William & Lady Gladstone) On B5125 just E of Hawarden village. Large garden and picturesque ruined castle. *Adm £1.50 Chd/OAPs £1. Suns April 20, May 18 (2-6)*

Pen-y-Bryn ♿✿✿ (Mr & Mrs R B Attenburrow) Llangollen. Signs at t-lights on A5 in centre of Llangollen. Walking distance or field parking. 2-acre garden on wooded plateau overlooking town; panoramic views; on site of old hall with established trees, shrubs and rhododendrons, walled garden, water feature, extensive lawns and herbaceous borders. TEAS. *Adm £1.50 Chd free (Share to Friends of Llangollen International Musical Eisteddfod®). Wed May 28, Sun June 8 (2-6)*

Pen-y-Wern ♿✿✿ (Dr & Mrs Forbes) Pontblyddyn, 5m SE of Mold, 7m NW of Wrexham. On E side of A541, ½ way between Pontblyddyn and Caergwrle. 2½-acre terraced country-house garden incl interesting small gardens. Shrubs, conifers, grasses and herbaceous borders; rose garden spectacular in June/July. Magnificent copper beech with canopy circumference of 250ft and other splendid trees. TEAS. *Adm £1.50 Chd 50p (Share to Hope Parish Church®). Sun July 13 (2-6)*

River House ♿✿✿ (Mrs Gwydyr-Jones) Erbistock. 5m S of Wrexham. On A528 Wrexham-Shrewsbury rd, ¼m before Overton Bridge (opp turning A539 to Ruabon). Small garden with unusual shrubs and plants. *Adm £1 Chd free. Sun May 25 (2-6)*

Three Chimneys ✿✿ (Mr & Mrs Hollington) 3m SW of Wrexham via Rhostyllen. From Wrexham A5152 fork R at Black Lion onto B5097. From Ruabon B5605 turn L onto B5426 signed Minera. Turn R ½m over bridge, L at Water Tower. Garden ¼m on L opp post box. Forester's garden of 1 acre; maples, conifers, cornus and sorbus species and varieties. Many small trees used in the manner of a herbaceous border. Very unusual and interesting. *Adm £1.50 Chd 50p. Sun May 18 (2-6) Sat, Sun Oct 18, 19 (1-5)*

Tir-y-Fron ♿✿✿ (Mr & Mrs P R Manuel) Llangollen Rd, Ruabon. 5m from Wrexham, take A539 from Ruabon By-Pass, signed Llangollen, turn R on brow of hill after 200yds. 1¾-acre garden with shrubs and herbaceous plants surrounded by mature trees with quarry. Offa's Dyke separates garden from drive. TEAS (Share to Llangollen Canal Boat Trust©). *Adm £1.50 Chd free. Sat, Sun June 14, 15 (2-6)*

¶**Tri Thy** ♿✿✿ (Norma Restall & Daughters) Pontybodkin nr Mold. Signposted off Chester to Corwen A5104 at Pontybodkin. Follow Craft Centre signs. ⅓-acre garden 500ft above sea level. Created within old farm buildings and surrounding land. Shrubs, herbaceous, roses and water feature. TEAS. *Adm £1.50 Chd 50p. Sun July 13 (2-6)*

Welsh College of Horticulture ♿ Northop. Village of Northop is 3m from Mold and close to the A55 expressway. Mature gardens incorporating many national award winning features. Commercial sections. Garden Centre and retail sections where produce and garden sundries can be purchased. A Golf Course is being constructed for the teaching of Greenkeeping Skills. Car parking. TEA. *Adm £1 OAPs & Chd 50p. Sun July 6 (12-5)*

SYMBOLS USED IN THIS BOOK (See also Page 17)

‡   Following a garden name in the Dates of Opening list indicates that those gardens sharing the same symbol are nearby and open on the same day.

‡‡   Indicates a second series of nearby gardens open on the same day.

¶   Opening for the first time.

✿   Plants/produce for sale if available.

♿   Gardens with at least the main features accessible by wheelchair.

✿   No dogs except guide dogs but otherwise dogs are usually admitted, provided they are kept on a lead. Dogs are not admitted to houses.

●   These gardens advertise their own dates in this publication although they do not nominate specific days for the NGS. Not all the money collected by these gardens comes to the NGS but they do make a guaranteed contribution.

■   These gardens nominate specific days for the NGS and advertise their own dates in this publication.

▲   These gardens open regularly to the public but they do not advertise their own dates in this publication. For further details, contact the garden directly.

The Glamorgans

Hon County Organiser:	Mrs Christopher Cory, Penllyn Castle, Cowbridge, South Glamorgan CF7 7RQ Tel 01446 772780
Assistant County Organiser:	Mrs L H W Williams, Llanvithyn House, Llancarfan, South Glamorgan Tel 01446 781232

DATES OF OPENING

April 13 Sunday
Merthyr Mawr House, Bridgend
April 20 Sunday
Penllyn Castle, Cowbridge
April 27 Sunday
Trehedyn House,
Peterston-Super-Ely
May 18 Sunday
9 Willowbrook Gardens, Mayals,
Swansea
May 25 Sunday
Llanvithyn House, Llancarfan
June 1 Sunday
Springside, Pen-y-Turnpike, Dinas
Powys
June 8 Sunday
Marleigh Lodge, Old St Mellons
June 15 Sunday
The Clock House, Llandaff

June 21 Saturday
Cwmpennar Gardens, Mountain
Ash
June 22 Sunday
Cwmpennar Gardens, Mountain
Ash
June 29 Sunday
11 Eastcliff, Southgate, Swansea
Pontygwaith Farm, Edwardsville
July 6 Sunday
Fonmon Castle, nr Barry
July 19 Saturday
10 Daniel Close, Sully
July 20 Sunday
6 Alma Road, Penylan, Cardiff
10 Daniel Close, Sully
Pontygwaith Farm, Edwardsville
July 21 Monday
10 Daniel Close, Sully
July 22 Tuesday
10 Daniel Close, Sully

July 23 Wednesday
10 Daniel Close, Sully
July 24 Thursday
10 Daniel Close, Sully
July 25 Friday
10 Daniel Close, Sully
July 27 Sunday
Gelly Farm, Cymmer

By appointment only
For telephone numbers and other details see garden descriptions. Private visits welcomed

11 Arno Road, Little Coldbrook
Garth Madryn, Penderyn, Aberdare
7, St Peters Terrace, Cockett,
Swansea
19, Westfield Road, Glyncoch,
Pontypridd

DESCRIPTIONS OF GARDENS

6 Alma Road ✿✸ (Mr Melvyn Rees) Penylan, Cardiff. N from city centre, off Marlborough Rd. Take Cardiff E junction 29 from M4, Llanedeyrn exit from Eastern Avenue, then towards Cyncoed and down Penylan Rd. Redesigned S-facing terraced house garden 30′ × 15′ with many species from the S and E hemispheres, incl Dicksonia Antarctica; some redesign this yr. Generally Japanese look; railway sleepers used as paving material with gravel infill. TEAS. *Adm £1 Chd 50p (Share to Alzheimers Disease Society®). Sun July 20 (2-6). Private visits welcome, please* Tel 01222 482200

11 Arno Road ✸ (Mrs D Palmer) Little Coldbrook. From A4050 Cardiff to Barry, take roundabout marked Barry Docks and Sully. Then 2nd R into Coldbrook Rd, 2nd L into Langlands Rd, then 6th R into Norwood Cresc; 1st L into Arno Rd. 40ft × 30ft informal plantsman's garden with ponds, herbaceous plants, gravelled area planted with low growing plants. As featured on Radio Wales 'Gardening Matters' Aug '95. TEAS. *Adm £1. Private visits welcome weekends and Wednesdays May to Oct (2-5), please* Tel 01446 743642

The Clock House ⎣✿✸ (Prof & Mrs Bryan Hibbard) Cathedral Close, Llandaff, 2m W of Cardiff. Follow signs to Cathedral via A4119. Bus: Cardiff alight Maltsters Arms. Small walled garden; fine old trees; wide variety of shrubs and plants; important collection of shrub, species and old roses. TEA. *Adm £2 Acc chd free. Sun June 15 (2-6)*

Cwmpennar Gardens ✿✸ Mountain Ash 1m. From A4059 turn R 100yds N of the traffic lights; follow sign to Cefnpennar, uphill for ¾m. Car park 100yds past bus shelter in Cwmpennar. Three of the gardens are contiguous, the fourth at entrance to Cwmpennar 100yds from others. Gardens high on mountain side in one-time coal mining village in rural surroundings. Tynewydd awarded 1st prize in gdn competition for Rhondda-Cynon-Taff. Gardens with variety of features, landscapes and unusual plants. TEAS. Glamorgan Wildlife Trust Sales stall. *Combined adm £2 Chd £1 (Share to St Illtyd's Church Restoration Fund®). Sat, Sun June 21, 22 (2-6)*
　The Cottage (Judge & Mrs Hugh Jones)
　Ivy Cottage (Mr & Mrs D H Phillips)
　¶Tynewydd (Mr & Mrs B Davies)
　Woodview (Miss A & Miss R Bebb)

10 Daniel Close ✿✸ (Mrs Christine Richards) Sully. Via Penarth Sully Barry Rd. Sully Church in small layby on South Rd. Take Cog Rd, pass Sully Inn, 1st R into Bassett Rd, 1st R into Dispenser Rd. L into Daniel Close, bear R, house in L-hand corner. Small suburban garden mainly of summer interest; many unusual plants in containers; arbour with climbing plants, trees, shrubs, perennials. Pond, small waterfall; small orchid collection. TEA. *Adm £1 Chd 25p. Sat to Fri July 19 to 25 (12-8). Please* Tel 01222 531214

11 Eastcliff ⎣✿✸ (Mrs Gill James) Southgate. Take the Swansea to Gower road and travel 6m to Pennard. Go through the village of Southgate and take the 2nd exit off the roundabout. Garden 200yds on the L. Seaside garden approx ⅓ acre and developed in a series of island and bordered beds for spring and summer interest. A large number of white and silver plants. Unusual plants and shrubs. TEAS. *Adm £1.50 Chd free. Sun June 29 (2-5). Also private visits welcome, please* **Tel 01792 233310**

Fonmon Castle Ᏸ፠ (Sir Brooke Boothby) nr Barry. Take rd Cardiff-Llantwit Major, marked for Cardiff Airport. Take turning W of Penmark for Fonmon village, bear R round pond. Gate ¼m on. Medium-sized garden. Walled kitchen garden; flowering shrubs; good trees; fuchsias. Ancient castle (shown Tues & Weds April to Sept (2-5)). TEAS. *Adm £1.50 Chd 50p. Sun July 6 (2-6).* **Tel 01446 710206**

Garth Madryn ፠፠ (Sue & Chris Williams) Church Rd. Penderyn, Aberdare. From Heads of the Valley Rd at Hirwaun follow signs to Brecon along Hirwaun by-pass. At Penderyn, turn L before Chapel and School. 3rd house on R. ½-acre mixed garden in the Brecon Beacons National Park. Collectors garden full of unusual plants featuring conifer beds, gravel garden, long herbaceous borders, island beds, formal and wildlife ponds. Huge collection of hardy geraniums, rubus and aquilegias. Extensive area of unusual plants for sale especially hardy geraniums. *Adm £1 Chd free. Private visits welcome April to September weekdays and some weekends (10-6).* Please **Tel 01685 811298**

Gelly Farm ፠፠ (Mrs A Appleton, Mrs L Howells, Mrs S Howells) Cymmer. 10m N E of Port Talbot, on A4107, ½m beyond Cymmer, towards Treorchy, turning off rd on R. 4 varied gardens grouped around the farmyard of a historically listed working hill farmstead on the slopes of a steep valley. Wildlife pond. Display of prize poultry, historical and other exhibitions. TEAS £1. *Adm £1.50 Chd free (Share to The Royal Agricultural Benevolent Institution®). Sun July 27 (2-6)*

Llanvithyn House ፠፠ (Mr & Mrs L H W Williams) Llancarfan 1.8m S of A48 at Bonvilston, sign for Llancarfan 100yds W of Bonvilston Garage, 1m N of Llancarfan. Medium-size garden on site of C6 monastery. C17 gatehouse. Lawns, interesting trees, shrubs, borders. TEAS if fine. *Adm £1.50 Chd 25p. Sun May 25 (2-6)*

Marleigh Lodge Ᏸ፠፠ (Mr & Mrs J C Rees) Old St Melons. A48 Cardiff-Newport. 5m from Cardiff turn L at White Hart Inn. Marleigh Lodge stands directly ahead between Began Rd and Druidstone Rd. 1½-acre family garden. Trees, rhododendrons, azaleas, camellias, flowering shrubs, water features. Herb garden. TEA. *Adm £1.50 Chd 50p. Sun June 8 (2-6). Private visits welcome May to Aug, please* **Tel 01222 794918**

Merthyr Mawr House ፠፠ (Mr & Mrs Murray McLaggan) Merthyr Mawr. 2m SW of Bridgend. Large garden with flowering shrubs, magnolias, scree and walled vegetable garden; bluebell wood with ruined C14 chapel; swallow hole. TEA. *Adm £1.50 Chd £1 (Share to Merthyr Mawr Church Steeple Fund©). Sun April 13 (2-6)*

Penllyn Castle Ᏸ፠፠ (Mrs Christopher Cory) 3m NW of Cowbridge. From A48 turn N at Pentre Meyrick. Turn 1st R and at T-junction straight ahead through gate, leaving

church on L. Large garden with fine views; old trees and some new planting; spring shrubs (rhododendrons and magnolias) and bulbs. TEAS. *Adm £1.50 Chd 50p. Sun April 20 (2-6)*

Pontygwaith Farm Ᏸ፠ (Mr & Mrs R J G Pearce) Edwardsville. Take A4054 Old Cardiff to Merthyr Rd. Travel N for approx 3m through Quaker's Yard and Edwardsville. 1m out of Edwardsville turn sharp L by old bus shelter. Garden at bottom of hill. Medium-sized garden; surrounding C17 farmhouse adjacent to Trevithick's Tramway; situated in picturesque wooded valley; fish pond, lawns, perennial borders. TEAS. *Adm £1 Chd 50p. Suns June 29, July 20 (2-6). Private visits welcome, please* **Tel 01443 411137**

¶7 St Peters Terrace ፠ (Mr & Mrs Tony Ridler) Cockett, Swansea. 4m W of Swansea behind Cockett Rd (A4216) between railway bridge and church. Young, ⅓-acre designers garden divided into series of formal enclosed areas. TEA. *Adm £1. Private visits welcome, please* **Tel 01792 588217**

Springside ፠፠ (Prof & Mrs Michael Laurence) Dinas Powys. From Cardiff take B4055 to Penarth and Dinas Powys as far as the Leckwith (Cardiff Distributor Rd) roundabout. Then take B4267 to Llandough, up Leckwith Hill past Leckwith Village, take R-hand fork in rd into Pen-y-Turnpike as far as the 30mph sign. Turn R immed into Springside. Undulating 2-acre garden recently rescued after 30yrs of wilderness. Spacious, with views and newly planted trees: small ponds and old village water supply returned to nature, where children must be supervised; vegetable garden. Parking in the grounds only available in dry weather. TEA. *Adm £2 Chd 50p (Share to Dinas Powys Orchestra©). Sun June 1 (2-6)*

Trehedyn House Ᏸ (Mr & Mrs Desmond Williams) Peterston-Super-Ely. A 48 Cardiff to Cowbridge. Turn R at Sycamore Cross (½way between St Nicholas and Bonvilston). Take 2nd L. Garden ½m on L. Medium-sized garden. Interesting trees, shrubs, borders, bulbs and spring planting. TEA. *Adm £1.50 Chd 50p. Sun April 27 (2-6)*

19 Westfield Road ፠፠ (Mr & Mrs Brian Dockerill) Glyncoch Pontypridd. From Pontypridd travel 1.5m N along B4273. Take L turn by school. At top of hill follow rd to L. Take first R and R again into Westfield Rd. Enthusiasts collection of over 2,500 different varieties of plants, many unusual, grown in ½-acre garden designed as a series of interlinked enclosures each of different character. TEA. *Adm £1 Chd 50p. Prevented by limited parking from having specific open day, we welcome visitors by appt through the yr, please* **Tel 01443 402999**

9 Willowbrook Gardens ፠ (Dr & Mrs Gallagher) Mayals, 4m W of Swansea on A4067 (Mumbles) rd to Blackpill; take B4436 (Mayals) rd; 1st R leads to Westport Ave along W boundary of Clyne Park; 1st L into cul-de-sac. ½-acre informal garden designed to give natural effect with balance of form and colour between various areas linked by lawns; unusual trees suited to small suburban garden, esp conifers and maples; rock and water garden. TEAS. *Adm £1.50 Chd 30p. Sun May 18 (1.30-6); also private visits welcome, please* **Tel 01792 403268**

Gwent (Monmouthshire, Newport and Caerphilly)

Hon County Organiser:	Mrs Joanna Kerr, Glebe House, Llanfair Kilgeddin, Abergavenny, Gwent NP7 9BE Tel 01873 840422
Asst Hon County Organiser:	Mrs Catriona Boyle, Penpergwm Lodge, Abergavenny, Gwent NP7 9AS Tel 01873 840208

DATES OF OPENING

March 30 Sunday
Veddw House, The Veddw,
  Devauden
May 4 Sunday
Penpergwm Lodge, nr
  Abergavenny
Veddw House, The Veddw,
  Devauden
May 11 Sunday
Great Campston, Llanfihangel
  Crucorney
Penpergwm Lodge, nr
  Abergavenny
May 18 Sunday
The Nurtons, Tintern
Penpergwm Lodge, nr
  Abergavenny
May 25 Sunday
Lower House Farm, Nantyderry ‡
Penpergwm Lodge, nr
  Abergavenny ‡
Wyndcliffe Court, St Arvans,
  Chepstow ‡‡
Veddw House, The Veddw,
  Devauden ‡‡
May 26 Monday
Llan-y-Nant, Coed Morgan, nr
  Abergavenny ‡
Lower House Farm, Nantyderry ‡
June 1 Sunday
The Graig, nr Raglan
Penpergwm Lodge, nr
  Abergavenny

The Volland, Lower Machen
June 8 Sunday
Penpergwm Lodge, nr
  Abergavenny
June 15 Sunday
Penpergwm Lodge, nr
  Abergavenny ‡
Trostrey Lodge, Bettws
  Newydd ‡
June 21 Saturday
Grace Dieu Court, Dingestow
June 22 Sunday
Clytha Park, nr Abergavenny ‡
Grace Dieu Court, Dingestow
Penpergwm Lodge, nr
  Abergavenny ‡
Veddw House, The Veddw,
  Devauden
June 29 Sunday
Court St Lawrence, nr Usk
Llanfair Court, nr Abergavenny ‡
The Nurtons, Tintern
Penpergwm Lodge, nr
  Abergavenny ‡
July 5 Saturday
Great Campston, Llanfihangel
  Crucorney
July 6 Sunday
Great Campston, Llanfihangel
  Crucorney
Great Killough, nr Abergavenny
July 13 Sunday
Glebe House, Llanvair Kilgeddin ‡
Orchard House, Coed Morgan, nr
  Abergavenny ‡

July 20 Sunday
Tredegar House & Park, Newport
July 27 Sunday
The Nurtons, Tintern
August 24 Sunday
Lower House Farm, Nantyderry
Veddw House, The Veddw,
  Devauden
August 25 Monday
Lower House Farm, Nantyderry
August 31 Sunday
Castle House, Usk
September 7 Sunday
Great Campston, Llanfihangel
  Crucorney
Tredegar House & Park, Newport
September 14 Sunday
The Nurtons, Tintern
October 5 Sunday
Chwarelau Farm, Llanfapley, nr
  Abergavenny
October 12 Sunday
Llanover, nr Abergavenny

Regular openings
For details see garden description

The Nurtons, Tintern
Penpergwm Lodge, nr Abergavenny
Tredegar House & Park, Newport
Veddw House, The Veddw Devauden

DESCRIPTIONS OF GARDENS

Castle House &⊛ (Mr & Mrs J H L Humphreys) Usk; 200yds from Usk centre; turn up lane opp fire station. Medium-sized garden of orderly disorder with herb garden and vegetables set around ruins of Usk Castle and medieval gatehouse which is open by appt. TEAS. *Adm £2 Chd free. Sat June 28 as part of Usk Gardens Day (donation to NGS) (10-6). For NGS Sun Aug 31 (2-6). Private visits also welcome, please* **Tel 01291 672563**

Chwarelau ⊛ (Mr & Mrs Maurice Trowbridge) On B4233 3½m E of Abergavenny. Medium-sized garden with magnificent views, approached down 200yd drive fringed by ornamental trees and shrubs. Lovely autumn colour; fruits and berries. TEAS. *Adm £1.50 Chd free. Sun Oct 5 (2-6)*

Clytha Park & (Sir Richard Hanbury-Tenison) ½ way between Abergavenny and Raglan on old rd (not A40). 5 acres; C18 layout; trees, shrubs; lake. Teas in aid of G.N.T.A. *Adm £1.50 Chd 50p. Sun June 22 (2-6)*

Court St Lawrence &⊛ (Mrs G D Inkin) Llangovan, 6m SW of Monmouth, 5m NE of Usk, between Pen-y-Clawdd and Llangovan. 5 acres of garden and woodland with trees, shrubs, lake, roses etc. TEAS, plants and produce stalls in aid of St David's Foundation, Newport. *Adm £1.50 Chd 50p. Sun June 29 (2-6)*

> **Regular Openers.** Open throughout the year. They are listed at the end of the Diary Section under 'Regular Openers'.

¶**Glebe House** ⟨symbols⟩ (Mr & Mrs Murray Kerr) Llanvair Kilgeddin. Midway between Abergavenny and Usk on B4598, 5m from each. Approx 1½-acre garden of mixed herbaceous and shrub borders with unusual and interesting plants, orchard and vegetable garden surrounded by wonderful rural aspects of Usk Valley. TEAS. *Adm £1.50 Chd free. Sun July 13 (2-6)*

Grace Dieu Court ⟨symbols⟩ (Mr & Mrs David McIntyre) Dingestow. 1½m NW of Dingestow Village which is N of old Raglan-Monmouth rd (not dual carriageway). 3-acre open country garden in rolling countryside. Started from scratch in 1986. Mostly roses as shrubs, climbers and hedges; 2 lge ponds; herbaceous border, young specimen trees, shrubs and fine old oaks. TEAS. *Adm £1.50 Chd 50p. Sat, Sun June 21, 22 (2-6)*

The Graig ⟨symbols⟩ (Mrs Rainforth) Pen-y-Clawdd, SW of Monmouth. Turn S from Raglan-Monmouth rd (not motorway) at sign to Pen-y-Clawdd. Bus: Newport-Monmouth, alight Keen's shop, ½m. Mixed cottage garden with interesting shrubs and roses and kitchen garden. TEAS. *Adm £1.50 Chd free. Sun June 1 (2-6). Private visits welcome, please* **Tel 01600 740270**

Great Campston ⟨symbols⟩ (Mr & Mrs A D Gill) 7m NE of Abergavenny; 2m towards Grosmont off A465 at Llanfihangel Crucorney. Drive on R just before brow of hill. Pretty 2-acre garden set in wonderful surroundings. Designed and planted from scratch by Mrs Gill, a garden designer; wide variety of interesting plants and trees enhanced by lovely stone walls, paving and summer house with fantastic views. The house stands 750ft above sea level on S facing hillside with spring fed stream feeding 2 ponds. TEAS. *Adm £2 Chd 50p (Share to 'Mind'®). Sun May 11, Sat, Sun July 5, 6, Sun Sept 7 (2-6). Private visits welcome, please* **Tel 01873 890633**

Great Killough ⟨symbols⟩ (Mr & Mrs John F Ingledew) Llantilio Crossenny, 6m E of Abergavenny. S of B4233. 3-acre garden created in the 1960s to complement mediaeval house. TEAS. *Adm £1.50 Chd free (Share to Barnardo's®). Sun July 6 (2-6)*

Llanfair Court ⟨symbols⟩ (Sir William Crawshay) 5m SE of Abergavenny. Route old A40 and B4598. Medium-sized garden, herbaceous border, flowering shrubs, roses, water garden; modern sculpture. TEAS. *Adm £1.50 Chd 50p. Sun June 29 (2-6)*

Llanover ⟨symbols⟩ (Robin Herbert, Esq) 4m S of Abergavenny. Bus: Abergavenny-Pontypool, alight drive gates. Large water garden; many rare trees, good autumn colour. TEAS. *Adm £2 Chd 50p. Sun Oct 12 (2-6)*

Llan-y-Nant ⟨symbols⟩ (Mr & Mrs Charles Pitchford) Coed Morgan. 4m from Abergavenny, 5m from Raglan on old A40 (now B4598) Raglan to Abergavenny rd. Turn up lane opp 'Chart House' inn; pass Monmouthshire Hunt Kennels 500yds on R. 3 acres of garden and woodlands. Lawn, beds, shrubs, herbs, alpines and kitchen garden. Small lake with wild life. TEAS. *Adm £1.50 Chd 50p. Mon May 26 (2-6)*

Lower House Farm ⟨symbols⟩ (Mr & Mrs Glynne Clay) Nantyderry, 7m SE of Abergavenny. From Usk-Abergavenny rd, B4598, turn off at Chain Bridge ¼m on R. Medium-sized garden designed for all-yr interest; mixed borders, fern island, herb bed, paved area, unusual plants. Late flowering perennials. Featured in magazines, on T.V. and in NGS video 1. TEAS. *Adm £1.50 Chd 50p (Share to All Saints Church, Kemeys Commander©). Suns, Mons May 25, 26; Aug 24, 25 (2-6). Private visits also welcome, please* **Tel 01873 880257**

■ **The Nurtons** ⟨symbols⟩ (Adrian & Elsa Wood) Tintern. On A466 opp Old Station, Tintern. 2-acre plantsman's garden of considerable botanical interest. Herbaceous borders, herb garden, rockery, shade beds, wildlife pond, mature trees. New areas being developed. 'Wye Valley Herbs' Nursery sells a range of unusual herbaceous plants incl full range of herbs. Teas nearby in Tintern. Garden and nursery open daily (10.30-5) March to end Oct. *Adm £1.50 Chd free. (Share to Gwent Wildlife Trust®). For NGS Suns May 18, June 29, July 27, Sept 14 (10.30-5). Private visits also welcome, please* **Tel 01291 689253**

Orchard House ⟨symbols⟩ (Mr & Mrs B R Hood) Coed Morgan. 1½m N of old Raglan-Abergavenny rd. Approx 6m from Abergavenny. Turn opp King of Prussia or The Charthouse. A garden of approx 1½ acres with mixed borders of unusual herbaceous plants and shrubs, rosebeds and lawn. TEAS in aid of St David's Church. *Adm £1.50 Chd 50p. Sun July 13 (2-6). Private visits welcome April to Sept, please* **Tel 01873 840289**

■ **Penpergwm Lodge** ⟨symbols⟩ (Mr & Mrs Simon Boyle) 3m SE of Abergavenny. From Abergavenny take B4598 towards Usk, after 2½m turn L opp King of Prussia Inn. Entrance 150yds on L. A 3-acre formal garden with mature trees, hedges & lawns; interesting potager, mixed unusual plants & vegetables; apple & pear pergola and S-facing terraces with sunloving plants. Nursery specialising in unusual hardy perennials. Home of Catriona Boyle's School of Gardening, now in its 11th yr. TEAS and plants in aid of St Cadoc's Church on NGS day only (Share to NGS on other days). *Adm £1.50 Chd free. Thurs, Fris, Sats March 27 to Oct 4, and all Suns in May, June (2-6). For NGS Sun June 8 (2-6). Private visits and parties welcome, please* **Tel 01873 840208**

■ **Tredegar House & Park** ⟨symbols⟩ (Newport County Borough Council) 2m SW of Newport Town Centre. Signposted from A48 (Cardiff rd) and M4 junction 28. Series of walled formal gardens dating from the early C18 surrounding one of the most magnificent late C17 houses (also open). Orangery Garden recently restored to early C18 appearance with coloured mineral parterres, espaliered fruit trees, box hedging etc. Deep C19 herbaceous borders line the central cedar garden. On NGS days private gardens around **Home Farm Cottage** and **Curator's Cottage** are open, with orchard area and glasshouses. Restored Edwardian sunken garden also open. TEAS. *Adm £2 Chd 50p (Share to The Friends of Tredegar House and Park®). For NGS Suns July 20, Sept 7 (11-6). House, Gardens etc open Easter to end of Oct, for details, please* **Tel 01633 815880**

Trostrey Lodge ✿ (Mr & Mrs Roger Pemberton) Bettws Newydd. Half way between Raglan and Abergavenny on old road (not A40). Turning to Bettws Newydd opposite Clytha gates, 1m on R. 'This other Eden, demi-paradise' is how one authority has described this walled garden. High concentration of interesting old-fashioned flowers, roses, vines and herbs, all bordered by rosemary, box, lavender and rugosas. It is set within a decorative orchard, surrounded by fine landscape in one of the prettiest parts of Usk Valley. Local dairy ice creams. *Adm £1.50 Chd free. Sun June 15 (2-6)*

■ **Veddw House** ⚘✿ (Anne Wareham & Charles Hawes) Devauden is approx midway between Chepstow and Monmouth on B4293. Signed from inn on the green. 4 acre garden; emphasis on good garden pictures with colour harmonies and contrasts. Formal vegetable garden with old roses and clematis; hardy geranium walk; small themed gardens; ruin, wild garden; conservatory. Unique ornaments of wood and enamel. Lovely views. Woodland walks with interesting artefacts. *Adm £1.50 Chd 50p*

(Share to Heart Research Foundation for Wales®). Every Sun June 1 to Sept 14 incl (2-6). For NGS Suns March 30, May 4, 25, Aug 24 (2-6). Parties welcome by appt, please **Tel 01291 650836**

The Volland ♿⚘✿ (Mr & Mrs William Graham) Lower Machen. Between Newport and Caerphilly, 10mins from junction 28 (M4) W of Lower Machen Village, 1st R before county boundary. 1½-acres of interesting shrubs, trees and herbaceous plants; fern rockery under restoration. Natural garden - a continued fight against ground elder! TEAS. *Adm £1.50 Chd free. Sun June 1 (2-6)*

Wyndcliffe Court ♿✿ (HAP Clay Esq) St Arvans. 3m N of Chepstow, turn at Wyndcliffe signpost. Bus: Chepstow-Monmouth; alight St Arvans, Wyndcliffe stop, ¼m. Medium-sized garden; herbaceous borders; views, topiary, shrubs. Mentioned in The Historic Gardens of Wales. TEA. *Adm £1.50 Chd free. Sun May 25 (2-6). Private visits welcome, please* **Tel 0129162 2352**

Gwynedd

Hon County Organiser:
Anglesey, North Caernarfonshire
Aberconwy

Mrs B S Osborne, Foxbrush, Port Dinorwic, Felinheli, Gwynedd LL56 4JZ
Tel 01248 670463

Hon County Organiser:
South Caernarfonshire &
Merionethshire

Mrs W N Jones, Waen Fechan, Islaw'r Dref, Dolgellau LL40 1TS
Tel 01341 423479

DATES OF OPENING

March 16 Sunday
Bryniau, Boduan
March 28 Friday
Penrhyn Castle, nr Bangor
March 30 Sunday
Bont Fechan Farm, Llanystumdwy
Bryniau, Boduan
Crug Farm, nr Caernarfon ‡
Foxbrush, Aber Pwll, Port Dinorwic ‡
April 13 Sunday
Bryniau, Boduan
April 27 Sunday
Gilfach, Rowen, nr Conwy
May 4 Sunday
Bryniau, Boduan
Crug Farm, nr Caernarfon
Haul-a-Gwynt, Wylfa Head
May 5 Monday
Crug Farm, nr Caernarfon
May 8 Thursday
Plas Newydd, Anglesey
May 11 Sunday
Foxbrush, Aber Pwll, Port Dinorwic

May 18 Sunday
Bont Fechan Farm, Llanystumdwy
Maenan Hall, Llanrwst
May 25 Sunday
Bryn Eisteddfod, Glan Conwy
Bryn Golygfa, Bontddu
Bryniau, Boduan
Glandderwen, Bontddu
Pen-y-Parc, Beaumaris
Rhyd, Trefor, nr Holyhead
St John the Baptist & St George, Carmel
May 26 Monday
Bryn Golygfa, Bontddu
Glandderwen, Bontddu
June 1 Sunday
Trysglwyn Fawr, Amlwch
June 15 Sunday
Bryniau, Boduan
Foxbrush, Aber Pwll, Port Dinorwic
Henllys Lodge, Beaumaris
June 29 Sunday
Crug Farm, nr Caernarfon
Gilfach, Rowen, nr Conwy
Tyn-y-Cefn, Dolwen, nr Ffestiniog

July 6 Sunday
Afallon, Bontddu
Bryniau, Boduan
Glandderwen, Bontddu
Gwyndy Bach, Llandrygarn
July 7 Monday
Afallon, Bontddu
Glandderwen, Bontddu
July 13 Sunday
Henllys Lodge, Beaumaris
July 20 Sunday
Rhyd, Trefor, nr Holyhead
July 27 Sunday
Bryniau, Boduan
Haul-a-Gwynt, Wylfa Head
Tyn-y-Cefn, Dolwen, nr Ffestiniog
August 17 Sunday
Bont Fechan Farm, Llanystumdwy
Maenan Hall, Llanrwst
August 23 Saturday
Gilfach, Rowen, nr Conwy
August 24 Sunday
Bryniau, Boduan
Crug Farm, nr Caernarfon
Tyn-y-Cefn, Dolwen, nr Ffestiniog
September 7 Sunday
Haul-a-Gwynt, Wylfa Head

September 14 Sunday
Bryniau, Boduan
October 5 Sunday
Bryniau, Boduan
October 26 Sunday
Bryniau, Boduan

Plas Muriau, Bettws-y-Coed
Plas Penhelig, Aberdovey

Hen Ysgoldy, Llanfrothen
Llys-y-Gwynt, Llandegai
Pencarreg, Glyn Garth, Menai Bridge

By Appointment only
For telephone numbers and other details see garden descriptions. Private visits welcomed

Regular Openings
For details see garden description

Bryn Meifod, Glan Conwy
Farchynys Cottage, Bontddu

Bryn Castell, Llanddona, Anglesey
Bryn-y-Bont, Nantmor
Cefn Bere, Dolgellau
Haulfryn, Llanberis

| **By Appointment Gardens.** |
| These owners do not have a fixed opening day usually because they cannot accommodate large numbers or have insufficient parking space. |

DESCRIPTIONS OF GARDENS

Afallon ✿ (Mr & Mrs Edward O Williams) Bontddu. 5m W of Dolgellau. Take A496 to Bontddu. Garden is N, 50yds past Bontddu Hall Hotel. 1-acre cottage garden open for 1st time. Summer flowers, clipped yew hedges, variety of trees and shrubs. *Adm £1 Chd free. Sun, Mon July 6, 7 (11- 6)*

Bont Fechan Farm ♿✿ (Mr & Mrs J D Bean) Llanystumdwy. 2m from Criccieth on the A497 to Pwllheli on the L-hand side of the main rd. Small garden with rockery, pond, herbaceous border, steps to river, large variety of plants. Nicely planted tubs. TEAS. *Adm 75p Chd 25p. Suns March 30, May 18, Aug 17 (11-5). Private visits welcome, please* **Tel 01766 522604**

Bryn Castell ✿ (Lady Gibson) Wern. 3m NW of Beaumaris. First L opp telephone box before entering village. ¼m down single track rd towards Wern-y-Wylan. 2 acres semi-wild gardens surrounding remote farmhouse with beautiful views. Pond and bog garden, wildflower lawns with bulbs and orchids; cottage garden with old roses and herbaceous plants; conservatory with vine. TEAS in aid of CRUSE. *Adm £1 Chd free. Private visits welcome by appt, please* **Tel 01248 810399**

Bryn Eisteddfod ♿✿ (Dr Michael Senior) Glan Conwy. 1½m SE Llandudno 3m W Colwyn Bay; up the hill (Bryn-r-Maen direction) from Glan Conwy Corner where A470 joins A55. 8 acres of landscaped grounds incl mature shrubbery, arboretum, old walled 'Dutch' garden, large lawn with ha-ha. Extensive views over Conwy Valley, Snowdonia National Park, Conwy Castle, town and estuary. TEAS. *Adm £1 Chd 50p. Sun May 25 (2-5)*

Bryn Golygfa ✿✿ (Mr R Alexander) Dolgellau. 5m W of Dolgellau. Take A496 to Bontddu; garden is N 100yds past Bontddu Hall Hotel. Small garden on steep hillside; mixed planting incl rhododendrons and alpines. *Adm £1 Chd free. Sun, Mon May 25, 26 (11-6). Private visits and parties welcome mid-May to mid-Aug, please* **Tel 01341 430260**

Bryn Meifod ✿✿ (Dr & Mrs K Lever) Graig Glan Conwy. Just off A470 1½m S of Glan Conwy. Follow signs for Aberconwy Nursery. ¾-acre garden developed over 25yrs but extensively replanted in the last 10yrs. Unusual trees and shrubs, scree and peat beds. Good autumn colours. Wide ranging collection of alpines especially autumn gentians. Extensive views towards Snowdonia and the Carneddau. Nursery adjacent. *Collection Box. Fri in April, May June and Sept (2-5), please* **Tel 01492 580875**

Bryn-y-Bont ✿ (Miss J Entwisle) Nantmor. 2½m S of Beddgelert, turn L over Aberglaslyn Bridge into A4085, 500yds turn L up hill, 2nd house on R. Small garden created since 1978 on S facing wooded hillside over looking Glaslyn Vale. Water garden, mixed borders and small woodland. Featured on TV and Radio. *Adm £1.50 Chd free. Private visits and small parties welcome, please* **Tel 01766 890448**

Bryniau ✿ (P W Wright & J E Humphreys) Boduan. ½m down lane opp. St Buan's Church, Boduan, which is half-way between Nefyn and Pwllheli on the A497. New garden created since 1988 on almost pure sand. Over 80 types of trees; hundreds of shrubs, many unusual, showing that with a little effort, one can grow virtually anything anywhere. Broadcast on BBC Gardeners World, Radio Wales, Radio Cymru, S4C Clwb Garddio. Plants and woodcraft for sale. TEAS. *Adm £1 Chd free. Suns March 16, 30, April 13, May 4, 25, June 15, July 6, 27, Aug 24, Sept 14, Oct 5, 26 (11-6) and private visits welcome, please* **Tel 01758 7213 38**

Cefn Bere ✿ (Mr & Mrs Maldwyn Thomas) Cae Deintur, Dolgellau. Turn L at top of main bridge on Bala-Barmouth Rd (not the by-pass); turn R within 20yds; 2nd R behind school and first L half way up short hill. Small garden; extensive collection of alpines, bulbs and rare plants. Tea Dolgellau. *Collecting box. Individuals and parties of up to 25 welcome, spring, summer and autumn months, please* **Tel Dolgellau 01341 422768**

Crug Farm ✿✿ (Mr & Mrs B Wynn-Jones) Griffiths Crossing. 2m NE of Caernarfon ¼m off main A487 Caernarfon to Bangor Road. Follow signs from roundabout to Bethel. Plantsman's garden; ideally situated; 2 to 3 acres; grounds to old country house. Gardens filled with choice, unusual collections of climbers, and herbaceous plants; over 300 species of hardy geraniums. Featured in 'The Garden' and on BBC TV Gardeners World. Only partly suitable wheelchairs. TEAS in aid of local charities. *Collecting box for walled display garden open Thurs, Fri, Sat, Suns & Bank Hols Feb 22 to Sept 28 (10-6). See calendar for openings of private gardens. Adm £1 Chd free. Natural Rock garden only open Suns & Mons March 30, May 4, 5, Suns June 29, Aug 24 (10-6). Private parties welcome, please* **Tel 01248 670232**

Farchynys Cottage ⚹ (Mrs G Townshend) Bontddu. On A496 Dolgellau-Barmouth rd; well-signed W of Bontddu village. 4 acres; informal country garden on steep wooded hillside; unusual shrubs and trees; azaleas, over 75 species of rhododendron, giant liriodendron-tulipifera. Best mid-May, mid-June. *Adm £1 Chd free. Open daily except Sats, May 1st to Sept 30. Parties welcome, please* **Tel 01341 423479**

Foxbrush ⅏⚘ (Mr & Mrs B S Osborne) Aber Pwll, Port Dinorwic, Felinheli. On Bangor to Caernarfon Road, entering village opp layby with Felinheli sign post. Fascinating 3-acre country garden on site of old mill and created around winding river; rare and interesting plants; ponds and small wooded area. Extensive plant collections incl rhododendrons, ferns, primula, alpines, clematis and roses; 45ft long pergola; fan-shaped knot garden with traditional and unusual herbs; coaches welcome. A winner 1995 RHS/Today Gardening Family of the Year. Featured on S4C Club Garddio. TEAS. *Adm £1 incl C16 cottage musuem Chd free. Suns March 30, May 11, June 15 (12-5). Also private visits and parties welcome, please* **Tel 01248 670463**

Gilfach ⅏⚹ (James & Isoline Greenhalgh) Rowen. At Xrds 10yds E of Rowen (4m S of Conwy) S towards Llanrwst, past Rowen School on L; turn up 2nd drive on L, signposted. 1-acre country garden on S-facing slope overlooking Conwy Valley; set in 35 acres farm and woodland; mature shrubs; herbaceous border; small pool. Partly suitable wheelchairs which are welcome. Magnificent views of River Conwy and mountains. TEAS. *Adm £1 Chd free. Suns April 27, June 29, Sat Aug 23 (11-5)*

Glandderwen (A M Reynolds Esq) 5m W of Dolgellau. Take A496 to Bontddu. Garden is on S 100yds past Bontddu Hall Hotel. ½-acre on N bank of Mawddach Estuary facing Cader Idris; set amid large oaks; shrubs, trees; steep and rocky nature. *Adm £1 Chd free. Sun, Mon, May 25, 26 July 6, 7 (11-6). Private visits and parties welcome May 1 to Sept 30, please* **Tel 01341 430229**

Gwyndy Bach ⅏⚹⚘ (Keith & Rosa Andrew) Llandrygarn. From Llangefni take the B5109 towards Bodedern, the cottage is exactly 5m out on the L. A ¾-acre artist's garden set amidst rugged Anglesey landscape. Romantically planted in intimate 'rooms' with interesting plants and shrubs, old roses and secluded lily pond. Studio attached. TEAS. *Adm £1 Chd free. Sun July 6 (11-5.30). Also open by appt June and July, please* **Tel 01407 720651**

¶**Haul-a-Gwynt** ⅏⚘ (M P Markwald) Wylfa Head. On the A5025 2m from Cemaes Bay travelling towards Holyhead. Turn R at Wylfa Power Station sign. At main gate (now signed Magnox, turn R for ¼m to Nature Trail car park on R. Please park here unless disabled. Immed opp car park is Tyn-y-Maes and Haul-a-Gwynt House sign. Private lane 100yds to house. ¾ acre of lovely countryside bounded by natural stone walls, sheltering 200 varieties of flowering shrubs, climbers and trees, the majority named. Fish pond and waterfall, natural pond, large domed greenhouse and alpine rockery. TEA in restored farm labourer's cottage. *Adm £1 Chd free. Suns May 4, July 27, Sept 7 (11-5). Private visits welcome, please* **Tel 01407 710058**

Haulfryn ⅏⚘ (Adrian & Diane Anthoine) Church Lane. ⸮ min walk from centre of Llanberis, up lane between gar age and church. Garden approx 1 acre. Commenced 1987 from rough sheep pasture at foot of Snowdon. Numerous tree plantings, natural rock outcrop; variety of ericaceous shrubs, old roses and mixed herbaceous borders bounded by a natural mountain stream. Partly suitable wheel chairs. TEAS. *Adm £1 Chd free. Private visits welcome please* **Tel 01286 870446**

Hen Ysgoldy ⚹ (Mr Brian Archard) Llanfrothen. From Garreg via B4410, after ½m L; garden 200yds on R Natural garden with streams and established trees, incl magnolias, eucalyptus and embothrium. Shrubs incl a variety of azaleas and rhododendrons, mixed borders planted for colour and interest all-yr. *Adm £1.50 Chd free Private visits and parties welcome April 1 to Aug 31 please* **Tel 01766 771231**

Henllys Lodge ⅏⚹⚘ (Mr & Mrs K H Lane) Beaumaris Past Beaumaris Castle, ½m turn L, 1st L again. Lodge a entrance to Henllys Hall Hotel drive. Approx 1-acre country garden, planted in traditional cottage style using perennials, shrubs, old roses and featuring extensive collection of hardy geraniums. Small woodland area. Stunning views across Menai Straits. TEAS. *Adm £1 Chd free Suns June 15, July 13 (12-5.30). Private visits and parties welcome, please* **Tel 01248 810106**

Llys-y-Gwynt ⅏⚘ (Jennifer Rickards & John Evans) Llandegai. 3m S of Bangor and 300yds from Llandygai Roundabout. Just off Pentir, Bethal, Caernarfon rd 200yds from junction with A5 and 100yds from entrance to Esso Service Station and Travel Lodge. 2-acre rambling garden; well established trees and shrubs and magnificent views; pond, N-facing rockery; large Bronze Age burial cairn. Planting with emphasis on wind resistance, yr round interest and encouraging wild life. *Adm £1 Chd free. Private visits welcome, please* **Tel 01248 353863**

Maenan Hall ⚘ (The Hon Christopher McLaren) Exactly 2m N of Llanrwst on E side of A470, ¼m S of Priory Hotel. Gardens created since 1956 by the late Christopher Lady Aberconway and then present owner; 10 acres lawns, shrub, rose and walled gardens; rhododendron dell; many species of beautiful and interesting plants shrubs and trees set amongst mature oaks and other hardwoods; fine views of mountains across Conway valley. Home-made TEAS. *Adm £1.80 Chd 50p (Share to St David's Hospice Foundation® May 18; Welsh National Opera® Aug 17). Suns May 18, Aug 17 (10-5). Last entry 4pm*

Pen-y-Parc (Mrs E E Marsh) Beaumaris. A545 Menai Bridge-Beaumaris rd; after Anglesey Boatyard 1st L; after Golf Club 1st drive on L. NOT easy for wheelchairs. ⸮ acres; beautiful grounds, magnificent views over Menai Strait; azaleas, rhododendrons and heathers; interesting terrain with rock outcrops used to advantage for recently planted conifer and rock gardens; small lake in natural setting; 2 further enclosed gardens. We would like to share the pleasure of this garden. TEA. *Adm £1 Chd 50p Sun May 25 (11-5)*

Pencarreg & (Miss G Jones) Glyn Garth. 1½m NE of A545 Menai Bridge towards Beaumaris, Glan Y Menai Drive is turning on R, Pencarreg is 100yds on R. Parking in lay-by on main rd, limited parking on courtyard for small cars and disabled. Planted for all-yr interest and colour with common and unusual shrubs. Small stream. Garden terminates at cliff edge and this has been skilfully planted. Views to the Menai Straits and the Carneddi Mountains in the distance. Featured in 3 television programmes. *Collecting Box (Share to Snowdonia National Park Society©). Private visits welcome all year, please* **Tel 01248 713545**

▲**Penrhyn Castle** & (The National Trust) 3m E of Bangor on A5122. Buses from Llandudno, Caernarvon. Betws-y-Coed; alight: Grand Lodge Gate. Large gardens; fine trees, shrubs, wild garden, good views. Castle rebuilt in 1830 for 1st Lord Penrhyn, incorporating part of C15 building on C8 site of home of Welsh Princes. Exhibition of National Trust Countryside; museum of locomotives and quarry rolling stock. NT Shop. TEAS and light lunches. *Adm £3 Chd £1.50 (Garden and Exhibition only). For NGS Fri March 28 (11-5). Last adm ½ hr prior to closing. Private visits welcome, please* **Tel 01248 353084**

Plas Muriau ✇✿ (Lorna & Tony Scharer) Betws-y-Coed. On A470 approx ¼m N of Waterloo Bridge, Betws-y-Coed; entrance by minor junction to Capel Garmon. A large garden dating from the 1870s recently restored. About 1 acre open to visitors. A structured garden within a woodland setting, with maginificent views. Unusual perennials and herbs, wild flowers, bulbs and roses. Many unusual plants for sale at adjacent nursery, Gwydir Plants. *Adm £1. Fri and Sats Easter to July incl (11-5) or by arrangement at nursery or by appt. Please,* **Tel 01690 710201**

▲**Plas Newydd** &✇ (The Marquess of Anglesey; The National Trust) Isle of Anglesey. 1m SW of Llanfairpwll and A5, on A4080. Gardens with massed shrubs, fine trees, and lawns sloping down to Menai Strait. Magnificent views to Snowdonia. C18 house by James Wyatt contains Rex Whistler's largest wall painting; also Military Museum. TEAS and light lunches. *Adm garden only £2, Chd £1, Family Adm £10.50. For NGS Thurs May 8 (11-5.30) last entry 5pm*

Plas Penhelig (Mr & Mrs A C Richardson) Aberdovey, between 2 railway bridges. Driveway to hotel by island and car park. 14 acres overlooking estuary, exceptional views. Particularly lovely in spring: bulbs, daffodils, rhododendrons, azaleas; rock and water gardens, mature tree heathers, magnolias, euphorbias; herbaceous borders, rose garden; wild and woodland flowers encouraged in large orchard; formal walled garden with herbaceous borders, large range of greenhouses, peaches, herbs. TEAS. *Adm £1.50 Chd 50p. Wed to Sun incl: April 1 to mid-Oct (2.30-5.30). Collecting box*

¶**Rhyd** &✇✿ (Ann & Jeff Hubble) Trefor, nr Holyhead. From Bodedern 2¼m along B5109 towards Llangefni, turn L. 2½ acres of gardens etc with many facets, herbaceous beds with some rare and unusual plants; many varieties of rhododendron, clematis and climbing roses, trees and shrubs; conservatory, ponds, rockery, pergola and nature walk (good footwear needed). Garden bordered by stream. Partly suitable wheelchairs. TEAS. *Adm £1 Chd free. Suns May 25, July 20 (11-5)*

¶**St John the Baptist & St George** (Bishop Abbot Demetrius) Carmel. On the A487 to Groeslon follow signs to Carmel. At village centre turn L and L again at Xrds. Holy community in the making under the authority of The Orthodox Catholic Church of America. This is not a garden in the traditional sense but a spiritual retreat from the stresses and strains of modern life, surrounded on all sides by space and rural tranquillity. We are privileged to share a glimpse of a more contemplative life. TEA. *Adm £1 Chd free. Sun May 25 (2-5)*

Trysglwyn Fawr & (Lord & Lady Stanley of Alderley) Rhosybol. Take the road S from Amlwch to Llanerchymedd. After 2m having passed the Parys Mountain mine shaft on your R, turn L, Trysglwyn Fawr is 1,000yds down that rd on your L. 1-acre garden overlooking farm land to fine view of Snowdonia. Mixed flower and shrub beds; vegetable garden, fruit garden and conservatory; farm walk showing amenity woodland and ponds. Planted during last 23yrs. TEA. *Adm £1 Chd free. Sun June 1 (1-5)*

¶**Tyn-y-Cefn** ✇✿ (Robert & Sheila Woodier) Ffestiniog. On the A496 3m from Maentwrog, 2m from Tanygrisiau [OS 695439]. Scenic setting in Snowdonia National Park for large garden with cottage garden atmosphere. Informal plantings of mixed beds and borders incl trees, shrubs, old-fashioned roses, climbers and many unusual plants. TEAS. *Adm £1. Suns June 29 July 27, Aug 24 (10-6). Private visits welcome, please* **Tel 01766 831810**

1927–1997

This year the National Gardens Scheme is celebrating its 70th Anniversary.

Please help us celebrate by visiting a garden in 1997.

Powys

Hon County Organisers:
(North – Montgomeryshire)   Captain R Watson, Westwinds, Kerry, Newtown, Powys Tel 01686 670605
(South – Brecknock & Radnor) Miss Shan Egerton, Pen-y-Maes, Hay on Wye, Hereford HR3 5PP
                              Tel 01497 820423
Assistant County Organiser: (South) Lady Milford, Llanstephan House, Llanstephan, Brecon. Powys LD3 OYR
                              Tel 01982 560693
Hon County Treasurer: (North) Captain R Watson
Hon County Treasuer: (South) Lady Milford

DATES OF OPENING

April 20 Sunday
Hill Crest, Brooks, Welshpool
April 27 Sunday
Llansantffraed House, Bwlch,
Brecon
April 30 Wednesday
Llansantffraed House, Bwlch,
Brecon
May 1 Thursday
The Bushes, Berriew
May 3 Saturday
Tan-y-Llyn, Nurseries, Meifod
May 4 Sunday
8 Baskerville Court, Clyro
Hill Crest, Brooks, Welshpool
Tan-y-Llyn, Nurseries, Meifod
May 5 Monday
Belan-yr-Argae, nr Welshpool
May 10 Saturday
Cae Hywel,
Llansantffraid-ym-Mechain
Glansevern Hall, Berriew,
Welshpool
May 11 Sunday
Cae Hywel,
Llansantffraid-ym-Mechain
May 15 Thursday
The Bushes, Berriew
May 18 Sunday
Bronhyddon,
Llansantffraid-ym-Mechain
Glanwye, Builth Wells
Gliffaes Country House Hotel,
Crickhowell
Hill Crest, Brooks, Welshpool
May 26 Monday
Belan-yr-Argae, nr Welshpool
Llysdinam, Newbridge-on-Wye
May 28 Wednesday
Powis Castle Gardens,
Welshpool
June 1 Sunday
Bodynfoel Hall, Llanfechain
The Bushes, Berriew
Cui Parc, Talybont-on-Usk
Gregynog, Tregynon
Hill Crest, Brooks, Welshpool
June 5 Thursday
The Bushes, Berriew

June 7 Saturday
Glansevern, Berriew, Welshpool
Tan-y-Llyn Nurseries, Meifod
June 8 Sunday
Cil Cottage, nr Meifod ‡
Maesllwch Castle,
Glasbury-on-Wye
Tan-y-Llyn Nurseries, Meifod ‡
June 15 Sunday
Ashford House, Talybont-on-Usk
Hill Crest, Brooks, Welshpool
Point Farm, Newtown
June 19 Thursday
The Bushes, Berriew
June 21 Saturday
The Millers House, Welshpool
June 22 Sunday
Crossways, Newcastle-on-Clun
Glanusk Park, Crickhowell
June 28 Saturday
Glansevern Hall, Berriew,
Welshpool
June 29 Sunday
Abernant, Fron
Broadheath House, Presteigne ‡
Llangorse Gardens
The Walled Garden, Knill, nr
Presteigne ‡
July 2 Wednesday
Llangorse Gardens
July 3 Thursday
The Bushes, Berriew
July 5 Saturday
Glansevern Hall, Berriew,
Welshpool
Tan-y-Llyn Nurseries, Meifod
Upper Dolley, Dolley Green,
Presteigne
July 6 Sunday
Hill Crest, Brooks, Welshpool
Tan-y-Llyn Nurseries, Meifod
Treberfydd, nr Bwlch
Upper Dolley, Dolley Green,
Presteigne
July 13 Sunday
Pen-y-Maes, Hay on Wye
July 17 Thursday
The Bushes Berriew
July 20 Sunday
8 Baskerville Court, Clyro
Fraithwen, Tregynon, Newtown

Hill Crest, Brooks, Welshpool
July 27 Sunday
Treholford, Cathedine, Brecon
August 2 Saturday
Tan-y-Llyn Nurseries, Meifod
August 3 Sunday
Hill Crest, Brooks, Welshpool
Talybont Gardens
Tan-y-Llyn Nurseries, Meifod
August 7 Thursday
The Bushes, Berriew
August 10 Sunday
Llysdinam, Newbridge-on-Wye
Point Farm, Newton
August 17 Sunday
Hill Crest, Brooks, Welshpool
August 21 Thursday
The Bushes, Berriew
August 24 Sunday
8 Baskerville Court, Clyro
September 4 Thursday
The Bushes, Berriew
September 6 Saturday
Tan-y-Llyn Nurseries, Meifod
September 7 Sunday
The Bushes, Berriew
Hill Crest, Brooks, Welshpool
Tan-y-Llyn Nurseries, Meifod
September 21 Sunday
Hill Crest, Brooks, Welshpool
October 12 Sunday
Gliffaes Country House Hotel,
Crickhowell

Regular openings
For details see garden description
Ashford House, Talybont-on-Usk
Diamond Cottage, Buttington
Mill Cottage, Abbeycwmhir

By appointment only
*For telephone numbers and other
details see garden descriptions.
Private visits welcomed*

Maenllwyd Isaf, Abermule

DESCRIPTIONS OF GARDENS

¶Abernant ✗❀ (J A & B M Gleave) Fron. Midway between Welshpool and Newtown on the A483. The garden is approached over a steep humpback bridge; straight ahead through gate. Approx 2.5 acre garden incl orchard. There is also a woodland area to the rear. Garden comprises lawns, pond, rose garden, rockery, ornamental shrubs, trees and ferns. TEA. *Adm £1.50 OAP's £1 Chd free. (Share to Welsh Historic Gardens Trust®) Sun June 29 (2-5)*

■ Ashford House ❀ (Mr & Mrs D A Anderson) Brecon. ¾m E of Talybont on Usk on B4558 signed from A40 through village. Walled garden of about 1 acre surrounded by woodland and wild garden approx 4 acres altogether. Mixed shrub and herbaceous borders; small formal garden; meadow garden and pond; alpine house and beds; vegetables. The whole garden has gradually been restored and developed since 1979. Bring and buy plant stall. Suitable in parts for wheelchairs. TEAS. *Adm £1.50 Chd free (Share to Save the Children®). Open Tues April 1 to Sept 30 (2-6). For NGS Sun June 15 (2-6). Also by appt, please* **Tel 01874 676 271**

■8 Baskerville Court ✗❀ (Mr & Mrs S Smith) Clyro, nr Hay-on-Wye. Leave A438 Hereford to Brecon rd at Clyro. Baskerville Court is nr church and behind Baskerville Arms. Small steeply terraced garden full of interesting and unusual plants imaginatively planted, incl alpines and heathers. Pergola and conservatory with magnificent views of the Black Mountains and Kilvert's Church. Teas at Baskerville Arms. *Adm £1.50 Chd free. Suns May 4, July 20, Aug 24 (11-5)*

Belan-yr-Argae ⅃ (Ivy Pritchard Evans) Cefn-Coch. 14m SW of Welshpool via Llanfair Caereinion and Cefn Coch and 12m NW of Newtown via Tregynon and Adfa. Garden attached to an old-fashioned farm comprising formal and wild gardens with pools, unusual plants, shrubs and trees, all set in approx ½ acre. Yr-round interest. TEA. *Adm £1.50 Chd free (Share to ADFA CM Chapel©). Mons May 5, 26 (2-6). Private visits welcome May 5 onwards, please* **Tel 01938 810658**

Bodynfoel Hall ⅃❀ (Maj Bonnor-Maurice) Llanfechain, 10m N of Welshpool. Via A490 to Llanfyllin. Take B4393 to Llanfechain, follow signs. Approx 3½ acres; gardens and woodland; lakes; young and mature trees; shrub roses and heather bank. TEAS. *Adm £1 OAPs 50p Chd free. Sun June 1 (2-6)* **Tel 01691 648486**

Broadheath House ⅃❀ (Mr & Mrs D McDowell) 1m E of Presteigne on B4362. 2½-acre garden designed by Sir Clough William-Ellis. Sunken rose garden, ponds, enclosed yew garden, newly planted kitchen garden and orchard. Walk to Hindwell Brook. TEAS in loggia. *Adm £1.50 Combined adm with* **The Walled Garden** *£2.50 Chd free (Share to East Radnor Day Centre, Presteigne®). Sun June 29 (2-5)*

Bronhyddon ❀ (Mr & Mrs R Jones-Perrott) Llansantffraid-ym-Mechain. 10m N Welshpool on A495 on E side in centre of village. Long drive; parking in fields below house. Wood having been almost clear felled now

planted with choice young trees & shrubs on acid soil on S facing slope. Grass rides have been made and in spring is a mass of bluebells and foxgloves; a mature stand has anemones, snowdrops & primroses. Both areas lead out of small garden in front of house with elegant Regency verandahs & balconies. TEAS. *Adm £1 Chd free. Sun May 18 (2-6)*

The Bushes ✗❀ (Hywel & Eileen Williams) Pantyffridd Berriew. 8m Welshpool on B4390 Berriew (3m) to Manafon. Set in the picturesque Rhiew Valley, this pretty ⅔-acre garden surrounds the old stone cottage on a S-facing site. Designed into terraced colour co-ordinated 'rooms' and planted with wide variety of perennials, shrub and climbers, pools, cobbled and paved areas; scented and new gravel garden. TEAS. *Adm £1.50 Chd free (Share to Cystic Fibrosis Trust®). Suns June 1, Sept 7 (1.30-5.30). 1st and 3rd Thurs May 1 to Sept 4 incl (1.30-5.30). Private visits also welcome May 16 to Sept 12, please* **Tel 01686 650338**

Cae Hywel ❀ (Miss Judith M Jones) Llansantffraid-ym-Mechain, 10m N of Welshpool. On A495; on E (Oswestry) side of village. Car park in village. 1 acre; S facing slope on different levels; rock garden; herb garden; interesting shrubs, trees and plants. Partly suitable for wheelchairs. TEAS. *Adm £1 Chd free. Sat, Sun May 10, 11 (2-5)*

¶Cil Cottage ✗(Mr & Mrs Goolden) Meifod. 7m Welshpool, 4m Meifod. Take A490 out of Welshpool past turning to Dingle Nursery entrance A490. Up hill to caravan park, down hill L turn into Cil Rd. 1m from garden, signposted off A490 or 495 Llansantffraid to Meifod rd, turn L A490 to Welshpool. Garden is well signposted. 2m after turn. 1½-2 acre cottage garden situated beside R Vyrnwy, comprising riverside area and walk, scree garden and stream: studio open for silk art work. TEAS. *Adm £1 Chd under 12 free. (Share to British Heart Foundation®). Partly suitable wheelchairs. Sun June 8 (12-6)*

■ Crossways ✗❀ (Mrs & Mr Smith) Newcastle on Clun, Shropshire. From Kerry take the B4368 signposted Clun. Travel past The Anchor for 1.5m then turn L at Xrds signposted Crossways, continue for 1m, cottage is at top of T-junction. Map ref. [205 859]. From Craven Arms take B4368 to Newcastle on Clun continue through village on B4368 for Newtown. 4m out of village turn R at Xrds signposted Crossways and continue. 1-acre cottage garden and nursery 1400ft on Shropshire/Wales border. Ponds, wildlife and woodland area, herbaceous beds and borders, rock garden. Small nursery, open Suns April 1 to Oct 31 (11-6). TEAS in aid of Shropshire and Mid-Wales Air Ambulance. *Adm £1. For NGS Sun June 22 (2-6). Private visits welcome, please* **Tel 01686 670890**

¶Cui Parc (Sir Andrew & Lady Large) Talybont-on-Usk. ¼m W of Talybont-on-Usk. On W side of lane leading S from Cross Oak. Follow signs from village. Well-established varied 3-acre garden with mixed border, lawns, roses, azaleas, rhododendrons and fully mature trees. Woodland garden by stream. Vegetable garden with cordon and espalier apples and pears; also plum and cherry trees. Recently planted orchard with old and rare local varieties of apple. A cider orchard is being re-established around a few remaining venerable old trees. TEAS.

Adm £1.50 Chd free. (Share to Riding for the Disabled®)
Sun June 1 (2-6)

Diamond Cottage ⚘❀ (Mr & Mrs D T Dorril) Buttington. From Welshpool on A458 3m turn R into Heldre Lane. From Shrewsbury, turn L past 'Little Chef' Trewern into Sale Lane. Then follow signs. 1.7-acre garden on steep N facing slope at 700ft. Unusual herbaceous plants and shrubs; wooded dingle with stream; vegetable garden, patio and pools. Extensive views to Berwyn Mountains. TEAS. *Adm £1.20 Chd free. Tues April 1, 8, 15, 22, 29, May 6, 13, 20, 27; June 3, 10, 17, 24; July 1, 8, 15, 22, 29; Aug 5, 12, 19, 26; Spt 2, 9, 16 (2-6). Private visits welcome April to Sept, please* Tel 01938 570570

Fraithwen ⚘❀ (Mr & Mrs David Thomas) Tregynon. 6m N of Newtown on B4389 midway between villages of Bettws Cedewain and Tregynon. 1-acre garden created in the last 10yrs; herbaceous borders, rockeries and ponds packed with interesting, unusual and rare plants and shrubs for colour throughout the year. Also on display antique horse-drawn machinery and implements. As featured in 'Womans Weekly'. Partially suitable for wheelchairs. TEAS. *Adm £1.50 Chd free (Share to Bettws Community Hall®). Sun July 20 (2-6). Private parties welcome, please* Tel 01686 650307

■ **Glansevern Hall Gardens** ⚸❀ (Mr & Mrs R N Thomas) Berriew. 4m SW of Powis Castle, Welshpool, on A483 at Berriew. 13-acre mature garden situated nr banks of R Severn. Centred on Glansevern Hall, a Greek Revival house of 1801. Noted for variety of unusual tree species; much new planting; lake with island; woodland walk; large rock garden and grotto. Walled rose garden; water features. TEAS. Free car/coach park. *Adm £2 Chd free. Fris, Sats, May to Sept. For NGS Sats May 10, June 7, 28, July 5 (2-6)*

Glanusk Park ⚸⚘ (The Viscountess De L'Isle) Garden 2m W of Crickhowell. A40, 12m from Brecon; 8m from Abergavenny. Large garden within beautiful park; fine trees and R. Usk. Formal garden with roses and fountain; water garden and pool. Original house destroyed during World War II. TEAS. *Adm £1.50 Chd free. Sun June 22 (2-5)*

Glanwye ⚸❀ (Mr & Mrs David Vaughan, G & H Kidston) 2m E Builth Wells on A470. Large garden, rhododendrons, azaleas; herbaceous borders, extensive yew hedges, lawns, long woodland walk with bluebells and other woodland flowers. Magnificent views of upper Wye Valley. Illustrated in 'Some Borderland Gardens' by B & A Palmer. Cream TEAS. *Adm £1.50 Chd free (Share to Llanddewi Cwm and Alltmawr Church®). Sun May 18 (2-5)*

■ **Gliffaes Country House Hotel** ⚸ (Mr & Mrs Brabner) 3m W of Crickhowell on A40. Large garden; spring bulbs; azaleas & rhododendrons, new ornamental pond; heathers; shrubs; ornamental trees; fine maples; autumn colour; fine position high above R. Usk. Cream Teas available at hotel. *April to Dec. For NGS Adm £1.50 Chd free (collecting box). Suns May 18, Oct 12 (2-5)*

Gregynog ⚸⚘❀ (University of Wales) Tregynon, 7m N of Newtown. A483 Welshpool to Newtown Rd, turn W at

B4389 for Bettws Cedewain, 1m through village gates or left. Large garden; fine banks, rhododendrons and azaleas; dell with specimen shrubs; formal garden; colour-coded walks starting from car park. Descriptive leaflet available. Early C19 black and white house; site inhabited since C12. TEAS. *Adm £1.50 Chd 50p 12/16 yrs. Sun June 1 (2-6)*

Hill Crest ❀ (Mr J D & Mrs P Horton) Brooks. 9m W of Welshpool. Turn R to Berriew, then L by Lion Hotel through village towards Bettws Cedewain. Turn R after 3m to Brooks then 1m up hill on L. 8m E from Newtown Through Bettws Cedewain. Take Brooks Rd, after 3m turn L. House at top of hill on L. Approx 1 acre of mixed shrub borders, alpines and pool; hillside arboretum with rhododendron walk, pine, spruce conifers and deciduous wooded area planted with daffodils. *Adm £1 Chd 10p Open 1st and 3rd Sun April 20 to Sept 21. Suns May 4, 18, June 1, 15, July 6, 20, Aug, 3, 17, Sept 7, 21 (1-5) Private visits welcome all year, please* Tel 01686 640541

Llangorse Gardens ❀ Llangorse is on B4560 4m off A40 at Bwlch, 6½m from Brecon and 4½m from Talgarth Park in village. TEAS in aid of Llangorse Church. *Adm £1.50 Chd free. Sun June 29, Wed July 2 (2-6)*
　The Neuadd (Mr & Mrs P Johnson) Informal garden of approx 1 acre with mixed borders of interesting trees, shrubs and herbaceous plants, emphasis on good foliage and unusual forms of cottage garden and native plants; small vegetable and fruit garden meadow gardens and copse. Maintained by owners on organic lines to encourage wild life. *Private visits welcome, please* Tel 01874 658 670
　The Old Vicarage ⚸⚘ (Major & Mrs J B Anderson) Small family garden maintained by owners with interesting herbaceous and shrub borders; lawns, trees and vegetables. Plants usually for sale in aid of NGS. *Private visits welcome Spring to Oct, please* Tel 01874 658639

¶**Llansantffraed House** ⚸⚘❀ (Mrs A Inglis) Bwlch, Brecon. On A40 at junction to Talybont-on-Usk, 6m E of Brecon, 2m W of Bwlch next to Llansantffraed Church. ½ acre sloping lawns, shrubs and trees with huge yew hedges. Masses of spring bulbs; old-fashioned wall of aubretia, alyssum and alpines. TEA in conservatory overlooking the Usk and Brecon Beacons. *Adm £1 Chd free (Share to Llansantffraed Church®) Sun, Wed April 27, 30 (2-6)*

Llysdinam ⚸❀ (Lady Delia Venables-Llewelyn & Llysdinam Charitable Trust) Newbridge-on-Wye, SW of Llandrindod Wells. Turn W off A479 at Newbridge-on-Wye; right immed after crossing R Wye; entrance up hill. Large garden. Azaleas; rhododendrons, water garden and herbaceous borders; shrubs; woodland garden; kitchen garden fine view of Wye Valley. TEAS in aid of NSPCC. *Adm £. Chd free. Mon May 26, Sun Aug 10 (2-6). Private parties welcome, please* Tel 01597 860 200

Maenllwyd Isaf ⚸⚘ (Mrs Denise Hatchard) Abermule 5m NE of Newtown & 10m S of Welshpool. On B4368 Abermule to Craven Arms, 1½m from Abermule. 3 acres unusual shrubs and plants; goldfish pool; 'wild' pool R Mule. C16 listed house. *Adm £1 Chd free (Share to*

Winged Fellowship Trust®). Private visits welcome all year. Gardening clubs etc welcome, please **Tel 01686 30204**

Maesllwch Castle 🌣 (Walter de Winton Esq) Glasbury-on-Wye. Turn off A438 immed N of Glasbury Bridge. Through Glasbury, ½m turn R at church. Medium-sized, garden owner maintained. Exceptional views from terrace across R Wye to Black Mountains. Woodland walk to old walled garden now used for young trees. Fine trees, C18 ingko tree. TEA Adm £1.50 Chd free (Share to All Saints Church, Glasbury®). Sun June 8 (2-5)

Mill Cottage 🌣 (Mr & Mrs B D Parfitt) Abbeycwmhir. 8m of Llandrindod Wells. Turning L off A483, 1m N of Crossgates Roundabout, then 3½m on L, signposted Abeycwmhir. ⅓-acre garden of unusual and rare shrubs, small trees and climbers. Numerous ericaceae. Narrow paths and steps; limited parking. TEA. Adm £1 Chd 50p. Sat to Sun incl, May 24 to June 1, July 5 to 13, August 2 to 10 (mid-day to dusk)

The Millers House 🌣🌣 (Mr & Mrs Mark Kneale) Welshpool. About 1¼m NW of Welshpool on rd to Guilsfield A490; turn R into Windmill Lane; 4th cottage on L. 1½-acre country garden begun in 1988. Superb views. Mixed shrub and herbaceous borders, roses, climbers, pool. Ornamental and fruit trees incl a planting of 12 hardy eucalyptus. TEAS in aid of Welshpool Methodist Church. Adm £1.25 Chd free. Sat June 21 (2-6). Private visits welcome, please **Tel 01938 555432**

Pen-y-Maes 🌣🌣 (Miss S Egerton) 1m W of Hay on Wye on B4350 towards Brecon. Entrance on L. 2-acre garden, mainly herbaceous. Walled kitchen garden with geometric beds of vegetables and flowers. Shrub roses, herbs and espaliered pears. Featured in Gardens Illustrated Oct 1993. TEAS. Adm £1.50 Chd free. Sun July 13 (2-5)

Point Farm 🌣🌣🌣 (Mr & Mrs F Podmore) Bryn Lane, Newtown. Head N across river from town centre. Take R-and rd into Commercial St off roundabout. L at fork into Canfair Rd L at hospital for 1½m along Bryn Lane. At 750' the ½-acre garden set in unspoilt views of the countryside. Patio, pergola, herbaceous plants and shrub beds, colour co-ordinated for informal interest. Soft fruits, raised vegetable garden with 15' × 25' greenhouse with peach and apricot trees, vegetables and tender plants. TEAS. Adm £1 Acc chd free and raffle by Aberhafesp WI and Happy Circle. Suns June 15, Aug 10 (2-6). Private visits welcome, please **Tel 01686 625709**

Powis Castle Gardens 🌣🌣 (The National Trust) Welshpool. Turn off A483 ¾m out of Welshpool, up Red Lane for ¼m. Gardens laid out in 1720 with most famous hanging terraces in the world; enormous yew hedges; lead statuary, large wild garden. Part of garden suitable for wheelchairs, top terrace only. Wheelchairs available free of charge. TEA in tea rooms. Adm (garden only) £4 Chd £2. For NGS Wed May 28 (11-6) last entry 5.30

Talybont Gardens 🌣🌣🌣 Talybont-on-Usk. ½m from turning off A40. 6m E of Brecon, signed Talybont. Teas in village. Combined adm £1.50 Chd free. Sun Aug 3 (2-6)
　Cartrefle (Mrs J F Fox) Small compact garden with

variety of trees, shrubs, vegetables, flower beds and abundance of flowers in pots and tubs; water garden feature
　Lonicera (Mr & Mrs G Davies) Garden of varied interest incl several small feature gardens extending to approx ¼ acre; modern rose garden with dwarf conifers; herbaceous and woody perennials; colourful summer bedding displays; window boxes, hanging baskets and patio tubs forming extensive house frontage display; greenhouses. Teas in village. (Share to Arthritis & Rheumatism Council®)

Tan-y-Llyn 🌣🌣 (Callum Johnston & Brenda Moor) Meifod. From Oswestry on the A495 turn L in village, cross R Vyrnwy and climb hill for ½m bearing R at Y-junction. Map ref. [167125]. 3-acre sheltered garden and orchard in Montgomeryshire hills. Informally terraced; laid out to complement the proportions of existing hillside. Thorn grove, herb garden; extensive collection of container plants. Nursery specialising in alpines, herbaceous plants and herbs. TEAS. Events, demonstrations and exhibitions. Adm £1 Chd free. Sats, Suns May 3, 4, June 7, 8, July 5, 6, Aug 2, 3, Sept 6, 7 (2-5)

Treberfydd 🌣 (Lt Col & Mrs D Garnons Williams) Bwlch. 2¼m W of Bwlch. From A40 at Bwlch turning marked Llangorse then L for Pennorth. From Brecon, leave A40 at Llanhamlach. 2¼m to sign Llangasty Church but go over cattle grid to house. Large garden; lawns, roses, trees, rock garden. Plants for sale at commercial nursery. TEAS. Adm £1.50 Chd free (Share to Llangasty Church®). Sun July 6 (2-6)

Treholford 🌣 (Mr & Mrs J A V Blackham) Cathedine. Turn off A40 between Crickhowell and Brecon at Bwlch for Llangorse. 2m on R. 6-acre garden overlooking Llangorse Lake; lawns with specimen trees, rock garden, pools and greenhouses incl a cacti house; walled kitchen garden with box hedges and rose arches. TEAS. Adm £1.50 Chd free (Share to St Michael's Church, Cathedine®). Sun July 27 (2-5). Private visits welcome, please **Tel 01874 730278**

Upper Dolley 🌣🌣🌣 (Mrs B P Muggleton) Dolley Green. Take B4356 W out of Presteigne towards Whitton. At Dolley Green, 2m from Presteigne, turn L down 'No Through Road' by red brick church; Upper Dolley is 100yds on L. From Knighton take B4355 to turning for Whitton, B4357. Turn L at Whitton B4356 to brick church; turn R. 2-acre country garden with open views of Lugg Valley; variety of borders with many shrub roses and large natural pond; C16 Grade 2 listed house (not open). Cream TEAS and plants in aid of Bible Society. Adm £1 Chd 50p. Sat, Sun July 5, 6 (2-6). Private visits welcome June, July, Aug, please **Tel 01547 560273**

The Walled Garden 🌣 (Miss C M Mills) Knill, 3m from Kington and Presteigne. Off B4362 Walton-Presteigne rd to Knill village; right over cattle grid; keep right down drive. 4 acres; walled garden; river; bog garden; primulas; shrub and climbing roses. Nr C13 Church in lovely valley. TEAS at **Broadheath House**. Adm £1.50 Chd free. Combined adm with **Broadheath** £2.50 Chd free. Sun June 29 (2-5). Private visits welcome any day (10-7) adm £1.50, please **Tel 01544 267411**

Index to Gardens

This index lists all gardens alphabetically and gives the counties in which they are to be found. Refer to the relevan county pages where the garden and its details will be found, again in alphabetical order. The following unorthodo: county abbreviations are used: C & W—Cheshire and Wirral; G, N&C—Gloucestershire (North & Central); G, S&B— Gloucestershire (South) & Bristol; L & R—Leicestershire and Rutland; W & WM—Warwickshire & West Midlands C/C—Ceredigion/Cardiganshire; C & P—Carmarthenshire & Pembrokeshire; D & C—Denbighshire & Colwyn; F & W— Flintshire & Wrexham. An * denotes a garden which will not be in its normal alphabetical order as it is a group garde and will be found under the Group Garden name but still within the county indicated.

A

D

Index to Advertisers

THE BLUE CROSS

The Blue Cross is, first and foremost, a charity for companion animals and their owners. It was founded in 1897, and today our 3 Hospitals and Clinic give over 60,000 free veterinary treatments annually. Every year, our 11 Adoption Centres find loving new homes for over 8,000 cats and dogs.

The Blue Cross Hospital at Victoria first opened in 1906, and despite two World Wars, has never closed its doors to the needs of London's companion animals. Today the Blue Cross pledge that "no animal will ever be turned away" is at serious risk. An ageing population and its continuing needs is placing greater demands on The Blue Cross.

In our Centenary Year of 1997, the need for our work is as great as ever. Please help The Blue Cross to continue to help the thousands of animals which come to us each year by making a donation of whatever you can afford.

The Blue Cross
Shilton Road
Burford
Oxon OX18 4PF

Tel: 01993 822651

Registered Charity
No: 224392

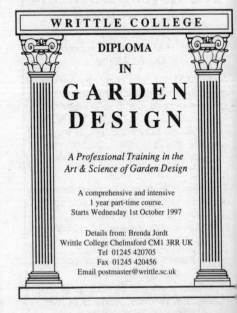

367

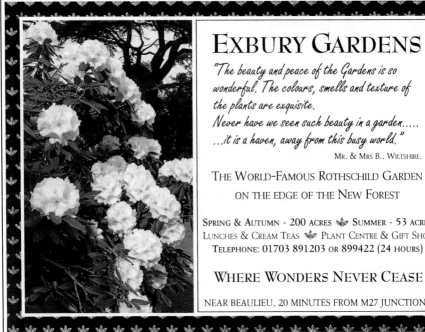

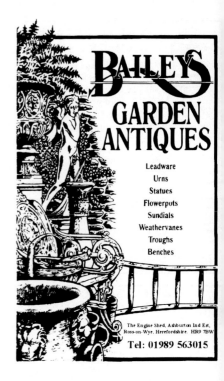